ERN MILITARY AIRCRAFT

MODERN MILITARY AIRCRAFT

THE WORLD'S FIGHTING AIRCRAFT: 1945 TO THE PRESENT DAY

GENERAL EDITOR: JIM WINCHESTER

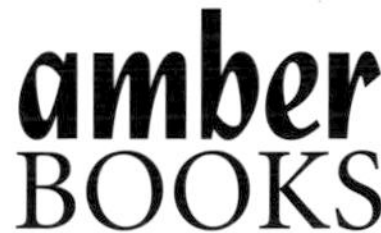

First published in 2010

Reprinted in 2013

Published by
Amber Books Ltd
74–77 White Lion Street
London N1 9PF
United Kingdom
Website: www.amberbooks.co.uk
Appstore: itunes.com/apps/amberbooksltd
Facebook: www.facebook.com/amberbooks
Twitter: @amberbooks

ISBN 978-1-907446-40-5

Printed and bound in China

10 9 8 7 6 5 4 3 2

This material was originally published as part of the reference set *Aircraft of the World*

Contents

Introduction

The genesis of today's military aircraft lies in the last years of World War Two. Jet engines, nuclear weapons, guided missiles and supersonic speeds were all concepts that were employed, evaluated or at least understood by 1945.

For pure combat aircraft, success was measured first in pure speed, then agility, and now no new fighter or bomber is developed without low observability or stealth taken into account. This is achieved with radar absorbent materials, jamming systems and careful airframe shaping. Only a few nations can afford all-aspect stealth of the sort that protects against both surface-to-air and air-to-air threats. Even stealth does not confer invulnerability, and it brings compromises, such as reduced weapons options.

Above: Very few modern military aircraft are designed with only one role. The C-17 can perform both strategic airlift missions and tactical operations from unpaved airfields, something its predecessor the C-141 could never do.

Helicopters, little more than toys during the war, have evolved from simple passenger and utility machines to highly sophisticated attack aircraft, replacing most light fixed wing combat aircraft over the battlefield. After many false starts and failed concepts, one hybrid aircraft with features of both fixed- and rotary-winged machines, the V-22 Osprey, has reached operational status.

Tankers and early warning radar aircraft emerged from technology that was in its infancy in 1945. Thirsty jet bombers and their escorts needed aerial refuelling to reach distant targets and stay on patrol. In the days of 24-hour airborne alerts, the USAF's Strategic Air Command operated hundreds of tankers alongside bombers and fighters. Airborne early warning (AEW) aircraft were developed firstly to protect carrier groups by extending their radar coverage, then to plug gaps in land-based coverage. Today AWACS aircraft perform many duties alongside other platforms in what is called ISR (Intelligence, Surveillance and Reconnaissance).

Compared to their World War II counterparts, which were largely derived from airliner designs, post-war cargo aircraft have become characterised by level floors, vehicle ramps and turboprop or turbofan engines. Airlift is vital in modern war for the supply of expeditionary forces at both the strategic and tactical levels.

Every air arm needs its trainers, and these range from simple light aircraft to supersonic jets with a credible secondary attack capability. As high-end fighters become ever more expensive, relatively simple combat aircraft have a growing niche in those air forces unable to afford the latest products from Lockheed Martin, Eurofighter or Sukhoi.

Below: The Eurofighter Typhoon is also capable of multiple roles, or even changing roles in a single mission. These Italian Typhoons are configured for air combat training.

AERMACCHI

MB.339

● Advanced trainer ● Light strike ● Frecce Tricolori aerobatic aircraft

A beautiful aircraft and a delight to fly, the Aermacchi MB.339 is the standard Italian air force trainer which has also been developed into a potent light-attack warplane. It is familiar on the air show circuit thanks to its appearances with the Italian national aerobatic team Frecce Tricolori, whose dramatic flight manoeuvres have entertained crowds in 32 countries.

▲ *The MB.339 has followed in the footsteps of the older MB.326 as a well-harmonised jet trainer. It is not as advanced as the BAe Hawk series, but is a better performer than the MB.326.*

PHOTO FILE

AERMACCHI MB.339

Tip tanks ▶
Like the MB.326, the MB.339 has wingtip fuel tanks. The attack-dedicated MB.339C has larger tip tanks.

▼ Prototype 'K'
The MB.339K only exists as a prototype. This was a single-seat dedicated light-attack variant with a limited air-to-air capability.

▲ Neat cockpit
The MB.339 has a neat cockpit of conventional layout. Unusually, the ejection seat has two handles on either side for firing.

▼ Straight wing
Unlike the higher performance Hawk and Alpha Jet, the MB.339 has a straight wing with a swept leading edge. This gives more stable handling.

▲ Italian air force
The largest user of the MB.339 is the Italian air force. Pilots complete 180 hours on the MB.339 after flying the SF.260 light trainer. They then convert to fast jets.

FACTS AND FIGURES

- ➤ The MB.339 introduced a 33-cm (13-in.) stepped SICAMB/Martin-Baker Mk 10 'zero-zero' ejection seat.
- ➤ Lockheed sought to sell licence-built MB.339s to the US as the 'T-bird II'.
- ➤ Just one of many export customers, Eritrea bought six MB.339Cs in March 1996.
- ➤ Six Argentine MB.339A fighter trainers were used as warplanes against the British in the 1982 Falklands War.
- ➤ The MB.339K is a single-seat version designed exclusively for light attack.
- ➤ Operators of the MB.339 include Dubai, Ghana, Malaysia, Nigeria and Peru.

PROFILE

Aermacchi's fast trainer

Based upon Aermacchi's earlier MB.326 used by 12 nations, the MB.339 looks 'hot' but has very docile handling qualities. This makes it ideal for flight instruction yet highly adaptable for combat duties. The MB.326 is first and foremost a trainer which has taught thousands of fast-jet students how to fly. In service with seven air forces, it was an unsuccessful competitor in the Pentagon's JPATS competition for a new primary trainer for the US Air Force and Navy.

But the MB.339 has considerable military potential, and a single-seat attack version has been evaluated. The two-seat 'lead-in fighter trainer' variant is designed to carry a wide variety of weapons to teach future fighter pilots how to fire them, and can be used as an effective light-attack and anti-shipping strike aircraft. The MB.339C has been ordered by the Royal New Zealand Air Force, which purchased 18 in May 1990 to replace the successful but ageing British Strikemaster. The single-seat MB.339K is unlikely to see operational service.

Above: The Italian air force aerobatic team, the Frecce Tricolori, show just how impressive the performance of the MB.339 can be in the hands of expertly trained pilots.

Below: The MB.339 has a landing speed of around 180 km/h (110 m.p.h.), making life simple for students converting from small trainers. Visibility from the rear cockpit is good.

MB.339A

Type: tandem two-seat trainer and close-support aircraft

Powerplant: one 17.78-kN (3,990-lb.-thrust) Piaggio-built Rolls-Royce Viper 632043 turbojet

Maximum speed: 898 km/h (552 m.p.h.)

Range: 1760 km (1,091 mi.)

Service ceiling: 14,630 m (48,000 ft.)

Weights: empty 3215 kg (7,073 lb.); loaded 5895 kg (13,970 lb.)

Armament: provision for two 30-mm or multi-barrel 7.62-mm (.30 cal.) guns, AS.11/AS.12 or Magic missiles, or up to 1935 kg of bombs (including two 340-kg (750-lb.) bombs on inboard pylons) or fuel tanks

Dimensions:

span	10.86 m (36 ft.)
length	10.97 m (36 ft.)
height	3.99 m (13 ft.)
wing area	19.30 m² (208 sq. ft.)

MB.339PAN

The Gruppo Pattuglia Aerobatica Nazionale, better known as the Frecce Tricolori, have used the MB.339PAN since 1982. This is a special version for the team, with the tip tanks removed for agility.

This flamboyant colour scheme is reserved for the team. The normal paintwork for the air force's MB.339s is a light grey with high-visibility 'dayglo' panels.

Compared to the MB.326, forward vision for the instructor in the rear seat is greatly improved. Both cockpits have full pressurisation and dual controls. A gunsight can also be fitted to the rear cockpit to allow an instructor to monitor his student's shooting during weapon training.

Systems fitted to the MB.339C version include laser rangefinder, Kaiser head-up display and weapon aiming computer.

The main undercarriage retracts into the wing. It has an anti-skid braking system and is capable of operation from semi-prepared surfaces.

Twin ventral strakes are fitted to the rear fuselage to enhance stability at high angles of attack.

Despite its age and lack of power, Aermacchi opted for the Rolls-Royce Viper turbojet.

ACTION DATA

MAXIMUM SPEED

Advanced trainers convert pilots from flying basic trainers, which typically have a maximum speed of around 500 km/h (300 m.p.h.), to jet fighters, which usually have a maximum speed at sea level of over 1000 km/h (600 m.p.h.). These speeds allow them to perform light-attack missions with a reasonable amount of success.

MB.339A	898 km/h (557 m.p.h.)
L-39 ALBATROS	850 km/h (527 m.p.h.)
ALPHA JET	916 km/h (568 m.p.h.)

WEAPONS

Secondary light-attack capability is vital to many small air forces, and all the main designs have some ability to drop light bombs or missiles, either for weapon training or operational use. The MB.339 can fire anti-ship missiles or rocket pods.

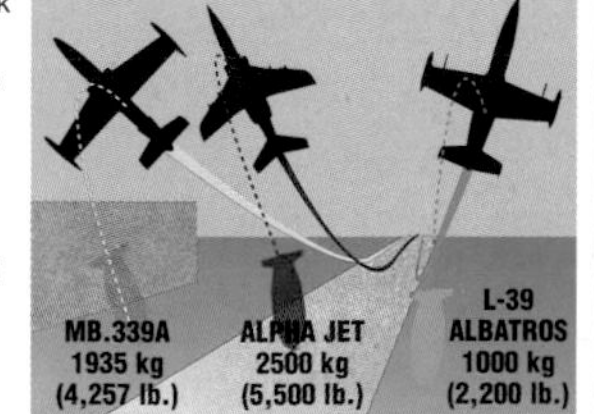

MAXIMUM TAKE-OFF WEIGHT

The MB.339 is less capable than the best advanced trainers, such as the Alpha Jet and the Hawk, but more capable than the cheapest, and its maximum take-off weight reflects this. The Alpha Jet has twin engines and a high standard of equipment, giving it a high take-off weight.

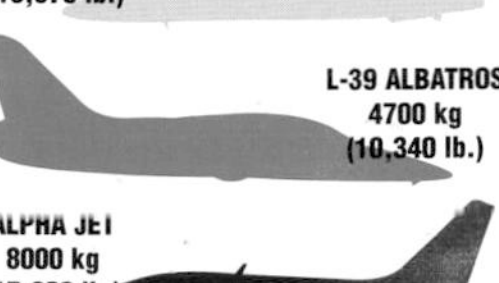

ALPHA JET
8000 kg
(17,600 lb.)

Aermacchi light civil and training aircraft

MB.308: This light two-seat sport aircraft was developed in the early 1950s. It was powered by a Continental C90 four-cylinder air-cooled engine and had a wooden fuselage.

MB.320: The MB.320 was a six-seat twin-engined touring machine with a wooden wing. Most of the fuselage behind the nose was also of wooden construction to reduce costs.

MB.323: Powered by a Pratt & Whitney radial air-cooled piston engine, the MB.323 was a basic trainer seating two in tandem. Although it was a fine design, it never entered service.

MB.326: The MB.326 was a very popular design which achieved wide export success as well as being licence-built in Australia and Brazil. It also used the Rolls-Royce Viper turbojet engine.

AERO

L-39/L-59 ALBATROS

● Czech-built trainer ● More than 2800 built ● Ground-attack variants

The L-39 Albatros, successor to Aero's earlier L-29, continues to be Russia's standard trainer. More than 2000 L-39s were delivered to the former Soviet Union between 1973 and 1989. The type has also sold well outside the former Eastern Bloc. Serving with the air forces of at least 16 other countries, the Albatros has been progressively modernised, and resulted in the more capable L-59 and a number of proposals for other variants.

▲ *Aero built 3,600 L-29 Delfins to fill the training requirements of the Warsaw Pact countries. The company was eager to produce a successor, and flew a prototype L-39 in 1968.*

PHOTO FILE

AERO L-39/L-59 ALBATROS

Trainer with teeth ▶
An L-39ZA of the Slovak air force. This ground-attack version has a secondary reconnaissance role and can carry a centreline camera pod. L-39ZA/ARTs with Elbit avionics were produced for Thailand.

▼ Greater capability
The improved L-39MS has a stronger fuselage, a new engine, upgraded avionics, powered controls and larger tip-tanks.

▲ More than 20 years' service
The L-39 first took to the air in 1968 and entered service in 1974. The Soviets alone ordered 2,094.

▼ L-39MS demonstrator
The first L-59s were designated L-39MS. Five were delivered to the Czech air force.

Export success ▶
Most customers for the Albatros came from Soviet allies, although since the end of the Cold War other countries, like Tunisia, have purchased the type.

FACTS AND FIGURES

- By removing the rear seat and fitting target-towing equipment, Aero created the L-39V for use with a KT-04 target.
- Czechoslovak L-39s were divided between the Czech and Slovak air forces in 1992.
- The second biggest customer, after the Soviets, was Libya with 181 machines.
- The L-39ZO replaced Warsaw Pact MiG-17s, MiG-21s and Su-7s in the weapons training role.
- A two-seat trainer variant of the L-159, the L-159T, is planned by Aero.
- The Czech air force has ordered 72 L-159s.

PROFILE

Trainer for WarPac and the world

By adding an undernose GSh-23 23-mm gun pod to the L-39ZO trainer, Aero created the L-39ZA ground-attack and reconnaissance platform. Wing pylons have a capacity of 1500 kg (3,300 lb.).

Many versions of the L–39 have been produced since the original L-39C entered service with the Czechoslovak air force in 1974. The L-39ZO has a built-in cannon and four wing hardpoints, plus a stronger undercarriage. The -39V is a target tug and the ZA is a ground-attack version. They are all powered by the 16.9-kN (4,400-lb.-thrust) AI-25 turbofan.

Aero built a version of the ZA with Israeli avionics, including a head-up display, and navigation/attack system, for Thailand. Another derivative, the L-139 with a Garrett TFE731 engine and other new systems and equipment, was developed to meet the American JPATS trainer specification.

By 1990 Aero had developed a new model powered by a DV-2 engine. The increased thrust gives the L-59 (known initially as L-39MS) greatly improved performance. The aircraft has a more sophisticated cockpit for advanced training, including weapons delivery techniques. It was also designed to be easier to maintain. Egypt was the first export customer, ordering 48, and Tunisia has bought 12.For the Czech air force, Aero is producing the L-159, a single-seat attack version with a 28-kN (6,300-lb.-thrust) Garrett F124 engine.

L-59E Albatros

Type: advanced trainer and light attack aircraft

Powerplant: one 21.57-kN (4,850-lb.-thrust) Povazski Strojarne/ZMK DV-2 turbofan

Maximum speed: 875 km/h (543 m.p.h.) at 5000 m (16,500 ft.)

Climb rate: 1500 m/min (4,920 f.p.m.) at sea level

Range: 1210 km (750 mi.) at 5000 m (16,500 ft.)

Service ceiling: 11,730 m (38,470 ft.)

Weights: empty 4030 kg (8,866 lb.); maximum take-off 7000 kg (15,400 lb.)

Armament: one GSh-23 23-mm cannon, plus up to 1500 kg (3,300 lb.) of rockets, bombs and air-to-air missiles

Dimensions:

	span	9.54 m (31 ft. 4 in.)
	length	12.20 m (40 ft.)
	height	4.77 m (15 ft. 8 in.)
	wing area	18.80 m² (202 sq. ft.)

L-39C ALBATROS

This L-39C basic and advanced trainer appeared at the 1990 Battle of Britain Salute at Boscombe Down. A factory demonstrator, it gave a spirited display in this colourful paint scheme.

The L-39C's optional underwing stations are for external fuel tanks. On the L-39ZO, ZA, MS and L-59, four are fitted and are intended for air-to-ground ordnance or camera equipment.

Flown in 1968 and placed in production in 1972, the L-39 is a generation behind types like the BAe Hawk. It is probably more comparable with the Aermacchi MB.326.

The L-39's Ivchenko turbofan is fed by two high-set air intakes behind the cockpit. Their position was chosen to minimise the FOD (foreign object damage) ingestion.

The L-39's undercarriage is robust enough for use on semi-prepared strips.

The L-39C is the basic training variant of the Albatros. The pilot and instructor sit in tandem in separate cockpits. Each has a Czech-designed ejection seat.

A major change in the L-59, apart from a new engine, was a multi-mode pulse-Doppler radar installed in the nose. This greatly increased the aircraft's capability.

Since the end of the Cold War and the break-up of the Eastern Bloc, a number of aircraft from the former Warsaw Pact and its allies have found their way into private hands in the West. For example, an L-39 now registered in Britain was flown by the air forces of Chad and Libya.

Most L-39 variants are powered by a single Ivchenko AI-25TL turbofan. This produces 16.87 kN (4,400 lb. of thrust). The L-39MS/L-59 introduced a Lotarev DV-2 engine of 21.57 kN (4,850 lb.-thrust).

A feature of the L-39, except for the L-39MS/L-59, is an electrically-operated variable-incidence tailplane. Elevators are also fitted, although these are manually actuated with a small trim tab.

COMBAT DATA

THRUST

With considerably more thrust than the other machines, the L-59E has enough power to be a very useful attack aircraft, as well as one of the world's best jet trainers.

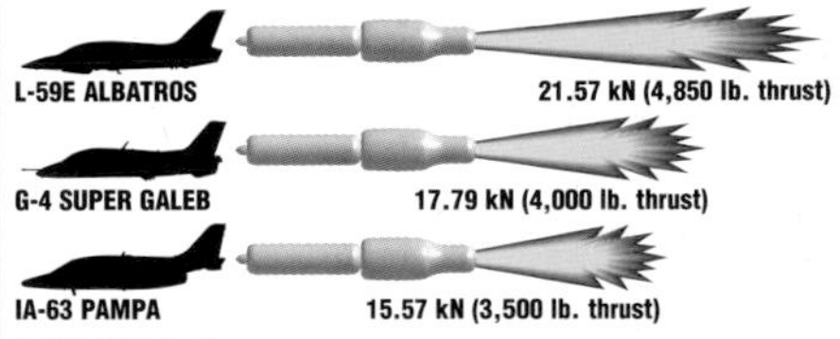

ORDNANCE

In the weapons training and light attack roles the L-59E is again the most capable aircraft. It can carry a considerably larger weapon load than its competitors.

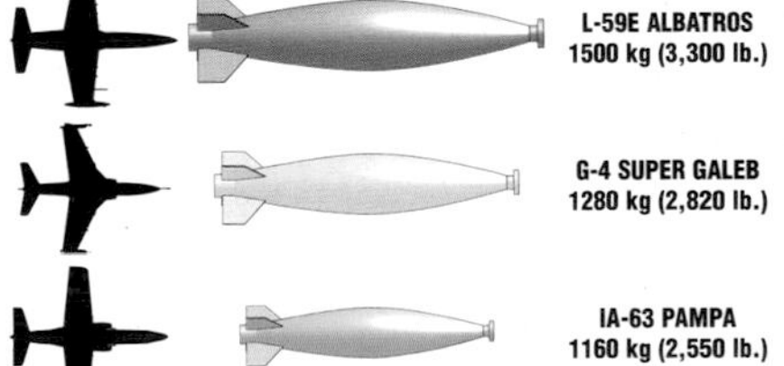

CLIMB RATE

Argentina's FAMF/FMA IA-63 Pampa is able to climb as quickly as the L-59E, but is struggling to find export sales. The L-59E has stunned air show crowds with its performance.

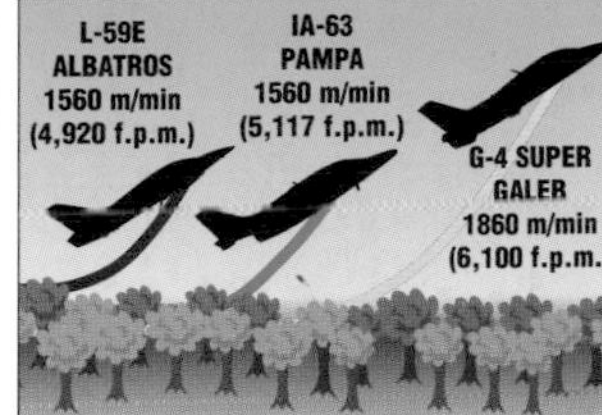

Ex-military trainers in private hands

DE HAVILLAND VAMPIRE T.Mk 55: This ex-Swiss air force aircraft wears the colours of a Sea Vampire T.Mk 22. Private owners often repaint their aircraft in unauthentic markings.

HAWKER HUNTER T.Mk 68: Some ex-military jets are used as executive aircraft. This British-registered Hunter is used by its owner to fly to his holiday home in Majorca.

HUNTING JET PROVOST T.Mk 5P: This ex-RAF Jet Provost carries advertising for an accessory retailer. Flying ex-military jets is expensive and sponsorship helps to cover costs.

LOCKHEED T-33A SHOOTING STAR: Based at Duxford in Cambridgeshire, this ex-USAF trainer carries the US registration N33VC to avoid having to be certificated in the UK.

AÉROSPATIALE (WESTLAND)

SA 330 PUMA

● All-weather transport helicopter ● Gulf and Bosnia veteran

Building on its experience with the earlier, larger Super Frelon, Sud Aviation (later Aérospatiale) answered the French army's call for an all-weather medium transport helicopter with the Puma. France and later Britain ordered sizeable fleets. Civil operators, too, found uses for what was to be the first all-weather helicopter in the West. Military and civil exports have flourished and the Puma is still in service more than 40 years later.

▲ *Despite their advancing years, Pumas are still widely used by the world's armed forces, including those of its original customers, France and the U.K. RAF examples took part in the First Gulf War.*

PHOTO FILE

AÉROSPATIALE (WESTLAND) SA 330 PUMA

◄ Still in active service
France deployed Pumas to the former Yugoslavia for use by the U.N. This example fires self-protection flares.

▼ Civilian sales
A Japanese civil SA 330 with flotation gear fitted to the nose and sponsons. This would inflate if the aircraft ditched.

◄ Say aaah!
A Puma will fit in the hold of a C-5 Galaxy—once its rotors have been removed. This RAF Puma is en route to the Persian Gulf in 1991.

◄ Oilfield support
Once the Puma had been equipped with radar for night/all-weather flying, operators in the oil industry became valued customers. Bristow Helicopters supports rigs in the North Sea.

◄ Early prototype
The SA 330A prototype first flew in 1965. This is the fifth of eight prototypes ordered in June 1963. In 1968 the last of this batch was delivered to the U.K. for evaluation.

FACTS AND FIGURES

- ➤ SA 330Js and Ls were the first Western helicopters certified for all-weather flight including operations in icing conditions.
- ➤ Aérospatiale replaced the Puma with the more powerful Super Puma from 1981.
- ➤ In the 1982 Falklands War Argentina used Pumas to move radars from site to site.
- ➤ The RAF's Pumas have given over 35 years' service.
- ➤ The Puma prototype had two 970-kW (1,300-hp.) engines; SA 330Ls have two with 1175kW (1,575 hp.) power.
- ➤ Romanian Pumas have been armed with 9M14 (AT-3) anti-tank missiles.

PROFILE

First all-weather Western chopper

To fill a French army requirement for an all-weather medium-lift transport helicopter, Sud Aviation (later to become part of Aérospatiale) designed the SA 330.

This, France's first attempt to build a medium helicopter without outside technical contributions, was a resounding success, though the all-weather capability did not come until after several years of development.

The first deliveries of SA 330Bs to the French army took place in 1969, the type becoming operational the following year.

Meanwhile, the last pre-production Puma was being modified by Westland for the RAF. After promising tests, a joint production agreement was reached and the British firm built 48 SA 330Es (Puma HC.Mk 1s).

Aérospatiale went on to build 686 SA 330s (before switching production to the Super Puma in 1981) in successively improved versions for numerous export customers. These included civil operators, especially those in the oilfield support industry once the all-weather capability was available in the SA 330J and L. Between 1970 and 1984, Aérospatiale sold 126 civil models in all.

Romanian company IAR began license production in 1977 and by 1994 had built over 200. Production of the IAR-330L continues at the IAR Ghimbav plant near Brasov.

Left: The French Orchidée battlefield surveillance radar program was shelved in 1990, but was revived during Operation Desert Storm. The system was carried aboard a Puma.

Above: The U.K. Defence Research Agency at RAE Boscombe Down operated this Puma HC.Mk 1 for several years.

SA 330L Puma

Type: Medium transport helicopter.

Powerplant: Two 1175kW (1,575-hp.) Turboméca Turmo IVC turboshafts.

Maximum speed: 294 km/h (182 m.p.h.)

Service ceiling: 6000 m (19,700 ft.)

Range: 572 km (355 mi.) at cruising speed.

Accommodation: Up to 20 fully equipped troops or 3200 kg (7,000 lb.) of cargo.

Weapons: Optional provision for various combinations of weapons including cannons, machine guns, rockets and missiles.

Weights: Empty 3615 kg (7,953 lb.); max takeoff 7400 kg (16,280 lb.)

Dimensions:

Main rotor diameter	15 m (49 ft. 3 in.)
Length	18.15m (59 ft. 6 in.)
Height	5.14 m (16 ft. 10 in.)
Rotor disc area	176.7 m² (1,901 sq. ft.)

SA 330H PUMA

The SA 330H is known to the French air force as the SA 330Ba. 1515 was based in the French Caribbean with Overseas Transport Squadron No. 58 in 1983.

The fully articulated main rotor with four aluminum blades on the initial production SA 330s were replaced by a new rotor with composite blades in the SA 330J and L.

Turboméca's Turmo turboshaft engine was also used in the SA.321 Super Frelon heavy transport helicopter of the early 1960s.

The tail rotor has five blades to absorb the power of the two engines while maintaining low noise levels.

Dual flight controls are standard on the Puma, which flies with two flight deck crew. There are two independent hydraulic systems.

The Puma's tricycle landing gear is semi-retractable and there is provision for pop-out flotation gear.

The main cabin of the Puma was designed to hold 18 passengers. In the military transport role 3200 kg (7,000 lb.) can be carried (or 2500 kg/5,500 lb. on an internal hoist). RAF Pumas have a door-mounted rescue hoist with a 575 kg (1,265-lb.) capacity.

Though painted in a predominantly green camouflage color scheme, this Puma also carries large patches of Day-Glo paint work, indicating a search-and-rescue role.

ACTION DATA

SPEED

Late-production Pumas have a good top speed compared to other helicopters in a similar category. Both the Sea King and Mi-8 are, however, slightly larger aircraft.

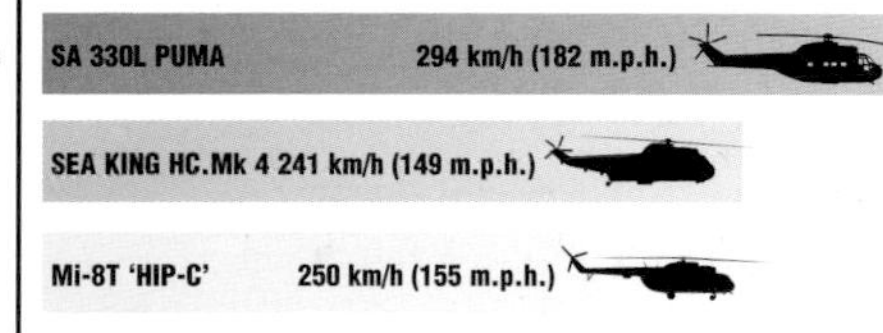

RANGE

Though smaller than the Sea King and Mi-8, the Puma has a good range with its maximum load aboard. With over 90 miles more range, Pumas can lift almost as much as larger types.

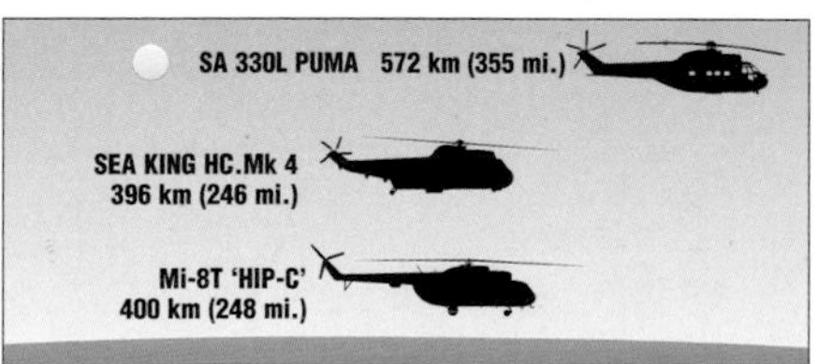

PAYLOAD

Its ability to lift over three tons combined with its relatively compact size makes the Puma ideal for the tactical transport role and also oil rig support sorties.

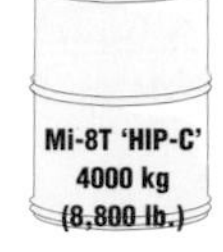

Military Pumas show their colors

ROYAL AIR FORCE SA 330E (PUMA HC.MK 1): XW229 was painted in tiger stripes for a NATO Tiger Meet while with No. 230 Squadron based in West Germany in the 1980s.

IRISH AIR CORPS SA 330J: The single SA 330J used by the Irish Air Corps is a converted civil example. It has the standard weather radar set and is used for troop and VIP transport.

BELGIAN GENDARMERIE SA 330H: Assigned to NATO in time of war are three civil-registered upgraded export model SA 330Hs, normally used for VIP transport and flown by army pilots.

Aérospatiale (SOCATA)

TB 30B Epsilon

● **Piston-engined trainer** ● **Armée de l'Air service** ● **Turbine version**

Derived from the TB 10 Tobago, the TB 30 Epsilon was proposed in both TB 30A and TB 30B versions with 194-kW (260-hp.) and 224-kW (300-hp.) engines. France's Armée de l'Air selected the 30B as its new basic trainer in June 1979; the first prototype flew the following December. Fully aerobatic, the Epsilon is designed to prepare students for more advanced training in the Alpha Jet.

▲ *Though the Epsilon sold in large numbers to the Armée de l'Air, exports have been limited. A turbine-engined variant, the Oméga, followed but has failed to find a buyer in the highly competitive trainer market in a period of shrinking defence budgets.*

Photo File

Aérospatiale (SOCATA) TB 30B Epsilon

▼ **Epsilon prototype**
After the first TB 30 prototype had flown in 1979, the design was fitted with a new tail and modified wings. VO are the last two letters of the aircraft's civil registration F-WZVO.

▲ **Turbine-powered TB 30C**
SOCATA's Epsilon prototype was fitted with a Turboméca TP319 turboprop as the TB 30C. Further modified, this became the Oméga.

TB 31 Oméga ▶
SOCATA developed the Oméga as a private venture, the first example flying in 1989.

◀ **Retractable gear**
A retractable undercarriage was a feature of the TB 20 Trinidad that was carried over to the TB 30.

African exports ▶
Former French colony Togo was one of two Epsilon export customers. Three aircraft were delivered in 1986, followed by an attrition replacement in 1987.

Facts and Figures

- SOCATA's TB 31 Oméga prototype first flew on 30 April 1989 and was a rebuild of the original Epsilon prototype.
- The Oméga features Martin-Baker ejection seats and *g* limits of +7/-3.5.
- Togo's four Epsilons are the only TB 30Bs to feature underwing hardpoints.
- Portuguese Epsilons feature a cathode ray tube (CRT) display for radio and navigation data.
- Between the Epsilon and Oméga there is 60 per cent component commonality.
- Total Epsilon sales totalled 172, including two demonstrators.

PROFILE

France's basic trainers

In addition to the 150 TB 30Bs bought by the French air force, Aérospatiale's SOCATA subsidiary produced one for Portugal, where OGMA assembled a further 17. They are used for the first 120 hours of pilot training.

The French aircraft are operated by the Armée de l'Air's basic flying training school at Cognac, where trainees spend 66.5 hours flying the Epsilon as part of their 23-week course. *G* limits of +6.7/-3.35 allow aerobatic manoeuvres to be carried out.

An export version of the Epsilon can carry a wide range of armament on its four underwing hardpoints, including machine-gun pods, rocket or grenade launchers or two 125-kg bombs. Togo is the only operator, with four delivered, the last in 1987.

The original TB 30B prototype was flown in 1985 with a Turboméca TP319 turboprop, before being modified and fitted with a 364-kW (488-hp.) TP319-1A2 Arrius as the TB 31 Oméga. With its new canopy and space for ejection seats, the Oméga offered higher performance than the Epsilon, including a top speed of 519 km/h (322 m.p.h.). However, the French air force selected the Tucano to replace its Magister trainers and SOCATA has so far failed to find a launch customer.

Above: Colourful tenth anniversary markings are worn by this Armée de l'Air Epsilon seen in 1994.

Below: Portugal's air force ordered 18 Epsilons in 1987. The first was delivered in January 1989, and the rest were assembled in Portugal by OGMA.

TB 30B Epsilon

Type: two-seat basic primary/basic trainer

Powerplant: one 224-kW (300-hp.) Lycoming AEIO-540-L1B5D flat-six piston engine

Maximum speed: 380 km/h (236 m.p.h.)

Endurance: 3 hours 45 min

Climb rate: 564 m/min (1,850 f.p.m.)

Service ceiling: 7010 m (23,000 ft.)

Weights: empty equipped 932 kg (2,050 lb.); maximum take-off and landing 1250 kg (2,750 lb.)

Armament: (export) up to 300 kg (660 lb.) of bombs, machine-gun pods or grenade launchers

Dimensions:

span	7.92 m (26 ft.)
length	7.59 m (24 ft. 10 in.)
height	2.66 m (8 ft. 9 in.)
wing area	9.00 m² (97 sq. ft.)

TB 30B EPSILON

Groupement Ecole 315 at Cognac/Châteaubernard took delivery of its first Epsilons in 1984. Employing the type as an *ab initio* pilot trainer, the unit had 150 of the aircraft by late 1989.

Unlike the high-performance Oméga, the Epsilon is not fitted with ejection seats and has a framed canopy. The cockpit is arranged to prepare student pilots for conversion to the Alpha Jet advanced trainer.

That the Epsilon is a derivative of the TB 10 Tobago four/five-seat light plane is most evident in the tailfin design. Changes introduced on the second prototype included increased wing span and rounded wingtips. Development of the TB 30 began in 1977 to an Armée de l'Air requirement.

The Epsilon's fuselage is a light alloy semi-monocoque structure. Fixed surfaces are metal skinned, while the elevators and rudder are covered with polyester fabric.

One of Lycoming's (later AlliedSignal's) large and successful family of air-cooled flat-configuration piston engines powers the Epsilon.

Epsilons built for export can carry a variety of stores on four underwing pylons; up to 80 kg (176 lb.) each on outer hardpoints and 160 kg (352 lb.) each on inner pylons.

The rear instructor's seat in this dual-control aircraft is raised 70 mm (3 in.) to improve visibility. The two-part canopy slides to the rear. Aft of the cabin is a small baggage compartment.

COMBAT DATA

POWER

Chile's ENAER Pillán shares the Epsilon's AlliedSignal (Lycoming) air-cooled, flat-six engine of 224 kW (300 hp.). SIAI-Marchetti's SF.260, derived from a civil light aircraft, has a smaller engine.

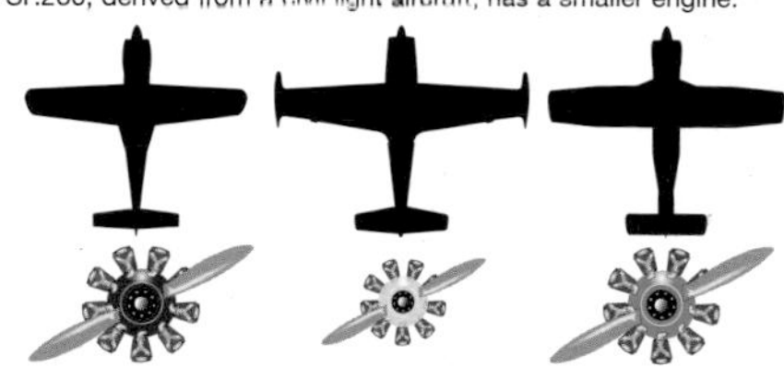

TB 30B EPSILON 224 kW (300 hp.) | SF.260W WARRIOR 194 kW (260 hp.) | T-35A PILLÁN 224 kW (300 hp.)

MAXIMUM CLIMB RATE

Climb rate is an area in which the Epsilon outperforms the other types, thanks to its good power-to-weight ratio. This also gives the type superior manoeuvrability.

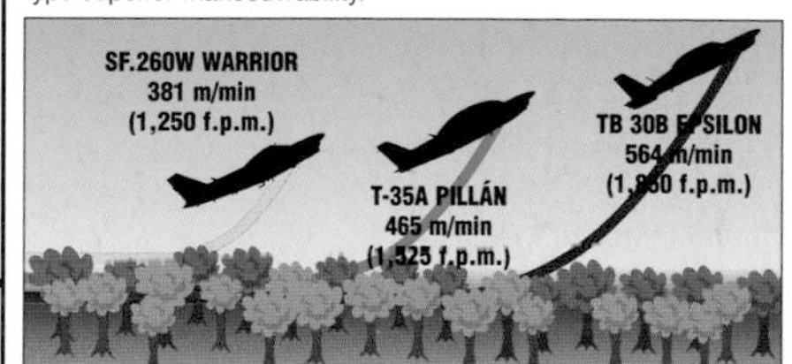

MAXIMUM ORDNANCE

The Pillán has strengthened wings able to carry almost 500 kg (1,102 lb.) of stores. Both the Epsilon and Warrior are restricted to 300 kg (661 lb.), though the Epsilon has four hardpoints stressed to hold 480 kg (1,058 lb.).

Turbine-powered trainers today

■ EMBRAER TUCANO: Brazil's turbine-powered EMB-312 has sold well in export markets and served as the basis for the Shorts-built, Garrett-engined Tucano sold to the RAF, Kenya and Kuwait.

■ ENAER T-35DT AUCÁN: Like the Oméga, the Aucán was a derivative of a piston-engined trainer, the Pillán. Chilean company ENAER developed the Pillán from the Piper PA-28 Dakota.

■ PILATUS PC-9: One of the Tucano's main competitors has been the Swiss PC-9. In 1997 the type was chosen by the USAF and US Navy to fill the need for a trainer to replace the T-34C and T-37B.

AGUSTA (SIAI-MARCHETTI) S.211

● **Advanced jet trainer** ● **Light attack aircraft** ● **Low cost**

Developed originally by SIAI-Marchetti, the S.211 joined a new stable of military trainers in January 1997 when ownership of the company was transferred from Agusta to Aermacchi. First flying in April 1981, by 1988 it had been sold to four countries. An upgraded version, known as the S.211A, lost out to Beechcraft's modified Pilatus PC-9 in the JPATS competition to supply a new primary trainer for both the US Air Force and Navy.

▲ *Besides its principal role as a trainer, the S.211 is also fully combat-capable, a feature that has contributed to its adoption by a number of air forces looking for a versatile dual-role aircraft.*

PHOTO FILE

AGUSTA (SIAI-MARCHETTI) S.211

◀ **JPATS**
An uprated S.211A was unsuccessfully shortlisted for the US Joint Primary Aircraft Training System (JPATS).

▼ **Lightweight performer**
Although a jet, the S.211 weighs little more than turboprop trainers, yet can out-perform them in most respects.

◀ **Service in the Far East**
S.211s were acquired by three Far Eastern nations – Brunei, the Philippines and Singapore – which operate them as trainers.

▼ **For export only**
Despite being of Italian origin, the S.211 has not been adopted by the country's own air force.

▲ **First flight**
Work began on the project in June 1977, with the first prototype, registered I-SITF, taking to the air on 10 April 1981.

FACTS AND FIGURES

- The Republic of Haiti, in the Caribbean, acquired a small number of S.211s in 1985. They were sold five years later.
- The S.211 was developed as a private venture by SIAI-Marchetti.
- JPATS S.211As were required to have a 14,400-hour fatigue life.
- Pratt & Whitney's JT15D turbojet engine also powers the USAF's Beech T-1A Jayhawk trainer.
- JPATS S.211A construction would have been split 50-50, with assembly in the US.
- Agusta proposed an S.211 variant with an improved navigation/attack system.

PROFILE

Lightweight, low-cost trainer

Economical operating costs and jet performance were the goal of the S.211. Weight is kept low by the extensive use of composite materials in its construction, and its reasonably high performance is accompanied by safe stalling and spinning characteristics, which are essential in a trainer.

In its alternative attack role, the S.211 can carry a useful ordnance load, including a wide range of rockets and gun pods, on four wing stations. Sales have proved disappointing, with only the Philippines, Singapore and Haiti having bought a total of 52 aircraft by 1988. Since then, Brunei has been the only other customer. Most of Singapore's 30 S.211s were assembled locally, and the Philippine Aerospace Development Corporation was responsible for assembling 14 of the 18 aircraft delivered to the Philippine air force.The improved variant, the S.211A, was developed in partnership with Grumman and put forward unsuccessfully for the US JPATS competition. It featured a 14.2-kN (3,195-lb.-thrust) JT15D-5C engine for a higher top speed of 766 km/h (475 m.p.h.). Climb rate, range, service ceiling and *g* loadings were all improved, and weapon load was increased to 1090 kg (2,400 lb.).

Left: One of the three SIAI-Marchetti company demonstrators, wearing this distinctive desert camouflage, is seen poised for touch-down.

Below: Serialled I-SIJF, the second prototype flew three months after the first machine. Both aircraft wore this distinctive SIAI-Marchetti company livery.

S.211

Type: basic trainer and light strike aircraft

Powerplant: one 11.12-kN (2,500-lb.-thrust) Pratt & Whitney Canada JT15D-4C turbofan

Maximum speed: 667 km/h (414 m.p.h.) at 7620 m (25,000 ft.)

Initial climb rate: 1280 m/min (4,200 f.p.m.)

Range: 1168 km (724 mi.) on internal fuel

Service ceiling: 12,200 m (40,000 ft.)

Weights: empty 1850 kg (4,070 lb.), maximum take-off 3150 kg (6,930 lb.)

Armament: two 20-mm or four 12.7-mm (.50 in.) or 7.62-mm (.30 in.) gun pods, four rocket launchers, or up to 600 kg (1,320 lb.) of bombs

Dimensions:

span	8.43 m	(27 ft. 8 in.)
length	9.31 m	(30 ft. 6 in.)
height	3.80 m	(12 ft. 6 in.)
wing area	12.60 m²	(136 sq. ft.)

S.211

The Philippines acquired 18 S.211s, of which four were built in Italy, the remainder being assembled locally. All were assigned to the 100th Training Wing at Fernando, Luzon.

Following in the footsteps of other modern jet trainers, the S.211 features a high-mounted tandem cockpit that, in addition to offering excellent visibility, provides space for full navigation and communication equipment. Both pilot and instructor sit on Martin Baker ejection seats, which are designed to punch through the canopy.

A mid-mounted supercritical wing gives the S.211 exceptional performance and manoeuvrability at high load. The ailerons feature a blunt trailing edge to enhance their effectiveness and control response.

Philippine aircraft are operated by one squadron. Half of them were delivered in natural metal and wear orange bands on the nose, rear fuselage and wings.

The main flight controls are mechanical, being operated by push rods. Secondary systems, such as the undercarriage and wheel brakes, are actuated hydraulically.

Fuel is carried internally in the wings and fuselage, with a total capacity of 802 litres (212 gal.). The aircraft can also be equipped with twin wing tanks containing 132 litres (35 gal.) each, which are normally used for ferry flights.

Powering the S.211 is a single Pratt & Whitney JT15D-4C twin spool turbofan, previously used only on business jet aircraft. Of advanced design, this engine has a good bypass ratio and gives excellent fuel consumption.

ACTION DATA

CLIMB RATE

Current jet trainers possess excellent performance and manoeuvrability. The S.211, although capable in its own right, is not quite in the same league of performance as the C.101 Aviojet or MB-339, both of which are used by their respective countries' national air display teams.

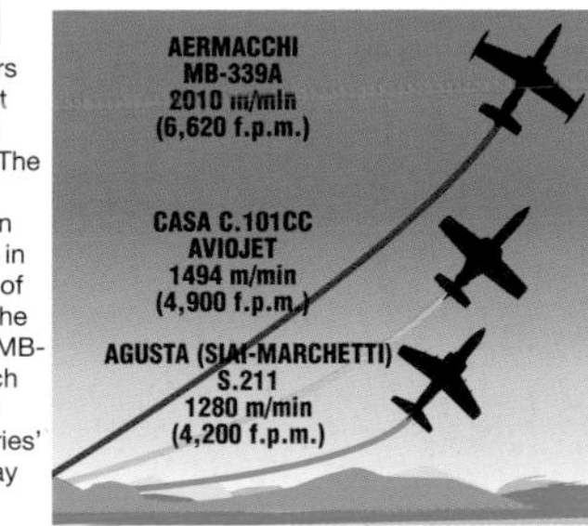

THRUST

Not quite as powerful as rivals such as the CASA Aviojet or MB-339, the S.211 nevertheless has an exceptional power-to-weight ratio, being one of the lightest operational jet trainers around. All three aircraft were designed as low-cost machines.

***G* LIMIT**

Today, the vast majority of combat trainers in service have been designed to withstand high *g* loadings, thereby providing performance as close as possible to that of front-line aircraft. The S.211 is capable of pulling more than 6 *g*.

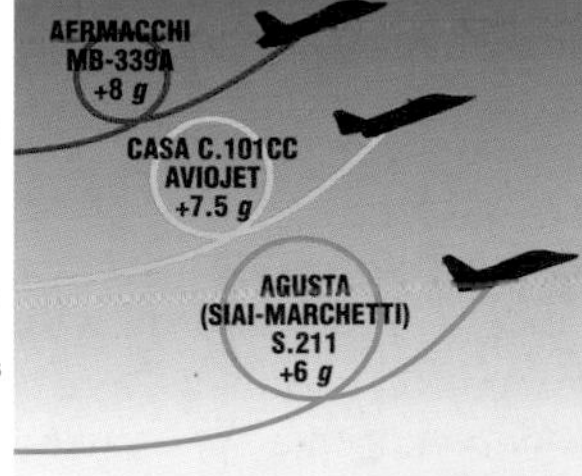

European training/light attack aircraft

■ **AERO L-39 ALBATROSS:** Originating from former Czechoslovakia, the L-39 has proved a highly successful light attack/training aircraft.

■ **BAe HAWK T.Mk 1:** RAF Hawks serve with training and weapons conversions units, and some are configured for the air defence role.

■ **CASA C.101CC AVIOJET:** This dedicated attack version of the C.101 trainer first flew in November 1983.

■ **DASSAULT/DORNIER ALPHA JET:** Jointly developed by France and Germany, the Alpha Jet remains in service with both countries' air forces.

AIDC

AT-3 TSU CHIANG

● **Basic trainer** ● **First jet developed in Taiwan** ● **Display mount**

After building a version of the Pazmany PL-1 trainer, the Aero Industry Development Center (AIDC) produced its own turboprop basic trainer, the T-CH-1 Chung Tsing. In the early 1970s the AIDC started building more than 200 F-5 fighters for the Taiwan air force, and in 1975 it started work on its own jet aircraft design. Flown for the first time in September 1980, the AT-3 is the Taiwanese air force's standard basic trainer.

▲ *Considerable pride in the development of the AT-3 is reflected in the formation of a display team equipped with the type. The team is based at the Air Force Academy at Kangshan.*

PHOTO FILE

AIDC AT-3 TSU CHIANG

Learning curve ▶
The Tsu Chiang is proving to be an excellent training tool for introducing potential front-line pilots to advanced fast jet aircraft.

▲ Clear view
Visibility for the pupil and instructor, vital in training aircraft, is achieved with a large canopy.

Dedicated attack ▶
The single-seat version (above) developed for the close support role is known as the AT-3B.

▼ Basic design
Though offering little in the way of advanced design features, the AT-3 was a major step forward for the Taiwanese aviation industry.

▲ Air-to-air
Though a basic trainer, when required the AT-3 can be fitted with wingtip launch rails for Sidewinder air-to-air missiles and pylons for the delivery of a wide range of bombs and rockets.

FACTS AND FIGURES

- The first flight of the AT-3 took place on 16 September 1980 at the AIDC test facility in Taiwan.
- A contract was placed for 60 aircraft by the ROCAF who are the prime operators.
- For attack duties a single-seat close air-support version was developed.
- Seven external stores pylons are available to carry a wide range of bombs and missiles.
- Fewer than four hours of maintenance is needed on the AT-3 after a one-hour flight.
- An attack version designated A-3 Lui Meng was developed but then halted.

PROFILE

Taiwanese jet trainer

Although a fairly conventional aircraft, the AT-3 represented an ambitious step on the part of the AIDC. It also helped pave the way for the company to develop its own supersonic fighter design in the shape of the Ching-Kuo, when the US government prohibited the export of advanced fighters to the country.

Of the 60 AT-3s delivered between 1984 and 1990, 20 have been modified as AT-3B attack aircraft. Equipped with a version of the F-16's APG-66 radar and fire-control system, they have a weapons bay under the rear cockpit which can carry machine-gun packs.

Other stores can be carried on a fuselage centreline pylon and four wing pylons, and there are wingtip rails for air-to-air missiles. Another attack variant, the single-seat A-3 Lui Meng, was built in prototype form only. The appearance of the AT-3B led to the original model being redesignated the AT-3A. It serves with the Taiwan air force (ROCAF) academy, and pilot cadets fly it for the first part of their jet training. The attack version equips the air force's No. 71 Squadron at Tainan.

Above: Taiwanese air force student pilots receive 120 hours' instruction on the AT-3 before advancing to a front-line squadron.

Above: The bright colours of this AT-3 signify its allocation to the Taiwanese display team based at Kangshan.

AT-3B Tsu Chiang

Type: two-seat basic trainer

Powerplant: two 15.57-kN (3,500-lb.-thrust) Garrett TF3 731-2-2L turbofan engines

Maximum speed: 904 km/h (561 m.p.h.) at 11,000 m (36,000 ft.)

Initial climb rate: 3078 m/min (10,100 f.p.m.)

Range: 2279 km (1,413 mi.)

Service ceiling: 14,625 m (48,000 ft.)

Weights: empty 3856 kg (8,483 lb.); take-off 7938 kg (17,464 lb.)

Armament: two wingtip AAMs; 2721 kg (5,986 lb.) of bombs can be fitted

Dimensions:

span	10.46 m (34 ft. 4 in.)
length	12.90 m (42 ft. 4 in.)
height	4.36 m (14 ft. 4 in.)
wing area	21.93 m² (235 sq. ft.)

AT-3 Tsu Chiang

The first military jet developed in Taiwan, the AT-3 is proving to be highly suitable as a fast jet trainer. A single-seat attack version has also been developed and is in limited service with the ROCAF.

The pilots are seated on zero-zero ejection seats which allow the crew to escape from the aircraft at ground level if necessary.

The two turbofan engines are easy to maintain, helping the AT-3 to be operated in the bustling environment of a flight training academy.

Of conventional construction, the AT-3 consists of a light-alloy structure with heavy plate machine skinning over the semi-monocoque fuselage.

Visibility from the cockpit is exceptional. The large canopy and the raised position of the ejection seats allow excellent crew co-ordination.

Although the AT-3 is only a trainer, a state-of-the-art radar is installed which is compatible with later aircraft on to which the student progresses.

A well-equipped cockpit instrument panel is fitted for each pilot featuring multi-functional displays, and for attack duties a sophisticated head-up display.

In a more offensive role, the AT-3 can be fitted with wingtip missiles for air combat. Pylons can also be attached to the wings to allow bombs to be carried.

The high visibility day-glo patches on this AT-3 signify that this aircraft serves in the flight training role, preparing cadets for fast-jet operations.

ACTION DATA

RANGE

The long range of the AT-3B is a reflection of the aircraft's dual role as a battlefield attack type. Restricted to purely training duties, the Spanish Aviojet offers a more modest range and consequently has no secondary attack role in Spanish service. Although the largest of the three the T-4's range is only fair.

AT-3B 2279 km (1,413 mi.)
C.101CC AVIOJET 519 km (322 mi.)
T-4 1297 km (804 mi.)

MAXIMUM SPEED

The twin-engine layout of the AT-3 allows a high performance to be achieved, which undoubtedly eases conversion to front-line jets for the Taiwanese pilots. Although Japan's T-4 is the best performer, this is reflected in the high cost of the aircraft which has reduced its export potential.

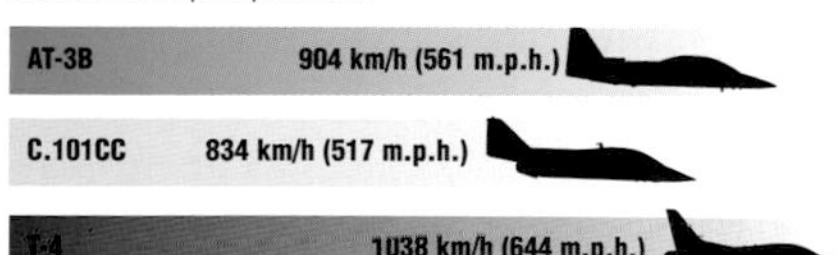

SERVICE CEILING

With the normal limited thrust of typical training types, a surprisingly good performance is achieved by the AT-3B. By operating at a high altitude a saving in fuel is possible, while increasing the safety margin for the pilot.

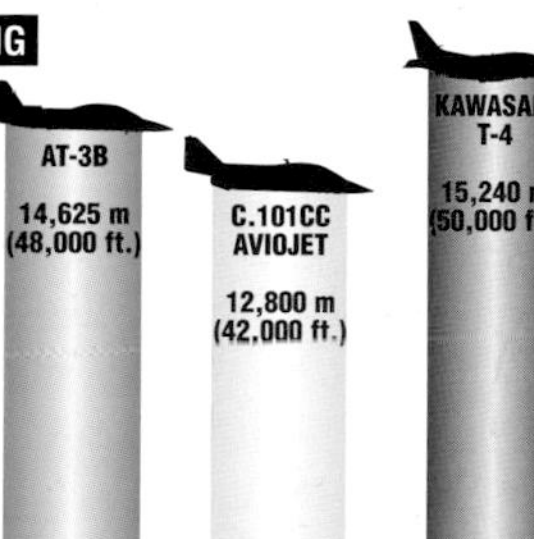

Defending the Republic

T-CH-1 CHUNG TSING: The first military aircraft of indigenous Taiwanese design, the T-CH-1 was heavily influenced by the T-28 Trojan. A reconnaissance variant is still in service.

F-104G STARFIGHTER: Purchased from surplus European stocks, the F-104 has been progressively updated. The aircraft will remain in front-line service for the foreseeable future.

F-5E TIGER II: First delivered in 1973, the F-5E at present is the most potent aircraft in the Taiwanese inventory, the twin-seat F-5F is also in service in a dual trainer-attack role.

AIRTECH

CN.235

● Twin turboprop tactical transport ● Excellent STOL performance

▲ *Airborne troops drop from doors fitted to both sides of the fuselage of a CN.235M military transport. The aircraft can carry and deliver up to 46 fully equipped paratroopers.*

It looks like a mini-Hercules, and performs like one. Designed and built in Spain and Indonesia, the Airtech CN.235 is a highly capable, very successful short-range tactical transport. Intended to operate from short, semi-prepared fields, this twin-turboprop machine has proven itself a highly effective and economical aircraft, suitable for a variety of uses from cargo-hauling through casualty evacuation and VIP transport to armed maritime patrol.

PHOTO FILE

AIRTECH CN.235

Airborne assault ▶
The CN.235's high swept tail and large rear loading ramp were designed to allow the delivery of cargo by parachute.

▼ Armée de l'Air
The French air force operates eight CN.235s alongside larger Transall C-160s and Hercules.

▲ Saudi CN.235
Saudi Arabia is one of the smaller operators of Airtech's CN.235, with just two transport and two luxury-interior VIP versions.

▼ U.S. powerplants
Like all CN.235s, this United Arab Emirates aircraft is powered by two General Electric CT7-9C four-blade turboprop engines.

Coastal persuasion ▶
The CN.235MPA Persuader is a maritime patroller that has search radar, FLIR surveillance sensors, and six wing pylons for armament.

FACTS AND FIGURES

- ➤ The first CN.235s to be delivered began coming off the Indonesian production lines in December 1986.
- ➤ Military CN.235s can land on airstrips less than 500 m (1,650 ft.) in length.
- ➤ As a commuter airliner, the CN.235 can carry up to 44 passengers.
- ➤ The coastal patrol CN.235MPA can carry up to 3500 kg (7,700 lb.) of torpedoes or anti-ship missiles on six underwing pylons.
- ➤ In the medevac role the CN.235 can carry 24 stretchers and four attendants.
- ➤ The cargo bay is 9.65 m (31.8 ft.) long and has a deck area of 22.82 m² (246 sq. ft.).

PROFILE

Multi-role Spanish-Indonesian airlifter

Spain's Construcciones Aeronauticas SA, or CASA, is one of the oldest aircraft manufacturing companies in the world. Founded in 1923, it seems an unlikely complement to Indonesia, one of the world's newer aviation nations. But in partnership with Industri Pesawat Terbang Nusantara, or IPTN, it has set up the joint company known as Airtech, specifically to develop and produce the twin turboprop CN.235 light/medium short-haul transport, and a successful partnership it has become.

Development work began in 1980. First flown on 11 November 1983 in Spain and on December 30 of that year in Indonesia, the CN.235 follows the standard layout of a modern military transport, with circular-section pressurized fuselage, high wing and tail, and rear loading ramp.

The CN-235's excellent rough-field STOL performance has seen it achieve considerable success on the export market. By the mid 1990s, more than 200 had been sold to at least 17 military customers and another 30 or more to civil operators.

The majority of CN.235s sold have been tactical transports, but a number have been fitted out as VIP transports, and the CN.235MPA Persuader is a specialized maritime patrol variant.

Above: South Korea has taken delivery of 12 CN.235s, and is one of more than 17 countries that operate the aircraft.

Right: The Moroccan air force operates six CN.235s in the general transport role, plus one example for VIP duties.

CN.235M Series 100

Type: short-range military transport

Powerplant: two 1394.5-kW (1,870-hp.) General Electric CT7-9C turboprops

Maximum cruise speed: 460 km/h (285 m.p.h.) at 4500 m (14,750 ft.)

Maximum climb rate: 579 m/min (1,900 f.p.m.)

Range: 1500 km (930 mi.) with max payload; 4355 km (2,700 mi.) with 3550-kg (7,810-lb.) payload

Service ceiling: 8110 m (26,600 ft.)

Maximum takeoff weight: 16,500 kg (54,120 lb.)

Payload: 48 troops or 46 paratroops or 24 stretchers or 6000 kg (13,200 lb.) of cargo

Dimensions:

span	25.81 m (84 ft. 7 in.)
length	21.35 m (70 ft.)
height	8.18 m (26 ft. 10 in.)
wing area	59.10 m² (636 sq. ft.)

CN.235M

Standard military version of the CN.235, seen here in Spanish colors. The Spanish air force operates 26 of these aircraft.

The CN.235 has a conventional cockpit, and is usually flown by a two-person flight crew of pilot and copilot.

From the 31st production aircraft the CN.235 has been fitted with a more powerful variant of the General Electric CT7 turboprop.

The high-lift wing is of conventional alloy, but the leading- and trailing-edge flaps are made from advanced composite materials.

The landing gear is carried on sponsons on the fuselage sides, and does not intrude into the cargo compartment. It is suitable for operation from semi-prepared surfaces.

The fuselage is of conventional semi-monocoque construction, and is largely built from aluminum alloys.

The upswept tail and tall fin was incorporated into the design to allow the large rear cargo door.

The lower part of the divided rear door swings down to serve as a cargo ramp for loading larger cargoes, such as NATO standard containers. The ramp can be opened in flight to allow parachute delivery of equipment.

ACTION DATA

PAYLOAD

The CN.235 has several rivals in the short-range tactical transport field. It has a larger payload than the similar-sized Canadian DHC-8M, but it cannot match the much bulkier Italian Alenia G222.

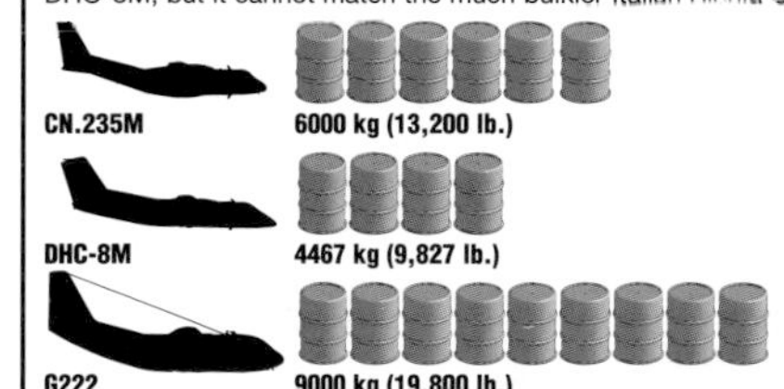

TAKEOFF DISTANCE

While the CN.235 is a good short-field performer it needs more runway than the DHC-8M, which sacrifices cargo load for performance. The far more powerful G222 performs even better.

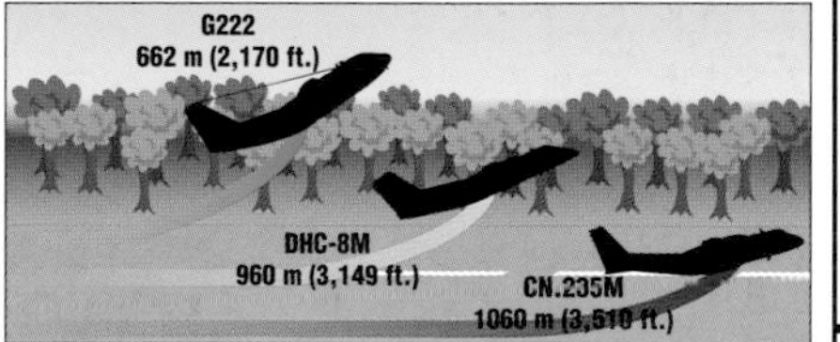

RANGE

The CN.235 has a longer range with maximum load than its rivals when carrying a full load, although the G222's capacious fuselage can lift around three tons more than the Spanish/Indonesian transport. The Canadian DHC-8 was designed as a passenger carrier, and so does not perform as well when carrying heavy freight loads.

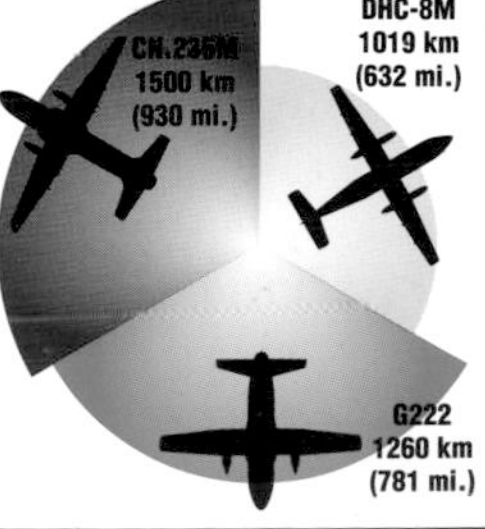

Roles of the CN.235

VERSATILITY: The CN.235's roller-equipped cargo bay can carry a variety of fittings depending on the aircraft's mission.

MEDEVAC: The CN.235's circular section pressure fuselage with rear loading ramp is easy to convert to a 24-stretcher ambulance configuration.

MARITIME PATROL: The CN.235MPA has added radar, night vision and electronic sensors, and can carry weapons.

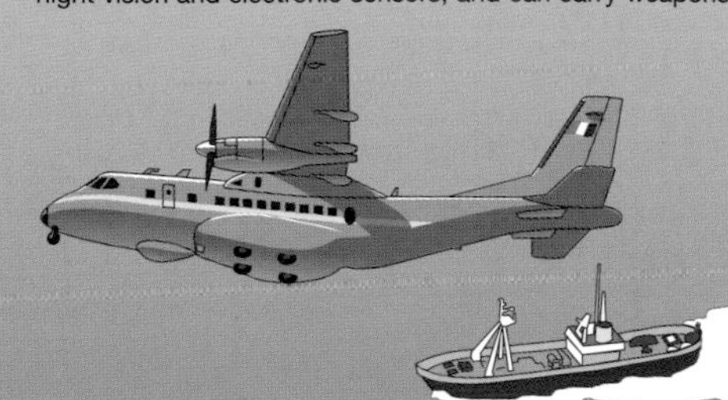

TRANSPORT: The CN.235 can carry troops or cargo in standard LD3 containers, or a mix of both.

ALENIA (AERITALIA)

G222

● Italian twin-engined tactical transport ● Operators worldwide

Originally designed by Fiat in the 1960s and flown for the first time in July 1970, the G222 had to fulfil the Italian air force's requirement for an aircraft that was able to cope with short, semi-prepared airstrips, mountainous terrain and extreme weather. The Aeronautica Militare Italiana (AMI) remains the type's biggest user, but the G222's ruggedness and adaptability have also won orders from other military operators and development continues.

▲ *An Italian M151 jeep is driven onto a G222 transport. Although only 100 examples of Italy's standard tactical lifter have been built, around half have been exported to seven other air arms.*

PHOTO FILE

ALENIA (AERITALIA) G222

▲ Cargo capacity
The G222 can lift a maximum payload of nine tons. It can air-drop palletised cargo or up to 32 fully-equipped paratroops.

▲ Export success
Ten customers have bought the G222 and use the transport aircraft in a variety of roles.

C-27 Spartan ▶
The USAF operates the C-27 Spartan in Central America.

◀ Calibration craft
Surprisingly agile for an aircraft of its size, the G222 is a popular Italian air show performer. This example is a G222RM instrument calibration aircraft and is one of four built for the Italian air force.

Short take-off ▶
The G222 excels at flying into and out of short, rough airstrips. It can take off in less than 1000 m (3,200 ft.).

FACTS AND FIGURES

- After operational evaluation by the Italian air force, a production G222 was flown in late 1975 and 46 machines were ordered.
- A NATO competition in the mid-1960s resulted in the G222.
- Two prototypes (MM582 and 583) were flown on 18 July 1970 and 22 July 1971.
- A collaborative manufacturing effort between Italian aerospace firms produced components for the G222.
- Four versions are in service with the Aeronautica Militare Italiana.
- Libyan Rolls-Royce Tyne-powered G222s use engines from ex-RAF Belfasts.

PROFILE

Italian tactical airlifter

Many G222s were delivered in special configurations for the Italian air force. Four were completed as flight inspection aircraft, with equipment to analyse the accuracy of radio navigation aids. A further eight were built as aerial firefighters and two as electronic warfare machines. One has been modified as a maritime patrol aircraft for the Italian customs service. The standard military transport can also be adapted to other roles. Quick-change kits turn it into an aeromedical aircraft, and in this form it has been used to support Red Cross operations as far afield as Kampuchea and Peru. Export customers include Argentina, Dubai, Nigeria, Somalia and Venezuela, and 20 were completed with Rolls-Royce Tyne engines for Libya. In 1990 the USAF selected the G222 to support US forces in Latin America. These aircraft were assembled by Alenia and sent to Chrysler Aerospace for installation of mission equipment.

In 1996 Alenia and Lockheed agreed to develop a modernised version as the C-27J, with upgraded systems similar to those installed in the latest four-engined, high-technology C-130J Hercules.

Above: Italy operates the G222SAA (Sistema Aeronautico Antincendio) firefighting version. The G222RM (Radio Misure) calibrates airfield radios and radars.

Below: Alongside the regular transport, the Italian air force operates three specialised versions. This is the G222VS (Versione Speciale), which is equipped with various antennas for the electronic warfare role.

G222TCM

The AMI bought 46 aircraft and operates the largest number of G222s. This is a standard transport, wearing the markings of 46a Aerobrigata Trasporti Medi (Medium Air Transport Wing), based at Pisa-San Giusto.

The G222 normally carries a crew of three – a pilot, co-pilot and a flight engineer/radio operator. A loadmaster can also be carried in the cargo hold.

Under licence from General Electric, Fiat produced the T64-GE-P4D engine for the G222. Libyan aircraft are powered by Rolls-Royce Tyne engines.

The cargo hold can carry a maximum of 44 troops or 32 paratroops or 9000 kg (19,800 lb.) of freight. Both the flightdeck and hold are partially pressurised (and air-conditioned) to give an environment which is equivalent to that at1200 m (4,000 ft.) when flying at 6000 m (19,700 ft.).

De-icing strips line the leading edges of all wing and tail surfaces. The leading edges of the propeller blades and the spinners are de-iced electrically. A mixture of hot air and electrical heating keeps the engine intakes clear of ice.

Paratroops are usually deployed via two doors, one on either side of the rear fuselage, but can use the rear doors if necessary.

As on most modern tactical airlifters, the upswept rear fuselage of the G222 contains rear loading doors which can be opened in flight for air-dropping cargo.

G222TCM

Type: light/medium tactical transport

Powerplant: two 2535-kW (3,400-hp.) Fiat-built General Electric T64-GE-P4D turboprops

Maximum speed: 540 km/h (335 m.p.h.)

Initial climb rate: 520 m/min (1,700 f.p.m.)

Take-off run: 662 m (2,170 ft.) at maximum take-off weight

Range: 1371 km (850 mi.) with maximum payload

Service ceiling: 7620 m (25,000 ft.)

Weights: empty 15,400 kg (33,880 lb.); maximum take-off 28,000 kg (61,600 lb.)

Payload: maximum 9000 kg (19,800 lb.)

Dimensions:

span	28.70 m (94 ft. 2 in.)
length	22.70 m (74 ft. 5 in.)
height	9.80 m (32 ft. 2 in.)
wing area	82.00 m² (882 sq. ft.)

ACTION DATA

MAXIMUM PAYLOAD

In service use performance considerations are likely to restrict the Antonov An-72 and Kawasaki C-1 to loads of a similar weight to those of the G222.

G222TCM 9000 kg (19,800 lb.)

An-72AT 'COALER-C' 10,000 kg (22,000 lb.)

C-1 11,900 kg (26,200 lb.)

TAKE-OFF RUN

Outstanding short take-off performance is a feature of the C-1, but it is not as rugged as the G222 or An-72 and is therefore restricted to better prepared airstrips. In addition, the jets are again weight restricted, while the G222 performs as shown with a full payload.

G222TCM 662 m (2,170 ft.)

An-72AT 'COALER-C' 930 m (3,050 ft.)

C-1 640 m (2,100 ft.)

RANGE

With maximum payload and maximum fuel, the efficient turboprop engines of the G222 allow it to outperform its jet rivals in range. With full payload, the jet transports – especially the 'Coaler-C' – offer only limited range, which is fine in a tactical scenario but restricts their overall versatility. The jets have the advantage of flying faster sectors, however.

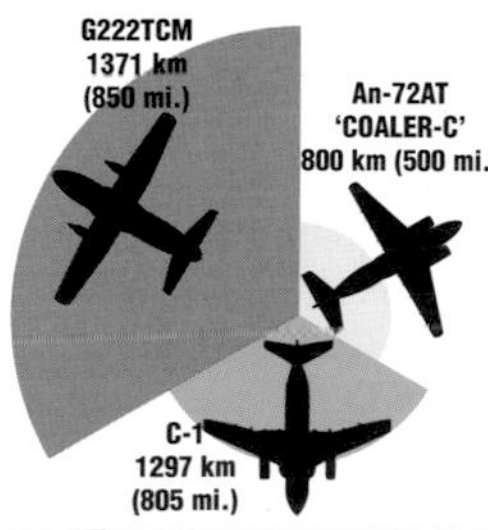

International G222 operators

ARGENTINA: Comando de Aviacion del Ejercito (Argentine Army Aviation Command) took delivery of three G222s in 1977. They played no part in the Falklands War.

DUBAI: Part of the United Arab Emirates, Dubai was the first export customer for the G222. Only one aircraft was delivered, in November 1976, and this remains in service.

LIBYA: Libya's 20 G222s were fitted with Rolls-Royce Tyne turboprops to overcome the American embargo on supplying T64 engines. They were used during the intervention in Chad.

SOMALIA: Somalia originally ordered six G222s, but only two were delivered, in 1980. They suffered from shortages of spares and were both destroyed during the 1993 civil war.

AMX INTERNATIONAL

AMX

● Tactical striker ● Light-attack aircraft ● Reconnaissance

Deemed good enough to replace two able old warriors, the Fiat G.91 and Lockheed F-104 in Italian air force service, the Aeritalia/Aermacchi AMX was originally conceived as a small multi-role light-attack aircraft in 1976. EMBRAER of Brazil joined the Italian concern and this collaboration eventually proved fruitful. The aircraft entered service with Italy's 51 Stormo in October 1989 and Brazil's 1 Esquadrao in October 1989.

▲ *Showing that it can help make light fighters, as well as trainers and executive aircraft, has been an important factor for EMBRAER. It makes the air intakes, pylons, wings and reconnaissance pallet.*

PHOTO FILE

AMX INTERNATIONAL AMX

▲ Night mission
Provision for forward-looking infrared or passive night goggles gives the AMX night strike capability, which would be much further enhanced by a TIALD pod.

▲ Light fighter
For nations such as Italy, the AMX is a good compromise between light-strike advanced trainers like the MB.339 and heavy-strike aircraft like the Tornado.

▲ Maximum load
Optimized for tactical strike, the AMX usually carries cluster bombs, rocket pods or Skyshark dispenser weapons.

◀ Two-seater
The AMX-T two-seat conversion trainer is fully combat capable, though it has shorter range than the single-seater.

Modern design ▶
Despite its plain appearance, the AMX is a modern design, with low maintenance requirements and good reliability. The aircraft can stand at 15 minutes readiness for 30 days with limited servicing.

FACTS AND FIGURES

- Series production of the AMX began in July 1986, and the first aircraft rolled out on 29 March 1988.
- Brazilian AMXs have two 30-mm cannon, and Italian ones have one 20-mm Vulcan.
- An engine problem resulted in the crash of the prototype AMX on 1 June 1984.
- The AMX can carry weapons on seven hardpoints and boost this figure to 12 by using multiple stores carriers.
- Brazilian AMXs carry the MAA-1 Piranha missile for self defense.
- A proposed electronic warfare AMX with HARM missiles has not been developed.

PROFILE

AMX Latin light striker

Designed from the outset to undertake the strike role, the AMX International is the result of European and South American collaboration to build a wholly new airplane for the Italian air force, and has proven remarkably successful. The Italian requirement was made known in 1977 and, rather than buy 'off-the-shelf' or opt for a refurbished older type, the decision was taken to design a new aircraft.

Both the larger Italian aerospace manufacturers pooled resources in April 1978 and Brazil joined in July 1981, with the object of securing the Italian design as a follow-up to the MB.326.

The AMX began flight testing in May 1984. Trials set out to establish that the planned low-level delivery of a variety of ordnance (up to 2722 kg (5,988 lb.)) over a 370-km (230-mi.) range was a viable alternative to big and expensive hardware. This was indeed proven but the AMX lacks radar and has no all-weather capability. But with the AMX/A-1 in service in Italy and Brazil, and a trainer version, the AMX-T, undergoing flight-tests, the development program promises some interesting new models, with an anti-shipping or electronic warfare variant still possible.

Another highly successful collaborative program for Italy and Brazil, the AMX has yet to win export orders in the face of severe competition from the Hawk 200.

Brazil's AMXs are the most modern strike aircraft in Latin America, and the type may well be ordered by other nations in the region. It offers a performance capability between Brazil's F-5s and Mirage IIIs.

AMX

Type: close support fighter-bomber.

Powerplant: one 49.10-kN (11,000-lb.-thrust) Rolls-Royce Spey Mk 107 turbofan.

Max speed: 914 km/h (567 m.p.h.)

Service ceiling: 13,000 m (42,640 ft.)

Range: 890 km (552 mi.)

Weights: empty 6700 kg (14,740 lb.); loaded 12,500 kg (27,500 lb.)

Weapons: one M61-A1 20-mm cannon or two DEFA 554 30-mm cannon; and up to a 2722-kg (5,988-lb.) bomb load.

Dimensions:		
	span	8.87 m (29 ft.)
	length	13.23 m (43 ft.)
	height	4.55 m (15 ft.)
	wing area	21 m² (226 sq. ft.)

AMX

The Fuerza Aera Braziliana designated the AMX as the A-1. The first Brazilian unit was 1 Esquadrao of 16 Grupo de Aviaco de Caca at Santa Cruz.

The wing has spoilers in front of the ailerons, which augment the ailerons as well as act as lift-dumpers and airbrakes. The wing has leading-edge flaps and trailing-edge Fowler flaps to give short-field takeoff capability.

The wingtip store station is for defensive air-to-air missiles, such as the Sidewinder.

An OMI/Selenia head-up display and Alenia multi-function display help ease pilot workload. The cockpit has HOTAS (Hands on throttle and stick) controls.

Italian AMXs have a small FIAR Pointer radar based on the ELTA EL/M, and any future advanced variants will probably have a FIAR Grifo multi-mode system. Brazilian aircraft will probably receive the SCP-01 radar soon.

The canopy is a one-piece sideways hinging unit, which allows excellent all-round vision. The pilot sits on a Martin-Baker ejection seat.

AMX is powered by a single Rolls-Royce Spey 168 turbofan built under license in Italy. This reliable engine is similar to the model which was used in the Buccaneer.

Low-intensity strip lights are fitted to the rear fuselage to aid formation flying at night.

ACTION DATA

AIM-9L SIDEWINDER

Used by several NATO countries, the AIM-9L is one of the most advanced Sidewinder models, able to attack targets from the front if they are flying fast enough. The AMX carries a pair of Sidewinders on wingtip pylons. Sidewinder has an 11-kg (24-lb.) blast fragmentation warhead triggered by a laser proximity fuse.

GBU-12

Paveway II GBU-12 is a laser-guided 500-lb. (227 kg.) bomb, which is extremely accurate. It homes in on reflected laser energy from a designator. Although the AMX has no laser designator, it is earmarked to receive a podded system such as the GEC TIALD or Thomson-CSF ATLIS to allow the pilot to mark targets.

MK-83

A conventional unguided 'dumb' bomb, the Mk 83 is a steel-cased 447-kg (1,000-lb.) weapon filled with 202 kg (450 lb.) of H-6 explosive. Used in conventional mode, the bomb is fitted with M904 nose fuses and M905 tail fuses. It can be fitted with a Ballute type tail section for delivery as a retarded bomb and is normally carried underwing.

Brazil's fighter-bombers

EMBRAER XAVANTE: The Xavante, a license-built Aermacchi MB.326, is an advanced trainer with light-strike capability and armed with machine guns, cluster bombs and rocket pods. About 100 remain in service. The Xavante can also be equipped with a Vinten camera pod for performing reconnaissance missions.

NORTHROP F-5E: Used in the light-attack role, Brazil is planning to upgrade its F-5s with the same SCP-01 radar and OMI/Alenia HUD as used in the AMX. They have already been supplied with air-to-air refueling probes. Brazil's 36 F-5Es are based at Santa Cruz and Canoas.

MIRAGE IIIDBR: The nation's primary interceptor, the Mirage III has also been upgraded with canards and new avionics. They are armed with Matra R530 missiles and DEFA 30-mm cannon. With the introduction of AMX, it is unlikely that the Mirage will be used in air-to-ground roles despite its capability.

ANTONOV

AN-2 'COLT'

● Biplane utility aircraft ● Post-war design ● More than 18,000 built

When the first An-2 flew in August 1947, nobody could have predicted that it would become the best-selling post-war aircraft. Yet it has remained in production for more than 40 years and at least 18,000 examples have been built in Russia, Poland and China. The biplane configuration that makes it look so old-fashioned in the jet age gives it outstanding short take-off performance and low-speed handling qualities.

▲ *Entering service in 1948, the An-2 immediately became the standard utility type for Aeroflot and the armed forces. More than 10,000, mainly Polish-built examples, have been delivered.*

PHOTO FILE

ANTONOV AN-2 'COLT'

◀ Sturdy design
Just like the wartime C-47 transport, the An-2 has been an economical, rugged aircraft.

▼ Fedya, the spotter aircraft
The An-2F Fedya had a new rear fuselage for a tactical observer and a 12.7-mm (0.5-in) machine gun in a dorsal cupola.

▼ Soviet colours
Naturally, the Soviet armed forces have been the biggest users of the An-2 in its various versions. Since the break-up of the Soviet Union, Russia operates the largest fleet of 'Colts', with more than 300 examples in the utility role.

▼ 'Scimitar' blades
Early production aircraft were fitted with a 3.6-m (11-ft 10-in) V-509A propeller with four scimitar-like blades. The usual propeller on later aircraft was a 3.35-m (11-ft) example with straight blades.

◀ Atmosphere sampler
An-2ZA had a heated compartment for a scientific observer, faired into the tailfin and accessed from the fuselage. The aircraft's ASh-62IR engine was fitted with a turbocharger to maintain 634 kW (850 hp) at its operating ceiling of 9500 m (31,170

FACTS AND FIGURES

- Originally, An-2s had a two-man crew: a pilot and flight engineer. The pilot was not allowed to touch the engine controls.
- 'Anusha' (or 'little Anna') is a common nickname for the An-2 in Eastern Europe.
- Some Chinese Y-5s were built with Pratt & Whitney PT6A turboprops.
- During its design, consideration was given to a welded tube and fabric structure to allow local repairs.
- An-2s have been fitted with glider tow hooks; all are easily fitted with skis.
- For parachute training, the cargo door is removed and a static line fitted.

PROFILE

Irreplaceable 'little Anna'

Tasked with designing a replacement for the Po-2 agricultural aircraft, Antonov chose the biplane configuration because it gave the aeroplane manoeuvrability and compactness. The An-2 was soon in production for a host of uses, from airline transport and paratroop training to crop-spraying and ambulance work.

By 1959, around 5450 An-2s had been built in the Soviet Union, when production was transferred to Poland. Since then, WSK-PZL has built more than 12,000 (mostly for the Soviet Union), including several locally developed variants.

Meanwhile, Nanchang had flown the first Chinese-built An-2 in 1957, under the designation Y-5. Shijiazhuang took over Chinese production in 1968, bringing the total aircraft built in the country to around 1000, including the Y-5B modified agricultural model.

Thousands of An-2s remain in service around the world. Fitted with wheels, skis or floats, they are used for water-bombing, aerial survey, glider towing and a host of other military roles, although the majority were completed as agricultural aircraft. A turboprop conversion designated An-3 was flown, but plans to convert large numbers of An-2s were abandoned.

Above: Since 1959, An-2 production has been concentrated at the PZL-Mielec plant in Poland.

Below: Among the many nations to have received versions of the An-2, Egypt chose to finish its aircraft in appropriate desert colours.

An-2P 'Colt'

Type: biplane utility aircraft

Powerplant: one 746-kW (1,000-hp) Shvetsov ASh-621R nine-cylinder air-cooled radial engine

Maximum speed: 258 km/h (160 mph) at 1750 m (5,740 ft)

Climb rate: 210 m/min (689 fpm) at sea level

Range: 900 km (560 miles) at 1000 m (3,280 ft) with 500-kg (1,100-lb) payload

Service ceiling: 4400 m (14,425 ft)

Weights: empty 3450 kg (7,606 lb); maximum take-off 5500 kg (12,125 lb)

Accommodation: two crew plus 12 passengers or 2140 kg (4,700 lb) of cargo

Dimensions:

	span	18.18 m (59 ft 8 in)
	length	12.74 m (41 ft 9 in)
	height	6.10 m (20 ft)
	wing area	71.52 m² (770 sq ft)

Y-5

Manufactured under Soviet licence, the An-2 was built in China for 30 years for both civil and military duties. The first of 948 examples from Nanchang and Shijiazhuang (SAP) factories flew on 7 December 1957.

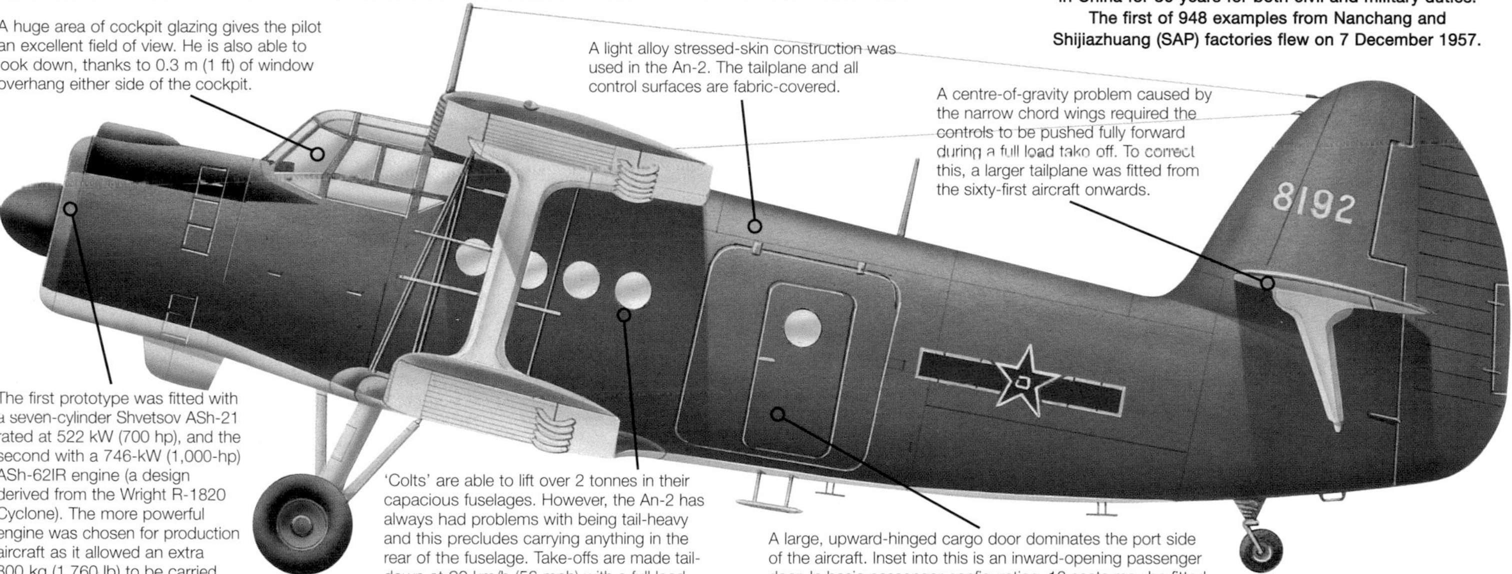

A huge area of cockpit glazing gives the pilot an excellent field of view. He is also able to look down, thanks to 0.3 m (1 ft) of window overhang either side of the cockpit.

A light alloy stressed-skin construction was used in the An-2. The tailplane and all control surfaces are fabric-covered.

A centre-of-gravity problem caused by the narrow chord wings required the controls to be pushed fully forward during a full load take off. To correct this, a larger tailplane was fitted from the sixty-first aircraft onwards.

The first prototype was fitted with a seven-cylinder Shvetsov ASh-21 rated at 522 kW (700 hp), and the second with a 746-kW (1,000-hp) ASh-62IR engine (a design derived from the Wright R-1820 Cyclone). The more powerful engine was chosen for production aircraft as it allowed an extra 800 kg (1,760 lb) to be carried.

'Colts' are able to lift over 2 tonnes in their capacious fuselages. However, the An-2 has always had problems with being tail-heavy and this precludes carrying anything in the rear of the fuselage. Take-offs are made tail-down at 90 km/h (56 mph) with a full load.

A large, upward-hinged cargo door dominates the port side of the aircraft. Inset into this is an inward-opening passenger door. In basic passenger configuration, 12 seats may be fitted.

'Colts' in worldwide service

NORTH KOREAN Y-5: 'Red 44' is finished in the all-over matt black worn by Chinese-built Y-5s involved in night-time covert operations over South Korea.

POLISH An-2V: Seen in Polish markings, this float-equipped An-2V further illustrates the versatility of the 'Colt'. Floats tended to be fitted at factory or major depot level, rather than in the field.

SOVIET An-2TD: This parachute training version of the An-2 carries the markings of DOSAAF, the huge paramilitary grouping which organized all sporting aviation in the Soviet Union.

ACTION DATA

ECONOMIC CRUISING SPEED

Speed is not a major consideration in the design of any of these utility aircraft. Short take-off and landing (STOL) performance and load-carrying ability are more important parameters, together with economy of operation.

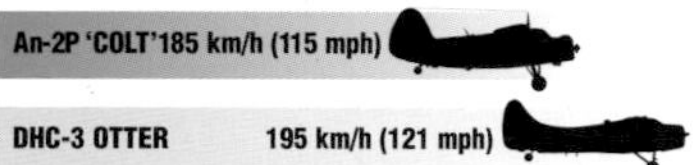

PASSENGERS

The An-2 is a large design for a single-engined aircraft, equipped with a sizeable fuselage for 12 seats in standard passenger configuration, or more than 2000 kg (4,400 lb) of cargo in the freight transport role. A comparable Western design is the de Havilland Canada Otter, although this cannot carry the same payload as the 'Colt'.

An-2P 'COLT' 12 passengers

DHC-3 OTTER 10 passengers

Do 28D-1 SKYSERVANT 12 passengers

RANGE

Where the An-2 has been left behind by some more recent Western designs is in its range performance. The twin-engined Skyservant has a range twice that of the An-2. Recently, DHC-3s have been fitted with the ASh-62 engine to improve performance.

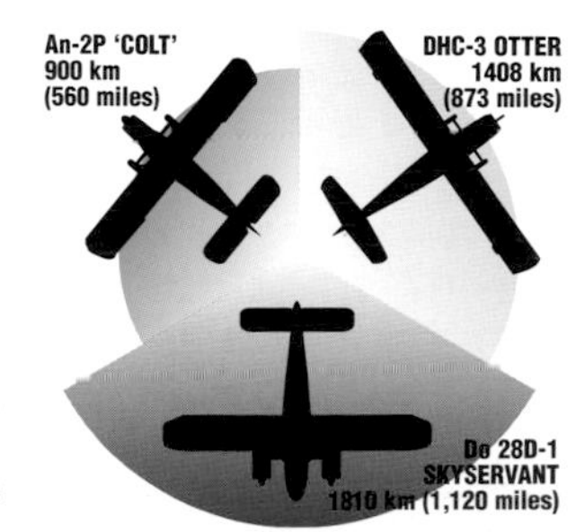

ANTONOV

AN-12 'CUB'

● Tactical airlifter ● Flying command post ● Electronic warfare

Antonov's An-12 'Cub' is a big, tough, practical transport often called the 'Soviet C-130' because it closely resembles the West's Lockheed Hercules. The Ukrainian-designed An-12 is a high-wing, four-engined, rear-loading freighter that won wide acceptance in the Soviet military, served the airlines and was copied in China. This versatile machine also operated in Afghanistan and worked as an electronic warfare jammer and testbed.

▲ *Like the C-130, the An-12 was the first transport properly designed for the forces that used it, featuring a high wing, turboprops, rough-field capability, large rear loading doors and a wide fuselage. The utility of such machines has ensured that the An-12 is still in service today.*

PHOTO FILE

ANTONOV AN-12 'CUB'

▲ Driver's seat
The An-12 cockpit is a spartan place to work, but it is well laid out and offers the pilot a good view for landing.

▲ Soft landing
With its long flaps and low-pressure tyres, the An-12 can easily touch down safely on rough strips at high weights.

Himalaya flyer ▶
India's An-12s operate in the Himalayan range, but the lack of pressurisation in the hold often limits their operations there.

▲ Still going strong
The An-12 still remained in service in the mid-1990s: this Aeroflot machine is flying from Zhukovskii.

Aeroflot visitor ▶
Intercepted by an A-7 from the carrier USS Midway*, this An-12 was on a reconnaissance mission.*

FACTS AND FIGURES

➤ Many An-12s have been converted for duty as test and research platforms, including engine testbed work.

➤ When production ended in 1973, about 900 An-12s had been built in the USSR.

➤ The prototype Antonov An-12 made its maiden flight in 1958.

➤ China produces the An-12, known as the Y-8, in Xian and has exported the type to Sri Lanka and Sudan.

➤ Afghan rebels succeeded in downing an An-12 with Stinger missiles.

➤ Four tonnes of electronic warfare gear is carried by the 'Cub-C' jammer.

PROFILE

Supreme Soviet tactical airlifter

Antonov's An-12 'Cub' is the hard-working transport which pilots say cannot be replaced. Although this burly, turboprop heavyweight has been out of production for a quarter of a century (its American equivalent, the C-130, is still being built), pilots agree that plans to replace the 'Cub' with jet transports were premature.

The 'Cub' is an enduring presence in the former Soviet Union and is still relied upon to transport military supplies, while also being used for secondary missions. In addition, Aeroflot continues to operate a small number of An-12 civil freighters.

The An-12 is not fully pressurised like the C-130 and uses a different method of rear loading, which sometimes requires additional ground equipment. The An-12 cannot land on a rough, unpaved surface near the battlefield in the short distance of 1500 m (4,920 ft.) that is required by the C-130. But when support equipment is available and airfields are used, the An-12 is a champion freight-hauler for a plane of its class.

Aeroflot found the An-12 essential, as a large area of the USSR was totally inaccessible to more conventional aircraft.

The Czech Republic and Slovakia both retained an An-12 each after the division of Czechoslovakia. Although the Slovak An-12 ('2209') is used, the Czechs have retired their aircraft despite having no replacement.

Y-8

The Shaanxi Y-8 is a Chinese-built version of the An-12. Amazingly, this aircraft is still in production and the latest version, the Y-8C, was first flown in 1990 and is widely used by Chinese operators.

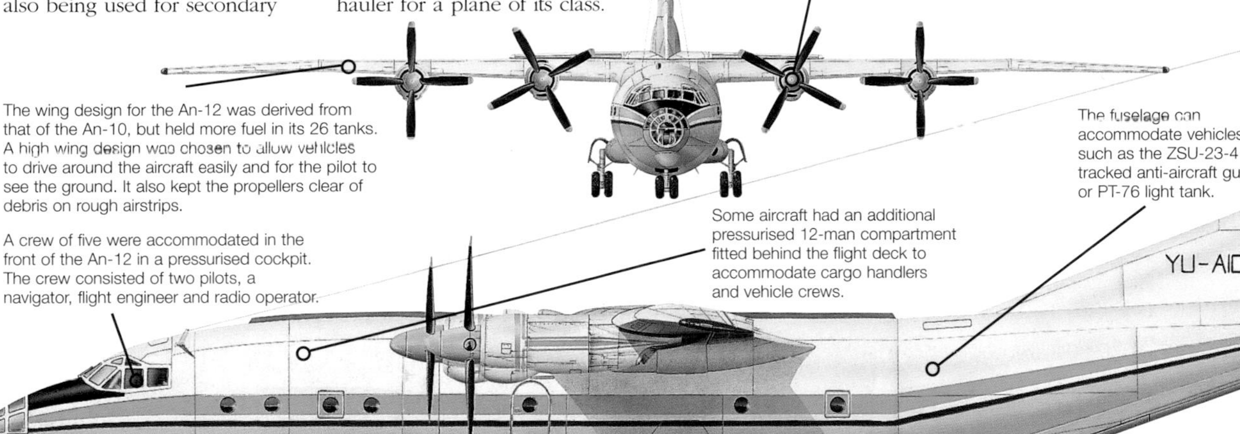

An-12 'Cub'

Type: passenger/cargo transport

Powerplant: four 2983-kW (3,940-hp.) Ivchenko AI-20K turboprop engines

Maximum speed: 670 km/h (416 m.p.h.)

Cruising speed: 550 km/h 342 m.p.h.) at 7620 m (25,000 ft.)

Range: 5700 km (3,542 mi.)

Service ceiling: 10,200 m (33,500 ft.)

Weights: normal take-off 54,000 kg (119,050 lb.); maximum take-off 61,000 kg (134,482 lb.)

Armament: (on some military An-12s) two 'NR-23' 23-mm cannons in a rear turret

Dimensions:
span 38.00 m (124 ft. 8 in.)
length 33.10 m (108 ft. 7 in.)
height 10.53 m (34 ft. 7 in.)
wing area 121.70 m² (1,310 sq. ft.)

COMBAT DATA

MAXIMUM CRUISING SPEED

With turboprop engines and a bulky fuselage, tactical transports are not designed for speed. The more streamlined fuselage of the An-12 gives it a slightly higher speed than the C-130, but in practice most transports rarely reach their maximum speed.

An-12 'CUB' 670 km/h (416 m.p.h.)
C-130 HERCULES 595 km/h (370 m.p.h.)
C.160 513 km/h (319 m.p.h.)

LOAD

The Antonov has impressive load-carrying capability, and can haul more than a C-130. Perhaps the only weakness of the An-12 is that loading the aircraft is slower than a C-130 or a Transall C.160 due to the absence of a rear loading ramp. The Transall is only a twin-engined design but still manages to carry a fair payload.

An-12 'CUB' 20,000 kg (44,092 lb.)
C-130 HERCULES 16,194 kg (35,702 lb.)
C.160 16,000 kg (35,274 lb.)

RANGE

The An-12 has less range than a C-130, but it still has an adequate radius of action for a tactical transport, especially considering that operations in Europe do not require long stretches without refuelling. Jamming An-12s could stay on station for long stretches at a time.

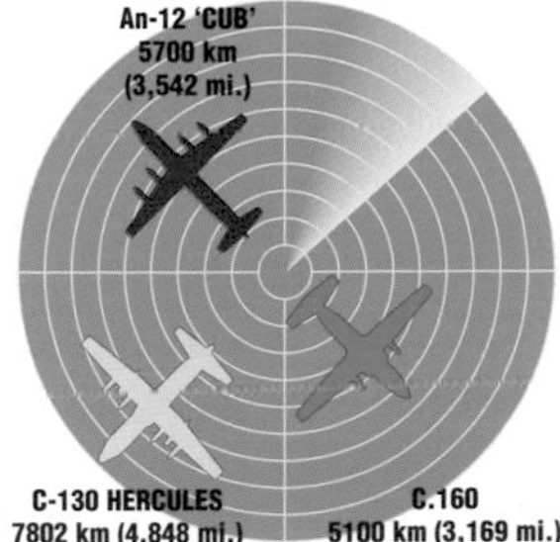

An-12 missions

BOMBING RAID: India converted several of its An-12BPs to serve as makeshift bombers; 16 tons of palletised bombs were pushed out of the rear doors.

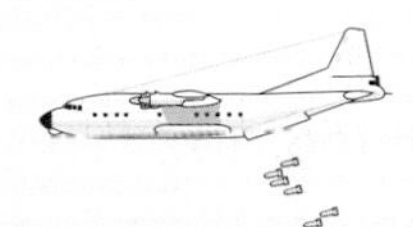

TARGET TANK: The object of the An-12 mission was to attack Pakistani troops and armour during the 1971 conflict.

EJECTION TEST: The An-12 has also been fitted with a special tail cone used for firing ejection seats to test their effectiveness.

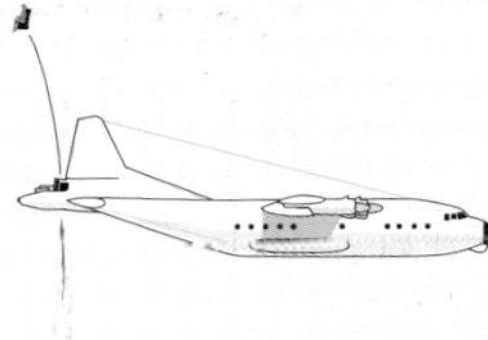

ELECTRONIC JAMMER: An electronic warfare variant known to NATO as 'Cub-C' has active jamming gear for blocking communications and radar, and can also dispense 'chaff' barriers to give false returns on radar.

ANTONOV

AN-22 ANTEI 'COCK'

● Strategic airlifter ● Multiple record-breaker ● Turboprop power

▲ Designed to move heavy and outsized loads around the vast expanse of the Soviet Union, the An-22 'Cock' has served reliably in the harshest of environments.

Antonov's design bureau, based at Kiev in the Ukraine, is renowned for producing some of the world's biggest aeroplanes. The An-22, with its maximum take-off weight of 250 tonnes (275 tons) including an 80-tonne (88-ton) payload, was certainly the largest of its day. At one stage Antonov was working on designs for even bigger versions, one of which would have carried 724 passengers on two decks, but An-22 production was halted in 1974.

PHOTO FILE

ANTONOV AN-22 ANTEI 'COCK'

Huge transport ▶
Ground personnel lend scale to the An-22. Everything about the aircraft is huge, including its 6.20-m (20-ft 4-in) diameter contra-rotating propellers, which are the world's largest mechanically coupled units.

◀ Gull-winged grace
With its distinctive gull wing the 'Cock' is a graceful shape once airborne. This aircraft has its starboard propellers feathered.

▼ Airline service
This Antei, in common with roughly half of those produced, wears civilian markings. In spite of this Aeroflot identity, all An-22s seem to be tasked with military duties.

◀ Antei air drop
A variety of loads may be air-dropped from the An-22's twin rear doors. The 'Cock' is strictly a freighter.

▼ Take-off
Two An-22s line up to take off. The aircraft's specialist abilities remain as valuable as ever.

▲ Missile loading
Missile systems and main battle tanks are standard military loads for the 'Cock'. Folding doors allow straight-in vehicle loading.

FACTS AND FIGURES

- In 1966 the prototype An-22 set 12 world load and height records; they were bettered by another An-22 in 1967.
- I.J. Davidov took the Antei aloft for the first time on 27 February 1965.
- When production ended in 1974, it is estimated that 66 An-22s had been built.
- A 75,000-tonne (82,673-ton) press was used in the manufacture of the main fuselage frames and principal wing components.
- Undercarriage tyre pressures can be altered in flight to suit runway conditions.
- One An-22 in Russian air force service has been seen in three-tone camouflage.

PROFILE

Gull-winged tank transporter

First flown in February 1965, the An-22 was similar in configuration to the An-12 'Cub', although much bigger and with twin tailfins to improve control and to keep the tail section to a practical height. The pressurized forward fuselage can seat 29 passengers, but the 'Cock' was built to carry freight rather than people.

The An-22's titanium-floored main hold has two travelling cranes and two winches to assist with loading and unloading. With 33 m (108 ft) of usable length and a 4.40-m (14-ft 5-in) square cross-section, the cabin can accommodate main battle tanks and other similar heavy loads. With a 45-tonne (50-ton) payload the Antei is capable of travelling more than 10,000 km (6,200 miles).

Of the estimated 66 An-22s produced, 55 remain in the inventory, but fewer than this are still in service. Most carry Aeroflot markings, although their main role is as military transports.

A few An-22s have been adapted to carry wings for the An-124 – a later Antonov contender for the title of world's biggest aircraft – from Tashkent to the assembly line in Kiev. The advantage of this method over the 'Super Guppy' style of aircraft used by Airbus is that the wing, mounted on pylons above the fuselage, generates additional lift.

Above: A classic shot of an An-22 operating from a snow-covered airfield. The aircraft is capable of flying from rough strips.

Below: This An-22 saved its An-124 successor from embarrassment by flying a spare engine for it to the 1988 Farnborough Air Show.

An-22M Antei 'Cock'

Type: strategic military transport

Powerplant: four 11,186-kW (15,000-hp) Kuznetsov NK-12MA turboprops

Maximum speed: 740 km/h (460 mph)

Take-off run: 1300 m (4,265 ft) at maximum take-off weight from a concrete surface

Range: 5000 km (3,100 miles) with maximum payload; 10,950 km (6,800 miles) with 45,000-kg (99,208-lb) payload

Service ceiling: 7500 m (24,600 ft)

Weights: empty 114,000 kg (251,327 lb); maximum take-off 250,000 kg (551,156 lb)

Payload: maximum 80,000 kg (176,370 lb)

Dimensions:	span	64.40 m (211 ft 3 in)
	length	57.90 m (190 ft)
	height	12.53 m (41 ft 1 in)
	wing area	345.00 m² (3,714 sq ft)

AN-22 ANTEI 'COCK'

The An-22 was the Soviet's main heavylift aircraft when it entered service. It has since been supplemented by the An-124 and An-225 but remains a vital transport aircraft.

Having produced the basic An-22 design by scaling up the successful An-12, it was decided to fit twin fin and rudder assemblies. This allowed better control in asymmetric flight, when one or both engines on the same side are inoperable.

When designing the An-22, Antonov was unwilling to take on the complexities of building a complete pressurized fuselage. As a result, only the forward section of the cabin, with seating for passengers, is pressurized.

Some of the most powerful turboprop engines ever built power the An-22. The basic NK-12 was developed by a mainly German team, headed by an Austrian engineer. Design of the powerplant is credited to Kuznetsov.

Even in profile the pronounced droop of the Antei's outer wings is evident. The main wing box forms a fuel tank with a capacity of 55,800 litres (14,740 US gal), or 43,000 kg (94,800 lb), of fuel. The tank runs from almost one wingtip to the other. Pressure refuelling points are mounted in the undercarriage fairings.

There are two doors at the rear of the cabin. The lower one opens to ground level for easy loading and also contains tracks which allow the cabin cranes to move out onto the opened ramp.

Large fairings on either side of the lower fuselage contain the 12-wheeled main landing gear. Six wheels are used on each side, mounted in rows of three twin-wheeled bogies. Auxiliary power units and systems controlling cabin air are also contained in the fairings.

ACTION DATA

PAYLOAD

Although it cannot match the payload capabilities of the Galaxy, the An-22 has proved to be an excellent airlifter with good field performance. It can carry a far greater payload than its second US rival, the Lockheed C-141B StarLifter.

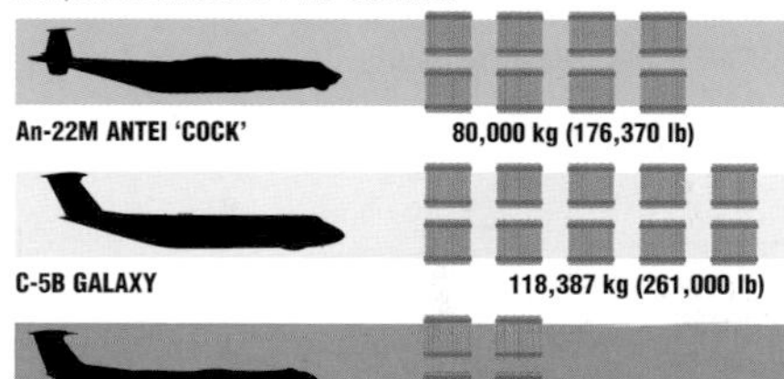

RANGE

These figures show range with maximum payload. Again, the C-5B is the leader, but the An-22 offers better range than the C-141B with almost twice the payload. This ability makes the Antei a highly versatile aircraft.

An-22M ANTEI 'COCK' 5000 km (3,728 miles)

C-5B GALAXY 5526 km (3,434 miles)

C-141B STARLIFTER 4725 km (2,936 miles)

TAKE-OFF RUN

For operations from short strips while carrying heavy loads, the An-22 excels among these types. Frontline airfields may not be able to offer the services of major air bases and may have shortened runways because of bomb damage.

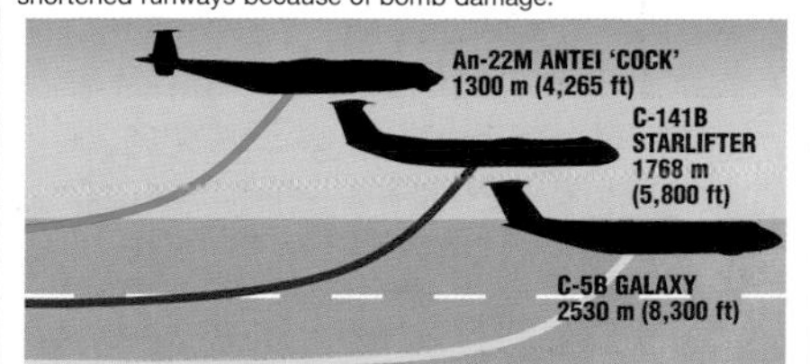

Airlifters by Antonov

■ **An-12 'CUB':** Roughly equivalent to the Lockheed C-130 Hercules, the An-12 is in widespread service. The An-22 used much of the design philosophy of the An-12.

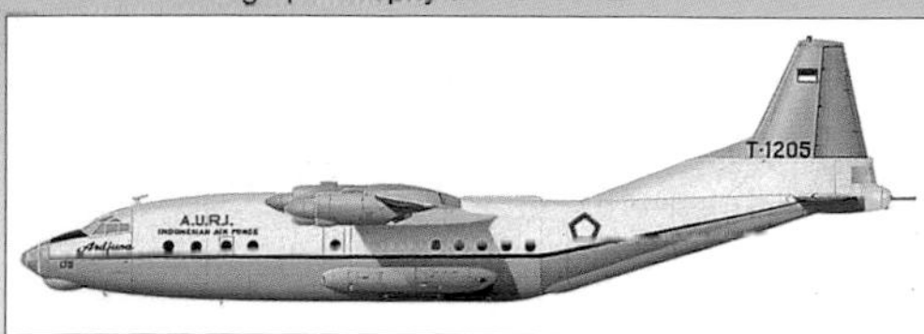

■ **An-26 'CURL':** An improved version of the An-24, the An-26 was originally intended as a light, tactical transport but has since been developed into a number of specialized variants.

■ **An-74 'COALER-B':** Developed from the An-72 turbofan-powered short take-off and landing airlifter, the An-74 is optimized for Arctic and Antarctic operations.

ANTONOV

AN-24 'COKE'/AN-26 'CURL'

● Twin-turboprops ● Personnel transport ● Tactical airlifters

Designed to satisfy an Aeroflot requirement for a turboprop transport, the An-24 'Coke' also sold in some numbers to military operators as both a passenger and freight carrier. It led directly to development of the An-26 'Curl', a dedicated military tactical transport, which has proven itself to be a rugged and capable performer. In China, unlicensed production of both aircraft has been carried out under the designation Xian Y-7.

▲ *Antonov's twins serve in some numbers with both military and paramilitary operators. The majority of An-24s are passenger transports without rear loading ramp doors.*

PHOTO FILE

ANTONOV AN-24 'COKE'/AN-26 'CURL'

Czech 'Curl' ▶
This aircraft demonstrates the distinctive bubble observation window of the type.

▼ Paradropping
With its large rear door and blister observation window, the An-26 is optimised for the parachute deployment of troops.

▲ Jet APU
The jet exhaust of the APU is clearly seen within the polished section of the starboard engine nacelle of this Czech An-26.

Abraded underside ▼
During rough-field operations debris is thrown up at the underside of the fuselage, as shown by this weathered aircraft.

▼ African 'Coke'
At least five An-24s were supplied to Sudan, but all seem to have been withdrawn from use.

FACTS AND FIGURES

➤ Very few operators use the An-24 in a freight role; most use the aircraft as a 50-seat passenger transport.

➤ Under the designation An-24P, one 'Coke' was modified for fire-bombing.

➤ Antonov claims a corrosion life of 30,000 hours for the An-24 fuselage.

➤ The An-26 was the first Soviet-designed transport aircraft to have a fully pressurised hold.

➤ During 1996, Russia had 20 Elint-dedicated An-26s on strength.

➤ Angola's and Mozambique's air forces have used An-26s as attack aircraft.

PROFILE

Antonov's lightweight airlifters

Having first flown on 20 December 1959, the An-24 'Coke' was a direct competitor to the F27 Friendship. Both aircraft were fundamentally airliners, but both sought military customers, in which quest the 'Coke' came off best. Antonov designed the An-24 with the emphasis on strength and reliability, rather than on lightweight and economical operations.

Early aircraft featured a gas turbine auxiliary power unit (APU) in the rear of the starboard engine nacelle, but this was replaced in the An-24RV by a small turbojet which improved take-off performance. This installation was also a feature of the An-24RT dedicated freighter.

Designed as a tactical airlifter, the An-26 has enjoyed far greater success. It has greater power, an upswept rear fuselage which incorporates a large cargo door, and is fully equipped for the rapid loading and off-loading of freight, light vehicles or paratroops.

Unusually, the An-26 has a second skin of titanium beneath the fuselage, to protect it during rough field operations. The aircraft has also been developed into a number of special versions, especially for the electronic intelligence, signals intelligence and electronic warfare (Elint, Sigint and EW) roles. All machines in this category are given the NATO designation 'Curl-B'.

Left: Early in 1996, the Libyan Arab Republic Air Force had eight An-26s on strength as transports.

Above: Hungary flies the An-24V in the conventional passenger role, alongside An-26 tactical airlifters, as illustrated.

AN-24RV 'COKE'

When it was formed in 1992, the Czech air force received a number of An-24s from the former Czechoslovak air force. The aircraft are generally used as staff transports.

In addition to its five An-24RVs, in March 1996 the Czech air force also had in service four An-26s and a single, Elint-dedicated An-26Z-1M 'Curl-B'.

A flight crew of three is required to operate the An-24. The aircraft represents a departure from previous Soviet design philosophy by having a radar nose instead of the extensively glazed navigator's position normally associated with Soviet transports.

Mounted high on the wing, the powerful turboprops and their propellers are kept away from flying debris. An-24RT and RV machines have an auxiliary turbojet replacing the APU in the starboard nacelle. This provides all electrical power on take-off, allowing the main engines to deliver more thrust to the propellers, as well as providing residual thrust.

In cross-section, the fuselage of both the An-24 and An-26 takes the form of a rounded triangle. This allows maximum floor width, while retaining a nearly circular cross-section which is structurally desirable for a pressurised cabin.

Most military An-24s are flown as pure passenger transports and are designated An-24V, or RV with turbojet APU. A cargo variant was produced as the An-24T (An-24RT) with rear loading and twin ventral fins, but it found few customers.

As a passenger transport, the An-24 was supplied with a small entry door in the port rear fuselage. The ventral fins fitted to An-24Ts were sometimes applied to An-24Vs, as on this example.

An-26B 'Curl-A'

Type: twin-turboprop tactical transport

Powerplant: two 2103-kW (2,820-hp.) ZMDB Progress AI-24VT turboprops and one 7.85-kN (1,765-lb.-thrust) Soyuz RU-19A-300 turbojet

Maximum speed: 540 km/h (335 m.p.h.) at 5000 m (16,000 ft.)

Maximum climb rate: 480 m/min (1,575 f.p.m.)

Range: 2550 km (1,580 mi.) with maximum fuel or 1100 km (680 mi.) with maximum payload

Service ceiling: 7500 m (24,600 ft.)

Weights: empty 15,400 kg (33,880 lb.), maximum take-off 24,400 kg (53,680 lb.)

Accommodation: 40 passengers on tip-up seats or 5500 kg (12,100 lb.) of cargo

Dimensions:
- span 29.20 m (95 ft. 9 in.)
- length 23.80 m (78 ft 1 in.)
- height 8.58 m (28 ft. 2 in.)
- wing area 74.98 m² (807 sq. ft.)

COMBAT DATA

MAXIMUM PAYLOAD

Although it has a lighter maximum payload than these contemporary designs, the An-26 has a carefully designed hold which helps prevent it becoming space-limited. Many transports are full before they reach their maximum payload weight.

CRUISING SPEED

When normal operational cruising speeds at altitude are compared, Fokker's F27 Mk 4000 Troopship is by far the fastest. It is not as rugged as the other types, however, and has gained a limited market. All three types have their origins in commercial designs.

An-26B 'CURL-A' 440 km/h (273 m.p.h.)

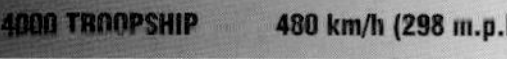

ANDOVER C.Mk 1 415 km/h (257 m.p.h.)

F27 Mk 4000 TROOPSHIP 480 km/h (298 m.p.h.)

RANGE

Range with maximum payload is a useful guide to the potential operating ranges of transport aircraft. A maximum payload is rarely carried, but, under most circumstances, the An-26B is likely to offer far superior performance.

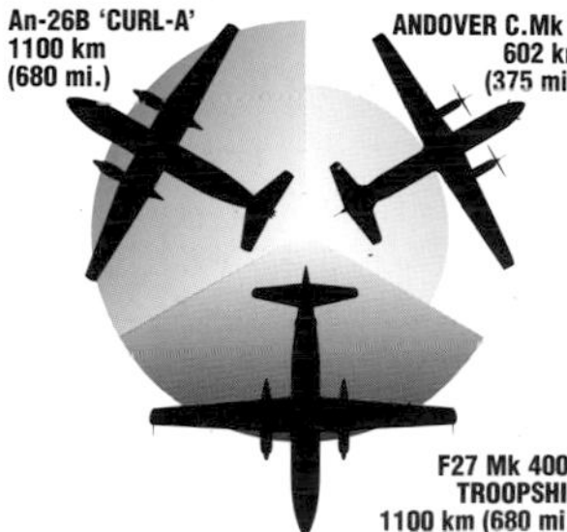

'Curl' colours

AFGHANISTAN: In 1978 the first of about 20 An-26s and a number of An-24s was delivered to the Afghan air force. Some were destroyed by rocket fire, but the survivors remain airworthy.

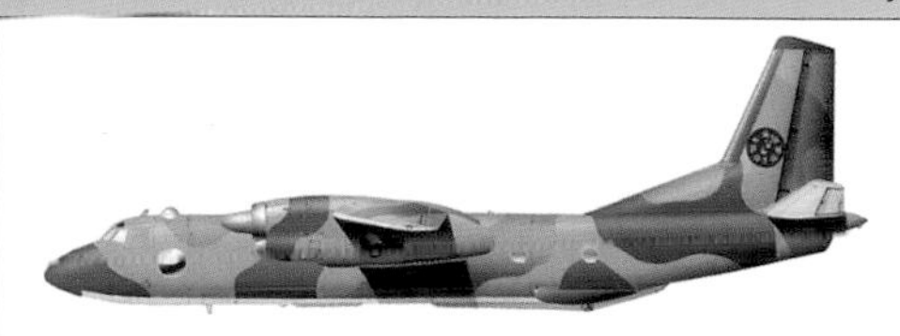

MALI: An-26s were first received in 1983 and continue to fly alongside a number of An-24s. 'Cokes' and 'Curls' have proved popular among African nations.

YUGOSLAVIA: After the divisions within Yugoslavia, the An-26 fleet now flies with Serbian forces. Having stood at 15 in the mid-1980s, numbers totalled 25 by 1996.

ANTONOV

AN-30 'CLANK'/AN-32 'CLINE'

● Twin turboprop ● Aerial survey and transport ● 'Open Skies' flights

No organisation has been responsible for a wider range of transport aircraft than the Ukraine's Antonov design bureau. Developed from the An-24RT, the An-30 is a specialised aerial survey aircraft used in small numbers by Russia and a handful of the former Soviet allies. The An-32, on the other hand, is a widely operated tactical transport. With its powerful engines it is particularly useful in hot, mountainous countries.

▲ *A versatile family of medium-range aircraft has been built up around the An-32. Meanwhile, modifications to the An-30 have taken it beyond the simple photographic survey mission capability.*

ANTONOV AN-30 'CLANK'/AN-32 'CLINE'

▼ Fire-killer
Firefighting An-32Ps have a total water capacity of 8000 kg, which is carried in removable tanks. They can also carry rain-making equipment.

▲ Nose job
A weather radar is contained within the solid nose of the An-32; this replaces the glazed nose of the An-30. The high-mounted engines are also unique to the An-32.

▲ 'Open Skies'
The Czech Republic uses this An-30 for 'Open Skies' overflights of other nations.

▼ Indian air force
India was the first customer to take delivery of the An-32 and received its first aircraft in 1984.

▲ Glass nose
Nose glazing has been a feature of many former Soviet designs. This is usually to aid navigation over the vast, featureless tracts of the former USSR and also, on the An-30, for photography.

FACTS AND FIGURES

- A computer aboard the An-30 is programmed with the route and controls the aircraft during surveys.
- In basic fit the An-30 cabin has four camera apertures and a light-meter.
- An-30s are also used for mineral prospecting and environmental studies.
- Western experts first received details about the An-32 in May 1977 and it appeared at the Paris Air Show that year.
- 'Cline' is the NATO reporting name of the An-32; 'Clank' is that of the An-30.
- An air ambulance version of the An-32 is equipped with an operating theatre.

PROFILE

Exceptional Antonovs

Externally, the most obvious difference between the An-30 and An-24RT, from which it was developed, is the glazed nose and raised cockpit canopy of the 'Clank'. Internally, though, the later model carries survey cameras along with a darkroom and map-making equipment, or other geographical survey equipment. An even more specialised version is the An-30M Sky Cleaner. This has fuselage-mounted pods which dispense granular carbon dioxide into clouds in order to produce rain over drought-stricken regions or forest fires.

The An-32 was developed specifically for operations in hot-and-high conditions. In addition to much more powerful engines than the An-30's 2103-kW (2,820-hp.) AI-24VTs, it has a new wing with triple-slot curved flaps and automatic leading-edge slats.

The type's ability to operate from airfields as high as 4500 m (14,750 ft.) above sea level, plus rough-field landing gear and a self-contained mechanised loading system, makes it an ideal tactical transport, fire-fighting, ambulance and agricultural aircraft. As a result of its outstanding performance and the difficult conditions in the country, the An-32 is the standard tactical transport of the Indian air force, which has named it the Sutlej.

Right: An-30 pilots have a far better field of view than their An-24 colleagues. The raised cockpit was primarily installed to provide more space for the navigator and survey equipment

Right: Bulgaria flies the An-30 in its basic survey role. Antonov designed the aircraft specifically for survey work in relation to map production.

An-32 'Cline'

Type: short-/medium-range transport

Powerplant: two 3760-kW (5,040-hp.) ZMKB Progress AI-20D Series 5 turboprops

Maximum cruising speed: 530 km/h (329 m.p.h.)

Climb rate: 640 m/min (2,100 f.p.m.)

Range: 2520 km (1,580 mi.) with maximum fuel

Service ceiling: 9400 m (30,840 ft.)

Weights: empty 16,800 kg (36,960 lb.); maximum take-off 27,000 kg (59,400 lb.)

Payload: 42 to 50 passengers or 6700 kg (14,740 lb.)

Dimensions:

span	29.20 m (95 ft. 9 in.)
length	23.78 m (78 ft.)
height	8.75 m (28 ft. 8 in.)
wing area	74.98 m² (807 sq. ft.)

AN-32 'CLINE'

India was a natural customer for the 'Cline', with its mountainous terrain and high temperatures. The Indian contract was fulfilled by Antonov from its GAZ 473 factory at Kiev before any other deliveries began.

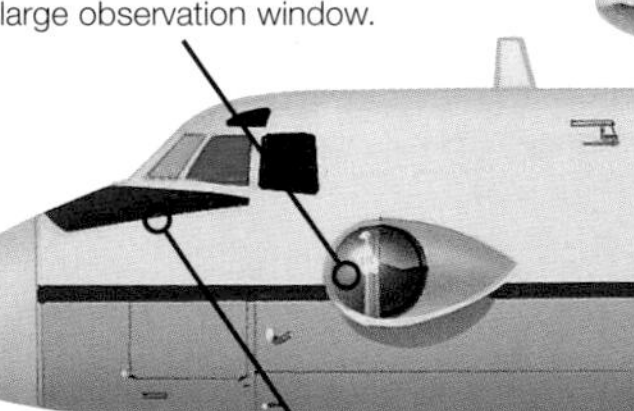

Without lower glazing through which to view navigational landmarks on the ground, accurate navigation becomes difficult. The An-32 and some An-24 and -26 aircraft have a large observation window.

By mounting the powerful AI-20 engines above the wing, the propellers inlets remained clear of runway debris. An-32s are expected to operate from rough airfields and foreign object damage could be disastrous under marginal take-off conditions.

Very deep nacelles characterise the An-32. These house the retracted main undercarriage and the high-set engines. The right-hand nacelle also contains a small auxiliary turbojet.

A 3000-kg capacity hoist is fixed in the cabin to aid freight handling, together with a removable roller conveyor. The cabin can accommodate 12 pallets, 50 passengers or 42 parachutists.

An-32s may be called upon to operate in icy, mountainous conditions. As indicated by the substantial de-icing boots on all leading edges, this was one area of improvement over the An-26.

A crew of three, consisting of pilot, co-pilot and navigator, fly the aircraft from a pressurised and air-conditioned cabin. A flight engineer may also be carried.

Two huge ventral fins are carried beneath the tail. These aid directional stability and provide some protection from the slipstream for paratroops.

ACTION DATA

PAYLOAD

Although the An-32 can carry less than the G222 and C.160, when taking off at high altitude with a full payload it retains its take-off performance. Both of its competitors must carry less fuel or cargo in order to operate from similar altitudes.

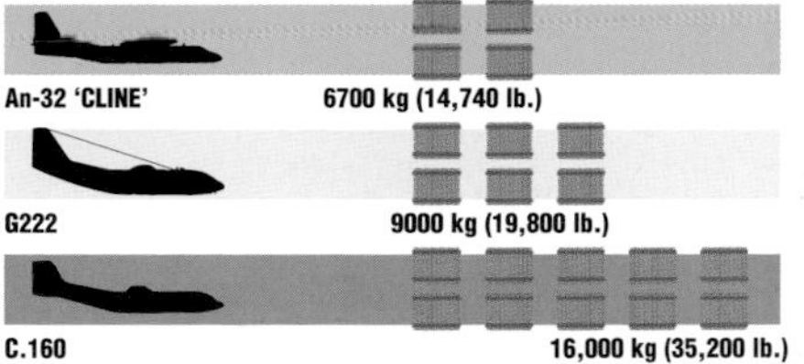

RANGE

With maximum fuel the An-32 exhibits good range. A full fuel load is likely to be at the expense of some payload, however. Despite this, range remains a creditable 1200 km (745 mi.) with a full payload.

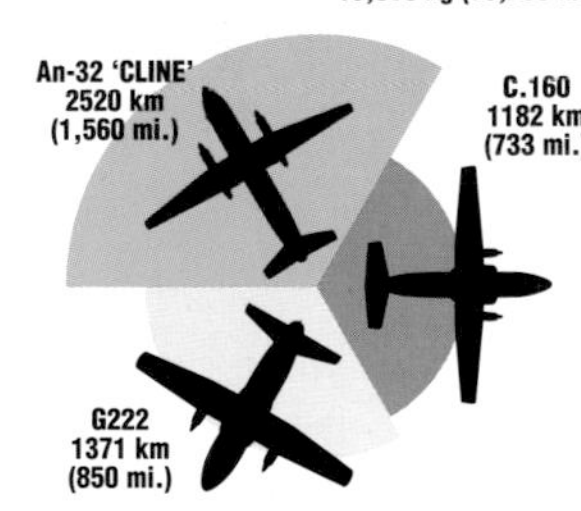

TAKE-OFF DISTANCE

At sea level the take-off performance of the An-32 is not particularly spectacular, since it does not have the STOL features of the other aircraft. Under hot-and-high conditions, however, its lift-off performance is excellent.

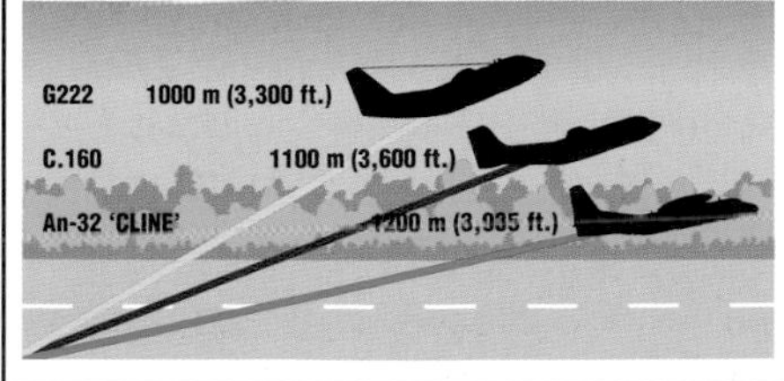

'Clanks' and 'Clines' in service

An-30 'CLANK': This is a camouflaged aircraft in Romanian air force service. Several eastern European air forces fly An-30s and some may serve in Vietnam.

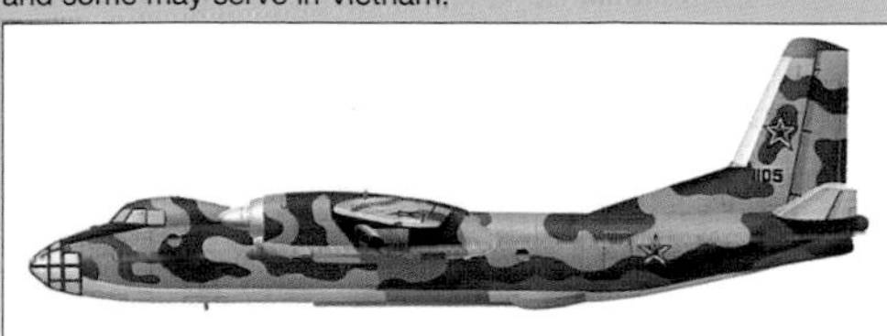

An-30 'CLANK': Many aircraft flying in Aeroflot colours are used on military operations and aircraft such as this one are probably committed to the military in times of crisis.

An-32 'CLINE': Solid nose, high-set engines, forward bubble observation window and enlarged ventral fins distinguish the An-32 from the earlier An-30, -26 and -24.

Antonov

An-124 Ruslan 'Condor'

● **Giant airlifter** ● **Fly-by-wire controls** ● **Humanitarian missions**

▲ *Ruslan continues to draw a crowd wherever it goes. Here it is seen on approach to Farnborough for its first appearance at the international airshow. The aircraft has proven to be of immense value to Russian forces.*

A true giant of the air, the Antonov An-124 Ruslan, known as the 'Condor' in the West, is the largest production aircraft in the world, dwarfing even the Lockheed C-5 Galaxy. In fact, this aircraft is so large that the cockpit is almost 9 m (30 ft.) high when the aircraft is on the ground. The An-124 is a successful military airlifter of great strategic importance because of its ability to carry tanks, missiles and heavy equipment over long ranges.

PHOTO FILE

Antonov An-124 Ruslan 'Condor'

◀ **Nose loader**

Although the An-124's nose takes a full seven minutes to open, it enables loading of the aircraft from either end. A ramp allows easy and rapid loading of vehicles. Both front and rear ramps are stressed for a 70,000-kg (154,000-lb.) main battle tank (MBT).

▲ **Lotarev turbofans**

The Lotarev bureau developed the D-18T engines. These were the first large Soviet turbofans.

Aeroflot airlifter ▶

Like the An-22 'Cock', which the AN-124 was designed to replace, many examples of the Ruslan fly in civilian Aeroflot markings. It seems that the majority are assigned military tasks, however.

▼ **Multi-wheel landing**

Seen on approach, the multi-wheel main landing gear and twin nosewheel units of the An-124 are apparent.

▲ **Civil charter**

Several 'Condors' are available for charter throughout the world. A huge crane is required to maneuver and load this payload.

FACTS AND FIGURES

- ➤ In 1990, a Ruslan carried 451 passengers when hauling Bangledeshi refugees from Amman to Dhaka.
- ➤ The prototype An-124 Ruslan made its maiden flight on 26 December 1982.
- ➤ About 40 An-124s have been manufactured for civil and military use.
- ➤ Four years of argument ensued before Aeroflot and the Russian air force could agree on the An-124's fuselage section.
- ➤ An An-124 carried 171,219 kg (376,682 lb.) of cargo to 10,750 m (35,250 ft.).
- ➤ The An-124 inspired the world's only larger transport, the six-engine An-225.

PROFILE

High-capacity Ukrainian airlifter

Named Ruslan after Pushkin's famous giant and known to NATO as 'Condor', the Antonov An-124 is one of the most impressive aircraft ever built. Developed to meet a joint airline and military need for a heavy lifter, this behemoth transport has a number of features to ease the loading of its cavernous hold.

These features include a rear loading ramp and an upward-hinging visor-type nose, which allows loading from both ends simultaneously. The interior of this transport is so voluminous that 3000-kg (6,600-lb.) capacity winches and 10,000-kg (22,000-lb.) capacity travelling cranes are part of its regular on-board equipment. The aircraft can be made to kneel, giving its hold a floor slope of up to 3.5 degrees to assist in loading and unloading. The flight deck and an upper cabin, which accommodates 88 passengers, is fully pressurized, while the cargo hold is only lightly pressurized. A relatively high-tech airplane of exceptionally clean and efficient design, the An-124 has a fly-by-wire control system and uses composite materials in its structure, bringing about a significant weight saving. Despite its enormous size, the Ruslan is designed to operate from semi-prepared strips, including hard-packed snow or even ice-covered lakes.

Above: Production of the An-124 continues at a rate of two to three per year. No other military customers have come forward, and cargo airlines seem content to charter aircraft as required.

Below: Admiring onlookers lend scale to the huge Ruslan. The aircraft flies regularly to airfields around the world.

An-124 Ruslan 'Condor'

Type: four-engine strategic transport

Powerplant: four 229.47-kN (51,622-lb.-thrust) ZMDB Progress D-18T turbofan engines

Maximum speed: 865 km/h (536 m.p.h.)

Cruising speed: 800 km/h (496 m.p.h.) to 850 km/h (527 m.p.h.)

Range: 16,500 km (10,230 mi.) with max. fuel

Service ceiling: approx. 11,000 m (36,080 ft.)

Weights: empty 175,000 kg (385,000 lb.); maximum take-off 405,000 kg (891,000 lb.)

Accommodation: 6 crew; 88 passengers and up to 150,000 kg (330,000 lb.) of freight

Dimensions: span 73.30 m (240 ft. 5 in.)
length 69.10 m (226 ft. 7 in.)
height 20.78 m (68 ft. 2 in.)
wing area 628 m² (6,757 sq. ft.)

AN-124 RUSLAN 'CONDOR'

Most An-124s wear a color scheme similar to this, whether they are nominally in military or civilian service. This aircraft carries Aeroflot markings.

Hinging at this point, the entire nose section of the aircraft swings upward and over the cockpit. The nose loading ramp is triple hinged.

Antonov produced a wing of exceptional design for the An-124. It features full-span leading-edge slats, huge three-section flaps, four airbrakes inboard and eight spoilers outboard, as well as two-piece ailerons.

Ten fuel tanks are contained within the sealed wing box. Between them they hold 229,999 kg (505,998 lb.) of fuel. In 1987, a 'Condor' set a 20,151-km (124,934-mi.) closed-circuit distance record in 25 hours and 30 minutes.

Using an unusual pear-shaped fuselage cross-section, Antonov was able to produce a cargo hold that is 4.40 m (14 ft. 5 in.) high, 6.40 m (21 ft.) wide and has a usable length of 36 m (118 ft.). This latter figure does not include the rear loading ramp, which is also stressed for load carrying.

At the rear of the aircraft, a pair of clamshell doors open hydraulically, allowing the deployment of a rear loading ramp. This may be fixed at an intermediate position for loading from truck-bed height.

ACTION DATA

PAYLOAD

Antonov's An-124 has the largest payload of any military airlifter. It carries considerably more than the Lockheed C-5B Galaxy, which is its closest rival. The An-225 is a considerably larger aircraft than the Ruslan, but the single example built now lies derelict.

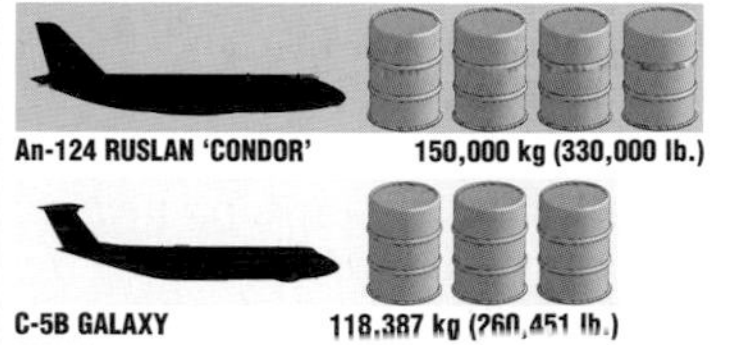

Aviation giants

ANTONOV AN-225 MRIYA 'COSSACK': Although it has recently been used as a spares source for An-124s, the An-225 was the heaviest and largest (apart from wingspan) aircraft ever produced. It was designed to carry the Buran spacecraft.

HUGHES H-4 HERCULES: Howard Hughes' 'Spruce Goose' is still able to boast the largest wingspan of any aircraft. It flew only once, for a distance of about one mile, and represented the ultimate large passenger flying boat airliner.

LOCKHEED C-5 GALAXY: Before the An-124, the C-5 was the largest aircraft, with the exception of wingspan. The An-124 is now the world's largest production aircraft and has carried a 53 per cent greater payload than the C-5B to 2000 m (6,550 ft.).

ATLAS CHEETAH

● Mirage III upgrade ● South Africa's indigenous fighter

Familiar on the outside, the high-tech Atlas Cheetah fighter is new on the inside. Developed from the Mirage III at a time when South Africa had little choice but to improve its existing aircraft, the Cheetah retains the exterior of the famous French fighter. But, within, it is modernized for combat against any opposition. With this aircraft, the South African Air Force (SAAF) remains a first-class fighting arm today.

▲ *Based on the Mirage III fighter-bomber, the Cheetah introduces modern weapon systems, avionics and aerodynamics into a proven airframe to produce a highly capable combat aircraft.*

PHOTO FILE

ATLAS CHEETAH

◀ **To the Moon, Atlas**
The first Cheetahs to be delivered were two-seat Cheetah Ds converted from Mirage IIIDZs and D2Zs. In total, 16 Cheetah Ds were produced, some of them from Mirages and Kfirs supplied secretly by Israel. The Cheetah closely resembles the Kfir C7.

▼ **Operational role**
The Cheetah Ds have full weapons capability. One of their wartime roles would be laser designation for Cheetah Cs.

▲ **Operational conversion**
Initially, the two-seat version was used mainly to convert new pilots to the Cheetah. They were first used by No. 89 Combat Flying School.

◀ **African attacker**
The Cheetah D is the most potent attack aircraft in the southern part of Africa and carries many locally made weapons.

▲ **Hot landings**
Like the Mirage, the Cheetah has a high landing speed; a braking chute reduces the landing run.

FACTS AND FIGURES

- The Cheetah was revealed to the public on 16 July 1986.
- The Atlas Cheetah became operational in 1987, while South Africa was still under an international arms embargo.
- The Israelis supplied much expertise and help in the development of the Cheetah.
- The Cheetah's cruciform braking parachute is easier to manufacture and pack than round chutes.
- Improved instruments, weapons and navigation systems are incorporated.
- The Cheetah was modified from the highly successful French Mirage III.

PROFILE

Modern day African warrior

In July 1968 the South African manufacturer Atlas unveiled a much-modified Dassault Mirage III, renamed Cheetah. Developed with Israel's help, the Cheetah resembles that country's Kfir fighter. South Africa has now converted about 38 single- and two-seat Mirage IIIs into Cheetahs, and is using them as the front-line cutting edge of its air combat force.

In addition, to the two cannon found on single-seat versions, the Cheetah carries a remarkable variety of smart air-to-air and air-to-ground weapons guided by an indigenous designator pod.

This pouring of a new wine into a familiar bottle has produced a first-rate warplane with superb performance. The pilot of the Cheetah sits at the controls of a formidable craft, capable of holding its own in any battle. The Cheetah is also a delight to fly, and pilots revel in being turned loose to fling this powerful ship around the sky.

Recognized by its new wing with its dogtoothed leading edge and by its canard foreplanes, the Cheetah is expected to be in service for years to come.

Aerodynamic modifications include Kfir-style small nose side-strakes and canards mounted behind the engine intakes. These give the aircraft excellent agility.

The most obvious distinguishing feature of the Cheetah is the longer nose, giving the Cheetah C an overall length of 15.62 m (51 ft. 3 in.) compared to 15.03 m (49 ft. 3 in.) for the Mirage III.

The two-tone gray color scheme with a diamond on the upper side was first introduced on the Cheetah C, although it is worn by at least one Cheetah D. The first Cheetahs were Cheetah Ds, followed by the single-seat Cheetah E, which was withdrawn from service in 1992. One Cheetah R reconnaissance version was also built. The Cheetah C is the most sophisticated of the Cheetah variants and was only unveiled in the early 1990s. A dedicated air defense variant, the C also retains significant ground-attack capability.

The canard foreplanes enhance maneuverability and low-speed handling, which improves safety on the landing approach.

CHEETAH C

Most of South Africa's Cheetahs are flown by No. 2 Squadron, The Flying Cheetah, based at AFB Louis Trichardt in the northeastern part of the country.

The longer nose of the Cheetah C probably houses an Israeli-designed EL/M-2032 radar. This can pick up an air-to-air target at 20 miles and can track targets while scanning for others.

Improvements introduced on the Cheetah include a fixed refueling probe for refueling from Boeing 707 tankers, and a one-piece windscreen for greater visibility. The ejection seat is the same Martin-Baker Mk 6 fitted to the Mirage III.

The Cheetah's air-to-air armament consists of short-range Kentron V3C Darter AAMs, which can be aimed using the pilot's helmet-mounted sight. Medium-range AAMs are now being developed.

Today the Cheetah C is powered by the Atar 9k-50 engine, but these may be replaced by MiG-29 or Mirage F-1 powerplants.

Cheetah EZ

Type: single- or two-seat fighter

Powerplant: one SNECMA Atar 9C turbojet engine rated at 41.97 kN (9,440 lb. thrust) dry and 60.80 kN (13,675 lb. thrust) with afterburner

Maximum speed: 2338 km/h (1,450 m.p.h.) at 12,000 m (39,400 ft.)

Cruising speed: 956 km/h (593 m.p.h.) at 11,000 m (34,000 ft.)

Range: 1200 km (745 mi.)

Service ceiling: 17,000 m (55,750 ft.)

Weapons: two DEFA 30-mm (1.18-in.) cannons (single-seat aircraft only); plus up to 4000 kg (8,800 lb.) of other weapons

Weights: empty approx. 7400 kg (16,280 lb.); maximum take-off approx. 16,500 kg (36,300 lb.)

Dimensions:

span	8.22 m (27 ft.)
length	15.65 m (51 ft. 3 in.)
height	4.55 m (14 ft. 11 in.)
wing area	34.80 m² (374 sq. ft)

ACTION DATA

SPEED

The basic Mirage airframe of the Cheetah is very clean, giving the aircraft Mach 2 performance for short periods and making it noticeably faster than the F-16. There have been studies into replacing the old Atar 9 engine with the RD-33 of the MiG-29.

CHEETAH E	2338 km/h (1,450 m.p.h.)
MiG-29 'FULCRUM A'	2445 km/h (1,516 m.p.h.)
F-16C	2124 km/h (1,317 m.p.h.)

WEAPONS

The Cheetah, Fulcrum and Fighting Falcon were all designed to be good air-to-air fighters but each has a significant ground-attack capability.The Cheetah typically carries eight 227-kg (500-lb.) bombs, but can also be equipped with LGBs, ASMs, cluster bombs and rockets. The two-seaters do not have the internal cannon.

CHEETAH E	MiG-29 'FULCRUM A'	F-16C FIGHTING FALCON
2 x 30-mm (1.18-in.) cannon, 4000 kg (8,800 lb.) of bombs	1 x 30-mm (1.18-in.) cannon, 3000 kg (6,600 lb.) of ordnance	1 x 20-mm (0.78-in.) cannon, 6894 kg (15,070 lb.) of bombs

CEILING

The origins of the Cheetah in the Mirage III are reflected in the high altitude performance of the Cheetah. The more modern twin-engine MiG-29 has the same maximum altitude as the Cheetah, while the F-16, with one engine and the smallest wing area of the three aircraft, has the lowest ceiling.

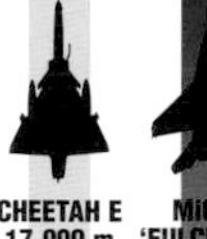

CHEETAH E	17,000 m (55,750 ft.)
MiG-29 'FULCRUM A'	17,000 m (55,750 ft.)
F-16C FIGHTING FALCON	15,240 m (50,000 ft.)

World-class Atlas aircraft

■ **IMPALA:** The first jet combat aircraft built in South Africa was the Atlas Impala Mk 1, a license-built version of the Aermacchi MB.326. The Impala Mk 2 was the single-seat attack version.

■ **AM-3C BOSBOK:** The Bosbok (Bushbuck) was originally a Lockheed design, but the license was passed to Aermacchi and then to Atlas. They were used as spotters for the army.

■ **XH-1 ALPHA:** The Alpha was a prototype aircraft designed to test the systems for the Rooivalk. It was basically an Alouette III with a new fuselage and cockpit and a 20-mm cannon.

■ **CHS-2 ROOIVALK:** The Rooivalk (Red Kestrel) is a dedicated attack helicopter with a secondary air-to-air (anti-helicopter) role. It has not yet been ordered by the SAAF.

ATLAS

IMPALA

● Licence-built MB.326 ● Two variants ● Active service in Africa

Atlas Aircraft of South Africa was formed in 1965 specifically to build the Aermacchi MB.326M trainer. The first kit-set example flew in 1966, and Atlas soon started manufacturing the aircraft as the Impala, completing a total of 151. In 1970, Aermacchi flew the first MB.326KC single-seat attack version. Atlas started building it in 1974 as the Impala Mk 2 for the South African Air Force, at the time embroiled in counter-insurgency campaigns.

▲ *Of the top-selling MB.326 family, South Africa's Impalas have perhaps seen the most action, having been used extensively in the skies over Angola and Namibia.*

PHOTO FILE

ATLAS IMPALA

▼ Prototype Mk 2
In all, 100 Mk 2s were built, including the first seven by Aermacchi, plus a further 15 kits of components. This aircraft, serialled 1000, was the first, entering service in 1974.

▲ Versatile design
The MB.326 design has proved highly versatile and has been widely exported and licence built in several countries.

▼ Maximum local content
This, the 28th Impala Mk 2, was the sixth produced without Italian parts. Underwing rocket pods are carried.

▼ Over south-west Africa
Impalas saw extensive service in South Africa's bush wars in Angola and Namibia.

▲ Kit-set beginnings
In the 1960s, Aermacchi supplied Atlas with 16 kits for a version of the MB.326GB suitable for training and the COIN role. This was known to the Italian company as the MB.326M and to Atlas as the Impala Mk 1. A further 135 aircraft followed.

FACTS AND FIGURES

- In March 1996, Impalas were in service with No. 8 Squadron and a No. 85 Combat Flying training unit.
- Impala production totalled 251, of which 151 were two-seat Mk 1s.
- Angolan missions included night intruder raids on supply convoys.
- An Impala returned from a raid on Angola with an unexploded SA-9 surface-to-air missile lodged in its jetpipe.
- In early 1996, 20 Mk 1 and 40 Mk 2 aircraft remained in SAAF service.
- SAAF Cheetah pilots must complete 700 hours on the Impala before selection.

PROFILE

Impalas in Angolan skies

Replacing the de Havilland Vampire in the South African Air Force, the Impala Mk 1 entered service from 1966. It was used mainly as a trainer for fighter pilots who had completed their initial training on North American Harvards (now being replaced by PC-7s). From 1968, it also equipped the South African Air Force's 'Silver Falcons' display team. Like the Mk 1s, the first Impala 2s were built from kits, but again Atlas steadily increased the proportion of local content in the aircraft. The 100 aircraft delivered differed from the original MB.326K, which was powered by a 19.57-kN (4,400-lb.-thrust) Viper 680, in using the same engine as the Mk 1. The Mk 2 was used extensively for ground-attack and close-support missions in Namibia and Angola. In addition to the two built-in guns, it carried 120-kg (260-lb.) and 250-kg (550-lb.) bombs, rocket launchers and tactical reconnaissance pods, often with auxiliary fuel tanks. Probably the most enduring contribution made by the Impala programme to South Africa's fortunes was its role in establishing the local aircraft industry when many states refused to sell arms to the country.

Above: A tactical camouflage scheme adorns the Mk 2s in recognition of their counter-insurgency (COIN) role.

Below: Two-seat Impala Mk 1s were generally finished in this all-over silver scheme. Aircraft 499 was among the second batch of 40 aircraft built using Italian components.

Impala Mk 2

Type: advanced training, COIN and armed reconnaissance aircraft

Powerplant: one 15.17-kN (3,400-lb.-thrust) Rolls-Royce Viper 20 Mk 540 turbojet

Maximum speed: 890 km/h (552 m.p.h.) at 1525 m (5,000 ft.)

Climb rate: 1981 m/min (6,500 f.p.m.)

Range: 130–1040 km (80–650 mi.), depending on weapons load and mission profile

Service ceiling: 14,325 m (47,000 ft.)

Weights: empty 2964 kg (6,520 lb.); maximum take-off 5897 kg (12,973 lb.)

Armament: two 30-mm cannon plus up to 1814 kg (4,000 lb.) of stores

Dimensions:

span	10.15 m (33 ft. 4 in.)
length	10.67 m (35 ft.)
height	3.72 m (12 ft. 3 in.)
wing area	19.35 m² (208 sq. ft.)

IMPALA MK 2

This licence-built MB.326KC served with the SAAF's No. 4 Squadron, a unit of the Active Citizen Force, based at Lanseria/Durban. Around 40 were still in SAAF service in March 1996.

The Impala Mk 2's pilot was strapped into a Martin-Baker zero-zero rocket ejection seat. Impala losses over Namibia and Angola were comparatively light.

To create a single-seat version of the MB.326 trainer, Aermacchi made minimal changes to the airframe, simply fitting a smaller cockpit canopy and fairing over the rear seat. An extra fuel tank filled part of the redundant space.

In the COIN role, the Impala Mk 1 often carried two 12.7-mm (.50 cal.) machine-gun pods and two 80-mm rocket pods. Mk 2s were used for armed reconnaissance, with an underwing camera pod and drop-tank.

From the outset, the MB.326 was powered by Rolls-Royce's highly successful Bristol Siddeley-designed Viper turbojet, which was fitted to several Western trainer/light-attack types. Whereas Aermacchi fitted a more powerful version of this engine to the single-seat MB.326K, Atlas retained the variant used in the trainer.

Although the SAAF adopted their current national marking, incorporating the springbok, after World War II they retained the red, white and blue fin flash, a legacy of the RAF, for some years.

Two 30-mm DEFA cannon added a ground-strafing capability to the COIN abilities of the single-seat Impala Mk 2. SAAF aircraft have also carried machine-gun pods under the wings.

Drop-tanks of up to 227 litres (60 gal.) capacity can be fitted on the underwing pylons to increase combat radius in the COIN role. The ordnance load limit is 1814 kg (4,000 lb.) on four pylons.

COMBAT DATA

MAXIMUM SPEED

The Impala, the design of which dates back to the MB.326 of the 1950s, is showing its age in terms of performance. Its maximum speed is less than that of both the MB.339, a development of the MB.326, and the Hawk Mk 200.

IMPALA Mk 2	890 km/h (552 m.p.h.)
MB.339K	900 km/h (558 m.p.h.)
HAWK Mk 208	1017 km/h (630 m.p.h.)

ORDNANCE LOAD

The Impala's ordnance load is a little less than that of the later MB.339, but considerably less than the Hawk 200's. The Hawk, in its single-seat guise, has developed into a considerably more capable aircraft than the original two-seat trainer variant. Not only can it carry a heavier load, but also a wider array of weapons.

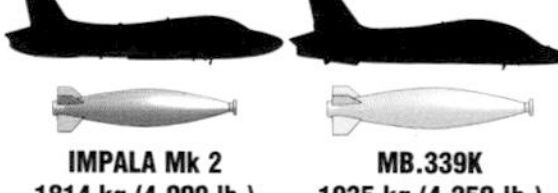

IMPALA Mk 2	MB.339K	HAWK Mk 208
1814 kg (4,000 lb.)	1935 kg (4,250 lb.)	3175 kg (7,000 lb.)

COMBAT RADIUS

While the Hawk 200 has a limited combat radius in a low-level mission with a 'typically' moderate ordnance load, it would be able to fly further than both the Impala and MB.339 with comparable loads. The MB.339 has twice the combat radius, but with half the weapons load on its wing pylons.

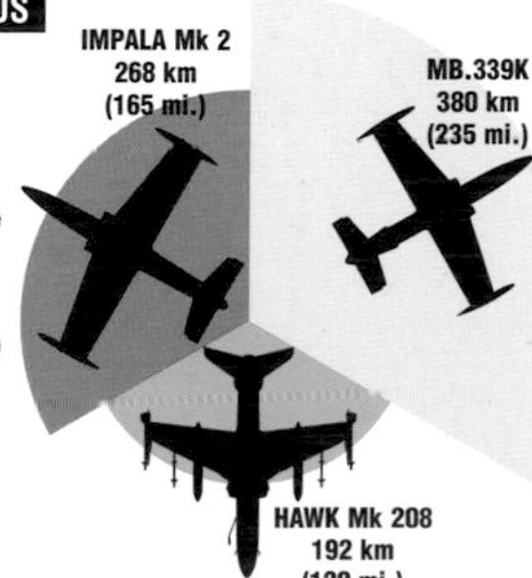

South African Air Force aircraft

■ **AÉROSPATIALE ALOUETTE III:** First delivered to the South African Air Force in 1967, this widely-exported Alouette remains in use in the communications and training roles.

■ **ATLAS CHEETAH:** A home-grown development of the Mirage III, the Cheetah uses Israeli avionics and radar as well as South African-designed equipment. Around 60 are in service.

■ **DASSAULT MIRAGE F.1:** Fewer than 30 F.1s remain in service with the SAAF, in the air defence and ground-attack roles. First delivered in 1975, they soon scored kills over Angolan MiGs.

AVRO

SHACKLETON AEW

● Long serving ● UK's sole AEW asset for 20 years ● Piston engined

▲ Thorough maintenance of the highest quality kept the Shackletons in service for 20 years longer than had been expected, with the highest levels of serviceability at all times.

The first Boeing E-3D Sentry AEW.Mk 1 arrived at RAF Waddington on 26 March 1991. The Shackleton AEW.Mk 2s of No. 8 Squadron, along with their antiquated radar system which used 1940s technology, could finally be retired. The United Kingdom had maintained a limited Airborne Early Warning (AEW) screen with the Shackleton since 1971, thanks to the skill and ingenuity of the crews. Its intended Nimrod AEW replacement of the mid-1980s was cancelled.

PHOTO FILE

AVRO SHACKLETON AEW

◀ **Famous ancestor**
This view clearly shows the similarity between the Lancaster and the Shackleton. The latter, however, was a larger machine.

▼ **'Ermintrude' in action**
No. 8 Squadron named all of its aircraft after characters in the children's television series The Magic Roundabout.

◀ **Lumps and bumps**
This near-silhouette shows the plethora of antennas and the large 'guppy' radome beneath the forward fuselage that are associated with the AEW systems.

Griffon power ▶
Six-bladed, contra-rotating propellers were a distinctive feature of the Shackleton.

◀ **AEW original**
The first Shackleton AEW.Mk 2 made its maiden flight on 30 September 1971. The conversions were based on the MR.Mk 2, as the newer MR.Mk 3s were at the end of their fatigue lives.

FACTS AND FIGURES

- The first MR.Mk 2 entered service in late 1952; the last MR.Mk 2, as an AEW.Mk 2, retired 39 years later.
- In April 1990 a Shackleton was lost when it flew into a hill in the Outer Hebrides.
- All AEW Shackletons retained a search and rescue capability.
- The majority of No. 8 Squadron's initial aircrew complement was made up of ex-Fleet Air Arm Gannet personnel.
- The RAF had planned to retire its Shackletons from 1980 onwards.
- Budget cuts early in the programme reduced the operational force to six.

PROFILE

Avro's last operational design

When the Shackleton AEW.Mk 2 was finally retired from RAF service, several Spitfires benefited from engine and other components donated by the venerable Avro aircraft, such was their age.

Even the most ardent Shackleton supporter admits that by the early 1980s the aircraft of No. 8 Squadron belonged to another era. It was a testimony to the quality of the original design and to the skill of its crews that the Shackleton remained viable as long as it did. It was the RAF's last front-line piston-engined aircraft.

In 1971 the Royal Navy was preparing to lose its aircraft-carriers and fixed-wing air power. This meant there would be no AEW coverage available to Royal Navy ships, as the shipborne Fairey Gannet AEW.Mk 3 would no longer be in service.

In order to provide naval forces and the UK's air defence system with the cheapest possible AEW cover, the Gannets' APS-20 radars were removed and rebuilt to improved APS-20F(I) standard, then fitted to 12 Shackleton MR.Mk 2 airframes. The resulting aircraft served throughout the blighted Nimrod AEW.Mk 3 programme and continued to operate until 1991.

Left: This AEW.Mk 2, WL745, originally appeared wearing the letter 'O', which was applied when it was a MR.Mk 2 serving with No. 204 Squadron.

Below: As the Nimrod AEW aircraft proved impractical, the situation for the antique Shackleton became increasingly desperate.

Shackleton AEW.Mk 2

Type: airborne early warning aircraft

Powerplant: four 1831-kW (2,455-hp) Rolls-Royce Griffon 57A V-12 piston engines

Maximum speed: 439 km/h (273 mph)

Endurance: maximum 15 hours

Initial climb rate: 259 m/min (850 fpm)

Range: 4908 km (3,050 miles)

Service ceiling: 7010 m (23,000 ft)

Weights: empty 25,855 kg (57,000 lb); maximum take-off 44,452 kg (98,000 lb)

Accommodation: typical crew of 10 consisting of four on the flight deck and six mission specialists

Dimensions:		
	span	36.58 m (120 ft 2 in)
	length	26.62 m (87 ft 4 in)
	height	5.10 m (16 ft 9 in)
	wing area	132.00 m² (1,421 sq ft)

SHACKLETON AEW.MK 2

'Dougal' flew with the RAF's only Shackleton AEW.Mk 2 squadron, No. 8. The aircraft were briefly based at Kinloss, but spent most of their careers flying from RAF Lossiemouth.

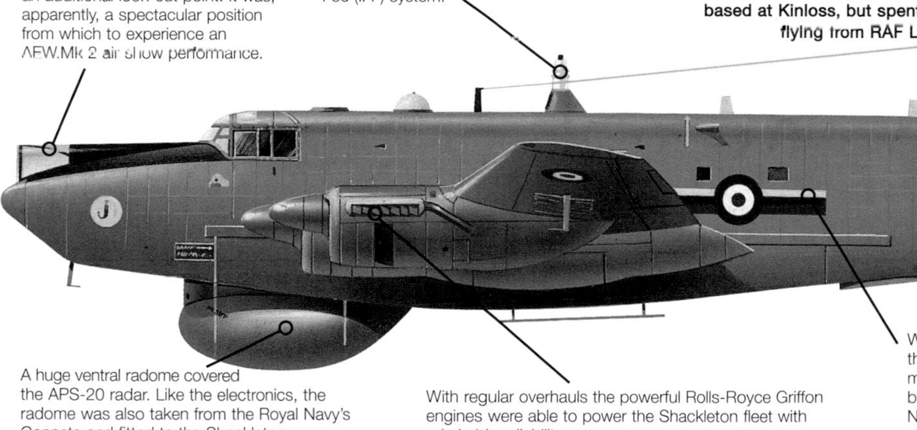

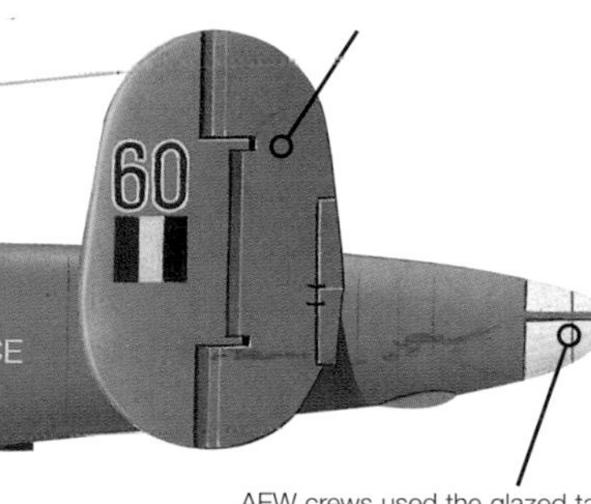

In the MR.Mk 2 this position was occupied by the forward gunner, but in the unarmed AEW.Mk 2 it was used as a navigation position and an additional look-out point. It was, apparently, a spectacular position from which to experience an AEW.Mk 2 air show performance.

While the casual observer might have been forgiven for thinking that the AEW.Mk 2 had a funnel, this unusual antenna actually served the APX-7 Identification Friend or Foe (IFF) system.

Avro designer Roy Chadwick was responsible for the entire line of bombers which led to the Shackleton. All used a similar and distinctive tail layout.

A huge ventral radome covered the APS-20 radar. Like the electronics, the radome was also taken from the Royal Navy's Gannets and fitted to the Shackleton.

With regular overhauls the powerful Rolls-Royce Griffon engines were able to power the Shackleton fleet with admirable reliability.

When the AEW.Mk 2s first entered service they retained the white upper fuselage of the maritime variants. This was soon replaced by an overall grey scheme, brightened by No. 8's colourful markings and the obligatory character painted on the forward fuselage.

AEW crews used the glazed tail position as a further observation point. Although the radome covered part of the bomb-bay, the remainder of the bay was used to stow a selection of search and rescue (SAR) equipment, including life rafts for the secondary SAR role.

ACTION DATA

MAXIMUM SPEED

Although long patrols are carried out at the most economical speed, a rapid transit to station is highly desirable. This helps to avoid gaps in AEW coverage as a result of unserviceability or other problems.

Aircraft	Maximum speed
SHACKLETON AEW.Mk 2	439 km/h (273 mph)
SENTRY AEW.Mk 1	853 km/h (530 mph)
NIMROD AEW.Mk 3	925 km/h (575 mph)

SERVICE CEILING

An ability to operate for long periods at high altitude is useful for any AEW platform as radar range increases with altitude. The service ceiling of the Shackleton is well below the operational ceiling of the Sentry, while the Nimrod outperforms both.

Aircraft	Service ceiling
SHACKLETON AEW.Mk 2	7010 m (23,000 ft)
SENTRY AEW.Mk 1	8840 m (29,000 ft)
NIMROD AEW.Mk.3	12,800 m (41,995 ft)

ENDURANCE

The endurance of the Shackleton is truly exceptional. The endurance of the Sentry AEW.Mk 1 is, however, accomplished at 1600 km (1,000 miles) from base and can be extended to the limits of crew fatigue by air-to-air refuelling.

SHACKLETON AEW.Mk 2
15 hours

SENTRY AEW.Mk 1
11 hours

NIMROD AEW.Mk 3
10 hours

Shackleton family line

■ LANCASTER: Developed from the disappointing, twin-engined Manchester, the Lancaster became a classic bomber design. This machine was one of the last flying, and served with the Aéronavale as a B.I(FE) maritime reconnaissance aircraft.

■ LINCOLN: Originally known as the Lancaster Mk IV and V, the Lincoln was based on the Lancaster layout but was a much larger aircraft, with more powerful engines. It began being replaced by the Canberra from 1951.

■ SHACKLETON MR: This Shackleton MR.Mk 3 is typical of the last Shackletons built. All aircraft in the series were developed from the Lincoln. The use of auxiliary Viper turbojets caused the MR.Mk 3s to reach the end of their fatigue lives prematurely.

AVRO

VULCAN

● Strategic missile carrier ● Delta-wing bomber

▲ *First flown in 1955, the Avro Vulcan was to spearhead British nuclear and conventional bombing capability for more than a quarter of a century.*

A major component of the free world's Cold War nuclear forces, the majestic Vulcan ruled the skies for more than two decades. This enormous delta-winged jet was one of the most graceful and beautiful flying machines ever committed to the grim reality of nuclear deterrence. The Vulcan also excelled, however, as a conventional bomber, tanker and reconnaissance platform.

PHOTO FILE

AVRO VULCAN

▲ **Switch to low level**
Development of Soviet air defences meant that in the 1960s the Vulcan's attack profile was changed to low-level penetration, and the men crewing the big bomber had to learn new skills.

▲ **'Iron' bomber**
Although designed for high-level nuclear strike, the Vulcan was a capable conventional bomber. The maximum bombload of '500-pounders' was over nine tons.

▲ **Stand-off strike**
The Blue Steel nuclear missile meant that the Vulcan could attack key strategic targets up to 350 km (210 miles) away.

◀ **Target Falklands**
Armourers load 454-kg (1,000-lb) bombs into the belly of a 'Black Buck' Vulcan from the British base on Ascension Island.

◀ **Conventional bomber**
With weapons bay doors open, an Avro Vulcan banks away at the end of a bomb run.

FACTS AND FIGURES

- Early Vulcans were painted a stunning pure white to reflect nuclear 'flash'.
- The four Olympus engines produced as much power as 18 railway locomotives.
- Vulcan pilots had ejection seats, but in an emergency the other three crewmen had to bail out through hatches.
- The Vulcan's pilot sat 5 m (16 ft) up and used a periscope to steer on the ground.
- The Vulcan could outmanoeuvre F-15s in high-altitude mock dogfights.
- Vulcans flew 12,650 km (7,860 miles) to bomb the Falklands, the longest straight-line combat missions in history at the time.

PROFILE

Vulcan to the fore

The Avro 698 Vulcan was the world's first large aircraft with a delta, or triangular-shaped, wing, and it opened up new frontiers in aerodynamic design. When the Vulcan joined Britain's bomber force, it marked a giant leap forward in technology. In addition to its impressive performance, the Vulcan gave the world a new look: it was one of the most exquisite and best-loved aircraft ever to take to the skies.

The prospect of atomic war was a far from pleasing one, however, and the Vulcan's grisly assignment was to prepare for the worst and to retaliate if a nuclear attack came. This serious business was at first carried out with heavy and awkward atomic and hydrogen bombs, and later with a far-reaching, nuclear-tipped missile called the Blue Steel.

As a conventional bomber, the five-man Vulcan achieved dramatic success in the 1982 Falklands War. Vulcans also served as strategic radar reconnaissance aircraft before their retirement from service in the late 1980s.

The Vulcan's unique delta wing made it highly manoeuvrable for such a large machine.

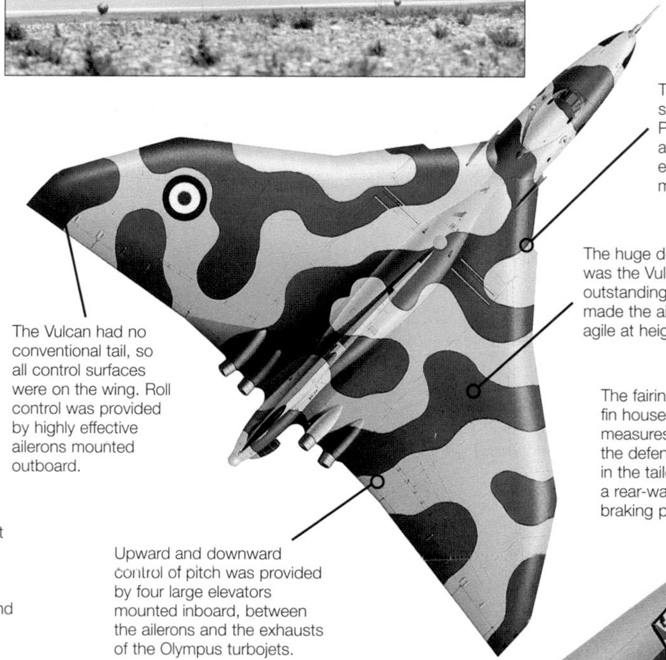

The prototype Vulcans had straight-wing leading edges. Production wings were kinked, a feature which helped to eliminate buffeting in high-*g* manoeuvring at altitude.

The huge delta wing was the Vulcan's most outstanding feature, which made the aircraft highly agile at height.

The Vulcan had no conventional tail, so all control surfaces were on the wing. Roll control was provided by highly effective ailerons mounted outboard.

The fairing on the tip of the fin housed a passive counter-measures antenna, but most of the defensive electronics were in the tailcone. This also housed a rear-warning radar and twin braking parachutes.

Upward and downward control of pitch was provided by four large elevators mounted inboard, between the ailerons and the exhausts of the Olympus turbojets.

VULCAN B.MK 2

Vulcans were in the process of being retired when they were called into action during the Falklands War. They were used to bomb Port Stanley airfield in the longest raids that had ever been flown up to that time.

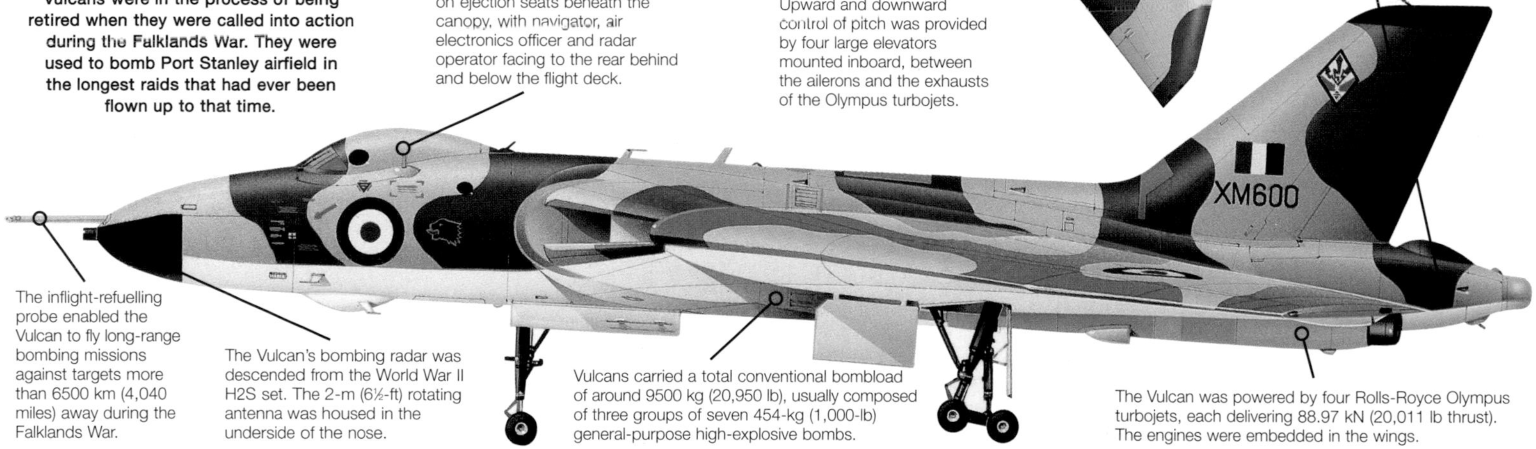

The Vulcan flew with a crew of five. The pilot and co-pilot sat on ejection seats beneath the canopy, with navigator, air electronics officer and radar operator facing to the rear behind and below the flight deck.

XM600

The inflight-refuelling probe enabled the Vulcan to fly long-range bombing missions against targets more than 6500 km (4,040 miles) away during the Falklands War.

The Vulcan's bombing radar was descended from the World War II H2S set. The 2-m (6½-ft) rotating antenna was housed in the underside of the nose.

Vulcans carried a total conventional bombload of around 9500 kg (20,950 lb), usually composed of three groups of seven 454-kg (1,000-lb) general-purpose high-explosive bombs.

The Vulcan was powered by four Rolls-Royce Olympus turbojets, each delivering 88.97 kN (20,011 lb thrust). The engines were embedded in the wings.

Vulcan B.Mk 2

Type: five-seat long-range bomber

Powerplant: four 88.97-kN (20,011-lb-thrust) Bristol (Rolls-Royce) Olympus turbojet engines

Maximum speed: 1038 km/h (645 mph) at 6096 m (20,000 ft)

Range: 5550 km (3,450 miles) on low-level mission with full bombload

Weight: maximum take-off 90,720 kg (200,000 lb)

Armament: Blue Danube hydrogen bomb, Blue Steel nuclear cruise missile or 21,454 kg (47,300 lb) of conventional bombs

Dimensions:

span	33.83 m (111 ft)
length	30.50 m (100 ft 1 in)
height	8.29 m (27 ft 2 in)
wing area	368.30 m² (3,964 sq ft)

COMBAT DATA

MAXIMUM SPEED

The first generation of strategic jet bombers were as fast as the fighters of the period, and were very hard to catch, particularly when flying high-level missions.

VULCAN B.Mk 2	1038 km/h (645 mph)
B-52 STRATOFORTRESS	1015 km/h (631 mph)
M-4 'BISON'	1100 km/h (684 mph)

SERVICE CEILING

Bombers tend to have big wings, which enables them to operate at high altitude more effectively than fighters. The Vulcan's huge wing gave it a particular advantage. Even at the end of its career, a well-flown Vulcan at 12,000 m (39,370 ft) could prove a handful even for an F-15 Eagle during mock dogfights.

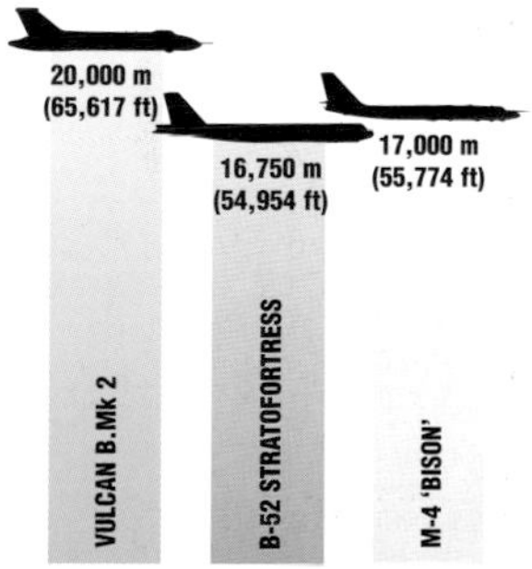

VULCAN B.Mk 2	20,000 m (65,617 ft)
B-52 STRATOFORTRESS	16,750 m (54,954 ft)
M-4 'BISON'	17,000 m (55,774 ft)

Vulcan nuclear strike profile

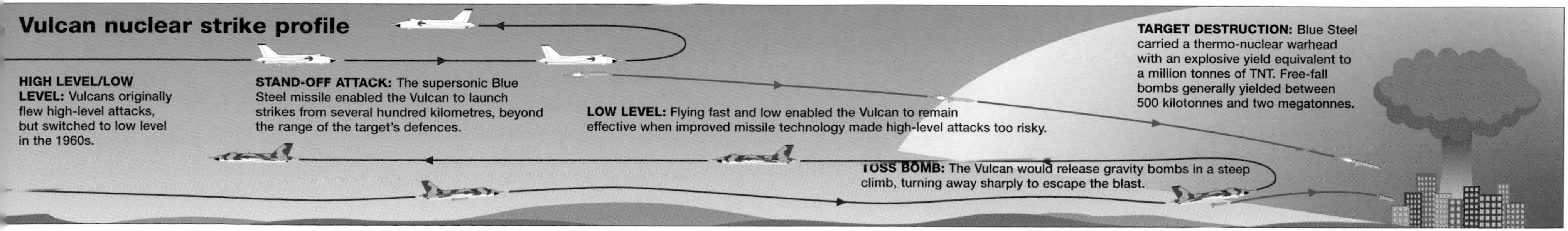

HIGH LEVEL/LOW LEVEL: Vulcans originally flew high-level attacks, but switched to low level in the 1960s.

STAND-OFF ATTACK: The supersonic Blue Steel missile enabled the Vulcan to launch strikes from several hundred kilometres, beyond the range of the target's defences.

LOW LEVEL: Flying fast and low enabled the Vulcan to remain effective when improved missile technology made high-level attacks too risky.

TARGET DESTRUCTION: Blue Steel carried a thermo-nuclear warhead with an explosive yield equivalent to a million tonnes of TNT. Free-fall bombs generally yielded between 500 kilotonnes and two megatonnes.

TOSS BOMB: The Vulcan would release gravity bombs in a steep climb, turning away sharply to escape the blast.

Avro Canada

CF-100 Canuck

● All-weather fighter ● Operational trainer ● ECM platform

When a pilot strapped into the CF-100 Canuck, he knew he was flying an excellent, all-weather warplane that was also Canada's first jet fighter. Avro Canada manufactured this two-man, twin-engined machine for the express purpose of defending North America from bomber attack. Designed in the late 1940s, this ship was one of the most popular aircraft ever to equip a squadron. The Canuck survived in squadron service until the early 1980s, by which time it had been relegated to second-line duties, including ECM missions.

▲ *The CF-100 defended the North American continent from attack. After the cancellation of its intended successor, the CF-105 Arrow, the Canuck remained in service with the Canadian air force in various roles for nearly 30 years.*

Photo File

Avro Canada CF-100 Canuck

▲ All-weather radar
Early CF-100s carried the Westinghouse APG-33 radar in the nose and eight machine guns in a ventral pack. Later versions carried an APG-40 radar.

High-performance jet ▶
The straight-wing layout of the CF-100 provided a very stable platform. Thanks to its powerful Orenda turbojets, it was also fast enough to exceed the sound barrier in a shallow dive; the first Canadian designed fighter to do so.

Air-to-air rockets ▶
The CF-100 Mk 4 introduced rocket armament, comprising 29 unguided 70-mm (2.75-in) rockets in each wingtip, plus 48 rockets in the ventral tray.

▲ Defence initiative
The Royal Canadian Air Force and the Avro Canada CF-100 Canuck participated in the joint defence of the North American continent with the US Air Defence Command, under the NORAD scheme.

▲ Missile armament
The Mk 3 was modified for testing the Velvet Glove missile. This weapon combination never became operational.

◀ Jet-assisted take-off
The CF-100 had provision for JATO bottles under the rear fuselage, although these were rarely used in squadron service.

Facts and Figures

- Four CF-100 squadrons were based in Europe, providing NATO allies with valuable all-weather defence.
- Some 692 Canucks were built for Canada and 53 were exported to Belgium.
- Painted all black, the CF-100 prototype made its maiden flight in January 1950.
- Belgium's sole CF-100 squadron was stationed at Beauvechain and was also committed to NATO defence.
- In 1952 a CF-100 became the first straight-wing fighter to exceed Mach 1.
- In the back seat was a radar operator using the APG-40 fire-control system.

PROFILE

Canada's first supersonic jet

Avro Canada began to design its first jet in 1946 and flew the CF-100 in 1950. This long-range interceptor became the backbone of Canada's contribution to the defence of North America and Western Europe.

Although it lacked the swept wings that became standard on most combat aircraft, the CF-100 was a fine all-weather fighter, its stability making it an excellent weapon platform and easy to fly on instruments. Pilots also found the Canuck (a slang term for a Canadian) an easy aircraft to handle at lower speeds when landing or manoeuvring in the airfield pattern. While it was not a dogfighter, for a 90-degree attack on a bomber formation using air-to-air rocket projectiles the CF-100 proved potent.

The Canuck flew alongside American interceptors such as the Northrop F-89 Scorpion and Lockheed F-94 Starfire, but these were never to earn the affection that Canadians bestowed on their airplane.

The definitive model of the CF-100 was the Mk 5, which introduced uprated powerplants and enhanced aerodynamics. The only export customer for the Canuck was Belgium, which received 53 Mk 5s. All served with the 1st All-Weather Interceptor Wing based at Beauvechain. A number of Canadian CF-100s were also based in Europe, some being used for electronic warfare.

Above: Unguided air-to-air rockets were first introduced on the CF-100 Mk 4 and proved to be a great improvement over the machine-gun armament of the Mk 3. A total of 116 rockets could be carried.

Above: The twin Canadian-built Orenda turbojets were non-afterburning, but provided a useful amount of thrust, as well as fuel efficiency and reliability for long-range patrol missions.

CF-100 Canuck Mk 5

Type: two-seat all-weather fighter

Powerplant: two 32.36-kN (7,278-lb-thrust) Orenda 11 or 14 turbojet engines

Maximum speed: 1046 km/h (650 mph) at 3050 m (10,000 ft)

Range: 3220 km (2,000 miles)

Service ceiling: 16,460 m (54,000 ft)

Combat radius: 1046 km (650 mph)

Weights: empty 10,478 kg (23,100 lb); maximum take-off 16,783 kg (37,000 lb)

Armament: 29 x 70-mm (2.75-in) 'Mighty Mouse' folding-fin aircraft rockets (FFAR) in each wingtip pod (48 additional FFAR or eight machine guns on some versions)

Dimensions:

span	17.68 m (58 ft)
length	16.48 m (54 ft 1 in)
height	4.74 m (15 ft 7 in)
wing area	54.90 m² (591 sq ft)

CF-100 CANUCK MK 5

This Canuck served in Europe with No. 440 Squadron, based at Zweibrucken, Germany. The squadron's aircraft later received a camouflaged colour scheme.

All CF-100 variants carried two crewmembers: the pilot in front and the navigator/weapons systems operator behind. Fifty dedicated training versions, the Mk 3CT and 3DT, were converted from standard Mk 3s.

The Avro Canada CF-100 Mk 1 prototype used Rolls-Royce Avon turbojets, replaced on production models by the Canadian Orenda 2 turbojet. On later versions the more powerful Orenda 8, 11 and 14 were used.

The definitive CF-100 Mk 5 model introduced a larger tailplane and increased wingspan, coupled with more powerful Orenda 14 turbojets, to improve high-altitude performance. Non-afterburning, each engine could provide 32.36 kN (7,278 lb thrust).

The Canuck Mk 5 shown here carried an all-weather APG-40 radar for the tracking of enemy bomber formations.

In the capacious ventral cavity under the forward fuselage, the Mk 5 could carry eight 12.7-mm (0.5-in) Colt-Browning machine guns or, alternatively, a tray containing 48 additional 70-mm (2.75-in) rockets.

Streamlined rocket pods mounted on each wingtip were first introduced on the CF-100 Mk 4. Each pod contained 29 unguided 70-mm (2.75-in) rockets, particularly effective in collision-course attacks on bomber formations. Alternatively, fuel tanks could be carried on the wingtip mounts.

Simple construction utilising tough materials gave the Canuck an exceptionally long flying life: the Royal Canadian Air Force's last few CF-100s were withdrawn as recently as 1981. Pilots enjoyed the plane's unrivalled stability and forgiving handling characteristics.

COMBAT DATA

MAXIMUM SPEED

Straight-wing, all-weather fighters were heavy and ungainly machines compared to lightweight air-superiority fighters such as the F-104 and MiG-17, but were just as deadly in their own role.

CF-100 CANUCK Mk 5	1046 km/h (650 mph)
F-89 SCORPION	1023 km/h (636 mph)
METEOR NF.Mk 11	960 km/h (597 mph)

ARMAMENT

Old-fashioned machine-gun armament was something of a weakness in the 1950s. Many MiG-15s in Korea returned to base after being hit by bullets from F-86 Sabres.

CF-100 CANUCK Mk 5	8 x 12.7-mm (0.5-in) MGs, 50 x 70-mm rockets
F-89 SCORPION	6 x 20-mm (0.79-in) cannon, 52 x 70-mm rockets
METEOR NF.Mk 11	4 x 20-mm cannon

RANGE

For defending the North American continent, the CF-100 had a good range performance to catch incoming bombers over the ocean.

CF-100 CANUCK Mk 5	3220 km (2,000 miles)
F-89 SCORPION	2200 km (1,379 miles)
METEOR NF.Mk 11	1480 km (917 miles)

Canadian-built jets

■ **CANADAIR SILVER STAR:** A licenced-built version of the Lockheed T-33 with a Nene engine, this aircraft served as an advanced trainer with the RCAF in Canada and Europe.

■ **CANADAIR SABRE:** A Canadian-built F-86, the Sabre served with no fewer than 16 RCAF squadrons until replaced by the CF-100. The Sabre served in Europe and the UK in the early 1950s.

■ **AVRO CANADA CF-105 ARROW:** The intended replacement for the CF-100, the Arrow would have been the most potent interceptor of the 1960s but for its cancellation in February 1959.

■ **CANADAIR CF-104:** Canada began to licence-produce the Lockheed Starfighter after the cancellation of the CF-105. Later, these aircraft were tasked with strike/reconnaissance.

BEECH C-12

● **Multi-role turboprop light transport** ● **Derived from civil design**

Initially supplied to the US Army and USAF in 1975 as a light transport, the Beech C-12 is today in service with all three US services and 18 other air arms (in some cases in its civil guise) in a wide variety of roles. The Beech B200 Super King Air, from which the C-12 is derived, was developed from the commercial Model 100 in the early 1970s. The new type featured a T-tail, longer wings and many internal refinements. Later versions have further improvements.

▲ *Beechcraft's C-12F replaced the CT-39 Sabreliner as an operational support aircraft and featured more powerful engines, a cargo door and improved passenger facilities.*

PHOTO FILE

BEECH C-12

▼ **Special duties**
Not all C-12s supplied to air arms are used as transports. Some are camouflaged and used for aerial surveillance and other tasks.

▲ **Navy transports**
A total of 78 Beech A200Cs was purchased by the US Navy and Marine Corps as UC-12Bs. They first entered service in 1980 as personnel and utility transports.

▼ **Mission support**
Designated UC-12J, this bigger and more powerful Beech 1900C is one of six used by the US Air National Guard for mission support from 1987.

▲ **Army Hurons**
The US Army employs its C-12A/C/D Hurons in the utility role, supporting Army units and US embassies around the world.

Upgraded aircraft ▶
When the US Army took delivery of the more powerful C-12C/Ds with PT6A-41 turboprops it upgraded its large fleet of C-12As to the same standard. This C-12D features increased-span wings and cargo doors.

FACTS AND FIGURES

- ➤ It took Beechcraft four years to develop the Model 200 Super King Air/C-12 with its large T-tail, from the Model 100.
- ➤ The first C-12 entered service with the US Army at Fort Monroe in July 1975.
- ➤ Two USAF C-12s are operated by US Customs for anti-smuggling surveillance.
- ➤ Extensive aerial arrays identify the RC-12 variants used by the US Army for electronics special missions.
- ➤ The Beech B200C/C-12F can fly faster, higher and further than the A200 model.
- ➤ Cargo doors and provision of wingtip fuel tanks are features of the C-12D.

PROFILE

Military utility 'off the shelf'

Beech developed its Super King Air 200 over a four-year period from 1969, using the successful King Air 100 executive turboprop transport as a basis. It had more powerful engines, a T-tail and increased wingspan as well as equipment changes. It was bigger, faster and more capable than the King Airs already in service with the US Army as the U-21. A contract was placed for 34 of the new aircraft as C-12s, for the US Army and USAF. In most respects these were standard Super King Airs from the production line, but with modified avionics and equipment to meet military requirements as staff transports.

In 1978 the US Navy bought the first of 78 C-12s for use as personnel and utility transports. In order to accommodate freight items these UC-12Bs had a large cargo door (1.32 m/4-ft. 4-in. by 1.32 m/4-ft. 4-in.) on the port side. They also had 634-kW (850-hp.) Pratt & Whitney PT6A-41 engines and a taller undercarriage assembly.

Above: A number of South American air arms, including that of Argentina, have purchased Super King Airs as affordable surveillance and maritime patrol platforms.

The US Army converted a number of its new C-12Ds for special electronic missions and battlefield surveillance as RC-12s. These have a large array of aerials and pods.

Below: This UC-12B was operated by the US Marine Corps headquarters and based at the Naval Air Facility at Washington, DC.

C-12F

Type: utility transport

Powerplant: two 634-kW (850-hp.) Pratt & Whitney Canada PT6A-42 turboprops

Maximum speed: 545 km/h (338 m.p.h.) at 7620 m (25,000 ft.)

Initial climb rate: 747 m/min (2,450 f.p.m.)

Range: 3641 km (2,260 mi.) with maximum fuel at 10,670 m (35,000 ft.)

Service ceiling: more than 10,670 m (35,000 ft.)

Weights: operating empty 3656 kg (8,043 lb.); maximum take-off 5670 kg (12,464 lb.)

Accommodation: two pilots, plus eight passengers or 1201 kg (2,642 lb.) of cargo

Dimensions:

span	16.61 m (54 ft. 6 in.)
length	13.36 m (43 ft. 10 in.)
height	4.52 m (14 ft. 10 in.)
wing area	28.15 m² (303 sq. ft.)

SUPER KING AIR B200

Ireland's Air Corps is one of 18 air arms apart from the US services that has operated Beech C-12/Super King Airs. Three B200s were used for maritime patrol missions and as transports and multi-engine trainers.

The semi-monocoque fuselage structure of the Super King Air 200 is of light alloy. The cabin is air-conditioned and fully pressurised. Large windows along the fuselage and on the flight deck give good visibility.

Accommodation is provided for two pilots and up to 10 passengers in the standard transport layout. When mission equipment is carried for maritime patrol, accommodation is reduced to a maximum of six, depending upon the duration of the flight.

The B200 has a cantilever T-tail structure of light alloy, with swept vertical and horizontal surfaces. The fixed incidence tailplane has de-icing 'boots' on the leading edges. Each elevator has a trim tab.

Two Pratt & Whitney Canada PT6A turboprops each drive a three-bladed, metal, constant-speed fully-feathering and reversible propeller.

The tricycle undercarriage has twin main wheels on each leg that retract forwards into the engine nacelle. The nose leg has a single, steerable wheel that retracts rearwards into the nose section.

This standard Super King Air 200 has a passenger entry door at the rear of the cabin on the port side. It has integral steps built into the back of the door that lower to the ground. Some USAF, US Navy and US Army C-12s have large (1.32-m/4-ft. 4-in. high and 1.32-m/4-ft. 4-in. wide) cargo access doors.

ACTION DATA

PASSENGERS

The usefulness of the C-12F as a liaison transport is limited by its size. This role is largely the preserve of larger, 19-seat machines like the C-12J (derived from the Beech 1900) and C-26A Metro, both civil designs that have been adapted for military roles.

- C-12F: 8 passengers
- C-12J: 19 passengers
- C-26A METRO: 19 passengers

MAXIMUM CRUISING SPEED

Though the C-12J is a larger aircraft it lacks the high cruising speed of the smaller C-12F. The Fairchild C-26A has a similar speed performance to the Beechcraft C-12F.

- C-12F: 536 km/h (338 m.p.h.)
- C-12J: 471 km/h (292 m.p.h.)
- C-26A METRO: 515 km/h (319 m.p.h.)

TAKE-OFF RUN TO 15 M (50 FT.)

Both the 19-seaters here require almost 1000 m (3,300 ft.) in which to get airborne and attain a height of 15 m (50 ft.). The smaller C-12F uses just under 800 m (2,600 ft.) of runway to do the same, making it more useful from smaller airports. Take-off performance varies according to the load being carried. Heavier loads need longer runways.

- C-12F: 786 m (2,580 ft.)
- C-12J: 991 m (3,250 ft.)
- C-26A METRO: 991 m (3,250 ft.)

USAF/ANG light transports

BRITISH AEROSPACE C-29A: BAe's well-known 125 Series 800A executive jet was adopted by the USAF in the late 1980s for the Combat Flight Inspection and Navigation (C-FIN) role.

FAIRCHILD C-26A: When the US Air National Guard (ANG) needed a new operational support transport aircraft, the Metro 3, a 19-seater regional airliner was chosen in 1988.

GATES LEARJET C-21A: In the early 1980s the then Military Airlift Command operated the CT-39 Sabreliner for high-priority, time-sensitive cargos. The Learjet replaced these from 1984.

SHORTS C-23: For the distribution of spare parts around Europe, USAFE bought 18 Shorts 330 Sherpas (C-23As). Ten were later bought for the ANG, while the Army bought ex-civil C-23Bs.

BEECH
T-1A JAYHAWK

● Civil design ● Tanker-trainer ● Military 'biz-jet'

Cutting an unusual shape in the sky with its all white colour scheme and swept-back wings, the T-1 Jayhawk is fast becoming the standard training tool for the United States Air Force. The shortage of T-38 Talon trainers coupled with a shrinking defence budget saw the United States Air Force undertake the unusual step of purchasing a civilian business jet for its training purposes. The aircraft required only minor modification.

▲ *Despite its civilian origins the Beech T-1 Jayhawk has proved suitable for the rigours of military training. Crews have found the aircraft a forgiving teaching tool.*

PHOTO FILE

BEECH T-1A JAYHAWK

▲ Classic lines
The Jayhawk displays the low-set wings and the rear-mounted engines that have become the hallmarks of current 'biz-jets.'

▲ Bright future
Having been in service for only a relatively short period of time, the Beech Jayhawk is expected to have a long military career with the USAF.

Japanese use ▶
By early 1994 Japan's Air Self-Defence Force had also purchased the improved American Jayhawk to use as a light utility transport aircraft.

▼ Improved design
One of the military modifications specified involved the wings of the Jayhawk being strengthened in order to withstand the damaging effects of a heavy birdstrike. The pilot's cockpit glazing was also improved as a precaution.

▲ Training for all
The type having passed its trials with 'flying-colours' the USAF quickly ordered 148 Jayhawks. A final total of 180 examples is anticipated.

FACTS AND FIGURES

- The T-1A Jayhawk provides the USAF with an advanced trainer for instructing future tanker/transport pilots.
- A shortage of T-38 Talons saw the adoption of the Jayhawk in US service.
- Increased fuel capacity is one of the major changes to military Jayhawks.
- During training flights a senior instructor pilot is accompanied by at least four students to reduce operating costs.
- Jayhawks are the first aircraft delivered under the new pilot training programme.
- The Jayhawk is based on the civilian Beech Jet 400.

PROFILE

America's pilot provider

The Beech T-1 Jayhawk is now entering service in increasing numbers and providing the USAF with a unique training tool. In line with the current trend of using civilian aircraft for military applications, future USAF tanker and transport pilots now receive training at Reese AFB at a much reduced cost to the American taxpayer. One source of economies is that several trainees can be taken on each sortie under the guidance of one senior instructor pilot.

Alterations to the aircraft were required before it entered military service. These saw an increase in the strength of the wing leading edges and a revised cockpit windscreen. To reduce maintenance demands a single refuelling point was also installed on the aircraft. USAF examples are limited to the training role and therefore feature six fewer windows in the cabin area because of their reduced seating capacity.

In a somewhat ironic move given the original Mitsubishi design of the Jayhawk, the Japanese Air Self-Defence Force (JASDF) followed the American example and bought the aircraft for the training role. Beginning in early 1994, the JASDF took delivery of three Beech 400Ts (equivalent to the T-1A) to use for pilot training. These aircraft are equipped with extra fuel tanks and thrust reversers to simulate the handling of large transport aircraft for their pupil pilots.

Above: America's training fleet has worn a host of colour schemes, but the overall white is now used.

Above: Having completed another sortie, a student enters the landing circuit at Reese AFB, where the first aircraft was delivered in 1992.

T-1A Jayhawk

Type: advanced jet trainer/utility jet

Powerplant: two 12.9-kN (2,900-lb.-thrust) Pratt & Whitney Canada JT15D-5B turbojets

Maximum speed: 854 km/h (529 m.p.h.) at 8840 m (29,000 ft.); cruising speed 828 km/h (513 m.p.h.) at 11,890 m (39,000 ft.)

Range: 3575 km (2,340 mi.) with four passengers and maximum internal fuel load

Service ceiling: 12,495 m (41,000 ft.)

Weights: empty 4588 kg (10,094 lb.); maximum take-off 7157 kg (15,745 lb.)

Accommodation: one instructor pilot; four students

Dimensions:

span		13.25 m (43 ft. 5 in.)
length		14.75 m (48 ft. 4 in.)
height		4.19 m (13 ft. 9 in.)
wing area		22.43 m² (241 sq. ft.)

T-1A JAYHAWK

This T-1A Jayhawk is based at Reese AFB in Texas, operating under the TTTS (Tanker/Transport Trainer System). The aircraft is proving to be an extremely practical training tool. Future orders for additional aircraft are currently being considered by the USAF.

Pilots destined for the vast transport and tanker fleet of the United States Air Force are instructed on the Jayhawk in an effort to develop the necessary skills required for handling large aircraft. This has resulted in a huge saving in training costs.

A high-set tail allows the Jayhawk excellent handling qualities at high altitudes where most operational training takes place. Very few modifications were made to the flight control systems of the aircraft.

Avionics equipment in the nose of the aircraft was relocated to the cockpit, also added was a turbulence-detection radar.

To improve the safety record of the aircraft the wings of USAF Jayhawks were strengthened, along with the pilot's windscreen.

A distinguishing feature of the aircraft is its small undercarriage. This was seen as a weight-saving measure but also allows the aircraft to be maintained without requiring gantries.

Positioned high on the rear fuselage are the Pratt & Whitney Canada JT15D turbofan engines. These received little modification prior to the entry of the Jayhawk into military service. Maintenance personnel have found the aircraft to be extremely reliable.

ACTION DATA

MAXIMUM SPEED

Matched against other military trainers the T-1 Jayhawk offers a maximum speed that is far in excess of its propeller-powered equivalents. Despite this performance, high speed is seldom used on training flights.

T-1A JAYHAWK	854 km/h (529 m.p.h.)
C-12F	545 km/h (338 m.p.h.)
KING AIR C90A	457 km/h (283 m.p.h.)

RANGE

Additional fuel tanks were a requirement before the USAF would accept the Jayhawk into service. Despite the addition of wing tip tanks to the Beech C-12 variants the huge range of the Jayhawk cannot be equalled by its contemporaries.

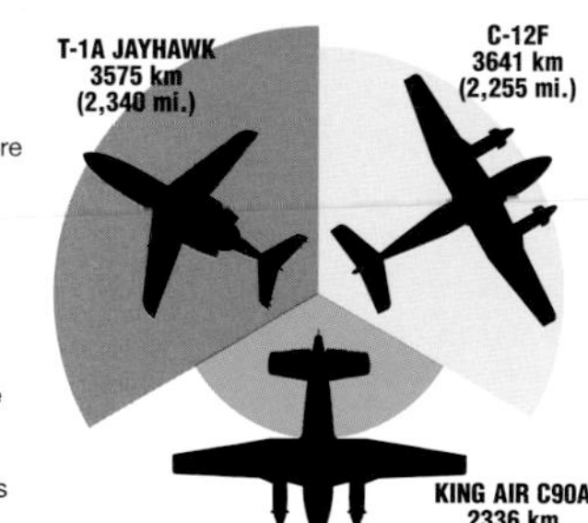

MAXIMUM TAKE OFF WEIGHT

In its role as a training aircraft the Jayhawk requires a large take-off weight. Despite its relatively small size the Jayhawk matches this need surprisingly well. Compared to the King Air, which is also used in the utility role, the Jayhawk compares very favourably.

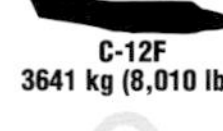

T-1A JAYHAWK	C-12F	KING AIR C90A
7157 kg (15,745 lb.)	3641 kg (8,010 lb.)	2336 kg (5,139 lb.)

Serving their country

CESSNA CITATION: Operational with the Spanish Navy, the Citation is used as a navigation trainer and light transport aircraft. One model is used for reconnaissance duties.

GRUMMAN GULFSTREAM: The large dimensions of the Gulfstream III have made it an ideal platform for liaison and VIP duties. This example serves with the Danish air force.

NORTH AMERICAN SABRELINER: Currently reaching the end of its service with the United States armed forces, the T-39 Sabreliner continues to serve with South American air arms.

BELL

UH-1B/C IROQUOIS

● Airborne jeep ● Multi-role helicopter ● NATO workhorse

Bell's Model 204 formed the basis for one of the most successful series of helicopters ever built. Flown for the first time in October 1956, it was designated XH-40, then HU-1, by the US Army (who called it the 'Huey'), before a designation change to HU-1A Iroquois. The HU-1B introduced a more powerful engine and the HU-1C had a new rotor system. Later still the HU- designation was changed to UH-. Variants were built by Agusta in Italy.

▲ *A door-gunner rides 'shotgun' with his M60 as a pair of 'Hueys' fly over the Delta region in Vietnam. To many people, the war in Southeast Asia was symbolized by images of the UH-1.*

PHOTO FILE

BELL UH-1B/C IROQUOIS

▲ High-speed bird
Several test configurations were used on the 'Huey', increasing the speed to 402 km/h (250 mph).

▲ Navy rescue
This TH-1L uses its sling hoist during a demonstration at Ellyson Field, Pensacola, Florida.

▼ Overseas success
Built under licence by Agusta in Italy as the AB 204, this 'Huey' serves in the anti-submarine role. Early versions of the UH-1 remain in service throughout Europe.

▲ Weapons platform
An Italian example demonstrates the offensive capabilities of the UH-1 by lifting off with two pylon-mounted machine guns and 21 rockets.

Anti-tank missiles ▶
The 'Huey' was employed in the development of the first air-to-ground missile for the US Army, which was used in Vietnam.

FACTS AND FIGURES

- ➤ Four prototype YUH-1Bs were ordered in June 1959, with the first flight taking place in the following April.
- ➤ A total of 1010 UH-1Bs were produced in Italy, Japan and the United States.
- ➤ The YUH-1B set an unofficial world speed record of 357 km/h (222 mph) in May 1964.
- ➤ Differences between the B and C models included a modified rotor system, wider rotor blades and a larger fin.
- ➤ The 'Huey' was the first helicopter to see widespread use as a gunship.
- ➤ The Royal Australian Air Force was the first non-US customer for eight UH-1Bs.

PROFILE

Bell's ubiquitous 'Huey'

The turbine engine was one of the keys to the Model 204's success. Mounted on the cabin roof just behind the gearbox, it left the cabin unencumbered and provided the performance required by the US Army.

Early UH-1Bs retained the UH-1A's 716-kW (960-hp) T53 engine, but an 820-kW (1,100-hp) powerplant soon became the standard. The new model was delivered from March 1961 and could be armed with rocket pods and machine guns carried on the sides of the cabin. UH-1Bs were also built by Fuji in Japan and Agusta in Italy. Agusta models included the AB 204AS anti-submarine variant for the Italian and Spanish navies, plus civil AB 204Bs with Lycoming T53, General Electric T58 or Rolls-Royce Gnome engines.

The UH-1C, which flew in September 1965, used a new rotor system with 'door hinges' and wider blades. This provided more lift, enabling the fuel load to be increased and improving the machine's manoeuvrability and speed. Variants of the UH-1C, with new designations, were used by the US Air Force, Navy and Marine Corps in the training, rescue and assault roles.

Below: The glossy overall olive drab, with a yellow tail band and white lettering, soon gave way to dull green when the 'Huey' entered combat.

Above: This is one of six test YH-40s seen during a proving flight. There were few differences between these and the first production 'Hueys'.

UH-1C

Type: single-engined multi-role utility helicopter

Powerplant: one 820-kW (1,100-hp) Lycoming T53-L-11 turboshaft engine

Maximum speed: 238 km/h (148 mph) at sea level

Initial climb rate: 427 m/min (1,400 fpm)

Range: 615 km (382 miles) with auxiliary fuel

Service ceiling: 3505 m (11,500 ft)

Weights: empty 2300 kg (5,070 kg); maximum take-off 4309 kg (9,500 lb)

Dimensions:

rotor diameter	13.41 m (44 ft)
length	12.98 m (42 ft 7 in)
height	3.84 m (12 ft 7 in)
rotor disc area	141.26 m² (1,521 sq ft)

TH-1L

Pictured in red and white training colours, this TH-1L, the navy designation for the 'Huey', is used for pilot training. This involves flying from aircraft carriers and over-water navigation.

The cabin could hold nine passengers and crew, and offered excellent all-round visibility. The machine was often flown with the doors removed to allow rapid exit.

One Lycoming T53-L-5 engine powered the UH-1D, although its output was improved in later variants. Licence-built models were powered by Rolls-Royce engines.

Originally on the left side of the tail boom, the tail rotor in later licence-built variants was positioned on the right-hand side. The tail size was also increased because of the uprated engines.

Two skids supported the UH-1 on the ground. Although less complex than wheeled landing gear, their use restricted the helicopter's movement once it had landed.

The bulbous design of the fuselage allowed the carriage of stores on external pylons, so as not to restrict the internal load.

Troop-carrying 'Hueys' were often called 'slicks' because their airframes were devoid of the external equipment which reduced performance; this name has been used throughout the UH-1's service.

A tail skid, designed to protect the rear rotor blades from striking the ground during landing, was positioned on the end of the boom.

COMBAT DATA

POWER

Although the Huey was the first practical transport helicopter to see widespread military use, the power of the early models was found to be lacking in the roles with which the helicopter was tasked. Later variants were fitted with improved engines.

MAXIMUM PAYLOAD

The early variants of the UH-1, although capable of lifting an acceptable load, required improvement. The advent of more powerful engines in later variants allowed an increased payload, although this was still restricted by the cabin size. The knowledge that was gained during the development of the 'Huey' was incorporated into the purpose-built Blackhawk.

MAXIMUM SPEED

The UH-1B's relatively light load meant that its performance was superior to that of later models, which became much heavier because of operational and design changes. The twin-engined Blackhawk offered improved performance in a streamlined fuselage while retaining the capability to carry large loads.

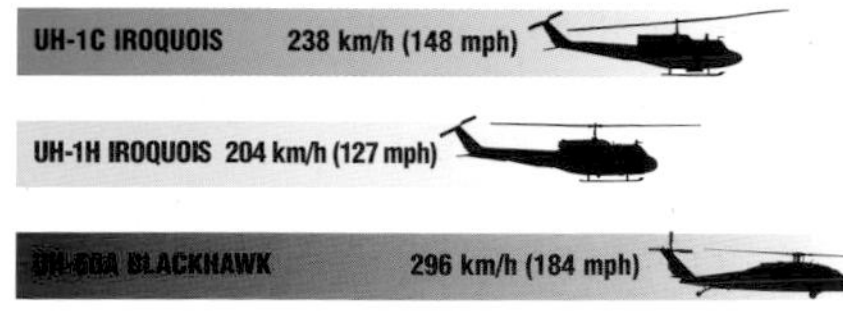

Improving the breed

■ **UH-1H:** An improvement of the UH-1B design, advances included increased lifting capability and an enlarged cabin area. This variant serves with the Taiwan air force.

■ **MODEL 212:** Offering the reliability of an improved twin engine and a weather radar located in the nose, this Singaporean example serves with the local VIP flight.

■ **MODEL 214ST:** Possessing little commonality with earlier designs, this Venezuelan 'Huey' features a stretched cabin, improved performance and composite rotor blades.

BELL/BOEING

V-22 OSPREY

● Assault transport ● Vertical take-off ● Multiple roles

US Marines have a phrase for it: they call it 'Vertical Envelopment'. The idea is to bypass a defended coast by flying troops over the top, fast, landing them in the enemy rear before the foe can react. And nothing can move Marines as fast as the revolutionary V-22 Osprey, which flies like an aeroplane but takes off and lands like a helicopter.

▲ *The prototype V-22 Osprey is seen transitioning to horizontal flight. It is this unique ability which will revolutionise the speed of US Marine Corps amphibious assaults.*

PHOTO FILE

BELL/BOEING V-22 OSPREY

▲ Osprey's forerunner
The Bell XV-15 was the culmination of a long line of experimental convertiplanes, and was the direct ancestor of the V-22.

Sea trials ▶
The Osprey has shown that it can operate from any deck large enough to give sideways clearance to the twin rotors.

Global reach ▶
The V-22 can be refuelled in flight. It can be deployed over intercontinental distances in less than a day – which is something that no helicopter can do.

▲ High-tech
The Osprey comes equipped with a modern 'glass' cockpit, dominated by multi-function controls and computerised video displays.

Marine ◀ assault
The most enthusiastic supporters of the V-22 are the US Marines, who see the aircraft as adding greatly to the ability with which they can carry out amphibious assaults.

▲ Folding wings
The Osprey takes up a lot of space, which is at a premium aboard even the largest carrier. To make more room, the rotors fold and the wing swivels in line with the fuselage.

FACTS AND FIGURES

- ➤ The V-22 first flew on 19 March 1989, taking off vertically from Bell's research facility at Arlington, Texas.
- ➤ First transition from vertical to horizontal flight took place on 14 September 1989.
- ➤ The V-22 has twice the speed and twice the range of a comparable helicopter.
- ➤ V-22s can be deployed anywhere in the world within 36 hours.
- ➤ A typical helicopter needs three times as much maintenance as the V-22.
- ➤ Ospreys can carry a seven-ton load slung beneath the fuselage at speeds of up to 375 km/h (235 m.p.h.).

PROFILE

High-speed assault

A Marine commander assaulting a defended shoreline needs to get his troops and equipment ashore fast. But landing craft are slow and make easy targets, and helicopters are horribly vulnerable to enemy fire. Until now, the only way to minimise the time the helicopters are at risk has been to launch them from as close to shore as possible, but that exposes the irreplaceable assault ships to danger from the enemy's long-range artillery and missiles.

The Osprey has changed all that. With its rotors pointing upwards, it can take off and land vertically on ship or ashore. But tilting the rotors forwards converts them into propellers, allowing the Osprey to fly twice as fast as the fastest helicopter.

Operating in conjunction with speedy air-cushion landing craft, the V-22 can deliver troops or weapons over much greater distances than a helicopter. An amphibious task force commander can now launch his attack from over the horizon, and still have his troops ashore in a shorter time than would have been possible with helicopters and landing craft.

The tremendous width of the Osprey's rotor blades is clear in this photo of a landing on a 'Wasp'-class assault ship.

The V-22's prop-rotors are 11.58 m (38 ft.) in diameter. Immensely strong to resist combat damage, one provides enough lift to keep the aircraft in the air alone if necessary.

The wing is fitted on a pivot. Swung fore and aft and with the rotors folded, an Osprey takes up no more room than a large helicopter.

MV-22A Osprey

Type: two-crew multi-role convertiplane transport

Powerplant: two 4593-kW (6,150-hp.) Allison T406-AD-400 turboprops

Maximum speed: 556 km/h (345 mi.) at sea level

Combat radius: 1880 km (1,168 mi.) search and rescue; 1000 km (620 mi.) amphibious assault

Rate of climb: 332 m/min (1,100 f.p.m.) vertically

Service ceiling: 8000 m (26,250 ft.)

Weights: empty 14,433 kg (31,820 lb.); loaded 24,948 kg (55,000 lb.)

Payload: up to 25 fully equipped troops or 4500 kg (9,920 lb.) cargo internally, or 6800 kg (15,000 lb.) external load

Dimensions:

span (inc rotors)	25.76 m (84 ft. 6 in.)
length	17.32 m (56 ft. 10 in.)
height	6.63 m (21 ft. 9 in.)
rotor area	210 m² (2,260 sq. ft.)

XV-22 Osprey

Although facing Congressional opposition, the V-22 has been described by senior Marine officers as 'our number one aviation priority'.

Test aircraft are often fitted with sensitive flight testing instruments to measure the aircraft's performance in all areas of the flight regime.

The Osprey is manned by a pilot and co-pilot. They control the aircraft by means of an electronic fly-by-wire system.

The Osprey's engines are immensely powerful, in order to lift the aircraft free of the ground without any aerodynamic assistance.

The huge paddle-bladed prop-rotors are a compromise between long helicopter-type rotors and much smaller aircraft-type propellers.

Osprey's twin tail is set high on a boom, in order to leave room for the rear door and loading ramp.

The extensive use of composite material means that the V-22 is about 25 per cent lighter than a metal aircraft of comparable size and lifting power.

ACTION DATA

TAKE-OFF PROCEDURE

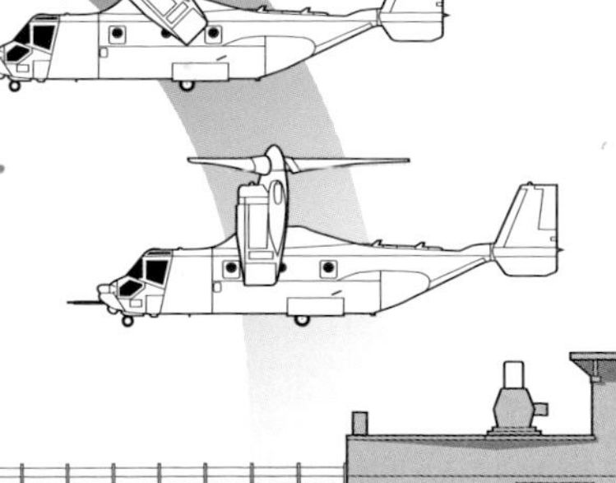

Osprey can take off vertically or with a short take-off run. Transition from vertical flight to horizontal is automatic. As the aircraft's forward speed increases, control is switched from the aircraft's rotors (as in a helicopter) to the conventional flaps and ailerons (as in an aircraft).

PAYLOAD EFFICIENCY

A CH-53 helicopter can carry up to 55 troops in the assault role.

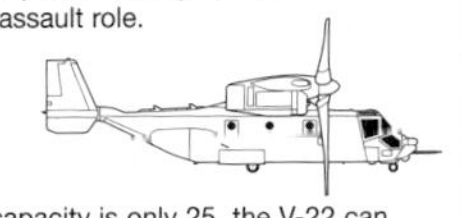

Although its capacity is only 25, the V-22 can make three trips to a helicopter's one, landing 75 troops in the same time that the CH-53 lands 55.

Landing comparison

MARINE ASSAULT: An amphibious assault using Ospreys and air-cushion landing craft can stand offshore a safe distance from enemy defences, and still land troops more quickly than helicopters and landing craft.

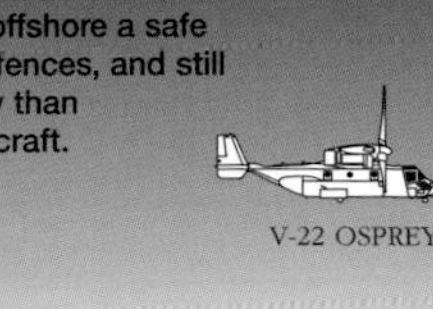

ENEMY THREAT: Most modern artillery pieces have a range of between 17 and 30 km 10 and 20 mi.), putting at risk any vessel coming within that range.

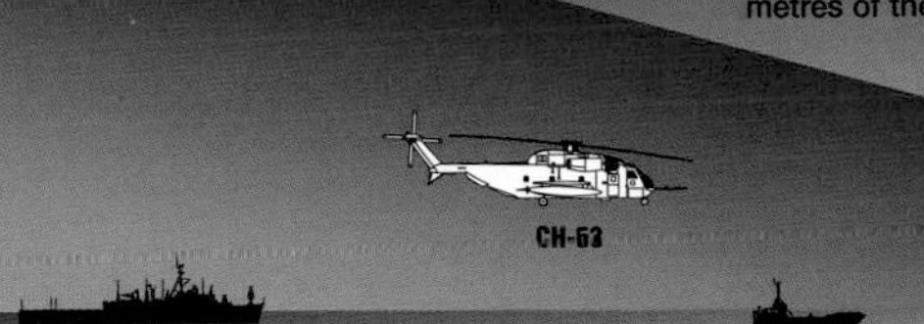

CLOSE RANGE: Conventional assaults are limited by the slow speed of conventional landing craft. To get troops ashore in under an hour, the assault fleet has to be within a few thousand metres of the coast, well within artillery range.

LARGE ASSAULT SHIP

AIR-CUSHION LANDING CRAFT

LANDING CRAFT

OBJECTIVE: THE BEACH

Blackburn

Buccaneer

● Low-level strike ● Anti-ship attack ● First Gulf War laser-bomber

One of those classics of aviation, the Blackburn Buccaneer was a warplane that pilots loved to fly and which was highly respected by its opponents. In its heyday it was the world's most advanced low-level, high-speed strike aircraft. Even at the end of its career it remained an immensely strong machine, capable of carrying just about any tactical bomb, rocket or missile used in modern air combat.

▲ *Blasting off from HMS* Ark Royal*, a Buccaneer sets off on a strike. The aircraft was designed to be a powerful threat to the Soviet navy, especially its 'Sverdlov'-class cruisers.*

Blackburn Buccaneer

▲ **Touchdown**
Early Buccaneers were powered by unreliable Gyron Junior engines. This made the final moments of a carrier landing somewhat perilous, if a pilot had to apply power to 'go around' again.

▼ **Bombs away**
Long-range bombing attacks were the Buccaneer's trademark. Although this bomb is conventional, the 'toss' delivery was designed for a nuclear weapon.

◀ **Bush striker**
South Africa was the only export success for the Buccaneer. These aircraft were used in action in long-range strikes, often at treetop height. They also carried South Africa's secret nuclear bombs; many experts estimated that five bombs existed.

▲ **Test aircraft**
This brightly coloured example, XW986, was operated on test flights for many years by Britain's Royal Aircraft Establishment.

▼ **At home on the floor**
The Buccaneer was designed to perform at very low altitude. Pilots took full advantage of this, and often carried out practice attacks while flying as low as 15 m (50 ft).

FACTS AND FIGURES

- The prototype Blackburn N.A. 39 made its initial flight on 30 April 1958.
- The 209th and last Buccaneer was delivered to the RAF on 6 October 1977.
- No. 801 Squadron of the Royal Navy was the first operational unit, embarking on HMS ***Ark Royal*** in January 1962.
- Buccaneers serving with RAF Germany were equipped with nuclear bombs.
- Buccaneers served as laser designators in the Gulf War in 1991.
- South African Buccaneers were acquired for maritime strike, but saw action in the guerrilla war in Namibia and Angola.

PROFILE

The king of long-range strike

Conceived in 1952, the Buccaneer was revolutionary – a carrier warplane designed to attack enemy warships at wavetop level, staying beneath hostile radar coverage. After surface-to-air missiles were introduced in the late 1950s, the Buccaneer was not just an innovation, but also a necessity. Seven versions of this brilliant strike warplane were built for Britain and South Africa. Buccaneers were designed to operate from the aircraft-carriers of the Royal Navy, but spent most of their career flying from land bases.

Developed in great secrecy, the Buccaneer was a powerful machine with superb low-level performance. Although designed with seaborne attacks in mind, its tough airframe was ideal for coping with the rapidly weaving high-*g* flight paths demanded by the terrain-following nature of its primary low-level attack role.

Despite being consigned to history, the final chapter of the Buccaneer story was written during Operation Desert Storm, when the sturdy old bombers were used with great success to designate targets for laser-guided weapons dropped from Tornados of the Royal Air Force.

Armed with a wing-mounted practice bomb pod, an RAF Buccaneer heads towards a bombing range. In well-trained hands the Buccaneer was a very accurate ground-attacker.

The thick wing gave a smooth ride at low level, and was excellent for carrying heavy stores like the Martel missile.

Rolls-Royce Spey turbofans replaced the Gyron Junior engines of the first Buccaneers. The Gyron Junior had poor reliability, and was less economical than the Spey.

BUCCANEER S.MK 2B

RAF Buccaneers based in Germany in the 1970s and 1980s wore this green-grey colour scheme. The Buccaneer carried a variety of bombs, including 'Paveway' laser-guided weapons, for this role.

'Upper surface blowing' using engine bleed air to increase lift over the wings was a novel feature of the Buccaneer design.

The bulged rear fuselage was designed to take advantage of the 'area rule' phenomenon, used to reduce transonic drag.

The long range of the Buccaneer could be extended even further by using air-to-air refuelling.

The aircraft's nose housed the 'Blue Parrot' attack radar, optimized for surface search.

The bomb-bay had a rotating door to minimize drag. It could carry four 500-kg (1,100-lb) bombs, or a nuclear weapon. Late in the aircraft's career, it usually held a fuel tank.

American ALQ-101 countermeasures pods were fitted to the wing hardpoints to jam hostile radars.

The Buccaneer featured unique 'clamshell' airbrakes that opened out sideways into the airstream.

Anti-shipping 'toss bombing' attack

The Buccaneer flies at low maximum speed at low level, in order to remain below the enemy's radar coverage for as long as possible.

About 5 km (3 miles) from the target, the Buccaneer pulls up sharply, releasing its weapons as it climbs.

Pulling over the top, the pilot dives away at full thrust to keep radar exposure to a minimum.

The bomb arcs towards its target. Its high-speed 'toss-bombing' profile gives the free-fall weapon a range of more than 4 km (2½ miles). Accurate enough when using nuclear weapons, it requires laser designation to ensure a hit with conventional bombs.

Royal Navy tactics called for several Buccaneers to attack simultaneously, presenting enemy air defences with the impossible task of coping with a shower of bombs arriving from a number of directions.

Buccaneer S.Mk 2

Type: two-seat carrier-capable low-level strike aircraft

Powerplant: two 49.38-kN (11,106-lb-thrust) Rolls-Royce RB.168-1A Spey Mk 101 turbofans

Maximum speed: 1038 km/h (645 mph) at 50 m (164 ft)

Combat radius: 1750 km (1,087 miles) (hi-lo-hi)

Service ceiling: 13,000 m (42,650 ft)

Weights: empty 13,600 kg (29,983 lb); loaded 28,123 kg (62,000 lb)

Armament: 7250 kg (15,984 lb) of bombs, rockets, anti-ship or air-to-surface missiles

Dimensions:

span	13.41 m (44 ft)
length	19.33 m (63 ft 5 in)
height	4.95 m (16 ft 3 in)
wing area	47.82 m² (515 sq ft)

COMBAT DATA

SPEED AT SEA LEVEL

The Buccaneer's powerful engines and immensely strong airframe were designed for the lowest of low-level flight. It was one of the fastest combat jets in the world when carrying a heavy warload in the thick, resistant air at sea level.

RANGE

Buccaneers carried a large amount of fuel in their portly fuselages. When later variants dropped internal bomb-carrying capacity in favour of a bomb-bay fuel tank, they were more capable of longer range strikes than most other carrier-capable jets.

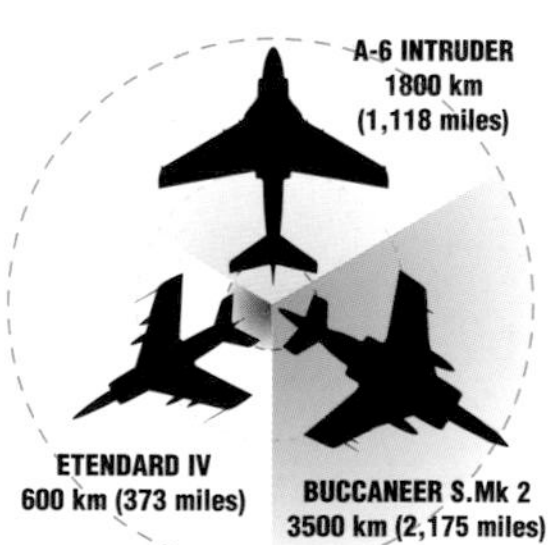

ARMAMENT

Originally designed to carry a relatively small bombload internally at high near-sonic speeds, the Buccaneer was soon found to be capable of hoisting a much greater tonnage of weaponry on four underwing hardpoints. It could match the American Grumman A-6 Intruder, although it lacked the American jet's sophisticated all-weather weapons delivery avionics.

BUCCANEER S.Mk 2
7250 kg (15,984 lb)

ETENDARD IV
1400 kg (3,086 lb)

A-6 INTRUDER
8000 kg (16,637 lb)

BOEING

B-47 STRATOJET

● All-jet bomber ● Swept-wing design ● Bicycle undercarriage

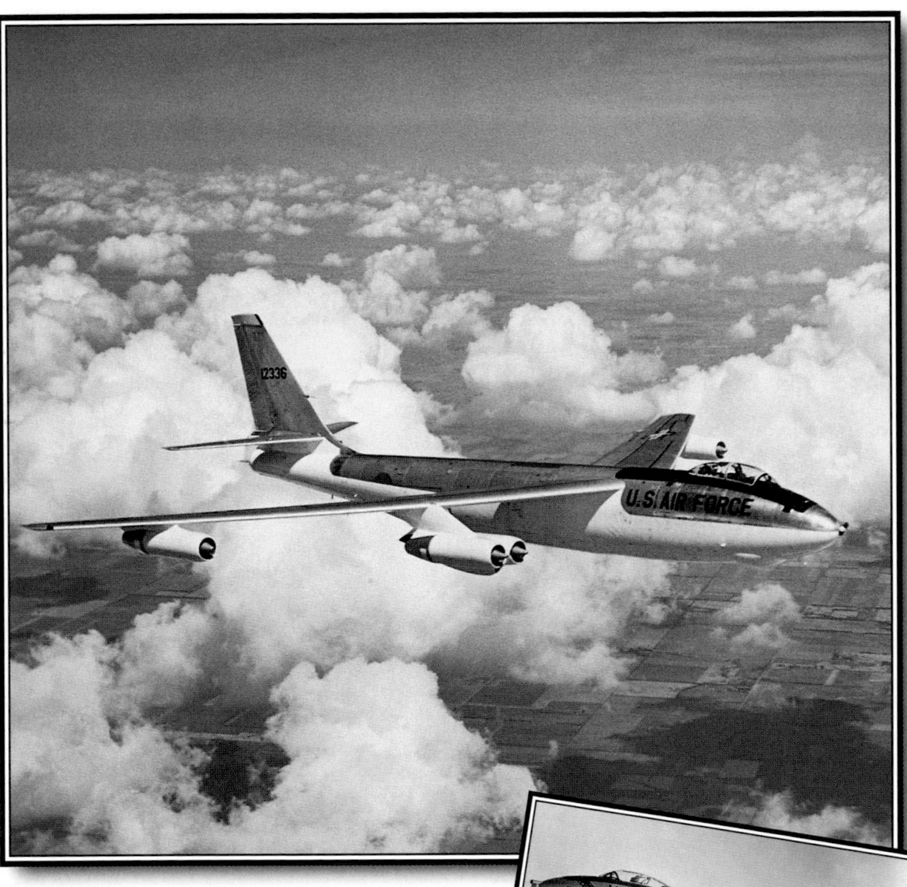

Graceful and beautiful, the Boeing B-47 Stratojet was an aircraft with a deadly mission. For years, the B-47 was the backbone of the US Strategic Air Command (SAC), poised and ready to leap into the skies carrying a lethal cargo of atomic bombs in response to a nuclear attack. SAC had nearly 2000 Stratojets in service in the mid-1950s, the most potent bomber force ever assembled.

▲ *Operating from distant bases was part of the SAC requirement; to some crews of the B-47 it meant the cold conditions of Alaska. Here a crew prepare its aircraft for take-off.*

PHOTO FILE

BOEING B-47 STRATOJET

Constant vigil ▶
With the need to launch at a moment's notice, B-47 crews were required to maintain a 24-hour alert. Here a Stratojet pilot waits for the call that will launch his bomber into the night's sky. Practice operations were undertaken at all hours.

◀ Combined operations
The nose of a KC-97 tanker partly obscures a B-47 positioned behind. These aircraft operated in close co-operation: the tanker supplied fuel to the bomber, allowing the Stratojet to strike targets at a greater distance. SAC pioneered routine IFR operations.

Long range ▶
A B-47 commander brings his aircraft in to formate with a KC-97 tanker. The refuelling receptacle was positioned on the nose of the bomber.

▲ Fighter handling
B-47 pilots found the bomber had exceptional handling for formation flying. It was also able to accomplish loops and rolls.

Late variants ▶
A late production Stratojet displays the bomber's unusual undercarriage design.

FACTS AND FIGURES

- ➤ The first B-47 flew on 17 December 1947, the anniversary of the Wright Brothers' first powered flight in 1903.
- ➤ A Stratojet set a transatlantic speed record from the United States to England.
- ➤ The first B-47 production contract was for 10 aircraft, costing $30 million in all.
- ➤ Production of the B-47 had amounted to 2041 of all variants when assembly work ended in February 1957.
- ➤ Some 440 Stratojets were built for non-bombing duties such as reconnaissance.
- ➤ The B-47 strongly influenced the design of the Boeing B-52 Stratofortress.

PROFILE

SAC's first jet bomber

The Boeing B-47 Stratojet defeated several rivals to become the US Air Force's choice as its principal strategic bomber of the 1950s. Stratojets began to arrive at SAC bases in October 1951. The Stratojet was the first swept-wing jet bomber ever produced. It was appealing to the eye and had breathtaking performance, but the cramped cockpit arrangement was awkward and crew fatigue on long missions was a problem.

Many B-47s stayed on nuclear alert, ready to launch with their deadly cargo of atomic bombs. Some B-47s participated in Reflex deployments between the United States and Great Britain, in support of worldwide strategic readiness. In 1959, Stratojets participated in Operation Oil Burner, practising low-level strike runs to penetrate below enemy radar detection while still accurately delivering nuclear weapons to their strategic targets.

Despite the fact that it was stressful on crews, the B-47 was much-loved by nearly all who maintained and flew it. Eventually replaced by the B-52 Stratofortress, the B-47 remained in operation with SAC until the 1960s. The last bomber version was retired on 11 February 1966, but the reconnaissance RB-47 variants were to remain on duty with the 55th SRW until 29 December 1967.

Above: A sight repeated right across the continental United States: two SAC Stratojets await their alert call to action.

Outrigger wheels were positioned within the outer engine pylons to provide some degree of lateral stability on the ground. These were vital during landings in cross-winds.

Located at the rear of the fuselage were twin 20-mm (0.79-in) cannon. They replaced the earlier 12.7-mm (0.5 in) machine guns which had offered little protection.

B-47E Stratojet

Type: long-range strategic bomber

Powerplant: six General Electric J47-GE-25/25A turbojets, each developing 32.03 kN (7,204 lb thrust) with water injection

Maximum speed: 975 km/h (606 mph) at 4970 m (16,300 ft)

Cruising speed: 806 km/h (501 mph) at 11,735 m (38,500 ft)

Ceiling: 12,345 m (40,500 ft)

Range: 6437 km (4,000 miles)

Weights: empty 36,630 kg (80,755 lb); maximum take-off 89,893 kg (198,180 lb)

Armament: two M24A1 20-mm (0.79-in) cannon, each with 350 rounds of ammunition, in radar-directed, remotely controlled tail turret, plus up to 9071 kg (20,000 lb) of bombs carried internally

Dimensions:		
	span	35.36 m (116 ft)
	length	33.48 m (109 ft 10 in)
	height	8.51 m (27 ft 11 in)
	wing area	132.66 m² (1,428 sq ft)

B-47E-I Stratojet

This B-47 Stratojet displays the late scheme of white anti-flash undersides, used to protect aircraft from the explosion of their own atomic bombs. SAC's blue ribbon insignia is painted on the nose.

The two pilots sat in tandem under a Plexiglass canopy. Visibility was excellent, although the second pilot's forward view was restricted.

The 35-degree swept-back wing was thin and had an extremely high aspect ratio. It proved to have very fine aerodynamic efficiency. The wings were constructed so that, during manoeuvres, they could flex up to 3 m (10 ft), allowing the bomber to accomplish loops and barrel rolls during certain attack procedures.

Because of the thin wings, fuel was carried in two main tanks positioned above and to the rear of the weapons bay. After testing, the bomb-bay was made smaller than that of the early A models, reflecting advances in bomb design.

A tandem or 'bicycle' arrangement was used for the main undercarriage, each set of wheels being installed either side of the bomb bay.

Later B-47E models did away with the internal jet-assisted take-off (JATO) units. Instead, the units were incorporated on an external rack which could be jettisoned following take-off. By using this procedure a larger bombload could be carried.

Stratojet bombing mission

1 In-flight refuelling: So that the B-47 Stratojet could attack targets at great distance, the aircraft would refuel from a KC-97 tanker aircraft.

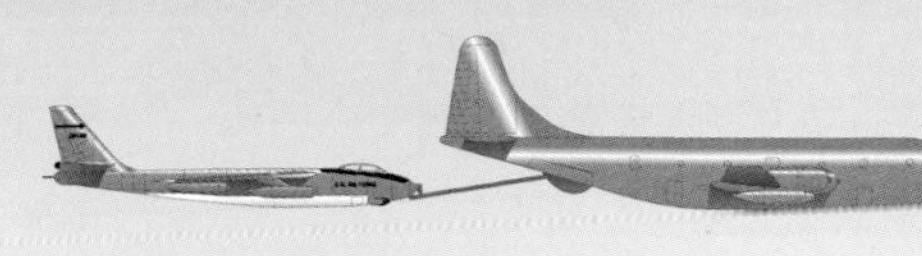

2 High performance: In its day the B-47 was able to outrun enemy fighters, although some SAC reconnaissance versions did return to base after missions having received damage from MiG-15s.

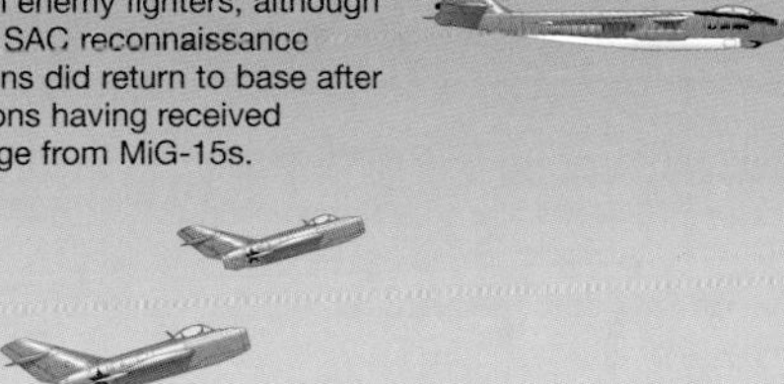

3 Bomb run: Capable of delivering a vast range of weapons, the Stratojet would use a variety of manoeuvres to avoid nuclear blast when dropping its ordnance.

ANDYR

KADENA AB

A possible mission planned from Kadena AB, Okinawa, could have been against the strategic bomber base at Andyr in the Soviet Eastern District. This would have meant a round trip of 9656 km (6,000 miles) over a duration of 11 hours with two in-flight refuellings by a KC-97. The mission profile would have been a simple climb to optimum cruising altitude of around 9750 m (32,000 ft) followed by a flight more or less direct to the target. However, no evasive action was deemed necessary. Similar attack profiles would also have been flown in Europe.

Boeing

B-50/KB-50 Superfortress

● Nuclear role ● Boeing's last piston-engined bomber ● Tanker conversions

For a brief period the Boeing B-50 Superfortress was the backbone of the US Strategic Air Command (SAC). A heavy bomber, tasked with the delivery of the first nuclear bombs in the US Cold War arsenal, it was developed from the B-29, but incorporated new materials and much more powerful engines. In 1949 the B-50 set a record by flying nonstop around the world, and in the 1950s it stood alert, armed with nuclear weapons, for several years.

▲ *As the ultimate development of the B-29, the B-50 was the last of the USAF's piston-engined bombers. It also performed pioneering work as a tanker, but was rapidly overtaken by the jet age.*

PHOTO FILE

Boeing B-50/KB-50 Superfortress

Triple-point tanker ▶
An F-100 Super Sabre, an F-101 Voodoo and a B-66 Destroyer refuel simultaneously from the three hoses of a KB-50.

▲ Tanker conversions
Replacing the underwing fuel tanks with jet engines and adding hose units produced the KB-50.

▲ Final role
All KB-50Ks (such as the one pictured above) were converted from TB-50Hs.

▲ The first B-50
Boeing changed the B-29D designation to B-50A to ensure funding for the 'new' bomber.

Pure bomber ▶
The B-50D had a single-piece nose section and 2650-litre (700-US gallon) underwing fuel tanks.

FACTS AND FIGURES

- ➤ The B-50 can be distinguished from the similar B-29 by its taller tailfin and underwing fuel tanks.
- ➤ In total, 350 production B-50s and one prototype were built for the US Air Force.
- ➤ Boeing's B-50 made its maiden flight on 25 June 1947.
- ➤ After being delivered to SAC, more than 6000 work hours were needed to modify the B-50 to accommodate nuclear bombs.
- ➤ The B-50 began reaching SAC squadrons in June 1948.
- ➤ B-50s were briefly grounded because of rudder hinge problems.

PROFILE

Boeing's last piston-engined bomber

The Boeing B-50 began life as an improved B-29. Too late for World War II but just in time for the Cold War, the B-50 was capable of hauling atomic bombs and was expected to fly long-range missions. On 2 March 1949 the B-50 'Lucky Lady II' completed the first nonstop round-the-world flight, covering a distance of 37,742 km (23,452 miles) in 94 hours and 1 minute.

The B-50 was plagued by early problems. Its bomb-bay, as initially designed, was inadequate for the heavy, plutonium-based Type III nuclear bombs of the 1940s. It had the largest and most powerful reciprocating engine ever installed in an operational warplane and was prone to engine malfunctions. Early B-50s also suffered from metal fatigue. All of these problems were eventually solved, but, by this time, SAC was receiving the more capable B-36, B-47 and B-52 bombers.

Many B-50s undertook reconnaissance missions around the periphery of the Soviet Union, while others were used to train SAC crews, or acted as weather reconnaissance machines. The majority of B-50s were converted into tankers, and the last aircraft flew during the Vietnam War.

Above: Seen in February 1955, this WB-50D is one of 36 B-50D bombers stripped of weapons systems and used for weather reconnaissance. The last one was replaced by a WB-47 in 1967.

Above: Serial number 49-391 was the last B-50D to be built and is seen here after being converted to a KB-50J. Even with jet boost the KB-50 struggled to keep up with contemporary military jets. The last KB-50 left service in 1965.

B-50A Superfortress

Type: four-engined heavy bomber

Powerplant: four 2610-kW (3,500-hp) Pratt & Whitney R-4360-35 Wasp Major turbocharged radial piston engines

Maximum speed: 620 km/h (385 mph)

Cruising speed: 378 km/h (235 mph)

Range: 7483 km (4,650 miles)

Service ceiling: 11,278 m (37,000 ft)

Weights: empty 36,764 kg (81,051 lb); maximum take-off 76,389 kg (168,409 lb)

Armament: 12 12.7-mm (0.5-in) machine guns and one 20-mm (0.79-in) cannon; 9072-kg (20,000-lb) bombload

Dimensions:

span	43.05 m (141 ft 3 in)
length	30.18 m (99 ft)
height	9.96 m (32 ft 8 in)
wing area	161.55 m² (1,739 sq ft)

RB-50B

All of the B-50Bs, except the first, were converted to RB-50B reconnaissance platforms. All of these ended their days as KB-50J tankers after 43 had been modified for even more specialized reconnaissance operations.

Like its B-29 predecessor, the B-50 had four remotely controlled gun turrets. The upper nose turret was fitted with four 12.7-mm (0.5-in) machine guns and each of the other turrets contained two similar weapons. The tail position was fitted with two machine guns and a 20-mm (0.79-in) cannon.

Constructed from a new type of aluminium known as 75 ST, instead of the 24 ST used on the B-29, the B-50's wing was nearly identical to that of the B-29, but 16 per cent stronger and more than 272 kg (600 lb) lighter.

An internal pressure bulkhead between the rear cabin and bomb-bay was situated at the position of this fuselage band. Crewmembers moved between the front and rear pressure cabins via a pressurized tunnel above the bomb-bay.

As it was heavier than the B-29, the B-50 required a larger fin to maintain directional stability. The vertical tail could be folded down so that the aircraft could be stored in an average-sized USAF hangar.

Four-row 28-cylinder R-4360 engines produced a 59 per cent power increase over those of the B-29.

After conversion to RB-50B standard, the rear bomb-bay could accommodate extra crewmembers, plus cameras and electronic equipment.

As a range-improving feature, 57 B-50As and all RB-50Bs were equipped with the British hose refuelling system. The receptacle for the tanker's hose was situated in a fairing on the right-hand side beneath the tailplane. The system facilitated the nonstop B-50A circumnavigation of the world.

COMBAT DATA

MAXIMUM BOMBLOAD

A 9979-kg (22,000-lb) bombload for the Lincoln was an unusual mission using a single 'earthquake bomb'. Its bombload was usually similar to that of the B-50A. The Tu-4 was a Soviet copy of the B-29.

B-50A SUPERFORTRESS 9072 kg (20,000 lb)

LINCOLN B.Mk II 9979 kg (22,000 lb)

Tu-4 'BULL' 8000 kg (17,637 lb)

SERVICE CEILING

Both the Avro Lincoln and B-50A represented extreme developments of wartime designs. While they offered good performance, they could not match that of all-new designs.

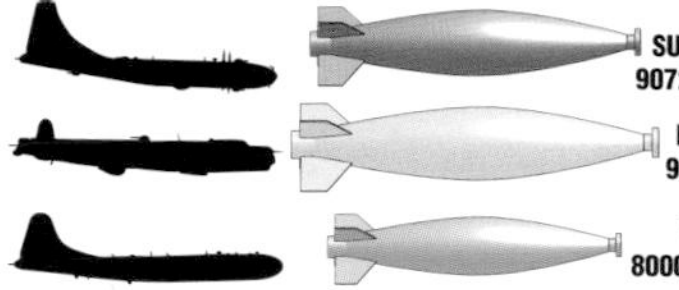
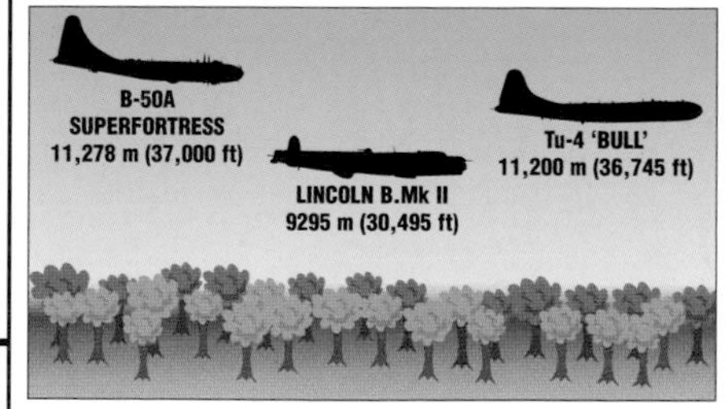

RANGE

Although the B-50A offered long range, the range of the 'D' version was exceptional. The Lincoln could achieve the figure shown only when carrying a reduced bombload of 3000 kg (6,614 lb). Tupolev could not match the range of the B-50 with its Tu-4.

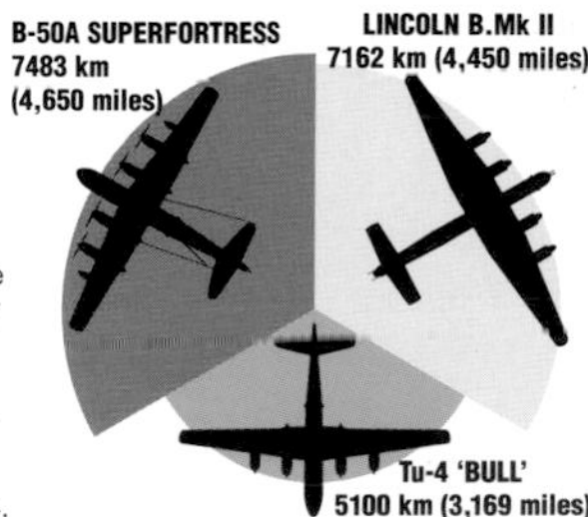

B-50 in action

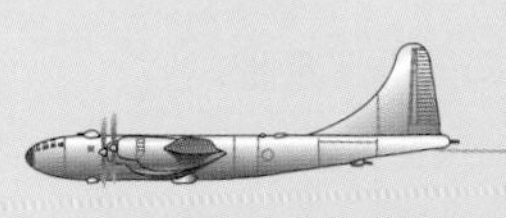

IN-FLIGHT REFUELLING: Early methods of air-to-air refuelling were complicated and could often be dangerous.

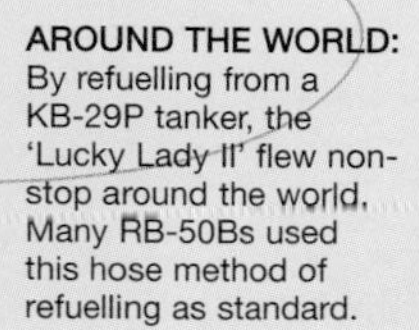

AROUND THE WORLD: By refuelling from a KB-29P tanker, the 'Lucky Lady II' flew non-stop around the world. Many RB-50Bs used this hose method of refuelling as standard.

NUCLEAR BOMBING: The primary role of the B-50A/D was the long-range delivery of free-fall nuclear weapons. The aircraft were soon considered obsolete in this role, however.

THREE-POINT TANKER: KB-50J/K aircraft could trail three hoses and simultaneously refuel three probe-equipped aircraft. Here two FJ4 Furies and an F-8 Crusader are being refuelled.

BOEING

B-52 STRATOFORTRESS (SAC)

● **Eight-engined nuclear bomber** ● **Still in service**

Stratofortresses were the mighty sword of the USAF's Strategic Air Command (SAC). From 1955 until 1991 the B-52 was on 'nuclear alert', sitting at the end of the runway armed with nuclear bombs and with crew poised nearby. SAC crews knew that a ballistic missile launched by a Soviet submarine could reach their base within 25 minutes. If they were to fight back, this was all the time they had to get into the air on what could be a one-way mission.

▲ *By 1958 the B-52 was the most important component in the world's most powerful military force. US foreign policy was based on deterrence; SAC could deliver a nuclear weapon anywhere.*

PHOTO FILE

BOEING B-52 STRATOFORTRESS (SAC)

▼ Hound Dog carrier
As ICBMs (intercontinental ballistic missiles) became more important, the B-52 took on the launching of stand-off weapons such as the jet-powered AGM-28 Hound Dog missile,

▲ Air-to-air refuelling
SAC also operated a large fleet of Boeing KC-135 tankers, which provided its 'anywhere in the world' capability.

▼ Tandem seating
The first two B-52s had a tandem two-seat cockpit, unlike production aircraft, which had a side-by-side arrangement.

Nuclear deterrence ▶
B-52s eventually lost their primary role in the SAC deterrent to ICBMs. This B-52 is pictured flying over an Atlas missile in California.

◀ Tailless but airborne
On loan to Boeing at the time, this B-52H lost most of its 12-m (40-ft) tailfin on a low-level test flight. Amazingly, it landed safely.

FACTS AND FIGURES

- ➤ The second B-52 built, YB-52 serial number 49-23, was the first to fly and is now at the USAF Museum in Ohio.
- ➤ The prototype for the B-52 series made its first flight on 15 April 1952.
- ➤ B-52Ds over Vietnam carried a load equivalent to eight World War II B-17Gs.
- ➤ In January 1957 three B-52Bs flew nonstop around the world (39,147 km/ 24,325 miles) in 45 hours and 19 minutes.
- ➤ The three pre-production B-52As built in 1954 cost a huge $29 million each.
- ➤ The 744th and last B-52 bomber entered service with SAC on 26 October 1962.

PROFILE

SAC's ultimate nuclear bomber

Boeing's B-52 Stratofortress was designed to drop atomic bombs from the stratosphere. The biggest USAF bomber of its era, the eight-engine B-52 dropped real 'nukes' during atmospheric tests in the Pacific in 1956 and 1962. For nearly four decades B-52 crews stood ready to drop nuclear bombs in anger, if necessary. Indeed, until the late 1960s aircraft equipped with live nuclear weapons were maintained on airborne alert.

With the advent of surface-to-air missiles in the 1960s the B-52 successfully shifted from high- to low-level weapon delivery, but the war in Vietnam brought a different mission – high-level tactical bombing with old-fashioned 'iron' bombs.

Built in seven production versions, the B-52 has been in service for more than 40 years and has outlived Strategic Air Command itself. Although its importance as a weapon system has been steadily downgraded, a number are projected to remain in service until at least 2020, making it the longest-serving warplane in history.

Twenty-seven RB-52Bs were built from 1955 and were able to carry a pod in the bomb-bay with four to six camera positions and/or electronic reconnaissance equipment and two operators. The 'convertible' concept was abandoned in 1956.

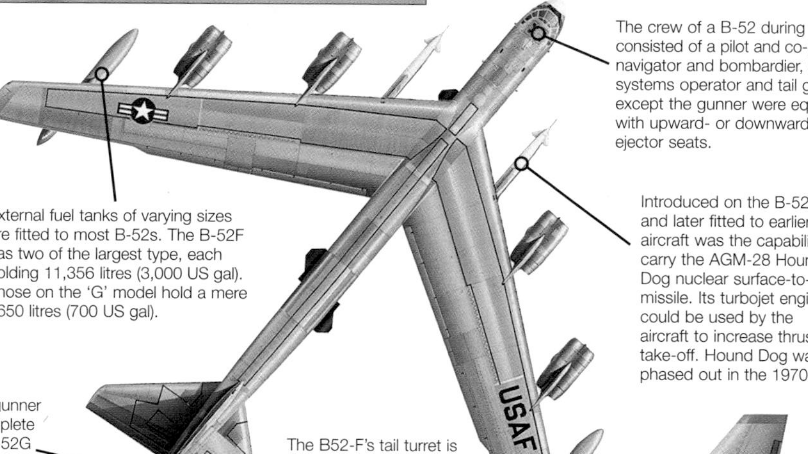

The crew of a B-52 during the 1960s consisted of a pilot and co-pilot, route navigator and bombardier, defensive systems operator and tail gunner. All except the gunner were equipped with upward- or downward-firing ejector seats.

External fuel tanks of varying sizes are fitted to most B-52s. The B-52F has two of the largest type, each holding 11,356 litres (3,000 US gal). Those on the 'G' model hold a mere 2650 litres (700 US gal).

Introduced on the B-52G and later fitted to earlier aircraft was the capability to carry the AGM-28 Hound Dog nuclear surface-to-air missile. Its turbojet engine could be used by the aircraft to increase thrust on take-off. Hound Dog was phased out in the 1970s.

In an emergency the tail gunner is able to jettison the complete turret to escape. In the B-52G and H the gunner was moved from the turret to a cockpit position, firing his guns remotely.

B-52D Stratofortress

Type: six-seat strategic bomber

Powerplant: eight 53.82-kN (12,105-lb-thrust) Pratt & Whitney J57-P-19W turbojet engines

Maximum speed: 893 km/h (555 mph) at altitude

Climb rate: 750 m/min (2,460 fpm)

Combat range: 11,730 km (7,290 miles)

Service ceiling: 11,600 m (38,000 ft)

Weights: empty 74,893 kg (165,111 lb); maximum 204,117 kg (450,000 lb)

Armament: four 12.7-mm (0.5-in) machine guns in tail turret and up to 27,215 kg (60,000 lb) of bombs internally and on external racks

Dimensions:		
	span	56.39 m (185 ft)
	length	47.73 m (156 ft 7 in)
	height	14.73 m (48 ft 4 in)
	wing area	371.60 m² (4,000 sq ft)

B-52F STRATOFORTRESS

Phased out in the early 1970s, B-52Fs were the first SAC bombers to serve over Vietnam; 57-0169 of the 320th Bomb Wing flew 68 missions over Vietnam from Guam and is shown here after its return to the States.

The B52-F's tail turret is fitted with four 12.7-mm (0.5-in) radar-guided machine guns. Some early models were built with a pair of 20-mm (0.79-in) cannon instead. The ultimate 'H' model used a Vulcan 20-mm rotary cannon in this position. Tail guns were deleted from the remaining B-52s in the mid-1990s.

Early production B-52s had a conventional side-by-side cockpit for the two pilots, with two other crewmembers seated behind facing aft. The fifth and sixth crewmen sat on a lower level facing forward.

All B-52s except the 'H' model are powered by eight Pratt & Whitney J57 turbojets as fitted to numerous other types, such as F-8 and F-100 fighters, A-3 bombers and U-2 reconnaissance aircraft.

B-52s carry an enormous amount of fuel – around 147,112 litres (38,863 US gal) – in large internal tanks in the fuselage and wings. The J57-powered models also carry water tanks for the water injection system used by the engines during take-off to increase thrust.

The radome under the cockpit contains the bombing radar scanner.

The main undercarriage is made up of four two-wheel steerable trucks, which may be slewed in unison to allow cross-wind landings. Outriggers support the wings.

COMBAT DATA

UNIT COST

The rising cost of military aircraft was largely a result of advancing technology. The larger the order for a new aircraft, the lower the unit cost. The three experimental B-52As cost a huge $29 million each, while the mass-produced B-52Es were a 'mere' $6 million.

B-52E STRATOFORTRESS $6.00 m

B-29A SUPERFORTRESS $0.64 m

B-47E STRATOJET $1.87 m

RANGE

Interestingly, the B-47E actually had a shorter range than the World War II-vintage B-29. However, the B-47 was a much faster aircraft and could be refuelled in the air. The much larger B-52 had a considerably enhanced fuel capacity compared to the others.

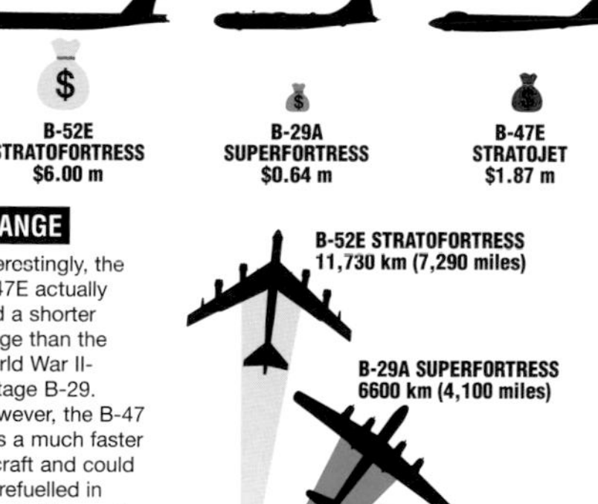

MAXIMUM SPEED

At the end of World War II the B-29 was one of the fastest four-engined bombers. The jet age increased speeds considerably, the B-47 being able to hold its own against fighters of the early 1950s. Speed was less important by the time the B-52 was produced; range and load-carrying capacity were paramount.

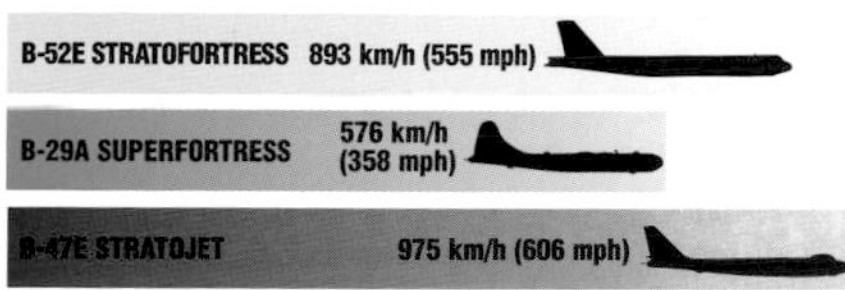

Boeing's strategic bombers

B-17 FLYING FORTRESS: Taking to the air in 1935, the B-17 was built in enormous numbers after the United States entered World War II. Most of its missions took place over Europe.

B-29 SUPERFORTRESS: The B-29 was an advanced aircraft when it first flew in 1942. It was to bear the brunt of the bombing campaign over Japan; one delivered the first atomic bomb.

B-50 SUPERFORTRESS: Production of this more powerful development of the B-29 began in 1945. Although they saw action over Korea, most were converted to tankers as the KB-50.

B-47 STRATOJET: Predecessor of the B-52 and the first swept-wing jet bomber built in any numbers, the six-engined B-47 served SAC from 1951. At its peak 1800 were in service.

BOEING

B-52G/H STRATOFORTRESS

● Strategic bomber ● Nuclear/conventional weapons ● Global reach

Conceived as the giant silver sword of the United States Air Force Strategic Air Command the B-52 Stratofortress was the biggest purely jet-powered bomber of its time, and has been flying for almost 50 years. Flown for decades on atomic alert, its only combat use has been the massive conventional bombing campaigns in Southeast Asia and the Persian Gulf.

▲ *Displaying its enormous wingspan a B-52 gets airborne trailing a thick plume of smoke as its eight turbojet engines strain at full power to lift its 229,000 kg (504,860 lb.) into the air.*

PHOTO FILE

BOEING B-52G/H STRATOFORTRESS

◀ Sting in the tail

Most versions of the B-52 had a fearsome rear defence of four '50-calibre' guns. These were aimed using the radar mounted above.

◀ Extending the range

By using inflight refuelling, the B-52 can cover any part of the globe from just a few bases. This veteran is seen on its way to Vietnam in 1972.

Modern day warrior ▶

Two fully-laden B-52Gs launch from Riyadh in Saudi Arabia for another mission against massed Iraqi armoured divisions during the Gulf War of 1991.

◀ Nuclear deterrence

The B-52 has an important role as a launch platform for nuclear missiles. Here a SRAM is launched from the massive weapons bay.

A fistful of throttles ▶

The B-52's cockpit is dominated by the central engine control panel. Every dial and lever is multiplied eight-fold.

FACTS AND FIGURES

- The B-52 has a crew of five, including two pilots, navigator, electronic warfare officer and bombardier.
- Boeing manufactured 744 'Buffs' and finished the last aircraft in October 1962.
- A B-52 can reach any target in the world within 18 hours.
- During Operation Desert Storm, B-52s flew 1624 missions, and dropped 5,829,000 kg (12,850,740 lb.) of bombs.
- Each B-52 contains 90 km (56 mi.) of electrical wiring.
- In 1959, three B-52Bs flew non-stop around the world in under 50 hours.

PROFILE

America's 'Big Stick'

The longest-serving front-line warplane in history, the B-52 Stratofortress was the right aircraft at the right time. It first flew on 15 April 1952 and became the backbone of the West's nuclear preparedness; had the need arisen, hundreds of B-52s would have headed for Russia to drop hydrogen bombs on key strategic targets.

The special 'Big Belly B-52D' could also carry 108 conventional bombs, and during the Vietnam War 129 B-52s, of several models, carried out the December 1972 'Christmas bombing', designed to force North Vietnam to the conference table. Since then, the B-52 has been extensively modified. New engines and electronics have extended the life of the 'Buff' (Big Ugly Fat Fella) into the 1990s. B-52Gs flew the longest combat missions in history during Operation Desert Storm, from Louisiana to the Middle East. Today, B-52Hs have both nuclear and conventional roles.

The 'Buff' is one of the best-loved of all aircraft and can operate at high level or at very low level on terrain-avoidance under-the-radar missions.

During the first Gulf War B-52s pounded Iraqi targets from as far afield as England and Diego Garcia in the Indian Ocean.

'Buffs' can mount up to 24 340-kg (750-lb.) or 454-kg 1,000-lb.) high-explosive or cluster bombs on wing pylons.

B-52H Stratofortress

Type: five-seat long-range strategic bomber

Powerplant: eight 75.62-kN (17,014-lb. thrust) Pratt & Whitney TF33-P-3 turbofans

Maximum speed: 958 km/h (595 m.p.h.) at 3096 m (10,160 ft.)

Range: 16,000 km (9942 mi.)

Service ceiling: 16,765 m (55,000 ft.)

Weights: empty 138,799 kg (306,000 lb.); loaded 229,000 kg (504,860 lb.)

Armament: one 20-mm M61A1 tail cannon; 81 454-kg (1,000-lb.) bombs, or 20 AGM-86 or AGM-129 cruise missiles, or four to six nuclear bombs

Dimensions:

span	56.39 m (185 ft.)
length	49.05 m (160 ft. 11 in.)
height	12.40 m (40 ft. 8 in.)
wing area	272.3 m² (2,932 sq. ft.)

B-52H STRATOFORTRESS

Known in the USAF as the 'Cadillac', the B-52H is significantly upgraded compared to the early Stratofortresses. With more modern turbofan engines it outperforms its predecessors in both range and payload. Built to carry nuclear-tipped ballistic missiles, it is still a vital weapon in the USAF arsenal.

23RD BOMBARDMENT SQ.

The radar-directed rear guns are controlled remotely by a gunner who aims via a screen in the forward cockpit.

The immensely strong wings of the B-52 not only support the eight engines but are also filled with fuel, giving the 'Buff' enormous range.

The B-52's wings can flex several metres up and down. Outriggers under the wingtips stop them from hitting the runway when carrying a full load of fuel and weaponry.

The flight deck of the B-52 has two levels. The upper deck houses the two pilots. Behind them sit the electronic warfare officer, who handles all the countermeasures equipment, and the tail gunner, who fires by remote control.

On the lower level, facing forwards, are two navigators. One handles the route navigation, while the other operates the upgraded radar and weapon control systems.

The enormous bomb-bays of the B-52 can accommodate clips of a wide range of armament, ranging from 227-kg (500-lb.) bombs to giant nuclear weapons.

USAF 00033

0033

The B-52 has a bicycle-type main undercarriage. This caters for crosswind landings and take-offs by crabbing, so that the aircraft's fuselage slews down the runway.

The longest raid in history

On the first night of the first Gulf War, B-52Gs took off from Barksdale AFB in Louisiana, flew to northern Saudi Arabia and launched cruise missiles against Iraqi targets. They then flew all the way back to their base, having flown non-stop for more than 35 hours.

Barksdale AFB is a major Strategic Air Command facility, and is the location of the USAF 8th Air Force headquarters.

BARKSDALE AFB

The B-52s were refuelled by tankers flying from Lajes in the Azores.

The Mediterranean flight path was chosen to avoid overflying other countries as much as possible.

Launching from northern Saudi airspace, the B-52s attacked key military targets in northern Iraq, around the oil centres of Kirkuk and Mosul.

COMBAT DATA

BOMBLOAD

The B-52H can carry a vast array of weaponry. Its load can include up to 20 nuclear cruise missiles or 81 free-fall bombs as well as anti-ship missiles or conventional cruise missiles. Designed during the Cold War, the B-52 carries its bombload over a great range and would have penetrated into the heart of the Soviet Union if necessary.

VICTOR 16,000 kg (35,275 lb.)

B-52H STRATOFORTRESS 38,250 kg (84,330 lb.)

Tu-95 'BEAR' 20,000 kg (44,100 lb.)

BOEING

C/KC-97 STRATOFREIGHTER

● B-29 development ● In-flight refuelling tanker ● Transport

By combining major sections of the B-29 with an all-new upper fuselage, Boeing produced the Model 367, which was first flown on 9 November 1944. Known to the US Air Force as the XC-97 Stratofreighter, this aircraft was to be the first in a long line of transports, tankers and tanker/transports based on the C-97. The refuelling techniques adopted from the KB-29P and refined on the KC-97 remain much the same on Boeing's modern KC-135.

▲ *Using the wings and other major components of the B-29, Boeing was able to develop a large transport which was to become the basis of the USAF tanker fleet.*

PHOTO FILE

BOEING C/KC-97 STRATOFREIGHTER

▼ Israeli transport

A YC-97 was supplied to Israel as payment for the cost of maintaining US aircraft, and one KC-97F and eight KC-97Gs were delivered later. They flew military missions in civilian markings.

▲ Fast-jet refuelling

KC-97Ls remained in US Air National Guard service until 1977. Many of them were fitted with auxiliary J47 turbojet engines so that they could reach the speeds required for refuelling fighters.

Tanker transport versatility ▶

The KC-97G gave the USAF an aircraft which was capable of carrying freight or passengers without removing its refuelling system. This was the most common model.

▼ Nose radome

When the C-97A entered service it introduced a distinctive chin radome, which housed an AN/APS-42 search radar. All subsequent aircraft featured radar.

▲ Wartime prototype

The first of three XC-97s flew in 1944. Its clamshell rear cargo doors and ramp can be clearly seen in this picture.

FACTS AND FIGURES

- On 9 January 1945 the first XC-97, carrying a 9072-kg (20,000-lb) payload, flew from Seattle to Washington DC in 6 hours and 3 minutes.
- With its pressurized cabin, the XC-97 was able to cruise at 9144 m (30,000 ft).
- The YC-97 used engine nacelles developed for, but never fitted to, the B-29.
- A single YC-97A flew in the Berlin airlift, carrying cargo such as coal, which was loaded by conveyor belt.
- MC-97C was the designation of casualty evacuation aircraft in the Korean War.
- New systems allowed the KC-97G to dispense with a radio operator.

PROFILE

Booming success for Boeing

Boeing chose the simplest structural route in order to produce the C-97. The lower fuselage lobe was of similar diameter to that of the B-29, while the upper fuselage also had a circular cross-section but was of greater diameter. Combining these gave Boeing two circular-section cabins to pressurize, which was a much easier proposition than it would face if producing an elliptical pressurized fuselage of the same size.

In January 1942 a US Army Air Force order resulted in the construction of three XC-97 prototypes, which led, in turn, to the production of 10 YC-97 service test aircraft. These were to prove the C-97 concept and eventually led to production of 50 C-97As.

Although the C-97A proved to be an exceptional freighter, various efforts were made to improve it, including trials with three experimental KC-97As fitted with refuelling booms taken from KB-29Ps. The aircraft proved to be a highly capable tanker, with the KC-97G becoming the most widely built model of the series.

Several KC-97 variants were made and the ultimate KC-97L served with Air National Guard units until 1977.

Above: Between March and August 1965, the KC-97Gs of the Wisconsin Air National Guard were brought up to KC-97L standard.

Below: Ten service test aircraft were ordered in July 1945 for US Army Air Force trials. They had a larger fuel capacity than the XC-97.

KC-97G Stratofreighter

Type: long-range transport and in-flight refuelling tanker

Powerplant: four 2610-kW (3,500-hp) Pratt & Whitney R-4360-59B radial piston engines

Maximum speed: 604 km/h (375 mph)

Cruising speed: 483 km/h (300 mph)

Climb rate: 50 min to 6096 m (20,000 ft)

Range: 6920 km (4,300 miles)

Operating ceiling: 9205 m (30,200 ft)

Weights: empty 37,421 kg (82,500 lb); maximum take-off 79,379 kg (175,000 lb)

Accommodation: 96 troops or 69 stretcher patients, plus refuelling system

Dimensions:		
	span	43.05 m (141 ft 3 in)
	length	33.63 m (110 ft 4 in)
	height	11.66 m (38 ft 3 in)
	wing area	164.34 m² (1,769 sq ft)

KC-97L STRATOFREIGHTER

J47 turbojets were introduced under the wings of the KC-97L by the Illinois Air National Guard. This aircraft belonged to the 108th Air Refueling Squadron (ARS) and was the first conversion from KC-97G standard.

Each of the 28-cylinder Pratt & Whitney radials provided 2610 kW (3,500 hp) and turned a four-bladed propeller. The C-97A was able to transport two propellers on special racks beneath the forward fuselage.

General Electric J47-GE-25 turbojets became available for the KC-97 when the jet-augmented B-50 models went out of service. The modified version was originally known as the JKC-97G.

This high B-50-style fin was introduced from the YC-97A onwards. The aircraft also introduced other changes, including a lighter wing, larger flaps and reverse pitch propellers.

Like the KC-97G from which it was converted, the KC-97L had additional fuel cells on the main cabin floor, as well as a substantial freight capacity.

Most KC-97Gs and Ls were used almost exclusively in the tanker role. Their rear clamshell doors were replaced by the boom operator's position and observation windows.

Many KB-50s relinquished parts of their fuel pumping system as well as their jet engines to the KC-97L. The aircraft had a refined version of the Boeing-developed flying boom used on the KB-29P. The boom of the modern KC-135 has changed very little.

ACTION DATA

CRUISING SPEED

The KC-97G had a slower cruising speed than contemporary transport aircraft in USAF service. This proved to be a problem when the Stratofreighter was required to refuel fighters and other jet aircraft. As a result, J47 turbojets were fitted.

KC-97G STRATOFREIGHTER 483 km/h (300 mph)

C-121C 523 km/h (325 mph)

C-118A 507 km/h (315 mph)

RANGE

Exceptional range was demonstrated by the KC-97G, especially when flying in the transport role. The aircraft was capable of being used over vast distances without removal of its tanking equipment.

KC-97G STRATOFREIGHTER 6920 km (4,300 miles)

C-121C 3920 km (2,436 miles)

C-118A 4710 km (2,927 miles)

PASSENGERS

Lockheed's C-121C and Douglas's C-118A, based on the Super Constellation and DC-6 airliners, respectively, were able to fly only as transports. The C-121C had greater seating capacity than the KC-97G. The Stratofreighter retained all of its tanking equipment, however, and allowed the extra flexibility of combined transport and tanking missions with reduced payload.

Boeing tanker chronology

KB-29P SUPERFORTRESS: Boeing pioneered the use of the flying-boom refuelling system on the KB-29P.

KB-50: Some 136 B-50s were modified to tanker configuration. Here an early conversion from a B-50D refuels two F-100 Super Sabres.

KC-135 STRATOTANKER: Boeing's KC-135 has become a classic military aircraft design and will be in service for many years.

MODEL 707: As second-hand 707 airliners became available, several air arms cheaply converted them into tankers.

BOEING

E-4

● Airborne command post ● Four built ● Based on the 747 airliner

▲ Boeing received its first E-4 contract in 1973, and delivered the first aircraft the following year after an internal refit by E-Systems. The first upgraded E-4B was redelivered in 1980.

Known as the AABNCPs (Advanced Airborne National Command Posts), or National Emergency Airborne Command Posts (NEACPs or 'Kneecaps'), the E-4 'Doomsday Planes' were always associated with the prospect of nuclear attack during the Cold War. The four USAF E-4Bs continue to provide an aerial command centre for US leaders in the event of not only nuclear war, but any major conflict or crisis.

PHOTO FILE

BOEING E-4

▼ **Continuing role**
Despite the end of the Cold War, the E-4 has a continuing role during national emergencies.

▲ **Communications gear**
In terms of its communications systems, the E-4B is the world's best-equipped aircraft. Thirteen external communications systems, covering seven wavebands, use power from a 1200-kVa electrical system powered by an engine-driven generator.

▼ **'Air Force One'**
The most recent 747s delivered to the USAF were two VC-25A Presidential transports based on Boeing's 747-200B airliner. The callsign 'Air Force One' is used when the President is aboard.

▲ **Advanced technology**
The E-4B's highly advanced range of communications systems are optimised for maximum reliability.

▲ **Maximum endurance by IFR**
The E-4s have in-flight refuelling capability via a receptacle above the nose of the aircraft.

FACTS AND FIGURES

- Four E-4Bs belong to the 1st Air Command and Control Squadron of the 55th Wing at Offutt AFB, Nebraska.
- E-4s are limited to 72 hours' endurance by their engines' lubricating oil capacity.
- The E-4 made its first flight without mission equipment on 13 June 1973.
- Including the VC-25s, the USAF operates six 747s; plans to buy ex-airline 747s for the National Guard were cancelled.
- Originally, the airborne command post requirement called for six E-4s.
- The E-4's systems are held in 1613 'black boxes' – three times the number in an E-3.

PROFILE

Presidential 'Doomsday Plane'

Right: Three of the four E-4Bs were delivered as E-4As, without the dorsal antenna.

Until recently an E-4 was kept on alert at Andrews Air Force Base, Maryland – a short helicopter journey from the White House. In the event of an attack on the United States, the President and his staff would have boarded the E-4 to direct American forces from the comparative safety of the air.

The E-4 uses the familiar Boeing 747 airliner's fuselage to accommodate the President (in his role as Commander-in-Chief of US forces) and key members of his battle staff. They reside in the flying equivalent of the White House's Situation Room.

This 'war readiness aircraft' is equipped with nuclear thermal shielding, protection against EMP (electromagnetic pulse) and a large variety of communications systems, covering seven wavebands from super-high to very-low frequency. If necessary, the aircraft can broadcast to the US population over the national radio network or link up to commercial telephone networks to send emergency messages.

Initially, the E-4As of the mid-1970s used equipment from EC-135J Project 'Looking Glass' command post aircraft. But when the current E-4B entered service in 1980 it had considerably more equipment, including SHF (super-high frequency) satellite communications gear in a distinctive dorsal blister. The result was a command post and flying 'situation room' aircraft.

Although the Cold War has ended, the E-4 remains available for deployment worldwide in times of crisis.

Above: Whenever the US President travels abroad, an aircraft from the E-4 fleet accompanies 'Air Force One' at a discreet distance in case an emergency situation arises.

E-4B

Type: national emergency airborne command post (NEACP)

Powerplant: four 233.53-kN (52,500-lb.-thrust) General Electric F103-PW-100 (CF6-50-E2) turbofans

Cruising speed: (typical) 933 km/h (578 m.p.h.) at 6096 m (20,000 ft.)

Endurance: 12 hours (without in-flight refuelling); 72 hours (with in-flight refuelling)

Ferry range: 12,600 km (7,812 mi.)

Cruise ceiling: 13,715 m (45,000 ft.)

Weights: max. take-off 362,874 kg (799,992 lb.)

Accommodation: two flight crews, each of four plus; total accommodation for 94 crewmembers, including a battle staff of 30

Dimensions:		
	span	59.64 m (195 ft. 7 in.)
	length	70.51 m (231 ft. 4 in.)
	height	19.33 m (63 ft. 5 in.)
	wing area	510.95 m² (5,498 sq. ft.)

E-4B

73-1676 was one of three E-4As delivered in the mid-1970s and was upgraded shortly after delivery to E-4B standard. All equip the 1st Air Command and Control Squadron, based at Offutt Air Force Base, Nebraska.

The E-4B carries two flight crews on potentially long missions, each consisting of an aircraft commander (pilot), co-pilot, navigator and flight engineer. A special navigation station and crew rest area are provided on the upper deck, behind the cockpit.

The most obvious external identification feature of the E-4B is the dorsal fairing on top of the forward fuselage. This contains the satellite/super-high frequency (SHF) antenna. The aircraft has nuclear thermal shielding and protection against EMP weapons.

The main deck is divided between a flight crew section and four operating compartments for the President and his battle staff. These are the NCA (National Command Authority) area (similar in role to the White House Situation Room), conference room, battle staff area and C³I (command, control, communications and intelligence) area.

When the Boeing 747 was selected to fill the SS-481B Support System requirement in 1973, it was chosen because of its size and the fact that it was an 'off-the shelf' design. Airframe costs were therefore kept to a minimum. The E-4s are painted in this all-over anti-flash white finish.

UNITED STATES OF AMERICA

31676

One of the 46 external antennas is an 8-km (5-mi.) long, retractable very-low frequency (VLF) aerial trailing behind the aircraft. VLF is used to communicate with submerged submarines.

E-4Bs are powered by four General Electric CF6 turbofans (military designation F103). The first two aircraft were delivered with Pratt & Whitney JT9Ds (F105s).

In times of crisis

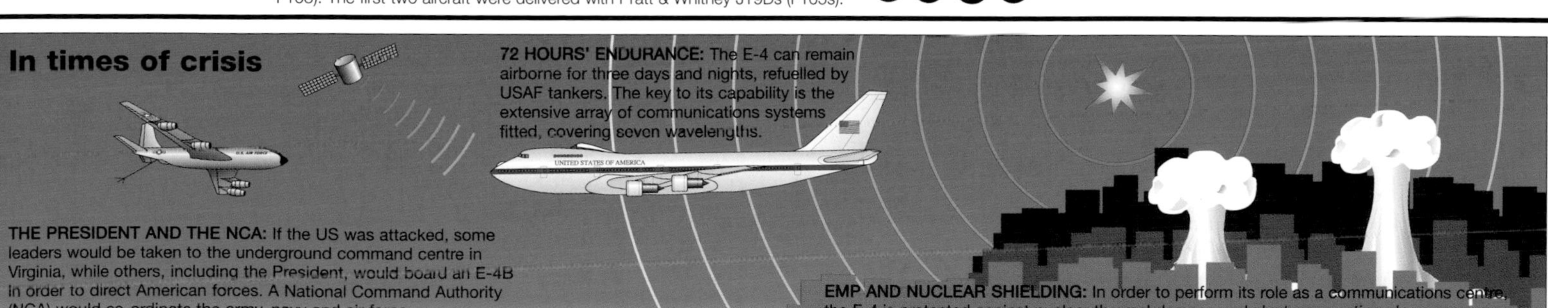

72 HOURS' ENDURANCE: The E-4 can remain airborne for three days and nights, refuelled by USAF tankers. The key to its capability is the extensive array of communications systems fitted, covering seven wavelengths.

THE PRESIDENT AND THE NCA: If the US was attacked, some leaders would be taken to the underground command centre in Virginia, while others, including the President, would board an E-4B in order to direct American forces. A National Command Authority (NCA) would co-ordinate the army, navy and air force.

EMP AND NUCLEAR SHIELDING: In order to perform its role as a communications centre, the E-4 is protected against nuclear thermal damage and electromagnetic pulse weapons.

EARLY COMMAND POSTS

BOEING EC-135C/J: E-4s replaced various versions of the EC-135 (itself based on the KC-135B tanker), which had performed the Project 'Looking Glass' task since 1961. 'Looking Glass' was the Strategic Air Command's (SAC) commitment to have a command post in the air at all times to direct SAC's manned and ballistic missile assets in time of war.

Boeing
E-6 Mercury

● Global mission ● Submarine communications ● Last of the 707s

Maintaining communication links with American missile submarines at sea is the unique job of the Boeing E-6 Mercury. The E-6, formerly known as Hermes, was the final version of the Boeing 707 off the production line in Renton, Washington. The 707 airframe, which was originally designed in the 1950s, encloses the hi-tech communications system known by the nickname TACAMO (Take Charge and Move Out).

▲ *Equipped with the latest communications systems, the E-6 Mercury will remain a vital component in the US chain of command well into the next century. A crew of 18 operators is required to control the systems.*

PHOTO FILE

Boeing E-6 Mercury

▲ Mercury roll-out
An admiring crowd gives scale to the first production E-6, showing the huge size of this special communications aircraft.

▲ On the flightdeck
Cockpit systems are similar to those of the standard 707, except for the F108-CF-100 engine controls and the highly accurate navigation equipment. Air-refuelled missions may last up to 72 hours, and a relief aircrew is carried for these extended flights.

▲ Communicating from Mercury
Relief systems operators may also be accommodated, since the E-6 has eight bunks. An area is also set aside for the in-flight repair of faulty systems.

▲ Winging through the clouds
Missions are carried out at high altitude and over long ranges. The CFM engines are more powerful than the similar units fitted to the E-3 Sentry.

Wingtip sensor array ▶
High-frequency communication probes are fixed under the wing, and the wingtips are fitted with pods containing ultra-high frequency satellite receivers.

FACTS AND FIGURES

- ➤ The maiden flight of the series prototype aircraft took place on 19 February 1987; the aircraft have seen combat.
- ➤ On 2 August 1989 the first operational E-6 Mercury entered service.
- ➤ Two squadrons, each with eight E-6s, are operated by the US Navy.
- ➤ The E-6 carries extra bunks for relief crewmembers because of its long endurance flights of up to 72 hours.
- ➤ Boeing manufactured 18 E-6s for service with the US Navy.
- ➤ Training for Mercury pilots is carried out in Waco, Texas, by civilian contractors.

PROFILE

Co-ordinating the submarine fleet

For several years the US Navy used the EC-130Q Hercules in the TACAMO role, which maintains low-frequency communications between American commanders and their nuclear submarines. However, a more modern aircraft, especially one that could provide extra space and improved crew comfort, was required as a replacement for the ageing Hercules. Navy experts decided that the Boeing 707-320 airliner offered the most suitable basis for the new aircraft, and issued a contract in 1983.

The 707 airframe, from which the E-6 was developed, provided maximum commonality with the E-3 Sentry AWACS (Airborne Warning and Communications System) aircraft, for ease of servicing. The huge CFM56 engines, chosen because of their outstanding fuel efficiency, resulted in ultra-long endurance while on patrol. In fact, since it can be refuelled aloft, the endurance of the Mercury is limited only by its engine oil capacity. To communicate with submarines, the Mercury uses two trailing wire antennas which are hardened against the effects of nuclear blast and are deployed from its tailcone (1220 m (4,000 ft.) long) and underfuselage (7925 m (26,000 ft.) long). When the aircraft flies a tight orbit these antennas hang vertically down and allow communications to be transmitted to submarines towing their own aerial array. After defence cuts in the 1990s, and as the threat of nuclear war becomes increasingly unlikely, the Navy has more E-6s than it needs and may assign some of them to secondary duties such as training or transport.

Above: Departing Renton for the short flight to Boeing Field in Seattle, the US Navy's first Mercury flew in 1987. The first two operational aircraft flew into NAS Barbers Point, Hawaii in August 1989 to serve with VQ-3 squadron in the Pacific theatre.

Above: Just visible at the extreme rear of this E-6's fuselage is the orange tip of the VLF trailing wire antennas. A tight orbit is flown to keep the wires vertical during use.

E-6A Mercury

Type: strategic communications aircraft

Powerplant: four 106.76-kN (24,000-lb.-thrust) CFM International F108-CF-100 (CFM56-2A-2) turbofan engines

Maximum speed: 981 km/h (608 m.p.h.)

Maximum cruising speed: 842 km/h (522 m.p.h.)

Range: 11,760 km (7,291 mi.)

Service ceiling: 12,800 m (42,000 ft.)

Weights: empty 78,378 kg (172,431 lb.); maximum take-off 155,128 kg (341,281 lb.)

Dimensions:

span	45.16 m (148 ft. 2 in.)
length	46.61 m (152 ft. 11 in.)
height	12.93 m (42 ft. 5 in.)
wing area	283.35 m² (3,049 sq. ft.)

E-6A Mercury

Some US Navy E-6s have been seen in this grey and white colour scheme, but most operational aircraft are painted an overall white. All Mercurys carry minimum markings.

A flight crew of four is standard, and they are the only crewmembers who have an outside view. The fuselage has no windows, apart from tiny portholes in the emergency escape doors.

The crew rest areas, with bunks, galley and a toilet, are housed in the forward section of the fuselage. Such amenities are vital if the crew is to remain efficient on missions of up to three days.

Efficiency and reliability were the main factors behind the choice of CFM International engines. Internal fuel capacity is an enormous 70,308 kg (154,678 lb.) enough for a 10½-hour mission at 1850 km (1,150 mi.) from base.

In addition to the satellite communications downlink equipment, the wingtip pods also contain electronic support measures systems.

Five communications stations are situated in the fuselage above the wing. A vast array of radio equipment is carried, including secure voice communications, which even allow secure communication between crew members via the intercom.

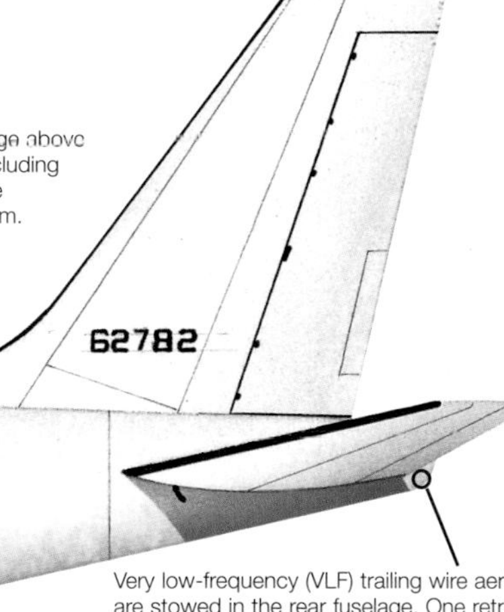

Very low-frequency (VLF) trailing wire aerials are stowed in the rear fuselage. One retracts into the tailcone while the other is stored within the rear fuselage.

Airborne relay station

TALKING TO SUBS: The E-6 is primarily tasked with providing communication links with the US Navy's ballistic missile-firing submarine fleet in a post-nuclear strike environment.

SECONDARY ROLE: As well as the wartime submarine communications role, the E-6 fleet has a secondary task of providing back-up VLF communications in parts of the world out of the range of ground-based transmitters.

RELAYING MESSAGES: Supported by the USAF's KC-135 tanker fleet, the Mercury can relay communications between ground stations, satellites, an E-4 command post aircraft and the submerged submarine fleet.

COMBAT DATA

RANGE

Aircraft of this type are often required to fly long distances on detachment to various parts of the world. Once there, they use air-to-air refuelling to stay airborne for long periods.

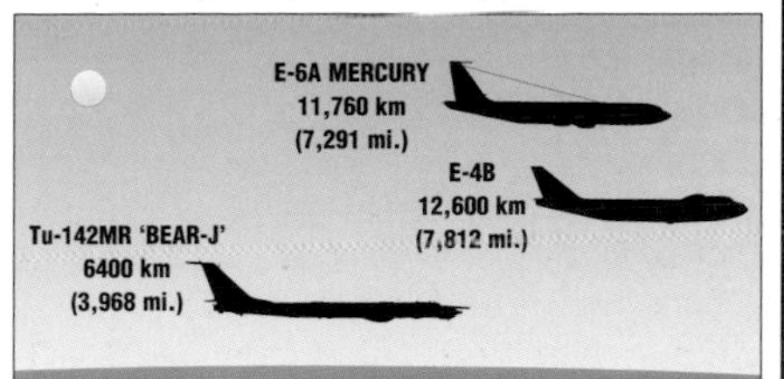

BOEING

E-3 AWACS SENTRY

● **Flying radar station** ● **Commands and controls the air battle**

Boeing's E-3 Sentry is a flying radar station. This aerial headquarters patrols the skies and scans the military situation below, monitoring friendly and hostile aircraft. Inside the metal cocoon of the E-3's fuselage, technical experts work magic with radar and electronics to detect enemy warplanes, plot their course, and guide friendly fighters to shoot them down.

▲ *A number of E-3 AWACS are assigned to NATO. Radar operators, communications technicians and battle analysts from each member state serve aboard each Sentry aircraft.*

PHOTO FILE

BOEING E-3 AWACS SENTRY

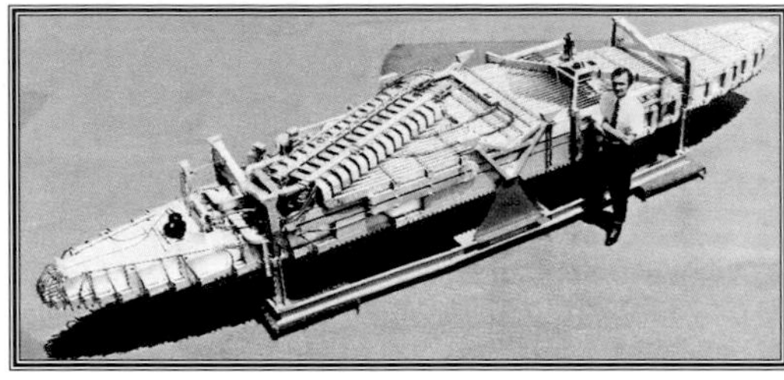

▲ **Giant radar**
This is the huge antenna for the APY-2 radar. On one side is the radar itself; on the other is the IFF equipment for detecting whether aircraft are friendly or hostile.

▲ **Flight deck**
E-3 pilots may expect to spend a good deal of time at their stations: AWACS missions often last 10 hours or more, flying basically a racetrack orbit.

▼ **Operator station**
The cabin of the E-3 is packed with consoles. From here, operators monitor air traffic on large screens which display output from the long-range radar.

▲ **Long endurance**
Inflight refuelling allows the E-3 to stay aloft for a day or more. On very long missions extra flight crew are carried to avoid over-exhaustion.

◀ **NATO's air force**
In addition to American, British and French E-3s, NATO also has its own AWACS squadron, crewed by airmen from the member nations.

FACTS AND FIGURES

- ➤ The Boeing E-3 Sentry took to the air for the first time on 5 February 1972.
- ➤ Originally, the Sentry was expected to be an eight-engined aircraft.
- ➤ The AWACS radar can see over the horizon, detecting enemy aircraft hundreds of kilometres away.
- ➤ In all, 68 AWACS were built for the US, NATO, Saudi Arabia, Britain and France.
- ➤ The disc-shaped radar dome atop the AWACS is larger than many aircraft.
- ➤ The Sentry was the last version of the Boeing 707, which went out of production in 1991 after 37 years.

PROFILE

Eye in the sky

Getting the edge over the enemy by using a large aircraft for surveillance was a hot idea in 1955 when the Lockheed Super Constellation became the first Airborne Warning and Control System (AWACS). Today's E-3 is a modern AWACS aircraft which flies at jet speeds carrying up to 17 technicians who use the latest hi-tech wizardry. To the pilots up front, the E-3 is an upscale version of the Boeing 707, the great and beautiful aircraft which revolutionised air travel. But to the technicians who sit out back, the E-3 AWACS is the eyes and ears of the battlefield commander, watching, analysing and directing. During Operation Desert Storm, 30 air-to-air victories were scored by Allied fighters who were guided into action by AWACS crews. With its long range and endurance, the E-3 Sentry can spy on an entire battlefield or, if necessary, an entire nation as they.did keeping tabs on the conflict in Bosnia.

Versions of the Sentry built for the UK, France and Saudi Arabia have much fatter and far more fuel-efficient engines than their USAF cousins.

British and French aircraft have a refuelling probe above the flight deck. The standard American boom receptacle is also retained.

Royal Air Force Sentries are equipped with wingtip ESM pods which house a Loral passive radar detection system.

The APY radar operates in various modes, including over-the-horizon, pulse-Doppler, passive and maritime.

E-3A AWACS SENTRY

Introduced into USAF service in 1977, the Sentry was selected to equip a multinational NATO unit based in Germany under Luxembourg registration. The first of 18 aircraft was delivered to the NATO Airborne Early Warning Force in 1981.

Key to the E-3's capability is the Westinghouse AN/APY-1 or -2 radar. Its huge antenna, mounted above the fuselage, rotates six times per minute.

E-3s generally carry a mission crew of 16, under the overall mission commander. These include radar operators, communications specialists and weapons controllers.

AWACS has a flight deck crew of four, comprising pilot/aircraft commander, co-pilot, navigator and flight engineer.

USAF and NATO Sentries are powered by four Pratt & Whitney TF-33 turbofans. British, French and Saudi E-3s are powered by larger and more fuel-efficient CFM-56 engines.

In order to control the air battle, AWACS is fitted with 13 HF, VHF and UHF communications links controlled by the computerised and digitised J-TIDS (Joint Tactical Information Distribution System).

E-3A AWACS Sentry

Type: airborne warning and control system

Powerplant: (USAF and NATO aircraft) four 93.36-kN (21,000-lb.-thrust) Pratt & Whitney TF-33-P-100/100A turbofans

Maximum speed: 853 km/h (550 m.p.h.) at 6096 m (25,000 ft.)

Normal operating speed: 563 km/h (350 m.p.h.) at 12,192 m (40,000 ft.)

Endurance: six hours, flying at 12,192 m (40,000 ft.), 1609 km (1,000 mi.) from base

Service ceiling: 8850 m (29,000 ft.)

Weights: empty 77,966 kg (172,000 lb.); loaded 147,420 kg (325,000 lb.)

Dimensions:

span	44.42 m (145 ft. 9 in.)
length	46.61 m (152 ft. 11 in.)
span	12.73 m (42 ft. 5 in.)
wing area	283.3 m² (3,050 sq. ft.)

COMBAT DATA

ENDURANCE

The E-3 Sentry's exceptional endurance means that it is capable of flying unrefuelled surveillance missions lasting six hours at distances in excess of 1600 km (1,000 mi.) from its home base.

E-2 HAWKEYE 6.25 hours

E-3 AWACS SENTRY More than 11 hours

A-50 'MAINSTAY' 8 hours

OPERATING ALTITUDE

The Sentry has a surprisingly modest service ceiling, being bettered by the smaller propeller-driven Hawkeye. Even so, at its working operating heights above 8000 m (25,000 ft.) the E-3 can 'see' for several hundred kilometres.

E-2 HAWKEYE 90,000 m (30,800 ft.)

E-3 AWACS SENTRY 85,000 m (29,000 ft.)

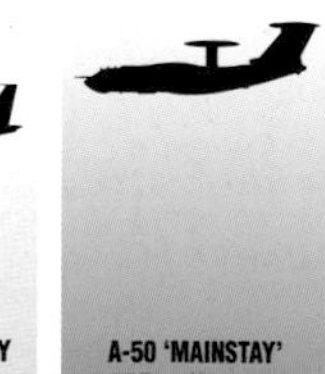

A-50 'MAINSTAY' 10,000 m (31,000 ft.)

RADAR RANGE

The Sentry's most important attribute is its amazing radar. Capable of detecting several thousand targets at extremely long range, it can also simultaneously direct and control 100 or more allied aircraft making intercepts.

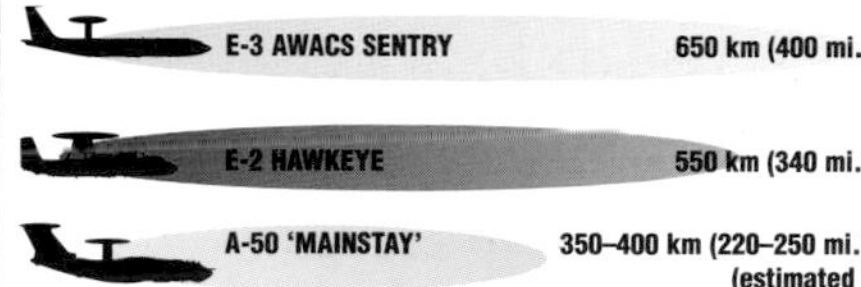

Multi-mode radar control

PDNS: Pulse-Doppler Non-elevation Scan is the basic radar mode, used to measure the distance of airborne targets several hundred miles away.

MARITIME: Advanced signal processing systems allows AWACS to pick-out ship-sized targets amid the chaotic clutter of radar returns from the surface of the sea.

INTERLEAVED: AWACS can switch between modes several times per second. This allows the big aircraft to scan for aircraft and surface targets simultaneously.

BOEING

EC/RC-135

● Strategic reconnaissance ● Intelligence gatherer ● Command post

For decades the Boeing RC-135, the aerial espionage cousin of the KC-135 tanker, has been in the vanguard of the secret world of reconnaissance, giving its crews hours of boring routine interrupted by seconds of sheer terror. During tensions with the Soviet Union, the 'spy in the sky' RC-135 often flew within a kilometre of Moscow's territory. The EC-135 is similar, but is packed with radios to act as a flying command post during a nuclear war.

▲ *The EC-135 is based on the same aircraft as the RC-135, but contains different equipment. Most of this is for communications with other US military forces. There is usually a General on board who can control the war from the air.*

PHOTO FILE

BOEING EC/RC-135

◀ **High-tech telephonist**
The job of most of the crew on the EC-135 is to make communication connections with ground stations or other aircraft.

▼ **Command post**
The airframe of the EC-135 is festooned with antennas for the many radios.

▼ **Missile watchers**
The two RC-135S Cobra Ball aircraft specialise in tracking and photographing missiles. A unique feature is the black painted wing, which reduces glare for photography of re-entry vehicles. Aerials are used to gather data from missile launchers.

▼ **Inflight refuelling**
Tanking is vital to the RC-135's ability to stay on station for many hours at a time.

▼ **The 'Hoover'**
This RC-135U is known as the 'Hoover' because of its ability to 'suck up' every electronic signal. Only two remain in service, flying from Offut AFB, Nevada.

FACTS AND FIGURES

- ➤ The systems operators in the RC-135 are known as Ravens.
- ➤ The first RC-135 reconnaissance craft became operational in August 1966.
- ➤ Strategic Air Command RC-135s flew more than 6200 intelligence-gathering sorties during the Vietnam War.
- ➤ EC-135s have a trailing antenna which can be reeled out to a length of 10 km for communication with submarines.
- ➤ Several EC-135s carried a special nose radome to track the Apollo spacecraft.
- ➤ The RC-135S can hunt for enemy mobile missile launchers in wartime.

PROFILE

America's super snooper

The Boeing RC-135 strategic reconnaissance aircraft is the offspring of the Boeing KC-135 Stratotanker and is closely related to the spectacularly successful Boeing 707 airliner. Designed as an electronic eavesdropper, the RC-135 collects SIGINT (signals intelligence), including an enemy's radar emissions, radio communications or missile telemetry.

The closely related EC-135 was an airborne command post for Strategic Air Command, and the E-6 Mercury still provides the same service for the US Navy's missile submarines. RC-135s of the US Air Force's 55th Wing deploy worldwide to snoop on potential adversaries in global trouble spots. During the Cold War, they flew closer to the USSR more often than any other Western aircraft. During Operation Desert Storm, the RC-135 gathered vital intelligence on Saddam Hussein's forces. Using radios, radar and electronic equipment to spy on potential opponents, the RC-135 continues to be vital to the overseas interests of the United States.

Below: The nose of the RC-135 is covered with bulges containing intelligence-gathering equipment.

Above: Despite the end of the Cold War, the RC-135 fleet is as important as ever to the United States. During the wars in Vietnam and the Gulf it proved it was just as good at collecting intelligence in a tactical war, as it was in the type of superpower stand-off for which it had been designed.

RC-135V

Type: multi-engine long-range reconnaissance aircraft

Powerplant: four 80.07-kN (17,960-lb.-thrust) Pratt & Whitney TF-33-P-9 (JT3D-3B) turbojets

Maximum speed: 990 km/h (614 m.p.h.) at 10,000 m (33,000 ft.)

Operational radius: 4300 km (2,666 mi.)

Service ceiling: 12,375 m (40,600 ft.)

Weights: empty 47,650 kg (104,830 lb.); loaded 144,000 kg (316,880 lb.)

Accommodation: reconnaissance versions of the Stratotanker carry electronic sensors and monitoring crews of up to 35

Dimensions:		
	span	39.88 m (131 ft.)
	length	41.53 m (136 ft.)
	height	12.70 m (42 ft.)
	wing area	226 m² (2,432 sq. ft.)

RC-135V

Known collectively by the codename Rivet Joint, the US Air Force has a fleet of 14 RC-135Vs and RC-135Ws for gathering electronic intelligence. Together they keep watch on potentially hostile nations on a global basis from bases around the world.

Large cheek fairings on either side of the fuselage contain flat antennas. These 'listen out' across a wide range of frequencies for signals which are analysed by the onboard crew.

The crew of the RC-135 is large: there are two pilots and two navigators on the flight deck, with about 17 systems operators in the cabin.

As well as 'listening' with extraordinary sensitivity, the RC-135 can also 'talk' thanks to satellite communications aerials fitted on the spine.

The elongated nose contains a side-looking radar, which provides an accurate picture of the coastline for precise navigation. This is very important when snooping close to a hostile country's airspace.

The RC-135V has a mass of large aerials under the fuselage. These are highly sensitive to electronic signals, and are used to pick up and record radars and communications.

Four Pratt & Whitney TF-33 turbofans provide adequate power and economic operation, but will be replaced in the next few years by more modern engines. Missile warning/jamming gear is often carried just above the engines to protect the RC-135.

This bulge is inherited from the KC-135 tanker from which the RC-135 is derived. In the tanker it is used to mount the refuelling boom, but in the RC-135 it incorporates yet more antennas. Some RC-135s also have a downward-facing camera in the bulge.

RC-135 missions

COMINT: Communications intelligence is the interception and recording of military communications. RC-135s may carry foreign language specialists to help in this work.

ELINT: Electronic intelligence gathering is the detection, location and classification of radars. The information may be passed to attack aircraft which can steer around potentially dangerous radars.

TELINT: The Cobra Ball aircraft gather telemetry intelligence. This entails recording signals from foreign missile tests and photographing the re-entry vehicles.

COMBAT DATA

MAXIMUM SPEED

Compared to the main British and Russian intelligence gatherers, the RC-135 is faster. Although in the deadly game of strategic reconnaissance, endurance and equipment capability are the telling factors.

RC-135V 990 km/h (614 m.p.h.)

NIMROD R.Mk 1 925 km/h (574 m.p.h.)

Tu-95 'BEAR' 815 km/h (505 m.p.h.)

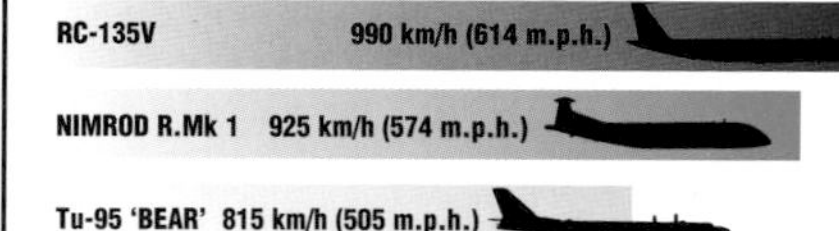

SERVICE CEILING

The three aircraft have similar ceilings. Operations are normally undertaken at around 10,000 m (33,000 ft.), at which height they are high enough to 'peer' a long way into the target territory.

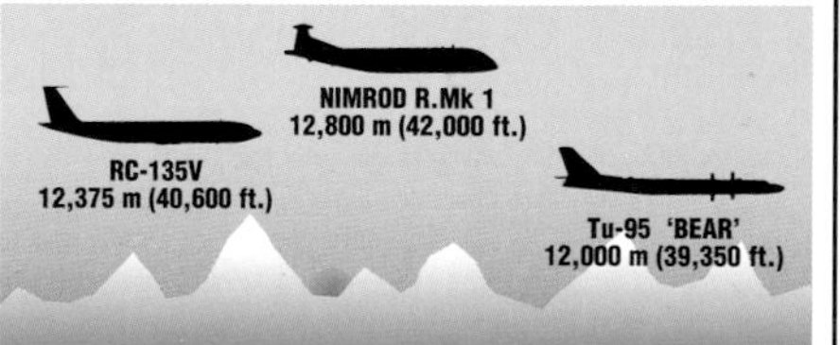

RANGE

Designed as a long-range bomber, the Tu-95 'Bear' has exceptional endurance. For longer missions RC-135s are supported by aerial tankers providing inflight refuelling to prolong the sorties.

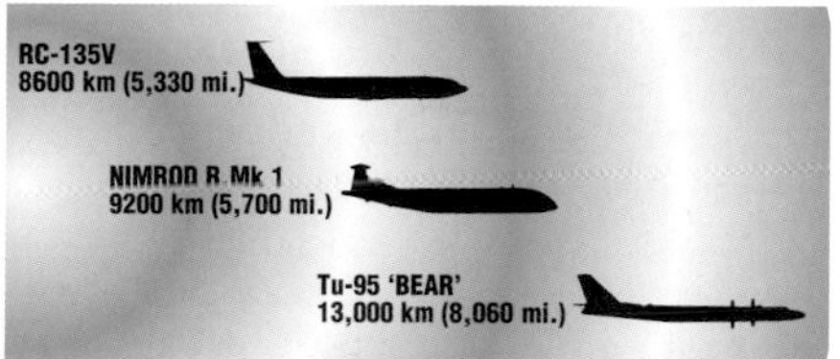

BOEING

KC-135 STRATOTANKER

● USAF tanker ● Passenger and cargo capability ● Long serving

▲ *Flying the KC-135 requires great skill and courage. The crew must either rendezvous with receivers at long range and at high altitude, or maintain an accurate course so that the receiver aircraft can fly to them.*

Taking a huge risk, Boeing proposed, built and funded a military jet tanker/transport prototype in 1954. The aircraft was ordered into production as the KC-135, and one of the greatest success stories in military aviation had begun. Stratotankers have since served around the world, supporting all types of USAF missions, and have been involved in combat operations over Vietnam and in the Gulf War.

PHOTO FILE

BOEING KC-135 STRATOTANKER

◀ Producing Stratotankers

KC-135 production was a priority as the USAF was equipped with increasing numbers of fast, jet-powered bombers which were supported by propeller-driven tankers that could not keep up with them.

▲ New developments

A KC-135A in its original natural metal colour is refuelled by the KC-135R development aircraft. New engines gave the 'R' improved performance.

▲ French tanker

French C-135Fs were adapted to the probe-and-drogue system of refuelling.

▼ A-7D top-up

Tactical jets are able to fly much longer attack missions with pre- and post-strike refuellings.

◀ Flying 'gas station'

A pristine KC-135A, with its large cargo door visible on the forward fuselage, is seen early in its life.

FACTS AND FIGURES

- ➤ When the 93rd Air Refuelling Squadron of the 93rd Bomb Wing received the KC-135 in 1957, each tanker cost $3,670,000.
- ➤ KC-135s powered by the old J57 turbojet are nicknamed 'stovepipe' aircraft.
- ➤ A 54,000-piece kit is required to convert a KC-135A to KC-135R standard.
- ➤ On 19 November 1988, 'Cherokee Rose', a KC-135R, established 16 time-to-height records in four weight classes.
- ➤ New refuelling pods allow KC-135s to support probe-equipped receivers.
- ➤ The US Air National Guard received its first jet tankers, KC-135As, in 1975.

PROFILE

Boeing's immortal jet tanker

Boeing and the USAF confidently expect that the KC-135 will be refuelling bombers, fighters, reconnaissance aircraft and transports beyond the year 2025.

The aircraft, which began as the private-venture Boeing Model 367-80 (or 'Dash-Eighty'), has been constantly updated, keeping pace with modern technology and remaining as safe and efficient now as it was on 15 July 1954 when the 'Dash-Eighty' first flew.

The addition of a Boeing-developed refuelling boom and a slightly wider fuselage produced the Model 717, known to the USAF as the Boeing KC 135 Stratotanker. Few modifications, the most important being a taller fin, were needed during the production of 732 aircraft. All of the surviving airframes have undergone a continuous evolution.

A host of special variants was produced, including the KC-135Q, a specialised supporter of the SR-71A; the KC-135E, a KC-135A re-engined with TF33 engines from old 707 airliners; and the KC-135R, which was powered by F108 engines and had a 150 per cent increase in fuel available for transfer at a radius of 4630 km (2,870 mi.).

France was the only export customer for the Stratotanker and bought 12, designated the C-135F, to support its Mirage IV fleet. In USAF service the KC-135 will fly for many more years performing its unglamorous but vital role.

Above: These Early Strategic Air Command KC-135As maintain operational readiness. They have the original short fin.

Below: The amount of time spent on station for a vital asset such as the E-3 Sentry may be increased from hours to a few days with regular KC-135 refuellings.

KC-135A Stratotanker

Type: long-range tanker transport

Powerplant: four 61.16-kN (13,760-lb.-thrust) Pratt & Whitney J57-P-59W turbojets

Maximum speed: 982 km/h (609 m.p.h.)

Cruising speed: 856 km/h (531 m.p.h.) at high altitude

Range: ferry range 14,806 km (9,180 mi.); radius to offload 10,886 kg (23,950 lb.) of fuel 5552 km (3,442 mi.); radius to offload 54,432 kg (11,975 lb.) of fuel 1850 km (1,147 mi.)

Service ceiling: 13,715 m (45,000 ft.)

Weights: operating empty 48,220 kg (106,084 lb.); maximum take-off 143,335 kg (315,337 lb.)

Dimensions:

span	39.88 m (130 ft. 9 in.)
length	41.53 m (136 ft. 3 in.)
height	12.70 m (41 ft. 8 in.)
wing area	226.03 m² (2,431 sq. ft.)

KC-135R Stratotanker

Strategic Air Command began to receive the KC-135R in July 1984 and it represented a big leap in performance over earlier variants. The grey colour of this early delivery aircraft has largely been replaced by a dark-green over grey or overall mid-grey scheme.

A large door on the left forward fuselage hinges upwards to allow cargo or passengers to be loaded. Up to 37,650 kg (82,000 lb.) of palletised freight may be accommodated.

CFM International F108-CF-100 turbofans, each of 97.86-kN (22,015-lb.-thrust), power the KC-135R. This extra thrust provides an all-round performance improvement, including an impressive take-off, with the KC-135R becoming airborne 61 m (200 ft.) before the KC-135A has left the runway.

All of the Stratotanker's refuelling systems are mounted below floor level, which gives the aircraft great flexibility by allowing the carriage of cargo or up to 80 passengers, or any combination of the two.

In order to keep the KC-135 in service for as long as possible, a programme was initiated in 1975 to re-skin the lower wings. The airframe fatigue life was increased by 27,000 hours.

Upgraded aircraft, beginning with the KC-135E programme, have increased-span tailplanes which were taken from 707 airliners.

Using a small control column the boom operator 'flies' the boom towards the receiver aircraft. The 'boomer' lies on his or her stomach on a couch.

Boeing's air-refuelling boom has control surfaces similar to those of an aircraft. It is also telescopic, so that a safe distance may be maintained between the tanker and the receiver.

U.S. AIR FORCE

10310

Tanking tactics

TWO RACE TRACKS: Flights of fighters set up a race-track at 90 degrees to the track of the tankers. Each flight waiting its turn to refuel.

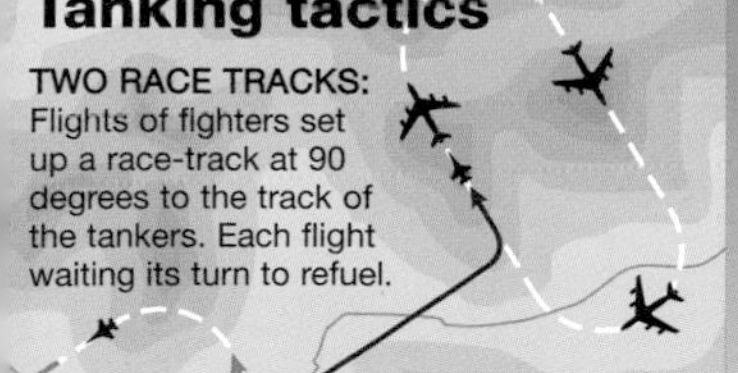

ACTIVE LEVEL: A series of tankers stack at 325 metre intervals above an active refuelling level. When the active tanker can give no more fuel it leaves the pattern and the remaining tankers all move down by one level.

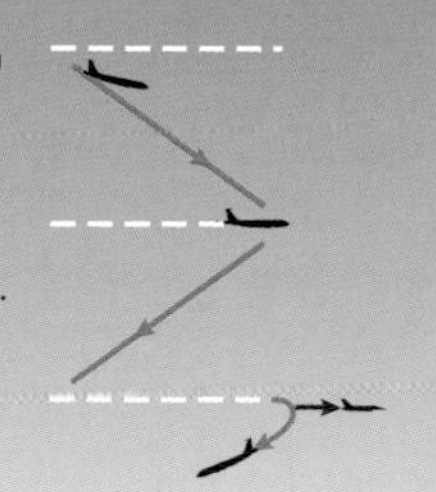

LAST TANKER, LAST FLIGHT: If all goes according to plan, the last tanker in the stack should refuel the last flight of fighters and still have enough fuel remaining for the return to base.

TANKERS RETURN, FIGHTERS FLY ON: As the tankers return to base, the fully fueled fighters are free to penetrate deeply into enemy territory. A similar operation may be mounted to get them home.

ACTION DATA

MAXIMUM FUEL LOAD

Although the Stratotanker carries less fuel than the other two, it retains a useful cargo capability. The TriStar K.Mk 1 is restricted to the carriage of passengers, while 'Midas' has no transport capability.

KC-135R STRATOTANKER	Il-78 'MIDAS'	TRISTAR K.Mk 1
92,212 kg (202,866 lb.)	118,000 kg (259,600 lb.)	142,111 kg (312,644 lb.)

Boeing/Grumman

E-8 J-STARS

● Stand-off surveillance ● Battlefield intelligence ● Gulf War veteran

▲ *Seventeen mission crew-members operate consoles displaying colour-coded images of enemy terrain and vehicles. A mission crew commander is usually a lieutenant colonel or colonel.*

Grumman's E-8 is a command post in the sky, able to detect, locate, track and classify enemy ground formations at long range. Flying for 12 hours at a time near the battlefield, this modified Boeing 707 uses Joint STARS (Surveillance Target Attack Radar System) to watch events unfold and to gather data. Rushed into service in the first Gulf War, the contribution made by the E-8 was enormous.

PHOTO FILE

Boeing/Grumman E-8 J-STARS

Tested in action

The two E-8A prototypes were hastily deployed and saw active service in the first Gulf War despite still being part-way through their test programme. Production E-8Cs have improved avionics.

▲ Production deliveries

Production E-8C serial number 90-0175 is one of a fleet of E-8s ordered by the USAF/US Army.

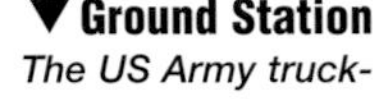

▼ Ground Station

The US Army truck-mounted Ground Station Module relays data from J-STARS to tactical operations centres on the ground for use by Army commanders.

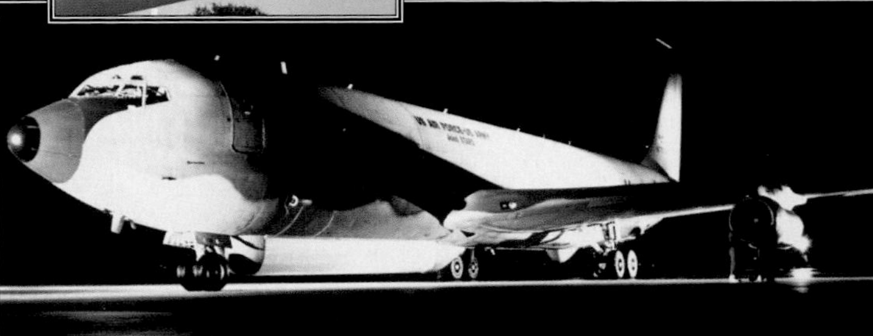

▲ Gulf War operations

In the Gulf the two E-8A prototypes were flown by the 4411th Joint STARS Squadron and were useful in locating 'Scud' missile sites.

◀ Fighter escorts

With no weapons or defensive systems, E-8 J-STARS are usually escorted by F-15 Eagles on HVACAP (high-value asset combat air patrol) during a mission.

FACTS AND FIGURES

- ➤ USAF plans call for Joint STARS aircraft to be assigned to the 93rd Airborne Surveillance Control Wing at Robins AFB.
- ➤ The first production E-8 (the third ship, an E-8C) appeared on 22 March 1996.
- ➤ An eight-hour sortie can cover an area of one million sq. km (400,000 sq. mi.).
- ➤ The first two E-8s were not modified to receive air-to-air refuelling, though later aircraft will be equipped for this.
- ➤ The two Desert Storm E-8s flew 54 missions and logged 535 flight hours.
- ➤ One E-8B airframe was delivered before the cheaper E-8C version was chosen.

PROFILE

Army eyes over the battlefield

Although still being developed, two E-8 Joint STARS aircraft were rushed to Riyadh, Saudi Arabia, in 1990. Their job was to provide Operation Desert Storm commanders with a 'real-time' method of tracking the enemy's armour and other military vehicles.

The sophisticated SLAR (side-looking airborne radar) aboard this converted Boeing 707 airliner is able to distinguish even stationary objects on the ground over a distance of 250 km (155 mi.), giving commanders an unprecedented ability to follow the enemy's every move on the battlefield.

E-8 development began in the late-1980s when advances in radar technology made it possible to design this 'air-to-ground' equivalent of the already proven E-3 AWACS (Airborne Warning and Command System) 'air-to-air' command centre. Operated jointly by the USAF and US Army, improved versions of this Grumman-modified airframe have also been on duty over the Balkans on behalf of United Nations forces. Cruising at 800 km/h (496 m.p.h.), the E-8 Joint STARS aircraft maintain continuous C^3I (command, control, communications and intelligence) operations monitoring hundreds of ground targets at a time.

The USAF and US Army have a requirement for 20 E-8Cs. Whether all these aircraft will be funded remains to be seen. One factor in the progress of the conversion programme has been the availability of suitable secondhand 707 airframes.

E-8A J-STARS

Type: multi-crew battlefield command and control aircraft

Powerplant: four 84.53-kN (18,960-lb.-thrust) Pratt & Whitney JT3D-7 turbofan engines

Maximum cruising speed: 973 km/h (603 m.p.h.) at 7620 m (25,000 ft.)

Endurance: 11 hours, or 20 hours with one inflight refuelling

Range: 9266 km (5,745 mi.)

Service ceiling: 12,800 m (39,000 ft.)

Weights: maximum take-off 151,315 kg (332,893 lb.)

Accommodation: pilot, co-pilot, flight engineer, navigator, plus 10 mission crewmembers

Dimensions:

span	44.42 m (145 ft. 8 in.)
length	46.61 m (152 ft. 10 in.)
height	12.93 m (42 ft. 5 in.)
wing area	283.35 m² (3,046 sq. ft.)

E-8A J-STARS

N8411 was the second E-8A airframe and was allocated the military serial number 86-0417. Production machines are designated E-8C and are converted from Boeing 707 ex-airliners.

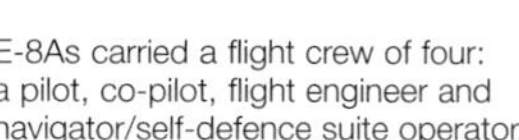

The plan to use newly constructed Boeing 707-320C airframes for the production E-8B was changed on cost grounds; converted airliners are being used instead, the result being the E-8C.

E-8Bs were to be powered by new GE/SNECMA F108 turbofan engines, as fitted to re-engined KC-135R tanker aircraft. However, efforts to cut costs have resulted in the E-8C with rebuilt TF33 engines.

E-8As carried a flight crew of four: a pilot, co-pilot, flight engineer and navigator/self-defence suite operator.

The 7.93-m (26-ft.) 'canoe' fairing below the fuselage contains the Norden synthetic aperture radar that forms the heart of the J-STARS system.

E-8As carried ten operator consoles. E-8Cs have 17 consoles and one dedicated to defensive electronics. The standard mission crew is 21, but this can be increased to 34 for longer missions.

The teardrop fairing known as the 'fiddle' was only fitted to E-8As. It contained the Flight Test Data Link used over long distances during Desert Storm to convey information to central command in Riyadh.

The E-8 airframe is that of the Boeing 707-320C, the final version of the famous airliner. These lack the ventral fin of earlier models.

US AIR FORCE-US ARMY Joint STARS

N8411

E-8 USAF 60417

J-STARS surveillance

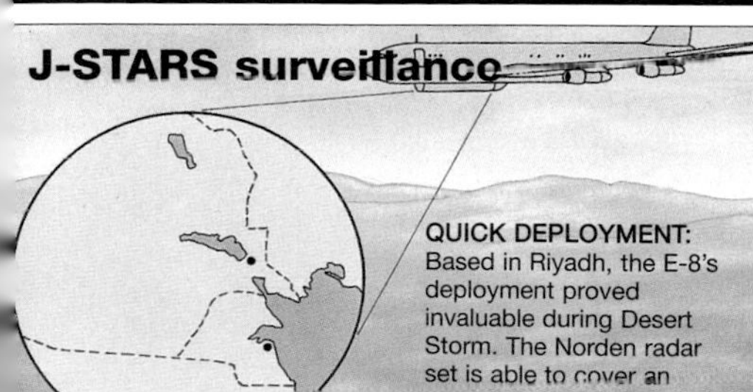

QUICK DEPLOYMENT: Based in Riyadh, the E-8's deployment proved invaluable during Desert Storm. The Norden radar set is able to cover an area of 50,000 km² (19,000 sq. mi.).

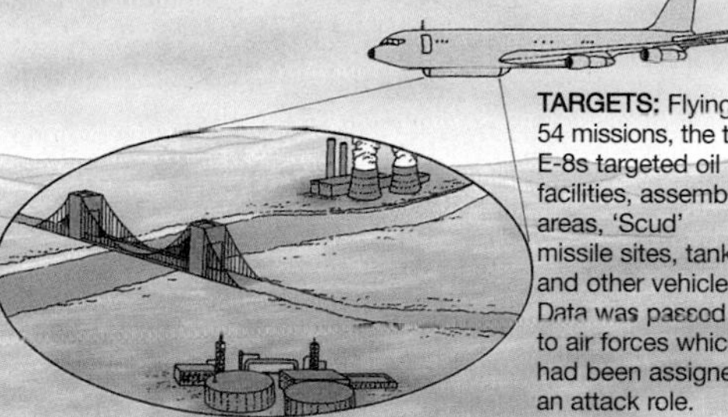

TARGETS: Flying 54 missions, the two E-8s targeted oil facilities, assembly areas, 'Scud' missile sites, tanks and other vehicles. Data was passed on to air forces which had been assigned an attack role.

GROUND STATION MODULE: The US Army's GSM receives relayed information from the J-STARS about the enemy's movements and passes this on to ground forces.

COMBAT DATA

MISSION ENDURANCE

The E-8 can stay aloft for 11 hours before needing to refuel using the standard USAF air-to-air refuelling system. Flights of up to 72 hours' duration are possible, onboard supplies and crew fatigue being the governing factors. All three types are also capable of air-to-air refuelling.

E-4
12 hours

E-6 MERCURY
10½ hours

E-8 J-STARS
11 hours

BRITISH AEROSPACE

SEA HARRIER FRS.MK 1

● **V/STOL fighter** ● **Anti-shipping strike** ● **Carrier air defence**

▲ *India has so far been the only export customer for the Sea Harrier, and operates these capable aircraft from its aircraft-carriers* Viraat *and* Vikrant*. Royal Navy Sea Harriers currently serve aboard the carriers* Invincible, Illustrious *and* Ark Royal, *sharing the ship's flight deck with Sea King helicopters.*

First ordered by the Royal Navy as a multi-role, carrier-borne fighter in 1975, the Sea Harrier went on to prove itself in various missions in the Falklands conflict. It was not taken seriously at first, but the Sea Harrier has proved capable of undertaking reconnaissance, anti-ship missile attacks and air defence missions with efficiency. It has been exported to India, and recently upgraded by Britain with more advanced radar and missiles.

PHOTO FILE

BRITISH AEROSPACE SEA HARRIER FRS.MK 1

▼ **Sidewinder armament**
On Royal Navy combat air patrol missions the Sea Harrier's principal air-to-air weapon is the AIM-9L Sidewinder infra-red homing missile.

▲ **Royal Navy's defender**
The key to the success of the Sea Harrier is the excellent integrated avionics and head-up display system. Pilots claim it is still one of the best in service in a fighter aircraft.

▼ **Long-range patrol**
These five Sea Harriers carry a typical long-range air combat training load of Sidewinder acquisition rounds and underwing drop-tanks.

▲ **Fleet training**
Prospective Sea Harrier pilots were trained on two-seat Sea Harrier T.Mk 4s for flight technique and Blue Fox radar-equipped Hunter T.Mk 8Ns for advanced intercept training.

Thrust-vectoring manoeuvrability ▶
The key to the Sea Harrier's success lies in its unmatched ability to alter the direction of its engine nozzles in flight and outmanoeuvre faster aircraft.

FACTS AND FIGURES

- In Royal Navy service the Sea Harrier filled the gap left when the McDonnell Douglas Phantom FGR.Mk 2 was retired.
- The Sea Harrier can carry the Sea Eagle anti-ship missile or a nuclear bomb.
- India operates 26 Sea Harrier Mk 51s armed with MATRA 550 missiles.
- The first operational Sea Harrier Squadron was No. 800 aboard HMS *Invincible* in 1980.
- Six Sea Harriers were lost in the Falklands, but none during air combat.
- Royal Navy FRS.Mk 1s have been upgraded to F/A.Mk 2 standard.

PROFILE

Vertical take-off superfighter

A first-class naval strike fighter in its own right, the Sea Harrier was originally developed from the RAF's own Harrier GR.Mk 3. Rather than being a land-based aircraft, the Sea Harrier was designed from the outset to serve aboard the Royal Navy's 20000-tonne ASW carriers.

Soon after its 1980 service entry with the fleet, the Sea Harrier became involved in the 1982 Falklands War, performing faultlessly in air defence, strike and reconnaissance duties. Embarking for the South Atlantic first aboard HMS *Hermes* and later aboard HMS *Invincible*, the two squadrons of Sea Harriers equipped with the Blue Fox radar and Sidewinder missile returned after their successful 'Operation Corporate' with 22 aerial victories and no aerial combat losses. Sea Harriers continue to be the Royal Navy's sole fixed-wing combat asset, but now also serve in numbers aboard the aircraft-carriers of the Indian navy as FRS.Mk 51s. The Indian navy may adopt an Israeli radar and advanced active radar missile for its Sea Harriers to acquire long-range air-to-air engagement capability.

For pilot training the Sea Harrier utilises a specially built land-based replica of the Royal Navy's carrier deck 'ski-jumps', used during short take-offs with increased payloads.

Sea Harrier FRS.Mk 1

Type: carrier-based V/STOL fleet defence fighter and strike aircraft

Powerplant: one 9752-kN (21,950-lb.-thrust) Rolls-Royce Pegasus Mk 104

Maximum speed: 1328 km/h (735 m.p.h.)

Combat radius: 750 km (465 mi.) with four AIM-9L Sidewinder AAMs

Service ceiling: 15,545 m (51,000 ft.)

Weights: maximum take-off weight 11,884 kg (26,145 lb.)

Armament: underfuselage mounts for two 30-mm ADEN cannon; maximum ordnance of 3629 kg (7,984 lb.) on underwing pylons

Dimensions:

span	7.70 m (25 ft. 3 in.)
length	14.50 m (47 ft. 7 in.)
height	3.71 m (12 ft. 2 in.)
wing area	18.68 m² (201 sq. ft.)

For naval operations the Sea Harrier has all its easily corroded magnesium components replaced.

The Sea Harrier's cockpit is raised to provide room for extra marine avionics. The FRS.Mk 1 also features weather-proof protective coatings on important components.

The naval Harrier carries an advanced Blue Fox all-weather radar in the nose. This can detect fighters up to 40 km (25 mi.) and ships up to 150 km (90 mi.) distant, but cannot 'look down' to search for aircraft flying low over water.

SEA HARRIER FRS.MK 1

This Sea Harrier is in the colours of No. 801 Squadron, based at RNAS Yeovilton, known to the Royal Navy as HMS *Heron*. The code '000' shows that it is the aircraft assigned to the squadron commander.

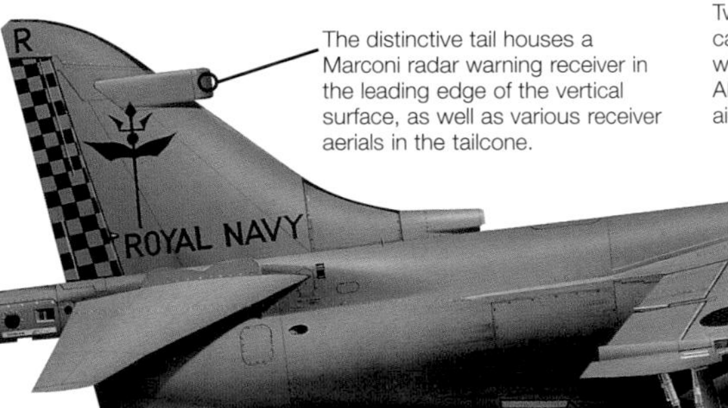

The distinctive tail houses a Marconi radar warning receiver in the leading edge of the vertical surface, as well as various receiver aerials in the tailcone.

Two ADEN 30-mm cannon pods are carried under the fuselage. Under the wings each outer pylon mounts twin AIM-9L Sidewinder heat-seeking air-to-air dogfight missiles.

A single Rolls-Royce Pegasus Mk 104 turbofan with two swivelling exhausts either side of the fuselage creates 9752 kN (21,950 lb. thrust).

The unusual bicycle undercarriage with wing-mounted outriggers provides the plane with stable vertical landings on aircraft-carrier decks in all weathers.

COMBAT DATA

MAXIMUM SPEED

The Sea Harrier and the Matador are from the same family of aircraft and therefore have a similar top speed. The 'Forger' is slower despite having one engine dedicated to forward speed.

SEA HARRIER FRS.Mk 1 1328 km/h (735 m.p.h.)

AV-8S MATADOR 1176 km/h (729 m.p.h.)

YAK-38 'FORGER' 1009 km/h (626 m.p.h.)

CLIMB RATE

At sea level the Sea Harrier has a blistering climb rate, ideal for a quick launch from a carrier to intercept incoming aircraft. The Yak-38 takes much longer to reach operating altitude.

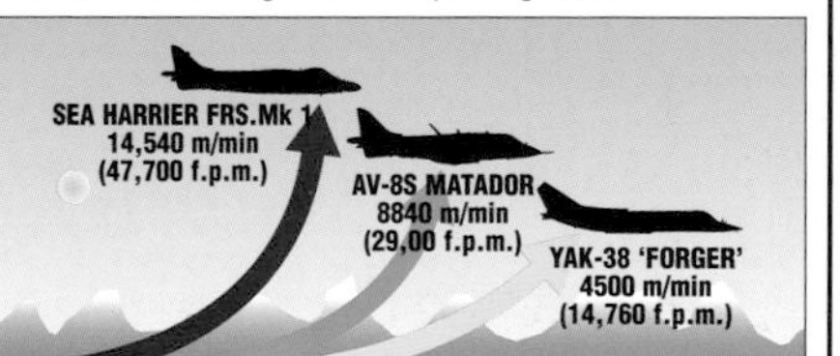

BOMBLOAD

Although it is powered by three engines the Yak-38 can only manage to carry a relatively light warload. The Sea Harrier can be equipped with a wide variety and a fair weight of weapons.

SEA HARRIER FRS.Mk 1
3629 kg (7,984 lb.)

AV-8S MATADOR
2404 kg (5,289 lb.)

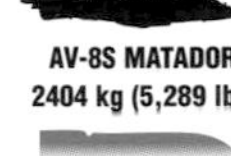

YAK-38 'FORGER'
2000 kg (4,400 lb.)

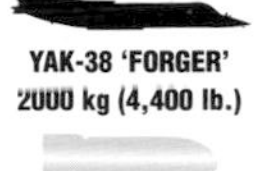

In the Falklands

AIRFIELD DESTRUCTION: Avoiding Argentinian fighters and 35-mm anti-aircraft guns, Sea Harriers flew low over Goose Green, hitting a stationary FMA Pucará with cluster bombs.

SIDEWINDER STRIKE: The Israeli-built Dagger was faster than the Sea Harrier, but a combination of pilot skill and the deadly Sidewinder missile accounted for 11 Dagger kills.

SURPRISE ATTACK: Sea Harriers ambushed Argentinian Agusta 109 and Puma helicopters over Mount Kent, strafing them.

BRITISH AEROSPACE

HAWK

● **Advanced jet trainer** ● **Light multi-mission fighter**

The Hawk is one of the most successful advanced trainers in the world. Used by the Royal Air Force and 14 other air arms worldwide, this lithe and exciting jet is also a carrier-capable advanced trainer for the US Navy and is being developed into a versatile family of lightweight fighters. But the Hawk is also a high-flying ambassador of goodwill: the all-red Hawks of the RAF's Red Arrows have entertained more than 50 million spectators in the past 18 years.

▲ *Steam rises from the catapult as a T-45 Goshawk is prepared for launch. The US Navy's carrier-capable version of the Hawk brings to 15 the number of countries using this best-selling trainer.*

PHOTO FILE

BRITISH AEROSPACE HAWK

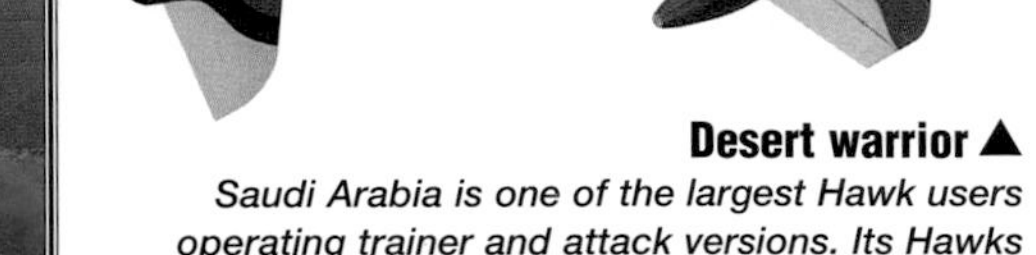

Desert warrior ▲

Saudi Arabia is one of the largest Hawk users operating trainer and attack versions. Its Hawks wear a disruptive brown/sand coloured camouflage scheme, enabling them to blend into the desert.

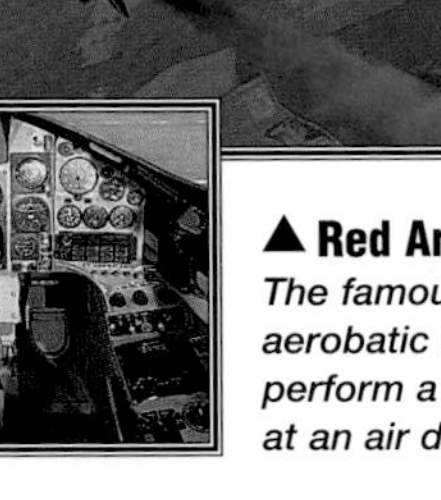

▲ Red Arrows

The famous Red Arrows aerobatic display team perform a formation loop at an air display.

▲ Pilot's classroom

The comfortable Hawk cockpit combines the simplicity of the aircraft that students would be familiar with from basic training with features of advanced combat jets that they all aspire to fly.

◀ Aerobat

The RAF use the Hawk as an advanced trainer with a secondary role as a light fighter armed with heat-seeking missiles, and an externally fitted 30-mm gunpod.

▼ Gulf warrior

During the Gulf War, Kuwaiti Hawks took part in light strike sorties against Iraqi positions inside Kuwait. This trainer Hawk is in service with the neighbouring state of Abu Dhabi.

▲ Alpine trainer

The Swiss air force selected the Hawk to replace ageing de Havilland Vampire trainers. The Hawk will take pilots from flying the turboprop PC-7 to the mighty F/A-18 Hornet.

FACTS AND FIGURES

- The Hawk made its maiden flight on 21 August 1971.
- Eighty-eight Hawks were modified to carry the Sidewinder missile and were designated Hawk T.Mk 1A.
- The Red Arrows display team has operated the Hawk since 1979.
- RAF No. 100 Squadrons uses the Hawk for target-towing duties. The towing equipment is attached under the fuselage.
- The Hawk trainer has been exported to the Middle East, Africa, Europe and the Far East.
- Finland purchased over 50 Hawk Mk 51s which were assembled by Valmet.

PROFILE

The world's favourite trainer

British Aerospace (originally Hawker Siddeley) developed the beautiful, capable Hawk to replace the RAF's standard trainer, the Gnat. As a trainer the Hawk is simple and practical, yet offers the high performance associated with military jets. Several air forces now use the Hawk to train pilots, and after a protracted period of development the US Navy is employing the McDonnell-built T-45 Goshawk trainer version.

Pilots found that flying this sleek jet was almost like flying the hottest, fastest fighter. Inevitably, fighter versions followed. Now the Hawk can be used as a trainer or fighter by a small air force unable to afford more expensive jets.

Although hardly in the category of a MiG-25 or an F-15, the Hawk is potent as a lightweight fighter and would give a good account of itself in battle. The Hawk 100 two-seater is a trainer with full military capabilities. Half-a-dozen nations are using versions of the Hawk 200, a single-seater which is a pure combat version fitted with the APG-66H multi-mode radar.

Blasting a target with SNEB rockets is part of the tactical weapons course for RAF pilots. The Hawk can carry four rocket pods.

This aircraft is seen in the grey-green colours of the early 1980s. Current weapons trainers are painted all-over grey.

The leading edge of the Hawk's wing is swept back at 26°.

Hawk T.Mk 1A

Type: two-seat trainer/light fighter

Powerplant: one 23.34-kN (5,200-lb.-thrust) Rolls-Royce/Turboméca Adour Mk 151-01 turbofan

Maximum speed: 1040 km/h (645 m.p.h.) at sea level

Range: 2500 km (1,800 mi.) with two drop-tanks; combat radius 1038 km (620 mi.) with a 1361-kg (3,000-lb.) warload

Service ceiling: 14,000 m (46,000 ft.)

Weights: empty 3990 kg (8,800 lb.); maximum 7755 kg (16,200 lb.)

Armament: two AIM-9L Sidewinder air-to-air missiles plus up to 500 kg (1,100 lb.) ordnance; maximum load 3000 kg (6,600 lb.)

Dimensions:

span	9.39 m (30 ft. 9 in.)
length	11.17 m (35 ft. 4 in.)
height	3.99 m (13 ft.)
wing area	16.69 m² (180 sq. ft.)

HAWK T.MK 1

The first customer for the Hawk was the RAF, which uses the type for advanced jet and tactical weapons training. RAF Hawks now use a new gloss-black colour scheme to make them more visible.

The Hawk cockpit has two Martin Baker ejection seats. The raised rear seat gives an instructor a good view of his student in action.

A Micro-Detonating Cord (MDC) runs through the top of the canopy. This shatters a fraction before the ejection seat is fired.

The Hawk is powered by a non-afterburning Rolls-Royce Adour turbofan engine, which has proved reliable and economical in service.

The airframe of the Hawk is immensely strong. It is stressed to 9*g*, the same as an F-16 or a MiG-29 fighter.

Hawks are clear-weather aircraft; basic versions lack radar.

The Hawk can carry a variety of external stores, from the tanks and rocket pods seen here to cannon packs and air-to-air missiles.

The airbrake fairs neatly into the Hawk's belly. It is of great value in training prospective fighter pilots the techniques of combat manoeuvring.

COMBAT DATA

MAXIMUM SPEED

Current advanced trainers are usually capable of high subsonic speeds. Their light weight and good power-to-weight ratios generally mean that they are very quick to accelerate, and give them the ability to perform as well as faster and more powerful machines.

HAWK T.Mk 1	1040 km/h (645 m.p.h.)
ALPHA JET E	1000 km/h (620 m.p.h.)
MB.339C	817 km/h (510 m.p.h.)

COMBAT RADIUS

Although the small size of trainers prevents them from carrying a great deal of fuel, their small, efficient engines mean that even when carrying a useful warload (typically, two 454-kg bombs and two air-to-air missiles) aircraft like the Hawk can strike at targets at considerable range. This extra capability allows the Hawk to turn from trainer to attack duties.

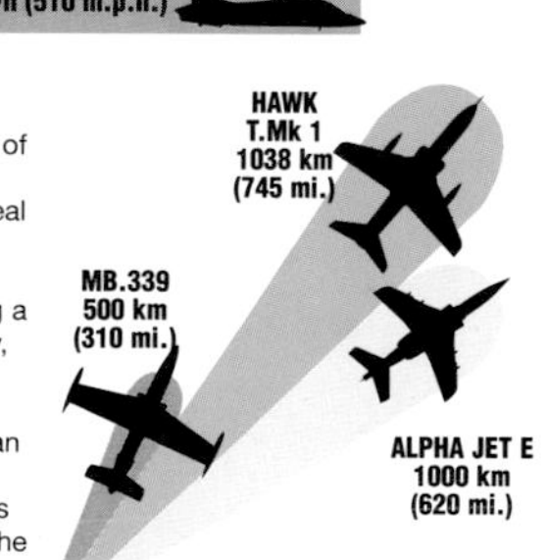

ARMAMENT

HAWK T.Mk 1	3000 kg (6,600 lb.)
ALPHA JET E	2500 kg (5,500 lb.)
MB.339	2000 kg (4,400 lb.)

They cannot match the latest front-line jets for sheer armament-lifting ability, but advanced combat trainers usually have a fairly respectable weapons load, and form an effective reserve force to more powerful combat jets.

A family of Hawks

■ **HAWK T.Mk 1** is the basic two-seat trainer version, capable of fast-jet training missions as well as weapons training. This version can carry a wide variety of weapons, but has no sensors and only basic avionics.

■ **HAWK 100** is a more advanced two-seat trainer and light-strike aircraft, with optional forward-looking infra red systems. The cockpit is more advanced than the standard version, and the wing has extra pylons.

■ **HAWK 200** is the most advanced and deadly of the family. Although no bigger than other Hawks, it can be equipped with a full array of sensors, including radar and a laser rangefinder, and can deliver a wide range of weaponry.

■ **T-45 GOSHAWK** has been selected by the US Navy as its combat trainer for the 21st century. Based on the Hawk, it has upgraded systems, an arrester hook and tougher landing gear to withstand carrier launches and landings.

CASA

C.101 AVIOJET

● Spanish twin-jet trainer ● German/US design help ● Exports

Designed as a trainer and light strike aircraft to replace the Hispano HA200 and HA220 Saeta, the C.101 flew for the first time in June 1977. Since then it has been sold to Chile, Honduras and Jordan and, naturally, to the Spanish air force as its primary trainer. While its main role is to take trainee pilots all the way from primary training to the operational conversion stage, a built-in provision for armament makes it a useful strike aircraft.

▲ *An impressive array of weapons including a cannon, bombs, rockets and napalm are displayed before the C.101 prototype. A secondary strike role has impressed export customers.*

PHOTO FILE

CASA C.101 AVIOJET

◄ Royal Jordanian C.101

Jordan was the last C.101 customer, in 1987, taking delivery of 16 C.101CC-04s at a cost of US$90 million, including spares and training. Used for training, they have an attack capability.

▼ Chilean A-36 Halcón

CASA granted ENAER a licence to build the C.101CC-02 as the Halcón (Hawk) attack aircraft, armed with BAe Sea Eagle anti-ship missiles.

▲ On the attack

The first attack C.101 variant was the dual-role C.101BB attack/trainer, which features six wing hardpoints and an optional DEFA 30-mm cannon.

▼ Exports to South America

Chile took delivery of four CASA-built and eight ENAER-built C.101BBs, designating them T-36. Ranging radar was fitted in the aircraft's nose.

▲ Colourful prototype

Bearing a civil registration EC-ZZZ, carried from 1982, the C.101 pylon-equipped prototype displays a colourful demonstration scheme. Ventral fins are a feature of exported aircraft.

FACTS AND FIGURES

- CASA unsuccessfully proposed a C.101 variant for the US Joint Primary Aircraft Training System (JPATS) requirement.
- Total C.101 production comprised 149 aircraft, including prototypes.
- Once Chile's A-36s were delivered, the T-36s were relegated to pilot training.
- In a reciprocal deal, Chile licence-built the C.101 while CASA assembled 41 Pillán trainers for the Spanish air force.
- The AGM-65 Maverick air-to-surface missile is compatible with the C.101DD.
- Germany's MBB designed the Aviojet's rear fuselage and tail section.

PROFILE

Blackbird: the Iberian instructor

In its initial C.101EB form for the Spanish air force, the Aviojet was an unarmed trainer designated E.25 Mirlo (Blackbird). The 88 delivered equip the central flying school and training and trials units, as well as the 'Team Aguila' aerobatic display team.

To improve performance at high altitudes, the C.101BB attack/trainer has a more powerful engine. It also carries a ranging radar, has up to six weapons pylons and can have a 30-mm cannon or two 12.7-mm (.50 cal.) machine-guns in a fuselage bay below the rear cockpit. In addition, this bay can be used for reconnaissance or electronic warfare equipment.

Both Chile and Honduras opted for the C.101BB. ENAER built eight of the Chilean air force's 12 T-36s, and has gone on to produce all but one of its 23 C.101CCs, a dedicated attack version which is designated A-36 Halcón (Hawk) in Chilean service. Honduras purchased four C.101CCs and the Royal Jordanian Air Force bought 16.

Above: Spain took delivery of 88 C.101EB-01s from 1980. After initial training on the E.25, pilots receive weapons tuition on the SF-5Bs.

A developed version, the C.101DD, was flown in May 1985 with an uprated engine and more sophisticated navigation/attack systems, like a head-up display (HUD) and hands-on-throttle-and-stick (HOTAS) controls. So far, it has failed to find a customer.

Above: In 1985, CASA flew the C.101DD advanced trainer with uprated engines and new avionics and cockpit systems. By 1996, a launch customer had yet to be found.

C.101CC Aviojet

Type: advanced trainer and light attack aircraft

Powerplant: one 19.13-kN (4,300-lb.-thrust) Garrett TFE731-5-1J turbofan

Maximum speed: 834 km/h (517 m.p.h.) at 4575 m (15,000 ft.)

Climb rate: 6 mins 30 secs to 7620 m (25,000 ft.)

Combat radius: 600 km (370 mi.) on lo-lo-lo mission with cannon and two Maverick missiles

Service ceiling: 12,800 m (42,000 ft.)

Weights: empty equipped 3500 kg (7,700 lb.); maximum take-off 6300 kg (13,860 lb.)

Armament: one 30-mm cannon or two 12.7-mm (.50 cal.) machine-guns, plus up to 2250 kg (4,950 lb.) of assorted unguided and guided weapons

Dimensions:		
	span	10.60 m (34 ft. 9 in.)
	length	12.50 m (41 ft.)
	height	4.25 m (13 ft. 11 in.)
	wing area	20 m² (215 sq. ft.)

E.25 Mirlo

Mirlo (Blackbird) XE.25-04 was the fourth C.101EB-01 prototype, flying in April 1978. In 1986, it was based at Torrejón with Grupo 54, a trials unit formally known as Escuadrón 406.

Two Martin-Baker E10C ejection seats are fired by a single handle situated between the crewman's knees. The E10C is a 'zero-zero' seat, able to be used at up to 15,240 m (50,000 ft.) at 1110 km/h (688 m.p.h.). Staggered command ejection by the instructor is possible.

An internal windscreen is fitted between the two cockpits. In the event of a bird strike, the instructor in the rear seat is protected from debris and air blast and can maintain control of the aircraft.

Two of Garrett's TFE731 turbofans power the C.101 family. Spanish E.25s use the TFE731-2-2J variant rated at a modest 15.6 kN (3,500 lb. thrust). Export models optimised for ground attack operate at higher weights and have additional power (up to 19.13 kN/4343 lb. thrust in the C.101CC).

Fuel tanks are situated behind the cockpit and in the wings. Total fuel tank capacity is 1259 litres, of which 1222 litres are usable.

For ease of design and building, the C.101 is of modular construction, which also affords cost benefits. During design, ample internal space was left for electronic equipment to meet future needs.

The C.101's nose landing gear retracts forward into the front portion of the nose. The rest of the nose carries radio and avionics equipment.

An equipment bay below the rear cockpit is employed for the storage of oxygen and some avionics. On armed aircraft, it may hold a cannon pack or electronic countermeasures (ECM) equipment.

Designed with help from Northrop in the US, the C.101's mainplane has 5° of dihedral and no de-icing provision. Export aircraft have three hardpoints per wing.

ACTION DATA

THRUST

In its improved C.101CC variant, the Aviojet's engines deliver a far better thrust figure than the original C.101EB training version. This makes the aircraft suitable for the attack role.

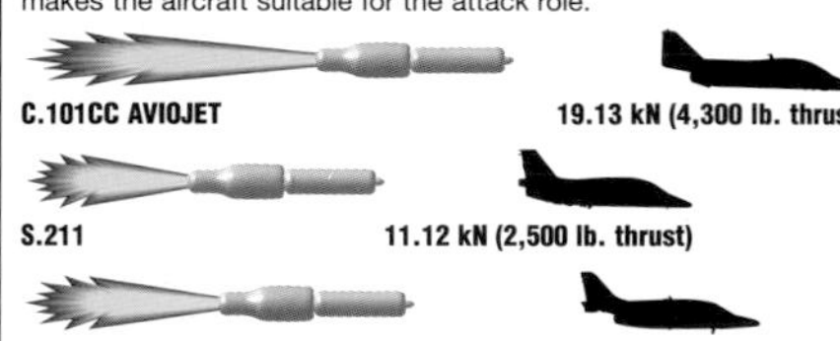

G LIMITS

Modular construction gives the Aviojet a surprisingly strong airframe, making it capable of higher-*g* manoeuvres than either the IA-63 or the S.211. Aerobatic ability is an important feature of any training jet. In the attack role, with a weapon load, *g* limits are considerably reduced to -1/+5.5 at maximum take-off weight.

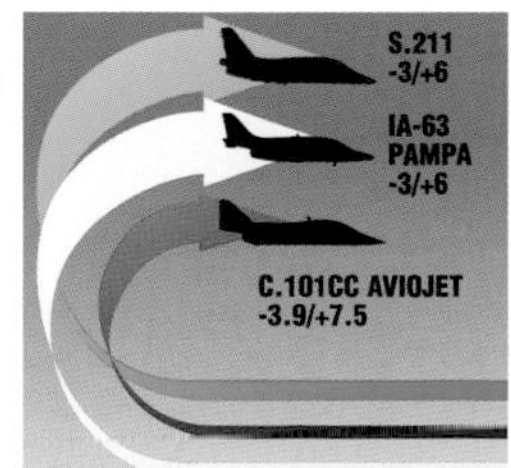

CLIMB RATE

The C.101's straight wing gives the aircraft a good climb rate, but limits its top speed. The Argentine FMA IA-63 also has straight wings, while the SIAI-Marchetti S.211 has swept wings.

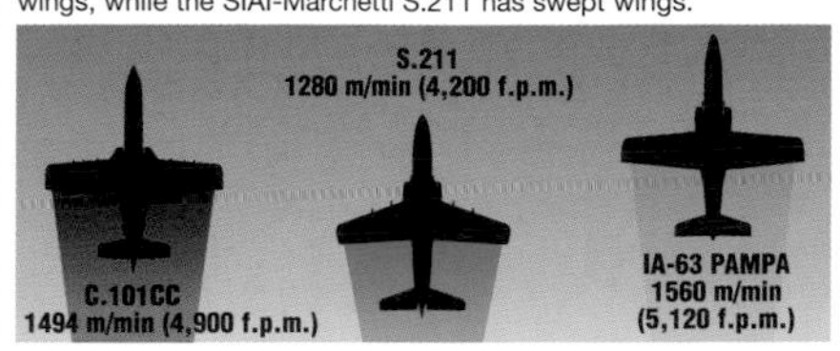

CASA training aircraft

■ **1.131 JUNGMANN:** Among several German types for which production licences were obtained was the Bücker Jungmann trainer.

■ **1.133 JUNGMEISTER:** As well as 500 Bü 131s, CASA built about 50 Bü 133 single-seat trainers for the Spanish air force.

■ **C.212E1 AVIOCAR:** Known as the TE.12B in Spanish air force service, this variant of the Aviocar is employed as dual-control trainer.

■ **C.223 FLAMINGO:** Hispano (later part of CASA) built this version of the German SIAT (later MBB) light training aircraft from 1972.

CASA

C.212 AVIOCAR

● Twin turboprop ● STOL transport ● SAR, VIP and reconnaissance

As its name suggests, the Aviocar was designed with utility in mind. It turned out to be an extraordinarily useful aircraft, with big rear doors that provide unrestricted access to the square section fuselage. In addition to the original military transport and commercial passenger versions, later models have been adapted to fill a wide variety of roles. Well over 400 have been sold, and the aircraft was built by IPTN in Indonesia as well as in Spain.

▲ *In its C.212-200 form the Aviocar is a far more capable aircraft than the original version. Maximum cargo load is increased from 2000 kg (4,400 lb.) to 2820 kg (6,200 lb.). Here a Jeep and crew enter via the rear door, ready for rapid offloading into combat.*

PHOTO FILE

CASA C.212 AVIOCAR

◀ Saving lives
The Spanish air force bought seven aircraft for the SAR role. Similar aircraft were purchased by Mexico, Sweden, Sudan and Venezuela. A search radar is mounted in the extended nose.

▼ Fully loaded
In an offensive role, the Aviocar may be armed with a range of weapons to suit a number of missions. Here the aircraft is shown with a Sea Skua anti-ship missile and Stingray light torpedo, in addition to gun and rocket pods.

▲ Continued development
The 300 series feature winglets and other changes. The US Air Force have used at least four on secret missions.

Far Eastern popularity ▶
Malaysian Aviocars are built by Nurtanio. The Indonesian company builds the C.212 under license from CASA.

Worthy successor ▶
When the Spanish air force needed a replacement for its DC-3 and Ju 52/3m transports, CASA responded with the C.212. Its rugged construction and versatility have made it successful at home and on the export market.

FACTS AND FIGURES

- ➤ Reverse thrust was applied while the prototype was still airborne at the Paris airshow in 1971, damaging the wing.
- ➤ The C.212-100 could carry 16 troops with a flight crew of two.
- ➤ Of almost 450 in total, around 130 Aviocars have been built by Nurtanio.
- ➤ Top secret missions, possibly into Northern Iraq, have been flown by U.S. Air Force Aviocars.
- ➤ The Aviocar was built for operations from unprepared runways.
- ➤ To land from an altitude of 15 m (50 ft.) the Aviocar requires only a 462-m (1,500-ft.) run.

PROFILE

Multi-role STOL transport

There have been three basic production models of the Aviocar since the first Series 100 flew in 1971. The Series 200, flown in 1978, has more powerful engines and a higher gross weight, while the Series 300 added more payload as well as improving performance. There is also a version of the Series 300 with PT6 turboprop engines.

As a transport, the Series 300 can carry up to 26 passengers, 25 fully equipped troops or 24 paratroops plus an instructor/ jumpmaster. Alternatively, it can be loaded with nearly three tons of cargo, and the rear doors can be opened for low-level cargo dropping. Photographic versions have space for a darkroom as well as cameras.

Other missions for which the Aviocar has been adapted include anti-submarine warfare and maritime patrol. Operators as far afield as Sweden and Argentina have bought maritime models, which have a surveillance radar in the nose or a submarine detection radar under the fuselage. Weapons on these more aggressive variants include the Stingray torpedo, Sea Skua anti-ship missile and gun or rocket pods.

There have also been a handful equipped for electronic intelligence gathering and electronic countermeasures. These carry equipment for the interception and jamming of signals from hostile radars. One example was also used by the U.S. Army to test sensors for use in anti-drug operations.

Above: The Chilean navy purchased C.212-100s. Variants of the 300 may also be in service.

Below: Swedish maritime patrol Aviocars are designated Tp 89 in service. Aircraft used for fisheries protection have side-looking radar and pollution detecting sensors.

C.212 Series 300

Type: utility transport

Powerplant: two 671-kW (900-hp.) Garrett TPE331-10-511C turboprops

Maximum speed: 370 km/h (229 m.p.h.)

Initial climb rate: 474 m/min (1,555 f.p.m.)

Range: 1433 km (890 mi.)

Service ceiling: 7925 m (26,000 ft.)

Maximum payload: 2820 kg (6,200 lb.)

Weights: empty 4280 kg (9,416 lb.); loaded 8000 kg (16,940 lb.)

Dimensions:

span	20.25 m (66 ft. 5 in.)
length	16.15 m (53 ft.)
height	6.30 m (20 ft. 8 in.)
wing area	41 m² (441 sq. ft.)

C.212-200 AVIOCAR

This aircraft belongs to the Venezuelan navy and is configured for the maritime patrol role. SAR is a secondary role for these Aviocars.

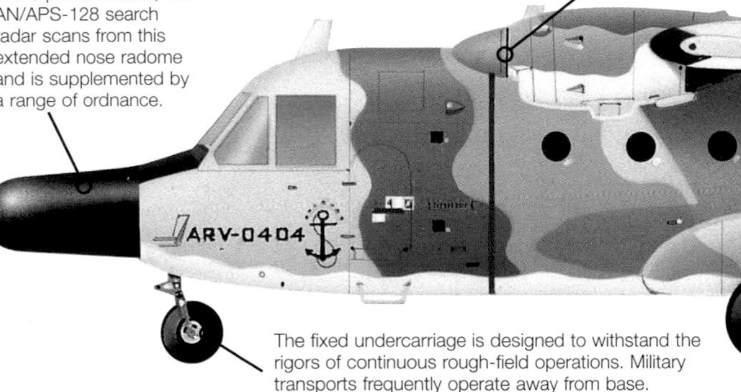

In the patrol version, the AN/APS-128 search radar scans from this extended nose radome and is supplemented by a range of ordnance.

Two Garrett TPE331 turboprops, producing 671 kW (900 hp.) each, drive four-blade propellers to give the Aviocar its exceptional range and STOL capabilities.

Attaching the wing at the fuselage shoulder allows the engines to be mounted away from any debris thrown from the airstrip. It also gives an unobstructed cabin.

The high set tail has become a classic feature of transport aircraft design. It allows for easy and rapid loading of troops and their equipment.

ARMADA

ARV-0404

Vehicles are loaded using the built-in ramp. When retracted this forms the rear door of the aircraft, which may be opened inflight for dropping of paratroopers or supplies.

In the maritime patrol and SAR variants the cabin contains special mission avionics and rescue equipment. In the transport role the C.212-200 carries up to 18 troops.

The fixed undercarriage is designed to withstand the rigors of continuous rough-field operations. Military transports frequently operate away from base.

ACTION DATA

SPEED

The heavier but considerably more powerful Sherpa is closely matched with the Aviocar. The smaller, lighter and older Twin Otter lags farther behind the others in terms of speed, but it boasts a phenomenal STOL performance.

C.212-300 AVIOCAR	370 km/h (229 m.p.h.)
C-23B SHERPA	372 km/h (231 m.p.h.)
DHC-6 TWIN OTTER	350 km/h (217 m.p.h.)

PAYLOAD

Carrying a cargo 272 kg (600 lb.) greater than that of the C.212, the Sherpa appears to be the better aircraft. Its range, however, is less than the superb 1433-km (890-mi.) range of the Aviocar.

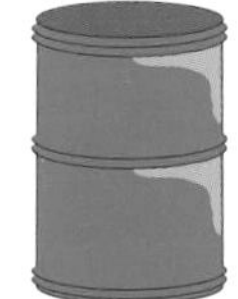

C.212-300 AVIOCAR	C-23B SHERPA	DHC-6 TWIN OTTER
2820 kg (6,200 lb.)	3221 kg (7,306 lb.)	1941 kg (4,270 lb.)

TAKE-OFF RUN

Although it is a smaller aircraft, the take-off performance of the DHC-6 is remarkable. Operating from damaged or unprepared airstrips, the C.212 has a huge advantage over the C-23B.

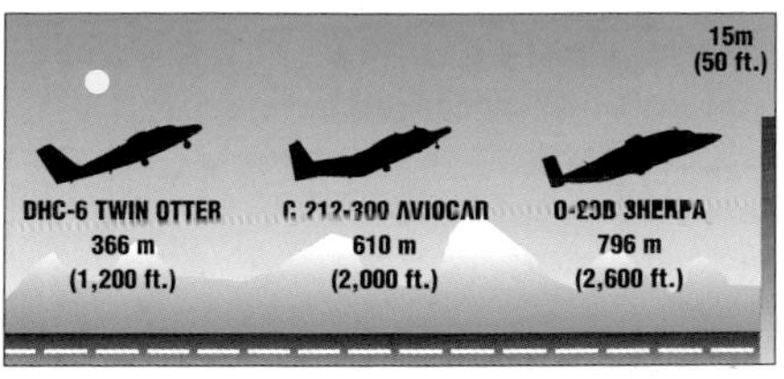

Military twin turboprop transports

■ **BAe JETSTREAM T.Mk 1:** Used by the RAF as a trainer, the Jetstream is capable of cruising at 454 km/h (281 m.p.h.).

■ **SHORTS SC-7 SKYVAN:** First flown in 1963, the Skyvan is a useful transport and patrol aircraft with impressive STOL performance.

■ **FAIRCHILD C-26:** Replacing Convair C-131s in the US Air National Guard, the C-26 features advanced avionics.

■ **ASTA (GAF) NOMAD:** Recent structural problems have caused the withdrawal of many Nomads from service.

CESSNA

T-37

● US Air Force primary trainer ● In service for over 40 years

Nicknamed the 'Tweet' or 'Tweety Bird' after an appealing cartoon character, the Cessna T-37 has been the USAF's primary training aircraft since the mid-1950s. The visually pleasing design has not changed externally in 40 years, although the instruments and equipment beneath its skin have been constantly improved. Genuinely loved and admired, the T-37 will still be training most USAF pilots well into the 21st century.

▲ *Cessna stuck to conventional wisdom by designing its T-37 trainer with side-by-side seats. Like many air arms, the USAF is now turning to a tandem arrangement for basic training.*

PHOTO FILE

CESSNA T-37

▼ First jet experience

The T-37B is the first jet aircraft flown by most USAF pilots. Primary training takes between 80 and 85 hours of flight time, after which the student will graduate to advanced training on the T-38 Talon.

▲ Mass production

Around 1000 T-37s were built to meet the USAF's high demand for pilots during the 1950s and 1960s.

1980s upgrade ▶

Cancellation of the T-46A programme left the USAF without a successor to the T-37B and from 1989 it began to upgrade surviving Tweets for continued service. The T-37 began to be replaced by the T-6 Texan II from 2001.

▲ Trainer with teeth

Cessna developed an armed version of the T-37 for light attack as the A-37 Dragonfly. Sidewinder missiles were not part of the standard armament.

▼ Foreign 'Tweets'

The T-37's excellent handling qualities make it the perfect mount for precision flying. T-37s are used by the Portuguese national aerobatic team.

FACTS AND FIGURES

- ➤ Many student pilots briefly fly a propeller aircraft before advancing to primary training in the T-37.
- ➤ The USAF currently has about 550 T-37Bs in training squadrons.
- ➤ The prototype for the T-37 series made its first flight on 12 October 1954.
- ➤ Cessna began designing the T-37 as a private venture, aimed at introducing jet power to the primary training mission.
- ➤ In total, 1269 T-37s were manufactured for the US Air Force and for export.
- ➤ Cessna flew the first production T-37 on 27 September 1955.

PROFILE

Long-serving USAF trainer

Tens of thousands of USAF pilots have their first experience of jet flying in the T-37 'Tweet'. The T-37 was designed in 1952 to meet a USAF requirement for a jet-powered primary trainer and first flew on 12 October 1954. It was a very practical trainer design seating two side-by-side, with a low and wide-tracked undercarriage to ease landing and ground handling.

Cessna built 534 T-37As, and from 1959 switched production to the T-37B model with uprated J69 engines and improved navigation and communications equipment. Provision was also made for wingtip fuel tanks. In all, 466 T-37Bs were built, including some for export, and all surviving A-models were brought up to T-37B standard.

The T-37C was the ultimate 'Tweet' and was never used by the USAF. Built solely for export, some 269 T-37Cs were sold to 10 foreign operators.

'Tweets' were to have been replaced during the mid-1980s by Fairchild T-46As but this new design was abandoned, and instead Sabreliner Corporation began supplying modification kits to the USAF which allowed T-37s to be rebuilt for extended service. The long-serving T-37 eventually began to be replaced by the Raytheon T-6A Texan II turboprop from 2001.

Above: The Pakistan air force is one of the eight current operators of the T-37C. The others are Chile, Colombia, Greece, Jordan, Peru, Thailand and Turkey.

Below: Most USAF T-37s are based in Texas where flying conditions are ideal for much of the year.

T-37B

Type: two-seat primary trainer

Powerplant: two 4.56-kN (1,026-lb. thrust) Continental J69-T-25 turbojet engines

Maximum speed: 685 km/h (426 m.p.h.)

Cruising speed: 612 km/h (380 m.p.h.)

Initial climb rate: 1027 m/min (3,369 f.p.m.)

Range: 972 km (604 m.p.h.)

Weights: empty 1755 kg (3,869 lb.); maximum take-off 2933 kg (6,466 lb.)

Accommodation: instructor (right) and student (left) in side-by-side seating

Dimensions:

span	10.30 m (33 ft. 10 in.)
length	8.92 m (29 ft. 3 in.)
height	2.68 m (8 ft. 10 in.)
wing area	17.09 m² (184 sq. ft.)

T-37C

Turkey's air force, the Türk Hava Kuvvetleri (THK) received 20 ex-USAF T-37Bs and 50 new-build T-37Cs. Based at Cigli, they are operated by 122 Filo (squadron) of the Häva Okullari Komutanligi (Air Training Command).

Turkish student pilots commence their primary flying training with 123 Filo at Gaziemir with a 10/15-hour course on propeller-driven Cessna T-41Ds and Beech T-34As. At Cigli, they complete a 90/100-hour basic training course on the T-37 before moving to the co-located 121 Filo for advanced training on Lockheed T-33 Shooting Stars and Northrop T-38 Talons.

The T-37's tailplane is set one-third of the way up the vertical fin to clear the efflux from the jet engines. As angle of attack increases, the tailplane remains in the relatively undisturbed airstream, thus preventing the aircraft from entering a deep stall.

T-37Cs have an armament training and light attack capability thanks to a single hardpoint under each wing. This can carry a multi-purpose pod containing a 12.7-mm (.50 cal.) machine-gun, two 70-mm folding-fin rockets and four 1.36-kg (3-lb.) practice bombs.

Four-digit codes on THK aircraft comprise the base identification number, followed by a three-number suffix which repeats the last three digits of the aircraft's serial.

Power is provided by two small J69 engines, which are licence-built versions of the French Turboméca Marboré used in the Fouga Magister. Buried in the wingroots and built by Continental, they deliver a total of over 9 kN (2025 lb.) thrust.

Wide track undercarriage makes the T-37 easy and stable to taxi. However, its relatively short stroke means that a tail bumper is necessary to protect the rear fuselage during take-off rotation and landing.

ACTION DATA

MAXIMUM SPEED

The single-engined Czech L-29, and the T-37B, have a comparable top speed, but both are out-paced by the French Magister. A higher top speed enables the French aircraft to transit to and from its training area more quickly, thus increasing training time.

T-37B 685 km/h (426 m.p.h.)

CM 170-1 MAGISTER 715 km/h (444 m.p.h.)

L-29 DELFIN 'MAYA' 679 km/h (422 m.p.h.)

CLIMB RATE

The twin-engined T-37B and Magister have a far superior climb rate to that of the L-29. The American trainer outclimbs the Magister on account of its more powerful engines which give a superior thrust-to-weight ratio.

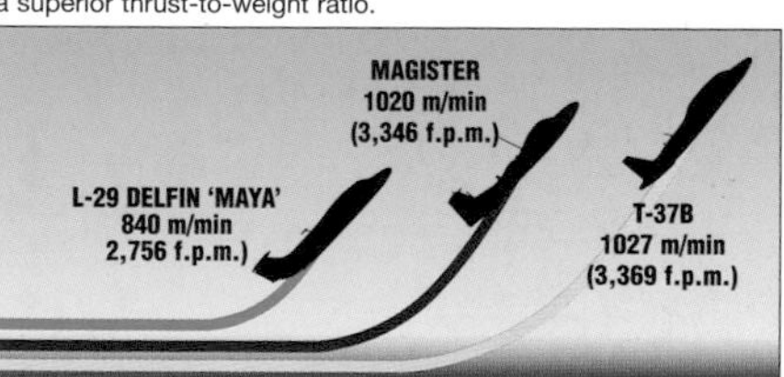

RANGE

With a standard fuel load, the T-37B can fly further or longer than either of its rivals. For a given flight condition, such as cruise, both twin-engined types can reduce their thrust settings to fly more economically than the single-engined L-29. Wingtip tanks were fitted to all three types to increase range.

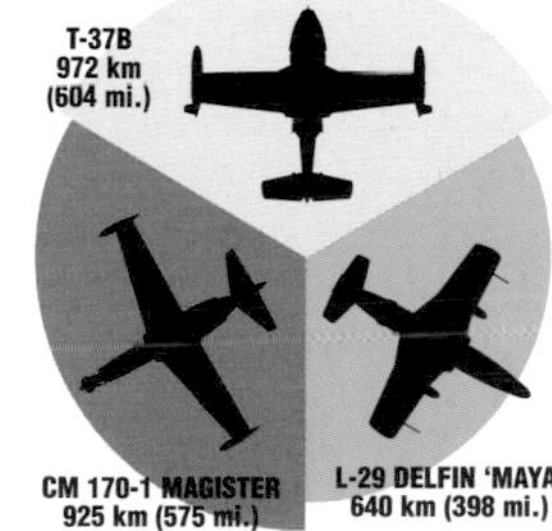

'Tweet' operators: American and export

USA: Since 1991 surviving USAF T-37Bs (which numbered 632 in 1989) have been cycled through an upgrade for continued service, until their eventual replacement in 2001.

CHILE: Chile received 22 ex-USAF T-37Bs and 12 T-37C trainers during the 1960s. Some 20-plus survivors serve with the training school 'Capitán Avalos' at Santiago-El Bosque air base.

PAKISTAN: Pakistan's air force received a total of 37 new-build T-37Cs and 28 ex-USAF T-37Bs. Two are used by instructors for the 'Sherdils' ('Lionhearts') aerobatic team.

CHENGDU

F-7

● Chinese-built MiG-21 derivative ● Updated variants ● Exports

Flown for the first time in January 1966, the Shenyang J-7 was a Chinese version of the Soviet MiG-21 'Fishbed'. By then Shenyang was working on the J-8, so development was transferred to Chengdu, where derivatives have been in production ever since. The J-7I, designated F-7B for export, was produced in small numbers before giving way to the J-7II, with an improved WP-7B engine. With Western avionics the J-7II became the F-7M Airguard. Development continues with the F-7MG, aimed at the export market.

▲ *Although essentially an updated MiG-21, the F-7M and F-7MG make use of Western avionics to enhance their capabilities. GEC-Marconi has been heavily involved.*

PHOTO FILE

CHENGDU F-7

▲ Named for export
Chengdu named the F-7M 'Airguard', with the Pakistani F-7P becoming 'Skybolt'. Neither name was adopted by other export customers.

▲ Two-seat trainer
In addition to the single-seat F-7, a two-seat version known as the JJ-7/FT-7 has been built. This FT-7P carries air-to-air missiles. It is primarily used as a trainer but can also adopt a secondary role as a fighter, if necessary.

◀ Low-cost warplane
Because of its simplicity and low unit cost, the F-7 has proved an ideal aircraft for small Third World air forces such as that of Sri Lanka.

▼ In Chinese service
The Air Force of the People's Liberation Army (AFPLA) continues to operate the J-7/JJ-7 in the fighter and training roles.

▲ F-7MG at Air Show China '96
Chengdu stated in 1996 that two of the updated F-7MGs had been built. Pakistan was expected to take delivery of the first service examples in 1997.

FACTS AND FIGURES

- ➤ Chengdu's all-weather J-7III, based on the MiG-21MF 'Fishbed-J', was built in limited numbers and not exported.
- ➤ The US-supported Super-7 project ended after 1989's Tiananmen Square massacre.
- ➤ Double-delta wings on the F-7MG offer an improved turn rate.
- ➤ The 'M' in F-7M signifies 'Marconi'; 'G' in F-7MG derives from the Chinese character 'Gai', meaning improved.
- ➤ Chengdu plans to install a new Western or Russian engine in the F-7MG in the future.
- ➤ Pakistan's first F-7Ps briefly had the name 'Skybolt' on their forward fuselages.

PROFILE

China's home-made 'Fishbeds'

Albania and Tanzania used the original J-7 as the F-7A, while F-7Bs were supplied to Egypt, Iraq and Sri Lanka. Bangladesh, Iran, Myanmar and Zimbabwe all received the F-7M Airguard, which is also used by the main export customer for the series, Pakistan. The F-7P variant was developed specifically to meet Pakistan's requirements.

Before the 1989 Tiananmen Square massacre in Beijing, Chengdu was collaborating with the American manufacturer Grumman on a Super-7 derivative for Pakistan. It was intended to use a US engine and carry the APG-66 radar used by the F-16, plus Sidewinder missiles. However, the US government suspended the collaboration.

Production of the two-seat JJ-7/FT-7 trainer variant is carried out at Guizhou. Another variant for the Chinese air force is the all-weather J-7III. Flown for the first time in April 1984, the III is powered by an up-rated 64.72-kN (14,650-lb.-thrust) Wopen WP-13 engine and also carries a new radar.

The latest version of the J-7 is the F-7MG which has a new wing, Western avionics and much improved weaponry.

Above: The Bangladeshi air force's F-7s currently fly with two units, Nos. 5 and 35 Squadrons.

Below: An updated version of the F-7 has been designated F-7MG in the Chinese inventory and features redesigned outer wings.

F-7M Airguard

Type: single-seat close support fighter

Powerplant: one 59.82-kN (13,460-lb.-thrust) Liyang Wopen WP-7B(BM) afterburning turbojet

Maximum speed: 2175 km/h (1,349 m.p.h.) above 12,500 m (41,000 ft.)

Endurance: 45 min on combat air patrol at 10,975 m (36,000 ft.) with three 500-litre (132-gal.) drop tanks

Initial climb rate: 10,800 m/min (35,425 f.p.m.)

Service ceiling: 18,200 m (60,000 ft.)

Weights: empty 5275 kg (11,605 lb.), normal take-off 7531 kg (16,570 lb.)

Armament: two NORINCO 30-mm cannon plus wing pylons for two PL-2, PL-5B, PL-7 or Magic air-to-air missiles, rocket pods or 500-kg (1,100-lb.) bombs on the inboard pylons

Dimensions:

span	7.15 m (23 ft. 6 in.)
length	13.95 m (45 ft. 9 in.)
height	4.10 m (13 ft. 6 in.)
wing area	23 m² (247 sq. ft.)

F-7P

An F-7P of the Pakistani air force, this machine was with No. 20 Squadron, based at Rafiqi, in 1991. It wears the air defence grey colour scheme with toned-down national markings.

Many export F-7s, including Pakistan's F-7Ps, have been fitted with Martin-Baker Mk 10 zero-zero ejection seats. Whereas early J-7I aircraft had single-piece canopies (as on the MiG-21F-13), later machines have more conventional two-piece units.

With a theoretical top speed of Mach 2.05 (with a full fuel load), the F-7P also has an excellent turn performance owing to its high power-to-weight ratio and low wing loading.

Known as the J-7 (for Jianjiji-7, or 'Fighter Aircraft Number Seven'), this development of the MiG-21 received the designation F-7 for export markets.

The engine air intake in the nose of the aircraft features a variable shockcone, as in the MiG-21. Computer-controlled, this is fully variable and houses a basic radar set. Western companies, including GEC-Marconi, supplied most of the avionics and other systems.

In Pakistani service, F-7P ordnance usually consists of a single centreline fuel tank and two AIM-9P Sidewinder or MATRA Magic air-to-air missiles. Four pylons are sometimes employed, and the aircraft has a limited air-to-ground capability.

Chengdu F-7Ps are powered by a single Wopen WP-7B afterburning turbojet producing 59.8 kN (13,460 lb. thrust). This engine is a copy of the Soviet Tumanskii R-11 found in early production MiG-21s.

COMBAT DATA

MAXIMUM SPEED

The Airguard and MiG-21bis 'Fishbed-L' share the same top speed as well as a common basic design. Northrop's F-5E Tiger II, though twin-engined, is designed for slightly slower speeds.

F-7M AIRGUARD	2175 km/h (1,349 m.p.h.)
MiG-21bis 'FISHBED-L'	2175 km/h (1,349 m.p.h.)
F-5E TIGER II	1700 km/h (1,054 m.p.h.)

THRUST

F-7s use an engine of earlier design than that of the MiG-21bis, producing less thrust. The F-5E's twin engines are comparatively small, producing just over two thirds the power.

F-7M AIRGUARD	59.82 kN (13,460 LB.)
MiG-21bis 'FISHBED-L'	69.65 kN (15,670 LB.)
F-5E TIGER II	44.40 kN (10,000 LB.)

INITIAL CLIMB RATE

In terms of its initial climb rate the MiG-21bis is the best performer of these types. Chengdu's F-7M has an inferior power-to-weight ratio and a climb rate little better than that of the F-5E.

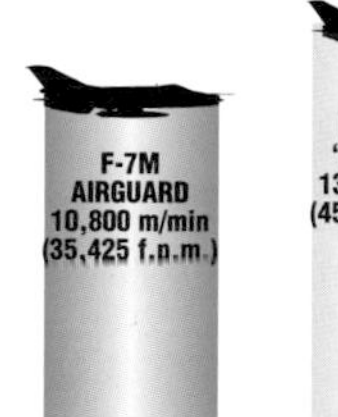

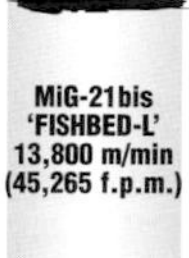

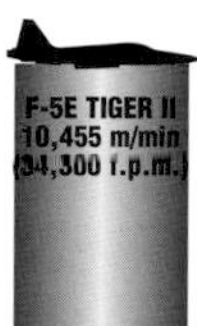

China's modern jet fighters

CHENGDU J-7 'FISHBED': Early J-7s were broadly equivalent to the MiG-21F-13 and were built under licence from 1961.

CHENGDU/GRUMMAN SUPER-7: For sale to Pakistan, the cancelled Super-7 featured an American APG-66 radar and engine.

SHENYANG J-8I 'FINBACK': An all-weather version of the J-8 twin-engined fighter of 1968, the J-8I was produced from the mid-1980s.

SHENYANG J-8IIM 'FINBACK': After cancellation of the improved J-8II (with US radar), China used a Russian radar in the J-8IIM.

CNIAR/SOKO

IAR-93/J-22 ORAO

● Lightweight attack ● Conversion trainer ● Troubled development

Designed jointly by Romania's CNIAR (now Avioane) and SOKO of Yugoslavia (now Bosnia), the twin-engined IAR-93/J-22 Orao has been built in single- and two-seat versions, both with and without afterburners. There were plans to upgrade the aircraft, but the two countries that collaborated to produce the IAR-93/J-22 Orao have undergone major upheavals in recent years, making these changes impossible.

▲ *Produced and designed equally by Romania and the former Yugoslavia, the IAR-93/Orao (Eagle) is a small, attractive twin-jet and is reminiscent of the larger SEPECAT Jaguar.*

PHOTO FILE

CNIAR/SOKO IAR-93/J-22 ORAO

▼ Packing a punch
With five weapons pylons and two twin-barrelled cannon, the Orao has impressive armament options.

▲ Tandem trainer
The 10 IAR-93A trainers featured an extended forward fuselage and sideways-opening canopies. However, they were found to be lacking in power and range.

▼ Robust structure
Designed from the outset to survive damage and for operating from rough airstrips, the Orao is a simple, but robust, design. It is fitted with a strong, twin-wheeled main undercarriage built by Messier-Hispano-Bugatti.

▼ Cold War service
Entering service in the early 1980s, the IAR-93 has survived the political upheavals in Romania.

Reconnaissance role ▶
Non-afterburning J-22 Orao 1s have been relegated to surveillance duties. This example, carrying a centreline camera pod, served with the Yugoslav air force and was based near Zagreb.

FACTS AND FIGURES

- ➤ Romanian and Yugoslavian single-seat prototypes made simultaneous first flights on 31 October 1974.
- ➤ Early Orao 1s are now used for tactical reconnaissance and are designated IJ-22.
- ➤ The J-22 prototype is currently displayed in the museum at Belgrade airport.
- ➤ On 22 November 1984 a pre-production Orao became the first Yugoslav-built aircraft to exceed the speed of sound.
- ➤ Following the break-up of Yugoslavia, the Orao 2 is now operated by Serbia.
- ➤ Romania ordered 165 IAR-93Bs, including a number of two-seaters.

PROFILE

Lightweight strike-fighter collaboration

Single-seat prototypes of the IAR-93/Orao flew in October 1974, followed by two-seat prototypes in January 1977. The first production version was the IAR-93A/Orao 1, with non-afterburning engines, which was built in both single-seat tactical reconnaissance and two-seat operational trainer versions.

Afterburning engines were used for the Orao 2 and IAR-93B attack aircraft, first flown in 1983 and 1985, respectively. Most were single-seaters, but the Orao 2 was also built in a two-seat configuration.

A third version developed in Yugoslavia is the Orao 2D. This is a two seat version of the Orao 2 and is used as a conversion trainer. The remaining two-seat Orao 1s were modified to the same standard, while the single-seaters were fitted with camera pods for reconnaissance.

The overthrow of the Communist government in Romania meant that plans to modernise the aircraft were left in limbo, and progress was halted in the former Yugoslavia when the SOKO factory at Mostar in Bosnia was demolished during fighting.

Above: Second-generation Orao 2s overcome the lack of power and range with afterburning engines and enlarged integral fuel tanks.

Oraos remain in service with the Serbian air force, and some were used operationally by the Serb forces in Bosnia before the imposition of the no-fly zone. The IAR-93B has remained in production after the revolution in Romania.

Below: This early IAR-93A, with four wing fences, wears the original Romanian air force insignia. This has since been replaced by a roundel.

IAR-93A

First flying in 1981, the IAR-93A was the first Romanian production version. CNIAR built 26 single-seat versions. They have been replaced in the attack role by the IAR-93B with afterburning engines.

Lacking a head-up display (HUD) and the latest avionics, the IAR-93A had fairly basic equipment. The updated Yugoslavian Orao 2 features a far more capable cockpit, with a Thomson-CSF HUD and other avionics from Honeywell and Collins. The pilot sits on a Martin-Baker Mk 10 ejection seat beneath a rearwards-opening canopy.

All operational versions of the J-22/IAR-93 have five weapons pylons: four on the wings and one beneath the fuselage. A wide variety of air-to-ground munitions can be carried, up to a total of 2800 kg (6,173 lb.). Orao 2s are capable of carrying the AGM-65 and AS-7 'Kerry' missiles.

The shoulder-mounted wing is of similar planform to that of the SEPECAT Jaguar. The early versions, such as this IAR 93A, did not have the leading-edge root extensions which gave later models better wing efficiency and manoeuvrability.

The strakes on the nose of the IAR-93A distinguish it from the prototypes and pre-production aircraft. The Orao 2 has a ranging radar in the dielectric nosecone.

A high degree of foreign-designed and imported equipment is used in the aircraft, including two Soviet GSh-23L twin-barrelled cannon in the forward fuselage.

All versions of the J-22 Orao and early versions of the IAR-93 have ventral fins. The IAR-93B is easily identifiable, however, as these fins were removed.

After problems and delays with the afterburning version of the Viper engine, the IAR-93A was fitted with two non-afterburning 17.79-kN (4,000 lb.) units. These engines did not provide the power to produce the desired performance.

J-22 Orao 2

Type: close-support and ground-attack aircraft

Powerplant: two 17.79 kN (4,000 lb.) Turbomecanica/ORAO-built Rolls-Royce Viper Mk 633-41 afterburning turbojets

Maximum speed: 1160 km/h (721 m.p.h.) at sea level

Climb rate: 4500 m/min (14,764 f.p.m.)

Range: 260–380 km (162–236 mi.) depending on load and mission profile

Service ceiling: 13,200 m (43,300 ft.)

Weights: empty 5700 kg (12,566 lb.); maximum take-off 11,200 kg (24,692 lb.)

Armament: two 23-mm cannon, plus up to 2800 kg (6,173 lb.) of bombs, rockets and air-to-surface missiles

Dimensions:

span	9.3 m (30 ft. 6 in.)
length	14.90 m (48 ft. 11 in.)
height	4.50 m (14 ft. 9 in.)
wing area	26 m² (312 sq. ft.)

ACTION DATA

THRUST

Twin engines give greater chances of survival, especially after hits by ground-fire. As a consequence, all three of these aircraft feature twin afterburning engines. The lighter airframe of the IAR-93B requires less power than the F-1 to carry a similar load.

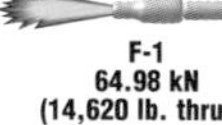

IAR-93B 44.48 kN (10,000 lb. thrust)
JAGUAR GR.Mk 1A 71.5 kN (16,080 lb. thrust)
F-1 64.98 kN (14,620 lb. thrust)

ARMAMENT

The IAR-93 can be loaded with a wide range of both Western and Eastern Bloc ordnance and can carry a reasonable load for a lightweight attack aircraft. The more powerful Jaguar can carry significantly more than the F-1 and the IAR-93B.

IAR-93B: 2 x 23-mm cannon, 2800-kg (6,173-lb.) bombload

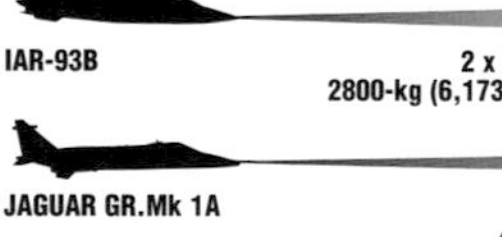

JAGUAR GR.Mk 1A: 2 x 30-mm cannon, 4536-kg (10,000-lb.) bombload

F-1: 1 x 20-mm cannon, 2722-kg (6,000-lb.) bombload

COMBAT RADIUS

Although the IAR-93 resembles the Jaguar, it does not have the same capabilities. Both the F-1 and the IAR-93 are intended for operations close to the front line and possess poor range for modern combat aircraft.

SOKO-built aircraft

■ **G-4 SUPER GALEB:** This two-seat advanced trainer was designed to replace the G-2A Galeb and T-33 in this role.

■ **J-1 JASTREB:** Derived from the Galeb trainer, which saw service in the war in Bosnia, the Jastreb has been gradually replaced by the Orao.

■ **J-20 KRAGUJ:** Retired from Yugoslav service in 1990 after 20 years of operations, this close-support aircraft now serves with Slovenia.

■ **SA 342 PARTIZAN:** SOKO licence-built the Gazelle as the Partizan. It is used for liaison, anti-tank and anti-helicopter duties.

CONVAIR
B-36 FICON

● Giant strategic bomber ● Reconnaissance mother-ship

▲ The B-36 was massive, yet its incredible weight rested on just single mainwheels. These weren't quite the biggest wheels ever carried by an aircraft, but they dwarfed ground crew.

The B-36 was America's most spectacular Cold War deterrent; 383 of these bombers were the backbone of the mighty Strategic Air Command from 1948 to 1959. The largest warplanes ever to fly in the West, they carried the biggest hydrogen bombs ever built and girdled the globe on nuclear alert or highly dangerous spying missions. At one stage they even carried their own fighter aircraft.

PHOTO FILE

CONVAIR B-36 FICON

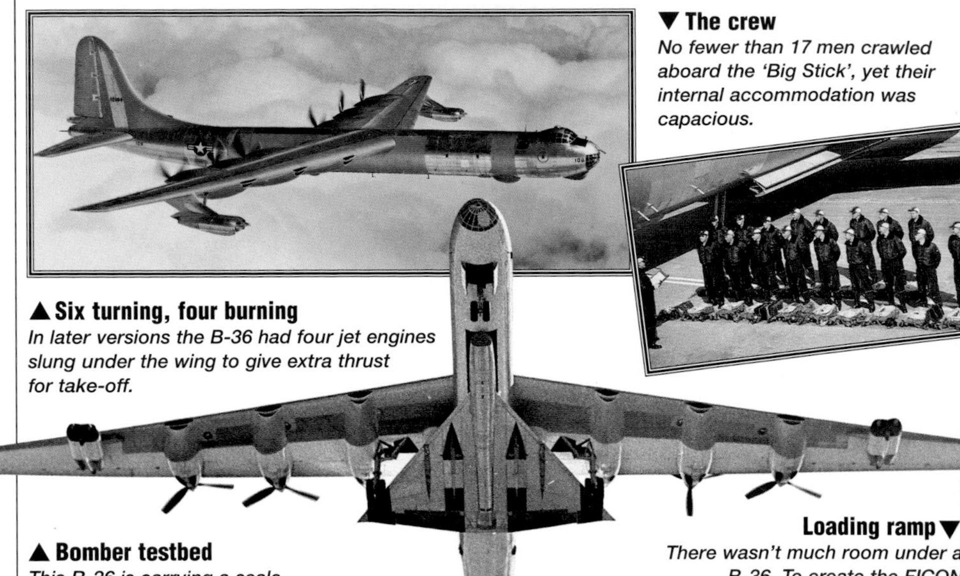

▼ The crew
No fewer than 17 men crawled aboard the 'Big Stick', yet their internal accommodation was capacious.

▲ Six turning, four burning
In later versions the B-36 had four jet engines slung under the wing to give extra thrust for take-off.

▲ Bomber testbed
This B-36 is carrying a scale model of the Convair B-58 Hustler for aerodynamic drop tests.

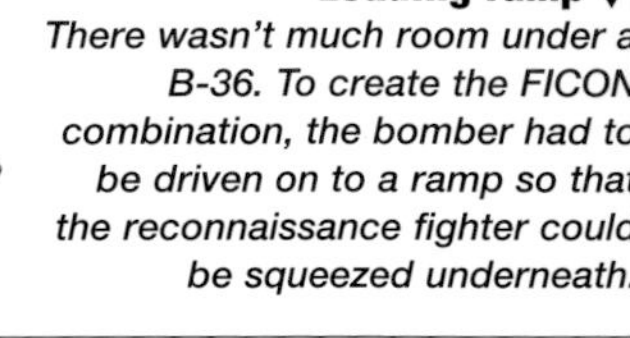

Loading ramp ▼
There wasn't much room under a B-36. To create the FICON combination, the bomber had to be driven on to a ramp so that the reconnaissance fighter could be squeezed underneath.

▲ Wingtip fighter
Before the FICON project, the USAF tested the B-36 with F-84 fighters towed from the wingtips using this strange attachment.

FACTS AND FIGURES

- ➤ A few B-36s were modified to carry a fighter in the bomb-bay.
- ➤ Convair developed a huge airlifter from the B-36, the experimental XC-99, but the giant transport never entered service.
- ➤ The B-36's radar and communications systems used 3000 vacuum tubes.
- ➤ To the men who flew it, the B-36 never had a name. The appropriate nickname 'Peacemaker' was assigned to this mammoth bomber years after it went out of service.
- ➤ B-36 missions lasted for so long that it was said to be equipped with a calender rather than clocks.

PROFILE

A deadly combination

Originally designed to drop bombs on Germany from bases in America, the big B-36 began as a six-engined bomber but soon had four jets added, making it a 10-engine behemoth by the time it entered service in 1948. It was tasked to rip out the heart of the Soviet Union with a retaliatory attack, using hydrogen bombs like the Mk 17, which weighed more than a DC-3 transport and was the largest bomb ever deployed by the US military.

When the B-36 flew overhead, it blotted out the sun. In slang, it was called the 'aluminum overcast'. The bomber was so long that crewmen used a powered dolly to transport themselves through the middle of the aircraft between nose and tail.

At high altitude, the vast wings of the B-36 clawed so much air that the bomber was more manoeuvrable than jet fighters. Missions in this incredible giant lasted as long as 40 hours. No other American bomber ever approached the B-36's size, weight, and bomb-carrying capacity.

The NB-36H carried a nuclear reactor to test its effect on the aircraft. The next step would have been a nuclear-powered bomber.

B-36D Peacemaker

Type: intercontinental strategic bomber

Powerplant: six 2834-kW (3800-hp) Pratt & Whitney R-4360-53 radial piston engines and four 23.13-kN (5204-lb-thrust) General Electric J47-GE-19 turbojets

Maximum speed: 700 km/h (435 mph) at 11,000 m (36,000 ft)

Range: 10,944 km (6800 miles) with a 4500-kg (9921-lb) bombload

Service ceiling: 14,780 m (48,490 ft)

Weights: empty 77,581 kg (171,037 lb); loaded 185,976 kg (410,007 lb)

Armament: 16 20-mm cannon in nose, tail and six fuselage turrets, plus bombload of up to 39,000 kg (85,980 lb)

Dimensions:

span	70.10 m (230 ft)
length	49.40 m (162 ft 1 in)
height	14.22 m (46 ft 8 in)
wing area	443.32 m² (4772 sq ft)

GRB-36 FICON

With its enormous size, the B-36 was a natural to act as a mother-ship for a secret strategic reconnaissance programme. A small reconnaissance fighter was carried over a long distance to its target, dropped off to go in and get the pictures, and then hauled back home to the US.

To give the huge bomber an extra burst of speed over the target area, the B-36 was fitted with four J47 turbojets to augment the six huge piston engines driving the propellers.

The aircraft carried by the GRB-36 was the Republic GRF-84F, a special version of the USAF's main tactical camera ship.

Operational bombers had two pairs of gun turrets in the rear fuselage, operated remotely from observation posts by dedicated gunners. When not threatened by the enemy, the guns were retracted and covered by sliding panels.

The FICON (Fighter Conveyor) combination went operational in 1955, but only a handful of missions were flown. The operating unit was the 91st Strategic Reconnaissance Squadron.

The Thunderflash fighter was held on a complicated trapeze which swung down from the bomb-bay. The doors of the bomb-bay were cut away so that the fighter could fit in snugly.

The B-36 was covered with aerials and radomes for electronic equipment and bombing radars. Many variants had huge reconnaissance cameras wedged into the bomb-bays.

B-36s were normally festooned with defensive guns, the standard bomber featuring no less than 16 20-mm cannon, including two in the tail. The FICON aircraft had them all removed to save precious weight.

COMBAT DATA

MAXIMUM SPEED

B-52 STRATOFORTRESS (1952)	965 km/h (600 mph)
B-36 PEACEMAKER (1946)	700 km/h (435 mph)
B-29 SUPERFORTRESS (1942)	570 km/h (354 mph)

Less than a decade spanned the first flights of the Boeing B-29, the Convair B-36 and the Boeing B-52, yet in that time maximum speed almost doubled. All three bombers used their big wings and immense engine power to outperform interceptors at height.

SERVICE CEILING

Bombing from high altitude was seen as the only protection against fighters in the days before guided missiles. The B-36 FICON used another technique – its onboard fighter flew the last, most dangerous part of the mission.

B-29 SUPERFORTRESS	9750 m (31,998 ft)
B-36 PEACEMAKER	14,780 m (48,490 ft)
B-52 STRATOFORTRESS	16,750 m (54,954 ft)

WEIGHTS

The need for massive fuel loads for intercontinental range, and the equally pressing need for huge carrying capacity to deploy the awesome first-generation hydrogen bombs, saw the maximum weights of heavy bombers skyrocket in the decade between the B-29 and the B-52.

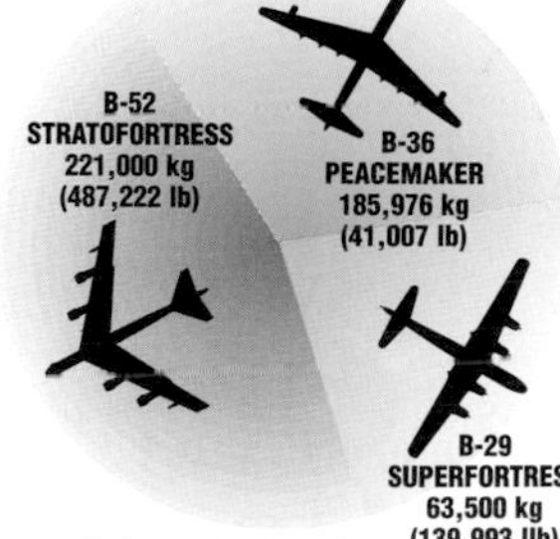

B-52 STRATOFORTRESS	221,000 kg (487,222 lb)
B-36 PEACEMAKER	185,976 kg (41,007 lb)
B-29 SUPERFORTRESS	63,500 kg (139,993 llb)

Maximum take-off weights

Inside the B-36

The B-36 was basically a long tube. The two crew compartments (green) were linked by a crew tunnel with a trolley on rails.

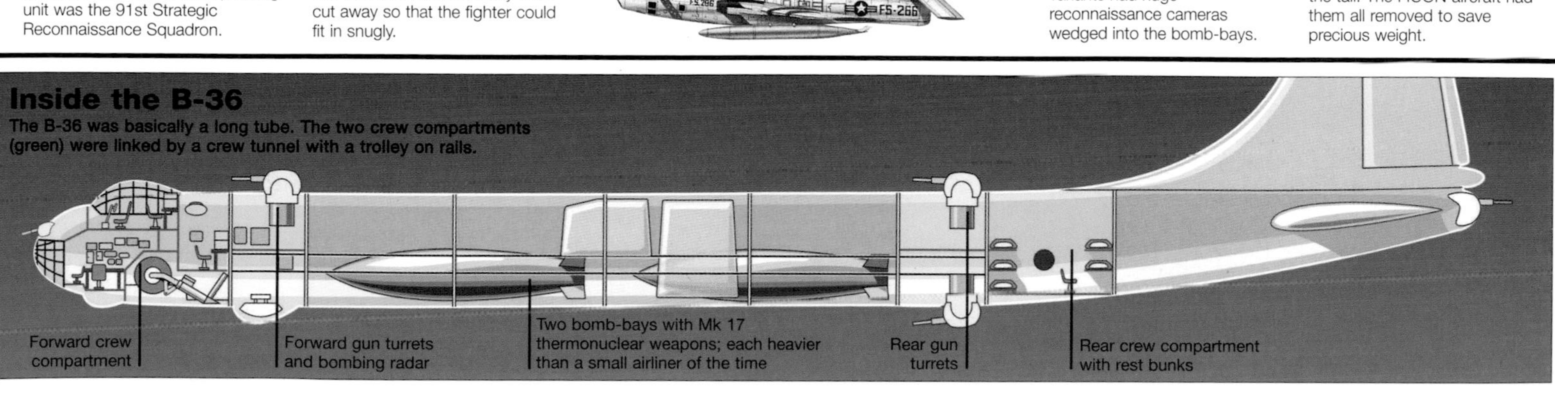

CONVAIR B-58 HUSTLER

● Supersonic strategic bomber ● Delta wing ● Nuclear-armed

▲ The B-58 was a technological wonder, with blistering performance. Its operational flexibility was limited, however, to the strategic role by its unusual combined fuel- and weapon-pod concept.

Brilliant but brief – that was the career of the Convair B-58 Hustler of the USAF's Strategic Air Command. From area-rule fuselage through crew escape capsules to its revolutionary J79 engines, everything about the B-58 pushed back the frontiers; it was a towering engineering achievement. Had it gone into battle, the Mach 2-capable Hustler, with its immense performance and advanced podded weapons, would have been able to penetrate Soviet defences with impunity.

PHOTO FILE

CONVAIR B-58 HUSTLER

▲ Brake chute

Hustlers landed fast – a typical touchdown speed with a high fuel load remaining was around 350 km/h (217 mph). A braking parachute was often used to prolong the life of the wheelbrakes.

▲ Fast mover

Without its huge fuel and weapon pod the B-58 looked like a fighter, and performed like one, too. With afterburner selected, the Hustler could climb at around 11,500 m (37,730 ft) per minute.

Flying capsules ▶

The three-man crew sat in individual cockpits. They liked their personal escape capsules, but disliked the lack of adequate air-conditioning.

▼ Big delta

The B-58 was the biggest delta ever to enter USAF service and followed Convair's delta fighters, the F-102 and F-106 series.

▲ High altitude

Hustlers performed very well at altitude, and could climb to around 20,000 m (25,610 ft). This enabled them to escape the attentions of most fighters, but the shooting down of the U-2 spyplane in 1960 by a surface-to-air missile showed that high altitude did not guarantee safety.

FACTS AND FIGURES

- The B-58's first flight took place on 11 November 1956, and it became operational in 1960.
- A B-58 carried a five-tonne bombload to a record height of 26,018 m (85,460 ft).
- The Hustler could fly at 1128 km/h (700 mph) at low level, never climbing above 155 m (510 ft).
- The first SAC Hustler wing set 19 world records, including supersonic flights to or from London, Tokyo and Paris.
- Before it could get aloft a fully loaded Hustler had to exceed 400 km/h (250 mph).
- A bear was ejected from a B-58 at 1400 km/h (870 mph) in order to test the escape system.

PROFILE

Twice the speed of sound – in a bomber!

The Convair B-58 Hustler was the world's first supersonic strategic bomber. Designed around the same delta-wing shape used on Convair's highly successful F-102 and F-106 fighters, the Hustler could fly nonstop for 18 hours – carrying a nuclear weapon to any target on the globe. This aircraft was, very simply, the most sensational in its category.

The B-58's four afterburning turbojets could maintain the big bomber at top speed for more than an hour before throttling back. The Hustler's refinements included pilot, bombardier-navigator and systems operator seated in tandem in three cockpits; a two-component droppable weapons/fuel pod under the fuselage that housed any of three weapon systems; and an air-to-surface missile, nuclear bombs or electronic countermeasures gear.

When the advent of the surface-to-air missile brought aerial warfare down to sea level, the high-flying B-58 dropped successfully to low-altitude operations. But one feature stayed up in the stratosphere – its operating costs. The type was retired for economy reasons in 1970 after a decade during which the Hustler equipped two of the USAF's Strategic Air Command bomber wings.

The Hustler had a short operational career, but it must have been a considerable headache for Soviet air-defence planners. It was the most advanced bomber to enter service in the 1960s, as the Myasishchev M-50 and North American XB-70 Valkyrie failed to proceed beyond trials.

Refuelling in the B-58 was much easier than in most aircraft, as the delta wing gave excellent stability and the refuelling port was straight in front of the pilot's canopy.

The J79 turbojet was a mainstay of the inventory in the 1960s; it also powered the F-4 Phantom, the F-104 Starfighter and the US Navy's RA-5 Vigilante.

The B-58 fleet usually had a natural metal finish, as camouflage was not needed for an aircraft that would rarely be seen from above in action.

The huge delta wing had no flaps. Control was provided by elevons – combined elevators and ailerons.

B-58A Hustler

Type: three-seat supersonic bomber

Powerplant: four 69.39-kN (15,607-lb-thrust) General Electric J79-GE-5B afterburning turbojets

Maximum speed: 1128 km/h (700 mph) at sea level; 2218 km/h (1,376 mph) or Mach 2.1 at high altitude

Range: 8250 km (5,126 miles) on internal and pod fuel

Service ceiling: 17,336 m (56,877 ft) with operational load

Weights: empty 25,202 kg (55,560 lb); take-off 73,937 kg (163,003 lb) (80,250 kg/176,921 lb after inflight refuelling)

Armament: up to 8823 kg (19,450 lb) in underfuselage pod with any six types of nuclear bomb including B43 and B61; one 20-mm (0.79-in) General Electric T-171 (M61A1) tail gun

Dimensions:

span	17.32 m (56 ft 10 in)
length	29.49 m (96 ft 9 in)
height	9.58 m (31 ft 5 in)
wing area	143.35 m² (1,543 sq ft)

B-58A HUSTLER

The 116 B-58s equipped two wings of Strategic Air Command, serving from 1960 to 1970, during which time the type set several speed and payload records.

The crew sat in individual cockpits, with the navigator behind the pilot and the defensive systems operator in the rear cockpit.

Four external hardpoints could be fitted with 3200 kg (7,055 lb) of nuclear or conventional bombs.

A powerful attack radar system was mounted in the nose. The navigator also had a computerized navigation system.

The rocket-powered BLU-2/B-2 and MB-1C pods contained fuel and weapons. The pod weapons bay could carry five nuclear bombs.

Since B-58 landings were usually fast and hard, the 16 tyres were filled with high-pressure nitrogen.

Chasing a B-58 was a dangerous business because a Vulcan M61 20-mm (0.79-in) cannon was mounted in the tail. This was radar-controlled and remotely operated by the defensive systems operator in the third cockpit.

COMBAT DATA

MAXIMUM SPEED

The B-58 was the fastest bomber of its time, and was quicker than the Soviet 'Backfire' which appeared two decades later. The strategic bomber version of the F-111 fighter which entered service in the late 1960s was faster, but it could maintain its top speed for only a few minutes; the Hustler could keep going at Mach 2 for more than an hour.

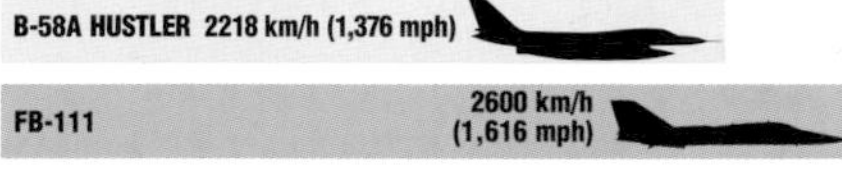

UNREFUELLED RANGE

The B-58 Hustler had superb range for such a powerful machine. It could strike considerably further than the FB-111 which replaced it in the supersonic wings of the USAF Strategic Air Command, and outperformed the 'Backfire' which entered service 10 years after the last B-58 landed for good.

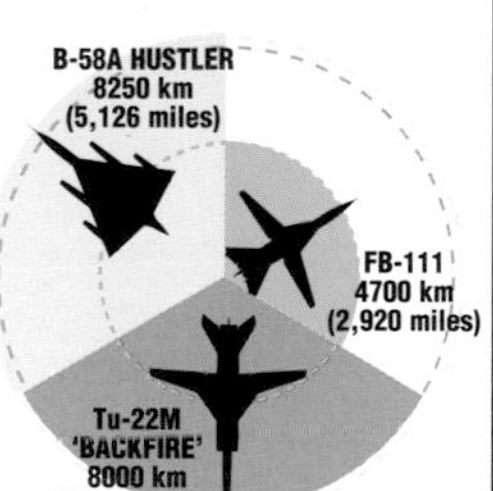

BOMBLOAD

The massive power which ensured great supersonic performance could be used to hoist heavy loads of conventional weapons. The B-58 was never really envisaged as a conventional bomber, however, and lacked the fittings to carry the kind of immense loads the other two bombers could, in theory, manage.

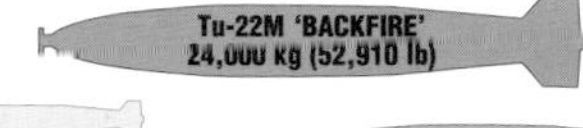

Supersonic strikers

MYASISHCHEV 'BOUNDER': Roughly contemporary with the Hustler, the Soviet jet was larger but slower, and had limited range.

NORTH AMERICAN XB-70: First flown in 1964, the XB-70 was a Mach 3 bomber. Astronomical costs meant that it never entered production.

GENERAL DYNAMICS FB-111: Entering service in 1969, the FB-111 replaced the B-58. It was faster, except when carrying a full load.

TUPOLEV Tu-22M 'BACKFIRE': Very similar in performance to the B-58, the swing-wing 'Backfire' became operational 20 years after the Hustler.

ROCKWELL B-1: The original B-1A prototype could reach Mach 2.5. The B-1B, which entered service in 1985, could fly at only half that speed.

Convair

F-102 Delta Dagger

● Supersonic fighter ● Delta-wing pioneer ● Long service career

▲ With its first attempt at the F-102, seen here, Convair was unable to get the aircraft to fly with anything like the required performance. A radical redesign followed, turning the aircraft into a world-class interceptor.

No spectacle in aviation was more dramatic than the F-102 taking off. Hurtling down the runway and lifting off with its afterburner throwing back a stabbing tongue of fire, the F-102 shattered the eardrums with its deafening roar. Once aloft, the F-102 climbed like a homesick angel, blazing into the stratosphere to intercept enemy bombers and shoot them down.

PHOTO FILE

Convair F-102 Delta Dagger

▲ **Delta X-plane**
To test the delta wing of the F-102, Convair built the XF-92 as a pure research craft. It was a hasty lash-up to get captured German delta-wing technology into the air as fast as possible.

▲ **Pure delta**
The wing of the F-102 was almost a perfect triangle, although the wingtip was very slightly cropped. Here a Falcon missile is being fired from the internal weapons bay.

Target drone ▲
Most surviving F-102s were turned into pilotless drones and blown up in missile tests.

▲ **Deuce on guard**
The F-102 enjoyed a successful career as the USAF's main interceptor in the late 1950s. This aircraft was one which guarded German skies.

▲ **Atlantic defenders**
The F-102 lasted in service in Iceland until 1973. Much of its time it shadowed Soviet 'Bear' reconnaissance aircraft over the unwelcoming waves of the North Atlantic.

▼ **Sad end for a noble warrior**
Still wearing the camouflage which it had worn on combat duty in Vietnam, this F-102 is a drone, about to meet its fate in a missile test.

FACTS AND FIGURES

- In all, 990 Convair F-102s were built, including 111 two-seat TF-102As.
- The YF-102 prototype first flew on 24 October 1953.
- The Delta Dagger planned to use nuclear-tipped Falcon air-to-air missiles to stop Soviet bombers.
- The F-102 was one of the first jet aircraft to use onboard computers.
- With its afterburner lit, the Convair was more than 80 times as powerful as a Bf 109 fighter of World War II.
- F-102s went to Turkey and Greece as part of assistance programmes to NATO.

PROFILE

Defender of America's skies

The Convair F-102 was the first supersonic warplane with a delta- or triangle-shaped wing. Designed to defend North America against the bomber attack dreaded by so many during the Cold War, the F-102 combined a 'wasp waist' fuselage shape, technically called 'area rule', with blade-like wings and tail to become one of the fastest fighters of its era.

Although it was a fighter, the F-102 carried no gun. It was armed with an almost unbelievable battery of rockets, including a Falcon missile with an atomic warhead intended to break up bomber formations.

Pilots called this magnificent aircraft the 'Deuce'. It was huge and powerful, and a pleasure to fly. F-102s served briefly in Vietnam where, late in its career, this great plane was miscast in a limited war setting. A few F-102s flew with Greece and Turkey, the only foreign users of one of the best-loved and most memorable aircraft in history and which led to the highly successful F-106 Delta Dart fighter.

Left: Along with its successor, the F-106 Delta Dart, the Delta Dagger was regarded as one of the most beautiful fighters ever built.

Not so beautiful was the TF-102A trainer, which had two seats side-by-side in a cumbersome new front end.

F-102A Delta Dagger

Type: single-seat interceptor

Powerplant: one 49.72-kN (11,183-lb-thrust) Pratt & Whitney J57-P-23 turbojet, increasing to 76.51 kN (17,208 lb thrust) with afterburning

Maximum speed: 1328 km/h (825 mph) at 12,190 m (40,000 ft)

Combat radius: 870 km (541 miles) with full weapons load

Service ceiling: 16,500 m (54,134 ft)

Weights: normal loaded 12,565 kg (27,700 lb); maximum 14,290 kg (31,504 lb)

Armament: three Falcon heat-seeking missiles and one Nuclear Falcon, or three radar and three heat-seeking air-to-air missiles; up to 24 unguided 70-mm (2.75-in) rockets

Dimensions:		
	span	11.62 m (38 ft 1 in)
	length	20.84 m (68 ft 4 in)
	height	6.46 m (21 ft 2 in)
	wing area	61.45 m² (661 sq ft)

F-102 DELTA DAGGER

The needle-nosed 'Deuce' was the first interceptor to be developed as part of an overall air defence weapon system, known as WS201A. The F-102 was considered just the airframe portion of this system, to which was added the radar and missile subsystems.

In addition to the Falcon missiles, the F-102 carried 24 unguided rockets. These were carried in tubes buried within the weapon bay doors. They were rarely used and eventually deleted.

The addition of drop-tanks gave the F-102 greatly increased range. It could now make ferry flights of more than 2000 km (1,240 miles).

The 'Bulldog' badge was for the 525th Fighter Interceptor Squadron, based at Bitburg AB.

The radar component of the Hughes MG-10 fire-control system could track several airborne targets simultaneously at ranges of up to 50 km (31 miles), and lock-on to individual aircraft at around 25 km (16 miles).

U.S. AIR FORCE FC-111

Most F-102s wore this gull-grey camouflage, although some adopted a green and brown scheme for service in the Vietnam War.

Falcon missiles usually had a high-explosive warhead, but some F-102s also carried a nuclear-tipped version.

Putting the weapons in an internal bay was a vital factor in the F-102's speed. If they had been on outside pylons, the drag would have degraded performance.

The first F-102 design was disappointing in service, and was revised to incorporate 'area rule'. This produced a pinched waist, or 'Coke bottle' shape. To make the tail fatter in area to conform with the new design, large bulges were added each side of the rear fuselage. These were known, for obvious reasons, as 'Marilyns'.

COMBAT DATA

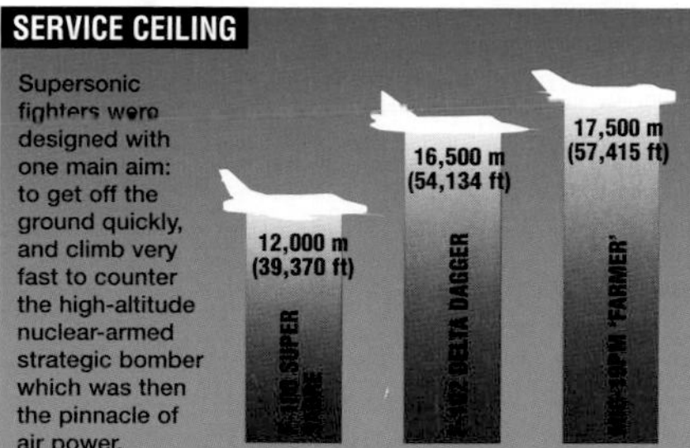

INTERCEPT ARMAMENT

The F-102 was designed as a bomber interceptor, and was possibly the first fighter designed without a gun. Instead, it was armed with Falcon air-to-air missiles, the earliest successful weapons of their type. The MiG-19 could not match the F-102's firepower.

F-102 DELTA DAGGER: 6 x AIM-4 Falcon missiles or 2 x AIM-26 Falcons with nuclear warheads

F-100 SUPER SABRE: 4 x 20-mm (0.79-in) cannon, 2 x AIM-9 Sidewinder missiles

MiG-19 'FARMER': 4 x AA-1 'Alkali' missiles

MAXIMUM SPEED

MiG-19 'FARMER'	1450 km/h (901 mph)
F-100 SUPER SABRE	1390 km/h (864 mph)
F-102 DELTA DAGGER	1328 km/h (825 mph)

The first generation of supersonic jets were capable of flying at speeds between 1.3 and 1.4 times the speed of sound. Although never achieving the kind of performance which had been expected of it, the delta-winged F-102 was nevertheless in the same league as its contemporaries.

Launching the Falcon

ENCLOSED WEAPONS BAYS: To reduce drag to the barest minimum, the missiles were all carried internally. The capacious bays could hold up to six air-to-air missiles. This fashion has recently been revived with the F-22, albeit to make the aircraft more stealthy.

WEAPONS DEPLOYED: The F-102 had three weapon bays, each holding two Falcons in tandem. Here one of the side bays is opened. Usually three heat-seeking Falcons were carried with three radar-homing missiles.

MISSILE LAUNCH: With the bays open, the missile trapezes were lowered into the airstream to allow the weapon to fire straight off the rail. The doors to the bay would immediately shut.

U.S. AIR FORCE

CONVAIR

F-106 DELTA DART

● Interceptor ● Nuclear rocket armed ● Air defender

Though it never fired a shot in combat, the F-106 Delta Dart is one of the most fondly remembered fighters to serve in the US Air Force. Building on experience from its predecessor, the F-102A Delta Dagger, the F-106 carried the flame as the guardian of North America at the Cold War's height. Its job was simple: as an all-weather interceptor it was to detect, identify and destroy Russian bombers carrying atomic weapons to American cities.

▲ *Convair's Delta fighters were extremely capable, complex and costly machines. The Dart was far more useful than the Dagger, which had grave development problems and was never reliable.*

PHOTO FILE

CONVAIR F-106 DELTA DART

▼ Sharp shape
In the quest for all-out speed and climb rate, the F-106 was designed with sharp lines and a thin wing section. Variable air intake geometry was also used.

▲ Red defender
Operating at altitude, with little need for concealment, the F-106 was often painted in bright colours, including orange and red schemes. These colours were designed to make them more conspicuous when operating over polar icefields.

▼ Delta wing
The Delta Dart's only similar feature to the Delta Dagger was its wing. The fuselage had to be considerably revised to cope with the 50 per cent extra thrust of its afterburning J75 engine. The cockpit was moved forward and the tailfin and rudder were redesigned.

Taking on gas ▲
The Pratt & Whitney J75 engine was powerful but thirsty, and tanking from KC-135s was a common task for F-106 pilots when on distant patrols.

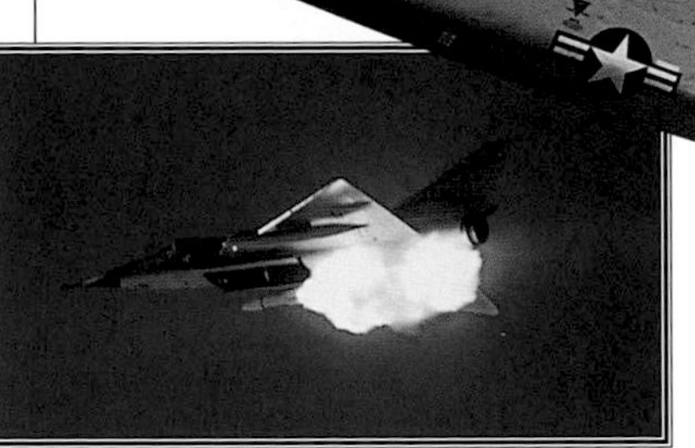

◀ Genie launch
The nuclear-tipped Genie was an unguided rocket, intended to be fired into bomber formations.

FACTS AND FIGURES

- ➤ The J75 turbojet was chosen after plans to use the Wright J67 Olympus were sidetracked by technical problems.
- ➤ The YF-106A prototype made its first flight on 26 December 1956.
- ➤ The F-106B had a second crewmember seated behind the pilot.
- ➤ In 1961 the last of 277 F-106As and 63 two-seat F-106Bs was delivered to the US Air Force.
- ➤ An advanced version with new radar, the F-106C, was only evaluated.
- ➤ The final operator was the 177th Fighter Group in Atlantic City in 1987.

PROFILE

America's delta defender

When it was introduced in the late 1950s, the F-106 was one of the fastest fighters in the world. It had twice the speed of the preceding F-102, and met all requirements of Aerospace Defense Command for a manned interceptor to defend North America. Linked via its complex MA-1 electronic fire-control system through a digital data-link into the nationwide SAGE (semi-automatic ground environment) air defence system, the F-106 was more than the sum of its 'black boxes' and missiles. Improvements to the F-106 included the addition of a gun in a neat installation in the missile bay, causing a slight bulge.

From the time it entered service at Geiger Field, Washington, in 1959, the F-106 was the backbone of North American air defence and was the favourite of many pilots who flew it. The Delta Dart served for much longer than intended and was never actually replaced, despite a continued threat by bombers and cruise missiles. Retirement of the last F-106 by the New Jersey Air National Guard in 1988 marked the end of the F-106 as a fighter. However, 200 airframes have been converted into QF-106 unmanned target drones.

Above: Despite its age, the F-106 remained in the USAF's inventory long after more modern tactical fighters entered service.

Below: Patrols over Alaska were an important task for F-106 crews, as Soviet bombers could have threatened the United States by flying from bases in northeastern Siberia.

F-106A Delta Dart

Type: single-seat interceptor

Powerplant: one Pratt & Whitney J75-P-17 turbojet rated at 76.5 kN (17,206 lb) dry thrust and 108.99 kN (24,513 lb thrust) with afterburning

Maximum speed: Mach 2.25 or 2400 km/h (1,491 mph) at 12,190 m (40,000 ft)

Range: 1850 km (1,150 miles)

Service ceiling: 17,680 m (58,000 ft)

Weights: empty 10,800 kg (23,810 lb); loaded 16,012 kg (35,300 lb); maximum take-off weight 17,350 kg (38,250 lb)

Armament: one M61A-1 20-mm cannon, four AIM-4E and/or AIM-4G Falcon air-to-air missiles, plus two AIR-2B Genie nuclear rockets

Dimensions:		
	span	11.67 m (38 ft 3 in)
	length	21.55 m (70 ft 8 in)
	height	6.18 m (20 ft 3 in)
	wing area	697.80 m² (7,511 sq ft)

F-106A Delta Dart

The F-106 was the primary air defence aircraft of the USAF between 1959 and the late 1970s, when the F-15C Eagle began entering service in numbers. Air National Guard Delta Darts were replaced by the F-16 Fighting Falcon.

Delta wings were a common feature of late 1950s fighters such as the MiG-21 and Mirage. The delta offers good performance in transonic flight, but is often less useful at low airspeeds and high alpha.

The Delta Dart carried its weaponry in an internal bay, a most unusual feature. A semi-retractable M61 cannon, also fitted in the bay, was introduced in 1973 following the experience of fighter pilots in Vietnam.

The F-106 had a powerful search radar and also an infra-red search-and-track system, a feature lacking on many of today's fighters.

One of the main features from the Dagger requiring redesign was the air intake, which was insufficient to cope with the mass flow of the huge J75 engine.

A highly advanced avionics suite was integrated with the ground-based NORAD air defence system.

The F-106 usually carried a pair of underwing fuel tanks.

The J75 engine was also used in the F-105 Thunderchief attack aircraft. It was one of the most powerful jet fighter engines of its day.

COMBAT DATA

MAXIMUM SPEED

All the interceptors of the 1960s could reach Mach 2 for a short time using afterburner. They could not go far beyond this speed because of kinetic heating causing damage to the alloy airframe.

F-106A DELTA DART	2400 km/h (1,491 mph)
Su-15 'FLAGON'	2653 km/h (1,649 mph)
LIGHTNING	2414 km/h (1,500 mph)

RANGE

Interceptors are required to reach high altitude in a very short time, fire their weapons and return to base. These aircraft were designed for performance and not long range.

LIGHTNING 1440 km/h (895 miles)

Su-15 'FLAGON' 1000 km (621 miles)

F-106A DELTA DART 1850 km (1,150 miles)

CLIMB RATE

The Lightning and Su-15 'Flagon' could outclimb the heavier Delta Dart, which had more weapons and advanced avionics and carried a great deal more fuel. Most interceptors have to trade fuel load for rate of climb.

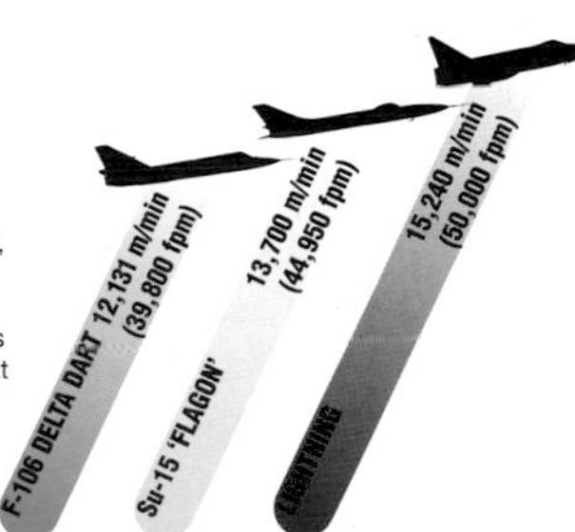

Air defence of North America

BOMBER ALERT: F-106s are scrambled to catch Soviet bombers out at sea before they can unleash their deadly cruise missiles. The area over the F-106 bases is defended by long-range Hawk and Nike missiles.

MISSILE DEFENCE: Air defence missiles handled most of the threat inshore.

BEAR ATTACK: At high altitude the long-range Tu-95 'Bear' was the main manned aircraft threat to the United States.

FIGHTER CONTROL: The NORAD air defence controller vectors an F-106 towards the incoming bomber. The controller will give the pilot instructions, or the F-106's avionics will automatically compute an intercept solution.

DASSAULT

ATLANTIQUE 2

● **Maritime patrol** ● **Anti-submarine** ● **Shipping strike**

Developed on a multinational basis for NATO, the Atlantic was created to shadow and, if necessary, attack the Soviet Union's imposing naval fleet. The Dassault Atlantic (Atlantique) has evolved into two generations of highly capable maritime patrol aircraft. Today's second-generation Atlantique 2 makes use of advanced technology to cope with undersea and surface warfare threats of many kinds, threats which persist even after the end of the Cold War.

▲ *Always a force to be reckoned with at sea, the multinational Atlantique 2 has matured into a sophisticated sub-killer with a highly secret sideline in intelligence-gathering.*

PHOTO FILE

DASSAULT ATLANTIQUE 2

◀ 'Nouvelle Génération'
The latest version of this long-serving warplane is one of the world's most sophisticated maritime aircraft. Designed to hunt submarines, it can also carry a wide variety of high-performance anti-ship and anti-radar missiles.

European defender ▶
Designed originally by Breguet, the Atlantic was built by and is in service with four European nations. Only France operates the new Atlantique 2.

Heavy load ▶
This Aéronavale Atlantic displays the aircraft's capacious weapons bay which typically holds air-launched torpedoes and depth charges. The smaller doors aft of the bay are used to launch flares and sonobuoys.

▲ Computer cockpit
Every part of the Atlantique 2's avionics has been upgraded along with pilot-friendly screen displays replacing the plethora of dials and switches found on the original Atlantic.

◀ Flexibility
A typical mission load comprises torpedoes, air-to-surface missiles and more than 100 sonobuoys.

FACTS AND FIGURES

- The Breguet Br.1150, which became the Atlantic, entered service with the French and German navies in December 1965.
- Originally the ANG (Atlantic Nouvelle Génération), the Atlantique 2 entered service in 1989.
- French Navy Atlantique 2s will serve well into the 21st century.
- The Atlantique 2 can detect and attack ships or submarines with missiles, depth charges, bombs or torpedoes.
- The Atlantique 2 has a chin-mounted infra-red turret and revised wing and fin-tip antennas.
- Other proposed variants include the Atlantic 3 with upgraded engines.

PROFILE

NATO's multinational sub-hunter

The Dassault Atlantic was the result of thinking which dates back to the 1950s, when it was felt that long-range overwater patrol might best be carried out by a standard aircraft shared among the Western European Allies.

The Atlantic 1 first flew on 21 October 1961, and while it was not accepted by all Allied countries it became the backbone of maritime operations in France, Germany and Italy, and has also been adopted by Pakistan.

With its very thin wing and enormous fuselage, the Atlantic has the staying power for anti-submarine and other patrol missions of up to 18 hours. The pilots have great power and flexibility at their disposal, and crew members have ample space for work and occasional respite. The Atlantique 2, used only by France, has new avionics, sensors and equipment giving an old design 21st century capabilities.

One of the more important additions is the infra-red sensor in a chin-mounted turret. Further changes are contemplated for Atlantic 3 and Europatrol versions, which may be built for service in the coming decades.

Above: The Atlantique Nouvelle Génération, or Atlantique 2, is identifiable by its chin turret and the antennas at the tip of the revised vertical tail.

Left: Although slower than its main contemporaries the Atlantique 2 combines impressive endurance with a modern and highly capable weapons lift.

Atlantique 2

Type: 12-seat long-range maritime patrol aircraft

Powerplant: two 4226-kW (5,670 hp.) thrust Rolls-Royce/ SNECMA Type 21 turboprops for take-off and emergency

Maximum speed: 648 km/h (402 m.p.h.)

Ferry range: 9000 km (5,580 mi.)

Service ceiling: 9150 m (30,000 ft.)

Weights: empty 25,700 kg (56,540 lb.); loaded 46,200 kg (101,640 lb.)

Armament: 2500 kg (5,500 lb.) of bombs, mines, depth charges or torpedoes internally and 3500 kg (7,700 lb.) externally; four AM39 Exocets may be carried on underwing pylons

Dimensions:

span		37.30 m (122 ft. 4 in.)
length		33.63 m (110 ft. 4 in.)
height		10.89 m (35 ft. 9 in.)
wing area		120.34 m² (1,295 sq. ft.)

ATLANTIQUE 2

Long after production of the original Atlantic had ceased, the French navy commissioned the improved Atlantique 2. It is similar in appearance to the original, but has improved sensors and avionics.

The Atlantique has a conventional flight deck with pilot, co-pilot and flight engineer. An observer can be carried in the glazed nose.

The tactical compartment in the fuselage houses the tactical co-ordinator, radio navigator, radar operator and two acoustic sensor operators.

The small fin on the back of the Atlantique is a direction-finding aerial. On the original Atlantic, this stretched right back and blended into the tailfin.

Two visual observers can be carried in a rear compartment, looking through port and starboard bubble windows.

The small radome at the tip of the Atlantique 2's tail houses an ECM antenna, designed to detect and identify enemy radar transmissions.

For anti-ship missions, the Atlantique is armed with up to four AM39 Exocet missiles.

The Atlantique can carry most NATO ASW weaponry internally. A typical load comprises eight air-launched torpedoes and four depth charges.

A smaller bay behind the main weapons bay houses sonobuoys and smoke markers. The Atlantique normally carries 100 buoys and 160 markers and flares.

The long tailboom houses a magnetic anomaly detector (MAD) sensor, which tracks down submarines by the effect they have on the local magnetic field.

MARINE

COMBAT DATA

MAXIMUM SPEED

An anti-submarine mission might take place hundreds of miles out to sea, so the ability to transit fast and in comfort is essential. The Atlantique's two Rolls-Royce designed turboprops are efficient, but cannot match the more powerful propulsion units of the Atlantique's main rivals.

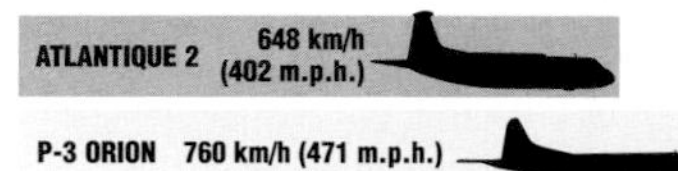

NIMROD MR.Mk 2 925 km/h (574 m.p.h.)

FERRY RANGE

From the start the original Atlantic was designed with a very efficient wing for maximum economy when cruising over long distances. This gives the aircraft a very long range, enabling it to mount patrols up to two hours long at ranges of 3300 km from its base.

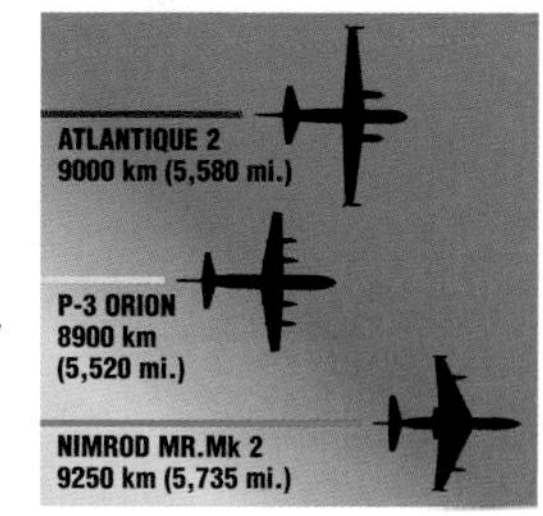

ENDURANCE

The key to successful anti-submarine warfare is endurance. Smaller than the Nimrod or the Orion, the Atlantique 2 uses less fuel. It can remain in the air for 18 hours, although crew fatigue usually limits mission length to between 10 and 12 hours.

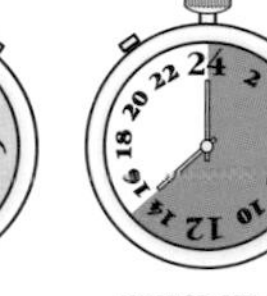

ATLANTIQUE 2 18 hours

P-3 ORION 17 hours

NIMROD MR.Mk 2 15 hours

Submarine attack

1 DETECTION: Atlantics carry more than 100 sonobuoys which listen passively for the sound of submarines or send out their own sound waves to locate the target by its echoes.

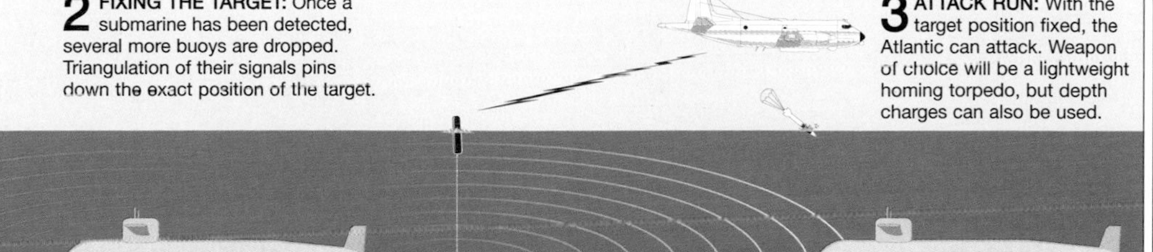

2 FIXING THE TARGET: Once a submarine has been detected, several more buoys are dropped. Triangulation of their signals pins down the exact position of the target.

3 ATTACK RUN: With the target position fixed, the Atlantic can attack. Weapon of choice will be a lightweight homing torpedo, but depth charges can also be used.

DASSAULT

MIRAGE 2000

● Air superiority ● Low-level attack ● Agile dogfighter

In 'clean' condition, whipping through the air without a clutter of weapons under its wings, the Dassault Mirage 2000 is one of the best-looking fighters ever built. This third-generation Mirage dates from 1978 and carries powerful radar, cannon, missiles and avionics. French pilots praise the delta-wing fighter mostly for its agility, claiming that an able pilot can fling the Mirage 2000 around as tightly as fighters like the F-16 or MiG-29.

▲ *Although it is called a Mirage, the 2000 shares only a shape and a name with its older brothers. It is far more capable than any previous Dassault fighter, notably in terms of its weapons fit.*

PHOTO FILE

DASSAULT MIRAGE 2000

▼ Magic attack
For dogfighting, the Mirage 2000 is armed with the MATRA Magic infra-red missile, a short-range heat-seeker.

Strike role ▶
The Mirage 2000 can fire armour-piercing AS30L laser-guided missiles for pinpoint attacks on surface targets. AS30s were used with great success by the French air force during the Gulf War.

▲ Filling up
Without external tanks, the Mirage 2000 needs a fill-up from an aerial tanker to stay on combat air patrol for any length of time.

◀ Reliable turbojet
Power for the Mirage 2000 comes from a single SNECMA M53 turbojet. This relatively simple engine is reliable and performs well at most speeds.

Long-range missile ▶
The advanced MATRA Mica missile will give Mirage 2000s the ability to carry out medium- and long-range 'fire-and-forget' engagements against other aircraft.

FACTS AND FIGURES

- ➤ The RDF radar was test-flown in an old Mystère fighter-bomber, and the M53 engine in a Caravelle airliner testbed.
- ➤ The French fighter wing at Dijon began receiving its first aircraft in April 1983.
- ➤ The two-seat Mirage 2000B trainer made its maiden flight on 7 August 1983.
- ➤ India operates the Mirage 2000H fighter, armed with MATRA 530D missiles; it is known locally as the 'Thunderbolt'.
- ➤ Finland, Iraq, Jordan and Switzerland all considered buying the Mirage 2000.
- ➤ The Mirage 2000s serving with Abu Dhabi are fitted with Sidewinder missiles.

PROFILE

Dassault's deadliest fighter

The brilliant engineers at Avions Marcel Dassault began work on the Mirage 2000 in 1972. Three years later, France's Armée de l'Air sought a new fighter and backed development of this arrow-like craft.

Now standard equipment in the French fighter arm, the Mirage 2000 has a large wing with 'relaxed stability' and automatic flight control system, making this warplane extremely agile and giving better handling than traditional deltas. Lacking a horizontal tail, the Mirage 2000 uses elevons at the trailing edge of its wing. The result is one of the world's most successful delta-winged fighters.

This is very much a pilot's aircraft – a 'Top Gun' in the world of modern dogfighting, especially when armed with the Magic 2 missile. The Mirage 2000 has become a popular export item, serving with Abu Dhabi, Egypt, France, Greece, India and Peru. Known for its air-to-air prowess, the Mirage 2000 also has considerable air-to-ground capability. A successful two-seat trainer variant has also been developed into France's Mirage 2000N nuclear strike aircraft.

The Mirage 2000 showed its mettle in the Gulf War, although it was never engaged in combat. It might have been exported more widely if it had not been so much more expensive than the F-16.

Like earlier Mirages, the Mirage 2000 has large elevons for roll and pitch control. Carbon-fibre spoilers are mounted on the forward section of the wing. Trim change is made automatically by the flight-control computer.

The wing has a leading edge consisting of two large slats, which are deployed during high angle-of-attack manoeuvres.

Mirage 2000C

Type: single-seat fighter

Powerplant: one SNECMA M53-P2 turbofan rated at 64.33 kN (14,475 lb. thrust) dry and 95.12 kN (21,400 lb. thrust) with afterburning

Maximum speed: Mach 2.2 or 2338 km/h (1,453 m.p.h.) at 11,000 m (36,000 ft.)

Ferry range: 3335 km (2,072 mi.)

Service ceiling: 18,000 m (59,000 ft.)

Weights: empty 7500 kg (16,535 lb.); loaded 17,000 kg (37,479 lb.)

Armament: two DEFA 554 30-mm cannon with 125 rounds per gun; MATRA Magic 2 air-to-air missiles; up to 4500 kg (9,920 lb.) of bombs, rockets or ARMAT anti-radiation missiles

Dimensions:		
	span	9.13 m (29 ft. 11 in.)
	length	14.36 m (47 ft. 1 in.)
	height	5.20 m (17 ft. 1 in.)
	wing area	41 m² (441 sq. ft.)

MIRAGE 2000P

The Peruvian air force was the third customer for the Mirage 2000, with 12 aircraft serving with Escuadron 412 at Base Aérea Meriano Melgar, La Joya. The unit operates in the ground-attack and air-defence roles.

The large avionics suite is carried in the fuselage spine. It includes a SAGEM ULIS 52 inertial navigation platform and the sophisticated CERVAL radar warning receiver.

The airframe is mostly of traditional alloys, but certain structural areas are made from titanium and steel, and extensive use is made of boron/epoxy and carbon-fibre panels.

The cockpit of the latest Mirage 2000 variants features four multi-function display screens, an advanced head-up display and a threat warning screen.

The radar is a Thomson-CSF RDM multi-mode set, with ground mapping, air-search and interception, maritime attack and terrain avoidance modes.

A fixed strake is fitted on the engine inlet fairing. This controls fuselage air vortices at high angles of attack.

A pair of DEFA 544 30-mm cannon, each with 125 rounds of ammunition, is housed in the wingroots. This gun can fire bursts at 1,800 rounds per minute for air-to-air engagements and at 1,100 rpm for air-to-ground firing.

COMBAT DATA

MAXIMUM SPEED

The Mirage 2000 is faster than its great rival, the F-16, since the American jet lacks the variable intakon which maximise supersonic performance. The MiG-29 is faster still, primarily thanks to the vastly greater power available from its twin engines.

MIRAGE 2000	2338 km/h (1,453 m.p.h.)
F-16 FIGHTING FALCON	2124 km/h (1,320 m.p.h.)
MiG-29 'FULCRUM'	2445 km/h (1,519 m.p.h.)

COMBAT RANGE

Modern fighter aircraft have considerably greater ranges than their immediate predecessors, and fighters like the Mirage 2000 can carry significant strike loads over great distances. However, the extended use of afterburning cuts their range considerably.

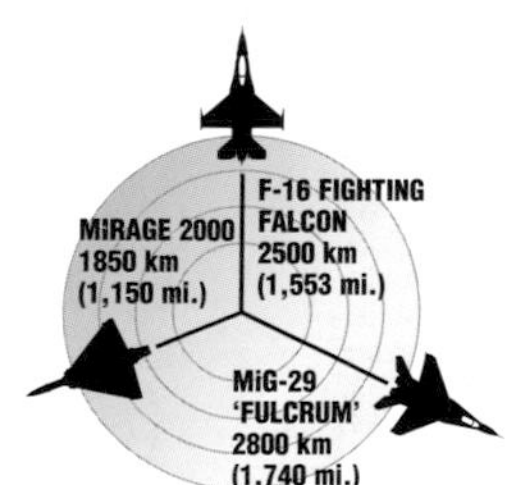

INITIAL CLIMB RATE

The Mirage is one of the fastest-climbing fighters in the world. It cannot match the MiG-29, again thanks to the immense power of the Russian fighter's twin jets. It can, however, climb faster than the American Fighting Falcon, although it cannot carry as heavy or varied a weapons load.

Multi-mission Mirage

1 INTERCEPTOR: The Mirage 2000 was designed to defend France from air attack, and its first mission is to deter enemy bombers.

The Mirage has an exceptional climb rate, and can reach a height of 15,000 m (49,200 ft.) within four minutes of take-off. This means it should be able to intercept any bomber currently in service.

2 GROUND ATTACK: Modern fighters are extremely expensive, and are expected to be able to perform more than one task. The Mirage 2000 is a highly capable ground-attack aircraft, and has also been adapted to the nuclear strike role.

3 AIR SUPERIORITY: The Mirage's excellent radar and modern missiles mean that in well-trained hands it is a formidable and hard-hitting fighter.

The Mirage 2000 is highly manoeuvrable. French air force pilots claim that in a dogfight it is a match for any potential enemy, up to and including the superb MiG-29 'Fulcrum'.

DASSAULT RAFALE

● Lightweight fighter ● Multi-role ● High-technology construction

▲ With pilots such as Guy Mitaux-Maurouard at the controls, Rafale has thrilled crowds at major air shows with its exceptional agility. The first flight of the technology demonstrator was in 1986.

Dassault's Rafale is a proud symbol of France's independent spirit. Refusing to rely upon other nations, the French are staking their military readiness on this superb machine, one of the best-performing combat aircraft in the sky today. Because nothing was spared in putting 21st-century technology into this futuristic fighting jet, the Rafale can outclimb, outmanoeuvre and outfight just about any warplane now in service.

PHOTO FILE

DASSAULT RAFALE

▲ Carrier fighter
France's navy was desperate to replace its ageing F-8 Crusaders with the Rafale M.

▲ 'Discreet' warplane
Air force operational versions of the aircraft are known as the Rafale D, the 'D' standing for 'Discret'. This word is meant to emphasise the stealthiness of the fighter.

▼ Engine testbed
The Rafale A testbed aircraft at one point featured two different engines: a French-built M88 in the left-hand side of the fuselage, and a US-built F404 to the right.

▲ The Rafale family
The three operational variants will be the two-seat Rafale B (leading) and single-seat Rafale C (foreground) for the air force, and the Rafale M (background) for the navy.

◄ Agility unlimited
Rafale's power and fly-by-wire electronics make it outstandingly agile, able to defeat any current service fighter in a low-speed dogfight.

FACTS AND FIGURES

- ➤ Composites and new materials make up 50 per cent of Rafale's weight.
- ➤ The twin-engine Rafale has 16 times as much power as the Mistral, an early French jet fighter.
- ➤ To decrease combat workload, most Air Force Rafales will have a crew of two.
- ➤ Rafale was the result of France dropping out of the European Fighter Aircraft project in August 1985.
- ➤ The prototype Rafale A made 865 test flights before being retired with honours.
- ➤ Naval Rafales will serve aboard the nuclear carrier *Charles de Gaulle*.

PROFILE

Multi-mission workhorse

The Dassault Rafale is the air combatant of tomorrow, created by today's top scientists. Very soon, one- and two-seat Rafales will rise to take command of the sky, as France's navy and air force press these dart-shaped jets into action from carrier decks and airfields. Thanks to its advanced propulsion and flight controls, the Rafale can switch paths abruptly in mid-air. The pilot can steer in one direction and point his nose to shoot in another, making it look as if the Rafale is flying sideways. Or it can snap into a 180° turn in less space than any other fighter. With this super agility, a Rafale pilot can rapidly get the aim on his opponent. The pilot's head need never leave his quarry as he manipulates his aircraft into firing position using his head-up display and voice- activated controls. Then he can launch several missiles or close in for the kill with his rapid-fire 30-mm cannon. The duel is likely to be over in seconds, with the Rafale the easy victor.

The French air force is getting a mix of one- and two-seat Rafales. The two-seaters will be used for both training and for difficult strike missions where the extra crew member is vital.

Fitted just forward by the main delta wing are the all-moving swept foreplanes. Constructed mainly of carbon-fibre, they give added manoeuvrability.

Rafale will be equipped with SPECTRA – Système pour la Protection Electronique Contra Tous les Rayonnements Adversés – a highly automated electronic protection system which includes radar warning and infra-red warning sensors, as well as radar jammers and chaff and flare dispensers.

Rafale is powered by a pair of SNECMA M88-3 lightweight turbofans, each delivering around 86.99 kN (19, 570 lb.) of thrust with afterburning.

Rafale D

Type: single-seat air combat fighter

Powerplant: two 86.99-kN (19,570-lb. thrust) SNECMA M88-3 turbofans with afterburning

Maximum speed: 2125 km/h (1,320 m.p.h.) at 11,000 m (36,000 ft.)

Combat radius: 1100 km (684 mi.) with typical weapons load; 1500 km (932 mi.) air-to-air

Service ceiling: 15,200 m (49,870 ft.)

Weights: empty about 9100 kg (20,060 lb.); maximum loaded 21,500 kg (47,399 lb.)

Armament: one 30-mm GIAT-built DEFA M791B cannon; up to 6000 kg (13,230 lb.) of air-to-air and air-to-ground ordnance

Dimensions:	span	19.90 m (65 ft. 3 in.)
	length	15.30 m (50 ft. 2 in.)
	height	6.91 m (22 ft. 8 in.)
	wing area	46 m² (495 sq. ft.)

RAFALE M

Designed to replace the ancient Vought F-8 Crusader aboard French carriers, the Rafale M will also be used as an anti-shipping strike and reconnaissance fighter, eventually also replacing the Super Etendard.

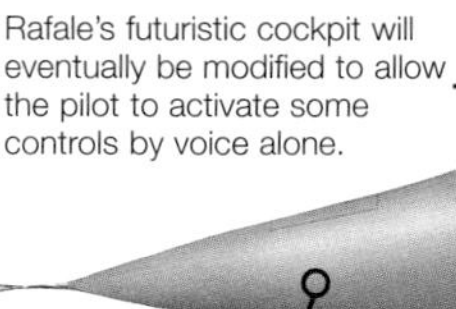

Rafale's futuristic cockpit will eventually be modified to allow the pilot to activate some controls by voice alone.

All Rafale variants will be equipped with an electronically-scanned multi-function radar with full air-to-air and air-to-ground capability.

The naval version of Rafale has a unique nose gear. Compressed before launch, it extends explosively, kicking the fighter's nose into the air as it leaves the deck.

In the air-to-air role, the Rafale can be armed with up to eight MATRA MICA advanced air-to-air missiles, or with six MICAs and two short-range Magic 2 dogfight missiles on wingtip launch rails.

COMBAT DATA

MAXIMUM SPEED

The current generation of fighters are not as fast as their immediate predecessors, but thanks to advances in engine efficiency they can maintain high speed for much longer periods, restricting the need for fuel-guzzling afterburners.

RAFALE 2125 km/h (1,320 m.p.h.)

EF 2000 2125 km/h (1,320 m.p.h.)

F-22 RAPTOR 2000 km/h (1,243 m.p.h.)

INTERCEPT RANGE

The Rafale and its contemporaries will be expected to fly many differing missions. In the intercept or long-range air-superiority role, they will be able to fly very long distances to reach their targets.

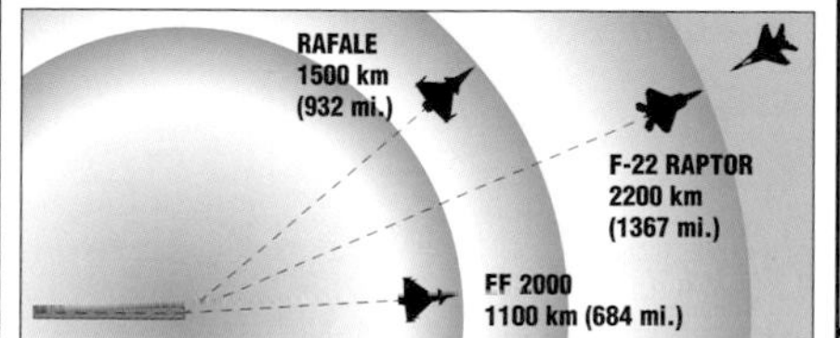

STEALTH

Stealth technology has revolutionised air warfare for those who can afford it, and all new fighters incorporate the expensive new features. Operational Rafales will be very stealthy, if not as elusive as the costly American F-22.

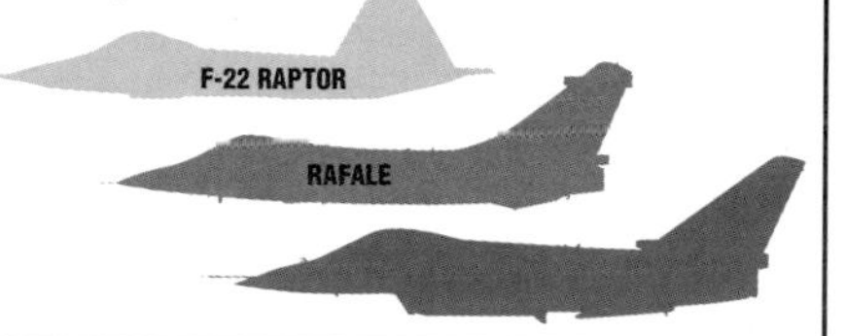

Rafale M – jumping from the carrier

RUN-UP: With the nosewheel strut compressed to its minimum extent, the Rafale runs up its engines to full power and then is hurled down the deck by a powerful steam catapult.

SKI-JUMP: The carrier *Charles de Gaulle* will be equipped with a small ski-jump at the end of the catapult, which pushes the Rafale into the air. The ramp will retract to allow other types to be launched.

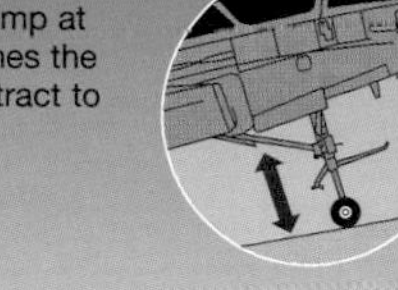

JUMP STRUT: As the aircraft hits the ramp, the compressed nose gear springs out to its maximum extent, literally jumping the fighter into the air at its most efficient low-speed angle of attack.

DASSAULT

SUPER ETENDARD

● **Carrier-based jet** ● **Anti-ship strike** ● **Maritime reconnaissance**

Dassault's Super Etendard is a sleek, arrow-like aircraft which has achieved a superb military record with French and Argentine naval forces. The carrier-based Super Etendard can meet many challenges, including reconnaissance in its unarmed photo version. Most importantly, it can deliver the famous Exocet anti-ship missile with devastating results, using the aircraft's Thomson-CSF/EMD Agave multi-mode radar.

▲ *Despite the age of the basic airframe design, the Super Etendard is a potent machine thanks to its avionics. It made history with the first ever air attack using a sea-skimming anti-ship missile.*

PHOTO FILE

DASSAULT SUPER ETENDARD

▲ Buddy refuel
To extend its range, the Super Etendard can refuel from another aircraft fitted with a 'buddy' refuelling pack.

▼ Etendard replacement
The Aéronavale had proposed a navalised Jaguar for its strike squadrons, but this was cancelled and the Super Etendard entered production in the late 1970s.

▲ Nuclear missile
For nuclear strikes, the Super Etendard is equipped with a single ASMP short-range nuclear stand-off missile. A fuel tank is carried on the port side to balance the weight.

▲ Argentina's revenge
Exocet-armed Super Etendards sank the destroyer HMS Sheffield *and the supply vessel* Atlantic Conveyer *in the Falklands war, despite being new in service.*

▼ Agave nose
Distinguishing it from the previous Etendard IV, the Super Etendard has the Agave attack radar in its nose. This system detects maritime targets for the Exocet missile.

FACTS AND FIGURES

➤ Reconnaissance versions can carry a Douglas 'buddy pack' and serve as air-refuelling tankers.

➤ Seventy-one Super Etendards were built for France and 14 for Argentina.

➤ More than 525,000 man-hours go into the production of a single Super Etendard.

➤ In the Falklands War, Argentine Super Etendards flew 580 sorties without a single aircraft being lost.

➤ The first flight of a Super Etendard prototype took place on 28 October 1974.

➤ The French navy first took delivery of the production aircraft on 28 June 1978.

PROFILE

Dassault's terror of the seas

From its first flight in 1974, the Super Etendard was an impressive machine for its small size. An updated version of the earlier Etendard IV, the Super Etendard featured a multi-mode attack radar, revised wing and more powerful Atar engine.

The Super Etendard served well with France, but this fine aircraft is mainly remembered as Argentina's cutting edge in the 1982 Falklands conflict. Best known was the sinking of the British destroyer HMS *Sheffield* by an Exocet, and the subsequent sinking of the supply vessel *Atlantic Conveyor* which was carrying many helicopters for the land forces.

Iraq leased five Super Etendards with Exocets to attack Iranian oil tanker traffic in the Persian Gulf, causing havoc and marine insurance rates to skyrocket. French Super Etendards finally went to war in 1995, when one was hit by an SA-7 over Bosnia while flying a reconnaissance mission but managed to fly back home.

Uprated with a new avionics suite and the ability to use the ASMP (Air-Sol Moyenne Portée) nuclear missile, the Super Etendard remain in service with France. In 1999 they began to be replaced as the first Rafale Ms entered service. The recently strengthened airframe could last until 2008.

Left: With new flaps and wing leading edge, the Super Etendard has the same performance as its predecessor, the Etendard IV, despite the extra weight.

Above: Aéronavale Super Etendards fly from the carriers Foch *and* Clemenceau.

Super Etendard

Type: single-seat carrier-based strike fighter

Powerplant: one 49.04-kN (11,000-lb.-thrust) SNECMA Atar 8K-50 turbojet

Maximum speed: 1380 km/h (856 m.p.h.) at high altitude

Combat radius: 850 km (527 mi.)

Service ceiling: 13,700 m (44,936 ft.)

Weights: empty 6500 kg (14,300 lb.); maximum take-off 12,000 kg (26,400 lb.)

Armament: underfuselage and underwing attachments for a variety of weapons, including AM39 Exocet or ASMP air-to-surface missiles, or AN52 tactical nuclear bombs; Sidewinder or MATRA Magic air-to-air missiles and rocket pods can also be carried

Dimensions:		
	span	9.60 m (31 ft.)
	length	14.31 m (47 ft.)
	height	3.86 m (13 ft.)
	wing area	28.40 m² (306 sq. ft.)

SUPER ETENDARD

The 11 Flottille of the Aéronavale operates Super Etendards from the carriers *Clemenceau* and *Foch*, which carry 20 Super Etendards. Unit 11F is based at Landivisiau and the sister unit 17F at Hyères.

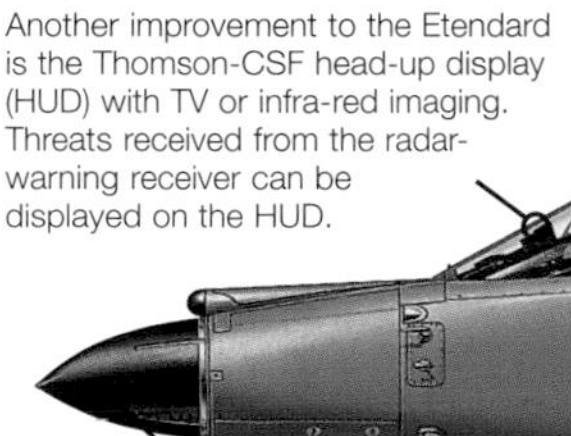

The Super Etendard wing uses blown flaps to allow take-offs from the short decks of the current French carriers.

The fuselage is of area-ruled design for supersonic flight.

Up to 3300 litres (500 gal.) of fuel are stored in the wing tanks. The four wing pylons can carry rocket pods, ECM pods or MATRA Magic missiles.

The cockpit has an improved HOTAS layout and VCN 65 electronic countermeasures display.

Another improvement to the Etendard is the Thomson-CSF head-up display (HUD) with TV or infra-red imaging. Threats received from the radar-warning receiver can be displayed on the HUD.

Aéronavale Etendards are now being updated with a new Anemone radar with ground mapping and search functions. The improved UAT 90 weapons computer is linked to the radar system.

One Exocet or ASMP missile can be carried with a fuel tank under the port wing, or an Exocet under each wing.

Power is provided by an ATAR turbojet, a slightly more powerful version of the original Etendard engine.

COMBAT DATA

MAXIMUM SPEED

Naval jet strike aircraft require range rather than speed. Designed to attack at sea level, high subsonic performance is more important than high speed at altitude.

SUPER ETENDARD	1380 km/h (856 m.p.h.)
A-4M	1038 km/h (644 m.p.h.)
A-7 CORSAIR	1123 km/h (696 m.p.h.)

ARMAMENT

The Super Etendard is a small aircraft, and carries a fairly light warload. For its size, the A-4M carries a hefty armament, although not usually a missile like the Exocet.

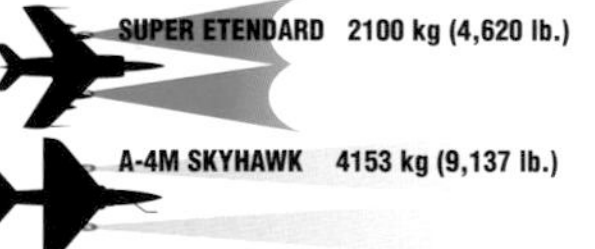

COMBAT RADIUS

For such a small aircraft, the Super Etendard has impressive range, greater than the small A-4 and less than the larger A-7 with its efficient TF41 engine. Naval strike aircraft often have a short combat radius when flying at low level, which consumes more fuel than high-altitude flight.

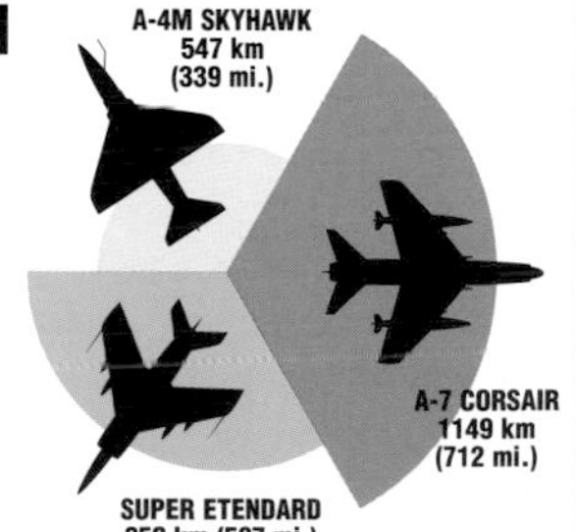

Exocet attack

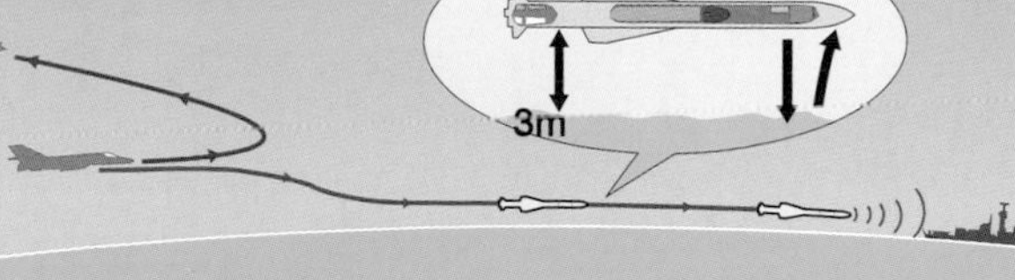

1 WEAPON LAUNCH: The ship's approximate position is confirmed by radar and passed to the missile's navigation computer.

2 SEA SKIMMER: Exocet has a radar altimeter which keeps the weapon at a set height, as little as 2 m (6 ft.). This height can be changed according to the target's height and the sea state.

3m

3 RADAR LOCK: When only a few kilometres from the ship, Exocet's radar searches for the target, aiming for a point halfway along the hull.

4 DECOY: If a ship can launch chaff rockets in time, it can fool Exocet into aiming for the centre of the combined radar return from the ship and the chaff cloud.

DASSAULT/DORNIER ALPHAJET

● Advanced weapon trainer ● Light strike ● 'Hind' hunter

The AlphaJet is an advanced trainer providing 'lead-in' instruction to pilots who will fly high-performance fighters. It is better known to the public for aerobatic displays with several nations, including single-ship performances in Belgium and formation exhibits by France's Patrouille de France. But the AlphaJet should not be dismissed as a 'feel good' aircraft: it is also a potent combat weapon.

▲ The AlphaJet has been one of the most successful trainers, giving fierce competition to the BAe Hawk. Now in Luftwaffe service only in limited numbers, it is still an effective light strike aircraft.

PHOTO FILE

DASSAULT/DORNIER ALPHAJET

▲ Tactical fighter
French AlphaJets are advanced trainers, but armed with SNEB rockets and cluster bombs they have light-attack capability.

▲ Patrouille de France
The national aerobatic team of France flies the AlphaJet, which replaced the Fouga Magister as the team's aircraft. The crisp handling and high speed endear it to the pilots.

▲ African Alphas
Export success in Africa for the AlphaJet included sales to Cameroon, Ivory Coast, Egypt and Morocco. The rival Hawk won sales in Zimbabwe.

'Hind' killer ▶
The Luftwaffe used 175 AlphaJets in the light-attack role. Armed with a 27-mm Mauser cannon, they were seen as an answer to the threat from Soviet Mi-24 'Hind' helicopter gunships.

▲ Twin-engine trainer ▼
Over 500 AlphaJets have been sold. Part of the attraction of the AlphaJet over rival trainers is the safety of its twin-engine design.

FACTS AND FIGURES

- French AlphaJet trainers have rounded noses for good spin performance, while German attack craft have pointed noses.
- The first AlphaJet flew at Istres, France, on 26 October 1973.
- All but one of Belgium's 33 AlphaJets were assembled by SABCA at Gosselies.
- A German attack version with a supercritical wing flew for the first time on 15 November 1980.
- Egypt assembled 26 AlphaJet trainers at Helwan from September 1982 onwards.
- The first close support AlphaJet made its initial flight on 12 April 1978.

PROFILE

Strike trainer with the killer touch

A beautiful aircraft with both peaceful and warlike purposes, the Dassault/Dornier AlphaJet is the result of Franco-German efforts in the 1960s to develop an advanced jet trainer for the air forces of both countries.

The original purpose was sidetracked when Germany chose to continue training pilots in the US and decided to use the AlphaJet as a light-attack craft. Other nations, especially those with tight budgets in the military field, also sought the AlphaJet as a warplane or, in some instances, in both roles. Eleven countries now fly the aircraft.Several versions emerged from Dassault-Breguet and Dornier, including a pure trainer for French use, a close-support variant, the dual-role AlphaJet 2, and the proposed Lancier with advanced instruments.

Several nations emulate Qatar, which trains pilots in the AlphaJet but would form an attack unit, crewed by instructors, in time of war. The versatility and performance of the AlphaJet has won it high praise from pilots and maintainers alike.

Like the rival Hawk, the AlphaJet can be a dangerous threat when fully armed. It can even carry the potent AS.30 laser-guided air-to-ground missile.

The rear seat is raised well above the front seat, giving the instructor an excellent view of the student's cockpit.

The proposed Lancier advanced trainer would have used twin multi-function cockpit displays, and advanced infra-red detection and radar systems.

Extra fuel can be carried in two 310- or 450-litre (82- or 120-gal.) underwing tanks.

AlphaJet E

Type: two-seat trainer and light-attack aircraft

Powerplant: two SNECMA/Turbomeca Larzac 04-C6 each rated at 13.24 kN (2,976 lb. thrust)

Maximum speed: 1000 km/h (621 m.p.h.) at 10,000 m (33,000 ft.)

Combat radius: 670 km (415 mi.)

Service ceiling: 14,630 m (48,000 ft.)

Weights: empty 3345 kg (7,359 lb.); loaded 8000 kg (17,600 lb.)

Armament: up to 2500 kg (5,500 lb.) of bombs, rockets or drop-tanks; one belly-mounted 27-mm Mauser MK 27 cannon pod (Germany); one 30-mm DEFA 553 cannon pod (France)

Dimensions: span 9.11 m (30 ft.)
length 11.75 m (38 ft.)
height 4.19 m (14 ft.)
wing area 17.50 m² (188 sq. ft.)

ALPHAJET E

The Force Aerienne Belge uses AlphaJets in the advanced trainer role, serving with Nos 7, 9, 11 and 33 squadrons based at Brustem. No. 9 squadron is responsible for specialised instructor training.

Luftwaffe AlphaJets have advanced avionics, including a Lear-Siegler twin-gyro navigation system, Litton Doppler radar and a Kaiser head-up display.

German AlphaJets are fitted with American-made Stencel ejection seats, but French aircraft use Martin-Baker seats.

The wing has single-slotted Fowler flaps and outer-wing leading-edge extensions, allowing approach speeds of just 200 km/h (125 m.p.h.).

Despite wearing a tactical camouflage colour scheme, Belgian AlphaJets operate only as unarmed trainers.

AT 01

The undercarriage is fitted with low-pressure tyres, allowing the AlphaJet to operate from rough 'tactical' sites near the front, just like its predecessor, the Fiat G91.

Many AlphaJets employ a podded DEFA 30-mm cannon with 150 rounds of ammunition for weapons training.

Although the AlphaJet has two engines, each has enough power to enable the aircraft to climb on one alone. This is a very useful asset in an aircraft flown at low level by junior pilots.

COMBAT DATA

MAXIMUM SPEED

Although a little slower than the lighter British Aerospace Hawk, the AlphaJet is capable of a useful turn of speed, its best performance being achieved at sea level. Both the AlphaJet and its great rival are swept-wing aircraft, and are faster than the straight-winged Italian Aermacchi M.B.339.

ALPHAJET E	1000 km/h (620 m.p.h.)
HAWK	1038 km/h (643 m.p.h.)
M.B.339C	900 km/h (558 m.p.h.)

CLIMB RATE

The AlphaJet's twin-jet power gives it a slight advantage over the single-engined Hawk, which is most clearly demonstrated in its improved climb performance. The M.B.339 has less available power than the other two jets, and cannot get aloft as quickly.

HAWK 2850 m/min 9,350 f.p.m.)
ALPHAJET E 3660 m/min (12,005 f.p.m.)
M.B.339C 2225 m/min (7,300 f.p.m.)

COMBAT RADIUS

Trainers spend much of their time flying at low level, and on weapons training or light-attack flights will rarely climb very high. The AlphaJet has a reasonable strike radius, but the Hawk can carry a heavier load over greater distances and at faster speeds than either of the Franco/German and Italian jets.

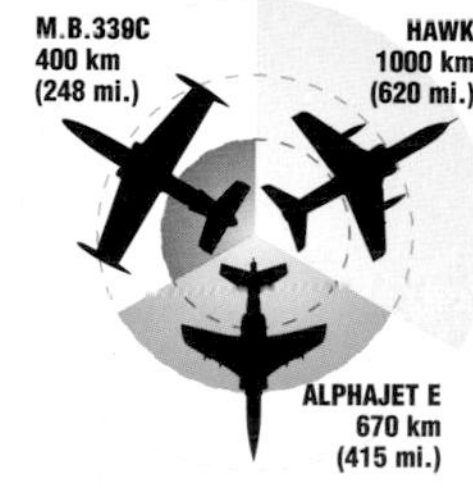

Advanced flight and weapons trainers

BRITISH AEROSPACE HAWK: Britain's Hawk is slightly more capable than the AlphaJet, but both are among the best of their kind. The two jets have competed fiercely on the export market, where both have gained considerable sales success.

NORTHROP T-38 TALON: In service with the USAF, the T-38 was the first aircraft designed as a supersonic trainer. Exported to only two countries, the T-38 is expensive to operate but provides a unique training environment.

AERMACCHI M.B.339: Less complex and a little less capable than the AlphaJet, Italy's M.B.339 is cheaper than its advanced rivals, and has been sold to a number of countries. It was built in both basic and combat-capable versions.

RS-48

DASSAULT-BREGUET ATLANTIC

● Anti-submarine ● Anti-ship ● Maritime patrol aircraft

A NATO requirement of the late 1950s for a long-range maritime reconnaissance aircraft was met by Breguet with the Br.1150 Atlantic. The European consortium which was formed to build it included several companies whose names have been consigned to aviation history, such as Aeritalia, Breguet and MBB. But the Atlantic, refurbished and modernized, soldiers on and will continue to patrol the seas well into the twenty-first century.

▲ *Comprehensive systems upgrades have kept the Atlantic in service and it is still a very effective maritime aircraft. Fewer than 100 were built, but survivors remain flying in the arduous, low-level marine environment.*

PHOTO FILE

DASSAULT-BREGUET ATLANTIC

Martel missiles ▶
Anglo-French AS.37 Martel guided missiles, carried on the underwing pylons, give the Atlantic an effective anti-surface vessel capability.

▲ Long-term Italian service
Italy received 18 Atlantics, with deliveries commencing in June 1972. They have been upgraded with Atlantique and Nimrod systems.

▲ Low-visibility
In the current trend, this Italian aircraft is finished in a low-visibility colour scheme. It also carries a non-standard spine antenna.

▲ Atlantic configuration
The aircraft's spine fairing, MAD boom and fin-mounted radome are clearly visible on this Aéronavale Atlantic.

▼ Valkenburg's Atlantics
No. 321 Squadron of the Royal Netherlands Navy received nine Atlantics, which were based at Valkenburg. The aircraft have now been retired.

FACTS AND FIGURES

- ➤ Breguet beat 24 designs from manufacturers in nine countries to win the NATO maritime patrol competition.
- ➤ Italy did not join the constructors' consortium until 1968.
- ➤ An international consortium was also established to build the Tyne engines.
- ➤ Some reports suggest that the Atlantic can deliver nuclear depth charges, each with a yield of 40 kilotons.
- ➤ Improvements to German Atlantics have extended their life to 10,000 hours.
- ➤ Three aircraft sold to Pakistan in 1975 continue to serve with No. 29 Squadron.

PROFILE

Venerable ocean patroller

Breguet flew the Atlantic for the first time from its Toulouse factory in October 1961. A successor to the Lockheed P-2 Neptune which was in European service, it was equipped with similar anti-submarine warfare systems, although it had a French radar, American sonar equipment and British-designed turboprop engines. The fuselage contains an unpressurized lower section in which the weapons are carried, and a magnetic anomaly detector (MAD) for sensing the presence of submarines is situated in the tailboom.

Several of the 40 Atlantics built for the French navy remain in service at colonial bases, although most are being replaced by the second-generation Atlantique 2. Three of the French navy's aircraft were supplied to Pakistan in the mid-1970s.

Six of the 20 Atlantics acquired by Germany were modified for electronic reconnaissance, and the rest have been updated with new radar, sonar and electronic warfare equipment.

Italy's 18 Atlantics were the last to be delivered. Supplied from 1972 to 1974, they were upgraded between 1988 and 1992 with systems designed for the Atlantique. The Netherlands navy chose to replace its six remaining aircraft of the nine originally supplied with Lockheed P-3C Orions.

Above: One of Germany's Atlantics shows its retracted radar radome and sonobuoy launch tubes.

Below: Most Atlantics, including this Italian aircraft, have spent their entire careers in this dark-grey over white colour scheme. Italian machines are used to patrol the Mediterranean.

Atlantic 1

Type: maritime reconnaissance and anti-submarine aircraft

Powerplant: two 4549-kW (6,100-hp) Rolls-Royce Tyne RTy20.Mk 21 turboprops

Maximum speed: 658 km/h (409 mph)

Endurance: 18 hours

Service ceiling: 10,000 m (32,808 ft)

Weights: empty 25,000 kg (55,116 lb); maximum take-off 44,500 kg (98,106 lb)

Armament: a maximum of 3500 kg (7,716 lb) of torpedoes, depth charges and missiles in the weapons bay and on four wing pylons

Dimensions:

span	36.30 m (119 ft 1 in)
length	31.75 m (104 ft 2 in)
height	11.33 m (37 ft 2 in)
wing area	120.34 m² (1,295 sq ft)

BR.1150 ATLANTIC 1

This very early French aircraft bears the painted signature of Louis Breguet on the tailfin. Most of the 40 first-generation Atlantics supplied to the Aéronavale have been replaced by the Atlantique.

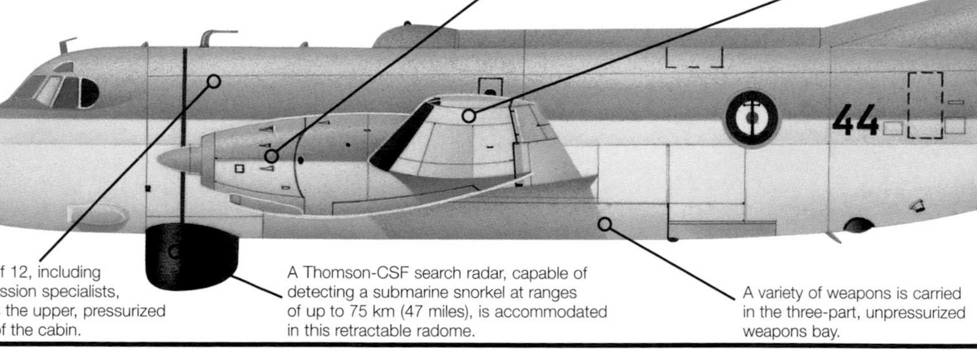

Powerful Rolls-Royce Tyne turboprops help to give the Atlantic its long endurance and ensure a performance which is far superior to that of previous piston-engined designs.

High aspect ratio wings provide good long-range cruising performance. A metal honeycomb sandwich wing skinning is designed to minimize leaks from the integral wing fuel tanks.

Electronic countermeasures (ECM) equipment is carried in this fin-top radome. All first-generation Atlantics, except for the first prototype, have this distinctive feature.

A crew of 12, including seven mission specialists, occupies the upper, pressurized section of the cabin.

A Thomson-CSF search radar, capable of detecting a submarine snorkel at ranges of up to 75 km (47 miles), is accommodated in this retractable radome.

A variety of weapons is carried in the three-part, unpressurized weapons bay.

A long tailcone extension contains the MAD boom. The equipment is positioned well away from the fuselage to avoid interference from the airframe structure.

COMBAT DATA

MAXIMUM SPEED

A typical long-endurance patrol flight is flown at the most economical cruising speed. However, maritime patrol aircraft often need to respond to a threat or emergency situation which requires them to arrive on station as soon as possible.

ATLANTIC 1 658 km/h (409 mph)

P-3B ORION 766 km/h (476 mph)

NIMROD MR.Mk 1 926 km/h (575 mph)

WEAPON LOAD

Operating at great distances from base, the maritime patrol aircraft commander is unable to make frequent landings to re-arm. A large, hard-hitting weapon load is therefore important if the aircraft is to demonstrate effective combat persistence.

ATLANTIC 1 3500 kg (7,716 lb)

P-3B ORION 6804 kg (15,000 lb)

NIMROD MR.Mk 1 3400 kg (7,496 lb)

ENDURANCE

Many missions involve long searches over vast tracts of ocean, hunting for elusive targets, followed by prolonged offensive operations against a submarine or surface vessel.

ATLANTIC 1 18 hours

P-3B ORION 17 hours

NIMROD MR.Mk 1 12 hours

Current Atlantic operators

GERMANY: This aircraft is one of the modified electronic intelligence-gathering aircraft which are flown by the German navy. They are also capable of jamming enemy transmissions.

ITALY: Two units operate the Italian Atlantics, including the 30° Stormo (Wing) of the 86° Gruppo (Squadron), based at Cagliari-Elmas in Sardinia.

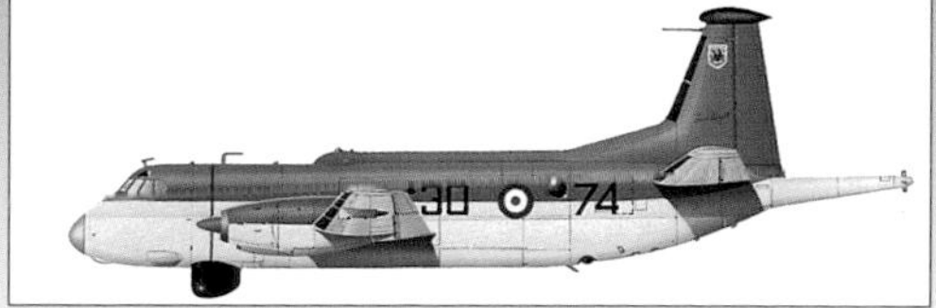

PAKISTAN: At one time reports suggested that Pakistan's Atlantics had been returned to France because of a lack of skilled servicing personnel, but they continue to fly from Sharea Faisal.

Dassault Breguet Etendard IV

● Carrier-based ● Attack and reconnaissance versions ● Long serving

▲ *The Etendard IV was originally intended as a close-support aircraft for the French air force. Instead this versatile machine was developed to become the Aéronavale's carrier attack warplane of the 1960s and 1970s.*

Along with the Etendard VI, which was designed in the mid-1950s as a light-attack aircraft for NATO air forces, Dassault developed a series of aircraft for other roles. After the Fiat G91 was selected to meet the NATO requirement in January 1958, the French navy picked the Etendard IV to equip its two new aircraft carriers. The original Etendard IV was then developed to produce IVM (Marine) attack and IVP photographic reconnaissance versions.

PHOTO FILE

Dassault Breguet Etendard IV

▼ IVP reconnaissance version
The IVP's five OMERA cameras (three in the nose and two in a ventral pack) replaced the IVM's attack avionics and guns.

▲ French carriers
Etendards served aboard the French navy's two carriers: the Clémenceau *and the* Foch*.*

▼ Two-tone grey camouflage
This Etendard IVP of 16F shows the newly applied two-tone camouflage in 1985.

▼ Landing speed
Wing high-lift devices, such as flaps and slats, reduced the Etendard IV's landing speed to 219 km/h (136 mph).

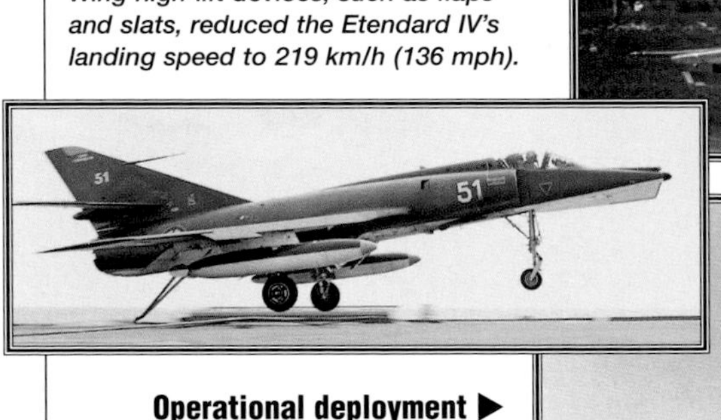

Operational deployment ▶
Entering service in 1962, Etendard IVs supported operations in Djibouti, Lebanon and the former Yugoslavia. This rocket-armed IVM is seen aboard Foch *in 1979.*

FACTS AND FIGURES

- ➤ Based on the Etendard, Dassault developed the Super Etendard with radar and more sophisticated weaponry.
- ➤ Internal rockets would have been carried by the Etendard IV development.
- ➤ Dassault planned tactical reconnaissance, naval and trainer variants.
- ➤ While the French air force selected the Mirage III, the navy adopted the larger Etendard IVM.
- ➤ Wingspan could be reduced by wing-folding to 7.8 m (25 ft 7 in).
- ➤ The highly manoeuvrable Etendard IVM could enter a loop at only 463 km/h (288 mph).

PROFILE

Locked and loaded for France

Delivered between 1961 and 1965, the 69 Etendard IVMs and 21 IVPs built operated from the aircraft carriers *Foch* and *Clémenceau* until the early 1990s. For attack missions, the IVP could carry an AS-30 missile plus bombs or rockets under each wing. It had an Aïda fire-control radar in the nose, along with an infrared sensor and a guidance antenna for the AS-30.

The IVM was used as an interceptor, too, adding four Sidewinder missiles under the wings. One of the two 30-mm (1.18-in) cannon carried in the belly was usually replaced by Tacan navigation equipment.

In the nose of the IVP were three reconnaissance cameras, and two more were installed in place of the guns in the lower fuselage. It was also equipped for buddy refuelling.

The IVM survived longer in service than the IVP, acting as a tanker for the Super Etendard, which replaced the IVM as well as carrying out reconnaissance missions.

Above: Although the Etendard IVM attack version was long retired, the IVP continued to serve on board Aéronavale carriers until 1996 in the air-to-air refuelling and reconnaissance roles.

Above: This display of weapons carried by the IVM includes AS.20, AS.30 and AIM-9B missiles, 68-mm (2.68-in) SNEB rocket pods and free-fall bombs. The removable ventral gun pack houses two 30-mm (1.18-in) DEFA cannon.

Etendard IVM

Type: single-seat carrier-based attack aircraft

Powerplant: one 43.13-kN (9,700-lb-thrust) SNECMA Atar 88 non-afterburning single-shaft turbojet

Maximum speed: 1096 km/h (681 mph) at sea level

Initial climb rate: 6000 m/min (19,680 fpm)

Combat radius: 298 km (185 miles) (low-level attack); 805 km (500 miles) (medium-level attack profile)

Service ceiling: 15,500 m (50,850 ft)

Weapons: two DEFA 30-mm (1.18-in) cannon; plus up to 1360-kg (3,000-lb) weapon load

Weights: empty equipped 6110 kg (13,470 lb); maximum take-off 10,253 kg (22,605 lb)

Dimensions:	span	9.60 m (31 ft 6 in)
	length	14.43 m (47 ft 4 in)
	height	4.32 m (14 ft 2 in)
	wing area	28.99 m² (312 sq ft)

ETENDARD IVM

This is an IVM of Escadrille de Servitude 59S, based at Hyères on the Mediterranean coast, during October 1981. The unit served as the Etendard carrier training unit and chose as its badge a seagull attempting to land on a swimming turtle.

The IVM's attack avionics comprise a small Aïda radar and a Saab toss-bombing computer. Aïda provided detection and ranging of targets within a small narrow cone directly ahead of the Etendard.

The Etendard IV's small wing makes only a small fold necessary; only the tips fold.

Simple semi-circular lateral intakes feed the Etendard IV's Atar turbojet. A small splitter ramp ahead of each intake removes boundary layer air from the forward fuselage.

Pitch control comes from all-moving tailplanes mounted high up on the vertical fin. Additional control is provided by large elevators inset into the tailplanes.

The pilot sits in an armoured, pressurized cockpit on a French-built Martin-Baker Mk 4 ejection seat. The high seat position gives a good view over the nose on approach to the carrier.

The IVM is fitted with a retractable refuelling probe directly in front of the cockpit. The large vertical blade fairing contains the guidance aerial for the now-obsolete AS.20 radio-guided air-to-surface missile.

The Etendard almost always carried a pair of 600-litre (159-US gal) fuel tanks to boost its relatively poor range. These further reduced the already modest warload.

The Etendard IV has a V-shaped arrestor hook.

ACTION DATA

SPEED

A fast approach to the target and an even more rapid escape are desirable for all-attack aircraft. The Buccaneer has a slight advantage owing to its twin engines.

ETENDARD IVM	1096 km/h (681 mph)
A-4M SKYHAWK II	1100 km/h (683 mph)
BUCCANEER S.Mk 1	1164 km/h (723 mph)

WEAPONS

An incredibly large bombload is carried by the unusually small Skyhawk. The Etendard carries the smallest weapon load, but if nuclear devices were used this would be of little consequence.

ETENDARD IV	A-4M SKYHAWK II	BUCCANEER S.Mk 1
1360 kg (3,000 lb)	4145 kg (9,140 lb)	3630 kg (8,000 lb)

COMBAT RADIUS

Larger aircraft often have longer range. This is true of the Buccaneer, although by modern standards all three types are modest performers in this respect.

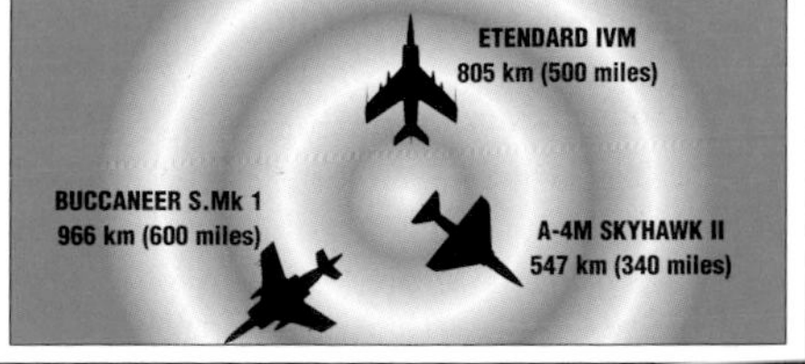

Multi-mission warplane

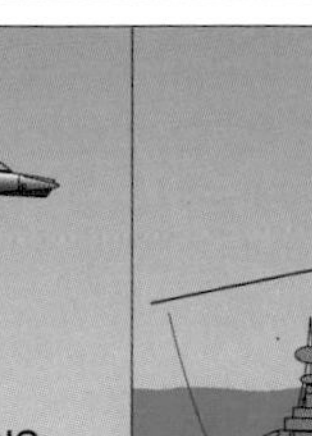

BUDDY-BUDDY REFUELLING: Equipped with an underfuselage refuelling pod, the Etendard IVP still serves as the Aéronavale's carrier tanker.

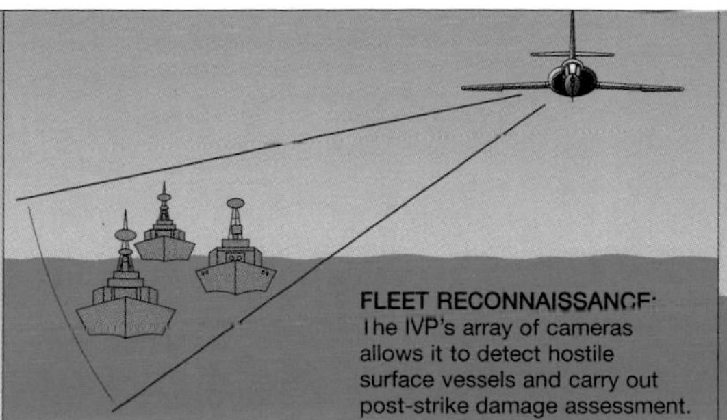

FLEET RECONNAISSANCE: The IVP's array of cameras allows it to detect hostile surface vessels and carry out post-strike damage assessment.

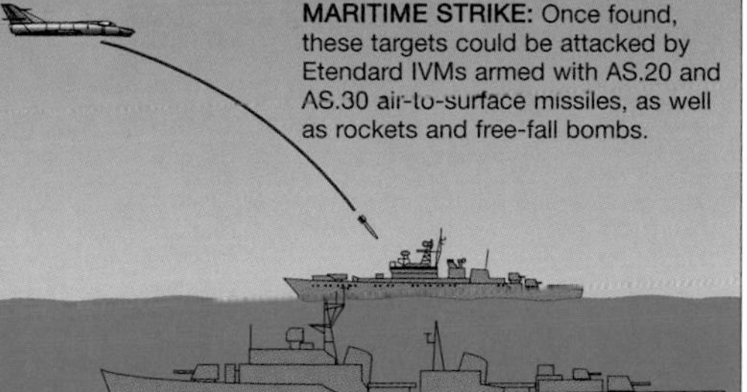

MARITIME STRIKE: Once found, these targets could be attacked by Etendard IVMs armed with AS.20 and AS.30 air-to-surface missiles, as well as rockets and free-fall bombs.

DASSAULT-BREGUET

MIRAGE III/5

● Mach 2 delta-wing jet ● Reconnaissance ● Ground-attack fighter

A shining jewel in the crown of French aircraft design, the Dassault Mirage III is a pioneering supersonic delta-winged jet that cemented the reputation of Dassault as a premier manufacturer of world-class jet fighters. With its perfect blend of speed, sophistication and simplicity, this Mach 2 delta became the backbone of France's air arm in the 1960s and still serves a dozen nations.

▲ *The Mirage has seen more combat than most jets, with mixed results. In the hands of well-trained pilots, however, it has proved to be a lethal fighting machine, as good as any fighter in the world.*

PHOTO FILE

DASSAULT-BREGUET MIRAGE III/5

Flying lab ▶
The Milan was an experimental high-agility version of the Mirage III with forward-swept nose-mounted canard foreplanes.

▲ Maritime strike
A number of Pakistan's Mirage 5s have been upgraded to 5PA3 standard featuring the Agave radar for use with Exocet anti-ship missiles.

◀ Eye in the sky
Equipped with nose-mounted cameras, the Mirage IIIR is a superb reconnaissance aircraft. Its high speed and stable handling at low level made it very popular with pilots.

▲ Ground-attack warload
Mirage armament includes MATRA 530 missiles, rockets, cannon and bombs.

▲ Air defender
Australia was one of 20 nations to operate variants of the Mirage III. Sidewinder-armed Mirages served in the air defence role until 1989.

◀ On the road
The Swiss air force is also a user of the Mirage III. Swiss pilots are trained to operate from small mountain airfields or even from straight stretches of highway.

FACTS AND FIGURES

- ➤ The prototype Mirage III made its maiden flight on 17 December 1956.
- ➤ The Mirage III was one of Western Europe's first Mach 2 fighters.
- ➤ The Mirage 5/50 series was conceived as an 'economy' Mirage III with no radar and a modified cockpit.
- ➤ Between 1956 and 1992, 1422 Mirage III, 5 and 50 aircraft were manufactured.
- ➤ Mirages can deliver a wide variety of air-to-surface weaponry, up to the size of Exocet anti-ship missiles.
- ➤ Some Mirage IIIs in Israeli service have notched up at least 10 combat kills.

PROFILE

Dassault's deadliest delta

The Mirage III is the progenitor of a family of interceptors and fighters which have in common an instantly identifiable delta wing and an almost incredible capability to fly and fight. This creation of Avions Marcel Dassault is also one of the most beautiful aircraft ever to take to the skies, and never fails to turn heads whenever it appears.

At least three-dozen versions of the Mirage III family have appeared since its first flight nearly four decades ago, including two-seat models and aircraft intended for strike/attack and reconnaissance in addition to the primary job of air-to-air combat. The Mirage IIIE strike fighter was a component of France's independent nuclear force until 1988.

Mirages have fought in many wars, most famously with the Israeli forces in 1967 when the aircraft shot down large numbers of MiG-21s. Twenty nations have operated Mirage IIIs as well as its Mirage 5 and 50 variants. Many are still flying, having been upgraded and improved to remain highly effective combat aircraft even in the type's fifth decade.

Celebrating the unit's seventieth anniversary, this Mirage 5 of No. 2 Squadron, Belgian air force, sports a vivid colour scheme. Belgium retired its Mirage force in 1993.

A special badge and paint scheme for a French air force Mirage, celebrating the Republic's bicentenary.

The Mirage's delta wing means that it has no conventional tailplane. Roll and pitch are controlled by the 'elevons' – combined elevators and ailerons – on the wing trailing edge.

Mirage IIIE

Type: single-seat fighter

Powerplant: one SNECMA 41.97-kN (9,440-lb-thrust) Atar 9C-3 (60.80 kN/13,674-lb-thrust with afterburning) and provision for one jettisonable 14.71-kN (3,308-lb-thrust) SEPR 844 rocket booster

Maximum speed: 2350 km/h (1,460 mph) or Mach 2.1

Range: 2400 km (1,491 miles)

Service ceiling: 14,440 m (47,375 ft)

Weights: empty 7050 kg (15,543 lb); loaded 13,700 kg (30,203 lb)

Armament: 30-mm (1.18-in) DEFA 552 cannon with 125 rounds; Nord 5103, MATRA R.511, MATRA T.53 or Hughes AIM-26 Falcon missiles

Dimensions:		
	span	8.22 m (27 ft)
	length	15.03 m (49 ft 4 in)
	height	4.50 m (14 ft 9 in)
	wing area	35.00 m² (377 sq ft)

MIRAGE IIICJ

The Mirage III really made its name in 1967, when the Israeli air force gained a stunning victory over Arab forces. Mirage pilots became the highest-scoring jet aces since the Korean War.

A British Martin-Baker ejection seat is fitted to most Mirages, although some use American-designed seats.

Israeli Mirages originally used the French Atar turbojet, but when Israel built its own Mirages it fitted the more powerful American J-79 engine, as fitted to the F-4 Phantom.

Pilot visibility ahead and to the side is good, although the rear view is limited especially when compared with more recent fighters such as the F-16 and MiG-29.

Early Mirages had fairly primitive radar sets giving range information only. Most have been upgraded with multi-mode systems such as the Israeli Elta series.

Mirage IIIs carry a pair of DEFA 30-mm (1.18-in) cannon beneath the intakes. These are potent weapons in dogfights and ground-attack missions.

In the air-combat role, Israeli Mirages usually carried two drop-tanks and two Sidewinder or Python missiles as well as two 30-mm (1.18-in) cannon.

COMBAT DATA

MAXIMUM SPEED

MIRAGE III	2350 km/h (1,460 mph)
MiG-21 'FISHBED'	2175 km/h (1,351 mph)
DRAKEN	2150 km/h (1,336 mph)

The Mirage III was one of the earliest of the Mach 2-capable jets which first appeared in the mid- to late 1950s. Even today, nearly 40 years later, it is one of the world's best high-speed performers at altitude.

ARMAMENT

The appearance of the Mach 2 fighter coincided with the development of effective air-to-air missiles. The Mirage carried fewer weapons than some of its contemporaries, but unlike its rivals was capable of engaging beyond visual range with a single medium-range radar-guided Nord 5103 or MATRA R.511 missile.

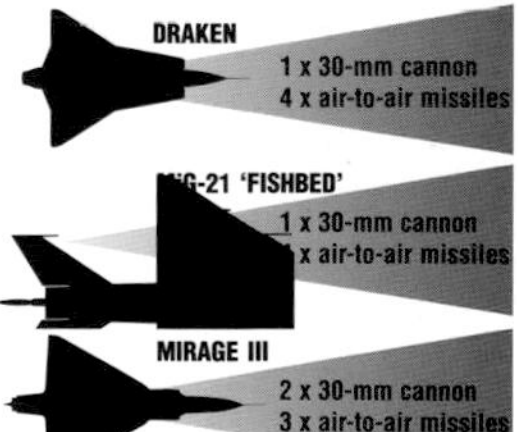

INTERCEPT RADIUS

Mirage III carries more than 2900 litres (766 US gal) of fuel internally. Two external drop-tanks of up to 1700 litres (500 US gal) more than doubles the load, giving the Mirage III a ferry range in excess of 4000 km (2485 miles). A more normal underwing load of two 625- or 1100-litre (165- or 290-US gal) tanks gives an operating radius of more than 1000 km (620 miles) on intercept missions. This is considerably better than most of the Mirage's contemporaries.

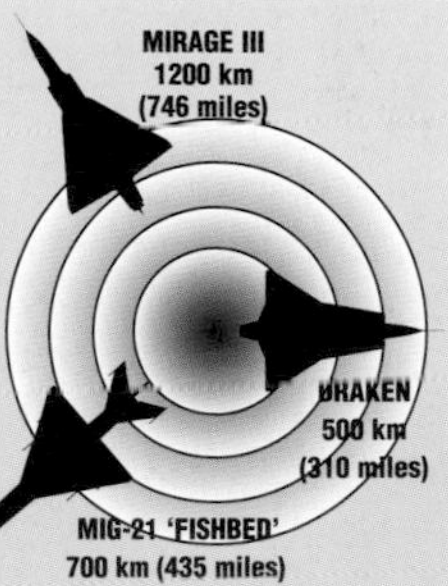

The delta wing advantage

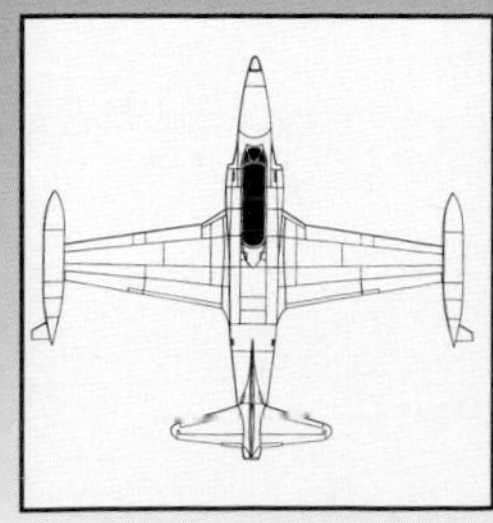

STRAIGHT WING: From the earliest days of flight, aircraft wings have generally been straight. This provides maximum lift at low speeds. With the advent of the jet engine, however, aircraft began to have the power to push much closer to the speed of sound, and straight-winged machines began to encounter problems with compression and drag.

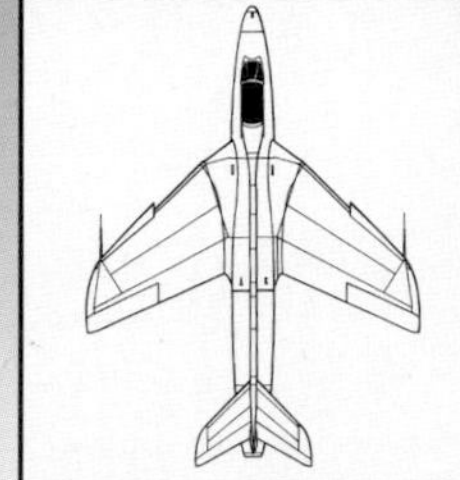

SWEPT WING: Pioneering work in the 1940s showed that sweeping the wing back enabled an aircraft to travel much faster, delaying the compression of the fast-moving air which causes turbulence and increases drag immensely. By making the wings much thinner and sweeping back even further, fighters were able to penetrate the 'sound barrier'.

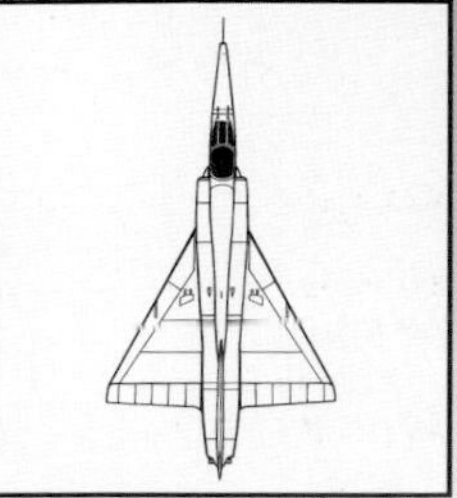

DELTA WING: German aviation pioneer Alexander Lippisch discovered in the 1930s that a triangular wing, looking like the Greek letter delta, could be made much thinner in cross-section. This offered significant advantages at supersonic speeds and high altitudes. The disadvantage was in landing, where deltas come in very fast and with a nose-high attitude.

DASSAULT-BREGUET

MIRAGE III/5/50

● 1960s design ● Fighter/attack/reconnaissance ● Upgrades

Between the late 1950s and 1992, Dassault and foreign licensees built more than 1,400 Mirage IIIs, 5s and 50s for 20 air forces. The same combination of performance, versatility and low cost that won the delta-winged fighter so many orders in the first place has encouraged several operators to embark on upgrade programmes. New avionics and weapons, plus airframe modifications, should keep them competitive well into the 21st century.

▲ *Although many larger operators have replaced their Mirage fleets, smaller users have seen a future in the type. Upgrading existing aircraft allows considerable cost savings.*

PHOTO FILE

DASSAULT-BREGUET MIRAGE III/5/50

▼ Colombia's Mirages and Kfirs
As well as IAI Kfirs, Colombia operates Mirage 5COAs upgraded with IAI help. Canards and IFR probes are features.

▲ Chasing exports
Finishing this Mirage 50 demonstrator (a former Mir IIIR) in desert camouflage made it clear that Dassau was seeking customers in the Middle East. However the type has sold exclusively in South America.

▼ Venezuela
Dassault converted surviving Venezuelan Mirage IIIs and 5s to Mirage 50EV standard with Cyrano IV radar and Atar 09K-50 engines.

▲ Belgium's ill-fated Elkan Mirages
Mirage Safety Improvement Programme (MIRSIP) was the name given to an ambitious plan for the country's locally built Mirage 5s. Although post-Cold War defence cuts saw the type retired by Belgium, some Elkans were exported to Chile.

Brazil's F-103Es ▶
Mirage IIIEBRs flown by the Brazilian air force are known as F-103Es. The first were delivered in 1972. In 1989 work began on refitting these aircraft with canards and improved gun and missile armament.

FACTS AND FIGURES

- ➤ Plans by Colombia to re-engine its Mirages with American J79 or F404 engines were cancelled on cost grounds.
- ➤ Dassault's Mirage prototype, a much smaller aircraft, flew in 1956.
- ➤ Mirage 5s were originally called 5Js; they were intended for Israel.
- ➤ With an eye to the upgrade market, Dassault built Mirage 50M, 3EX and 3NG prototypes to demonstrate new systems.
- ➤ The first Mirage 5 took to the air in May 1967; the Mirage 50 in April 1979.
- ➤ The Mirage 3NG offered fly-by-wire controls and Mirage 2000 systems, but did not sell.

PROFILE

Dassault's delta lives on

The Mirage IIIE, the main export model of the original series, remains in service with Argentina, Brazil, Pakistan and Switzerland. The latter two also fly the IIIR reconnaissance variant, along with France and South Africa. Abu Dhabi, Argentina, Chile, Colombia, Egypt, Gabon, Libya, Pakistan, Peru and Zaire still use the Mirage 5; Chile and Venezuela fly Mirage 50s.

More than half the air forces operating the various models have selected Dassault upgrades. New avionics options include head-up displays, inertial navigation systems, hands on throttle and stick (HOTAS) controls, and a multi-mode radar and/or laser rangefinder. Canard foreplanes improve take-off and manoeuvring performance.

Chile added new radars and air-to-air missiles to its Mirage 50s with the help of Israel Aircraft Industries to produce the Pantera, and bought 15 ex-Belgian Mirage 5s upgraded to Elkan standard.

IAI has helped Colombia and Argentina upgrade their Mirages, the Colombian aircraft having Kfir-style canards as well as improved avionics.

Above: Switzerland's Mirage IIISs are tasked with air defence. Survivors have been upgraded with canards, new avionics and other changes.

The Mirage family will survive for many years to come, thanks to upgrade packages that produce a modern warplane at a fraction of a new aircraft's price.

Below: Peru's Mirage 5Ps and 5P3s have been refurbished by Dassault with distinctive fixed in-flight-refuelling probes, Magic 2 air-to-air missiles and new avionics. The avonics include a new radar-warning receiver (RWR).

Mirage 50M

Type: single-seat interceptor/fighter-bomber

Powerplant: one 70.82-kN (15,930-lb.-thrust) SNECMA Atar 09K-50 afterburning turbojet

Maximum speed: 2338 km/h (1,450 m.p.h.) at 12,000 m (39,000 ft.)

Initial climb rate: 11,160 m/min (36,614 f.p.m.)

Combat radius: 1315 km (815 mi.) on a hi-hi-hi interception mission with two air-to-air missiles and three drop tanks

Service ceiling: 18,000 m (59,000 ft.)

Weights: empty equipped 7150 kg (15,730 lb.); maximum take-off 14,700 kg (32,340 lb.)

Armament: up to 4000 kg (8,800 lb.) of ordnance

Dimensions:		
	span	8.22 m (26 ft. 11 in.)
	length	15.56 m (51 ft. 1 in.)
	height	4.50 m (14 ft. 9 in.)
	wing area	35 m² (377 sq. ft.)

Mirage 50C

This aircraft was among the first Mirage 50s built, as part of an order for six 50s delivered to the Chilean air force in 1982 and 1983. All were operated by 4 Escuadron of Brigada Aérea 4 at Santiago.

ENAER began a programme to upgrade the Chilean 50C fleet to Pantera (Panther) standard in the mid-1980s. With assistance from Israel Aircraft Industries (IAI), the airframe is being changed (including the addition of canard foreplanes) and new avionics are being fitted, resulting in effectively an Atar-engined Kfir. Funding problems have slowed the programme.

Canard foreplanes attached to the engine air intakes are a commonly specified addition to upgraded Mirage IIIs, 5s and 50s. On the Pantera, IAI-designed fixed canards are employed; they dramatically reduce take-off runs and improve manoeuvrability.

Local technological expertise has been used in the Pantera, namely a Chilean-designed RWR (Caiquen III) and Eclipse chaff/flare dispensers, the former developed by ENAER (Empresa Nacional de Aeronáutica de Chile). A number of Mirage upgrade programmes have been undertaken locally to save money and take advantage of technology transfer.

Chile originally took delivery of eight ex-Armée de l'Air Mirage 5Fs, bought back by Dassault and rebuilt to 50FC standard. Six new-build Mirage 50Cs, with nose radar, followed, along with a pair of two-seat 50DCs, the latter with Atar 09C engines (as fitted to Mirage IIIs and 5s).

As built, Chile's Mirage 50s were believed to be equipped with Agave multi-mode radar. As part of the Pantera upgrade a 1-m (3-ft.) plug is inserted in the nose ahead of the cockpit to make room for avionics equipment, including a new Elbit EL/M-2001B radar.

Drop tanks of 600-litre (160-gal.) capacity are a common Mirage store. Rebuilt aircraft are often able to carry later, more capable variants of standard weapons systems, including air-to-air missiles. Agave radar-equipped machines can often carry Exocet anti-ship missiles.

Mirage 50s derive their designation from the SNECMA Atar 09K-50 engine fitted to what is otherwise a standard Mirage III/5 airframe. The afterburning 09K-50 was originally fitted to the Mirage F1 and offers more thrust.

COMBAT DATA

COMBAT RADIUS

Range has never been a strength of the Mirage family, though the 5 performs better in this respect than the Mikoyan-Gurevich MiG-27. SEPECAT's Jaguar has 50 per cent greater range.

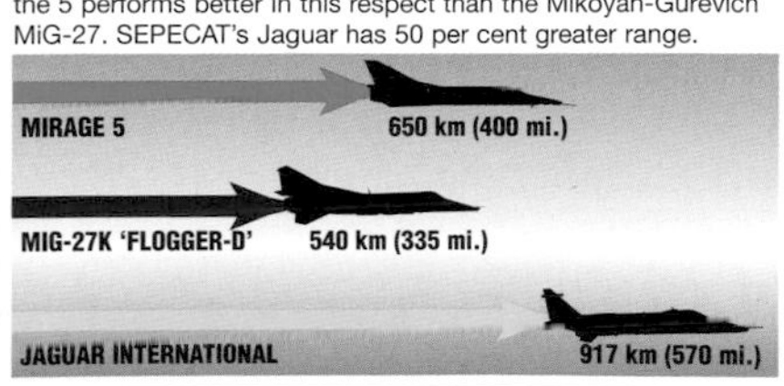

Mirage IIIS rocket-assisted take-off

FROM CONFINED SPACES: Switzerland's air force faces unique challenges in its day-to-day operations in a small country that has limited areas of flat land on which to construct airfields. Its Mirages use thrust augmentation in order to take off from short runways.

RATO BOTTLES: Standard fit on Switzerland's Mirage IIIS/RS and BS are six rocket-assisted take-off (RATO) bottles under the wing centre-section. With the aircraft's engine producing maximum thrust, the bottles are lit and burn for a set duration.

SPECTACULAR TAKE-OFF: When used on a lightly loaded aircraft the result is spectacular. This aircraft is seen during an air show climbing almost vertically from the runway after a reduced take-off run with a minimal load.

DASSAULT-BREGUET

MIRAGE F1

● **Air defence** ● **Ground attack** ● **Reconnaissance**

France's Dassault Mirage F1 comes from a company with decades of experience in designing affordable high-performance jet fighters. When the first F1 flew on 20 March 1969, it immediately demonstrated improvements over its predecessor, the delta-wing Mirage III. The F1 introduced more fuel economy, better avionics and increased agility. Although now an ageing design, the F1 will remain a viable frontline aircraft well into the twenty-first century.

▲ *Following the extremely popular Mirage III on Dassault's production lines, the Mirage F1 was a great advance on the pioneering delta-wing fighter, and it also achieved export success.*

PHOTO FILE

DASSAULT-BREGUET MIRAGE F1

◀ **Spy in the sky**
The Mirage F1CR is France's primary tactical reconnaissance aircraft. It can carry a variety of radar, infrared and optical sensors.

▼ **Global reach**
The F1C-200 has a fixed refuelling probe, which with the support of Boeing C-135FR tankers enables the interceptor to deploy almost anywhere in Africa or the Middle East.

▼ **Reliable power**
The Atar turbojet has been continually developed over more than four decades. The version in the F1 needs servicing every 300 hours, with a full overhaul being required after 900 hours of use.

▼ **French defender**
The Mirage F1 was France's main air defence interceptor for more than 15 years, from the middle of the 1970s until it was replaced in the role by the more advanced Mirage 2000.

◀ **Mirage with a tail**
The conventional wing and tailplane layout of the F1 was a temporary break in Dassault's delta-wing tradition.

FACTS AND FIGURES

- ➤ Most F1s use Cyrano IV air-to-air radar to detect intruders and aid in engaging enemy warplanes.
- ➤ In France, the F1 replaced the SNCASO Vautour IIN all-weather interceptor.
- ➤ The reconnaissance Mirage F1CR first flew on 20 November 1981.
- ➤ Users of the F1 have included Ecuador, Iraq, Jordan, Kuwait, Qatar, Libya, Morocco, South Africa and Spain.
- ➤ At least one Angolan MiG was shot down by a South African Mirage F1.
- ➤ In the Gulf War, an Iraqi F1 flew into the ground while chasing an EF-111A Raven.

PROFILE

Dassault's gallic guardian

Mirage is the beautiful and evocative word chosen by Avions Marcel Dassault (which became Dassault-Breguet) as the name for its modern jet combat planes. The classic Mirage of the 1970s, which has given superb service for more than two decades, is the Mirage F1.

Battle tested, the Mirage F1 has been a bastion of France's air defence capability for many years. Equally successful as a ground-attack and a reconnaissance airplane, it is respected by its allies and feared by its enemies.

The first of more than 220 aircraft for the French air force were ordered in 1969, with the initial production fighter being delivered on 14 May 1973. The first operational unit was 30 Escadre de Chasse, which converted to the type on December of that year.

It has also been a great success in the export market, having been sold to 10 air forces. South African F1As were adapted as strike aircraft with secondary air-to-air duties. It was used by both sides during the Gulf War, although eight of Iraq's Mirage F1EQ fighters were downed by American and Saudi F-15 Eagles.

Primary armament of the original Mirage F1 was a single Matra 530 missile with two Matra R.550 Magic dogfight missiles on wingtip rails.

The F1's cockpit is reasonably roomy by the standards of its time, but it lacks the all-round visibility now common.

The instrument panel is old-fashioned, with small analog instruments and a shielded radar scope.

The Mirage's high-lift wing gives much better low-speed agility than the previous delta form, while maintaining excellent high-speed and high-altitude performance.

Mirage F1C

Powerplant: One 70.43-kN (15,840-lb-thrust) SNECM Atar 9k-5 afterburning turbojet

Max speed: 2334 km/h (1,450 mph) or Mach 2.2 at high altitude

Initial climb rate: 12,777 m/min (41,918 fpm)

Ceiling: 20,000 m (65,600 ft)

Range: 2594 km (1,612 miles) with drop tanks and light combat load

Weights: empty 7384 kg (16,280 lb); maximum 15,168 kg (33,440 lb)

Weapons: two 30-mm (1.18-in) DEFA 553 cannon with 270 rounds; two Matra Super 530 radar missiles and/or two Matra R.550 Magic infrared missiles; up to 3622 kg (7,986 lb) of ordnance

Dimensions:		
	span	8.23 m (27 ft)
	length	14.94 m (49 ft)
	height	4.57 m (15 ft)
	wing area	24.99 m² (269 sq ft)

MIRAGE F1CE

Spain was one of the first export users of the F1, ordering 15 F1CE interceptors in 1972. All of Spain's 73 Mirages are assigned to the Ala de Caza (Fighter Wing) 14.

Fighters and multi-role variants of the Mirage F1 carry pitot probes on the tips of their nose radomes. These gather data from the clean airflow ahead of the aircraft for the aircraft's primary flight instruments, including the airspeed indicator and altimeter.

The Mirage F1 has semi-circular air intakes with a variable shock cone centre body, which regulates air flow to the engine at supersonic speeds. The fighter's two 30-mm (1.18-in) cannon are housed in the lower intake trunking.

Like most aircraft of its generation, the Mirage F1 is of all-metal monocoque construction, with no significant use of advanced alloys or composite materials.

14-15

C14-15

The distinctively long and slender Mirage radome covers the antenna of its Cyrano radar. This is a multi-function system capable of air-to-air and air-to-ground operation.

Many NATO squadrons with big cats in their squadron badges take part in multinational exercises known as 'Tiger Meets'. Aircraft such as this Ala 14 machine participating in these events often receive temporary 'Tiger stripe' decoration.

ACTION DATA

SPEED

The Mirage F1 is no slouch, being capable of reaching Mach 2.2 at altitude. The contemporary MiG-23 is much more powerful and has a slight advantage, while the agile American F-16 is slower.

MIRAGE F1 2334 km/h (1,450 mph)

MiG-23 2485 km/h (1,544 mph)

F-16A 2120 km/h (1,317 mph)

SERVICE CEILING

Although it has excellent low-level performance, the Mirage F1 really excels at high altitude. Its service ceiling is better than most other fighters, and is outclassed only by immensely powerful machines such as the MiG-25 'Foxbat'.

F-16A 18,245 m (59,860 ft)

MIRAGE F1 20,000 m (65,600 ft)

MiG-23 17,500 m (57,400 ft)

AIR-TO-AIR WEAPONS

Most modern fighters carry a range of weapons. Larger missiles can destroy enemy aircraft at well beyond visual range, while smaller, more agile weapons are used in dogfights.

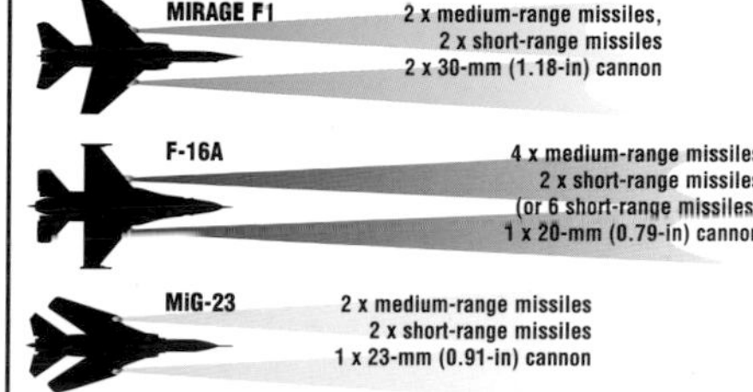

Matra Magic in action

SHORT-RANGE ENGAGEMENT: The F1's main close-combat weapon is the Matra R.550 Magic missile, which has a range of up to 5 km (3 miles).

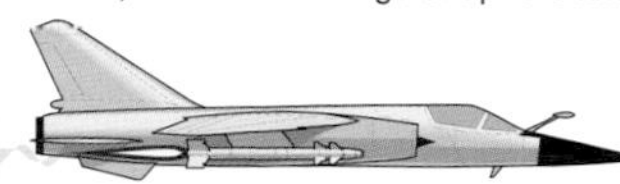

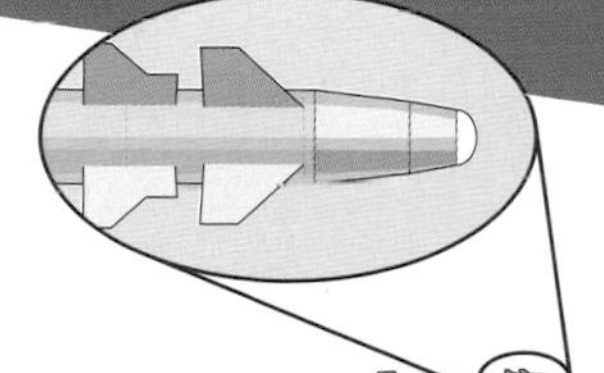

HEAT SOURCE: All aircraft generate heat. The most obvious source is from the jet exhaust, which acts as a beacon to heat-seeking missiles.

HEAT SEEKER: Magic is guided by detecting and homing in on infra red radiation, or heat. Once the missile has detected and locked onto a target, it is ready to be launched.

HOMING IN: A highly sensitive infra-red detector mounted on gimbals in the missile's nose automatically points towards the source of heat. Control fins are slaved to the seeker, automatically steering the weapon towards the target.

IN FOR THE KILL: A proximity fuse detonates the 13-kg (29-lb) high-explosive/fragmentation warhead when within lethal range.

Dassault-Breguet

Mirage IV

● Supersonic nuclear bomber ● Strategic reconnaissance platform

▲ The Mirage IV remained a potent long-range strike aircraft for more than 35 years, thanks to its performance, allied with effective upgrades and the ability to carry advanced new weapons.

France's Mirage IV was the aerial component of its 'Force de Frappe', or nuclear deterrent. A delta-winged aircraft based on the well-proven Mirage III design, but very much enlarged, the Mirage IV was flown by a crew of two, with pilot and navigator sitting in tandem cockpits. This supersonic striker was designed for one job – to carry an atomic weapon to Russia, possibly on a one-way trip.

PHOTO FILE

Dassault-Breguet **Mirage IV**

▲ Production line ▼

The Mirage IVA production line delivered aircraft between December 1963 and November 1966. By that year, a force of nine squadrons was operational, each with four aircraft on alert status (below).

▲ Big brother

The Mirage IV dwarfed the rest of the Mirage family. It was three times as heavy as these early Mirages and twice as heavy as the latest two-seat nuclear strike Mirage, the 2000N.

Stand-off attack ▶

The Air-Sol-Moyen-Portée (ASMP) missile became the Mirage IV's primary weapon. With a range of over 250 km (155 miles), it allowed the Mirage to strike from a distance.

▲ Rocket launch

The Mirage IV needed a fairly long runway to take off. To assist on short airstrips, the big delta could be fitted with rocket-assisted take-off packs.

◀ Silver machine

The polished metal of the original Mirage IV was a sign of the high-level delivery profile used in the 1960s. Like most bombers of the era, when its mission profile went down to low level a striped camouflage scheme was applied.

FACTS AND FIGURES

- The Mirage IV was expected to fly supersonic at low level only on its final run-in to the target.
- The ASMP stand-off missile was armed with a 300-kiloton TN81 warhead.
- A few radar-equipped Mirage IVs were assigned to reconnaissance duties.
- The Mirage IV could operate from a short runway, boosted into the air by six rockets under each wing.
- Production of the Mirage IV was completed in March 1968.
- EB 1/91 'Gascogne' and EB 2/91 'Bretagne' were the last Mirage IV units. The strike variant was retired in 1996.

PROFILE

France's supersonic nuclear bomber

The Mirage IV was a Mirage III scaled up by a factor of approximately two to become a strategic nuclear bomber. It was an aircraft which was designed to fly so fast and so high that it could not be successfully intercepted by any fighter. Even now, decades after its first flight on 17 June 1959, the aircraft's performance is scarcely matched.

The Mirage IV became operational in 1964, when four squadrons totalling 62 aircraft enabled President de Gaulle to declare France separate from NATO and independent in world affairs.

The Mirage's original warload consisted of a 60-kiloton yield AN-22 free-fall nuclear bomb semi-recessed into the underside of the fuselage. When the Mirage was switched to low-level missions in the late 1960s, the AN-22 was fitted with a parachute retardation system.

Four aircraft were adapted for strategic reconnaissance, with a CT 52 reconnaissance pod fitting into the belly recess. The pod was usually equipped with six cameras and a mapping camera. An infra-red linescan camera could also be fitted for low-level all-weather missions.

Although clearly a great warplane, the Mirage IV never had the range to make a comfortable round trip to Russian targets, and pilots accepted that their missions might be one-way. Silo-based missiles have taken over the job of nuclear readiness, and the Mirage IV has now been retired, with the last reconnaissance variants being struck off the inventory in 2005.

The Mirage IV was a survivor from an era when delta-winged bombers were the cutting edge of major air forces. The Mirage was smaller than the Vulcan, B-58 and Myasishchev delta designs of the period, but was a good solution to the limited needs of the Force de Frappe.

Mirage IVA

Type: two-seat long-range bomber

Powerplant: two SNECMA Atar 9K-50 engines each rated at 70.61 kN (15,880 lb thrust) with afterburning

Maximum speed: Mach 2.20 or 2338 km/h (1,453 mph) 'clean' at 11,000 m (36,090 ft); 1350 km/h (839 mph) at sea level

Range: 4000 km (2,485 miles)

Service ceiling: 20,000 m (65,617 ft)

Weights: empty 14,500 kg (31,967 lb); loaded 31,600 kg (69,666 lb)

Armament: ASMP nuclear missile or six conventional bombs or four AS.37 Martel anti-radar missiles or one CT 52 sensor pod

Dimensions:		
	span	11.85 m (38 ft 11 in)
	length	23.50 m (77 ft 1 in))
	height	5.65 m (18 ft 6 in)
	wing area	78.00 m² (840 sq ft)

MIRAGE IVP

Nine squadrons were originally equipped with the Mirage IV. They remained on nuclear alert duty for more than 30 years until eventually being replaced by the Mirage 2000N.

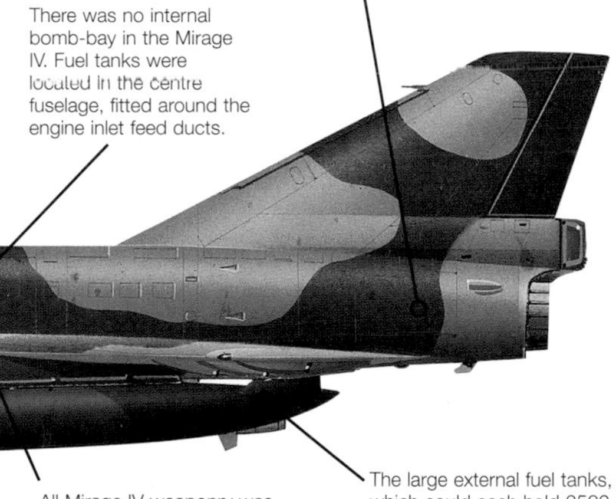

The Mirage IV was unusual in that its inflight-refuelling probe was located at the very front of the nose.

The navigator's main references were his radar screen and instruments, so the rear cockpit had only two small windows and a periscope to allow him a view below the aircraft.

Large airbrakes were mounted on the upper surfaces of the wingroot. The centre of the wing leading edge had a notch to control airflow over the wing upper surface.

There was no internal bomb-bay in the Mirage IV. Fuel tanks were located in the centre fuselage, fitted around the engine inlet feed ducts.

The twin Atar engines gave the Mirage IV twice as much power as most other Mirage variants. A brakechute was stored in the housing above the jetpipes.

A retractable spotlight was fitted to allow the crew to carry out night inflight-refuelling. An OMERA camera is located just ahead of it for post-strike damage assessment.

Both pilot and navigator were provided with Hispano-built Martin Baker BM.4 ejection seats. The pilot's cockpit had a two-panel 'knife edge' windscreen, reminiscent of American Convair fighter designs.

Unusually for a low-level strike aircraft, the Mirage IV had its radar mounted in the belly, not the nose. The navigator operated the Thomson-CSF Cerval radar warning system.

All Mirage IV weaponry was located on the external centre pylon. Jamming pods could be carried on wing outboard pylons.

The large external fuel tanks, which could each hold 2500 litres (660 US gal) of fuel, could be retained at supersonic speeds.

COMBAT DATA

MAXIMUM SPEED

The Mirage IV is very fast and can climb very high. Its only rival in the 1960s was the slightly earlier Convair B-58 Hustler, which was marginally slower. The American jet was much more powerful, however, and could carry a heavier bombload at supersonic speeds for much longer periods. The contemporary Soviet Tupolev was much slower, but could also carry more weapons.

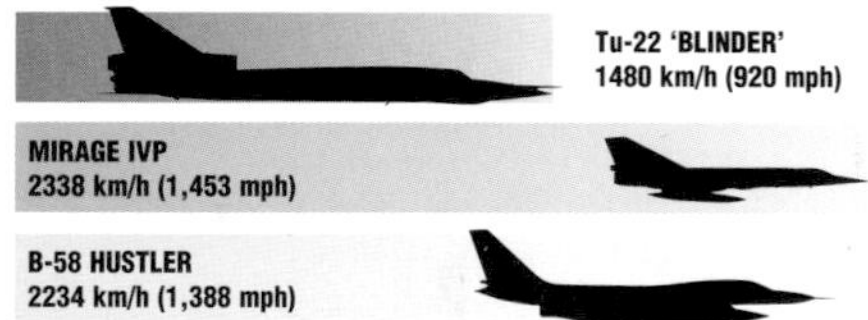

COMBAT RADIUS

The Mirage's major weakness was always its marginal range. Even with its internal and external fuel tanks, the prospect of making a successful mission deep into Soviet territory was slim at best. Aerial refuelling is essential for successful Mirage operations.

MIRAGE IVP
1250 km
(777 miles)

B-58 HUSTLER
4000 km
(2,485 miles)

Tu-22 'BLINDER'
3000 km
(1,864 miles)

WEAPONS LOAD

Although the Mirage IV can lift a fair weight of bombs, its normal nuclear load of one 60-kiloton weapon was not very large by comparison with the multi-megaton yields carried by the Hustler and 'Blinder'. The adoption of the ASMP missile with its larger warhead means that, even though the Mirage IVP is close to retirement, it is still a potent delivery system.

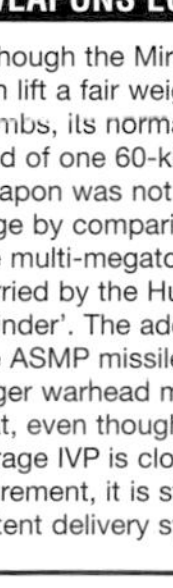

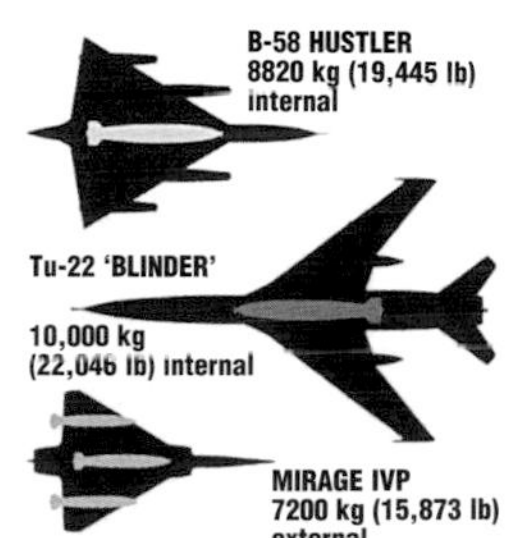

France's nuclear triad

▼ SEA-BASED DETERRENT: France has six nuclear-powered ballistic missile submarines. The least accurate component of the triad, the underwater launch platforms are also the most secure.

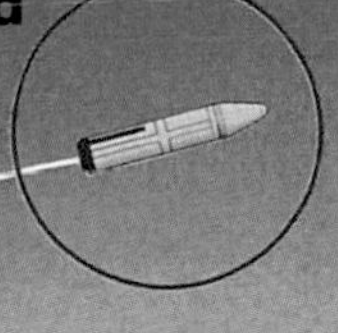

◀ M-4 MISSILE: Roughly equivalent to the American Poseidon, the M-4 has a range of between 4500 and 6000 km (2,800 and 3,730 miles).

◀ S-3 MISSILE: Carrying a 1.2-megaton warhead and with a range of 3500 km (2,175 miles), the S-3 is the most powerful component of the triad.

▶ ASMP: The Air-Sol-Moyen-Portée missile is a supersonic ramjet with a range of up to 250 km (155 miles) carrying a 300-kiloton warhead.

▲ LAND-BASED DETERRENT: Eighteen land-based missiles are very accurate, but are vulnerable to enemy action.

▲ AIRBORNE DETERRENT: Two squadrons of Mirage IVPs formed the smallest but most flexible portion of the deterrent triad.

DASSAULT-BREGUET

MIRAGE 4000

● **Interceptor and attack prototype** ● **Mach 2 performance**

Built as a private venture experimental prototype by Dassault-Breguet, the twin-engined Super Mirage 4000 drew on the experience gained in the development of the single-engined Mirage 2000 fighter. Capable of a speed exceeding Mach 2, it had the potential to be a worldbeater in its class. Budgetary cutbacks and the very high price tag of the new Mirage meant that it was not placed in production, despite its capability.

▲ *Powered by two SNECMA M.53 engines, as fitted to the smaller Mirage 2000, the 4000 prototype attained a speed of Mach 2.2 with ease on its sixth flight in April 1979.*

PHOTO FILE

DASSAULT-BREGUET MIRAGE 4000

▼ Composite construction
In order to save weight, extensive use was made of carbon fibre and boron composites in structures including the fin, rudder, elevons and foreplanes.

▲ Mirage 2000 and 4000 prototypes
The prototypes of the Mirage 2000 and 4000 flew within a year of each other, the former in March 1978.

▲ Mock-up first
Prior to assembly of the prototype, a full-scale mock-up was built. It was unveiled in December 1977.

▼ Eight-tonne bombload
The Mirage 4000 was able to carry over 8000 kg (17,600 lb.) of bombs, missiles and other equipment.

▲ Delta wings
The third-generation Mirages returned to the delta-wing design pioneered in the Mirage III/5 family of the 1960s.

FACTS AND FIGURES

- The Mirage 4000 design was heavily influenced by the cancelled Mirage F2 low-level attack aircraft.
- As many as 14 air-to-air missiles could be carried at once by the Mirage 4000.
- The prototype broke the speed of sound on its first flight, achieving Mach 1.2.
- Although a very capable aircraft, the 4000 offered little more than the smaller 2000, at considerably greater cost.
- Despite funding from Saudi Arabia, the type lost out to the F-15 and Tornado.
- Airbrakes are fitted above each wingroot leading edge.

PROFILE

Dassault's big delta prototype

Flying for the first time on 9 March 1979, the Mirage 4000 was a twin-engined interceptor and low-altitude attack prototype in the 20-tonne class. With a delta wing planform and canard foreplanes the Mirage 4000 employed fly-by-wire controls, but was a comparatively simple design with ease of maintenance on forward airfields in mind.

Its overall dimensions put it midway between the size of the F-14 Tomcat and the F/A-18 Hornet. The aircraft's twin engines provided a thrust-to-weight ratio greater than 1:1 in its original interceptor form.

The generous nose profile enabled the installation of a 80-cm (31-in.) radar dish which offered an effective range of 120 km (75 mi.).

Computer projection placed this apparently outstanding performance ahead of any other fighter in its class. Indeed, when the project was first announced in December 1975 the makers boldly assured potential export customers of the Mirage 4000's superiority over any similar aircraft in production or under development.

Although an operational version was envisaged, Dassault hoped to sell the type in export markets as well as to the Armée de l'Air as a replacement for the Mirage IV bomber, but orders did not materialise. What was destined to be the sole prototype has been used as a 'chase plane' during flight tests of the new Dassault Rafale advanced combat aircraft, the successor to the Mirage family.

Above: At an early stage of development the Mirage 4000 was known as the Super Mirage Delta.

Above: The prototype featured desert camouflage while flying in the Middle East. Despite the success of earlier Mirages in that region, the price tag of the 4000 deterred buyers.

Mirage 4000

Type: single-seat multi-role combat aircraft

Powerplant: two 95.13-kN (21,400-lb. thrust) SNECMA M.53 afterburning turbofans

Maximum speed: 2655 km/h (1,650 m.p.h.)

Initial climb rate: 18,300 m/min (60,039 f.p.m.)

Combat radius: 1850 km (1,150 mi.)

Service ceiling: 20,000 m (65,600 ft.)

Weights: combat 16,100 kg (35,494 lb.)

Armament: over 8000 kg (17,630 lb.) of external stores including bombs, rockets, air-to-air and air-to-surface missiles and cluster munitions

Dimensions:

span	12.00 m (39 ft. 4 in.)
length	18.70 m (61 ft. 4 in.)
wing area	73 m² (786 sq. ft.)

MIRAGE 4000

The prototype Mirage 4000 took to the air for the first time in early 1979. Despite an aggressive sales campaign by the makers, the prototype remains the sole example.

The powerful 80-cm RDM multi-mode radar is the same as that fitted to the Mirage 2000C interceptor.

A two-seat version of the Mirage 4000 was under study by Dassault-Breguet, but was not built.

Dassault-Breguet hoped for sales of the 4000 in the Middle East. For sales tours in the region it therefore carried a 'desert' camouflage.

To provide extra fuel capacity, the tailfin of the 4000 contains a fuel tank; other tanks are found in the wings and fuselage. External tanks can also be carried.

The Mirage 4000's flight-control system has been used as a technology demonstrator for the Rafale combat aircraft.

Provision was made for two DEFA 30-mm cannon and up to 11 pylons for external stores, including weapons and fuel tanks.

MATRA Magic missiles were among the variety of air-to-air weapons which the 4000 could carry for self-defence.

Power was provided by two SNECMA M.53 turbofan engines, which gave the 4000 a thrust-to-weight ratio in the same class as that of the F-15 or Sukhoi Su-27.

COMBAT DATA

MAXIMUM SPEED

A top speed of over Mach 2 is a necessity for a modern, long-range, high-altitude interceptor designed to defeat waves of bombers or cruise missiles. The F-15 and Su-27 represent the most capable interceptors in service.

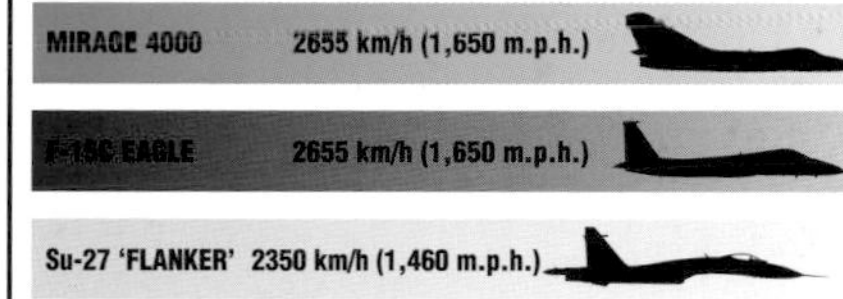

RANGE

The range of the Sukhoi Su-27 reflects the size and fuel-carrying capacity of an aircraft designed to defend the vast area of the Soviet Union. The first export customer for the Su-27, China, has similarly large areas to patrol. The F-15 and Mirage 4000 carry the same fuel load, with tanks, as an Su-27 carries internally.

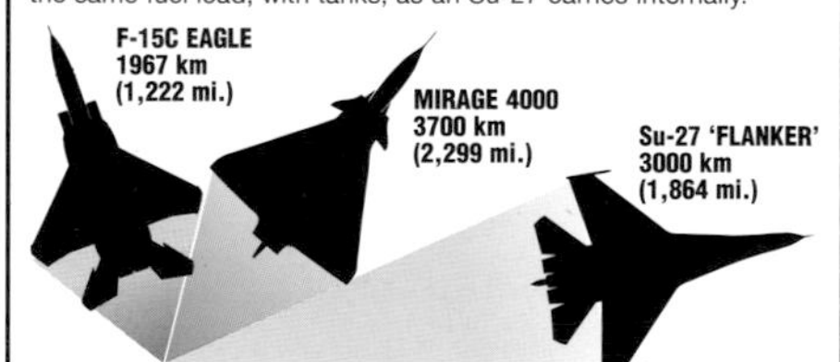
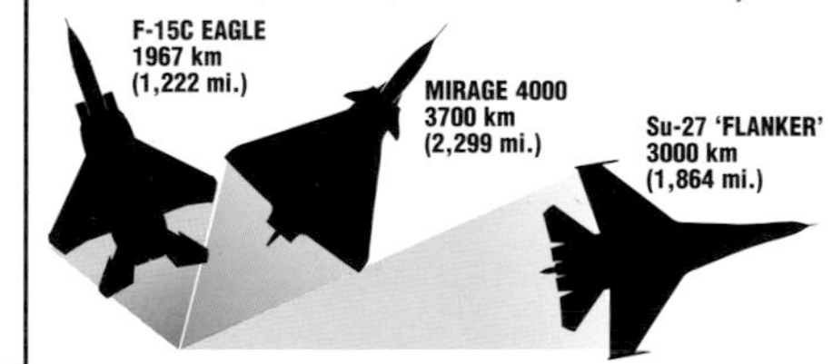

CLIMB RATE

Interceptors need to be able to climb quickly to the altitude of attacking aircraft. A power-to-weight ratio better than 1:1 allows excellent rates of climb. All three types have twin engines which give the aircraft exceptional power.

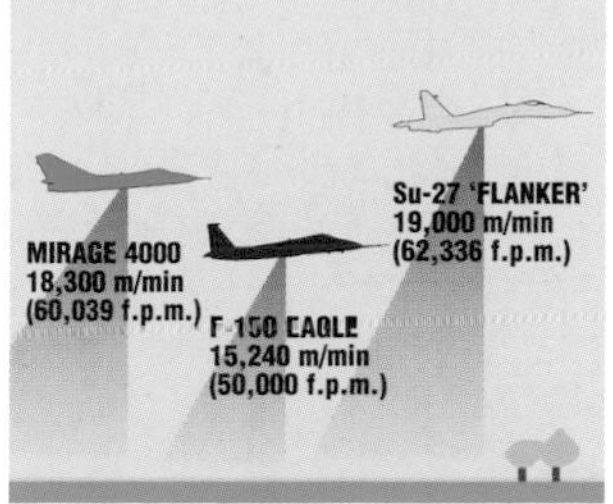

The Dassault Mirage family

MIRAGE III/5: This Mach 2 delta-wing fighter and fighter-bomber provided the core of the French air forces in the 1960s and 1970s and won large foreign orders.

MIRAGE IV: This was a scaled-up, twin-engined bomber version of the Mirage delta, designed with a nuclear capability. The prototype first flew in 1959.

MIRAGE F1: The second-generation Mirage multi-role aircraft intended to replace the Mirage III and 5, the F1 discarded the delta wing for a more conventional layout.

MIRAGE 2000: Fly-by-wire controls solved the handling problems found in delta-winged aircraft. The prototype flew in 1978, and fighter, attack and reconnaissance versions followed.

DE HAVILLAND

DH.110 SEA VIXEN

● Carrier fighter ● All-weather interceptor ● Attack fighter

With its twin engines and armed with missiles, the Sea Vixen replaced the single-engined, gun-equipped Sea Venom aboard Royal Navy aircraft-carriers. At the time of its selection it represented a major step forward for the Fleet Air Arm, and its career came to an end only when the navy was forced to give up its flat-top carriers. Yet by the time it entered service naval fighter design had moved into the era of the Mach 2 Phantom.

▲ *The Sea Vixen's powerful radar and missile armament was a great leap forward, and together with the Scimitar and Buccaneer it provided the backbone of the Royal Navy's carrier force in the 1960s.*

PHOTO FILE

DE HAVILLAND DH.110 SEA VIXEN

▲ Air-to-air missile armament
The FAW.Mk 1 introduced guided missiles to the Royal Navy, with the de Havilland Firestreak. Up to four of these could be carried in addition to internal rockets.

Take-off ▶
The Sea Vixen was regarded as a safe aircraft, but the observer had little chance to escape if the aircraft ditched after take-off. The catapult strop can be seen under the aircraft, falling into the sea.

▲ Refuelling the Buccaneer
As well as receiving fuel, the Sea Vixen could fill up other aircraft from its own refuelling pods.

▲ Improved interceptor
The FAW.Mk 2 was a great improvement, with new infra-red guided Red Top missiles, air-to-surface missiles and additional fuel in the tailbooms.

◀ Fleet fighter
At its peak the Sea Vixen served with a Royal Navy display team, known as 'Simon's Sircus', and performed at air shows.

FACTS AND FIGURES

- ➤ The Sea Vixen FAW.Mk 2 first flew on 8 March 1963 and was received by the first squadrons later in the year.
- ➤ The prototype Sea Vixen first flew on 26 September 1951 after long delays.
- ➤ Sea Vixen FAW.Mk 2s were used by Nos 890, 892, 893 and 899 air squadrons.
- ➤ Sea Vixens from HMS *Eagle* intercepted Soviet Tu-16 'Badger' bombers near a NATO exercise in 1968.
- ➤ A specification (N 40/46) for the Sea Vixen was issued as early as 1945.
- ➤ With AI.18 radar and Firestreak missiles, the Sea Vixen was an all-weather fighter.

PROFILE

The fighter that came too late

Delays ruined the career of the Sea Vixen. The first DH.110 prototype flew in 1951, but was destroyed in a crash, which delayed the navy order. It was also not chosen as the Royal Air Force's new fighter, losing out to the Javelin in 1952. By 1955 a naval version had flown, but it was 1960 before the first Sea Vixen FAW.Mk 1s went to sea.

One feature that marked the Sea Vixen as a modern fighter for its day was its armament of four Firestreak infra-red homing missiles. Another was the large nose radome. The radar was responsible for one of the most unusual characteristics of the Sea Vixen: lack of a canopy for the observer. His compartment was on the right side of the fuselage, and was enclosed to make the most of the dim screen of the radar display.

The FAW.Mk 2 Sea Vixen was armed with the new Red Top missile and had longer tailbooms which extended ahead of the wing leading edges in order to carry more fuel. Although they did not see combat, Sea Vixens were the main armament of Britain's aircraft-carriers until the early 1970s. The last Sea Vixen squadron disbanded in 1972.

Above: An FAW.Mk 1 leaps into the air from a land base, carrying four dummy Firestreak missiles and the outer pylon fuel tanks that were a standard feature.

Right: The first British fighter without internal guns, the Sea Vixen carried 28 51-mm (2-in) rockets instead.

Sea Vixen FAW.Mk 2

Type: two-seat all-weather shipboard interceptor fighter

Powerplant: two 49.96-kN (11,237-lb-thrust) Rolls-Royce Avon RA.28 Mk 208 15-stage axial-flow turbojets

Maximum speed: 1030 km/h (640 mph) at altitude

Initial climb rate: 3050 m/min (10,000 fpm)

Range: 2260 km (1,404 miles)

Service ceiling: 14,630 m (48,000 ft)

Weights: maximum take-off 16,783 kg (37,000 lb)

Armament: 28 51-mm (2-in) rockets in underfuselage Microcell pack, plus 2000 kg (4,400 lb) of weapons on four underwing pylons

Dimensions:

span	15.24 m (50 ft)
length	16.94 m (55 ft 7 in)
height	3.28 m (10 ft 9 in)
wing area	60.19 m² (648 sq ft)

SEA VIXEN FAW.MK 2

This Sea Vixen served with No. 892 Squadron of the Royal Navy, and was detached to the 'Simon's Sircus' display team during 1968. The five Sea Vixens carried smoke-generating equipment and painted fuel tanks.

The pilot had a good view from his offset bubble canopy, but the radar operator was 'buried' in the opposite fuselage side.

The outer two out of six wing stores hardpoints were almost always used for the carriage of external fuel tanks to improve the Sea Vixen's already impressive range. The drop-tanks could be jettisoned to improve the aircraft's performance.

A wide range of defensive and attack stores could be carried on the remaining four pylons, typically Red Top or Firestreak air-to-air missiles, 454-kg (1,000-lb) bombs, Bullpup air-to-surface missiles or 96 additional 51-mm (2-in) rockets in four Microcell packs.

The large area wing was reminiscent of that on the de Havilland DH.108, the first British aircraft to exceed the speed of sound.

The distinctive twin-boom layout was inherited from the earlier Vampire and Venom fighters, and provided good stability.

The Sea Vixen's main sensor was the AI.18 radar in the nose. The radome hinged to starboard for maintenance.

A single refuelling probe projected from the wing leading edge. Refuelling pods could be carried on underwing pylons.

Twin Microcell glass-reinforced plastic packs in the bottom of the fuselage each contained 14 unguided 51-mm (2-in) rockets, but these were rarely used.

For carrier operations the Sea Vixen carried a hydraulically operated arrestor hook between the Rolls-Royce Avon engine tailpipes.

COMBAT DATA

MAXIMUM SPEED

Although it had immense power, the Sea Vixen also suffered from high drag, and was only supersonic in a dive. The F-8 was a much faster machine thanks to its J79 engine and sleek airframe.

RANGE

The large fuselage could hold lots of fuel and the Sea Vixen therefore had long range. The F3H also had a good range, but only because its poor engines were not able to convert the fuel to power quickly enough.

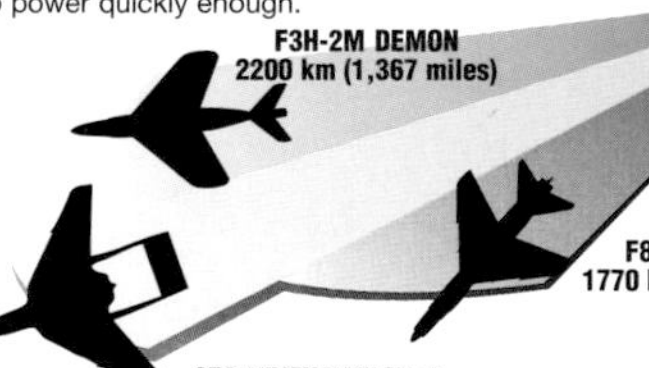

ARMAMENT

Designers in the late 1950s were obsessed with building fighters capable of launching guided missiles. The Crusader could fire the only radar-guided version of Sidewinder, the AIM-9C.

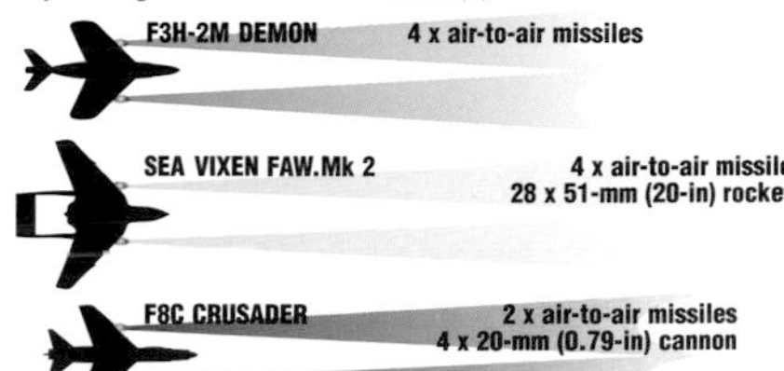

Fleet Air Arm fast jets

BLACKBURN BUCCANEER: A specially designed low-level high-speed strike aircraft, the Buccaneer also served with the RAF.

DE HAVILLAND SEA VENOM: The Royal Navy's first all-weather jet fighter, the Sea Venom served from the mid-1950s until 1960.

McDONNELL DOUGLAS PHANTOM: The US-built but Rolls-Royce Spey-powered Phantom was the Royal Navy's best carrier-based fighter.

SUPERMARINE SCIMITAR: Entering service in 1957, the twin-engined Scimitar was the FAA's first swept-wing single-seat fighter.

Douglas AC-47 'Spooky'

● C-47 conversion ● Vietnam War gunship ● Minigun armament

▲ By the time C-47s were undergoing conversion to 'Spooky' standard in the mid-1960s, the venerable but versatile Skytrains were all at least 20 years old.

Experiments with the 'gunship' concept began in the United States in the early 1960s, as a means of bringing accurate, concentrated fire to bear on an enemy position from the air. Some USAF generals were sceptical at first, concerned that an aircraft in such a position would be vulnerable to enemy fire. As soon as the first armed C-47s began to fly combat missions in Vietnam in late 1964, however, the concept proved its worth.

PHOTO FILE

Douglas AC-47 'Spooky'

Widely employed ▶
Two units were equipped with 'Spooky' – 4th Air Commando Squadron (at Da Nang, Pleiku, Phu Cat and Nha Trang) and 14th Air Commando Squadron (at Nha Trang, Phan Rang, Bien Hoa and Binh Thuy).

◀ Eight crew members
'Spooky' missions were manned by seven USAF personnel and a Vietnamese observer.

▲ Psy-war operations
As well as AC-47s, the USAF used a small number of EC-47s for leaflet-dropping missions.

▲ Southeast Asia camouflage
In common with most other tactical types in the Southeast Asian theatre, the 'Magic Dragons' were finished in three-tone colours with light-coloured under surfaces.

Minigun pods ▶
General Electric's SUU-11 gun pods were intended for underwing mountings on smaller COIN aircraft, but were adapted for use in the AC-47. Each was manned by a gunner.

FACTS AND FIGURES

- The 'Puff the Magic Dragon' nickname came from a popular song of the same name released in the 1960s.
- In 1965 prices, the first 20 AC-47Ds were converted for US $4,288,975.
- For target illumination at night, each AC-47 carried 56 hand-dropped flares.
- During its first 11 days of use the first AC-47 flew seven training and 16 combat missions; 179,710 rounds were fired.
- The aircraft captain in the left-hand pilot's seat could aim and fire all the guns.
- By the end of 1965, AC-47s were based in Thailand for service over Laos.

PROFILE

'Puff the Magic Dragon'

Originally known as the FC-47 (suggesting a 'fighter' variant), the gun toting version of the long-serving 'Gooney Bird' transport was soon known by the more appropriate AC-47 designation and by the code name 'Spooky'.

The gunship concept, of which the AC-47D was the first example, was based on a large fixed-wing aircraft flying in a pylon turn to bring fire down on a target using fuselage-mounted sideways-firing rotary Miniguns. From the outset, 'Spooky' was seen as a night weapon, flares being used to illuminate targets. The first night mission was flown on 23/24 December 1964 and was deemed successful. AC-47s were able to loiter for long periods over suspected Viet Cong ground positions.

Soon nicknamed 'Puff the Magic Dragon' after a song of the same name, the AC-47D paved the way for further gunship development, based on the C-119 and C-130. Once these were in service, most AC-47s were transferred to the VNAF.

Above: Around 25 C-47s were converted to AC-47D standard, the first entering service with the 4th Air Commando Squadron in late 1965.

Right: Among other 'special mission' C-47s to serve in Southeast Asia were a small number of EC-47N electronic reconnaissance platforms.

AC-47D 'Spooky'

Type: counter-insurgency gunship

Powerplant: two 820-kW (1,100-hp) Pratt & Whitney R-1830-90D Twin Wasp radial piston engines

Maximum speed: 257 km/h (160 mph)

Initial climb rate: 3050 m (10,000 ft) in 9.5 min

Normal range: 2575 km (1,600 miles)

Service ceiling: (typical) 914 m (3,000 ft)

Weights: empty 8226 kg (18,135 lb); maximum 14,061 kg (31,000 lb)

Armament: three fuselage-mounted 7.62-mm (0.3-in) General Electric SUU-11A Miniguns, each with a 6000 round-per-minute rate of fire

Dimensions:		
	span	29.11 m (95 ft 6 in)
	length	19.43 m (63 ft 9 in)
	height	17.00 m (55 ft 9 in)
	wing area	91.69 m² (987 sq ft)

AC-47D 'Spooky'

The USAF's 4th Commando Air Squadron based at Tan Son Nhut Air Base was charged with introducing the AC-47, doing so in late 1964. Delays had been experienced in the supply of Miniguns.

On 8 February 1965 a 'Magic Dragon' was sent to the Bong Son area in the face of a Viet Cong offensive in the Central Highlands. In under five hours, the gunship poured 20,500 rounds of 7.62-mm (0.3-in) ammunition into a hilltop where the VC were dug in. More than 300 soldiers were killed.

For night operations, 'Spooky' was fitted with a flare dispensing system to illuminate targets for the attentions of the gunners and their Miniguns. Originally it had been intended to convert Convair C-131s for the role, but the Douglas transport was available in larger numbers.

Fire-control equipment in the AC-47D was almost nonexistent. The pilot used a gunsight mounted in the port cockpit window, through which he viewed the target.

Gunship aircraft operated at relatively low altitudes and were camouflaged to reduce their vulnerability in their new role. By the late 1960s, aircraft were carrying a three-tone green and brown Southeast Asia colour scheme, with white unit codes on the tailfin.

Initial AC-47 conversions were fitted with four air-cooled 12.7-mm (0.5-in) machine guns. These were soon replaced by three far more effective General Electric SUU-11A six-barrelled rotary Miniguns of 7.62-mm (0.3-in) calibre. One of these was mounted in the cargo doorway, the other two in the rearmost cabin windows.

GUNSHIP FIREPOWER

'SHADOW' and 'STINGER': To increase the firepower available to gunship units, the USAF chose the C-119 Packet as the basis for its next generation of 'Magic Dragon'. The first of 52 were delivered in 1968, the AC-119G featuring four Minigun pods and new sensors, including a illuminator light set and night observation gear. More conversions followed; 26 AC-119Ks had underwing jet booster engines and two 20-mm (0.79-in) rotary cannon added.

'SPECTRE': During 1967 an AC-130A prototype was converted and tested in Vietnam. Night flying aids and improved sensors helped guide the aircraft, which boasted no fewer than four Miniguns and four 20-mm (0.79-in) rotary cannon. Successful trials led to seven more C-130A conversions. These were put to work 'truck hunting' along the Ho Chi Minh Trail. Later examples carried a 40-mm (1.57-in) Bofors cannon, side-looking radar and a laser designator.

Special missions transports over Vietnam

DOUGLAS EC-47: As well as the gunship role, C-47s in Southeast Asia were assigned electronic intelligence and 'psy-war' tasks.

FAIRCHILD UC-123K PROVIDER: Fitted with spray bars, C-123s were used on Ranch Hand defoliant-spraying missions.

LOCKHEED DC-130E HERCULES: USAF C-130s (like this USN example) launched and directed spy drones over targets in the North.

LOCKHEED HC-130H HERCULES: Specially-equipped 'Herks' co-ordinated combat rescue missions to retrieve downed aircrew.

Douglas

A-1 Skyraider (Korea)

● Strike fighter ● Piston-engine attack ● Carrier aircraft

▲ *Nicknamed the 'Spad' by its adoring pilots, the Skyraider proved that the age of the jet was not complete. Delivering ordnance with pinpoint accuracy long after the last jets had gone home, the Skyraider also proved better able to absorb massive battle damage.*

Able to deliver an incredible array of ordnance, the Skyraider's origins began with the Douglas Dauntless of World War II fame. Incredibly strong with a good performance, the A-1 long outlived its anticipated life until people believed that the only replacement for the Skyraider was another Skyraider! It was in the Korean War that the early models of the aircraft began to prove that, carrier- or land-based, the Skyraider had few equals in combat.

PHOTO FILE

Douglas A-1 Skyraider

▼ Airfield beat-up

Even with a load of bombs and rockets, the Skyraider could still thunder less than 30 m (100 ft) above the runway at around 550 km/h (342 mph). Pilots loved the aircraft's low-level performance.

▲ Rocket raider

A favourite Skyraider tactic was unguided rocket attacks. Up to a dozen 127-mm (5-in) rockets could be carried, or two massive 30-cm (11.8-in) 'Tiny Tim' weapons, as well as the powerful 20-mm (0.79-in) cannon.

First of many ▶

A few early Skyraiders were finished in bare metal, but most were painted dark blue.

▼ Hooking up

With the ability to make lower speed approaches than a jet, the AD-1 was easier to land on deck.

'Tiny Tim' ▶

With its speedbrakes deployed just behind the wing, this AD-1 reveals its load, including a pair of huge 'Tiny Tim' rockets. The AD-4 could carry more than its own weight.

FACTS AND FIGURES

- In a raid in May 1951, AD-1s flying from USS ***Princeton*** used aerial torpedoes to burst a North Korean dam at Hwachon.
- The XBT2D of 1945 was the first US single-seater dive/torpedo bomber.
- The Skyraider was able to carry more ordnance than a wartime B-17 Fortress.
- In 1952, a US pilot successfully landed his Skyraider after having been blinded by a shell hit.
- Skyraiders were also used in Vietnam, where two aircraft shot down MiG-17s.
- In Korea, the Skyraiders carried every weapon in the US Navy arsenal.

PROFILE

'Spad' goes to war in Korea

Making its maiden flight on 18 March 1945 as the XBT2D-1, the aircraft that became the Skyraider was designed by the legendary Ed Heinemann. In 1946 it looked set for a peaceful and probably brief career as an 'old-fashioned' piston-engined attack aircraft in the new jet age. The Skyraider's career was in fact anything but mundane, thanks to its fine showing in the Korean War. Proving that 'low and slow' still produced results in ground-attack work, the AD squadrons of the US Navy and Marine Corps gave outstanding air support to United Nations ground forces.

By integrating air strikes with the faster jets which acted as escorts, the Skyraider pilots flying off Task Force 77's carriers could go in unmolested by enemy air attack. The main hazard was from ground fire, a fact of life faced equally by land-based Marine Corps AD units. Combat flying in the Skyraider gave pilots the reassurance that their aircraft could take a great deal of punishment and still fly home.

The AD-1 first entered Navy service in November 1946 and it soon became clear that the basic design was immensely versatile. Being such a large aircraft (for a single-seater), the Skyraider could accommodate a second seat and the necessary equipment inside the fuselage for a radar/ECM operator. This version, the AD-1Q, covered 35 airframes out of the total 242 AD-1 Skyraiders built.

Left: The Skyraider was also fitted with underwing radar. A few XBT2D destroyers were completed with an underwing searchlight and room for a second crewmember.

Above: Although considered obsolete just after its inception, the Skyraider was still fighting in Chad as late as 1979.

AD-1 Skyraider

Type: single-seat ground-attack aircraft

Powerplant: one 2252-kW (3,020-hp) Wright R-3350-26W Cyclone radial engine

Maximum speed: 498 km/h (309 mph)

Range: 1448 km (900 miles)

Service ceiling: 9753 m (32,000 ft)

Weights: empty 4577 kg (10,091 lb); loaded 8178 kg (18,029 lb)

Armament: four 20-mm (0.79-in) cannon in wings, plus mixed ordnance including bombs, napalm and unguided folded-fin aircraft rockets on centreline and wing stores stations

Dimensions:

	span	15.24 m (50 ft)
	length	11.63 m (38 ft 2 in)
	height	4.7 m (15 ft 5 in)
	wing area	37.16 m² (400 sq ft)

AD-1 Skyraider

The mainstay of the US Navy's carrier-borne attack force in Korea, the AD-1 entered service in 1946 and was only finally retired in 1968 during the Vietnam War.

The large cockpit was a typical feature of late American piston fighters. Topped by a bubble canopy offering excellent visibility, it had no ejector seat and pilots 'bailed out' manually.

The single 1470-litre (388-US gal) fuel tank was located just behind the pilot, next to the radio and avionics racks. The large twin speedbrakes were located on the fuselage sides just behind it.

Much of the Skyraider's success was due to the superb Wright R-3350 two-row radial engine, which was powerful and reliable.

Massive strength was built into the wing. Several Skyraiders made it home after taking hits from flak shells of up to 37 mm (1.46 in).

The AD-1 was equipped with a sturdy tailhook for arrester landings on carriers. The distinctive Skyraider tail shape was one feature that hardly changed between versions.

COMBAT DATA

MAXIMUM SPEED

For a piston-engined fighter-bomber, the AD-1 was quite fast; however, even the early jets could outrun it. The wartime Il-10 could not match post-war aircraft.

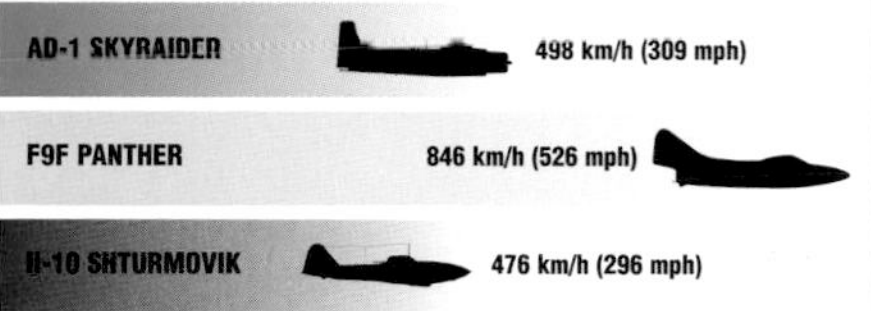

ARMAMENT

Few jet fighters could match an AD-1's weapon load until the mid-1960s, and most did not have the same firepower from their guns either. The Il-10 was designed for anti-armour attack and usually carried eight rockets in addition to its powerful cannons.

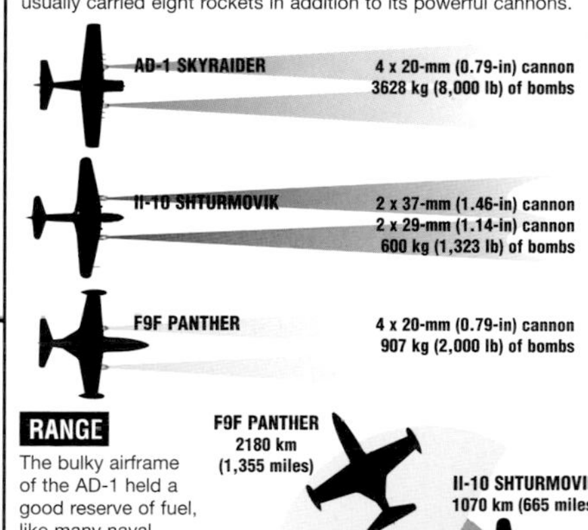

RANGE

The bulky airframe of the AD-1 held a good reserve of fuel, like many naval aircraft. The Il-10 was designed for tactical support from front-line airfields and had short range. Early jets usually had short range and most were inferior to the AD-1.

F9F PANTHER 2180 km (1,355 miles)

Il-10 SHTURMOVIK 1070 km (665 miles)

AD-1 SKYRAIDER 1448 km (900 miles)

Deck landing signals for carrier pilots

TOO LOW: The most dangerous condition was too low, as the pilot risked striking the carrier's stern.

TOO HIGH: Both hands raised told the pilot that he was too high to make a safe approach to the deck.

ONE WING HIGH: If the pilot had too much bank on, the deck officer gave a 'one wing high' signal to him.

WAVE-OFF: This signal told the pilot to terminate the approach because it looked unsafe to the deck officer.

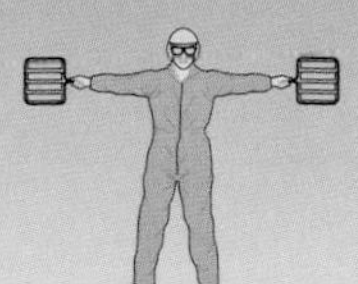

SAFE TO LAND: If the aircraft had wings level at the right height, the deck officer gave the pilot this signal.

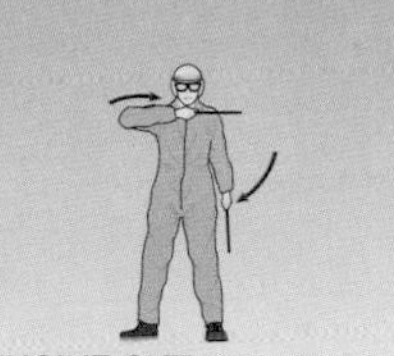

ENGINE CUT: Once he saw the arrestor catch the tail-hook, the deck officer gave the signal to 'cut engines'.

DOUGLAS

A-1 SKYRAIDER (VIETNAM)

● Vietnam warbird ● Versatile strike fighter ● Rescue support

Near the end of its long American career, the Douglas A-1 Skyraider became a Vietnam rescue craft, known by its call-sign 'Sandy'. The A-1 pilot's task was complex: he had to locate and protect shot-down air crew while directing rescue helicopters and other support aircraft to make a pick-up, all in the face of strenuous efforts by the North Vietnamese to prevent the rescue. In spite of the fact that it was old, noisy and rather slow, the hard-hitting Skyraider was more than able to do the job.

▲ *Major Bernie Fisher carried out an amazing rescue in Vietnam in 1966, actually landing his A-1 in the A Shau valley to pick up his squadron buddy, Major Datford Myers.*

PHOTO FILE

DOUGLAS A-1 SKYRAIDER (VIETNAM)

◀ Primed to fight
Rockets hang from the wings of a Skyraider. The red tapes are flags attached to safety pins, which prevented weapons being armed by accident during handling on the ground. The white phosphorus rockets were used as target-markers.

▲ Jungle colours
The jungle camouflage of this Skyraider had some chance of fooling North Vietnamese MiG fighters, but it was little protection against the main enemy – anti-aircraft fire.

▲ Rescue team
A pair of 'Sandys' escort an OV-10 Bronco. The OV-10 acted as a forward air-control station, coordinating the rescue and target-spotting. A-1 pilots and controllers worked very closely together.

▲ Navy mission
Powerful piston engines roar into life as Navy A-1s prepare for a mission. The naval ancestry of the Skyraider can be seen in the folding wings, designed to take up less deck space on a carrier.

▼ Built like a tank
Pilots also called the A-1 the 'Spad', as its chunky appearance was reminiscent of the robust biplane fighter used by the United States during World War I.

FACTS AND FIGURES

- Between 1945 and 1956, 3180 Skyraiders were built.
- The maiden flight of the A-1 was made at Mines Field, California, on 18 March 1945.
- The last wartime use of aerial torpedoes occurred when Skyraiders attacked the Yalu River dams in the Korean War.
- In Vietnam, propeller-driven A-1 Skyraiders shot down two jet-propelled MiG-17 fighters.
- Some Vietnamese air force pilots logged over 4000 combat hours in the Skyraider.
- Skyraiders were still engaged in a shooting war in Chad as late as 1979.

PROFILE

Pilot pick-up in Vietnam

American fliers rescued in Vietnam in 1969 were glad that Ed Heinemann designed the Douglas A-1 (AD) Skyraider in a hotel room in 1944. One of the last great piston-engined combat planes, the Skyraider was big, tough, and an incredible performer. Known by their callsign 'Sandy', Skyraiders were the key element in the US air force rescue organization in Southeast Asia. Directing and protecting the rescue force, the ageing bombers also kept the enemy away from aircrew stranded on the ground.

The rescue mission in Vietnam was tailor-made for a heavy, sturdy combat aircraft which carried enough fuel to loiter for extended periods and enough bombs to wreck the enemy's day.

Two Skyraider pilots were awarded the Medal of Honor for Vietnam action, and a 'Jolly Green' rescue helicopter escorted by A-1s became a familiar sight. 'Sandy' pilots managed 300 rescues from 1965 until turning the job over to the A-7D Corsair II in 1972.

The A-1E was a multi-role variant of the Skyraider. Originally designated AD-5, it was easily identifiable by its enlarged side-by-side cockpit. Fitted out for transport it could carry 12 passengers.

A-1H Skyraider

Type: single-seat carrier-based attack bomber

Powerplant: one 2013-kW (2,700-hp) Wright R-3350-26WA 18-cylinder radial piston engine

Maximum speed: 518 km/h (322 mph)

Range: 2000 km (1,243 miles)

Service ceiling: 8685 m (28,494 ft)

Weights: empty 5429 kg (11,969 lb); loaded 11,340 kg (25,000 lb)

Armament: four wing-mounted 20-mm (0.79-in) M3 cannon with 200 rounds per gun plus up to 3629 kg (8,000 lb) of bombs or rockets on one under-fuselage and 14 underwing hardpoints

Dimensions:		
	span	15.25 m (50 ft)
	length	11.84 m (38 ft 10 in)
	height	4.78 m (15 ft 7 in)
	wing area	37.19 m² (400 sq ft)

The original ground-attack Skyraider was fitted with a pair of 20-mm (0.79-in) cannon, but by the end of the aircraft's production run four cannon were standard, and most aircraft involved in Vietnam had them.

A-1H SKYRAIDER

At the beginning of the Vietnam War the A-1 was still serving aboard US Navy carriers. This example was flown by the commander of VA-52 aboard the USS *Ticonderoga* in the early 1960s.

The 18-cylinder Wright R-3350 engine could survive serious battle damage. It kicked out a lot of oil, however, much of which was deposited on the fuselage.

Fuel was carried in one large tank in the fuselage behind the pilot. When external tanks were added, the A-1 could loiter over a rescue scene for several hours.

With 14 underwing hardpoints, the Skyraider could carry a fearsome variety of weaponry. Typical loads included bombs, rockets and smoke markers up to a total weight of more than 3600 kg (7937 lb).

In the early stages of the war Navy A-1s were used to bomb conventional targets in North Vietnam. For rescue missions, a wider range of weaponry could be carried.

Designed as a torpedo- and dive-bomber, the Skyraider was fitted with huge divebrakes on the sides of and below the fuselage.

The folding wings, tailhook and sturdy undercarriage were naval features that were found on all Skyraider variants.

COMBAT DATA

MAXIMUM SPEED

The Skyraider was a World War II aircraft, and in terms of pure speed was no match for the jet-powered A-4 of the early 1950s, let alone the sheer Mach 2 power of the Phantom II of 1960. But speed is not everything in combat, and the A-1 had virtues the other two classic fighters lacked.

A-1 SKYRAIDER 518 km/h (322 mph)

A-4 SKYHAWK 1040 km/h (646 mph)

F-4 PHANTOM 2300 km/h (1429 mph)

MISSION FLEXIBILITY

The Skyraider may not have been able to carry as much weight of ordnance as the more powerful jets, but with 14 hardpoints under the wings and one under the fuselage it could carry and deliver a greater variety of weapons on a single mission than almost any other fighting plane giving the A-1 the flexibility to fly different missions.

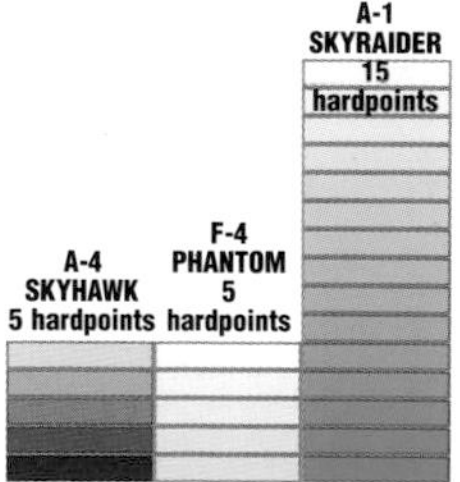

LOITER TIME

Compared to a jet, piston engines are extremely economical. The Skyraider might have been slow, but it could fly out to a rescue site, call in some fast jets to make an attack, direct the rescue helicopters to make the pick-up while the jets refuelled, call in the fast movers again, then escort the whole force clear of enemy territory – all on a single load of fuel.

A-1 SKYRAIDER 7 hours

A-4 SKYHAWK 4 hours

F-4 PHANTOM 3 hours

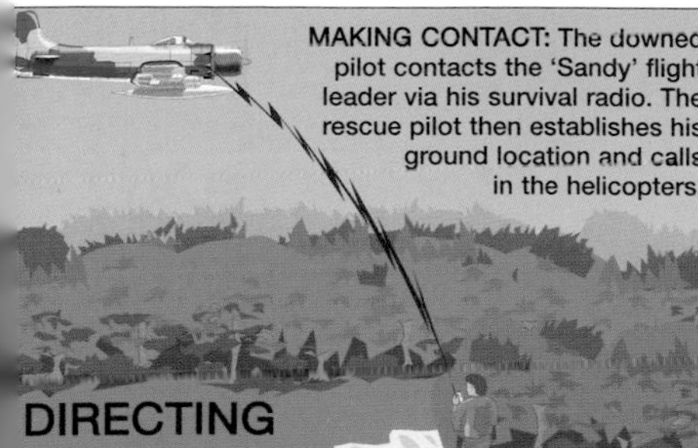

MAKING CONTACT: The downed pilot contacts the 'Sandy' flight leader via his survival radio. The rescue pilot then establishes his ground location and calls in the helicopters.

DRIVING OFF THE ENEMY: The 'Sandy' Skyraider deliberately draws fire to locate enemy positions. Any enemy troops approaching too close to the person to be rescued are engaged with cannon, bombs and rockets.

RESCUE: As the 'Jolly Green Giant' rescue helicopter makes the pick-up, 'Sandy' stands guard from above, ensuring that enemy ground forces cannot interfere.

DOUGLAS

C-54 SKYMASTER

● Four-engined long-range transport ● Three hundred in Operation 'Vittles'

When the Soviets sealed off Berlin in 1948, the large, four-engined Douglas C-54 Skymaster was the right aircraft at the right time. The Berlin Airlift began in late June 1948, the first major confrontation of the Cold War. The Allies had a variety of aircraft types at their disposal, in particular the C-47. Its age, however, was beginning to show, and it was the more capable C-54 that was to become the mainstay of the airlift.

▲ *At the peak of the round-the-clock supply of Berlin, flights in and out of Tempelhof, Tegel and Gatow took place every 90 seconds. An aircraft remained on the ground in Berlin for just 30 minutes.*

PHOTO FILE

DOUGLAS C-54 SKYMASTER

Presidential Skymaster ▶
President Truman used this VC-54C, known as the 'Sacred Cow', to visit 55 countries between 1944 and 1947. It was retired in 1961.

▲ Backbone of the Airlift
Over 300 USAF Skymasters took part in the Berlin Airlift, drawn from units based around the world.

▼ Navy and Marine Corps
R5D was the designation given to Navy and Marine Corps Skymasters; more than 200 were delivered during World War II.

▲ In almost all weathers
Tempelhof airport, Berlin, was covered in snow on 1 March 1949. High winds, poor visibility and icy conditions forced flights to stop the night before.

Operation 'Vittles' ▶
USAF participation in the airlift was codenamed 'Vittles'. Here a Skymaster, loaded with supplies, is on its final run into Tempelhof.

FACTS AND FIGURES

- ➤ US, British and Commonwealth transports carried 545,651 tonnes (601,477 tons) of food to the people of Berlin.
- ➤ The total tonnage of cargo airlifted was equivalent to one tonne per Berliner.
- ➤ The RAF's airlift flights were codenamed Operation 'Plainfare'.
- ➤ The airlift's single-day record of 12,940 tonnes (14,264 tons) in 1398 sorties was set during the 'Easter Parade' of April 1949.
- ➤ Berlin, 160 km (100 miles) into East German territory, was served by three air corridors.
- ➤ Over 1000 C-54s were built for the US Air Force in all, plus over 200 for the Navy.

PROFILE

Mainstay of the Berlin Airlift

A lifeline of transport aircraft kept Berlin alive during the 1948/49 Russian blockade. At the time, the Berlin Airlift was the largest major humanitarian operation ever undertaken by air. Many Allied aircraft flew supplies into Berlin, but the Douglas C-54 Skymaster was perhaps the best known.

The C-54 entered service with the USAAF in 1942, the earliest examples coming off the DC-4 production line after it was commandeered when the United States entered World War II.

Much of the Berlin Airlift consisted of flying food from Western Europe into the surrounded German city. As no supplies of any type were able to reach Berlin by road, some aircraft were modified to carry other commodities such as coal and fuel oil.

Flying conditions were often hazardous. The pilot of a C-54 flying into Berlin knew that a transport was taking off or landing every few minutes, that the weather could deteriorate to zero-zero conditions without warning and that the Soviets might harass or even shoot at Skymasters as they attempted the difficult, short-field landing at Tempelhof airport. After over 2.3 million tonnes of cargo had been airlifted, the blockade ended on 30 September 1949.

Left: Eight squadrons of USAF C-54s served in the Berlin Airlift, replacing C-47s from late 1948. As well as being more reliable, they had a greater payload.

Right: The Military Air Transport Service (MATS) combined the long-range transport elements of the US Air Force and Navy.

C-54A Skymaster

Type: four-engined long-range transport

Powerplant: four 962-kW (1,290-hp) Pratt & Whitney R-2000-9 Twin Wasp radial piston engine

Maximum speed: 427 km/h (265 mph)

Climb rate: 3048 m (10,000 ft) in 14.8 min

Range: 4828 km (3,000 miles) with 4082-kg (9,000-lb) payload

Service ceiling: 6706 m (22,000 ft)

Weights: empty 19,641 kg (43,300 lb); maximum take-off 30,844 kg (68,000 lb)

Accommodation: flight crew of six and up to 10,000 kg (22,046 lb) of freight

Dimensions:

span	35.81 m (117 ft 5 in)
length	28.60 m (93 ft 10 in)
height	8.38 m (27 ft 6 in)
wing area	135.63 m² (1,460 sq ft)

C-54D SKYMASTER

42-72581 is a C-54D, the most produced variant of the Skymaster. All 380 were built at Douglas's Chicago plant in 1944/45.

Wartime C-54s carried an olive drab camouflage colour scheme. After hostilities ceased an unpainted natural metal finish was adopted across the fleet.

While the civil DC-4 carried up to 40 passengers by day, late-build C-54s were able to seat up to 76 passengers. The C-54A had troop benches instead of seats.

C-54s were favoured over C-47s during the Airlift as they required less maintenance.

Typically the crew consisted of six: pilot, co-pilot, navigator, radio operator and two relief crewmembers.

Four Pratt & Whitney R-2000-9 Twin Wasps powered all C-54s. This was an enlarged development of the R-1830 fitted to the C-47 and numerous other aircraft.

Post-1945, a 'buzz' number was used to quickly identify an aircraft. It consisted of the last three digits of the serial number and a two-letter code; 'CJ' was the code for the C-54.

Skymasters were able to carry 10 tonnes of freight. This was loaded, usually on pallets, through the enlarged port-side cargo door.

ACTION DATA

MAXIMUM PAYLOAD

The C-54 replaced the C-47 because of its larger payload capacity and the fact that it was easier to maintain. Similarly, the RAF began to use the more suitable Hastings instead of Yorks and Dakotas.

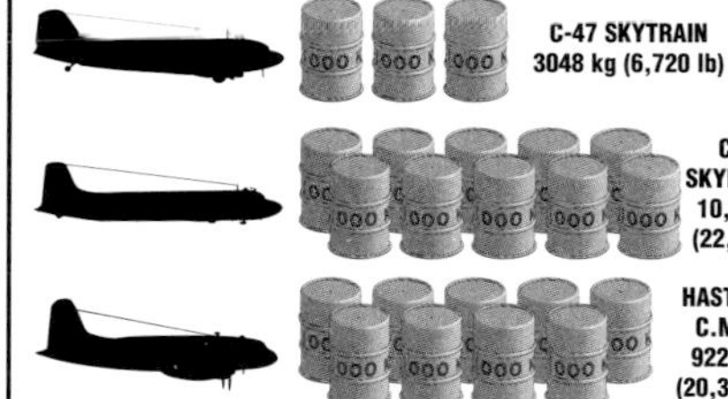

NUMBERS BUILT

The standard Allied transport of World War II, the C-47 was built in huge numbers in several factories. The C-54 was also used by the Allies and other countries, especially after 1945.

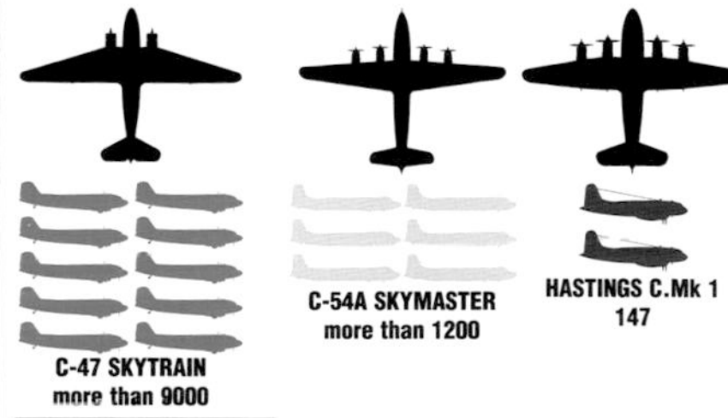

MAXIMUM SPEED

The most modern of the three designs, the Hastings benefited from more powerful engines. The C-54 used four similar engines to the two fitted to the C-47 but was a much larger aircraft.

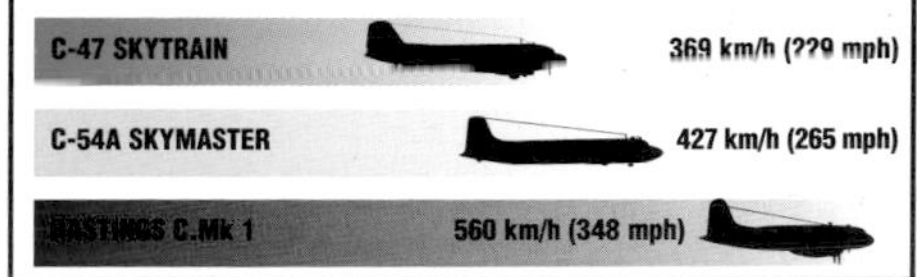

Lifeline to Berlin

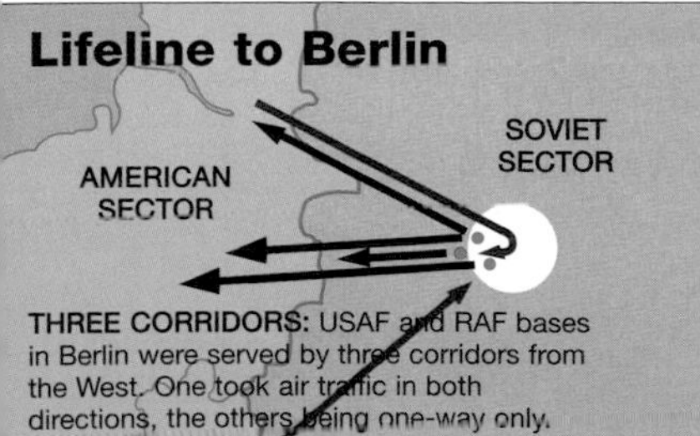

THREE CORRIDORS: USAF and RAF bases in Berlin were served by three corridors from the West. One took air traffic in both directions, the others being one-way only.

HAZARDOUS CONDITIONS: Pilots had to endure bad weather as well as the hazards involved in flying through the confined air space of the corridors and over Berlin.

BUZZED BY THE RUSSIANS: Another potential hazard was presented by the Russians, who sent fighters, such as Yak-9s, to harass the airlift aircraft.

DOUGLAS

A-3 SKYWARRIOR

● Largest carrier aircraft ● Nuclear bomber ● Long service

Nicknamed the 'Whale' by its crews, the Douglas A-3 Skywarrior was an impressive aircraft by all accounts. It began to enter service in the mid-1950s and, ultimately, enjoyed a colourful and long service career; the final examples were retired from the US Naval Reserve during the early 1990s. Skywarriors proved their worth during the Vietnam War, and were among the first aircraft to drop bombs in anger over North Vietnam in 1965.

▲ *Designed as a carrier-borne nuclear bomber, the A-3 achieved only modest success in its intended role. It blossomed, however, as a tanker, reconnaissance and Elint aircraft.*

PHOTO FILE

DOUGLAS A-3 SKYWARRIOR

▲ Skywarrior up North
This rare picture shows an A-3B attacking a ground target over North Vietnam.

▲ Aboard ship
Folding wings were an absolute necessity for operations at sea, and enabled the massive A-3s to be 'parked' on deck with relative ease.

Assisted take-offs ▶
This early A3D-1, seen here in 1954, was equipped with JATO (Jet-Assisted Take-Off) bottles in an effort to improve the type's short-field performance.

◀ Dual-role variant
Identified by the distinctive blister fairing below the cockpit, the EKA-3B was a combined electronic warfare/tanker variant which saw extensive service in Vietnam.

Rear gun turret ▶
As originally delivered, the bomber variants had twin cannon mounted in a tail turret designed by Westinghouse. In service the guns were often removed, and, on later versions, the turret was omitted entirely.

FACTS AND FIGURES

- In 1957 two Skywarriors flew from San Francisco to Hawaii in a record time of 4 hours and 31 minutes.
- The first operational cruise of the A-3 was with VAH-1 on USS *Forrestal* in 1957.
- As late as 1987 EA-3Bs were still serving with frontline US Navy units.
- During the Cuban missile crisis in 1962, a single A-3 unit, VAP-62, flew a variety of missions and later received an award.
- The A-3 actually outserved its intended replacement, the A-5 Vigilante.
- Many examples served as testbeds at NAS Point Mugu in California.

PROFILE

'Whales' in the Navy

Elegant but having a deadly purpose, the A-3 was designed as a carrier-borne nuclear bomber, but the Skywarrior did not serve for long in its intended role. By the time it had entered service the US Navy had begun to relinquish the strategic mission, instead preferring to concentrate on using its air assets in the context of limited wars.

When war broke out in Southeast Asia, 'Whales' flew round-the-clock sorties from carrier decks. They initially acted as conventional bombers, attacking targets in North Vietnam. Designer Ed Heinemann had campaigned from the start to keep weight to a minimum and this proved advantageous; the large A-3s could operate from both the bigger carriers and the small World War II vintage Essex-class wooden-decked ships.

From late 1966, frontline A-3s began to adopt other roles such as tanking, reconnaissance and intelligence gathering. As the war in Southeast Asia continued, the Skywarriors still performed sterling work, and many crews returning from sorties over the North welcomed the sight of a KA-3B tanker. The advent of specialist Intruder variants caused the A-3 slowly to disappear from carrier decks.

Above: When first delivered to US Navy heavy attack squadrons, A-3s were painted overall dark blue. This soon changed to the familiar grey and white scheme.

Above: With its landing gear and tailhook deployed, this A-3B is just about to 'trap' aboard the USS Forrestal. *The weight of the A-3 meant that the arrestor gear had to be very strong.*

EA-3B Skywarrior

Type: carrier-borne and land-based electronic reconnaissance platform

Powerplant: two 55.16-kN (12,406-lb-thrust) Pratt & Whitney J57-P-10 turbojets

Maximum speed: 982 km/h (610 mph)

Cruising speed: 837 km/h (520 mph)

Range: 4667 km (2,900 miles)

Service ceiling: 12,495 m (41,000 ft)

Weights: empty 17,856 kg (39,366 lb); loaded 33,112 kg (73,000 lb)

Accommodation: crew of seven: pilot, co-pilot and navigator, plus four electronic systems operators

Dimensions:		
	span	22.10 m (72 ft 6 in)
	length	23.27 m (76 ft 4 in)
	height	6.95 m (22 ft 10 in)
	wing area	75.43 m² (812 sq ft)

A-3B Skywarrior

Seen wearing the markings of VAH-2, this Skywarrior is shown as it would have appeared in 1965, on board the USS *Coral Sea* in the Gulf of Tonkin. At this time, it was configured as an A-3B bomber/tanker.

The raised cockpit included seating for three crew. Only one set of flight controls was fitted, at the pilot's station on the port side. Next to him sat the bombardier/navigator. Behind the pilot, facing aft, was a third seat, originally occupied by a gunner who operated the twin cannon on early variants.

Above the refuelling probe, this A-3 carries the unit insignia of Heavy Attack Squadron (VAH) 2. This unit had the distinction of being the first to take 'Whales' to Vietnam, and commenced flying bombing missions on 29 March 1965.

As the largest aircraft ever to be deployed aboard ship, the Skywarrior took up a substantial amount of space. The wings folded outboard of the engines to lie almost flat, and the tail hinged to starboard for stowage below deck.

Over the years, A-3s were seen with a variety of different nose profiles. Later aircraft had a flat-tipped radome housing the AN/ASB-12 radar system.

Skywarriors converted for the in-flight refuelling role had a fuel tank fitted into the rear section of the bomb bay. Most converted A-3s retained bombing capability.

Under the rear fuselage was the buddy refuelling pack, with a single hose reel. US Navy aircraft used the British-developed probe-and-drogue refuelling system in Vietnam.

Twin speed brakes were fitted to the rear fuselage, directly below the horizontal tailplane, and were hydraulically actuated.

COMBAT DATA

MAXIMUM SPEED

Early examples of the A-3 were originally powered by anaemic Westinghouse J40s, although these were soon replaced by more powerful engines. At maximum speed, the A-3 was slower than its B-66 cousin and its electronic warfare successor, the EA-6B.

Aircraft	Speed
EA-3B SKYWARRIOR	982 km/h (610 mph)
EB-66C DESTROYER	1032 km/h (641 mph)
EA-6B PROWLER	1003 km/h (623 mph)

MAXIMUM THRUST

As the largest aircraft ever to operate from carrier decks on a regular basis, the A-3 needed as much thrust as it could get. It was thus more powerful than the very similar USAF Douglas B-66 Destroyer, which was purely land-based. The EA-6B Prowler was not as large or as heavy, and did not require as much thrust.

Aircraft	Thrust
EA-3B SKYWARRIOR	110 kN (24,740 lb thrust)
EB-66C DESTROYER	91 kN (20,467 lb thrust)
EA-6B PROWLER	100 kN (22,491 lb thrust)

SERVICE CEILING

Intended as a nuclear bomber, the Skywarrior was designed to fly at high altitudes where it would be immune to attack from ground forces. All three aircraft – the A-3, Destroyer and Grumman EA-6B Prowler – served in Vietnam and, ironically, were often casualties of ground fire.

Aircraft	Service ceiling
EA-3B SKYWARRIOR	12,495 m (41,000 ft)
EB-66C DESTROYER	10,880 m (35,696 ft)
EA-6B PROWLER	11,460 m (37,598 ft)

Douglas carrier aircraft of the 1950s

DOUGLAS A-1H SKYRAIDER: One of the best loved of all aircraft, the venerable 'Spad' was the US Navy's principal medium attack aircraft during the 1950s and 1960s.

DOUGLAS A-4C SKYHAWK: Designed as the smallest aircraft to carry a nuclear weapon, the A-4 served with both the US Navy and Marines, and was exported to many countries.

DOUGLAS F4D (F-6) SKYRAY: Nicknamed the 'Ford', the Skyray entered service in 1951, but was already obsolescent. By 1962 only three frontline units remained equipped with the type.

DOUGLAS

F4D SKYRAY

● Tail-less design ● Fleet defence

Designed at the height of the Cold War, the bat-winged, fast-climbing Douglas F4D Skyray's mission was to guard the US Fleet against attack by Soviet bombers. Today, those who flew this great jet, one of the most advanced interceptors of its time, praise the Skyray as a little-appreciated legend. Only a few hundred US Navy and Marine pilots actually flew the 'Ford', but it was much-loved and performed its duties superbly.

▲ *The Skyray was typical of the second generation of jet fighters, possessing exceptional performance, but being tricky to fly. The accident rate was high, especially during carrier operations.*

PHOTO FILE

DOUGLAS F4D SKYRAY

◀ Lippisch delta
The configuration of the Skyray owed much to German aerodynamics' expert Dr Lippisch, who had devised the layout of the Me 163.

▼ Fleet defender
The first line of the fleet's defence was the Skyray. The early Sidewinder missile was just coming into service with the F4D.

▼ Deck approach
Coming in slow with the hook down, the F4D was quite a handful. Early naval jets approached the deck at twice the speed of wartime fighters.

▼ Clean design
Although the Skyray looked beautiful and handled well, the design had control and powerplant problems.

◀ Mixed weapons
Late in its career the F4D was cleared to carry the Sidewinder heat-seeking missile, while retaining rocket and gun armament. The underfuselage pod was the NAVPAC, containing extra navigation equipment.

FACTS AND FIGURES

- Skyrays of Navy squadron VF(AW)-3 twice won the NORAD (North American Air Defense Command) Trophy.
- The first XF4D-1 Skyray prototype made its maiden flight on 23 January 1951.
- The Westinghouse XJ40 turbojet engine was powerful but unreliable.
- The XJ40-powered 'Ford' set a world speed record of 1211.746 km/h (752.944 mph) on 3 October 1953.
- The Skyray was also flown with the Allison J35 turbojet engines.
- In May 1958, US Marine Colonel Edward LeFaivre seized five world climb records.

PROFILE

The tail-less wonder

Douglas's star designer Ed Heinemann used German tail-less delta research when he created this carrier-based interceptor, even though the manta-like wing was not a genuine delta. The sleek, unorthodox Skyray had a fantastic rate of climb – just what was needed to 'scramble' against high-flying bombers. The F4D Skyray was the only Navy aircraft to serve in the US Air Force's Air Defense Command, charged with fending off the first blows of a World War III that never came.

Just 419 F4Ds (redesignated F-6A in 1962) were built. Technical problems and rapid advances in technology limited the aircraft's service life to the period between 1956 and 1962; however, 11 US Navy, six Marine and three Reserve squadrons used this remarkable interceptor during its brief tour of duty. Navy pilots operated this aircraft from carriers, flew it under difficult operational conditions, and found it to be a superb performer with fine handling qualities.

Above: Like most contemporary fighters in the 1950s, the F4D had no end of minor problems. The inlets had to be extensively redesigned to prevent compressor stalls.

Below: The tail-less delta was a short-lived phenomenon in US aircraft design, also appearing in the F-102.

The trailing-edge control surfaces acted as combined elevators and ailerons for roll and pitch. The outer stores pylon could carry a 19-round 70-mm (2.76-in) rocket pod.

The outer wing folded up to allow the Skyray to fit onto aircraft carrier lifts. The cannon were mounted in pairs in the wing, with 70 rounds per gun.

F4D-1 Skyray

Type: single-seat all-weather interceptor fighter

Powerplant: one Pratt & Whitney J57-P-8A turbojet rated at 45.38 kN (10,205 lb thrust) dry and 71.18 kN (16,009 lb thrust) with afterburning

Maximum speed: 1162 km/h (722 mph)

Cruising speed: 837 km/h (520 mph)

Range: 1930 km (1,200 miles)

Service ceiling: 16,764 m (55,000 ft)

Weights: empty 7268 kg (16,023 lb); normal loaded 9983 kg (22,009 lb); maximum take-off 12,300 kg (27,117 lb)

Armament: four internal 20-mm (0.79-in) cannon, plus up to 1814 kg (4,000 lb) of bombs, rocket pods, AIM-9 Sidewinder air-to-air missiles or auxiliary fuel tanks mounted on seven external hardpoints

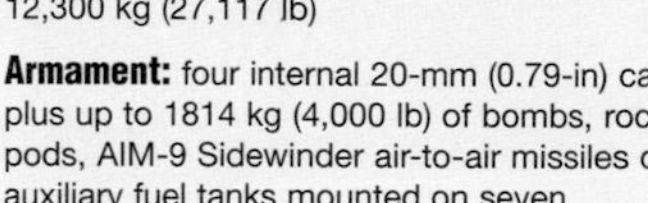

Dimensions:		
	span	10.21 m (33 ft 6 in)
	length	13.79 m (45 ft 3 in)
	height	3.96 m (13 ft)
	wing area	51.75 m² (557 sq ft)

F4D-1 SKYRAY

VF-162 'Hunters' was the shortest lived F4D unit, receiving the type in September 1962 and turning to the new F-8 Crusader only two years later, after a single cruise deployment aboard USS *Intrepid*.

Like many early jet fighters, the F4D had particularly poor cockpit visibility, especially to the rear.

Large fuel cells were mounted in the blended wing and fuselage junction, with 1200 litres (317 US gal) in each side.

The Skyray was equipped with an APQ-50 radar system, giving limited target range information. An Aero 13F weapon fire-control package was located behind the radar scanner dish.

Inlets in the wingroots were a common feature of early 1950s aircraft, notably the Hawker Sea Hawk, a British contemporary, and the large 'V' bombers.

Unusually, the Skyray also had a tailwheel as well as a tailhook, to compensate for its high nose attitude on landing and take-off.

COMBAT DATA

MAXIMUM SPEED

The Skyray was closely matched by contemporary fighters, all of which had limited power from their engines. A few years later, fighters were flying at Mach 2 with afterburner engaged.

Aircraft	Speed
MIG-17 'FRESCO'	1145 km/h (711 mph)
SCIMITAR	1143 km/h (710 mph)
F4D-1 SKYRAY	1118 km/h (695 mph)

ARMAMENT

The Scimitar and Skyray both outgunned the MiG-17, which was designed with a relatively light armament in typical Russian fashion. The era of missile armament was just beginning.

Aircraft	Armament
MIG-17 'FRESCO'	3 x 23-mm (0.91-in) cannon, 500 kg (1,100 lb) of bombs
SCIMITAR	4 x 30-mm (1.18-in) cannon, 1814 kg (4,000 lb) of bombs
F4D-1 SKYRAY	4 x 20-mm (0.79-in) cannon, 1814 kg (4,000 lb) of bombs

RANGE

Unusually for a Russian fighter, the MiG-17 had quite long range. The F4D was not far behind thanks to its capacious fuselage fuel tanks, a necessity for a naval fighter.

Aircraft	Range
F4D-1 SKYRAY	1930 km (1,200 miles)
SCIMITAR	966 km (600 miles)
MIG-17 'FRESCO'	2250 km (1,398 miles)

Naval fighters of the 1950s

■ **HAWKER SEA HAWK:** The straight-wing Sea Hawk was a conservative design, but served as late as the 1970s in Indian service.

■ **MCDONNELL F3H DEMON:** Plagued by problems with low engine power, the Demon was armed with early series Sparrow missiles.

■ **NORTH AMERICAN FJ-4 FURY:** Effectively a navalized F-86, the FJ4 was powered by a licence-built version of the British Sapphire turbojet.

■ **SUPERMARINE SCIMITAR:** The Fleet Air Arm's first swept-wing jet, the Scimitar could carry nuclear weapons and Bullpup missiles.

EMBRAER
EMB-312 Tucano

● Two-seat turboprop trainer ● Brazilian origin ● Fourteen operators

Initially developed to meet a Brazilian air force requirement and flown for the first time in August 1980, the Tucano has proved extremely successful. It sold well in its original form, powered by a 559-kW (750-hp.) PT6 engine, and has also been developed to use much more powerful engines. It has been built in two other countries. The latest development is a single-seat light attack and two-seat trainer version, again produced for the Brazilian air force and known as the ALX.

▲ One reason for the Tucano's success is that its cockpit layout and controls were designed from the outset to offer 'jet-like' training experience at speeds only marginally slower than those of a jet.

PHOTO FILE

EMBRAER EMB-312 Tucano

▼ Amazon warrior
A one-tonne warload gives the Tucano a useful weapons training and secondary attack capability.

▲ Prestigious British order
The RAF operates extensively modified Tucanos which are built under licence by Short.

▲ British Tucanos
Short-built Tucanos have considerably better performance than their Brazilian counterparts. They have been sold to Kenya and Kuwait.

▲ South American exports
The Tucano has been especially successful in South America. Among the operators are Colombia and Paraguay.

Drug hunter ▶
Brazilian Tucanos are primarily used as trainers, but some are armed and used in the covert fight against drug smuggling.

FACTS AND FIGURES

- ➤ Development of the Tucano began in 1978 in response to a Brazilian air force requirement for a T-37 replacement.
- ➤ Brazil's Air Force Academy received its first T-27 Tucano in September 1983.
- ➤ Egypt supplied 80 of its licence-built Tucanos to Iraq.
- ➤ 'Escuadron de Fumaca', the Brazilian national aerobatic team, replaced its Harvards with the Tucano.
- ➤ Firm orders for 623 aircraft, excluding demonstrators, have been received.
- ➤ The Super Tucano is 1.37 m (4 ft. 6 in.) longer than the standard machine.

PROFILE

South American trainer design

As the Tucano entered Brazilian air force service during September 1983, EMBRAER was already receiving its first export order, from Egypt for 134 aircraft. Most were built in Egypt, and the majority were supplied to Iraq.

This was just the first of a flood of orders. Argentina, Colombia, Honduras, Paraguay, Peru and Venezuela all operate the type in South America and Iran in Asia. Many more machines were acquired by two European air forces, Britain and France, bringing the number of operators to more than a dozen.

The RAF bought 130 Tucano T.Mk 1s produced under licence by Short. These aircraft were strengthened and re-engined with an 820-kW (1,100-hp.) Garrett TPE331. Short also built armed versions for Kenya (T.Mk 51) and Kuwait (T.Mk 52). France bought 80 copies of the Brazilian Tucano fitted with a ventral airbrake, increased airframe life and French-manufactured avionics.

More recently, the Super Tucano, with a 1190-kW (1,595-hp.) PT6A-68 engine, was one of the unsuccessful finalists in the US competition to find a new trainer for the USAF and Navy. Using this new engine, the ALX light attack aircraft, with a head-up display, enhanced navigation systems and five hardpoints for weapons is being developed.

With its four wing hardpoints, the Tucano is able to carry a variety of weapons. Both single- and two-seat dedicated attack variants are planned, based on the uprated Super Tucano.

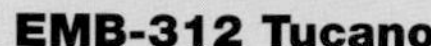

EMB-312 Tucano

Type: two-seat turboprop trainer

Powerplant: one 559-kW (750-hp.) Pratt & Whitney PT6A-25C turboprop

Maximum speed: 448 km/h (273 m.p.h.)

Endurance: 5 hours with internal fuel

Initial climb rate: 680 m/min (2,230 f.p.m.)

Range: 1844 km (1,143 mi.) with internal fuel

Service ceiling: 9145 m (30,000 ft.)

Weights: basic empty 1810 kg (3,982 lb.); normal take-off 2550 kg (5,610 lb.); maximum take-off 3175 kg (6,985 lb.)

Weapons load: 1000 kg (2,200 lb.) of light bombs, gun and rocket pods

Dimensions:

wing span	11.14 m (36 ft. 6 in.)
length	9.86 m (32 ft. 4 in.)
height	3.40 m (43 ft. 6 in.)
wing area	19.40 m² (209 sq. ft.)

TUCANO T.MK 1

Two RAF Flying Training Schools (FTS) have been disbanded since the Tucano entered service. Only No. 1 FTS remains and ZF203 is currently on strength with the unit at Linton-on-Ouse, North Yorkshire.

A four-bladed Hartzell propeller drives the Tucano. It is fully feathering and offers reverse pitch to shorten the landing roll and for improved ground manoeuvrability.

A stronger canopy was required for RAF service to withstand birdstrikes when flown at low level. The two-piece Lucas canopy is able to withstand a 1-kg (2-lb.) strike at 444 km/h (275 m.p.h.).

The lightweight Martin-Baker 8LC Mk 1 ejection seats are suitable for ejection at zero altitude and speeds down to 130 km/h (80 m.p.h.). The seats may be fired through the canopy.

Dunlop produces the brakes, tyres and wheels of the Short aircraft. The nose undercarriage retracts backwards and the main units inwards.

Although it looks very similar to the EMB-312, the Short-built S312 has only 20 per cent commonality with the Brazilian aircraft. One significant recognition feature is the pair of large exhausts for the TPE331-12B engine.

A great deal of work was required to modify the cockpit to British standard. In its final form it is very similar to the RAF's Hawk advanced trainers.

Like the Brazilian aircraft, the T.Mk 1 is largely made of aluminium. The Short machine is strengthened to give an increased airframe life of 12,000 hours with increased manoeuvre loads. The wing leading edges are strengthened for improved birdstrike resistance.

COMBAT DATA

POWER

With its higher power the Turbo Orlik should be the more versatile aircraft, but engine problems have caused protracted development. The Tucano offers jet-like performance at a fraction of the cost of a jet-powered aircraft.

EMB-312 TUCANO 559 kW (750 hp.)

PC-7 TURBO TRAINER 485 kW (650 hp.)

PZL-130TC TURBO ORLIK 798 kW (1,070 hp.)

WEAPON LOAD

Many primary trainers have a secondary light attack role. Turboprop machines are especially useful for counter-insurgency and border patrol missions, where their ability to loiter for long periods and their relatively low noise level are an advantage.

EMB-312 TUCANO 1000 kg (2,200 lb.)

PC-7 TURBO TRAINER 1040 kg (2,288 lb.)

PZL-130TC TURBO ORLIK 800 kg (1,760 lb.)

CLIMB RATE

With its higher power output, the PZL-130TC offers the greatest climb performance. The Tucano and PC-7 are evenly matched and fierce competitors in the international trainer market. The RAF's uprated Tucano has an even better climb rate.

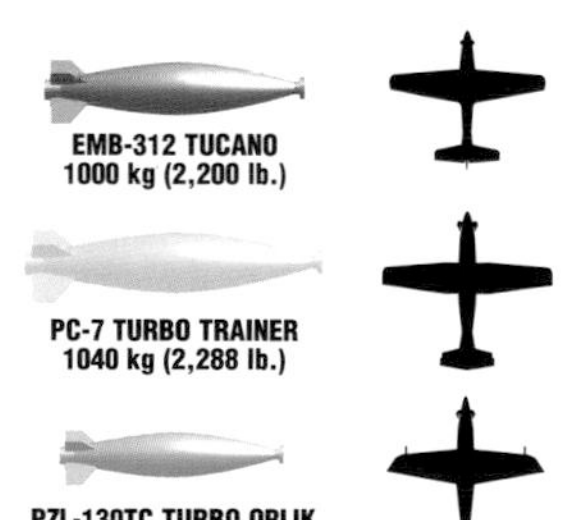

South American military trainers

NEIVA T-25 UNIVERSAL: After its first flight in 1966, the Brazilian air force ordered 150 T-25s to replace the North American Harvard.

ENAER T-35 PILLÁN: Piper developed the PA-28R-300 from the Saratoga as a primary trainer for licence production in Chile.

ENAER T-35DT TURBO PILLAN: This Allison turboprop-engined T-35, which first flew in 1986, has not found any customers.

FAMA/FMA IA 63 PAMPA: Now in service with the Argentine air force, the Pampa serves as a weapons trainer.

ENGLISH ELECTRIC

CANBERRA (BOMBER)

● High-altitude bomber ● Low-level interdictor and nuclear strike

▲ The interdictor Canberra B(I).Mk 8 and its export variants had a fighter-style canopy offset on the port side of the fuselage for the single pilot, while the navigator sat in the nose.

The English Electric (BAC) Canberra is one of the greatest aircraft of all time, although its short-span wings and a seemingly ordinary shape attracted little attention when it appeared in 1949. Like the de Havilland Mosquito of World War II, the Canberra was expected to fly fast and high enough to dispense with any need for defensive armament. Most Canberras were bombers or interdictors, although there were also reconnaissance and trainer versions.

PHOTO FILE

ENGLISH ELECTRIC CANBERRA

▲ Backbone of Bomber Command
The Canberra was the mainstay of the RAF's bomber fleet until the V-bombers entered service, taking over the strategic nuclear bombing role. These B.Mk 6s are from No. 9 Squadron.

▲ Accurate bomber
Canberras relied on ground stations for precise navigation and blind bombing. The bombardier had a glazed nose position for accurately aiming the bombs.

▲ Falklands War
It was Argentina rather than the RAF that used the Canberra in the Falklands War. One aircraft was shot down by Sea Harriers.

External bombs ▶
Regular bomber Canberras carried their bombs internally, but the interdictors, such as this B(I).Mk 6, used wing pylons.

◀ Vietnam warrior
Canberras were employed in many conflicts, including the Vietnam War, where the Royal Australian Air Force used the type alongside USAF aircraft on bombing raids. Note the wingtip bomb pylons.

FACTS AND FIGURES

- Out of 1352 production Canberras, 403 were built in the USA and 48 in Australia.
- The prototype Canberra (VN799) was flown for the first time on 13 May 1949 by Wing Commander Roland P. Beamont.
- Shorts developed and built the dedicated reconnaissance Canberra PR.Mk 9.
- The Martin B-57 Canberra was the first USAF jet bomber to drop a bomb in anger, in Vietnam in 1965.
- India was the biggest overseas customer, purchasing 71 Canberra intruders.
- RAF Canberras bombed Egyptian airfields during the Suez Crisis in 1956.

PROFILE

Britain's versatile bomber

Designed by W.E.W. 'Teddy' Petter and placed into Royal Air Force service in 1951, the Canberra began life as a modest technical advance, but almost immediately established a dominant position as the world's leading light bomber. Nothing else matched it: the Canberra could fly as fast as contemporary fighters and was just as agile. It could also carry a reasonable bombload to hit a target 1500 km (932 miles) away with uncanny accuracy, and bring its crew safely home.

Canberras flew with several engine types and in dozens of different roles. It was perfect for reconnaissance, both the ordinary photographic kind and the darker, more secret electronic ferreting missions of the Cold War. Other Canberras excelled as trainers and test ships. The Americans purchased the plane as the Martin B-57, and many other nations have flown the type in its four decades of service.

A Canberra powered by Bristol Olympus turbojets set a world altitude record of 20,079 m (65,876 ft) in August 1955, then reached 21,336 m (70,000 ft) two years later. In every area of performance, the Canberra was a superstar.

Above: The interdictor B(I).Mk 8 version could carry a belly pack of four ADEN cannon for strafing. Its main role, however, was as a tactical nuclear bomber.

Below: Peru bought both new and second-hand Canberras. It is the last operator of the type in the bomber role, and has used the aircraft during border clashes with Ecuador.

Canberra B.Mk 6

Type: light bomber, with electronic, photo-reconnaissance and target-tug derivatives

Powerplant: two 33.36-kN (7,503-lb-thrust) Rolls-Royce Avon Mk 109 turbojet engines

Maximum speed: 871 km/h (541 mph) at 12,190 m (39,993 ft)

Range: 5842 km (3630 miles)

Service ceiling: 14,630 m (48,000 ft)

Weights: empty 10,099 kg (22,264 lb); normal take-off 19,597 kg (43,204 lb); maximum take-off 24,041 kg (78,875 lb)

Armament: up to nine internal 454-kg (1,000-lb) bombs or other ordnance loads; two wing-mounted 454-kg (1,000-lb) bombs, gun pods, AS.30 or Martel missiles, or rocket launchers

Dimensions:

span	19.51 m (64 ft) (without wing-tip tanks)
length	19.96 m (65 ft 6 in)
height	4.75 m (15 ft 7 in)
wing area	89.19 m² (960 sq ft)

CANBERRA B.MK 52

Bomber versions of the English Electric Canberra were sold to several nations, including Argentina, Australia, Ecuador, Ethiopia, France, Germany, India, New Zealand, Peru, Rhodesia, South Africa and Venezuela. This aircraft was one of four purchased by Ethiopia. Designated B.Mk 52, the aircraft were based on the RAF's B.Mk 2 model with Avon 101 engines.

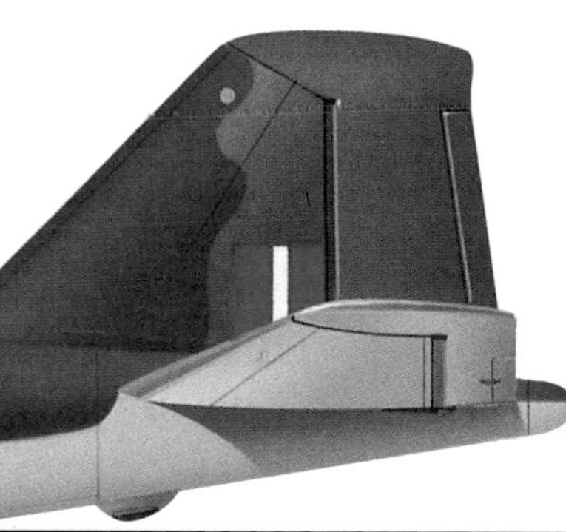

Key to the Canberra's exceptional range, altitude and load-carrying performance was the enormous slab-like wing. This had simple split flaps either side of the engine nacelles for low-speed flight, and incorporated finger-type airbrakes.

Internal fuel was usually augmented by tanks attached to the underside of the wingtips. Some aircraft, notably the B.Mk 20s used by Australia, could carry bombs on the tip-tank attachment points.

The Avon engines were mounted right at the front of the engine nacelles, with a long jetpipe leading back to the trailing-edge exhaust nozzles.

The Canberra was flown by a crew of three, comprising a single pilot on the flight deck and a navigator and bombardier sitting in the fuselage below and behind him. The bombardier could crawl past the pilot's seat to a prone position in the nose for visual bomb aiming.

The entire lower half of the central fuselage was available for the carriage of bombs. The standard maximum load was nine 454-kg (1,000-lb) weapons, held in three triplets. The area above the weapons bay was used to house the bulk of the aircraft's fuel load.

In the rear fuselage, just aft of the bomb-bay, was a camera pointing vertically downwards. This was used to record the bomb drop.

COMBAT DATA

MAXIMUM SPEED

In terms of speed and bombload the Canberra was a match for its two main rivals in Europe, the French Vautour IIB and the Russian Il-28. What the figures do not show is the extraordinary advantage it enjoyed in operational altitude.

WEAPONS

The Canberra had a useful conventional bombload, but in Germany and Cyprus its main weapon was the tactical nuclear bomb: US-made Mk 43s in Germany and British-developed 'Red Beards' in the Mediterranean.

Canberra B(I).Mk 8: nuclear strike

1 LOW LEVEL: The B(I).Mk 8s were based in Germany in support of NATO. Throughout the 1960s the only way to get anywhere near their WarPac targets was by flying low under the radar.

2 POP-UP: As the Canberra approached its target, it would pop up to a few hundred feet for the final run-in.

3 LAY-DOWN: The US-made Mk 43 tactical nuclear weapon was delivered in a low-level pass directly across the target.

4 PARA-RETARD: The bomb contained a braking parachute, which allowed the Canberra to escape before the nuclear explosion.

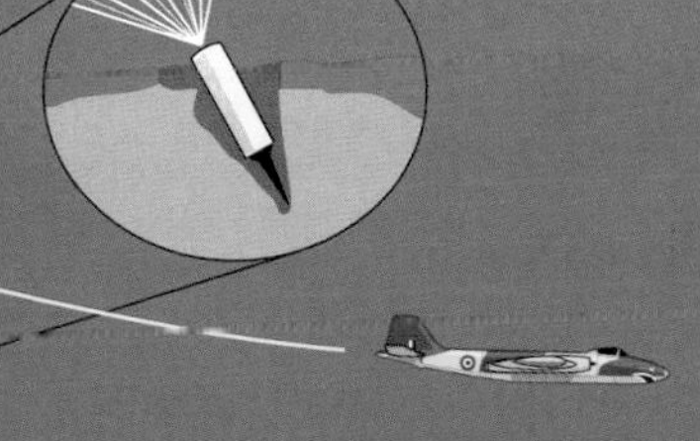

ENGLISH ELECTRIC

CANBERRA PR

● Long-range reconnaissance ● Secret spy flights? ● Still in service

▲ *Like other intelligence assets, much of the operational life of the RAF's Canberra reconnaissance fleet has been shrouded in secrecy. A small fleet remains in use after more than 50 years, a testimony to its continuing usefulness.*

In 2001 the RAF celebrated the 50th anniversary of continuous Canberra service, such is the continued viability of the type as a proven and adaptable reconnaissance platform. Like the wartime de Havilland Mosquito which it replaced, the Canberra has admirably filled both bomber and photo-reconnaissance roles for the RAF and foreign air forces alike. It is in the latter role, however, that the type has proved indispensable.

PHOTO FILE

ENGLISH ELECTRIC CANBERRA PR

▲ PR.Mk 7 from B.Mk 6

Derived from the B.Mk 6 bomber variant, the PR.Mk 7 was distinguished by its unusual glazed nose, which lacked the bomb aimer's optically flat panel. The silver finish was later replaced with camouflage, which in turn gave way to low-visibility hemp.

▲ 21st-century upgrade

The RAF's surviving Mk 9s have been upgraded to include a long-range oblique photography (LOROP) camera.

Canberra conversion ▶

For conversion training, the RAF uses a few T.Mk 4s and PR.Mk 7s.

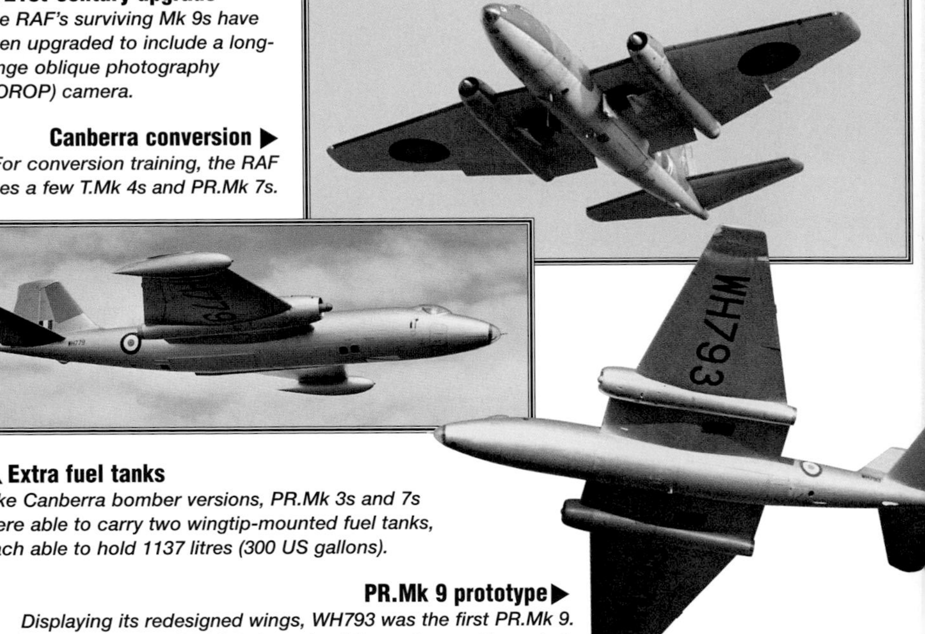

▲ Extra fuel tanks

Like Canberra bomber versions, PR.Mk 3s and 7s were able to carry two wingtip-mounted fuel tanks, each able to hold 1137 litres (300 US gallons).

PR.Mk 9 prototype ▶

Displaying its redesigned wings, WH793 was the first PR.Mk 9. Converted from a PR.Mk 7, it retained the earlier mark's cockpit.

FACTS AND FIGURES

- Canberra PR.Mk 3, WE139, now at the RAF Museum, won the speed section of the 1953 London – New Zealand Air Race.
- In late 1996 an RAF PR.Mk 9 was used to locate Rwandan refugees in Zaire.
- RAF PR.Mk 9s operate alongside Tornado GR.Mk 1As in the reconnaissance role.
- By 1996 Chile's last two PR.Mk 9s were believed grounded; India was still operating six PR.Mk 57s.
- In peacetime, RAF Canberras are used to map military installations and ranges.
- In 1996 No. 39 Squadron began the mapping of Kenya using PR.Mk 9s.

PROFILE

Long-serving camera ship

By the time Mosquito PR.Mk 34s and 35s were retired in the early 1950s, the RAF had chosen to develop a reconnaissance version of the Canberra light bomber under Specification PR.31/46. Thus the Canberra PR.Mk 3 prototype flew on 19 March 1950. Based on the B.Mk 2 bomber, the Mk 3 was stretched 35.5 cm (14 in) in order to accommodate extra fuel tanks and camera equipment. Thirty-five examples were built for the RAF and were followed by 74 PR.Mk 7s, derived from the longer-range B.Mk 6 and first flown in 1953.

It is alleged that an RAF PR.Mk 7 made a high-altitude flight over the Soviet Union in 1954 to obtain vital targeting information for the RAF's nuclear V-Force bombers.

New, longer-span wings and more powerful Avon engines on the PR.Mk 9 greatly improved altitude performance. This variant entered service in 1960, serving the RAF in Germany, Cyprus, Malta and Singapore. During the 1962 Cuban missile crisis RAF PR.Mk 9s tracked Soviet shipping movements. Most recently the RAF's last five Mk 9s have made intelligence-gathering flights over Bosnia. Canberra PRs have been exported to India, Venezuela and, finally, to Chile.

Above: This PR.Mk 7 was captured on film en route to an exercise in Sicily, Italy. The RAF's No. 1 PRU retains two Mk 7s for training, while India continues to use a few PR.Mk 57s.

Above: Signifying the unit's early history as a bomber squadron, the 'winged bomb' tail-fin badge on this Mk 9 is that of No. 39 Squadron, RAF. This aircraft is today preserved as a gate guard at RAF Wyton.

Canberra PR.Mk 9

Type: high-altitude, long-range photographic reconnaissance aircraft

Powerplant: two 50-kN (11,246-lb-thrust) Rolls-Royce Avon Mk 206 turbojets

Maximum speed: 900 km/h (559 miles) at 12,192 m (40,000 ft)

Initial climb rate: 3660 m/min (12,008 fpm)

Range: 8160 km (5,070 miles)

Service ceiling: over 18,300 m (66,039 ft) (maximum operational altitude over 21,000 m/69,000 ft)

Weights: empty about 13,608 kg (30,000 lb); maximum take-off 26,081 kg (57,500 lb)

Dimensions:

span	20.68 m (67 ft 10 in)
length	20.32 m (66 ft 8 in)
height	4.75 m (15 ft 7 in)
wing area	97.08 m² (1,045 sq ft)

CANBERRA PR.MK 9

No. 1 Photographic Reconnaissance Unit (now part of No. 39 Squadron) is the RAF's last frontline Canberra operator. XH131 is one of their small fleet of PR.Mk 9s and was one of a batch of 23 built by Short Brothers between 1958 and 1960.

All Canberras were powered by Rolls-Royce's ever-reliable Avon turbojets. PR.Mk 9s are the most powerful Canberras built. Their Rolls-Royce Avon Mk 206s are rated at 50 kN (11,2465 lb thrust), compared to the PR.Mk 7's 33.4-kN(7,512-lb-thrust) Avon Mk 109s.

A distinctive feature of the Mk 9's longer span wing is the increased chord inboard of the engines. An integral fuel tank in each wing holds 3865 litres (1,021 US gal) of fuel. PR.Mk 9s may also carry wing-tip fuel tanks, but these are rarely used.

As part of the continued upgrading of the surviving PR.Mk 9s, a radar warning receiver (RWR) was fitted in fin- and tail-mounted fairings to provide visual and audible alert of the presence of illuminating radars.

Both crew members have Martin Baker ejection seats. The navigator occupies a compartment forward of the cockpit, his seat blasting through a frangible hatch above.

Among the various sensors fitted is the port-facing F.96 oblique camera, mounted behind optically flat glass and equipped with either a 61-cm (24-in) or 122-cm (48-in) lens.

In place of a weapons bay reconnaissance Canberras have a camera bay in which various types of camera and infra-red linescan equipment are installed.

In the early 1980s low-visibility 'hemp' colours were introduced on several RAF aircraft types, including the reconnaissance Canberras, Nimrod maritime patrol aircraft and Victor and VC 10 in-flight refuellers.

ACTION DATA

THRUST

Martin's RB-57F was a radical development of the Canberra designed to operate at higher altitudes. As well as new long-span wings, larger turbofan engines were installed.

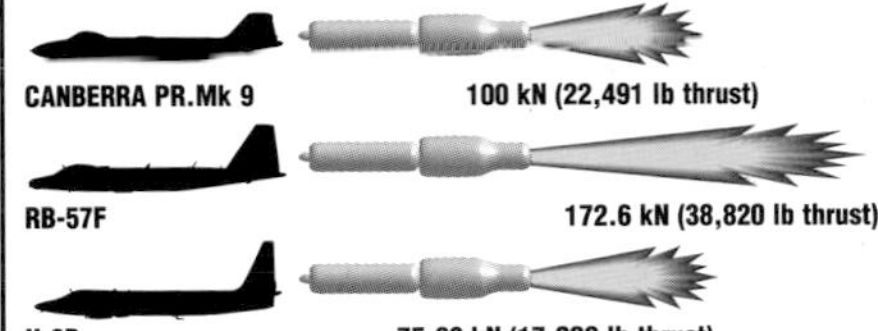

CEILING

Early versions of Lockheed's U-2 spy plane could operate at altitudes above 24 km (78,740 ft), well above the Canberra and RB-57F. Altitude gives spy aircraft a margin for safety on hazardous missions.

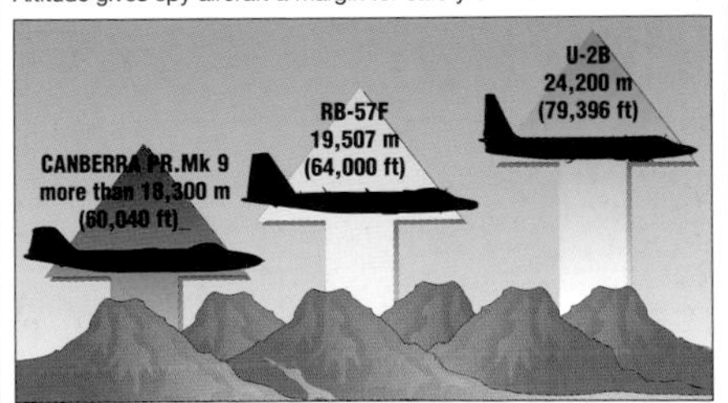

RANGE

Canberra PR.Mk 9s, with their increased fuel tankage, have a prodigious range performance, similar to that of early U-2s. Though able to operate at high altitudes, the RB-57F was hampered by poor range. Long range allows an intelligence-gathering aircraft to make positioning flights far from home bases and carry out missions deep into hostile territory.

CANBERRA PR.Mk 9 8160 km (5,070 miles)

RB-57F 4747 km (2,950 miles)

U-2B over 7290 km (4,530 miles)

Canberra's cameras

SPECIALISED CAMERA FIT: Fitted with cameras optimized for tactical reconnaissance, the RAF's Canberra PR.Mk 9s are used largely for daytime survey work fitted with a variety of cameras with varying focal length lenses. For night/all-weather work, an infra-red (IR) linescan unit is used to spot targets obscured by cloud, showing relative temperatures of objects in the target area. The IR linescan equipment used by the Canberras came from retired Phantom FGR.Mk 2s.

TACTICAL RECONNAISSANCE/SURVEY

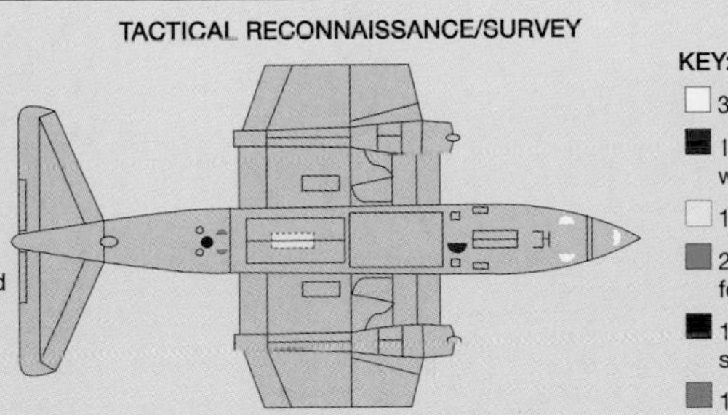

NIGHT/ALL-WEATHER RECONNAISSANCE

KEY:
- 3 x F.95 cameras
- 1 x F.96 port-facing oblique wide-angle format camera
- 1 x F.49 Mk 4 survey camera
- 2 x F.96 cameras with long focal length lenses
- 1 x F.96 vertical camera with short focal length lens
- 1 x IR linescan unit

ENGLISH ELECTRIC
LIGHTNING

● Mach 2 interceptor ● Superfast climber ● Point defender

Flying the English Electric Lightning was like being saddled to a skyrocket. This great interceptor, with its sharply swept-back wings and tail, guarded Britain against air attack for many years. The Lightning was a creature of raw power and brute force – it had the incredible ability to climb to 10,000 m (32,808 ft) in two minutes – and was regarded with great affection by pilots who flew it.

▲ *Blistering performance and a single seat are the stuff fighter pilots dream of, and performance was what the Lightning offered in plenty. Even in its old age, to fly the beefy twin jet was the most sought-after posting in the Royal Air Force.*

PHOTO FILE

ENGLISH ELECTRIC LIGHTNING

◀ Rapid reaction
The Lightning was a very fast-reacting interceptor. Even as the big jet reached old age in the 1990s, only fighters such as the F-15 and Su-27 could match its superb climb performance.

▲ Overwing tanks
A unique feature of the Lightning was the use of overwing fuel tanks. They were often carried to extend the aircraft's meagre range.

▼ Export Lightnings
Kuwait and Saudi Arabia were the Lightning's only export customers. The two Gulf air forces used its intercept capability to defend their desert airspace.

▲ Two-seat trainer
The Lightning was quite a handful to fly. To familiarize pilots with its tricks, a wide-nosed two-seat trainer was developed, housing student and instructor side by side.

◀ Supersonic prototype
This is the English Electric P.1A – forerunner of the Lightning. Distinguished by its rounded-triangle intake, lack of radar and short fin, the type's sharply swept wings were then unique.

FACTS AND FIGURES

- ➤ The prototype P.1A made its first flight on 4 August 1954.
- ➤ A small test aircraft was used to evaluate the Lightning's wing configuration.
- ➤ The P.1B Lightning prototype was the first British fighter to fly at twice the speed of sound, on 25 November 1958.
- ➤ In all, 337 Lightnings were manufactured, including test craft and export models for Kuwait and Saudi Arabia.
- ➤ Improved Lightning variants were planned but never built.
- ➤ The Lightning was the last all-British supersonic fighter.

PROFILE

Britain's front line

The Lightning was aptly named indeed. This classic fighter really was a bolt out of the blue, able to hurtle skywards at enormous speed to confront any intruder.

During the Cold War, Lightning pilots frequently turned back Soviet reconnaissance aircraft heading for Britain's shores; in a real shooting war, this swift flying machine would have detected, intercepted and fired its Firestreak or Red Top missiles on approaching bombers and cruise missiles, sending many falling in flames.

From the cockpit, this was a racehorse of the skies. Few other fighters were as fast or as formidable. Pilots cherished the Lightning; although not easy to handle at low speed near the airfield and hampered by limited visibility, the Lightning's quirks were easy to 'learn' and it was a sensational performer once aloft.

Had the Lightning been challenged by another fighter, it would have proven itself to be remarkably manoeuvrable as well as lethal, using its air-to-air missiles or 30-mm (1.18-in) ADEN cannon.

A Vulcan leads a quartet of Lightnings, encapsulating British air power in the 1960s.

Built for speed, the Lightning featured a wing of incredible sweepback. Later models had a small kink added to improve handling.

RAF squadrons in the 1960s were renowned for applying colourful markings to their aircraft. No. 56 Squadron, known as the 'Firebirds', featured its traditional Phoenix badge and red/white chequerboard on its Lightnings.

Lightning F.Mk 6

Type: single-seat air-defence fighter

Powerplant: two 72.77-kN (16,367-lb-thrust) Rolls-Royce Avon 302 afterburning turbojets

Maximum speed: Mach 2.3 or 2415 km/h (1,500 mph) at 12,000 m

Range: 1200 km (746 miles)

Service ceiling: 16,500 m (54,134 ft)

Weights: empty 12,700 kg (28,000 lb); loaded 22,500 kg (73,820 lb)

Armament: two ADEN 30-mm (1.18-in) cannon with 120 rounds each; two Red Top or Firestreak heat-seeking missiles; 2500 kg (5,512 lb) of under- and over-wing stores (export variants only)

Dimensions:

span	10.62 m (34 ft 10 in)
length	16.84 m (55 ft 3 in)
height	5.97 m (19 ft 7 in)
wing area	35.31 m² (380 sq ft)

COMBAT DATA

MAXIMUM SPEED

LIGHTNING	2415 km/h (1,500 mph)
J 35 DRAKEN	2100 km/h (1,305 mph)
MIRAGE III	2330 km/h (1,448 mph)

Mach 2.5 is about the limit at which an aircraft can fly without being built from exotic – and very expensive – materials. As a result, fighters which entered service in the late 1950s are just as fast as aircraft built three decades later.

CLIMB RATE

The Lightning was designed to intercept high-flying bombers. Its immense power gave it a phenomenal climb rate, which can be matched only by superfighters such as the American F-15 Eagle and the Russian Sukhoi Su-27 'Flanker'. Used for point defence the Lightning could reach incoming bombers within minutes of take-off.

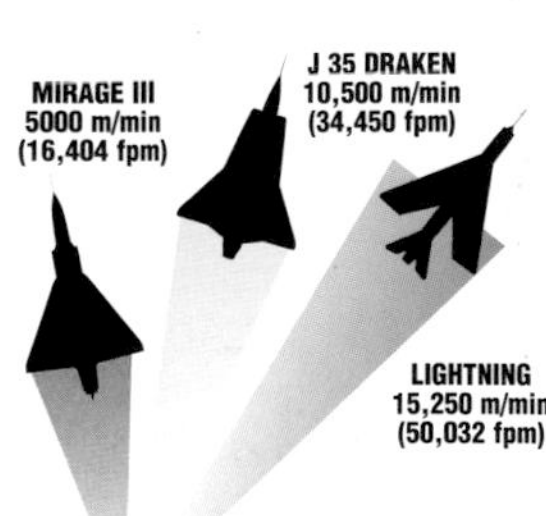

COMBAT RADIUS

To get such superb performance from what was a big and heavy machine for its time, the Lightning used fuel at a great rate. Its short range was fine for interception duties, but for longer missions could be a real handicap.

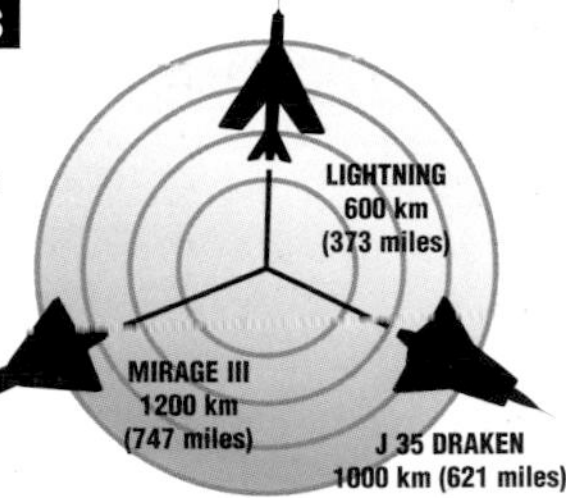

LIGHTNING F.MK 1A

Britain's best-loved fighter of the post-war period, the Lightning was an outstanding warplane, a joy to fly and a firm favourite of air show crowds.

Although popular with its pilots, the Lightning was not an easy aircraft to fly. The cockpit was fairly cramped, and instruments and controls were of 1950s vintage.

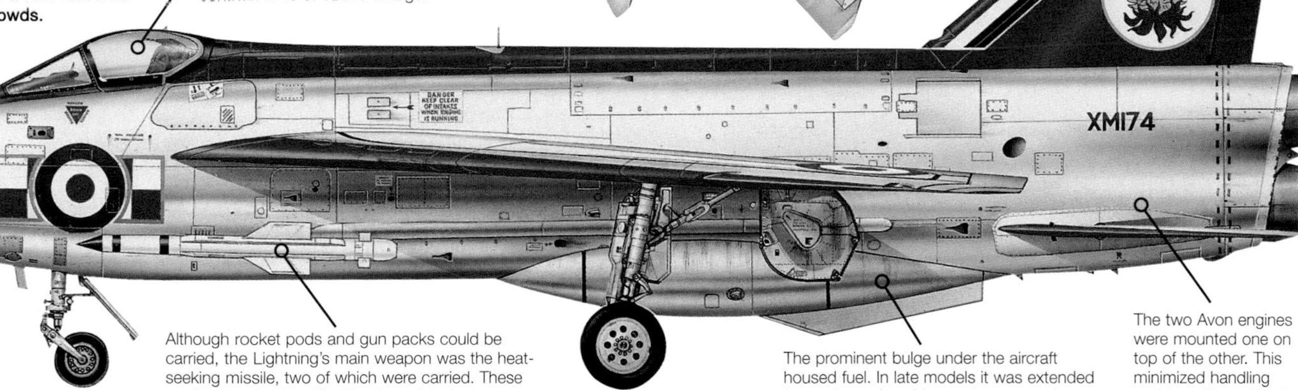

The Lightning was fitted with an air-to-air radar in the nosecone. This was located in the middle of the air intake.

Although rocket pods and gun packs could be carried, the Lightning's main weapon was the heat-seeking missile, two of which were carried. These are Firestreaks, identified by the pointed nose.

The prominent bulge under the aircraft housed fuel. In late models it was extended forwards, and could mount a gun pack.

The two Avon engines were mounted one on top of the other. This minimized handling problems if one failed.

Mach 2 Pioneers

■ **SAAB J 35 DRAKEN:** This Swedish contemporary of the Lightning was just as startling in its own way. Its most distinguishing feature was its unique double-delta wings.

■ **LOCKHEED F-104 STARFIGHTER:** Like the Lightning, the F-104 was designed as a fast-climbing high-speed interceptor. It was a smaller and less powerful machine.

■ **DASSAULT MIRAGE III:** The delta-winged Mirage was Europe's first Mach 2 service jet. Much lighter than the Lightning, it was a great export success.

■ **MiG-21:** Entering service in 1957, the MiG-21 was a mainstay of Soviet aviation. Exported to many countries, it has been built in larger numbers than any other supersonic fighter.

Eurofighter

EF 2000

● **Agile fighter** ● **Ground attacker** ● **Multinational**

Embodying everything that aeronautical science has learned in the 20th century, the EF 2000 is destined to be the Top Gun of the 21st century. Developed by four nations, it will be one of the cornerstones of European air defence over the next 25 years. This is the fighter of tomorrow, bristling with the products of advanced science, relying on new technology for hi-tech victory in aerial combat.

▲ *Fast, agile and highly potent, the Eurofighter EF 2000 uses extremely advanced technology to provide Europe with one of the most flexible of the latest generation of superfighters.*

PHOTO FILE

Eurofighter EF 2000

▲ **Euro-power**
EFA's EJ200 engines are produced by a highly experienced consortium led by Rolls-Royce and MTU.

▼ **Forward control**
The rear-mounted delta wing and 'canard' foreplanes give the EFA incredible manoeuvrability at low and high speeds and altitudes.

▲ **Europe's defender**
Launched in a media spectacular, the EFA will provide the backbone of European air defence as well as deadly-accurate strike capability for the next 30 years.

▲ **High-tech warrior**
It doesn't look exotic, but the EFA incorporates the latest advances in airframe and engine design with new avionics, stealth and weapons technology.

◀ **Multi-role, multinational fighter**
Designed to meet exacting British, German, Italian and Spanish air force requirements, the EF 2000 will be a true multi-purpose fighter.

FACTS AND FIGURES

- ➤ The Eurofighter flies twice as fast as a 9-mm pistol bullet.
- ➤ Not only fast and high-flying, the futuristic EFA performs high-angle manoeuvres for victory in a close-up dogfight.
- ➤ Eurofighter simultaneously tracks a dozen targets, and engages six at once.
- ➤ Eurofighter design features were tested on British Aerospace's Experimental Aircraft Programme (EAP) demonstrator in the late 1980s.
- ➤ In common with most new-generation fighters, EF 2000 uses canards – small wings near the nose – to improve performance.

PROFILE

Defender of Europe's skies

Hard proof that Europe has a vision and that its nations can co-operate to produce the ultimate fighter for common defence, this purposeful, high-performance delta-winged jet offers significant advances in engines, radar, combat systems and weaponry. From nose to tail, the Eurofighter is one of the most advanced fighters in the skies today, equally at home as a highly agile interceptor and as a precision ground attacker.

It has not been easy for experts in Britain, Germany, Italy and Spain to develop their new warplane. The original Eurofighter was even more capable than that now being built, but following considerable German opposition to the original price tag the consortium agreed to build a much less costly design now known as the EF 2000.

Even so, the EF 2000's advanced new radar, infra-red sensors and avionics mean that it is the best multi-role fighter flying today, which will form the backbone of Europe's fighter resources for many years.

The EAP trials confirmed that the canard layout and fly-by-wire controls would produce a superb fighter.

'Canard' foreplanes are primarily used to provide increased lift on take-off and at low speeds. This translates into greatly increased agility in dogfights.

Fuel-efficient EJ200 turbofan engines will allow the Eurofighter to cruise supersonically without the need for afterburning, greatly enhancing the fighter's range at high speed.

EF 2000's delta wing is very effective at high speeds and high altitudes, but slow-speed performance is equally good, thanks to computer-controlled fly-by-wire technology.

The Eurofighter has no conventional tailplanes, climbing and diving being controlled by a combination of the aircraft's foreplanes and the control surfaces at the wing trailing edge.

EF 2000

No single aircraft can perform every military role, but the EF 2000 will come closer than most. Agile, with good radar and a heavy weapons load, it will be called on to fight enemies both in the air and on the ground.

The advanced cockpit has been designed to reduce pilot workload. High-technology features include multi-function video displays, and some non-essential functions will be voice-activated.

ZH588

Eurofighter will enter service with the Marconi-developed ECR-90 radar. This will have lookup/lookdown air-to-air capability, and will be able to search for, track and engage multiple targets.

A passive infra-red search-and-track sensor mounted just to the left of the cockpit can detect and track multiple targets without any give-away radar signals.

Although weighing less than 10 tons, the EFA can carry more than six tons of weapons or fuel on nine hardpoints.

Eurofighter is designed to be armed with fire-and-forget active radar AMRAAM missiles and heat-seeking ASRAAM dogfight weapons, but will also be able to carry earlier-generation missiles such as the AIM-7 Sparrow and AIM-9 Sidewinder.

EF 2000

Type: high-performance jet fighter

Powerplant: two 60.02-kN (13,500-lb. thrust) Eurojet EJ200 engines, increased to 90.03 kN (20,257-lb. thrust) with afterburning

Maximum speed: Mach 2.0+, or 2125 km/h (1320 m.p.h.) at 6096 m (20,000 ft.)

Combat radius: up to 556 km (345 mi.) with full weapons load

Weights: empty 9750 kg (21,495 lb.); loaded 21,000 kg (46,297 lb.)

Armament: 6500 kg (14,330 lb.) of ordnance including up to eight missiles such as Sky Flash, ASRAAM, AMRAAM or Sidewinder, plus a 27-mm rapid-fire cannon

Dimensions:

	span	10.50 m (34 ft. 5 in.)
	length	14.50 m (47 ft. 7 in.)
	height	4.00 m (13 ft. 1 in.)
	wing area	50 m² (538 sq. ft.)

COMBAT DATA

MAXIMUM SPEED

The Eurofighter EF 2000 is one of the fastest of the latest generation of combat jets. However, although the phenomenally expensive American F-22 is slower, it can maintain supersonic speeds for longer periods.

EF 2000	Mach 2.0
JAS 39 GRIPEN	Mach 1.8
F-22 RAPTOR	Mach

COMBAT RADIUS

EF 2000 is at a disadvantage in terms of combat radius. The single-engined Gripen is smaller and less fuel-hungry, and the F-22 is much larger and carries a bigger fuel load. But for most tactical purposes the EFA has enough range for its missions.

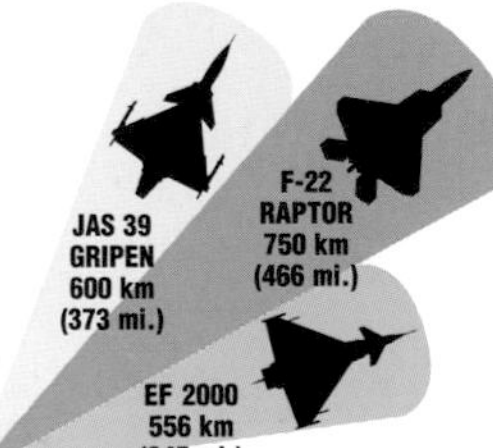

ARMAMENT

Most modern fighters carry a very large weapons load. Both the EF 2000 and the Gripen have been designed to be dual air-to-air and air-to-ground capable. The F-22 has the capability, but is more dedicated to the air-superiority role.

EF 2000
27-mm cannon
8–10 short- and medium-range AAM
6500 kg (14,330 lb.) of weapons and stores

JAS 39 GRIPEN
27-mm cannon
6-8 short- and medium-range AAM
6500 kg (14,330 lb.) of weapons and stores

F-22 RAPTOR
20-mm cannon
AIM-120 AMRAAM and AIM-9 Sidewinders carried internally
10,000 kg (22,046 lb.) of air-to-surface weapons

Tomorrow's fighters today

SUKHOI Su-27 'FLANKER'

This is arguably the best fighter currently in service. The Eurofighter was designed to outperform advanced versions currently under development.

DASSAULT RAFALE

Developed after the French withdrew from the Eurofighter programme, the Rafale is a French national project. It is similar in design to the EFA, but is somewhat lighter.

SAAB JAS 39 GRIPEN

A product of Sweden's highly respected Saab concern, the Gripen is also a tail-less delta with canard foreplanes but is much smaller, and is powered by a single engine.

LOCKHEED F-22 RAPTOR

The F-22 incorporates a great deal of stealth technology, and is the most capable of the new batch of fighter designs. But that performance comes at phenomenal cost.

FAIRCHILD

A-10 THUNDERBOLT II

● CAS and anti-armour aircraft ● Gulf War veteran ● Forward air control

▲ *Plans for the withdrawal of the A-10 from the USAF inventory were well advanced by 1990, but events in the Persian Gulf meant that the retirement of the 'Warthog' was postponed.*

Built to attack the Warsaw Pact's main battle tanks, the Fairchild A-10 Thunderbolt II was named after a Fairchild Republic product from another era, the P-47 Thunderbolt of World War II. The twin-engined, single-seat A-10 'Warthog' showed its excellent air-to-ground capability in the unlikely setting of the Middle East during the first and second Gulf Wars, despite a proposed change of role for the A-10 in line with changes in USAF policy.

PHOTO FILE

FAIRCHILD A-10 THUNDERBOLT II

◀ Second prototype
The two YA-10A prototypes flew for the first time in 1972. The second one is seen here carrying 'dumb' iron bombs. Service aircraft carry the Maverick air-to-surface missile as their primary anti-tank weapon.

▼ Vulnerability issue
Since the A-10's introduction debates have raged about the vulnerability of this relatively slow aircraft. As a result, the F-16 was chosen to replace it.

▲ Camouflage
Since the first Gulf War, all-over grey paintwork has replaced the grey/green scheme.

▲ Avenger cannon
The cannon is so powerful that it can be fired only in short bursts as it dramatically slows down the aircraft.

Countermeasures ▶
Even though it is relatively unsophisticated, the A-10 carries an electronic jamming pod.

FACTS AND FIGURES

- ➤ A-10s entered service in April 1976; 144 aircraft were committed to the Persian Gulf war zone in 1990/91.
- ➤ The first A-10 prototype made its initial flight on 10 May 1972.
- ➤ A-10s shot down two Iraqi helicopters during the first Gulf War.
- ➤ Although almost as large as the multi-crewed B-25 Mitchell bomber of World War II, the A-10 is flown by a single pilot.
- ➤ In 1994 plans to export 50 surplus A-10s to Turkey were cancelled.
- ➤ At its maximum rate of fire, a 30-round burst from the GAU-8 takes half a second.

PROFILE

Forward air control in the 'Warthog'

More than 100 A-10s were committed to the 1991 Gulf War and performed admirably in the air-to-ground and FAC roles.

The need for a close air support (CAS)/anti-armour aircraft was one of the lessons learned in the Vietnam conflict. The machine needed to be able to fly from rough forward airstrips, carry heavy weapon loads and withstand battle damage. Speed was not a major consideration.

Fairchild's A-10A was the design chosen to fill this 'A-X' requirement. A sturdy, somewhat heavy, single-seat attack aircraft, the A-10 was said to be too slow; it flew at subsonic speeds in an era when fast anti-aircraft missiles were rapidly appearing on the scene.

Despite this, 713 A-10s were built, and the first entered service in 1976. Units in the continental US, Alaska, Europe and Korea were equipped with the type. However, the end of the Cold War meant that this specialist aircraft was no longer a vital requirement, and it was to be replaced by the Lockheed Martin F-16. Surplus A-10s began to take over from the well-worn Rockwell OV-10 Broncos in the forward air control (FAC) role, with a number being redesignated OA-10A.

OA-10A Thunderbolt II

Type: single-seat anti-tank and FAC aircraft

Powerplant: two 40.3-kN (9,042-lb.-thrust) General Electric TF34-GE-100 turbofan engines

Maximum speed: 682 km/h (438 m.p.h.) at sea level

Maximum climb rate: 1828 m/min (6,000 f.p.m.)

Combat radius: 885 km (550 mi.)

Service ceiling: 10,575 m (34,690 ft.)

Weights: empty 10,977 kg (21,500 lb.); loaded 21,500 kg (49,900 lb.)

Armament: one General Electric GAU-8/A 30-mm cannon, plus up to 7258 kg (15,950 lb.) of weapons; forward air control load consists of up to 12 LAU-68 seven-tube rocket pods, two AIM-9 Sidewinder air-to-air missiles and ECM pod

Dimensions:		
	span	17.53 m (57 ft.)
	length	16.25 m (53 ft.)
	height	4.47 m (15 ft.)
	wing area	47.01 m² (506 sq. ft.)

An AN/ALQ-184 electronic countermeasures (ECM) pod is a common fitting on both FAC OA-10s and tank-busting A-10s.

Split ailerons give the A-10 an exceptional rate of roll for the rapid low-level manoeuvres required for the anti-tank and FAC roles.

All A-10As have been redesignated OA-10A without undergoing any modifications, apart from changes to cockpit lighting to make them compatible with NVG equipment.

A-10A THUNDERBOLT II

The 706th Tactical Fighter Squadron, 926th Tactical Fighter Group, operated A-10As during Operation Desert Storm. After the Gulf War, the unit took on squadron/wing status and F-16C/Ds.

Survivability was one of the key considerations of the A-10's designers. The aircraft is able to fly on one engine or with one tailfin missing. The pilot sits in a titanium 'tub' as protection from ground fire.

Two General Electric TF34 turbofans power the A-10 and are high-mounted in pods to the rear of the aircraft to avoid debris when using rough airstrips. The nacelle design results in a low infra-red signature, which reduces vulnerability to heat-seeking missiles. This design also makes maintenance easier as access to the engine is less restricted than in other types.

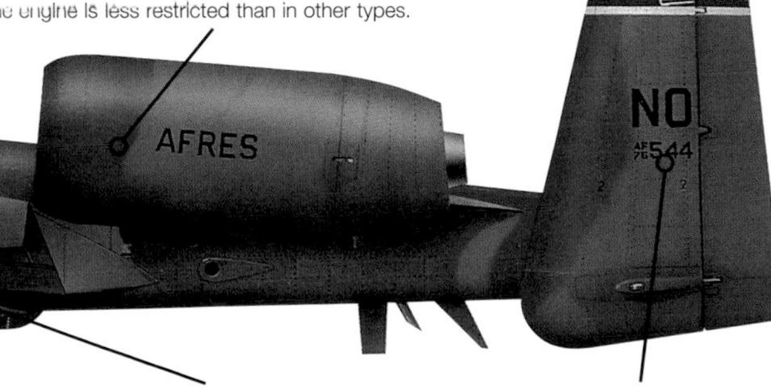

In its original 'tank-busting' role the A-10's main weapon was the General Electric GAU-8/A Avenger 30-mm seven-barrelled Gatling-type cannon.

For the FAC role the OA-10 carries few weapons apart from two rocket pods for target marking and AIM-9 Sidewinder air-to-air missiles. The pilot is provided with NVG (night-vision goggles) for a night-time capability.

The main undercarriage retracts forwards into an underwing bay. In theory, once the aircraft's weapon load has been dropped, a safe wheels-up landing can be made with minimal wing damage.

This A-10 carries the 'NO' tailcode of the 926th Fighter Wing, based in New Orleans. In September 1996 it received A/OA-10As once again to take on the attack/FAC training role.

ACTION DATA

WEAPON LOAD

The A-10A had an unmatched load-carrying ability in the CAS role, almost twice that of the Soviet's equivalent aircraft, the Sukhoi Su-25. The V/STOL Harrier is able to lift heavier loads with a short take-off than it can when taking off vertically.

A-10A THUNDERBOLT II	Su-25K 'FROGFOOT-A'	HARRIER GR.Mk 7
7258 kg (15,950 lb.)	4400 kg (9,680 lb.)	4173 kg (9,180 lb.)

MAXIMUM SPEED

The Thunderbolt II has been criticised throughout its operational career as being too slow and vulnerable for its CAS role. Both the 'Frogfoot' and Harrier are capable of speeds of around 1000 km/h (620 m.p.h.) at sea level without a load.

A-10A	682 km/h (438 m.p.h.)
Su-25K 'FROGFOOT-A'	975 km/h (604 m.p.h.)
HARRIER GR.Mk 7	1065 km/h (660 m.p.h.)

TAKE-OFF DISTANCE

The STOL ability of the Harrier gives it an unbeatably short take-off run, although this limits the aircraft's load-carrying ability. At maximum take-off weight both the A-10 and Su-25 require about 1200 metres of runway to get airborne.

HARRIER GR.Mk 7	Su-25K 'FROGFOOT-A'	A-10A THUNDERBOLT II
405 m (1,328 ft.)	1200 m (3,936 ft.)	1220 m (4,000 ft.)

AGM-65 Maverick anti-tank strike

1 'POP-UP' APPROACH: When near the target, the pilot pops up from low altitude in his A-10 and acquires the target either visually or via the cockpit TV screen. The image on the screen is produced by the camera fitted in the missile's nose.

2 MAVERICK LAUNCH: During a shallow dive the pilot launches the Maverick, keeping the target in view to maximise the missile's speed and height.

3 TERMINAL PHASE: As it approaches the target the Maverick glides in, using the image produced by its TV camera. The missile is able follow slow-moving targets.

FAIRCHILD

A-10 THUNDERBOLT II

● Tank-buster supreme ● Close air support ● Forward air control

Friendly troops are about to be crushed into the dirt by enemy tanks. Suddenly, help appears. Over the battlefield roar Fairchild A-10 Thunderbolt II anti-tank warplanes, known to everybody as 'Warthogs'. Within minutes, the A-10s unleash a withering barrage of gunfire and a hail of missiles, leaving the tanks a twisted mass of smoking steel and halting the enemy in his tracks.

▲ *The A-10 showed its worth in the First Gulf War, when 'experts' had written it off as good only for forward air control. Flying under ideal conditions, the 'Warthog' ripped through Iraq's armour with deadly efficiency.*

PHOTO FILE

FAIRCHILD A-10 THUNDERBOLT II

▲ Two-seater

A single two-seat night and adverse weather A-10B was built for evaluation, but was not followed up. The A-10 remains a fair weather machine, with relatively simple avionics and no attack radar.

▲ The flying gun ▼

The A-10 was built around the awesome GAU-8 Avenger 30-mm (1.18-in) cannon. Firing 30-round bursts of depleted uranium shells at up to 4200 rounds per minute, it is the most powerful gun ever fitted to a combat aircraft.

▲ Friendly fire

Two British Army Warrior personnel carriers were blasted by Mavericks from A-10s in a Gulf War 'friendly fire' incident. This highlighted the importance of forward air controllers.

▲ Fully loaded

In addition to its mighty gun, the A-10 can carry a wide range of air-to-ground weapons, of which the AGM-65 Maverick is the most important.

Gulf tank-killer ▶

Some 200 A-10s of the 23rd and 354th Tactical Fighter Wings were sent to the Gulf, second only to the F-16 in terms of numbers deployed.

FACTS AND FIGURES

- ➤ In its primary role the A-10 smashed more than 1000 Iraqi tanks, 1200 guns and 2000 military vehicles in the Gulf.
- ➤ Nearly 200 A-10s were sent to the Gulf, and equipped three fighter wings.
- ➤ A-10s flew more than 8500 combat sorties during Operation Desert Storm.
- ➤ The A-10's seven-barrel GAU-8 cannon is the most powerful gun ever carried by a tactical aircraft.
- ➤ The GAU-8 cannon can destroy any known main battle tank.
- ➤ OA-10s were used to control other fighters on 'Fast FAC' missions.

PROFILE

Warthog goes tank-busting

During the 1991 Gulf War, the slow, ugly but nimble A-10 proved itself a devastating weapon against the tanks of Iraq's Republican Guard. Second only to the F-16 in the numbers of aircraft deployed to Saudi Arabia, the 'Warthog' ranged the deserts of Kuwait and Iraq, using its devastating GAU-8 gun and pinpoint-accurate Maverick missiles to smash tanks, artillery pieces, military vehicles, radar sites and missile launchers.

They even downed two helicopters, scoring the only gun-kills of the air war.

Some idea of the A-10's worth can be gained from the performance of just two pilots. Captain Eric Solomonson and Lieutenant John Marks of the USAF's 23rd Tactical Fighter Wing accounted for 23 Iraqi tanks in a single day. Altogether, Warthog pilots destroyed more than 4500 tanks, vehicles and artillery pieces in the course of the war. There were those who had claimed the A-10 was too slow for the modern battlefield, but the war against Saddam showed that, although other jets fly higher and faster, nothing could match the Warthog for destroying tanks on the ground.

The Vietnam War demonstrated just how unsuitable for strike missions some US fighters were. Consequently, the A-10 was designed with its armament and defence measures as a priority.

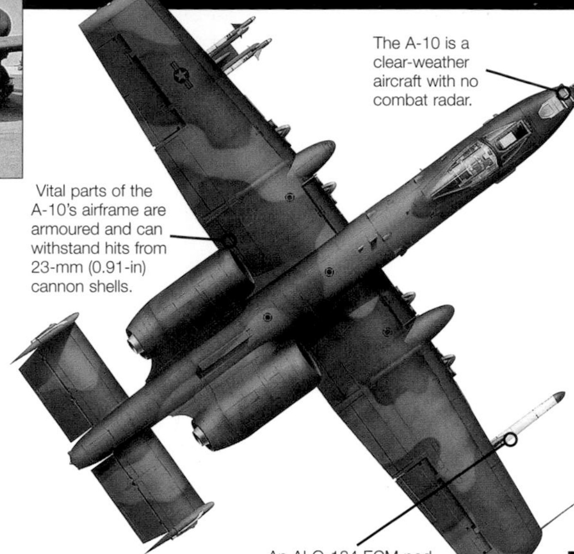

The A-10 is a clear-weather aircraft with no combat radar.

Vital parts of the A-10's airframe are armoured and can withstand hits from 23-mm (0.91-in) cannon shells.

An ALQ-184 ECM pod, designed to jam enemy gun and missile radars, is carried for self-defence.

A-10A Thunderbolt II

Type: single-seat anti-tank aircraft

Powerplant: two 40.31-kN (9,066-lb-thrust) General Electric TF34-GE-100 non-afterburning turbofans

Maximum speed: 682 km/h (424 mph)

Ferry range: 4000 km (2,485 miles)

Service ceiling: 10,575 m (34,695 ft)

Weights: empty 10,977 kg (24,200 lb); loaded 21,500 kg (47,400 lb)

Armament: one General Electric GAU-8/A 30-mm (1.18-in) cannon with 1350 rounds plus up to 7258 kg (16,000 lb) of mixed ordnance including laser-guided bombs, cluster bombs and AGM-65 Maverick missiles on 11 weapons pylons

Dimensions:

span	17.53 m (57 ft 6 in)
length	16.25 m (53 ft 4 in)
height	4.47 m (14 ft 8 in)
wing area	47.01 m² (506 sq ft)

OA-10A THUNDERBOLT II

Although most of the A-10s deployed to the Gulf were 'shooters', the 23rd Tactical Air Support Squadron based at King Fahd Airport flew OA-10As as Forward Air Controllers.

The high-set bubble canopy gives the A-10 a superb view of the battlefield, while a titanium armour 'bathtub' protects the pilot from ground fire.

The controls are linked to traditional cables as well as hydraulics for an emergency back-up in case of damage.

The A-10's controls are linked to traditional cables as well as hydraulics for an emergency back-up in case of damage.

The TF-34 engines are high-mounted for avoiding debris when using tactical airstrips. They have a relatively low infra-red signature and are powerful enough for the A-10 to fly on one engine.

Pave Penny is a laser tracker system mounted under the nose. It detects reflected laser energy from designated targets.

Although Sidewinder missiles are carried for self-defence, the only weapons used on the FAC mission are rockets, which mark targets for other attack aircraft.

The undercarriage retracts into nacelles in the leading edge of the wing. The wheels are slightly exposed, so that the A-10 can better survive a belly landing.

The twin fins look archaic, but they help screen jet heat signature, and as the A-10 can fly with one fin shot away they also give a damaged aircraft more chance of getting home.

COMBAT DATA

WEAPONS LOAD

Slower than its Soviet equivalent, the Su-25 'Frogfoot', the A-10 has a heavier weapons load. Both are extremely versatile and carry a wide variety of weaponry on multiple stores stations beneath the wings and fuselage. However, the A-10 has been replaced in front-line service by the F-16, which is much faster, more agile, and carries a heavier weapons load.

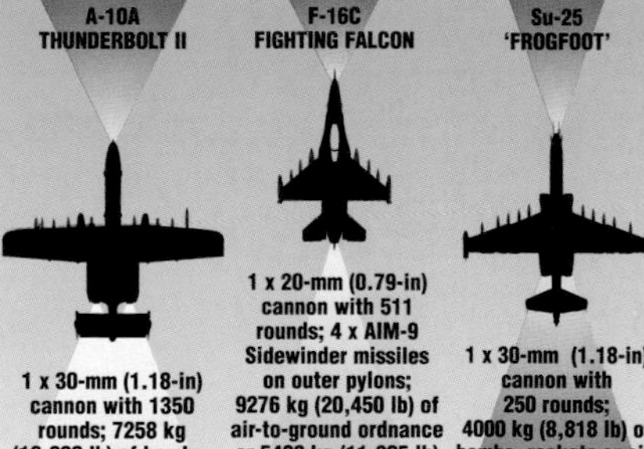

The Avenger cannon in action

GUN ENGAGEMENT: A-10s usually engage enemy armour with their guns from a shallow dive. The GAU-8 is effective against ground targets at ranges of up to 3 km (2 miles).

BURST FIRE: The A-10 pilot can select between 2100 and 4200 rounds per minute. At high rate, a typical 30-round burst lasts less than half a second.

ARMOUR PIERCING: The depleted (non-radioactive) uranium armour-piercing shells weigh around 500 g (18 oz), and have a secondary incendiary effect.

MULTI-BARREL CANNON: The GAU-8 Avenger is a seven-barrel electrically driven Gatling-type gun.

AMMUNITION DRUM: The massive reload drum contains up to 1350 rounds the size of beer bottles.

AMMUNITION LOAD: A typical load contains armour-piercing and high-explosive incendiary rounds.

MISSILE LOAD: In spite of the immense power of its cannon, the A-10's primary anti-armour weapon is the infra-red-guided Maverick missile, which has a range of between 25 and 40 km (15 and 25 miles).

FMA

IA-58 PUCÁRÁ

● **Robust structure** ● **Counter-insurgency** ● **Hard-hitting turboprop**

The FMA Pucará, built by Fabrica Militar de Aviones, is an ideal military aircraft for small countries. Argentina developed this twin-turboprop anticipating that an aircraft would be required to undertake anti-guerrilla and counter-insurgency (COIN) operations. Repeatedly upgraded and improved, the Pucará had limited success in the Falklands War. The COIN aircraft is better suited for counter-drug work in Colombia.

▲ *Argentina's hard-hitting Pucará is one of the best counter-insurgency planes ever built. It did not show its true potential in the Falklands War as many of the aircraft were destroyed on the ground.*

PHOTO FILE

FMA IA-58 PUCARÁ

▲ RAF evaluation
One of the Argentine Pucarás captured by British forces in the Falklands was flown and evaluated by test pilots at the UK test centre at Boscombe Down.

▲ Silver Pucarás
These four Argentine Pucarás are wearing the original silver colour scheme. Subsequently most have been camouflaged.

▲ COIN formation
This pair of IA-58As are armed with nose-mounted 20-mm Hispano DCA-804 cannon and pylon-mounted rockets and bombs.

▲ Arms assortment
In addition to the fixed cannon in the nose, the Pucará can carry up to 1620 kg (3,565 lb.) of mixed weapons and tanks on underfuselage and underwing racks.

◄ Fast striker
With an unusual configuration that necessitates carrying stores externally, increasing drag, the Pucará still has a top speed of over 500 km/h (310 m.p.h.).

FACTS AND FIGURES

- ➤ The first aircraft, designed in 1966 and named the AX-2 Delfin, completed its maiden flight on 20 August 1969.
- ➤ The prototype was powered by two 674-kW Garrett TPE331-U-303 turboprops.
- ➤ The first production Pucará took to the air on 8 November 1974.
- ➤ Pucarás were ordered by eight countries but only Argentina, Colombia, Sri Lanka and Uruguay took delivery.
- ➤ In the Falklands a Pucará shot down a British Army Westland Scout helicopter.
- ➤ Most of the Pucarás in the Falklands were destroyed on the ground.

PROFILE

Close support in the Pucará

Named after the stone forts built by indigenous South American tribes, the Pucará is a manoeuvrable and rugged aircraft able to operate from small, rough airstrips – as short as 80 metres when boosted by JATO (Jet-Assisted Take-Off) bottles. With this ability to fight from primitive backwater bases, in the 1970s the Pucará proved that it would have been useful to US forces serving in Vietnam.

In fact, the Pucará dates back to the early 1960s and is a unique design. A tall, retractable tricycle undercarriage provides ample space for weapons and the generous propeller ground clearance needed for flights from unpaved ground. The two crewmembers are strapped into Martin-Baker Mk 6 ejection seats, with the rear-seat positioned 25 cm higher. In practice, many missions are flown by a single pilot. Without exception, pilots are pleased with the stability and responsiveness of the Pucará.

The IA-58 has been successful against lightly armed rebels in Argentina, but during the Falklands War nearly all of the aircraft flown to the islands were lost to sabotage, or were captured by the advancing British Army.

Above: The view from the cockpit is excellent, with the seats positioned in a staggered arrangement. Both crewmembers have a rearview mirror and unobstructed and almost undistorted vision.

Above: This Pucará, in landing configuration, shows its fully extended flaps and tall, stalky tricycle undercarriage. The legs are long to give good ground clearance on irregular surfaces.

IA-58A Pucará

Type: two-seat close air support and reconnaissance aircraft

Powerplant: two 729-kW (975-hp.) Turboméca Astazou XVIG turboprop engines

Maximum speed: approx. 500 km/h (310 m.p.h.) at sea level

Range: 1500 km (930 mi.)

Service ceiling: 10,000 m (33,000 ft.)

Weights: empty 4020 kg (8,800 lb.); maximum take-off 6800 kg (14,960 lb.)

Armament: two 20-mm Hispano cannon under the nose and four 7.62-mm (.30 cal.) Browning machine-guns abreast of the cockpit, plus up to 1620 kg (3,565 lb.) of external bombs or rockets

Dimensions:

span	14.50 m (47 ft. 6 in.)
length	14.25 m (46 ft. 9 in.)
height	5.36 m (17 ft. 7 in.)
wing area	30.30 m² (326 sq. ft.)

IA-58A PUCARÁ

Uruguay received six IA-58As prior to the Falklands War in 1982. They equipped the Grupo de Aviación 2 of Brigada Aérea II at Durazno.

The tall, all-metal T-tail has a fixed tailplane with manually driven control surfaces and electric trim tabs on the trailing edges.

The moulded Plexiglas canopy covers both cockpits in a single unit that hinges upwards from the rear. Martin-Baker APO6A ejector seats, which can be used at zero speed and at zero height, are fitted.

The crew are protected by armoured plate glass in the canopy.

Two 20-mm Hispano DCA-804 cannon are carried in the nose, each equipped with up to 270 rounds.

The French Ratier Forest three-blade propellers have fully feathering blades of solid forged duralumin.

Fuselage attachments can carry tandem pylons, and stores pylons are permanently attached under the wings at the junction between the rectangular centre section and the outer panels. These carry triplets of 110-kg (242-lb.) high-explosive bombs.

Most of the rear fuselage is empty apart from control rods leading to the tail surfaces, air bottles and radio/electronics racks. The centre section contains a large fuel tank and the machine-guns and cannon.

COMBAT DATA

MAXIMUM SPEED

Not surprisingly, the twin turbojet-powered Cessna A-37 Dragonfly is appreciably faster than the twin turboprop Pucará. The two turboprop aircraft can operate closer to the frontline due to their STOL performance.

- IA-58A 500 km/h (310 m.p.h.)
- A-37 DRAGONFLY 843 km/h (523 m.p.h.)
- OV-10 452 km/h (280 m.p.h.)

ARMAMENT LOAD

Although the Dragonfly is only equipped with a single 7.62-mm Minigun it also has eight underwing hardpoints to carry a large weight of bombs and rockets. The Pucará and Bronco can only carry two-thirds of the A-37's munitions load in a combat situation.

IA-58A PUCARÁ 1620 kg (3,565 lb.)

A-37 DRAGONFLY 2268 kg (4,990 lb.)

OV-10 BRONCO 1633 kg (3,593 lb.)

COMBAT RADIUS

The Pucará's combat radius with a 1000-kg (2,200-lb.) warload flying at low level is 400 km (250 mi.), rising to 650 km (400 mi.) flying a hi-lo-hi profile. The A-37's radius with a similar warload is much less if flown at low level and 370 km (230 mi.) on a hi-lo-hi attack. With its lower overall performance, the OV-10 has a reasonable combat radius with a full weapons load.

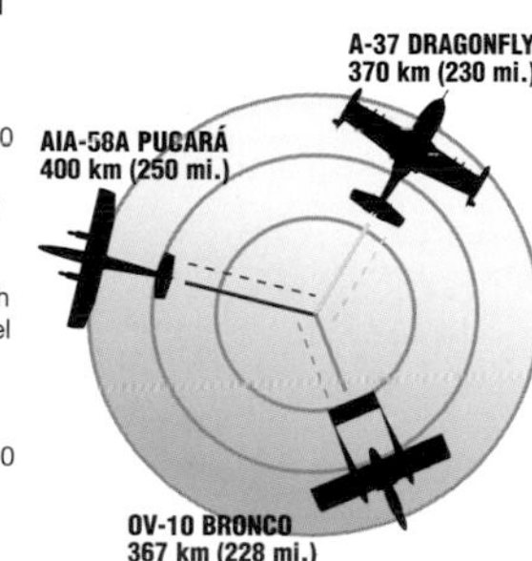

Falklands wipe-out

HELICOPTER DOWNED: In April 1982 the Argentine air force flew 25 Pucarás to newly captured Port Stanley and Goose Green. They found strong British resistance and the only success was the downing of a British army Scout helicopter.

BOMB TARGETS: As early as 1 May 1982 an Argentine Pucará about to take off was blasted by a cluster bomb released by a Sea Harrier. Worse was to come. On 15 May six aircraft were destroyed on Pebble Island by a raiding force of the SAS. Several more were shot down by infantry arms and missiles, and one by a Sea Harrier's guns. The remaining Pucarás were captured.

FOKKER F50

● Transport duties ● Missile attack ● Intelligence gathering

Fokker used its 50-seat twin-turboprop airliner as the basis for a range of military models. Using similar equipment to that carried by derivatives of its predecessor, the F27, they were designed to meet a wide variety of requirements, from transport and maritime patrol, to electronic surveillance and airborne early warning. However, targeting the aircraft at a very crowded market resulted in few production orders.

▲ *Utilising successful building techniques developed on the F27, the F50 incorporates all the latest advances in airframe technology, coupling this with a sophisticated radar system.*

PHOTO FILE

FOKKER F50

▼ Far East operations
Singapore operates four F50s, replacing Shorts Skyvans, in the transport role. Five Maritime Enforcer examples are to follow these aircraft into service to patrol coastal waters.

▲ More capability
Its lengthened fuselage is helping the F50 prove to be an even more capable aircraft than the F27 Fellowship that it is replacing.

Search radar ▶
A blister containing a 360-degree search radar is positioned on the underside of the fuselage. This allows the aircraft to locate ships at great distances in all weathers.

▲ Ship killer
The Enforcer Mk 2 has provision for four torpedoes or depth charges, along with Exocet, Harpoon, Sea Eagle or Sea Skua anti-ship missiles.

Airliner guise ▶
Resplendent in a high-visibility gloss white scheme, this F50 operates as a VIP transport for high-ranking officers in the Dutch air force.

FACTS AND FIGURES

- The Republic of China (Taiwan) air force was the first customer for the Fokker 50 transport aircraft in 1992.
- First flight of the Fokker 50 occurred on 28 December 1985.
- The aircraft is basically a lengthened, re-engined development of the F27.
- The aircraft was initially intended purely for the civil airline market, but has seen numerous military applications.
- A complete F-16 engine can be carried within the F50's fuselage.
- Fokker has developed an electronic reconnaissance version of the F50.

PROFILE

Airliner to ship-killer

Taiwan was the first nation to acquire the military Fokker 50, purchasing three examples for use as general transports. Singapore bought another four to replace its ageing Skyvans, but the more specialised variants of this former airliner have found few takers.

For naval operations, there was the unarmed Maritime Mk 2 for coastal surveillance, and the Maritime Enforcer Mk 2, which flew for the first time in 1992. Both these types carried a surface search radar but the Enforcer had added provision for the carriage of external stores. The Republic of Singapore Air Force eventually bought five Enforcers.

These machines could be armed with a choice of American, Italian or British torpedoes, with depth bombs available as alternatives if customers wished. For operations against surface ships, the armament options included a pair of Exocet, Maverick, Harpoon, Sea Skua or Sea Eagle missiles.Other military variants of the Fokker 50 are the Black Crow signals intelligence aircraft, the radar-carrying Sentinel for overland reconnaissance, the Troopship Mk 3 transport and an airborne early-warning aircraft dubbed 'Kingbird'. More successful was a transport version of the stretched Fokker 60. Used by the Dutch air force, it can carry up to 50 paratroops and can readily be converted for the medical evacuation role.

Left: Now wearing a more 'warlike' camouflage, this Dutch F50 operates on combat support missions. Later variants will have an improved ECM suite fitted to the wing tips.

Right: With the ability to fly long patrols over coastal waters and, if the need arises, to attack hostile shipping, the F50 may yet achieve substantial sales, as many nations need to upgrade their maritime fleets.

Maritime Enforcer Mk 2

Type: armed maritime patrol aircraft

Powerplant: two 1864-kW (2,500-hp.) Pratt & Whitney Canada PW 125B

Maximum speed: 480 km/h (298 m.p.h.); patrol speed 277 km/h (172 m.p.h.) at 610 m (2,000 ft.)

Combat radius: 2224 km (1,379 mi.)

Range: 6820 km (4,230 mi.)

Service ceiling: 7620 m (25,000 ft.)

Weights: empty 12,520 kg (29,300 lb.); maximum take-off 19,900 kg (47,400 lb.)

Armament: four Sting Ray torpedoes, depth bombs, two or four Harpoon anti-ship missiles

Dimensions:

span	29.00 m (95 ft. 2 in.)
length	25.24 m (82 ft. 9 in.)
height	8.31 m (27 ft. 3 in.)
wing area	70 m² (753 sq. ft.)

F50

Singapore was an early customer for the Fokker 50, receiving four transport examples in early 1994. These operate with No. 121 Sqn, replacing old Skyvans; an additional purchase of three aircraft seems likely.

An advanced cockpit is provided for the two pilots with multi-function displays and FLIR available for particular customers. Pilots have found the aircraft a delight to fly.

The F50 was equipped with improved engines to increase performance. This particular variant is fitted with two Pratt & Whitney turboprops which are linked to an advanced six-bladed composite propeller blade system, a combination that is proving very satisfactory.

The increased fuselage length allows the F50 to carry either more specialised avionics for maritime operations, or more cargo in its transport guise.

Retained from the earlier F27 Friendship, the large fillet positioned ahead of the tail offers the F50 superb lateral stability, a quality of particular value during a search pattern.

Maritime attack versions of the F50 are fitted with fuselage hardpoints that allow the aircraft to carry anti-ship missiles.

A large access door is retained from the airliner versions. This is positioned on the rear fuselage to facilitate the loading and unloading of cargo.

The tall tail of the F50 offers the aircraft excellent handling characteristics, particularly at low level during long patrol missions over the ocean.

COMBAT DATA

MAXIMUM RANGE

With the need to patrol for long distances over the oceans, range is of vital importance for maritime aircraft. Leader in this field is the Nimrod.The small size of the Enforcer means that only a relatively modest internal fuel load can be carried.

CP-140 AURORA 8339 km (5,170 mi.)

NIMROD MR.Mk 2 9266 km (5,745 mi.)

F50 MARITIME ENFORCER 6820 km (4,230 mi.)

MAXIMUM SPEED

With its four jet engines the Nimrod easily out-performs many other maritime patrol aircraft. Powered only by two turbo-props the Enforcer's speed is much less.

Aircraft	Speed
CP-140 AURORA	732 km/h (454 m.p.h.)
NIMROD MR.Mk 2	926 km/h (574 m.p.h.)
F50	480 km/h (298 m.p.h.)

WEAPON LOAD

Mines, depth charges and anti-ship missiles all need to be carried by maritime aircraft. For its size, the F50 Enforcer can carry a reasonable amount of ordnance, though it is a lot less capable in this respect than the CP-140.

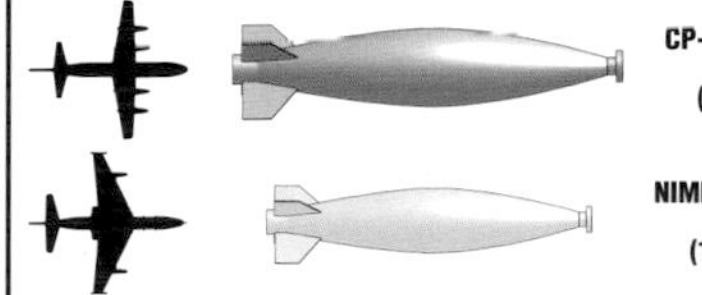

Aircraft	Weapon load
CP-140 AURORA	9072 kg (8,778 lb.)
NIMROD MR.Mk 2	6124 kg (19,958 lb.)
F50 MARITIME ENFORCER	3990 kg (13,473 lb.)

Patrolling the oceans on propellers

ATLANTIQUE 2: Continually upgraded, Dassault's Atlantique operates with many NATO forces and Pakistan.

EMB-111: Despite its small size, Embraer's maritime patrol aircraft is proving very successful in South America.

S-2 TRACKER: Now fitted with improved avionics, the Grumman Tracker continues to serve with smaller nations.

GENERAL DYNAMICS FB-111A

● Two-seat 'swing-wing' bomber ● Nuclear weapons delivery

A bold attempt to combine the roles of fighter and strike bomber in an aircraft that would be equally at home on a carrier deck or a land base, the F-111 took some years to develop into a first-line combat aircraft. In the 1970s, General Dynamics began an updating program that kept the F-111 current through the last years of the Cold War. The FB-111A nuclear bomber was developed for Strategic Air Command – just in case.

▲ *The key to the FB-111's range, speed and heavy lift capacity was the aircraft's variable geometry 'swing wings'. These are unswept during take-off and landing, then swept back for high speed.*

PHOTO FILE

GENERAL DYNAMICS FB-111A

▲ Weapons bay
The internal weapons bay could be used for either extra fuel or short-range nuclear missiles.

▲ Two crew members
The crew consisted of a pilot and weapons systems officer, the latter was responsible for navigation and weapon delivery.

▼ Afterburners for speed
Two Pratt & Whitney TF30 afterburning turbofans provided power for high speed.

▲ 'Aardvark' and 'Earth Pig'
Its ungainly appearance on the ground has earned the F/FB-111 at least two nicknames.

Huge load capacity ▶
Each wing on the FB-111 could be fitted with up to four pylons for carrying weapons or fuel up to a maximum weight of 16,973 kg (37,420 lb). Bombs would usually be carried on the inner pylons.

FACTS AND FIGURES

- ➤ The aircraft uses terrain-following radar that enables it to be flown completely 'hands off'.
- ➤ The original F-111s were the first swing-wing aircraft to enter service.
- ➤ Part of the FB-111's main undercarriage door is also used as an air brake.
- ➤ Dumping unused fuel into the afterburner exhaust of an F/FB-111 results in a spectacular flame, or 'torching'.
- ➤ The prototype FB-111A was converted from the eighteenth F-111A constructed.
- ➤ The FB-111A had longer wings and stronger undercarriage than the F-111A.

PROFILE

SAC's atomic 'Aardvark'

Politics and defence budgets balanced the future of the General Dynamics F-111 on a knife edge more than once. Costly and controversial, the aircraft was shunned by foreign governments, but after two combat tours in Vietnam, its potential was recognized. General Dynamics embarked on a comprehensive upgrading, the success of which ensured that the 'Vark' remained one of the world's most potent combat aircraft.

Cancellation of Strategic Air Command's (SAC) new spearhead, the Rockwell B-1A, in the 1970s led to a potential nuclear-strike shortfall if the ageing B-52 fleet was grounded for any reason. An alternative had to be found and the FB-111A was the USAF's answer. An order for 263 of this strategic bomber version was placed.

When the B-1 was reinstated, however, the FB-111 order was reduced to 76. The first FB-111A made its maiden flight on 13 July 1968. With the end of the Cold War, the FB-111 fleet was retired, some aircraft being converted to F-111Gs armed with conventional weapons and used mainly for training. By 1993, all had been retired to cut costs, 15 being sold to Australia to supplement its F-111C fleet.

On long-range missions only one AGM-69 SRAM would have been carried; the rest of the weapons bay was taken up by an auxiliary fuel tank.

The F-111G and FB-111 shared the longer span wing for additional range. The F-111G was basically an FB-111 airframe converted for the training role. A large bombload could be carried under the wing in addition to the internal bomb-bay load.

The 76 FB-111As were converted from airframes of the F-111K aircraft originally ordered by the Royal Air Force, but later cancelled.

The F-111's weak point was its engines, the TF30 suffered ongoing reliability problems and also sometimes 'flamed out' when afterburner was engaged.

FB-111A

Type: Two-seat nuclear/conventional strike bomber

Powerplant: Two 89.81-kN (20,200-lb-thrust) Pratt & Whitney TF30-7 afterburning turbofan engines

Max speed: 2649 km/h (1,646 mph) 'clean' at 10,973 m (36,000 ft)

Service ceiling: 18,288 m (60,000 ft)

Range: more than 4700 km (2,920 miles)

Weights: empty 21,714 kg (47,872 lb); loaded 57,922 kg (127,697 lb)

Weapons: up to six AGM-69 short-range attack missiles or 16,973 kg (37,420 lb) of free-fall nuclear weapons

Dimensions:	
span	21.34 m (70 ft)
length	23.16 m (76 ft)
height	5.18 m (17 ft)
wing area (spread)	51.10 m² (550 sq ft)

F-111G

The 428th FS, part of the USAF's 27th Fighter Wing at Cannon Air Force Base, New Mexico, was the only operator of the F-111G, mainly in the training role.

The 'bump' on the upper nose just in front of the cockpit, housing the astrotracker, was a feature unique to the FB-111A/F-111G. The long nose led to the 'Aardvark' nickname.

If the crew needs to eject from an FB-111, the entire cockpit becomes an escape capsule that blasts away from the aircraft and descends by parachute. At maximum speed, the limiting part of the airframe is the canopy perspex, which would melt after only a few minutes due to air friction.

The 'CC' code on the fin of this aircraft is that of Cannon Air Force Base, New Mexico. The blue fin-top stripe denotes the 428th Fighter Squadron.

The main nose radar was the AN/APQ-161, with a secondary AN/APQ-171 terrain-following system.

The wing glove was moveable to accommodate the wing sweep.

The F-111Gs were the first F-111s painted in 'gunship gray', beginning in 1990.

ACTION DATA

SPEED

Although the FB-111 is a heavy aircraft, its TF30 turbofans provide over 176.44 kN (39,683 lb thrust) – enough to make it one of the fastest combat aircraft ever. Bomber designs of the 1960s were based around a high penetration speed to give a better survival rate against enemy fighters and surface-to-air missiles.

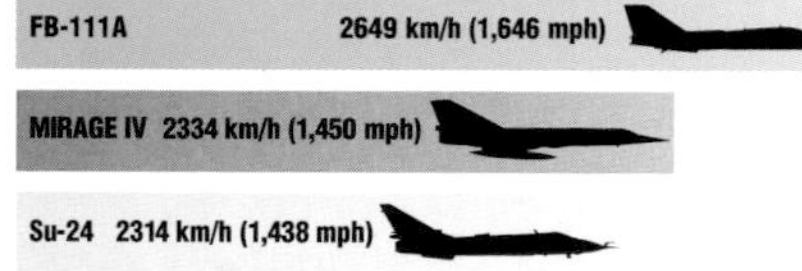

RANGE

Designed for nuclear strikes against targets deep inside the Soviet Union, both the FB-111A and the Mirage IV required long range. Although powered by fuel-guzzling engines, the FB-111A could penetrate more than 2010 km (1,250 miles) into the Soviet Union thanks to its large fuel capacity. The Su-24 is a more modern design and does not require the reach of its Cold War adversaries.

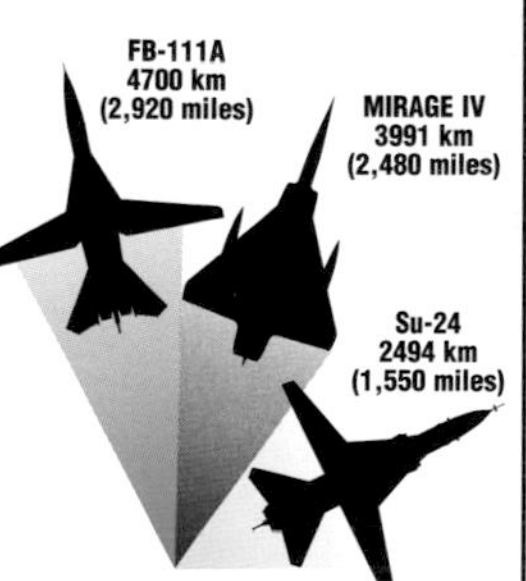

WEAPONS

Again, the FB-111's size is a major factor in determining its payload. Its internal and external weapon points, along with its immensely powerful engines, give the FB-111A twice the bomb carrying capacity over the Mirage IV and the Su-24. On long-range missions, however, the FB-111A would have carried just one SRAM missile to allow extra fuel to be carried.

FB-111 nuclear strike

LOW-LEVEL: Using its highly accurate astro-navigation system and terrain-following radar an FB-111 approaches its target at just 61 m (200 ft).

DEFENCE SUPPRESSION: From medium altitude an accompanying FB-111 makes an AGM-69 SRAM attack on a surface-to-air missile position.

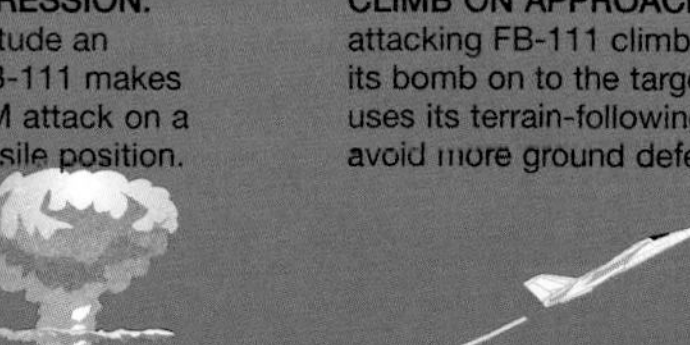

CLIMB ON APPROACH: As the attacking FB-111 climbs to 'toss' its bomb on to the target, another uses its terrain-following radar to avoid more ground defences.

TOSS BOMBING: With the bomb released at the top of the climb, it can fly several miles to its target.

GENERAL DYNAMICS

F-111F

● Swing-wing strike fighter ● Gulf War precision laser-bomber

The F-111F was the ultimate combat variant of the amazing General Dynamics F-111. Known to its pilots as the 'Aardvark', the F-111 has a slender fuselage, side-by-side seating and 'swing' wings. In its day it was a revolutionary warplane of unrivalled all-weather striking power, and the modern F-111F, with a Pave Tack targeting device bulging in its belly, could hit targets with uncanny accuracy.

▲ A Gulf War F-111 pilot checks the mighty TF30 turbofan. The F-111 was a superb performer in the Gulf, showing that after 20 years it remained almost unique in its long-range strike capability.

PHOTO FILE

GENERAL DYNAMICS F-111F

▲ **Massive payload**
Few attack aircraft had as many armament options as the 'Aardvark'. Together with the F-15E, it was the only aircraft capable of delivering the GBU-28 'bunker buster' used to devastating effect in the Gulf War.

▼ **In-flight refuelling**
The F-111 was designed to strike deep into Russia from bases in England. Fuelling in flight extended its range still further.

◀ **Precision strike**
Key to the F-111's performance is its ability to carry a heavy load of laser-guided bombs, which are able to strike to within centimetres of a designated target.

Desert strike ▲
Carrying a large load of 'iron bombs', an F-111F heads for a target somewhere in Iraq.

▼ **Capsule cockpit**
Instead of having ejection seats, the entire cockpit of the F-111 detaches as a parachute-retarded escape capsule.

▲ **Take-off position**
The F-111's wings sweep forward for take-off and landing.

FACTS AND FIGURES

- ➤ The first F-111A made its maiden flight on 21 December 1964.
- ➤ The F-111 was originally called the TFX (Tactical Fighter Experimental).
- ➤ After a tragic start, F-111s returned to Vietnam in 1972 and flew 4030 successful sorties in five months.
- ➤ The F-111F, with more powerful engines, improved avionics and Pave Tack, served with the USAF until July 1996.
- ➤ One F-111F was lost during the air attack on Libya in April 1986.
- ➤ The 66 F-111Fs at Taif in Saudi Arabia flew 4000 sorties during the Gulf War.

PROFILE

'Aardvark' – the laser-bomber

The F-111 supersonic fighter-bomber was the world's first operational aircraft with a variable-sweep wing, and for two decades was the most advanced strike bomber. Introduced in 1968, it has flown in a number of versions, including the nuclear-armed FB-111A strategic bomber and the EF-111 electronic warfare aircraft.

The complex F-111 suffered a tortuous development process, culminating in the F-111F. Although the earlier F-111D had more advanced electronics, the 'F' model was much more reliable. Above all, it had more powerful and fuel-efficient engines than previous variants.

The F-111F has seen more action than other 'Aardvarks'. It performed well in a long-range counter-terrorist strike against Libya in 1986. During Operation Desert Storm the F-111F was a workhorse, accurately delivering more precision ordnance than any other warplane.

When they were retired in 1996 the F-111Fs were replaced by F-15E Eagles. The remaining airframes are in storage and could be returned to operational status in a time of crisis.

A typical mission load included a pair of 'Paveway' 1000-kg (2,200-lb.) laser-guided bombs, two AIM-9 'Sidewinder' missiles for self-defence, and the huge AVQ-26 Pave Tack laser-designation turret mounted under the fuselage.

Paveway III bombs have an advanced proportional guidance system, and are distinguishable from earlier laser-guided weapons by their long fixed noses.

The wing is swept to the forward position of 16° for landing and back to 72.5° for high speed.

The F-111F could carry up to 14228 kg of ordnance on its underwing and under-fuselage hardpoints, including air-to-air missiles and Vulcan cannon pods.

F-111F

Type: two-seat tactical strike fighter

Powerplant: two 111.65-kN (25,050-lb.-thrust) Pratt & Whitney TF30-P-100 afterburning turbofans

Maximum speed: Mach 1.2 or 1468 km/h (910 m.p.h.) at sea level; 2655 km/h (1,646 m.p.h.) clean at altitude

Radius of action: more than 2200 km (1,365 mi.)

Service ceiling: 18,300 m (60,000 ft.)

Weights: empty 21,500 kg (47,300 lb.); loaded 45,360 kg (99,792 lb.)

Armament: up to 14,228 kg (31,302 lb.) of ordnance, including bombs, missiles or gun pods. Normal tactical load of two or four precision-guided weapons plus AIM-9 Sidewinder missiles

Dimensions:	span	19.20 m (63 ft.)
	length	22.40 m (73 ft. 6 in.)
	height	5.21 m (17 ft.)
	wing area	48.77 m² (525 sq. ft.)

F-111F

The F-111Fs of the 48th Tactical Fighter Wing, based at RAF Lakenheath, were sent to the Taif airfield in Saudi Arabia during the 1991 Gulf War. They were arguably the most accurate and lethal bombers of the war.

The F-111 is one of the fastest aircraft in the world at low level. The main factor limiting an F-111 pilot who wishes to run his aircraft flat-out is that the canopy would melt due to air friction heating after 10 minutes.

The F-111 may have a fighter designation, but it was an out-and-out attack aircraft. Pilot visibility to the rear is poor, but thanks to the downward slope of the nose the forward visibility is excellent for a fast strike aircraft.

The complex system of moving wing glove and variable inlets are designed to cope with the conflicting requirements of Mach 2 flight and variable-geometry wings.

The F-111 has a fuel emergency jettison pipe between the afterburner nozzles. Dumping fuel with afterburner on results in a spectacular 'torch'.

The multimode APQ-144 attack radar and the APQ-146 terrain-following radar allows the aircraft to fly terrain-hugging attacks at low level day or night, whatever the weather.

The Pave Tack pod housed in the weapons bay has a stabilised turret containing an infra-red sensor and a laser designator. It enabled the F-111F to drop laser-guided munitions autonomously at night.

The GBU-24 is a BLU-109 907-kg (2,000-lb.) steel-jacketed penetration bomb fitted with a Paveway III laser-guidance kit.

The ALQ-131 jamming pod mounted on the rear fuselage gives the F-111F additional defence against hostile radar.

Chaff and flare dispensers are fitted on the underside of the tail. These were designed to decoy enemy radar-guided and heat-seeking missiles.

COMBAT DATA

SPEED AT LOW LEVEL

The F-111F had one of the longest operational service lives of any modern combat jet and was also one of the world's fastest jets, especially at low level. With its wings swept back it could penetrate the air more cleanly, suffering less turbulence than most of its rivals.

F-15E EAGLE 1400 km/h (1,678 m.p.h.)

F-111F 1468 km/h (910 m.p.h.)

Su-24 'FENCER' 1320 km/h (818 m.p.h.)

RANGE ON INTERNAL FUEL

The F-111F was designed at the height of the Cold War, and from the start was tasked with penetration missions. These involved flying very fast and very low through enemy air defences, striking at key command and communications targets deep inside enemy territory.

WEAPONS LOAD

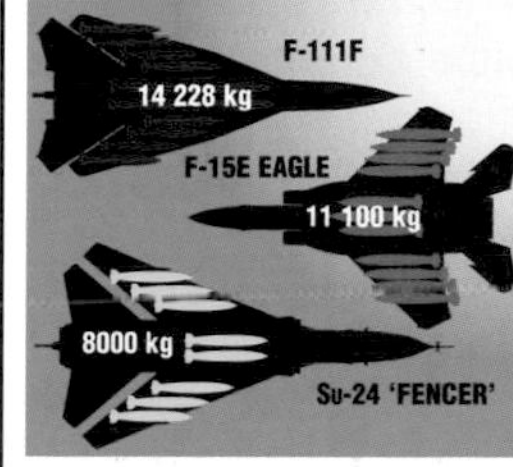

The F-111F's internal bomb-bay was designed to carry two nuclear bombs or missiles. However, it usually housed a cannon pod or a Pave Tack guidance pod. But the bomb-bay was only part of the story. More than 14 tons of weaponry could be carried on six swivelling underwing pylons.

Pave Tack attack

DETECTION: An F-111F crew could detect their target visually via the infra-red sensor mounted in the Pave Tack turret under the fuselage. This allowed the attackers to acquire aiming points by day or by night at ranges of several kilometres.

WEAPONS RELEASE: The fire-control computer calculated the optimum point for dropping weapons. Releasing the bomb in a climb 'tossed' it further than would be possible in a level release or a diving attack.

ILLUMINATION: As the bomber turned away, the Pave Tack turret swivelled to keep the target in sight. Just before the weapon arrived, the F-111F illuminated the target with a laser beam onto which the bomb steered with deadly accuracy.

GLOSTER JAVELIN

● Delta fighter ● Missile-armed pioneer ● Air defence

The Cold War nuclear threat demanded that NATO air forces deploy radar-equipped interceptors able to halt attacking Soviet bombers far from the West's vulnerable cities. Britain's Gloster Javelin, the world's first twin-jet, delta-winged interceptor, was designed for the job. A two-man long-range interceptor, the Javelin was a little slow and difficult to fly, but its radar and missile combination made it one of the most advanced fighters of the 1950s.

▲ *The Javelin was an important machine for Britain, as it took the RAF into the era of all-weather missile-armed fighters. If it had been upgraded as planned with an advanced 'thin wing', it could have served into the 1980s.*

PHOTO FILE

GLOSTER JAVELIN

▲ Base overflight

The RAF was proud of its latest fighter. In 1956 these gun-armed FAW.Mk 1 (Fighter All Weather) aircraft flew a display for the press over their base in Hampshire.

▲ Aerobatics

The Javelin was a heavy, solidly built aircraft, but it was still capable of performing smooth aerobatics: especially the FAW.Mk 8 variant of 1958, which had Sapphire engines of increased power.

Heavyweight ▶

Javelins were monsters compared to the Meteors and Vampires that they replaced.

▲ Firestreak armed

The Javelin FAW.Mk 7 was the first RAF fighter which could use the Firestreak infra-red missile. This later armed the Lightning.

▼ Gate guardian

Britain still has some Javelins, but only as 'gate guardians' on RAF stations. Although short of performance all through its relatively brief career, the Javelin was well regarded by its users for its power, long range and potent missile armament.

FACTS AND FIGURES

- ➤ An early version, known as the Gloster GA.Mk 5, first flew on 26 November 1951.
- ➤ The Javelin prototype took to the skies for its initial flight on 22 July 1954.
- ➤ In February 1956 No. 46 Squadron of the Royal Air Force became the first user of the Javelin.
- ➤ The FAW.Mk 8 was the final Javelin, making its first flight on 9 May 1958.
- ➤ Modifications to the Javelin's wing improved the aircraft's fuel capacity and its weapons-carrying potential.
- ➤ In a production run of only four years 343 Javelins were delivered.

PROFILE

Gloster's mighty delta-winged fighter

Air combat at high speed in poor weather was the aim when the Gloster Javelin became operational in 1956. It had the same role as Meteor night fighters or the American F-94 Starfire – to detect, intercept, identify and destroy bombers. The Javelin was designed to make any air attack so costly that no aggressor would attempt it.

On paper, it was a perfect design – a delta wing for high-altitude performance, but with a high-set tail to reduce the approach angle on landing. In reality, the Javelin's performance was middling and it was a maintenance nightmare – but crews loved it.

The production Javelin was considered quite advanced for its time. Its air-intercept radar was gradually improved, and the Firestreak missile was added to its arsenal. In the end the Javelin gave RAF squadrons a formidable if imperfect weapon, to bolster Britain's defence against atomic attack.

Eight Javelin variants came out of the factory, each offering distinct improvements over its predecessors. In service for more than a decade, the Javelin stood guard until 1967, when it was finally retired from service.

Above: Based in Germany and the Far East, the RAF's Javelins had a vital role in projecting an all-weather air defence capability. They were replaced by the far more capable Lightning.

Above: Like any high-tailed delta, the Javelin needed a careful hand on the controls when landing.

The Javelin's simple, round jet intakes were designed for subsonic efficiency. Giving the fighter extra speed would have called for a major redesign.

Javelin FAW.Mk 7

Type: two-seat all-weather fighter

Powerplant: two 48.94-kN (11,007-lb-thrust) Armstrong Siddeley Sapphire 203 turbojets

Maximum speed: 1130 km/h (702 mph) at sea level

Range: 1600 km (994 miles)

Service ceiling: 16,000 m (52,493 ft)

Weights: empty 14,324 kg (31,579 lb); loaded 19,578 kg (43,162 lb)

Armament: two 30-mm (1.18-in) ADEN cannon in each wing; four de Havilland Firestreak heat-seeking air-to-air missiles

Dimensions:

span	15.85 m (52 ft)
length	17.15 m (56 ft 3 in)
height	4.88 m (16 ft)
wing area	86.12 m² (927 sq ft)

JAVELIN FAW.Mk 5

The Javelin served with 14 squadrons of the Royal Air Force, including No. 11 Squadron, which used various marks from 1960 to 1966.

Both pilot and navigator sat on Martin-Baker ejection seats. The navigator operated the radar set.

The wide fuselage was built as one unit with integral engines. The shape of the Javelin was one of its limitations, with drag being far too high.

The FAW.Mk 4 variant was the first to have a variable-incidence tailplane. The massive fin made the Javelin easy to recognize.

All-round visibility from the high-set cockpit was quite good for an aircraft of the 1950s.

The all-important radar system was British in the FAW.Mk 1, but American in the FAW.Mks 2 and 6.

The original four-cannon armament was fitted in the wings. Only two cannon were fitted when the aircraft was carrying the Firestreak.

Extra fuel was required by the RAF, and the Javelin FAW.Mk 5 had a belly tank for extended range.

Armstrong Siddeley's Sapphire turbojet was steadily improved; early versions were prone to flameouts and lacked power.

COMBAT DATA

MAXIMUM SPEED

The Javelin contrasted strongly with its counterparts from the Soviet Union and the United States. Its bulky fuselage and thick wing limited it to high subsonic speeds, where the huge Tupolev Tu-28 and the delta-winged Convair F-102 single-seater both had supersonic dash performance.

JAVELIN FAW.Mk 7 — 1130 km/h (702 mph)

Tu-28 'FIDDLER' — 1600 km/h (994 mph)

F-102 DELTA DAGGER — 1328 km/h (825 mph)

RANGE

The Javelin offered little in the way of increased range over its immediate predecessors, but it was good enough to protect the relatively small air space of the United Kingdom. Superpower air defenders were faced with vastly greater areas to protect, and their interceptors consequently had greater range.

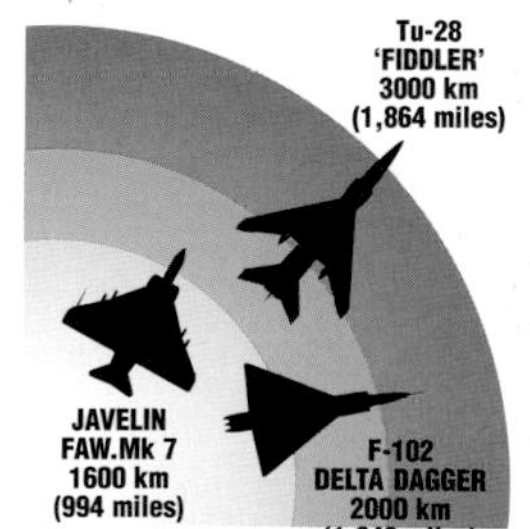

WEAPONS

The late 1950s saw the first large-scale deployment of guided air-to-air missiles. The American Falcon had similar performance but greater range than the British Firestreak, while the larger Soviet 'Ash' missile was capable of making intercepts at much greater distances.

JAVELIN FAW.Mk 7: 2 x 30-mm (1.18-in) cannon, 4 x Firestreak infra-red guided missiles

Tu-28 'FIDDLER': 4 x AA-5 'Ash' radar or infra-red guided missiles

F-102 DELTA DAGGER: 6 x AIM-4 or AIM-26 Falcon radar or infra-red guided missiles with conventional or nuclear warheads

Night and all-weather fighters of the 1950s

■ **DOUGLAS F3D SKYKNIGHT:** This carrier-based, purpose-designed two-seat all-weather jet fighter made the first jet-versus-jet kill at night during the Korean War.

■ **NORTHROP F-89 SCORPION:** The USAF's purpose-designed all-weather jet, the rocket-armed F-89 entered service in 1951 and was operational until the late 1950s.

■ **AVRO CF-100:** The first combat jet designed and built in Canada, the CF-100 became operational in 1952. It was the first straight-wing fighter to exceed Mach 1 in a dive.

■ **YAKOVLEV Yak-25:** Codenamed 'Flashlight' by NATO, the Yak-25 was the Soviet Union's first all-weather jet. It became operational in 1952 and served for more than two decades.

■ **DE HAVILLAND SEA VIXEN:** This striking twin-boom jet was Britain's carrier-borne equivalent of the Javelin. It served until replaced by the F-4 Phantom in the late 1960s.

Grumman

A-6 Intruder

● Classic naval aircraft ● Three decades of service ● Many upgrades

▲ *A familiar sight on US carrier decks in both Navy and Marine Corps markings, the A-6 proved a highly capable aircraft in many combat actions.*

On 28 February 1997 a ceremony was held at NAS (Naval Air Station) Whidbey Island to celebrate the retirement of the A-6 Intruder from the US Navy. The aircraft had provided more than three decades of service, most recently by A-6E variants equipped with advanced laser and infra-red (IR) targeting systems. In the course of its career the A-6 was involved in several combat actions and fought superbly during the first Gulf War.

Photo File

Grumman A-6 Intruder

▲ HARM compatibility
From 1990 the A-6E was given AGM-88 HARM (High-Speed Anti-Radiation Missile) capability.

◀ Into the storm
Wearing mission symbols and heavily armed, this A-6E prepares for launch on a Desert Storm raid.

▲ Intruder's last war
Both A-6E strike aircraft and KA-6D tankers were involved in the 1991 Gulf War.

▼ Tacit Rainbow
Designed to attack enemy radars, the AGM-136 Tacit Rainbow was tested on this A-6E.

▲ Protecting the Kurds
After the Gulf War Intruders were involved in Operation 'Provide Comfort' – the protection of Kurdish people returning to Northern Iraq.

Facts and Figures

- VA-75 squadron introduced the Intruder into service in 1963 and was the last unit to fly the type in 1997.
- Neither the advanced A-6F nor the cheaper A-6G entered production.
- F/A-18C/D Hornets currently undertake the missions once flown by Intruders.
- Several US Marine Corps A-6Es were passed to the Navy when the Marines retired their A-6s.
- The US Navy and Marines Corps intend to replace their A-6Es with F/A-18E/Fs.
- Some 240 A-6As became A-6Es; 12 were built per year between 1972 and 1977.

PROFILE

At the front line to the last

New avionics and radar were primary features of the A-6E Intruder when it first flew in 1970. In order to achieve rapid procurement of the new model within a limited budget, the US Navy began a programme of upgrading A-6As to the higher standard while new A-6Es were being built.

Further upgrades were added to the Intruder, including a navigation system that was used in the F-14A Tomcat. The most important modification, however, was the addition of a Target Recognition Attack Multi-sensor (TRAM) turret beneath the nose. This contained laser, IR and video sensors, allowing accurate targeting and compatibility with smart, laser-guided munitions.

A programme to fit the A-6 fleet with new composite wings was started in 1988. In addition, the capability to fire stand-off missiles, including the AGM-84E SLAM, was added in the early 1990s, making the last of the Intruders highly capable attack platforms.

Short-sighted US Navy officials cancelled the formidable A-6F in favour of the A-12. This was later scrapped.

A removable air-to-air refuelling probe was normally mounted on the centreline, aft of the nose radome. Refuelling was possible from KA-6Ds and other hose-equipped tankers.

Early in the Intruder programme, it was realised that the rear fuselage-mounted airbrakes interfered with airflow around the tail. Hence split airbrakes were employed at each wingtip.

For stowage aboard the carrier, the Intruder's wings were folded hydraulically at a hinge line just outboard of the outer pylon.

A-6E Intruder

Type: all-weather shipborne attack aircraft

Powerplant: two 41.40-kN (9,040-lb.-thrust) Pratt & Whitney J52-P-8B turbojets

Maximum speed: 1037 km/h (643 m.p.h.) clean at sea level

Maximum climb rate: 2323 m/min (7,620 f.p.m.)

Range: 1627 km (1,008 mi.) with maximum military load; ferry range 5222 km (3,240 mi.)

Service ceiling: 12,925 m (42,400 ft.)

Weights: empty 12,132 kg (26,690 lb.); maximum for catapult launch 26,580 kg (58,478 lb.)

Armament: a maximum of 8165 kg (17,963 lb.) ordnance and external fuel

Dimensions:

span	16.15 m (53 ft.)
length	16.69 m (54 ft. 9 in.)
height	4.93 m (16 ft. 2 in.)
wing area	49.13 m² (529 sq. ft.)

A-6E INTRUDER

In service with VA-42 'Green Pawns', this A-6E wears the low-visibility camouflage which was common at the end of the type's career. VA-42 was the Atlantic Fleet Replenishment Squadron.

Both the pilot and navigator sat on Martin-Baker GRU-7 ejector seats. The bombardier/navigator was positioned to starboard, slightly below and behind the pilot, and was responsible for operating the attack systems.

Intruders proved vulnerable to small-arms fire over Vietnam, a problem which was to surface again when the type was used at low level in the Gulf. The prominent exhausts could also attract heat-seeking surface-to-air missiles.

FLIR and laser-designator systems were located in the TRAM turret, at the heart of the A-6E's attack avionics.

Shown here with a load of 18 Mk 82 227-kg (500-lb.) bombs, the A-6E was also able to carry stand-off weapons such as the AGM-84E SLAM.

Single-piece, all-moving tailplanes provided pitch control and all flying controls were hydraulically powered. The pipe beneath the rudder hinge line allowed fuel to be jettisoned from the fuselage tanks.

COMBAT DATA

THRUST

With its afterburning engines, the F/A-18C is a more powerful aircraft than the A-6E or A-7E which it has replaced. It has shorter range than the A-6E, however.

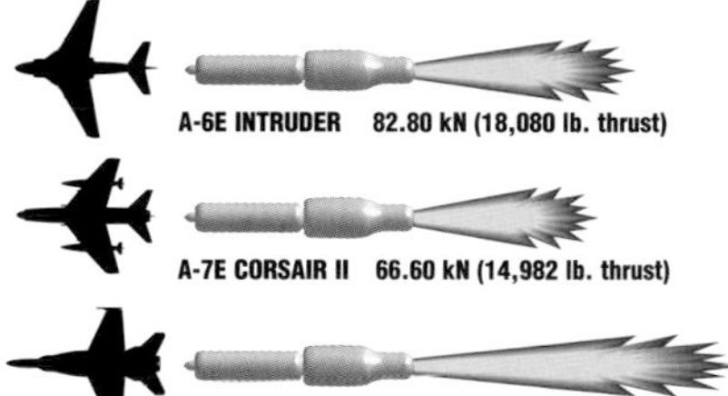

BOMBLOAD

As a dedicated attack aircraft, the A-6E could carry a formidable bombload. The A-7E was the US Navy's second attack platform, but did not have the weapons-carrying ability of the A-6E.

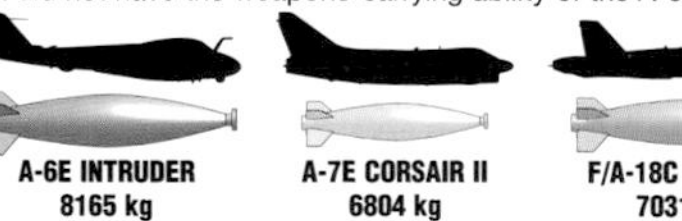

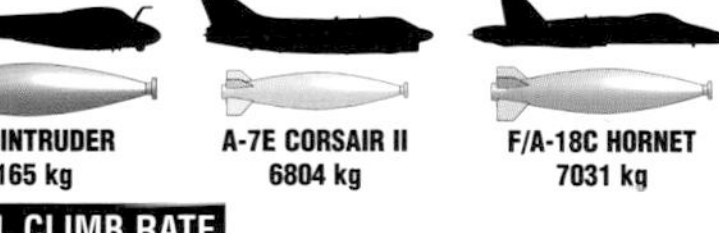

INITIAL CLIMB RATE

Comparing aircraft in clean condition, the F/A-18C has by far the most impressive climb rate. When the F/A-18E/F is introduced, the Navy hopes to overcome the range deficiencies of the F/A-18C/D.

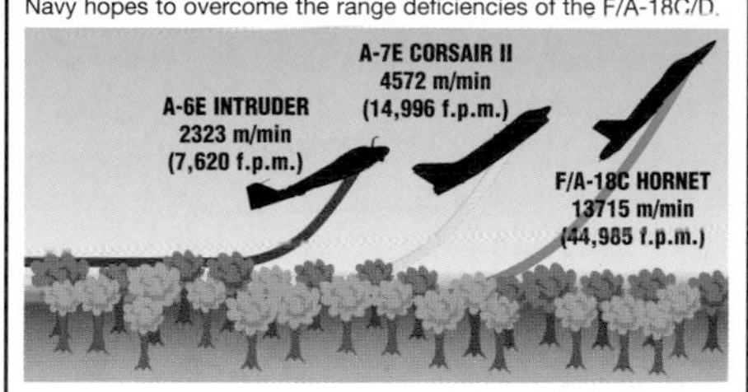

TRAM attack

Gyro-stabilisation allows the TRAM turret to remain locked on to the target, even as the aircraft overflies it.

1 TARGETING INFORMATION: Using its Forward-Looking Infra-Red (FLIR) and laser-targeting systems, the A-6E is able to calculate precise targeting information for dumb or laser-guided munitions.

2 OVER THE TARGET: FLIR allows the A-6E to attack the hottest parts of a target; the engine room of a ship or a moving tank. The TRAM turret rotates to keep the target designated and in view of the IR system.

3 POST-STRIKE ASSESSMENT: After the attack the FLIR is able to look backwards from the turret. TV-like pictures are produced, which are viewed in the cockpit and recorded by an onboard video recorder for damage assessment.

GRUMMAN

A-6 INTRUDER

● **Two-seat attack** ● **First Gulf War veteran** ● **Carrier- and land-based**

One of the primary weapon systems of the 1991 Gulf conflict, the 1960s vintage American A-6 Intruder provided tactical bombing and close support airpower from aircraft-carriers and land bases. Initially the Intruders were used at low level, but Iraqi anti-aircraft fire quickly brought about a change in tactics. From medium altitude A-6s were able to wreak havoc unmolested in the last major conflict of the Intruder's long career.

▲ *Lieutenant Colonel Leif Larsen stands in front of his VMA(AW)-533 aircraft. The A-6 fleet (A-6Es and KA-6Ds of the US Navy and Marine Corps A-6Es) was heavily used during Operation Desert Storm.*

PHOTO FILE

GRUMMAN A-6 INTRUDER

◀ **Folding wings**
This A-6E demonstrates the Intruder's ability to fold its wings for stowage aboard a carrier. Carrier aircraft must be lashed down when parked on a carrier deck in case bad weather is encountered.

▲ **Retirement on the horizon**
After the 1991 Gulf War the Marine Corps replaced its A-6s with F/A-18s. The US Navy's replacement for the A-6 was the cancelled A-12 Avenger II.

▲ **Intruder refuels Prowler**
US Navy KA-6D tanker variants of the Intruder saw service in the Gulf. This one is refuelling an EA-6B.

▲ **Refuelling**
An A-6 takes on fuel from a USAF KC-135 tanker. The majority of the Coalition's tanker force was American, although other refuellers included aircraft from the RAF and the French air force.

▲ **Precision-guided munitions**
Carrier crewmen load a laser-guided bomb aboard an A-6 prior to a mission. Intruders also delivered a large tonnage of 'iron bombs'.

FACTS AND FIGURES

- A total of seven US aircraft-carriers participated in the 'Desert Shield' build-up and subsequent war.
- Five A-6 Intruders were lost in the Persian Gulf; two crewmen were killed.
- The Marine Corps flew A-6s in Vietnam and the Gulf, but has now retired its fleet.
- Two years before the war the US Navy cancelled the A-6F – an improved Intruder with new radar and turbofan engines.
- Intruders flew 6444 combat sorties from 17 January until 24 February 1991.
- The US Navy has now replaced its A-6s with the new enlarged F/A-18E/F Hornet.

PROFILE

First Gulf War tactical bomber

At dawn on 17 January 1991, the first full day of war, Saddam Hussein's guns sought out many Allied warplanes. Among them were the low-flying A-6 Intruders from no fewer than six US Navy aircraft-carriers, part of the largest sea armada in decades.

The twin-engined, two-seat Grumman A-6 all-weather attack aircraft first flew in 1960. The A-6E was an improved version of the Vietnam-era A-6.

Throughout the 1991 Gulf conflict US Navy A-6s attacked airfields, dams, transport facilities and other targets using a mixture of 'iron' bombs and precision-guided munitions. In addition, land-based Marine Intruders provided air support for ground forces.

Initially low-level attack, a method developed for war in Europe and Korea, was used. But this was a risky tactic against Iraq. An A-6 Intruder shot down on the first night of the war was hit by concentrated anti-aircraft fire encountered at low altitude. Following early losses the Intruders switched to medium altitude, where they were much less vulnerable.

The tanker version of the Intruder, the carrier-based KA-6D, was also in action in the Gulf, providing vital refuelling support to the US Navy. Only the EA-6B Prowler variant remains in service.

Above: Modified USAF tankers were able to refuel US Navy aircraft, such as these A-6 Intruders, during the Gulf War. This greatly improved operational flexibility.

Left: Both US Navy and Marine Corps Intruders were in action during Desert Storm. Navy A-6Es and KA-6Ds operated from aircraft-carriers and Marine A-6Es were based at Bahrain.

A-6E Intruder

Type: two-seat all-weather attack aircraft

Powerplant: two 41.37-kN (9,305-lb-thrust) Pratt & Whitney J52-P-8B turbojets

Maximum speed: 1037 km/h (644 mph) 'clean'

Range: 1627 km (1,011 miles) with maximum warload

Service ceiling: 12,925 m (42,405 ft)

Weights: empty 12,525 kg (27,613 lb); maximum take-off 26,580 kg (16,516 lb) (carrier launch) or 27,397 kg (60,400 lb) (land take-off)

Armament: up to 8165 kg (18,000 lb) of bombs and/or missiles, including AGM-65 Maverick, AGM-84 Harpoon/SLAM and AGM-88 HARM

Dimensions:		
	span	16.15 m (53 ft)
	length	16.69 m (54 ft 9 in)
	height	4.93 m (16 ft 2 in)
	wing area	49.13 m² (529 sq ft)

A-6E Intruder

This A-6E served with Marine All-Weather Attack Squadron 533 'Hawks' during Operation Desert Storm, when it was based at Sheikh Isa in Bahrain.

Split trailing-edge airbrakes are fitted on each wingtip. The complex wing has spoilers, flaperons and leading-edge slats.

The generous load-carrying capacity of over eight tons includes both 'dumb' bombs, precision-guided munitions (PGMs) and auxiliary fuel tanks.

The two-man crew consists of a pilot and a bombardier/navigator. The main part of the avionics suite is the Norden AN/APQ-148 multi mode radar.

The main wings of the A-6 fold at about mid-span to ease stowage aboard aircraft-carriers.

During the Gulf conflict VMA(AW)-533's squadron hawk emblem was modified to include a laser-guided bomb.

The Target Recognition and Attack Multi-sensor (TRAM) turret contains a forward-looking infra-red (FLIR) sensor and a laser designator.

A-6Es use two non-afterburning Pratt & Whitney J52 turbojets of the type fitted to the A-4 Skyhawk. Plans for a re-engined F404 turbofan-powered version were abandoned.

Maximum internal fuel capacity is 8873 litres (2,344 US gal), to which can be added up to five tanks of 1135 litres (300 US gal) or 1514 litres (400 US gal) capacity each. An air-to-air refuelling probe is fitted forward of the cockpit.

COMBAT DATA

MAXIMUM SPEED

The swept-wing Jaguar, with its afterburning turbofans, has by far the highest top speed among these Gulf War attack aircraft. Like the A-6, the Jaguar was initially deployed on low-level strikes.

A-6E INTRUDER 1037 km/h (644 mph)

JAGUAR GR.Mk 1A 1338 km/h (831 mph)

AV-8B HARRIER 1065 km/h (662 mph)

BOMBLOAD

The carrier-based A-6 has an excellent load-carrying capacity. This can be made up of weapons, fuel and other equipment. The AV-8B's bombload is limited by its V/STOL capability.

A-6E INTRUDER 8165 kg (18,000 lb)

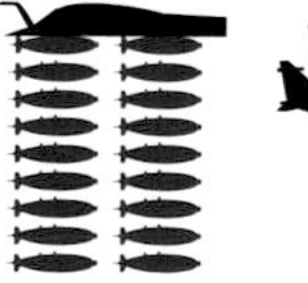

JAGUAR GR.Mk 1A 4534 kg (9,996 lb)

AV-8B HARRIER 4173 kg (9,200 lb)

FERRY RANGE

Ferry range is important when an aircraft is required to deploy a long distance from its base. It determines the number of air-to-air refuellings necessary during the journey.

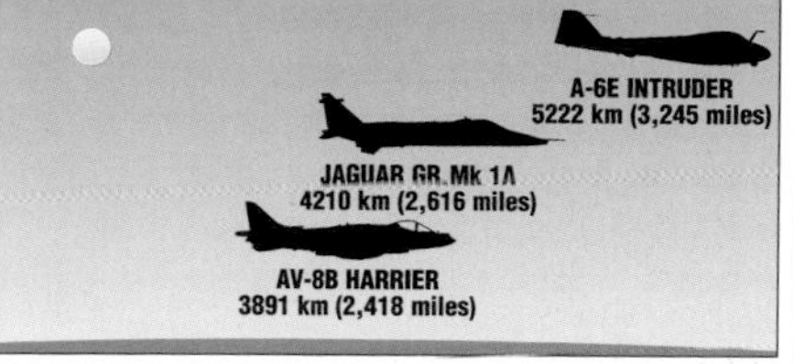

Sinking Iraqi gunboats

FAST PATROL BOAT THREAT: Iraq's small navy in the Persian Gulf included captured Kuwaiti 'TNC45'-class patrol boats equipped with Exocet anti-ship missiles. This threat was met by Royal Navy Lynx helicopters.

PATROL BOATS ENGAGED: On 8 February 1991 a Lynx from a Royal Navy destroyer engaged two patrol boats, but fired all of its Sea Skua anti-ship missiles without destroying them both.

ASSISTANCE REQUESTED: The Lynx radioed its ship which, in turn, summoned help from US Navy A-6s armed with Rockeye cluster bombs. These attacked the boat that was still afloat and destroyed it.

GRUMMAN

C-2A GREYHOUND

● COD aircraft ● Derived from the E-2 Hawkeye ● Twin turboprop

During the 1960s Grumman built the Greyhound for hauling supplies and people from land bases to the decks of the US Navy's aircraft-carriers. This is known in jargon as the COD (carrier on-board delivery) mission. The Greyhound draws its fundamental design features from the better-known Grumman E-2 Hawkeye airborne early-warning aircraft. It is a superb aircraft with a fine record of safety and performance.

▲ *The US Navy's C-2 Greyhound fleet was delivered in two batches, beginning in the mid-1960s and ending in the late 1980s. Most of the original batch have now been retired.*

PHOTO FILE

GRUMMAN C-2A GREYHOUND

▼ Atlantic and Pacific C-2s
Two transport units are equipped with C-2s and are based in the US. A detachment is also stationed in Japan. Training is carried out at NAS Norfolk, Virginia.

▲ Carrier on-board delivery
COD squadrons are attached to Hawkeye-equipped airborne early warning wings.

◀ Folding wings for easy stowage
The Greyhound has the same wing as the E-2 Hawkeye. Wing folding is a necessity for aircraft moving within the confines of a fleet carrier.

▼ Mail call
One of the Greyhound's most important deliveries, at least from the sailors' point of view, is the cargo of mail for crews.

▼ Different cargoes
As well as ferrying personnel, the C-2 delivers weapons for the carrier's combat aircraft. Among the weapons shown here are three AIM-54 Phoenix air-to-air missiles for an F-14 Tomcat.

FACTS AND FIGURES

- The Greyhound prototype completed its maiden flight on 18 November 1964.
- Fifty-eight Greyhounds were produced in two batches – between 1964 and 1968 and between 1985 and 1989.
- A proposal to re-open the Greyhound production line was rejected in 1991.
- Plans to replace the Greyhound with a version of the Lockheed S-3A Viking met with only limited success.
- The C-2A replaced the Grumman C-1A Trader, which was based on the S-2.
- Grumman considered a jet-powered version of the C-2 but it was never built.

PROFILE

Delivery van of the US Fleet

The Grumman C-2A Greyhound was developed in the early 1960s by mating a deeper, more capacious fuselage to the basic wings and tail of the E-2 Hawkeye. The result was a highly effective transport for the essential task of delivering supplies to aircraft-carriers at sea.

Although it is equipped with a tailhook and folding wings for carrier operations, the Greyhound is not intended to be stationed aboard a carrier. Instead, it is operated by a shore-based squadron placed in a strategic location to resupply ships at sea. The C-2A Greyhound is also successful in its secondary duty as a training aircraft, and has been used for training Hawkeye crews.

Before the cockpits of combat aircraft were opened up to women in 1993, the Greyhound was one of the very few carrier-capable aeroplanes to be flown by female pilots. Unlike the crews of fighters and bombers, these transport pilots fly a real-world mission every time they take off and land. Great care has to be taken when landing the Greyhound on an aircraft-carrier because its large wingspan leaves little room for manoeuvre on a crowded deck. But, for its size, the Greyhound is relatively easy to fly.

Above: Carrying the 'RG' tailcode of the since-disestablished VRC-50, this Greyhound was based at Cubi Point in the Philippines.

Below: This photograph of 162153, one of the batch built in the 1980s, shows the wing and tail design to good effect. These are shared by the E-2 Hawkeye.

C-2A Greyhound

Type: twin-engine carrier onboard delivery (COD) transport

Powerplant: two 3663-kW (4,900-hp.) Allison T56-A-425 turboprop engines

Maximum speed: 574 km/h (356 m.p.h.)

Range: 1930 km (1,792 mi.)

Service ceiling: 10,210 m (33,500 ft.)

Weights: empty 16,486 kg (36,269 lb.); maximum take-off 26,081 kg (57,378 lb.)

Accommodation: two pilots, up to 39 passengers or 20 stretchers plus four attendants or up to 6800 kg (14,960 lb.) of palletised cargo

Dimensions:

span	24.56 m	(80 ft. 6 in.)
length	17.32 m	(56 ft. 10 in.)
height	4.84 m	(15 ft. 10 in.)
wing area	65.03 m²	(700 sq. ft.)

C-2A GREYHOUND

Aircraft 155124 was one of the original batch of 19 Greyhounds delivered from the mid-1960s. 'JM' is the tailcode of Fleet Logistics Support Squadron 24 (VR-24), 'Lifting Eagles', based at Sigonella, Italy.

In all, including prototypes, 58 Greyhounds have been delivered to the US Navy. The 39 built in the 1980s differ from earlier C-2s in having uprated engines and an auxiliary power unit fitted.

The Greyhound's engines are the same 3663-kW (4,900-hp.) Allison T56-A-425 turbines as those fitted to the E-2C Hawkeye. This commonality between the two aircraft eases maintenance and reduces the need to carry different spare parts in the cramped confines of an aircraft-carrier.

Redesigned for the transport role, the Greyhound's fuselage is considerably larger than that of the Hawkeye. When configured for passengers, the Greyhound can carry up to 39 people. Twenty stretchers can also be installed.

Mission profiles for the Greyhound centre on its role for the delivery of high-priority cargo and passengers to and from carriers at sea. Its range of 1900 km (1,180 mi.) when fully loaded is far greater than that of land-based helicopters.

The tail design is another feature shared with the E-2. Four fins are required to provide sufficient tail area, but must still fit within the cramped confines of the carrier hangar. All except the port inner fin have a rudder fitted.

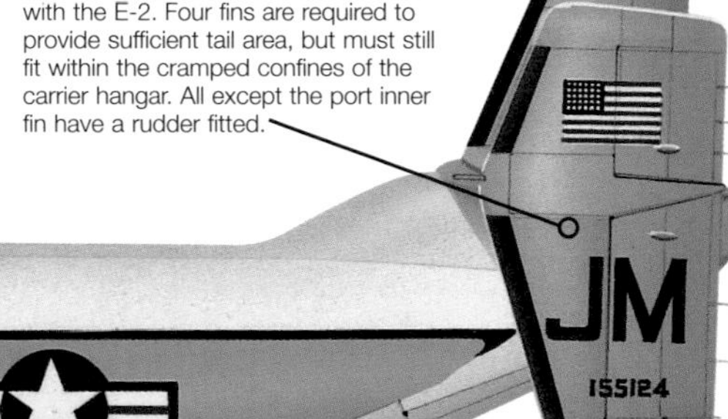

For the loading of bulky items like aircraft engines and weapons, the C-2 has a rear ramp. An arrester hook is fitted for carrier landings.

ACTION DATA

LOAD CAPACITY

The tilt-rotor Osprey, if funded, will greatly enhance the COD capabilities of the fleet. It has almost twice the capacity of the C-2. For land-based operations the C-2 has a maximum load of 6800 kg. The Viking, based on the S-3 ASW aircraft, has a limited capacity.

C-2A GREYHOUND 6800 kg (14,960 lb.)

V-22A OSPREY 9072 kg (19,958 lb.)

US-3A VIKING 2600 kg (5,720 lb.)

RANGE

When fully loaded and making a short take-off, the Osprey has an impressive range performance – an improvement on that of the C-2. The US-3A also has an excellent range.

C-2A GREYHOUND 1930 km (1,197 mi.)

US-3A VIKING 3700 km (2,294 mi.)

V-22A OSPREY 3336 km (2,068 mi.)

TAKE-OFF RUN

The Viking has the shorter take-off distance of the two fixed-wing aircraft. The Osprey tilt-rotor has a vertical take-off capability, but uses a short take-off run when carrying all but the smallest payloads.

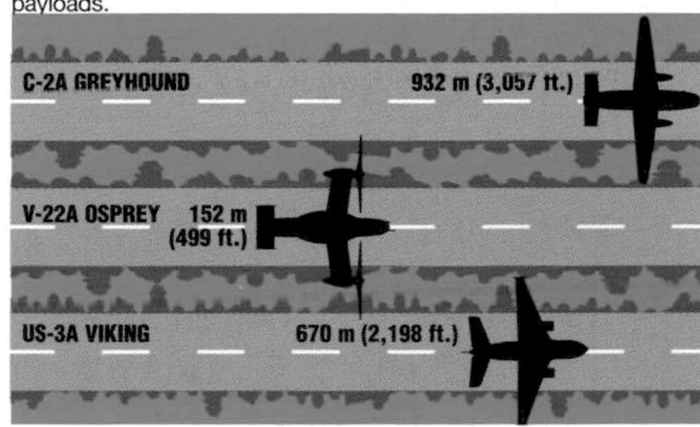

Carrier on-board delivery aircraft

GRUMMAN TBM-3R AVENGER: As well as carrying personnel, COD Avengers delivered nuclear weapon components in times of crisis.

GRUMMAN C-1 TRADER: The Trader was a variant of the S-2 Tracker, which had its ASW equipment removed to make room for freight.

GRUMMAN US-3A VIKING: To supplement the C-2 fleet, a small number of anti-submarine S-3A Vikings have been converted for COD tasks.

FAIREY GANNET COD.Mk 4: In common with American COD designs, the British Gannet COD.Mk 4 was based on an existing design.

GRUMMAN

E-2 HAWKEYE

● **Combat proven** ● **Airborne early warning** ● **Fighter controller**

▲ *Throughout 22 years of service the E-2 Hawkeye has become an indispensable part of US naval operations. The latest E-2C Group II aircraft are far more capable and are likely to remain in use for some time.*

Designed as a flying radar station, the Hawkeye is the US Navy's eye in the sky. Sometimes called 'the affordable AWACS' (Airborne Warning and Control System), it is just what the US Navy requires to guard its aircraft-carrier battle groups and to direct friendly warplanes when the action begins. This twin-engined aircraft, with its long, slender wing, huge tail, and saucer-shaped rotodome, is now a familiar sight in every US Navy carrier air wing.

PHOTO FILE

GRUMMAN E-2 HAWKEYE

▲ **Rotodome**

An E-2C from USS Constellation *shows off its enormous radar rotodome.*

▼ **Fuel venting**

An anonymous E-2, probably flying a research and development mission, dumps fuel from the rear-mounted fuel vent pipe.

Catapult launch ▶

The Hawkeye runs its engines up to full power before the steam catapult hurls it from the carrier deck at take-off speed.

▼ **Feet-dry Hawkeye**

All US Navy E-2s have a permanent shore base and most export customers fly their E-2s solely from airbases. This aircraft flies from NAS Norfolk, Virginia.

▲ **Folded Hawkeye**

With its wings folded the Hawkeye presents a more compact shape for stowage aboard the crowded decks of an aircraft-carrier.

FACTS AND FIGURES

- The Hawkeye was the last propeller-driven naval aircraft built by Grumman, the world's primary naval aircraft builder.
- In December 1971 Israel purchased four Hawkeyes equipped with APS-125 radar.
- Other users of the Hawkeye include Egypt, Japan, Singapore and Taiwan.
- The Hawkeye made its first flight from Grumman's Peconic River, Long Island, facility on 21 October 1960.
- The Hawkeye is now back in production, equipped with the AN/APS-145 radar.
- Hawkeyes are launched ahead of other carrier aircraft and are the last to return.

PROFILE

Eyes of the fleet

Japan received the first of its E-2s in 1982 and it is known as Daya (kite) in Japanese service. Several countries fly the E-2, including Egypt, Israel and Singapore.

Nicknamed the 'Hummer' by its crews, the E-2 Hawkeye was designed to replace the earlier E-1B Tracer, the first radar plane in the fleet. The Hawkeye, with turboprop engines, a higher speed and a higher ceiling, was a great improvement over its predecessor. The Hawkeye introduced a General Electric APS-96 radar, the antenna of which revolves at six revolutions per minute inside the disc shaped radome. The first production Hawkeyes began reaching squadron VAW-110 'Firebirds' based at North Island, California, in 1964. In Vietnam, the Hawkeye performed its primary mission of protecting aircraft-carriers with its radar 'eyes', but it also served as a flying headquarters for F-4 Phantom IIs and F-8 Crusaders on combat air patrols.

The Hawkeye's radar unit has changed again, to APS-138, APS-139 and APS-145. The APS-145, now being retrofitted to aircraft in the fleet, offers better resistance to jamming. Although it is now getting old, the present E-2C Hawkeye is an up-to-date, state-of-the-art military fighting machine.

Avionics systems create a vast amount of heat and must be kept cool to maintain their efficiency. A large dorsal radiator cools the fluid of the E-2's cooling system.

Remaining on station for four hours, 300 km (186 mi.) from the carrier and without inflight refuelling, the Hawkeye requires long endurance. This is achieved by its long, slender wings.

E-2C Hawkeye

Type: carrier-based airborne early warning aircraft

Powerplant: two 3661-kW (4,910-hp.) Allison T56-A425 turboprop engines

Maximum speed: 598 km/h (374 m.p.h.)

Endurance: 6 hours 6 min

Ferry range: 2583 km (1,602 mi.)

Service ceiling: 9390 m (30,000 ft.)

Weight: maximum take-off 23556 kg (51,900 lb.)

Accommodation: crew of five; fuel load of 5624 kg (12,399 lb.)

Dimensions:

span	24.56 m (80 ft. 7 in.)
length	17.54 m (57 ft. 7 in.)
height	5.58 m (18 ft. 3 in.)
wing area	65.03 m² (2,593 sq. ft.)

E-2C HAWKEYE

This aircraft belongs to VAW-126 'Seahawks', part of CVW-3, aboard the USS *John F. Kennedy*. The unit is home based at NAS Norfolk, Virginia, and proved invaluable during Operation Desert Storm.

A crew of five is normally carried, including pilot and co-pilot, a combat information centre officer, air control officer and radar operator.

With a diameter of 7.32 m (24 ft.) the rotodome houses the AN/APS-139 radar and 'identification friend or foe' systems. It is lowered on jacks for parking on the carrier.

A four-fin tail arrangement was required to give the Hawkeye sufficient directional stability, but the tail had to be small enough to fit in a carrier's hangar.

Very strong undercarriage units are features of all ship-borne aircraft designed to be launched by steam catapult. This bar on the nosewheel leg connects with the catapult shuttle on the deck.

Although the original E-2C was powered by the 3661-kW (4,910-hp.) T56-A-425, the latest E-2C Group IIs are fitted with the even more powerful 3803-kW (5,096-hp.) T56-A-427.

US Navy E-2Cs have been slow to take on the low-visibility markings of the rest of the fleet, retaining colourful squadron markings and grey and white camouflage.

COMBAT DATA

SERVICE CEILING

The Hawkeye requires a good service ceiling because the higher the radar is, the further it can see. The E-2 is being fitted with the exceptional AN/APS-145 radar, giving it stunning performance.

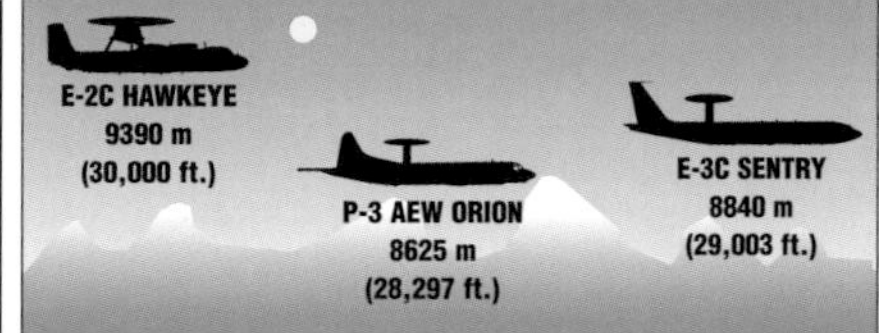

RADAR RANGE

Using the latest AN/APS-145 radar the P-3 AEW will be able to locate low-flying aircraft targets at very long range. In its E-3D and E-3F variants the Sentry is much more capable than the E-3C.

E-2C HAWKEYE 480 km (300 mi.)

P-3 AEW ORION 556 km (345 mi.)

E-3C SENTRY 470 km (291 mi.)

CREW

As it is a small aircraft the E-2C carries few crew. This means a necessary reliance on automation and a heavy workload for operators. In larger aircraft there are more crew to divide the work between.

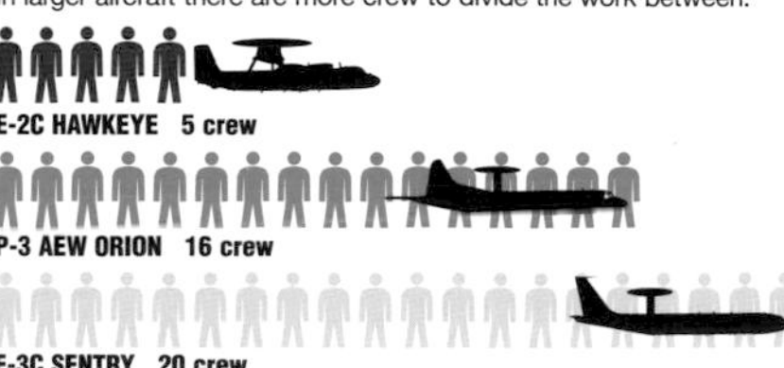

Controlling the air war

OVER THE HORIZON: Acting as an extension of the aircraft-carrier's own radar, the E-2C is able to monitor possible threats at greater distances.

AIRBORNE CONTROLLER: When the E-2 detects enemy aircraft or anti-ship missiles (ASMs) it alerts F-14 Tomcats, which are sent on barrier combat air patrol to intercept.

F-14

E-2

9150 m (30,000 ft.)

Tu-22M

ASM

AIRCRAFT-CARRIER

RANGE km 900 800 700 600 500 400 300 200 100

miles 500 400 300 200 100

GRUMMAN

EA-6B PROWLER

● **Electronic warfare aircraft** ● **In combat from Vietnam to the Gulf**

▲ *The jamming systems of the EA-6B are some of the most sophisticated in the world. A handful of these aircraft can 'black out' an area the size of France with their powerful electronic systems.*

Based on the Grumman A-6 Intruder, the EA-6B Prowler harnesses the electron to 'clean up' combat zones so that friendly warplanes can attack in safety. The Prowler takes a pilot and three operators into action with a powerhouse of 'black boxes', intent on jamming an enemy's radar. But it does more than jam; with its HARM missiles, the EA-6 is a fearsome radar-killer in its own right.

PHOTO FILE

GRUMMAN EA-6B PROWLER

▲ ADVCAP Prowler
In 1990 the advanced capability (ADVCAP) variant of the EA-6B was introduced. This is fitted with a global positioning kit for pinpoint navigation, and chaff, flare and self-protection jamming systems.

▼ Electronic power
The Prowler's systems are never turned on when it is on deck, as they emit enough energy to microwave anyone passing by.

Folding wings ▶
With its wings folded up, the EA-6 has a narrow profile. Under the fixed wingroot is the massive TJS jamming pod, containing a high-powered noise generator and a tracking receiver. Operating power is generated by a wind turbine on the pod's nose.

▲ Catapult launch
The EA-6B is a heavy machine, and a catapult launch is essential for it to reach flying speed. If for any reason the launch fails, the four-man crew will instantly eject as the aircraft clears the deck.

▼ Gulf strike mission
Prowlers were vital components in the first Gulf war, protecting the massive Coalition air offensive which destroyed Saddam Hussein's air defences.

FACTS AND FIGURES

- ➤ The first EA-6 Prowler flew at Calverton, New York, on 25 May 1968.
- ➤ The Prowler has a black radiation warning symbol on its nose so that deck crews do not get 'fried' inadvertently.
- ➤ Home port for Navy EA-6Bs is Whidbey Island Naval Air Station, north of Seattle.
- ➤ The Prowler has been through five electronics upgrade programmes.
- ➤ When the EF-111 Raven fleet was retired in 1998, EA-6Bs were deployed in their place.
- ➤ The HARM missile used by some Prowlers has a launch weight of 361 kg (749 lb.).

PROFILE

Jamming with the fleet

The Prowler is one of the most expensive aircraft in the US Navy inventory. The huge cost of the EA-6B is offset, however, by the lives and aircraft saved by the protection it can provide.

Prowlers are in short supply and are sorely needed. Modern air power demands electronic warfare aircraft, and the US Navy developed the Grumman EA-6B to give its Carrier Air Wings a trump card in today's hi-tech warfare. The Prowler fought in Vietnam (1972), and in every action since – Grenada (1983), Libya (1986), both Gulf Wars, Bosnia (1995) and Afghanistan. The final Prowler was delivered in 1991 and the final 'upgrade' programme curtailed two years later. The Prowler is 1.37 metres longer than the A-6 Intruder and substantially heavier. It sends out jamming transmissions from underwing pods, and analyses hostile signals received by equipment in a bulge on its tail.

Although well into middle age, the Prowler remains one of the best electronic warriors and saw service in Afghanistan and the 2003 Gulf War. Prowlers replaced US Air Force EF-111 Ravens even though Prowlers are slower and lack the Raven's 'reach' to accompany strike aircraft on some missions.

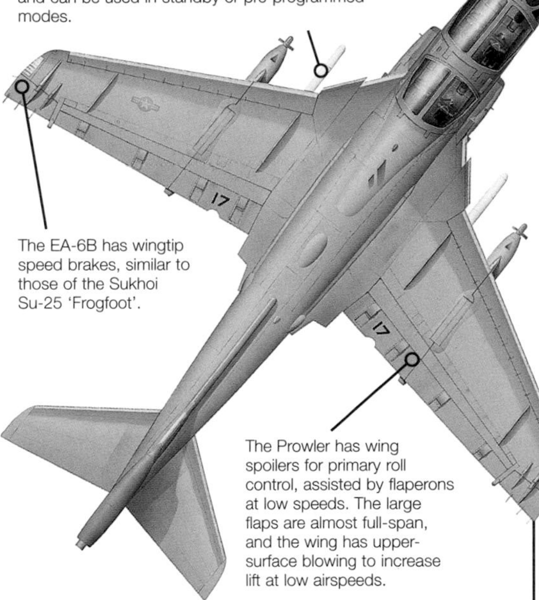

The large HARM missile has a passive seeker head and can be used in standby or pre-programmed modes.

The EA-6B has wingtip speed brakes, similar to those of the Sukhoi Su-25 'Frogfoot'.

The Prowler has wing spoilers for primary roll control, assisted by flaperons at low speeds. The large flaps are almost full-span, and the wing has upper-surface blowing to increase lift at low airspeeds.

EA-6B PROWLER

This EA-6B 'ICAP-II' Prowler flies with VMAQ-2, one of four US Marine Corps squadrons based at the Marine Corps Air Station, Cherry Point. The unit is fully carrier-capable and often deploys with the fleet.

The pilot sits in the front port cockpit, surrounded by three electronic countermeasures officers (ECMOs). ECMO one sits by his side and operates the navigation, radar and communications equipment, with ECMO two and three operating the tactical jamming suite.

ECMO two operates the ground-mapping Norden APS-130 radar system, a downgraded version of the A-6E's APQ-156 with attack functions deleted.

The large pod on top of the tail fin houses the system integration receiver, which detects hostile radar emissions and sends them to a central computer for threat analysis.

Self-protection jamming to decoy enemy radar-guided missiles is provided by a deception jamming suite. The antenna for this is located next to the refuelling probe.

The ICAP-II improvement programme allows the pair of underwing TJS pods to jam in any one of seven frequency bands. They can also simultaneously interfere with more than one enemy radar, even when they are using widely different frequencies.

The Prowler can carry an internal fuel load of 6995 kg (15,390 lb.), with 4547 kg (10,000 lb.) in underwing tanks.

A large avionics pallet and fuel tanks occupy the fuselage area behind the engines. The J52 turbojet was also used in the McDonnell Douglas A-4 Skyhawk.

The aft-facing cylindrical pod on the fin is the ALQ-136 deception countermeasures system, known as the 'beercan' to crews.

EA-6B Prowler

Type: four-seat electronic warfare aircraft

Powerplant: two Pratt & Whitney 49.80-kN (9,300-lb.-thrust) J52-P-408 turbojets

Maximum speed: 1048 km/h (650 m.p.h.) in 'clean' condition at sea level

Range: 1770 km (1,097 mi.)

Service ceiling: 12,550 m (41,164 ft.)

Weights: empty 14,588 kg (32,028 lb.); loaded 24,703 kg (54,347 lb.)

Payload: four AGM-88A HARM (High-speed Anti-Radiation Missiles), AN/ALQ-99 emitter pods, or Aero 1-D 1136-litre (300-gal.) drop-tanks; some with AN/ALQ-149 jamming system

Dimensions:

span	16.15 m (53 ft.)
length	18.24 m (60 ft.)
height	4.95 m (16 ft.)
wing area	49.13 m² (529 sq. ft.)

COMBAT DATA

MAXIMUM SPEED

The Prowler was derived from a subsonic carrier bomber which was able to fly and fight in all weathers, by day or night. The EA-6 lacks the Mach 2 performance of the EF-111, but since its main function in to escort formations of heavily-laden strike aircraft at subsonic speeds this is no real handicap.

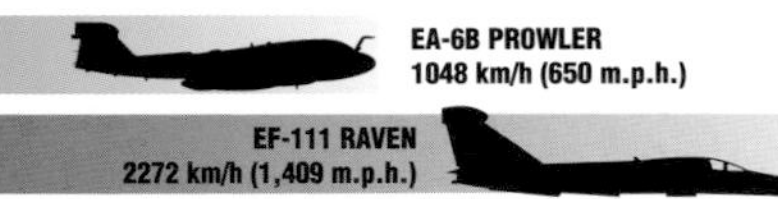

RANGE

The EA-6 has a shorter range than its land-based equivalents. Nevertheless, thanks to its ability to launch from a carrier anywhere on the world's oceans it can reach a much greater range of potential targets than aircraft like the EF-111, which can only operate from a few high-tech air bases.

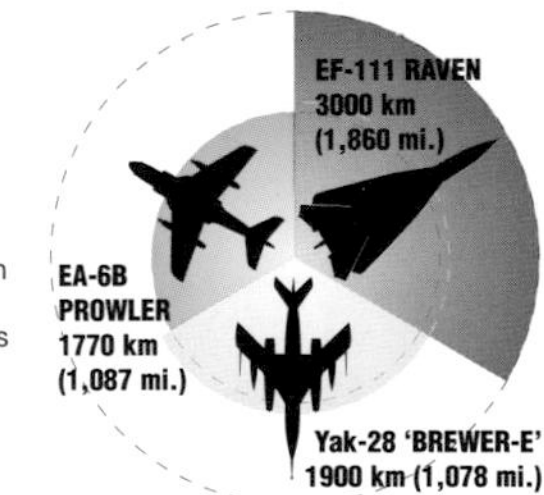

ELECTRONIC WARFARE CAPABILITY

The Prowler and the EF-111 have a similar electronics fit, but the 'Spark Vark' is a more recent adaptation, and greater computerisation means that one electronic warfare officer can do the job of three aboard the Prowler. Both are a great deal more sophisticated than the 'Brewer', which was operational with Soviet forces until the break-up of the USSR.

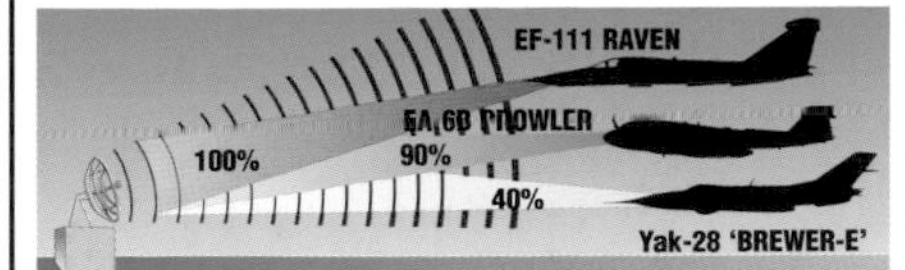

Location of enemy radar transmitters

Prowlers will often operate in pairs, both to produce wider and more powerful jamming transmissions and, as depicted here, to locate and fix enemy radar sites.

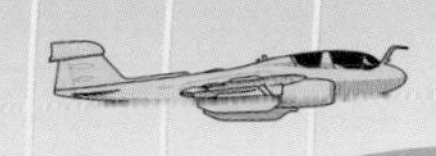

LEAD PROWLER: ➤ One aircraft flies close enough to the enemy to persuade him to activate his radar. The 'senso' notes the exact bearing of the enemy transmitter.

◄ TRAILING PROWLER: Close enough to pick up the enemy radar, but far enough behind for any radar beams to be too weak to return an echo to the enemy, the second Prowler also notes the bearing of the radar site.

MISSION ACCOMPLISHED: Once the two Prowlers have noted the radar's bearing, they can turn away before coming within range of enemy missile defences.

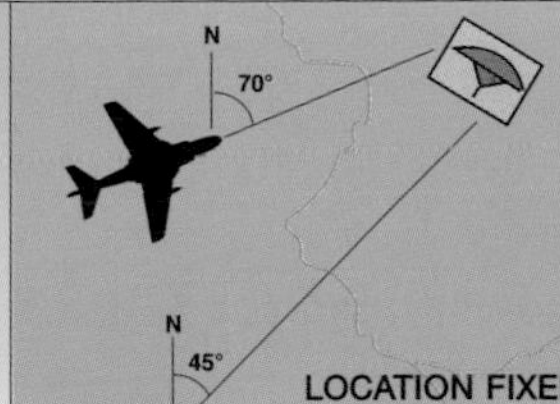

LOCATION FIXED: A simple triangulation calculation exactly fixes the location of the enemy radar.

Grumman

F9F Panther

● Early navy jet ● Korean War MiG-killer ● Tactical fighter-bomber

The F9F Panther brought the jet age to the US Navy. Although not the USN's first carrier jet, it was the first to reach widespread service and to win real popularity among the Navy and Marine pilots who flew in it. There were reconnaissance and target-drone Panthers, too, but this superbly tough warplane is best remembered as the most important carrier-borne jet fighter of the Korean War.

▲ *The Panther gained many 'firsts' for the US Navy. It was the first USN jet to go to war, the first to use a blown flap and the first to try an inflight-refuelling system.*

PHOTO FILE

Grumman F9F Panther

▼ Wingtip tanks
Besides being useful perches for the deck crews, the Panther's tip tanks helped to improve the aircraft's rather poor rate of roll.

▲ Swinging guns ▶
This experimental Emerson gun installation was tested, but, like similar projects in Russia by MiG, it was not used in squadron service.

Prototype ▶
Despite being lost in an accident, the first Panther prototype showed promise.

▼ Rocket ship
A favourite armament of Korean War Panthers was six high-velocity aircraft rockets, used against surface targets.

▼ Carrier operations ▶
Although the Panther was basically sound, it had a high landing speed and poor control in certain conditions, providing the US Navy with valuable experience of jet operations at sea.

FACTS AND FIGURES

- ➤ The first flight by a Panther prototype was an inadvertent 'hop' during taxi tests on 21 November 1947.
- ➤ The Navy's first jet-versus-jet 'kill' was a MiG-15 downed on 9 November 1950.
- ➤ Panthers flew 78,000 combat sorties in the Korean 'police action'.
- ➤ The only foreign air arm to receive F9Fs was the Argentine air force, which acquired 24 Panthers in 1958.
- ➤ Panthers shot down two North Korean Yak-9 prop-driven fighters.
- ➤ In total, 1385 Panthers were built by Grumman between 1947 and 1953.

PROFILE

The first Navy jet to go to war

Panthers were usually finished in an all-midnight blue paint scheme. This colour was used on all versions of the aircraft, including the ground attack and reconnaissance variants.

The F9F Panther was the most successful of the first generation of US Navy jets. Originally proposed as a four-jet combat craft, which the navy sensibly rejected, the single-engined Panther was a sturdy warplane which performed well, but required nurturing over time.

Panthers flew in US Navy squadrons with three choices of powerplant (J33, J42 and J48) before the USN settled on the F9F-5 propelled by a J48, based on the Rolls-Royce Tay.

The Panther flew for the first time in 1947, and was the first carrier-based jet fighter to see combat. Extensively used on ground-attack duties in Korea, the Panther was a fine warplane in the hands of a trained pilot. Its structural strength, a trademark of the 'Grumman Iron Works', helped Marines enormously when they flew Panthers through gunfire to attack ground troops in Korea. But in spite of the fact that a Panther gained the US Navy's first jet kill, a MiG-15 in November 1950, the F9F was seriously outclassed by the swept-wing F-86 Sabre and MiG-15 which were entering service.

The last operational Panther was retired in October 1958, but the old fighter continued as a training machine and target tug well into the 1960s.

The thick wingroot, with its engine intakes built into it, was typical of Grumman's famously strong engineering. The folding hinge was unusually close inboard to the fuselage.

F9F-5 Panther

Type: single-seat carrier-based fighter and attack aircraft

Powerplant: one 31.14-kN (7,004-lb-thrust) Pratt & Whitney J48-P-6 turbojet (licence-built Rolls-Royce Tay)

Maximum speed: 932 km/h (579 mph) at 6706 m (22,000 ft)

Range: 2100 km (1,305 miles)

Service ceiling: 13,000 m (42,650 ft)

Weights: empty 4603 kg (10,148 lb); loaded 8492 kg (18,722 lb)

Armament: four 20-mm (0.79-in) Browning M3 cannon each with 190 rounds; up to 1360 kg (3,000 lb) of underwing bombs or rocket projectiles

Dimensions:	span	11.58 m (38 ft)
	length	11.84 m (38 ft 10 in)
	height	3.73 m (12 ft 3 in)
	wing area	23.23 m² (250 sq ft)

F9F-2 PANTHER

This Grumman F9F Panther was used by VMF-311, a US Marine Corps squadron flying ground-attack missions in support of UN forces in Korea.

The 'panther's head' paint scheme was a personal badge.

The Panther suffered instability problems which were never entirely cured. With the hydraulic control boost inoperative, aileron stick forces were very high.

The deep, sturdy fuselage was so shaped because the J42 engine was of centrifugal design. The shape was useful, however, as it gave a very large volume for internal fuel – twice as much as the British Hawker Sea Hawk.

An internal 95-litre (25-US gal) tank of water/methanol was fitted beneath the fin, to give extra engine thrust.

WL

MARINES

VMF-311

Four 20-mm (0.79-in) cannon were mounted in the nose, which could be slid forward to gain access for reloading.

Panthers had two ventral airbrakes, mounted left and right on the front fuselage.

Although ostensibly a fighter, the Panther usually delivered air-to-ground munitions such as HVAR rockets or bombs.

The strong tailhook and high landing speed caused at least two Panthers to rip their tails off on landing.

COMBAT DATA

MAXIMUM SPEED

Although heavy and very strongly built to withstand the rigours of carrier operations, the Panther was not much slower than the first generation of straight winged land-based jets. But by the early 1950s all had been outclassed by the new swept-wing fighters.

F9F-5 PANTHER 932 km/h (579 mph)

F-80C SHOOTING STAR 956 km/h (594 mph)

METEOR F.Mk 8 950 km/h (590 mph)

RANGE

Carrier aircraft generally have longer ranges than their land-based counterparts. This is an operational necessity: there are few conveniently placed diversionary fields in the wide expanses of the ocean. For the naval pilot the choice is simple: you make it back to the carrier, or you learn to swim.

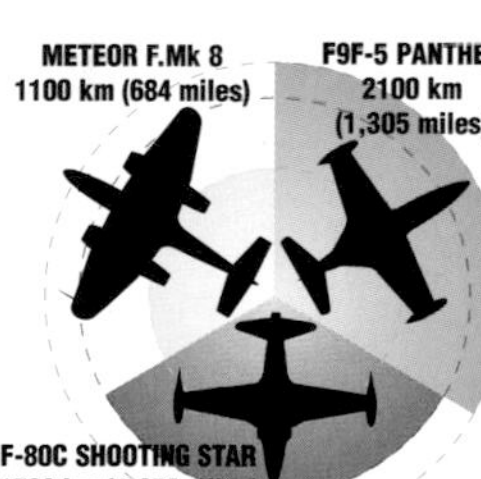

ARMAMENT

The US Navy was much quicker than the US Air Force to adopt the heavy cannon armament which had been accepted as standard elsewhere in the last years of World War II. In addition to its cannon, the Panther was able to carry a considerable load of air-to-ground ordnance.

Fighters from the 'Grumman Iron Works'

■ **F3F:** The first Grumman carrier fighters in the 1930s established all of the company's characteristics, with toughness and agility foremost.

■ **F6F HELLCAT:** Swarms of these big, beefy fighters wrested control of the Pacific skies from the fighters of Imperial Japan.

■ **F8F BEARCAT:** The last of the great Grumman prop-fighters, the Bearcat missed World War II. It served into the 1950s.

■ **F9F COUGAR:** A swept-wing adaptation of the Panther, the Cougar served well into the 1960s, ending as an advanced trainer.

■ **F-14 TOMCAT:** Possibly the last Grumman fighter, the Tomcat has been the US Navy's main airborne defender since the 1970s.

GRUMMAN

F-14 TOMCAT

● **Naval interceptor** ● **Long-range defence** ● **Upgraded systems**

US Navy warships relied on the capabilities of the F-14 Tomcat to protect them from air attack. No job is more challenging: the pilot and radar intercept officer of an F-14 knew that they might be attacking bombers or cruise missiles at great distances. To defend their aircraft-carrier and the other vessels in the Fleet, the Tomcat crew had to seize every advantage offered by the F-14's long-range missiles and far-reaching radar.

▲ *Highly trained crews and considerable combat success have given the Tomcat a legendary reputation. The last Tomcats in US Navy service were retired in 2006.*

PHOTO FILE

GRUMMAN F-14 TOMCAT

▲ Tomcat complement
Most aircraft-carriers carried a squadron of about 20 Tomcats as part of their standard air wing complement.

▲ Carrier return
After a long mission, possibly involving the extreme stress of air-to-air combat and with little fuel remaining, the pilot had to safely land the F-14 on a rolling, pitching carrier deck.

▲ Inner fighter screen
Any attacker which managed to pass through the screen of defending Tomcats would have faced the shorter-ranged F/A-18C Hornet.

▲ Hawkeye co-ordination
An integral part of the Fleet defence system is the E-2 Hawkeye, which is able to find targets beyond the range of the F-14's radar and direct the battle.

▼ Air-to-air refuelling
Tomcats worked in combination with other naval air assets, including KA-6D tankers.

FACTS AND FIGURES

- ➤ The Tomcat's Hughes AWG-9 radar could track 24 targets at once and attack six simultaneously.
- ➤ Late Tomcats had more powerful engines and advanced avionics.
- ➤ The Tomcat could carry more than 7348 kg (16,200 lb) of internal fuel.
- ➤ Production of the F-14 Tomcat totalled 712 aircraft, including 80 for pre-revolutionary Iran.
- ➤ The prototype F-14 Tomcat completed its maiden flight on 21 December 1970.
- ➤ Late-model Tomcats used the General Electric F110-GE-400 turbofan.

PROFILE

Defending the carrier battle group

Flying this super interceptor, the F-14 pilot and back-seater had one of the most important and thrilling jobs in the US Navy. The F-14 Tomcat was the combat champion of the 'outer air battle' – the furious action that erupts when the carrier battle group is threatened with attack.

A long-range interceptor with powerful radar and missiles is really the only answer when the adversary may be a fast, sea-skimming attack aircraft, a high-flying strategic bomber or an unmanned missile. With a Top Gun crew handling its controls and avionics, the F-14 Tomcat could detect, identify, engage and destroy the adversary before that adversary posed any real threat to the carrier battle group.

The F-14 remained one of the world's most formidable warplanes into the 1990s, even though early versions have served for more than 20 years. It was one of the first jets in service with a computer-controlled, automatic variable geometry wing – unswept for slow-speed flight and close combat and swept back when high speed is required. The Tomcat was the only fighter to use the Phoenix missile, which had a superb capability to shoot down attackers at long distance.

Above: The primary long-range weapon of the F-14 is the AIM-54 Phoenix missile, which, in its AIM-54C form, has a range of 148 km (92 miles). To engage targets at such extreme ranges the missile must carry a great deal of fuel, which results in a heavy weapon.

Above: With its long-range kill capability the Tomcat has inspired the phrase 'reach out and touch someone'. This aircraft is ready for a catapult launch.

F-14A Tomcat

Type: two-seat shipboard interceptor

Powerplant: two 92.97-kN (20,910-lb-thrust) Pratt & Whitney TF30-P-412A afterburning turbofans

Maximum speed: 2485 km/h (1,544 mph) at high altitude

Combat radius: 1233 km (766 miles)

Range: 3220 km (2,000 miles)

Service ceiling: 16,150 m (52,986 ft)

Weights: empty 18,191 kg (40,104 lb); maximum take-off 32,098 kg (70,764 lb)

Armament: one M61A1 20-mm cannon with 676 rounds, plus six AIM-7 Sparrow and four AIM-9 Sidewinder missiles, or six AIM-54 Phoenix and two AIM-9 missiles or other weapons weighing up to 6577 kg (14,500 lb)

Dimensions:

span (unswept)	19.54 m (64 ft 1 in)
span (swept)	11.65 m (38 ft 3 in)
length	19.10 m (62 ft 8 in)
height	4.88 m (16 ft)
wing area	52.49 m² (565 sq ft)

F-14D(R) Tomcat

US Navy fighter squadron VF-2 flew the Tomcat for more than 30 years. The squadron is known as the 'Bounty Hunters' and served aboard a number of carriers, including USS *Constellation*.

An AN/APG-71 radar gives the F-14D even greater detection and processing abilities than the AWG-9-equipped F-14A. F-14D(R) aircraft were rebuilt from F-14As.

Most Tomcats are fitted with the Martin-Baker GRU-7A ejection seat, but the F-14D has been equipped with the NACES (Naval Aircrew Escape System) ejection seat in order to match the T-45 and F/A-18C/D.

For close-in missile combat the F-14D normally carries two AIM-9M dogfight missiles on the outboard shoulder pylons. These heat-seeking missiles are capable of engaging a target from any aspect.

Two AIM-7 Sparrow missiles are normally carried on the wing pylons. These medium-range, semi-active, radar-guided missiles are being supplanted by the fire-and-forget AIM-120.

An electronic countermeasures antenna fairing and fuel dump pipe are located at the extreme rear of the Tomcat's fuselage. The ALE-39 chaff/flare dispenser is fitted beneath this section.

Twin pods under the nose of the F-14D house the AN/AAS infra-red search-and-track system on the left and AN/AXX-1 television camera system on the right.

Originally developed to equip the ill-fated F-111B, the AIM-54 Phoenix air-to-air missile has remained unique to the F-14.

Auxiliary drop-tanks are available for attachment to hardpoints beneath the engine pods. Each contains 1011 litres (267 US gal) of fuel.

General Electric F110-PW-400 turbofans of 122.8 kN (27,619 lb thrust) give the F-14D 30 per cent lower fuel consumption in afterburning mode and a 50 per cent increase in intercept radius over the F-14A.

COMBAT DATA

MAXIMUM SPEED

Ironically, the re-engined, updated F-14D fell short of its more recent competitors in terms of speed. In the pure interceptor role, however, range, detection ability and firepower are more important.

F-14D TOMCAT	1997 km/h (1,241 mph)
MiG-29K	2300 km/h (1,429 mph)
Su-33 'FLANKER-D'	2300 km/h (1,429 mph)

WEAPON LOAD

With the change to F-14D standard, the Tomcat's ground-attack capabilities were enhanced. The ship-based Flanker has only limited strike capability, especially when compared to the MiG-29K.

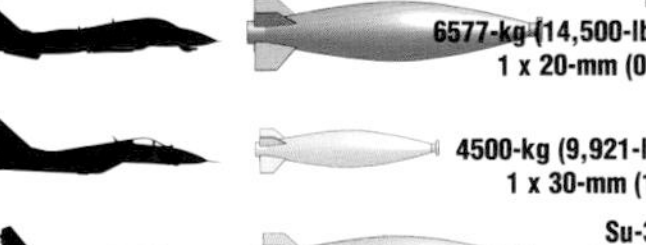

RANGE

Each of these aircraft has exceptional range performance, although the figure shown here for the Tomcat is on internal fuel only and can be improved with drop-tanks and air-to-air refuelling. In addition, the extended search range of the AN/APG-71 radar and the two-person crew of the F-14D make it even more effective.

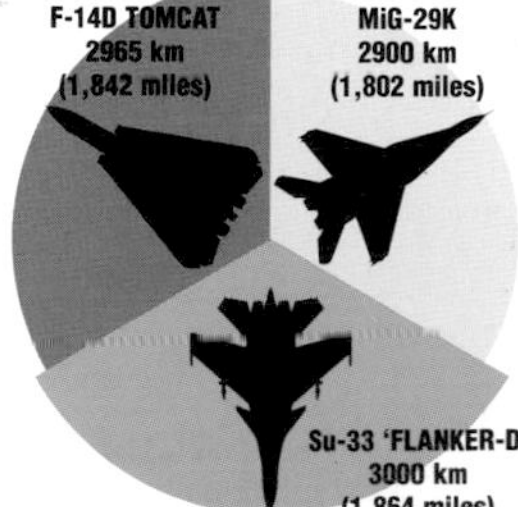

Forty years of fleet defence

McDONNELL F3H DEMON: First delivered to the US Navy in 1954, the F3H Demon was an all-weather fighter and night fighter. Early aircraft were twin-engined.

LTV F-8 CRUSADER: With its variable incidence wing the F-8 was able to offer exceptional performance combined with low carrier landing speeds.

McDONNELL DOUGLAS F-4 PHANTOM II: Many navy pilots preferred the F-8, with its cannon armament, to the all-missile F-4, but the Phantom II was to achieve huge success.

GENERAL DYNAMICS F-111B: Grumman's F-14 inherited its Hughes APG-9 radar and Phoenix missiles from the troublesome F-111B, which became too heavy to be a naval fighter.

Grumman

F-14A Tomcat

● Long-range fleet interceptor ● Recon platform ● Fighter bomber

With its high speed and ultra-long-range weapons, the Tomcat is the main defender of the US fleet and can operate hundreds of miles away from the carrier. Its AWG-9 radar can engage six targets at once and its Phoenix missiles can kill hostile bombers 150 km away before they can launch their attacks. The Tomcat is one of the world's true 'Top Guns'.

▲ *Tomcat aircrew are an elite within an elite. The pilot and backseat Naval Flight Officer act as a carefully co-ordinated team to wring the best from the awesome combination of performance, sophistication and firepower at their command.*

Photo File

Grumman F-14A Tomcat

▲ Power to protect
The F-14's high-thrust TF-30 turbofans and swing wing allow it to operate from short carrier decks. Take-offs are made using a powerful steam catapult.

▲ Fleet defender
The main threat to US Navy carriers is posed by long-range bombers armed with sea-skimming missiles. Only the Tomcat can intercept the bombers before they get within lethal range.

▼ Detecting the enemy
As well as its own radar, the F-14 operates with an E-2 Hawkeye, a flying radar station with a huge rotating antenna above the fuselage.

Deadly performer ▶
The F-14 has Mach 2+ performance, a sparkling rate of climb and good manoeuvrability – all the hallmarks of a great fighter.

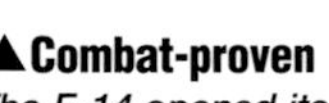

▲ Combat-proven
The F-14 opened its score on 19 August 1981, when F-14 pilots Lt Larry Muszynski (above left) and Cdr Hank Kleeman of VF-41 'Black Aces' squadron destroyed a pair of marauding Libyan Sukhoi Su-22 'Fitters'. Two MiG-23s fell to F-14s in a similar incident during 1989.

Facts and Figures

- The Tomcat's AWG-9 radar can detect, track and engage targets at ranges of more than 150 km (93 mi.).
- One Tomcat can engage the same number of targets as three F/A-18 Hornets.
- The AIM-54C Phoenix is the world's longest-range air-to-air missile.
- The Tomcat's high magnification TV camera enables visual target identification at more than 50 km (30 mi.).
- Forming the outer edge of a battle group's defences, the Tomcat can engage enemy bombers and missiles more than 800 km (497 mi.) out from its home carrier.

PROFILE

Defender of the fleet

The Tomcat has been one of the great superfighters of the world since its first squadron took to the skies in 1972. It packs a massive punch, performs superbly and is the warplane of choice for many aspiring military pilots. Nothing is more calculated to worry an enemy than to know Tomcats are on his track.

And yet this tremendous fighting machine can operate from a 110-m (360-ft.) strip of aircraft carrier deck, in all weathers and around the clock.

Working with E-2C Hawkeye radar planes and using air-to-air refuelling, a squadron of Tomcats can sanitise the airspace 650 km (404 mi.) out from the Carrier Battle Group, allowing no hostile aircraft to threaten the warships below.

Even sea-skimming missiles can be killed by Tomcats using their Phoenix and AMRAAM missiles.

The fact is that Tomcats and their aircrews have to be good – they are protecting a 10-warship, $15-billion battle group manned by 10,000 sailors projecting as much firepower as the United Kingdom's entire armed forces.

The F-14's swing wings allow it to combine high-speed performance and supersonic manoeuvrability with docile low-speed handling.

This Tomcat is armed with two short-range Sidewinder missiles outboard with four longer-range Sparrows inboard.

F-14A Tomcat

Type: two-seat long-range shipboard fleet defence interceptor, tactical reconnaissance aircraft and fighter-bomber

Powerplant: two 92.97-kN (20,920-lb.-thrust) Pratt & Whitney TF-30 turbofans with afterburning

Maximum speed: 2485 km/h (1,544 m.p.h.)

Combat radius: 525 km (326 mi.) on internal fuel; 1210 km (752 mi.) with two 409-litre (90-gal.) tanks

Service ceiling: 15,515 m (50,900 ft.)

Weights: empty 18,191 kg (40,104 lb.); maximum take-off 32,098 kg (70,764 lb.)

Armament: one 20-mm Vulcan cannon, six AIM-54 Phoenix missiles or six AIM-7 Sparrow plus four AIM-9 Sidewinder missiles

Dimensions:

span	19.54 m (64 ft. 1 in.)	
	(11.65 m/38 ft. 3 in. swept)	
length	19.10 m (62 ft. 8 in.)	
height	4.88 m (16 ft.)	
wing area	52.49 m² (565 sq. ft.)	

F-14A TOMCAT

An F-14A Tomcat of VF-143, an Atlantic Fleet fighter squadron nicknamed the 'Pukin' Dogs'. This world famous unit fought in Korea, Vietnam and the Gulf War, and has flown the Tomcat for 20 years.

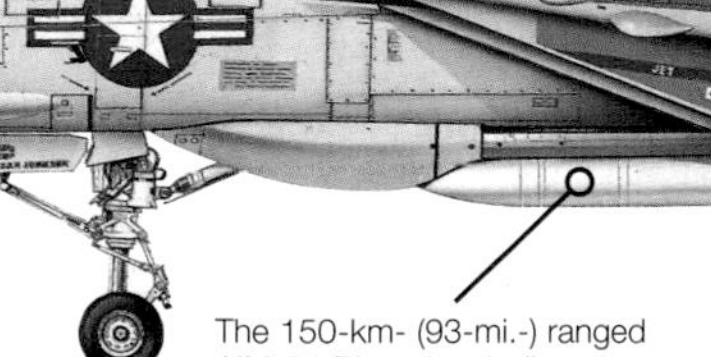

The Tomcat carries a crew of two – pilot up front and Naval Flight Officer behind, controlling the radar and weapons systems.

The key to the F-14's success lies in its powerful Hughes AN/AWG-9 radar, which can detect fighter-sized targets at very long range, and even allows the F-14 to shoot down cruise missiles.

The 150-km- (93-mi.-) ranged AIM-54 Phoenix missile steers itself towards the target using an onboard inertial navigation system, then homes in using its own onboard radar.

The Tomcat can extend its range or endurance by using inflight refuelling, or by carrying external fuel tanks.

The F-14's powerful TF-30 turbofans give the aircraft superb performance and economy, but have proved troublesome and unreliable.

Highly colourful squadron markings have given way to a subdued low-visibility grey camouflage on all US Navy aircraft.

COMBAT DATA

REACH

The Tomcat's fuel capacity and highly efficient turbofan engines allow it to operate further out from the carrier than its F/A-18 Hornet counterpart. Once at its patrol station it can see further and reach further with its Phoenix, destroying enemy fighters before they can launch their own missiles against the fleet or the Tomcat itself.

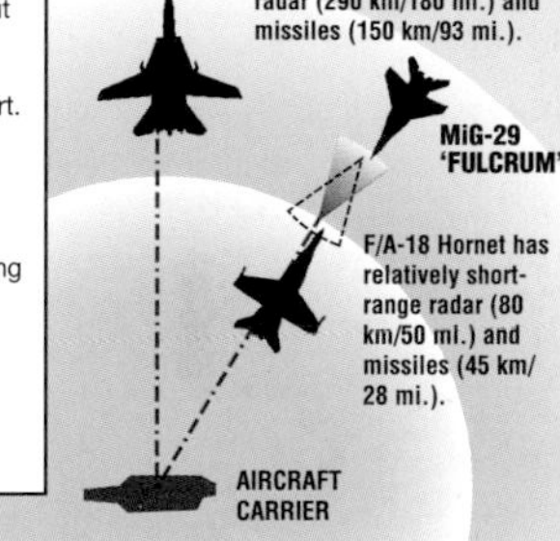

SIMULTANEOUS ENGAGEMENT

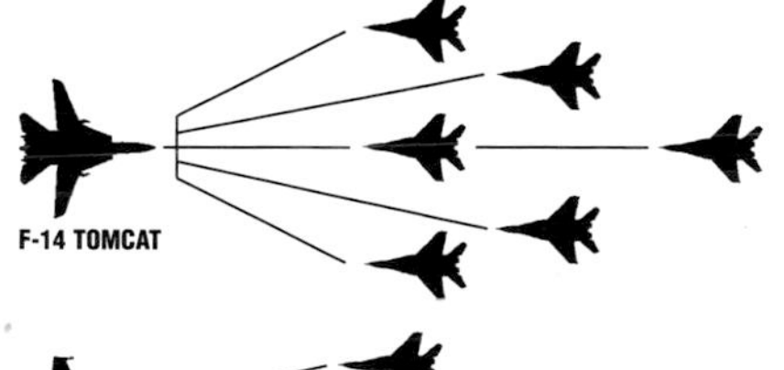

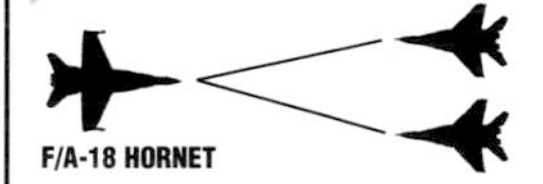

The F-14 can simultaneously engage up to six targets flying at different altitudes, airspeeds and in different directions. Because the Phoenix missile has its own radar it is independent after launch. The F/A-18 can fire only two Sparrows at a time against targets which are close together. Unlike the Phoenix, the Sparrow requires the Hornet to continue flying towards the enemy using its radar, making it vulnerable to a return missile shot.

Weapons of the Tomcat

■ **AIM-9 SIDEWINDER:** The highly agile Sidewinder is used against manoeuvring targets. It homes in on heat from the enemy's jetpipes. **Range 8 km (5 mi.).**

■ **AIM-7 SPARROW:** The Sparrow homes on radar energy reflected from the target, which must be illuminated by the F-14's radar for the whole of its flight. **Range 45 km (28 mi.).**

■ **AIM-54 PHOENIX:** Weighing in at almost 450 kg, costing $2m and with a range in excess of 150 km (93 mi.), the AIM-54 is the world's biggest, most costly and longest-ranged air-to-air missile. A Tomcat can launch six AIM-54s simultaneously against separate targets. The missile's onboard radar lets the F-14 turn away after launch. **Range 150 km (93 mi.).**

■ **BOMBCAT:** The Tomcat can carry a range of 'dumb' (unguided) bombs for use against ground targets. Tomcat squadrons began training in the bombing role in 1991.

Grumman

S-2E/F/G/UP Tracker

● 1950s design ● US and foreign service ● Turbine conversions

The first carrier-borne anti-submarine aircraft to combine the 'hunter' and 'killer' functions, detecting and tracking submarines and attacking them with bombs and depth charges, the S-2 Tracker entered US Navy service in 1954. The Tracker seemed an ideal counter to the Soviet Union's vast fleet of attack submarines threatening US warships. Many were exported and a few remain in service, some fitted with new engines and avionics.

▲ *While originally intended as a carrierborne aircraft, most S-2s that are still in service are land-based and equip the navies of smaller nations which require an affordable ASW platform.*

PHOTO FILE

Grumman S-2E/F/G/UP Tracker

▼ Folding wings
Designed to operate aboard aircraft-carriers, the S-2 has folding wings to ease storage below deck. Until recently Canada operated its S-2s in this low-visibility dark grey colour scheme.

▲ Prototype Turbo Tracker
Built as an S2F-3S (S-2E after 1962) and retired by the US Navy years before its designation changed, this S-2T still carries US Navy markings. Taiwan's conversions were completed under a USN Foreign Military Sales contract.

▼ Argentine S-2A
Having retired its S-2As, Argentina is having its S-2Es refurbished by Israel Aircraft Industries.

▲ Republic of China naval service
Taiwan's original fleet of S-2Es and Fs has been retired or converted. This example has now received turbine engines.

◀ Fire-bomber S-2F1T
Marsh Aviation offers turboprop conversions for both civil fire-bomber and military aircraft.

FACTS AND FIGURES

- The first S2F Tracker completed its maiden flight from Long Island, New York, on 4 December 1952.
- Navy crews nicknamed the Tracker the 'Stoof' after its S2F designation.
- The first S-2G conversion was undertaken by Martin, the rest by the Navy using kits.
- In all, 1269 Trackers were built, including 100 under licence by de Havilland Aircraft of Canada.
- The S-2G variant was modified to carry Bullpup air-to-surface missiles.
- Marsh S-2 turboprop conversions employ a five-bladed propeller.

PROFILE

Breathing new life into the 'Stoof'

By the early 1960s, the S-2 had been in US Navy service for almost 10 years. In 1962 the new S-2E variant was introduced. This benefited from AQA-3 'Jezebel' passive long-range acoustic search equipment used in conjunction with a 'Julie' active acoustic echo-ranging by explosive charge device. The equipment was installed in the lengthened S-2D airframe, which offered more internal room than earlier versions.

The S-2F (an S-2B with 'Jezebel' and 'Julie' fitted) followed. In 1972, 50 S-3Es were converted to the more capable S-2G, an interim aircraft pending the introduction of the all-new Lockheed S-3 Viking. These were the last carrier-borne USN Trackers and made their final cruise in 1975.

The Tracker was eagerly snapped up by foreign navies, with surplus S-2Es and Gs going to Australia, Turkey and various Asian and South American nations. An affordable anti-submarine platform, the Tracker has become a candidate for major upgrades with new engines and avionics gear. Argentina, Brazil and Taiwan have taken delivery of rebuilt Turbo Trackers.

Above: Taiwan's Trackers carry one of two colour schemes, either grey or two-tone blue and dark grey. All were surplus ex-US Navy aircraft.

Right: Brazil continues to fly S-2Es and re-engined S-2Ts from its carrier Minas Gerais. *Operated by the air force, they are designated P-16E and P-16T.*

S-2T TURBO TRACKER

Taiwan ordered 32 S-2T conversions, the first two of which were carried out by Grumman and delivered in 1989. The remainder were tackled in Taiwan using kit sets of parts.

Tracker variants from the S-2D onwards had a lengthened forward fuselage with accommodation for two pilots and two radar operators. New navigation systems and radios are fitted as part of the S-2T conversion.

A key change made in the S-2T is the replacement of the original Wright R-1820 Cyclone 9 piston engines with 1227-kW (1,645-hp.) Garrett TPE331 turboprops, which produce about 10 per cent more power. Pratt & Whitney Canada PT6As have also been offered in other conversion packages.

The new engines and their Dowty advanced technology four-bladed propellers boost top speed to 500 km/h (310 m.p.h.) at 1525 m (5,000 ft.) and the payload by 500 kg (1,100 lb.). Cruising speed, field length, single-engined performance and time-between-overhauls are also improved.

As well as having new engines, the Tracker has improved avionics. These include the magnetic anomaly detector (MAD) and radar as well as the acoustic receivers and processors.

The later versions of the Tracker (from S-2D) had a longer wing span, enlarged tail surfaces and greater fuel capacity.

S-2E Tracker

Type: carrier-borne anti-submarine warfare aircraft

Powerplant: two 1137-kW (1,525-hp.) Wright R-1820-82WA Cyclone radial piston engines.

Maximum speed: 426 km/h (264 m.p.h.) at sea level

Patrol speed: 241 km/h (149 m.p.h.) at 455 m (1,500 ft.)

Endurance: 9 hours with maximum fuel and 10 per cent reserves

Weights: empty 8505 kg (18,711 lb.); maximum take-off 13,222 kg (29,088 lb.)

Armament: one Mk 47 or Mk 101 nuclear depth charge or similar in weapons bay, 60 depth charges in fuselage, 32 sonobuoys in engine nacelles, plus a variety of bombs, rockets or torpedoes on six underwing hardpoints

Dimensions:

span	22.12 m (72 ft. 7 in.)
length	13.26 m (43 ft. 6 in.)
height	5.05 m (16 ft. 7 in.)
wing area	46.08 m² (496 sq. ft.)

ACTION DATA

PATROL SPEED

Contemporary carrier-borne ASW types include the Fairey Gannet and Breguet Alizé, only the latter of which remains in service along with a small numbers of Trackers. A great deal of ship-borne ASW work is now carried out by helicopters like the Sea King.

S-2E TRACKER	241 km/h (149 m.p.h.)
BR.1150 ALIZÉ	232 km/h (144 m.p.h.)
SEA KING Mk 42B	90 km/h (56 m.p.h.)

ENDURANCE

Larger fixed-wing aircraft have a considerably longer endurance than helicopters and operate at greater distances from the carrier or land base. The Alizé is smaller than the Tracker and thus carries less fuel, hence its shorter endurance.

S-2E TRACKER
9 hours

BR.1150 ALIZÉ
7 hours 35 min

SEA KING Mk 42B
3 hours

CLIMB RATE

A better climb rate than any fixed-wing aircraft is inherent in the design of a helicopter, due to its ability to rise vertically. The Tracker and Alizé have comparable climb rates, which are fairly typical for this type and size of aircraft.

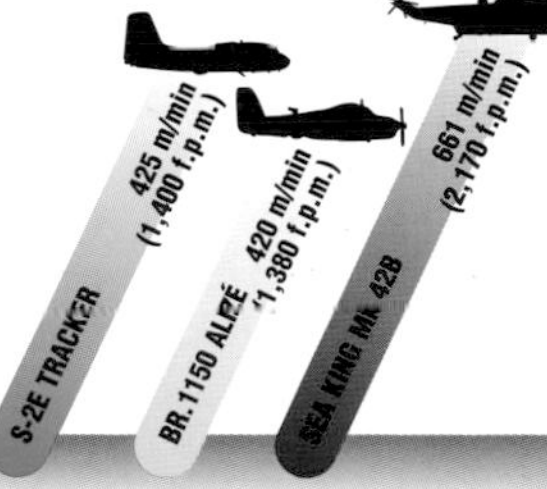

Post-war US Navy ASW aircraft

GRUMMAN AF GUARDIAN: A replacement for the TBM Avenger, there were two versions of the AF, the radar-equipped AF-2W 'hunter' (below) and the weapon-carrying AF-2S 'killer'.

GRUMMAN TBM-3E: Famous during World War II as a torpedo-bomber, the TBM was used after the war by the US Navy as an anti-submarine aircraft equipped with radar.

LOCKHEED S-3 VIKING: The only carrier-borne type ever produced by Lockheed, the jet-powered Viking replaced the S-2 from 1974 and is still in service.

GRUMMAN/GENERAL DYNAMICS

EF-111A RAVEN

● **Supersonic electronic warfare aircraft** ● **Converted F-111A**

▲ *The Raven's role was 'non-lethal defence suppression', which involves jamming enemy radar defences, but the aircraft did not carry air-to-surface weapons to destroy them. That task is left to F-16Cs armed with AGM-88 HARM anti-radar missiles.*

The EF-111 Raven was until recently the USAF's 'secret weapon' – an electronic wizard that jams and confounds enemy radar and communications. Converted from the famous F-111A 'Aardvark' this big, variable-sweep veteran carried no weapons but relied on the magic of electrons to clear a path through enemy defences for other warplanes. The Raven saw action during the 1991 Gulf War.

PHOTO FILE

GRUMMAN/GENERAL DYNAMICS EF-111A RAVEN

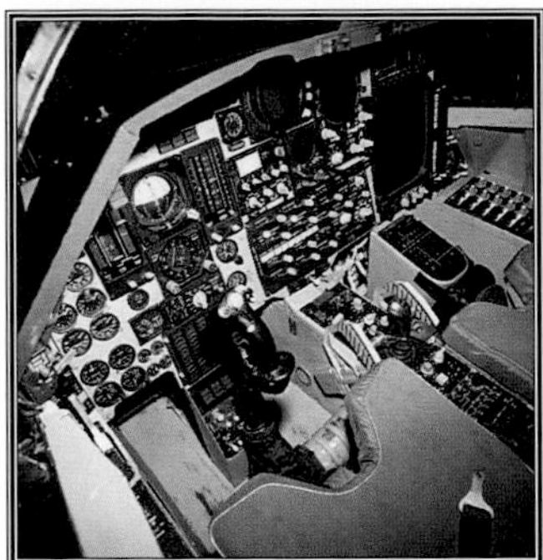

◀ **Jammer's cockpit**
Dominating the control panel in front of the electronic warfare officer's right hand station is a large tactical situation display screen providing threat information.

Air-to-air refuelling ▶
As with the F-111 'tanking' was used to extend the already long range of the EF-111. Here a KC-10 is about to refuel a Raven.

◀ **Afterburners lit**
The immensely powerful TF30-powered F-111 was the ideal platform for a tactical jammer as it was able to keep up with F-111 strike aircraft on long-range missions such as those to Libya and Iraq.

▼ **Two-tone grey**
The Raven fleet was always painted in this two-tone grey colour scheme, the darker shade is on the upper surfaces of the aircraft. This makes it less conspicuous when viewed from above.

▲ **'Electric Fox' and 'Spark Vark'**
After the F-111 'Aardvark', the EF-111 was known as the 'Spark Vark'. The type was also called the 'Electric Fox' before 'Raven' was coined by the USAF.

FACTS AND FIGURES

- ➤ Skilful manoeuvring by an EF-111 pilot caused an Iraqi Mirage F.1 to crash into the ground early in the first Gulf War.
- ➤ The EF-111 has only one set of pilot's controls compared to the F-111's two.
- ➤ An EF-111 aerodynamic prototype flew in 1975 and the first full conversion in 1977.
- ➤ Though EF-111s used a similar ALQ-99 system to the four-seat EA-6B, greater automation allowed just one operator.
- ➤ The EA-6B differs from the Raven in being armed with anti-radar missiles.
- ➤ The last EF-111s were replaced with a version of the F-15E Strike Eagle.

PROFILE

Supersonic radar jammer

The 1973 Yom Kippur War demonstrated that tactical aircraft were extremely vulnerable to an enemy's large integrated air defence system of the type favoured by the Soviets and Warsaw Pact states. The USAF's Tactical Air Command (TAC) had invested little in electronic warfare and was about to retire its EB-66 stand-off jammers.

Grumman had experience with tactical radar jamming systems, having combined the ALQ-99 system with the A-6 Intruder attack aircraft to create the EA-6B Prowler carrier-based jammer.

TAC, however, needed a faster platform on which to mount this system so that it could keep up with its 'strike packages'. It therefore chose the long-range, Mach 2-capable General Dynamics F-111.

The EF-111 combined the proven airframe of a fast, sturdy, long-range strike aircraft with a 'package' of electronic equipment which would enable bombers to reach their targets.

By late-1985 Grumman had converted 42 redundant F-111As. Their first use 'in anger' came the following year, supporting the US raids on Libya. At the start of the first Gulf War, the Raven was one of the first aircraft to challenge Iraq's air defences.

The USAF's fleet of Ravens was retired in 1998, after a long-running deployment in the Southern no-fly zone over Iraq.

Above: EF-111A serial number 66-0041 was the second F-111A to be converted to Raven standard, but the first to have a full electronics suite installed.

Left: EF-111As drawn from units of the 66th Electronic Combat Wing from RAF Upper Heyford, Oxfordshire, and the 388th Tactical Fighter Wing from Mountain Home AFB, Idaho, performed a vital role in Operation Desert Storm, based at Incirlik, Turkey and Taif, Saudi Arabia, respectively.

EF-111A Raven

Type: two-seat supersonic electronic warfare aircraft

Powerplant: two 82.28-kN (18,460-lb.-thrust) Pratt & Whitney TF30-P-3 afterburning turbofan engines

Maximum speed: 2272 km/h (1,408 m.p.h.)

Combat radius: 1495 km (927 mi.)

Service ceiling: 13,715 m (45,000 ft.)

Weights: empty 25,072 kg (55,158 lb.); loaded 40,347 kg (88,763 lb.)

Armament: usually none, but able to carry two AIM-9 Sidewinder air-to-air missiles

Equipment: AN/ALQ-99E tactical jamming suite (TJS) consisting of a System Integrated Receiver (of hostile radar emissions) and jamming transmitters; self-defence avionics; mapping radar and terrain-following radar

Dimensions:

span (spread)	19.20 m (63 ft.)
span (swept)	9.74 m (32 ft.)
length	23.16 m (70 ft.)
wing area	48.77 m² (525 sq. ft.)

EF-111A Raven

This Raven belonged to the 430th Electronic Combat Squadron, 27th Fighter Wing, at Cannon Air Force Base, New Mexico. The last unit to fly the EF-111A operationally was the 429th Electronic Countermeasures Squadron.

The 168-kg (370-lb.) 'football' pod on the top of the fin holds 264 kg (580 lb.) of receiver antennas and related equipment, including an infra-red warning system.

The crew consists of a pilot and an electronic warfare officer, the latter in place of the weapons systems officer of the F-111.

Up to four wing pylons can be fitted, two on each wing, for the carriage of such items as fuel tanks and datalink pods.

The only armament carried by the EF-111 is a pair of AIM-9 Sidewinders for self-defence. Its best means of defence, however, remains its sheer speed and acceleration.

The main jamming equipment is housed in the former weapons bay, the 10 transmitters filling a 4.9-m (16-ft.) long 'canoe' fairing. These cover seven frequency bands.

The Raven retains both the F-111A's APQ-160 attack radar and APQ-110 terrain-following radar equipment.

The EF-111A uses the basic airframe of the F-111A, including the engines, two Pratt & Whitney TF30-P-3 turbofans.

COMBAT DATA

MAXIMUM SPEED

Based on the Mach 2-capable F-111A strike aircraft, the Raven possessed a similarly impressive performance. The Su-24MP is also based on a supersonic attack aircraft.

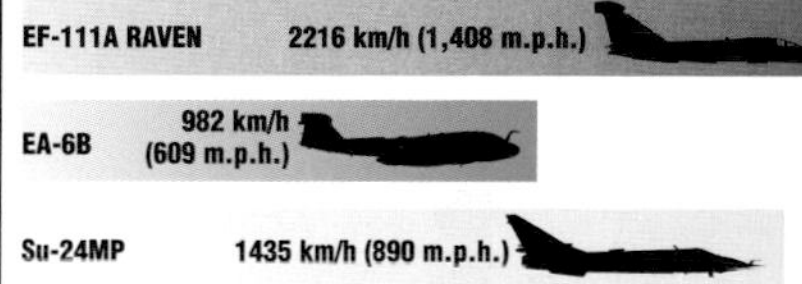

DEFENSIVE ARMAMENT

While the EA-6B is capable of carrying up to four AGM-88 HARM anti-radar missiles, it is not equipped with defensive weaponry. The AIM-9 Sidewinder has a considerably better range than the R-60.

2 x AIM-9 Sidewinder missiles — EF-111A RAVEN

None — EA-6B PROWLER

2 x R-60 air-to-air missiles — Su-24MP 'FENCER-F'

RANGE

The F-111 family has an unrivalled range performance in the supersonic deep strike role. All three types may be refuelled in the air.

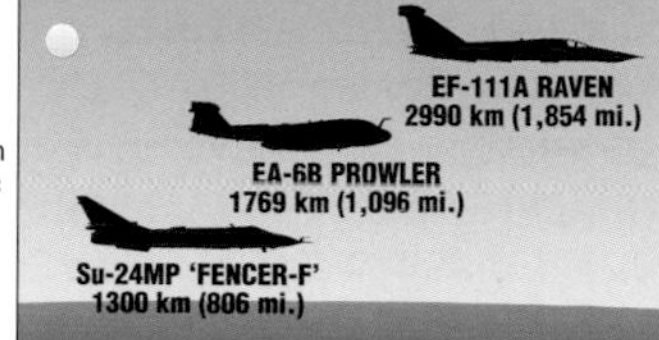

The EF-111A's mission

1 Ravens can undertake radar jamming from a distant (stand-off) position or as a strike escort, accompanying a wave of attacking fighter-bombers.

2 One or more EF-111s precedes the strike 'package', detecting hostile radar emissions and transmitting 'noise' so that the enemy is unable to detect the attackers.

3 Without the capacity to detect an attack, the enemy cannot direct anti-aircraft fire or fighters on to the strike force.

HANDLEY PAGE VICTOR

● Nuclear bomber ● Missile carrier ● V-bomber

▲ Despite the genius of its design, the Victor's lengthy development and the advent of advanced surface-to-air missiles meant that it actually flew as a bomber for only a small part of its career.

Handley Page's Victor was one of the great post-war jet bombers. This giant, crescent-winged jet belonged to the trio of Britain's epoch-making V-bombers, the others being the Avro Vulcan and Vickers Valiant, and in many ways was the most advanced of the three. It brought powerful new capabilities to the job of strategic bombing, previously carried out by propeller-driven aircraft. After the Cold War the Victor served as a tanker.

PHOTO FILE

HANDLEY PAGE VICTOR

▲ Crescent wing
The crescent shape wing was unique, designed to maintain the same critical Mach number over the whole area.

▲ Blue Steel alert
This Victor carries a Blue Steel missile in its weapons bay. The missile used liquid fuel and required extensive preparation before flight.

▲ First of the Victors
The last of the V-bombers to enter service, the Victor prototype finally flew in 1952. The nose was slightly lengthened and the tailplane shortened in the production aircraft.

▲ Missile armed
To maintain the credibility of Britain's deterrent, the Victor often carried live Blue Steels on patrols.

Gleaming white ▶
The Victor's all-white paint scheme was intended to reflect the flash from its own nuclear weapons.

FACTS AND FIGURES

- ➤ On 1 June 1957 a Victor exceeded Mach 1 in a shallow dive, the largest aircraft ever to fly supersonic at that time.
- ➤ The prototype Victor first flew on 24 December 1952, but crashed in 1954.
- ➤ Victors could carry the 'Grand Slam' bomb used by the wartime Lancaster.
- ➤ For defence, Victors were fitted with a top-secret electronics countermeasures system called 'Red Steer'.
- ➤ An escape capsule was originally considered for the Victor design.
- ➤ Victors fired Blue Steels in trials in the desert near Woomera, Australia.

PROFILE

The crescent-winged avenger

Designed to carry nuclear bombs to the Soviet Union, the Victor suffered from a protracted development compared to its rivals, only entering service in 1958, 12 years after design had started. The Victor had a larger bomb-carrying capacity than the other V-bombers and would have been at the vanguard of a strategic strike if war had come. It was equipped with the Blue Steel nuclear-tipped stand-off missile, but the weapon was never used outside trials.

The Victor was in many ways a very advanced aircraft. Its wing was crescent-shaped, with the angle of sweep being highest inboard and decreasing outboard. This idea had first been studied by the German manufacturer Junkers at the end of World War II. Handley Page built the HP.88 research aircraft to test this radical design, and it proved its worth when a Victor was dived supersonically in tests. The nose shape, which looks as if it was designed to fly in space, remains highly unusual even today.

Painted a bright white for nuclear warfare, the Victor fleet acquired grey and green upper surfaces when the RAF began practising conventional and nuclear low-level bombing. Some Victors became reconnaissance aircraft, but a larger number finished their days as tanker aircraft.

Below: Like the Vulcan, the Victor needed more power and a bigger wing to be a real success, and the B.Mk 2 was fitted with Rolls-Royce Conway turbojets. Thirty of this version were built, many being converted for reconnaissance.

Above: Despite its potential, the Victor had a short career as a bomber, entering squadron service in 1958 and standing down in 1968.

Victor B.Mk 2

Type: five-seat long-range strategic bomber

Powerplant: four 91.64-kN (20,611-lb-thrust) Rolls-Royce Conway RCo.17 Mk 201 turbofan engines and two 35.60-kN (8,010-lb-thrust) de Havilland Spectre rocket motors

Maximum speed: Mach 0.98 or 1038 km/h (645 mph) at 12,200 m (40,026 ft)

Range: 6500 km (4,039 miles)

Service ceiling: 16,765 m (55,000 ft)

Weights: empty approx. 51,820 kg (114,244 lb); maximum loaded approx. 10,115 kg (22,300 lb)

Armament: one Avro Blue Steel Mk 1 stand-off missile; or 35 to 48 454-kg (1,000-lb) conventional bombs

Dimensions:

span	36.57 m (120 ft)
length	35.03 m (114 ft 11 in)
height	8.57 m (28 ft 1 in)
wing area	241.30 m² (2,597 sq ft)

VICTOR B.MK 2

The Victor was the only V-bomber never to be used as a bomber in war. A total of 86 Victors were built, the final aircraft leaving the production line in May 1963.

The large bulged pods in the wings contained additional fuel to that in the main wing tanks.

Like its V-bomber brethren, the Victor's turbojets were buried in the wingroots. This was an elegant solution in terms of aerodynamics, but a source of irritation to the engineers servicing the engines.

The wing was swept at 48° inboard, 35° in the centre and 27° in the outboard section.

Victors were crewed by two pilots, navigator-radar, navigator-plotter and electronic warfare operators. Only the pilots sat on ejector seats. A rear-facing periscope for the crew was fitted in the rear of the flight deck.

Much of the centre fuselage was occupied by the massive bomb-bay. The Handley Page designers had also planned large wing pylons, which would have given the Victor a payload similar to that of a B-52 over short ranges, but these were never needed for the nuclear role.

The Victor had a pair of airbrakes on the rear fuselage. This part of the fuselage also contained a freight compartment and fuel tanks. The bulge in front of the fin contained an air intake and heat exchanger.

For protection from fighter attack, the Victor had a rear-facing radar in the tailcone. It was also fitted with some very powerful jamming equipment designed to confuse fighter radars.

COMBAT DATA

SERVICE CEILING

All the V-bombers had excellent high-altitude performance, which was their primary defence against fighter attack. The MiG-17 could only just reach 16,000 m (52,493 ft). In later years fighter ceilings improved and this advantage was lost. Bombers then had to resort to low-altitude weapons delivery.

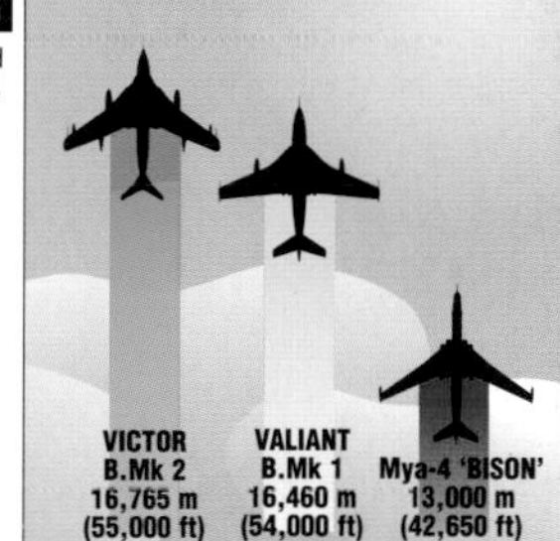

MAXIMUM SPEED

The crescent wing and very streamlined fuselage gave the Victor a high speed. It was as fast as many Soviet jet fighters of the early 1950s. The earlier Valiant and Mya-4 had much straighter wings which limited their top speed. Eventually fighter speeds increased significantly and easily outstripped those of bombers.

VICTOR B.Mk 2 1038 km/h (645 mph)

VALIANT B.Mk 1 912 km/h (567 mph)

Mya-4 'BISON' 900 km/h (559 mph)

WEAPON LOAD

The standard load of a Victor was 15 tonnes (16.5 tons), which compared very favourably to most bombers of the time. The Victor could actually lift considerably more at the expense of range. The Valiant was the first of the V-Bombers and was fairly quickly superseded by the Vulcan and Victor.

VICTOR B.Mk 2 15,876 kg (35,000 lb)

VALIANT B.Mk 1 9525 kg (21,000 lb)

Mya-4 'BISON' 10,000 kg (22,046 lb)

Nuclear bombers of the Cold War

■ **AVRO VULCAN:** The most successful of the RAF's V-Bombers, the Vulcan also started life as a nuclear bomber. In service until the 1980s, a few saw action in the Falklands War.

■ **BOEING B-52 STRATOFORTRESS:** Boeing's giant, eight-engined B-52 was the backbone of USAF's Strategic Air Command from the 1960s into the 1980s.

■ **TUPOLEV Tu-16 'BADGER':** The smaller cousin of the Tu-95, the twin turbojet-powered Tu-16 was built in large numbers by the Soviet Union. Nuclear and conventional versions exist.

■ **TUPOLEV Tu-95 'BEAR':** The largest turboprop bomber ever built, the Tu-95 shocked the West with its speed when it appeared in the 1950s. It remains in service in Russia.

HAWKER

HUNTER F.MKS 1-5

● Second generation RAF jet ● First British swept-wing fighter

With the Hawker Hunter the RAF had a jet fighter that represented a major improvement over the first-generation Gloster Meteors and de Havilland Vampires which were serving in the early 1950s. Popular with pilots as it had almost flawless handling qualities and few limitations, the Hunter was very robust and saw almost two decades of frontline service. However, the early marks had various performance problems that needed to be rectified.

▲ *The engine air intake proposed for the nose of the original design was moved to the wingroots on either side of the fuselage. Radar ranging equipment replaced it.*

PHOTO FILE

HAWKER HUNTER F.MKS 1-5

◀ Overseas sales
Sweden's air force bought 120 Hunter F.Mk 50s (an export version of the F.Mk 4) in 1955.

▼ Gun problems
Early Hunters had gun firing problems that caused their engines to surge.

▼ Airbrakes
The fitting of a 'barn-door' style airbrake below the Hunter's rear fuselage solved a major combat stability problem.

▼ Weapons
Hunter F.Mk 4s were later able to carry eight rocket packs on underwing pylons.

▼ Classic lines
Throughout its development the Hunter retained its sleek swept wings, tail and fuselage profile.

▲ Sapphire engine
This Hunter F.Mk 2 and F.Mk 5 were powered by an Armstrong Siddeley Sapphire turbojet and were 19.05 cm (7½ in) longer than the original F.Mk 1.

FACTS AND FIGURES

- The prototype Hunter was first flown in July 1951, the production F.Mk 1 entering service in 1954.
- More than 650 Hunters of Marks 1-5 were built; only 150 were Sapphire-powered.
- Flaps were used as airbrakes initially, but this caused control problems.
- The prototype Hunter was fitted with reheat and other improvements to make an attempt on the world air speed record.
- The Hunter F.Mk 3 set a new world speed record of 1171 km/h (728 mph) in 1953.
- The first Hunter F.Mk 1 display team was formed by No. 54 Squadron in 1956.

PROFILE

First of the successful Hunters

After the North American XP-86 swept-wing fighter first flew at the end of 1947, Britain found itself falling behind in fighter development. The Gloster Meteor and DH Vampire lacked the potential of the new 'second generation' swept-wing jet fighters.

The RAF had an urgent need for a swept-wing design to replace the first jet fighters, with an armament of four cannon, an endurance of one hour and a level speed of Mach 0.94 being specified. It was to be powered by either a Rolls-Royce Avon or an Armstrong Siddeley Sapphire axial-flow turbojet. Before the first prototype Hunter, the Hawker P.1067, was flown in July 1951, a contract for 113 aircraft had been placed. These initial Hunter F.Mk 1s had many problems that prevented their introduction into service for more than a year after many of them were built.

The Rolls-Royce Avon engines had bad surge characteristics in combat at high altitude, made worse when the guns were fired. Manual controls proved to be inadequate and had to be replaced by powered controls, and the use of the flaps as airbrakes caused further instability. Solutions were found for these shortcomings, however, and the Hunter F.Mk 1 entered service in July 1954.

After these setbacks the design, control characteristics, power, range and armament were all improved in later marks.

Ammunition link collectors and underwing pylons have been omitted from this No. 56 Squadron F.Mk 1.

An all-metal, all-swept tail unit was fitted. The tailplane, with fully powered elevators, was mounted on the fin above the jet pipe.

An 'acorn' fairing was located at the junction of the rudder and elevators to prevent tail buffet at high subsonic speeds. A 'non-flying' tail was standard on all Hunters built up to the Swedish air force's F.Mk 6.

Hunter F.Mk 5

Type: single-seat interceptor fighter

Powerplant: one 35.59-kN (8,005-lb-thrust) Armstrong Siddeley Sapphire 101 turbojet

Maximum speed: 978 km/h (608 mph) at 11,000 m (36,089 ft)

Initial climb rate: 8 min 12 sec to 13,720 m (45,000 ft)

Range: 689 km (428 miles)

Service ceiling: 15,240 m (50,000 ft)

Weights: empty 5689 kg (12,542 lb); loaded 'clean' 7756 kg (17,100 lb); maximum take-off weight 10,886 kg (24,000 lb)

Armament: four 30-mm (1.18-in) ADEN cannon

Dimensions:		
	span	10.29 m (33 ft 9 in)
	length	13.98 m (45 ft 10 in)
	height	4.01 m (13 ft 2 in)
	wing area	33.42 m² (360 sq ft)

HUNTER F.MK 1

WW645 was the last Hunter Mark 1 built for the RAF. It flew with No. 43 Squadron, the 'Fighting Cocks', at RAF Leuchars from mid-1954 until autumn 1957. By then the unit had re-equipped with Hunter F.Mk 6s.

Four Hispano 20-mm (0.79-in) cannon equipped the Hunter F.Mk 1, rather than two of the new 30-mm (1.18-in) ADEN cannon that were not ready for service when the Hunter F.Mk 1 was built.

Hunters had an all-metal semi-monocoque stressed-skin fuselage that was manufactured in three sections. The single-piece, sliding cockpit canopy covered a fully automatic Martin-Baker Mk 2H ejector seat with the Duplex drogue system.

The Hunter had a detachable rear fuselage for ready access to the engine. The rear section included the removable jet-pipe, and the base of the fin and tail.

The mid-set wing widened as it joined the fuselage to incorporate the engine air intakes. The wing was swept nearly 40° at 25 per cent chord. The wide track undercarriage main wheels retracted into the wing.

Production Hunters had a forward end hinged airbrake on the underside of the rear fuselage. It could be lowered to an angle of 67°, presenting a large surface area to the slipstream and slowing down the aircraft effectively.

COMBAT DATA

THRUST

The first Hunters to enter service were a little short on thrust compared to the twin-engined Meteor F.Mk 8, but represented a major advance over the single-engined Canadair-built F-86 Sabre.

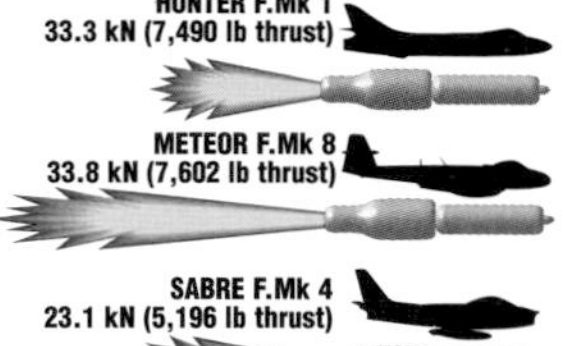

MAXIMUM SPEED

While the first Hunters were faster than the RAF's Meteor F.Mk 8s, they were at least 100 km/h (62 miles) slower than the Sabre F.Mk 4s. This lack of speed was addressed in later Hunter variants, which employed powerplants rated at around 44.48 kN (10,004 lb thrust).

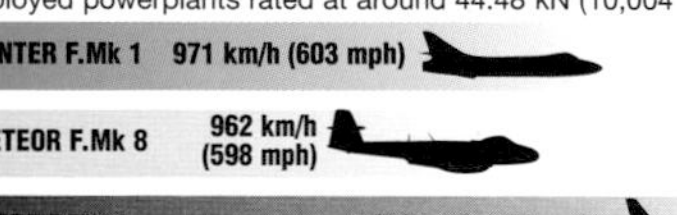

Hunter derivatives that never were

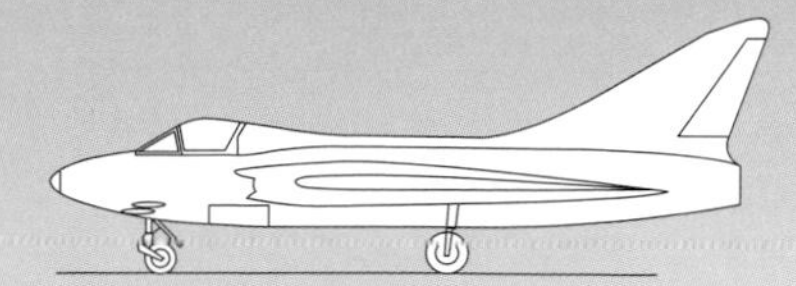

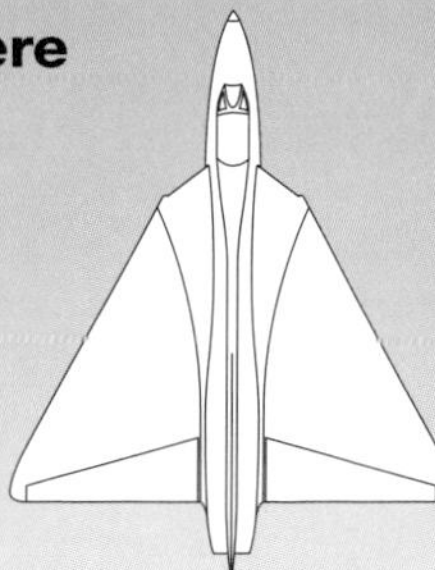

P.1091: This delta-winged Hunter derivative was proposed in 1951 and had an afterburning version of the Sapphire turbojet installed. It was expected to achieve a top speed of Mach 0.98.

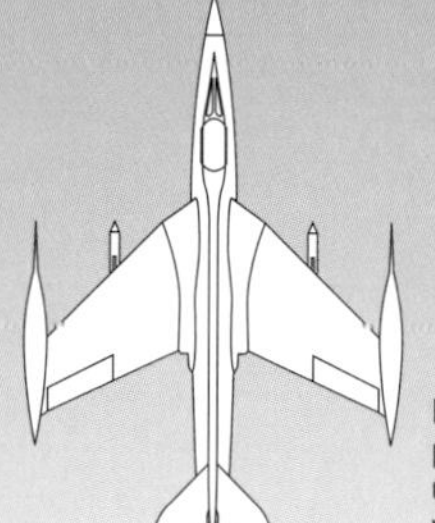

P.1100: With an afterburning Rolls-Royce Avon engine and two rocket boosters, the P.1100 was expected to reach Mach 1.5. This 1955 proposal was to be armed with two ADEN guns and two Firestreak missiles.

P.1128: Two Bristol Orpheus turbojets would have powered this 1957 passenger transport proposal, which used standard Hunter wings and undercarriage. The cabin would have accommodated five or six passengers.

Hawker Siddeley

Harrier GR.Mk 1/GR.Mk 3

● Pioneering 'Jump Jet' ● V/STOL close support ● Ground attack

The Hawker Siddeley Harrier was a great aviation breakthrough. Designed in the late 1950s by Sydney Camm, the Harrier became the world's first V/STOL (vertical/short take-off and landing) combat aircraft. No other warplane could rise vertically like a helicopter and also fly level like a conventional fighter-bomber. For years the early Harrier, called the 'Jump Jet' for its ability to spring abruptly skyward, enjoyed a monopoly in the vertical flight arena.

▲ *The Harrier's astonishing ability to take off and land vertically liberated its users from the tyranny of the runway, basing aircraft anywhere from car parks to forest clearings.*

PHOTO FILE

Hawker Siddeley Harrier GR.Mk 1/GR.Mk 3

▲ Hard hitter
Although it could not carry as much armament as a more conventional ground-attack jet, the Harrier still packed a considerable punch, especially with SNEB high-explosive rockets.

▲ Harrier at war
Harrier's V/STOL ability meant that RAF ground-attack variants could operate alongside Sea Harriers from Royal Navy decks during the Falklands War.

▲ Export to America
The Harrier was one of the few foreign aircraft ever bought by the Americans. The US Marine Corps operated 110 Harriers as the AV-8A.

▼ Reinforcement specialist
Harriers were often assigned to British mobile forces, and were regularly used on exercises to reinforce Norway and NATO's northern flank.

▲ Marine Corps warrior
In spite of its relatively poor range and weapons load, the US Marine Corps saw the Harrier, or AV-8, as the best solution to the need for very close support during amphibious assaults.

FACTS AND FIGURES

- The prototype for the Harrier series, known as the P.1127, first flew on 21 October 1960.
- On 7 March 1964 a pre-production version, the Kestrel, had its maiden flight.
- The RAF ordered 132 Harrier GR.Mk 1 single-seaters and 19 T.Mk 2 trainers.
- The 'Jump Jet' entered service on the RAF's fifty-first birthday, 1 April 1969.
- The US Marine Corps overcame Pentagon resistance to order Harriers, and started flying AV-8s in 1971.
- The first generation of GR.Mk 1s and 3s have been replaced by modern variants.

PROFILE

Upwardly mobile

The Harrier GR.Mk 1 – the predecessor of today's advanced Harriers and the inspiration for the advanced F-35 JSF – has a special place in aviation history. When Britain's Royal Air Force began flying this first operational Harrier in 1969, it showed that you could fight a war without conventional airfields.

Harrier GR.Mk 1s served with remarkable success – and an enviable safety record – with RAF Germany. For 20 years bomb-laden Harriers standing ready to fight were key participants in the Cold War.

The notion of a V/STOL combat plane, proven during the years when GR.Mk 1s served in Germany, had wide appeal. The US Marine Corps picked up the idea and, although there were some troubles initially, the Marines had enough confidence in the concept to sponsor advanced new versions of the Harrier.

Pilots did not master the Harrier easily, but, once they invested the effort, they commanded an aircraft with unique and exciting performance. It was also agile: in a dogfight the Harrier could hold its own with any fighter in the sky.

Above: The Royal Air Force operated one Harrier squadron in Britain and three in Germany. The original 71 Harrier GR.Mk 1s were followed by 40 GR.Mk 3s, which had a more powerful engine.

Below: The Harrier proved the concept of using high-performance jets at sea without the need for conventional aircraft-carriers. Here an early Harrier uses its vectored thrust to make a vertical landing on the helicopter cruiser HMS Blake.

Harrier GR.Mk 1

Type: single-seat V/STOL ground-attack/reconnaissance aircraft

Powerplant: one 84.52-kN (19,010-lb-thrust) Rolls-Royce (Bristol Siddeley) Pegasus Mk 101 vectored-thrust turbofan

Maximum speed: 1186 km/h (9737 mph)

Range with one air refuelling: 5560 km (3,455 miles)

Service ceiling: 15,240 m (50,000 ft)

Weights: basic operating weight 5580 kg (12,302 lb); maximum take-off 11,340 kg (25,000 lb)

Armament: up to a maximum of 2268 kg (5,000 lb) of stores on underfuselage and underwing hardpoints, including a 30-mm (1.18-in) ADEN gun pod, bombs, rockets, flares and a five-camera reconnaissance pod

Dimensions:	span	7.70 m (25 ft 3 in)
	length	13.87 m (45 ft 6 in)
	height	3.45 m (11 ft 4 in)
	wing area	18.68 m² (201 sq ft)

HARRIER GR.MK 3

No. 3 Squadron is one of the oldest units in the world, having been in existence since 1912. It was the fourth and last RAF squadron to convert to the original Harrier, flying the type between 1972 and 1988 from its base at Guterstöh.

The view ahead from the Harrier's cockpit is excellent, although all-round visibility is poor.

Harrier pilots sit on a Martin-Baker Mk 9D rocket-powered ejection seat. This can blast a pilot to safety at all speeds and altitudes.

The key to the Harrier's V/STOL performance is the system used to vector engine thrust. The Pegasus has four swivelling jet nozzles which provide lift when pointing downwards and conventional thrust when pointing to the rear.

In common with most modern combat aircraft, the Harrier ended its career after being fitted with a radar-warning receiver which was able to detect and classify hostile radar transmissions.

The extended nose of the Harrier GR.Mk 3 houses the Ferranti laser-rangefinder and marked target seeker, which can search for and detect energy reflected from a target by a ground-based designator.

A single Rolls-Royce Pegasus engine powers the Harrier.This is one of the most powerful jet engines currently used in combat aircraft: in the GR.Mk 3 it delivered nearly 10 tonnes (11 tons) of thrust *without* afterburning.

Two 30-mm (1.18-in) ADEN cannon, each with 150 rounds, are mounted in pods slung beneath the Harrier's fuselage. These are very accurate and can be used against both ground and air targets.

The MATRA SNEB rocket pod contains 19 unguided rocket projectiles with 'flip-out' stabilizing fins. Available with both HEAT and fragmentation warheads, the 68-mm (2.68-in) rockets are effective against most armoured targets.

At hovering speeds, when aerodynamic surfaces have no effect, the Harrier is controlled by 'puffer' jets in the nose, tail and wingtips. These operate on high pressure air bled from the engine.

COMBAT DATA

MAXIMUM SPEED

The Harrier was not built for supersonic speed, but its subsonic performance was excellent, thanks to the immense power of its Pegasus engine. It had good acceleration, but the GR.Mk 3 with more equipment and greater weight was a little slower than the original Harrier GR.Mk 1 of 1969.

HARRIER GR.Mk 3	1160 km/h (721 mph)
A-4M SKYHAWK	1078 km/h (670 mph)
G91Y	1110 km/h (690 mph)

COMBAT RADIUS

The Harrier was criticized for its lack of range, but its combat radius was about average for light-attack aircraft used in the 1960s and 1970s. It could outperform the Fiat G91Y, designed a decade earlier, but was not as good as the amazing A-4 Skyhawk of the 1950s. However, neither of the older jets could fly vertically.

BOMBLOAD

Another area of criticism was the Harrier's relatively light weapons load. Again, this was slightly unjustified: most of the preceding generation of attack aircraft were limited to an even smaller load, with only exceptional designs such as the Skyhawk being able to carry more.

Development of the early Harriers

■ **P.1127 PROTOTYPE:** First flown in 1961, the Hawker Siddeley P.1127 proved the V/STOL fighter-bomber concept. An enlarged version known as the Kestrel was used for tri-partite trials in Britain, Germany and the United States.

■ **HARRIER GR.Mk 1/AV-8A:** The first production Harriers were larger and heavier than the prototypes, and went into service in Britain, Spain and the United States. The American and Spanish Harriers had the more powerful engine of the RAF's GR.Mk 3.

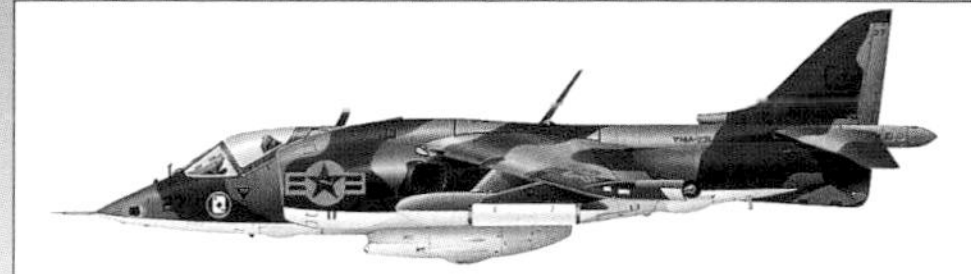

■ **HARRIER GR.Mk 3:** The more powerful GR.Mk 3 was fitted with better attack systems. Forty-seven US Marine AV-8A Harriers, which served until 1987, were upgraded to AV-8C standard, with strengthened airframe, better avionics and communications.

HAWKER SIDDELEY

NIMROD R.MK 1

● RAF electronic intelligence aircraft ● Three examples in service

▲ *The Nimrod is a heavily modified version of the Comet airliner, and further modification to R.Mk 1P standard has only served to add to the number of protuberances and aerials on the basic airframe. However, they serve the serious task of collecting electronic signals from potentially hostile forces.*

Three specialised and highly classified conversions of the Nimrod maritime reconnaissance aircraft gather electronic intelligence (Elint) on hostile powers for the Royal Air Force. Packed with sophisticated sensors and designated Nimrod R.Mk 1, they entered service in May 1974 and fly with No. 51 Squadron. Although their operations are shrouded in secrecy, they were used during both the 1982 Falklands and 1991 Gulf conflicts.

PHOTO FILE

HAWKER SIDDELEY NIMROD R.MK 1

Combat operations ▶
R.Mk 1P operations are highly secretive, but it is thought that they flew combat Elint-gathering missions from Chile during the 1982 Falklands War.

◀ 'New' Nimrod R.Mk 1P
Following the crash of one of its R.Mk 1Ps (XW666) in May 1995, the RAF received a 'new' Nimrod R.Mk 1 (XV249) in May 1997.

New base ▶
No. 51 Squadron's R.Mk 1Ps were at RAF Wyton for more than 20 years, but are now based at Waddington.

◀ Experienced crew
Packed with highly sophisticated sensors,the Nimrod R.Mk 1 is believed to fly regularly with more than 25 crew, many of whom are experienced sensor operators chosen for their discretion as well as their skill.

Elint and nav sensors ▶
The R.Mk 1P's sensors comprise a wide range of receivers to pick up signals. A comprehensive navigation suite was also fitted for extremely accurate flight around the borders of the former USSR.

FACTS AND FIGURES

- ➤ Originally, three R.Mk 1 aircraft were converted from Nimrod MR.Mk 1 airframes (XW664, XW665 and XW666).
- ➤ XW666 was lost in May 1995, after engine failure over the Moray Firth.
- ➤ All of XW666's sensitive equipment was recovered from the sea.
- ➤ A Battle Honour was awarded to No. 51 Squadron for its combat service during the Falklands conflict.
- ➤ Nimrod R.Mk 1Ps share their Waddington base with E-3D Sentry AEW.Mk 1s.
- ➤ An endurance of 19 hours is possible with one refuelling.

PROFILE

Highly secretive RAF 'ferret'

A version of the Nimrod maritime reconnaissance aircraft, the Nimrod R.Mk 1P is a specialised electronic intelligence-gathering aircraft. The type was developed in the early 1970s for use during the Cold War. Its role was to patrol just outside Warsaw Pact airspace in order to record the signals from ground and airborne radars and other emitters, as well as monitoring communications traffic. The R.Mk 1s carry more radio-frequency sensors than the maritime reconnaissance Nimrods. They have multiple antennas on the fuselage and wing tanks, but do not have the tail-mounted magnetic anomaly detector (MAD). With the addition of refuelling probes for operations in the South Atlantic in 1982, they became designated R.Mk 1P, and there have been other modifications since.

Generally carrying a crew of 25 or more, the R.Mk 1Ps are believed to have operated from bases on the South American mainland during the Falklands War in 1982. They were also used operationally during the Gulf War in 1991, when they were based at RAF Akrotiri in Cyprus. Since 1995 they have been based at RAF Waddington, alongside the RAF's force of E-3D Sentry airborne early warning aircraft.

Above: The main feature that distinguishes the Nimrod R.Mk 1P from its maritime counterpart is the lack of a MAD boom at the tail.

Above: Entering service in 1974 the RAF's R.Mk 1Ps were used extensively to probe Soviet defences during the Cold War. These missions remain shrouded in secrecy.

Nimrod R.Mk 1P

Type: electronic intelligence aircraft

Powerplant: four 54.00-kN (12,150-lb. thrust) Rolls-Royce RB168-20 Spey Mk 250 turbofans

Maximum speed: 926 km/h (575 m.p.h.)

Endurance: typically 12 hours; maximum 15 hours without refuelling and 19 hours with one in-flight refuelling

Ferry range: 5000 km (3,107 mi.)

Service ceiling: 12,800 m (42,000 ft.)

Weights: typical empty 39,010 kg (86,000 lb.); normal maximum take-off 80,514 kg (176,709 lb.)

Accommodation: 25 to 28 crew

Dimensions:

span	35.00 m (114 ft. 10 in.)
length	36.60 m (120 ft. 1 in.)
height	9.08 m (29 ft. 9 in.)
wing area	197.04 m² (2,121 sq. ft.)

NIMROD R.MK 1P

Three standard Nimrod MR aircraft were delivered to RAF Wyton in 1971 for fitting out with mission equipment. Flight trials took place during 1973 and the type entered operational service in May 1974.

All three Nimrod R.Mk 1s gained a refuelling probe for combat operations in the Falklands in 1982, thus adding a 'P' to their designation. Tanker support is invaluable for the R.Mk 1's long-endurance sorties.

During Cold War operations, Nimrod R.Mk 1s frequently operated in international airspace around the peripheries of the Soviet Union, making extremely accurate navigation essential. Accordingly, they received a Delco AN/ASN-119 Carousel Mk IVA inertial navigation system and an upgraded EKCO 290 weather radar.

The R.Mk 1P's fuselage is covered with various aerials and antennas which serve its sensors. The main receivers cover the widest possible range of frequencies, with DF (direction finding) and ranging, and are thus able to record and locate the source of hostile radar and radio emissions The aircraft almost certainly have a computerised 'threat library', allowing a detailed 'map' of potential enemy radar stations, fighter radars, navaids and air defence systems to be built up.

In addition to their mission and navigation equipment, the R.Mk 1Ps have also received Loral ARI.18240/1 wingtip pods containing ESM (electronic support measures) gear. Increased equipment internally has led to the deletion of several cabin windows, and in recent years the aircraft have started carrying BOZ chaff/flare dispensers.

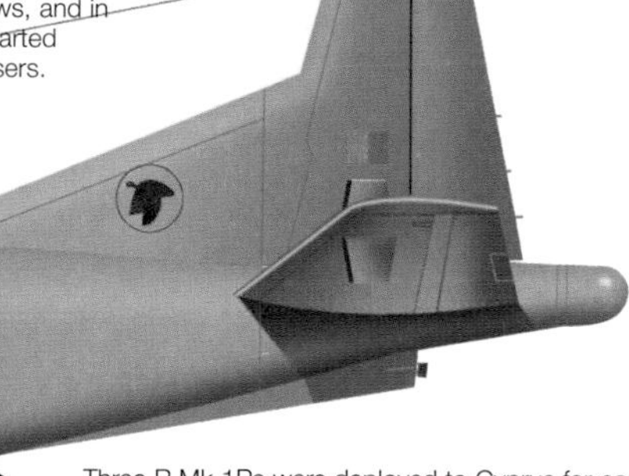

Three R.Mk 1Ps were deployed to Cyprus for combat operations during Desert Storm in 1991. However, their role was fictitiously reported as 'radar and radio aid calibration'.

COMBAT DATA

MAXIMUM SPEED

The Nimrod and RC-135 are much faster than the turboprop-powered 'Coot'. The Nimrod is marginally faster than the RC-135, and has a far better unrefuelled endurance, thanks to its more economical Spey turbofan engines. The R.Mk 1P can fly on just one engine to conserve fuel on long-endurance missions.

Aircraft	Maximum speed
NIMROD R.Mk 1P	926 km/h (575 m.p.h.)
RC-135C STRATOTANKER	901 km/h (560 m.p.h.)
Il-20DSR 'COOT-A'	674 km/h (419 m.p.h.)

Nimrod variants

MR.Mk 1: The prototype Nimrod first flew in 1967 and was followed by 46 production MR.Mk 1s which entered RAF service in 1969. The type eventually equipped five squadrons.

MR.Mk 2: From 1975, the remaining 35 MR.Mk 1s were upgraded to MR.Mk 2 standard with improved mission equipment. The first example was redelivered to the RAF in 1979.

AEW.Mk 3: Developed during the 1980s to fulfil the airborne early warning role, the Nimrod AEW.Mk 3 was cancelled because of technical difficulties and spiralling costs.

NIMROD 2000: The Nimrod remains the RAF's standard maritime recce aircraft. Around 20 have recently been upgraded with new engines, mission equipment and armament.

HAWKER SIDDELEY

NIMROD MR

● Anti-submarine ● Search and rescue ● Maritime patrol

Prowling the oceans of the world, the Nimrod is uniquely qualified to oversee surface shipping and to hunt down hostile submarines. Descended from the Comet jetliner, but in such modified form that when it first appeared it was in many ways a totally new design, the Nimrod is the world's only four-jet maritime patroller, able to detect and sink submarines, or mount anti-shipping strikes with Harpoon missiles. Much of its time is spent in a humanitarian role, however, mounting and coordinating search-and-rescue operations after accidents at sea.

▲ *The Nimrod is a complete anti-submarine and anti-ship battle station. Its unique four-jet configuration allows the aircraft to chase a contact faster than any other maritime aircraft.*

PHOTO FILE

HAWKER SIDDELEY NIMROD MR

◀ **Filling up**

The Nimrod fleet was hastily modified with air-to-air refuelling probes during the Falklands War in 1982. This allowed the Nimrod to make long surface search patrols into the South Atlantic, with missions often lasting well over 12 hours.

To the rescue ▶

If a shipping disaster occurs, Nimrods are sent to locate the ship and monitor the scene, guiding in rescue ships or helicopters.

Sidewinder armed ▶

The Nimrod received the capability to fire Sidewinders during the Falklands War. The aircraft never used them in anger.

▼ **Close watch**

Following up a radar contact, the Nimrod closes for a visual check on this 'Kotlin'-class destroyer.

▲ **Electronic support**

The Loral electronic support measures pod allows the Nimrod to analyse radar and radio transmissions. This information can then be programmed into a special computer 'threat library'.

FACTS AND FIGURES

- The first Nimrod was an aerodynamic prototype which flew on 23 May 1967.
- The Nimrod first entered service with the RAF in October 1969.
- Seven aircraft were used in the unsuccessful effort to develop an airborne early-warning version of the Nimrod.
- The Nimrod needs 1465 m (4,806 ft) of runway to take off and 1615 m (5,298 ft) to land.
- During Operation Desert Storm, Nimrods flew patrols from Seeb airfield, Oman.
- All Nimrod aircraft were upgraded in the mid-1970s; after the 1982 Falklands War all acquired air-refuelling probes.

PROFILE

The mighty ocean hunter

In 1964, Hawker Siddeley (now part of British Aerospace) began work on a naval reconnaissance aircraft based on the Comet 4C to replace the Royal Air Force's worn-out Shackletons. The Nimrod has a distinctive bulged fuselage, a fin-tip radome and a tailboom for magnetic anomaly detection (MAD) gear. It is far from pretty, but is perhaps the world's best maritime ASW (anti-submarine warfare) aircraft, superior in performance to the Lockheed P-3 Orion and Breguet Atlantic. From 1969 onwards, the Nimrod has served the RAF valiantly. Improvements to the basic design came with both the 1982 Falklands conflict and the 1991 Gulf War.

A trio of Nimrods went to the RAF for the very different job of ELINT (electronics intelligence) gathering, snooping on an enemy's activity with hi-tech 'black boxes'. One of the three was lost in an accident in 1995. A planned airborne early-warning version of the Nimrod – in effect, a flying radar station – never overcame technical difficulties, and Britain purchased Boeing's E-3 Sentry AWACS instead.

The Nimrod is now getting old and is progressing towards retirement, but it will remain on active duty well into the twenty-first century.

A replacement for Nimrod is currently under consideration, but it will not be easy to find an aircraft with the combination of superb mission equipment, long-range performance and tough low-level maritime flying.

Nimrod MR.Mk 2

Type: long-range maritime patrol aircraft

Powerplant: four Rolls-Royce RB.168-20 Spey Mk 250s each rated at 54.00 kN (12,145 lb thrust) dry

Maximum speed: 926 km/h (575 mph)

Cruising speed: 880 km/h (547 mph)

Ferry range: 9266 km (5,758 miles)

Service ceiling: 12,800 m (41,995 ft)

Weights: empty 38,937 kg (85,841 lb); loaded 87,091 kg (192,003 lb)

Armament: capability for Sting Ray torpedoes, Harpoon or Sidewinder missiles

Accommodation: crew typically 12 to 16; GEC central tactical system, Thorn EMI Searchwater radar; acoustics sensors; advanced communications equipment

Dimensions:	span	35.00 m (114 ft 10 in)
	length	38.63 m (126 ft 9 in)
	height	9.08 m (29 ft 9 in)
	wing area	197.04 m² (2,121 sq ft)

The four Rolls-Royce Spey turbofans are similar to the engines formerly used in the RAF's Buccaneers and Phantoms.

The fin-tip radome also houses electronic support measures equipment. The tailplane has now been modified with small finlets.

Nimrods can also carry an underwing BOZ jamming pod for self-defence, in place of the Sidewinder rail.

NIMROD MR.MK 2

Entering service in 1969, the Nimrod has seen much service in its long career, from patrolling icy North Atlantic waters to combat in the Falklands and the Gulf.

Nimrod's Searchwater radar performs very well, with good range and discrimination. It can spot a small periscope in choppy water, and pick up a small ship at very long distances.

The flight deck accommodates two pilots, a navigator and a flight engineer.

Two teams of systems operators are housed in the rear cabin. The 'wet' team is responsible for anti-submarine engagements, while the 'dry' team handles surface searches and actions.

MAD gear is carried in the tailboom. This equipment detects large objects made of iron or steel, such as a submarine's hull. It is a short-range system used just before an attack is made.

The lower, unpressurized section of the Nimrod's distinctive 'double-bubble' fuselage houses a capacious weapons bay.

Most of the large weapon load is carried in an internal bomb-bay, but Harpoon missiles are carried on wing hardpoints.

ACTION DATA

MAXIMUM/PATROL SPEED

The Nimrod's jet engines enable it to reach patrol areas faster than any other maritime aircraft. Once there, it can shut down two of its four engines and loiter for up to 15 hours at a time. The American Orion and the Franco/German Atlantic can also stay on station for long periods, but being propeller-driven they lack the Nimrod's ultimate speed and spend much more time in transit.

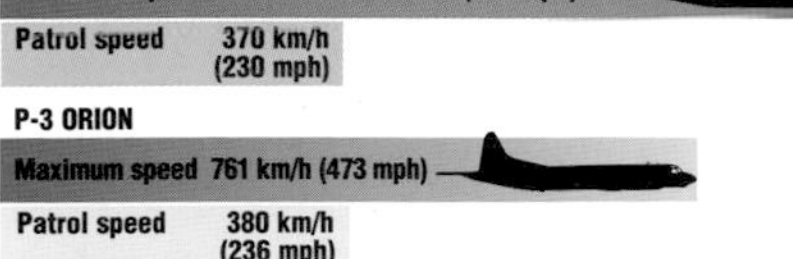

ATLANTIC
Maximum speed 660 km/h (410 mph)
Patrol speed 315 km/h (196 mph)

Sting Ray engagement

The Nimrod's primary anti-submarine weapon is the Sting Ray lightweight torpedo. Sting Ray can be launched from ships as well as aircraft, and combines a computerized guidance system with a powerful shaped-charge explosive designed to punch through the double hulls of Soviet Cold War-era submarines.

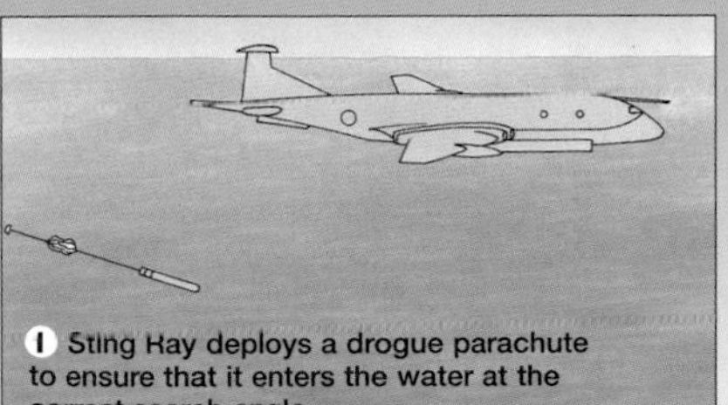

1 Sting Ray deploys a drogue parachute to ensure that it enters the water at the correct search angle.

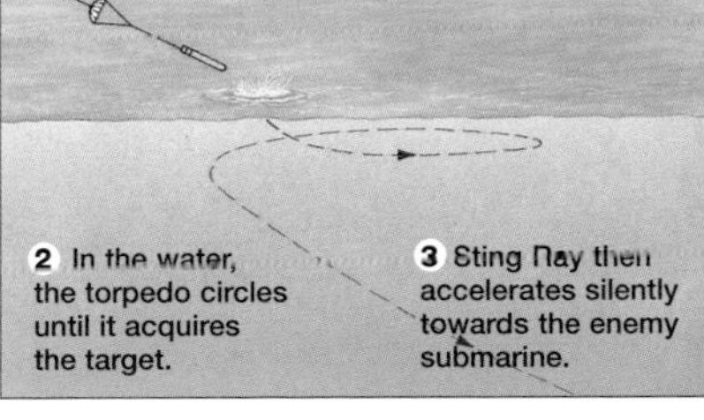

2 In the water, the torpedo circles until it acquires the target.

3 Sting Ray then accelerates silently towards the enemy submarine.

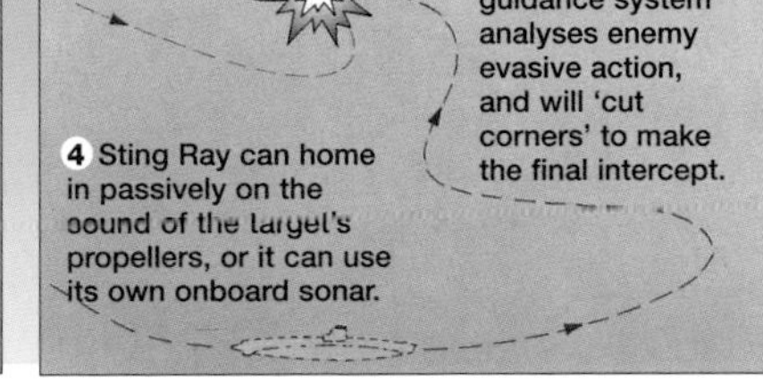

4 Sting Ray can home in passively on the sound of the target's propellers, or it can use its own onboard sonar.

5 The torpedo guidance system analyses enemy evasive action, and will 'cut corners' to make the final intercept.

ILYUSHIN

IL-20/22 'COOT'

● Intelligence-gatherer ● Il-18 derivative ● Russia and Ukraine

Flown for the first time in July 1957 as a 75-passenger airliner, the Il-18 'Coot' entered service with Aeroflot in April 1959. Later versions used more powerful engines to carry more passengers and additional fuel; more than 700 were built. Most were used by Aeroflot, others being exported. Military derivatives include the Il-20 'Coot-A' and Il-22 'Coot-B', top secret variants used for intelligence-gathering and command post duties.

▲ As in the West, the Soviet Union chose to modify an existing airframe for the Elint/reconnaissance role, choosing the reliable and sufficiently roomy Il-18 turboprop airliner.

PHOTO FILE

ILYUSHIN IL-20/22 'COOT'

◄ Snooping flight
Elint and Sigint aircraft often shadow large 'enemy formations' of the type found during military exercises by Western forces.

▼ Airliner roots
Retention of its cabin windows betrays the origins of this Il-20 as an Il-18 airliner.

▼ Developed in the 1970s
First observed by the West in 1978, about 40 Il-20DSRs were converted. Other variants include the Il-22 'Coot-B' command post aircraft.

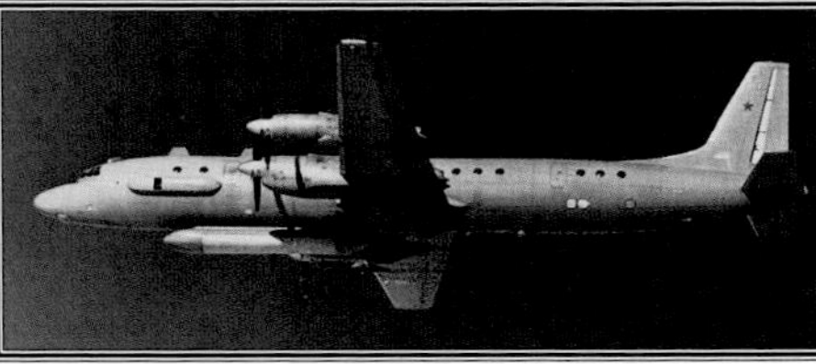

▼ Covert snapshot
Presumably at considerable risk to the photographer, this shot of an Il-20 was taken through an airfield's perimeter fence.

▲ Close up
Encounters between Western interceptors and 'snooping' Soviet intelligence aircraft have yielded close-up photographs like this one, useful to Western analysts.

FACTS AND FIGURES

- The Il-24N is an Il-20DSR derivative for fishery observation, retaining the SLAR but with Elint equipment deleted.
- About 20 Il-22s were operated by the CIS after the splitting-up of the USSR.
- One Il-22 'Coot-B' based in Belarus flies in Aeroflot colours.
- Il-22s are identified by a fin-top bullet fairing, a long container below the fuselage and numerous blade aerials.
- Il-20DSRs have a similar cruising speed to the Il-18M – around 625 km/h (388 m.p.h.).
- Il-20s are believed to have performed a secondary weather reconnaissance role.

PROFILE

Listening in on the West

Designated 'Coot-A' by NATO, the original Il-20 is an electronic intelligence (Elint) and reconnaissance version of the Il-18D. It carries a large fairing for a side-looking airborne radar (SLAR) under its fuselage, and pods for optical sensors are mounted on the forward fuselage sides. There are big blade antennas on top of the forward fuselage, and a series of three blister fairings on the fuselage underside, aft of the SLAR housing.

The aircraft are most often encountered by Western fighters 'scrambled' to intercept them on a 'snooping' flight, or while they are shadowing a large military exercise in order to glean information from intercepted communications.

The Il-22 'Coot-B' has a fin-tip pod plus many blade antennas above and below the fuselage. It is believed to be used as a communications relay aircraft and command post. Most 'Coots' are converted airliners, the Il-22s often being repainted in Aeroflot airline markings after conversion. At least one has been seen since the end of the Cold War in Ukrainian air force colours. 'Coot-As' fly with Russia and the Ukraine.

Above: This unknown variant of the Il-18 is equipped as a flying laboratory and features dielectric panniers and electro-optical sensors.

Below: Before the end of the Cold War, this was the closest that the West got to Il-20s and Il-22s – interception by an air defence fighter.

Il-20DSR 'Coot-A'

Type: Elint/Sigint/reconnaissance platform

Powerplant: four 3169-kW (4,250-hp.) Ivchenko AI-20M turboprops

Accommodation: flight crew of 4 or 5, plus 20 mission specialists

Dimensions:

span	37.42 m (122 ft. 9 in.)
length	35.90 m (117 ft. 9 in.)
height	10.17 m (33 ft. 4 in.)
wing area	140 m² (1,507 sq. ft.)

IL-20DSR 'COOT-A'

About 40 Il-18s were converted in the 1970s to Il-20DSR electronic intelligence (Elint) and signals intelligence (Sigint) platforms for the Soviet forces.

Square-section pods approximately 4.4 m long are fitted to both fuselage sides. They have a small door near the forward end for a camera or other optical sensor.

A major feature of the Il-20DSR is the side-looking airborne radar (SLAR) fairing under the forward fuselage. It is approximately 10.25 m (33 ft. 8 in.) long and 1.15 m (3 ft. 9 in.) in diameter. In addition to this, most aircraft also carry 12 to 15 extra antennas, the functions of which are not entirely clear to Western observers.

Powerplants on the Il-20 are four standard Ivchenko AI-20Ms rated at 3169 kW (4,250-hp.), which drive AV-68I four-bladed reversible propellers. These engines, like similar Western designs, date from the 1950s.

Like civil Il-18Ds, the 'Coot-A' has a flight crew of four or five, including two pilots, a navigator, radio operator and flight engineer. A mission crew of about 20 is carried in the main cabin to operate the aircraft's systems.

To avoid drawing attention to their special mission, Elint aircraft tend to carry low-visibility colour schemes, for example all-over grey or an unpainted 'natural metal' finish.

Originally converted from Il-18s for the Soviet armed forces, since the end of the Cold War the Il-20 fleet has been divided between the Russian Federation and Ukraine. Each state is believed to operate at least five aircraft, including three used by Russian naval aviation.

Weather reconnaissance in the West

BOEING WB-47E STRATOJET: This conversion of the B-47E bomber was employed by the MATS Air Weather Service until 1969.

BOEING WC-135B STRATOLIFTER: This C-135B was one of 11 converted for weather reconnaissance by Hayes International.

LOCKHEED HERCULES W.Mk 2: A sole Hercules C.Mk 1 was converted to W.Mk 2 standard for RAF service.

LOCKHEED WP-3D ORION: The US Department of Commerce operates two Orions from Florida on 'hurricane hunting' duties.

ACTION DATA

CREW

Mission specialists operate the top secret sensors and signals processing equipment aboard these Elint aircraft, the exact numbers varying according to the precise nature of a given mission. The RAF's BAe Nimrod R.Mk 1s have a comparatively large crew, but the USAF's RC-135V 'Rivet Rider' has just 21 crew.

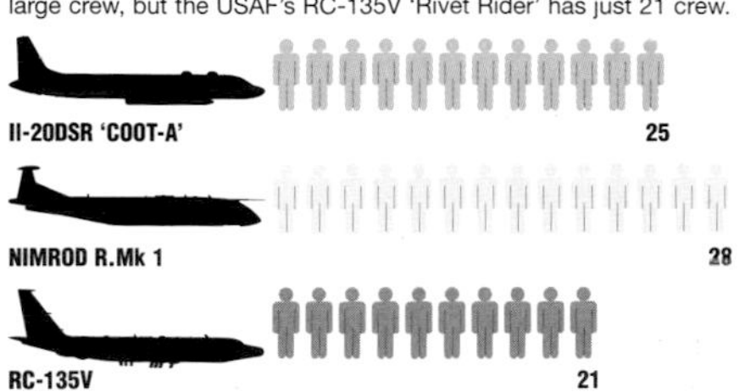

ILYUSHIN

IL-28 'BEAGLE'

● Early jet bomber ● Torpedo strike ● Middle East war veteran

Still in service half a century after it was designed, the Il-28 was a stunning aircraft when it first flew, the equal of the British Canberra. The 'Beagle' was exported to many nations, and hundreds were based in Warsaw Pact countries. In service with Egypt and Syria, the Il-28 saw action against Israel in 1967, and also fought in Nigeria. Built under licence in China, the Il-28 still flies in very small numbers in support roles.

▲ *Lacking a suitable replacement, China built the Il-28 long after it was obsolete, even exporting one to Albania, where it may still be flying. Like the British Canberra, it survived because large twin-engined jets are extremely useful for tasks such as target towing.*

PHOTO FILE

ILYUSHIN IL-28 'BEAGLE'

Bombsight ▶
The Il-28's bomb-aimer sat in a glazed nose and aimed his weapons visually with an OPB-5S bombsight, set to the right of the cockpit.

▼ Advanced design
Due to the success of the basic design the Il-28 was hardly changed during its career. Unusually, the main wing was unswept, but the tail was swept. In trials, it easily beat the rival Tu-78 prototype.

▼ Indonesian sailor
Torpedo-bombing Il-28s and the training Il-28U were used by Indonesia. The front cockpit accommodated the instructor, who could override his pupil if required.

◀ German Beagle
East Germany used 'Beagles' until the late 1970s. This aircraft has had its 23-mm (0.91-in) tail guns deleted as a weight-saving measure.

▼ African warrior
Nigeria used the Il-28 in its civil war. Poor maintenance meant that the aircraft were grounded for the majority of their lives, and the type has now been retired by all the user nations of Africa.

▲ Czech relic
Known as the B-228 in Czech service, the Il-28 served first as a light bomber, then as a target tug without armament. The wing-tip pods were not always fuel tanks; many Il-28s had ECM equipment fitted in these pods. Il-28s can still be seen at air museums in Prague and Monino, near Moscow.

FACTS AND FIGURES

- ➤ Israeli air strikes in the 1967 war claimed many Egyptian and Syrian Il-28s before they had even got off the ground.
- ➤ The prototype was initially fitted with Soviet-built Jumo 004 turbojets.
- ➤ Aeroflot used civilianized Il-28s (Il-20s) to fly newspaper matrices to Siberia.
- ➤ In flight trials against the Tu-78, three randomly picked crews all said they preferred flying the Il-28.
- ➤ Albania purchased a single H-5, which may still be flying, from China.
- ➤ Il-28Ts carried two 553-mm (21.7 in.) torpedoes in the internal bomb-bay.

PROFILE

Bombing in the 'Beagle'

Ilyushin's Il-28 was the mainstay of the Warsaw Pact tactical bomber force in the early Cold War period. Design began in 1947, benefiting from advanced British engine technology (the Rolls-Royce Nene engine) which had just been sold to the Soviet Union.

The aircraft first flew in 1948, entering squadron service in 1950. More than 1500 had been built by 1955, including minelaying and torpedo-bombing Il-28Ts for the naval air arm (AVMF) and Il-28U conversion trainers. The 'Beagle' was fast and carried an effective warload, including the TN nuclear weapon. The Il-28 reconnaissance version also flew in 1950, followed by the long-range nuclear strike Il-28D and other versions for target towing, electronic warfare and systems development.

The success of the 'Beagle' was widely recognized abroad, with sales to most Eastern bloc states, Egypt, Finland, Indonesia, Somalia and Yemen. China licence-built the Il-28 as the Hongzhaji-5 (H-5) and even exported this version, which remains in service today. Its half-century of service includes action in the Arab-Israeli war of 1967, the Afghan war, and probably in the Iran-Iraq and Somali-Ethiopian wars.

Above: In an effort to get hundreds of Il-28s into service as soon as possible, the airframe was built in sections which were then bolted together.

Above: Had the Cold War ever turned hot, the Il-28 would have been committed in huge numbers, probably armed with tactical nuclear weapons as well as flying electronic warfare and tactical reconnaissance missions.

Il-28 'Beagle'

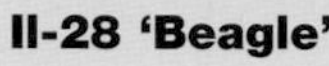

Type: three-seat twin-jet light bomber, torpedo bomber and reconnaissance aircraft

Powerplant: two 26.87-kN (6,403-lb-thrust) Klimov VK-1 (Rolls-Royce Nene) turbojets

Maximum speed: 900 km/h (559 mph) at 4500 m (14,764 ft)

Initial climb rate: 770 m/min (2,526 fpm) to 5000 m (16,404 ft)

Combat radius: 1135 km (705 miles)

Service ceiling: 12,300 m (40,354 ft)

Weights: empty 12,890 kg (28,418 lb); maximum take-off 23,200 kg (51,147 lb)

Armament: two 23-mm (0.91-in) cannon in nose (fixed) and two in tail turret; 3000 kg (6,614 lb) of bombs

Dimensions:		
	span	21.45 m (70 ft 4 in)
	length	17.65 m (57 ft 11 in)
	height	6.70 m (22 ft)
	wing area	60.8 m² (654 sq ft)

H-5

Built under licence in China as the H-5, the Il-28 still serves the People's Liberation Army Air Force and Romanian air force. More than 2,000 were built in China and 500 were imported from the Soviet Union.

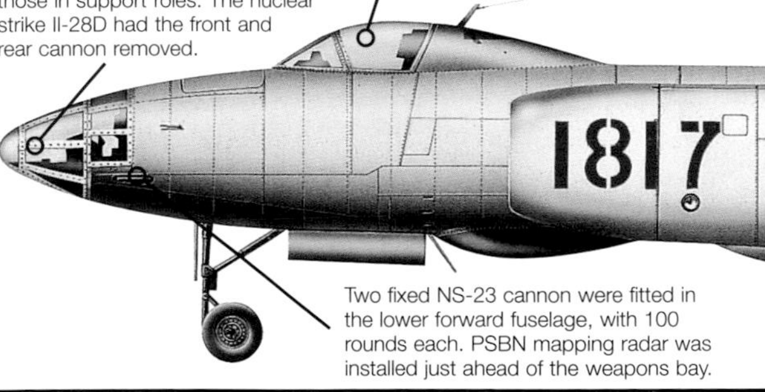

De-icing using hot air was fitted to the wing leading-edges of the wing and tailplane. The wing actually had a very small dihedral. Tip tanks containing 333 litres (88 US gal) were later fitted as standard.

VK-1 turbojets were also used in the Tu-14 bomber, MiG-17 fighter and (as the Rolls-Royce Nene) in the Hawker Sea Hawk.

The pilot sat in a fighter-style cockpit with the canopy hinging to the right. Both pilot and navigator/bombardier sat on ejection seats. The equipment fit included radar-warning receiver, instrument landing system, gun camera, autopilot, VHF Omni-Range, distance measuring equipment and radar altimeter.

All Il-28s retained a glazed nose, even those in support roles. The nuclear strike Il-28D had the front and rear cannon removed.

The fuselage construction was conventional, except that the airframe was built in separate halves, complete with equipment, then joined later to save time. The sections were bolted together, which was heavy, but quick and cheap.

Two fixed NS-23 cannon were fitted in the lower forward fuselage, with 100 rounds each. PSBN mapping radar was installed just ahead of the weapons bay.

To save weight, the gunner's cockpit was constructed entirely of magnesium, with armoured ammunition boxes and feeds. The structure (minus NR-23 guns) weighed only 375 kg (827 lb). The gunner was cut off from the other crewmembers.

COMBAT DATA

MAXIMUM SPEED

Jet bombers were already travelling much faster than post-war fighters by 1950, making them potentially very difficult to intercept. Great advances in engine technology were the main reason.

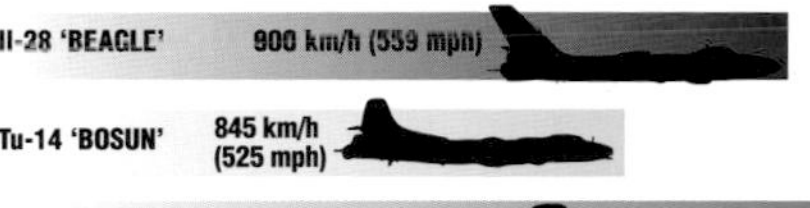

WEAPON LOAD

Tactical nuclear payloads were very common for the Canberra, but less so for the Tupolev and Ilyushin, which both had very respectable payloads. The Canberra's gun armament was all forward-facing, as its speed meant that it had little use for tail guns.

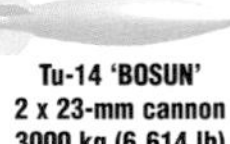

Il-28 'BEAGLE'	Tu-14 'BOSUN'	CANBERRA B(I).Mk 8
4 X 23-mm cannon	2 x 23-mm cannon	4 x 20-mm cannon
3000 kg (6,614 lb) of bombs	3000 kg (6,614 lb) of bombs	2270 kg (5,004 lb) of bombs

RANGE

The Tu-14 was designed as a naval strike aircraft (albeit operating from land bases and not ships), and therefore had long range. Despite its excellent performance, the Soviets ordered the Il-28 instead. The Canberra and Il-28 were both designed as tactical bombers, and therefore had shorter range. Neither aircraft was refuelled in flight, although the Canberra was able to carry underwing fuel tanks. High fuel consumption was a feature of early jet engines such as the VK-1.

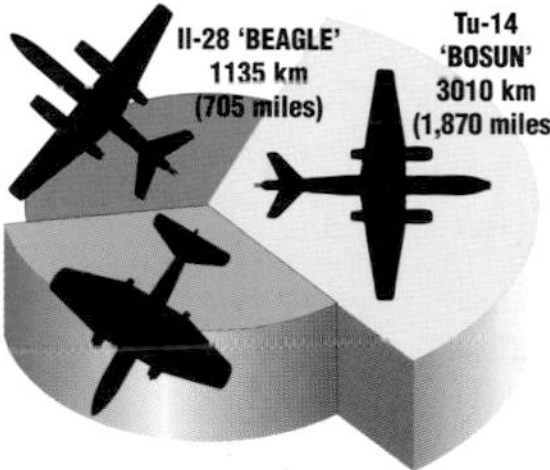

Jet bombers of the 1950s

NORTH AMERICAN B-45 TORNADO: Using four engines in pairs, the B-45 was an extremely ugly aircraft, but had a long range and heavy payload. Later Tornados had more advanced engines and systems, and the reconnaissance version carried 12 cameras.

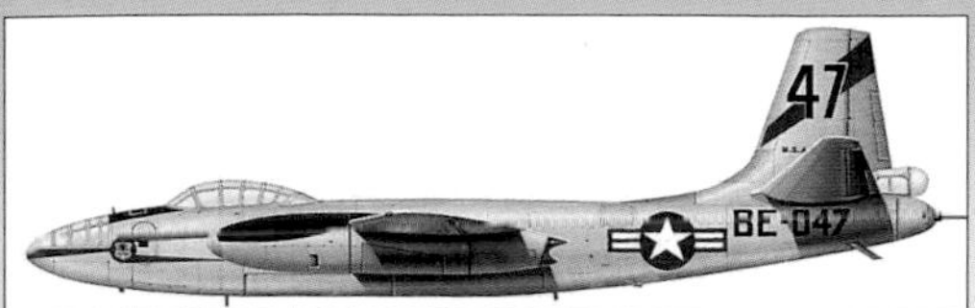

ENGLISH ELECTRIC CANBERRA B.Mk 2: The B.Mk 2, the first operational version of the Canberra, was very successful. Many were based in RAF Germany, armed with tactical nuclear weapons. The B.Mk 6 was essentially the same aircraft with uprated engines.

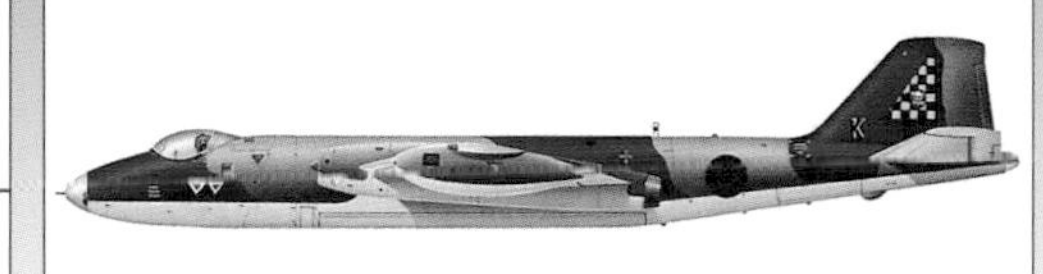

SUD-OUEST VAUTOUR: Designed as an all-weather fighter and ground-attack aircraft as well as a light bomber, the Vautour was used with spectacular success by Israel during raids against Arab airfields in 1967, and was only retired in the late 1970s.

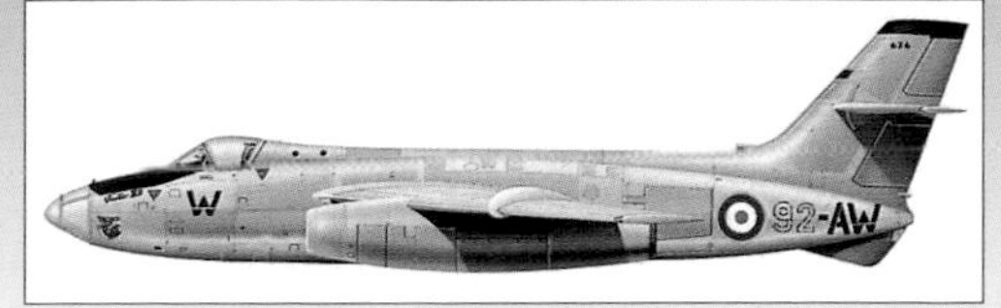

Ilyushin

Il-38 'May'

● Sub hunter ● Maritime patroller ● Based on Il-18 airliner

Just as the American P-3 Orion was developed from the Lockheed Electra and the British Nimrod from the de Havilland Comet, the Soviet Il-38 was derived from the Il-18, an airliner and military transport that first flew in 1957. The 'May' has a longer fuselage and the wings are mounted farther forward. Stores bays are ahead of and behind the wing structure and there is a long magnetic anomaly detector (MAD) stinger extending from the tail.

▲ *The 'May' is one of Russia's two main sub hunters and maritime patrollers. Around 50 are estimated to remain in service with the Russian navy, as well as in India and the Ukraine.*

Photo File

Ilyushin Il-38 'May'

▼ Airliner roots
Like its Western counterparts, the Nimrod and Orion, the Il-38 is developed from an airliner, the 122-seat Il-18 "Coot."

▲ Deployment
'Mays' have been deployed under Soviet control all over the world, from the Baltic, to Yemen, Libya, Syria, northern Asia, Vietnam and Egypt.

▼ 'May' in the tropics
The only export customer has been the Indian navy. Entering service in 1977 with No. 315 Squadron was the first of five Il-38s. These are based at INS Hansa, at Dabolim. Interestingly, India also operates eight Tu-142 'Bear-Fs'.

▲ Shadowing the US fleet
An A-6 Intruder intercepts a snooping 'May'. One of the Il-38's missions is to keep a close watch on the activities of U.S. Navy carrier battle groups.

◀ Caught in the act
A Swedish interceptor snaps an Il-38 dropping a sonobouy. The 'May' carries two types of this acoustic sensor: passive and active. Ejected in a predetermined pattern, they are designed to pinpoint the location of hostile submarines.

Facts and Figures

- In order to adjust the center of gravity of the heavier Il-38 compared to its parent Il-18, the wings are set farther forwards.
- Yemen and the former USSR signed a treaty allowing 'Mays' to fly from Yemen.
- Four pressure refueling points serve the Il-38's 30,000-litre (7,926-gal.) fuel tanks.
- Shrouded in secrecy for some time was the conversion of 22 'Mays' to airborne command posts as the Il-20 'Coot-B'.
- The Il-20 'Coot-A' is an electronic intelligence rebuild of the Il-38.
- Eight engine-driven generators supply electrical power for the avionics.

PROFILE

Soviet eye above the seas

As well as the tail-mounted MAD sensor, which detects the small variations in the earth's magnetic field caused by passing submarines, the 'May' carries a big 'Wet Eye' search radar under the forward fuselage. It can remain on patrol for up to 12 hours at a time, fly at speeds as low as 190 km/h (118 m.p.h.), and land in as little as 850 m (2,790 ft.) using reverse thrust from its propellers.

In addition to the two pilots and flight engineer on the flight deck, the aircraft carries a crew of nine systems operators in the main cabin. Their job is to monitor the displays showing targets detected by the radar and MAD sensors, and to track submarines using sonobuoys dispensed from the stores bays. Contacts may be destroyed using depth charges, torpedoes or missiles.

Only one export customer for the 'May' was found and a handful of Il-38s are operated by the Indian navy's No. 315 Squadron from its base at Dabolim. Before the Soviet Union disintegrated, 'Mays' were also deployed to bases in Yemen, Libya and Syria. And during the early 1970s, Soviet aircraft were flown in Egyptian markings from bases located in Egypt.

The bulk of the former Soviet Il-38s (about 59 aircraft in 1993) remain in service with the AV-MF, the air arm of the Russian navy. Lack of significant upgrades for the 'May' and continuing production of the Tu-142 seem to indicate that the latter is Russia's preferred maritime patrol and ASW aircraft.

Il-38 'May'

Type: medium-range anti-submarine and maritime patrol aircraft

Powerplant: four 3169-kW (4,250-hp.) ZMDB Progress AI-20M turboprops

Maximum speed: 722 km/h (448 m.p.h.) at 6400 m (21,000 ft.)

Take-off run: 1300 m (4,264 ft.)

Endurance: 12 hours

Weapons: Attack weapons and sonobuoys carried in two lower-fuselage bays.

Weight: 63,500 kg (140,000 lb.) max. take-off

Dimensions:

span	37.42 m (122 ft. 9 in.)
length	39.60 m (131 ft.)
height	10.16 m (133 ft. 4 in.)
wing area	140 m² (1,506 sq. ft.)

Compared to its Western counterparts, the P-3 Orion, Atlantique and Nimrod, the Il-38 does not appear to have been upgraded with sophisticated sensors such as low-light level TV, FLIR or electronic surveillance measures equipment.

A massive radome dominates the Il-38's forward fuselage. It houses a search radar, NATO codename 'Wet Eye', which is used for detecting submarine periscopes and surface vessels.

Four powerful and efficient turboprops power the Il-38. Identical to those fitted on the Il-18D 'Coot' airliner, they give the 'May' a respectable top speed of 722 km/h (448 m.p.h.), and a patrol endurance of 12 hours.

IL-38 'MAY'

Former Soviet Il-38s are now flown by Russia's naval air arm (AV-MF). Only one export customer was found. India received five aircraft.

'Mays' have only been seen in this overall gray camouflage scheme. Apart from national markings (the Soviet red star) and small identification numbers, the aircraft is entirely devoid of other markings.

The Il-38 carries three flight crew. Separated from the flight deck by a pressure bulkhead is the main cabin, which houses the equipment and operating consoles for nine mission specialists.

In modifying the Il-18 airliner for the sub-hunting role, Ilyushin stretched the fuselage by about 12 feet. The weight of the special mission equipment so affected the aircraft's center of gravity, that the wings were moved forward to compensate.

The Il-38 has two weapons bays fore and aft of the wing spars. These can carry torpedoes, depth charges, mines and sonobuoys.

The Il-38's featureless fuselage contains few windows. Observation blisters allow the crew to photograph ships and intercepting aircraft.

The MAD (magnetic anomaly detector) projecting aft of the tail is used to give the general location of hostile submarines. The device picks up the disturbance in the Earth's magnetic field caused by a large metallic mass such as a submarine.

ACTION DATA

SPEED

Maritime patrol aircraft frequently have to reach a distant part of the ocean quickly, perhaps to check a contact or to assist in a rescue. The P-3C arrives first, but the Il-38 is not far behind.

IL-38 'MAY'	722 km/h (448 m.p.h.)
ATLANTIQUE 2	648 km/h (402 m.p.h.)
P-3C ORION	761 km/h (472 m.p.h.)

ENDURANCE

Patrol aircraft must spend a long time on station. The less fuel-efficient 'May' loses out to the other aircraft. The Orion achieves its endurance by shutting down two engines.

IL-38 "MAY"
12 hours

ATLANTIQUE 2
18 hours

P-3C ORION
17 ½ hours

WEAPONS

Having found an enemy target, it must be destroyed with depth charges, torpedoes or missiles. The smaller load of the Il-38 relates to its lack of external weapons stowage.

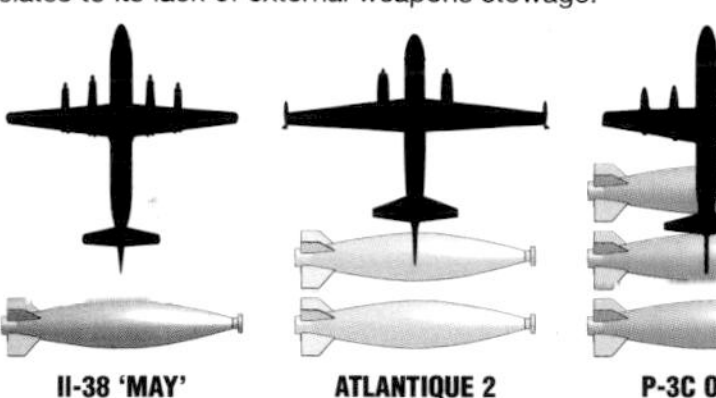

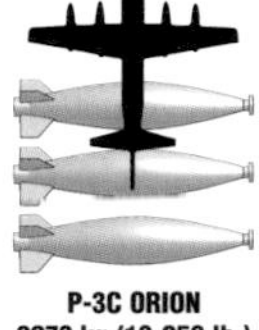

IL-38 'MAY'	ATLANTIQUE 2	P-3C ORION
3000 kg (6,600 lb.)	6000 kg (13,200 lb.)	9072 kg (19,958 lb.)

From airliner to maritime patroller

■ **PILATUS BRITTEN-NORMAN MARITIME DEFENDER:** This version of the original Islander has proved popular with smaller air forces.

■ **BRITISH AEROSPACE NIMROD:** Developed from the world's first jet airliner, the superb Nimrod will serve for many years to come.

■ **LOCKHEED CP-140 AURORA:** Lockheed redesigned the Electra to build the Orion and Canada adopted its own CP-140 variant.

■ **AIRTECH (CASA/IPTN) CN-235 MPA:** In competition with the Maritime Defender, this more modern aircraft is becoming popular.

ILYUSHIN

IL-76 'CANDID'

● Tactical transport ● Strategic airlift ● Airborne command post

Capable of carrying a 40-tonne payload onto a battlefield airstrip, the massive Il-76 is one of the world's most impressive transports. Even larger than the Lockheed StarLifter, the Il-76 has short-field capability, long range and can carry huge loads. Despite being designed for the military transport role, the Il-76 has also been converted into an airborne command post and a water-bomber, and is also used by many civilian operators.

▲ *Like most Soviet aircraft, the Il-76 is extremely rugged; in the words of an RAF C-130 pilot, 'the thing is built like a bridge'. It remains the principal equipment of the Russian military transport force.*

PHOTO FILE

ILYUSHIN IL-76 'CANDID'

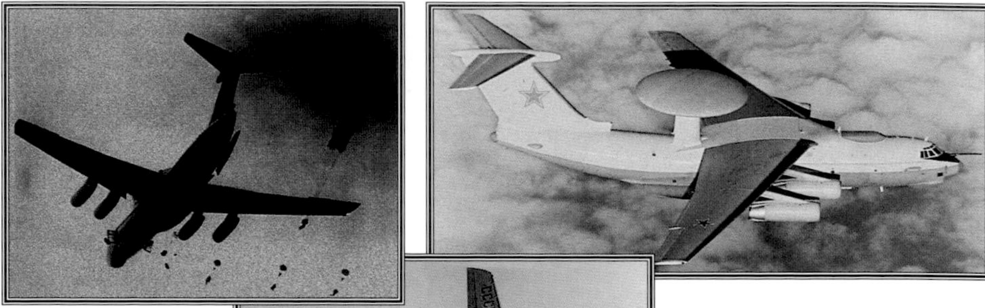

▲ Para drop
The Soviet army's paratroop force relies on the Il-76M to go to war. The aircraft can deploy 125 fully-equipped paratroops at a time. They exit the aircraft over the rear ramp to avoid the engine efflux.

▲ Early warning
The Il-76 carried out trials for the Soviet Il-78 'Midas' airborne early warning aircraft, which is comparable to the Boeing E-3.

◀ Record breaker
In 1975 an Il-76 flew a 60-ton payload for 2000 km (1,240 mi.) at 875 km/h (543 m.p.h.).

▼ Aeroflot colours
Despite its airline colour scheme, the Il-76 was mostly dedicated to military service; many Aeroflot aircraft flew to in Kabul in Afghanistan to offload Soviet garrison troops.

▲ Ramp loading
Unlike most of the An-12s it was designed to replace, the Il-76 has an integral rear door and ramp for fast loading.

FACTS AND FIGURES

- ➤ The Il-76 has been exported to Algeria, China, Cuba, Hungary, India, Iraq, Libya, North Korea and Syria.
- ➤ In Indian service the Il-76 is called 'Gajaraj' (cock elephant).
- ➤ The Il-76MDK allows trainee cosmonauts to experience weightless conditions.
- ➤ The 'Candid' can be converted into the Il-76DMP firefighter, carrying 42,000 litres (11,000 gal.) of water or retardant.
- ➤ The Il-76 transport can airdrop light tanks, pallets and amphibious vehicles.
- ➤ The new Il-76MF, carrying a 52,000-kg (114,000-lb.) payload, first flew on 1 August 1995.

PROFILE

Russia's military heavyweight lifter

Designed to replace the turboprop An-12, the Il-76 first flew in 1971 and entered service with a development squadron in 1974. Series production began in 1975 in Tashkent, and by 1993 more than 750 had been built, with production then continuing at the rate of one aircraft per week.

Immensely strong, the Il-76 has a titanium floor in the hold, a multi-wheel undercarriage, a wing fitted with various high-lift devices and four powerful Lotarev turbofans to allow short take-offs from rough airstrips. The 'TD' variant has uprated engines for 'hot-and-high' performance, and other Il-76s have been converted for airborne early warning and as command and control aircraft and tankers.

Military Il-76s differ from their civilian brothers by having a prominent rear gun turret with two 23-mm cannon, chaff and flare dispensers, and small fairings for electronic countermeasures gear. With the delays in the An-70 programme, the Il-76 remains a vital aircraft to the Russian tactical airlift force.

An adaptable aircraft, the Il-76 has also found use with Aeroflot as a freight transport and airliner. At least one, equipped with buffet kitchen, sleeping area and various cold-weather modifications is used in support of Russian Antarctic operations.

Il-76M 'Candid-B'

Type: medium military transport, command post, tanker (Il-78) and AEW aircraft (A-50)

Powerplant: four 117.68-kN (26,575-lb.-thrust) PNPP Soloviev D-30KP-1 turbofans

Maximum speed: 850 km/h (527 m.p.h.)

Maximum cruising speed: 800 km/h (496 m.p.h.) at 12,000 m (39,350 ft.)

Range: 5000 km (3,100 mi.) with maximum payload of 40,000 kg (105,600 lb.)

Service ceiling: 15,500 m (50,850 ft.)

Weights: max. take-off 190,000 kg (418,000 lb.)

Armament: optional two 23-mm GSh-23L twin-barrelled cannon in tail turret

Dimensions:

span	50.50 m (165 ft. 8 in.)
length	46.59 m (152 ft. 10 in.)
height	14 76 m (47 ft. 5 in.)
wing area	300 m² (3,228 sq. ft.)

The undercarriage doors close when the wheels are down to prevent the entry of mud, snow and ice. Braking is hydraulic and the tyre pressure can be altered from the cabin. Two packs of 96 50-mm flares can be carried on the landing gear fairings and a further two on each fuselage side.

Power is supplied by four reliable Lotarev turbofans, replaced on the stretched Il-76MF by Aviadvigatel PS-90ANs. The new MF's fuselage length is increased by 6.6 m (22 ft.).

The wing is high mounted and built in five pieces with a fail-safe, multi-spar construction.

Il-76TD 'Candid'

The Russian air force operates around 300 Il-76 transports, plus an additional number of testbeds, labs, AEW aircraft, tankers, Il-76VPK naval command posts and various electronic aircraft.

The cockpit seats a crew of seven, including two freight handlers. The glazed nose houses a navigator for negotiating combat landings without the use of the chin radar. All systems are designed for all-weather, day or night operations.

The 'Candid' has a hold with reinforced titanium flooring and folding roller conveyors. In the roof are two travelling lifter cranes each with two hoists of 2500-kg (5,500-lb.) capacity. At the front of the hold are twin winches for loading cargo. The hold can accommodate up to three specially designed modules for medical evacuation, passenger transport, supply or maintenance.

The large fuselage hold is fully pressurised and accommodates 140 troops or 125 armed paratroops. Alternatively freight containers, cranes, trucks, APCs, artillery or light tanks can be carried.

The tail ramp can be used as an additional hoist, with a 30,000-kg (66,000-lb.) capacity for loading heavier caterpillar-tracked vehicles.

The military-tasked Il-76 generally carries a tail turret containing two 23-mm twin-barrelled guns.

COMBAT DATA

MAXIMUM CRUISING SPEED

The C-141 is more streamlined and can cruise at a higher speed than the Il-76. The Polaris is based on the A310 airliner. All three would normally cruise at between 800 and 880 km/h (495 and 545 m.p.h.).

Il-76M	800 km/h (496 m.p.h.)
C-141B STARLIFTER	910 km/h (564 m.p.h.)
CC-150 POLARIS	850 km/h (527 m.p.h.)

PAYLOAD

The StarLifter and Il-76 are of similar design and perform similar tasks, both being able to carry around 40000 kg of cargo. The CC-150 cannot transport as much or such a range of freight.

IL-76M 'CANDID-B'	C-141B STARLIFTER	CC-150 POLARIS
40,000 kg (88,000 lb.)	41,222 kg (90,688 lb.)	33,780 kg (74,316 lb.)

RANGE WITH PAYLOAD

The Il-76 and StarLifter are used to transport troops and equipment on a global scale. They both regularly extend their range by the use of air-to-air refuelling to allow quick deployment.

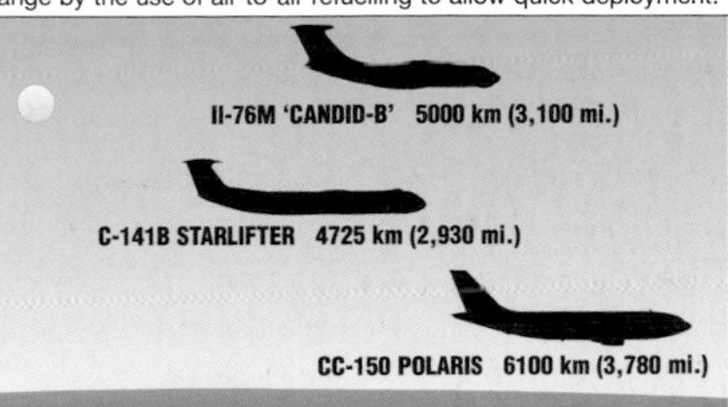

Red star airlifters

■ **ILYUSHIN Il-14 'CRATE':** Now thoroughly obsolete, the Il-14 enjoyed great success as the standard Eastern Bloc military transport aircraft throughout the 1950s and 1960s.

■ **ANTONOV An-26 'CURL':** Derived from the An-24, the An-26 is a very successful transport aircraft which has found widespread use in both military and civilian markets.

■ **ANTONOV An-72 'COALER':** This turbofan-powered STOL transport was designed to replace the turboprop An-26. It can carry freight, troops or paratroops, with entrance via a rear ramp.

ILYUSHIN/BERIEV

IL-78 'MIDAS'/A-50 'MAINSTAY'

● Flying tanker ● Airborne command post ● Transport aircraft

As the effectiveness of Boeing's E-3 Sentry AWACS (Airborne Warning and Control System) aircraft became apparent, Soviet designers began working on an equivalent. The Ilyushin Il-76 'Candid' formed the basis of Beriev's A-50 response to the requirement, while Ilyushin itself had been working on a further modification of the Il-76, this time to tanker configuration. The definitive Il-78M emerged as a useful three-point in-flight refuelling tanker.

▲ *With the ending of the Cold War, Russian crews unloading baggage from their Il-78 'Midas' aircraft at a British airfield have become a common sight.*

PHOTO FILE

ILYUSHIN IL-78/A-50

▼ Early warning
Beriev developed a specialised airborne early warning aircraft from the Ilyushin Il-76 transport aircraft.

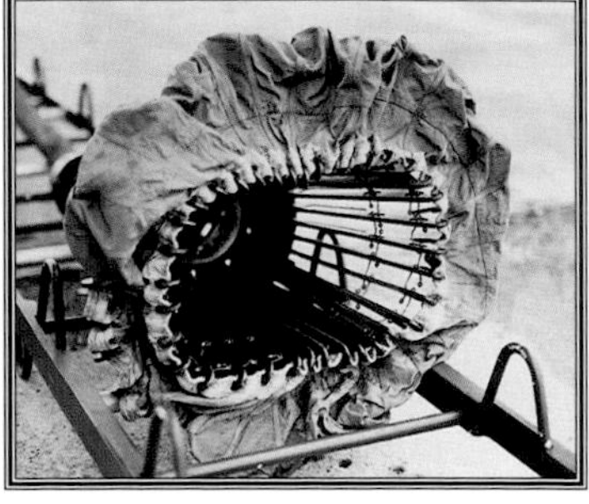

▲ Fuelling the fighters
In its tanker role the Il-78M can refuel three aircraft at the same time, using hose and drogue units like the one illustrated here.

◀ On the approach
The high-set tail and multi-wheeled undercarriage allow the 'Midas' to have a relatively short landing run. In this view the three refuelling points under the wings and rear fuselage are seen.

Watching and waiting ▶
Orbiting at high altitude, the A-50 'Mainstay' is charged with directing Su-27 'Flankers' and MiG-29 'Fulcrums' on intercept missions.

◀ Funding problems
Russian technology is now regarded as being the equal of its Western counterparts, but recent funding problems look set to hinder development of the A-50.

FACTS AND FIGURES

- The Il-78 'Midas' is a three-point tanker which carries the fuel internally on two pallet-mounted tanks.
- Ten mission operators are carried within the fuselage of the A-50 'Mainstay'.
- 'Midas' tankers were given a civilian airliner colour scheme.
- During the Gulf War 'Mainstays' operated over the Black Sea observing American air strikes flown from Turkey.
- The 'Mainstay' is said to be inferior to NATO's E-3 Sentry.
- China is seeking to purchase A-50s to support its 'Flanker' fleet.

PROFILE

The Soviets' all-seeing eye

During 1978, work began on a replacement for the primitive Tu-126 'Moss' AWACS platform in service with the Soviet forces. An all-new radar system, with its associated computer equipment and other sensors, was to be incorporated into the Il-76 airframe by Beriev.

Production of the A-50 'Mainstay' began in 1983 and, although there were a number of early problems, the aircraft has matured into an effective radar and command asset. It has demonstrated simultaneous operations with MiG-31 interceptors, Tu-22M bombers and submarines. A less capable aircraft, which retains the glazed nose of the Il-76, is known as the Be-976 and is used to support missile test programmes.

In an unrelated programme, Ilyushin converted an Il-76 to act as the prototype of the Il-78 'Midas' in-flight refuelling tanker. With some 28 tonnes (28 tons) of fuel in cylindrical tanks within the hold, the aircraft was initially equipped with a single hose drum unit (HDU) crudely attached to its rear fuselage. After 10 years of development 'Midas' finally entered service in 1987 and further modifications have seen the development of the much-improved Il-78M with two additional HDUs beneath the wings.

Above: The 'Midas' is the principal Russian air-to-air refuelling platform. It uses a probe and drogue system like most European air arms.

Below: Operational use of the A-50 has remained limited. Despite this Russia claims to have 12 examples flying.

A-50 'Mainstay'

Type: airborne early warning and control aircraft

Powerplant: four 117.68 kN (26,475-lb.-thrust) PNPP 'Aviadvigatel' (Soloviev) D-30KP turbofans

Maximum speed: 850 km/h (527 m.p.h.) at optimum altitude

Cruising speed: 800 km/h (496 m.p.h.)

Endurance: 4 hours

Radar detection range: 350–400 km (217–249 m.p.h.)

Operational ceiling: 10,000 m (32,000 ft.)

Accommodation: five flight crew; 10 mission specialists

Dimensions:

span	50.50 m (165 ft. 8 in.)
length	46.59 m (152 ft. 10 in.)
height	14.76 m (48 ft. 5 in.)
wing area	300 m² (3,228 sq. ft.)

A-50 'MAINSTAY'

Having observed America's success with the Boeing E-3 AWACS, the Russian air force requested an aircraft with similar capabilities. Despite its capabilities the A-50 faces budgetary restrictions.

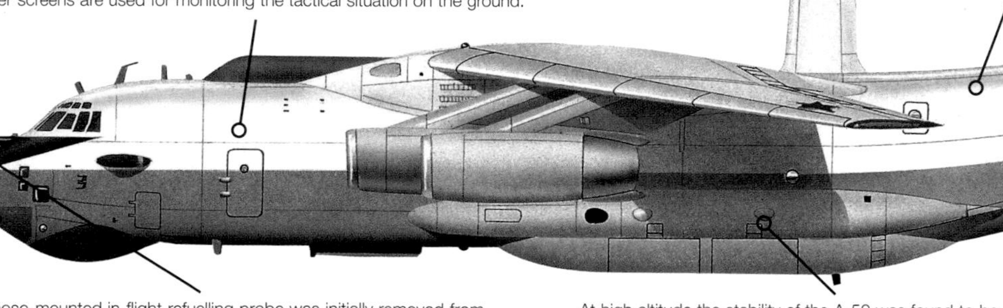

Two A-50 'Mainstays' flew round-the-clock monitoring flights during the Gulf War from orbits high over the Black Sea. They observed combat strikes and US cruise missile launches.

Influenced by the design of America's E-3 Sentry, the 'Mainstay's' main radar is positioned in a rotodome mounted above the fuselage.

Crews used to operating in the Tu-126 'Moss' have found the conditions within the A-50 particularly unpleasant, because of the high noise levels.

Within the fuselage a single large screen is used for controlling fighters, smaller screens are used for monitoring the tactical situation on the ground.

The nose-mounted in-flight refuelling probe was initially removed from the developmental 'Mainstay' because of problems encountered with the airflow across the aircraft during the fuel transfer phase.

At high altitude the stability of the A-50 was found to be relatively poor. Additional finlets were added to the lower fuselage above the undercarriage bays to alleviate the problem.

Deleted from both the AEW and tanker variants is the rear tail turret. On this particular variant, the A-50 'Mainstay', the glazing is retained but additional avionics radomes are installed. This allows the aircraft to detect any rearward-approaching enemy aircraft. During flight operations this position is unmanned.

ACTION DATA

MAXIMUM TAKE OFF WEIGHT

The need to lift all the required radar equipment associated with airborne control requires the 'Mainstay' to have a large take-off weight. Offering an improvement over the Boeing Sentry, the 'Mainstay' is fitted with more bulky equipment.

MAXIMUM SPEED

Weighed down as they are with heavy equipment, tairborne control aircraft can never reach high speeds. They normally orbit over friendly territory well protected by escort fighters, so their operational speeds are related to their radar capabilities.

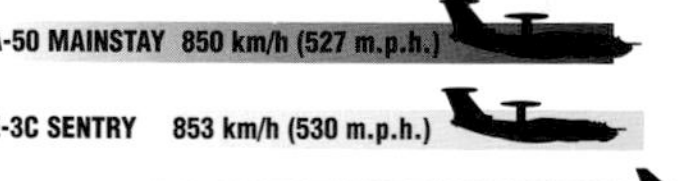

OPERATIONAL CEILING

Operating at high altitude allows the the aircraft to extend the range of their radar and contact friendly fighters for intercept duties at greater distances. One of the highest flying in its class, the 'Mainstay' operates at a much higher altitude than the Sentry but is unable to equal the E-4B.

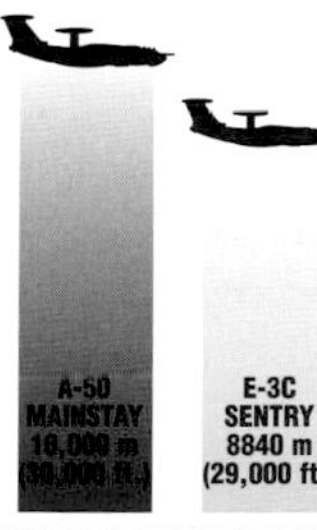

Controlling the skies

■ **E-3A AWACS:** Operated by the US Air Force and NATO, the AWACS is the West's primary airborne control aircraft.

■ **E-3F SENTRY:** The turbofan-powered E-3D and E-3F are the most capable European-owned AEW aircraft in service.

■ **Tu-126 'MOSS':** Derived from an airliner, the 'Moss' was the first Soviet aircraft to be fitted with a radar rotodome.

ISRAEL AIRCRAFT INDUSTRIES

KFIR

● Multi-role fighter ● 'Top Gun' aggressor ● Combat veteran

The Kfir (Lion Cub) has cemented a worldwide reputation for Israel Aircraft Industries, an aggressive and innovative builder of hi-tech warplanes in a very small country. The Kfir, based on France's remarkable Mirage III, appeared in the mid-1970s and became a key weapon in the Israeli arsenal, as well as a successful export product. Although originally designed as an interceptor, it has been developed into one of the world's finest strike aircraft. To fighter pilots the Kfir is fast, nimble and potent – enjoyable to fly, and proven in combat in the Lebanon.

▲ *The Kfir is a generation ahead of early Mirage models. It has a more powerful engine and a much more modern cockpit, including advanced head-up and multi-mode displays.*

PHOTO FILE

IAI KFIR

▼ Strike jet
Although designed as a fighter, the Kfir is extremely versatile and has given Israel excellent service as a strike fighter-bomber.

▲ Marine aggressors
The Kfir was used in aggressor training by the US Navy and Marine Corps.

▼ Canard nose
The canard foreplanes are the most obvious difference between the Kfirs and the Mirage family, which are far less capable.

◀ On patrol
Armed with four missiles and two cannon, the Kfir is still a dangerous foe, despite the age of the Mirage airframe on which it was based.

▼ IAI factory
This is the Kfir-C2's assembly line in Israel. The success of the Kfir family has been a very valuable source of work for the company.

FACTS AND FIGURES

- ➤ Israel hastened development of the Kfir by testing the Technolog, a two-seat Mirage III with canards.
- ➤ The Kfir was not shown in public until Israel unveiled the aircraft in 1975.
- ➤ The US prevented Israel from exporting J79-powered Kfirs to Taiwan.
- ➤ Israel lent two squadrons of Kfirs to the US Navy and the US Marines, used for dissimilar air combat training.
- ➤ To avoid a US embargo, Israel developed a Kfir powered by an Atar engine.
- ➤ Israel successfully exported the Kfir to Ecuador and Colombia.

PROFILE

The Lion Cub from Israel

Israel operated the tailless, delta-winged Mirage III long before the revolutionary design of this French fighter was proved in combat. The Mirage was one of the great successes of the 1967 Six Day War, but when France embargoed a shipment of 50 aircraft, Israel became determined to offset its reliance on overseas suppliers.

This process began when agents of Mossad, the Israeli secret intelligence service, stole plans for the Mirage III, which were used to produce the Nesher, a pirated Israeli Mirage.

Then, in great secrecy, Israeli engineers worked on a programme called Black Curtain to adapt the Mirage III airframe to take a more powerful American-designed J79 engine. In 1975, this produced the Kfir. Although it originally resembled the Mirage 5, a version first seen in 1976 introduced small, swept-back foreplanes which improved handling, agility and low-speed performance.

From 1983 Israel began operating the Kfir-C7, which is an upgraded aircraft fitted with advanced radar and avionics and a boosted engine. A highly capable interceptor, it is also as good a ground attack aircraft as can be found anywhere in the world.

The Kfir was a potent addition to the Israeli air force, and performed well during the battles over Lebanon in 1982. Although used primarily in the ground attack role, it scored several kills against Syrian MiG-23s.

One of the many changes to the Mirage design was the pronounced 'dogtooth' in the wing leading edge.

Kfirs built after 1983 have an engine overspeed capability. This allows the J79 to give even more boost under combat conditions, although at the expense of engine life.

Kfir-C7

Type: single-seat interceptor, fighter and fighter-bomber

Powerplant: one 79.63-kN (17,864-lb.-thrust) (83.36 kN/18,700-lb-thrust) with emergency boost afterburning General Electric J79-J1E turbojet

Maximum speed: Mach 2.3 or 2440 km/h (1,523 m.p.h.) above 11,000 m (36,000 ft.)

Combat radius: 880 km (546 mi.)

Service ceiling: 17,680 m (58,000 ft.) or 22,860 m (75,000 ft.) in a zoom climb

Weights: empty 7285 kg (16,027 lb.); maximum loaded 16,500 kg (36,300 lb.)

Armament: two 30-mm DEFA cannon with 280 rounds; up to 6085 kg (13,400 lb.) of bombs, rockets or missiles

Dimensions:

span	8.22 m (27 ft.)
length	15.65 m (51 ft.)
height	4.55 m (15 ft.)
wing area	34.80 m² (374 sq. ft.)

KFIR-C2

Ecuador was one of two main export customers for the Kfir. The aircraft are primarily used as interceptors, and equip Escuadrón de Combate 2113, part of Grupo 211, based at Taura.

Small strakes are fitted to the nose just behind the radar. These generate vortices for increased control at high angles of attack.

Ecuador's aircraft are nominally Kfir-C2s, but have been upgraded with many of the advanced avionics systems of the Israeli Kfir-C7.

The intake design of the Kfir series was modified to cope with the greater mass flow of the J79 engine.

The Kfir can carry a huge variety of weapon stores, including Shafrir and Python dogfight missiles, Shrike anti-radar missiles, Maverick air-to-surface missiles, and various types of bombs.

The dorsal airscoop on the Kfir is necessary to provide cooling air for the J79 engine, which generates much more heat than the Atar engine powering the original Mirage.

The Kfir-C2 has a relatively simple ranging radar, as the aircraft is primarily a ground-attack type and only carries infra-red missiles.

The Kfir is powered by a single General Electric J79-J1E augmented turbojet, the most powerful variant of this American-designed engine.

COMBAT DATA

MAXIMUM SPEED

A combination of light weight, clean design and a powerful engine gives the Kfir a small edge in maximum speed over the lightweight MiG-21 and the far heavier F-4 Phantom.

KFIR-C7 2440 km/h (1,513 m.p.h.)

F-4 PHANTOM 2390 km/h (1,482 m.p.h.)

MiG-21 'FISHBED' 2230 km/h (1,383 m.p.h.)

CLIMB RATE

Although the Kfir is generally used as a ground attack aircraft, it is no mean performer as an interceptor. It cannot match the Phantom in a climb – even though the American jet is much heavier, the power of two J79s instead of one puts the F-4 in front – but the Kfir still climbs very fast, and it easily outpaces the older, lighter and less powerful MiG-21.

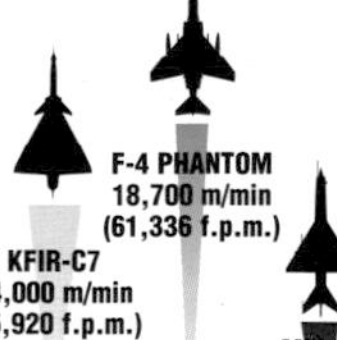

ARMAMENT

The large delta wing and powerful engine give the Kfir excellent striking power, allowing it to lift almost as much as the F-4 and far more than the much less versatile MiG-21 'Fishbed'.

History of a Lion Cub

■ **MIRAGE ANCESTOR:** The classic Dassault Mirage III was used to great effect as an air-superiority fighter by Israel during their amazing triumph in the Six Day War of 1967.

■ **PIRATE COPY:** Driven to desperate measures by an arms embargo, the Israelis built Mirage copies with stolen plans. Some were sold to Argentina and used in the Falklands.

■ **AMERICAN POWER:** Fitting a larger and more powerful American-designed General Electric J79 engine into a Mirage airframe, IAI produced the first Kfir in the early 1970s.

■ **AERODYNAMIC REFINEMENT:** The canard foreplanes are the most obvious feature of the Kfir-C2, designed to improve the delta-winged fighter's low-speed handling.

■ **STATE OF THE ART:** New radar, cockpit, avionics and a boosted engine have turned the Kfir-C7 into one of the most potent ground-attack fighters in service today.

KAWASAKI C-1

● Twin-jet transport ● JASDF service ● Engine testbed

Designed in the late 1960s as a medium transport to replace the C-46 Commando in Japanese Air Self-Defence Force (JASDF) service, the C-1 has a typical military transport configuration. Kawasaki flew the first example in November 1970, and delivered 31 aircraft in October 1981. Proposed tanker, reconnaissance and other military variants were abandoned, but one C-1 has been used for research into blown flying surfaces for improved field performance.

▲ *A competent, medium-ranged military transport, the C-1 has served with the JASDF for 22 years. No export customers were found and only 31 aircraft were built.*

PHOTO FILE

KAWASAKI C-1

▼ STOL testing
Four 47.07-kN (10,600-lb.-thrust) turbofans and a powerful flap blowing system allow a landing distance of only 853 m (2,800 ft.).

▲ Kawasaki camouflage
Deliveries of the C-1 were completed in 1981, and by 1982 all were camouflaged.

▲ Silver C-1
Sleekly-podded turbofans and large fairings over the flap hinges are characteristics of the C-1 design. All were originally natural metal.

▲ Rear ramp and clamshells
Kawasaki followed the accepted formula for tactical airlifter design, fitting the C-1 with a rear loading ramp and clamshell doors.

Two squadrons ▶
The stylised bird marking of the 402 Hikotai also appears on the unit's NAMC YS-11s. The C-130H is Japan's other principal airlifter.

FACTS AND FIGURES

- The C-1 needs only 439 m (1,440 ft.) to take off and only 853 m (2,800 ft.) to reach a height of 15 m (50 ft.).
- Nihon Aeroplane Manufacturing Company began designing the C-1 in 1966.
- Two prototypes completed C-1 test flying in March 1973.
- Five long-range versions were built with an additional 4732-litre (1,250-gal.) wing tank.
- Kawasaki was responsible for final assembly and testing of the C-1.
- One of the potential replacements for the C-1 is the C-17A Globemaster III.

PROFILE

Japanese STOL transport

With its high wing, fuselage-mounted undercarriage sponsons and hydraulically-actuated rear loading ramp, the C-1 Asuka resembles other tactical transport aircraft. Designed to provide maximum internal cargo space for troops, vehicles and freight, it is powered by turbofan engines but carries a smaller payload than the Lockheed C-130 Hercules or Transall C.160.

Construction of the C-1 was a collaborative effort involving the four major Japanese aircraft manufacturers, with Fuji, Mitsubishi and Nihon all contributing major sub-assemblies. The Asuka was used to equip two Japanese Air Self-Defence Force (JASDF) transport squadrons, the 402nd based at Iruma and the 403rd at Miho. One C-1, known as the EC-1, was modified as an electronic warfare training aircraft, with massive bulges and radomes to house the necessary sensors. Another was used as a testbed for the T-4 trainer's Ishikawajima-Harima F3 engine and the MITI/NAL FJR710 high-bypass turbofan.

Another modified C-1, the National Aerospace Laboratory Asuka, a quiet short take-off and landing (QSTOL) research aircraft, uses the FJR710/600S powerplant. Although the C-1 was designed to a JASDF specification, its limited payload has ultimately restricted its versatility in service and a replacement is being sought.

Above: For air-dropping freight or paratroops, the rear loading ramp and clamshell doors can be opened in flight. Typical loads include a 105-mm howitzer, three jeeps, a 2.54-tonne (2½-ton) lorry or two 0.76-tonne (¾-ton) trucks. Alternatively, three standard freight pallets may be accommodated.

Below: This take-off shot shows the C-1's extensive flaps and leading-edge slats to advantage.

C-1

Type: tactical military transport aircraft

Powerplant: two 64.5-kN (14,500-lb.-thrust) Pratt & Whitney JT8D-M-9 turbofans

Maximum speed: 806 km/h (500 m.p.h.) at 7620 m (25,000 ft.)

Range: 1297 km (800 mi.) with 7900-kg (17,400-lb.) payload

Service ceiling: 11,580 m (38,000 ft.)

Weights: empty 24,300 kg (53,460 lb.); maximum take-off 45,000 kg (99,000 lb.)

Accommodation: five crew plus 60 fully-equipped troops, 45 paratroops, 36 stretchers with attendants or 11,900 kg (26,200 lb.) of cargo

Dimensions:

span	30.60 m (100 ft. 4 in.)
length	29.00 m (95 ft. 2 in.)
height	9.99 m (32 ft. 9 in.)
wing area	120.5 m² (1,297 sq. ft.)

EC-1

Extensively modified, this EC-1 is nominally used for electronic countermeasures (ECM) training with the 501st Hikotai. It is likely to have an additional electronic intelligence (Elint) role.

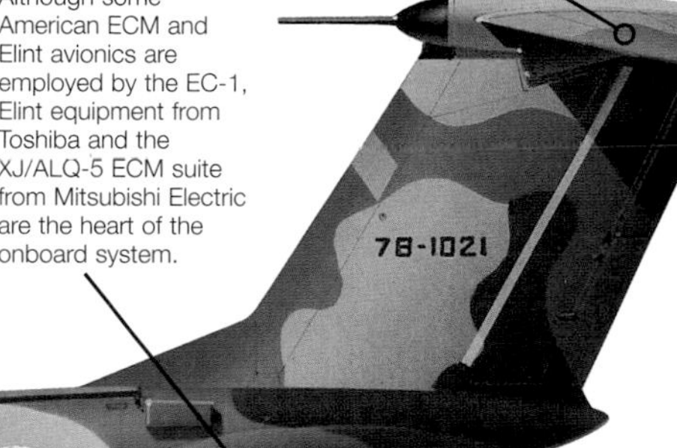

Large fairings festoon the EC-1, the most unusual being the giant radomes on the nose and beneath the tail. Kawasaki modified the 21st C-1 airframe to this standard, to meet a 1983 Defence Agency contract.

Setting the wings high up on the fuselage ensures that the wing carry through structure does not affect cabin volume. The outer wings were built by Fuji, with Nihon producing the engine pods and control surfaces.

Although some American ECM and Elint avionics are employed by the EC-1, Elint equipment from Toshiba and the XJ/ALQ-5 ECM suite from Mitsubishi Electric are the heart of the onboard system.

Contrary to the solution adopted by Lockheed for the tail unit on its C-130, Kawasaki used a high-set horizontal surface on the C-1. This keeps the tailplane clear of the jet wash.

Using the upswept tail arrangement that has become characteristic of tactical transports, the C-1 offers easy loading. Three separate hydraulic units operate the aircraft's systems, one of which is dedicated solely to the rear ramp.

COMBAT DATA

PAYLOAD

While the C-1 can carry a greater payload than the An-72C, it does not have the capacity required by a primary airlift asset. The YC-14 can lift a maximum of 12,247 kg (27,000 lb.) for STOL operations, but carries over 35,000 kg (77,000 lb.) normally.

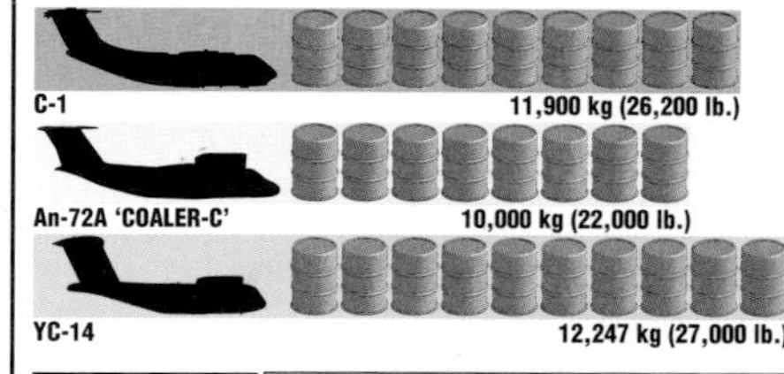

TAKE-OFF RUN

With maximum payload the C-1 requires a respectable 914-metre run to clear a 15-metre obstacle. Antonov's An-72C needs a longer runway to attain a height of 10.7 metres, while Boeing's incredible YC-14 requires just 305 metres to become airborne.

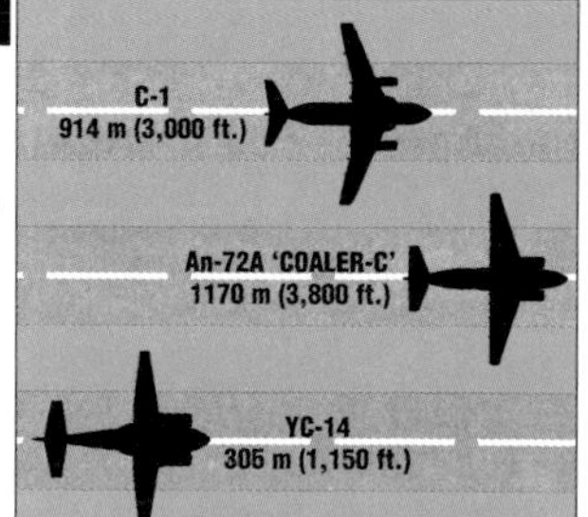

MAXIMUM RANGE

Japan's C-1 has adequate range compared to other contemporary types. However, its range is sufficient for tactical in-theatre operations, and five examples of an extended-range version were built. Greater range would give the fleet added versatility.

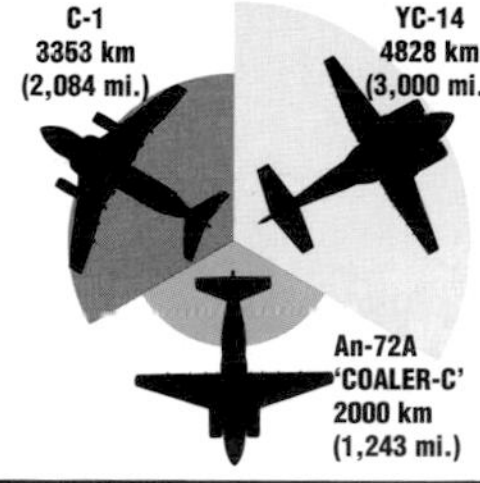

Electronic transports

■ **BEECH RC-12 'GUARDRAIL':** Several variants of the RC-12, most dedicated to communications intelligence, have been used by the US Army. The latest version is the RC-12P.

■ **BOEING RC-135 'RIVET JOINT':** Ordered as RC-135Bs, the 'Rivet Joint' strategic reconnaissance aircraft were delivered as RC-135Cs and updated to RC-135Vs.

■ **LOCKHEED EC-130E 'RIVET RIDER':** Highly modified EC-130Es are used as Airborne Battlefield Command and Control Centres and also flew broadcast duties during the Gulf War.

■ **NAMC YS-11E:** Three YS-11s were modified for electronic warfare training as YS-11Es. The aircraft shown has since been modified to YS-11EA standard for the Elint role.

KAWASAKI

T-4

● **Modern jet trainer** ● **Indigenous design** ● **Highly versatile**

Japan's T-4 was developed as a replacement for the Japanese Air Self-Defence Force's Lockheed T-33 and Fuji T-1 trainers. The new aircraft is sourced almost entirely from Japanese industry and offers excellent performance in the training role, as well as providing a useful liaison capability. Production deliveries began in September 1988 and since 1996 the T-4 has been the mount of the famous 'Blue Impulse' aerobatic team.

▲ *Kawasaki's T-4 is the standard medium jet trainer of the Japanese Air Self-Defence Force (JASDF) and looks likely to continue in service well into the 21st century.*

PHOTO FILE

KAWASAKI T-4

▼ Joint-venture
The T-4 is a collaboration between Kawasaki, Mitsubishi and Fuji. Kawasaki is the lead contractor.

▲ Japanese exclusive
A T-4 prototype in flight. The type equips several JASDF units, though no export orders have so far been secured.

Aerobatic performer ▶
In addition to various training wings, the Japanese aerobatic team 'Blue Impulse' also flies the T-4, as seen here.

▼ First prototype
Identified by its red and white pitot head, the first prototype T-4 (66-5601) sits at rest. The first flight took place on 29 July 1985.

'Blue Impulse' ▶
The acclaimed aerobatic team has only recently re-equipped with the T-4 after operating the Mitsubishi T-2 for several years. Here one of its aircraft makes a low 'n' slow flypast with its gear lowered.

FACTS AND FIGURES

- Fuji builds the rear fuselage, supercritical-section wings and tail unit of the T-4.
- Some T-4s used by front-line squadrons are camouflaged.
- T-4s have replaced the T-33 in F-1, F-4 and F-15 units.
- Training T-4s are flown by 31 and 32 Flying Training Squadrons of the 1st Air Wing at Hamamatsu, Tokyo.
- Mitsubishi has responsibility for the centre fuselage and air intakes.
- Kawasaki has so far made no provision for the T-4 to be armed.

PROFILE

Indigenously designed trainer

Pilots from Japan might consider themselves proud to have been trained on a fully indigenous aircraft. On 4 September 1981, Kawasaki was chosen as prime contractor for the T-4. Although production aircraft are assembled by Kawasaki, the company shares manufacturing responsibility with Fuji and Mitsubishi.

Four XT-4 prototypes were funded, the first flying on 29 July 1985. Almost three years of testing followed, before the first production aircraft was delivered in 1988, and by 31 March 1996, 171 out of a total requirement for 200 aircraft had been delivered. Similar in configuration to the Franco-German Alpha Jet, the T-4 offers greater versatility thanks to its in-built baggage compartment. This centre-fuselage hold allows the aircraft to fulfil its secondary liaison and high-speed, light transport duties. Many front-line JASDF squadrons have one or two T-4s on strength for use in this liaison role, or as 'hacks'.

Other missions within the capabilities of the T-4 include target-towing, electronic countermeasures (ECM) training and air sampling, with special equipment carried on three external pylons.

Despite its versatility and excellent manoeuvrability, Kawasaki's T-4 has yet to find an export customer, but nevertheless is set to serve the JASDF for years to come.

Above: The T-4 features relatively large trailing edge flaps allowing a low approach and landing speed.

Above: Underwing hardpoints enable the T-4 to carry 450-kg (990-lb.) drop tanks. Additionally, a centre-line pylon permits the carriage of a target winch, ECM pod, or chaff flare dispenser.

T-4

Type: two-seat tandem intermediate jet trainer and liaison aircraft

Powerplant: two 16.28-kN (3,660-lb.-thrust) Ishikawajima-Harima turbofan engines

Maximum speed: 1038 km/h (644 m.p.h.) at sea level

Initial climb rate: 3048 m/min (10,000 f.p.m.)

Take-off run: 610 m (2,000 ft.)

Range: 1297 km (800 mi.) (on internal fuel)

Service ceiling: 15,420 m (50,600 ft.)

Weights: empty 3790 kg (8,338 lb.); maximum take-off 7500 kg (16,500 lb.)

Dimensions:

span	9.94 m (32 ft. 7 in.)
length	13.00 m (42 ft. 8 in.)
height	4.60 m (15 ft. 1 in.)
wing area	21 m² (226 sq. ft.)

T-4

This particular T-4, serial number 56-5601, was the first of four prototypes, originally designated XT-4 and is seen here wearing the markings of the Air Proving Wing.

The T-4 is jointly manufactured by three different companies, Fuji, Kawasaki and Mitsubishi. Kawasaki builds only the forward fuselage but is responsible for all flight testing.

Like many modern jet trainers, the T-4 features a raised, staggered cockpit offering excellent visibility for both pupil and instructor. The large canopy features a wraparound windscreen and separate main unit which hinges to starboard for entry/exit.

Conventional in design, the relatively high-set wing gives the T-4 excellent high-subsonic manoeuvrability and docile handling characteristics. Although it is not configured for combat, hardpoints under the wings permit the carriage of various external stores.

Many modern jet trainers feature a relatively large vertical tail structure and the Kawasaki T-4 is no exception. The low-set tailplane (below the main wing) was designed to avoid adverse effects should the aircraft accidentally go into a spin.

Japan's newest intermediate jet trainer was designed to withstand hard and heavy landings; consequently, the undercarriage is extremely strong and has anti-skid brakes, which are located on the main units.

Being of twin-engined configuration, the T-4 enjoys a distinct performance advantage over many other single-engined, contemporary jet trainers. Its two Ishikawajima-Harima turbofans put out a considerable amount (32.56 kN/7,320 lb. thrust) of thrust.

ACTION DATA

THRUST

In comparison with the Polish PZL I-22 and the older Dassault/Dornier Alpha Jet, the T-4 has more than adequate thrust and performance, thanks to its small but powerful locally designed and built F-3 IHI turbofans.

T-4 32.6 kN (7,320 lb. thrust)
ALPHA JET E 26.5 kN (5,960 lb. thrust)
I-22 IRYDA 21.6 kN (4,860 lb. thrust)

CLIMB RATE

Although powerful for its size, the T-4's overall performance is somewhat less than that of the Alpha Jet. All three types can out-perform several current front-line combat aircraft, however.

T-4 3048 m/min (10,000 f.p.m.)
ALPHA JET E 3660 m/min (12,000 f.p.m.)
I-22 IRYDA 1500 m/min (4,900 f.p.m.)

g LIMITS

Modern advanced trainers are capable of pulling higher-*g* manoeuvres than their predecessors without coming apart. This allows pilots to develop their skills and awareness before being assigned to front-line combat units.

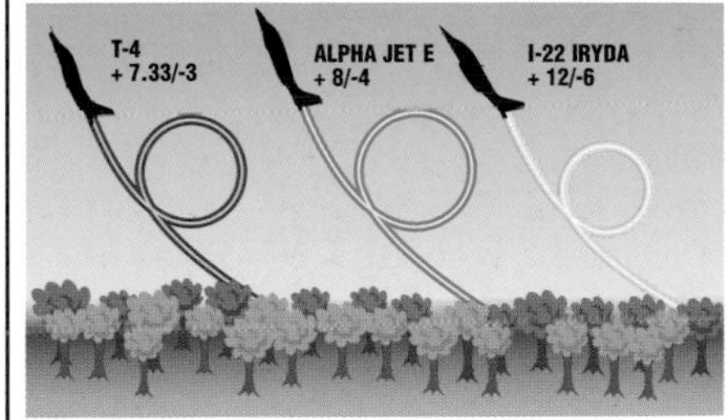

Asian jet trainer designs

AIDC AT-3 TSU CHIANG: The first military jet developed by Taiwan, the AT-3 performs both basic training and light attack roles.

CNAMC/PAC K-8 KARAKORUM: Jointly financed by China and Pakistan, the K-8 serves as a basic jet trainer with both air forces.

FUJI T-1A/B: This was Japan's first indigenous jet trainer, though it is now largely out of service, having been replaced by the T-4.

MITSUBISHI T-2: The T-2 serves as the JASDF's standard advanced trainer and shares many components with the F-1 fighter variant.

LOCKHEED

C-130A-E HERCULES

● **Versatile airlifter** ● **Widely exported** ● **Still going strong**

▲ *Not revolutionary when it first appeared, the C-130 was, nevertheless, the first transport aircraft to incorporate all the latest technological features in a single package.*

Designed from 1951 for the US Air Force's Tactical Air Command, the C-130 set a new pattern for military transport aircraft. Previous types usually had piston engines, tailwheel landing gear and side doors. The Hercules used turboprops for improved performance, a high-set wing to avoid encroaching on the cargo space and to provide excellent STOL capability, and a sturdy tricycle landing gear to allow it to operate from unpaved airstrips.

PHOTO FILE

LOCKHEED C-130A-E HERCULES

◀ **Hotrod Hercules**
A lack of external wing tanks were a distinguishing feature of the C-130B. With uprated engines, this variant was the fastest of all production Hercules. Canada acquired 24 of the type.

Relief flights ▶
Since the mid-1950s, when they first entered service, C-130s have flown thousands of humanitarian missions around the world.

◀ **First of the many**
Displaying the small nose radome, the original prototype YC13-A (serialled 53-3396) takes off on an early flight. Early production C-130As were virtually identical to the prototypes.

▲ **Caught on the ground**
Seen after being hit by Viet Cong mortar, a USAF C-130 burns at Dak To. Viet Cong sappers did more damage to C-130s than anti-aircraft fire in 'Nam.

▼ **Arctic operations**
Among the rarest of all Hercules were the ski-equipped C-130Ds flown by the New York Air National Guard. These aircraft were used to supply radar stations located in the Arctic.

FACTS AND FIGURES

- The first Hercules actually to fly was the second prototype YC-130A, which took to the air on 23 August 1954.
- C-130As were the only variants to be delivered with three-bladed propellers.
- The longer-ranged C-130E was bought by nine countries outside the United States.
- In Vietnam, the Hercules played a vital part in delivering supplies to the besieged US Marine bases at Khe Sahn.
- Many early USAF C130-As were converted into extremely capable gunships.
- All seven of the C-130Bs delivered to South Africa in 1962 remain in service.

PROFIL

Backbone of world's air forces

Produced by Lockheed's Skunk Works, the first prototype Hercules flew in August 1954. Deliveries of the first major production version, the C-130A, began in December 1955, with 231 completed.

Another 18 were converted to AC-130A gunship configuration, with four 20-mm (0.79-in) and four 7.62-mm (0.3-in) guns for close air support in Vietnam and Laos. Later gunship platforms based on the C-130E model had improved armament comprising twin 40-mm (1.57-in) guns in place of the 20-mm ones, and, ultimately, an enormous 105-mm (4.13-in) howitzer.

The C130-B introduced four-bladed propellers as standard and incorporated numerous other improvements. It was bought by the USAF and several other countries. Aircraft in US service were adapted for a variety of different roles such as search and rescue for the Coast Guard, drone control, weather reconnaissance, satellite recovery and intelligence gathering. Other variants included KC-130F tankers for the US Marine Corps.

Approximately 12 C-130A models modified with ski undercarriage were designated C-130D and used for operations in the Arctic, supplying the DEW (Distant Early Warning) radar stations. The next major production variant was the C-130E tailored towards Military Airlift Command operations, as opposed to the previous versions which had been tactical.

This model was bought in larger numbers by overseas countries. Like the C-130B, it spawned numerous sub-variants, including the MC-130E Rivet Clamp aircraft used for special operations. Others included the specialist EC-130Es, which played a key role right up to the time of the First Gulf War.

Left: External fuel tanks located between the engines were an identifying feature of the C-130E.

Above: An outstanding attribute of the C-130 is its ability to carry large loads into small airfields. Here, a Cessna T37 fuselage is manhandled into the enormous cabin.

C-130A Hercules

Type: four-engined military transport aircraft

Powerplant: four 2796-kW (3,749-hp) Allison T56-A9 turboprop engines

Maximum speed: 616 km/h (383 mph)

Cruising speed: 528 km/h (328 mph)

Initial climb rate: 783 m/min (2,569 fpm)

Range: 4110 km (2,554 miles)

Service ceiling: 12,590 m (41,306 ft)

Weights: empty 26,911 kg (59,329 lb); loaded 48,988 kg (108,000 lb)

Dimensions:

span	40.41 m (132 ft 7 in)
length	29.79 m (97 ft 9 in)
height	11.66 m (38 ft 3 in)
wing area	162.12 m² (1,745 sq ft)

C-130B Hercules

Christened *Fat Albert*, this aircraft was originally built as a C-130B. It was converted to KC-130F tanker status, before being acquired by the US Navy display team – the 'Blue Angels' – for use in the support role.

The spacious, high-set cockpit offered superb visibility and was a huge improvement over the flight decks of previous transports. In addition, it was quiet and vibration-free.

Uprated Allison T56-A-7 engines powered the C-130B variant, driving Hamilton four-bladed propellers. It was the first variant to be so equipped.

Compared to the first production model of the Hercules, the C-130B had a much-strengthened structure, with the centre-section of the wing housing extra fuel tanks. This increased total fuel capacity and gave the aircraft greater range and endurance. At the same time, the extra fuel capacity resulted in the deletion of the underwing tanks of the C-130A.

When converted to KC-130Fs, Marine Corps aircraft had extra fuel tanks placed in the cargo hold. Theoretically, the aircraft were able to fulfil a dual tanker/transport role, but in practice this proved difficult and time-consuming (the tanks took up a lot of space and had to be removed to permit the carriage of freight). This particular aircraft appears to have had the refuelling equipment removed.

An additional feature of the C-130B was its much-stengthened undercarriage, incorporating larger, low-pressure tyres. Extensive rough-field trials were conducted with the prototype and in combat in Vietnam the C-130Bs proved their worth, operating frequently from small airstrips.

Blue Angels

9806

UNITED STATES MARINES

ACTION DATA

MAXIMUM SPEED

Faster than the older piston-engined Fairchild C-123, the Hercules considerably raised the performance of military transports in the 1950s. The later Lockheed C-141 StarLifter offered jet performance and increased cargo capacity, but was not STOL-capable.

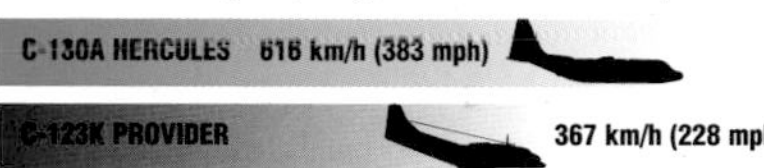

SERVICE CEILING

The rapid advance in aviation technology is clearly evident in the different capabilities of these three aircraft, which entered service within 15 years of each other. Although the C-141 StarLifter ushered in a new era of USAF jet-powered transports when it began operations in 1965, the older types were still considered indispensable.

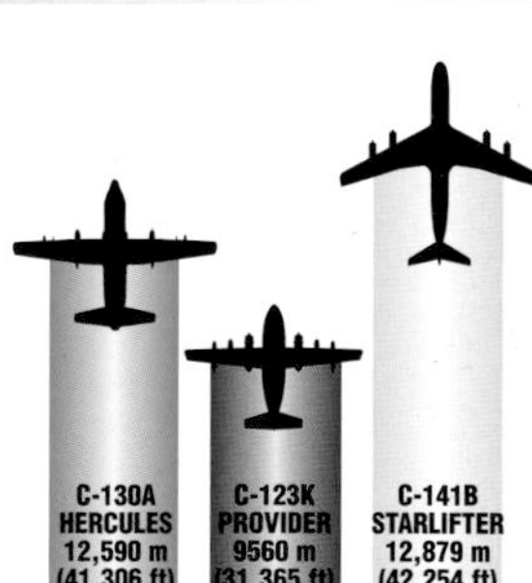

MAXIMUM PAYLOAD

Being able to carry much more, the C-141 should be the natural successor to both other types. It was the first aircraft to give the USAF truly global logistic support capabilities. However, the keys to the continuing success of the Hercules were its rough-field capability and simple design.

Delivering the goods

STOL SUPPLY: Experience in Vietnam dictated a steep landing approach and rapid take-off with as little time spent on the ground as possible. This was to avoid enemy fire and to get supplies in quickly.

LOW-ALTITUDE DROP: When delivering supplies from the air, the C-130 pilot would fly as close to the ground as possible, and the cargo, often attached to a pallet, would be extracted using a parachute and would slide to a stop while the Hercules quickly climbed away.

LOCKHEED

EC-121 WARNING STAR

● **Airborne early warning** ● **Fighter controller** ● **Cold War warrior**

Combining the elegance of the Super Constellation with the bumps and bulges created by ungainly radar equipment gave America the EC-121, Lockheed's flying radar station. The EC-121 Super Constellation (also known by a number of other military designations) guarded the US coastline in the 1950s and fought in Vietnam in the 1960s. It was the forerunner of today's airborne warning and control system (AWACS).

▲ *A victorious Phantom pilot explains to the crew of an EC-121 how he got a MiG 'kill' over North Vietnam thanks to their direction. Warning Stars performed a key role in the war.*

PHOTO FILE

LOCKHEED EC-121 WARNING STAR

◀ **Standing guard**
Painted in dull blue-grey, a US Navy WV-2 flies another long patrol over the world's oceans, searching for activity.

▼ **Still graceful**
At the start of its service, the Constellation was one of the most elegant aircraft in the US inventory. Despite the additional radomes, its beauty was still evident.

▼ **Radar specialists**
Intelligence operators gather information from within the confines of a Warning Star. The limited amount of space is clearly seen.

▲ **Operation College Eye**
During the Vietnam War, EC-121s operated as flying radar stations and airborne control platforms, offering assistance to any combat aircraft.

Combined operations ▶
Flying over a US carrier, the Warning Stars would often direct fighters from the ship to intercept approaching aircraft. Being airborne increased the radar detection range.

FACTS AND FIGURES

- Warning Stars were operated by the United States to provide early warning of approaching enemy aircraft.
- US Navy Warning Stars were the first examples in service, in October 1955.
- EC-121s flew weather reconnaissance missions until the early 1970s.
- During the air war in Vietnam, Warning Stars acted as fighter controllers, directing US jets towards the MiGs.
- Operations were flown from bases ranging from the Caribbean to Iceland.
- The last EC-121s were retired from USAF service in 1979.

PROFILE

Lockheed's graceful observer

With the beautiful shape of the Lockheed Super Constellation and the miracle of electronic gadgetry, the EC-121 Warning Star became one of the most important aircraft of the 1950s and the subsequent Vietnam War. The four-engined, low-wing Super Constellation carried technical specialists aloft on marathon patrols, searched the skies for enemy aircraft, and guided friendly fights into action against them.

The US Navy and US Air Force employed these fine aircraft as part of the United States' warning system for home defence and also in other corners of the world. Although the main purpose of the EC-121 was air warning and control, some of these aircraft were used to carry out other duties, including electronic reconnaissance. The only one ever lost in action was shot down on a reconnaissance flight near North Korea in 1969, with the loss of its 21-member crew.

In the 1970s, the EC-121 was replaced by Boeing's E-3 AWACS. Warning Stars can still be seen gracing the skies of the United States thanks to two fully restored examples.

Above: Wearing prominent Day-Glo rescue marking, this EC-121D lifts off for another patrol over the Arctic.

Right: Coming into land at Nellis AFB, Nevada, is this fully restored Warning Star. Privately owned, this aircraft is flown at airshows across the United States.

EC-121D Warning Star

Type: airborne early warning aircraft

Powerplant: four 2535-kW (3,400-hp) Wright R-335-34 radial piston engines

Maximum speed: 516 km/h (321 mph) in 6095 m (20,000 ft)

Endurance: up to 35 hours

Initial climb rate: 258 m/min (846 fpm)

Combat range: 7400 km (4,598 miles)

Service ceiling: 6280 m (20,604 ft)

Weights: empty 36,565 kg (80,612 lb); loaded 65,136 kg (143,600 lb)

Accommodation: five crew and 28 mission specialists

Dimensions:		
	span	37.49 m (123 ft)
	length	35.54 m (116 ft 7 in)
	height	8.23 m (27 ft)
	wing area	153.29 m² (1,650 sq ft)

WV-2 Warning Star

Designed from the outset as an early warning aircraft, the WV-2 was officially named the Warning Star, although 'Willy Victor' was the more common nickname. This example operated with the US Navy, and was deployed to numerous overseas bases during the 1960s, before finally being retired in 1965.

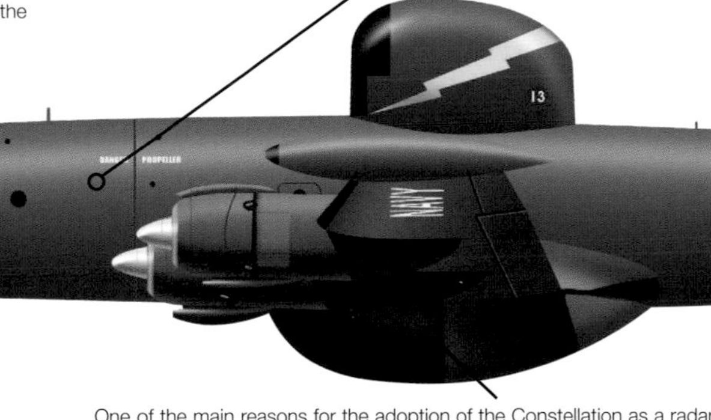

Despite the long-standing patrols that had to be maintained during operational flights, the Warning Star retained all the comforts of the airliner on which it was based. Crews found the flight deck roomy and well suited to the mission. Positioned behind the two pilots was the flight engineer and, farther back, the navigator and radio operator were situated.

Seated in the fuselage in two rows were electronics operators who collected and correlated the information received by the Warning Star's radar. During missions the radar specialists were able to supply information to other friendly aircraft and ships in the area.

Four squadrons were equipped with WV-2s. They maintained constant patrols over the North Atlantic, operating from bases in Iceland and Scotland. In September 1952, the WV-2s were redesignated EC-121Ks, in line with the USAF's designations.

One of the main reasons for the adoption of the Constellation as a radar warning aircraft was the need to position a radome on the underside of the fuselage. Adequate ground clearance was available on the Constellation because of its long undercarriage. This feature and the Constellation's long-range performance made the C-121 an ideal choice.

The rear of the aircraft was devoted to the crewmembers' comfort because of their large number. Four bunks and a toilet were positioned in the extreme rear of the fuselage. Meals could be prepared, reducing the fatigue or boredom that often set in during long, routine missions.

Cold War watchers

RB-47H STRATOJET: Developed from the bomber, the ERB-47H was capable of outrunning most intercepting fighters.

RB-50B SUPERFORTRESS: One of the first intelligence-gathering aircraft in operation was developed from the B-29.

P4M MERCATOR: Although limited in numbers, Martin's Mercator saw extensive use around Soviet borders.

ACTION DATA

MAXIMUM SPEED

When the Warning Stars first entered service, huge radomes were located on the outside of the airframes, restricting the speed of the EC-121s. As technology improved, the equipments could be fitted inside the aircraft, increasing the speed of the jet-powered RC-135.

Aircraft	Speed
EC-121D	516 km/h (321 mph)
RB-47H STRATOJET	956 km/h (594 mph)
RC-135C	990 km/h (615 mph)

COMBAT RANGE

The Warning Star retained the range of the Constellation airliner, despite the additional weight of its equipment. Early jet designs had range restricted by the performance of the first-generation jet engines.

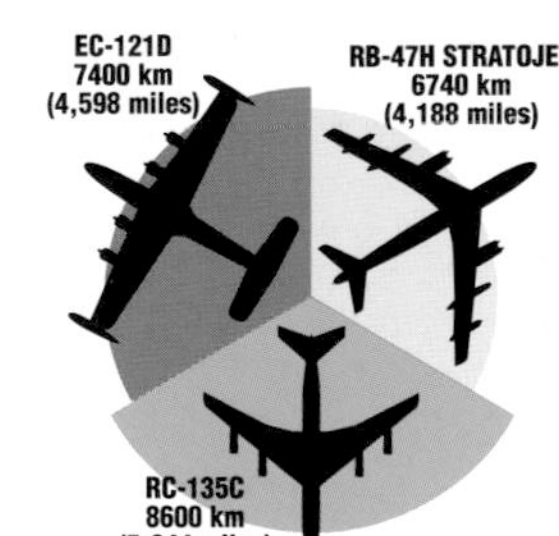

OPERATING WEIGHT

To improve the capabilities of the first early warning aircraft, more equipment was continually added to the airframces, which gradually increased their weight. Compared to late-model EC-121s, the early versions of the RC-135s were twice the weight.

EC-121D	RB-47H STRATOJET	RC-135C
65,136 kg (143,600 lb)	86,697 kg (191,134 lb)	144,000 kg (317,466 lb)

LOCKHEED AC-130 SPECTRE

● Massive firepower ● Dangerous missions ● Advanced sensors

▲ The AC-130 Spectre was the ultimate gunship in Vietnam. Used in the interdiction war against the Ho Chi Minh Trail, it proved devastatingly effective at destroying supply lorries travelling from North to South Vietnam.

One of the most fearsome weapons to emerge from the war in Vietnam was the AC-130 Hercules gunship. Clever and elusive Viet Cong guerrillas, who were difficult enough to defeat in daylight, seemed to command the shadows of the night. The Spectre's task was to use its advanced sensors and hi-tech communications equipment to learn about enemy troop movements, and fire heavy guns to halt the enemy's advance.

PHOTO FILE

LOCKHEED AC-130 SPECTRE

▲ Sideways firing

All guns faced to port. By flying a tight turning circle the AC-130 could concentrate its devastating firepower on a small area.

▲ Gun armament

Project Surprise Package replaced a pair of the AC-130A's aft 20-mm (0.79-in) cannon with twin 40-mm (1.57-in) Bofors guns. These could destroy a lorry with a single round.

Bigger and better ▶

Faster and better armed and equipped, the AC-130 replaced previous gunship versions of the C-47 and C-119 transports.

▲ 105-mm howitzer

A howitzer, the US Army's standard field gun, was the heaviest and most awesome weapon carried.

Spectre sensors ▶

To hunt trucks and other vehicles in the dark, the AC-130 was fitted with a comprehensive range of night-vision and target acquisition sensors.

FACTS AND FIGURES

- ➤ The AC-130 programme began on 20 December 1967 with a USAF order for C-130s to be modified into gunships.
- ➤ Combat trials showed that the AC-130 was better at destroying trucks than the A-26.
- ➤ During the 1969/70 campaign, AC-130s destroyed 3384 enemy vehicles.
- ➤ On 24 January 1971, an AC-130 crew set a record of 58 lorries destroyed and seven damaged during one mission.
- ➤ In 1970 AC-130 crews prevented the Chin Loa special forces camp being overrun.
- ➤ AC-130s were used most recently by US forces in Iraq.

PROFILE

Gunship over the Trail

Vietnam was the proving ground for the aerial gunship. After the success of the Douglas AC-47 and Fairchild AC-119, the 'ultimate' gunship appeared on the scene – the Lockheed AC-130 Spectre.

From a distance, this warplane looks like the C-130 transport aircraft upon which it is based, except that it is painted in dark colours to blend into the night. Close-up, the AC-130 can be seen to be a potent fighting machine. With the port side of its fuselage turned towards the ground and flying in a tight pylon turn above the battlefield, the Spectre can unleash a barrage of gunfire from cannon and machine guns.

The AC-130 is slow compared to jet warplanes, and is vulnerable to gun or missile fire from the ground. But when the enemy has light, mobile forces, such as the Viet Cong guerrillas moving in a convoy of lorries along a supply trail deep in the Vietnamese jungle, the AC-130 Spectre is a powerful and terrifying weapon.

The gunship mission is a difficult challenge for the men who fly it. The task requires incredible skill on the part of the pilot, perfect coordination among the members of a large and busy crew and extreme courage. The rigours of flying combat missions inside an orbiting gunship at night, with no windows, caused many aircrew to become violently ill even without enemy gunfire.

Introduced to knock out well-hidden vehicles at night, the AN/ASD-5 Black Crow sensor detects and locates the electro-magnetic signal impulses given out by a vehicle's ignition.

Unlike other early C-130s models, the gunships retained three-bladed propellers.

AC-130A Spectre

Type: multi-sensor ground attack gunship

Powerplant: four 3020-kW (4,050-hp) Allison T56-A-7 turboprop engines

Maximum speed: 612 km/h (380 mph) at 10,000 m (32,808 ft)

Range: 3685 km (2,290 miles)

Service ceiling: 11,000 m (36,089 ft)

Weights: empty est. 36,000 kg (79,366 lb); maximum take-off 79,389 kg (175,023 lb)

Armament: early aircraft carried four 7.62-mm (0.3-in) Miniguns and four 20-mm (0.79-in) M61A1 Vulcan six-barrelled rotary cannon; later the Vulcans were replaced by two 40-mm (1.57-in) Bofors guns and two 20-mm T-171 multi-barrelled cannon

Dimensions:		
	span	40.41 m (132 ft 7 in)
	length	29.79 m (97 ft 9 in)
	height	11.66 m (38 ft 3 in)
	wing area	162.11 m² (1,745 sq ft)

Introduced in 1973, the overall gunship grey paint scheme gradually replaced the sinister black undersides and three-tone camouflage.

AC-130A SPECTRE

After its Vietnam combat, 55-0011 joined the 711th Special Operations Squadron, an Air Force Reserve unit, and was given the name 'Night Stalker'. It was retired from service in the mid-1990s.

Illustrating the Hercules' versatility, this C-130 served as a transport from 1957 until 1969, when it was converted to AC-130A gunship standard. It was the prototype for both Pave Pronto and Surprise Package upgrades.

Spectres were tasked with finding and destroying North Vietnamese supply lorries hidden under the thick jungle canopy. Target acquisition and designation was provided by the Stabilized Tracking Set, which comprised a low-light-level TV, laser illuminator and laser designator/target ranger.

The Spectre acquired self-defence systems to counter the growing North Vietnamese air defence threat. ALQ-87 ECM pods, huge chaff and flare dispenser pods and engine exhaust shields were fitted to protect the aircraft from SA-7 surface-to-air missiles.

Armament on this AC-130A comprised a pair of belt-fed 20-mm (0.79-in) Vulcan cannon forwards, twin 7.62-mm (0.3-in) Miniguns amidships and a pair of clip-fed 40-mm (1.57-in) Bofors cannon aft.

AFRES

USAF 50011

Ground fire was an ever-present threat. During combat operations, an observer sat on the rear ramp and watched for muzzle flashes. The Spectre illuminated its search area with a trainable searchlight.

COMBAT DATA

MAXIMUM SPEED

After pioneering gunship operations over Vietnam, the AC-47 was soon replaced by the AC-119 and, ultimately, the formidable AC-130A. Each aircraft represented an advance in avionics, firepower and performance.

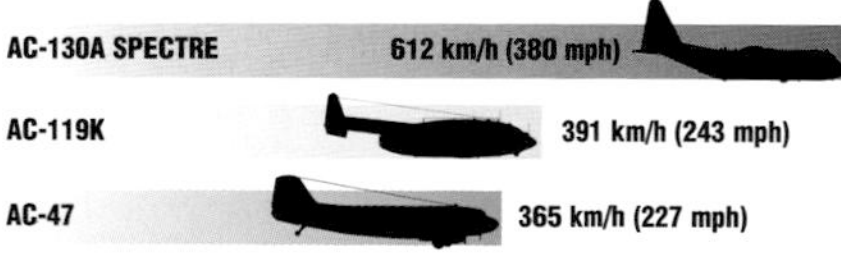

ARMAMENT

With its capacity for lifting heavy loads of freight, the Hercules was a natural choice for gunship conversion. It was able to carry heavy weaponry and thousands of rounds of ammunition.

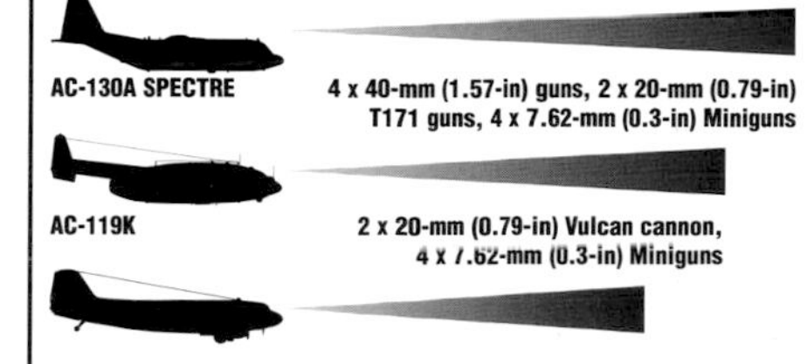

Spectre in action

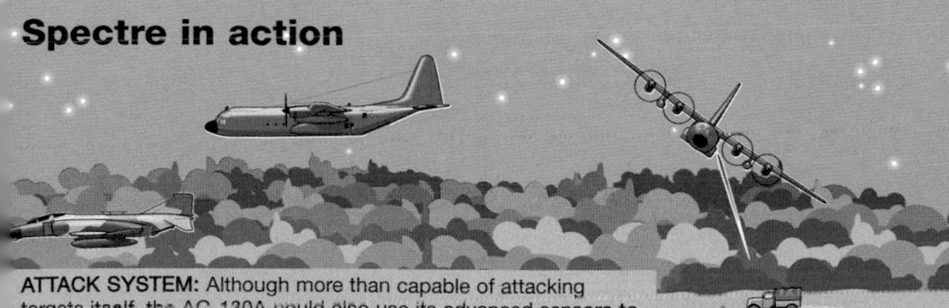

ATTACK SYSTEM: Although more than capable of attacking targets itself, the AC-130A could also use its advanced sensors to designate targets for F-4D Phantoms carrying laser-guided bombs.

1 SEARCHING THE TRAIL: Viet Cong lorries were difficult to find in the dense jungle of the Ho Chi Minh Trail. The AC-130A often remained on station for many hours, acquiring and attacking targets.

2 INVADER INTERDICTION: Few aircraft had the endurance or weapons load to fly all-night missions alongside the AC-130A. One aircraft particularly suitable for the task was the B-26K Invader.

LOCKHEED C-5 GALAXY

● Strategic transport ● Heavylift heavyweight

This monster aircraft, the world's biggest transport for two decades, hauled cargoes in American military actions from Vietnam onwards. Although not as large as the Antonov aircraft of today, the C-5 Galaxy has an unmatched service record for transporting the weaponry of war. To pilots, perched 10 m (30 ft.) off the ground before starting engines, the Galaxy is rated as the biggest and the best.

▲ *Slowly disappearing into the opened 'mouth' of a C-5 Galaxy, a mothballed F-5 fighter demonstrates the huge Lockheed transport's unrivalled ability to handle large loads.*

PHOTO FILE

LOCKHEED C-5 GALAXY

▼ **Global reach**
Inflight refuelling means that the C-5 can deliver its outsize loads anywhere in the world.

▲ **Rear loader**
The C-5's tail is upswept, enabling a huge rear-loading door and ramp to be fitted.

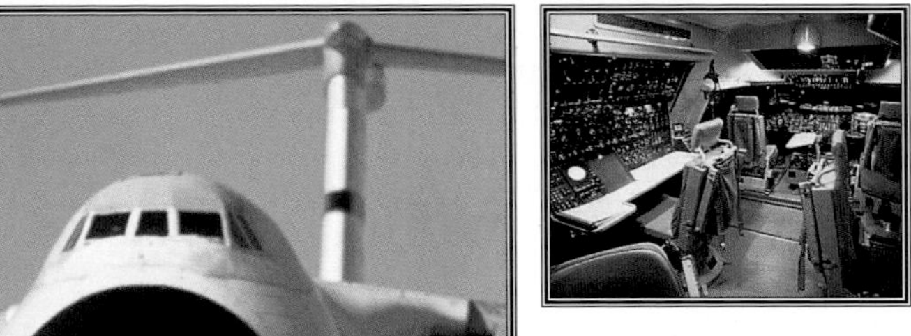

◄ **Flight deck**
The C-5 is flown by a pilot and co-pilot, with flight engineer and navigator facing outwards at the rear of the flight deck.

◄ **'Fat Albert'**
Nicknamed with back-handed affection by its crews, the C-5 was for two decades the biggest and heaviest aircraft in the world.

◄ **Easy to fly**
The Galaxy's four-man flight crew sit high in the upper decking of the forward fuselage. In spite of its size, the C-5 is reasonably easy, if a little sluggish, to fly.

FACTS AND FIGURES

- The C-5 was chosen by the Air Force over transports proposed by Boeing and Douglas.
- Eighty-one C-5A transports were built in 1967-71; 50 similar C-5Bs were built when production resumed between 1984-89.
- Many C-5 loadmasters have logged 20,000 flight hours, more than most airline pilots.
- The crash of a C-5A at Ramstein, Germany, on 29 August 1990 was the only loss of a transport plane during the massive Desert Shield airlift preparing for the Gulf War.
- Lockheed claims that the C-5's four engines have the same power as 48 railroad locomotives.

PROFILE

Giant from Georgia

The revolutionary thing about the Lockheed C-5 Galaxy is its sheer size. Many big aircraft have won fleeting cameo roles in history's cast of aviation characters, but few of the real giants actually register a full working day, all day, every day, doing a real job in the real world. The C-5 combines greatness with unromantic achievement.

At over 300 tonnes, the C-5 was the biggest and heaviest aeroplane in its class when test pilots thundered aloft in the first example on 30 June 1968. Since then, even larger Antonov transports have appeared in the former Soviet Union, but for its first two decades of operation the Galaxy was without rival.

The C-5 can carry almost any item in the US military inventory, from Abrams main battle tanks to over 360 fully-equipped paratroops. It was the backbone of the 1991 Desert Shield airlift, the entire force of 85 Galaxies being used to carry 42 per cent of all air-delivered cargo – nearly a quarter of a million tonnes.

The C-5 was vital to the success of the Gulf War. Its record-breaking effort saw the Galaxy lifting a heavier tonnage in the first 21 days of Desert Shield than was carried in the entire Berlin airlift.

There are three inboard and three outboard sets of slotted flaps on the trailing edge of the wing, with slotted slats on the outboard leading edge.

The tip of the C-5's nose houses a Bendix APS-133 digital colour weather radar. The entire nose hinges upwards for access to the hold.

The T-tail is fitted with hydraulically-actuated four-section elevators and a twin-section rudder. There are no trim tabs; the whole of the horizontal tail can be adjusted.

The original C-5A had considerable problems with wing fatigue, which was corrected in the C-5B. In the 1980s the entire fleet was given new, stronger wings at a cost of more than one billion dollars.

The bullet fairing at the top of the huge T-tail houses an air data recorder as well as a flight data and crash recorder – the so-called 'Black Box'.

C-5B Galaxy

Type: heavy, long-range logistic freighter

Powerplant: four 191.24-kN (41,000-lb.-thrust) General Electric TF39-GE-1C turbofans

Maximum speed: 760 km/h (570 m.p.h.) at 10,000 m (32,800 ft.)

Range: 6033 km (3,700 mi.) with max. payload

Service ceiling: 10,900 m (34,000 ft.)

Weights: empty 170,000 kg (375,000 lb.); loaded 380,000 kg (838,000 lb.)

Payload: Up to 120,200 kg (264,440 lb.) in main freight compartment plus 73 passengers or fully-equipped combat troops

Dimensions:

span	67.88 m (222 ft. 8 in.)
length	75.54 m (247 ft. 10 in.)
height	19.85 m (63 ft. 2 in.)
wing area	576 m² (6,200 sq. ft.)

C-5B GALAXY

First built in the 1960s, the C-5 went back into production as the improved C-5B in the 1980s. There are more than 120 C-5s in service with the US Air Force, 50 of which are 'B' models.

Aircraft of the Galaxy's size became possible only with the development of large, powerful jet engines. The C-5 is powered by four General Electric TF39-GE-1C twin-shaft high bypass turbofans, each delivering 191.24 kN (41,000 lb. of thrust).

The main landing gear of the Galaxy consists of four bogies each with six wheels, two forwards and four aft.

The massive hold can accommodate a wide variety of outsize loads, from helicopters and tanks to trucks and cargo containers. It can also carry over 360 fully-equipped troops.

COMBAT DATA

RANGE

The arrival of the Galaxy in the late 1960s meant that for the first time the US military had the capacity to deliver outsize loads anywhere in the world at jet speeds. The Galaxy can fly intercontinental distances even when carrying a payload of 118 tonnes (118 tons); the huge Antonov An-124 is its only rival. The An-124, known as 'Condor' to NATO but called 'Ruslan' after a fairytale giant by its makers, can carry even heavier loads, but not over such great distances.

Aircraft	Range
C-17 GLOBEMASTER III	5200 km (3,200 mi.)
C-5B GALAXY	6033 km (3,400 mi.)
An-124 RUSLAN	4400 km (2,700 mi.)

Heavylift specialist

ARMOURED TRANSPORT: Hoisting just one 60-tonne M1 Abrams main battle tank would be beyond most other transport aircraft, but the C-5 can carry it with ease, along with its crew and mechanics, three 20-tonne M2 Bradley infantry fighting vehicles plus their crews and mechanics – all in airline comfort in the passenger compartment on the top deck.

HELICOPTER MOVER: Galaxies were vital during Operation Desert Shield, especially when they were used to fly Apache gunship helicopters out to Saudi Arabia. The AH-64s were packed two by two, six at a time, and three C-5 trips could move a whole battalion. Once in the Gulf, the helicopters were re-assembled and operational within 24 hours.

Lockheed
C-141 StarLifter

● Strategic freighter ● Troop carrier ● Long-range heavy lifter

Lockheed's C-141 StarLifter is the heavy muscle of the American military air transport fleet. Although growing old and being replaced, slowly, by the McDonnell Douglas C-17 Globemaster III, the C-141 has logged millions of miles since entering service in the mid-1960s. As the principal long-range airlifter for US forces (helped by smaller numbers of the outsized C-5 Galaxy), the C-141 has carried equipment and freight to and from every crisis in recent history.

▲ *The USAF's first purpose-built, long-range jet cargo and troop transport, the C-141 StarLifter was designed with its own ground-based handling system.*

Photo File

Lockheed C-141 StarLifter

▲ Short-field performance
A large wing area and full deflection, 60 per cent span Fowler-type flaps allows a fully laden C-141 to clear a 15-m (50-ft.) obstacle with a roll of just 1731 m (5,675 ft.). It also has a very impressive short landing run.

▲ Clamshell doors
The C-141's large rear cargo doors allow vehicles and equipment to be loaded via a ramp that lowers to ground level.

▲ Inflight refuelling
The C-141B introduced air-to-air refuelling to the StarLifter, increasing it to a potential global range. It has a prominent fairing on the top of the forward fuselage to receive the boom from the refueller.

▲ First paradrop jet
The first paradrop from a jet transport aircraft was made from a C-141 in August 1965. It made its first heavy cargo drops from the ramp later in the year.

◀ Long range
Cruising at 800 km/h (500 m.p.h.), a fully laden C-141B StarLifter can fly nearly 5000 km (3,100 mi.) on internal fuel, and much further with inflight refuelling.

Facts and Figures

- The StarLifter first flew on 17 December 1963, 60 years after the Wright Brothers.
- The first operational C-141A was delivered to Tinker AFB, Oklahoma, in October 1964.
- The C-141B has a 7.11-m (23-ft.) longer fuselage and inflight refuelling capability.
- The C-141B can carry 205 passengers or 168 fully-equipped paratroopers.
- In 1984, C-141Bs carried tents, water, blankets and 118,000 kg (259,000 lb.) of foodstuffs to famine victims in Sudan.
- The last of 270 rebuilt C-141Bs was delivered to Military Air Command in 1982.

PROFILE

The USAF's strategic lifter

Famous for finally bringing home the Prisoners of War from Vietnam in 1973 and for dramatic paratroop drops in Panama in 1989, the C-141's main task is far less glamorous but equally as important. For over 30 years the C-141 StarLifter has supplied US military and sometimes civilian installations around the world with vital supplies and reinforcements. In times of crisis the C-141 can, in partnership with the massive C-5, fully equip an entire army in a matter of days anywhere in the world.

StarLifters began hauling supplies to Vietnam in the 1960s. A decade later, Lockheed won an ambitious contract to 'stretch' the 263-plane C-141A fleet by 7.11 m (23 ft.) and to add an air refuelling receptacle. The lengthened StarLifter, known as the C-141B, flew for the first time on 24 March 1977 and was put into service soon after. The improvements have given the StarLifter global reach and made it a familiar sight almost everywhere. Except for a couple of test aircraft, all of today's StarLifters are lengthened C-141B variants.

Wearing the original Military Airlift Command colour scheme, this is the first C-141B StarLifter. The scheme was later changed to the drab green and grey 'lizard' European camouflage. They have now been repainted in overall medium-grey.

The StarLifter is powered by four Pratt & Whitney TF33-P-7 turbofan engines, each rated at 93.42 kN (20,950 lb. thrust), mounted in underwing pods and fitted with clamshell-door thrust reversers.

A conventional two-spar, box-beam, cantilever high-wing is mounted on top of the fuselage with 25° sweepback. It has Fowler-type trailing-edge flaps and hinged spoilers on the upper and lower wing surfaces.

An all-metal, variable-incidence tailplane is mounted at the top of the fin. Elevators are controlled by dual hydraulic units with manual reverse.

C-141B StarLifter

Type: strategic airlifter (troop/cargo transport)

Powerplant: four 93.42-kN (20,950-lb.-thrust) Pratt & Whitney TF33-P-7 turbofan engines

Maximum speed: 933 km/h (578 m.p.h.)

Maximum cruising speed: 911 km/h (565 m.p.h.)

Range: 4773 km (2,960 mi.) with max. payload

Service ceiling: 12,879 m (42,250 ft.)

Weights: empty weight (C-141A) 60,678 kg (133,491 lb.); (C-141B) 67,187 kg (147,811 lb.); maximum take-off 155,585 kg (342,287 lb.)

Accommodation: has carried every cargo from vehicles to a whale; normal payload is 32,135 kg (70,697 lb.); maximum payload 41,223 kg (90,690 lb.)

Dimensions:

span	48.74 m (159 ft. 10 in.)
length	51.29 m (168 ft. 3 in.)
height	12.15 m (39 ft. 10 in.)
wing area	299.90 m² (3,227 sq. ft.)

C-141B STARLIFTER

The StarLifter was the USAF's first pure-jet transport designed to meet a Specific Operational Requirement for a strategic transport.

Modification of the C-141A to the C-141B involved the insertion of newly-fabricated fuselage sections ahead of and behind the wing, resulting in a stretch of 7.11 m (23 ft.). This gave an increase in the volume of cargo that could be carried. The C-141B also had a new, more streamlined wingroot fairing and inflight-refuelling capability.

The swept vertical fin and rudder has a prominent bullet fairing where it meets the horizontal tailplane. The rudder is hydraulically controlled by electric trim tabs.

The spacious cockpit accommodates a flight crew comprising two pilots, flight engineer and navigator. It contains modern instrumentation for all-weather operations around the world.

The raised area above the forward fuselage houses the inflight-refuelling receptacle, into which the tanker's boom is connected to pass fuel to the StarLifter.

The stretched C-141B can house three extra pallets, although the weight capacity is no greater. Volumetric limitations of the C-141 have therefore been overcome.

The nosewheel retracts rearwards into the fuselage and is enclosed by two doors.

The four-wheel bogie main undercarriage units retract forwards into fairings on the sides of the lower fuselage. To assist with short-field landings the aircraft has hydraulic, multiple-disc, anti-skid brakes.

The large rear ramp doors can be opened fully in flight for aerial load dropping, while a built-in loading ramp can be extended and lowered for vehicle access when on the ground.

COMBAT DATA

PAYLOAD

The USAF had a small number of Boeing 707s adapted as C-135s for interim cargo transport before the C-141 came into service. With no ramp or rear loading doors, the volume of freight was limited. The Russian Il-76 has a similar weight-lifting capacity to the C-141, but its smaller fuselage limits the size and volume that can be accommodated.

C-141 STARLIFTER 41,000 kg (90,200 lb.)

C-135A 37,650 kg (82,830 lb.)

Il-76 'CANDID' 40,000 kg (88,000 lb.)

Lockheed's 'Star' lifter

BULK CARRIER: The C-141's hold is of almost constant cross-section along its entire length. This gives a usable cargo volume of 322.79 m³ in the C-141B, enabling it to transport up to four military vehicles.

HEAVY LIFTER: In terms of tonne/miles per flying hour, one C-141 could equal four C-124 Globemasters. Just 18 StarLifters could have accomplished the same as 142 C-54 Skymasters in the Berlin Airlift of 1948/49.

CONVERTIBLE: An extensive array of internal equipment, including fold-away floor rollers, tie-down points and seat tracks, enables the passenger/cargo mix to be changed rapidly.

FAST FREIGHTER: In Vietnam, under combat conditions, the C-141 could offload in 17 minutes using its special handling equipment. A full palletised load could be installed in only 30 minutes and flown to its destination in half the time of the C-124 it replaced.

LOCKHEED

CP-140 AURORA

● **Anti-submarine platform** ● **Canadian service** ● **Special duties**

A special version of the famous P-3 Orion anti-submarine warfare (ASW) aircraft, Lockheed's CP-140 Aurora is optimised for the maritime patrol requirement of the Canadian Armed Forces (CAF). The CP-140A Arcturus is based on the same airframe, but without submarine detection gear or weapons, and is used for crew training and environmental and fisheries work. These aircraft are a familiar sight around the coastline of Canada.

▲ *The first CP-140 Aurora was handed over to the CAF at Greenwood, Nova Scotia. Seventeen more machines followed until 1981, finally replacing the 20-year-old Bristol Britannia-derived Argus.*

PHOTO FILE

LOCKHEED CP-140 AURORA

▼ Specialist weapons
The Aurora is unique among Orion variants with its ability to carry eight Mk 44/46 torpedoes, one of a number of specific requests from the Canadian Armed Forces.

▲ Anti-submarine sensors
The Aurora is fitted with the US Navy S-3A Viking's APS-116 search radar, ASQ-501 MAD and AN/AYK-10 computer. A full crew consists of 11.

◀ New missions
Canada's CP-140 fleet has become increasingly involved in anti-drug smuggling operations.

▼ Canadian colours
Initially delivered in patriotic red and white colours, the fleet later reverted to an all-over grey.

◀ CP-140 future upgrade
Paramax Systems has submitted a bid for a C$750-million upgrade of the acoustic sensors, radar, ESM and communication/navigation systems.

FACTS AND FIGURES

- ➤ Canada's four Aurora and Arcturus squadrons are based at two locations, Greenwood and Comox.
- ➤ The first CP-140 completed its maiden flight on 22 March 1979.
- ➤ The last Canadian Aurora was delivered in July 1981.
- ➤ Lockheed built 18 CP-140 Aurora and three CP-140A Arcturus aircraft for Canada's armed forces.
- ➤ The CP-140 Aurora replaced the piston-engined Canadair CP-107 Argus.
- ➤ A No. 405 'Eagle' Squadron CP-140 won the Fincastle ASW competition in 1996.

PROFILE

Canada's coastal patroller

A machine of the Cold War and a reminder of the days when the Soviet Union had more than 450 nuclear submarines, the Lockheed CP-140 Aurora was Canada's answer to the undersea threat. Although the Cold War has ended, the submarine fleets belonging to Russia and other nations must still be watched closely. The four-engined, turboprop-powered Aurora allows Canadian combat crews to guard their nation and to secure the ocean approaches hundreds of miles from the shoreline.

The CP-140 Aurora uses the proven airframe of the famous Lockheed P-3 Orion – the world's most popular ASW aircraft – and is equipped with an avionics system based on that of the Lockheed S-3A Viking. This includes radar, magnetic anomaly detection (MAD) gear, and a basic computer. The CP-140 crew can detect a submarine from a considerable distance and attack with a variety of weapons.

The CP-140A Arcturus looks like the Aurora but it is not armed. The Arcturus has been used to train hundreds of ASW crews for the Canadian forces, and is also very successful for environmental and fisheries patrol duties.

A proposed upgrade of some of its systems will allow the fleet to continue operations to 2010 and beyond.

Below: Like the Orion, the Aurora's distinctive tail spikes contain a magnetic anomaly detector for the location of submerged enemy submarines.

Above: The Aurora serves with the CAF in relatively large numbers. Eighteen are currently operational, in addition to three CP-140A environmental aircraft.

CP-140 Aurora

Type: long-range maritime reconnaissance and anti-submarine patrol aircraft

Powerplant: four 3661-kW (4,910-hp.) Allison T56-A-14 turboprops

Maximum cruising speed: 732 km/h (454 m.p.h.) at optimum altitude

Maximum range: 8339 km (5,170 mi.)

Combat radius: 1853 km (1,150 mi.)

Service ceiling: 8610 m (28,250 ft.)

Weights: empty 27,892 kg (61,690 lb.); maximum take-off 64,411 kg (141,704 lb.)

Armament: 9071 kg (19,955 lb.) of stores

Dimensions:

span	30.37 m (99 ft. 8 in.)
length	35.61 m (116 ft. 10 in.)
height	10.29 m (33 ft. 9 in.)
wing area	120.77 m² (1,300 sq. ft.)

CP-140 AURORA

The CAF operates CP-140s from Greenwood, Nova Scotia (Nos 404, 405, 415 Squadrons), and Comox in British Colombia (Nos 407 and 409 Squadrons). No. 409 is the reserve squadron and No. 404 is also tasked with training.

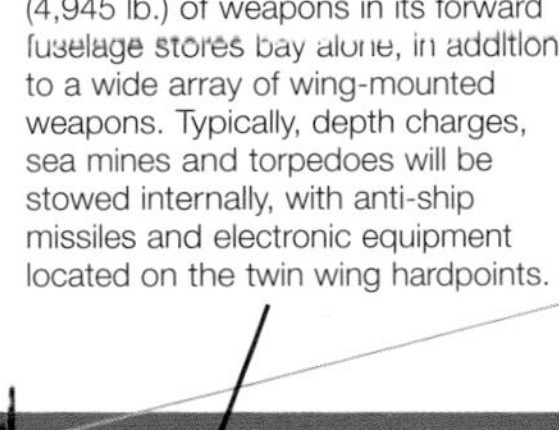

On a typical patrol the CP-140 will carry a crew of 11 on an ASW mission of approximately 8 hours' endurance. Each of the Aurora's four Allison turboprops provides at least 3661 kW of power.

The Aurora can carry 2247 kg (4,945 lb.) of weapons in its forward fuselage stores bay alone, in addition to a wide array of wing-mounted weapons. Typically, depth charges, sea mines and torpedoes will be stowed internally, with anti-ship missiles and electronic equipment located on the twin wing hardpoints.

A secondary role for the CAF's Aurora fleet is search and rescue, for which the weapons bay can be quickly adapted to carry a special search-and-rescue package. In terms of anti-submarine capability, the Aurora is generally deemed to have a superior tactical compartment layout to that of the Orion.

The Aurora's mission profile has been widened to include the post-Cold War roles of pollution monitoring, resources surveying, ice reconnaissance and Arctic surveillance. The Aurora is destined to remain in service into the 21st century.

A battery of anti-submarine sonobouy launching tubes is carried in the lower fuselage behind the wing. In addition, powerful searchlights may be fitted underwing.

The primary conventional submarine detector aid is the tail-mounted MAD boom. This is used to locate submerged vessels, by detecting their magnetic presence in the water.

COMBAT DATA

WEAPONS LOAD

A maritime patrol aircraft has to have sufficient ordnance to deliver a decisive punch against a target at very long range. The CP-140 is well armed compared to the other aircraft.

- CP-140 AURORA 9071 kg (19,955 lb.)
- Il-38 'MAY' 6000 kg (13,200 lb.)
- NIMROD MR.Mk 2 6124 kg (13,473 lb.)

MAXIMUM SPEED

High speed is a useful asset as it allows rapid transit to the combat zone or the scene of a rescue. The speed of the Nimrod enables it to search large areas relatively quickly. The CP-140 has a good top speed for a turboprop aircraft.

- CP-140 AURORA 732 km/h (454 m.p.h.)
- Il-38 'MAY' 722 km/h (448 m.p.h.)
- NIMROD MR.Mk 2 926 km/h (574 m.p.h.)

MAXIMUM RANGE

The Nimrod is used for long over-water missions and therefore requires a good range. The CAF tends to use its aircraft for coastal duties, and therefore range is less important. Illyushin's Il-38 is much shorter ranged than either of its competitors and sees only limited use.

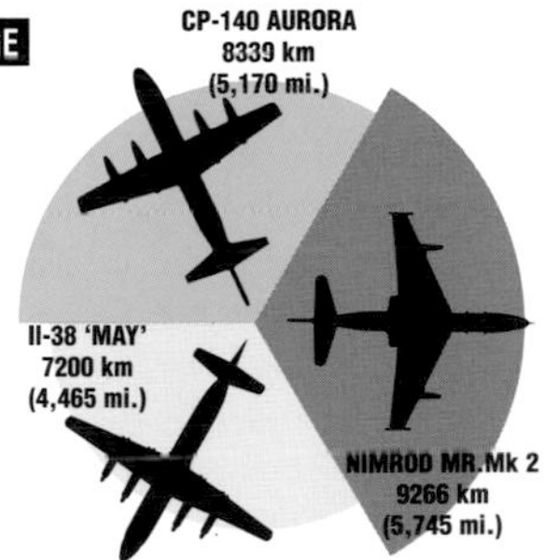

Canada's post-war maritime aircraft

LOCKHEED PV-1 VENTURA: The PV-1 Ventura served the CAF from the mid-war period and continued post-war as a target-tug before it was retired.

AVRO LANCASTER Mk 10MR: The veteran Lancaster Mk 10MR, built by Victory Aircraft of Canada, was the CAF's standard patrol aircraft of the 1950s.

LOCKHEED P-2 NEPTUNE: The widely exported P-2 Neptune served as an interim aircraft until the Argus was available. This P-2 flew with No. 404 Squadron.

CANADAIR CP-107 ARGUS: The CP-107 Argus was a Canadian-built patrol version of the British Bristol Britannia airliner. It was finally retired in 1981 when the Aurora arrived.

LOCKHEED

EC-130

● Electronic warfare Hercules variants ● Highly classified equipment

Under the designation EC-130, the USAF operates four special mission variants of the ubiquitous Hercules transport. One is an airborne control centre, while the other three have a much more sensitive role: electronic warfare. Although routinely seen on the outside, the inside is a secret world. To gain access to the interior of the aircraft a top-secret codeword is required, as the task of the EC-130E and EC-130H is to listen to and disrupt enemy communications.

▲ *The USAF operates an EC-130E version as an airborne battlefield command and control centre. Internal consoles can display digitised maps covering any area of the world.*

PHOTO FILE

LOCKHEED EC-130

EC-130H Compass Call ▶
The EC-130H is used for communications intrusion and jamming duties. Previously operated from Sembach in Germany, the 10 operational aircraft are now based at Davis-Monthan in Arizona.

▲ Jamming equipment
An array of wire antennas is suspended on a gantry under the tail. Blisters on the rear fuselage contain two further antennas.

▲ EC-130(RR) Rivet Rider
Working in conjunction with the EC-130H is the EC-130(RR) Rivet Rider, which is also tasked with jamming enemy communications. It can tap into and rebroadcast radio and TV transmissions for propaganda and psychological warfare missions.

▲ Rivet Rider antennas
The Rivet Rider is easily identified by a single, large axehead antenna under each wing.

TACAMO – TAke Charge And Move Out ▶
A US Navy C-130Q relays communications to its ballistic nuclear missile submarines.

FACTS AND FIGURES

- ➤ EC-130 crew often exceed the USAF's recommended maximum of 155 days away from home each year.
- ➤ Incredibly, the original C-130 airframe made its first flight on 23 August 1954.
- ➤ US Navy EC-130Q aircraft were replaced in 1989 with the Boeing E-6 Mercury.
- ➤ Comfy Levi, Rivet Rider and ABCCC EC-130Es and EC-130Hs were operational during Operation Desert Storm.
- ➤ The US Coast Guard operates an EC-130E as an electronic calibration aircraft.
- ➤ A major role during the Cold War was eavesdropping in the Berlin Corridor.

PROFILE

USAF electronic warriors

The EC-130 may look like a transport aircraft but it is a saboteur with wings, using the marvel of electronics to break up an enemy's military radio and television broadcasting.

The USAF operates several intelligence-gathering versions of the Hercules transport under the designation EC-130E. A Hercules version, unofficially designated EC-130E and now retired, operated from Frankfurt and gathered signals, electronic and communications intelligence. Another EC-130E version, the ABCCC, is an airborne battlefield control aircraft.

There are two types of intelligence-gathering EC-130Es, both operated by the 193rd Special Operations Squadron, based at Harrisburg in Philadelphia.

The EC-130E(CL) Comfy Levi undertakes Elint (electronic intelligence) and probably jamming missions under the codename 'Senior Scout'. Special mission equipment uses antennas that are fitted to removable undercarriage doors and fairings. Five of these aircraft carry sensor operators in the cargo hold, who use black boxes to intrude into an enemy's communications and extract information.

The most heavily-modified version, the EC-130E(RR) Rivet Rider, intrudes into enemy radio and television broadcasts and flies under the name 'Commando Solo'.

Above: For anti-drug trafficking duties, the US Coast Guard bought an early-warning EC-130V fitted with an APS-145 search radar. High costs, however, forced it out of service and the role was taken over by Customs Service P-3s. The EC-130 was reported to have gone to the USAF for an undisclosed 'black' programme.

Above: The huge blade antenna on the fin leading edge and the Vietnam-style camouflage distinguishes early Rivet Riders. The latest upgraded version wears a smart two-tone grey scheme.

EC-130H Hercules

Type: electronic warfare aircraft

Powerplant: four 3020-kW (4,050-hp.) Allison T56-A-15 turboprop engines

Maximum speed: 611 km/h (379 m.p.h.)

Range: 4100 km (2,540 mi.)

Service ceiling: 13,225 m (43,400 ft.)

Weights: empty 34,105 kg (75,031 lb.); maximum take-off 74,202 kg (163,244 lb.)

Accommodation: two pilots, navigator, electronic warfare officer, flight engineer, loadmaster and five electronic equipment operators

Dimensions:

span	40.41 m (133 ft.)
length	29.79 m (98 ft.)
height	11.66 m (38 ft.)
wing area	162.11 m² (1,744 sq. ft.)

EC-130E(RR) HERCULES

All EC-130E(RR)s are operated by the 193rd Special Operations Squadron, Pennsylvania Air National Guard. They are based at Harrisburg International Airport.

An in-flight refuelling receptacle is fitted above the cockpit. Refuelling capability means that crew fatigue is the limiting factor during a mission.

The Rivet Rider's mission is to disrupt enemy communications. It can broadcast on any frequency, including AM/FM radio, black and white and now colour TV, as well as short-wave (HF) and other communication bands.

EC-130Es are powered by four Allison T56-A-15 turboprops, as fitted to the standard C-130H transport variant.

The most prominent feature of the early Rivet Riders was the blade aerial ahead of the tailfin. This was believed to be related to TV broadcasting.

The dark 'European One' colour scheme, as shown here, replaced the earlier Vietnam 'Southeast Asia' camouflage.

The Rivet Rider has recently been extensively upgraded. The latest model differs considerably from the one shown here. Current versions have worldwide colour television broadcast capabilities. Externally, these aircraft have four bullet fairings on the fin and two large pods under the outer wings.

There are two retractable trailing antennas: a high-frequency one reeled horizontally behind the aircraft and a 304-metre AM-band antenna held in a near-vertical position by a weight.

Underwing stores include long-range fuel tanks, as on standard Hercules, a pod containing a trailing aerial and an 'axe-head' antenna.

COMBAT DATA

MAXIMUM SPEED

All manner of different aircraft have been used as ELINT platforms. The Soviet An-12 is broadly similar to the C-130 in size and configuration, whereas the C-47 is a cheap and reliable alternative.

EC-130E HERCULES	612 km/h (379 m.p.h.)
An-12 'CUB-C'	777 km/h (482 m.p.h.)
C-47	346 km/h (215 m.p.h.)

RANGE

A useful feature of the Hercules is its range. Long range allows long-distance ELINT missions to be carried out or, alternatively, shorter range flights can be made with longer 'loiter' times in the air over the 'target'.

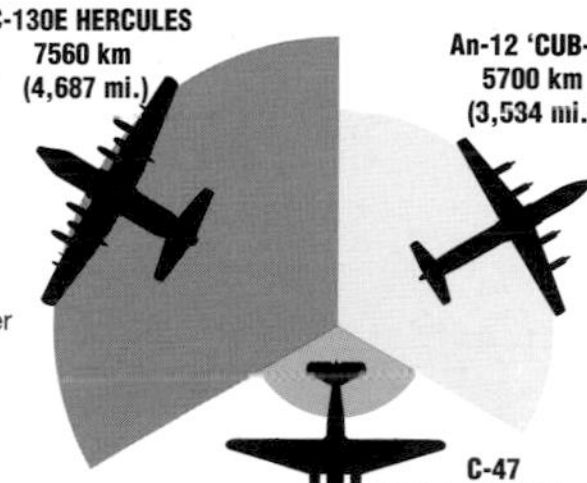

EC-130 Hercules missions

The C-130, with the minimum of modification to the basic airframe, has proved ideal for the various EC-130 roles.

1 COMMAND MODULE: The ABCCC is a regular Hercules transport fitted with a removable battle command module. This houses equipment for 16 mission specialists.

2 COMMUNICATIONS JAMMER: The EC-130E(RR) Rivet Rider is fitted with comprehensive jamming equipment in the tail, fuselage and wings to disrupt enemy communications.

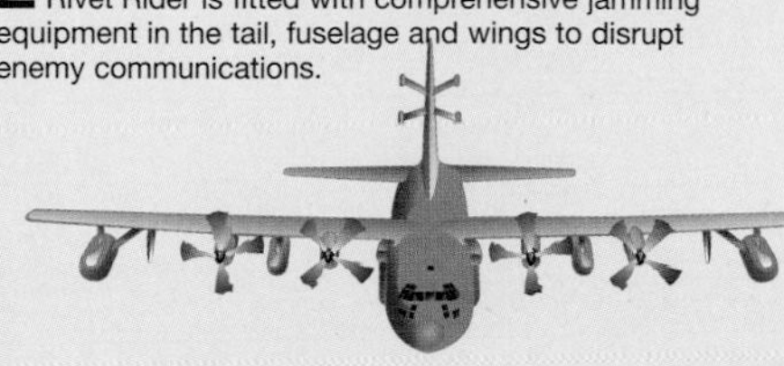

3 RADAR CALIBRATION: Air traffic search and control radars need to be constantly checked. The US Coast Guard uses the Hercules to calibrate these.

LOCKHEED

F-94 STARFIRE

● All-weather interceptor ● Cold War defender ● T-33 development

▲ For more than three years, from late 1949 until 1953, the F-94 was the USAF's only all-weather jet fighter. As such, it played a vital part in the Cold War, protecting the United States from a perceived Soviet threat.

In the 1950s the Lockheed F-94 Starfire was the first jet aircraft to combine weaponry with an air-to-air radar set. The F-94 was the USAF's first jet-powered, all-weather interceptor. This fighter, with its crew of pilot and radar operator, saw useful service in the Korean conflict (1950–53), but its reputation was made in guarding the North American continent from the threat of bomber attack during the volatile Cold War.

PHOTO FILE

LOCKHEED F-94 STARFIRE

▲ Swept tailplane
The modified tailplane of the F-94C is obvious here. Starfires devoid of rocket pods but carrying wingtip tanks were introduced from the 100th aircraft.

▲ First prototype
Modified from a TF-80C Shooting Star (later known as the T-33A), the first two YF-94s lacked some operational equipment and were used as test aircraft.

▲ From F-97A to F-94C
Initially designated F-97A due to an extensive redesign, 387 examples of the improved variant were delivered as F-94Cs between 1951 and 1954. The last examples were retired in 1959.

▲ Rippling rockets
An F-94C fires a salvo of highly accurate 70-mm (2.76-in) 'Mighty Mouse' rockets from its wing pods.

Afterburner aglow ▶
Radar and armament added considerable weight to the F-94, and an afterburner was essential to maintain performance.

FACTS AND FIGURES

- ➤ The F-94 was the world's first two-seat combat aircraft to exceed the speed of sound in a dive.
- ➤ The YF-94 prototype, piloted by Tony LeVier, first flew on 16 April 1949.
- ➤ The first 17 production F-94As were modified from T-33 airframes.
- ➤ The shootdown of an La-9 on 30 January 1953 was the first air victory achieved solely on cockpit instruments.
- ➤ In all, 854 Lockheed F-94 interceptors were built between 1948 and 1952.
- ➤ The F-94C became the first production fighter to use a braking parachute.

PROFILE

America's Cold War defender

When the Lockheed F-94 Starfire began to reach Air Defense Command squadrons in the early 1950s, many thought that it looked familiar. This was because the F-94 was a development of the Lockheed F-80 Shooting Star, the first operational US jet fighter. The F-80 also gave its design features to the famous T-33 trainer, the 'T-bird', from which the F-94 was derived.

The F-94 Starfire all-weather interceptor was created by adding radar, fitting a rear-seat observer and equipping the aircraft to detect and intercept approaching bombers.

The F-94 was rushed to Japan for action when it became clear that the enemy was employing both prop and jet warplanes in an effort to control the night sky. At the time, the F-94's radar was considered so secret that aircraft were not allowed to fly beyond enemy lines – but they still managed to down several warplanes. F-94s also served with more than two dozen air defence squadrons in the United States and Alaska. When sent aloft to intercept a bomber, the F-94 was given directions by a ground control intercept (GCI) operator using ground-based radar, as the aircraft's air-to-air radar was useful only over a distance of about 32 km (20 miles). Replaced by supersonic interceptors, the F-94 was retired less than a decade after it entered service.

The earlier-production F-94B bore a stronger resemblance to the TF-80C (later redesignated T-33) from which it was developed. The F-94C introduced a swept tailplane, a broader rear fuselage and wing-mounted rocket pods.

Introduced on the 100th aircraft and retrofitted to earlier machines, wing-mounted rocket pods held 12 rockets each and doubled the F-94C's armament.

The F-94C's long-range wingtip fuel tanks added 1893 litres to the Starfire's fuel load. Wing and fuselage tanks held 1385 litres, with the total capacity being much improved over the F-94A and B.

F-94B Starfire

Type: two-seat all-weather interceptor

Powerplant: one 26.69-kN (6,0003-lb-thrust) Allison J33-A-33 afterburning turbojet

Maximum speed: 975 km/h (606 mph) at sea level

Cruising speed: 727 km/h (452 mph) at sea level

Initial climb rate: 2088 m/min (6,850 fpm)

Maximum range: 1455 km (904 miles)

Service ceiling: 14,630 m (48,000 ft)

Weights: empty 4565 kg (10,064 lb); maximum take-off 7640 kg (16,843 lb)

Armament: four 12.7-mm (0.5-in) machine guns

Dimensions:		
	span	11.86 m (38 ft 11 in)
	length	12.22 m (40 ft 1 in)
	height	3.86 m (12 ft 8 in)
	wing area	21.81 m² (235 sq ft)

F-94C STARFIRE

51-5641 carries the markings of the 84th Fighter Interceptor Squadron, Air Defense Command (ADC), as seen at the 1954 Yuma, Arizona, gunnery meet.

Six 'Mighty Mouse' 70-mm (2.76-in) folding-fin aerial rockets (FFARs) were fitted behind four snap-action doors surrounding the radome. The weight of the nose radar and armament offset that of the afterburner, thus preventing a major change in the aircraft's centre of gravity.

The rear seat, which was occupied by a flying instructor in the T-33, was used by the radar operator. Both cockpits were fitted with ejection seats, F-94As and Bs had their cockpits widened after a number of pilots were injured during ejection.

'Buzz numbers' were introduced after 1945 to quickly identify low-flying aircraft. Each aircraft type had a two-letter code, the first of which identified its role. 'FA' was the F-94's code. This was followed by the last three digits of the aircraft's serial number.

An APG-32 radar and Hughes E-1 fire control system (in the F-94A and B) or an APG-40 and E-5 in the F-94C provided the all-weather capability of the F-94.

The initial production versions of the F-94 were powered by an afterburning version of the T-33's Allison J33 turbojet. The F-94C was fitted with a Pratt & Whitney J48, a licence-built version of the afterburning Rolls-Royce Tay turbojet.

The afterburner-equipped F-94 had a much fatter tailpipe than the T-33. This was enlarged further on the F-94C to accommodate the bigger J48 engine.

COMBAT DATA

MAXIMUM SPEED

All three of these jet designs were capable of speeds around 950 km/h (590 mph) – about the maximum speed of straight-winged aircraft. All subsequent designs had swept wings.

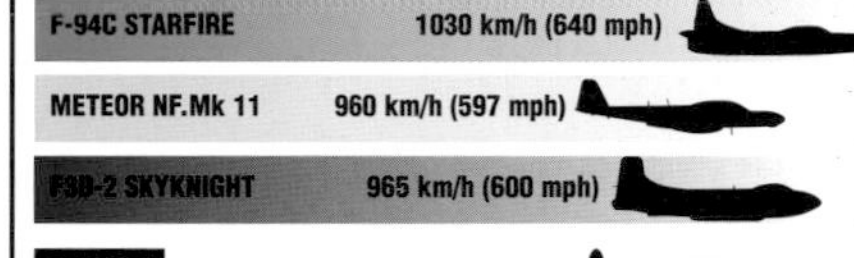

RANGE

By the time the Meteor night fighters were produced, their airframes were reaching the outer limits of development. Consequently, the aircraft was limited in its fuel capacity and its engines were outdated. Both of these factors affected its range performance.

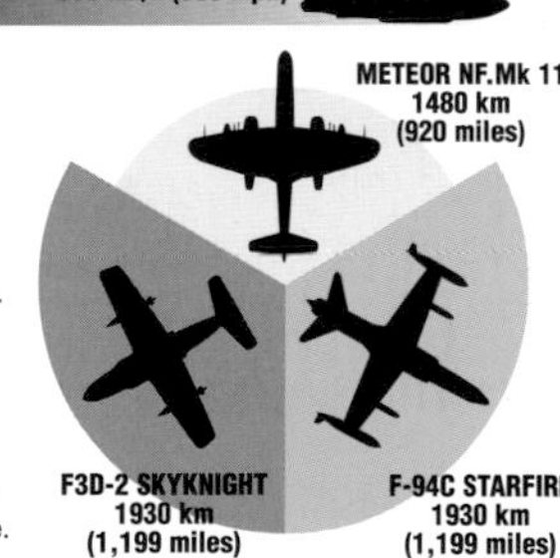

ARMAMENT

Once teething problems with the F-94C's rocket armament were solved, the system proved highly accurate and was a major improvement over the earlier F-94B's machine guns.

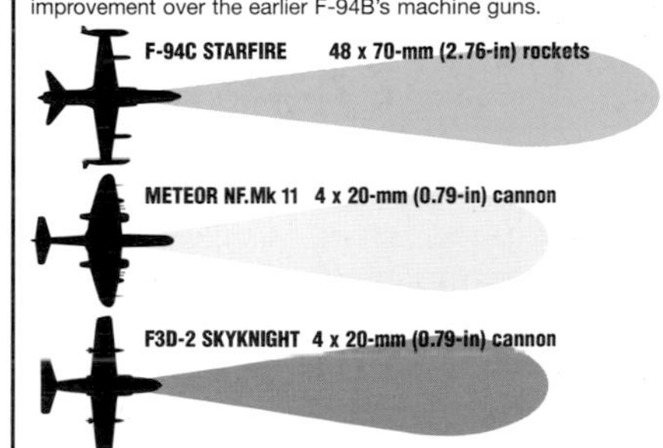

The USAF's first all-weather jets

■ **CURTISS XP-87 BLACKHAWK:** Cancelled in 1948, the XP-87 was one of two all-weather aircraft (along with the XP-89) ordered in 1945/46.

■ **NORTHROP F-89 SCORPION:** As a result of teething problems, the F-89 did not enter service until 1952.

■ **DOUGLAS F3D SKYKNIGHT:** The US Navy's F3D was inconclusively evaluated to fill the gap created by problems with the XP-87 and F-89.

■ **NORTH AMERICAN F-86D SABRE:** While the F-94 was an interim solution, the radar-equipped 'Sabre Dog' served from 1951 to 1965.

LOCKHEED

F-104 STARFIGHTER

● Interceptor ● Lightweight fighter ● Record holder

The Lockheed F-104A Starfighter was known as the 'Zipper' to pilots who flew the aircraft during its brief, unsuccessful US military career. But the sleek, futuristic fighter was not a failure. Designed with speed as its primary feature, the F-104A was a fast performer. It extended the boundaries of fighter performance in the 1950s, and brought Mach 2 capability to more than two dozen air forces around the world.

▲ *An F-104A pilot stands next to the powerful 20-mm (0.79-in) Vulcan cannon fitted to the USAF Starfighters and one of its ancestors, the nineteenth-century Gatling gun.*

PHOTO FILE

LOCKHEED F-104 STARFIGHTER

▲ Two-seat trainer
Conversion training was made easier by the introduction of the F-104B tandem-seat trainer.

▼ NASA test
The F-104's high speed made it useful for NASA, both in high-speed test flights and as a chase aircraft.

▲ Record breaker
The USAF set many performance records with its F-104As, especially for speed and altitude. But the operational success of the aircraft was less spectacular.

▲ Single engine
The Starfighter was powered by a single J79 engine, the same one that powered the later F-4 Phantom in twin-engined configuration.

Wingtip ▶ missiles
Originally designed for US Navy aircraft, the early versions of the Sidewinder missile were brought into USAF service with the F-104. They initially proved only marginally more reliable than the Starfighter.

FACTS AND FIGURES

- The first Starfighters were transferred from the US Air Defense Command to the Air National Guard.
- The Lockheed XF-104 Starfighter made its first flight on 4 March 1954.
- At its deepest point the F-104A wing was only 10.16 cm (4 in) thick.
- In history's first encounter between Mach 2 fighters in 1965, a Pakistani F-104A outran pursuing Indian MiG-21s.
- Improved F-104Cs were operated by Tactical Air Command into the mid-1960s.
- The F-104A was the first aircraft to hold simultaneous speed and altitude records.

PROFILE

First of the Starfighters

The Lockheed F-104 Starfighter was just what the public of the 1950s expected a supersonic fighter to look like. Long, sleek and with a rocket-like fuselage and tiny, impossibly sharp-edged wings, the aircraft looked as though it was itching to break the sound barrier even when sitting motionless on the ground.

Designed by the great 'Kelly' Johnson to be as small as possible, the F-104's wings were optimized for Mach 2 performance. At subsonic speeds where most combat takes place, however, the F-104 was at a disadvantage. Its small size meant that there was very little room for extra equipment, and it fell out of favour with the US Air Force. Still, its speed made it popular with air forces around the world.

The F-104 saw relatively little combat. USAF fighters flew uneventful patrols in Vietnam, while Pakistan's F-104As were involved in actions against India, and Taiwanese aircraft tussled with Chinese MiGs. But to most who flew it the F-104 was simply the incredibly fast fighter that was never needed in the Cold War.

Left: The USAF never really liked the concept of light fighters, preferring heavy, fast, expensive all-weather types such as the F-4 Phantom. The F-104 had more success in the new role as a tactical nuclear bomber in Europe.

Right: Designers went to great lengths to turn out very fast missile-armed interceptors in the mid-1950s. Pilots then discovered that agile, slower aircraft with reliable cannon were often more effective in real battles.

F-104A Starfighter

Type: single-seat supersonic fighter

Powerplant: one 65.83-kN (14,806-lb-thrust) afterburning General Electric J79-GE-11A turbojet

Maximum speed: 2100 km/h (1,305 mph) at 12,190 m (40,000 ft)

Combat radius: 800 km (497 miles)

Service ceiling: 16,764 m (55,000 ft)

Weights: 9880 kg (21,782 lb) loaded

Armament: one 20-mm (0.79-in) General Electric M61A1 Vulcan six-barrel rotary cannon with 725 rounds; two AIM-9 Sidewinder missiles and up to 1814 kg (4,000 lb) of bombs

Dimensions:		
	span	6.68 m (21 ft 11 in)
	length	16.69 m (54 ft 9 in)
	height	4.11 m (13 ft 6 in)
	wing area	18.22 m² (196 sq ft)

F-104C STARFIGHTER

The 479th TFW operated the F-104C from Da Nang in 1965 to provide cover for tactical operations. The Starfighter did not see extensive service in Vietnam, being too short on range to be a useful escort fighter.

Original F-104s had a downward-firing ejector seat, a feature more usually found in Soviet jets. The reason for this was that designers feared an upward-firing seat might hit the tailplane, which turned out not to be the case.

Visibility from the F-104 was surprisingly good for a fighter of the time. The area in front of the canopy was painted black to reduce glare for the pilot.

USAF F-104s were originally left in bare metal finish. Deployment to Southeast Asia, however, led to the adoption of a three-tone tactical camouflage.

The T-tail configuration was used to retain pitch control authority at transonic speed. This had been a problem in earlier designs flying close to the sound barrier.

The Starfighter was not originally designed to have radar, a decision that was soon changed. A simple range-only set was fitted, and later versions built abroad had greatly improved radars.

Designers of the F-104 regarded the missile as its main armament, but did not dispense with the gun, retaining a Vulcan 20-mm (0.79-in) rotary cannon.

The F-104C Starfighter was powered by an afterburning J79-GE-7. Later versions of the F-104 used even more powerful variants of this engine which went on to power the F-4.

The tiny 6-m (19-ft 8-in) wing was optimized for Mach 2 performance. It had large anhedral, or downward angle, which gave a very high rate of roll. The wing's leading edge had to be covered with a guard when the aircraft was on the ground to prevent injuries to the ground crews.

COMBAT DATA

MAXIMUM SPEED

The F-104, like the Lightning, had staggering speed and climb rate gained at the expense of versatility, range and weapon load.

F-104A STARFIGHTER 2100 km/h (1,305 mph)

MiG-21F 'FISHBED' 2000 km/h (1,243 mph)

LIGHTNING F.Mk 1 2414 km/h (1,500 mph)

AGILITY

Short wings with high wing loading meant that both the F-104 and the Lightning could be out-turned by the more agile MiG-21 with its delta wing.

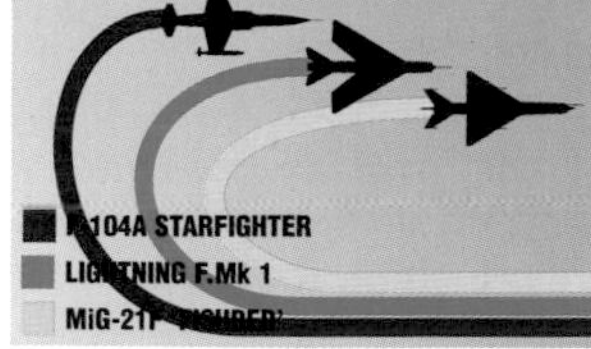

Early century series fighters

■ F-100 SUPER SABRE: The F-100 was the first American fighter to exceed Mach 1 in level flight. It saw extensive service in the Vietnam War as a tactical fighter-bomber.

■ F-101 VOODOO: Big, heavy and very complicated, the Voodoo was the antithesis of the F-104. It was a potent aircraft, with advanced fire-control and nuclear rocket armament.

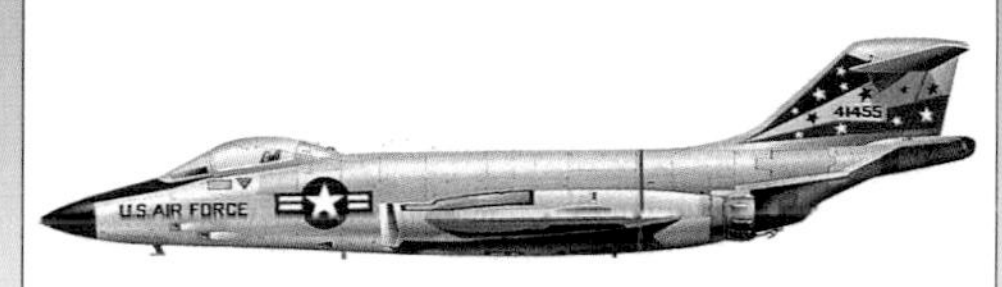

■ F-102 DELTA DAGGER: Another heavy and costly fighter, the F-102 was a problematic design at first, but like the F-104 it eventually matured into a more successful aircraft.

Lockheed

F-104G/S Starfighter

● Lightweight supersonic fighter ● Eight-nation building programme

Sharp, sleek and as fast as a flying bullet, the striking Lockheed F-104 Starfighter promised to be the ultimate interceptor. Small, light in weight and with stunning straight-line performance, the F-104 was never agile enough to become what its designers wanted. But it did evolve into a sophisticated all-weather ground-attack aircraft, which inspired mixed reactions in the men who flew it. They either loved the Starfighter, or loathed it.

▲ *The small size of the Starfighter belies its stunning performance and considerable combat capability.*

PHOTO FILE

Lockheed F-104G/S Starfighter

▲ **Super gun**
A brand-new gun was designed for the Starfighter and its contemporaries. The multi-barrel Vulcan cannon could fire an astonishing 6000 20-mm (0.79-in) rounds per minute.

▶ **High flyer**
Early F-104s were easily the hottest aircraft around. In 1958, the F-104 set new world speed and altitude records.

◀ **Rocket launch**
A German F-104 was fitted with a powerful rocket to blast it from a 'Zell', or zero-length launcher, straight into the air to flying speed.

◀ **Italian stallion**
Licence-built in Italy, the F-104S was a dedicated interceptor carrying Sparrow and Sidewinder missiles.

▲ **Mach 2**
The Starfighter's tiny wing was not efficient at low speeds, but it was more effective than a swept wing at twice the speed of sound.

Ship-killer ▶
The German Kriegsmarine flew the F-104G armed with the deadly Kormoran supersonic anti-ship missile.

FACTS AND FIGURES

- In 1958 Germany purchased the F-104G, sparking many NATO orders in what became known as 'the sale of the century'.
- The Luftwaffe lost 69 Starfighters in the warplane's first four years of service.
- The RF-104G was a dedicated photo-reconnaissance platform.
- In all, 2439 F-104s were built in eight countries between 1954 and 1979.
- The NF-104 was a rocket-powered variant that could zoom to 40,000 m (131,236 ft).
- Italy spent more than $530 million upgrading its Starfighters to F-104ASA standard from 1986 to late 1991.

PROFILE

Missile with a man in it

When it first flew just nine years after the end of World War II, the futuristic look of the Lockheed F-104 Starfighter was simply unbelievable. And its performance matched its rocket-like appearance: even today, so many years later, few aircraft can match the F104's speed and climb rate.

It takes more than that, however, to make a successful fighter. The Starfighter lacked agility, and required sure hands on the controls. As a result the jet had a brief and somewhat accident-prone career with the US Air Force. Instead, Starfighters were to make their mark in a very different role. The much-improved F-104G equipped the ground-attack squadrons of the rapidly growing Luftwaffe and seven other NATO air forces. Nearly 1500 aircraft were built multinationally, giving a much-needed boost to Europe's aviation industry.

Never the easiest aircraft to fly, in German service the F-104 developed an unjustified reputation as a 'widow-maker'. The truth was that accident rates were high for all aircraft of the period, and the Starfighter was actually safer than most of its contemporaries.

The Italian air force operated its upgraded Starfighters until 2004, until they were replaced by the Eurofighter Typhoon.

The F-104's final incarnation is as a very capable ground-attack fighter, built until 1979 by Fiat in Turin and operated by the Italian and Turkish air forces.

F-104G Starfighter

Type: single-seat multi-role fighter and fighter-bomber

Powerplant: one 70.29-kN (15,809-lb-thrust) General Electric J79-GE-11 turbojet with afterburning

Maximum speed: 2092 km/h (1,300 mph) at 12,200 m (40,026 ft)

Initial climb rate: 12,500 m/min (41,010 fpm)

Combat radius: 1200 km (746 miles)

Service ceiling: 16,750 m (54,054 ft)

Weights: empty 6388 kg (14,083 lb); maximum take-off 13,054 kg (28,779 lb)

Armament: one six-barrel M61 Vulcan 20-mm (0.79-in) cannon, two wing-tip AIM-9 Sidewinder heat-seeking air-to-air missiles, up to 1815 kg (4,000 lb) of ordnance on seven underwing and fuselage hardpoints

Dimensions:		
	span	6.68 m (21 ft 11 in)
	length	16.69 m (54 ft 9 in)
	height	4.11 m (13 ft 6 in)
	wing area	18.22 m² (196 sq ft)

The tiny wing that gave the Starfighter its supersonic performance was also its biggest drawback. It was too thin to be used as a fuel tank, and too small to provide much manoeuvrability.

To enable ejecting crew to avoid the Starfighter's high-set tailplane, its designers initially made the disastrous decision to fit a downward-firing ejector seat!

F-104G STARFIGHTER

The German Navy operated this F-104G in the anti-shipping role until early 1982. Based at Schleswig in northern Germany, it is seen carrying two Kormoran anti-ship missiles under the wings.

F-104Gs were retro-fitted with the highly effective British Martin-Baker ejector seat.

The F-104G (for Germany) was considerably more capable than early USAF versions. It was equipped with a NASARR multimode radar, enabling it to follow the terrain and fly high-speed, all-weather, low-level attacks.

Visibility from the Starfighter's cockpit was not great, but it was not needed in the interceptor role for which the aircraft was designed or for the ground-attack role to which it was converted.

The half-cones in the centre of each of the F-104's engine intakes are designed to improve the flow of air to the Starfighter's powerful General Electric J79-GE-11A engines.

Short range was a problem with the first Mach 2 jets. The F-104 quickly lost its wing-tip missiles to make room for extra streamlined fuel tanks, which greatly increased its endurance.

F-104 OPERATORS IN THE 1970s

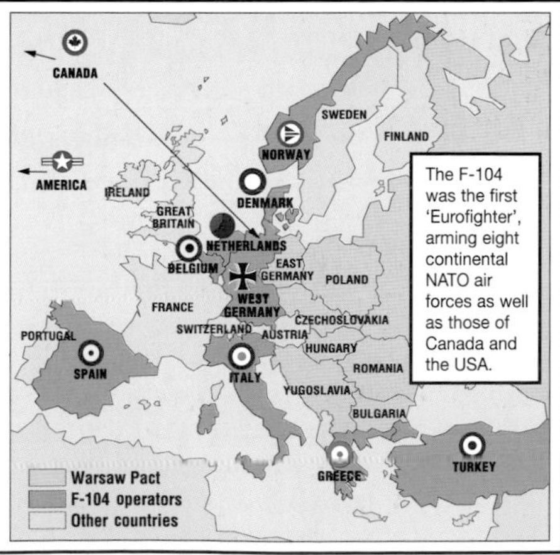

COMBAT DATA

MAXIMUM SPEED

F-104G STARFIGHTER	2092 km/h (1,300 mph)
MiG-21 'FISHBED'	2124 km/h (1,320 mph)
LIGHTNING F.Mk 2	2414 km/h (1,500 mph)

The F-104 was one of the first Mach 2 fighters. It was slower than either the lightweight Soviet MiG or the much more powerful British Lightning.

COMBAT RADIUS

The English Electric Lightning was a classic point-defence fighter. Larger and heavier than the F-104, it had a phenomenal rate of climb, but a relatively short range.

The MiG-21 was also used as a light supersonic machine. More agile than the F-104, it was notorious for its low endurance.

Despite its small size, the F-104 had a considerably longer range than British and Soviet jets.

Maximum range was achieved subsonically: at supersonic speeds, all three aircraft exhausted their fuel in minutes.

CANNONS

On the face of it, the F-104's single 20-mm gun armament cannon was less powerful than its contemporaries. But the six rotating barrels of the M61 Vulcan cannon made up for that by firing its explosive rounds at a rate of 6000 per minute, two or three times the rate of fire of the two 30-mm ADEN guns carried by the Lightning or the 23-mm twin-barrel GSh-23 used to arm the MiG-21. However, the ADEN 30-mm cannon is more likely to give a single-shot kill.

F-104G STARFIGHTER CANNON SHELL

MiG-21 'FISHBED' CANNON SHELL

LIGHTNING F.Mk 2 CANNON SHELL

LOCKHEED

F-117 NIGHTHAWK

● 'Stealth' fighter-bomber ● Fly-by-wire control ● Gulf War veteran

▲ *Two weapons bays in the F-117 are equipped with a trapeze to carry bombs weighing up to 907 kg (2,000 lb.). The usual weapon for raids on Iraq was the laser-guided GBU-27. AGM-65 Maverick or AGM-88 HARM missiles can also be carried.*

Developed in great secrecy, the F-117A Nighthawk quickly became one of the world's best known aircraft after its success in the first Gulf War. Making use of the stealth technology that renders the aircraft virtually invisible to radar, the USAF's F-117s attacked important targets in Iraq from the opening moments of Desert Storm. Not only did they reach Baghdad unseen, but they hit their assigned targets with pinpoint accuracy using laser bombs.

PHOTO FILE

LOCKHEED F-117 NIGHTHAWK

▲ Under cover of darkness

As during the first seven years of its existence, the F-117 flew almost exclusively at night to maintain the secrecy of its missions and capability.

▼ Baghdad bombers

Striking unexpectedly at night, F-117s flew missions against heavily defended positions in central Baghdad during both Gulf conflicts.

▲ Protective shelter

This Nighthawk is seen inside its hardened shelter, in which the F-117s spent much of their daylight hours between night attack missions.

▲ Rarely seen

There was little evidence at their bases at home or overseas that the Nighthawks were operating, other than the standard joke signs.

First major deployment ▶

Apart from the invasion of Panama in 1989, the first Gulf War was the first major use of the F-117A. Nighthawks were assigned nearly one-third of the Baghdad targets during the first 24 hours.

FACTS AND FIGURES

- Laser-guided bombs used by the F-117 are specially modified with 'clipped' fins so that they will fit in the weapons bay.
- The most missions flown by an F-117 pilot during Desert Storm was 23.
- Successive missions were flown over different routes to confuse the Iraqis.
- Khamis Mushait airfield was at an altitude of 2073 metres, which affected take-off and necessitated in-flight refuelling.
- On rare occasions F-117 missions were supported by EF-111s and F-4Gs.
- The 1271 sorties undertaken totalled around 7000 flight hours.

PROFILE

Unseen bomber of Baghdad

High-tech 'stealth' capabilities allowed the F-117A to operate undetected at night in Iraqi airspace until it reached Baghdad. Transferred in great secrecy from its home base in Nevada to Khamis Mushait in the south of Saudi Arabia, the F-117A spearheaded the opening of the air war by coalition forces in January 1991. The dual infra-red weapons delivery system and laser-guided bombs gave it the means to attack targets with the utmost precision. In addition to attacking important military areas in central Baghdad, the Nighthawks hit strategic targets such as communications facilities, bridges, airfields and command centres. In all, 1271 combat missions were flown by the F-117s, with each pilot averaging 21 sorties. Despite an estimated 3000 Iraqi anti-aircraft artillery (AAA) pieces and 60 surface-to-air missile (SAM) sites in the areas attacked, no F-117 was hit while dropping around 2000 laser-guided bombs (LGBs) onto targets deep inside Iraq. The normal flight-time for a Gulf War mission which included air-to-air refuelling was just over five hours.

In-flight refuelling played a vital part in most raids during the war, not least those flown by F-117s.

F-117A Nighthawk

Type: single-seat strike fighter

Powerplant: two 48.04-kN (10,800-lb. thrust) non-afterburning General Electric F404-GE F1D2 turbofans

Maximum speed: Mach 1 (estimated) or 1040 km/h (2,293 m.p.h.)

Combat radius: 1200 km (746 mi.) unrefuelled, with a 2250-kg (4,960-lb.) weapon load

Armament: up to 2268 kg (5,000 lb.) carried internally

Weights: empty 13,600 kg (29,983 lb.); maximum take-off 23,814 kg (52,500 lb.)

Dimensions:

span	13.2 m (43 ft. 4 in.)
length	20.08 m (65 ft. 11 in.)
height	3.78 m (12 ft. 5 in.)
wing area	about 105.9 m^2 (1,140 sq. ft.)

F-117A NIGHTHAWK

The 37th Tactical Fighter Wing, based at Tonopah Air Force Base, Nevada, is the sole F-117A operator, and sent 44 aircraft to the Gulf.

A receptacle incorporated in the spine running along the top of the Nighthawk's fuselage is used for in-flight refuelling, via the USAF's standard 'flying boom' system.

The F-117's wings are swept at 67°. This is again intended to reduce radar reflections as well as being for high-speed performance.

The pyramid-shaped cockpit canopy restricts the area around the pilot's shoulders and head. The cockpit itself is a modern 'all-glass' environment dominated by large video displays.

The F-117 is manufactured from aluminium and composites with radar-absorbing material (RAM) sprayed onto the surface and key points, such as the joints between each facet of the fuselage and the wing leading edges.

Tailfins are carefully positioned to keep radar reflections to a minimum and to help shield the engine exhausts from infra-red sensors of a pursuing fighter or missile.

All air data for the F-117's instruments are collected by four faceted plastic and metal sensor probes in the aircraft's nose.

37 TFW

Two imaging infra-red (IR) turrets (FLIR and DLIR) are recessed into the aircraft's nose. They are fully integrated with, and provide data for, the weapons release system.

Weapons are carried internally, to avoid the radar reflections associated with external stores. In the Gulf, F-117s were normally armed with 907-kg (2,000-lb.) laser-guided bombs.

The two General Electric turbofans are buried in the fuselage. The unique 'platypus' exhaust system mixes hot gasses with cold air, reducing the aircraft's infra-red signature.

The Nighthawk's sharply swept twin butterfly tailplanes act both as rudders and elevators. The 'ruddervators' work in opposition for yaw control and together for pitch control.

COMBAT DATA

MAXIMUM SPEED

Maximum speed and other performance parameters do not have the same relevance in an aircraft like the F-117. Its shape is optimised for stealth rather than speed.

F-117A 1040 km/h (646 m.p.h.)

F-15E EAGLE 2655 km/h (1,650 m.p.h.)

F-111F 2655 km/h (1,650 m.p.h.)

BOMBLOAD

The F-111F has been unequalled for its range and load-carrying capabilities for many years, and performed well in the Gulf. However, like other conventional aircraft, it was heavily reliant on its low-level speed and electronic countermeasures support.

F-117A NIGHTHAWK 2268-kg (5,000-lb.) bombload

F-15E EAGLE 11,113-kg (25,000-lb.) bombload

F-111F 14,228-kg (25,550-lb.) bombload

Black jets over Iraq

DESERT SHIELD: The Iraqi invasion of Kuwait and the decision by the coalition powers to come to Kuwait's aid gave the USAF its first opportunity to test the F-117 on a large scale.

TANKER SUPPORT: As the F-117s' Saudi base was situated at high altitude, the aircraft were required to take off with a reduced fuel load and 'top up' their tanks from a KC-135 once airborne.

STRATEGIC TARGETS: Among the F-117s' targets on the first night of Desert Storm were Iraqi Tu-16/H-6 bombers believed to be preparing for a chemical weapon raid.

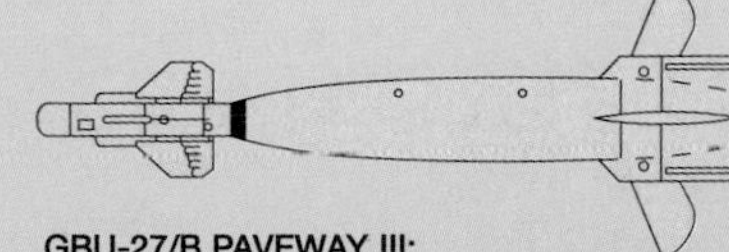

GBU-27/B PAVEWAY III: (above) This laser-guided bomb, seen here with tail wings deployed, was one of the F-117s' primary offensive weapons. It has a standard 907-kg (2,000-lb.) Mk 84 general-purpose warhead.

GBU-27A/B PAVEWAY III: (below) Seen here with wings stowed, this LGB variant has a 907-kg BLU-109 'I-2000' penetrator warhead for use against hardened targets. The F-117's weapons bay is limited to two LGBs.

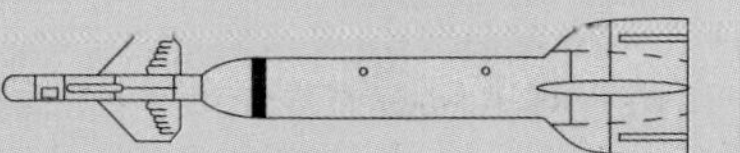

Lockheed

P-2 Neptune

● **Anti-submarine patrol aircraft** ● **Long service** ● **Export success**

One of the greats of naval aviation, the Lockheed P2V (P-2 from 1962) Neptune was the West's answer to the Soviet Union's awesome submarine threat during the first half of the Cold War. This superb land-based maritime patrol aircraft not only searched for submarines, but also filled an anti-surface vessel role. Neptunes performed various specialized duties for the United States and other nations, and some saw war service as late as 1982.

▲ *A veteran of wars in Southeast Asia and the South Atlantic, the P-2 was built in large numbers. More than 1000 served with US and foreign forces.*

PHOTO FILE

Lockheed **P-2 Neptune**

Neptune and its quarry ▶

The Neptune's anti-submarine weapons included rockets, bombs, mines, depth charges and torpedoes. It was never called upon to sink a submarine during the volatile years of the Cold War.

▼ Later colours

This VP-31 SP-2H wears the grey and white colours carried during the last years of US Navy service.

▲ Turbine engines on the P-2J

Between 1969 and 1979 Kawasaki built 82 Neptunes with General Electric T64 turboprop engines and improved avionics.

▼ Popular P2V-5

Built in larger numbers than any other version, P2V-5 production totalled 372. Most later had a MAD boom and jet boosters fitted.

'Midnight blue' P2V-2 ▶

This 'midnight blue' Neptune is typical of the earliest Neptune variants, before the addition of a raised cockpit, jet engines, tip-tanks and a MAD boom.

FACTS AND FIGURES

- ➤ During the 1950–53 Korean War P2Vs dropped secret agents behind enemy lines, even into Manchuria.
- ➤ In all, 1181 of these great planes were built; the prototype flew on 17 May 1945.
- ➤ Twelve modified P2Vs served briefly as carrier-based atomic bombers.
- ➤ In 1982 an Argentine Neptune guided the Super Etendard which sank the destroyer HMS *Sheffield* with an Exocet missile.
- ➤ The largest foreign P-2 fleet was Japan's, and included Japanese-built P-2Js.
- ➤ In Vietnam the US Army used AP-2Es to relay communications from secret agents.

PROFILE

Patrolling 'king of the sea'

With a crew of between seven and 12 men, depending on the model and mission, the Lockheed P2V Neptune spent most of its career stalking Soviet submarines. It also served in other capacities, including electronic intelligence, drone launching and electronic countermeasures training.

Perhaps the most famous achievement of this maritime patrol ship was a distance record that has stood the test of time. Piloted by Commander Thomas P. Davies, a P2V-1 named *The Truculent Turtle* flew 18,227 km (11,326 miles) from Perth, Australia, to Columbus, Ohio, in 55 hours and 17 minutes. This record demonstrated the Neptune's superb range and endurance.

The Neptune's ease of handling and manoeuvrability, with its unusually large rudder, and its spacious accommodation made it popular with Navy crews. Best remembered are the blue-painted Neptunes that prowled the world's oceans. With its maritime patrol capabilities and potential for other military duties, the Neptune was also widely exported, with customers including Australia, Argentina, Brazil, Britain and Canada.

Below: In 1952 P2V-5s entered service with four squadrons of RAF Coastal Command as the Neptune MR.Mk 1. The majority were later fitted with MAD (magnetic anomaly detector) 'stings' and a Plexiglass nose.

Above: The Royal Canadian Air Force took delivery of 25 P2V-7s in the mid-1950s. When they were replaced in the early 1970s by the CP-107 Argus, many were converted for civilian fire-fighting.

SP-2H Neptune

Type: long-range anti-submarine and maritime patrol aircraft

Powerplant: two 2610-kW (3,500-hp) Wright R-3350-32W Turbo-Compound radial piston engines and two 15.1-kN (3,396-lb-thrust) Westinghouse J34-WE-36 turbojets

Maximum speed: 648 km/h (403 mph) at 4265 m (13,993 ft)

Maximum range: 5930 km (3,685 miles)

Service ceiling: 6800 m (22,310 ft)

Weights: empty 22,650 kg (49,935 lb); maximum take-off 36,240 kg (79,896 lb)

Armament: two 12.7-mm (0.5-in) machine guns in dorsal turret, plus provision for underwing rockets and up to 3628 kg (8,000 lb) of weapons

Dimensions:		
	span	31.65 m (103 ft 10 in)
	length	27.94 m (91 ft 8 in)
	height	8.94 m (29 ft 4 in)
	wing area	92.90 m² (1,000 sq ft)

SP-2H NEPTUNE

Originally designated P2V-7S, the SP-2H was a conversion of the last Neptune production variant, the P2V-7. Aircraft 140967 carries the 'YB' tailcodes of Patrol Squadron 1 (VP-1) in the early 1960s.

A clear, bulged canopy, a smaller radome and wingtip tanks characterized the P-2H and its variants. Popular with US Navy ASW crews, a P-2 would often stay on patrol for up to 15 hours.

Neptunes from the P2V-5 onwards had mixed powerplants, consisting of two Wright R-3350 Cyclone 18 Turbo-Compound engines and two Westinghouse J34 turbojets. The J34s were carried in underwing pods.

The SP-2H had new submarine detection gear, codenamed 'Julie' and 'Jezebel', installed. Avionics and navigation equipment in the SP-2H weighed almost four times that of the original P2V-1. The dorsal turret was often removed on this variant.

The colour scheme worn by this aircraft was an intermediate livery between the early all-over 'midnight blue' and the white and grey used in later years.

Neptunes had a reputation for easy handling and manoeuvrability, the latter due to its unusually large rudder. In its heyday, the P-2 served with 35 patrol (VP) squadrons.

A large radome, forward of the weapons bay, contained an APS-20B radar scanner for the detection of surface targets. A searchlight was also installed in the nose of the starboard wing-tip fuel tank.

The P-2's tail was dominated by the MAD 'sting' and antennas associated with the aircraft's other detection systems. A 'tail bumper' was positioned directly below the tailplane to prevent damage if the tail touched the ground on take-off.

ACTION DATA

MAXIMUM SPEED

With its Turbo-Compound engines, which used the piston engines' exhausts as a source of extra thrust, and jet boosters, the P2V-7 (P-2H) had a good speed advantage over the RAF Shackleton and Soviet Be-6.

P2V-7 NEPTUNE	648 km/h (403 mph)
SHACKLETON MR.Mk 3	486 km/h (302 mph)
Be-6 'MADGE'	415 km/h (258 mph)

ARMAMENT

Although the later Neptune variants could carry a large weapons load, this was bettered by almost a tonne in the final maritime version of the Shackleton. Outdated gun armament was modest.

P2V-7 NEPTUNE	2 x 12.7-mm (0.5-in) machine guns; 3628-kg (8,000-lb) weapon load
SHACKLETON MR.Mk 3	2 x 20-mm (0.79-in) cannon; 4536-kg (10,000-lb) weapon load
Be-6 'MADGE'	5 x 23-mm (0.91-in) cannon; 4400-kg (9,700-lb) weapon load

RANGE

Both the Neptune and Shackleton were capable of impressive range, which also allowed longer loiter times while on patrol. The Beriev Be-6's range was 1000 km (620 miles) less than that of the Western machines, but it was not reliant upon land bases.

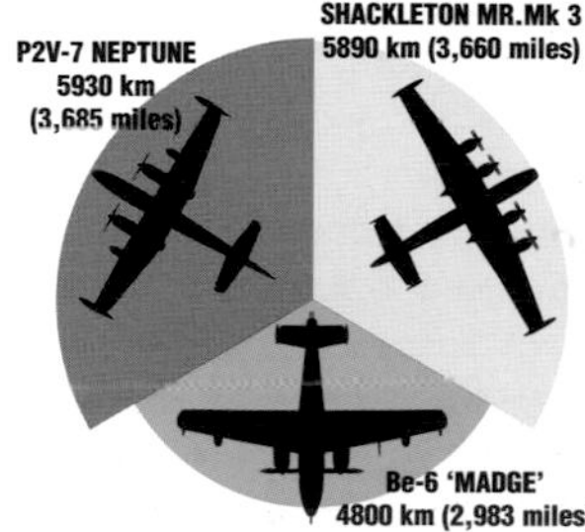

Neptunes in service worldwide

BRITISH STOP-GAP: This Neptune MR.Mk 1 wears the markings of No. 217 Squadron, one of four Coastal Command units equipped with Neptunes under the Mutual Defense Assistance Program. They were replaced by Avro Shackletons.

OVER THE HO CHI MINH TRAIL : US Navy unit VAH-21 operated the AP-2H as a 'gunship' from Cam Ranh Bay, South Vietnam. Armed with guns and grenade launchers, these aircraft attacked truck convoys resupplying the Viet Cong.

FALKLANDS VETERANS: Argentina acquired a number of P2V-5s from Great Britain and later operated SP-2Hs. A number of SP-2Hs were flown on support missions during the Falklands War. Argentina was one of the last P-2 operators.

LOCKHEED

P-3 ORION

● Maritime patrol ● Anti-submarine warfare ● Electronic listener

Adapting airliner designs to the maritime reconnaissance role has long been an inexpensive solution adopted by nations requiring an airborne sea-search capability. The Lockheed Orion, based on the civil Electra, offered four-engined reliability and the necessary range and 'loiter' time for hours of patrol duty. Capable of considerable modification and updating, the Orion has served the US Navy and other air arms for nearly four decades.

▲ *The four-turboprop Lockheed Orion maritime patrol aircraft has remained virtually unchanged in appearance from the initial P-3 to the US Navy's latest P-3C Update IV.*

PHOTO FILE

LOCKHEED P-3 ORION

▲ Overseas equipment

P-3s have been supplied to 13 air arms around the world, including Australia, Canada, the Netherlands (P-3C-II above) and Spain, in addition to the US Navy.

▲ Anti-submarine

When a submarine or ship is identified on the surface, it is visually identified and photographed using the fixed KA-74 camera and hand-held equipment.

▲ Updates

Older P-3s are being updated to incorporate the latest equipment. Australian P-3s, for example, are having new data processors and weapons fitted.

▲ Attack

Various offensive weapons can be carried on underwing pylons, including mines, rocket projectiles or Harpoon medium-range anti-ship missiles. In addition, the P-3 can carry torpedoes, mines and depth bombs internally.

◄ Maritime patrol

The Lockheed P-3 Orion's primary task is to detect, identify and track submarines. For this role it is equipped with a variety of sensors, including a sting-tail mounted MAD and electronics equipment.

FACTS AND FIGURES

- The first flight of the P-3 derivative of the Lockheed Electra airliner took place on 19 August 1958.
- P-3Cs delivered to Norway and South Korea are named Update IIIs.
- Orions have been in production for nearly 40 years, the most recent going to Korea.
- To keep its crew alert on long missions, the P-3 has two rest bunks and a dinette to serve food around the clock.
- EP-3 is an electronic intelligence-gathering (ELINT) version of the P-3C.
- US Coast Guard Orions are used for anti-smuggling patrols.

PROFILE

Lockheed's sub-hunter

One of the most enduring maritime reconnaissance aircraft in service today, the Lockheed P-3 Orion is a powerful submarine hunter. Equipped with an array of advanced sonics equipment including DIFAR (Directional Acoustics-Frequency Analysis and Recording) sonobuoy processing gear and APS-115 search radar, the P-3 can find a periscope in a choppy sea or listen to the noise of a propeller in deep water. The first P-3 flew in the summer of 1962.

The upgraded P-3B with better engines but similar mission avionics flew in 1965. The P-3C which first flew in 1968, and remains in service today, has achieved great export success with countries as far apart as New Zealand and Norway.

To undertake its new military role, the P-3 inherited good shortfield performance and handling as well as ample fuselage space. A flight crew of four flies the Orion, while a team of six operates the sonics, electronic surveillance and radar equipment in the centre fuselage section. Update programmes have kept the P-3 abreast of advances in military technology, and a new version has been offered to the RAF to replace its current Nimrod patrol aircraft.

The US Navy received large numbers of all three main production models: the P-3A/B from 1961 and P-3C from 1968. The latter version remains in service to this day, also equipping the forces of Australia, Canada, Japan, Norway, the Netherlands and Pakistan.

The tail unit is made from aluminium alloy. The tailplane has dihedral and there is a dorsal fin. The leading edges of the tailplane and fin have an electrical anti-icing system.

The pylons between the fuselage and inboard engines usually carry a Loral AN/ALQ-78A ESM pod.

P-3C Orion

Type: long-range anti-submarine patrol and early-warning aircraft

Powerplant: four 3661-kW (4,900-hp.) Allison T56-14 turboprop engines

Maximum speed: 761 km/h (472 m.p.h.)

Mission radius: 2494 km (1,546 mi.)

Service ceiling: 8625 m (28,290 ft.)

Weights: empty 27,890 kg (61,358 lb.); loaded 64,410 kg (141,702 lb.)

Armament: up to 9076 kg (19,967 lb.) of torpedoes, mines and depth charges internally, plus depth bombs, torpedoes, Harpoon anti-ship missiles on 10 pylons

Dimensions:

span	30.37 m (100 ft.)
length	35.61 m (117 ft.)
height	10.27 m (34 ft.)
wing area	120.77 m² (1,300 sq .ft.)

P-3C ORION

The land-based Lockheed P-3 Orion has been the premier maritime patrol and anti-submarine warfare aircraft with the US Navy and many other nations

The main cabin is the tactical centre and contains advanced electronic, magnetic and sonar detection systems. Computers and data processing equipment analyse inputs from the sensors.

Conventional aluminium-alloy construction fin and rudder are fitted, the latter being hydraulically-boosted.

The crew consists of 10 – four on the flight-deck, plus the tactical co-ordinator who has a team of five in the main cabin.

Four Allison T56A turboprops power the Orion, each driving four-bladed Hamilton Standard constant-speed propellers.

The tailcone has been adapted to house electronic equipment, namely the AN/ASQ-81 magnetic anomaly detector (MAD) for detecting and tracking submerged submarines.

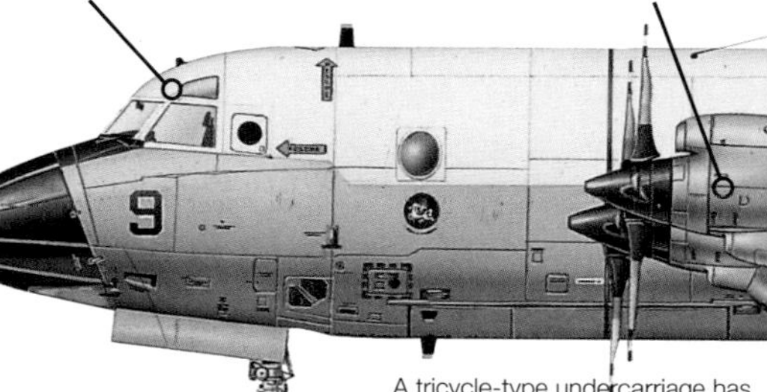

A tricycle-type undercarriage has hydraulically, forwards-retracting twin-, main- and nosewheels.

There are two weapons pylons permanently fitted outboard of the engines.

Launch tubes for sonobuoys and sound signals carried internally run along the rear, lower fuselage.

COMBAT DATA

ENDURANCE

The twin-engined Atlantic has a staggering 18 hours' endurance on its maximum fuel load, although this is at the expense of speed (315 km/h/195 m.p.h.). With a normal endurance of 13 hours at a patrol speed of 381 km/h (236 m.p.h.) the P-3C can increase this to over 17 hours by flying on two engines. The Russian Ilyushin Il-38 derivative of the Il-18 airliner has an endurance of 12 hours at a patrol speed of 400 km/h (248 m.p.h.).

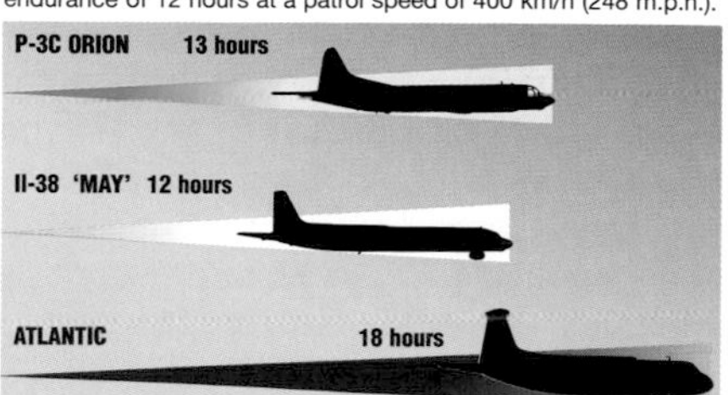

Ship attack

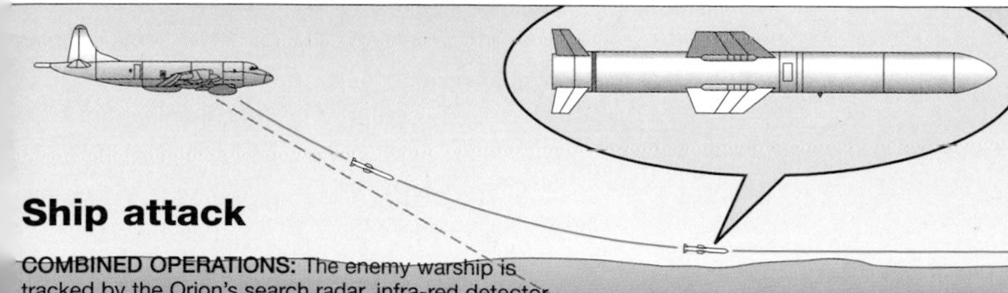

COMBINED OPERATIONS: The enemy warship is tracked by the Orion's search radar, infra-red detector and electronic support measures. In addition, a submarine uses its sonar devices to help the P-3C to fire its sea-skimming missile towards its target.

MISSILE: Fired from the P-3C, the subsonic, turbojet-powered Harpoon anti-ship missile uses a radar altimeter to remain just above the surface of the water.

ON TARGET: The missile's inertial guidance system is programmed to fly towards its target and an active radar controls its terminal guidance. The Harpoon then 'pops-up' before descending to impact the target with its warhead.

LOCKHEED

S/ES-3 VIKING

● Twin-jet anti-submarine ● Elint version ● Gulf War veteran

Although it may not be as glamorous as the F-14 and F/A-18 'fast jets' which also serve aboard the United States' super-carriers, the S-3 Viking has, arguably, a more crucial role. One of the biggest enemies of a carrier battle group is the submarine. The Viking's task is to find these undersea machines and stop them in their tracks.

For this role Lockheed packed sophisticated electronics and potent weapons into a surprisingly compact airframe.

▲ *The S-3's main task is outer-zone anti-submarine warfare (ASW). Inner-zone ASW is tackled by carrier-borne helicopters, such as the SH-3 Sea King and SH-60 Seahawk.*

PHOTO FILE

LOCKHEED S/ES-3 VIKING

◀ **Improved Viking**
Most surviving S-3As were converted to S-3B standard in the late-1980s, with the addition of Harpoon anti-ship missiles and new avionics. Number 159742 was the first conversion.

▲ **Carrier-borne transport**
Six US-3A COD aircraft deliver vital replenishment supplies to the Pacific Fleet.

▼ **'Bombed-up' Viking**
Vikings were active in the Gulf War, undertaking bombing missions against land targets and small vessels in the Persian Gulf.

▲ **ES-3A eavesdropper**
Packed with extra sensors and a third systems operator, the ES-3A is an electronic intelligence (Elint) variant of the Viking. Sixteen conversions are deployed in pairs aboard US carriers.

'Stinger' deployed ▶
With its boom extended, this Viking drops a torpedo. The weapons bay can hold up to 1814 kg (4,000 lb.) of ordnance, which, until recently, included nuclear depth charges.

FACTS AND FIGURES

➤ In partnership with Lockheed, Vought designed and built the wings, tail, landing gear and engine pods for the Viking.

➤ The US-3A COD transport aircraft have been stripped of their ASW gear.

➤ ES-3A Elint Vikings have replaced the last carrier-based EA-3B Skywarriors.

➤ Modified, so-called 'Brown Boy', Vikings were used to drop ground movement sensors in Bosnia.

➤ At one time the S-3A equipped 14 squadrons.

➤ In February 1974 the S-3 made its first carrier landing, on USS *Forrestal*.

PROFILE

US Fleet's Nordic sub-hunter

In 1964 the US Navy began its search for a replacement for the proven Grumman S-2 Tracker. Lockheed, a company with comparatively little experience in building carrier-borne aircraft, teamed with Vought to build the S-3 Viking.

After a January 1972 first flight, a further seven development airframes and 179 production aircraft were built. Operations began in 1974 and the last S-3As were delivered in 1978. A number have been modified for the carrier onboard delivery (COD) role as US-3As, and a dedicated in-flight refuelling version, the KS-3A, was trialled but did not go into production. There are also 16 ES-3A electronic intelligence variants operating in pairs from US Navy carriers.

The current ASW version is the S-3B, introduced in 1987. This aircraft features greatly improved avionics and a Harpoon air-to-surface missile capability.

This Viking is in its natural environment, in search of submarines. All S-3s are operated by the US Navy and represent the most capable carrier-borne anti-submarine force in the world.

S-3B Viking

Type: carrier-borne anti-submarine aircraft

Powerplant: two 41.2-kN (9,270-lb.-thrust) General Electric TF34-GE-2 turbofans

Maximum speed: 814 km/h (505 m.p.h.) at sea level

Ferry range: more than 5558 km (3,445 mi.)

Service ceiling: over 10,670 m (35,000 ft.)

Weights: empty 12,088 kg (26,594 lb.); maximum take-off 23,832 kg (52,430 lb.)

Armament: up to 3175 kg (6,985 lb.) of ordnance (up to 1814 kg/4,000 lb.) in internal weapons bays), including bombs, depth charges, torpedoes and AGM-84 Harpoon air-to-surface missiles

Dimensions:	span	20.93 m (68 ft. 8 in.)
	length	16.26 m (53 ft. 4 in.)
	height	6.93 m (22 ft. 9 in.)
	wing area	55.56 m² (554 sq. ft.)

S-3B VIKING

Air Antisubmarine Squadron 30 flew from the USS *Saratoga* during the Gulf War. Facing an enemy without submarines, VS-30 undertook bombing raids against Iraqi land targets.

Two General Electric TF34 turbofans provide the power for the S-3 family. Both main wings fold inwards and the vertical tail to the left on the Viking, to make it relatively compact and easy to manoeuvre on a crowded aircraft-carrier deck.

The chief sensors aboard the S-3 include a large APS-137(V)1 search radar in the nose, for the detection of surface vessels and submarine periscopes, and a retractable forward-looking infra-red (FLIR) turret under the forward fuselage.

Two 1136-litre auxiliary fuel tanks are often carried to improve range. An in-flight refuelling probe is also fitted. In the 'buddy' refuelling role a D-704 'probe-and-drogue' refuelling pod is carried on the port wing pylon.

Vikings have a crew of four. Two pilots sit side-by-side and handle flight control and navigation. Behind them are the mission crew of Tactical Co-ordinator ('Tacco') and Sensor Operator ('Senso'). All sit in ejection seats.

Apart from the FLIR turret and radar, the Viking's most important sensor is the magnetic anomaly detector (MAD) 'sting' deployed from the rear of the aircraft. This detects changes in the earth's magnetic field caused by a large metallic mass like a submarine.

The S-3B is virtually indistinguishable from the S-3A. However, the later version has a small chaff dispenser fitted to the rear fuselage.

As well as carrying 60 sonobuoys in the aft fuselage, the two internal weapons bays can hold bombs, torpedoes or depth charges. Harpoon missiles are carried on the wing pylons.

COMBAT DATA

MAXIMUM SPEED

Powered by turbofan engines, the Viking has an impressive top speed compared to propeller-driven aircraft – almost twice that of the S-2E. When the Viking is loaded this speed is appreciably reduced, but it can still reach its given patrol area faster than other carrier-borne, fixed-wing ASW machines.

Aircraft	Maximum speed
S-3B VIKING	814 km/h (505 m.p.h.)
S-2E TRACKER	426 km/h (264 m.p.h.)
Br.1150 ALIZÉ	323 km/h (200 m.p.h.)

ENDURANCE

The Viking has a shorter patrol endurance than the propeller-driven aircraft, but has the ability to be refuelled in the air, which greatly increases its flexibility. Vikings have a secondary in-flight refuelling role, for which they can be fitted with 'buddy' refuelling tanks. A tanker version of the Viking was also used until recently.

S-3B VIKING
7 hours 30 min

S-2E TRACKER
9 hours

Br.1150 ALIZÉ
7 hours 40 min

Multi-role Viking at work

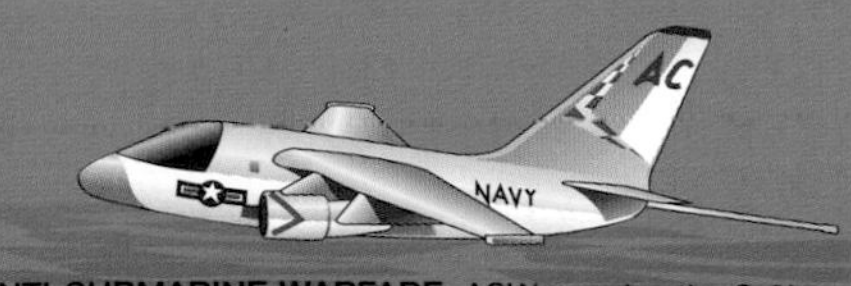

ANTI-SUBMARINE WARFARE: ASW remains the S-3's most important task. The S-3B is found aboard all of the US Navy's super-carriers, providing protection from the ever-present underwater threat. During the Gulf conflict the S-3 displayed its versatility, and was deployed as a bomber.

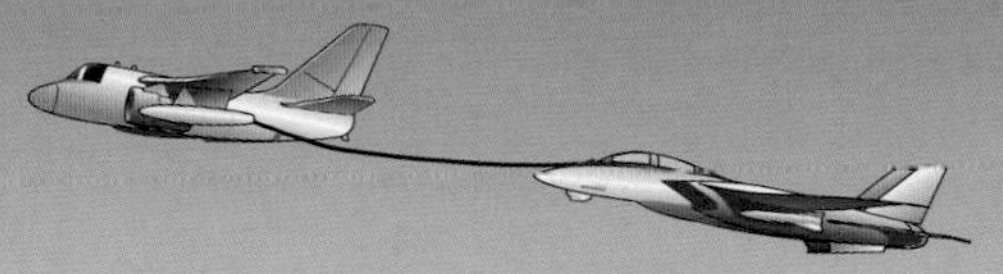

IN-FLIGHT REFUELLING: Development of a specialised KS-3A tanker variant of the Viking was abandoned and ASW Vikings were modified to carry 'buddy' IFR equipment. The 'probe-and-drogue' gear is carried in a pod attached to the port underwing pylon.

CARRIER ONBOARD DELIVERY: A small number of S-3As were modified as COD aircraft to supplement the Pacific Fleet's C-2 Greyhounds. Avionics equipment was removed to make space for passengers and cargo.

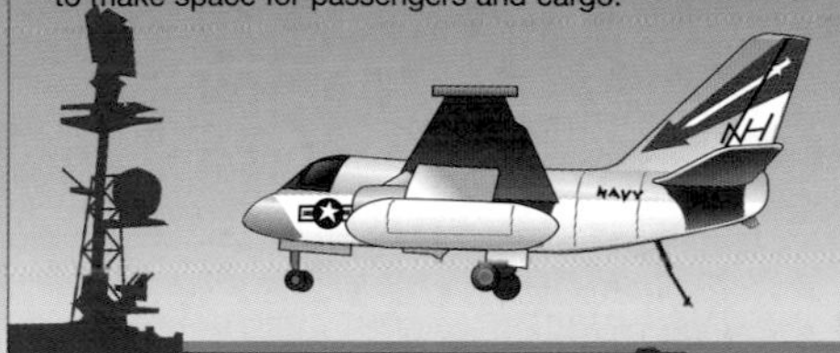

ELECTRONIC INTELLIGENCE: Elint is the role assigned to the small ES-3A fleet. A large collection of new sensors (and their associated antennas) was installed in the aircraft modified and these are used in pairs from carriers.

Lockheed

SR-71 Blackbird

● High-flying reconnaissance ● World's fastest jet

Lockheed's SR-71 Blackbird was the most spectacular performer ever to leave the ground under its own power and spread wings. Thirty years after entering service the Blackbird was briefly returned to service, but this superlative aircraft has now been permanently retired.

▲ *SR-71s operated at the extreme edge of the Earth's atmosphere, and their crews needed to wear space suits to have a chance of survival in the event of an emergency.*

PHOTO FILE

Lockheed SR-71 Blackbird

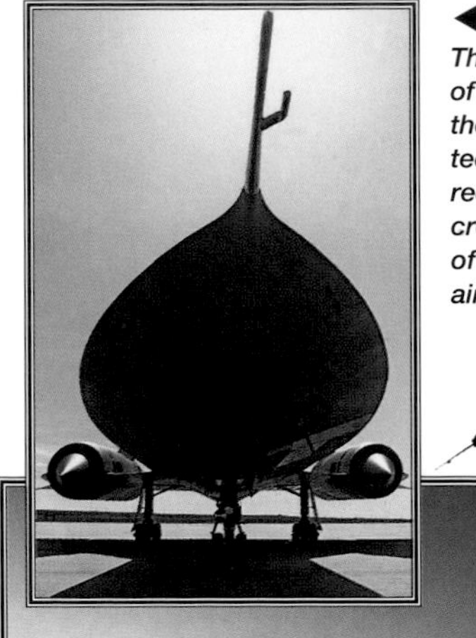

◀ Stealth pioneer
The SR-71's shape is one of the first examples of the use of stealth technology to reduce the radar cross-section of a combat aircraft.

Hypersonic fighter ▲
The original CIA spyplane was developed into an armed interceptor. The YF-12 was equipped with radar and missiles which were carried in an internal bay.

▲ 'Skunk Works'
This unique reconnaissance ship came from Lockheed's top-secret 'Skunk Works', where the U-2 was also developed and where high-performance aircraft are a tradition.

▲ Spy in the sky
In the SR-71's heyday, a pilot could set off from one of its three main bases and get a photograph of anywhere in the world within six hours.

Unique power and fuel ▶
The SR-71's engines were unique, running on JP7 low-volatility fuel. A fleet of KC-135Q tankers was required to keep the Blackbird in the air.

FACTS AND FIGURES

- The Blackbird crossed the USA at a record speed of 3419 km/h (2,124 mph) in 1990.
- The pressure suits worn by the crew were identical to those used by astronauts on the first four Space Shuttle missions.
- Blackbird missions over North Vietnam were the fastest ever flown in combat.
- One version of this spyplane carried the D-21 drone, launched in flight at supersonic speeds.
- At speed and altitude, friction caused the metal skin of the SR-71 to heat up to 200°C (392°F).

PROFILE

Eye in the sky

When it was first flown in the 1960s, the black, needle-nosed SR-71 was an amazing performer. Today, several decades later, the Blackbird's capability has still never been matched, and the superfast jet was pulled out of early retirement in the 1990s to resume reconnaissance flights.

One pilot who watched this incredible speedster return to flying condition called it a 'magic machine'. Yet the Blackbird was more than a spectacular flier. Using cameras and electronic sensors, the SR-71 was able to look down from above or peer sideways hundreds of kilometres into enemy territory with a clarity that no other reconnaissance aircraft could equal. Before the Cold War ended, the SR-71 flew in support of the NATO Allies, usually staying on its side of the border, but still able to spy on the other side.

The SR-71 had very powerful engines and used special fuel, requiring its own tankers for long missions.

Above: It took a lot of effort to keep the SR-71 and its space-suited pilots in the air. One estimate has put the cost of flying the Blackbird at more than $200,000 per hour.

Below: For many years the US Air Force would say only that the Blackbird cruised 'above 80,000 feet' (24,384 m). It is now known that the jet could reach at least 30,000 m (98,524 ft) without any difficulty, and could probably zoom even higher.

SR-71A Blackbird

Type: two-seat all-weather strategic reconnaissance aircraft with electronic, optical, infra-red or radar sensors

Powerplant: two Pratt & Whitney J58 turbo-ramjets each delivering 144.57-kN (32,516-lb-thrust) static with afterburners

Maximum speed: estimated at Mach 3.5 or more than 4000 km/h (2,485 mph); normal operating speed over Mach 3 or 3700 km/h (2,300 mph)

Range: more than 4000 km (2,485 miles) without refuelling; intercontinental with aerial refuelling

Operational ceiling: 25,900 m (84,974 ft); maximum ceiling estimated to be 30,960 m (101,575 ft)

Weights: empty 27,215 kg (60,000 lb); loaded 76,340 kg (168,300 lb)

Dimensions:

span	16.94 m (55 ft 7 in)
length	32.74 m (197 ft 5 in)
height	5.64 m (18 ft 6 in)
wing area	167.30 m² (1,801 sq ft)

SR-71A Blackbird

SR-71s were operated by the 9th Strategic Reconnaissance Wing, United States Air Force, Beale AFB, California, with detachments to Kadena on Okinawa and RAF Mildenhall in England.

The black paint is highly sophisticated, specially formulated to radiate excess heat while at the same time disrupting incoming radar energy. At operating temperatures and altitudes, it changes colour to blue.

To withstand the intense friction-generated heat at Mach 3, 93 per cent of the Blackbird's airframe is made of titanium.

The vertical tails are the only large, flat surfaces on the Blackbird. They are canted slightly inboard, in an attempt to deflect the large radar returns they would produce.

The component parts of the Blackbird fit very loosely, to allow for expansion at high temperatures. At rest on the ground fuel leaks out constantly, as the six large tanks in the fuselage and wings only seal at operating temperatures. There is little danger, however, as the fuel is very stable with an extremely high flash point.

The nose contains reconnaissance sensors. The entire unit is detachable so that different sensor combinations can quickly be fitted.

Separate cockpits house the pilot and reconnaissance systems officer, known as the RSO. The sensors are largely computer-controlled, but the RSO is responsible for monitoring their operation.

The Blackbird's tyres are filled with nitrogen and impregnated with powdered aluminium to enable them to withstand heat.

There are four compartments in the fuselage, which can house panoramic, long-range and infra-red cameras, electronic intelligence sensors and side-looking radars.

The huge J58 engines operate as ordinary jets at low speeds, switching to become ramjets at above 3220 km/h (2,000 mph).

ACTION DATA

SPEED

The only aircraft which even approaches the Blackbird's speed is the MiG-25, and it can only sustain Mach 3 for a few minutes, compared to the eight-hour supersonic missions regularly flown by the SR-71. The Anglo-French Concorde is the only other aircraft which could sustain supersonic flight for hours at a time.

SR-71 BLACKBIRD
Operational speed: over 3600 km/h (2,237 mph)

MiG-25R 'FOXBAT-B'
Maximum speed: 3000 km/h (1,864 mph)

U-2R
Maximum speed 700 km/h (435 mph)

Blackbird reconnaissance profile

1 TAKE-OFF: The Blackbird takes off with a light fuel load, climbing subsonically to rendezvous with a tanker about seven minutes later.

2 ACCELERATION: After filling up, the SR-71 dives briefly and accelerates to go supersonic. Then it climbs to around 25,000 m (82,000 ft) and Mach 3, where it cruises to the next refuelling or the reconnaissance target.

3 MISSION: As the Blackbird approaches the target, reconnaissance sensors are activated automatically by onboard computers tied in with the inertial and stellar navigation systems.

4 HIGH THREAT: The Blackbird avoids getting within range of enemy defences.

5 RETURN: Another tanker waits well away from the sensitive area, and the Blackbird descends to take on more fuel. For long-range missions the superfast jet might have to refuel three or four times.

LOCKHEED

U-2

● Spy aircraft ● 'Skunk Works' design ● Gary Powers shoot-down

Operated by the Air Force and the Central Intelligence Agency, the U-2 was designed at the height of the Cold War to penetrate heavily defended airspace and bring back photos and data on the enemy's most secret installations. The aircraft was built and flew its missions in great secrecy. When one was shot down over Russia, the U-2 became a household name. The type was used over Iraq in the 1990s and remains in service with NASA.

▲ *The U-2 program was kept a secret from the public for many years, but after the Gary Powers incident the veil was lifted – a little. This U-2 at an airshow has missile-tracking cameras on the spine.*

PHOTO FILE

LOCKHEED U-2

▲ Safety problems
Until a U-2A was rebuilt as a two-seat U-2CT conversion trainer in 1973, accidents were not infrequent. This aircraft crashed in Germany in 1975.

▲ First production model
About 40 of the U-2A model were built, along with seven U-2Bs, which had a more powerful engine and greater fuel capacity.

Blacked out ▶
Not to be confused with the later U-2R and TR-1 variants, this all-black U-2D was one of only five of this model to be made.

Cuban crisis ▶
U-2s were involved in the Cuban Missile Crisis in 1962 and flew over Cuba looking for Russian nuclear missiles. This U-2D was based in Florida in the early 1960s.

▲ Spies in the sky
Most of the earliest U-2s were operated by the CIA before being passed to the Air Force.

U-2 in the U.K. ▶
This U-2C was used in trials of a radar-locating system from UK bases in the mid 1970s.

FACTS AND FIGURES

- U-2Gs undertook trials to see if the type could operate from aircraft carriers.
- The only other country to use U-2s was Taiwan, a number of which were lost over mainland China.
- The U-2's wing worked well at high altitude, but made landings tricky.
- The U-2 was put back into production twice, and improved U-2R models have seen service over Bosnia and Iraq.
- NASA uses a version of the U-2 called the ER-2 for earth resources mapping.
- The U-2 pilot used an external mirror to check if he was leaving a contrail.

PROFILE

Cold War spies

The Experimental Department of Lockheed Aircraft Corporation was known as the 'Skunk Works'. The first, and arguably the most famous, of their secret projects was the U-2. Designed in record time under the direction of the Works' director, Clarence 'Kelly' Johnson, it met a joint Central Intelligence Agency (CIA)/USAF requirement for an espionage reconnaissance aircraft.

Work began in 1954, on what was essentially a powered glider. The 'Dragon Lady', as it became known, first flew in 1955 and entered service in the late 1950s, crewed by CIA personnel. The U, for Utility, designation was used by the Department of Defense to hide the true role of the aircraft. Flights over the Soviet Union were made until 1 May 1960, when one was shot down over Sverdlovsk. From then on flights were restricted to spy sorties over non-Soviet territory and secondary tasks like high-altitude sampling, the USAF eventually taking over their operation.

Up to 1960 around 54 had been built in all. In 1967, a second-generation aircraft, the U-2R, flew for the first time and remains in service today.

The traditional matt-black finish became synonymous with the U-2. Few markings or national insignia were carried, other than a serial number, though this was often bogus.

Two 'slipper' fuel tanks with a capacity of 477 litres (105 gallons) each were fitted to U-2Bs and Cs to improve range performance. Total fuel capacity was 6956 litres (1530 gallons). Range was over 7275 km (4520 miles).

A rearward-facing radar warning receiver (RWR) was fitted inside a fairing on the trailing edge of the starboard wing. This warns the pilot of the presence of hostile radar associated with a surface-to-air missile site or fighter aircraft.

This camouflage scheme was worn by aircraft used on the 1975 ALSS trials flown from RAF Wethersfield, codenamed 'Constant Treat'.

The key to the U-2's altitude and range performance was its long-span wings. It was effectively a powered glider, with its high aspect ratio wing and lightweight structure.

U-2B

Type: single-seat high-altitude reconnaissance aircraft

Powerplant: one non-afterburning 75.65-kN (17,000-lb-thrust) J75-P-13B turbojet

Maximum speed: more than 853 km/h (530 mph) at 42,000 ft)

Initial climb rate: 1524 m/min (5000 fpm)

Range: more than 6840 km (4520 miles)

Service ceiling: 24,080 m (79,000 ft)

Weapons: none

Weights: empty 5888 kg (12,980 lb); loaded 10,478 kg (23,100 lb)

Dimensions:		
	span	24.38 m (80 ft)
	length	15.14 m (49 ft 8 in)
	height	4.62 m (15 ft 2 in)
	wing area	447.42 m² (600 sq ft)

U-2C

56-6700 was built in the late 1950s as a U-2A. Converted to a U-2C, it was involved in the Pave Onyx Advanced Location and Strike System trials in 1975, with ALSS orbiting aircraft precisely located hostile radar sites.

To save weight the first U-2s were not fitted with an ejection seat, though they were added later. The type has a reputation for being difficult to handle on landing.

The Q-bay behind the pilot housed the principal sensors and/or cameras. A smaller bay was built into the nose of the aircraft.

Communications, navigation and mission equipment was housed in the long dorsal spine of the U-2C. U-2Fs were similar but had a refueling receptacle at the front.

The U-2A used a Pratt & Whitney J57 turbojet, however all subsequent variants were fitted with a larger J75, of the type fitted, with an afterburner, to the F-105 Thunderchief.

For the Pave Onyx program, the Q-bay had a bulged dielectric lower hatch for the 18 ALSS electronic intelligence antennas.

Jettisonable wheels, known as 'pogos', were mounted under the wings to support them during taxi and take-off.

To shield the exhaust from infrared sensors or missile seeker heads, a 'sugar scoop' was fitted to the lower portion of the jetpipe.

INTERCEPTED: The Soviets were aware of the spy flights and did all they could to destroy a U-2. They were lucky to hit Powers's aircraft with an SA-2. Much propaganda was made of Powers's capture and arms talks were disrupted. He was tried as a spy, and later returned to the United States in a swap with a Russian agent.

SPY FLIGHT PLAN: Gary Powers's U-2 took off from Peshawar, Pakistan, to fly over the Soviet missile test base at Sverdlovsk. His route avoided known SA-2 missile sites and the plan was to carry on to Bodø in Norway rather than return over a predictable flight path.

The U-2 incident

SECRET MISSION: On 1 May 1960, CIA U-2 pilot Francis Gary Powers took off from a secret base in Pakistan to fly over and photograph several strategic bases in the Soviet Union. He would fly at 22,860 m (75,000 ft), out of the range of surface-to-air missiles.

TARGET SVERDLOVSK: For the photo run, Powers had to concentrate on flying straight and level over the target. MiG-15 fighters climbed to intercept the U-2, but could not reach its height.

SHOT DOWN: Possibly because of a technical problem, the U-2 came within range of SA-2 missiles and was hit. Powers ejected and was captured. A missile also destroyed a MiG-15.

LOCKHEED U-2R

● **High-altitude reconnaissance** ● **Earth resources survey**

Today's high-flying Lockheed U-2R is an improvement on the Cold War's most famous reconnaissance plane, updated with microchip technology. The U-2R is easy to spot with its huge, sailplane-like wing. Painted black and flown by a pilot in an astronaut-style pressure suit, this remarkable craft can loiter for hours higher than most planes can fly, gathering intelligence with its cameras and electronic sensors.

▲ *Clarence L. 'Kelly' Johnson was one of the best-known aircraft designers. He was responsible for the U-2 series, the F-104 Starfighter and the SR-71 'Blackbird'. Here he is seen in front of a NASA ER-2, a special version of the U-2R.*

PHOTO FILE

LOCKHEED U-2R

◀ Dragon Lady
The sinister black paint and elegant manoeuvres of the U-2 earned it this nickname. Its huge wings carry it to extreme altitude, from where its sensors can peer sideways many miles into denied territory. With radars, cameras or electronic receivers onboard, little escapes the watchful eye of the U-2R.

The first generation ▶
Today's U-2R is based on the original U-2, which was developed by Lockheed's famous 'Skunk Works' under the direction of Clarence L. Johnson.

▶ Delicate wings
The wings are very fragile, and the pilot has to take great care not to overstress them.

▲ Motor glider
The U-2 has often been likened to a giant glider with a jet engine. Like gliders, the Dragon Lady is very efficient in the air, but is also very tricky to land. A second pilot drives behind the U-2 and gives a running commentary of the approach to aid the pilot.

◀ Black paint
The U-2 is coated with a special paint containing iron. This makes the aircraft difficult to see on radar.

FACTS AND FIGURES

➤ The original U-2 prototype, for the series that preceded today's U-2R, first flew on 4 August 1955.

➤ The prototype of the enlarged U-2R initially flew on 28 August 1967.

➤ A total of 49 U-2Rs and TR-1s were built in two batches.

➤ Lockheed's production line was reopened in November 1979 for the TR-1 (now also known as the U-2R).

➤ The U-2R and TR-1 employ ASARS-2 battlefield surveillance radar.

➤ Some U-2Rs have a satellite communication system.

PROFILE

Lockheed's black dragon

First introduced in the Vietnam era, the U-2R is similar to but bigger and more powerful than the U-2 in which Francis Gary Powers was shot down over Russia on 1 May 1960. A few identical aircraft used for battlefield surveillance in the 1980s were known by the designation TR-1.

The 'Dragon Lady', as this unique aircraft is sometimes called, is designed to monitor potential enemy forces or to police arms agreements. It carries photographic, radar and electronic sensors in a long, detachable nose cone, in the fuselage and in wingpods. The sensor fit is changed depending on the mission.

Although the basic design is nearly 50 years old, the U-2R still flies higher than all but a handful of aircraft. It is difficult to fly, with a cramped cockpit and challenging handling properties. It lands and takes off using an odd bicycle-style landing gear with outrigger wheels at the wingtips which detach and fall away after take-off. Recent missions have involved flights over Bosnia, which helped locate mass graves.

NASA uses two ER-2s, which are based on the U-2R airframe. They are employed for high-altitude research into the ozone layer and for monitoring the earth's crust.

U-2R

Type: single-seat high-altitude reconnaissance aircraft

Powerplant: one 75.61-kN (16,950-lb.-thrust) Pratt & Whitney J75-P-13B turbojet engine

Maximum speed: Mach 0.8 or 960 km/h (595 m.p.h.) at sea level

Cruising speed: 692 km/h (429 m.p.h.) at 10,000 m (33,000 ft.)

Range: 10,060 km (6,237 mi.)

Service ceiling: 24,835 m (81,459 ft.)

Weights: empty 7031 kg (15,468 lb.); maximum take-off 18,733 kg (41,213 lb.)

Dimensions:		
	span	31.39 m (103 ft.)
	length	19.13 m (63 ft.)
	height	4.88 m (16 ft.)
	wing area	92.9 m² (1,000 sq. ft.)

U-2R

The U-2R's altitude performance and incredible endurance make it the perfect vehicle for maintaining a long watch on hostile territory. The small hand-built fleet is very important to the US Air Force, which has re-engined the aircraft. Radar reconnaissance and communications intelligence gathering are the U-2's main tasks, although the type still carries traditional cameras on some missions.

The U-2 has only a central mainwheel and a small tailwheel. When it lands, it topples over on to specially toughened wingtip skids. Groundcrew then come and fix the 'pogo' wheels back on to allow the aircraft to taxi.

For taxiing, the U-2 is fitted with outrigger wheels under each wing. On take-off these keep the wings level until the aircraft leaves the ground. These 'pogo' wheels then drop free.

The U-2R pilot has a mirror to look behind to see if the aircraft is leaving a contrail – a giveaway sign to those on the ground. If there is a trail, he can change speed or altitude to prevent it.

Power for the U-2R was provided by the Pratt & Whitney J75, but in the mid-1990s these were replaced by General Electric F101s, similar to the engine which powers the B-2 stealth bomber. The U-2R's designation changed to U-2S.

U-2Rs usually carry 'superpods' on each wing, used for the carriage of sensors. These are mainly electronic receivers for intercepting communications.

Immediately behind the cockpit is a large space known as the Q-bay. When the U-2R carries enormous downward-looking cameras, this is the only place big enough to fit them. The bottom door of the bay often has glass windows for the lenses.

The cockpit is fully pressurised, but if this failed at high altitude the pilot would die almost immediately without protection. For emergency situations, he wears a full pressure suit, very similar to that worn by astronauts flying the Space Shuttle.

The nose of the U-2R carries yet more sensors and is interchangeable. Two favourite noses are the ASARS-2 stand-off radar and the LOROP side-looking camera.

COMBAT DATA

SERVICE CEILING

The U-2 is renowned for its altitude capability and is only bettered by the Lockheed SR-71. However, the U-2's main advantage is its ability to remain in the same area at this incredible altitude for hours at a time, whereas the SR-71 has been and gone in a matter of seconds. The Russian M-55 'Mystic' has some of the U-2's capabilities, but cannot achieve the operational altitude of the 'Dragon Lady'. It is slightly faster, but the U-2R has a much greater endurance and can carry a far heavier load of sensors.

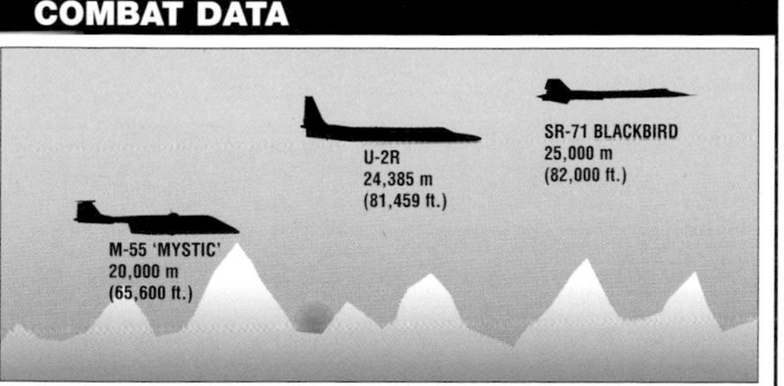

Stand-off reconnaissance

UPLINK: Some U-2s are fitted with the Senior Span pod on their backs. This digitally processes the intelligence gathered by the sensors, which can be relayed to a military communications satellite.

STAND-OFF: From high altitude the U-2's sensors can penetrate the target area without the need for the aircraft to enter hostile airspace.

ASARS RADAR: Among the U-2R's sensors is the ASARS-2 radar, which peers sideways from the aircraft's nose.

RADAR PICTURES: The radar produces pictures of military and industrial installations deep within foreign territory. These are recorded digitally and can be datalinked to ground stations.

DOWNLINK: The images are relayed down from the satellite straight into a command post anywhere in the world. This allows battle staff to view the U-2's intelligence the moment it is gathered.

LOCKHEED MARTIN

C-130H HERCULES

● **Four-engine turboprop transport** ● **Used worldwide**

There have been so many versions of the "Charlie One-Thirty" during its 40 years of service that it is hard to imagine it ever being grounded because of old age. Over the years it has undertaken dozens of useful tasks ranging from maritime patrol to secret agent support. Its main task, however, remains in the STOL transport role for which it was designed. The prototype first flew in August 1954, and the C-130H version was the biggest seller.

▲ *The 'Herc' was designed to meet a US Air Force requirement for a tactical transport able to use rough airstrips and carry 18 tonnes (24,950 lb.) of cargo, 92 ground troops or 64 paratroops.*

PHOTO FILE

LOCKHEED MARTIN C-130H HERCULES

▼ Desert airlift
The Gulf War of 1990-91 brought together numerous C-130s from several nations as part of the Coalition force.

▲ Providing relief
Worldwide, the C-130's airlift tasks today often involve mercy flights and supply drops.

First exports ▶
The first export customer was Australia, which received 12 C-130As in 1958 and later batches of both the E and H models.

▲ Stretched 'Dash-30s'
Originally known as the C-130H(S), C-130H-30s have been delivered to several air forces including those of Algeria, France, Indonesia and Saudi Arabia.

▼ Swedish 'Hercs' over Bosnia
Due to the country's neutrality, few units of Sweden's air force deploy overseas. An exception has been its C-130 unit, F7, which deployed to the former Yugoslavia.

FACTS AND FIGURES

- There is also a civilian version of the C-130, which is known as the L-100.
- US Air Force C-130s have seen combat in Vietnam, Grenada, Panama and the Persian Gulf.
- The US Navy tested a scale model of an amphibious version of the C-130.
- New Zealand's air force regularly uses its C-130Hs in Antarctica; the USAF also deploys ski-equipped 'Hs' to the Arctic.
- The first USAF C-130Hs were search-and-rescue HC-130Hs built in 1964.
- RAF Hercules are based on the C-130H with British radar and other equipment.

PROFILE

H-model Herky-bird

The C-130H was fitted with a redesigned and strengthened wing box, additional power (provided by uprated engines), and better brakes to distinguish it from the C-130E, the earlier main production variant of the Hercules. The first H model aircraft flew on November 19, 1964. Two years later, examples were delivered to the Royal New Zealand Air Force, the initial customer for the new model in Lockheed-Martin's already impressive catalog of aircraft.

The C-130H has since entered service with over 50 air forces around the world and although originally intended for export only, has also been ordered by the United States Air Force.

An important version of the C-130H was the Dash-30 which has a 4.57-m (15-ft.) fuselage extension to significantly increase payloads without any detrimental effect on performance. The first examples of this model were delivered to Indonesia in September 1980 and this stretched version has since found wide appeal.

Built-in adaptability has also enabled a number of other major modifications to be made to the basic C-130H for a variety of extra roles.

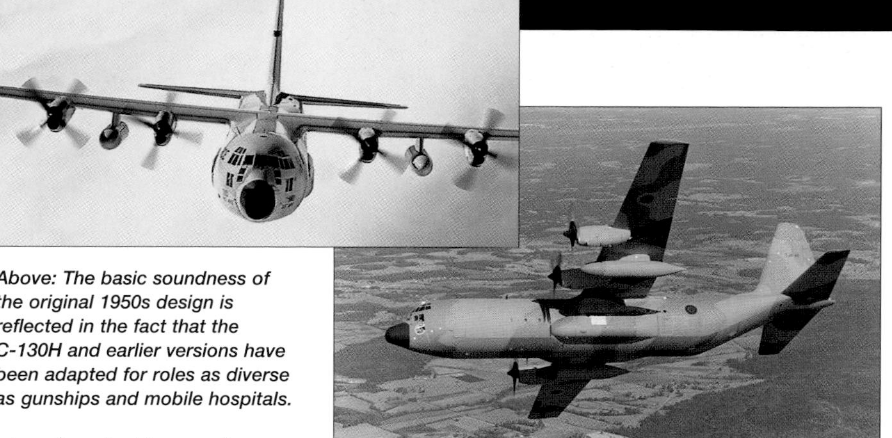

Above: The basic soundness of the original 1950s design is reflected in the fact that the C-130H and earlier versions have been adapted for roles as diverse as gunships and mobile hospitals.

Above: Cameroon, another operator of the C-130H-30, has its aircraft painted in a sand camouflage scheme. These aircraft often carry civilians during the Haj pilgrimage season.

C-130H

Type: medium-range STOL transport

Powerplant: four 3362-kW (4,500-hp.) Allison T56-A-15 turboprop engines

Maximum speed: 618 km/h (383 m.p.h.)

Service ceiling: 10,058 m (33,000 ft.)

Range: 3791 km (2,350 mi.) with max payload

Maximum payload: 19,350 kg (42,570 lb.)

Weights: empty 34,357 kg (75,585 lb.); loaded 79,380 kg (174,636 lb.)

Dimensions:

span	40.41 m (132 ft. 6 in.)
length	29.70 m (97 ft. 9 in.)
height	11.66 m (34 ft. 3 in.)
wing area	162.12 m² (1,744 sq. ft.)

C-130H HERCULES

The Algerian air force operates 12 C-130Hs that were delivered between 1981 and 1990, replacing Antonov An-12s, on the understanding that the aircraft would not be used on operations against Polisario guerillas.

The bulbous 'Pinocchio' nose of the C-130H contains a navigational radar set.

C-130 Hercules in the transport role generally fly with a crew of five: aircraft commander, co-pilot, flight engineer, navigator and loadmaster.

The new Allison T56-A-15 engines introduced on the C-130H removed the need for rocket-assisted take-off equipment as fitted to some earlier models. Four-blade propellers are standard.

External fuel tanks, each holding 5150 litres (1,360 gal.), are fitted between the engines of each wing and are standard on all C-130Hs.

Algerian air force C-130s carry quasi-civilian registrations that are used when the aircraft fly overseas. The camouflage is a USAF-style, Vietnam-era scheme.

The rear loading ramp gives access to a hold capable of accommodating over 19 tons of cargo. A Low-Altitude Parachute Extraction System (LAPES) is used to make drops in combat zones.

ACTION DATA

SPEED

The jet-powered Kawasaki C-1 has a higher top speed than the An-12 and C-130, both of which are powered by turboprop engines. While the C-130 has a considerably lower top speed than the An-12, it has a better range, especially with a maximum fuel load on board.

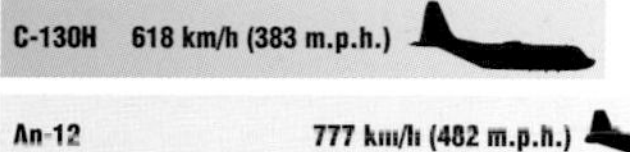

PAYLOAD

The C-130 and C-1 have a rear loading ramp, while the An-12 has a pair of clamshell doors. The C-130 and C-1 are able to lower their ramps in flight so that troops and equipment can be deployed, usually with the aid of parachutes. The C-130 and An-12 are large enough to carry a medium-sized armored vehicle.

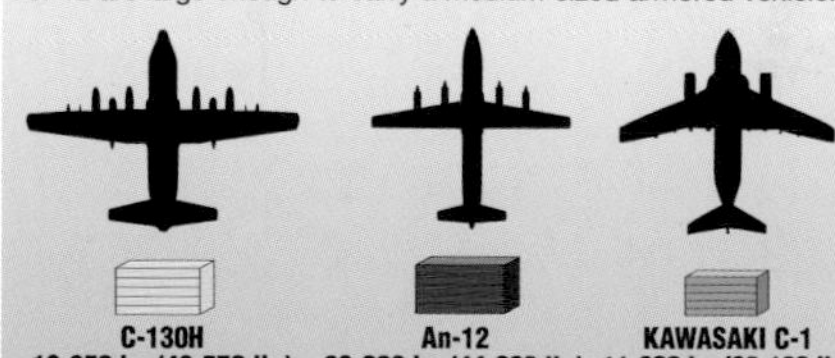

TAKE-OFF RUN

The engines on the jet-powered C-1 are positioned so that the exhaust is directed over the lower surface of the aircraft's flaps to provide more lift. Take-off distance is therefore shortened. Short take-off runs are particularly important for a tactical transport that needs to land in confined spaces near the battlefield.

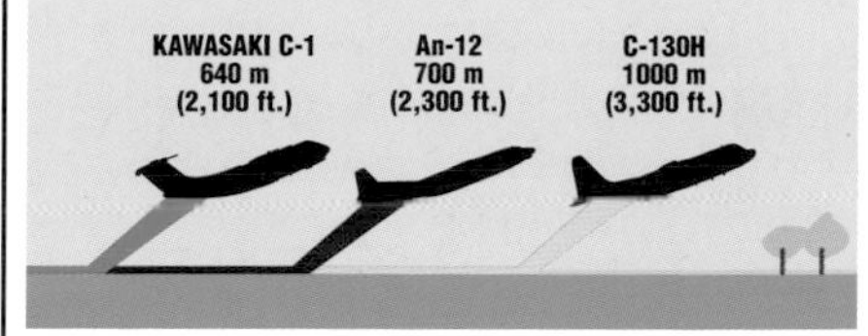

The many labours of Hercules

HERCULES W. MK 2 'SNOOPY': Modified in 1973 from a standard Hercules C Mk.1, XV208 replaced a Vickers Varsity operated by the RAF Meteorological Flight for weather research.

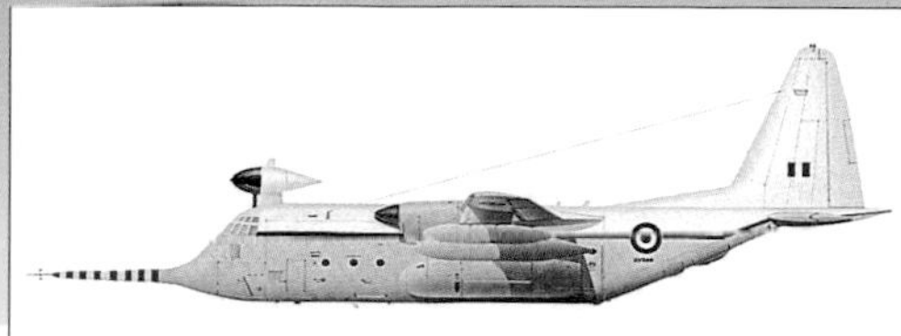

EC-130E: Codenamed 'Rivet Rider', four C-130Es were rebuilt by the USAF as airborne radio/television transmission stations to provide broadcasts in the event of a major disaster or emergency.

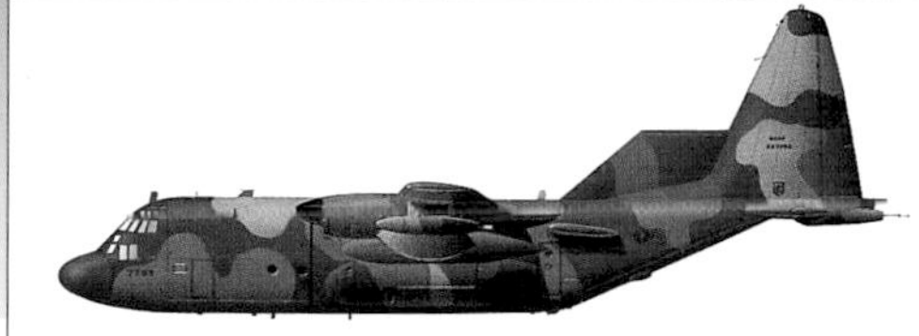

MC-130E: USAF MC-130s use the folding nose-mounted 'forks' of the Fulton recovery system to retrieve special operations personnel without having to land in hostile territory.

LOCKHEED MARTIN

F-16A FIGHTING FALCON

● Lightweight fighter ● Multi-mission capable ● 'The Electric Jet'

CAPT JOHN PEARSE

▲ The F-16 pilot has at his command the West's premier light-fighter. The view from the cockpit is outstanding, thanks to the massive one-piece bubble canopy.

The F-16 Fighting Falcon is 20 years old, but remains a star performer. A fast and potent dogfighter, it is equally at home destroying enemy tanks or positions at tree-top level. This relatively lightweight and inexpensive warplane introduced electronic flight controls and other hi-tech wizardry, and its radar, missiles and cannon make it a genuine 'Top Gun', respected by friend and foe alike.

PHOTO FILE

LOCKHEED MARTIN F-16A FIGHTING FALCON

◀ **Head-up fighting**
The F-16 pilot reclines at 30° and flies the fighter using a pressure-sensitive sidestick with his right hand.

▲ **Flying the flag**
Perhaps the best-known F-16s are those of the USAF's Thunderbirds team. The F-16 gives them excellent agility matched with noise and speed.

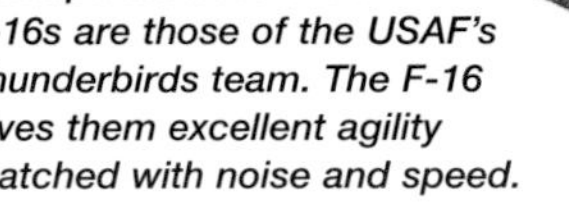

◀ **Combat success**
Israel has been using the Fighting Falcon since the early 1980s. The aircraft's combat debut came with the destruction of Iraq's Osirak nuclear facility in 1981, and over Lebanon in 1982 Israeli F-16s shot down 44 Syrian MiGs without loss.

▼ **Fighter and bomber**
Originally devised as a lightweight fighter, the F-16 emerged as a warplane capable of lifting just about every ground-attack store available.

▲ **Air defender**
Falcons can launch the latest AMRAAM air-to-air missile. Using this weapon, a USAF F-16 shot down a MiG-25 over Iraq.

FACTS AND FIGURES

- Lockheed acquired General Dynamics, who created the F-16, in March 1993.
- The company says it can build a new F-16 today for $20 million, less than half the price of an F-15E Strike Eagle.
- The F-16 ejection seat works safely at any speed and altitude.
- More than 4,000 F-16s serve in the US, NATO, Asia and Latin America.
- A delta-winged test version, the F-16XL, has wing area increased by 120 per cent.
- F-16 pilots flew 13,500 combat sorties in Operation Desert Storm, more than any other aircraft.

PROFILE

Lightweight superjet

The F-16 is proof that one aircraft can move back the boundaries of aviation. This marvellous warplane introduced lightweight computers, 'fly-by-wire' electronic controls and a breathtaking arsenal of hi-tech weaponry.

No longer new, the F-16 is a boon to those who fly it. Pilots say the F-16 is a super aircraft, without equal from the viewpoint of the airman at the controls.

Engineers saw the F-16 as a no-frills 'hot rod'. It gained weight with the addition of improved radar and weaponry, but is smaller and more nimble than many fighters. Used mainly to drop bombs, the Fighting Falcon can turn and fight with unbridled fury when provoked and was one of the first operational 'fly-by-wire' aircraft, its controls being electronically-operated and computer-controlled. The pilot sits in a seat which reclines at 30° to withstand high-*g* manoeuvres, allowing the gut-wrenching turns that give the F-16 an advantage over its rivals.

Despite its amazing agility, the F-16 is rock-steady when it needs to be – diving in to attack a target with gun or missiles. Here a two-seater lets fly with a Maverick missile, a favourite against tanks.

Halfway along its back the F-16 has a refuelling receptacle so that it can take on fuel in flight. This is now standard on most military fighting planes.

Nearly all F-16s are painted in shades of grey. This colour was found to be the most difficult to see across a wide range of different weather conditions.

F-16s are powered by a Pratt & Whitney F100 engine. It is extremely powerful, and very resistant to changes in airflow.

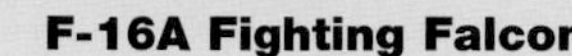

F-16A Fighting Falcon

Type: single-seat multi-role fighter

Powerplant: one 106.05-kN (23,800-lb. thrust) Pratt & Whitney F100-P-100 afterburning turbojet

Maximum speed: Mach 2.05 or 2173 km/h (1,350 m.p.h.) at 12,190 m (40,000 ft.)

Combat radius: 1300 km (808 mi.) with drop tanks

Service ceiling: 15,240 m (50,000 ft.)

Weights: empty 6607 kg (14,566 lb.); maximum take-off 14,968 kg (32,999 lb.)

Armament: one M61 Vulcan 20-mm cannon, up to 6900 kg (15,212 lb.) of air-to-air and air-to-ground weaponry

Dimensions:	span	9.45 m (31 ft.)
	length	15.03 m (49 ft. 4 in.)
	height	5.01 m (16 ft. 5 in.)
	wing area	27.87 m² (300 sq. ft.)

F-16A FIGHTING FALCON

In service with many nations, the F-16 can rightly be regarded as the world's standard fighter. This example is one of Pakistan's aircraft, which have shot down several Russian types along the border with Afghanistan.

With its curved surfaces blending the fuselage and wing together, and its fly-by-wire electric flight control system, the F-16 ushered in a new era of fighter design. The radical shape had far better aerodynamics than earlier designs, making the F-16 more agile for dogfighting.

The radar of the F-16 is as versatile as the aircraft. With a flick of a switch the pilot can change from air-to-air operation to air-to-ground. When dogfighting, the radar automatically follows the enemy and gives the pilot a steering cue on the large head-up display in front of him.

AIM-9 Sidewinders are the main air-to-air weapon of the F-16, seen here carried on the wingtips and on underwing pylons.

The AIM-9 is a heat-seeking missile, homing in on the heat of the enemy's exhaust. It is very difficult to counter and is far more manoeuvrable than an aircraft, so cannot be shaken off.

COMBAT DATA

AGILITY

The F-16 was a revelation when it first appeared, being the most agile fighter in the world. Both the Mirage 2000 and the MiG-29 were designed to try to match the smaller American jet's superb handling.

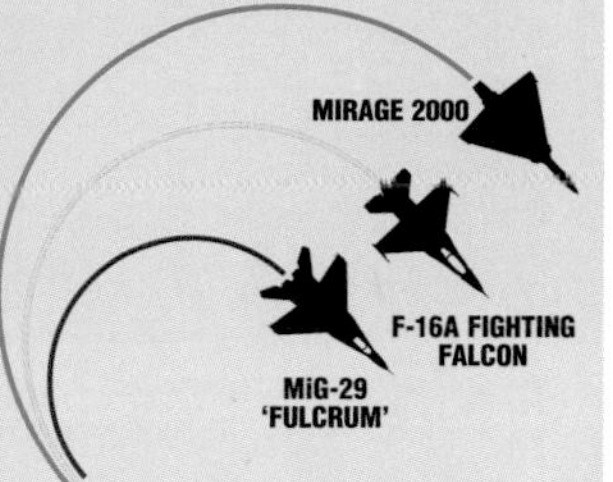

SPEED

Although capable of twice the speed of sound at altitude, it is the F-16's performance at lower level and its acceleration at lower speeds which make it such an outstanding fighter.

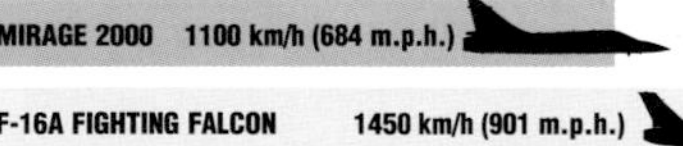

Speeds at sea level

Multi-role fighter

POINT DEFENCE: In the interceptor role, the F-16 can launch in next to no time, scream upwards and shoot down incoming bombers before they can launch their weapons.

CLOSE SUPPORT: Over the battlefield the F-16 can use a variety of bombs and missiles against enemy tanks and positions.

AIR SUPERIORITY: The F-16 can be used to keep the battle zone clear of enemy fighters.

DEFENCE SUPPRESSION: In this role, the F-16 uses high-tech missiles to kill enemy radars. This allows other friendly aircraft to operate in safety.

PRECISION STRIKE: With laser-guided bombs, the F-16 can attack strategic targets such as nuclear installations and power stations.

LOCKHEED MARTIN X-35/F-35 JSF

● Single-seat strike fighter ● Multi-service ● Service entry 2008

▲ US Congressional pressure produced the JSF: an amalgamation of the CALF (Common Affordable Lightweight Fighter) and JAST (Joint Advanced Strike Technology) programmes. The USN, USAF and USMC require 2852 examples.

The X-35, Lockheed Martin's winning contender in the Joint Strike Fighter contest, is the product of the biggest military aircraft procurement programme in history. The aircraft embodies a wide range of capabilities that will fulfil the requirements of the US Air Force, US Navy, US Marine Corps and the British armed forces well into the twenty-first century. Twenty-two development aircraft are currently in production.

PHOTO FILE

LOCKHEED MARTIN X-35/F-35 JSF

▲ Conventional demonstrator
The first version of the X-35 to fly was the conventional X-35A, which validated the basic handling characteristics.

▲ Ultra-manoeuvrable
A vectored engine nozzle and computer-controlled power-by-wire flight controls make the JSF virtually spin-proof.

Colour cockpit ▶
The F-35C cockpit will have full-colour displays and a sidestick.

▼ Lift fan and vectoring nozzle
To provide vertical lift (required in the naval JSF variant), the X-35 has a lift fan shaft-driven from the main engine – behind the cockpit – which means a separate lift engine is not required.

▲ Flexible refuelling options
The X-35 prototypes had a USAF-style boom and receptacle refuelling system, but British, US Navy and Marine Corps F-35s will have a retractable probe.

FACTS AND FIGURES

- Lockheed Martin's proposal used design data purchased from the Russian builder of V/STOL aircraft, Yakovlev.
- Boeing's unsuccessful design for the JSF was designated X-32.
- Export potential for the JSF has been identified in several countries, including Australia, Canada, Germany and Spain.
- General Electric/Rolls-Royce and Pratt & Whitney are both developing interchangeable engines for the JSF under a unique arrangement.
- By 2011 the JSF production rate is expected to reach 122 per year, with manufacturers in the UK producing various elements.

PROFILE

21st century strike-fighter

The Joint Strike Fighter (JSF) will replace Harriers and Hornets, F-16s and A-10s within the US services and will likely equal the F-16 for export sales. More than 3000 are to be built for the US and UK alone, but this may eventually reach more than 6000 examples, with many nations almost certain to select it as their next fighter.

The JSF programme began in 1994, and by 1997 two manufacturers had been selected to produce two demonstrators each to prove their designs. Boeing's X-32 used a similar propulsion system to the Harrier, in a tailless delta configuration with a huge air intake under the nose. Lockheed Martin's X-35 looked more conventional, but the X-35B variant featured a 'lift fan' arrangement, a thrust-vectoring jet pipe and roll-control ducts. The winning X-35 design was the first ever aircraft to perform a short take-off, level supersonic dash, and vertical landing, all in a single flight.

The details of the actual F-35 will differ considerably from the X-35s, as will the performance specifications. An estimate of the relative costs puts the USAF's conventional F-35A at $40 million, while the lift-fan and roll-control X-35B and C will be $50 million apiece. So far costs have been kept in check, but the most complicated, risky part of the programme has yet to be undertaken.

Left: One of the specific features of the X-35C is a stronger undercarriage able to take the added stresses of catapult take-offs and arrested landings.

The variant produced for the US Navy will have a larger wing area, 57.6 m² (620 sq ft) rather than 42.7 m² (460 sq ft), to allow greater range and better low-speed handling around the carrier.

F-35 JSF (STOVL)

Type: advanced STOVL strike-fighter

Powerplant: one approx 187 kN (42,075 lb) thrust Pratt & Whitney F135 or General Electric/Rolls-Royce F136 turbofan engine

Maximum speed: Mach 1.5

Combat radius: 1112 km (691 miles)

Service ceiling: over 15,240 m (50,000 ft)

Weights: 13,921 kg (30,697 lb) empty; 22,680 kg (50,000 lb) loaded

Armament: six AIM-120C AMRAAM or two AIM-120C AMRAAM and two 907-kg (2000 lb) JDAM in internal fuselage bay; provision for one 20-mm M61A2 rotary cannon; four underwing pylons with 2268 kg (5000 lb) capacity each

Dimensions:		
	span	10.66 m (35 ft)
	length	15.39 m (50 ft 6 in)
	height	4.07 m (13 ft 4 in)
	wing area	42.73 m² (460 sq ft)

F-35B JSF

This is an artist's impression of the carrier version (CV) of the F-35. It will have larger wings and tail surfaces, strengthened undercarriage, arrester hook and other naval features for deck operations.

The pilot's full-colour helmet-mounted display (HMD) will give him a 'through-the-floor' simulated display provided by three focal plane array sensors arranged to give a spherical field of view. This information is particularly useful during a vertical landing.

The use of a vectoring exhaust and a shaft-driven lift fan rather than a direct lift system avoids many of the problems associated with jet engines reingesting hot exhaust gases. Operations from carrier decks are also less hazardous for deck crew when using the lift fan system.

The F-35 has a noticeable bulge in its fuselage just in front of the air intakes. This works in conjunction with the swept-forward inlet lip to provide stealth.

Unlike other STOVL aircraft like the Harrier, the entire powered lift and propulsion system is controlled by computers, making the F-35 much easier to fly. As the aircraft transitions from wing-borne to jet-borne flight, the throttle and stick functions change automatically.

ACTION DATA

JSF REQUIREMENTS

The USAF currently has the largest initial requirement for JSF aircraft, as the type will replace the large fleet of F-16s amassed by Air Combat Command during the 1980s. The JSF also represents the US Navy's long-awaited A-6 replacement, while the STOVL version will take over from Harriers in both the USMC and Royal Navy.

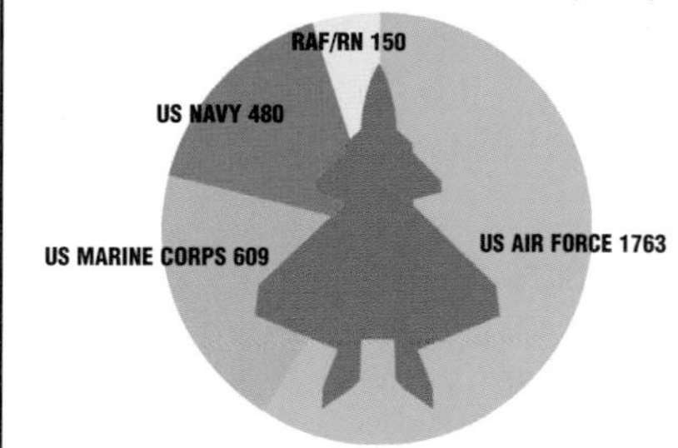

MAXIMUM THRUST

Few figures have been released regarding the JSF's final specification. The X-35 prototype had an engine which developed around 187-kN (42,075-lb-thrust); production aircraft are likely to be a little more powerful. The X-35 falls between the thrust figures of the Harrier and higher performance types such as the F-15.

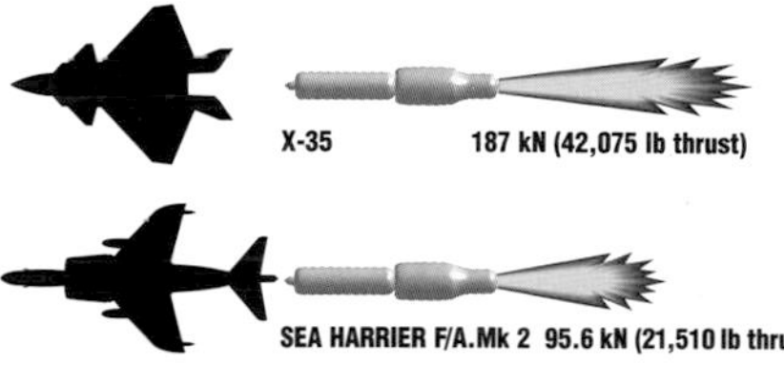

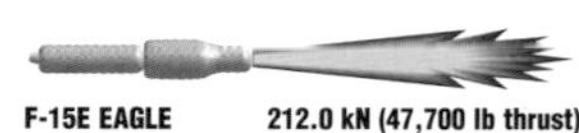

Replaced by the Joint Strike Fighter?

HARRIER II: The US Marine Corps will use the JSF to replace the AV-8B Harrier II. The RAF is also a potential customer.

SEA HARRIER: The Royal Navy is hoping to purchase up to 60 JSFs to operate from its aircraft-carriers.

F-16 FIGHTING FALCON: The largest single order for JSFs will come from the USAF, which requires 2036 to replace its large F-16 fleet.

F/A-18 HORNET: Marine Corps F/A-18s and Navy A-6s and F-14s will be replaced by a conventional carrier-based form of the JSF.

LOCKHEED MARTIN (ROCKWELL)

AC-130U SPECTRE

● **Airborne gunship** ● **Special Forces** ● **Improved model**

After its successful combat debut in Vietnam, the AC-130 Spectre became the standard USAF night attack gunship. The early 'Herc' gunships were subsequently upgraded, up-gunned and, more recently, replaced by newer airframes. The ultimate model is the AC-130U, which carries fewer guns than its predecessor but, with its computer-controlled 105-mm (4.13-in.) howitzer, can bring down devastating firepower on the enemy.

▲ *Ungainly in looks, the AC-130U is extremely simple in concept. The airborne gunship looks set to remain in the front line for the future, providing fire support for ground troops.*

PHOTO FILE

LOCKHEED MARTIN (ROCKWELL) AC-130U SPECTRE

◀ **State of the art**
The AC-130 was used to develop the gunship role in Vietnam. The AC-130U is equipped with the most advanced avionics available.

Old colours ▶
Early AC-130Us wore the old-style European One colour scheme. Later models wear an overall Gunship Gray camouflage.

◀ **Test flights**
Equipped with a nose-mounted probe, the prototype AC-130U undertook a long series of developmental flights. Crews found the aircraft was ideal for the role.

▼ **Special crews**
Because of the unique requirements of AC-130U operations, only the very best Hercules crews are selected to fly the specialised aircraft.

▲ **Broadside attack**
Retained on the latest Hercules gunship variant is the positioning of the cannon and guns along the port side of the fuselage. During combat missions the AC-130U maintains a circular orbit to maximise fire accuracy.

FACTS AND FIGURES

- Rockwell was awarded a $155 million contract to develop the new C-130 gunship for the USAF.
- The first AC-130U was rolled out on 20 December 1990.
- Flight trials were conducted at Edwards AFB during 1992–93.
- Thirteen aircraft were delivered to the 16th Special Operations Squadron at Hurlburt Field, Florida, in 1995.
- The radar of the AC-130U is derived from that of the F-15E Strike Eagle.
- The calibre of the guns aboard the aircraft ranges from 25 mm (1 in.) to 105 mm (4.13 in.).

PROFILE

Prowler of the battlefield

In the Vietnam air war, one of the more important developments was that of the aerial gunship. This involved heavily armed converted transport aircraft orbiting a point and delivering deadly firepower with great precision. From its origins in the crude 'Spooky' AC-47s left over from an earlier war, 'hosing' the target with multiple Miniguns, the gunship concept has developed into a highly sophisticated combination of sensors and weapons able to bring each round to the target. The AC-130A of the Vietnam era had up to eight machine-guns. The AC-130U developed by Rockwell International has only three guns – one 25-mm (1-in.) multi-barrelled cannon, a 40-mm (1.57-in.) Bofors and a 105-mm (4.13-in.) howitzer. However, the guns can be brought to bear with greater precision – even engaging two targets at once – by the four mission computers and the extremely accurate GPS-based navigation system. For self-defence, the AC-130U is equipped with powerful jammers, together with a number of radar-warning antennas. On the underside are three combined chaff/flare launchers.Although the AC-130U has yet to prove itself in combat, the other post-Vietnam version, the AC-130H, saw action in Grenada in 1983, Panama in 1989 and over Iraq during the Gulf War. It has gained a reputation as an efficient destroyer of enemy vehicles and troops.

Left: Retained on the new model is the 'Spectre' nose art. This dates back to the earliest days of gunship operations over Vietnam.

Above: The AC-130U can be distinguished from earlier models by the lack of the distinctive nose-mounted radome.

AC-130U Spectre

Type: aerial gunship

Powerplant: four 3363-kW (4,500-hp.) Allison T56-A-15 turboprops

Cruising speed: 602 km/h (373 m.p.h.)

Initial climb rate: 597 m/min (1,960 f.p.m.)

Range: 7876 km (4,883 mi.) with maximum fuel

Service ceiling: 10,060 m (33,000 ft.)

Weights: operating weight 34,356 kg (75,583 lb.); maximum take-off 79,380 kg (174,636 lb.)

Armament: GAU-12/U 25-mm (1-in.) cannon with 3000 rounds; 40-mm (1.57-in.) Bofors cannon; 105-mm (4.13-in) howitzer

Dimensions:

span	40.41 m (132 ft. 7 in.)
length	29.79 m (97 ft. 9 in.)
height	11.66 m (38 ft. 3 in.)
wing area	162.12 m² (1,744 sq. ft.)

AC-130U HERCULES

The gunship has proved itself in Vietnam and the Gulf War. The latest development of the Hercules gunship is the AC-130U, equipped with state-of-the-art avionics.

Dramatic improvements in the survivability for the crew have been made since the first AC-130A was developed. Crews are now surrounded by Spectra ceramic armour and the fuel is carried in explosion-suppressing fuel tanks.

AC-130Us are unique among the gunship Hercules variants in that they are based on the C-130H. They thus feature the strengthened wing box and derated 3363-kW (4,500-hp.) Allison T56-15 engines.

Required to operate over hostile territory, the AC-130U is equipped with an extensive array of electronic countermeasures equipment. This includes wing-mounted ALQ-172 jammers and less sophisticated chaff/flare dispensers.

The heavy punch of the AC-130U is provided by the 105-mm (4.13-in) howitzer and the 40-mm (1.57-in) Bofors cannon. They are positioned in the rear of the fuselage. Situated opposite these guns are racks for the vast amount of ammunition required.

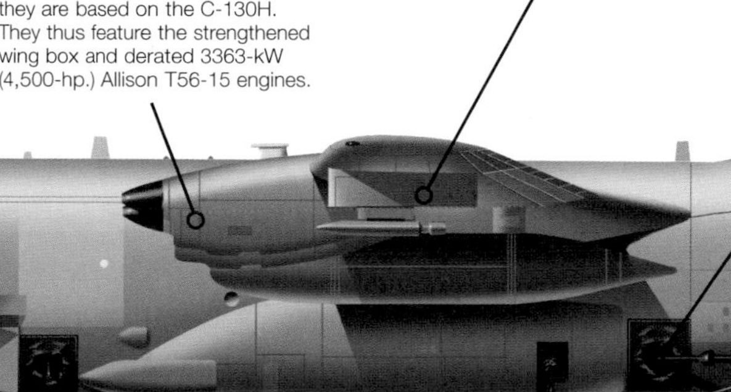

The observer's station is on the rear loading ramp. This crewman is equipped with a small clear dome from which to observe firing by the aircraft. Firing corrections can then be reported to the pilot.

GUNSHIP HISTORY

'STINGER': Having developed the concept of airborne artillery with the AC-47, the USAF looked round for a more suitable aircraft to lift the necessary equipment into the air. The result was the conversion of the large twin-boom C-119 Flying Boxcar. Emerging as the AC-119K 'Stinger' (pictured below), the aircraft was soon pressed into combat against the North Vietnamese. The 'Stinger' was highly successful in this role, although limitations of the design soon became apparent. The aircraft was extremely vulnerable to ground fire, and soon operations switched to night-time to offer some degree of protection.

'SPECTRE': Already a well proven transport aircraft, the Lockheed C-130 was soon adapted to the gunship role. Known as the AC-130A 'Spectre' (below), the design was one of the most valued aircraft in Vietnam for supporting ground forces. Equipped with Miniguns, the 'Spectre' proved to be the ideal platform for 'truck-busting' along the network of trails that the North Vietnamese used for transporting troops and materials. The 'Spectre' took part in some of the final missions of the war, and after returning to the United States remained in front-line service with the USAF Special Operations Squadrons.

Legendary Lockheed C-130s

■ AUSTRALIA: Providing the heavy lift element of Australia's air force are C-130Hs, which continue in front-line service.

■ FRANCE: Operated alongside France's C.160 Transalls, the Hercules has been used on countless French combat operations in Africa.

■ NEW ZEALAND: The C-130H has been in production for over 30 years. The first C-130H built was sold to New Zealand in 1965.

■ SAUDI ARABIA: Resplendent in an overall desert camouflage, Saudi Arabian C-130s are often used as VIP transports.

McDONNELL

F-101A/C VOODOO

● Long-range interceptor ● Reconnaissance ● Tactical nuclear strike

To pilots, the McDonnell Douglas F-101 Voodoo was a friendly monster. It was not a forgiving mount; in fact, it was one of the hardest-to-fly aircraft ever to serve in the US Air Force. But once a pilot learned its quirks, the Voodoo was an extravagant performer. Designed as a bomber escort, it became a tactical nuclear striker and an interceptor defending North America. But its greatest moments came in Southeast Asia, when reconnaissance versions flew history's fastest combat missions over North Vietnam.

▲ *Voodoo crews lived exciting lives, flying a tricky aircraft with startling performance in roles such as one-way nuclear strike sorties and high-speed reconnaissance flights at treetop height.*

PHOTO FILE

McDONNELL F-101A/C VOODOO

▲ Racing speed
When MiGs chased Voodoos in Vietnam, pilots usually selected afterburner and made a high-speed escape.

▲ More fuel
The original Voodoos used the standard USAF refuelling boom, but were unusual in having a probe for a drogue system as well.

◀ All stop
The Voodoo needed its brake chute, being fast and heavy. A field arrestor hook was also fitted for emergency landings at high speed.

◀ Escort fighter
The Voodoo was originally designed to fly long-range missions alongside nuclear bombers such as the B-47.

Flaps down ▶
The Voodoo was built to fly very fast, but its large split flaps and leading-edge flaps gave it good handling at low airspeed, even when fitted with large external fuel tanks.

FACTS AND FIGURES

- ➤ F-101A and F-101C models were designed to carry a nuclear weapon to the Soviet Union from air bases in Britain.
- ➤ A Korean War ace, Major Lonnie R. Moore, was killed in an F-101A crash.
- ➤ The RF-101C reconnaissance version was the only Voodoo to fight in Vietnam.
- ➤ The only export user of the Voodoo was Canada, which operated two batches of around 60 F-101B interceptors.
- ➤ In all, 480 two-seaters, known as TF-101B and F-101F, served as interceptors.
- ➤ Two-seat Voodoos in USAF service could carry the Genie nuclear air-to-air missile.

PROFILE

McDonnell's monster fighter

The Voodoo was possibly the first warplane to exceed supersonic speed on its first flight (on 29 September 1954), but it never became easy to fly. Tucking in the Voodoo's nosewheel was a challenge and the aircraft had a tendency to 'pitch up', for which various cures were attempted, never with success. It killed test pilots and challenged service pilots. It remained totally unforgiving throughout – but when used properly it was a world-beater.

Development of the F-101 Voodoo was drawn out because of its teething troubles, but its service career was also surprisingly long (1956–1987).

Daylight reconnaissance missions over Hanoi by the RF-101C routinely exceeded Mach 1.8, faster than any other aircraft has ever flown under fire. The two-seat F-101B interceptor, in both American and Canadian hands, was one of the most complex warplanes ever fielded, and was deemed a nightmare by mechanics – but it was able to intercept bombers thousands of kilometres from their targets.

The sleek shape of the F-101 was very close to the shape of the original XF-88 fighter design on which it was based. As with many designs of the 1950s, gains in performance were made at the cost of difficult handling.

The plan view is of a reconnaissance Voodoo, which differs from the fighter primarily in having a camera nose rather than radar.

Voodoos were usually either all-metal in colour or finished in grey, but the reconnaissance machines in Vietnam received a brown and green jungle paint scheme.

The wing was fitted with 'fences'. These reduced induced drag by limiting the outward flow of air over the upper surface.

F-101A Voodoo

Designed as escort fighters, Voodoos were quickly adapted to a new role as tactical nuclear bombers. This example served with the 81st Tactical Fighter Wing based in Suffolk in the late 1950s.

F-101As and Cs were equipped with a Hughes fire-control system, which linked a primitive computer to the radar system.

The Voodoo housed most of its fuel internally, in nine tanks running along the spine of the aircraft from behind the cockpit to the fin. Total capacity was 8123 litres (2,146 US gal).

Due to the wing-mounted intakes and the unusual fuselage shape, the Voodoo's main wing spar was not continuous; it divided around the intake ducts.

The airbrakes were mounted on the upper rear fuselage sides, just above the tailpipes. Single-seat Voodoos were powered by the J57-P-55 engine, and the afterburner nozzles were much shorter.

F-101 fighter variants carried three M39 20-mm (0.79-in) cannon, two on the port side and one on the starboard side of the fuselage.

The J57 engine was a very powerful one for its day. It was not without its problems initially, being prone to compressor stalls.

The high-set tail was the main cause of the Voodoo's unpleasant tendency to pitch up unexpectedly. The tailplane was an all-moving unit, with a VHF antenna on top of the fin.

F-101A Voodoo

Type: single-seat tactical fighter bomber

Powerplant: two Pratt & Whitney J57-P-13 turbojets each rated at 66.20 kN (14,889 lb thrust) with maximum afterburner

Maximum speed: Mach 1.9 or 1982 km/h (1,232 mph) at 10,000 m (32,808 ft)

Range: 3040 km (1,889 miles)

Service ceiling: 15,850 m (52,000 ft)

Weights: empty 11,617 kg (25,611 lb); loaded 23,135 kg (51,004 lb)

Armament: four 20-mm (0.79-in) cannon, 3050 kg (6,724 lb) of bombs, including tactical nuclear weapons

Dimensions:

span	12.09 m (39 ft 8 in)
length	20.54 m (67 ft 5 in)
height	5.48 m (18 ft)
wing area	34.19 m² (368 sq ft)

COMBAT DATA

MAXIMUM SPEED

F-101A VOODOO	1982 km/h (1,232 mph)
HUNTER	1144 km/h (711 mph)
MiG-21 'FISHBED'	2125 km/h (1,320 mph)

The Voodoo was one of the fastest fighters of its time, and considerably quicker than the contemporary British Hunter. The MiG-21 appeared several years later, and although faster at altitude it still could not match the sheer brute power of the Voodoo at low level.

RANGE

The Voodoo was a very big fighter, and could carry a large amount of fuel. This meant that it had a very long range, and it was therefore ideally suited to long-range missions; Voodoos based in Britain during the Cold War were tasked with low-level nuclear strike, and were expected to destroy targets deep into Eastern Europe.

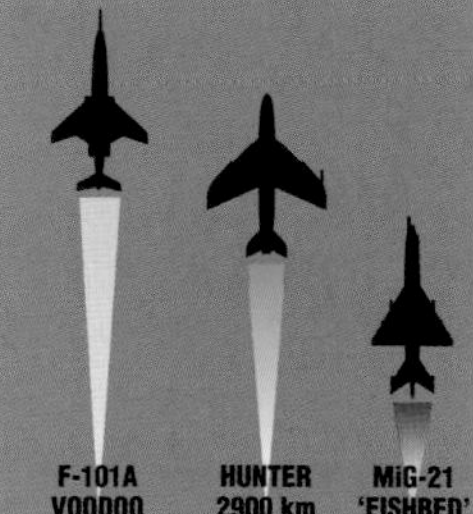

WARLOAD

F-101A VOODOO	HUNTER	MiG-21 'FISHBED'
3050 kg (6,724 lb)	1000 kg (2,205 lb)	1500 kg (3,307 lb)

The Voodoo carried a considerable bombload for a single-seat fighter of the 1950s. Its primary ground-attack mission called for the accurate delivery of large tactical nuclear weapons, but it could also deliver a wide variety of conventional weapons.

Voodoo 'over the shoulder' nuclear strike

1 HIGH-SPEED APPROACH: Armed with a Mk 7 nuclear bomb, the Voodoo's attack profile called for the approach to the target to be made at high speed and low level.

2 WEAPONS RELEASE: Approaching the target, the fighter pulls up into the first half of a loop, releasing the weapon in a climb of about 45° for maximum range.

3 BOMB FLIGHT: The bomb follows a high ballistic arc. It is not a very accurate delivery method, but is precise enough to hit a large target such as a railway junction or airfield, especially when using a nuclear weapon.

4 ESCAPE: At the top of the loop, the fighter rolls and dives away at full speed to get clear of the titanic blast effects when the nuclear weapon detonates.

McDONNELL DOUGLAS A-4 SKYHAWK

● Carrier-borne and land-based attack ● Defence suppression

▲ Close support missions over Vietnam were fraught with risk. Many Skyhawks returned to their carrier or base with damage sustained during a tangle with Communist anti-aircraft defences.

Skyhawk pilots in Vietnam went into battle relying on their ability and on their lightweight, nimble attack aircraft. The enemy waited, equipped with missiles, MiGs and thousands of anti-aircraft guns. The challenge for the Skyhawk pilot was to take off from a carrier deck or shore base, fly into hostile territory and attack a heavily defended target in North Vietnam. Navy and Marine Corps A-4s were among the most important attack aircraft of the war.

PHOTO FILE

McDONNELL DOUGLAS A-4 SKYHAWK

◀ With the Corps at Chu Lai
US Marine Corps A-4s flew close support missions from shore bases. A ground catapult system called SATS was used at Chu Lai.

▼ Heading back to the carrier
An A-4F of VA-144 'Roadrunners' returns to the USS Bonne Homme Richard. *Heavy losses were sustained over North Vietnam.*

▼ In action throughout Vietnam War
Although A-4s were replaced in carrier-based attack units from 1967, they continued to operate from small 'Essex'-class carriers.

▼ Iron Hand – the anti-radiation mission
Carrying a pair of AGM-45 Shrike anti-radiation missiles and a bomb, this A-4F, distinguished by its dorsal avionics hump, prepares for a 'cat shot'. Flak and surface-to-air missile suppression missions were among the most dangerous of those performed by A-4s.

◀ 20-mm cannon
An armourer replenishes a Skyhawk's Colt cannon ammunition. Cannon were effective for ground-attack strafing, but enemy SAMs soon made low-level missions too risky.

FACTS AND FIGURES

- ➤ An A-4 pilot killed while attacking missile sites was one of only two naval aviators awarded the Medal of Honor in Vietnam.
- ➤ 'Heinemann's Hot Rod' and 'Scooter' are just two of the A-4's many nicknames.
- ➤ The first A-4 entered US Navy service in 1955; action in Vietnam began in 1964.
- ➤ The Skyhawk was replaced by the Vought A-7 Corsair II as the US Navy's standard attack aircraft.
- ➤ Just before the Vietnam War, the US Army evaluated the A-4 for close air support.
- ➤ The Marine Corps used a few two-seat Skyhawks for combat observation duties.

PROFILE

'Scooters' over Indo-China

Edward Heinemann, Douglas's chief designer, wanted to produce a formidable warplane small enough to fit on an aircraft-carrier deck without having to fold its wings.

The A-4 Skyhawk was designed for a nuclear mission. Originally, it was intended to carry a single atomic bomb on a centreline rack beneath the fuselage, but the Navy and Marine Corps always saw the type with an additional role as a conventional bomber.

From the start of its flight test programme in the early 1950s, the A-4 carried a variety of conventional bombs, rockets and missiles. When the United States launched its first air strike against North Vietnam in August 1964, the 'Scooter' was there.

In the years that followed, A-4s flew from US Navy carriers and land bases (with the Navy and Marines) to support troops in South Vietnam and to hit targets in the North. Attacks were of two types: major strikes on predetermined targets, involving aircraft from more than one unit, and interdiction missions by small numbers of aircraft attacking targets of opportunity. Among the most risky roles was defence suppression, using cluster bombs and ARMs.

Although the A-4 was an air-to-surface machine, air-to-air encounters were not unheard of. One Skyhawk even shot down a MiG-17 with a Zuni air-to-ground rocket barrage.

After low-level attacks proved too risky, Communist targets were approached at high speed from high altitude, and bombed in shallow diving attacks.

Centreline and wing fuel tanks were often carried on A-4 missions, thereby reducing warload. In-flight refuelling was also possible via the nose-mounted air-to-air probe.

Essentially a 'cropped delta', the A-4's wing span was just 8.38 m (27 ft 6 in). This meant that a folding wing was not required for storage aboard an aircraft-carrier.

A-4E Skyhawk

Type: single-seat attack aircraft

Powerplant: one 41.37-kN (9,305-lb-thrust) Pratt & Whitney J52-P-8A turbojet engine

Maximum speed: 1083 km/h (673 mph) at sea level

Combat radius: 612 km (380 miles)

Range: 1480 km (920 miles)

Service ceiling: 11,400 m (37,402 ft)

Weights: empty 4581 kg (10,099 lb); maximum take-off 12,437 kg (27,419 lb)

Armament: two 20-mm (0.79-in) Mk 12 cannon, each with 200 (later 400) rounds, provision for up to four LAU-10A rocket pods containing Zuni air-to-ground projectiles; up to four Martin Marietta AGM-12A Bullpup-A air-to-surface guided missiles or up to 4491 kg (9,900 lb) of bombs

Dimensions:

span	8.38 m (27 ft 6 in)
fuselage length	12.29 m (40 ft 4 in)
height	4.57 m (15 ft)
wing area	24.16 m² (260 sq ft)

A-4E Skyhawk

BuNo. 149993 served with Attack Squadron 72 (VA-72) 'Blue Hawks' aboard the USS *Independence* in the South China Sea in May 1965. VA-72 was the first US Navy unit to operate Skyhawks, receiving A4D-1s in 1956.

The A-4E was the first Skyhawk variant optimized for air support and conventional bombing rather than the nuclear mission. New equipment included tactical air navigation (TACAN), Doppler navigation, a radio altimeter and new toss-bombing and low-altitude bombing systems.

Originally intended for the cancelled A4D-3 all-weather variant, the Pratt & Whitney J52 turbojet made its debut in the A-4E (designated A4D-5 during development). Its lower fuel consumption increased range by 27 per cent.

For a 'cat shot' from a carrier, the Skyhawk was connected to the catapult shuttle by cables attached to the main undercarriage. For Marine Corps land-based operations the Short Airfield Tactical Support (SATS) was used. This consisted of a 674-m (2,211-ft) (aluminium runway and required rocket-assisted take-offs (RATOs) plus arresting gear for landings.

This aircraft carries three 227-kg (500-lb) Mk 82 Snakeye high-drag bombs. The A-4 was able to carry a variety of weapons, up to a load capacity of around 4500 kg (9,920 lb). Two additional hardpoints were fitted on the A-4E and the aircraft's structure was strengthened to a catapult gross weight of 11,113 kg (25,000 lb).

COMBAT DATA

MAXIMUM SPEED AT SEA LEVEL

Although slower than the Skyhawk, the Vought A-7 had a considerably greater weapons load. Both the USAF and Navy operated the type in Vietnam. The twin-engined, two-seat Intruder was marginally quicker and a much more sophisticated aircraft.

Aircraft	Speed
A-4E SKYHAWK	1083 km/h (673 mph)
A-7D	1065 km/h (662 mph)
A-6A INTRUDER	1102 km/h (685 mph)

CLIMB RATE

Land-based A-7s and Intruders had a much better initial climb rate than the Skyhawk. Carrier-based aircraft are hampered by their limited launch speeds, which greatly restrict climb rate.

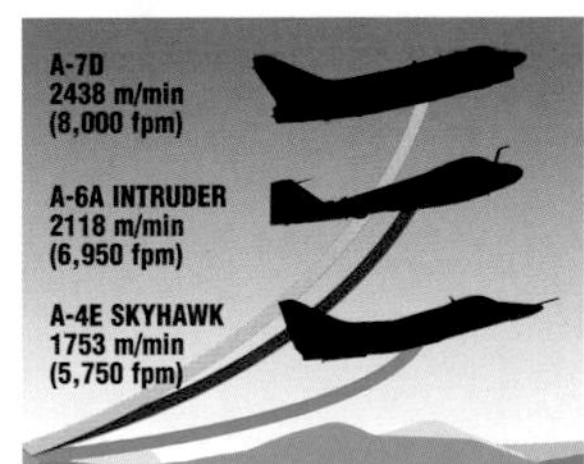

ARMAMENT

Operating from land bases, the A-7D was able to lift a much larger load than the A-4. This load-carrying capacity also impressed the Navy, which adopted the type from the late 1960s. The larger Grumman Intruder carried a correspondingly large weapon load.

A-4E SKYHAWK	3700-kg (8,157-lb) bombload; 2 x 20-mm (0.79-in) cannon
A-7D	6804-kg (15,000-lb) bombload; 1 x 20-mm (0.79-in) cannon
A-6A INTRUDER	6804-kg (15,000-lb) bombload

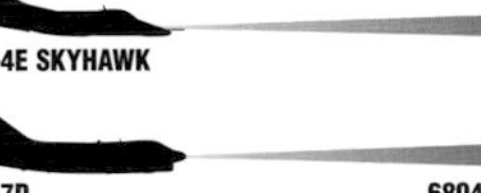

Skyhawks over 'Nam

MARINE CORPS 'SCOOTERS': USMC Skyhawks used the Short Airfield Tactical Support RATO take-off/arrested recovery system, which allowed them to operate from cramped airstrips such as Chu Lai.

OVER THE NORTH: Having taken off on a strike mission, A-4s often teamed up with an aircraft such as the A-6 Intruder pathfinder, and utilized its sophisticated navigation equipment to find the target.

HIGH-LEVEL APPROACH: After the flak SA-2 surface-to-air missile (SAM) threat had resulted in high losses during low-level 'pop-up' attacks, A-4 missions were made using a shallow high-speed pass following a high-speed, high-altitude approach.

McDonnell Douglas

A-4 Skyhawk II

● **Light attack** ● **1950s design** ● **Upgraded for the 21st century**

Originally called the A4D, the Douglas A-4 Skyhawk was conceived in the 1950s to carry an atomic weapon on a one-way mission if a third world war was declared. In practice, the Skyhawk provided the US Navy and Marines with an impressive, conventional light-attack aircraft for the next 20 years. The improved A-4M Skyhawk II flew in 1970 and more recently several nations have updated their early-model A-4s with new engines, avionics and weapons.

▲ *While no two-seat Skyhawk IIs were built, a number of early-model two-seaters have been included in the upgrade programmes carried out by the Malaysian and New Zealand air forces. The US Marine Corps also rebuilt a number of TA-4Fs to OA-4M standard for forward air control duties.*

PHOTO FILE

McDonnell Douglas A-4 Skyhawk II

▼ AGM-12 Bullpup
The main air-to-surface missile carried by Skyhawks before recent upgrades was the Bullpup.

▲ Singaporean two-seater
The Royal Singaporean Air Force TA-4S is a rebuilt A-4B and is unique in having two cockpits each with a separate canopy.

▲ Skyhawk II for the Marines
Entering service in the mid-1970s, the A-4M operated until about 1994 mainly in the close air support role. This example is firing an unguided Zuni rocket during exercises.

▲ From 'dumb bombs' to LGBs
The refurbished A-4s are able to deliver laser-guided bombs and missiles and later versions of heat-seeking air-to-air missiles like the Sidewinder.

Combat in the Gulf ▶
Twenty Kuwaiti A-4KUs escaped to Bahrain during the 1991 Iraqi invasion and later flew daylight attack missions from Dhahran, Saudi Arabia. Kuwait also has one two-seat TA-4KU remaining in service.

FACTS AND FIGURES

- New Zealand's A-4Ks contain the APG-66 radar, as fitted to the F-16, in the nose to improve capability.
- Designed by Ed Heinemann, the A-4 has been nicknamed 'Heinemann's Hot Rod'.
- On their first Gulf War mission, Kuwaiti A-4s mistakenly bombed Saudi Arabia.
- F404 turbofans fitted to Singapore's A-4s are heavier than the J52 but are more fuel efficient and cheaper to maintain.
- Pave Penny laser designators, used on USAF A-10s, may be fitted to RSAF A-4s.
- American companies Lockheed and Grumman have updated foreign A-4s.

PROFILE

Bantam bomber reborn

The A-4 Skyhawk became a classic of US naval aviation, but it began as an extraordinary design. Douglas' famous designer Ed Heinemann created the Skyhawk at half of the specified weight. When the 'bantam bomber' was ordered in 1952 it was remarkably light,but nothing had been stripped from the design or omitted. The Skyhawk was easy to fly and an effective attack aircraft, and because of its small size it did not require folding wings for use aboard carriers.

In Vietnam, Skyhawks performed traditional bombing raids and 'Iron Hand' missions against North Vietnamese surface-to-air missile sites.

Intended for production from 1954 until 1957, the Skyhawk was produced for a further 26 years in many variants. Significant numbers were exported, some operating from land bases. More recently, retired ex-Navy aircraft have been refurbished and sold overseas. Malaysia and Singapore operate updated former USN machines, while New Zealand's upgraded A-4s were delivered new in the 1970s.

Above: Malaysia bought 88 ex-US Navy A-4s in 1979, but abandoned a major upgrade. Grumman refurbished 40 examples which now carry Maverick and Sidewinder missiles.

Below: With the GE F404 fitted to Singapore's A-4S aircraft, Skyhawks have used three types of engine, including the Wright J65 fitted in very early marks and the Pratt &Whitney J52 in versions after the A-4E.

A-4S-1 Super Skyhawk

Type: single-seat attack aircraft

Powerplant: one 48.04-kN (10,800-lb. thrust) General Electric F404-GE-100D non-afterburning turbofan

Maximum speed: 1128 km/h (701 m.p.h.) at sea level

Initial climb rate: 3326 m/min (10,912 f.p.m.)

Range: 1158 km (720 mi.) with max. ordnance

Service ceiling: 12,190 m (40,000 ft.)

Weights: empty 4649 kg (10,249 lb.); maximum take-off 10,206 kg (22,500 lb.)

Armament: two Mk 12 20-mm cannon, plus external ordnance

Dimensions:		
	span	8.38 m (27 ft. 6 in.)
	length	12.72 m (14 ft. 9 in.)
	height	4.57 m (15 ft. 4 in.)
	wing area	24.14 m² (260 sq. ft.)

A-4M SKYHAWK II

US Marine Corps Attack Squadron 324 operated the first production A-4M Skyhawk IIs from 1971. By 1976 five USMC squadrons used the variant.

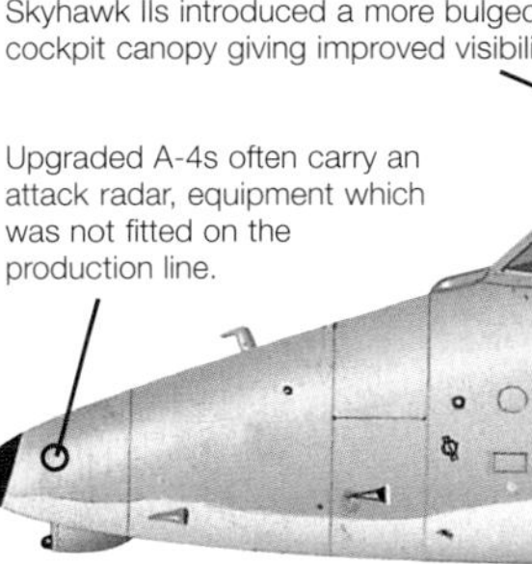

Skyhawk IIs introduced a more bulged cockpit canopy giving improved visibility.

Upgraded A-4s often carry an attack radar, equipment which was not fitted on the production line.

Intended to hold avionics, 'humps' were fitted to early versions of the Skyhawk, starting with the A-4F of 1966. Some upgraded A-4s have had these removed.

This A-4M carries the high-visibility markings common to US Navy and Marine aircraft in the 1970s. Today 'low-viz' colour schemes are more usual.

Skyhawk IIs have a later version of the Pratt & Whitney J52 turbojet engine. Singapore's 'Super Skyhawks' use a non-afterburning variant of the F-18's General Electric F404 turbofan.

Marine Corps aircraft generally carry a two-letter unit tailcode and the last four digits of the aircraft's 'BuNo', or serial number.

Two 20-mm Mk 12 cannon were fitted to the A-4M. Singaporean A-4S aircraft have been equipped with two 30-mm ADEN cannon, as carried by the SEPECAT Jaguar and the BAe Sea Harrier.

In its day the Skyhawk could carry a substantial weapons load. While this is modest by modern standards, upgraded A-4s can deliver much more up-to-date and effective weapons than before.

COMBAT DATA

MAXIMUM SPEED

The twin-engined A-5 is a relatively fast aircraft compared to the Skyhawk. The straight-winged A-10 was designed for low-speed close air support missions over a battlefield.

A-4M SKYHAWK II	1006 km/h (625 m.p.h.)
A-5 'FANTAN'	1190 km/h (739 m.p.h.)
A-10A	682 km/h (424 m.p.h.)

COMBAT RADIUS

The A-10's longer range is used to give it extended loiter time over a battlefield. The range of both the A-4 and A-10 can be extended by using air-to-air refuelling, unlike the A-5.

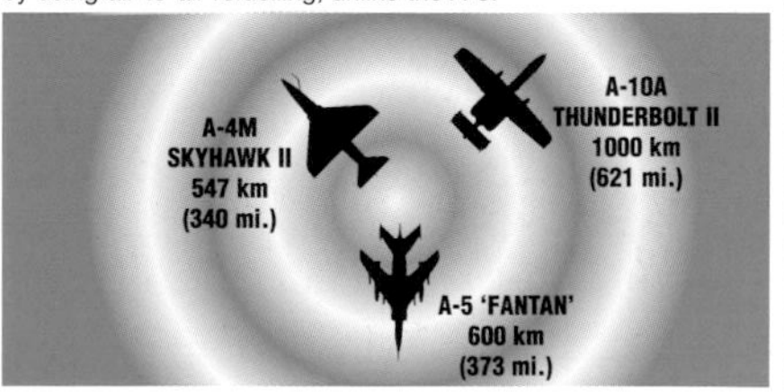

BOMBLOAD

The design of the A-5 was based on that of a lightweight fighter, and therefore could not carry as much ordnance as the A-4 and A-10 which were designed from the outset as attack aircraft.

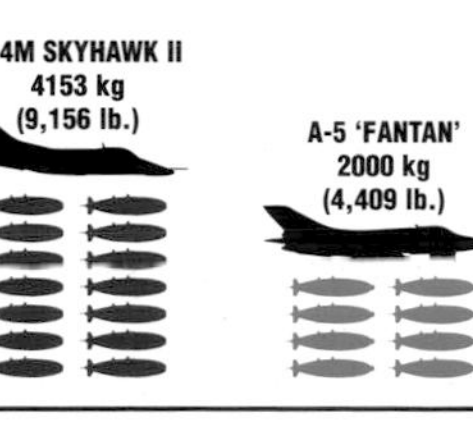

Fighter upgrade projects

■ F-5E TIGER IV: With the equipment installed in the Tiger IV, Northrop hopes to capture some of the market for updated F-5s.

■ MIRAGE 50CN PANTERA: Chile's Mirage 50Cs are being rebuilt with canards and new avionics with help from Israel Aircraft Industries.

■ F-4E KURNASS 2000: Originally intended to include new engines, this Israeli project is now restricted to an avionics and airframe upgrade.

■ MIG-21-2000: First flown in May 1995, the Israel Aircraft Industries MiG-21-2000 has a comprehensive Western avionics fit.

McDONNELL DOUGLAS

C-9 NIGHTINGALE

● VIP carrier ● Airborne ambulance ● Civilian design

After its successful introduction into the civil airline market during the mid-1960s, the McDonnell Douglas DC-9 was selected by the USAF in 1967 as its dedicated aeromedical evacuation aircraft. Experience in Vietnam showed just how vital such an aircraft was in modern war theatres. Ordering such an aircraft 'off-the-shelf' kept costs low, and the enduring nature of the type has ensured that it remains in service more than 30 years later.

▲ *Essentially based on the commercial DC-9 Series 30, the C-9A Nightingale has given sterling service to the USAF, yet it is often overshadowed by more glamorous aircraft.*

PHOTO FILE

McDONNELL DOUGLAS C-9 NIGHTINGALE

▼ Cargo carrier
When operated by the US Navy, the type is known as the C-9B Skytrain II. For this role it is equipped with a large cargo door.

▲ International rescue
With a large Red Cross on its tail, a C-9 Nightingale lands at the scene of another disaster.

Naval reserve ▶
After a review of its transport assets, the US Navy turned over its fleet of Skytrain IIs to the naval reserve. In time of war, however, the aircraft would be deployed to front-line naval bases.

◀ Angel in the air
The US Navy has operated the C-9B Skytrain II since the early seventies. The aircraft required minor modifications for military service but retained the grace of its civilian counterparts.

Great white bird ▶
Throughout their entire service life the aircraft have retained a smart white and grey colour scheme. This has proved to be very appropriate for missions involving high-ranking personnel or government figures.

FACTS AND FIGURES

- ➤ C-9A Nightingales flew home the American hostages released from Iran in 1981.
- ➤ One C-9A Nightingale is configured as a VIP transport within Europe.
- ➤ Flight crew consists of two pilots with a crew chief or loadmaster.
- ➤ On aeromedical missions, the C-9A Nightingale can accommodate 40 stretcher patients or 40 seated patients.
- ➤ One C-9A was lost in a mishap at Scott Field on 16 September 1971.
- ➤ In March 1981 C-9Bs replaced the long-serving C-118B Liftmaster in the USN.

PROFILE

America's airborne saviour

From Vietnam to the Gulf War, the C-9A Nightingale has become indispensable in support of front-line US troops. Up to 40 stretcher cases or 40 walking wounded can be accommodated along with trained medical staff on these vital evacuation flights.

Based on the DC-9 Series 30, the Nightingale entered service in June 1968. Modifications to the standard airliner included a new access door with an in-built hydraulic ramp for the loading of stretchers, and a specialist medical care compartment.

The USAF also received three C-9C VIP transport versions.

The success of the DC-9 in military service was soon appreciated by the US Navy which ordered the C-9B Skytrain II in an effort to modernise its small but important logistics support service. First entering service in 1972, a dozen aircraft were acquired along with two for the US Marine Corps. Also based on the Series 30, the C-9B features additional fuel capacity for extended range and can operate in all-cargo, all-passenger or mixed configuration. The aircraft were deployed to Saudi Arabia during the Gulf War.

Other military users include Kuwait and Italy which operate two examples on light transport and VIP duties.

Above: Operated on behalf of the special air missions airlift wing, this particular Nightingale is used as a personal VIP transport. The aircraft is especially configured for the role.

Above: Taxiing to the main runway, this C-9B Skytrain II operates with the US Navy on support duties. This example is capable of airlifting 107 naval personnel.

C-9A Nightingale

Type: transport/medical evacuation aircraft

Powerplant: two 64.5-kN (14,500-lb.-thrust) Pratt & Whitney JT8D-9 turbofan engines

Maximum cruising speed: 907 km/h (562 m.p.h.) at 7620 m (25,000 ft.)

Initial climb rate: 885 m/min (2,900 f.p.m.)

Range: ferry range 3327 km (2,060 mi.); range with full accommodation 2388 km (1,480 mi.)

Weights: empty 25,940 kg (57,068 lb.); maximum take-off 54,885 kg (120,747 lb.)

Accommodation: four crew; 30 to 40 stretcher patients with medical attendants

Dimensions:

span	28.47 m (93 ft. 5 in.)
length	36.37 m (119 ft. 3 in.)
height	8.38 m (27 ft. 6 in.)
wing area	92.97 m² (1,000 sq. ft.)

C-9B Skytrain II

Though not as glamorous as the fighters operated by the US Navy, the C-9B Skytrain II has proved to be the ideal aircraft for transporting personnel and cargo to various naval bases throughout the world.

A flight deck crew of three is used for standard operations. Positioned on the port side of the nose is a set of hydraulically-operated self-contained airstairs. Often flown by reserve crews, who are full-time commercial airline pilots, the aircraft has proved itself to be a highly versatile transport asset for the USN.

Despite being in military service, the C-9B Skytrain II retains a smart civil-looking colour scheme. Although it rarely enters a combat zone, the aircraft is equipped with an infra-red jammer on the tail. This reduces the risk of attack by missiles.

To allow the C-9B to undertake cargo operations the aircraft is equipped with a large cargo door. This is hydraulically raised to ease loading and is operated from within the cockpit.

With room for 107 passengers, sufficient safety equipment is of vital importance. For ditching at sea, the aircraft is equipped with four 25-man life rafts located at various positions along the fuselage.

The fuselage area of the C-9B Skytrain II can contain up to eight standard military freight pallets when in all-cargo configuration. For these operations the aircraft is fitted with a specially adapted cargo roller floor to reduce the loading and unloading times.

UNITED STATES NAVY
JK
9119

ACTION DATA

MAXIMUM SPEED

With the need to reach an emergency situation in the shortest period of time, the speed of the C-9A Nightingale is high compared to that of its contemporaries. Fastest of all the current military airliners is the CT-43A

C-9A NIGHTINGALE	907 km/h (562 m.p.h.)
Tu-134 'CRUSTY'	900 km/h (558 m.p.h.)
CT-43A	927 km/h (575 m.p.h.)

RANGE

Although equipped with additional fuel tanks to extend its range, the C-9 Nightingale still has a relatively short endurance. The Russian Tu-134 'Crusty' offers only a slightly increased range. Although its lack of range is a problem, the C-9 operates in concert with longer-range C-141s.

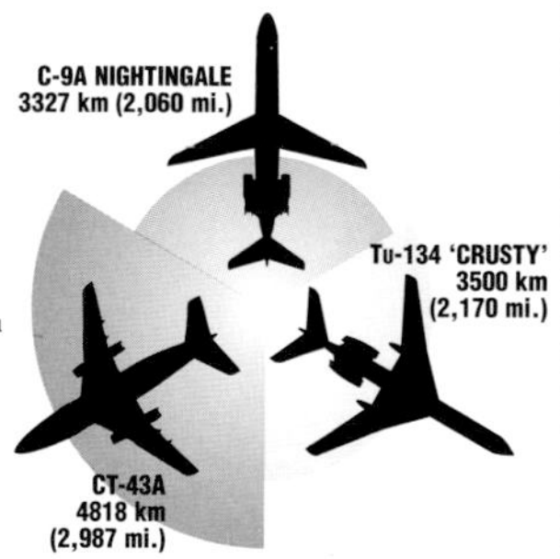

SERVICE CEILING

Designed originally for the civil airliner market, the C-9 Nightingale has retained its ability to operate at high altitudes. When operating with a full load of casualties its performance is significantly reduced, however. The highest performer is the Tu-134 'Crusty'.

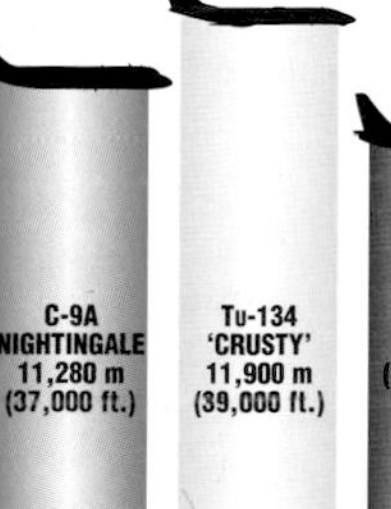

Airliners in military service

■ BOEING E-4B: Adapted from the Boeing 747 Jumbo, the military E-4B is used as an Advanced Airborne Command Post. The aircraft is equipped with highly sophisticated communications equipment. Four aircraft are currently in service.

■ BOEING KC-135A: Operated both as an airborne tanker and transport aircraft, the KC-135 has served with the USAF since the 1960s. Current upgrades of the aircraft involve the adoption of more fuel-efficient engines.

■ DOUGLAS EC-24A: Serving with the US Navy as an Electronic Warfare Support aircraft, the EC-24A is used against naval vessels to assess their ability to defend themselves against attack during military exercises.

McDonnell Douglas

C-17 Globemaster III

● Modern airlifter ● Next-generation technology ● Service proven

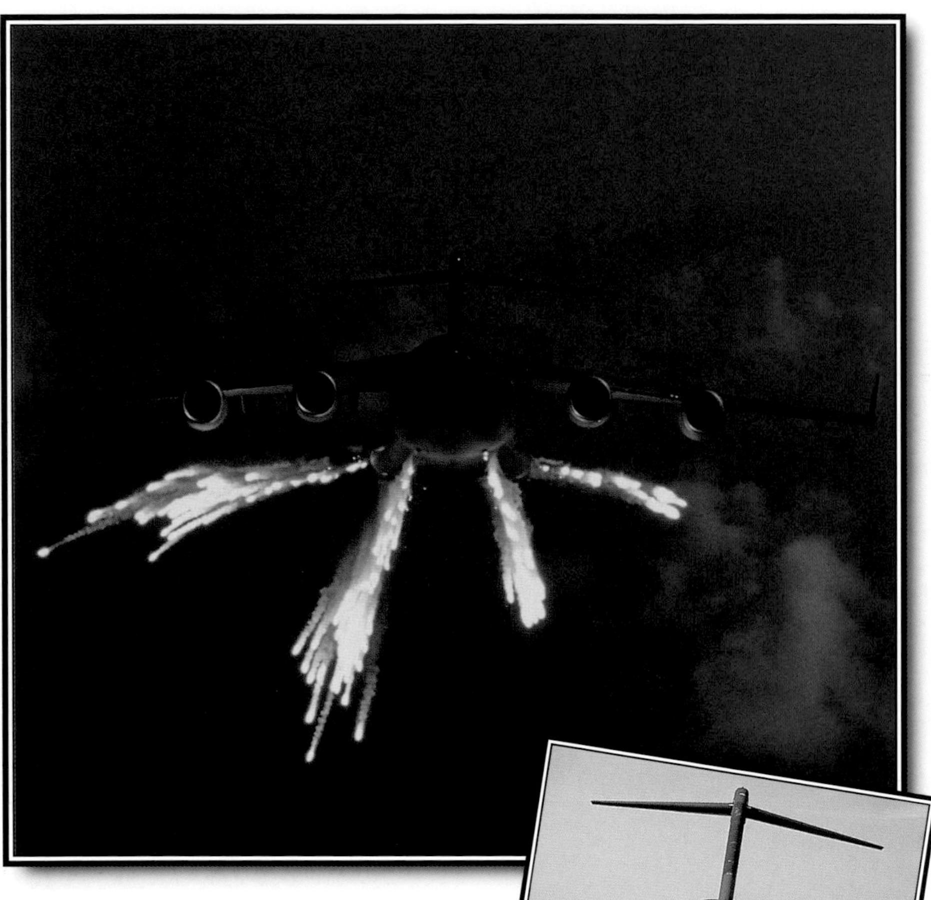

▲ Providing relief to crisis-hit regions and delivering military supplies around the world, the C-17 is said by pilots to handle more like a fighter than an airlifter in spite of its large size.

At first glance the C-17 could be mistaken as a run-of-the-mill transport, but those who have been inside the Globemaster III never forget it. This four-turbofan, hi-tech aircraft's interior is like a giant cavern. The C-17 can carry huge cargoes and can be 'turned around' quickly thanks to its 'roll-on, roll-off' capability. This is achieved by locating the ramp near ground level and using a palletised system with floor-mounted rollers for rapid loading.

PHOTO FILE

McDonnell Douglas C-17 Globemaster III

◀ **Squadron service**
Lockheed C-141B Starlifters began to make way for the Globemaster III at Charleston AFB in June 1993. The 17th Airlift Squadron was the first unit to receive production aircraft.

▼ **Fighter or freighter?**
For the first time on a transport aircraft, the C-17 introduced twin, fighter-style, head-up display units for the two flight crew.

▲ **Always ready**
The C-17, carrying heavy and bulky loads, can be rapidly deployed to unprepared airstrips, by night and day, and in all weathers.

▲ **Global reach**
Air-to-air refuelling, which allows worldwide transport missions, is vital for any airlifter.

▼ **Armoured mobility**
One of the C-17's load requirements was the ability to accommodate large armoured vehicles, such as this 28,349-kg (62,368-lb.) payload of an M110A2 self-propelled Howitzer and support vehicles.

FACTS AND FIGURES

- ➤ In honour of the Douglas C-74 and C-124, the Globemaster III name was given to the C-17 in February 1993.
- ➤ The USAF is aiming for 140 C-17s, 70 of which have currently received funding.
- ➤ The C-17 is the world's third most expensive aircraft, after the B-2 and E-3.
- ➤ The C-17's fin contains a tunnel which enables a crewmember to climb up inside for stabiliser maintenance.
- ➤ In 1993 C-17s flew their first operational mission from the US to Kenya.
- ➤ The C-17 prototype completed its first flight on 15 September 1991.

PROFILE

Transport for the 21st century

Combining long range, a capacity to carry heavy cargoes and the capability to land near the front line, the C-17 Globemaster III is the world's newest military transport. The high-wing aircraft is able to carry almost any cargo and it bears a slight resemblance to the airlifter it is replacing, the C-141 Starlifter. The C-17 boasts an ergonomic flightdeck (that is, one optimised for pilot comfort) with digital displays. The C-17's two pilots sit side-by-side and the plane is flown with a control stick instead of the yoke which is traditionally used on transport aircraft. The wing is swept at 25° and has winglets for fuel efficiency. The wing accounts for almost one-third of the aircraft's structural weight.

This fine aircraft is only just beginning to prove its global airlifting abilities. It is the hi-tech hauler of the future, and the USAF expects to establish a fleet of more than a hundred aircraft.

Left: A parachute fixed to a freight pallet drags cargo from the C-17's cabin as the Low-Altitude Parachute Extraction System (LAPES) is used.

Above: All aircraft likely to be deployed anywhere in the world must be able to operate in extreme conditions. This C-17 is undergoing cold weather trials.

C-17A Globemaster III

Type: long-range transport

Powerplant: four 185.49-kN (41,730-lb.-thrust) Pratt & Whitney F117-PW-100 turbofan engines

Maximum cruising speed: 648 km/h (402 m.p.h.) at low altitude

Ferry range: 8710 km (5,400 mi.)

Service ceiling: 13,715 m (45,000 ft.)

Weights: empty 122,016 kg (268,435 lb.); maximum take-off 263,083 kg (578,783 lb.)

Accommodation: two pilots, one loadmaster and up to 102 troops/paratroops in stowable seats or 48 stretchers with attendants, or up to 76,658 kg (169,000 lb.) of cargo including an M1 Abrams main battle tank

Dimensions:		
	span	50.29 m (164 ft. 11 in.)
	length	53.04 m (174 ft.)
	height	16.79 m (55 ft. 1 in.)
	wing area	353.02 m² (3,798 sq. ft.)

The C-17 carries a large amount of internal fuel. Six wing tanks are positioned between the main spars and fill almost the entire wing span, giving a capacity of 102,614 litres (27,110 gal.).

A front view of the C-17A shows how close to the wing the engines are positioned. This is a result of the complex propulsive-lift technology used to give the aircraft its short take-off and landing (STOL) capability.

Four F117-PW-100 turbofan engines give outstanding fuel economy and a combined maximum thrust of 742 kN (1662,920 lb. thrust). The engine is based on the PW2040 turbofan, which powers many Boeing 757s and has already achieved in excess of six-million flying hours in regular service.

C-17A Globemaster III

This C-17A is the first production aircraft and was used for tests at Edwards AFB. It was successfully tested at 100 per cent loading before its first flight and was subsequently used for in-flight load tests.

A flight crew of two fly the C-17A. Two extra seats are provided at the rear of the flightdeck to accommodate a relief aircrew on long flights.

Only one loadmaster is required to supervise and handle the C-17A's large payload, using an internal cargo handling system to load up to 18 standard 463L cargo pallets.

Each main undercarriage unit has six wheels and, when retracted, is accommodated in a fairing against the lower fuselage.

In common with many long-range airliners, the C-17A is fitted with winglets. These provide greater range and improved cruising characteristics.

When retracted, the rear loading ramp is able to carry heavy cargo, including two 463L pallets for air-dropping.

A quadruple-redundant fly-by-wire system operates the C-17A's 29 control surfaces. As well as the complex wing systems, these include the twin rudders, tailplanes and four elevators.

ACTION DATA

MAXIMUM PAYLOAD

Compared to other similarly sized four-jet transports, and particularly the C-141B which the C-17A is partly replacing, the Globemaster III offers exceptional payload capabilities.

C-17A GLOBEMASTER III 76,658 kg (169,000 lb.)

C-141B STARLIFTER 41,222 kg (90,688 lb.)

Il-76M 'CANDID-B' 40,000 kg (88,000 lb.)

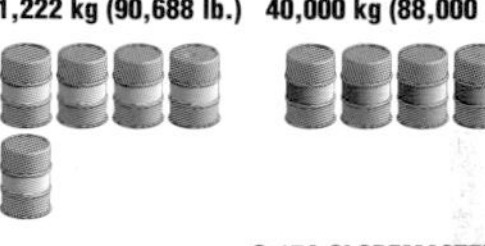

RANGE

McDonnell Douglas' C-17A has only slightly better range than that of the Il-76M, but the American aircraft achieves this figure with almost twice the payload. Air-to-air refuelling is an important part of the C-17A capability and is also available to extend the range of the C-141B.

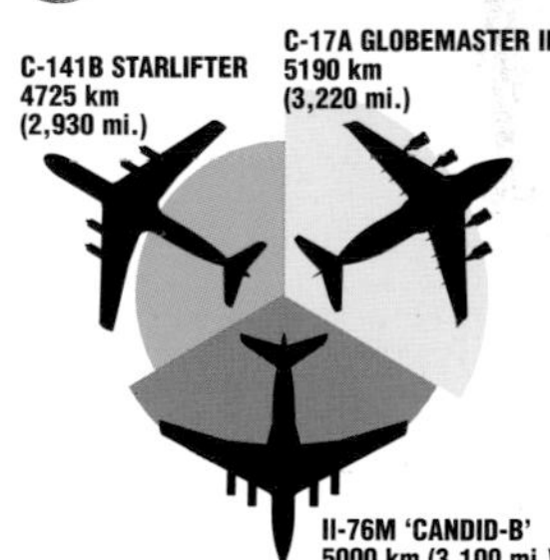

LANDING DISTANCE

Ilyushin used advanced systems to give the Il-76M excellent field performance, with a maximum payload only slightly below that of the C-141B. The C-17A is equally impressive, requiring twice the distance of the Il-76M for landing but with twice the payload.

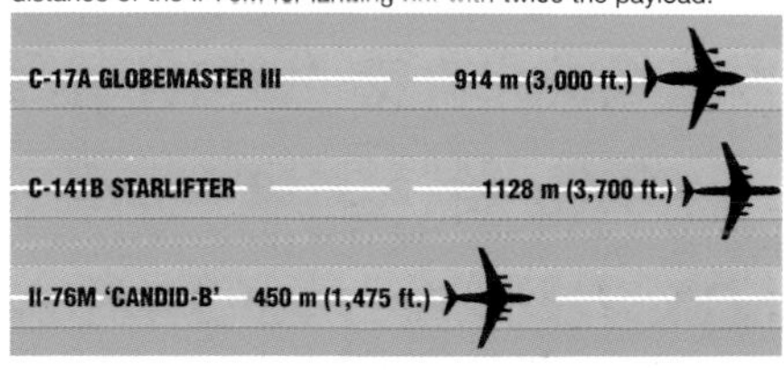

USAF's Douglas airlifter dynasty

■ C-54 SKYMASTER: Douglas flew the first C-54 in 1942 and more than 1000 were delivered to the US Army Air Force and Navy.

■ C-74 GLOBEMASTER I: Having flown for the first time in September 1945, many C-74s were cancelled at the end of the war.

■ C-124 GLOBEMASTER II: The C-124 was produced by fitting the C-74 with 2610-kW (3,500-hp.) engines, a deeper fuselage and nose doors.

■ C-133 CARGOMASTER: Only 35 of these advanced turboprop transports were built. They were retired in 1971 after fatigue problems.

McDONNELL DOUGLAS

F-4 PHANTOM II (USAF)

● Two-seat fighter-bomber ● War veteran ● Thirty years of service

Arguably the greatest warplane of its era, the McDonnell Douglas F-4 Phantom II was designed as a naval aircraft. When the US Air Force adopted the Phantom, airmen had to swallow their pride and fly a plane that the Navy had used first. The USAF was so impressed, however, that it bought more than 2000 examples; the 'Phabulous Phantom' was to form the backbone of Tactical Air Command for 20 years. Indeed, USAF F-4s both began and ended their service in a war zone – Vietnam in the 1960s and the Gulf in the 1990s.

▲ *Reputedly described by one USAF general as looking as though it was 'delivered upside-down', the Phantom could never be described as 'good-looking'. However, its years of mainly trouble-free service inspired admiration from those associated with it.*

PHOTO FILE

McDONNELL DOUGLAS F-4 PHANTOM II (USAF)

▲ F-4D takes on fuel
USAF Phantoms differed from Navy F-4s in using 'boom' air-to-air refuelling rather than the 'probe and drogue' system. The 'D' was the second USAF version, but the first purpose-designed for the Air Force.

▼ Reconnaissance Phantom
Over 500 RF-4Cs were delivered from 1964 to 1973, and except for the F-4E it was in production the longest. As built, the RF-4Cs were unarmed, although they could deliver an atomic weapon.

▼ Gun-toting F-4E
With its internal M61 cannon the F-4E was the last and most widely used version. Almost 1400 were built, with many being exported.

▲ Precision-guided weaponry
In Vietnam USAF F-4s pioneered the use of precision-guided munitions. Here an F-4E delivers a TV-guided GBU-15 glide bomb.

▼ Advanced 'Wild Weasel'
The F-4G was the USAF's last variant of the Phantom and was also the last in service. In all, 134 'Wild Weasels' were converted from F-4Es.

FACTS AND FIGURES

- ➤ While the Vietnam War was under way, the F-4E equipped the 'Thunderbirds' USAF flight display aerobatic team.
- ➤ All five US aces in Vietnam, three of whom served in the USAF, flew the F-4.
- ➤ In the F-4G, based on the F-4E, the M61 gun was replaced by a radar detector.
- ➤ Now displayed in Colorado, one F-4 shot down six Vietnamese MiGs; no other F-4 was credited with more than three.
- ➤ Over 5100 Phantoms were built, with the USAF being by far the largest operator.
- ➤ The M61 20-mm cannon in the F-4E had a rate of fire of 100 rounds per second.

PROFILE

Thirty years of USAF Phantoms

US Air Force generals were so impressed by the US Navy's F-4 that in March 1962 they decided that it would be the standard fighter for their tactical squadrons.

Three years later, F-4s began their campaign against MiG fighters in the skies over Hanoi. MiG-17s and MiG-21s were smaller, simpler and more nimble than the robust and ungraceful Phantom – but the F-4 entered each dogfight with brute force and power. The Vietnam War proved the merit of the Phantom, not just in air-to-air combat, but also in nearly every military job a jet aircraft could perform, including close support, bombing and reconnaissance.

While the first F-4C (from which a camera-equipped tactical reconnaissance RF-4C variant was also developed) was a minimum-change version of the Navy's F-4B, the F-4D introduced many improvements, mainly to enhance air-to-ground capability. 'Smart' weapons could now be delivered by F-4s.

The lack of an internal gun was addressed in the F-4E – the ultimate model – more than 800 of which entered USAF service. In all, more than 2200 F-4s flew with the Air Force, many operating in Vietnam.

The 'E'-model was to serve as the basis for the last USAF F-4s, the F-4G 'Wild Weasel' defence-suppression aircraft. These and RF-4Cs saw active duty in the 1990/91 Gulf War in the twilight of the Phantom's career. The last Phantoms were retired from the USAF in March 1996.

Above: Before their own Phantoms had been delivered, the USAF borrowed 29 US Navy F4H-1s. The first two carried 'F-110A' paintwork.

Right: Starting in 1967 the more capable F-4D replaced the F-4C in Vietnam. From the late 1970s many D variants went to Air National Guard and Reserve units, the last examples being retired in 1990. This aircraft wears the two-tone grey colour scheme adopted during the 1980s.

F-4E Phantom II

Type: two-seat multi-role fighter

Powerplant: two 79.6-kN (17,903-lb-thrust) General Electric J79-GE-17 afterburning turbojets

Maximum speed: 2304 km/h (1,432 mph) or Mach 2.17

Ferry range: 2593 km (1,611 miles)

Service ceiling: 18,975 m (62,254 ft)

Weights: empty 13,770 kg (30,358 lb); maximum loaded 28,055 kg (61,851 lb)

Armament: one M61A1 Vulcan 20-mm (0.79-in) cannon with 639 rounds and up to 7258 kg (16,000 lb) of ordnance, including four AIM-7 Sparrow and four AIM-9 Sidewinder missiles, plus a wide variety of bombs, rockets and precision-guided munitions

Dimensions:		
	span	11.68 m (38 ft 4 in)
	length	19.20 m (63 ft)
	height	5.00 m (16 ft 5 in)
	wing area	49.24 m² (530 sq ft)

F-4E Phantom II

67-0308 was delivered in September 1968 and in October went to the 388th Tactical Fighter Wing (TFW) at Korat Air Force Base, Thailand, the first unit to use the F-4E in the war zone. It returned to the United States in 1973.

All Phantoms had two crew and many had dual controls. USAF aircraft carry a pilot and Weapons System Officer (WSO, or 'Wizzo', or 'Bear' in the F-4G). Initially the USAF wanted to equip their F-4s with two qualified pilots, an expensive option which was later abandoned.

Vietnam-era camouflage retained gull-grey undersides as applied to USAF F-4s from the beginning, but added a mixture of greens and tan to the upper surface.

The reshaped nose of the F-4E housed a Westinghouse APQ-120 radar set, which had a smaller dish than earlier Phantom radars. The shark's teeth were a 388th TFW trademark.

JV
AF 70 308
Belly Loo
308

Shortcomings in the concept of a gunless fighter saw the installation of a General Electric M61 Vulcan six-barrel, 20-mm (0.79-in) rotary cannon in the nose of the F-4E.

Primary defensive armament for USAF Phantoms was the AIM-7 Sparrow medium-range and AIM-9 Sidewinder short-range air-to-air missiles; typically four of each were carried.

Pratt & Whitney J79 afterburning turbojet engines powered all USAF F-4s. In later years the F-4G's engines were modified to reduce smoke.

All F-4s carried a tailhook, a legacy of their carrier-borne origins. Land-based aircraft could use the hook if their braking systems or undercarriage failed.

COMBAT DATA

MAXIMUM SPEED

Although all Phantoms had very good performance, the F-4E with its uprated engines was the best performer. The Rolls-Royce-engined British FG.Mk 1 was slightly slower than the others.

F-4B PHANTOM II	2277 km/h (1,415 mph)
F-4E PHANTOM II	2304 km/h (1,432 mph)
PHANTOM FG.Mk 1	2230 km/h (1,386 mph)

ENGINE THRUST

The large, fuel-thirsty engines of the naval FG.Mk 1 gave it more thrust than the American marks. The later model F-4E has a slight edge over the older F-4B sub-type.

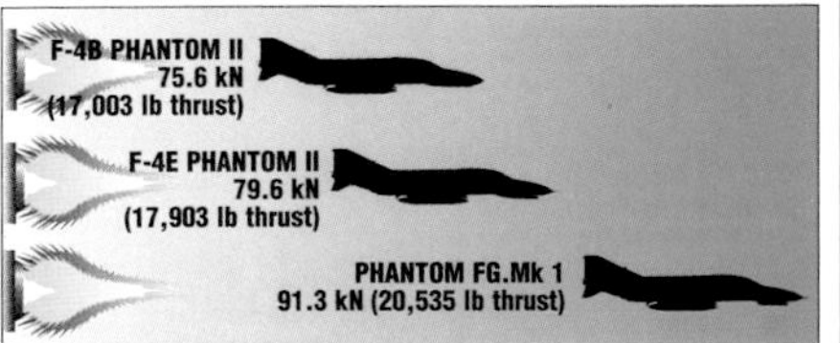

SERVICE CEILING

The land-based USAF Phantom IIs are in a league of their own when it comes to altitude. The British FG.Mk 1's heavier engines led to a fuselage redesign, producing slower speed, a reduced weapons load and a lower service ceiling.

F-4B PHANTOM II	F-4E PHANTOM II	PHANTOM FG Mk.1
18,900 m (62,008 ft)	18,975 m (62,254 ft)	18,288 m (60,000 ft)

Phantoms in Vietnam

HAM RUNG BRIDGE: On 27 April 1972 F-4s of the 8th TFW used laser-guided bombs to destroy this difficult target at Thanh Hoa.

JUNGLE DEFOLIATION ESCORT: F-4s escorted vulnerable C-123 Providers as they sprayed 'Agent Orange' defoliant over concealed Viet Cong positions.

RECONNAISSANCE: RF-4Cs flew high-speed, unarmed reconnaissance missions over North Vietnam, avoiding SA-2 missiles and gunfire.

McDONNELL DOUGLAS

F-4 PHANTOM II (US NAVY)

● Classic carrier fighter ● MiG-killer ● Ground-attack capability

McDonnell's F-4 Phantom II was developed to meet a US Navy need for an interceptor to defend its aircraft-carriers from attack. After the Phantom became operational, it grew into a multi-role warplane with many capabilities – all of them superior. The Phantom could fight MiGs and drop bombs. It was bigger, heavier, more powerful, faster and further-reaching than any other contemporary combat aircraft.

▲ *McDonnell's incredible warplane began life as a shipboard interceptor with the US Navy, and it is perhaps these examples which are the true classic Phantom variants.*

PHOTO FILE

McDONNELL DOUGLAS F-4 PHANTOM II

◀ More capable variant

By the early 1970s, most Navy units had re-equipped with the more capable F-4J, which boasted a number of improvements, including more powerful engines and a datalink system.

▼ Launch the Phantom

A trio of F-4Bs from VF-102 'Diamondbacks' prepares for launch from one of the bow catapults on the USS Enterprise. *Both the carrier and this squadron later saw combat in Southeast Asia.*

▲ Armament

Operating primarily as fleet defence fighters, USN F-4s were seen most often carrying Sparrow and Sidewinder AAMs. The wing fuel tanks were seldom fitted.

▲ Smoky engines

This flypast fully illustrates the characteristic smoke trails which were a Phantom trademark.

◀ Trapping aboard 'Connie'

After a routine combat air patrol, a VF-92 F-4J lands aboard USS Constellation *in 1974.*

FACTS AND FIGURES

- Only the larger US Navy carriers could operate Phantoms. The aircraft were too heavy for 'Essex'-class carriers.
- Unlike their USAF counterparts, Navy F-4s were never fitted with guns.
- Lieutenant Randy Cunningham was the USN's only Phantom ace in Vietnam.
- In 1967 a Zuni rocket was accidentally fired on the deck of USS *Forrestal;* the resulting fire claimed a number of F-4s.
- Some USN F-4Js were later refurbished and delivered to the RAF.
- Grumman F-14 Tomcats began to supplant Phantoms in the mid-1970s.

PROFILE

Elite of the US Navy

In the early 1960s, the Phantom was the hottest thing in the sky. To show off its new fighter, the US Navy flew the new craft faster and higher than any operational warplane had gone before. Typical was a world altitude record of 30,218 m (99,140 ft). In 1961 a specially prepared Phantom reached 2585.15 km/h (1,606.34 mph). Not surprisingly, the Phantom was already becoming vital to US naval aviation when the American role in Vietnam expanded during the mid-1960s.

Phantoms participated in the first US air strikes against North Vietnam and were still around at the end of the war a dozen years later. For the pilot and radar intercept officer of a Phantom, part of the challenge consisted of taking off from and landing on an aircraft-carrier deck, sometimes at night, sometimes in bad weather. High over Hanoi, Phantoms faced North Vietnamese MiG-17 and MiG-21 fighters and fought well.

The US Navy's only ace pilot of the war flew a Phantom.

Above: With afterburners blazing, a VF-41 Phantom hurtles skyward. This unit was one of several Atlantic Fleet squadrons deployed on combat cruises to the Gulf of Tonkin.

Other Phantoms were operated from land bases in South Vietnam by US Marine crews. Long after Vietnam, the Phantom retained a key position in US naval aviation until its eventual retirement in the 1980s.

Below: This quartet of F-4Bs, belonging to VF-21 'Freelancers', is shown posing for the camera. The wing fuel tanks are unusual.

F-4B Phantom II

Type: two-seat carrier-borne interceptor

Powerplant: two 79.65-kN (17,914-lb-thrust) General Electric J79-8A afterburning turbojets

Maximum speed: 2390 km/h (1,485 mph)

Combat radius: 1450 km (901 miles)

Range: 3700 km (2,299 miles)

Service ceiling: 21,640 m (71,000 ft)

Weights: empty 12,701 kg (28,000 lb); maximum take-off 24,766 kg (54,600 lb)

Armament: four AIM-7 Sparrow medium-range and four AIM-9 Sidewinder short-range air-to-air missiles, plus various air-to-ground stores

Dimensions:

	span	11.71 m (38 ft 5 in)
	length	17.75 m (58 ft 3 in)
	height	4.95 m (16 ft 3 in)
	wing area	49.24 m² (530 sq ft)

F-4B Phantom II

Carrying a full load of Mk 82 bombs, this F-4B is depicted as it would have appeared during its first Vietnam cruise with VF-84 'Jolly Rogers' on board the USS *Independence* in late 1965. During this cruise, the squadron lost three aircraft in combat.

Unlike USAF Phantoms, the F-4B could not be flown from the rear cockpit. In Navy parlance, the backseater was the RIO (Radar Intercept Officer), whose job it was to operate the weapons system.

Sufficient clearance for the twin J79 engines resulted in the distinctive bulky profile, which gave rise to the type's nickname 'Double Ugly'. Above the engines were the fuselage fuel cells.

Early in their service careers, F-4Bs featured slick fin-tips, although later most aircraft were retro-fitted with radar homing and warning receiver (RHAW) antennas housed in distinctive bullet fairings facing both fore and aft.

As the first major production Phantom variant, the F-4B featured a Westinghouse APQ-72 radar, which was state of the art in 1965. A small undernose pod housed an infra-red seeker, although this was removed from the F-4J.

The medium-range AIM-7 Sparrow air-to-air missile was designed as part of the F-4's weapons system. When it was working, the Sparrow was an excellent missile, although in Vietnam it was prone to malfunctioning.

Although used by the Navy primarily as an interceptor, the F-4B was wired to carry air-to-ground weapons. As the war in Southeast Asia intensified, USN Phantoms were often seen flying bombing missions over North Vietnam, especially when there were not sufficient attack aircraft available. Most F-4 crews despised bombing sorties.

COMBAT DATA

MAXIMUM SPEED

During the 1960s the F-4's main rival in the naval fighter stakes was the Vought F-8 Crusader. The Crusader was often overrated because it was a single-seat fighter with guns. The Phantom was considerably faster thanks to its powerful twin J79 turbojets.

F-4B PHANTOM II	2390 km/h (1,485 mph)
F-8J CRUSADER	1802 km/h (1,120 mph)
A-4E SKYHAWK	1083 km/h (673 mph)

COMBAT RADIUS

Operational radius was where the Phantom came up short. It was a thirsty beast and needed regular air-to-air refuelling. By contrast, the smaller Crusader and even smaller Skyhawk were longer-legged, an important factor when flying sorties deep into the heart of North Vietnam.

MAXIMUM WEIGHT

Among its many records, the Phantom had the distinction of being the heaviest fighter to have served aboard a carrier up to that time. This weight factor prolonged the career of the F-8, which continued to operate from the smaller wooden-deck carriers.

F-4B PHANTOM II
24,766 kg
(54,600 lb)

F-8J CRUSADER
12,474 kg
(27,500 lb)

A-4E SKYHAWK
7355 kg
(16,215 lb)

US Navy Phantom MiG-killers in Vietnam

■ VF-161: During Operation Linebacker in May 1972, two F-4Bs from VF-161 'Chargers' tangled with two MiG-19s, downing both. The victorious crews, Lts Brown, Bartholomy, Arwood and Bell, are seen back in the squadron ready room.

■ VF-92: 10 May 1972 saw a number of MiG-kills for US Navy Phantoms. Lt Curt Dose of VF-92 'Silver Kings' successfully despatched an NVAF MiG-17 with an AIM-9 Sidewinder, and is seen here describing his tangle.

■ VF-114: Seen in high spirits after his return to the USS *Kitty Hawk*, Lt Robert Hughes, and his RIO Lt (jg) Adolph Cruz, managed to shoot down a MIG-21 on 6 May 1972. Hughes's wingman also scored a kill during the same successful sortie.

McDONNELL DOUGLAS

F-4 PHANTOM II (VIETNAM)

● Vietnam warrior ● Fighter and bomber ● MiG-killer supreme

▲ *Lt Randy Cunningham and his RIO Lt Willie Driscoll scored their third, fourth and fifth kills on 10 May 1972 to become the Navy's only aces of the war in Southeast Asia.*

The Phantom broke all the rules. Fighters were supposed to be small, sleek single-seaters with guns; the Phantom was huge and had bent wings, a two-man crew and missile armament. It looked wrong, but it flew right. Strapped inside Phantom cockpits over Vietnam, naval aviators fought MiGs in raging air combat and, after early problems, came out on top almost every time.

PHOTO FILE

McDONNELL DOUGLAS F-4 PHANTOM II

▼ Top Guns of the 1960s
In the late 1960s the F-4 Phantom crew was considered the elite of the West's air forces. No service trained its crews better than the US Navy.

▲ Marines at sea
It wasn't just the Navy which flew the Phantom from aircraft-carriers. US Marine Corps squadrons shared the load of shipboard deployments.

▼ Catapult launch
An F-4J thunders from the deck on an unarmed training sortie. The undercarriage was immensely strong to absorb the pounding of carrier operations.

▲ Fighter-bomber
The Phantom was best known as a MiG-killer, but it did its fair share of ground-attacking as well. These aircraft are seen over Vietnam, dropping 227-kg (500-lb) bombs from the relative safety of medium altitude.

FACTS AND FIGURES

- Tests showed that pilots in Vietnam were more anxious about landing on the carrier than about fighting MiGs.
- Navy and Marine F-4B and F-4J fighters flew over 100,000 sorties in Vietnam.
- In early Vietnam combat, Phantom pilots were achieving only a 1:1 kill ratio.
- A Phantom weighs 4.68 times as much as the Hellcat carrier fighter of 1944.
- After the introduction of 'Top Gun' training, the kill ratio improved to as much as seven MiGs for each F-4 lost.
- On 10 May 1972 Navy F-4s from fighter squadron VF-96 downed six MiGs.

PROFILE

US Navy MiG-killers

Few human exploits compare with fighting in the F-4 Phantom. The big, powerful machine gave both pilot and radar officer the ride of their lives, blasting aloft with twice as much power as other fighters and going into battle armed to the teeth.

Randy Cunningham and Willie Driscoll were the first American aces in Vietnam, making three kills in the great air battles of 10 May. Their first kill, however, had come on 18 January while escorting an A-6 strike against Qhan Lang. After dodging surface-to-air missiles, they noticed two aircraft about four miles ahead.

'As we closed, I saw they were delta-winged MiG-21s, at about 500 feet [150 metres]. Just as I squeezed off a Sidewinder, my MiG broke into a hard turn. I could see my adversary's head thrashing around in the cockpit.'

After a series of manoeuvres, Cunningham found himself directly behind the MiG, and he fired again.

'Just as his wings levelled, the Sidewinder hit: the tail came off and the airplane went tumbling into the ground, creating a huge fireball.'

'Showtime 100' was the Phantom used by Randy Cunningham and Willie Driscoll on 10 May to score their three kills. The last was an epic battle against Colonel Tomb, reputedly the leading North Vietnamese ace. On the way home, 'Showtime 100' took a SAM hit and the crew had to bail out, but they were rescued safely.

Two crewmen meant an extra pair of eyes, which was a real advantage in a close-range, visual dogfight.

For air-to-air work the Phantom carried four short-range heat-seeking Sidewinders on the wing pylons.

F-4J Phantom II

Type: two-seat carrier-based multi-role fighter

Powerplant: two 79.63-kN (17,910-lb-thrust) General Electric J79-GE-10 turbojets with afterburners

Maximum speed: Mach 2.25 or 2390 km/h (1,485 mph)

Combat radius: 950 km (590 miles)

Service ceiling: 19,000 m (62,336 ft)

Weights: empty 13,250 kg (29,211 lb); loaded 27,655 kg (60,969 lb)

Armament: typically, four AIM-7 Sparrow radar missiles and four AIM-9 Sidewinder infra-red missiles; up to 1370 kg (3,020 lb) of bombs beneath fuselage and up to 5888 kg (12,980 lb) of bombs under wings

Dimensions:		
	span	11.71 m (38 ft 5 in)
	length	18.96 m (62 ft 2 in)
	height	5.03 m (16 ft 6 in)
	wing area	49.24 m² (530 sq ft)

F-4J PHANTOM II

By 1972, when Cunningham and Driscoll flew this aircraft to their three MiG victories, the F-4J was the standard shipboard fighter for the US Navy. Because of its size it could fly only from the larger carriers, and could not fit on the small 'Essex'-class ships.

In 1965, carrier fighter squadron VF-96 scored the US Navy's first MiG kill of the Vietnam War. That was the unit's only success until 1972, when its crews downed a further eight MiGs, including five by the ace team of Cunningham and Driscoll.

For protection, the F-4 was fitted with a radar-homing and warning system, which detected enemy-surveillance and fire-control radars. The antennas were housed in the tip of the fin.

The Phantom had a superb radar in the shape of the APG-59. This was the best in the world at the time, and could track both low- and high-altitude targets.

To launch, the F-4 was hooked to the catapult with a heavy cable bridle which fell away when the aircraft left the deck.

To highlight the secondary attack role of the Phantom, this aircraft carries cluster bombs.

The jetpipes of the Phantom were angled down to give an extra punch for carrier take-offs. The arrestor hook for stopping the aircraft was between the two engines.

COMBAT DATA

MAXIMUM SPEED

The Phantom's sheer power gave it tremendous speed, but it was very much a straight-line machine. Although by no means a dogfighter, the F-4's climbing, diving and acceleration ability were used to advantage against slower but much more agile opponents.

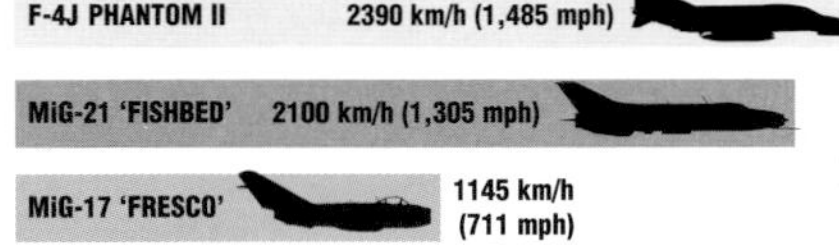

ARMAMENT

American rules of engagement in Vietnam meant that F-4 pilots had to visually identify the enemy before firing, negating their long-range missiles. And in a dogfight, the lack of a gun was a severe handicap which only good training could overcome.

F-4J PHANTOM II	MiG-21 'FISHBED'	MiG-17 'FRESCO'

4 x AIM-7 Sparrow missiles 4 x AIM-9 Sidewinder missiles	1 x twin-barrel 23-mm (0.91-in) cannon 4 x AA-2 'Atoll' missiles	3 x 23-mm (0.91-in) nose cannon

SERVICE CEILING

The combination of immense power and a large wing area meant that the F-4 could reach exceptionally high altitudes. With its missile armament, the F-4 made an excellent bomber interceptor. In Vietnam, however, its opponents were agile fighters, but Phantom pilots could usually get out of trouble with MiGs by outclimbing their less powerful opponents.

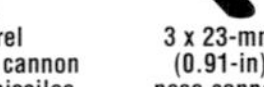

MiG-killers of 10 May 1972

THE NAVY TAKES ON THE MIGs: 10 May 1972 was the Navy Phantom's big day over Vietnam. Flying from USS *Constellation*, sister squadrons VF-92 'Silver Kings' and VF-96 'Fighting Falcons' blasted seven MiGs from the skies between them, while a VF-51 crew shot down another for the Navy. To make matters worse for the North Vietnamese, USAF Phantoms accounted for another three MiGs that fateful day.

■ FIRST KILL OF THE DAY: Lt Curt Dose (seen here demonstrating his dogfight) and Lt James McDevitt from VF-92 scored the first kill of 10 May after blasting their F-4s down the Kep runway near Hanoi to stir up the MiGs.

■ TWO MIGs IN ONE DAY: RIO Lt Thomas Blonski of UF-96 'Fighting Falcons' aboard the *Constellation* looks on as his pilot, Lt Matt Connelly, relives one of their duels with MiGs on 10 May. Two MiGs fell to their AIM-9 Sidewinders that day.

■ THE FOE: North Vietnamese MiG-17s shelter behind bunkers between missions. Although the faster MiG-21 was available, many experienced pilots, such as Colonel Tomb, favoured the nimble 'Fresco' for combat.

McDONNELL DOUGLAS

F-4 PHANTOM II

● Air superiority ● Long-range strike ● Modernised classic

▲ Like its classic adversary, the MiG-21, the F-4 is a highly versatile aircraft that sold in the thousands. An upgrade can cost as little as one-sixth of the cost of a new fighter, but can deliver performance that in many ways is as good as that of the latest tactical aircraft.

Although the last American Phantoms have been withdrawn from service, the amazing F-4 story continues all over the world. Several nations have decided that the best value for money in military aviation is to upgrade the mighty F-4 with new cockpits, avionics, engines and missiles, making the 40-year-old fighter as good as many new types.

PHOTO FILE

McDONNELL DOUGLAS F-4 PHANTOM II

◀ **'Wild Weasel'**
The last Phantoms in US service were the F-4G 'Wild Weasel' defence suppression aircraft. Armed with HARM missiles, they flew with distinction in the Gulf.

◀ **Turkish F-4s**
An upgrade by Israel Aircraft Industries for Turkey includes a new radar from Elta and advanced multi-function displays.

▼ **Kai upgrade for Japan**
Japan's F-4EJ Phantoms were upgraded with a new AN/APQ-172 radar, new cockpit displays and avionics, but externally look almost unchanged.

'Kurnass' Phantoms ▶
Israel has upgraded its Phantoms, calling the new version 'Kurnass' (hammer). These have seen action over South Lebanon.

◀ **Luftwaffe ICE**
The upgrade for 110 of the Luftwaffe's F-4Fs included a ring laser-gyro, APG-65 radar, smokeless engines, radar-warning receiver and the ability to fire four AMRAAM missiles.

FACTS AND FIGURES

- ➤ The powerplant for the F-4F ICE consists of two German-assembled J79-MTU-17A turbojet engines.
- ➤ Israel's Kurnass Phantoms can launch the large Popeye stand-off weapon.
- ➤ The F-4G has been retired, but no fully satisfactory replacement yet exists.
- ➤ Israel's Super Phantom prototype was fitted with Pratt & Whitney PW1120 engines in trials.
- ➤ Forty Luftwaffe F-4Fs were upgraded to a lower standard than ICE/KWS.
- ➤ Upgraded Phantoms will remain in service until at least 2008.

PROFILE

New life for the great Phantom

Though the time-honoured Phantom is now a very old design, the F-4F ICE (Improved Combat Efficiency) upgrade will be flying with the Luftwaffe well into the 21st century, until the Eurofighter Typhoon enters full service. Improved radar, long-range AMRAAM missiles and advanced multi-function cockpit displays to ease the pilot's workload are all features of the upgraded aircraft. It also has a revised control stick for the pilot and improved avionics.

While Germany is the world leader in breathing new life into the Phantom, advanced versions of this super aircraft are being flown in Japan, Korea, Israel and Turkey. The Israeli Phantom 2000 incorporates strengthening and new avionics, while the proposed Super Phantom was equipped with a canard wing and new engines for greatly superior performance and economy.

The combination of modifications like new avionics and engines makes the F-4 feel like a new aircraft.

Japan's F-4EJ Kai aircraft also has improved weapons, radar and avionics, and has the ability to deliver the ASM-1 anti-ship missile.

Pilots say that new models like the F-4F ICE can take on any fighter in the world in a long-range air-to-air duel and come out victorious.

The dials and knobs of the old F-4E cockpit are being replaced by TV-type displays.

F-4F ICE Phantom

The Luftwaffe's improved F-4F Phantoms are now entering service with JG 71 and JG 74. They are the only operational F-4s armed with AMRAAM missiles

The addition of new armament to the F-4 is one of the most important parts of the upgrade programmes, enabling it to deliver precision-guided munitions like Popeye and Paveway.

Most upgraded F-4s have a new radar-warning receiver. The ICE has a Litton system with receiver aerials in the wingtips.

Improved engines for the F-4 give little extra thrust, but offer much better fuel consumption and need far less maintenance.

The aerodynamics of the F-4 are a generation behind today's fighters. Generally, it is only worth upgrading Phantoms with relatively low airframe hours; many F-4s are too old to be worth modifying.

The pilot flies the new F-4 with a HOTAS (hands-on-throttle-and-stick) cockpit system. Elta of Israel is offering an advanced head-up display in its upgrades.

The multi-mode APG-65 radar is also used in the F-18 Hornet. It can perform in ground-mapping, search-and-track and dogfight modes.

The new F-4Fs will have special Frazer-Nash ejector rails, allowing the carriage of the AMRAAM fire-and-forget missile.

Unlike the MiG-21, most Phantom upgrades have not included major changes of engine; the proposed PW1120 engine for the Israeli Super Phantom was not adopted.

F-4F ICE Phantom

Type: two-seat fighter/fighter-bomber

Powerplant: two 79.63-kN (17,917-lb. thrust) GE J79-MTU-17A afterburning turbojets

Maximum speed: Mach 2.17 or 2304 km/h (1,432 m.p.h.) without weapons

Ferry range: 2593 km (1,611 m.p.h.)

Service ceiling: 18,975 m (62,250 ft.)

Weights: empty 14,556 kg (32,090 lb.); loaded 28,055 kg (61,850 lb.)

Armament: four AIM-120 AMRAAM or AIM-7 Sparrow medium-range radar-guided air-to-air missiles; AIM-9 Sidewinder heat-seeking missiles

Dimensions:		
	span	11.68 m (38 ft. 4 in.)
	length	18.96 m (62 ft. 2 in.)
	height	5.05 m (16 ft. 5 in.)
	wing area	49.24 m² (530 sq. ft.)

COMBAT DATA

TURN RATE

Increased thrust and reduced weight give the newer F-4s a better instantaneous and sustained turn rate than older F-4s, especially those with unslatted wings. The upgraded MiG-21 with an RD-33 engine could probably still out-turn the F-4.

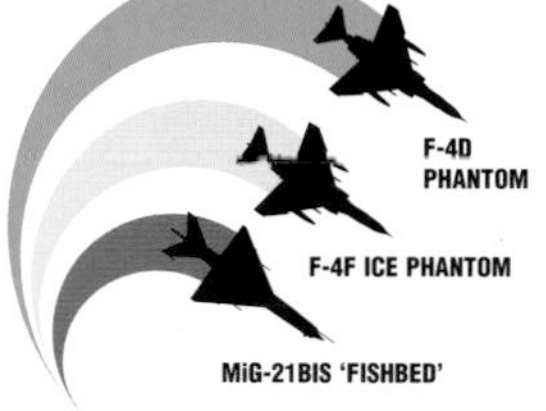

CLIMB RATE

Increased engine efficiency gives the new generation F-4s a superior climb rate to the older models. The F-4D had a slightly better rate than the standard MiG-21bis, thanks to its high thrust-to-weight ratio; the latest upgraded MiG-21s would probably have a better climb rate due to the power of the RD-33 engine. The F-4 ICE's climb rate would challenge many more modern fighters.

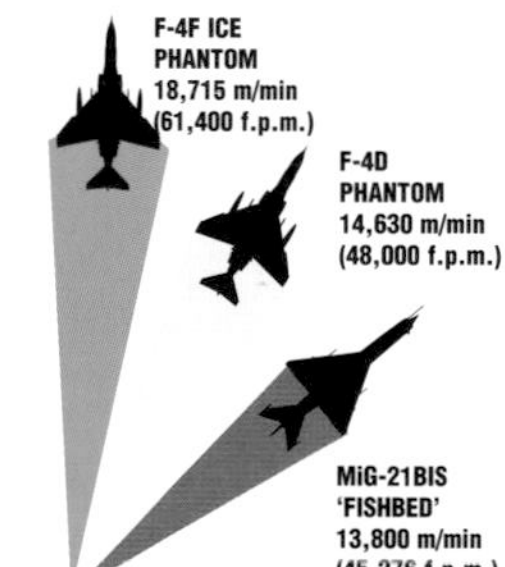

MISSILE RANGE

Like the MiG-21, the F-4 has been made vastly more capable with the addition of new fire-and-forget missiles, allowing the aircraft to turn away from its opponent as soon as it fires its weapons.

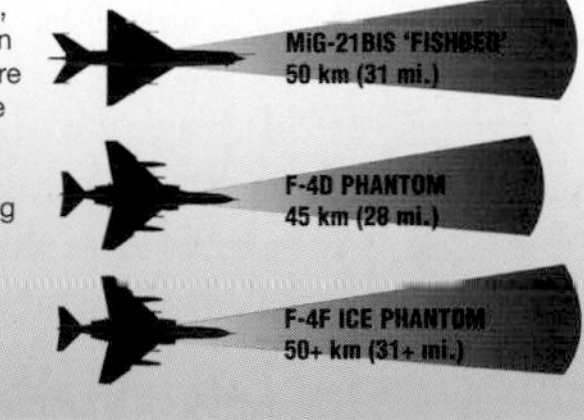

The Phantom generation

■ US NAVY F-4B: The first major F-4 variant was the US Navy's F-4B, an interceptor with ground-attack capability that saw widespread service in Vietnam and inspired the USAF F-4C.

■ EGYPTIAN F-4E: Egypt received 35 ex-USAF F-4Es. This variant had a slatted wing to enhance manoeuvrability, and an internal cannon as a result of combat in Vietnam.

■ JAPANESE F-4EJ: The last Phantom built was one of 140 F-4EJs licence-produced by Mitsubishi, serving in the air-defence role. They were fitted with Japanese-built radar.

McDONNELL DOUGLAS

F/A-18 HORNET

● Carrier fighter ● Multi-role strike ● Anti-ship/radar bomber

McDonnell Douglas' F/A-18 can vault from a carrier deck, bomb a target, and stay to dogfight the enemy's top guns. The US Navy is delighted with this versatile warplane, its first jet intended for double duty against air and ground enemies. Marines and overseas operators also love the Hornet. The coming F/A-18E/F is a bigger, more robust version of this superb fighter for carrier squadrons in the 21st century.

▲ *Being an F/A-18 Hornet pilot is perhaps the ultimate aviation job flying a single-seat high-performance jet from a carrier, tasked with both air-to-air combat and dropping bombs.*

PHOTO FILE

McDONNELL DOUGLAS F/A-18 HORNET

▲ Angels of thunder
The US Navy's elite 'Blue Angels' formation team flies the Hornet. It offers outstanding agility while thrilling air show crowds with explosively noisy power displays.

▲ Export success
Nations which have chosen to operate the Hornet include Australia, Canada and Spain.

◀ Fighting office
The Hornet had the first truly modern cockpit aboard a carrier jet, designed around large TV-style screens and a head-up display.

▼ Marine mud-mover
The Marine Corps uses the two-seat F/A-18D Hornet on night attack missions, armed with laser bombs and other 'smart' weapons.

▲ Carrier-borne versatility
The Hornet is one of the world's most capable and versatile warplanes, and yet it still finds room to combine its talents with the demanding requirements of operating from the carrier deck.

◀ Killer on the prowl
Armed with Sparrow and Sidewinder missiles, and with an internal cannon, the F/A-18 can fight and win against the world's best air-to-air combatants.

FACTS AND FIGURES

- ➤ Land-based F/A-18 Hornets make up the front line of defence in Australia, Canada, Finland, Kuwait and Spain.
- ➤ About 65 crack pilots apply for three or four annual vacancies with the US Navy's Hornet-equipped 'Blue Angels'.
- ➤ An RF-18 Hornet photo ship was tested but not adopted.
- ➤ NASA uses a much modified F/A-18 to explore manoeuvring at extremely high angles of attack.
- ➤ The digital cockpit of the sophisticated Hornet has been described as a cross between 'Star Wars' and a video game.
- ➤ First flight of an F/A-18 Hornet took place on 18 November 1978.

PROFILE

Multi-mission master

This magnificent fighting jet from McDonnell Douglas has established a place as the backbone of US Navy and Marine aviation; sailors and marines wanted the F/A-18 Hornet so badly they relinquished other aircraft to get it. Their faith is justified: the F/A-18 performed superbly in raids on Libya and in Operation Desert Storm.

To keep the F/A-18 on top in the crucible of air combat, they are improving the Hornet constantly. Better flight instruments and avionics have been added to new aircraft along with the capability to use far-reaching missiles. None of these changes detract from the manoeuvrability of the Hornet, an exceedingly agile adversary.

The future F/A-18E (single-seat) and F/A-18F (two-seat) will be 86 cm (2 ft. 10 in.) longer and carry 1360 kg (2,998 lb.) more fuel. Navy carrier air wings will soon boast as many as four Hornet squadrons, giving a formidable stirke and fighter capability. With the F/A-18 on board the US Navy can project power globally knowing it has the best aircraft in the world.

Defender of the frozen North – Canada has Hornets standing by to deter any attack across the vast areas that straddle the north of the country. The Hornet can react quickly to any intruder.

The ends of the Hornet's wings fold up so that the aircraft does not take up much room in the confines of the aircraft-carrier deck or hangar.

Long strakes ahead of the wing give the Hornet pilot outstanding control of his aircraft when flying very slowly.

F/A-18C Hornet

Type: carrier-based naval strike fighter

Powerplant: two 71.2-kN (16,020-lb. thrust) afterburning General Electric F404-GE-400 turbofans

Maximum speed: Mach 1.8 or 1915 km/h (1,190 m.p.h.) at 12,190 m (40,000 ft.)

Combat radius: 1060 km (659 mi.)

Service ceiling: 15,240 m (50,000 ft.)

Weights: empty 10,455 kg (23,049 lb.); loaded 22,328 kg (49,225 lb.)

Armament: one Martin Marietta M61A1 Vulcan 20-mm cannon; two AIM-9L Sidewinder missiles; 7000 kg (15,432 lb.) of ordnance

Dimensions:

span	11.43 m (37 ft. 6 in.)
length	17.07 m (56 ft.)
height	4.66 m (15 ft. 3 in.)
wing area	37.16 m² (400 sq. ft.)

F/A-18C HORNET

Popularly called the 'Swing Fighter' because it can swing between air-to-air fighting and ground attack with great ease, the Hornet can perform a wide range of missions, including radar-killing and 'Fast FAC' – guiding other attack aircraft to their targets.

Above the radar is the trusty M61 20-mm Vulcan cannon which is used for close-range air-to-air combat. A drum containing 570 rounds of ammunition is mounted below the gun and aft of the radar.

Under the rear fuselage of the Hornet is an arrester hook for carrier landings. When lowered, this hook catches wires which are strung across the deck of the carrier.

The Hornet's undercarriage is immensely strong, since it has to withstand the repeated 'controlled crashes' of carrier landings.

This Hornet carries a mixed load of weapons – Sidewinders and Sparrows for enemy fighters, and Mk 82 bombs for ground targets.

In the nose of the Hornet is the APG-73 radar, which is at the heart of the aircraft's versatility. It can see and track other aircraft at great distances, while also mapping the ground to make precision bombing easy.

COMBAT DATA

SPEED

F/A-18C	1915 km/h (1,190 m.p.h.)
MIRAGE 2000	2330 km/h (1,448 m.p.h.)
TORNADO GR.Mk 1	2300 km/h1,429 m.p.h.)

The Hornet is optimised for subsonic combat and weapons delivery, so while it is comfortably supersonic its simple intake design limits it to about 1.8 times the speed of sound.

LOW-LEVEL COMBAT RADIUS

Hornets have always had the reputation of being 'short-legged', even though they have longer range than the preceding F-4 Phantom. However, this is no real handicap in these days of aerial refuelling, and the F/A-18's superb fighting ability more than makes up for any minor defect, as shown in Operation Desert Storm.

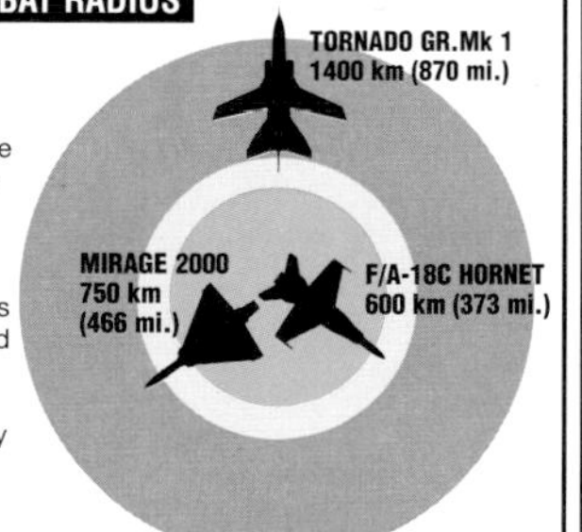

WEAPONS LOAD

Although the Hornet is one of the most manoeuvrablo fighters in the world, it carries almost as large a weapons load as a specialised bomber like the Tornado. And with its sophisticated targeting and laser designation system it is one of the most accurate bombers currently in service.

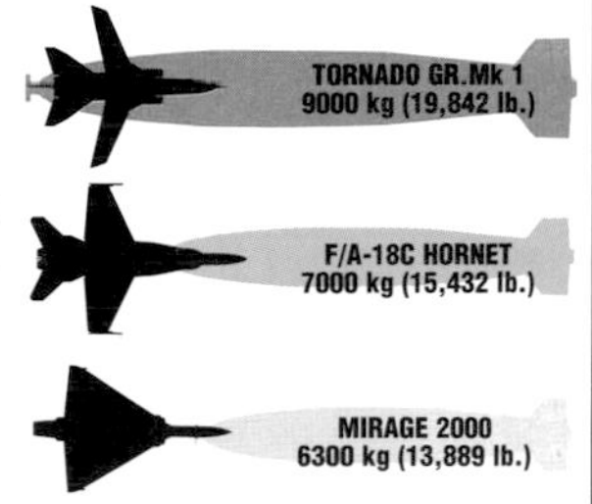

Killing radars with the Hornet

DETECTION ZONE

ATTACK FORCE

LETHAL ZONE

ENEMY MISSILES AND RADAR BATTERY

PRE-EMPTIVE SHOT: As the main attack force approaches the target, an F/A-18 lobs a HARM anti-radar missile over the top of the attack force. If any enemy radars are up and running, they will be destroyed immediately before the attackers enter the lethal zone.

ANTI-RADAR ESCORT: After the pre-emptive HARM missile has been fired, other HARM-carrying Hornets lead the attack force into the lethal zone. Any enemy radars that attempt to turn on are fired at by these strike escort aircraft.

MCDONNELL DOUGLAS

KC-10 EXTENDER

● USAF tanker ● Strategic transport role ● Gulf War veteran

▲ Supporting USAF aircraft deploying to bases all over the world, the Extender has become a symbol of US power projection. Forty-six KC-10As flew 25 per cent of the tanker missions over the Persian Gulf.

In a reversal of the Boeing KC-135 Stratotanker's production history, McDonnell Douglas built the KC-10A Extender tanker/transport after it had established the DC-10 airliner design. The aircraft has revolutionised USAF overseas deployments, with the ability not only to refuel formations of tactical jets, but also to carry their support equipment and personnel. The Extender is now a key element in USAF operations.

PHOTO FILE

MCDONNELL DOUGLAS KC-10 EXTENDER

▼ Gulf-bound Extender

During Desert Storm, 46 of the USAF's 59 surviving KC-10As were used to support coalition air power. The KC-10A enabled the deployment of US-based fighters.

▲ Refuelling options

The principal Extender tool is the 'flying boom', but for refuelling US Navy and other NATO aircraft a hose drum unit is also carried.

◀ KC-10A achievements

In September 1982, seven KC-10As met 20 C-141Bs over Goose Bay, Labrador, delivering an incredible 29,484 kg (64,865 lb.) of fuel to each. The C-141Bs went on to drop troops over West Germany.

▼ Premier tanker

The Extender can transfer 90,720 kg (200,000 lb.) of fuel to one or more receivers.

▲ Changing colours

Originally operated in a blue and white colour scheme the KC-10 fleet has appeared in number of different colours including lizard green, dark grey and the current light grey scheme.

FACTS AND FIGURES

➤ During its initial operational assessment, the KC-10A supported eight A-7Ds on a deployment to the UK.

➤ McDonnell Douglas based its KC-10A on the DC-10-30CF airframe.

➤ Royal Netherlands Air Force KDC-10 tankers are conversions of DC-10s.

➤ A typical KC-10A mission might involve accompanying and refuelling eight fighters, while carrying 25 cargo pallets.

➤ A digital fly-by-wire control system is fitted to the air-refuelling boom.

➤ A six-month evaluation was carried out on the KC-10A before it entered service.

PROFILE

USAF's tactical Extender

This 2nd Wing KC-10A, seen on take-off from Barksdale AFB in Louisiana, has its crew provided by the Air National Guard.

Ordered off-the-shelf as a version of the DC-10 airliner to satisfy a USAF requirement for a dual-role Advanced Tanker/Cargo Aircraft, KC-10A deliveries began in 1981. Unlike the KC-135, the Extender has a permanent probe-and-drogue refuelling system in addition to its flying boom, allowing the support of USAF and USN aircraft on the same mission.

Officially credited with the best USAF aircraft safety record (only one aircraft has been lost, in a ground fire), the KC-10A was involved in the 1986 raids on Libya, operations in Panama in 1989, and in the Gulf War.

While the KC-135 force is mostly tasked with the support of strategic bombers, the KC-10A mission is almost wholly tactical. The KC-10A currently forms part of the USAF's primary tactical force, which is capable of rapid deployment to foreign airfields.

The Extender offers an unrivalled combination of capabilities. A full payload of 76,843 kg (169,055 lb.) can be carried over a 7033-km (4,360-mi.) range.

Just prior to Desert Storm, an experiment to fit additional, British-built hose refuelling pods beneath each wingtip was completed, providing a three-point refuelling capability.

KC-10A Extender

Type: in-flight-refuelling tanker/strategic airlifter

Powerplant: three 233.53-kN (52,535-lb.-thrust) General Electric CF6-50C2 turbofans

Maximum speed: 982 km/h (609 m.p.h.) at 7620 m (25,000 ft.)

Range: 18,507 km (11,475 mi.) in ferry configuration

Service ceiling: 10,180 m (33,400 ft.)

Weights: operating empty 108,891 kg (240,100 lb.)as a tanker; maximum take-off 267,620 kg (588,764 lb.)

Max payload: 76,843 kg (169,055 lb.) cargo, plus max. internal fuel 161,508 kg (355,310 lb.)

Dimensions: span 47.34 m (155 ft. 3 in.)
length 55.35 m (181 ft. 7 in.)
height 17.70 m (58 ft.)
wing area 358.70 m² (3,860 sq. ft.)

No navigator is needed, thanks to the KC-10A's comprehensive navigation systems. On long-range missions, the flight deck accommodates a pilot, co-pilot and a flight engineer. The flight engineer has a secondary role as loadmaster when cargo is being carried.

Power for the Extender's long-range activities is provided by three General Electric turbofans, fitted with thrust reversers for shortening landing distances. For improving its own endurance, the KC-10A has a refuelling receptacle fitted.

The last KC-10A to be built carries a single Flight Refuelling Limited Mk 32B probe-and-drogue refuelling pod beneath each wing. The remainder of the fleet may be similarly equipped.

The KC-10A fuselage can accommodate up to 25 freight pallets, or mixed loads. A typical mixed load might be 75 seated troops and 17 pallets.

Manufactured by McDonnell Douglas, the Advanced Aerial Refuelling Boom (AARB) is located opposite an additional refuelling hose reel unit for probed aircraft.

KC-10A Extender

During the Libyan Crisis of 1986, Extenders were based at RAF Mildenhall, tasked with the support of the USAF strike force of F-111s.

The KC-10A has a 2.59-m (8-ft. 5-in.) by 3.56-m (11-ft. 8-in.) upward-hinged door in the fuselage side. Rollers and winches are fitted within the freight compartment.

Additional or emergency power is provided by a Garrett TSCP-700-4 auxiliary power unit.

Lacking the nuclear flash curtain and electro-magnetic pulse shielding of the KC-135, the KC-10A is unable to support strategic nuclear strikes.

For tanker missions, the lower fuselage carries fuel bladder cells, taking maximum usable capacity to a total of 206134 litres.

The KC-10A is favoured over the KC-135 by boom operators at least, for its comfortable aft-facing seating position in the rear fuselage.

COMBAT DATA

INTERNAL FUEL CAPACITY

A huge amount of internal fuel allows the KC-10A to refuel fighters several times on long missions, while retaining enough fuel for its own needs. The KC-135A does not fly such support-type missions, although the RAF's Tristar does.

KC-10A EXTENDER 161,508 kg (353,310 lb.)

TRISTAR K.Mk 1 142,111 kg (312,644 lb.)

KC-135A STRATOTANKER 86,047 kg (189,303 lb.)

Douglas airliners in military form

■ DC-3: From its world-beating DC-3, Douglas developed the C-47 Skytrain for military operations. A mainstay of the Allied transport fleet during World War II, the aircraft also served as a gunship in Vietnam. Several remain in service.

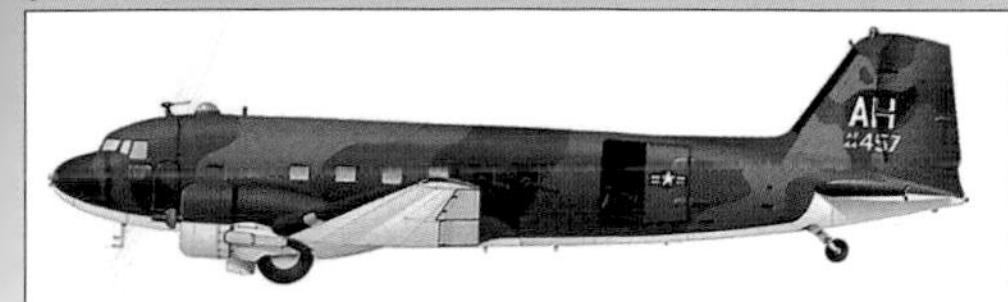

■ DC-6: While the USAF and US Navy both operated military versions of the DC-6, several other air forces flew DC-7 airliner conversions. A number of nations, mostly in South America, still had DC-7s on strength in the mid-1990s.

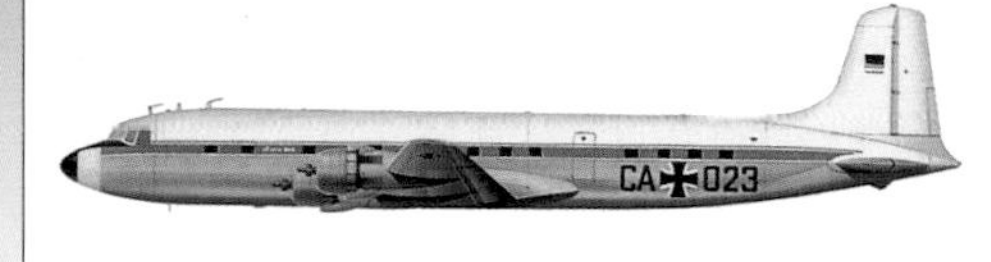

■ DC-9: McDonnell Douglas sold military variants of the DC-9 to the USAF as the C-9 Nightingale, primarily for use in the aeromedical evacuation role. The USN uses the C-9 Skytrain II on fleet logistic support duties.

McDONNELL DOUGLAS T-45 GOSHAWK

● US Navy trainer ● Navalized BAe Hawk ● Latest technology

When it wanted a new trainer, the Navy looked at several aircraft before deciding on Britain's well-established Hawk. Given the designation T-45 and named Goshawk, the aircraft is manufactured in the U.S. This well-known British jet is becoming the standard flying schoolhouse for all who earn the wings of gold worn by US Naval aviators. The T-45 replaces the Rockwell T-2 Buckeye and the Douglas TA-4J Skyhawk.

▲ *Many modifications to the basic Hawk produced the T-45. The nose undercarriage unit is a completely new, stronger unit and features twin wheels and a catapult launch bar.*

PHOTO FILE

McDONNELL DOUGLAS T-45 GOSHAWK

▼ Carrier launch
Steam rises from the catapult as a Goshawk crew prepare to leave the carrier. The T-45 launches at 224 km/h (139 m.p.h.).

▲ Trainer supreme
Sitting on a raised ejection seat, the instructor has an excellent view forward over the student's head. Carrier landings demand optimum visibility.

▲▼ Flying 'dirty' and flying 'clean'
The robust undercarriage, flaps, slats, airbrakes and arrestor hook are all deployed (above) in the landing configuration above while the aircraft is seen below in 'clean' cruising configuration.

▲ Complex wing design
Full-span hydraulically operated leading-edge slats were developed by McDonnell Douglas and are not found on the simpler wing of the BAe Hawk.

FACTS AND FIGURES

- ➤ Compared to previous U.S. Navy training, the cost saving T-45 system uses 42 per cent fewer aircraft.
- ➤ First squadron to with the T-45A is VT-21 Fighting Redhawks at Kingsville, Texas.
- ➤ French navy Rafale pilots will be trained in the US using the Goshawk.
- ➤ Compared with the British Hawk, the T-45 has an extra ventral fin and a tailfin heightened by about six inches.
- ➤ The T-45A will train about 600 new naval pilots each year.
- ➤ Each Navy T-45 is expected to make 16,000 carrier deck landings.

PROFILE

Navy trainer for the next century

Development of the T-45 Goshawk was criticized for taking a long time and costing plenty, but the result gives the U.S. Navy an advanced trainer second to none in the world. Looking very much like a fighter and performing in many ways like one, the T-45 Goshawk is an extensively altered version of the British Hawk, strengthened to permit operation on aircraft carriers.

The T-45 Goshawk is operated as a land-based trainer replacing both the intermediate and advanced trainers of the past and it also operates from aircraft carriers as part of the student pilot program.

Since the Goshawk began carrier trials in 1991, the Navy has been generally pleased with its performance and has moved – too slowly, according to critics – to place the Goshawk in service with training squadrons.

Initially flying from Kingsville, Texas, and now operating at four locations, the T-45 is be the first jet flown by Navy, Marine and Coast Guard aviators (after they fly the Beech T-34 Turbo Mentor) and student pilots fly it until they graduate with their wings.

SMURFS (Side-Mounted Unit horizontal Root tail Fins) help to limit aerodynamic interference between the deployed flaps and the tailplane.

All Hawk variants are fitted with a gas turbine starter unit for starting the engines and onboard systems. The unit exhausts through this distinctive aperture on the spine.

A HUD in the front cockpit can show navigation, flight instrument and weapon aiming data. Two underwing pylons may carry practice bombs.

T-45A Goshawk

Type: two-seat intermediate and advanced flight trainer

Powerplant: one 26.00-kN (5,850-lb.-thrust) Rolls-Royce/Turboméca F405-RR-401 turbofans

Maximum speed: 997 km/h (618 m.p.h.)

Rate of climb: 2128 m/min (7,000 f.p.m.) at sea level

Ferry range: 1854 km (1,147 mi.)

Service ceiling: 12,875 m (42,240 ft.)

Weights: empty 4, 251 kg (9,374 lb.); maximum take-off (5,773 kg (12,731 lb.)

Dimensions:

span	9.39 m	(30 ft. 9 in.)
length	11.97 m	(39 ft. 3 in.)
height	4.24 m	(13 ft. 11 in.)
wing area	16.69 m^2	(180 sq. ft.)

T-45A GOSHAWK

This aircraft belongs to VT-21 Red Hawks, Training Wing Two and was based at NAS Kingsville, Texas, in 1995 in standard high-visibility markings.

Student and instructor each sit on a Martin-Baker Mk 14 NACES (Naval Aircraft Common Ejection-Seat). The seat allows safe escape at zero height and zero air-speed.

Power comes from a single F405-RR-401 engine. With this engine the T-45 burns 55 per cent less fuel than its T-2 Buckeye predecessor.

All Goshawks will eventually be fitted with Cockpit 21. This development replaces the original instruments with two multi-function display screens in each cockpit.

With a launch weight of 5787 kg (13,675 lb.), the T-45's catapult launch bar withstands huge stress. The catapult launches the aircraft at flying speed even with the brakes on.

In order to accommodate the new nose undercarriage unit, a deeper nose section was designed. The nosewheel doors close once the leg is locked down.

The strengthened rear fuselage has two side-mounted airbrakes and a modified F/A-18 arrestor hook, which is capable of holding the T-45 in the event of an accidental snagging of the arrestor cable while the aircraft is still airborne.

ACTION DATA

SPEED

High speed is important for a jet trainer, both to give the student pilot a taste of fast-jet speeds and to shorten any time spent flying between home base and the training area. In the case of the Goshawk, for example, this might allow extra carrier training.

T-45A GOSHAWK 997 km/h (618 m.p.h.)

ALPHA JET E 1000 km/h (620 m.p.h.)

MB-339C 902 km/h (559 m.p.h.)

CLIMB RATE

Rate of climb is important in a similar way to maximum speed. Much training takes place at high altitude in order to give the student room for mistakes. The T-45 loses out here due to the extra weight of its unique naval systems.

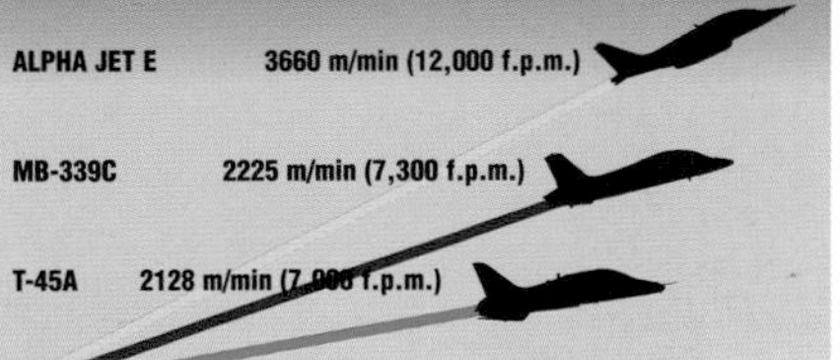

THRUST

Although some critics have suggested that the Goshawk is underpowered, its upgraded F405-RR-401 engine provides adequate thrust for carrier operations and is extremely fuel efficient. The MB-339C is unusual amongst modern trainers in having a turbojet engine that is much less fuel efficient.

ALPHA JET E 26.48 kN (5,960 lb. thrust)

MB-339C 19.57 kN (4,400 lb. thrust)

T-45A GOSHAWK 26.00 kN (5,850 lb. thrust)

Carrier-capable trainers

■ NORTH AMERICAN T-28B TROJAN: From 1952 the T-28 was the US Navy's standard on-and-off-ship basic trainer.

■ ROCKWELL T-2 BUCKEYE: Entering service in 1959, the T-2 is now being replaced in service by the T-45A Goshawk.

■ GRUMMAN TF-9J COUGAR: Developed from the 1950s fighter, the trainer variant continued in service into the 1970s.

■ McDONNELL DOUGLAS TA-4 SKYHAWK: A two-seat version of the highly successful attack jet.

McDonnell Douglas Helicopters

AH-64 Apache

● Armoured gunship ● Tank destroyer ● Infantry close-support

Equipped with video-type electronic aiming devices, Hellfire missiles and rapid-fire cannon, the AH-64 Apache is a new kind of warrior bringing a powerful punch to the battlefield. When a ground commander wants support he summons the Apache, a miracle helicopter which can rush into the fray in any weather, day or night, to pin down the foe and help friendly troops to fight and win.

▲ *Designed to fly and fight in the hostile airspace over a modern battlefield, the AH-64 is a potent weapons platform.*

Photo File

McDonnell Douglas Helicopters AH-64 Apache

▲ All-weather attacker
Fast, agile and very tough, the AH-64 uses its advanced sensors to fly and fight in all conditions.

Tank killer ▶
The Apache's primary weapon is the laser-guided Hellfire missile. It can destroy any known tank.

Combat reliability ▶
Apaches are complex machines, but they are designed to be serviced easily in the field.

▲ Chain Gun
The helicopter's powerful 30-mm (1.18-in) cannon is linked to the crew's helmets, aiming where the pilot or gunner is looking.

◀ See through fog
The Longbow Apache is equipped with millimetric radar which is capable of seeing through rain, fog and snow.

▼ Into action
The Apache was one of the stars in the Gulf War, its hi-tech weaponry proving lethal to a wide range of Iraqi targets.

Facts and Figures

- ➤ The Apache is designed to survive hits from 23-mm (0.91-in) cannon, and the cockpit to withstand hitting the ground at 13 m (42 ft 8 in) per second.
- ➤ The Apache uses a super-heated ceramic block to deceive heat-seeking missiles.
- ➤ Apache operators include Egypt, Greece, Israel, Saudi Arabia, the UAE and the USA.
- ➤ The Apache's 16 laser-guided Hellfire missiles can destroy a tank 20 km (12 miles) away.
- ➤ The Apache uses digital technology to pinpoint targets for commanders, other helicopters, tanks and vehicles.
- ➤ The Apache's Chain Gun weighs 56 kg (123 lb) and fires 625 rounds per minute.

PROFILE

Battlefield destroyer

It is important, when a battle is unfolding, to hit hard and disrupt the enemy's forces. The helicopter represents the new knight in shining armour to ground troops, who need the flexibility and striking power of their own aircraft overhead, and the AH-64 Apache is the undisputed champion of battlefield helicopters.

The Apache uses electronic wizardry to find its way and to aim its hi-tech missiles and cannon. The two pilots of the slender, mantis-like Apache can hug the earth when they need to, or navigate through smoke and rough weather to seek out enemy troops and tanks using night-vision equipment and hi-tech sensors.

Assisted by observation helicopters and staying in close contact with troops on the ground, the Apache is able to shoot with remarkable accuracy from a greater distance than most other combat helicopters.

In high-threat environments Apaches operate at low level, usually attacking from among the trees.

With its combination of speed, durability and accuracy, the Apache brings a new dimension to the ground commander's task of outsmarting and outfighting his adversary.

Communications and avionics systems are carried in armoured fairings on each side of the fuselage.

Power is provided by a pair of 1265-kW (1,696-hp) General Electric engines. Key propulsion components are armour-protected.

The four-bladed main rotor is of laminated steel, glass-reinforced plastic and composite construction.

AH-64A Apache

Israel's Defence Force was the first organization to acquire the Apache after the US Army.

The Israelis have a wealth of combat experience with gunships, and consider the AH-64 the best of its kind. It has the standard gunship layout of gunner in front and pilot behind.

Passive Night Vision (PNV) sensors in the nose include infra-red and TV cameras and a laser designation system.

The engines are fitted with 'Black Hole' infra-red suppression systems as protection against heat-seeking missiles.

The two-tail rotor blades cross at 55°, which reduces the amount of noise they generate.

Apaches carry up to 1,200 rounds of 30-mm ammunition for the Chain Gun. It can fire at up to 625 rounds per minute.

Stub wings carry up to 16 missiles or four pods containing 76 folding-fin 70-mm high-explosive rockets.

The structure of the AH-64 is designed to allow it to withstand hits from high-explosive rounds of up to 23-mm (0.91-in) calibre.

AH-64A Apache

Type: two-seat all-weather attack helicopter

Powerplant: two 1265-kW (1,696-hp) General Electric T700-GE-701 turboshaft engines

Maximum speed: never-exceed speed 365 km/h (227 mph); maximum cruise speed 297 km/h (185 mph)

Initial climb rate: 760 m/min (2500 ft/min)

Weights: empty 5165 kg (11,387 lb); normal mission weight 8000 kg (17,637 lb); maximum take-off 9525 kg (21,000 lb); maximum internal fuel weight 1157 kg (2,551 lb)

Armament: one 30-mm (1.18-in) M230 Chain Gun cannon with 1200 rounds, up to 16 AGM-114 Hellfire laser-guided missiles or up to 76 folding-fin rockets

Dimensions:

rotor diameter	19.55 m (64 ft 2 in)
fuselage length	14.97 m (49 ft 1 in)
height to top of rotor head	4.66 m (15 ft 3 in)
rotor area	168.11 m² (1,810 sq ft)

COMBAT DATA

HOVER CEILING

Both the Apache and the Havoc have more power than the Tiger, and can hover a kilometre higher than the Franco-German machine. This is not the absolute ceiling: sometimes the terrain and air temperature bounce the air from the rotors straight back up in what is called ground effect, and the extra air cushion can add one or two thousand metres to the hover limits.

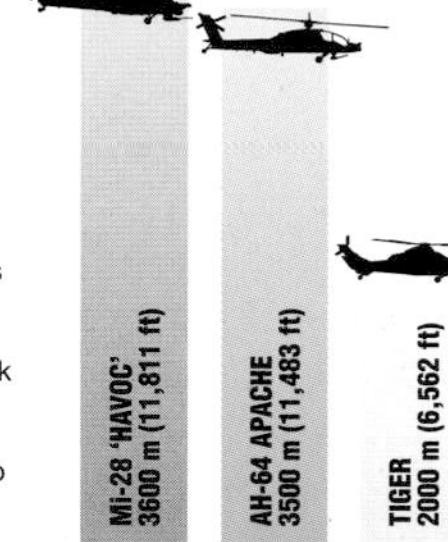

MAXIMUM SPEED

All three helicopters have a good turn of speed, with the Mi-28 having a very slight edge.

Mi-28 'HAVOC'	300 km/h (186 mph)
AH-64 APACHE	297 km/h (185 mph)
TIGER	280 km/h (174 mph)

COMBAT RADIUS

As attack helicopters operate from forward bases close to the fighting, they do not need long range. Fighting at close quarters means that being able to refuel and re-arm quickly is more important than being able to fly great distances.

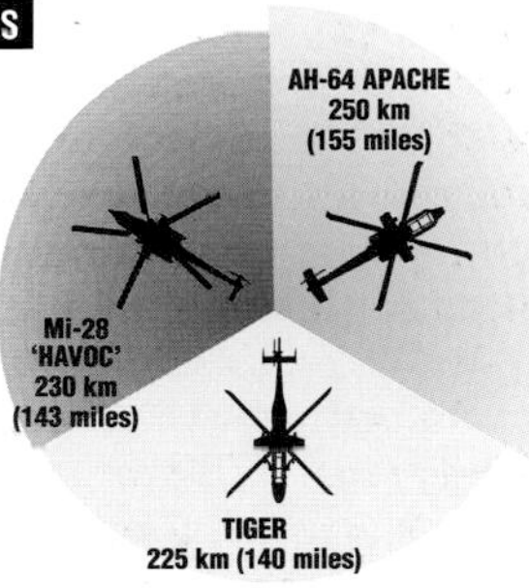

Gulf War battalion attack

1 TEMPORARY BASES: Forward Air Refuelling Points, or FARPs, are established close behind the forward echelons. One of the three AH-64 companies uses it to re-arm.

2 WAITING FOR ACTION: The second Apache company loiters in the air at a holding point some 20 km (12 miles) ahead of the FARP, waiting to replace the company in contact.

3 OPEN FIRE: As soon as an enemy column is located, the lead company moves forward to engage with guns, rockets and Hellfire missiles.

4 CONTINUED ATTACK: As each company exhausts its weapons, it moves back to the FARP and is replaced by the company at the holding point. The enemy is thus kept under continual fire.

McDONNELL DOUGLAS/BAe

AV-8B HARRIER II PLUS

● **Latest Harrier variant** ● **Air-to-air capability** ● **Export orders**

▲ *Outwardly almost indistinguishable from the standard AV-8B, the Harrier II Plus embodies many improvements, including a new radar, new weapons and an upgraded engine.*

Internationally recognised as one of the most potent and versatile warplanes in service, the original second-generation Harrier II was penalised by its lack of radar. In the UK, British Aerospace (BAe) had produced the Sea Harrier by adding radar to the basic Harrier, a trend that has been repeated with the Harrier II Plus. With the APG-65 radar from the F/A-18A Hornet, the Harrier II Plus has gained a formidable beyond-visual-range (BVR) capability.

PHOTO FILE

McDONNELL DOUGLAS/BAe AV-8B HARRIER II PLUS

▲ First rebuild

Unpainted and showing the various different structural materials, the first rebuilt Harrier II Plus performs a hover.

▼ European operators

Italy and Spain have procured the latest AV-8B. Both countries employ the aircraft primarily in the air defence role.

'Flying Tigers' ▶

The first unit of the US Marine Corps to receive the Harrier II Plus was VMA-542, which took delivery of its first example in 1993. One of its aircraft is seen here dropping Mk 82 Snakeye bombs during a training sortie.

◀ Variation in colours

Different paint schemes can be seen on the Harrier II Plus. Most sport two-tone Ghost Grey, though these two examples have much darker upper surfaces.

Reduction in orders ▶

Originally it was hoped that the entire USMC fleet would be upgraded to Harrier II Plus standard, but defence cutbacks during the 1990s have reduced the total to 99 aircraft.

FACTS AND FIGURES

- Since the first Harrier II Plus took to the air in 1992, engine failure has resulted in one of the prototypes crashing.
- A primary motivation for the programme was experience from the first Gulf War.
- All of the improved AV-8Bs were delivered by 2002.
- All the Harrier II Plus variants receive entirely new fuselages. This is cheaper than modifying the old ones.
- The introduction of the new aircraft has resulted in a true multi-role Harrier.
- Italy has been the first country to acquire trainers before single-seat variants.

PROFILE

Harrier II receives an update

Already a proven dogfighter with the short-range AIM-9 Sidewinder air-to-air missile (AAM), the Harrier II has now matured into an all-weather fighter, with the capability to engage BVR targets using AIM-7 Sparrow and AIM-120 AMRAAM radar-guided AAMs. The Harrier II Plus retains the close-support capability of its predecessor, but adds an important air defence role. In June 1987 McDonnell Douglas and BAe announced their intention to develop a radar-equipped Harrier as a private venture. By late 1990, Italy, Spain and the US had signed a joint agreement for Harrier II Plus funding. The first prototype flew on 22 September 1992.

Since then, the USMC has received 27 new aircraft, andanother 72 were converted from AV-8Bs. Spain has received eight machines, and Italy has received 16, with options on a further eight.

Above: Another feature has been to increase the number of wing pylons from six to eight, in line with the RAF's aircraft. The new APG-65 radar and AIM-120 AMRAAM can be carried.

Left: Pilots have welcomed the introduction of the new aircraft and one, serving with VMA-542 'Flying Tigers', went so far as to describe it as a 'quantum leap for the Marines'.

AV-8B Harrier II Plus

Type: single-seat air-defence/close-support V/STOL aircraft

Powerplant: one 105.9-kN (23,825-lb.-thrust) Rolls-Royce Pegasus vectored-thrust turbofan

Maximum speed: 1065 km/h (660 m.p.h.)

Endurance: 3 hours

Combat radius: 1101 km (683 mi.)

Range: 3035 km (1,882 mi.)

Weights: empty 6336 kg (13,939 lb.); loaded 14,061 kg (20,552 lb.)

Armament: one 25 mm GAU-12/A cannon plus 11 hardpoints for various external stores

Dimensions:

span	9.25 m	(30 ft. 4 in.)
length	14.55 m	(47 ft. 9 in.)
height	3.55 m	(11 ft. 8 in.)
wing area	21.37 m²	(230 sq. ft.)

AV-8B Harrier II Plus

BuNo.164553 was one of the first Harrier II Plus variants to be delivered, being taken on charge by VMA-542 'Flying Tigers' at NAS Cherry Point in North Carolina, which has been a centre of US Marine Corps Harrier operations since the early 1970s.

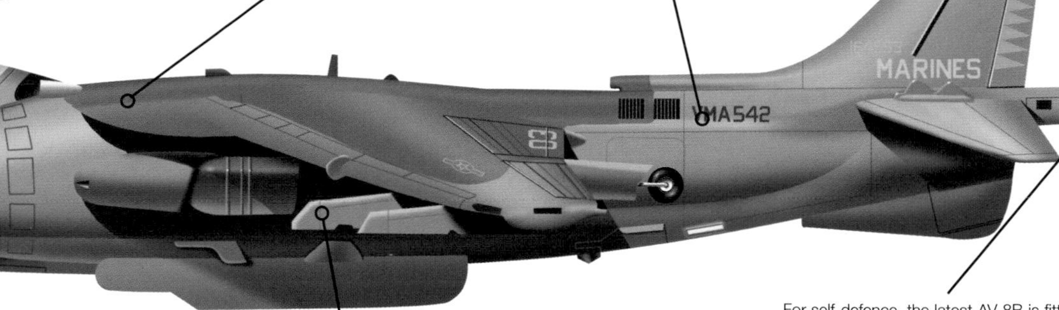

Unlike early Harriers, the second-generation aircraft have retractable refuelling probes, which can be fitted to the port side of the fuselage above the intake. They are not always fitted, as is shown on this particular example.

Compared to the original Hawker design, the AV-8B series makes greater use of composite materials and graphite epoxy. The fuselage is somewhat longer and also stronger, with a much longer fatigue life than that of the early variants.

The lack of an adequate radar remained a handicap of the Harrier force for many years. Fitting the APG-65 into the AV-8B has resulted in a vastly superior machine, and has turned it into an effective sea defence fighter, offering better capability than the British Sea Harrier.

One improvement of the Harrier II Plus has been to increase the number of underwing hardpoints from six to eight. The latest AV-8B is also capable of carrying the AIM-120 AMRAAM (Advanced Medium-Range Air-to-Air Missile).

For self-defence, the latest AV-8B is fitted with a forward- and aft-looking RWR (radar warning receiver), a Goodyear AN/ALE-39 chaff dispenser and a Doppler MAW (missile approach warning) radar. This last item is fitted to the protruding tail boom unit.

COMBAT DATA

MAXIMUM SPEED

As the only truly effective V/STOL combat aircraft in service, the Harrier II has an impressive turn of speed. It is quicker than the Russian Sukhoi Su-25, which was also designed for battlefield support, but the Jaguar A is quicker still.

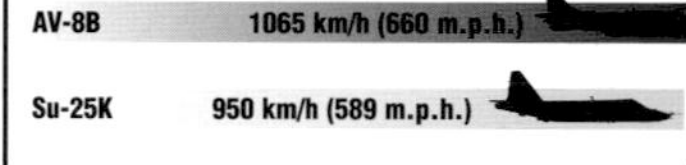

COMBAT RADIUS

Today's attack aircraft are designed to reach their targets at low level, in order to avoid tracking by enemy radar. Compared to the Jaguar and Su-25, the Harrier II Plus has a greater radius of action which is also a great improvement over the original Harrier.

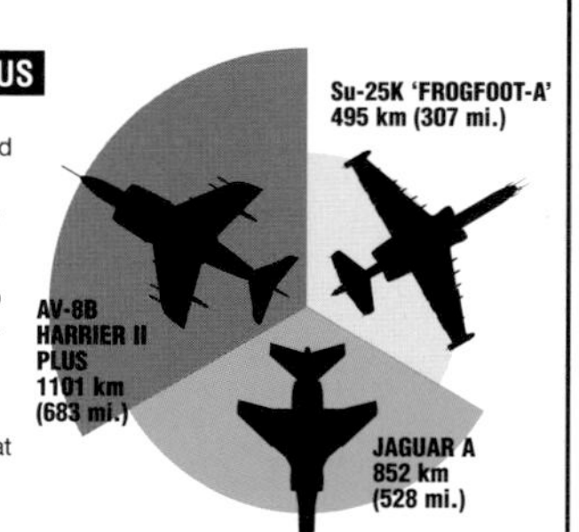

CLIMB RATE

With its twin afterburning Adour turbofans, the SEPECAT Jaguar A (for Attack) has a phenomenal climb rate. The Su-25K 'Frogfoot' is not far behind, nor is the Harrier II, both of which can carry a greater amount of external stores.

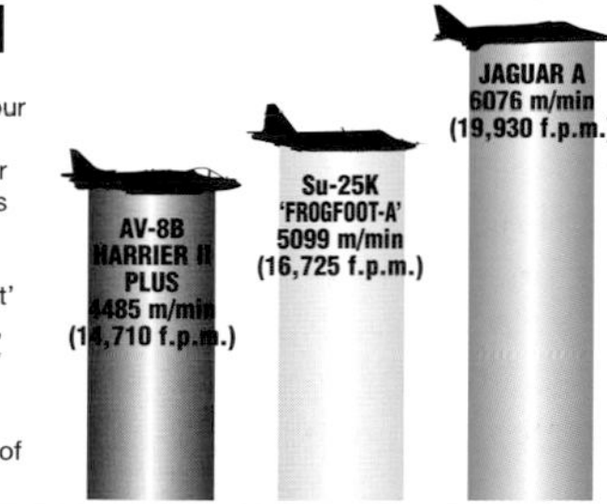

Evolution of the Harrier

■ **HAWKER P.1127:** Forerunner of what became known as the Harrier, the P.1127 performed its first hover in October 1960.

■ **HAWKER KESTREL FGA.Mk 1:** With the success of the P.1127, nine development aircraft, known as Kestrels, were procured.

■ **HAWKER SIDDELEY AV-8A HARRIER:** First-generation Harriers were acquired by the USMC. They have been replaced by AV-8Bs.

■ **HAWKER SIDDELEY HARRIER GR.Mk 3:** Representing the pinnacle of early Harrier development, the GR.Mk 3 served until 1993.

MIKOYAN-GUREVICH

MiG-15 'FAGOT'

● Swept-wing fighter ● Korean War warrior ● Sabre's foe

▲ *Crude and simple it may have been, but in many ways the MiG-15 was the best fighter in the world when it first flew in the late 1940s. In the hands of experienced Soviet pilots, it was a real threat to the West.*

In the history of war, few events have been as shocking as the surprise debut of the MiG-15 in Korea. Unprepared, the United States saw its aircraft suffer defeat after defeat until the F-86 Sabre was thrown into the fray. The duel between Sabre and MiG-15 became a classic military campaign. Although superior in some ways, the MiG-15 ultimately suffered a seven-to-one defeat by American Sabre pilots.

PHOTO FILE

MIKOYAN-GUREVICH MiG-15 'FAGOT'

▲ **Combat trainer**
Due to the success of the MiG-15UTI, China built a derivative based mainly on the MiG-17. Called the Chengdu JJ-5, more than 1000 have been produced, including this example flown by the Bangladesh air force.

▲ **Swept-wing pioneer**
The MiG-15 was designed using German research (captured by the USSR in 1945) into swept wings, and was one of the first operational jets of this type.

▲ **Founder of a family**
A Polish MiG-15, flanked here by two MiG-17s, is distinguishable by its lack of an afterburning tailpipe. The MiG-17 was a more powerful evolution of the basic design, which retained all the earlier jet's agility and fighting ability. The two-seat MiG-15UTI was used as a basic trainer by many Warsaw Pact nations.

▲ **Cold War defender**
The MiG-15 formed the backbone of Soviet and Warsaw Pact air forces for most of the 1950s.

Middle East survivor ▶
Egypt has long been a MiG user. Surviving two-seat MiG-15UTIs have been upgraded with Western avionics.

FACTS AND FIGURES

- ➤ The MiG-15 was initially given the NATO codename 'Falcon'. It was thought too favourable, and was changed to 'Fagot'.
- ➤ The first flight took place on 30 December 1947, three months after the XP-86 Sabre.
- ➤ Early MiG-15s had RD-45F engines; improved versions had the VK-1 engine.
- ➤ When the Korean War began, 1,200 MiG-15s were flying; Britain had only two aircraft with swept wings.
- ➤ The Allies in Korea offered $100,000 to any pilot who would defect in a MiG-15.
- ➤ Several MiG-15s now fly as 'warbirds' in private hands in the USA and the UK.

PROFILE

The first Cold War superfighter

The MiG-15, which first flew weeks after the F-86 Sabre, proved that the Soviet Union could design, produce and use a jet fighter as modern as any in the world. The MiG-15 had better climb, ceiling, rate of roll and turn radius than early F-86s, and only with late versions of the F-86F, introduced in 1953, did the Soviet fighter inescapably meet its superior. The Sabre's success against the MiG was due less to the aircraft than to the skill and tactics of American pilots.

Still, the MiG-15 was a triumph – the word MiG itself is recognized by more humans than any other aircraft name. The Mikoyan-Gurevich bureau's best-known product became one of the most numerous warplanes in the second half of the twentieth century, operated by dozens of countries.

Although no two-seat version of its arch-rival, the Sabre, succeeded, more than 1000 MiG-15UTI two-seaters have trained pilots the world over, and a small number remain in service with Third World nations.

The US Air Force acquired a MiG-15 during the Korean War, and tested it very thoroughly. Famed test pilot Chuck Yeager was impressed by the rugged Soviet-built jet.

MiG-15UTI 'Midget'

Type: two-seat advanced pilot and weapons trainer

Powerplant: one 26.48-kN (5,956-lb-thrust) VK-1 centrifugal-flow turbojet (derived from Rolls-Royce Nene)

Maximum speed: 1073 km/h (667 mph) at sea level

Range: 1424 km (885 miles)

Service ceiling: 15,600 m (51,181 ft)

Weights: empty 4000 kg (8,818 lb); loaded 5400 kg (11,905 lb)

Armament: often not fitted, or one 23-mm (0.91-in) cannon with 80 rounds or one 12.7-mm (0.5-in) cannon with 150 rounds, plus option of two 500-kg (1,100-lb) bombs carried underwing as an alternative to drop-tanks

Dimensions:		
	span	10.08 m (33 ft 1 in)
	length	10.04 m (33 ft)
	height	3.74 m (12 ft 3 in)
	wing area	20.60 m² (222 sq ft)

MiG-15UTI 'Midget'

Before most were destroyed on the ground during the 1991 Gulf War, Iraq operated a number of MiG-15s and MiG-17s, including two-seat MiG-15UTIs such as this one, which was based at the Rashid training college.

The pylon in the centre of the gaping air intake splits incoming air and ducts around the cockpit before it reaches the engine, buried in the rear fuselage.

As a trainer, the MiG-15 makes a good introduction to the flying characteristics of later MiGs. However, the instructor's view from the rear seat is limited.

MiG-15s were much more heavily armed than their American opponents in Korea, and MiG-15 trainers still carry a powerful 23-mm (0.91-in) cannon under the nose.

The huge wide-chord swept tailfin houses a gyro-compass in its base, and has room for a radar warning receiver.

The MiG-15's modestly swept wing can be fitted with a pair of underwing pylons for light bombs, rockets or drop-tanks.

Much of the MiG's performance was due to its engine. The Klimov VK-1 was based on the Rolls-Royce Nene supplied to the Soviet Union by Britain soon after World War II.

COMBAT DATA

CLIMB RATE

The F-86 was more powerful than the MiG, and from sea level was initially a faster-climbing machine. But it was also heavier, and at higher altitudes the Soviet-built jet had a considerable advantage. The F-80 was one of the first generation of jet fighters and lacked the performance of its swept-wing rivals.

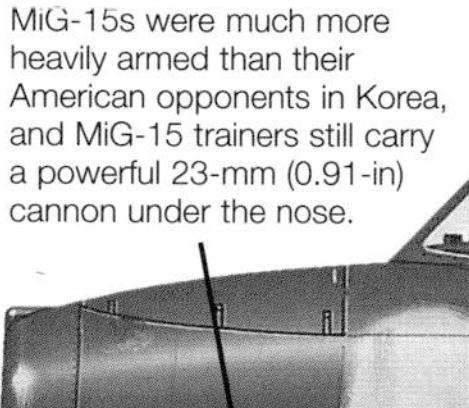
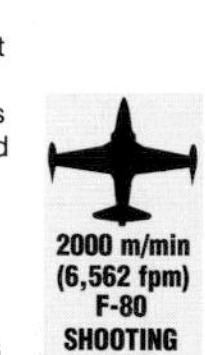
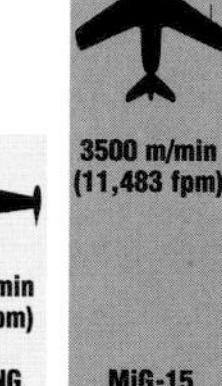
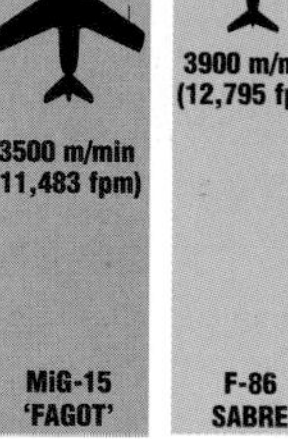

F-80 SHOOTING STAR	MiG-15 'FAGOT'	F-86 SABRE
2000 m/min (6,562 fpm)	3500 m/min (11,483 fpm)	3900 m/min (12,795 fpm)

MAXIMUM SPEED

MiG-15 'FAGOT'	1073 km/h (667 mph)
F-86 SABRE	1075 km/h (668 mph)
AF-80 SHOOTING STAR	960 km/h (597 mph)

Both the MiG and its great rival the Sabre were greatly superior to the previous generation of jets. The Sabre was marginally faster at high altitude, but the MiG probably handled a little better.

SERVICE CEILING

Once again, the MiG and the Sabre proved to be considerably more capable than the earlier generation of jets. The MiG's high ceiling was of particular value in the early days of the Korean War, when they often used it to climb high above American B-29 bombers and their fighter escorts.

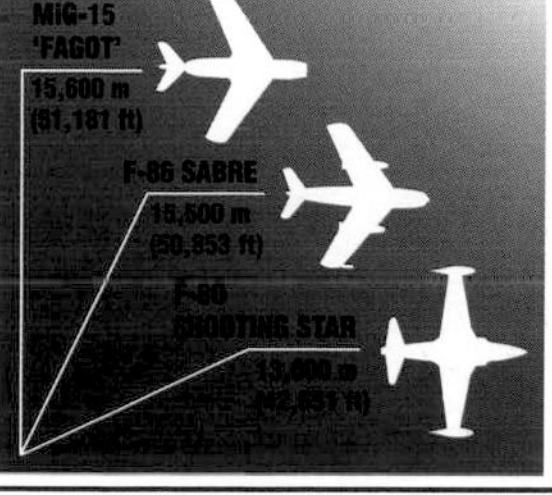

MiG shootdown!

The MiG had a better climb rate and acceleration and was more manoeuvrable at high altitude than its American opponent in Korea, the Sabre. But any advantage the Communists had was negated by the better-trained American pilots: in two years of fierce fighting, 780 MiG-15s were downed for the loss of 110 Sabres. In the last six months of the war F-86s achieved a kill ratio of nearly nine to one.

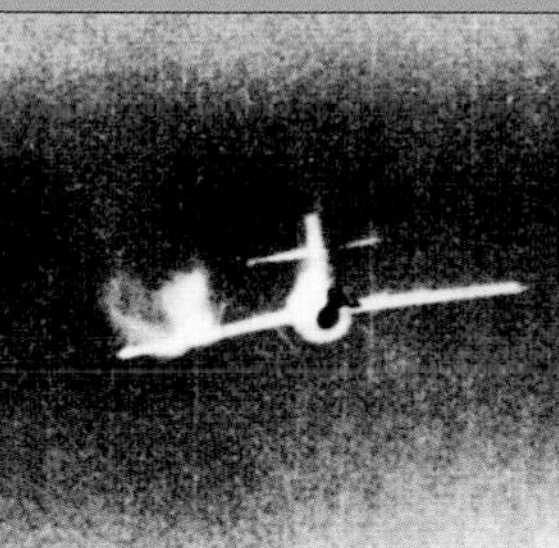

MIKOYAN-GUREVICH

MiG-17 'FRESCO'

● MiG-15 successor ● Interceptor/ground attack ● Huge production

In January 1950, barely a year after the MiG-15 had entered service, Mikoyan flew the first prototype of its successor. The new fighter, designated MiG-17 and named 'Fresco' by NATO, was to be one of the most widely exported of all Soviet military aircraft. More than 9000 were built, including approximately 900 produced in Poland as the LIM-5 and LIM-6. Several of the world's smaller air forces were still flying the type in the early 1990s.

▲ *Pilots were pleased that the high-speed stability and control problems of the MiG-15 had been solved in the MiG-17.*

PHOTO FILE

MIKOYAN-GUREVICH MiG-17 'FRESCO'

▼ Afterburning night-fighter
East Germany operated the radar-equipped, afterburning MiG-17PF 'Fresco-D' all-weather/night fighter.

▲ Afterburning variant
The MiG-17F 'Fresco-C', which introduced the afterburning VK-1F engine, quickly replaced the MiG-17 'Fresco' in service. It formed the basis of most export aircraft and Chinese and Polish production.

▲ MiG-17SN experimental
The side-mounted intakes of the SN allowed the whole nose section to be occupied by a rotating cannon assembly.

▼ Syrian defector
Two MiG-17Fs fell into Israeli hands when their Syrian pilots defected. They were extensively tested by the Israeli air force.

▲ Radar scanner and cannon
Using an installation similar to that of the MiG-15, the MiG-17PF's upper intake-lip radome housed an RP-1 Izumrud radar scanner. A third NR-23 cannon was installed in place of the N-37D and the fuselage was slightly lengthened.

FACTS AND FIGURES

- The first MiG-17, which was also known as the MiG-17, SI, I-330 or MiG-15bis-45°, flew on 13 January 1950.
- On 20 March 1950 the second MiG-17 prototype crashed.
- Flight testing of an afterburner-equipped MiG-17 began on 29 September 1951.
- More than 1700 MiG-17s have been exported, not including licensed production.
- Poland retired its last licence-built MiG-17s in 1991/92.
- A number of 'Frescos' are flown by a secret squadron of the USAF.

PROFILE

Multi-faceted 'Fresco'

Developed to improve on the MiG-15's handling, especially at high speeds, the MiG-17 featured a thinner, more swept wing, longer fuselage and a bigger tail. Deliveries started in 1952, and by 1953 almost all MiG-15 production lines had switched to the new design. The MiG-17P, with radar scanners in the nose and a slightly longer fuselage to make room for the additional equipment, was an interceptor version of the basic MiG-17.

The MiG-17F introduced an afterburning engine, and the PF was an afterburner-equipped counterpart of the MiG-17P. Until this point all MiG-17s had been armed with guns, but the PFU carried four AA-1 'Alkali' air-to-air missiles instead. This entered service in the late 1950s.

As newer fighters appeared, many MiG-17s switched to ground attack. The Polish-built LIM-5M used rockets to shorten its take-off run with an increased bombload, and a braking parachute to shorten landing distances. MiG-17Fs were also produced in China as Shenyang J-5s. Aircraft built for export were designated F-5 and FT-5.

This Soviet MiG-17F has the twin 600-litre (159-US gal) drop-tanks, a near-standard feature.

Hardest hitting of the 'Fresco-C's' weapons was the 37-mm (1.46-in) cannon mounted in a fairing on the lower starboard nose. The MiG-17P, PF and SP-2 MiG-17 all had variations of the standard armament.

Compared to the MiG-15, the 'Fresco' had one extra wing fence on each wing. The inner fence was moved inboard and the new fence was fitted outboard of the ailerons.

MiG-17F 'Fresco-C'

Type: single-seat fighter

Powerplant: one 33.2-kN (7,467-lb-thrust) Klimov VK-1F afterburning turbojet

Maximum speed: 1100 km/h (684 mph) at 3000 m (9,843 ft)

Initial climb rate: 3900 m/min (12,795 fpm)

Combat radius: 700 km (435 miles) on a hi-lo-hi mission with two 250-kg (550-lb) bombs

Service ceiling: 16,600 m (54,462 ft)

Weights: empty 3930 kg (8,664 lb); maximum take-off 6069 kg (13,380 lb)

Armament: two 23-mm (0.91-in) NR-23 and one 37-mm (1.46-in) N-37D cannon, plus 500 kg (1,100 lb) of bombs

Dimensions:

span	9.63 m (31 ft 7 in)
length	11.26 m (36 ft 11 in)
height	3.80 m (12 ft 6 in)
wing area	22.60 m² (243 sq ft)

MiG-17F 'FRESCO-C'

Indonesia received large numbers of Soviet aircraft in the 1960s. Among these were several MiG fighters, including the MiG-17Fs which flew with the aerobatic team of No. 11 Squadron, Indonesian air force.

Mikoyan-Gurevich developed its own aircraft escape systems and the MiG-17 had the third type of ejection seat produced by the company. The seat had a face blind, similar to that of contemporary Martin-Baker seats.

MiG found it necessary to increase the area of the vertical fin to 4.26 m² (46 sq ft). The company went to great lengths to ensure that none of the MiG-15's handling problems was inherited by the new fighter.

The six-petal afterburner nozzle of the MiG-17F varied in diameter from 540 to 624 mm (21¼ to 24½ in), according to power setting. Afterburning was initially limited to a three-minute burst up to 7000 m (22,966 ft).

Cannon armament was an important feature of early MiG jets and the MiG-17F carried twin NR-23 cannon low down on the port forward fuselage.

After testing the I-330 MiG-17 prototypes, MiG altered the airbrakes to give them an area of 1.76 m² (19 sq ft). This area was increased again in the 'Fresco-C', and its more powerful, larger airbrake actuator rams were covered by distinctive blister fairings.

COMBAT DATA

THRUST

Even with afterburning the 'Fresco-C' had less thrust than the non-afterburning Hunter F.Mk 6 and F-86H Sabre. The Hunter did not, however, have the development potential of the Soviet aircraft.

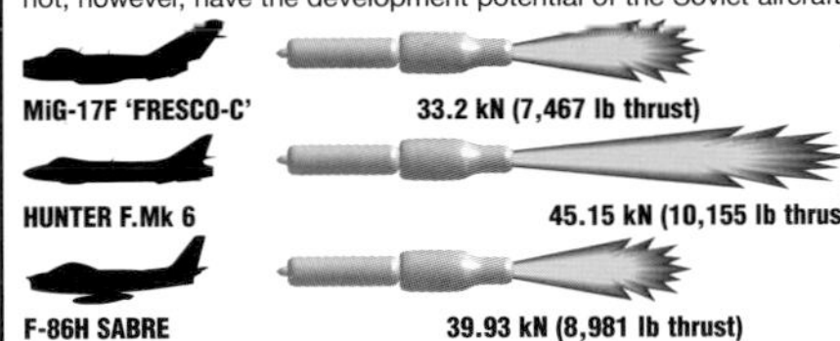

SERVICE CEILING

Both the Hunter and Sabre represented developments of older designs, and neither could equal the altitude performance of the MiG-17F. The MiG was to remain in widespread service as an effective combat aircraft long after its Western rivals.

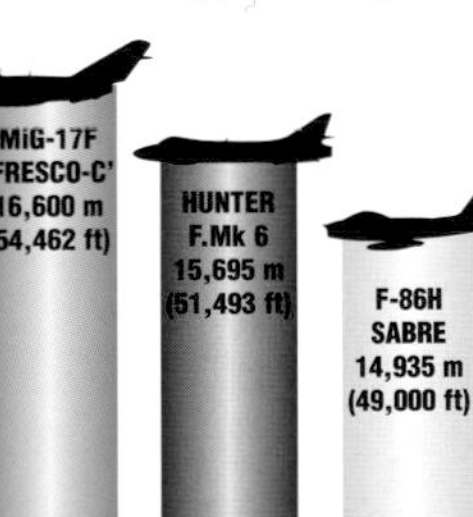

MiG fighter development

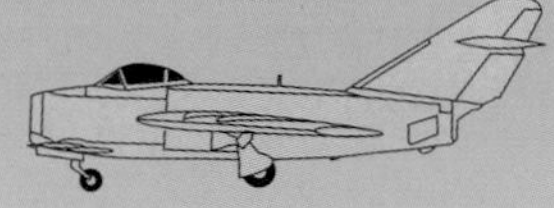

MIG-15 'FAGOT': Known also as the I-310, the MiG-15 came as a shock to the West when it was encountered over Korea in 1950. It was the world's first successful swept-wing fighter.

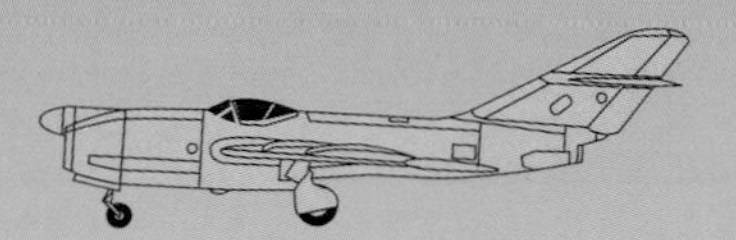

I-320: Designed in response to a 1948 requirement for a long-range radar-equipped fighter, the I-320 was a twin-engined development of the MiG-15. Three were built.

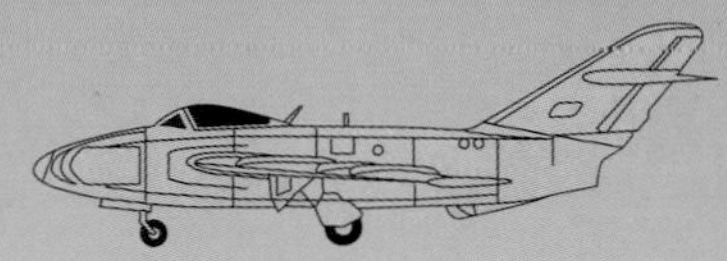

SN: A development of the MiG-17, the SN had guns installed in the nose that pivoted in the vertical plane. Side-mounted intakes were fitted. Performance was shown to suffer during trials.

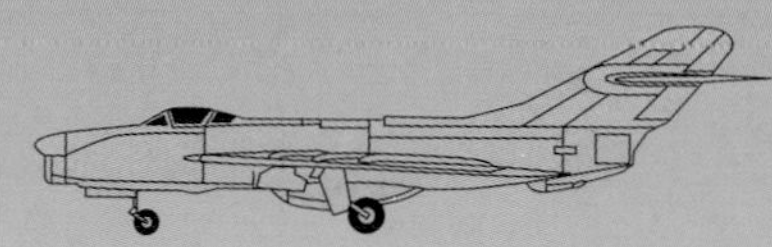

I-350: A supersonic, radar-equipped derivative of the MiG-17, the I-350 used a single, untested engine design. The unreliability of this powerplant led to the aircraft's cancellation.

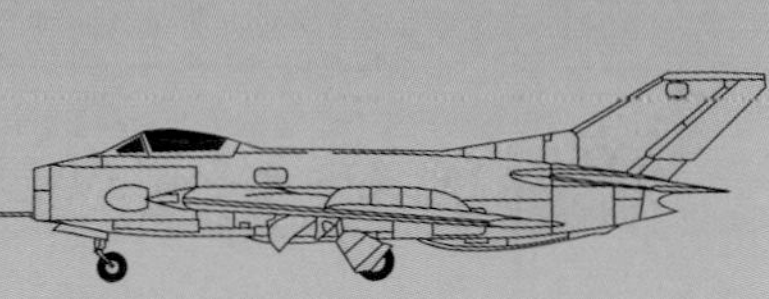

MiG-19 'FARMER': The Soviet air force's first supersonic fighter, the twin-engined MiG-19 was the last swept-wing MiG design before the delta-wing MiG-21. Large numbers were built.

MIKOYAN-GUREVICH

MIG-19 'FARMER'

● 1960s dogfighter ● Indo-Pak War veteran ● Supersonic interceptor

Entering service in 1955, the MiG-19 'Farmer' was Russia's first supersonic fighter. More than four decades later, this sleek Mikoyan-Gurevich aircraft remains a formidable opponent in a dogfight. The 'Farmer' has the traditional MiG agility and its cannon produce enormous firepower. Although quickly replaced in the Soviet Union, derivatives of the MiG-19 have found remarkable success in China, which has exported it to many countries.

▲ *The MiG-19 showed that Soviet aviation remained as advanced as that of the USA during the 1950s, taking fighter aircraft through the sound barrier with a design that still remains in service.*

PHOTO FILE

MIKOYAN-GUREVICH MIG-19 'FARMER'

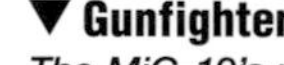

▼ Gunfighter

The MiG-19's powerful armament of three 30-mm (1.18-in) cannon outranged most of its opponents.

▲ Radar gunsight

Later MiG-19s, such as this 'M' version, had primitive ranging radar and also carried four simple 'beam-riding' air-to-air missiles.

▲ Wing fence

The large blade on top of the wing is called a 'fence' and is designed to reduce drag.

▼ Pakistan's finest

Pakistan uses the Chinese-built Shenyang F-6, a greatly improved copy of the MiG-19.

▲ Dogfight victim

This Chinese-built MiG-19 of the Pakistan air force is caught in a dogfight with an F-16. The MiG-19 cannot hold its own against modern fighters.

FACTS AND FIGURES

- About 2700 MiG-19s were manufactured, compared with 2294 examples of the contemporary American Super Sabre.
- Small numbers of Chinese-supplied MiG-19s fought in the Vietnam War.
- A few Soviet 'Farmers' had a 'Scan Odd' gun-ranging radar in the upper nose.
- A MiG-19 prototype, the I-350, may have beaten the North American F-100 past the sound barrier.
- The aircraft also served in Poland, Bulgaria, East Germany and Romania.
- The Chinese Shenyang F-6 version made its first flight in December 1961.

PROFILE

MiG goes supersonic

The Mikoyan-Gurevich design bureau confirmed its place in the front ranks of world aircraft design with its very impressive twin-engined MiG-19. The North American F-100 Super Sabre, flown on 25 May 1953, is traditionally regarded as the first fighter capable of supersonic speed in level flight; however, the production MiG-19, which took to the air the following year, was never far behind. And at Mach 1.33, it was much faster than its American counterpart.

The MiG-19 'Farmer' was not built in as large numbers as the earlier MiG-17 and later MiG-21, and production was transferred to Czechoslovakia in 1958. In the same year China began to build its version, the Shenyang F-6.

MiG-19s served Soviet Frontal Aviation squadrons through the 1960s, with later versions receiving radar and guided missiles. The Chinese-built F-6 became the backbone of the PLA air force, and this version was still in production as recently as 1990. It has been exported widely in the Third World, uprated with new ejection seats, avionics and Sidewinder missiles.

Above: The higher landing speeds of aircraft such as the MiG-19 made brakechutes a standard feature on fighters in the mid-1960s. Initially dismissed as inferior by American observers, the MiG-19 'Farmer' was later reappraised.

Above: Czechoslovakia produced large numbers of MiG-19s, designated the S-105. The aircraft's large ventral airbrake can clearly be seen in this picture.

MiG-19SF 'Farmer-C'

Type: single-seat day fighter-bomber

Powerplant: two 32.66-kN (7,346-lb-thrust) MNPK 'Soyuz' (Tumansky) RD-9BM afterburning turbojets

Maximum speed: 1452 km/h (902 mph) at high altitude

Ferry range: 2200 km (1,367 miles)

Service ceiling: 18,500 m (60,695 ft)

Weights: empty 5760 kg (12,700 lb); maximum take-off 9100 kg (20,062 lb)

Armament: two or three 30-mm (1.18-in) NR-30 cannon each with 73 rounds; provision for two bombs of up to 454 kg (1,000 lb) (usually 227-kg/500-lb) bombs carried), various single or multi-barrel pod rockets, two 767-litre (203-US gal) fuel tanks or four missiles

Dimensions:

Dimensions:	span	9.20 m (30 ft 2 in)
	length	12.60 m (41 ft 4 in)
	height	3.88 m (12 ft 9 in)
	wing area	25.00 m² (269 sq ft)

MiG-19S 'Farmer'

This carmine-red and blue-grey aircraft was part of a special aerobatic display team organized in the VVS Moscow Military District from 1958 until 1966.

The cockpit has relatively cluttered forward visibility due to the large gunsight. The ejection seat cannot be used safely at low airspeeds.

The MiG-19 has a highly swept wing in order to attain its supersonic speed. Four pylons on the wings could carry the K5M 'Alkali' missile. Pakistan's Shenyang J-6s carry the more effective American AIM-9P Sidewinder.

Like the MiG-15 and MiG-17, the MiG-19 had prominent wing fences to reduce induced drag. The MiG-19PM had no cannon but carried four underwing missiles.

The improved MiG-19S featured an all-moving tailplane as well as other refinements to the flying controls. The distinctive kink in the fin leading edge is a useful recognition feature to distinguish the MiG-19 from the similar MiG-17.

47

The first MiG-19s had three 23-mm NR-23 cannon, but these were upgraded to NR-30s in later production aircraft. The 30-mm gun caused devastating damage but had a short range and slow rate of fire.

Air was fed through a nose intake containing a splitter plate that separated the airflow to each engine. The air passed through the airframe in two tunnels under the cockpit, then to the engines.

The MiG-19PF had more powerful Mikulin engines and later versions used Tumansky RD-9B turbojets. The Wopen engine of the Chinese-built versions is almost identical.

COMBAT DATA

COMBAT RADIUS

Soviet designers have traditionally given their aircraft greater performance at the expense of range, by cutting fuel capacity. The low cost of MiGs compared to Western fighters meant that their short range could be compensated for by building more aircraft and bases around the edge of the Soviet Union. The latest MiG-29 was designed with the same tactical philosophy as the old MiG-19.

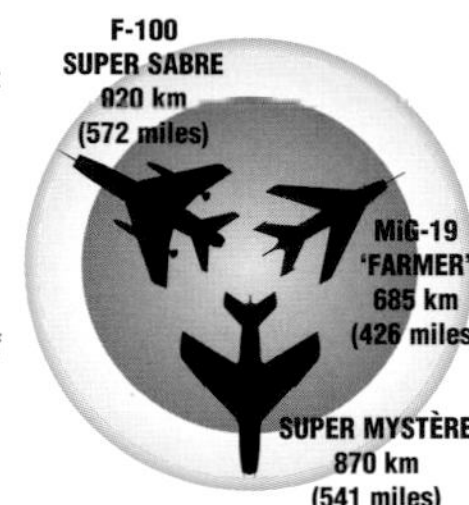

MAXIMUM SPEED

The MiG-19 could outrun any fighter of its day with reheat selected, easily faster than the Super Mystère or F-100.

F-100 SUPER SABRE 1390 km/h (864 mph)

MiG-19 'FARMER' 1462 km/h (908 mph)

SUPER MYSTÈRE

WEAPONS

Since the 1930s heavy cannon were a favoured feature of Russian designers. The three 23-mm (0.91-in) cannon of early MiG-19s were replaced by even harder hitting 30-mm (1.18-in) NR-30 cannon, which had a higher rate of fire.

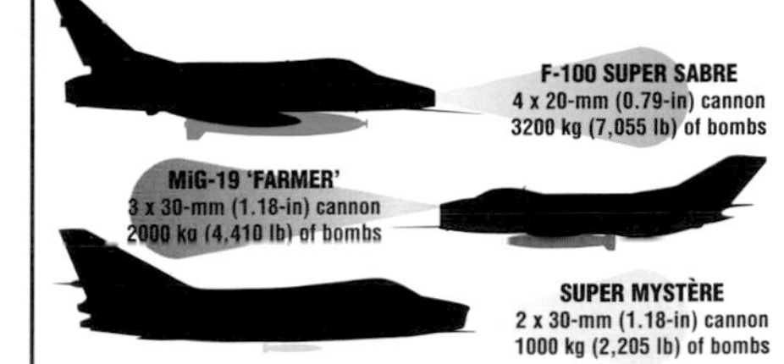

1954 MiG-19 'Farmer' 1452 km/h

1950 F-86 Sabre 1080 km/h (671 mph)

1945 Me 262 870 km/h (541 mph)

1940 Spitfire Mk I 595 km/h (370 mph)

The race for faster fighters

The 1940s Spitfire could reach around 595 km/h (370 mph), but by the end of the war the swept-wing Me 262 jet exceeded 870 km/h (541 mph). The American F-86E Sabre of the Korean War had a top speed of 1080 km/h (671 mph) in level flight. And by 1954 the twin afterburning engines of the MiG-19 blasted it past the sound barrier in level flight, touching 1452 km/h (902 mph).

Mikoyan-Gurevich

MiG-21 'Fishbed' (Early)

● First generation ● Outstanding performance ● Record-breaker

In the early 1950s, a small number of MiG design bureau members began to study a concept for an interceptor capable of reaching speeds of 2000 km/h (1,243 mph). Two designs of swept- and delta-wing configuration were chosen, known as Ye-2 and Ye-4, respectively. The delta-wing model was selected for production and this became the MiG-21F, which entered service with the VVS (Soviet air force) in 1959.

▲ *First-generation MiG-21s were somewhat limited as frontline interceptors, yet they were superb aerial performers. More importantly, they became the most numerous jet fighter.*

Photo File

Mikoyan-Gurevich MiG-21 'Fishbed' (Early)

◀ Vapour trails
An early MiG-21F-13 is seen during a climb. The smoke trailing from the wings appears to be caused by vortices but is, in fact, coming from the twin ARS-57 rocket-launchers which were fitted beneath the wings.

▼ Quickest and cleanest
Early MiG-21s had very clean lines, making them lithe-looking aircraft compared to their successors.

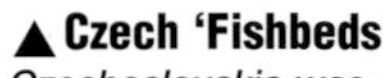

▲ Czech 'Fishbeds'
Czechoslovakia was one of the first countries to acquire a licence to build MiG-21s. Known as CS-106s, these lacked the transparent panels behind the cockpit canopy.

▼ Stopping aid
Despite being a very light aircraft, the MiG-21 still required a braking parachute to slow it down upon landing.

▲ Design limitations
Compared to Western fighters of the period, the MiG-21 was small, sleek and simple. This resulted in limited avionics and armament, and the early variants were barely acceptable as frontline fighters.

Facts and Figures

- ➤ With more than 10,000 built and service with 56 different air forces, the MiG-21 is the most widely built jet fighter.
- ➤ In 1961 a prototype, the Ye-6/3, set a world height record of 34,714 m (113,891 ft).
- ➤ A MiG-21F-13 was the first 'Fishbed' to be acquired by the USAF for evaluation.
- ➤ The exhilarating performance of the early variants led to one Indian pilot dubbing his as 'my supersonic sports car'.
- ➤ Chengdu F-7s are basically new-build first-generation MiG-21s.
- ➤ Western analysts first thought that the MiG-21 was the swept-wing Ye-2.

PROFILE

Supersonic interceptors

Small and narrow, with a tiny wing area, the MiG-21 was conceived as a short-range point defence interceptor, based on experience gained in the Korean War.

The origins of this fighter can be traced to two distinct families: the Ye-2 swept-wing proposal and the delta-wing Ye-4. Tests proved that the Ye-4 offered slight advantages in performance, fuel capacity and agility, thus it was chosen over its swept-wing rival. An improved derivative was designated the Ye-6T and this became the series production MiG-21F-13. These early aircraft entered widespread service from 1960 onwards. A very basic radar and armament fit were incorporated, but, right from the beginning, these early aircraft were destined to be interim machines, pending availability of more advanced MiG-21 variants.

This new supersonic jet, code-named 'Fishbed' by NATO, was utilized not only by the Soviet Union, but also by other nations such as Czechoslovakia (which acquired a licence to build it), and many other countries around the world. The basic design was also built in China without a licence and formed the basis of the Chengdu F-7 Airguard which is in widespread use today.

Above: Indonesia was one of the more unusual operators of the MiG-21. This early F model is now preserved at a museum in Jakarta.

Below: Among the last of the first-generation models in frontline service were those of the Finnish Ilmavoimat, which were finally retired in 1986.

MiG-21F-13 'Fishbed-C'

Type: single-seat air superiority fighter

Powerplant: one 60.58-kN (!3,625-lb-thrust) Tumanskii R-11F-300 twin-spool afterburning turbojet

Maximum speed: 2175 km/h (1,351 mph)

Endurance: 2 hrs 30 mins

Range: 1420 km (882 miles)

Service ceiling: 19,000 m (62,336 ft)

Weights: empty 4871 kg (10,739 lb); loaded 8625 kg (19,015 lb)

Armament: one 30-mm (1.18-in) NR-30 cannon, later replaced by a gun pack housing a GSh-23L or GP-9 twin-barrel cannon and two K-13A (AA-2 'Atoll') air-to air missiles

Dimensions:	span	7.15 m (23 ft 5 in)
	length	15.76 m (51 ft 8 in)
	height	4.10 m (13 ft 5 in)
	wing area	23.00 m² (248 sq ft)

MiG-21F-13 'Fishbed-C'

Romania received a batch of late-model MiG-21F-13s, including '902' shown here. As Romania had somewhat looser ties with the former Soviet Union, this resulted in Romanian 'Fishbeds' being a comparatively late delivery.

Despite its poor range, basic avionics suite and light armament, the MiG-21F was without doubt a true pilot's aircraft. Hydraulic controls and light weight made it an ideal aerobatic platform. By Western standards, the ergonomic layout of the cockpit was appalling, with the controls scattered and the interior tight and cramped.

Early Soviet machines had twin transparent panels mounted on either side behind the cockpit. These did little to improve visibility and were deleted, first from Czech-built MiG-21Fs, and then from all subsequent aircraft (such as this example).

A very small and crude ranging radar was housed inside the bullet fairing in the intake duct. This was linked to a rudimentary gunsight. The undernose pitot boom was a characteristic of the early variants.

With range severely limited, extra fuel was essential for combat sorties. A single centreline drop tank was often carried.

MiG-21Fs were often seen carrying a pair of K-13A short-range air-to-air missiles. These were essentially copies of the early AIM-9 Sidewinders used on Western aircraft.

Propulsion was by means of a single Tumanskii R-11 twin-spool turbojet. Full afterburner was seldom used as it seriously restricted the aeroplane's endurance to a matter of minutes.

COMBAT DATA

MAXIMUM SPEED

Lithe and little, the early MiG-21s were the fastest of all variants and quicker than rival Western designs, such as the Lockheed F-104 Starfighter which was designed to a similar specification. The Crusader was slower, but was a better equipped combat jet.

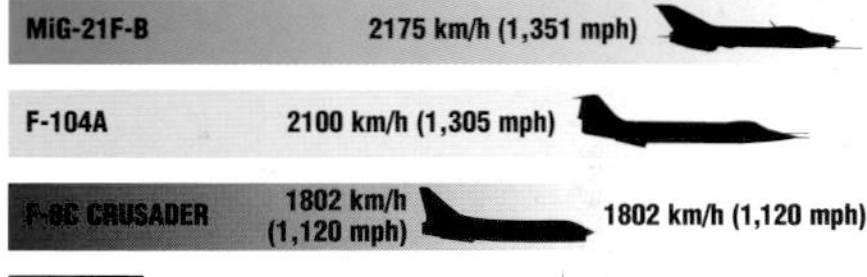

RANGE

Both MiG-21Fs and early Starfighters were notorious for their very poor range. Afterburner had to be used sparingly to extend endurance as much as possible. Navy aircraft such as the F-8 had to operate over greater distances and consequently had greater range.

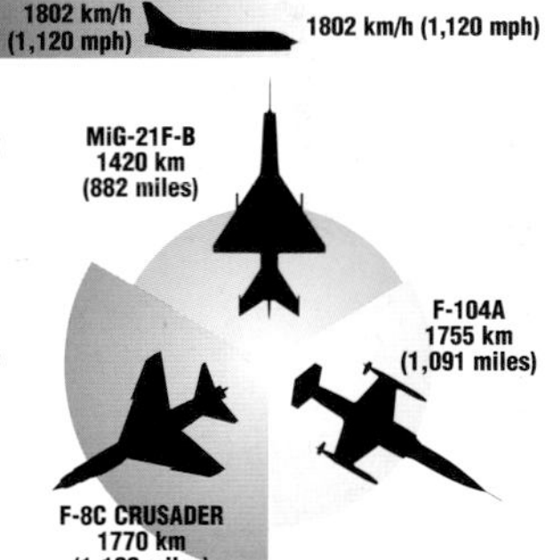

SERVICE CEILING

These early supersonic fighters were little more than manned missiles with wings and could reach altitudes previously unheard of. Early MiG-21s could reach almost 20,000 m (65,620 ft) and indeed one of the prototypes set the world height record in 1961. The Crusader, surprisingly, had a greater service ceiling than the F-104.

Early MiG-21s in service

MiG-21F-13, PEOPLE'S REPUBLIC OF CHINA: In the late 1950s, China and the Soviet Union shed ties. Production of the aircraft was begun in China under the designation J-7. These aircraft served alongside a handful of genuine MiG-21Fs.

MiG-21FL INDIAN AIR FORCE: India was another country which built MiG-21s under licence, though these were all second-generation machines, known as Type-77 in the Indian inventory. These are still in service today and have been upgraded.

MiG-21PF-31 AFGHAN REPUBLICAN AIR FORCE: Second-generation MiG-21PFs were also supplied to Afghanistan during the late 1960s and early 1970s. Since the Islamic revolution not much is known about their fate, although a few may still exist.

MIKOYAN-GUREVICH

MIG-21 'FISHBED' (SECOND GENERATION)

● **Supersonic interceptor** ● **More built than any other jet fighter**

A top-notch dogfighter, the MiG-21 has the flying properties demanded by pilots. It is light, nimble, fast, and armed to the teeth. Other fighters may have longer range, but the MiG-21 is the nasty triggerman of the skies, primed to strike and kill. Used by many nations and in many conflicts, this flying 'hot rod' deserves to be called the most successful jet fighter ever built.

▲ *Wearing pressure suits, these intrepid Soviet pilots prepare for a mission in their MiG-21s. In a zoom climb, the MiG could reach an altitude of more than 20,000 m (65,617 ft).*

PHOTO FILE

MIKOYAN-GUREVICH MIG-21 'FISHBED' (SECOND GENERATION)

◀ Reconnaissance fighter

MiG-21Rs, such as this Czech aircraft, carried a belly pod crammed with cameras and electronic sensors, together with extra avionics in the bulged dorsal spine.

▲ Steam-age cockpit

Unlike today's fighters, the MiG-21 had a cockpit jam-packed with dials and switches. Pilots loved it nonetheless.

Trainer ▶

The two-seat MiG-21U and the upgraded MiG-21US and UM were given the NATO code name 'Mongol'. They are mainly used for conversion and continuation training.

▼ Intake radar

The cone in the middle of the intake housed the antenna for the MiG's air-to-air radar.

Rocket take-off ▶

To get into the air as quickly as possible, the MiG-21 could augment the power of its single engine with a pair of strap-on rockets. These produced blistering take-offs and gut-churning climbs.

Defender of the Motherland ▶

Second-generation MiG-21s with upgraded avionics and engines first saw service with Soviet air defence forces. Large numbers remain in service with ex-Warsaw Pact forces.

FACTS AND FIGURES

- The MiG-21 racked up a seven to one victory streak against Americans over North Vietnam in 1967–68.
- The E-66 MiG-21 prototype zoom-climbed to an altitude of 34,714 m (113,891 ft).
- The MiG-21 has been operated by nearly 50 air forces in the last 35 years.
- At least 14 versions of the MiG-21 have been built.
- Israeli pilots in the 1970s said the MiG-21 was the best enemy fighter they had met.
- In 1979, 'Fishbeds' in frontline Soviet service outnumbered the fighter strength of all NATO air forces.

PROFILE

The world's most popular fighter

As American pilots were to learn over Hanoi, the 'Fishbed' (the West's nickname) was a serious adversary. Soviet aircraft often use crude construction techniques, but many, such as the MiG-21, compensate for a lack of glamour with hard-hitting combat power. One of the most manoeuvrable warplanes of its era, it could wriggle its way out of a trap and score the kill.

With its familiar clipped delta wing and nose intake (with a spike sticking out like the point of a nail), the Mikoyan-Gurevich MiG-21 was easy to recognize and instantly respected by any opponent. Conceived after the Korean War as an interceptor, the supersonic MiG filled many combat roles and has undergone frequent improvements in its powerplant and electronics.

In the right hands, the MiG-21 could turn the mighty F-4 Phantom into meat on the table. American fighters were more sophisticated and flew further, but none was a match for the MiG-21 in a close-quarter battle.

The 'Fishbed' was popular with pilots, although by modern standards the aircraft had poor radar and endurance.

The MiG-21 has been built in a bewildering number of variants, including two-seaters for training. The later fighter aircraft have a large humped spine which carries extra fuel.

The MiG-21 was what was called a 'tailed delta'. Combined with the powerful engine, this made the type one of the nimblest fighters of its era – more than a match in a close-in dogfight for the heavy Phantom, which opposed it in Vietnam and in the Middle East.

MiG-21MF 'Fishbed'

Type: single-seat interceptor and fighter

Powerplant: one 63.65-kN (14,316-lb-thrust) Tumanskii R-13 afterburning turbojet engine

Maximum speed: 2230 km/h (1,386 mph)

Range: 1480 km (917 miles)

Service ceiling: 18,500 m (60,696 ft)

Weights: empty 5350 kg (11,795 lb); loaded 9400 kg (20,723 lb)

Armament: one twin-barrel 23-mm (0.91-in) GSh-23 cannon with 200 rounds; four wing pylons for heat-seeking or radar-guided 'Atoll' air-to-air missiles; up to 2000 kg (4,409 lb) of bombs or rocket pods

Dimensions:		
	span	7.15 m (23 ft 5 in)
	length	15.76 m (51 ft 8 in)
	height	4.50 m (14 ft 9 in)
	wing area	23.00 m² (248 sq ft)

MiG-21FL 'Fishbed'

India is one of the most important users of the MiG-21, and has taken the aircraft into combat against Pakistan. India values its 'Fishbeds' so highly that it is upgrading them with new radars and modern systems.

Even though the Indian air force operates more modern combat aircraft, such as the Mirage 2000, its many MiG-21s are still a vital element in its order of battle.

When the MiG-21 was in its heyday, its pilots were the élite of the Soviet air defence forces.

Three different types of engine powered the MiG-21 through its production life, all made by MNPK 'Soyuz' (Tumanskii). The first aircraft had an R-11 of 60.56 kN (13,621 lb thrust), mid-period aircraft had the 63.65-kN (14,316-lb-thrust) R-13, and the final aircraft had the much better R-25 of 69.63 kN (15,661 lb thrust).

The MiG-21's main weapon was the AA-2 'Atoll' heat-seeking missile. This was a pirated copy of the West's Sidewinder.

This version of the 'Fishbed', the MiG-21FL, did not have any internal guns, but carried a 23-mm (0.91-in) cannon pack under the fuselage.

COMBAT DATA

MAXIMUM SPEED

MiG-21 'FISHBED' 2230 km/h (1,386 mph) 

F-4 PHANTOM 2300 km/h (1,429 mph)

LIGHTNING F.Mk 6 2415 km/h (1,501 mph)

The MiG-21 was one of the first fighters capable of twice the speed of sound, and is still one of the fastest fighters around. The contemporary Lightning and Phantom are faster, but both have two engines.

TIME TO 12,000 M (39,370 FT)

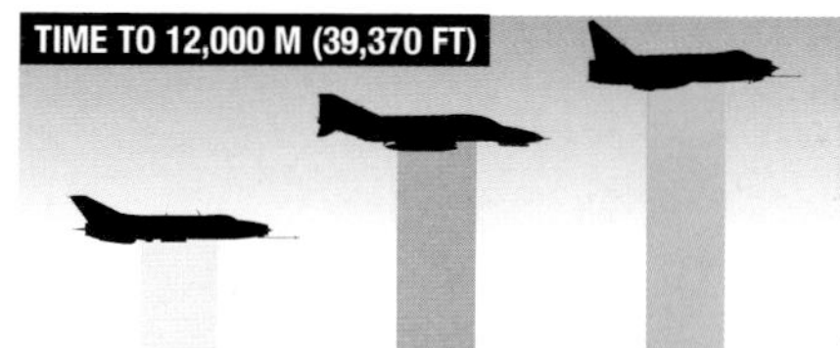

Designed as an interceptor, the MiG can get to a bomber's operating height in a matter of minutes. Only the brute power of the Lightning gives it an advantage. The Phantom is just as powerful, but is twice the size and weight of the Russian jet.

COMBAT RADIUS

Afterburning jets use a lot of fuel, and the first generation of Mach 2 fighters had poor endurance by modern standards. But the MiG-21 was designed as a fast-climbing point-defence weapon, and did not really need long range. Nor did it ever acquire an air-to-air refuelling capability.

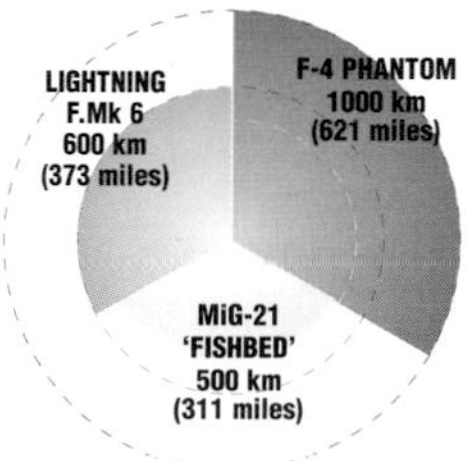

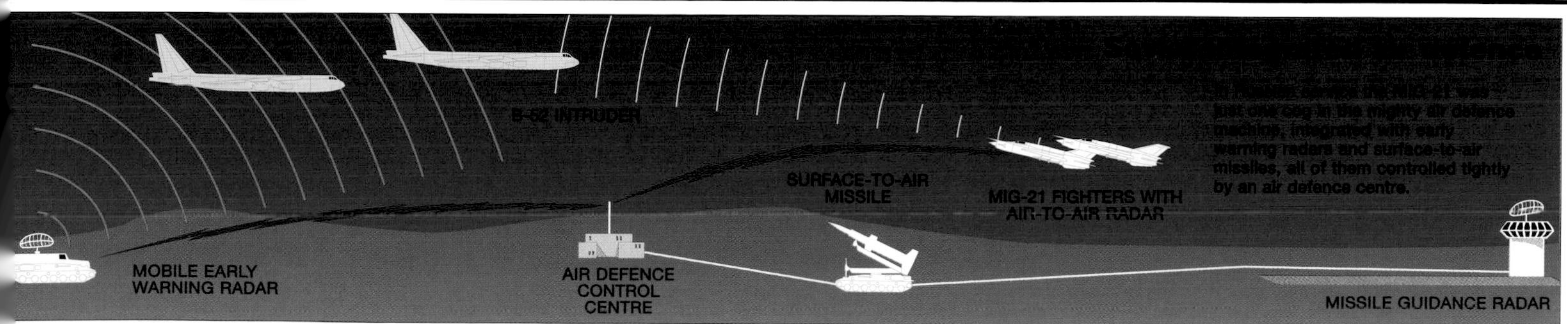

MIKOYAN-GUREVICH

MiG-23 'FLOGGER'

● Swing-wing fighter ● High-performance interceptor

▲ *Written off initially as a 'poor man's Phantom', the MiG-23 is not easy to fly. But it has extremely good acceleration, high top speed and simple-to-use avionics, and is highly adaptable.*

To most of the world, the word 'MiG' means 'Soviet fighter'. The MiG-23 'Flogger' is perhaps the least glamorous warplane bearing its famous name. Derided over the years as being ineffective, this tough and reliable swing-wing fighting jet has come in for a reappraisal. Available in interceptor and ground-attack versions, 'Floggers' have been built in large numbers and have seen action all over the world.

MIKOYAN-GUREVICH MiG-23 'FLOGGER'

▲ Polish air defender

Armed with a brace of R-60 missiles under the belly and wing-mounted R-23s, a Polish MiG-23 stands ready to scramble.

▲ Dogfight story

Soviet MiG-23 pilots re-live a training fight. Not the most agile of fighters, in experienced hands the 'Flogger' could nevertheless give a good account of itself.

Mixed MiG formation ▶

A 'Flogger' flies with two 'Fulcrums', slower but more agile successors to the MiG-23.

▼ Eastern favourite

The MiG-23MF was exported to Czechoslovakia, Germany, Hungary, Poland and Romania.

Bullet nose ▶

The sharp profile of the MiG-23 shows that it was meant to go very fast if need be. Later versions could even out-accelerate the Lockheed Martin F-16 Fighting Falcon.

▶ Mission ready ▲

A MiG-23 prepares for flight. Like most jets designed in the Soviet era, the MiG-23 can operate from semi-prepared strips, thanks to its swing wing and tough undercarriage.

FACTS AND FIGURES

- ➤ Development of the MiG-23, successor to the MiG-21, began in the early 1960s.
- ➤ The MiG-23 was first seen by the West at an air show near Moscow in June 1967.
- ➤ A typical MiG-23 carries 5380 litres (1,400 gal.) of internal fuel and up to 2370 litres (616 gal.) in external tanks.
- ➤ Its variable-geometry wing allows the MiG-23 to fly from short tactical runways.
- ➤ Two Libyan MiG-23s were shot down by US Navy F-14 Tomcats in 1989.
- ➤ Export MiG-23s have not done well in combat, due mainly to pilot inexperience and their downgraded avionics fit.

PROFILE

The variable-geometry 'Flogger'

More of a bully than a beauty, the MiG-23 'Flogger' is a contemporary of the West's F-4 Phantom. Both are powerful. Both are versatile. Both are rewarding aircraft from the pilot's point of view, and both succeed at their grim military business. Both make effective use of powerful engines, superb radar and muscular weapons-carrying capacity.

But while the Phantom is a two-seater with a fixed wing, most MiG-23s are single-seat aircraft with a variable-geometry wing which sweeps forward for good performance at low speeds and backward for high-speed flight.

The MiG-23 equipped nearly all allies of the former Soviet Union, and was still being refined and improved three decades after entering service. Its combat record was mixed. Arab forces lost large numbers of the aircraft to the Israelis, but this was more to do with disparity in training than any superiority of Western designs.

The MiG-23 may have been overshadowed by its successors, but the sheer numbers of this aircraft mean that it will remain an important combat type for many years to come.

No longer at the cutting edge of technology, the MiG-23 'Flogger' remains amenable to further development even as it gathers age, and it remains a hard-hitting weapon of war.

With its wing in the forward position, the MiG-23 can safely land slowly on rough surfaces. With the wing swung back, it can outrun almost anything in the skies.

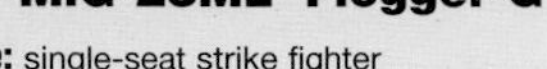

MiG-23ML 'Flogger-G'

Type: single-seat strike fighter

Powerplant: one Soyuz (Tumanskii) R-35-300 turbojet rated at 127.5 kN (22,050-lb.-thrust) with afterburner

Maximum speed: 2500 km/h (1,550 m.p.h.) at 12,500 m (41,000 ft.)

Range: 2800 km (1,736 mi.)

Service ceiling: 18,000 m (59,000 ft.)

Weights: empty 8200 kg (18,040 lb.); loaded 17,800 kg (39,160 lb.)

Armament: one 23-mm GSh-23L twin-barrel cannon; 2000 kg (4,400 lb.) of ordnance

Dimensions:	span	13.95 m (46 ft.)
	length	16.70 m (53 ft.)
	height	4.80 m (13 ft.)
	wing area	37.35 m² (402 sq. ft.)

MiG-23MS 'Flogger-E'

Libya has received large numbers of the MiG-23MS, and has used them in action over Chad and Egypt. Two were shot down during a confrontation with US Navy F-14 Tomcats in January 1989.

The fact that the MiG-23 was not designed to dogfight can be seen in its cockpit. Rearward visibility is very poor, even with mirrors fitted on the canopy arch.

The MiG-23 gains its speed from its small frontal area, coupled with the huge power of the Tumanskii R-29 turbojet, which has a massive jetpipe.

The MiG-23 was always constrained by the performance of its radar, which lacked a true 'lookdown' capability until the final 'ML' variant was introduced.

The air intake of most MiG-23s had moveable 'splitter plates' to control airflow when flying at high speeds. The plates are fixed in the MiG-27 (the ground-attack variant of the MiG-23), which operates at lower speeds.

Export MiG-23s are often armed with the basic infra-red K-13 missile, known in the West as the AA-2 'Atoll'. This is a copy of a very early version of the American AIM-9 Sidewinder.

All Russian fighters have large mudguards to allow flight from rough airstrips in snowy weather.

COMBAT DATA

MAXIMUM SPEED

Even today, some three decades after its first flight in 1967, the MiG-23 remains one of the fastest fighters in the world. Its immensely powerful Tumanskii turbojet propels the fighter to Mach 2.5 with wings swept back at 72°. With wings at a minimum sweep of 16°, speed is limited to the subsonic regime, with a maximum of 940 km/h (580 m.p.h.).

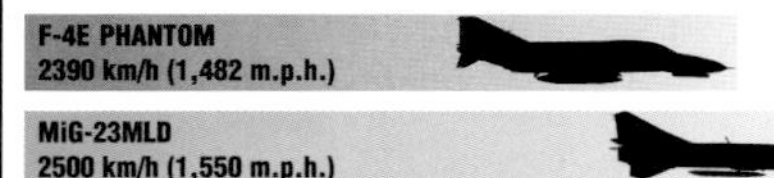

CLIMB RATE

Although powered by a potent engine, the MiG-23 cannot match the sheer brute twin-engined power of its great American rival. But the big and heavy Phantom cannot climb as high as the 'Flogger', nor can it accelerate as rapidly in level flight.

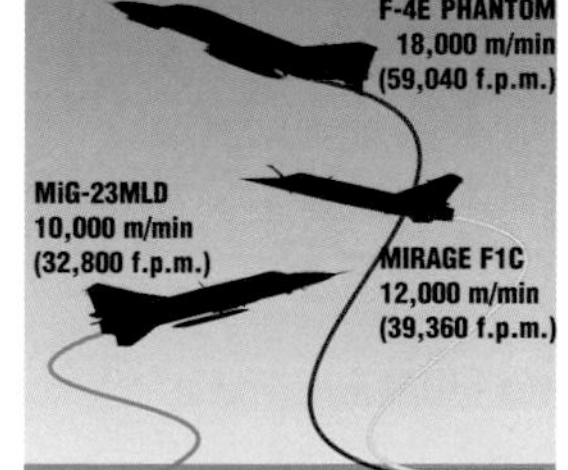

RANGE

No fast jet combat aircraft developed in the 1960s is notable for its range, although all have respectable ferry ranges. In combat, however, radius of action is dramatically reduced, and using the afterburner cuts endurance to a matter of minutes.

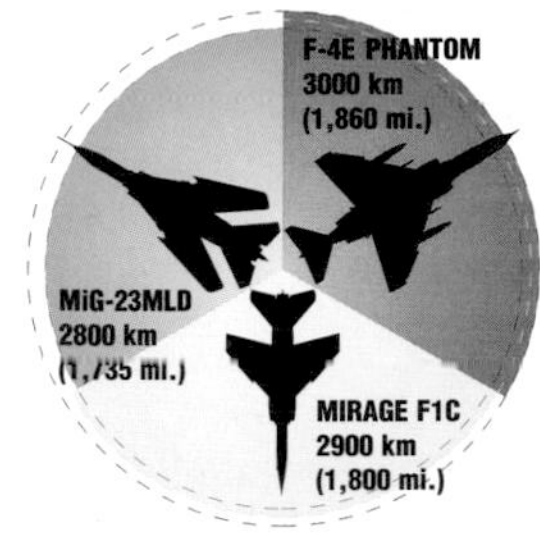

Swing-wing solutions

FULL WING SWING: The Panavia Tornado's wings swing from the wingroots, necessitating an extremely complex hinge construction built onto the fuselage. This allows all of the wing to be swept for high speeds and extended for low speeds, but presents a considerable engineering challenge and one that costs a great deal of time and money to perfect.

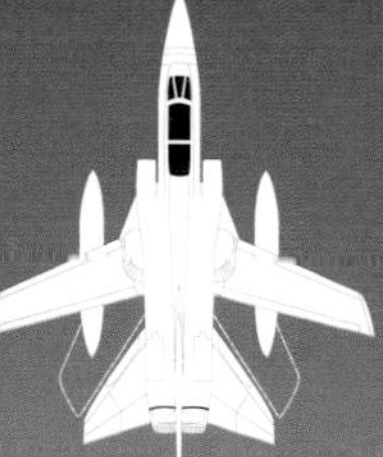

SWINGING FROM THE MIDDLE: The MiG-23 was one of the first operational variable-geometry aircraft. To simplify engineering problems, MiG's designers decided to move only those sections of the wing that were clear of the fuselage, leaving a small part fixed. That way, they could move the wing hinges away from the body of the plane, making for much less complex construction.

WINGTIP SWING: The huge Tupolev swing-wing bombers like the 'Backfire' and 'Blackjack' utilise the simplest swing wings, pivoting only the outer portions. While less efficient at low speeds than a fully moveable wing, they still significantly cut landing speeds. Fully swept, they are just as effective.

Mikoyan-Gurevich

MiG-25 'Foxbat'

● World's fastest fighter ● Mach 3-capable ● Soviet defender

▲ The MiG-25 is the world's fastest operational interceptor. It is also one of the biggest: this Indian pilot and ground crew are dwarfed by the huge machine.

For a decade the word 'Foxbat' struck terror into the hearts of NATO planners. The appearance of the needle-nosed Soviet interceptor, bristling with missiles, and its startling Mach 3, high-altitude performance signalled the dawn of a new era in Cold War aviation. As time passed the 'Foxbat' gave up some of its secrets, and analysts came to understand its strengths and weaknesses. However, while it is no longer the awesome warplane it once was, it is still an impressive machine.

Photo File

Mikoyan-Gurevich MiG-25 'Foxbat'

▲ **Brute force**
The MiG-25 achieves its amazing performance through sheer power rather than by any smart aerodynamics.

▼ **Export 'Foxbats'**
MiG-25s were exported to a few favoured nations, such as Libya (shown here), Syria, India, Iraq, Algeria and Bulgaria.

◀ **At full throttle**
One can almost feel the power of the twin Tumanskii R-15 engines as a MiG-25 launches. Between them the two mighty turbojets produce 219.68 kN (49,409 lb thrust) in full afterburn.

▲ **Trials aircraft**
This MiG-25, seen at Moscow's Zhukhovski trials base, is a flying laboratory; it has an open rear cockpit to test ejection seats at high supersonic speeds. The pilot flies from the front cockpit.

◀ **Windfall for the West**
In 1976 Soviet air force pilot Viktor Belenko defected in a MiG-25. Its arrival in Japan allowed Western experts to analyse this hitherto unknown quantity before it was returned to the Soviet Union.

Facts and Figures

- Viktor Belenko's defection to Japan in a MiG-25 in 1976 was considered the biggest spy coup of the Cold War.
- Soviet-piloted Egyptian MiG-25s flew against Israel between 1971 and 1975.
- At maximum speed, the MiG-25's canopy is too hot to touch with the naked hand.
- 'Foxbats' fly in Algeria, Azerbaijan, Belarus, Bulgaria, India, Iraq, Kazakhstan, Libya, Russia, Syria and the Ukraine.
- The MiG-25BM is designed to attack an enemy's air defence radars from great distance and height.

PROFILE

Three times the speed of sound

Although it is growing old now, the Mikoyan-Gurevich MiG-25 'Foxbat' is one of the most amazing performers ever built. The MiG-25 was a panic response to the American B-70 bomber of the 1960s, but after the B-70 was cancelled Moscow went ahead with this incredibly powerful, heavily armed interceptor, and 'Foxbat' became a scare word in the Pentagon after the first MiG-25 was glimpsed briefly in July 1967. Except for the (unarmed) SR-71 Blackbird, the West has never had a craft able to reach the speeds and altitudes where the 'Foxbat' routinely flies every day.

The pilot of the MiG-25 rides high in the cockpit of a truly massive single-seater. He can fly at more than 5 km (3 miles) higher than any of his Western contemporaries. He can close in for the kill at far greater speed, or complete his reconnaissance mission with overwhelming chances of success. The Israeli air force sought in vain to catch Soviet-piloted 'Foxbats' that once flew from Egypt, and the 'Foxbat' remains a potent force today. During the 1991 Gulf War, an Iraqi MiG-25 is believed to have claimed the only coalition aircraft (an F/A-18) shot down in an air-to-air battle.

There are many MiG-25s configured for reconnaissance, in a multitude of variants. This MiG-25RBK has a large side-looking radar in the nose.

MiG-25 'Foxbat-A'

Type: high-performance all-weather interceptor

Powerplant: two 109.84-kN (24,704-lb-thrust) Tumanskii R-31 afterburning turbojets

Maximum speed: up to Mach 3, although normally limited to Mach 2.8 or 3120 km/h (1,939 mph)

Range: 1700 km (1,056 miles) subsonic with internal fuel

Service ceiling: 24,000 m (78,740 ft)

Weights: empty 20,000 kg (44,092 lb); loaded 36,200 kg (79,807 lb)

Armament: four AA-6 'Acrid' long-range air-to-air missiles, or two AA-6 and two AA-7 'Apex' missiles; other missiles in other combinations

Dimensions:		
	span	13.95 m (45 ft 9 in)
	length	23.82 m (78 ft 2 in)
	height	6.10 m (20 ft)
	wing area	56.83 m² (612 sq ft)

The MiG-25's large highly swept wings, twin fins and variable intakes are a sophisticated combination which give maximum stability and manoeuvrability at high speeds.

The 'Foxbat' introduced the twin vertical tails now common on high-performance combat jets. A single tail with the same effect would have needed to be much larger and stronger.

MiG-25BM 'Foxbat-F'

Based on the multi-role MiG-25RB, the 'Foxbat-F' is a specialized defence suppression aircraft. Unlike American 'Wild Weasels', it is designed to attack enemy radars from high altitude at very long range.

The left fin cap houses the main VHF communications antenna. The starboard equivalent contains ECM and IFF gear.

Although painted to appear like a radar-equipped fighter, the MiG-25RB does not carry air-to-air electronics.

As the MiG-25 was designed for speed rather than dogfights, its cramped cockpit reflects a need for low drag rather than all-round visibility.

Part of the reason for the MiG-25's blistering performance is the immense power it gets from two huge Tumanskii turbojets. Each delivers more than 11 tonnes (12 tons) of thrust.

In place of the normal radar, the nose of the 'Foxbat-F' houses passive detection devices designed to pick up hostile radar transmissions.

As with most combat jets of the Soviet era, the MiG-25 has a rugged undercarriage, allowing it to operate from rougher fields than Western fighters.

As a defence suppression aircraft, the 'Foxbat-F' is armed with radar-homing missiles. The supersonic Kh-58 (NATO designation AS-11 'Kilter') has a range in excess of 50 km (31 miles).

The MiG-25 is mostly made from steel, rather than the hugely expensive titanium used in Western aircraft of similar performance.

High-altitude interceptor

MiG-25: The 'Foxbat' was designed to tackle the mighty B-70 Valkyrie and later to counter the SR-71 Blackbird, although it had little chance of catching the latter.

NORTH AMERICAN B-70: The monster Valkyrie was a high-altitude Mach 3 bomber. Even though it was cancelled, the Soviets continued with the development of the MiG-25.

BOEING B-52: The USAF's main strategic bomber was easy meat for the MiG-25 and MiG-21. However, when cruise missiles appeared on the B-52 the MiG-25 was hastily redesigned with a new radar which could detect and track these low-flying targets.

MiG-21: Early Soviet interceptors such as the MiG-21 and Su-15 had sufficient performance to kill the B-52, but could never have got near the B-70.

COMBAT DATA

SERVICE CEILING

SR-71 BLACKBIRD 30,000 m (98,425 ft)

MiG-25 'FOXBAT' 24,000 m (78,740 ft)

F-15 EAGLE 18,000 m (59,055 ft)

The sheer power of the MiG-25 allowed it to reach extreme heights, although it could not match the huge SR-71. It could fly higher than the American F-15, which although designed as a 'Foxbat' killer could reach the MiG only in a one-shot zoom climb.

MIKOYAN-GUREVICH

MiG-25R 'FOXBAT'

● Soviet spy plane ● Exported ● Mach-3 flights

Expanding on knowledge gained in the design of the interceptor version of the 'Foxbat', the Soviets realised that the MiG-25 would make an ideal reconnaissance platform. Still often deployed along the Russian borders, the aircraft is tasked with looking deep into NATO countries to monitor military exercises and the like. Cameras were used at first; later versions employ a large side-looking airborne radar (SLAR).

▲ *Maintenance personnel lend scale to the huge size of the Foxbat. A development of the fighter version, the MiG-25R will serve in the Russian air force for the foreseeable future.*

PHOTO FILE

MIKOYAN-GUREVICH MiG-25R 'FOXBAT'

◄ Border missions
Taking-off from an airfield in East Germany, a MiG-25RBF displays the small dielectric panels on the nose. These aircraft were active along NATO's borders.

▼ Stopping distance
Because of the enormous size of the MiG-25, two large braking chutes are deployed to slow the aircraft.

▲ Camera bay
Lowered for servicing is one of the five cameras installed on the MiG-25 which allow high-altitude images to be taken.

▼ Rare bird
This complex camouflage scheme of green, brown and sand shades is seen on a few examples.

▼ Indian operations
A highly capable aircraft, reconnaissance versions of the 'Foxbat' have not been widely exported because of their advanced systems.

FACTS AND FIGURES

- The reconnaissance version of the Foxbat first flew on 6 March 1964, six months before the fighter variant.
- Five cameras are fitted in the nose of the aircraft in vertical and oblique positions.
- The MiG-25RB operates in a dual reconnaissance-bomber role.
- A detachment of four pre-production models was deployed to Egypt under the designation X-500.
- For training future reconnaissance pilots a dedicated two-seat trainer exists.
- Overseas operators of the aircraft have included Algeria, India, Libya and Syria.

PROFILE

Soviet high-speed snooper

Highly regarded as a Soviet Mach-3 fighter, the 'Foxbat' first flew in its reconnaissance variant six months before the interceptor. The most noticeable change was a longer, slimmer nose, the fighter's radome having been removed. Other modifications were shorter span wings and the addition of a constant leading-edge taper to improve handling.

Following a protracted development phase, two main variants were identified by the West. The 'Foxbat-B' version employed five oblique cameras and a small side-looking airborne radar (SLAR), whilst the 'Foxbat-D' variant has no cameras fitted and relies on a much larger SLAR panel. Since the appearance of these aircraft, numerous upgrades of the type's reconnaissance systems have led to a host of sub-types becoming operational within the Soviet and Russian air forces. These have included reconnaissance/bomber versions. Requests for the aircraft from Soviet client states were initially turned down, but after a covert deployment to the Middle East during the 1970s the type became available for export. Algeria, India, Syria and Libya are all believed to continue operating MiG-25R/RB ('Foxbat-B') aircraft, but with assistance from Russian advisors or even Russian pilots.

Above: The huge twin Tumanskii engines of the MiG-25 are powered up prior to propelling this reconnaissance aircraft on another intelligence-gathering mission.

Above: India operates five MiG-25RBs, having lost one in an accident. They serve with No. 102 Squadron which also flies two MiG-25RUs, specialised training versions used to instruct future MiG-25RB pilots.

MiG-25RB 'Foxbat-B'

Type: high-speed, high-altitude reconnaissance fighter

Powerplant: two 109.83-kN (24,712-lb. thrust) Tumanskii R-15BD-300 afterburning turbojets

Maximum speed: 3000 km/h (1,864 m.p.h.) at 13,000 m (42,650 ft.)

Range: 2400 km (1,491 mi.) with underbelly tank

Service ceiling: 23,000 m (75,500 ft.)

Weights: normal take-off 37,100 kg (81,791 lb.); maximum take-off 41,200 kg (90,830 lb.)

Armament: Up to eight 500-kg (1,100-lb.) FAB-500 bombs

Dimensions:

span	13.38 m (43 ft. 11 in.)
length	19.58 m (64 ft. 3 in.)
height	6.50 m (21 ft. 4 in.)
wing area	58.90 m² (634 sq. ft.)

MiG-25RBF 'Foxbat-B'

Developed from the interceptor variant, the MiG-25RBF is the latest of a number of reconnaissance versions, many of which have been brought up-to-date with the addition of more sophisticated equipment.

Lacking the large distinguishing SLAR panels on the nose, the improved reconnaissance variants rely on dielectric panels symmetrically positioned around the nose of the aircraft to gather information.

The pilot is seated in a pressurised cockpit deep within the fuselage of the aircraft, restricting the field of view. Operating at high altitude with little risk of interception the pilot requires a minimum view of the outside world during a mission.

On early variants of the MiG-25R, wingtip mass-balances were fitted to improve the handling of the aircraft at high speed. Though standard, variants are often seen flying without them.

The twin tails allow the aircraft to be much more stable at high speeds, particularly during the photographic runs where the images obtained must be extremely clear.

Reconnaissance variants of the Foxbat have a smoother nose profile than interceptor versions, this aerodynamic change allowing them to reach higher speeds.

The vertical camera window is retained on this version, although most of the intelligence collected is obtained by the small dielectric panels on the nose.

Two Tumanskii turbojets power the 'Foxbat', these being improved versions originally employed in the interceptor variants. The high speed achieved by these engines allowed the Foxbat to outrun Israeli F-4 Phantoms and Mirages.

COMBAT DATA

MAXIMUM SPEED

For sheer speed the MiG-25 has become a legend within aerospace circles. The reconnaissance versions are the fastest of the MiG-25 variants and have frequently been flown over various nations' borders during missions, escaping before fighters could intercept. The RF-4 and Su-24 are not capable of such speeds.

Aircraft	Speed
MiG-25RB 'FOXBAT-B'	3000 km/h (1,864 m.p.h.)
Su-24MR 'FENCER-E'	2320 km/h (1,442 m.p.h.)
RF-4C PHANTOM II	2348 km/h (1,459 m.p.h.)

Middle East missions

SPY FLIGHT: Arriving in total secrecy during March 1971, two MiG-25Rs were deployed to Cairo West air base in Egypt, and were code-named X-500s.

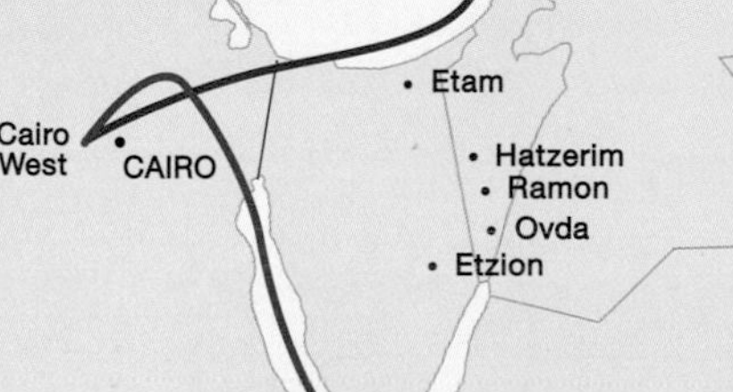

IMMUNE TO INTERCEPTION: Despite repeated attempts by Israeli F-4 Phantoms and Mirages, the Foxbats were never attacked during their flights. Flown by Soviet pilots throughout the deployment, the aircraft were operated under strict control from Moscow.

'Foxbat' variants at home and abroad

■ **MiG-25 'FOXBAT-A':** Still in front-line service with the Russian air force, this example displays a typical mixed war load of heat-seeking and radar-guided missiles.

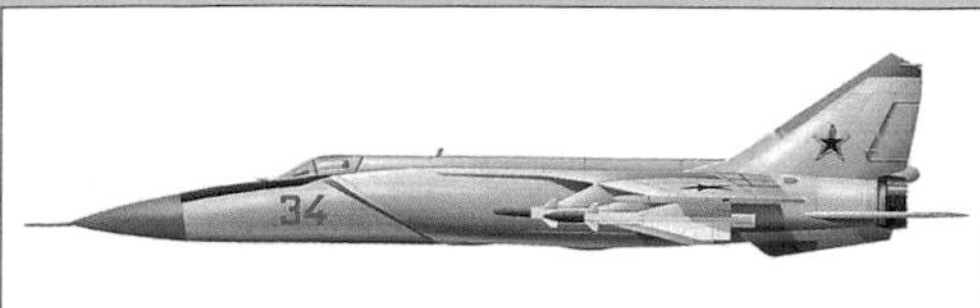

■ **MiG-25P 'FOXBAT':** An export fighter variant was supplied to a number of Soviet client states, including Syria, whose examples have seen considerable action in the Middle East.

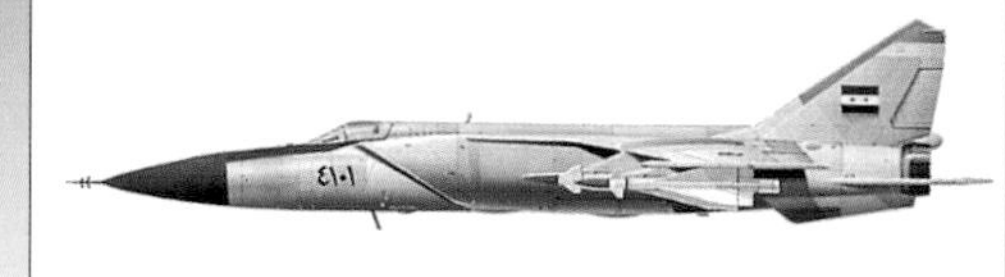

■ **MiG-25RU 'FOXBAT-C':** India operates a number of examples of the MiG-25 reconnaissance variant. Two two-seat training examples are used to convert pilots on to the type.

MIKOYAN

MIG-27 'FLOGGER-D/J'

● Ground attack ● Close air support ● Anti-shipping strike

Based on the MiG-23BM, the MiG-27 is a dedicated ground-attack aircraft and is equipped with a six-barrelled 30-mm cannon for use against ground targets. The undercarriage is strengthened so that it can carry the additional weight of air-to-surface stores, including nuclear weapons, and the air intakes are simplified. It is fitted with a comprehensive array of antennas and sensors for targeting and self-protection.

▲ *The MiG-27 was popular with the pilots who flew the aircraft in combat over Afghanistan, improving their operational techniques. Various modifications to the aircraft resulted from these operations.*

PHOTO FILE

MIKOYAN MIG-27 'FLOGGER-D/J'

◀ **The Indian Valiant**
India licence-builds the MiG-27M, and in Indian air force service it is known as the 'Bahadur' (Valiant).

▼ **Frontal aviation**
The MiG-27 has been an important asset to Russia's air armies since the mid-1970s.

▲ **Tactical deployment**
MiG-27s armed with tactical nuclear weapons were on strength at Soviet bases across East Germany until 1992.

▼ **Commonality**
The Soviet MiG-27 shared components with the MiG-23 but was dedicated to the ground-attack role.

▲ **Rough-field capability**
The rugged MiG-27 has been designed to operate from hastily prepared forward air bases with minimum ground support. Take-offs are kept as short as possible by using reheat.

FACTS AND FIGURES

- The Mikoyan MiG-27 was chiefly developed because of the Soviet's dissatisfaction with the MiG-23BN.
- For ground-strafing MiG-27s carry SPPU-22 gunpods with articulated barrels.
- To confuse enemy defences the MiG-27 has a powerful thermal jammer.
- The MiG-27 can be distinguished from the MiG-23BN by its fixed intakes and splitter plates 80 mm (3 in.) from the fuselage wall.
- Russian air force MiG-27s can carry the TN series of tactical nuclear weapons.
- The MiG-27K has an internal smoke emitter for laying battlefield screens.

PROFILE

'Ducknose', the strike fighter

Both the original MiG-27 and the MiG-27K were known in the West by the NATO designation 'Flogger-D'. However, the -27K had a new navigation and attack system, including a laser rangefinder in the nose, that made it capable of highly accurate blind bombing.

Further equipment improvements produced the MiG-27M, or 'Flogger-J'. This is equipped to launch missiles and precision-guided munitions. Later versions carried various additional systems, including forward-looking infra-red sensors and specialised navigation systems for the nuclear strike role.

Soviet forces used MiG-27s during the later stages of the war in Afghanistan in 1987–89. They were fitted with dispensers for chaff and flares to help protect them against surface-to-air missiles used by the Mujahideen guerillas.

The subsequent break-up of the Soviet Union left MiG-27s in the hands of several of the newly independent states, like the Ukraine. Other than these, however, the only MiG-27s to serve outside Russia are those operated by India, which actually built many of its own MiG-27Ms.

Above: The Russian air force is now beginning to phase out its older MiG-27s in favour of newer multi-role types. The aircraft remains a very important weapon for India, however.

Below: The original MiG-27K 'Flogger-D' has now been supplanted in the Russian air force by the improved MiG-27M 'Flogger-J' and '-J2', with provision to carry more precision-guided munitions.

MiG-27M 'Flogger-J'

Type: single-seat ground-attack and close air support aircraft

Powerplant: one 112.77-kN (25,370-lb.-thrust) MNPK Tumanskii R-29B-300 turbojet

Maximum speed: 1885 km/h (1,169 m.p.h.)

Initial climb rate: 12,000 m/min (39,360 f.p.m.)

Combat radius: 540 km (335 mi.) at low level

Service ceiling: 14,000 m (45,900 ft.)

Weights: maximum take-off 20,300 kg (44,660 lb.)

Armament: one GSh-6-30 six-barrel 30-mm gun, plus 5000 kg (11,000 lb.) of weapons on seven pylons

Dimensions:

span	13.97 m (45 ft. 10 in.)
length	17.08 m (56 ft.)
height	5.00 m (16 ft. 5 in.)
wing area	37.35 m² (402 sq. ft.)

MiG-27K 'Flogger-D'

In the 1980s the West's intelligence sources were confident that the MiG-27 had been widely exported to the Soviet's allies, including Syria (whose markings are shown below). However, India and the former Soviet republics are the only operators of the aircraft.

The MiG-27's broad, flat nose contains a small ranging radar and a laser rangefinder which are capable of locking on to laser energy from a marked target. The nose also holds air data probes and other antennas. The MiG-27 is known to the Russians as 'utkanos' (ducknose).

Large, heavy-duty armoured panels are scabbed onto the sides of the cockpit to protect the pilot from shrapnel and gunfire. The pilot's windscreen is also heavily armoured.

There are seven external stores pylons, including the centreline for carrying a 790-litre drop-tank. Other stores include: 23-mm gunpods; 20-, 130- or 240-mm rockets; 500-kg (1,100-lb.) bombs; bomblet dispensers; air-to-air and air-to-surface missiles including the Kh-29 and Kh-31.

The wing can be continuously swept or set to any of three pre-selected positions for different flight patterns. The hydraulically powered wings can be set to 16°, 45° or 72° sweep.

The tailcone contains a large brake chute normally deployed just prior to landing.

The sturdy forward undercarriage is designed for adverse terrain operations and features twin nosewheels, low-pressure tyres and mudguards.

A powerful GSh-6-30 Gatling gun, with six 30-mm barrels and provision for 260 rounds of ammunition, is housed in a bulge under the belly. The gun is especially useful for attacking ground targets and armoured vehicles.

A single Tumanskii turbojet with two-position afterburner provides up to 112.77 kN (25,370 lb.) thrust.

A stabilising ventral fin automatically folds up when the undercarriage is lowered.

COMBAT DATA

TAKE-OFF DISTANCE

Ground-attack aircraft can extend their time over the target by using forward air strips, which are often very short pieces of disused road or damaged airfields. The figures given are for maximum weapon load, typical for a front-line mission.

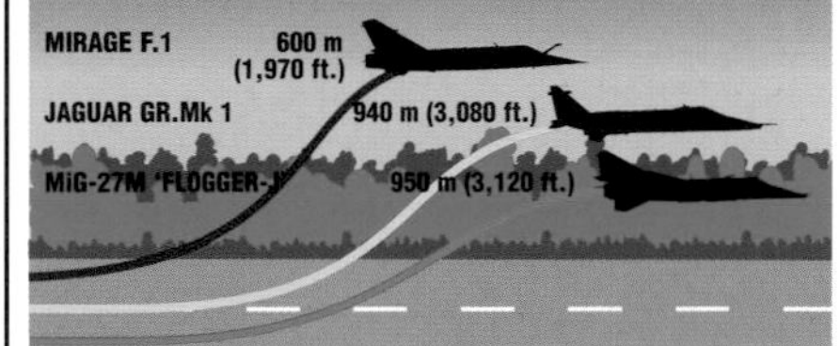

INTERNAL GUNS

Unlike dedicated air-defence aircraft, which are equipped with less devastating but higher velocity cannon, the MiG-27 and its rivals in the ground-attack role use 30-mm (1.18-in) cannon. These rounds are far heavier than those used by the air-defence machines.

MiG-27M 'FLOGGER-J' — 30-mm, 260 rounds

JAGUAR GR.Mk 1 — 30-mm, 300 rounds

MIRAGE F.1 — 30-mm, 250 rounds

COMBAT RADIUS

Equipped with two Kh-29 missiles and three 790-litre (210-gal.) drop-tanks, the MiG-27 has a useful range. With full weapon load, range is reduced to 225 km (140 mi.) with internal fuel only. The Jaguar has especially long range due to its efficient Adour engines.

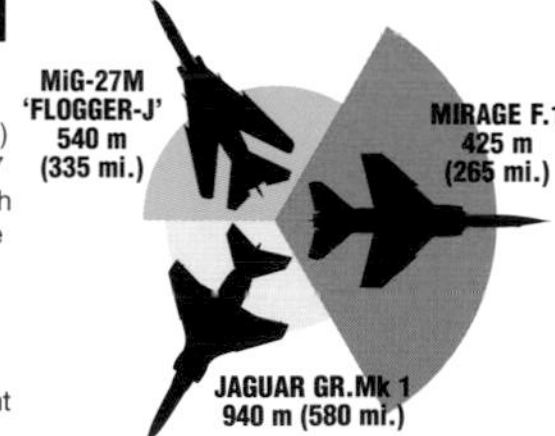

Combat missions

AIRFIELD STRIKE: Armed with 500-kg (1,100-lb.) bombs and KMGU bomblet dispensers, the MiG-27 is suited to low-level attacks.

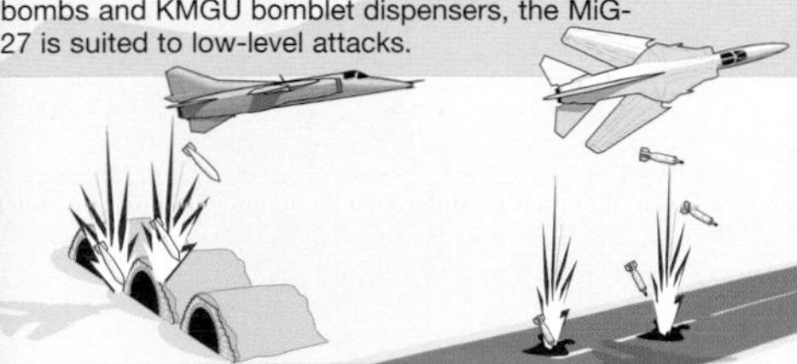

TANK BUSTING: The MiG-27 is a formidable anti-tank aircraft, using its 30-mm Gatling gun combined with Kh-29 precision-guided air-to-surface missiles. For self-protection it is equipped with chaff, smoke and flares.

ANTI-SHIPPING: Russian navy MiG-27Ms are equipped to carry the Kh-31 long-range ramjet-powered anti-ship missile. These aircraft are tasked with the protection of Russian shipping lanes and are based on the Kola Peninsula.

MIKOYAN

MiG-29 'FULCRUM'

● Multi-role fighter ● Highly agile ● Advanced weapon systems

The MiG-29 is a killer. This jet fighter from Russia is agile and potent, a challenge to America's best. Western fighters may be expensive limousines, but the 'Fulcrum', with its high manoeuvrability, resilient engines and excellent missiles, is like a hot racing car, not easy to fly but formidable in battle. And now the MiG-29K has been developed to fly from aircraft-carriers – even without the help of steam catapults!

▲ *The advent of the MiG-29 in the 1980s gave the highly professional Russian fighter pilot a combat aircraft second to none.*

PHOTO FILE

MIKOYAN MiG-29 'FULCRUM'

▼ **Afterburning power**

A MiG-29 'Fulcrum' blasts into the sky, twin Klimov/Sarkisov RD-33 turbofans blazing. It can get airborne in less than 250 m (800 ft.).

Supremely agile ▲

Although some of its systems are old-fashioned, the MiG's advanced aerodynamics and great power give it unsurpassed manoeuvrability.

▶ **Export success**

'Fulcrums' are being operated by the air forces of nearly 30 nations, including Slovakia.

▲ **Old enemies, new friends**

For 10 years the MiG was a threat to Western air forces, but it is now more likely to be encountered as a friend.

◀ **Rough-field performer**

As with most Soviet-designed aircraft, the MiG-29 is designed to operate from rough fields. Braking parachutes are used to bring the 15-ton fighter to a halt.

FACTS AND FIGURES

- For a 'stealthy' intercept the MiG-29 can use an infra-red imaging device rather than its radar.
- The MiG-29 has an outstanding ejection seat, the Zvezda K-36, which works even at Mach 2.5.
- The MiG's AA-10 'Alamo' missile can destroy enemies 40 km (25 mi.) away.
- When the air forces of East and West Germany combined, the MiG-29 was the only Russian combat type good enough to be retained by the 'new' Luftwaffe.
- Unlike Western fighters, the 'Fulcrum' readily performs the tailslide, the aircraft falling backwards at the apex of a vertical climb.

PROFILE

Mikoyan's fantastic 'Fulcrum'

Russia's Mikoyan-Gurevich bureau came up with a real winner when the MiG-29 burst on the scene in 1977. Using advanced technology to make the 'Fulcrum' a real slugger in medium-range and close-quarter combat, engineers created a fighter which is one of the world's most manoeuvrable. In the right hands a MiG-29 can fight and win a close-in, gloves-off dogfight against any warplane in service today.

Seen by the West as a rival to the F-16, the MiG-29 offers far superior detection capabilities, and the AA-10 and AA-11 missiles it carries are much better than their Western counterparts. However, it does not have much of an air-to-ground repertoire, although the second-generation MiG-29M can carry a wide array of precision weapons.

Though it offers super performance, the MiG-29 is practical, and less expensive than Western fighters. But the 'Fulcrum' never fails to command respect: in the heat of battle, it is always a lethal foe.

With the end of the Cold War, new customers are considering purchasing this superb fighter. The offer of a state-of-the-art machine at a bargain price is too good to refuse.

India is one of many countries to have bought the MiG-29. Its high performance and low cost has made it attractive to air forces worldwide.

Before the fall of the Soviet Union the MiG-29 was flown by many of the elite Guards Aviation Regiments.

The carrier version of the MiG-29 is thought to be based on the advanced 'Fulcrum-M', with more powerful engines, improved radar and avionics.

The MiG-29's wing and leading-edge extensions were designed at TsAGI, the Soviet equivalent of NASA. They are extremely efficient aerodynamically, and contribute to the 'Fulcrum's' superb performance.

MiG-29 'Fulcrum-A'

Type: single-seat multi-purpose fighter

Powerplant: two Klimov/Leningrad RD-33 afterburning bypass turbofan engines rated at 81.40-kN (11,100-lb.-thrust) static thrust

Max speed: Mach 2.2 or 2445 km/h (1,520 m.p.h.) at 10,000 m (32,800 ft.)

Range: 1200 km with an average weapons load

Service ceiling: 17,000 m (35,800 ft.)

Weights: empty 10,900 kg (24,000 lb.); maximum take-off 18,500 kg (40,800 lb.)

Armament: GSh-301 single-barrel lightweight 30-mm cannon, six to eight AA-8, AA-10 or AA-11 air-to-air missiles, or rocket pods and free-fall bombs for ground attack

Dimensions:

	span	11.36 m (37 ft. 4 in.)
	length	17.32 m (56 ft. 10 in.)
	height	4.73 m (15 ft. 7 in.)
	wing area	38 m² (410 sq. ft.)

COMBAT DATA

MAXIMUM SPEED

The MiG-29 is one of the fastest fighters in the world, although supersonic flight cuts its range considerably.

MiG-29 'FULCRUM'	2445 km/h (1,520 m.p.h.)
F/A-18	1915 km/h (1,200 m.p.h.)
MIRAGE 2000	2340 km/h (1,450 m.p.h.)

COMBAT RANGE

Thanks to more efficient engines and greater fuel capacity, the MiG-29 has twice the range of earlier Soviet tactical jets such as the MiG-21 and MiG-23. Even so, the 'Fulcrum' has a relatively short range compared to its Western contemporaries.

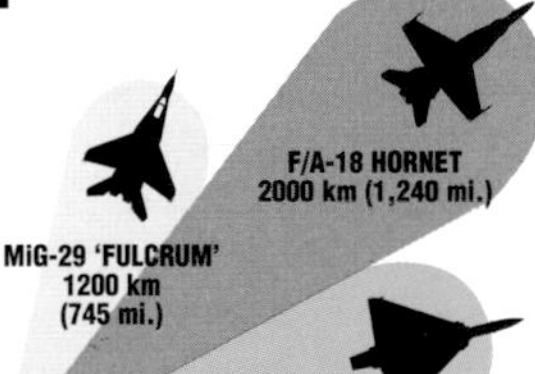

SERVICE CEILING

The MiG is not really an interceptor, but its high speed and good ceiling mean that it can be pressed into service to catch high-flying bombers and reconnaissance aircraft.

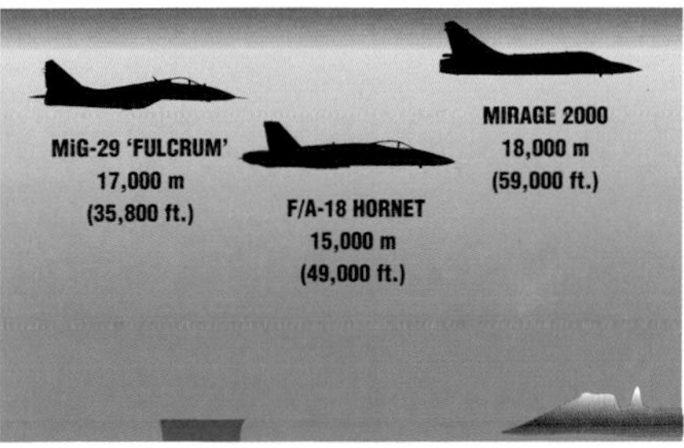

MIG-29K 'FULCRUM'

The MiG-29K is a dedicated maritime aircraft, and underwent trails on the carrier *Kuznetsov* during 1992/1993.

The ball in front of the MiG-29's cockpit houses the laser and infra-red sensors of the infra-red search-and-track system.

Although the 'Fulcrum' has a much less obstructed view from the cockpit than previous Soviet designs, it does not match its Western rivals such as the F-15 and F-16 for pilot visibility.

The MiG-29's radar is a multi-mode lookup/lookdown system. It is extremely powerful, although data handling is a little less sophisticated than in the latest Western systems.

MiG-29s are fitted with shields for their air intakes which close when the aircraft is on the ground. This is designed to prevent debris entering the engines in rough-field operation.

Standard weapons on the MiG-29 include the AA-10 'Alamo' for beyond-visual-range engagements and the exceptionally agile heat-seeking AA-11 'Archer' for dogfights.

The carrier-capable MiG-29K is fitted with folding wings and an arrester hook.

Infra-red tracker

HEAT SOURCE: All powered machinery generates infra-red energy in the form of heat. Jet engines are particularly powerful heat generators.

RANGE-FINDING: Once a target has been detected, the MiG-29 uses a laser beam to measure its distance and bearing. Weapons can then be locked on without the need for giveaway radar transmissions.

DETECTABLE ENERGY: The heat generated by the engines and by air friction on the aircraft's skin is broadcast for miles around. This heat is detectable by another aircraft equipped with a heat sensor. The MiG-29 an aircraft-sized heat source at more than 80 km (50 mi.).

MIKOYAN

MIG-31 'FOXHOUND'

● Long-range interceptor ● High-speed fighter ● Advanced radar

MiG's 'Foxhound' is at the cutting edge of Russian air defence. The world's largest and most powerful fighter, the MiG-31 was designed to use the latest radar and missile technology to find and destroy bombers or cruise missiles threatening Russia. Able to control intercepts for other aircraft and engage targets from sea level to the edge of space, the 'Foxhound' is still being improved, and the more potent MiG-31M may yet enter service.

▲ *Without equal in the West, the MiG-31 is a unique aircraft, developed to meet the requirement of defending what was the world's largest nation with a relatively small number of interceptor units.*

PHOTO FILE

MIKOYAN MIG-31 'FOXHOUND'

Guess from the West ▶
This drawing was produced by intelligence officers in the United States, based on satellite pictures of MiG-31 prototypes and reports from defecting MiG-25 pilot Victor Belenko. Despite early assessments, the MiG-31 is far more than a 'super-Foxbat'.

▲ Stealthy search
Like the MiG-29 and Su-27, but not most Western types, the MiG-31 can detect aircraft passively with its retractable infra-red search-and-track sensor.

▼ First appearance
'Foxhounds' began appearing over the Barents Sea in 1985. This example has the full armament fit of AA-9 'Amos' and AA-8 'Aphid' missiles.

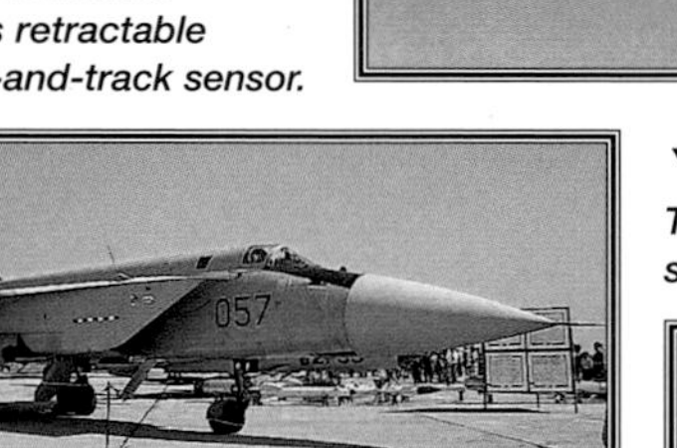

▲ Advanced Foxhound
The improved MiG-31M, easily recognisable by the four wing pylons for R-77 missiles and one-piece 'wrap-around' front canopy, is unlikely to be built in quantity.

▼ Mother of all radars
The mighty 'Zaslon' radar's beam can even be swung to the side of the aircraft if required.

FACTS AND FIGURES

➤ A fully loaded MiG-31 weighs as much as four unloaded MiG-29s, or two English Electric Canberra bombers.

➤ The MiG-31's GSh-23 cannon fires at a rate of 6000 rounds per minute.

➤ The SBI-16 (S-800) 'Zaslon' radar can engage several targets simultaneously.

➤ A MiG-31 prototype, the Ye-155, broke the payload-to-height record in 1977, climbing to 37,080 m (121,622 ft.) with 2000 kg (4,400 lb.).

➤ A MiG-31 shot down a low-level cruise missile from 20 km (12 mi.) away and 6 km (4 mi.) high.

PROFILE

Russia's fighting Foxhound

Developed as a specialised interceptor to defend Russia's extensive borders, the MiG-31 is arguably the most advanced air-defence aircraft ever built. Derived from the MiG-25 'Foxbat', the MiG-31 has the same blistering top speed as its ancestor, but also has a second crewmember who operates a massive phased-array 'Zaslon' radar (the first ever fitted to a fighter, and probably the most powerful). Also equipped with a search-and-track infra-red system, advanced datalink and the long-range AA-9 'Amos' missile, the 'Foxhound' can engage difficult targets (like cruise missiles) from almost surface level to maximum altitude, working in concert with other fighters and ground stations. Unlike the MiG-25, the MiG-31 has demonstrated impressive range, even allowing overflights of the North Pole.

The new MiG-31M has even more advanced defensive avionics, 'glass' cockpit displays, leading-edge root extensions and a new radar to allow it to fire active radar missiles. Despite its superb capabilities, the MiG-31M faces an uncertain future because of defence cuts.

Below: Despite being optimised for long-range engagements, the MiG-31 can take on short-range targets with missiles like the R-60 as well as with its 23-mm cannon.

Above: The MiG-31 can act as a fighter-control aircraft. Four aircraft in line formation can protect over 10,000 km² (3,680 sq, mi.) when used in this way.

One improvement in the MiG-31M is the addition of leading-edge root extensions, which improve the aircraft's high-alpha ability.

A distinct clue as to the MiG-31's ancestry, the wing consists of a welded steel and titanium box containing a very large fuel tank. This acts as a heat sink because at maximum speed the MiG-31's skin can reach 300°C (572°F).

MiG-31 'Foxhound'

Type: twin-engine high-performance interceptor

Powerplant: two PNPP (Soloviev) D-30F6 turbofan engines each rated at 93.19 kN (20,904-lb.-thrust) or 152.06 kN (34,111-lb.-thrust) with afterburner

Maximum speed: 3000 km/h (1,860 m.p.h.) at 17,500 m (57,400 ft.)

Ferry range: 3300 km (2,046 mi.)

Service ceiling: 20,600 m (67,568 ft.)

Weights: empty 21,825 kg (48,115 lb.); normal take-off 41,000 kg (101,640 lb.); maximum take-off 46,200 kg (191,851 lb.)

Armament: one GSh-6-23 six-barrelled 23-mm Gatling-type cannon with 250 rounds; various air-to-air missiles

Dimensions:		
	span	13.46 m (44 ft.)
	length	22.68 m (74 ft.)
	height	6.20 m (20 ft.)
	wing area	61.60 m² (663 sq. ft.)

MiG-31M 'Foxhound'

The seventh prototype MiG-31M, '057' may be the last of this unique aircraft to be built. The first fighter in the world equipped with a phased-array radar, the MiG-31 serves only with the Russian PVO air defence force.

Some MiG-31Ms have this ECM pod on the wingtip, with radomes on each end and on the outer side.

Half of the airframe is constructed from advanced steel, with one-third duralumin and 16 per cent titanium.

Visibility is somewhat limited for the backseater, whose attention is focused on a very large radar scope and multifunction displays. He sits on the K-36 ejection seat.

Power is provided by a pair of D-30 turbofans derived from the engine in the Tu-134 airliner. These offer considerably better fuel consumption (and have longer life) than the MiG-25's R-15 turbojets.

Another unusual feature of the MiG-31 is the tandem mainwheel configuration of the undercarriage designed for operating in the snowy Russian climate.

By using electronic beam control the size of the aerial can be maximised, giving greater range than conventional radars. The 'Zaslon' radar can detect a fighter at over 200 km (125 mi.).

COMBAT DATA

MAXIMUM SPEED

The MiG-31 is not quite as fast as its predecessor, the MiG-25, but it can easily outrun any other fighter in service. In practice, few fighters ever reach such speeds for more than a few minutes, and only then without their full load of fuel and weapons.

Aircraft	Speed
TORNADO F.Mk 3	2340 km/h (1,451 m.p.h.)
F-14A TOMCAT	2480 km/h (1,537 m.p.h.)
MiG-31 'FOXHOUND'	3000 km/h (1,860 m.p.h.)

ARMAMENT

Missiles like the R-33 (AA-9 'Amos') give the MiG-31 the ability to destroy enemy aircraft up to 110 km (70 mi.) away. Although it can carry eight missiles, six is a more usual load, with just two R-60s.

MiG-31 'FOXHOUND': 1 x 23-mm cannon; 4 x short-range R-60 AAMs; 4 x long-range R-33 AAMs

TORNADO F.Mk 3: 1 x 27-mm cannon; 4 x short-range Sidewinder AAMs; 4 x medium-range Skyflash AAMs

F-14A TOMCAT: 1 x 20-mm cannon; 2 x short-range Sidewinder AAMs; 2 x medium-range Sparrow AAMs; 2 x long-range Phoenix AAMs

RADAR RANGE

The powerful 'Zaslon' radar system has very long range, surpassing even the AWG-9 radar in the F-14. The Tomcat's radar can track more targets at the same time.

Aircraft	Range
MiG-31 'FOXHOUND'	200 km (125 mi.)
F-14A TOMCAT	180 km (111 mi.)
TORNADO F.Mk 3	185 km/h (115 mi.)

The ultimate air-defence team

BOMBER THREAT: By the early 1980s, the threat varied from high-flying cruise missile-armed B-52s to low-level aircraft like the FB-111A and Rockwell B-1 and ground-launched cruise missiles.

MINI-AWACS: MiG-31s can act like a small AWACS craft, with the leader of a four-aircraft formation linked to a ground radar station and AEW aircraft.

TARGET DATA TRANSFER: The MiG-31's PD-518 datalink can transfer target information to other air-defence aircraft like the Su-27 or MiG-29. Four MiG-31s can sweep an area 900 km (560 mi.) wide.

MIL

MI-8 'HIP'

● Assault transport ● Civil helicopter ● Gunship

▲One of the most enduring rotary designs ever, the Mi-8 has all the typical attributes of a Mil machine, combining strength and simplicity in a well-proven low-cost airframe.

A tough and resilient combat veteran, the Mil Mi-8 'Hip', and the closely related Mi-17, stands tall in its reputation as one of the most versatile helicopters in the world. The Mi-8 is the most widely used helicopter in service, and is cheap to run, easy to maintain and powerful. The 'Hip' is primarily a troop carrier and civil transport. Other roles include helicopter gunship, airborne command post, search and rescue and even communications jamming.

PHOTO FILE

MIL MI-8 'HIP'

▼Shooting from the hip
The 'Hip-E' gunship version is one of the world's most heavily armed helicopters, and has been used extensively in Chechnya.

▲Santa's sleigh
Even Santa Claus used the Mi-8 when travelling in distant areas of the Soviet Union. The Mi-8 was also vital to the Soviet oil industry, which explored in very remote areas.

Tourist flyer ▶
This Mi-8, belonging to Avialini Baltiski, flies tourists over St Petersburg on short pleasure flights in the summer.

▼Assault transport
This Mi-8 of the Indian air force is landing troops close to the front. Soviet Mi-8s made thousands of air assaults in Afghanistan, and large numbers were shot down.

▲KGB transport
Guarding the huge borders of the Soviet Union, the KGB needed a large number of Mi-8s to transport dog teams.

FACTS AND FIGURES

- ➤ More than 10,000 Mi-8s and Mi-17s have been built, with many hundreds being exported to more than 40 operators.
- ➤ The Mil Mi-17 is basically a Mi-8 with more power and a new tail rotor.
- ➤ The rare Mi-8PPA is a special communications jammer variant.
- ➤ The Mi-8 has fought in Afghanistan, Angola, Chechnya, Egypt, Mozambique and Nicaragua.
- ➤ The Czech Republic, Hungary and Russia use the 'Hip-G' command post version.
- ➤ The Mil Mi-14 'Haze' anti-submarine helicopter is derived from the Mi-8.

PROFILE

Helicopter workhorse to the world

Design of the Mi-8 'Hip' began in 1960. Unlike the earlier Mi-4 'Hound' which had its engine mounted in the nose, the Mi-8 has a more efficient shape with the turboshaft powerplant above the fuselage leaving maximum space for payload. Except on specialized models, large clamshell doors swing open at the rear fuselage.

Nearly a dozen versions of the Mi-8 and its upgraded Mi-17 derivative were used by Soviet forces and exported to Moscow's allies, and thousands of examples remain in service in Russia and around the world. Despite the age of the basic design, the type remains in production and sales continue. From the Arctic tundra of Finland to the tropical jungles of Peru, the 'Hip' is always a formidable performer, whether dropping into a landing zone with a load of troops or flying scheduled airline or cargo services to remote settlements.

Military Mi-8s are often equipped to a high specification, including additional cockpit armour, infra-red jammers, chaff and flare dispensers and exhaust gas diffusers. The Mi-17 improved upon the original Mi-8 by introducing a titanium rotor head for greater strength, improved efficiency engines and a new gearbox.

Mi-8s belonging to Interflug, former state airline of the DDR, have now all been retired.

The Mi-8 was cheap enough to produce in thousands, giving the Red Army mass airlift capability.

Mi-8T 'Hip-C'

Type: assault transport helicopter

Powerplant: two 1104-kW (1,480-hp) Klimov (Isotov) TV-2-117A turboshaft engines

Maximum speed: 250 km/h (155 mph) at sea level

Typical cruising speed: 208 km/h (129 mph)

Radius of action: 350 km (217 miles)

Ferry range: 930 km (578 miles)

Service ceiling: 4500 m (14,764 ft)

Weights: typical empty 7160 kg (15,875 lb); loaded 12,000 kg (26,455 lb)

Accommodation: up to 28 combat troops in a cabin area behind pilots; combinations of rockets or 250-kg (550-lb) bombs or UV-16-57 rocket pods (16 x 57-mm/2.24-in projectiles each) astride the fuselage

Dimensions:

main rotor diameter	21.29 m (69 ft 10 in)
length	25.24 m (82 ft 10 in)
height	5.65 m (18 ft 6 in)
main rotor disc area	356.00 m² (3,832 sq ft)

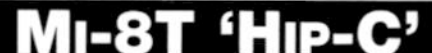

MI-8T 'HIP-C'

The Mi-8 remains in service in very large numbers with Aeroflot's successor airlines in the former Soviet Union, such as Baltiski, Baikal Avia, Orbi, Tajik Air and Tatarstan, as well as with many military air arms.

The Mi-8 has a traditional rotor head with flapping hinges and bearings. The improved titanium rotor head of the Mi-17 needs less maintenance and is more bullet resistant.

Although slightly redesigned, the Mi-8's large five-bladed main rotor was also used by the later Mi-24 gunship. Like all Mil designs, it rotates clockwise when viewed from above. The rotors have an automatic ice detection and thermal de-icing system, essential for operations in Russian conditions.

In the Mi-8 the tail rotor is on the starboard side of the tail, but on the port side of the Mi-17.

The Isotov TV-2 engines of the Mi-8 are very similar to the TV-3 engines in the Mi-24 and Mi-17. The TV-3 proved more reliable and economical and dramatically improved performance in 'hot-and-high' conditions.

The Mi-8 cockpit is surprisingly large. Israeli pilots flying captured examples in 1973 found that the machine had a totally different feel in flight to Western helicopters, and could easily outrun many of them.

Loading a Mi-8 is easy, thanks to the clamshell doors at the rear which can accommodate wide cargoes and allow infantry to exit very swiftly in an assault.

ACTION DATA

MAXIMUM SPEED

Typical top speeds for this type and size of helicopter tend to be around 250 km/h (155 mph). The Puma had a marginal edge in this respect, with a better power-to-weight ratio.

Mi-8T 'HIP-C'	250 km/h (155 mph)
SA 330H PUMA	280 km/h (174 mph)
COMMANDO Mk 2	226 km/h (140 mph)

TROOP CAPACITY

The Commando and Mi-8 can carry large numbers of troops. The Puma was designed to transport only a small platoon of infantry, and has a narrow fuselage compared to the much roomier Mi-8 and Commando.

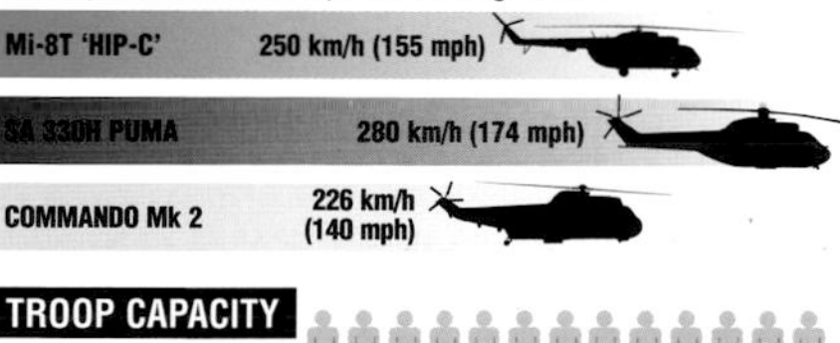

Mil's multi-role 'Hip'

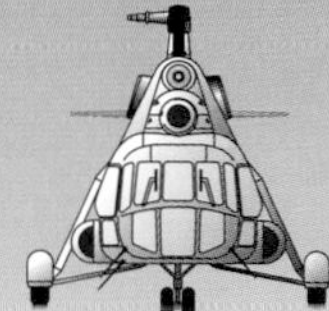

Mi-8 'HIP-A': The first Mi-8 was the single-engined prototype that lacked power and only had a four-bladed main rotor.

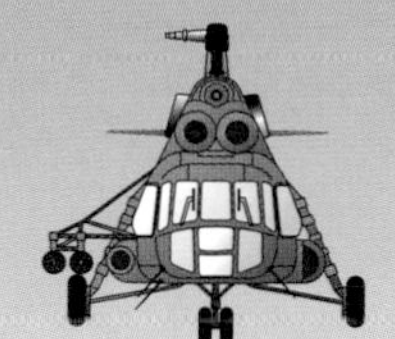

Mi-8 'HIP-C': With two engines and five main rotor blades, the Mi-8 'Hip-C' became the main assault helicopter of the USSR.

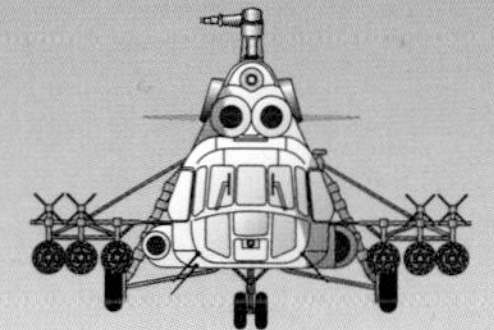

Mi-8 'HIP-E': Probably the most heavily armed helicopter in service, the 'Hip-E' carried up to six pods of 32 rockets.

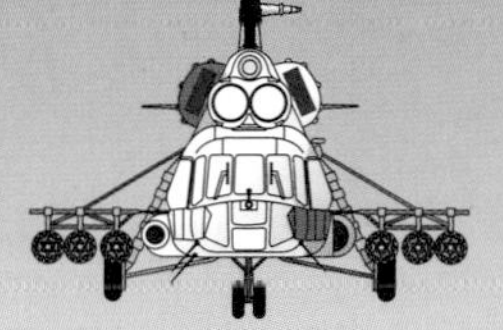

Mi-17 'HIP-H': The Mi-17 featured new engines, gearbox and rotor shaft and was a lot more powerful and economical than the Mi-8.

AWACS HIP: The Mi-17 was even converted to act as an airborne early warning and control machine with side-mounted radar aerials.

MIL

MI-14 'HAZE'

● Twin-engined shore-based ASW/SAR helicopter ● Exports

Based on the Mi-8 'Hip', the Mi-14 was developed as a land-based anti-submarine helicopter in the early 1970s. A boat hull and retractable landing gear were used to make it suitable for amphibious operations, with more powerful engines compensating for the additional weight. Flight tests started in September 1969. Specialised versions for minesweeping and search-and-rescue operations have also been produced.

▲ *Entering production in 1978, more than 240 Mi-14 'Haze-As' were built. The 'Haze' family has been the Soviet Bloc's principal source of shore-based ASW and SAR helicopters.*

PHOTO FILE

MIL MI-14 'HAZE'

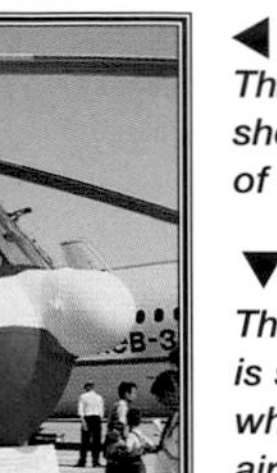

◀ Export potential
This Mi-14P was displayed at the Mosaero air show in 1995. It has a new nose radome in place of the undernose fairing and a searchlight.

▼ Amphibious 'Haze' at sea
The boat hull shape of the Mi-14's lower fuselage is supplemented by floating bags, which are useful when retrieving personnel in the SAR role or if the aircraft is forced to ditch.

▼ Upgraded Mi-14 demonstrator
To 'drum up' business, the Russian aviation industry is offering upgrades for existing airframes.

▼ Land based
As featured on other maritime helicopters such as the Sikorsky Sea King, the Mi-14 has a shaped hull to provide an amphibious capability.

▲ 'Haze' underside
This view of an Mi-14's underside shows the large weapons bay doors open and the MAD 'bird' deployed. Other apertures in the rear of the fuselage house dipping sonar and include parachutes for sonobuoys and flares.

FACTS AND FIGURES

- ➤ The Mi-14PL 'Haze-A' entered service in 1976, the Mi-14BT 'Haze-B' followed in 1986 and the Mi-14PS 'Haze-C' in 1992.
- ➤ Poland was the only export customer for the search-and-rescue Mi-14PS.
- ➤ East German Mi-14s were retired after the German reunification.
- ➤ The engine and gearbox from the Mi-17, itself developed from the Mi-8, was installed in the Mi-14.
- ➤ The SAR 'Haze-B' carries ten 20-place life-rafts and can tow these when filled.
- ➤ Mi-14PLs carry four crew: two pilots, a flight engineer and a systems operator.

PROFILE

Soviet ASW and SAR patroller

Equipped with a search radar, dipping sonar, dispensers for sonobuoys and flares and a towed magnetic anomaly detector (MAD), the original anti-submarine version of the 'Haze' was the Mi-14PL. The Mi-14PLM is a later variant with an improved engine and has the search radar moved to the bottom rear end of the fuselage.

For minesweeping, the Mi-14BT 'Haze-B' has a mine-activating sled in place of the MAD. Towed behind the helicopter, it carries either electrical cables or noise generators to detonate magnetic or acoustic mines. A searchlight on the tailboom enables the sled to be launched and recovered at night. The BT variant was used by the former East German navy, as well as the Soviet naval air arm, although only about 25 were built. The Luftwaffe did not keep the East German navy's six Mi-14BTs after reunification. Some have been converted to water bombers for use in civilian fire-fighting operations.

Above: Mi-14PL export markets included Bulgaria, Cuba, East Germany, Libya, North Korea, Poland, Syria and Yugoslavia.

The search-and-rescue version of this helicopter is known as the Mi-14PS 'Haze-C'. It has a more powerful winch and a wider main door, and is fitted with searchlights in the nose. The only users of the 'Haze-C' are Russia and Poland.

Below: The 'Haze' usually carries a flight crew of three, although the anti-submarine variants also have a systems operator for the sonar equipment and weapons.

Mi-14PL 'Haze-A'

Type: land-based anti-submarine helicopter

Powerplant: two 1434-kW (1,923-hp) Klimov (Isotov) TV3-117MT turboshafts

Maximum speed: 230 km/h (143 mph) at sea level

Climb rate: 468 m/min (1,535 fpm) at sea level

Endurance: 5 hours 55 min

Range: 1135 km (705 miles) with maximum fuel

Service ceiling: 4000 m (13,123 ft)

Weights: empty 8902 kg (19,626 lb); loaded 13,000 kg (28,660 lb); maximum take-off 14,000 kg (30,865 lb)

Armament: torpedoes and depth charges, as well as sonobuoys/smoke/flare floats

Dimensions:		
	main rotor diameter	21.29 m (69 ft 10 in)
	length	18.37 m (60 ft 3 in)
	height	9.63 m (31 ft 7 in)
	rotor disc area	362 m² (3,897 sq ft)

Mi-14PL 'Haze-A'

This Mi-14PL serves with the Polish navy, which also operates an Mi-14PX in the SAR training role and a small number of Mi-14PS 'Haze-C' dedicated SAR machines.

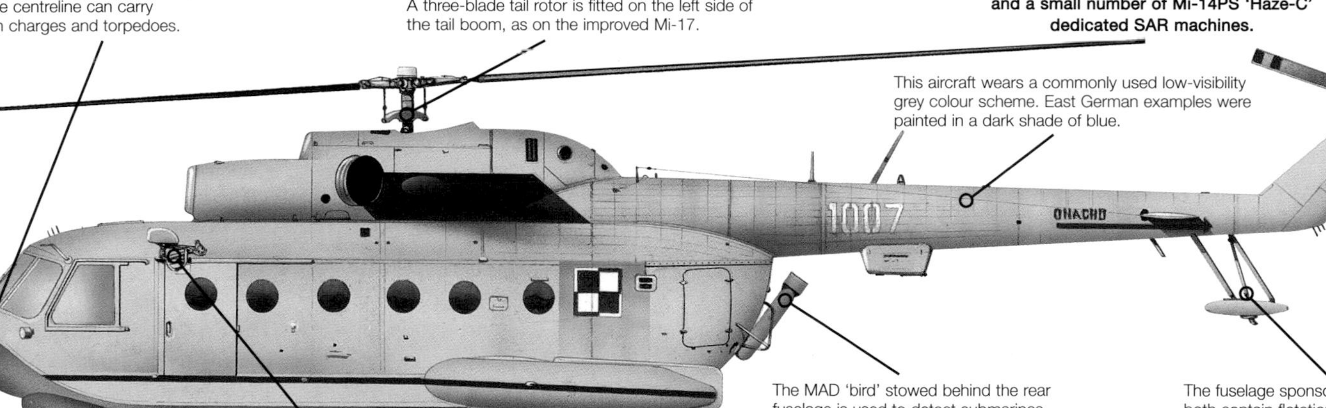

The underfuselage radome contains a Type 12-M search radar. A watertight weapons bay on the centreline can carry depth charges and torpedoes.

In common with the Mi-8 'Hip' from which it was developed, the Mi-14 has a five-blade main rotor. A three-blade tail rotor is fitted on the left side of the tail boom, as on the improved Mi-17.

This aircraft wears a commonly used low-visibility grey colour scheme. East German examples were painted in a dark shade of blue.

To assist during personnel recovery, a 150-kg (330-lb) hoist is fitted above the main cabin door.

The MAD 'bird' stowed behind the rear fuselage is used to detect submarines. Magnetic anomalies may be caused by the presence of a large metallic mass, such as a submarine.

The fuselage sponsons and tail float both contain flotation gear for use if the helicopter ditches at sea. The tail float prevents the tail rotor touching the water during an on-water landing.

COMBAT DATA

MAXIMUM SPEED

Aircraft such as the Mi-14 were not intended to be high-speed machines, range and endurance were more important factors. All three types are capable of speeds in the 250 km/h (155 mph) band.

Mi-14PL 'HAZE-A'	230 km/h (143 mph)
SA 321G SUPER FRELON	275 km/h (171 mph)
Ka-27PL 'HELIX-A'	250 km/h (155 mph)

ENDURANCE

The land-based Mi-14 has the best endurance of these representative types. 'Helix' is a smaller carrier-based machine, and the Super Frelon has three engines and a higher fuel consumption.

Mi-14PL 'HAZE-A'	5 hours 55 min
SA 321G SUPER FRELON	4 hours
Ka-27PL 'HELIX-A'	4 hours 30 min

FERRY RANGE

The endurance of each type is reflected by the range figure. The values quoted are for ferry range with a maximum fuel load and no weapons or other equipment on board. Range performance is particularly important when it comes to carrier-based aircraft.

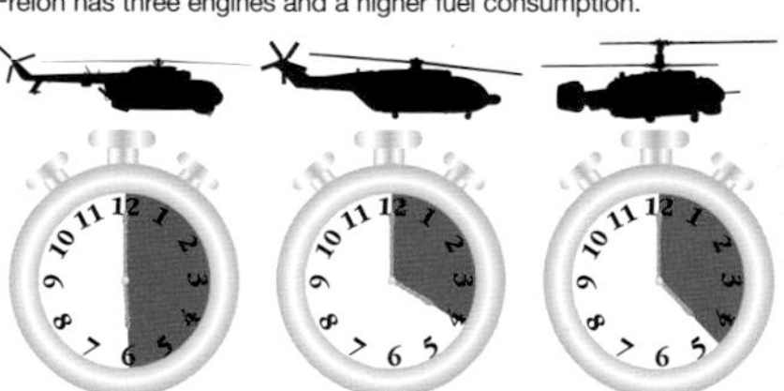

Anti-submarine helicopter designs

■ **AÉROSPATIALE SA 321 SUPER FRELON:** The SA 321G ASW variant of this three-engined machine entered Aéronavale service in 1965.

■ **KAMAN SH-2 SEASPRITE:** Derived from the UH-2, this ASW variant appeared in 1970 and remains in use with the US Navy.

■ **WESTLAND LYNX:** The first naval version of the Lynx did not fly until 1976. Widely exported, it is the Royal Navy's principal ASW machine.

■ **SIKORSKY SH-3 SEA KING:** Sikorsky's very successful S-61 design flew in 1959 and has been developed by Westland and Agusta.

Mil

Mi-24 'Hind-A'

● Soviet gunship/assault helicopter ● Exported ● Afghan action

Soviet helicopter pioneer Mikhail Mil's last helicopter design, the Mi-24, has been one of the most widely used military helicopters. The original Mi-24 prototype flew in 1970, and was used with two other prototypes to establish several speed, height and climb records. Initial production aircraft were given the NATO reporting name 'Hind-A', and were operated by a three-man crew, including a flight engineer as well as a co-pilot/gunner.

▲ *On its entry into Soviet service, the Mi-24 was unique. The West had no direct equivalent, which was considered disastrous at the time. The response was to develop the dedicated AH-64 Apache, a far more effective tank-killer.*

Photo File

Mil Mi-24 'Hind-A'

▲ Low-drag attributes
Cockpit glazing was designed to reduce drag and contributed to the Mi-24's excellent performance.

▲ Well armed
A variety of weapons (including anti-tank missiles, rockets and bombs) was carried on 'wings' behind the cabin. Each had a 250-kg (550-lb) capacity. The Mi-24 first saw action in Afghanistan.

▲ Inspired by HueyCobra
Mikhail Mil studied the American Bell 209 HueyCobra before proposing the Mi-24. The 'Hind' differed from the Cobra in having a troop-carrying capability.

▲ 'Hinds' in action
During the Soviet intervention in Afghanistan in the 1980s, 'Hind-As' and 'Hind-Ds' were used in the COIN role.

Museum piece ▶
Most early-model 'Hinds' are today relegated to the museums.

Facts and Figures

- Iraqi Mi-24s were credited with downing Iranian Cobra helicopters and even F-4 fighter-bombers during the Iran–Iraq War.
- An Mi-24 prototype flew for the first time in early 1970.
- A 'Hind-A' was modified to test systems for the later 'Hind-D'.
- Pre-production Mi-24s were known as 'Hind-B' in the West as they were not identified until after production 'Hind-As'.
- During the conflict in Afghanistan, Mi-24s were flown by Soviet and Afghan forces.
- As well as carrying weapons, the stub wings provide some lift.

PROFILE

Warsaw Pact armed assault chopper

Built to take troops to the thick of battlefield action, the Mi-24 gained from lessons learned by US forces in Vietnam. Big enough to carry eight troops, it was powerful and fast, and carried enough weapons to suppress hostile forces en route to the landing zone – a flying armoured personnel carrier.

Mil used the TV2-117 engines and dynamic system from the Mi-8 'Hip' so that design work could be concentrated on the weapons installation. As a result, the 'Hind-A' was in service with the Soviet forces in East Germany from 1973.

The TV2-117 engines were replaced by TV3-117s in later production aircraft, and the same powerplant was fitted to some earlier machines. 'Hind-As' with the later engine have the tail rotor repositioned on the left of the tail boom.

Although the 'Hind-A' was not exported as widely as some of the later gunship versions of the Mi-24, small numbers have served with the forces of Afghanistan (where the type saw its first action, mainly in the counterinsurgency role), Algeria, Libya and Vietnam.

The 'Hind-C' (Mi-24U) was a dedicated training version of the 'Hind-A' with dual controls but stripped of armament. It was one of these aircraft (designated 'A-10') that was used in 1975 to set eight world marks, including a number of speed records, with a female aircrew. From the mid-1970s, the redesigned 'Hind-D' replaced the A model on the production line.

Straight wings without anhedral identify this Mi-24 as a 'Hind-B' from the first production series.

Mi-24 'Hind-A'

Type: gunship/assault helicopter

Powerplant: two 1434-kW (1,923-hp) Isotov TV3-117MT turboshafts

Maximum speed: 320 km/h (199 mph)

Climb rate: 900 m/min (2,953 fpm) at sea level

Range: 750 km (466 miles)

Service ceiling: 4500 m (14,764 ft)

Weights: empty 8400 kg (18,519 lb); maximum take-off 12,500 kg (27,558 lb)

Armament: one 12.7-mm (0.5-in) machine gun and four AT-2 'Swatter' anti-tank missiles plus bombs or two rocket pods

Dimensions:

rotor diameter	17.30 m (56 ft 9 in)
length	17.51 m (57 ft 5 in)
height	6.50 m (21 ft 4 in)
rotor disc area	235.00 m² (2,530 sq ft)

MI-24 'HIND-A'

Libya was among four Soviet allies to receive the 'Hind-A', the others being Algeria, Afghanistan and Vietnam. It is believed that few, if any, 'Hind-As' remain in service.

It is believed that from the outset the 'Hind' was expected to have a dual role as both a gunship and an assault helicopter (thus replacing the Mi-8 'Hip'). However, Mi-24s have never been able to carry a full weapons load while carrying troops, and the dual role abilities of the type are limited.

Twin 1434-kW Isotov TV-3 turboshafts powered most Mi-24s, though early production batches were fitted with smaller TV-2s as installed in the Mi-8, on which the Mi-24 design was based.

Shrouded in flat plate glazing, the cockpit of the 'Hind-A' had three seats. The crew consisted of a gunner seated in the centre front, a flight engineer/co-pilot behind him to the rear, and the pilot offset to the left rear, next to the co-pilot. In the lower nose a 12.7-mm (0.5-in) machine gun was fitted in a flexible mounting.

Unlike the extensively redesigned 'Hind-D', the 'Hind-A' was only lightly armoured.

3037

DANGER

Each stub wing can carry two Falanga anti-tank missiles (known to NATO as AT-2 'Swatters') as well as four 32-round rocket pods. Various antennas on the aircraft were associated with radio equipment and defensive avionics, such as IFF (identification friend or foe).

While early production 'Hind-As' and some later 'Hind-Ds' had their tail rotors located on the starboard side of the tailfin, those on late 'Hind-As' were switched to the port side.

'Hinds' at home and abroad

Mi-24 'HIND-A': Algerian 'Hind-As' served alongside Mi-4s and Mi-8s. In 1996 the North African state continued to fly 'Hinds', although whether these were 'Hind-As' is unclear. Few export customers ordered the variant.

Mi-24D 'HIND-D': The 'Hind-D' was a major redesign of the Mi-24 intended to address the weaknesses of the 'Hind-A'. Early production examples of the new aircraft were delivered to Warsaw Pact countries, including East Germany.

Mi-24P 'HIND-F': Experience in Afghanistan led to replacing the 12.7-mm (0.5-in) nose-mounted machine gun with a twin-barrelled 30-mm (!.18-in) cannon on the Mi-24P. The USSR and GDR used this variant; the Mi-35P was an export derivative.

COMBAT DATA

MAXIMUM SPEED

As the 'Hind' was developed with new engines, a redesigned fuselage and more capable weapons, its top speed fluctuated. The first Mi-24Ds were marginally slower than the 'Hind-A', but by the time that the Mi-24P 'Hind-F' had appeared in service this had been addressed, the type having a small top speed margin over the Mi-24D 'Hind-D'.

Mi-24 'HIND-A'	320 km/h (199 mph)
Mi-24D 'HIND-D'	310 km/h (193 mph)
Mi-24P 'HIND-F'	335 km/h (208 mph)

MIL

MI-24 'HIND'

● Gunship ● Tank-buster ● Afghan war veteran

The Mil Mi-24 'Hind' is the hammer of the Russian army. A veteran of battles in Afghanistan and Angola, and most recently in Chechnya, the Mi-24 is a flying armoured personnel carrier, able to deliver a squad of soldiers and cover them with suppressive fire. Armed with a cannon and powerful laser-guided anti-armour missiles, and now fitted with the latest avionics and new engines, the 'Hind' is a highly potent attack helicopter.

▲ *The 'Hind' was regarded with awe by NATO when it appeared in the 1970s. Now regarded as a simple machine by Western standards, it is respected for its speed, strength and massive firepower.*

PHOTO FILE

MIL MI-24 'HIND'

▲ Twin cannon
The 'Hind-F' replaced the nose turret machine gun with a fixed twin-barrel 30-mm GSh cannon.

▲ Tank-buster
Standard armament in early 'Hinds' was UV-32 rocket pods and the AT-2 missile.

Battle wagon ▶
The 'Hind' proved its toughness in Afghanistan, where it often survived massive small-arms fire.

▲ German 'Hind'
The Luftwaffe has disposed of its Mi-24 fleet, acquired along with East Germany, mainly due to poor supplies of spares.

◀ Gunfighter
The 'Hind-D' carries the classic Mi-24 armament fit. A 12.7-mm multi-barrel gun turret shares the nose with an electro-optical guidance system to starboard and a missile guidance pod to port.

▲ Fast mover
The 'Hind' used its speed to advantage in attacks, acting much like a ground-attack jet fighter.

FACTS AND FIGURES

- ➤ The prototype for the Mi-24 series, fitted with a conventional cockpit, made its first flight in 1970.
- ➤ An Mi-24 set a helicopter world speed record of 368.4 km/h (228.9 mph).
- ➤ Mi-24s fought against South African troops during the Angolan war.
- ➤ Mujahideen guerrillas in Afghanistan shot down three Mi-24s at Jalalabad air base in five minutes using Stinger missiles.
- ➤ The 'Hind' is operated by more than two dozen countries.
- ➤ Two Mi-24s were flown to Pakistan by defecting Afghan air force pilots.

PROFILE

Russia's flying tank

First seen in the West in 1974, the 'Hind' was designed to carry eight men into frontline positions and support them with air-to-ground fire. The Mi-24 is very large and fast, but it is not as agile as Western battlefield helicopters. However, aircraft such as the American AH-64 Apache are designed to engage tanks from hidden hovering positions, which calls for low-speed manoeuvrability. The 'Hind', by contrast, is a purely offensive weapon, heavily armed and armoured, and designed to advance at high speed.

Most 'Hinds' are gunships, with a stepped tandem canopy housing a weapons operator in front and a pilot higher to the rear. Either can aim the gun with a magnifying sight in a bulge under the nose, which also contains a laser tracker for missiles.

Following combat experience in Afghanistan, Mil introduced an improved 'Hind' with a twin-barrelled GSh-23L 30-mm (1.18-in) cannon. This, together with its rockets and missiles, makes the 'Hind' very much a close-support weapon, with enormous firepower.

Like most Russian weapons the 'Hind' is a powerful machine, built to take battle damage and capable of operating in very harsh conditions. It will serve for many years yet, as the planned Mi-40 replacement has been cancelled.

The stub wings allow the 'Hind' to travel very fast by adding to the lift from the rotor, but by sticking out into the rotor downwash they inhibit low-speed and hovering handling.

Both cockpits have excellent armour protection and bulletproof glass canopies.

The five-bladed main rotor may be replaced by that of the more modern Mi-28 'Havoc', if the 'Hind' upgrade programme goes ahead.

The original 'Hind-A' had its tail rotor on the starboard side of the tail boom, but it was switched to port soon after production had started.

Mi-24D 'Hind-D'

Type: battlefield helicopter

Powerplant: two 1640-kW (2,199-hp) Klimov (Isotov) TV3-117 Series III turboshafts

Maximum speed: 310 km/h (193 mph)

Maximum cruising speed: 260 km/h (162 mph)

Range: 750 km (466 mph) with internal fuel

Service ceiling: 4500 m (14,764 ft)

Weights: empty 8400 kg (18,519 lb); loaded 12,500 kg (27,558 lb)

Armament: one four-barrel JakB 12.7-mm (0.5-in) Gatling gun in chin turret; four S-8 80-mm (3.15-in) rocket pods or up to 3460 kg (7,628 lb) of rockets or missiles

Dimensions:

span	6.54 m (21 ft 5 in)
main rotor diameter	17.30 m (56 ft 9 in)
length	19.79 m (64 ft 11 in)
height	6.50 m (21 ft 4 in)
main rotor disc area	235.00 m² (2,530 sq ft)

Mi-24H 'Hind-E'

This Mi-24 'Hind-E' serves with the Polish air force's 56th squadron at Inowroclaw, armed with the 'Shturm' AT-6 laser-guided anti-tank missile.

The Isotov turboshafts are powerful engines, but they are getting old. They may be replaced by engines used in the Mi-28 if Russia can find the money to upgrade its 'Hinds'.

All Mil helicopters have a clockwise rotating rotor. The rotor head was built to withstand heavy machine-gun fire.

Many 'Hinds' have an infra-red jammer fitted to counter shoulder-launched heat-seeking missiles such as Stinger and SA-14.

Large exhaust suppressors are fitted to some 'Hinds' to reduce infra-red signature.

Flare dispensers are often fitted to 'Hinds', usually on the tailboom. Lack of these units caused heavy losses to Stinger missiles in the Afghan war.

The tail rotor remains one of the weak points of the 'Hind'. The yellow warning strip has the Russian word for 'danger' painted on it, as ground crews often fail to spot it when it is rotating.

COMBAT DATA

MAXIMUM CRUISING SPEED

Mi-24D 'HIND-D'	260 km/h (162 mph)
AH-1F COBRA	227 km/h (141 mph)
LYNX AH.Mk 7	260 km/h (162 mph)

Specially prepared 'Hinds' established a number of helicopter speed records in the 1970s, and the production variant remains one of the fastest helicopters currently in service. An experimental version of Britain's Lynx has since taken the absolute helicopter speed record.

COMBAT RADIUS

Mi-24D 'HIND-D'	160 km (100 miles)
AH-1F COBRA	200 km (124 miles)
LYNX AH.Mk 7	270 km (168 miles)

The Mi-24 is a big and heavy machine, and with a full combat load its range is noticeably shorter than those of its rivals, although it can double its range by carrying drop-tanks in place of weaponry. As the 'Hind' is primarily a battlefield weapon, its lack of range is no real handicap.

ANTI-TANK WEAPONS

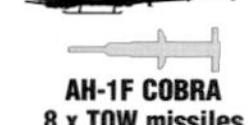

Mi-24D 'HIND-D'	4 x AT-2 'Swatter' or AT-6 'Spiral' missiles
AH-1F COBRA	8 x TOW missiles
LYNX AH.Mk 7	8 x TOW missiles

Although the 'Hind' carries fewer anti-tank weapons than its rivals, it should be remembered that it was not designed as an anti-tank platform. Its stub wings can be used to carry a much heavier weight of other weapons, including bombs, rockets, guns and even chemical weapons.

Gunship rivals

■ **BELL AH-1 COBRA:** This pioneering gunship helicopter introduced the now standard fighter-style cockpit, with a gunner in front and the pilot behind. Much smaller than the 'Hind', the Cobra is purely a fighting machine and has no passenger cabin.

■ **McDONNELL DOUGLAS AH-64 APACHE:** Much more manoeuvrable at low speeds than the 'Hind', the Apache is the West's premier gunship and anti-tank helicopter. Like the big Mil design, it is heavily armed and armoured.

■ **MIL Mi-28 'HAVOC':** Even more powerful than the 'Hind', the 'Havoc' dispenses with the earlier helicopter's passenger cabin. It is actively marketed by the Mil design bureau, but might not enter service with the financially strained Russian military.

MITSUBISHI

MU-2

● STOL design ● Built in Japan and USA ● Civil and military users

A fine light business transport, the Mitsubishi MU-2 has gained popularity in a wide range of civilian and military duties. Several versions of this twin-engined, high-wing aircraft are in operation, some with evocative names like Marquise and Solitaire. The MU-2 has a truly international flavour, with examples flying in at least 19 countries, and many of these Japanese aircraft were assembled at an American plant in Texas.

▲ *The design of the MU-2 began in Japan in the late 1950s, but the bulk of the production was carried out in Texas. The US represented the largest potential market for the aircraft.*

PHOTO FILE

MITSUBISHI MU-2

▲ High-speed MU-2M
Publicity for the MU-2M emphasised its 590 km/h (367 m.p.h.) speed.

▼ Reconnaissance MU-2C
Ordered by the Japanese Ground Self-Defence Force as the LR-1, this was an unpressurised version of the MU-2B and was fitted with cameras and radar.

▲ MU-2P becomes Solitaire
The MU-2P was built in the US as the Solitaire and had more powerful engines. With a crew of two, the cabin can carry six or seven passengers.

▼ Astazou power
The earliest MU-2As, which flew in 1963, were powered by Turboméca Astazou engines.

Long-fuselage Marquise ▶
The MU-2N, with its lengthened fuselage and four-bladed propellers, was fitted with more powerful Garrett turboprops and named Marquise.

FACTS AND FIGURES

- Rhein Flugzeugbau obtained rights from Mitsubishi to assemble and maintain MU-2s in Germany.
- The prototype aircraft made its first flight on 24 September 1963.
- In all, 831 Mitsubishi MU-2s were built; only 57 were for users in Japan.
- The MU-2 was initially sold in the US by Mooney, until Mitsubishi established its own plant in Texas.
- Japan's Air and Ground Self-Defence Forces ordered 53 military examples.
- MU-2Cs and Ks operated by the JGSDF can carry two 12.7-mm (.50 cal.) machine-guns.

PROFILE

Japan's little turbine twin

The Mitsubishi MU-2 was a result of plans in 1959 for a STOL (short take-off and landing) utility transport. Mitsubishi developed a twin-engined, high-wing aircraft with wingtip tanks as standard.

The MU-2 immediately proved efficient and economical to civilian purchasers, who used it as an executive transport and feeder airliner. A few were adapted for military duties, including airfield radar calibration, target-towing and search and rescue.

The MU-2 has gained a reputation as a relatively fast aircraft, although not an easy one to fly; it can 'get away' from any pilot who forgets that it is a high-performance machine.

Operators who want effective transport for key personnel praise the MU-2. The operating costs of this turboprop machine are 65 per cent of those of a jet aircraft with similar capacity. And with its short take-off run, the MU-2 can use smaller airfields that are not available to most jets.

Production ended in 1986 after 831 MU-2s in 15 different versions had been produced. Marquise and Solitaire production in the United States totalled 282.

Above: A stretched version, the MU-2G, was offered by Mitsubishi. The fuselage was lengthened by 1.88 m (6 ft. 2 in.) to increase seating.

Above: The majority of civil MU-2s were sold in the United States, although it had some sales success in Europe and Asia. This is a French-registered example.

MU-2C

Type: twin-engined STOL liaison aircraft

Powerplant: two 540-kW (725-hp.) Garrett TPE331-6-251M turboprops

Maximum cruising speed: 590 km/h (366 m.p.h.) at 4575 m (15,000 ft.)

Maximum rate of climb: 945 m/min (3,100 f.p.m.)

Maximum take-off distance: 520 m (1,706 ft.) to 15 m (50 ft.) altitude

Range: 2706 km (1,681 mi.)

Service ceiling: 10,110 m (33,170 ft.)

Weights: empty 2685 kg (5,919 lb.); maximum take-off 4500 kg (9,921 lb.)

Accommodation: two pilots and six or seven passengers

Dimensions:

span	11.94 m (39 ft. 2 in.)
length	10.13 m (33 ft. 3 in.)
height	3.94 m (12 ft. 11 in.)
wing area	16.55 m² (178 sq. ft.)

MU-2E

Derived from the MU-2K, the MU-2E serves with the Japanese Air Self-Defence Force under the designation MU-2S. Twenty-nine were built and are in use with the Air Rescue Wing at Iruma, with detachments elsewhere.

The Japanese Self-Defence Forces have been the only military operators of the MU-2, using the type in the SAR, training, reconnaissance, liaison, target-towing and radar calibration roles.

For its search-and-rescue role a Doppler search radar is fitted in the 'thimble' nose radome. The standard flight crew consists of one or two pilots. In this variant crew would also be carried as observers and to operate the radar.

Two 540-kW (725-hp.) Garrett TPE331-6-251M turboprops power the MU-2K and derivatives. Each drives a Hartzell fully-feathering, three-bladed, reversible-pitch, constant-speed propeller.

A sliding door is fitted to the MU-2E for air dropping dinghies to the victims of maritime disasters, downed aircrew and the like. Although most MU-2 variants are pressurised, this version is not due to its role and the need to deploy dinghies.

The wingtip fuel tanks have a total capacity of 682 litres (150 gal.). Tanks in the wings hold 697 litres (153 gal.), giving a total fuel load of 1379 litres (303-gal.). The MU-2E utilised the original short fuselage of the original production versions of the MU-2.

The observation windows below each wing are bulged to improve the crew's view. The fuselage is painted in a high-visibility colour scheme to make the aircraft easier to see.

ACTION DATA

MAXIMUM CRUISING SPEED

While some versions of the MU-2 were fast compared to their rivals, the MU-2N had a top speed closer to the 450 km/h average for turboprop twin-engined aircraft of the 1960s. All three aircraft have similar speed performances.

MU-2N	465 km/h (289 m.p.h.)
JETSTREAM SERIES 200	454 km/h (280 m.p.h.)
CONQUEST	426 km/h (265 m.p.h.)

RANGE

A range figure around 2300 km (1,430 mi.) was typical of the period. Range is an important consideration for buyers of executive aircraft which often fly long distances between cities.

MU-2N	2330 km (1,448 mi.)
JETSTREAM SERIES 200	2224 km (1,382 mi.)
CONQUEST	2995 km (1,861 mi.)

PASSENGER LOAD

Scottish Aviation's Jetstream (later built by British Aerospace) was able to carry a larger passenger load than both the MU-2N and the later Conquest. Limited size was a weakness of the MU-2 design.

MU-2N	11
JETSTREAM SERIES 200	16
CONQUEST	10

Other Mitsubishi aircraft

F-4EJ PHANTOM II: Mitsubishi licence-built 125 McDonnell Douglas F-4Es for the Japanese Air Self-Defence Force between 1971 and 1981.

T-2: Japan's first supersonic jet, the T-2 flew in July 1971. Used for the training role, the aircraft is powered by two Adour turbofans.

F-1: This fighter derivative of the T-2 flew in 1977. Its principal role is anti-shipping, for which it is equipped with missiles.

MU-300/DIAMOND: First flown as the MU-300 in 1978, the aircraft was marketed as the Diamond and later built in the US by Beech.

MITSUBISHI
T-2

● **Advanced/combat trainer** ● **Supersonic** ● **Multi-role aircraft**

Japan's first indigenous supersonic jet, Mitsubishi's T-2 was designed to meet a Japanese Air Self-Defence Force (JASDF) requirement for an advanced training aircraft. Gaining inspiration from the SEPECAT Jaguar, a T-2A combat trainer variant, armed with a 20-mm cannon and hardpoints under the fuselage and wings, was also built. It provided a basis for subsequent development of the Mitsubishi F-1 close-support supersonic fighter.

▲ *The T-2 trainer has proved a popular and efficient aircraft in JASDF service, and pilots benefit from its commonality with the Mitsubishi F-1 fighter.*

PHOTO FILE

MITSUBISHI T-2

Supersonic trainer ▶
Japanese officials were very impressed with the SEPECAT Jaguar, and when Mitsubishi designed the T-2 it incorporated many features which were similar to those of the European design.

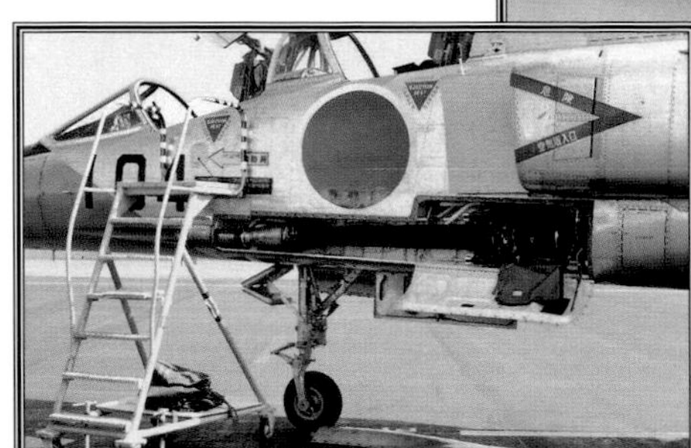

◀ Training for combat
The T-2A combat trainer is fitted with a 20-mm M61 multi-barrel Vulcan cannon under the cockpit floor. It also has weapons stations on the centreline and under the wings, plus wingtip points for Sidewinder missiles.

Long service ▶
First flown as the XT-2 on 20 July 1971, the type has been in JASDF service since March 1975.

◀ Jaguar look-alike
Similarities with the Jaguar are evident in this view of a T-2 carrying four underwing rocket pods. The aircraft was also fitted with the Jaguar's engines.

F-86 replacement ▶
Entering service with the 4th Air Wing at Matsushima, the T-2 replaced the ageing, licence-built F-86 Sabre and T-33 in the advanced training role. Ninety-six T-2s were built, including two F-1 development aircraft.

FACTS AND FIGURES

- ➤ Mitsubishi was announced as the winner of the competition in September 1967, beating Fuji and Kawasaki.
- ➤ The T-2s of the 'Blue Impulse' aerobatic team have a secondary air defence role.
- ➤ AIM-9L Sidewinder AAMs can be carried on the T-2A's wingtips.
- ➤ One T-2 was extensively modified as the T-2CCV control-configured vehicle with test equipment in the rear cockpit.
- ➤ The T-2 can carry up to 2000 kg (4,400 lb.) of ordnance.
- ➤ The first prototype F-1 was a modified T-2A with a blanked-off rear cockpit.

PROFILE

High-performance Japanese trainer

As its first excursion into supersonic military aircraft design, Japan produced this two-seat combat trainer, which was intended to train pilots who would go on to fly the Lockheed F-104J Starfighter and the McDonnell Douglas F-4EJ Phantom. Mitsubishi's T-2, which became renowned as the mount of the 'Blue Impulse' aerobatic team, was also designed to give Japanese industry vital engineering experience that would eventually contribute to a home-built fighter – the F-1, which was based on the T-2. More recently, this engineering knowledge has been used to produce the F-2 strike fighter development of Lockheed's F-16.

When it first came on the scene in 1971, the T-2 astonished those who had not expected to see fighter-like features in a trainer. Using a Japanese-built version of the Rolls-Royce/Turboméca Adour turbofan engine and incorporating many hi-tech features both inside and out, the T-2 is equipped with licence-built American avionics. The successful Japanese trainer has also proved to be highly useful as a testbed for exploring fly-by-wire technology and other advanced systems.

T-2/T-2A advanced and combat trainers are operated by the 4th Air Wing, based at Matsushima. Avionics systems include a J/AWG-11 nose-mounted search and ranging radar.

T-2A

Type: two-seat supersonic combat trainer

Powerplant: two Ishikawajima-Harima TF40-IHI-801A (Rolls-Royce/Turboméca Adour Mk 801A) turbofans, each rated at 22.75 kN (5,120-lb. thrust) dry and 32.49 kN (7,310-lb. thrust) with afterburning

Maximum speed: 1700 km/h (1,054 m.p.h.) at 10,975 m (36,000 ft.)

Service ceiling: 15,240 m (50,000 ft.)

Weights: empty 6307 kg (13,875 lb.); maximum take-off 12,800 kg (28,160 lb.)

Armament: one M61 20-mm Vulcan cannon, up to 2000 kg (4,400 lb.) of ordnance on one centreline and four underwing stations plus wingtip rails for AIM-9 Sidewinders

Dimensions:		
	span	7.88 m (25 ft. 10 in.)
	length	17.86 m (58 ft. 7 in.)
	height	4.39 m (14 ft. 5 in.)
	wing area	21.17 m² (228 sq. ft.)

T-2A

Japan's national aerobatic team, 'Blue Impulse', has up to six T-2s allocated to it at any one time.

'Blue Impulse' T-2s are painted in this elaborate colour scheme and carry smoke-generating equipment. Based at Matsushima, the team is part of the 4th Kokudan (Air Wing) The T-2 was adopted by the aerobatic team, which previously flew licence-built F-86F Sabres, in 1982.

The fuselage is of all-metal semi-monocoque construction, with titanium accounting for 10 per cent of the trainer's weight, mainly around the engine bays. Two airbrakes and a pair of ventral fins are located under the rear fuselage behind the wheel bays.

The T-2A has shoulder-mounted wings and fixed-geometry lateral air inlets for the pair of (licence-built) Rolls-Royce/Turboméca Adour afterburning turbofans.

The T-2A's wings have electrically-actuated flaps and no conventional ailerons. Lateral control is maintained by hydraulically-actuated, slotted spoilers which move differentially and are located in front of the flaps.

Instructor and pupil are accommodated in tandem under separate canopies in a pressurised and air-conditioned cockpit. The rear seat is elevated to give the instructor improved forward vision. Aerobatic displays are normally flown by a single pilot.

Avionics systems include Mitsubishi Electric J/AWG-11 search and ranging radar, J/ARC-51 UHF radio, Nippon Electric J/ARN-53 TACAN and Tokyo Communication J/APX-101 SIF/IFF (Identification Friend or Foe).

Armament comprises an M61 20-mm Vulcan cannon mounted on the left side of the fuselage under the cockpit. Early 'Blue Impulse' machines had the cannon port faired over.

All components of the tricycle landing gear retract into the fuselage, with the main units retracting forwards and the nosewheel rearwards.

A runway arrester hook is mounted beneath the rear fuselage and there is a brake parachute in the tailcone.

COMBAT DATA

MAXIMUM SPEED

Only two supersonic trainers have entered service in quantity, the T-2 and the Northrop T-38 Talon, of which the T-2 is by far the faster. Most air arms are not willing to pay the extra operating costs of a supersonic trainer and prefer high-performing subsonic types.

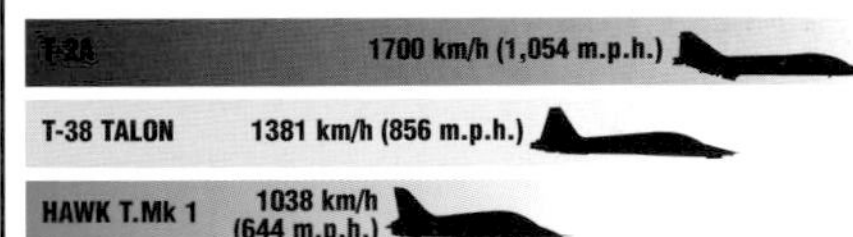

MAXIMUM CLIMB RATE

With its lower power, the Hawk has a slower rate of climb. It is, however, far more agile and its aerobatic capabilities more than compensate for its comparative lack of performance. The USAF is updating its T-38s to allow them to stay in service for several more years.

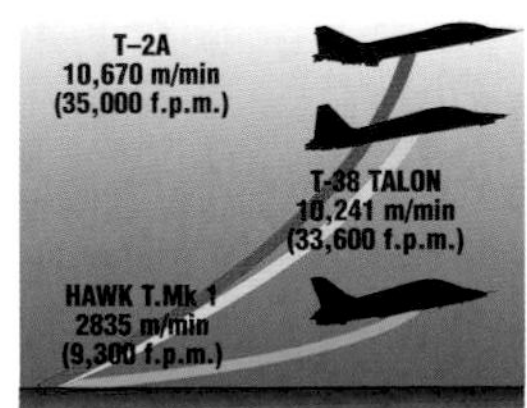

SERVICE CEILING

The Hawk and T-2 operate at similar altitudes, but the T-38 has a higher service ceiling. This has meant that it has been used for a number of special training and test roles, including training SR-71 and B-2 pilots.

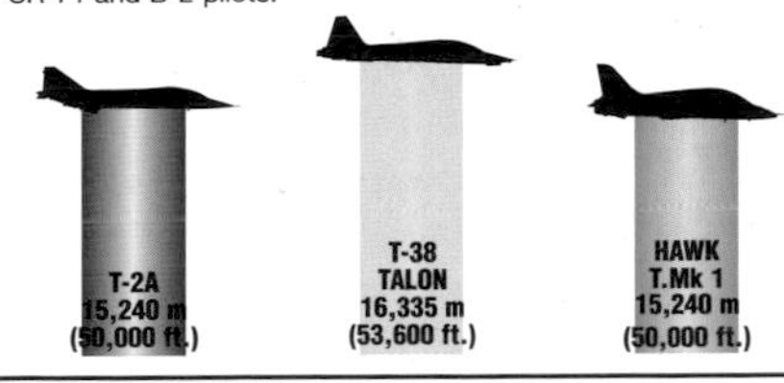

Japanese trainers

FUJI T-1: This indigenous basic and intermediate trainer, based on the F-86, was the first post-war jet aircraft designed in Japan.

FUJI T-3/BEECH T-34: The T-3 (developed from the Beechcraft T-34) provides the initial 75 hours of primary pilot training in the JASDF.

KAWASAKI T-4: Built as a T-33 replacement, the T-4 is an intermediate jet trainer. The JASDF has a requirement for 200 aircraft.

FUJI T-5: This primary/basic aerobatic trainer and utility aircraft serves with the Japanese Maritime Self-Defence Force.

Mitsubishi

F-1

● **Single-seat close-support fighter** ● **Design based on T-2 trainer**

Mitsubishi's F-1 is a hard-hitting combat aircraft that draws its main features from the earlier T-2 supersonic trainer. The F-1 was developed for close air support and anti-ship operations, performing these tasks admirably in the robust Japan Air Self-Defence Force (JASDF). Seventy-seven F-1s were built, with the surviving aircraft equipping three squadrons.

▲ *The F-1 was a straight development of the earlier T-2 trainer. In fact, their airframe dimensions are identical, with the rear cockpit canopy simply being faired over and extra avionics added.*

Photo File

Mitsubishi F-1

▲ Brake parachute deployed

The fuselage tailcone at the base of the rudder contains a single 5.5-metre diameter ring-slot-type braking parachute. Anti-skid brakes and an airfield arrester hook are also fitted.

▲ Licence-built Adour turbofans

The IHI-built Adour turbofans fitted to the F-1 are comparable to those that equip the French versions of the Jaguar, which has a maximum take-off weight of some 2000 kg (4,400 lb.) more.

◀ T-2 heritage

It is very apparent that the single-seat F-1 was based on the two-seat T-2.

▼ F-1 number one

The first production F-1, 70-8201, left the Mitsubishi factory in June 1977.

▲ Three squadrons

The Japan Air Self-Defence Force's three F-1 units are based at Misawa in the north (two squadrons) and Tsuiki in the west (one squadron).

Facts and Figures

- The F-1 was belatedly given extra air-to-air capability with provision for up to four AIM-9 Sidewinder missiles.
- Two F-1 prototypes used British-built Adour engines.
- Up to three 821-litre (220-gal.) fuel tanks can be carried externally by the F-1.
- The first production Mitsubishi F-1 aircraft made its maiden flight on 16 June 1977.
- The last of 77 F-1s was delivered by Mitsubishi in March 1987.
- Japan's anti-military stance means that no F-1s have been exported.

PROFILE

From trainer to anti-ship striker

An island nation, Japan works hard to protect its shores. The Mitsubishi F-1 was created because of the threatening nature of Soviet naval activity around the Japanese home islands in the 1970s and 1980s.

Following the success of the T-2 twin-turbofan trainer, Mitsubishi went ahead with this close-support fighter version, intended primarily to fly from land bases on defence missions against enemy shipping.

The F-1 has a comprehensive avionics fit, its principal weapon being the Japanese-developed Mitsubishi ASM-1 (Type 80) solid-propellant missile, which combines a similar range to that of the German Kormoran with a warhead comparable to the French Exocet. A secondary air-defence role is also fulfilled, and AIM-9 Sidewinders may be fitted for this purpose.

Very little is known of the F-1's overall performance, as limited information has been published in Japan and few foreign pilots have flown the aircraft. Published specifications suggest a fairly modest performance by modern standards, mainly due to its relatively low-powered engines and small fuel capacity.

The F-1 remained in service until the end of the twentieth century, when it began to be replaced by the Mitsubishi F-2 – an adaptation of the F-16 Fighting Falcon.

Above: Most F-1s carry a three-tone camouflage, consisting of dark green, olive drab and light tan on the upper surfaces with a light grey underside.

Above: Interviews with Japanese pilots suggest that the F-1's cockpit is 'optimised for the average Japanese physique' and has low stick forces and 'mild' control sensitivity.

F-1

Type: single-seat close-support fighter

Powerplant: two 32.49-kN (7,288-lb.-thrust) Ishikawajima-Harima TF40-IHI-801 (Rolls-Royce/ Turboméca Adour Mk 801A) afterburning turbofan engines

Maximum speed: 1700 km/h (1,054 m.p.h.) at 10,975 m (36,000 ft.)

Range: 2870 km (1,779 mi.)

Service ceiling: 15,240 m (50,000 ft.)

Weights: empty 6358 kg (13,988 lb.); maximum take-off 13,700 kg (30,140 lb.)

Armament: one JM61 Vulcan 20-mm rotary cannon and maximum of 2721 kg (6,000 lb.) of ordnance including four AIM-9L air-to-air missiles; two ASM-1 anti-ship missiles or combinations of other rockets and bombs

Dimensions:		
	span	7.88 m (26 ft.)
	length	17.86 m (59 ft.)
	height	4.39 m (14 ft.)
	wing area	21.17 m² (228 sq. ft.)

F-1

Aircraft 70-8203 carries the markings of 8 Hikotai (8th Squadron) of 3 Kokudan (3rd Air Wing) of the Northern Air Defence Command, based at Misawa Air Base on Honshu.

For self-defence the F-1 can carry two AIM-9L Sidewinder heat-seeking air-to-air missiles and has a Japanese-built M61 20-mm rotary cannon fitted in the forward fuselage.

When JASDF squadrons adopted individual markings in 1983, 8 Hikotai chose a black panther and the nickname 'The Panthers'.

Dimensionally identical to the T-2, the F-1 uses the rear cockpit to house the fire-control system, bombing computer, inertial navigation and radar-warning system.

An American-designed zero-zero ejection seat is fitted to the F-1, which uses canopy penetrators to shatter the cockpit canopy when the seat is activated.

F-1s use a J/AWG-12 dual-mode (air-to-air and air-to-ground) radar based on that fitted to Royal Air Force Phantom FGR.Mk 2s.

The principal weapon system for the F-1 is the Mitsubishi ASM-1 sea-skimming anti-ship missile, two of which may be carried. Each has a 150-kg (330-lb.) semi-armour-piercing warhead.

Two Rolls-Royce/Turboméca Adour afterburning turbofans, similar to those in early versions of the SEPECAT Jaguar, power the F-1.

COMBAT DATA

MAXIMUM SPEED

The F-1 was based on the Jaguar, which was designed to have a high penetration speed for ground attack. The A-6 and Super Etendard were both subsonic designs.

F-1 1700 km/h (1,054 m.p.h.)

SUPER ETENDARD 1380 km/h (856 m.p.h.)

A-6 INTRUDER 1037 km/h (643 m.p.h.)

COMBAT RADIUS

For the purpose of defending Japan, the F-1 did not need long range. The naval A-6 and Super Etendard both required much longer range to be effective rather than all-out speed.

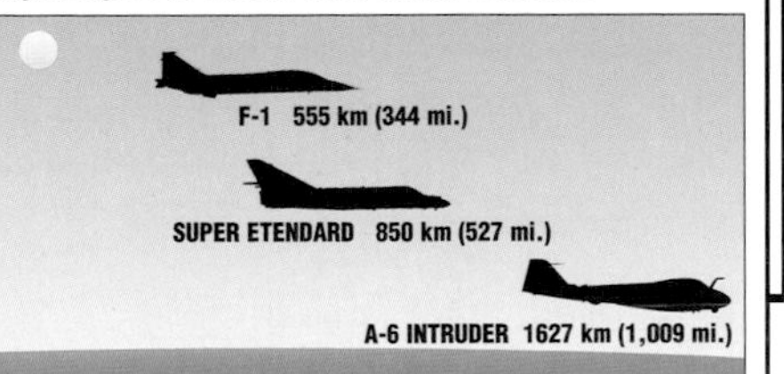

WEAPON RANGE

Harpoon is one of the longest ranged naval missiles produced in the West, and is superior to the Exocet and ASM-1. The F-1's ASM-1 missile has enough range to avoid defensive naval missiles.

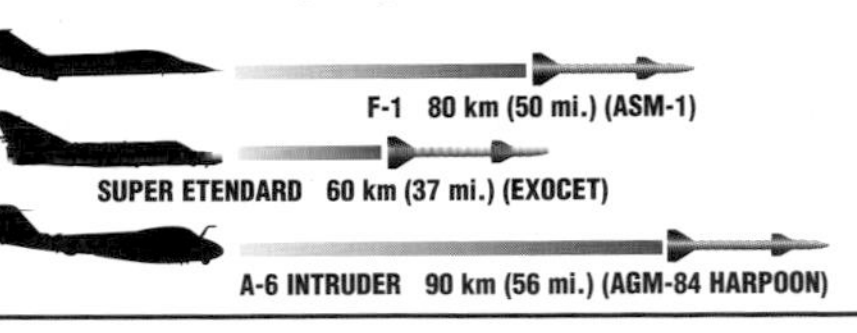

Fighters of the JASDF

McDONNELL DOUGLAS F-4EJ PHANTOM II: Japan continues to operate a number of Japanese-built F-4Es which are being upgraded. This is the RF-4EJ reconnaissance variant.

McDONNELL DOUGLAS F-15J EAGLE: Like the F-4EJ, most F-15Js were assembled in Japan by Mitsubishi. This is Japan's principal fighter aircraft.

MITSUBISHI/LOCKHEED F-2: Originally known as the FS-X, this high-performance fighter is a local development of the Lockheed (General Dynamics) F-16C and will replace the F-1.

Myasishchev

M-4 'Bison'

● Cold War bomber ● Shuttle-carrier ● Air-to-air refueller

▲ The M-4 'Bison' was one of the first jet-powered strategic bombers. Known to its operators as 'Molot', or 'Sledgehammer', it was flown by both Soviet Long Range Aviation and the Soviet navy.

When it first appeared the 'Bison' terrified experts in the West, although it never fulfilled its promise to give the Soviet Union a nuclear edge: designed during the Cold War as a strategic bomber, it lacked the range to attack North America. But it was a versatile design, and as a bomber, reconnaissance platform, tanker and transport it was to serve for four decades.

Photo File

Myasishchev M-4 'Bison'

▲ Under armed escort

A reconnaissance 'Bison' is intercepted by RAF Lightnings as it probes NATO's air defence network.

Scrub-down ▲

As it was designed as a nuclear bomber, the 'Bison's' ground crews frequently practised nuclear and chemical decontamination drills.

▼ Still flying

This 'Bison' remains in service as a testbed with the Myasishchev design bureau at Zhukovski.

▲ Maritime snooper

The 'Bison-C' has a large search radar in an extended nose. It has been used mainly for maritime reconnaissance.

On display ▶

This pristine 'Bison' is seen at a Russian air display. The huge doors hanging down show the unusual position of its bicycle undercarriage. The bomb-bay is located in the fuselage between the two sets of doors.

Facts and Figures

- The huge Myasishchev bomber was revealed to the world at a fly-by over Red Square on 1 May 1954.
- On 16 September 1959 a 'Bison' lifted a 55-tonne (60.6-ton) payload to 13,121 m (43,048 ft).
- The 'Bison' has small outrigger pods to keep the wingtips clear of the runway.
- 'Bison' tankers can refuel other planes at the rate of 2250 litres (594 US gal) per minute.
- More than 40 'Bisons' were chopped into pieces in the 1980s to fulfil a strategic arms reduction agreement.
- A 'Bison' modified to carry outsize loads is known as the VM-T Atlant.

PROFILE

Multi-mission Myasishchev

The Myasishchev M-4 Bison was created in 1949 after Stalin ordered Vladimir Myasishchev to create an intercontinental bomber to carry nuclear weapons to North America. Myasishchev considered a giant, eight-engined design which would have weighed an incredible 230,000 kg (507,063 lb), but decided on the four-engined 'Bison'. He hoped that improvements in engine technology, over time, would give the bomber global reach.

The United States, which had a colossal force of 2200 bombers, feared competition when the new Myasishchev bomber was unveiled in 1954. In truth, Moscow was already focusing on intercontinental missiles, and the West's concern was exaggerated.

Although often seen as a partial failure, the 'Bison' was an excellent design, and within its limitations of range and weapons capacity performed well. It was even more successful as a long-range maritime reconnaissance craft and tanker.

Today, the 'Bison' is most visible as the civil VM-T Atlant, used to carry outsized cargoes.

'Bison' bombers were among the many strategic weapon systems scrapped in the 1980s as part of the START nuclear arms reduction process. Under the terms of the treaty, wrecked bombers were left in the open so that they were visible to American spy satellites.

The original 'Bison-A' was designed around the huge first generation of nuclear bombs which needed a massive bomb-bay to carry them.

Just like the American Boeing B-47, the 'Bison' incorporated swept-wing technology captured from German scientists at the end of World War II.

All Soviet bombers built in the 1950s and 1960s have been armed with tail guns. 'Bison' bombers are equipped with a pair of radar-directed 23-mm (0.91-in) cannon.

M-4 'Bison-A'

Type: four-engined strategic bomber/tanker

Powerplant: four 85.32-kN (19,190-lb-thrust) Mikulin AM-3D turbojets

Maximum speed: 930 km/h (578 mph)

Range: 9400 km (5,841 miles)

Service ceiling: 14,000 m (45,932 ft)

Weights: empty 79,700 kg (175,708 lb); loaded 184,000 kg (405,651 lb)

Armament: up to 10 23-mm (0.91-in) cannon plus bombload of up to 9000 kg (19,842 lb)

Dimensions:		
	span	50.53 m (165 ft 9 in)
	length	47.67 m (156 ft 5 in)
	height	14.10 m (46 ft 3 in)
	wing area	340.20 m² (3,662 sq ft)

M-4 'Bison-A'

The Myasishchev 'Bison-A' was operated as a bomber by the Long Range Aviation branch of the Soviet air force. 'Bisons' were retained in this role until the early 1980s.

Today, the most important job for the 'Bison' is to carry outsize items of cargo, notably for the Russian space programme. The converted bombers carry their loads 'piggyback', and have twin fins in place of the bomber's single unit.

6303134

61

'Bison-A' was a strategic bomber, with a smooth nose containing radar. Later maritime reconnaissance variants had an extended nose with extensive glazing.

Underneath the nose of the 'Bison-A' was a large bombing radar. This provided accurate mapping which was fed into the weapon system.

The 'Bison' is powered by four Mikulin turbojets buried in the wingroots. In their time, these were the most powerful production engines in the world.

The 'Bison's' bomb-bay is located between its bicycle-type main gears. This limited the size of weapon which could be carried, and 'Bison' bombers were never armed with the huge air-to-surface missiles carried by competing Tupolev designs.

COMBAT DATA

SERVICE CEILING

The threat of high-performance surface-to-air missiles did not exist in the 1950s, so bombers of the period were designed to operate at very high altitude. Their large, efficient wings made them as agile as fighters when flying at 12,000 m (39,370 ft) or more.

BOMBLOAD

The 'Bison' and the similar, slightly smaller British Valiant had a heavy bombload by the standards of preceding propeller-driven warplanes, but they paled into insignificance behind the immense capacity of the American B-52.

B-52 STRATOFORTRESS	VALIANT	M-4 'BISON-A'
40,000 kg (88,185 lb)	9500 kg (20,944 lb)	9000 kg (19,842 lb)

The great fear: attack across the Pole

It is hard to remember in these changed days, but the world of the 1950s seemed a very dangerous place to those who lived in it. To millions of ordinary Americans, the 'Red Menace' was personified by what was believed to be a huge force of Soviet bombers, poised to launch thermonuclear destruction at a moment's notice.

TARGET FOR ATTACK: For the first time, major American cities were thought to be vulnerable to attack.

ACROSS THE POLE: The shortest route between the Soviet Union and North America lay across the unpopulated frozen wastes of the Arctic Ocean.

THE 'BOMBER GAP': Many Western analysts believed that the Soviets had thousands of long-range bombers such as the 'Bison' poised along the northern coasts of the Soviet Union. The fear was largely imaginary – there were never more than a couple of hundred bombers in service, and their long-range capability had been seriously overestimated.

MYASISHCHEV

M-17/M-55 'MYSTIC'

● Balloon interception ● Reconnaissance ● Geophysical survey

In 1982 Western intelligence reported the sighting of an unidentified Russian high-altitude reconnaissance aircraft. Satellite photographs of the Zhukhovskii flight test centre, known as Ramenskoye in the West, showed an aircraft with twin tail fins and long, unswept wings, suggesting that it was a Soviet counterpart of the American U-2. It was known as 'Ram-M', and several years passed before the mysterious aircraft was finally identified as the Myasishchev M-17.

▲ *Russia's answer to the U-2 has not achieved the success or infamy of its American equivalent. The M-17s and M-55s have performed useful environmental research, however.*

PHOTO FILE

MYASISHCHEV M-17/M-55 'MYSTIC'

Record breaker ▶
During 1990 the single-engined M-17 Stratosphera set a total of 25 speed/climb/height records.

▼ Environmental research
The M-55 Geofizika was developed to help to study the problems of ozone depletion.

M-55 Geofizika ▶
The M-55 can carry equipment for Earth-resource missions, agricultural surveying, ground mapping and ice reconnaissance.

▲ Air show star
Geofizika has appeared in the West at the Paris and Farnborough air shows.

Mystic power ▶
Two 88.30-kN (19,500-lb.-thrust) Soloviev D-30-10V turbofans power the M-55.

FACTS AND FIGURES

- ➤ Subject 34 was cancelled when the CIA stopped using high-altitude balloons as reconnaissance platforms.
- ➤ Eduard Chyeltsov flew the first M-17 Stratosphera on 26 May 1982.
- ➤ In 1992 an M-17 'Mystic-A' investigated the Antarctic ozone hole.
- ➤ Chyeltsov also flew the M-55 Geofizika on its maiden flight on 16 August 1988; at least three more have flown since.
- ➤ A projected M-55UTS trainer was to have a periscope to aid back-seat vision.
- ➤ The M-55 'Mystic-B' can climb to 21 km (13 mi.) in 35 minutes.

PROFILE

Master of the stratosphere

Originally planned in 1967 as an interceptor of high-altitude reconnaissance balloons under the designation Subject 34 and known as the Chaika (Gull), Myasishchev's new aircraft was first seen by NATO in the unarmed 'Mystic-A' form. Known as the Stratosphera in Russia, the M-17 retains some of its original mystery.

It resembles the U-2 in having a single engine with intakes on the sides of the forward fuselage, and was designed for a similar strategic reconnaissance role. But it has a greater wingspan and is slightly longer overall, with a shorter, deeper fuselage and a long tailplane carried on twin fins.

It was intended to replace the Yak-25RD, but one of the two M-17s that were built is now housed in a museum. The second aircraft has been used to investigate the ozone layer and pollution in the upper regions of the atmosphere.

Since 1994 a twin-engined version, the M-55 Geofizika ('Mystic-B'), has appeared at Western air shows. Designed specifically for environmental and geophysical research, it can carry a 1500-kg (3,300-lb.) payload and has an endurance of seven hours.

From its operational altitude of 21,500 m (70,500 ft.), the M-55 can photograph an area 120 km (75 mi.) wide, and can also glide for a distance of 200 km (125 mi.).

Above: According to Russian sources, development of the 'Mystic-B' as a strategic reconnaissance platform for military service is continuing.

Below: One of the two prototype M-17 Stratospheras (17103) survives in Aeroflot colours at the Monino aerospace museum near Moscow.

M-17 Stratosphera 'Mystic-A'

Type: single-seat high-altitude reconnaissance and research aircraft

Powerplant: one 68.65-kN (15,450-lb.-thrust) RKBM Rybinsk RD-36-51V turbojet

Maximum speed: 743 km/h (460 m.p.h.) at 20,000 m (65,600 ft.)

Endurance: 2 hours 25 min

Range: 1315 km (815 mi.)

Service ceiling: 21,550 m (70,700 ft.)

Weights: empty 11,900 kg (26,180 lb.); maximum take-off 19,950 kg (43,890 lb.)

Dimensions:

span	40.32 m (132 ft. 3 in.)
length	22.27 m (73 ft. 1 in.)
height	5.25 m (17 ft. 3 in.)
wing area	137.70 m² (1,482 sq. ft.)

ACTION DATA

MAXIMUM TAKE-OFF WEIGHT

With its high maximum take-off weight, the M-17 is capable of lifting heavier loads to altitude than either of its most direct rivals. It does not have the hi-tech avionics of the U-2R, however.

M-17 STRATOSPHERA 'MYSTIC-A' 19,950 kg (43,890 lb.)

U-2R 18,733 kg (41,213 lb.)

STRATO 2C 13,350 kg (29,370 lb.)

CEILING

Grob's all-composite Strato 2C uses specially tuned high-altitude piston engines to achieve its exceptional altitude capabilities. It is used solely as a research vehicle.

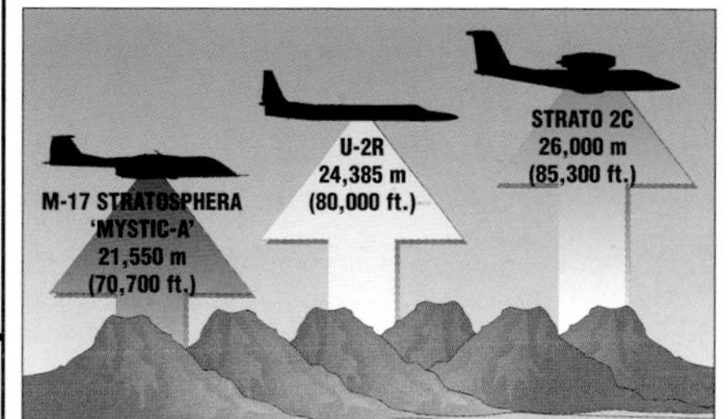

ENDURANCE

With its two-seat cabin the Strato 2C is equipped for missions of long duration. Its engines are extremely fuel-efficient but do not deliver the climb and speed performance of the jet aircraft.

M-17 STRATOSPHERA 'MYSTIC-A' 2 hours 25 min

U-2R 12 hours

STRATO 2C 48 hours

M-17 STRATOSPHERA 'MYSTIC-A'

Although it achieved a number of world records, the prospect of the M-17 becoming a Soviet counterpart of the U-2 faded. The aircraft moved on to investigation of the Antarctic ozone problem.

The M-17's single pilot is seated on a K-36L ejection seat, under an upward-hinging canopy. Carried just behind the pilot are two oxygen canisters.

Compared to the unusual inverted gull wing of the Subject 34 interceptor, the M-17's wing is much more conventional in layout. The engine is started by a turbo-starter and fed with fuel from five separate wing tanks, which hold a total of 10,000 litres (2,650 gal.).

The M-17s were built at Kumertau, Bashkiri, primarily from lightweight metals. The entire aircraft is comprehensively ice-protected for high-altitude operations. In normal conditions the reconnaissance-configured M-17 would have carried 1000 kg (2,200 lb.) of advanced cameras and sensors.

This M-17, serial CCCP-17401, was the aircraft used during trials and preparation work for the M-55. It flew missions to monitor Antarctica's atmosphere. A number of environmental slogans were subsequently added.

'Mystic-A' carries a PRNK-17 navigation system radio compass and an RSBN Kobalt radar. These were also used in the M-55 'Mystic-B'.

A novel feature of the M-17 'Mystic-A' is its retractable landing lights, stowed under the front of the tail booms.

Designed for high altitudes, the RD-36-51V is based on the engine core from which the MiG-31's powerplants were derived.

Both the M-17 Stratosphera 'Mystic-A' and M-55 Geofizika 'Mystic-B' feature an unusual twin-boom tail, with vertical surfaces bridged by a long horizontal stabiliser.

Changing roles of the 'Mystic'

Since its conception in 1967, the 'Mystic' has seen its role change from balloon interceptor to research platform.

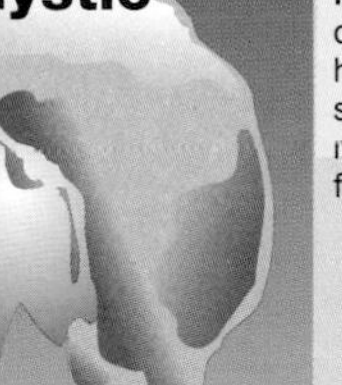

INTERCEPTOR: Armed with a turret-mounted GSh-23 cannon and two air-to-air missiles, the single-seat Subject 34 was intended to destroy spy balloons.

M-17 'MYSTIC-A': In its design role the M-17 would have flown high-altitude strategic reconnaissance missions over sensitive foreign installations.

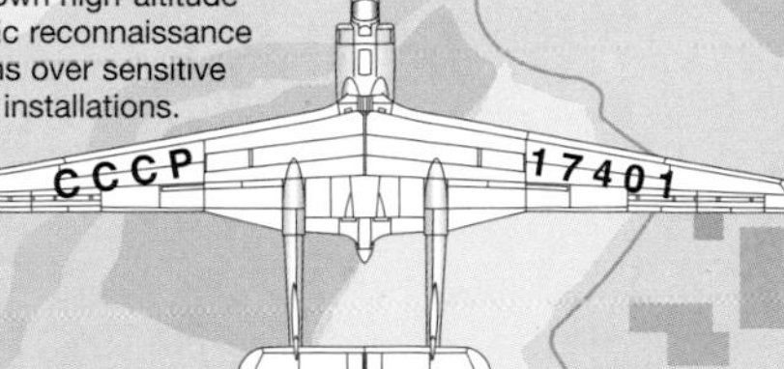

M-55 'MYSTIC-B': An unusual role adopted by the M-55 is the conversion of hail into rain by the use of chemicals. Such weather alteration avoids excessive crop damage, helping the struggling Russian economy.

NANCHANG A-5 'FANTAN'

● Ground attack ● Converted MiG ● Tactical fighter-bomber

Based loosely on the airframe of the Chinese-built MiG-19, the Nanchang A-5 'Fantan' (alias the Q-5) is a robust, capable warplane. The 'Fantan' airframe relies largely on technology of the 1950s, but incorporates more modern electronics, Sidewinder missiles and new ejection seats to ensure combat effectiveness. Although it is hardly at the cutting edge of fighter design, the A-5 has a very low price tag and suits the needs of Third World users.

▲ *The A-5 might seem crude and old-fashioned, but price is important. The aircraft is an excellent low-cost 'bomb truck' in contrast to the Pakistan air force's high-tech F-16s.*

PHOTO FILE

NANCHANG A-5 'FANTAN'

▲ Armed and dangerous
Fitted with AIM-9P Sidewinders, Pakistan's A-5s are no easy target for a fighter. The original MiG-19 was known as a very dangerous dogfighter. There is also a nuclear-capable version of the Q-5 which can carry a 20-kT weapon.

▲ Chinese weapon
The 'Fantan' is offered on the export market with a range of Chinese weapons like this short-range PL-5.

▲ Home defence
China is still the most numerous user, with hundreds of A-5s in service. China plans to introduce the F.10, derived from Israel's Lavi.

▲ Black Spiders
Operating the A-5 from the large Pakistan air force base at Peshawar in North Pakistan, No. 26 squadron is known as the 'Black Spiders'. The PAF also operates the Shenyang F-6.

Flying to fight ▶
This A-5 is equipped with 57-mm rocket pods, MATRA Magic air-to-air missiles, 100-kg (220-lb.) iron bombs and a pair of 760-litre (200-gal.) drop-tanks.

FACTS AND FIGURES

- ➤ Over 1000 'Fantans' have been built, including 52 for Pakistan, 40 for North Korea and 20 for Bangladesh.
- ➤ China's 'Fantans' were used in the border conflict with Vietnam in 1979.
- ➤ Although design work began in 1960, the prototype A-5 first flew on 4 June 1965.
- ➤ An extended-range version carrying fuel in the bomb-bay has about a 35 per cent greater combat radius.
- ➤ The latest A-5 uses Italian-designed avionics and has additional pylons.
- ➤ The A5 carries 2827 kg (6,220 lb.) of fuel and up to 1178 kg (2,592 lb.) in drop-tanks.

PROFILE

Ground attack at low prices

The Nanchang A-5 'Fantan' gives China a low-cost, supersonic strike aircraft, demonstrating the country's ability to improve an existing military aircraft.

Although the A-5 is based on the proven MiG-19, Chinese designers created a new, stretched fuselage, an internal bomb-bay and a pointed nose. With work beginning in the early 1960s the 'Fantan' was designed, tested and produced without Soviet help and has evolved into a bomber that is quite different from its Russian origins. The A-5 has less ability in a dogfight than its MiG cousin, but it carries more bombs, can fly further and is more accurate in its important duty of air-to-ground combat. The nuclear version of the 'Fantan' dropped a real atomic bomb during a test in 1970.

Export success has been considerable in the Third World due to the price tag. Pakistan's A-5s cost just $2.6 million each, about a quarter of the cost of a Jaguar or F-16A. Pakistan upgraded its A-5s with better avionics and Sidewinder missiles, and China is now offering improved versions with laser rangefinder, head-up display, an IFF (Identification Friend or Foe) system and radar-warning receiver.

The Pakistan air force A-5s have improved avionics and British Martin-Baker ejector seats.

The cannon armament is carried in the wingroots. Unlike most modern ground-attack fighters, the A-5 uses 23-mm weapons with 100 rounds each.

A-5 'Fantan'

Type: single-seat ground-attack fighter

Powerplant: two Liming (previously Shenyang) Wopen-6A turbojet engines each rated at 29.42 kN (6,600-lb.-thrust) dry and 36.78 kN (8,250-lb.-thrust) with afterburning

Maximum speed: Mach 1.12 or 1190 km/h (738 m.p.h.) at 11,000 m (36,000 ft.)

Combat radius: 400 km (250 mi.) to 600 km (375 mi.)

Range: 2000 km (1,240 mi.)

Service ceiling: 15,850 m (52,000 ft.)

Weights: empty 6375 kg (14,025 lb.); maximum take-off 11,830 kg (26,026 lb.)

Armament: two 23-mm cannon each with 100 rounds, plus tandem pairs of pylons carrying up to 500 kg (1.100 lb.) of stores

Dimensions:

	span	9.68 m (32 ft.)
	length	15.65 m (51 ft.)
	height	4.33 m (14 ft.)
	wing area	27.95 m² (300 sq. ft.)

A-5 'FANTAN'

Still one of the most numerous aircraft in the People's Liberation Army Air Force, the Nanchang A-5 will probably be at least partially replaced by the F-10 fighter-bomber, derived from the IAI Lavi.

The A-5M is equipped with the avionics from the Italian AMX, including laser-rangefinder, Alenia head-up display and inertial navigation.

The A-5's original Chinese ejection seats are another feature which customers often replace, as they are not guaranteed below 270 m (900 ft.) or above 280 km/h (179 m.p.h.).

Almost all A-5 users have their aircraft painted in a three-colour stripe camouflage paint scheme.

Like the MiG-19, the A-5 has an all-moving slab tailplane.

The main clue to the A-5's MiG-19 ancestry is the swept tail.

The A-5 never received a radar, despite the removal of the original nose intake allowing for this. Future aircraft, if there are any, will use this space for avionics or a rangefinder.

The inboard wing pylons can carry 760-litre (200-gal.) fuel tanks and the outboard pylons 3,790-litre (1,000-gal.) tanks.

One of the most inhibiting features of the A-5 is the Wopen turbojet that powers the aircraft. This engine is an uneconomical design and requires a major overhaul every 100 hours.

COMBAT DATA

MAXIMUM SPEED

The 'Fantan' is limited by its old technology Wopen turbojets and the increased girth of the airframe compared to the original design. However, most ground-attack aircraft travel at around 800 km/h in combat, and theoretical maximum speeds are seldom reached.

A-5 'FANTAN' 1190 km/h (738 m.p.h.)

A-7D CORSAIR 1123 km/h (696 m.p.h.)

JAGUAR GR.Mk 1 1699 km/h (1,053 m.p.h.)

COMBAT RADIUS

Another victim of the poor engine technology is the A-5's range, which might have been improved with Western engines. Short range is generally a typical feature of second-generation MiGs, which had quite good performance.

A-7D CORSAIR 1149 km (712 mi.)

A-5 'FANTAN' 600 km (372 mi.)

JAGUAR GR.Mk 1 852 km (528 mi.)

BOMBLOAD

The 'Fantan' has quite a low bombload compared to the Jaguar and A-7, but the amount of weight carried per dollar cost of the airframe is about equal.

A-5 'FANTAN' 2000 kg (4,400 lb.)

A-7D CORSAIR 9072 kg (19,958 lb.)

JAGUAR GR.Mk 1 4536 kg (9,979 lb.)

Many faces of the MiG-19

MiG-19PM: This MiG-19 version introduced the K-5 missile system, guided by an Izumrud radar in the nose. It could carry rocket packs.

SHENYANG J-6: China built a straight copy of the MiG-19 fighter, which is also used by Pakistan and fought in the 1965 war.

S-105: This aircraft was a Czech-built MiG-19PM which was built by Aero Vodochody between 1958 and 1963.

SM-12PMU: An experimental version, the SM-12 used a mixed powerplant of turbojets and a rocket motor which could be re-lit.

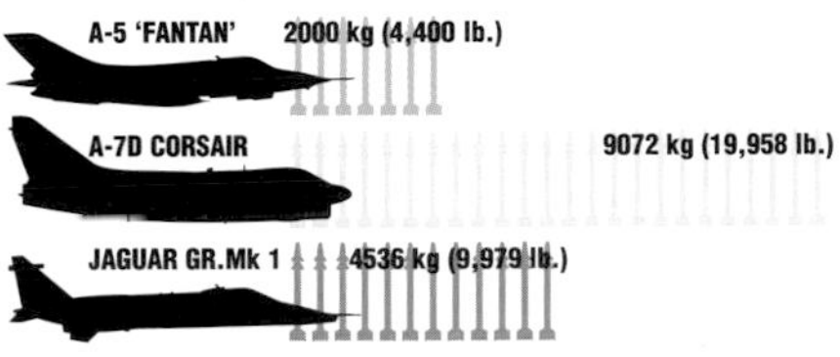

NORTH AMERICAN FJ FURY

● 1950s carrier-borne jet fighter ● F-86 design derivative

Beginning life as the straight-winged FJ-1, the North American Fury became the first jet fighter to go to sea under operational conditions. After the US Navy belatedly followed the USAF in using German research data to produce swept-wing fighters, the FJ Fury was reborn as a carrier-based equivalent of the F-86 Sabre. The swept-wing Fury was one of the Navy's first fighters to carry missiles and served widely in the 1950s.

▲ *Although there were initial concerns about the suitability of swept-wing designs for carrier operations, the performance of the USAF's F-86 Sabre persuaded the US Navy to adopt the FJ-2.*

PHOTO FILE

NORTH AMERICAN FJ FURY

◀ **'Navalized' Sabre**
The first swept-wing variant, the FJ-2, was effectively a navalized F-86F Sabre with folding wings and 20-mm (0.79-in) cannon armament.

▼ **Rocket motor boost**
To test a rocket installation, two FJ-4s were fitted with an AR-1 motor and nose instrumentation.

▼ **Air-to-air refuelling FJ-4s**
Like the FJ-3, the FJ-4B had an in-flight refuelling receptacle on the port wing and could carry 'buddy' refuelling gear.

▼ **VMF-232 'Red Devils'**
Marine Fighter Squadron 232's FJ-2s set a Navy-Marine flight record, flying 2558 hours in one month. Twenty-one aircraft and 52 pilots participated. The FJ-2 shared its 'slatted wing' with the F-86F Sabre.

▼ **FJ-4B attack-fighter**
This final Fury variant had six underwing pylons, for stores such as Bullpup air-to-surface missiles.

FACTS AND FIGURES

- After its first flight on 27 November 1946, the FJ-1 became the US Navy's first operational carrier jet.
- FJ-3Ms and FJ-4s were able to carry AAM-N-7 Sidewinder air-to-air missiles.
- Starting in January 1954, all 200 FJ-2s were delivered to Marine Corps fighter units.
- The final Fury variant, the FJ-4B, was equipped with the LABS low-altitude nuclear weapon delivery system.
- Furies remained in Naval Reserve service into the 1960s.
- In all, North American's Columbus, Ohio, plant delivered 1115 swept-wing Furies.

PROFILE

First operational jet carrier fighters

From the fat, straight-winged, dark blue FJ-1 to the sleek, swept-winged, grey and white FJ-4, the North American FJ Fury fighters of the US Navy and Marine Corps marked a decade of progress that began at the start of the jet age and continued to the brink of the supersonic era. Although the Fury never went to war, from the late 1940s to the Beirut crisis of 1958, the aircraft was armed and ready to fight if the need arose.

Thirty straight-winged FJ-1 Fury fighters were briefly the newest and fastest machines in the sky when they went aboard the carrier USS *Boxer* in 1948. Quickly overtaken by other jets (the Navy focusing on the straight-wing F9F Panther which became its standard fighter in the Korean War), the FJ-1 Fury was relegated to Reserve duty, then retired, in less than two years.

North American, meanwhile, had developed a faster, swept-wing aircraft, based on the FJ-1 and called the F-86 Sabre, for the USAF. The swept-wing FJ-2, FJ-3 and FJ-4 Fury fighters resulted from an effort to produce a navalized F-86. While the first FJ-2 was little more than a Sabre in blue paint, the FJ-3 and much improved FJ-4 missile-armed attack fighter introduced new engines and major airframe and equipment changes.

Above: The first Fury, XFJ-1 39053, took to the air on 27 November 1946. The 30 FJ-1s were destined to be 'fighter familiarization' aircraft, rather than combat types.

Above: FJ-3s of VF-21 Squadron fly over the USS Forrestal. *The last FJ-3s were delivered in 1956, a year after this new carrier was commissioned.*

FJ-4 Fury

Type: single-seat carrier-based fighter

Powerplant: one 34.25-kN (7,703-lb-thrust) Wright J65-W-16A turbojet engine

Maximum speed: 1094 km/h (680 mph) at sea level

Endurance: 859 km/h

Initial climb rate: 2334 m/min (7,657 fpm)

Range: 3250 km (2,019 miles)

Combat ceiling: 14,265 m (46,801 ft)

Weights: empty 5991 kg (13,208 lb); loaded 10,750 kg (23,700 lb)

Armament: four 20-mm cannon, plus up to 1360 kg (2,998 lb) of weapons (including bombs, rockets or four AAM-N-7 Sidewinder air-to-air missiles) on four wing pylons

Dimensions:	span	11.91 m (39 ft 1 in)
	length	11.07 m (36 ft 4 in)
	height	4.24 m (13 ft 11 in)
	wing area	31.49 m² (339 sq ft)

FJ-1 FURY

Carrying the markings of the only unit equipped with the FJ-1, Fighter Squadron VF-5A (later VF-51), this aircraft is one of 30 FJ-1s delivered. They were transferred to the Reserve after just 14 months of service.

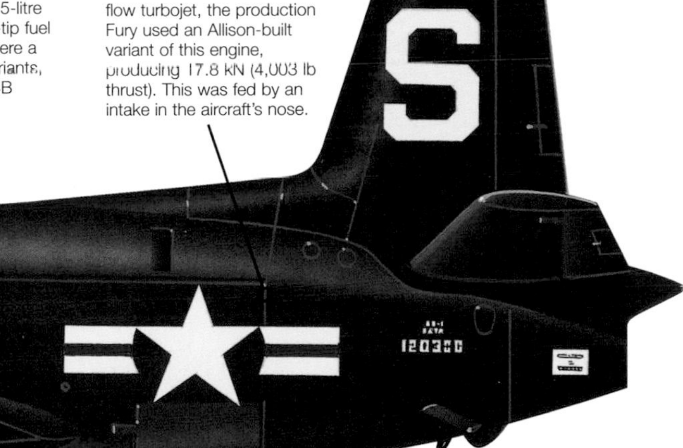

Fitted with six 12.7-mm (0.5-in) machine guns in the nose, the FJ-1 was the last US Navy aircraft to have 'half-inch' guns.

Like the McDonnell FH-1 Phantom which followed it, the FJ-1 was able to 'kneel' on the carrier deck by retracting its nose gear and resting on a tiny wheel. This facilitated stowage without wing folding.

To increase its somewhat limited range, the FJ-1 was soon fitted with 625-litre (165-US gal) wing-tip fuel tanks. Airbrakes were a feature of all FJ variants, especially the FJ-4B attack version.

Designed around the General Electric J35 axial-flow turbojet, the production Fury used an Allison-built variant of this engine, producing 17.8 kN (4,003 lb thrust). This was fed by an intake in the aircraft's nose.

ACTION DATA

THRUST

Although the afterburner had been introduced, naval jet fighter design in the 1950s was hampered by the lack of powerful engines. Supermarine overcame this by installing twin engines in the Scimitar.

FJ-4 FURY	34.25 kN (7,703 lb thrust)
SCIMITAR F.Mk 1	100.0 kN (22,491 lb thrust)
F3H-2 DEMON	43.1 kN (9,694 lb thrust)

MAXIMUM SPEED

Even though it had twin engines, the Scimitar was a heavy aircraft which limited its top speed. The McDonnell F3H Demon was a bigger machine than the Fury, but early examples were underpowered.

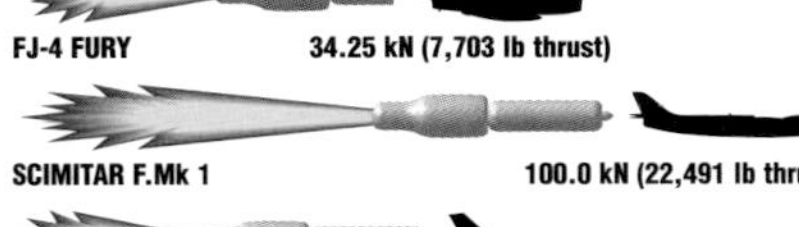

CLIMB RATE

Advances in wing and engine design and improved power-to-weight ratios were reflected in better climb rates of aircraft such as the Scimitar and the Demon.

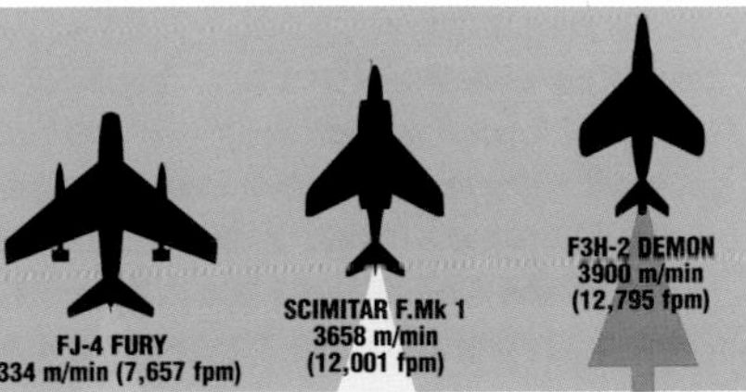

US Navy aircraft from North American

■ **SNJ TEXAN:** Like the USAAF and Allied air forces, the US Navy took delivery of hundreds of Texans for pilot training from the late 1930s.

■ **AJ SAVAGE:** Ordered as a carrier-borne nuclear strike aircraft in 1946, the AJ had two piston engines and a small turbojet in the tail.

■ **T2J BUCKEYE:** The T2J entered service as the US Navy's all-purpose trainer, in single- and twin-engined forms, from 1959.

■ **A3J VIGILANTE:** Known as the A-5 from 1962, the A3J entered service as an all-weather attack aircraft in 1961 aboard USS *Enterprise*.

North American F-86 Sabre

● Jet vs jet combat ● US vs Soviet pilots ● Multiple kills

Together, the F-86 Sabre and MiG-15 brought swept wings and the sonic bang to modern warfare. Developed at the same time, both aircraft were just supersonic in a dive. In 1950 the Sabre was rushed to Korea to confront the MiG in a new kind of combat with closing speeds and performance never before experienced. High over the Yalu River, Sabres and MiGs tested each other in the biggest jet-versus-jet battles in history.

▲ *Even in its initial form the F-86 was a match for the Soviet-flown MiG-15s. However, improved Sabres, such as the F-86E, soon dominated when the MiGs were flown by less experienced pilots.*

PHOTO FILE

North American F-86 Sabre

▲ MiG testing
Senior Lieutenant Kum Suk No took his MiG-15 to the Americans when he landed at Kimpo airfield as a defector. The MiG was first tested at Kadena in Japan by Chuck Yeager and later at Wright-Patterson in the USA, where it survives at the USAF museum.

▲ Dixon's tail
Lieutenant Colonel Dixon was about to fire at a MiG-15, when his F-86F was hit by anti-aircraft artillery fire.

▲ Victorious Sabre
This rare photograph was taken by the gun camera of an F-86 which had just peppered the MiG with 12.7-mm (0.5-in) machine-gun fire. The pilot ejected seconds later, leaving the MiG-15 to its fiery fate.

▲ Improved interceptor
As the F-86A was entering combat in Korea, North American was putting the F-86E into production. This improved model was superior to the MiG-15.

US air power for the United Nations ▶
Large numbers of US aircraft were committed to the United Nations' effort in Korea. This photograph shows several combat-ready F-86 Sabres.

FACTS AND FIGURES

- ➤ Design of both the Sabre and the MiG-15 was made possible by German swept-wing research.
- ➤ The first Sabres arrived at Kimpo airfield, near Seoul, Korea, in December 1950.
- ➤ Captain Joseph P. McConnell, a top Sabre ace, scored 16 victories in Korea.
- ➤ Late-model Sabres had a redesigned wing, known as the 6-3 wing, which improved manoeuvrability in combat.
- ➤ One downed F-86 was test-flown by the Soviets near Moscow.
- ➤ Total production of all versions of the Sabre exceeded 9000 aircraft.

PROFILE

Swept wings over Korea

America's Sabre pilots were well trained, confident and ready to face the MiG-15. Many of the pilots had flown combat in World War II, just five years earlier, and in 1950 they introduced the first US swept-wing jet into battle.

Mikoyan-Gurevich had produced an aircraft more than worthy of the Sabre's challenge, however, and the MiG-15 was capable of flying higher than the F-86 and was armed with cannon rather than the Sabre's six machine guns. Both fighters were fast and manoeuvrable. Ultimately, the result of each aerial battle was largely determined by the pilots.

Unknown to the Americans at the time, the first MiGs were flown by experienced Soviet pilots. It was only later, when Chinese and North Korean pilots took over, that the better training of the US pilots won through. As the Sabre gained the upper hand, the Americans claimed that 15 MiGs were shot down for every F-86 lost. After the war research revealed that the correct figure was actually seven to one, but this was still a remarkable statistic in the history of air-to-air combat.

A pair of Sabres takes off in search of MiGs. Many missions involved flying top cover for US fighter-bombers.

Low-level manoeuvrability was improved on the F-86A and E, with the use of leading-edge slats. These were a disadvantage at altitude, however, and they were deleted on the F-86F.

North American, in common with Mikoyan-Gurevich, relied on the work of German aeronautical engineers to produce the swept wings for its aircraft.

On the F-86E, the tailplane of the F-86A was replaced by an all-moving surface, which included larger, power-boosted elevators. The entire control system was given improved 'feel'.

Guided missile development was some way behind the technology of the jet aircraft and both the F-86 and MiG-15s were gun-armed in Korea.

F-86E SABRE

***Elenore 'E'* was flown by Major William T. Whisner of the 25th Fighter Interceptor Squadron, 51st Fighter Interceptor Wing.**

All Sabres flying over Korea had followed the instructions of the Far East Air Force (FEAF) by the summer of 1952, with the adoption of yellow theatre markings.

North American developed and built the ejection seat used in the F-86. Such escape systems were vital at the high speeds reached by the new jets.

Both the F-86A and E models were powered by the General Electric J47-GE-13 turbojet. The F-86F used the J47-GE-27, which improved time taken to reach 9144 m (30,000 ft) by almost one minute and added an extra 244 m (800 ft) to its maximum altitude.

Sabres always flew with drop-tanks. The extra fuel allowed a transit to North Korea and increased loiter time in the combat zone. The tanks were jettisoned as soon as MiGs were sighted.

F-86E Sabre

Type: single-seat fighter and fighter-bomber

Powerplant: one 23.13-kN (5,202-lb-thrust) General Electric J47-GE-13 turbojet engine

Maximum speed: 1086 km/h (675 mph) at 762 m (2,500 ft)

Initial climb rate: 2326 m/min (7,631 fpm)

Range: 1263 km (785 miles)

Service ceiling: 14,722 m (48,300 ft)

Weights: empty 4760 kg (10,494 lb); maximum take-off 4987 kg (10,994 lb)

Armament: six 12.7-mm (0.5-in) machine guns with 267 rounds per gun; provision for two 454-kg (1,000-lb) bombs or 16 127-mm (5-in) rocket projectiles

Dimensions:	span	11.31 m (37 ft 1in)
	length	11.43 m (37 ft 6 in)
	height	4.47 m (14 ft 8 in)
	wing area	26.76 m² (288 sq ft)

COMBAT DATA

ARMAMENT

With its cannon armament the MiG-15 had much greater firepower than the Sabre. Improvements in power and controllability, together with superior training, allowed the US pilots to overcome this, but immediately after the war a cannon-armed F-86 was developed.

F-86A SABRE	6 x 12.7-mm (0.5-in) machine guns
F-86H SABRE	4 x 20-mm (0.79-in) cannon
MiG-15 'FAGOT'	1 x 37-mm (1.46-in)cannon 2 x 23-mm (0.91-in) cannon

COMBAT ZONE: Only Sabres were allowed into the area known as 'MiG Alley'; other United Nation aircraft, even the jets, were considered to be too vulnerable. In response to this decision, the Soviets moved more MiGs into North Korea, making 'MiG Alley' a hotbed of air combat.

MiG-killing over Korea

LAUNCH: United Nation bases were scattered around the coast of Korea, but the base closest to the action was Kimpo, just south of the 38th Parallel.

TARGET MiG: With its good manoeuvrability, altitude advantage and heavy weaponry, the MiG-15 in Russian hands was a difficult opponent. The advantage was never clear-cut between the MiG and Sabre.

MiG IN SIGHT: This MiG is in a desperate situation, with the 'pipper' of an F-86's gunsight closing in on its tail. A simple radar allowed gun-ranging.

FIREBALL: Even though the F-86's armament was not as powerful as that of the MiG-15, a well-placed burst from its six machine guns could have a devastating effect on the Russian plane. Hits to the rear fuselage were most likely to damage vital systems.

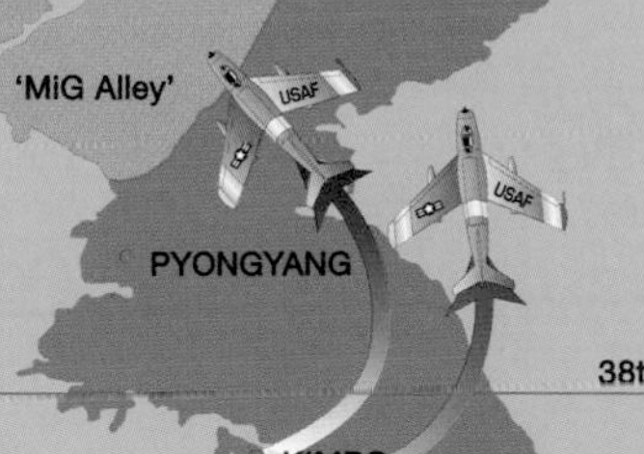

NORTH AMERICAN F-86D/H/K SABRE DOG

● All-weather operations ● Interceptor ● Ground attack

▲ Distinguished by its nose-mounted radome, the F-86D/H/K series turned the basic F-86 into a specialized and highly competent all-weather interceptor and attack aircraft.

To defend North America, the USAF worked frantically in the 1950s to develop fighter-interceptors which were able to fly and fight in any weather. As an interim measure, experts took the F-86 Sabre design from the Korean War and added radar and air-to-air rockets. This produced the F-86D Sabre Dog – an all-weather interceptor with a one-man crew. The Sabre Dog was developed into the F-86K/L by the addition of cannon armament.

PHOTO FILE

NORTH AMERICAN F-86D/H/K SABRE DOG

German Sabre Dog ▶
The F-86K, which was supplied to European air forces, was produced by replacing the rockets of the F-86D with four 20-mm cannon.

◀ Defending Southeast Asia
A number of F-86Ds were delivered to the air force of the then newly established Philippine republic, bolstering regional air defence.

NATO fighter ▶
Analogous to the F-16 programme, the F-86K became the standard fighter of several NATO air arms in Europe. It was paid for by the USAF.

Rocket pack
A retractable rocket-launching pack was fitted to the belly of the F-86D for air-to-air work.

European Sidewinders ▶
As new systems became available these were combined with the already advanced, complex avionics of the F-86D and K. New weapons included the AIM-9 Sidewinder, seen here on an F-86K, which was later licence-built in Europe.

FACTS AND FIGURES

- ➤ Production of Sabre Dog interceptors totalled 2626, including 120 export versions armed with cannon.
- ➤ An additional 121 aircraft were built for NATO use by Fiat in Italy.
- ➤ The Sabre Dog prototype first flew on 22 December 1949.
- ➤ In July 1952 mechanical faults were resolved in a modification programme called Project Pull Out.
- ➤ The F-86D's main flaw was a tendency for a sudden violent pitch downwards.
- ➤ A few Sabre Dogs were exported to Japan, South Korea and Thailand.

PROFILE

Developing the Sabre

The Sabre Dog interceptor version of the immortal North American F-86 Sabre was equipped with a distinctive nose radar unit and was flown by a pilot who was also tasked with the duties usually performed by a radar operator.

When approaching bombers were spotted on radar, an F-86D pilot was expected to rush to his aircraft and to get aloft within three minutes. He then followed instructions from a ground-control operator, who directed him to the bomber. In the later F-86L version, this process of scrambling and engaging enemy bombers was largely automated. Once within a short distance of the bombers, the pilot was expected to 'paint' them on his own radar and to attack them at a 90° angle with rocket projectiles. The export version of this interceptor was a much-simplified warplane and was armed with cannon, but it had the same task of tracking down and destroying enemy bombers.

In service, the Sabre Dog was initially plagued by technical problems, mainly with its radar, but it evolved into a mature combat aircraft.

Above: Seen high over Mount Fuji, Japan, this F-86D typifies the Sabre Dogs belonging to the USAF.

Above: Some countries, including Greece, received second-hand USAF F-86Ds. This one is fitted with Sidewinder launch rails.

No guns were fitted to the F-86D, but 24 70-mm (2.76-in) 'Mighty Mouse' rockets, each with a 3.4-kg (7½-lb) warhead, could be fired from this retractable rocket pack.

D model Sabres retained the standard slatted Sabre wing, but the fuselage was redesigned and was both longer and wider to accommodate the new engine and avionics.

Drop-tanks of 454-litre (120-US gal) capacity were a near-permanent fixture of the F-86D. Fuel was also carried in internal tanks below the intake trunking and in the inboard wing sections between the spars.

A retractable airbrake was positioned on either side of the rear fuselage. When closing head-on with a target, the pilot must be certain of the aircraft's ability to slow down quickly.

F-86D Sabre Dog

This aircraft wears the colourful markings typical of its era and belongs to the 94th Fighter Interceptor Squadron of the 1st Fighter Group. The squadron flew F-86Ds from 1953 to 1956.

Once the AN/APG-37 radar had detected a target within its 48-km (30-mile) range, the AN/APA-84 computer calculated an interception course.

A single strut braced the drop-tank outboard of the pylon in an installation similar to that on the MiG-15.

All Sabres had this distinctive fuel dump pipe, which allowed fuel to be jettisoned in an emergency. The pipe on the F-86D was longer, however, to keep fuel away from the afterburner section.

A very basic afterburner was fitted to the J47-GE-17 turbojet. In early aircraft this provided 23.14 kN (5,204 lb thrust), but later variants produced up to 34.04 kN (7,656 lb thrust).

F-86D Sabre Dog

Type: single-seat all-weather interceptor

Powerplant: one 33.4-kN (7,512-lb-thrust) General Electric J47-GE-17B or J47-GE-33 turbojet with afterburning

Maximum speed: 1138 km/h (707 mph) at sea level

Range: 1344 km (835 miles)

Service ceiling: 16,640 m (54,593 ft)

Weights: empty 5656 kg (12,469 lb); maximum take-off 7756 kg (17,099 lb)

Armament: 24 70-mm (2.76-in) 'Mighty Mouse' folding-fin aircraft rockets (FFAR) or (F-86K only) four 20-mm (0.79-in) cannon

Dimensions:

span	11.30 m (37 ft 1 in)
length	12.29 m (40 ft 4 in)
height	4.57 m (15 ft)
wing area	27.76 m² (299 sq ft)

COMBAT DATA

RANGE

A comparison of contemporary American all-weather interceptors reveals their complementary nature. The F-94C Starfire covers the middle ground between the large, heavily armed F-89D, providing long-range defence, and the shorter ranged but much higher performing F-86D.

SERVICE CEILING

All three aircraft provided air defence of the USA, and any aircraft making an attack would have done so from high altitude. Armed only with rockets, an interceptor would be forced to get very close to the target so altitude performance was of great importance.

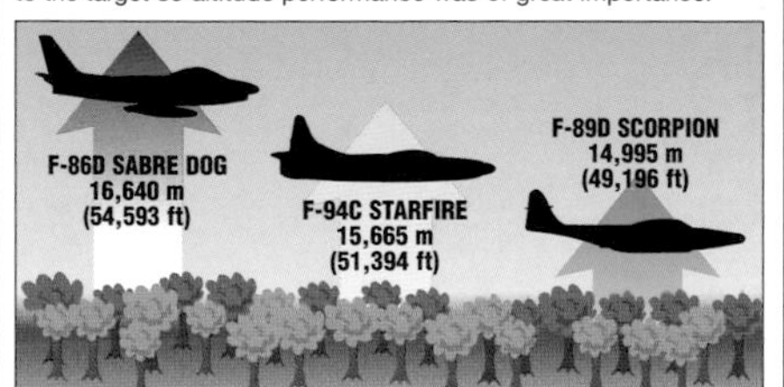

ARMAMENT

The primary armament was the unguided rocket, fired from retractable launchers, batteries in the aircraft nose or wing pods. As the first guided air-to-air missiles, such as the AIM-9 and Hughes Falcon, became available, these were also employed.

F-86D SABRE DOG — 24 x 70-mm (2.76-in) rockets

F-94C STARFIRE — 48 x 70-mm (2.76-in) rockets

F-89D SCORPION — 104 x 70-mm (2.76-in) rockets

Rocket-armed interceptors

DE HAVILLAND SEA VIXEN: Retractable launching batteries were built into the forward fuselage of the Sea Vixen, but were rarely used.

ENGLISH ELECTRIC (BAC) LIGHTNING: Provision was made for two retractable launchers, which were sealed shut when in service.

LOCKHEED F-94C STARFIRE: Each wing-tip pod held 12 rockets and a further 24 were carried in a ring of launchers around the nose.

NORTHROP F-89D SCORPION: Permanently attached wingtip pods held the Scorpion's powerful 104-rocket armament.

NORTH AMERICAN F-100 SUPER SABRE

● USAF's first supersonic jet ● Zero-length launches ● War service

Sabre 45 was the name given to North American's private efforts to produce a supersonic development of its highly successful F-86 Sabre. The name referred to the wing's 45° of sweep. This programme proved not to be as easy as envisaged, but after early problems the final product was to prove its worth, especially in Vietnam. Although it always had an accident rate higher than other types, the Super Sabre had plenty of fans among aviators.

▲ *In its heyday, the F-100 equipped 16 full USAF wings, assuming a fighter-bomber role as faster interceptor types became available. It was the USAF's first fighter to reach Mach 1 in level flight.*

PHOTO FILE

NORTH AMERICAN F-100 SUPER SABRE

◀ Zero-length launches
The final F-100Ds could be 'zero-length launched' from atom bomb-proof shelters using a 667-kN (150,017-lb-thrust) rocket booster.

▼ Two-seat combat trainer
An F-100C was modified as a two-seat TF-100C, the prototype for the F-100F; 339 were built.

◀ 'Thunderbirds'
The first F-100C fighter-bomber flew in September 1955. In all, 476 were built, some equipping the USAF's display team.

▼ Short-tail F-100A
The first 70 production F-100As had shorter fins, which caused roll control problems.

▲ Armée de l'Air 'Hun'
Super Sabres were exported to France, Taiwan, Denmark and Turkey, the last named being the final operator until the late 1980s. Ex-USAF examples are used as QF-100 target drones.

FACTS AND FIGURES

- ➤ Test pilot George Welch likened the effect of the first YF-100's afterburner to 'a kick from a well-fed mule'.
- ➤ More than 200 surplus F-100s were converted into QF-100 target drones.
- ➤ Between mid-1956 and mid-1970, more than 500 F-100Ds were lost in accidents.
- ➤ On 20 August 1955 a USAF colonel in an F-100C set the first world speed record over Mach 1 – 1323.03 km/h (822.09 mph).
- ➤ The first F-100 model flown overseas was the F-100C, using in-flight refuelling.
- ➤ USAF F-100s were deployed overseas to Germany and Japan in 1956.

PROFILE

First of the 'Century' fighters

Considering it suffered from so many inherent problems, including landing characteristics described by a pilot with 2000 hours on the type as 'a controlled crash', the F-100 is remembered with respect and some affection by a generation of aviators.

Its good features were viceless handling, a robust airframe and reliable systems. The Super Sabre was the latest product from the North American team that produced P-51 Mustangs and F-86 Sabres.

Attempts to build a supersonic Sabre had been killed by the limitations of its wing and engine. The latter problem was solved by Pratt & Whitney's JT3 (J57) turbojet, so, with USAF agreement, a new aircraft was designed. After the 24 April 1953 first flight, the Super Sabre went into production for the USAF as the F-100A day-fighter. However, a fatal crash caused by handling problems brought groundings and delays. A taller tail fin and longer wings were the solution.

Above: Demonstrating the afterburner fitted to its Pratt & Whitney J57 engine, this F-100 starts its take-off run. Poor fuel economy resulted in the aircraft carrying underwing fuel tanks.

From 1954, the F-100C fighter-bomber was built, and it was this and the much-improved D-model that were built in the biggest numbers – 1750 in all.

Above: Bullpup air-to-surface missiles could be fired from a number of modified F-100Ds. Some D-model 'Huns' were also wired to carry Sidewinder air-to-air missiles.

F-100D Super Sabre

Type: single-seat fighter-bomber

Powerplant: one 75.4-kN (16,958-lb-thrust) Pratt & Whitney J57-P-21A afterburning turbojet

Maximum speed: 1436 km/h (892 mph) at altitude

Initial climb rate: 5045 m/min (16,552 fpm) (clean)

Range: 2494 km (1,550 miles) with two drop-tanks

Service ceiling: 14,020 m (45,997 ft)

Weights: empty 9526 kg (21,000 lb); maximum take-off 15,800 kg (34,833 lb)

Armament: four M-39E 20-mm (0.79-in) cannon plus up to 3402 kg (7,500 lb) of external stores including bombs, napalm tanks, rockets and missiles

Dimensions:		
	span	11.82 m (38 ft 9 in)
	length	14.36 m (47 ft 1 in)
	height	4.94 m (16 ft 2 in)
	wing area	35.77 m² (385 sq ft)

F-100D SUPER SABRE

In the markings of the 481st TFS, this 'Hun' (as it was nicknamed – short for 'Hundred') was the personal aircraft of World War II P-47 ace Lieutenant Colonel Hal Comstock. It carries the skull insignia that adorned his P-47, and seven German kill markings.

This aircraft represents an F-100 in the early years of USAF involvement in the Vietnam War. Camouflage was later applied to all tactical aircraft in Southeast Asia. Note the bomb mission symbols painted on the nose.

A key feature of the F-100D was the redesigned wing. This had a kinked trailing edge incorporating broad, slotted landing flaps. These were much needed and appreciated by pilots used to the high-speed landing run of the F-100C. Extra internal tankage was provided. D-models were built at North American's Inglewood, California, and Columbus, Ohio, factories.

An afterburning version of Pratt & Whitney's J57 turbojet was fitted to the 'Hun'. This engine had already flown in such types as the B-52 bomber and the Navy's A-3 Skywarrior and F-8 Crusader, the latter also using an afterburning variant.

The most obvious identification feature of the D-model was its taller vertical tail, introduced to improve handling. This incorporated a deeper fairing for the fuel dump pipe (later used to mount the radar warning receiver antenna).

For ground-strafing and self-protection, four M39 20-mm (0.79-in) cannon were fitted in the nose of the F-100D. Two AIM-9 Sidewinder air-to-air missiles were also fitted on occasions. Air-to-ground ordnance totalling over three tonnes could be carried, including napalm, bombs, rockets and Bullpup missiles.

External fuel tanks, such as the 1268-litre (335-US gal) examples fitted to this aircraft, were necessary to give the Super Sabre an acceptable range figure. An in-flight refuelling probe could also be fitted under the right wing.

COMBAT DATA

MAXIMUM SPEED

The F-100 and MiG-19 faced each other across the Iron Curtain as the first supersonic types produced by the chief Cold War adversaries. The RAF's main fighter type was the subsonic Hunter.

F-100D SUPER SABRE 1436 km/h (892 mph)

MiG-19SF 'FARMER' 1454 km/h (903 mph)

HUNTER F.Mk 6 1004 km/h (624 mph)

ARMAMENT

Cannon armament was the primary means of air-to-air defence as these types were introduced. Missiles were still in their infancy. The F-100 had a prodigious bombload capacity.

F-100D SUPER SABRE 4 x 20-mm (0.79-in) cannon 3193 kg (7,039 lb) of bombs

MiG-19SF 'FARMER' 3 x 30-mm (1.18-in) cannon 500 kg (1,102 lb) of bombs

HUNTER F.Mk 6 4 x 30-mm (1.18-in) cannon 907 kg (2,000 lb) of bombs

RANGE

The Hunter had a good range performance compared to the other, faster types. All three needed to carry external fuel tanks for anything but the shortest sorties.

F-100D SUPER SABRE 2494 km (1,550 miles)

MiG-19SF 'FARMER' 2200 km (1,367 miles)

HUNTER F.Mk 6 2961 km (1,840 miles)

Sabre/Super Sabre family

■ **FJ FURY:** NA's first jet fighter was the US Navy's straight-winged Fury, which served as the basis for a swept-wing version and the F-86.

■ **F-86 SABRE:** The USAF's first swept-wing jet fighter, the Sabre was to see extensive service in the Korean War and served until 1965.

■ **YF-93:** Initially designated F-86C, the F-93 had an afterburning engine, but was hampered by the limitations of the Sabre wing design.

■ **YF-107A:** An all-weather interceptor/fighter-bomber F-100 development, initially known as the F-100B, the F-107 lost out to the F-105.

NORTHROP

B-2 SPIRIT

● **Unique flying wing** ● **Advanced technology stealth bomber**

The B-2 Spirit looks sinister because it has the dark mission of pressing into enemy territory in an atomic war. Northrop designed this charcoal-grey flying wing as the world's only stealth bomber, an invisible ghost to enemy radar operators. Long kept under a cloak of secrecy, the B-2 is out in the open today and is soon to be fully operational, with both nuclear and conventional bombing duties.

▲ *With its flowing, organic lines, the Northrop B-2 looks like no other aircraft in the world. But it offers power and combat capability unmatched by any other military aircraft.*

PHOTO FILE

NORTHROP B-2 SPIRIT

▲ **First flight**
Rolling out from the Northrop facility in Palmdale, the B-2 made its first flight, to Edwards Air Force Base, on 17 July 1989.

Stealth bomber revealed ▶
When the B-2 was first rolled out, photos were taken only from certain angles to keep its stealth features as secret as possible.

▲ **Flying wing**
The B-2 has no conventional fuselage; its entire structure is contained within a smoothly-blended delta wing with 'W'-shaped trailing edges.

▲ **Long experience**
Northrop has amassed a great deal of experience with flying wings; its first full-sized bombers, such as this XB-35, flew in the 1940s.

Compact power ▶
By doing away with the fuselage, the B-2's designers have produced a very powerful and capable aircraft with enormous range and payload, in a surprisingly small package.

FACTS AND FIGURES

- ➤ Two B-2s can complete a bombing raid which previously required 32 F-16s, 16 F-15s and 27 support aircraft.
- ➤ Before the B-2 ever flew, wind tunnel models were tested for 24,000 hours – a record.
- ➤ The radar-absorbing body of the B-2 contains 900 materials and a million parts.
- ➤ Almost invisible to radar, the B-2 was also made difficult to hear or see.
- ➤ The B-2 Spirit's engines are concealed deep within the structure to hide them from radar and heat-seeking sensors.
- ➤ The USAF's first B-2 was delivered exactly 90 years after the Wright brothers' first flight

PROFILE

Northrop's amazing Flying Wing

The boomerang-like Northrop B-2 Spirit began as one of the best-kept secrets in history. Its sleek shape and special materials foil radar detection. The stealthy B-2 also flies very well with no fuselage or tail, using the flying-wing concept pioneered by earlier Northrop aircraft.

The B-2 is a triumph of technology in many ways, able to leap halfway around the globe on a strategic mission with just two pilots, located side-by-side in the crew compartment bulge. If the Cold War had continued, the B-2's stealth qualities, four powerful turbofan engines and lethal bombload would have made it the spearhead of nuclear forces. In today's changing world, the B-2 is flexible enough to fly long-distance to a crisis zone with highly accurate conventional bombs.

The B-2 is also the most expensive warplane ever built, with a price tag of $2 billion, so only 20 of these remarkable bombers will be produced.

Above: In common with most stealth aircraft, the B-2 carries minimal markings: a serial number on the fuselage and a low-visibility star-and-bar on the wing.

Below: Control of an aircraft without a vertical stabiliser is difficult, and led to the downfall of earlier flying-wing projects. The B-2 gets around the problem by using the kind of modern computer control that was unavailable to the pioneers of tail-less flight.

B-2A Spirit

Type: two-seat long-range strategic bomber

Powerplant: four 84.52-kN (19,017-lb. thrust) General Electric F118-GE-100 turbofan engines

Maximum speed: approx. 960 km/h (597 m.p.h.) above 12,200 m (40,000 ft.)

Range: 12,225 km (7,596 mi.)

Service ceiling: over 16,920 m (53,440 ft.)

Weights: empty 79,380 kg (175,995 lb.); loaded 181,437 kg (400,000 lb.)

Armament: eight B61 or B83 nuclear bombs or 16 stand-off nuclear missiles on rotary launcher in bomb-bay or 80 Mk 82 227-kg (500-lb.) bombs or up to 22,600 kg (50,000 lb.) of other weapons

Dimensions:

span	52.43 m (172 ft.)
length	21.03 m (69 ft.)
height	5.18 m (17 ft.)
wing area	196 m² (2,110 sq. ft.)

B-2A SPIRIT

Developed under great secrecy and at huge expense, the B-2 Spirit is the world's most advanced strategic bomber.

The B-2 has an advanced two-man cockpit with provision for a third crew member/observer. High technology has done away with the flight engineer and bombardier of earlier bombers.

The B-2 is powered by four General Electric F118 non-afterburning turbofans. They are buried deep within the aircraft, keeping the highly radar-reflective fan blades away from enemy radar transmissions.

The engines exhaust through 'V'-shaped outlets set back and above the trailing edges to hide these heat sources from the ground.

The 33° sweep of the leading edge and the 'W' configuration of the trailing edge are designed to trap and deflect radar energy away from a hostile transmitter.

The Hughes AN/APQ-181 attack radar has phased array transmitters buried in the fuselage, so there is no need for a dish aerial and its bulbous radome.

Extensive use is made of graphite/epoxy materials in the aircraft's structure. These are not good reflectors of radar energy, and contribute to the bomber's stealthiness.

The B-2's undercarriage has been adapted from a commercial design, used on the Boeing 757 and 767 airliners.

Vapour trails are the enemy of any aircraft claiming to be stealthy. Chloro-fluorosulphonic acid is injected into the exhaust gases of the B-2 to inhibit the formation of contrails at high altitude.

COMBAT DATA

RANGE

Thanks to its large fuel capacity and highly efficient turbofan engines, the Northrop B-2 has a truly global range. Others can fly as far, but not with such a heavy warload or such economy. Airborne refuelling allows the B-2 to strike anywhere in the world from its home base.

B-2A SPIRIT 12,225 km (7,596 mi.)
Tu-160 'BLACKJACK' 14,000 km (8,700 mi.)
B-1B LANCER 12,000 km (7,500 mi.)
Unrefuelled range

WEAPONS

Although it is much smaller than the massive 'Blackjack', the B-2 can carry a much heavier load. The B-1B can carry far more, but a heavy warload strictly limits the Lancer's range.

B-2A SPIRIT
22,600-kg (50,000-lb.) maximum weapons load

B-1B LANCER
60,000-kg (132,000 lb.) maximum weapons load

Tu-160 'BLACKJACK'
estimated 16,500-kg (36,000 lb.) maximum weapons load

SPEED

Both the B-1B and the Tu-160 are designed to make the last portion of an attack at supersonic speeds, to give the maximum chance of survival. The B-2's stealthiness means that it does not need this highly expensive and fuel-hungry capability.

B-2A SPIRIT
Cruise: 750 km/h (466 m.p.h.)
Maximum: approx. 960 km/h (600 m.p.h.)

B-1B LANCER
Cruise: 960 km/h (600 m.p.h.)
Maximum: 1324 km/h (822 m.p.h.)

Tu-160 'BLACKJACK'
Cruise: 850 km/h (528 m.p.h.)
Maximum: 2000 km/h (1,240 m.p.h.)

Ancestry of the 'Flying Wing'

PIONEERS OF WINGLESS FLIGHT: Among the earliest pioneers were the German Horten brothers, whose radical Ho IX fighter evolved from pre-war gliders and which promised superb performance in 1945.

SCALE MODELS: American Jack Northrop had always been interested in flying wings, and his first designs for the US Air Force were scale designs exploring the potential of the configuration as a long-range bomber.

AHEAD OF ITS TIME: Northrop developed a full-size jet bomber to compete with the more conventional B-52, but control technology of the day meant that the resulting YB-49 of 1947 was not easy to handle in some conditions.

LIFTING BODIES: Between the demise of the XB-49 and the launch of the B-2, Northrop was involved in lifting bodies such as the X-24, shown here in 1969. These did away with wings, gaining lift from the shape of the fuselage.

Northrop

F-5A Freedom Fighter

● Lightweight fighter ● Flown by 13 nations ● Vietnam veteran

▲ Northrop's Freedom Fighter, as its name suggests, was a product of the Cold War. It was a means of providing an affordable yet capable aircraft for America's allies.

Designed in the late 1950s as a lightweight fighter for supply to friendly nations as part of the US Military Assistance Program, the F-5 remains a viable combat aircraft. Although the early examples are more than 30 years old, some late production aircraft are being upgraded with modern avionics. The type's advantages include supersonic performance and the ability to carry reasonable loads while maintaining economy of operation.

Photo File

Northrop F-5A Freedom Fighter

▼ **Scandinavian Freedom Fighter**
Norway operates seven F-5As and eight F-5Bs, upgraded under PAWS (Programme for Weapons and Systems Improvements), as lead-in trainers for its new F-16s.

▲ **In retirement**
The Netherlands was a major F-5 operator, until it introduced the F-16.

Blooded in Vietnam ▲
Skoshi Tiger F-5s were transferred to the Vietnamese air force (VNAF) in 1967. Here, an aircraft of the 522nd Fighter Squadron is seen in its revetment at Bien Hoa Air Base.

▲ **Canadian service**
Known in RCAF service as the CF-116, the Freedom Fighter served in both A and D versions from Cold Lake CFB, Alberta.

Refuelled in the air ▶
From the outset, the F-5 incorporated air-to-air refuelling. These aircraft are seen being 'tanked' by a KC-135A prior to deployment in Vietnam.

Facts and Figures

- Canada operated a small number of aircraft, designated CF-116A(R), fitted with Vinten 70-mm (2.76-in) nose cameras.
- Bristol Aerospace's upgrade for the CF-116 included HOTAS controls.
- A complete F-5A upgrade, as offered by Northrop, cost $4.5 million per airframe.
- The F-5A originated from the N-156 Fang proposal for a lightweight fighter, which also led to the USAF's T-38A trainer.
- F-5 development was funded under the Mutual Defense Aid Program.
- An F-5A has an eight-minute turnaround between missions, including refuelling.

PROFILE

Lightweight fighters for America's allies

Flown for the first time in May 1963, the F-5 entered service the following year with a USAF training squadron. A dozen of the first F-5As were sent to Vietnam in 1965, where they proved able to match the USAF's frontline fighters in some missions. They served with South Vietnam throughout the 10-year war with the North.

Air forces in Europe, the Middle East, South America and Southeast Asia acquired Freedom Fighters before production switched to the uprated Northrop F-5E Tiger II. The RF-5A was adapted as a camera-equipped photo-reconnaissance version.

F-5s were also built in Canada, where Canadair produced CF-5s for the RCAF (known as CF-116s in service) and the NF-5 for the Dutch. Many ex-Canadian F-5s went to Turkey, while Greece also acquired some NF-5s.

By the mid-1980s, more than 400 of the 1100-plus Freedom Fighters built were still in service with a dozen air forces. The remaining Canadian CF-5s had been upgraded for sale, and Spain's fleet was refurbished to serve as weapons trainers.

For long-range missions, the Freedom Fighter's wing-tip missile pylons can be replaced with fuel tanks.

F-5Cs were powered by two afterburning General Electric J85 turbojets. For low-speed operations, air louvre doors on the rear fuselage provided improved air flow.

Serving over Vietnam between October 1965 and April 1967, the USAF Skoshi Tigers flew 9985 missions, in which nine aircraft were lost. Around 17,000 general-purpose bombs had been dropped by the time these trials aircraft were handed over to South Vietnam.

F-5A Freedom Fighter

Type: lightweight fighter and fighter-bomber

Powerplant: two 18.15-kN (4,082-lb-thrust) General Electric J85-GE-13 afterburning turbojets

Maximum speed: 1487 km/h (924 mph) 'clean' at 10,975 m (36,000 ft)

Maximum climb rate: 8748 m/min (28,700 fpm) at sea level

Combat radius: 989 km (615 miles) on hi-lo-hi mission with two 240-kg (530-lb) bombs and maximum fuel

Service ceiling: 15,390 m (50,492 ft)

Weights: empty equipped 3667 kg (8,084 lb); maximum take-off 9379 kg (20,677 lb)

Armament: two 20-mm (0.79-in) M39 cannon and up to 1996 kg (4,400 lb) of air-to-ground ordnance

Dimensions:	span (with tip tanks)	7.87 m (25 ft 10 in)
	length	14.38 m (47 ft 2 in)
	height	4.01 m (13 ft 2 in)
	wing area	15.79 m² (170 sq ft)

F-5C FREEDOM FIGHTER

Serving with the 10th Fighter Commando Squadron, F-5C 64-13332 was based at Bien Hoa Air Base, South Vietnam. The 10th FCS, originally the 4503rd TFS (Provisional), was in combat for almost 18 months.

The F-5's cockpit afforded good pilot visibility. Seated on a rocket-powered ejection seat, USAF Freedom Fighter pilots over Vietnam were fortunate that their aircraft had an additional 90 kg (200 lb) of cockpit and engine armour, upgraded avionics and an improved jungle camouflage scheme.

Mounted in the nose are two 20-mm (0.79-in) M39A2 lightweight cannon, with 280 rounds of ammunition. A nose-mounted refuelling probe and night formation lights were also added to USAF Freedom Fighters. South Vietnamese RF-5As carried four KS-92 cameras in a modified nose.

Skoshi Tiger aircraft typically carried mission markings. Flying up to four times a day, the 10th FCS was kept busy on light attack duties.

Underwing, on jettisonable pylons specifically fitted for Vietnam service, the F-5C carried up to 2720 kg (6,000 lb) of rockets, gun pods, bombs or, as shown here, four 340-kg (750-lb) BLU-1 anti-personnel napalm tanks.

COMBAT DATA

MAXIMUM SPEED

Northrop's F-5 family has been extensively developed from the Freedom Fighter to the Tiger II and ill-fated Tigershark. The F-5E Tiger II introduced more powerful J85 engines, and the F-20 (originally F-5G) had a single afterburning turbofan.

F-5A FREEDOM FIGHTER 1487 km/h (924 mph)

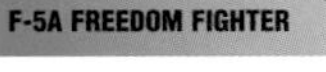

F-5E TIGER II 1700 km/h (1,056 mph)

F-20 TIGERSHARK 2124 km/h (1,320 mph)

MAXIMUM CLIMB RATE

Increased engine power and improved power-to-weight ratios contributed greatly to climb rates. A good climb rate allows a fighter aircraft to reach its patrol station quickly. The F-20 lost out to the F-16A ADF in the race to equip the US Air National Guard with a new air-defence fighter.

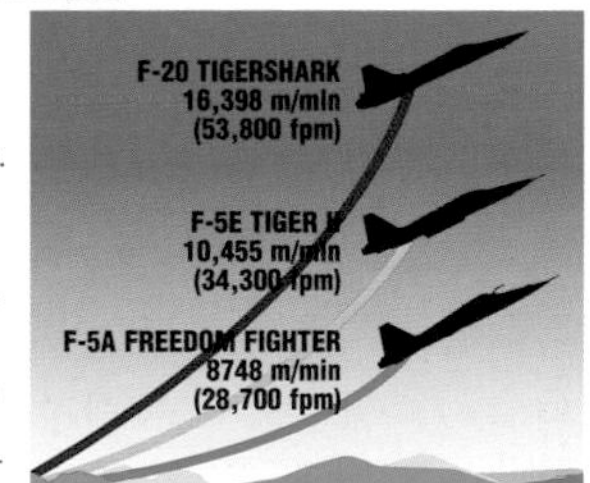

ARMAMENT

Greater engine power also allowed higher loads to be carried. When the F-20 appeared, its maximum weapons load was double that of the original F-5As.

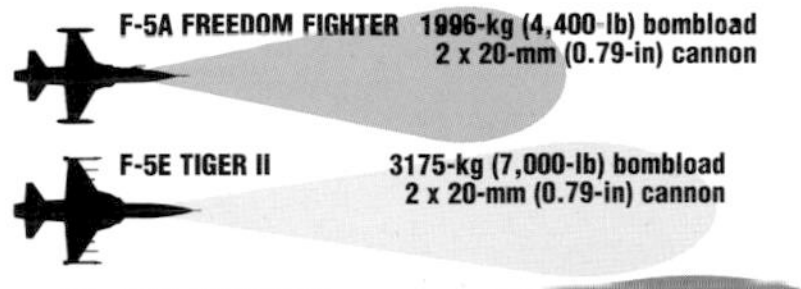

Freedom Fighter operators

ROYAL CANADIAN AIR FORCE: Canada recently retired its last CF-5s, which had been upgraded for use as CF-18 lead-in trainers with reworked wings and tail plus new avionics.

ELLINIKI AEROPORIA: Greece flies two Freedom Fighter squadrons, including ex-Dutch aircraft, from Thessaloniki, mainly for light ground-attack and advanced weapons training duties.

ROYAL THAI AIR FORCE: Thailand operates the original F-5A/B and RF-5A in small numbers in the ground attack role, alongside the later F-5E/F Tiger II.

NORTHROP

F/RF-5E TIGER II/F-20 TIGERSHARK

● Upgraded 'Freedom Fighter' ● Lightweight, low cost ● Exports

As a result of the great success of Northrop's first F-5 – the 'Freedom Fighter' – the company won the contest to build its replacement as America's affordable, lightweight fighter for the world. The Tiger II, with more power and an emphasis on air-to-air capability, was a vast improvement over its predecessor. The Tiger II was a big seller, but the same could not be said of the Tigershark, which failed against F-16 opposition.

▲ *The F-5 family answered a request from the US government for a relatively cheap fighter for export to smaller nations under the Mutual Assistance Plan (MAP).*

PHOTO FILE

NORTHROP F/RF-5E TIGER II/F-20 TIGERSHARK

▼ Ill-fated Tigershark
Three F-20s were built, and a fourth was started but never finished. Two were lost in fatal accidents due to pilot incapacity, and the third went to a museum.

▲ RF-5E Tigereye
Malaysia, Saudi Arabia and Singapore have taken delivery of this camera-equipped variant. Cameras are fitted in the nose, in place of the radar, and can include night-reconnaissance sensors.

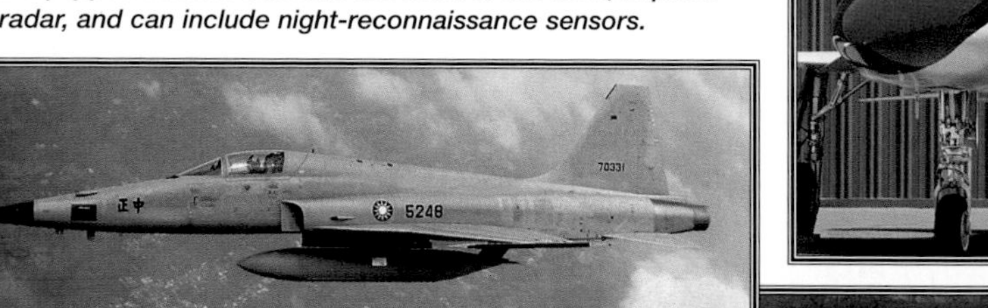

▲ Taiwanese Tiger IIs
The Republic of China operates a sizeable fleet of locally-built F-5Es and Fs.

▲ Popular upgrades
Northrop Grumman is among several companies offering avionics upgrade packages for Tiger IIs.

◀ Increased capability
In addition to a top speed in excess of Mach 2, the F-20 had an avionics fit comparable to that of the F-16A and improved weapons capability.

FACTS AND FIGURES

- Total F-5 production, including 'Freedom Fighters', T-38 Talons and overseas production, totalled 3840.
- Overseas F-5E/F production has taken place in Korea, Switzerland and Taiwan.
- Israel's F-5 upgrade is known as Tiger III; Northrop Grumman's is the Tiger IV.
- The first F-5E flew on 11 August 1972, from Edwards Air Force Base, four months ahead of schedule.
- Taiwan is considering re-engined F-5Es with new radar and AIM-120 missiles.
- Only 12 RF-5Es were built; Singapore converted six F-5Es to RF-5E standard.

PROFILE

Feline son of the 'Freedom Fighter'

Skoshi Tiger was the name given to the evaluation of the F-5E's predecessor, the F-5A 'Freedom Fighter', in combat in Vietnam in 1965. The F-5A (and two-seat F-5B) were lightweight, low-cost fighters intended for export to 'approved countries'.

When, in 1970, the USAF asked for proposals for a new international fighter aircraft, Northrop successfully suggested an updated F-5, the F-5E, which was dubbed Tiger II to perpetuate the name made famous in Vietnam.

Export sales have been numerous, with aircraft going to both existing F-5 customers and to new converts to this capable, yet affordable, tactical fighter. While the F-5A sold well to NATO countries, the Tiger II has been popular with Middle Eastern, Asian and South American states.

The re-engined F-20 (at first designated F-5G) flew in 1982, but failed to sell. F-5 production has ended, but upgrades will ensure long-term service.

The principal modification made to the F-5 design to produce the F-20 Tigershark, was replacing the two J85 turbojets with an F404 turbofan, as fitted to early F/A-18 Hornets.

F-5E Tiger II

Type: light tactical fighter

Powerplant: two 22.2-kN (4,000-lb.-thrust) General Electric J85-GE-21B afterburning turbojets

Maximum speed: 1700 km/h (1,054 m.p.h.) at 10,975 m (36,000 ft.)

Service ceiling: 15,590 m (51,100 ft.)

Weights: empty 4349 kg (9,568 lb.); maximum take-off 11,187 kg (24,611 lb.)

Armament: two M39A2 20-mm cannon in the nose, two AIM-9 Sidewinder air-to-air missiles on wing-tip launchers plus up to 3175 kg (6,985 lb.) of ordnance on fuselage and wing pylons

Dimensions:

span	8.13 m (26 ft. 8 in.)
length	14.45 m (47 ft. 5 in.)
height	4.08 m (60 ft. 9 in.)
wing area	17.28 m² (186 sq. ft.)

F-5E TIGER II

Once a renowned Hawker Hunter display team, Switzerland's Patrouille Suisse exchanged its elderly Hunters for Tiger IIs in 1994. J-3089 is one of the team's brightly-painted F-5Es based at Dubendorf Air Base.

Unlike earlier F-5s, the E model did not require wingtip fuel tanks but it did retain the rails for AIM-9 air-to-air missiles.

The F-5E was developed with emphasis on the air-to-air role, although ground-attack capability was not ignored. Indeed, the earliest customers, Iran and Saudi Arabia, both acquired the type for this role.

The standard radar of the F-5E was the Emerson Electric AN/APQ-159 search-and-track radar with a range of about 37 km (23 mi.).

Because the F-5E was designed as a counter to the Soviet MiG-21, it was also an ideal threat simulator for the USAF and US Navy Dissimilar Air Combat Training (DACT) schemes. The Navy continues to operate a small number of F-5Es in this role.

The two-seat conversion trainer version of the F-5E was the F-5F, which has tandem cockpits in a 1.02-m (3-ft.) longer fuselage (from the USAF's T-38 Talon). It retains the combat capabilities of the E model, but is fitted with just one 20-mm nose cannon.

The available upgrades concentrate on improving the aircraft's avionics and weapons capability. The leading suppliers are Northrop Grumman and Israel Aircraft Industries (IAI).

Two Pontiac (Colt-Browning) M39A2 20-mm cannon are fitted in the nose of a standard F-5E. The RF-5E Tigereye and two-seat F-5F use just one, fitted on the left hand side.

Switzerland took delivery of 98 F-5Es and 12 two-seat F-5Fs, a number of which were assembled at FFA's Emmen factory. Originally tasked with air defence, some have been re-roled as ground-attack aircraft and replace Hunters.

The two 22.2-kN (5,000-lb.-thrust) General Electric J85 afterburning turbojets have separate, but cross-feedable, fuel supplies. The electrically-operated louvre doors supply additional air to the engines during take-off and in flight below speeds of Mach 0.4-0.35.

COMBAT DATA

MAXIMUM SPEED

Among the world's most exported tactical fighters, the F-5E has an excellent speed performance which is only bettered by the MiG-21. Both the MiG and F-5E employ afterburning turbojet engines to achieve a high top speed. However, range tends to suffer as a result.

F-5E TIGER II 1700 km/h (1,054 m.p.h.)

MiG-21bis 'FISHBED' 2175 km/h (1,349 m.p.h.)

HAWK Mk 200 1065 km/h (660 m.p.h.)

ARMAMENT

The Tiger II represents a compromise between speed and range performance and lifting ability. Although limited to speeds of less than Mach 2 (unlike the MiG-21), the F-5 is able to lift more than 3 tons of ordnance. The smaller Hawk can also carry a good load.

F-5E TIGER II 2 x 20-mm cannon 3175 kg (6,985 lb.) of bombs

MiG-21bis 'FISHBED' 2000 kg (4,400 lb.) of bombs

HAWK Mk 200 2 x 25-mm cannon 3493 kg (7,685 lb.) of bombs

CLIMB RATE

The greater thrust of the MiG-21's powerful engine gives it the best climb rate. The Tiger II is not far behind, but the Hawk, powered by a non-afterburning engine, is significantly slower.

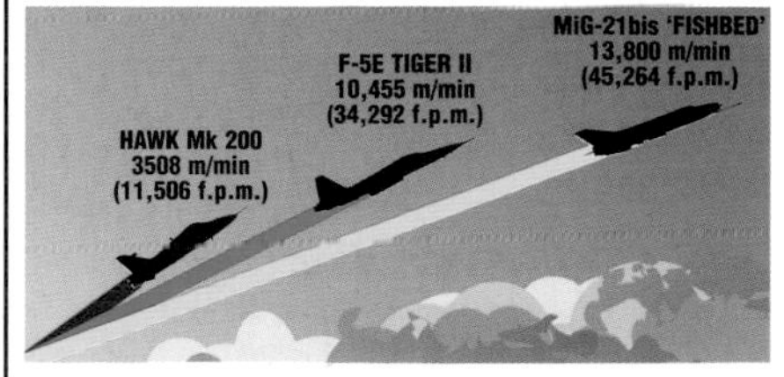

Mutual Assistance Plan fighters

REPUBLIC F-84F THUNDERSTREAK: This French air force Thunderstreak was among a number of members of the F-84 family supplied, in particular, to NATO nations.

NORTH AMERICAN F-100 SUPER SABRE: Under the Mutual Assistance Plan, new-build F-100s were supplied by the USAF to Denmark, France and Taiwan.

LOCKHEED F-104 STARFIGHTER: The 'missile with a man in it' was built for the USAF under MAP contract in variants, like the F-104G, which did not actually serve with the USAF.

NORTHROP F-89 SCORPION

● **All-weather interceptor** ● **North American defender** ● **Nuclear-capable**

Defending the icy wastes of the North American frontier, the much-maligned F-89 Scorpion was developed in the late 1940s and eventually soldiered on until 1969. Armed with Mighty Mouse collision-course rockets, the two-seat F-89D Scorpion interceptor provided protection against Soviet intrusion from Iceland to Alaska. Half a dozen production versions served the USAF, culminating in the definitive F-89J.

▲ *Problems with the F-102 Delta Dagger prolonged the service career of the Scorpion. The final variants were much improved and served on faithfully into the 1960s.*

PHOTO FILE

NORTHROP F-89 SCORPION

NORAD service ▶
During the 1950s, the F-89 played a pivotal role within NORAD, the North American Air Defense system.

◀ Rapid deployment
Scorpion missions were planned throughout by Air Force GCI (Ground Control Intercept) teams. Ground-based radars each covered 1600-km (994-mile) swathes.

▲ Long-range missions
Out-and-out interceptors, unlike the contemporary F-94, the Scorpions usually operated in pairs. For northern operations, F-89s carried large Dayglo orange panels on tail, wings and tanks.

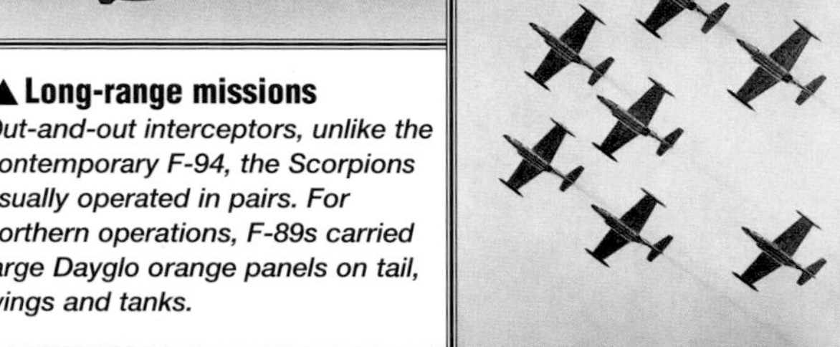

▼ Weapons upgrade
To maintain an edge over ever-improving Soviet bombers, the F-89's weapons progressed from nose-mounted cannon to a fully integrated missile system.

▲ Bomber attack
For destroying Soviet bomber formations over North America, the F-89D carried unguided rockets.

Cold War interceptor ▶
With a full weapons and fuel load, the F-89 could only just get airborne, even with the use of afterburning.

FACTS AND FIGURES

- ➤ The trailing-edge decelerons were very effective; when they deployed by mistake on one F-89 it literally fell from the sky.
- ➤ On training missions, the F-89 would regularly fly against the Lockheed T-33.
- ➤ The XF-89E was a testbed for the Allison J71 engine which later powered the B-66.
- ➤ Alaska-based aircraft would fly 1200 km (746 miles) nonstop to Edmonton, Canada, then on to Palmdale, California, for servicing.
- ➤ F-89s of the 57th FIS were tasked with the air defence of Iceland.
- ➤ In 1961 all Scorpions were relegated to Air National Guard use from the USAF.

PROFILE

Fighter with a sting

A frontline interceptor between 1954 and 1961, the F-89D was frequently scrambled to investigate intruders. This main production variant dispensed with the six 20-mm (0.79-in) cannon of previous models, in favour of an all-rocket armament.

One hit from a rocket was sufficient to take down a slow-moving bomber, and the pilot could select several firing options. Most potently, all 104 rockets could be released in just under four-tenths of a second. Usually flying in pairs, Scorpions had a considerable range, boosted when the sixteen 127-mm (5-in) underwing rockets were replaced with drop-tanks. At the heart of the F-89D's avionics package was the Hughes E-6 fire-control system, linked to the advanced AN/APA-84 computer.

During its heyday, the F-89D flew from bases in Canada, Iceland and the United States. Life for the crews was far from easy – flying under extreme conditions and aware that at any moment the air-base klaxon could sound, signalling a Soviet bomber assault from the north.

Above: As a dedicated bomber destroyer, the original weapons fit for the F-89 was 104 unguided rockets housed in wing-tip pods. Good stability was needed to cope with the buffet created on launching.

Below: Although possessing a good endurance and potent weapons load, the sluggish Scorpion was disliked by day-fighter pilots. The F-89Ds pictured carry underwing tanks for increased range.

F-89D Scorpion

Type: two-seat all-weather interceptor fighter

Powerplant: two 32.03-kN (7,204-lb-thrust) Allison J35-A-41 turbojets with Solar afterburners

Maximum speed: 1024 km/h (636 mph)

Initial climb rate: 2548 m/min (8,360 fpm)

Cruising speed: 787 km/h (489 mph)

Maximum range: 2200 km (1,367 miles)

Service ceiling: 14,996 m (49,200 ft)

Weights: empty 11,428 kg (25,194 lb); maximum take-off 19,160 kg (42,241 lb)

Armament: 104 70-mm (2.76-in) folding-fin unguided rockets in two wing-tip pods

Dimensions:

	span	18.19 m (59 ft 8 in)
	length	16.41 m (53 ft 10 in)
	height	5.36 m (17 ft 7 in)
	wing area	60.39 m² (650 sq ft)

F-89D SCORPION

This Northrop F-89D wears the colours of the 66th Fighter Interceptor Squadron (FIS), usually based in Alaska, and tasked with patrolling the Bering Straits between the Soviet Union and Alaska.

For the demanding conditions of Alaska, windscreen wipers were a necessity. Crews wore full survival gear, heavy parkas and fur-lined jackets. Prior to flight the cockpit was unheated.

In the backseat of the F-89D, the radar operator used a 250-kW (335-hp) APG-40 air intercept radar. Advanced for its day, the system allowed for near-autonomous final-stage intercepts.

Power was provided by twin Allison axial-flow turbojets, with a basic Solar afterburner system. Hydraulic hoists allowed the engines to be lowered for maintenance. The F-89 could make it home with just one engine functioning.

A high tailplane earned the Scorpion its name. Accidents involving ground crew slipping from tail or wing were commonplace. Aircraft stood on ground alert rather than in hangars.

U.S.AIR FORCE
111397
FV-397

Trailing-edge-mounted split decelerons acted as airbrakes when the aircraft was diving or formation-holding. Wing-tip pods held unguided folding-fin rockets forward and fuel aft. A typical patrol mission lasted two hours 15 minutes.

Before the 'D' model, F-89s carried six 20-mm (0.79-in) cannon in the nose. The F-89H introduced six wing-tip Falcon AAMs and 21 rockets, while the final F-89J used underwing Genie AAMs in addition to either wing-tip option of the earlier models.

A cumbersome wing made taxiing difficult, but provided great stability on the landing approach. Fuel was carried in four bulletproof tanks and 12 wing bladder tanks. Even without external tanks, the F-89D had an 11 per cent greater range than the F-89C.

COMBAT DATA

MAXIMUM SPEED

While criticized for its lack of speed, the Scorpion more than made up for this with stability, good landing characteristics and a heavy weapons load. In fact, it was not much slower than the F-86D.

F-89H SCORPION	1024 km/h (636 mph)
F-86D SABRE DOG	1138 km/h (707 mph)
F-102A DELTA DAGGER	1328 km/h (825 mph)

THRUST

With two turbojets, as opposed to its predecessor's single powerplant, the Scorpion had almost twice the thrust of the F-86D. Its primitive yet effective afterburner gave it a maximum thrust nearing that of its successor, the much larger Convair F-102A.

F-89H SCORPION	64.1 kN (14,420 lb thrust)
F-86D SABRE DOG	33.4 kN (7,512 lb thrust)
F-102A DELTA DAGGER	76.5 kN (17,206 lb thrust)

ARMAMENT

Throughout its service, the weapons system of the F-89 was continually upgraded. It was possible for the F-89H to carry six wingtip-mounted missiles, although four was a more usual load.

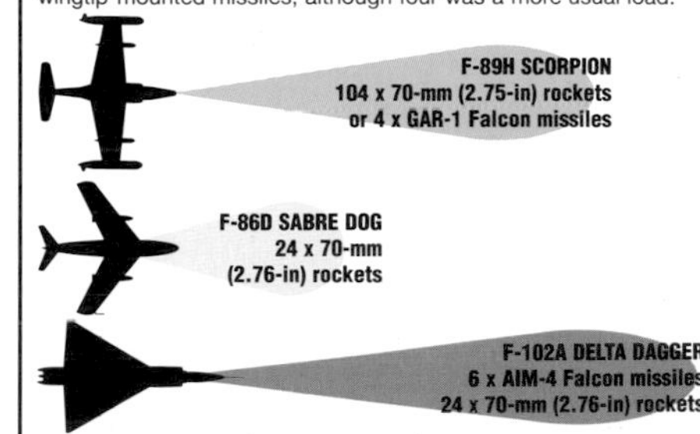

Bomber interception with the F-89J

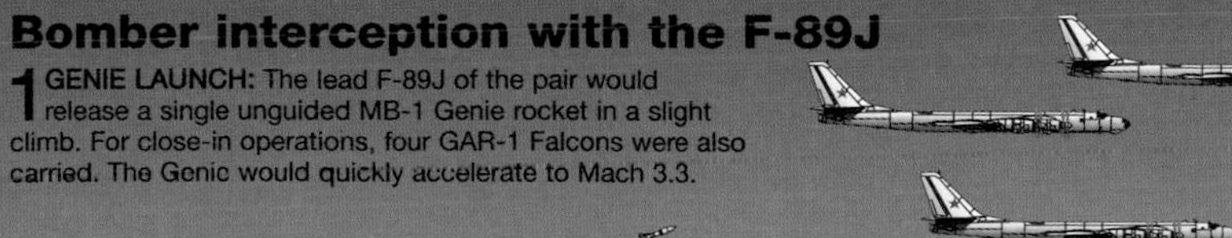

1 GENIE LAUNCH: The lead F-89J of the pair would release a single unguided MB-1 Genie rocket in a slight climb. For close-in operations, four GAR-1 Falcons were also carried. The Genie would quickly accelerate to Mach 3.3.

2 SCORPION TARGETS: The Genie had a 9-km (6-mile) range, and was intended to knock out slow-flying Soviet bomber formations. On release, the pilot would quickly turn around to escape, although the chances of the F-89 avoiding the nuclear blast seem remote.

3 ENGAGEMENT: In tests, the Genie's 1.5-kT nuclear warhead created a 0.8-km (½-mile) fireball. Bombers not destroyed would be crippled by the electromagnetic pulse of the explosion. A second F-89 would then destroy them with 70-mm (2.76-in) rockets.

PANAVIA

TORNADO ADV

● Long-range bomber interceptor ● Swing-wing ● Iraq and Bosnia

▲ The Tornado is the mainstay of Britain's long-range strike and air defence capability, and its pilots and navigators are among the best trained in the world.

Resulting from the marriage of the Tornado strike aircraft with the Sky Flash missile, the Tornado ADV (Air Defence Variant) is a long-range interceptor designed to defend British airspace by engaging bombers hundreds of kilometres out over the ocean. It has advanced radar and fire-control avionics, and with its great reach and ability to shoot down missile-carrying attackers beyond visual range it is superbly capable at its assigned task.

PHOTO FILE

PANAVIA TORNADO ADV

▲ Combat patrol
The ADV was designed to mount combat air patrols and to intercept bombers far from the British coast. It has a very long endurance, and a powerful and highly sophisticated radar.

Sidewinder-armed ▶
The Tornado's superb intercept capability has now been enhanced by the replacement of its long-serving Sky Flash and Sidewinder missiles with advanced AMRAAM and ASRAAM missiles.

▲ Low and fast
The Tornado was originally designed as a low-level strike fighter, and as such it is one of the fastest aircraft in the world. But the engines were built to deliver low-level thrust, and at altitude they do not perform as well as could be expected.

Export fighter ▲
Saudi Arabia is the only other ADV operator, using the type in conjunction with F-15 Eagles.

▲ Tornado family
The ADV was derived from this strike variant, but has a longer fuselage with additional fuel and a longer nose to accommodate the Foxhunter radar.

◀ Desert defender
Tornados defended Saudi airspace during the 1991 Gulf War, and made strikes deep into Iraqi airspace during the 2003 invasion of the country.

FACTS AND FIGURES

- In 1976, it was revealed that 165 of the 385 Tornados ordered by the Royal Air Force would be interceptors.
- First flight of the definitive Tornado F.Mk 3 interceptor was on 20 November 1985.
- The final ADV was delivered to the RAF's No. 56 Squadron on 24 March 1993.
- The Tornado F.Mk 3 introduced an extended afterburner which increases fuselage length by 36 cm (14 in).
- The ADV's intercept radar is the GEC-Marconi AI.Mk 24 Foxhunter.
- Six Saudi ADVs and 38 British F.Mk 3s are equipped with full dual controls.

PROFILE

Defender of the Realm

The Tornado Air Defence Variant, designated Tornado F.Mk 3 in RAF service, is one of the world's most capable long-range interceptors. The pilot and radar officer of the Tornado ADV are strapped into a slender, graceful fuselage with ample room and visibility, which has been stretched from the original Tornado ground-attack variant.

The Tornado is quite heavy relative to its size, but enjoys enough thrust to climb to combat altitude even while accelerating. An afterburner take-off in this powerful machine, which can be accomplished in as little as 765 m (2,510 ft), is an unforgettable experience.

Although fairly agile, the Tornado is no dogfighter, and would be no match for a superfighter such as the Sukhoi Su-27 in a 'turn and burn' struggle. But apart from its limitations in close-quarter combat, the Tornado ADV is a fine warplane well equipped to deal with any bomber pilot with hostile intentions.

This clean, powerful interceptor has been purchased by Saudi Arabia, which has a similar geographic need to engage invading warplanes from long distance. Plans for a purchase by Oman were cancelled, but Italy operated 24 aircraft on loan from the RAF from 1995–2003.

Britain's air defence team for the 1990s consists of the ADV and the Boeing E-3D AWACS. The E-3D would allocate targets for ADV crews.

The IWKA-Mauser 27-mm (1.06-in) cannon, mounted beneath the cockpit on the starboard side of the fuselage, can fire a 25-round burst of high-explosive rounds in under a second.

Saudi ADVs are painted in an all-grey paint scheme. The Saudi IDS strike aircraft carry a brown striped colour scheme to blend in with the desert.

The ADV has the advanced Hermes RHAW (Radar Homing and Warning Receiver) to warn the crew of enemy radar emissions.

Tornado F.Mk 3

Type: two-seat long-range interceptor

Powerplant: two Turbo-Union RB.199-34R Mk 104 turbofans each rated at 40.48 kN (9,104 lb thrust) dry and 73.48 kN (16,527 lb thrust) with afterburning

Maximum speed: 2338 km/h (1,453 mph) at 11,000 m (36,089 ft)

Intercept radius: 1800 km (1,118 miles) (subsonic) or 600 km (373 miles) (supersonic)

Service ceiling: 21,000 m (68,900 ft)

Weights: empty 14,500 kg (31,967 lb); loaded 27,986 kg (61,700 lb)

Armament: one 27-mm (1.06-in) IWKA-Mauser cannon; four BAe Sky Flash radar missiles; four AIM-9L Sidewinder heat-seeking missiles (in future, ADV may carry six AIM-120 AMRAAMs)

Dimensions:		
	span (swept)	8.60 m (28 ft 3 in)
	(spread)	13.90 m (45 ft 7 in)
	length	18.06 m (59 ft 3 in)
	height	5.70 m (18 ft 8 in)
	wing area	26.60 m² (286 sq ft)

TORNADO ADV

The Royal Saudi Air Force has three Tornado ADV squadrons, operating in the air defence role alongside McDonnell Douglas F-15Cs.

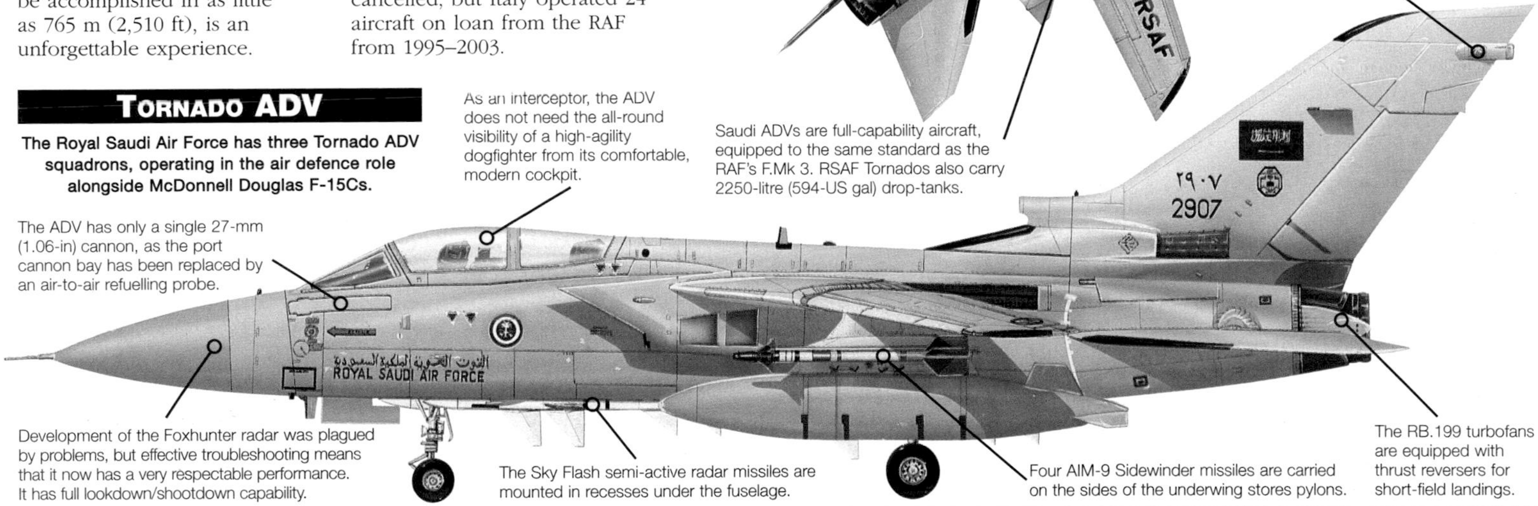

As an interceptor, the ADV does not need the all-round visibility of a high-agility dogfighter from its comfortable, modern cockpit.

Saudi ADVs are full-capability aircraft, equipped to the same standard as the RAF's F.Mk 3. RSAF Tornados also carry 2250-litre (594-US gal) drop-tanks.

The ADV has only a single 27-mm (1.06-in) cannon, as the port cannon bay has been replaced by an air-to-air refuelling probe.

Development of the Foxhunter radar was plagued by problems, but effective troubleshooting means that it now has a very respectable performance. It has full lookdown/shootdown capability.

The Sky Flash semi-active radar missiles are mounted in recesses under the fuselage.

Four AIM-9 Sidewinder missiles are carried on the sides of the underwing stores pylons.

The RB.199 turbofans are equipped with thrust reversers for short-field landings.

COMBAT DATA

MAXIMUM SPEED

The Tornado's clean design means that despite its engine problems, which manifest most obviously as slow acceleration, the aircraft is very fast at high level. It can outrun the larger F-14 Tomcat, although it is not in the same class as the massively powerful MiG-31.

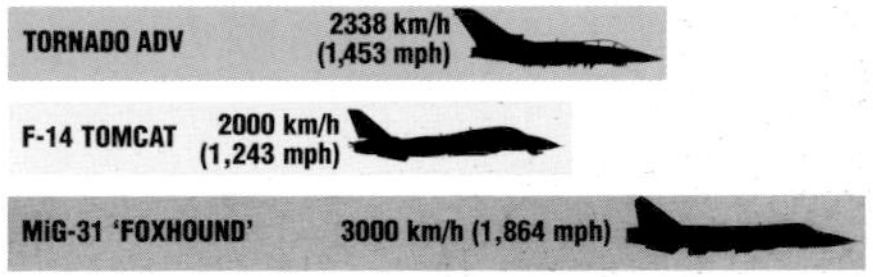

TORNADO ADV 2338 km/h (1,453 mph)

F-14 TOMCAT 2000 km/h (1,243 mph)

MiG-31 'FOXHOUND' 3000 km/h (1,864 mph)

INTERCEPT RADIUS

At optimum altitude, the Tornado's RB.199 turbofans are very fuel-efficient. Despite the fact that the relatively small Tornado carries so much less fuel than either the swing-wing Tomcat or enormous 'Foxhound', the Anglo/German/Italian jet has a much greater operational reach.

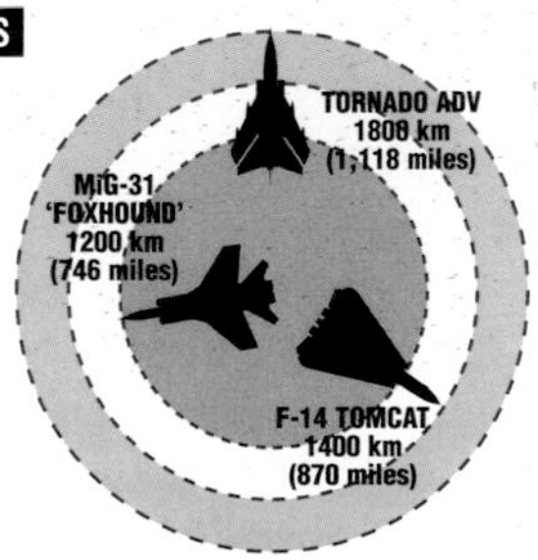

TORNADO ADV 1800 km (1,118 miles)

MiG-31 'FOXHOUND' 1200 km (746 miles)

F-14 TOMCAT 1400 km (870 miles)

SERVICE CEILING

The Tornado was designed for low-level flight. However, its efficient moving wing design enables it to climb very high, although it uses fuel rather rapidly at extreme altitude. The MiG-31 uses brute power to achieve similar performance, while the Tomcat is less capable.

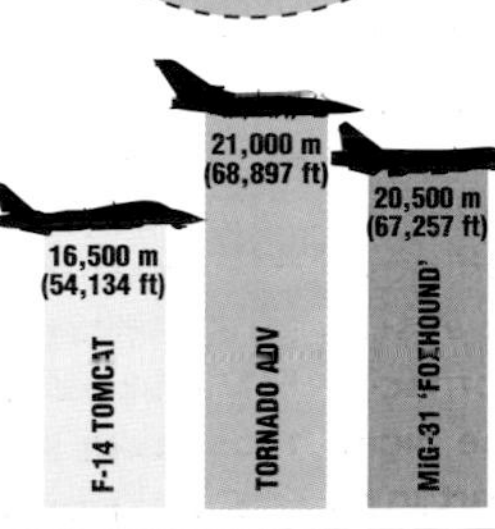

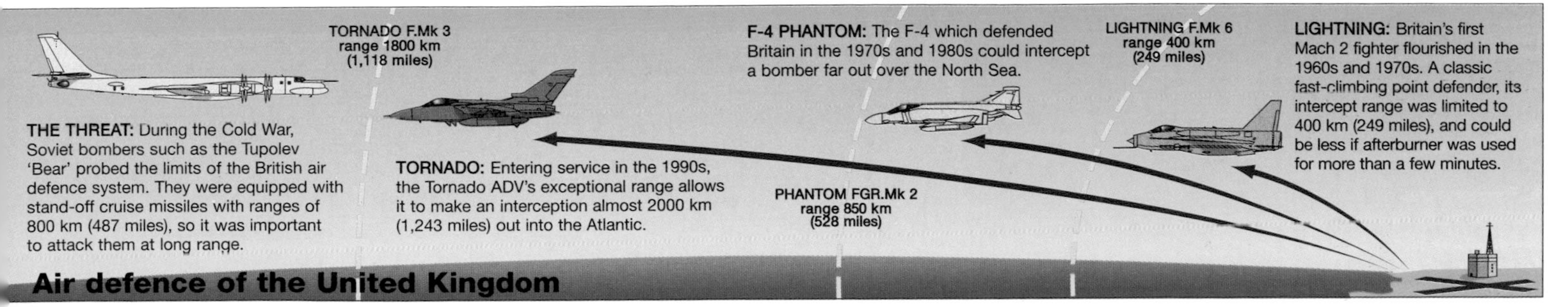

Air defence of the United Kingdom

TORNADO F.Mk 3 range 1800 km (1,118 miles)

THE THREAT: During the Cold War, Soviet bombers such as the Tupolev 'Bear' probed the limits of the British air defence system. They were equipped with stand-off cruise missiles with ranges of 800 km (487 miles), so it was important to attack them at long range.

TORNADO: Entering service in the 1990s, the Tornado ADV's exceptional range allows it to make an interception almost 2000 km (1,243 miles) out into the Atlantic.

PHANTOM FGR.Mk 2 range 850 km (528 miles)

F-4 PHANTOM: The F-4 which defended Britain in the 1970s and 1980s could intercept a bomber far out over the North Sea.

LIGHTNING F.Mk 6 range 400 km (249 miles)

LIGHTNING: Britain's first Mach 2 fighter flourished in the 1960s and 1970s. A classic fast-climbing point defender, its intercept range was limited to 400 km (249 miles), and could be less if afterburner was used for more than a few minutes.

Panavia

Tornado GR.Mk 1

● Multi-role strike fighter ● Dangerous low-level missions

They flew the most dangerous air missions of the 1991 Gulf War. Hurtling through the desert night, less than 60 m (200 ft) above the ground, their targets were the heavily defended runways of Iraq's military airfields. And the perilous nature of their role is reflected in the fact that the RAF's Tornado GR.Mk 1s suffered proportionally the highest losses of all the aircraft taking part in Operation Desert Storm.

▲ *Tornados are designed to fly very fast and very low. Just how low is evident in this view from the cockpit of a Tornado as it races a hundred feet up through a desert 'wadi'.*

Panavia Tornado GR.Mk 1

▲ On the deck
The most modern equipment helps the pilot at low altitude. Control is largely automatic, the aircraft's terrain-following radar ensuring that a constant ground clearance is maintained.

Multi-mission ▶
The nose of Tornado 'MiG-Eater' records three JP233 missions, 23 bombing missions and 14 laser-guided bombing missions.

▲ Low-level attack
Germany's MW-1 weapon dispenses a mixture of anti-armour and anti-personnel submunitions for attacks on ground targets. The similar British JP233 is a specialized airfield attack weapon that is designed to crater runway surfaces.

▼ Low-flying danger
Some crewmen, such as Jon Peters (inset), survived being shot down, getting out of their shattered Tornados only to suffer mistreatment at the hands of their captors.

▲ First mission
Strain shows on the faces of a returning Tornado crew after the first night's mission, along with relief at having survived unscathed.

FACTS AND FIGURES

- On the first three nights of the war Tornados flew 63 sorties, delivering JP233 runway attack munitions.
- Airfields hit included Al Asad, H-2, H-3, Shaibah, Tallil, Al Taqaddum and Ubaidah.
- Four Tornados were lost in the first five days, although only one carried JP233.
- Six RAF Tornados were lost in action, five crew being killed and seven captured.
- British Tornados flew a total of 1600 bombing missions during the war, or 1.4 per cent of the Coalition total.
- They delivered 100 JP233s, 4250 free-fall bombs and 950 laser-guided bombs.

PROFILE

1st Gulf War spearhead

In the words of Tornado pilot Flt. Lt. Ian Long: 'It was a very, very black night; probably one of the darkest I have ever flown on. Over the desert, especially over Iraq, there are no lights. You are flying very low, and all you see is the odd Bedouin camp flashing by.'

From the beginning of the First Gulf War, RAF and Saudi Tornados made their trademark high-speed attacks. Passing low over their target, the huge JP233 containers beneath the fuselage dispensed runway-cratering munitions and area-denial mines, designed to prevent repairs.

JP233 missions were among the most dangerous of the war. Five aircraft were lost to the full force of enemy anti aircraft artillery.

'It's absolutely terrifying. You're frightened of failure; you're frightened of dying. You're flying as low as you dare but not too low to drop your weapons. You put it over the target as low as possible, and then you get away as fast as you can.'

The problem was the size and multiple runways of the Iraqi air bases. It didn't take the Tornado pilots long to work out that destroying the taxiways leading to the runways was the most effective way of making the airfield unusable.

The lack of air opposition later in the war testified that the incredible courage of the crews was not wasted, and the Tornado force had done its job.

JP233 is no lightweight. At 6 m (20 ft) long and weighing 2335 kg (5,148 lb), it needs a powerful machine such as the Tornado to carry its twin dispensers.

All of the Tornado's wing stations were occupied by tanks or defence pods, with weapons carried under the fuselage. The only exception were two Sidewinders carried for self-defence.

The Tornado's small swing wing minimizes low-level, high-speed turbulence, giving its two-man crew a very comfortable ride.

Tornado GR.Mk 1

Type: two-seat multi-role combat aircraft

Powerplant: two 38.49-kN (8,657-lb-thrust) Turbo-Union RB.199 Mk 103 turbofans (71.59 kN / 16,102 lb thrust with afterburning)

Maximum speed: 1482 km/h (921 mph) at low level

Combat radius: 1400 km (870 miles) on a typical hi-lo-hi attack mission

Service ceiling: more than 15,250 m (50,030 ft)

Weights: empty 13,890 kg (30,622 lb); loaded 27,950 kg (61,619 lb)

Armament: two 27-mm (1.06-in) IWKA-Mauser cannon each with 180 rounds, 9000 kg (19,842 lb) of ordnance ranging from WE177B nuclear bomb, JP233 or MW-1 airfield attack weapons, ALARM or HARM anti-radar missiles, Paveway laser guided bombs, and 550-kg (1,216-lb) free-fall or retarded HE bombs

Dimensions:	span (swept)	8.60 m (28 ft 3 in)
	(spread)	13.91 m (45 ft 8 in)
	length	16.72 m (54 ft 10 in)
	height	5.95 m (19 ft 6 in)
	wing area	26.60 m² (286 sq ft)

TORNADO GR.MK 1 'MIG-EATER'

RAF Tornados in the Gulf were notable for their colourful nose art. 'MiG-Eater', depicted here, was based at Tabuk. It was one of the most heavily used Tornados, being flown on 40 missions.

Tornado carries the Sky Shadow electronic countermeasures pod. This detects and jams enemy fire-control radars across a wide range of frequencies.

The Tornado's multi-mode radar is its primary navigation and attack system. Behind the radar is the chisel-like housing for the laser seeker, used when dropping precision-guided munitions.

After the Iraqi airfields were neutralized, Tornados switched to laser-guided attacks, using British 500-kg (1,100-lb) bombs fitted with the Paveway II laser-guidance system. Two or three bombs were carried side by side on fuselage hardpoints.

The tip of the Tornado's large vertical tail houses a VHF communications aerial. A pair of Marconi radar-warning receivers, which detect enemy search radars, project fore and aft immediately beneath.

COMBAT DATA

ATTACK HEIGHTS

Iraq's air bases were the Tornado's primary target, and were attacked with a number of different weapons. The two most effective required very different attack techniques.

JP233: Attacking with the specialized airfield denial weapon entailed approaching from as low as 75 m (246 ft), which made the fighter vulnerable to small arms and hand-held missiles.

LASER-GUIDED BOMBS: These were dropped with deadly accuracy from as high as 6100 m (20,000 ft), as seen here, in almost complete safety from enemy defences.

Tornado mission

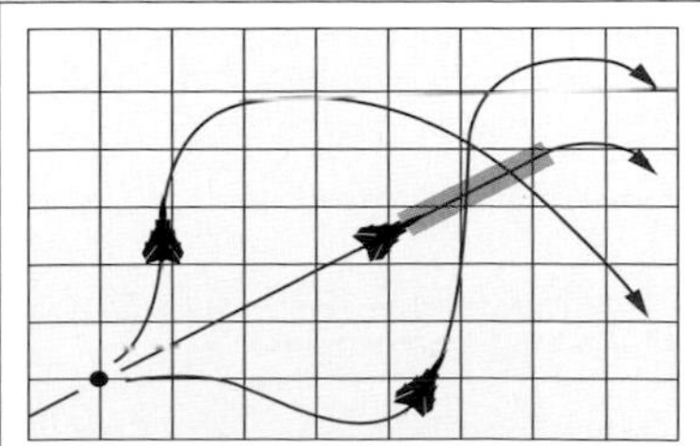

1 INITIAL POINT: About 10 km (6 miles) from the target the Tornado reaches the IP, or initial point. This is the start of the bomb run itself, which is completely automatic.

2 WEAPONS RELEASE: The computerized fire-control system continually monitors aircraft speed, height and position, calculating the exact moment at which to release weapons in order to hit the target.

3 LAYDOWN ATTACK: Usually involving multiples of four aircraft attacking several hundred metres apart at intervals of a few seconds, often from different directions, this makes target acquisition much more difficult for the enemy's air defences.

4 ESCAPE: Once the weapons have been released the Tornado runs out at full speed in a more or less straight line, in order to minimize the time spent in detection and weapons firing range of the target's defences.

The armament is designed to penetrate and crater the runway.

PANAVIA

TORNADO GR.MK 1B/GR.MK 4

● Low-level bomber ● Stand-off missiles ● Ship-killer

Although it is a well-proven strike aircraft, the Tornado's experiences in the first Gulf War highlighted its deficiencies. In a time of tightening defence budgets, a mid-life update was initiated for the Tornado to extend its service life. With an upgraded navigational suite and the ability to deliver stand-off weapons, the improved Tornados will remain the RAF's premier strike aircraft until the Typhoon is fully operational.

▲ *In a world of increasing technology, the cover of night is the final sanctuary for attacking aircraft. In this environment Tornado pilots are suitably equipped with night-vision goggles (NVG).*

PHOTO FILE

PANAVIA TORNADO GR.MK 1B/GR.MK 4

◀ Pilot's delight
Improved versions of the Tornado have retained all the well-respected handling qualities pilots have come to expect from the aircraft.

Ship-killer supreme ▶
In its maritime role the GR.Mk 1B Tornado is able to deliver the Sea Eagle anti-ship missile, which has a range of over 92 km (50 mi.).

More power ▶
Despite the type's excellent low-level performance, an uprated turbofan engine was installed in the new models.

▲ Covert intruder
With an improved avionics suite linked to stand-off missiles, the Tornado is able to destroy enemy positions from afar.

▼ Flight testing
In the hands of British test pilots, the Tornado GR.Mk 4 is proving to be an ideal interdiction aircraft. Overseas interest in the aircraft is increasing.

FACTS AND FIGURES

- The first flight of the Tornado GR.Mk 4 prototype took place on 29 May 1993 from BAe's Warton Aerospace facility.
- On 14 July 1994 government approval was given to upgrade 142 examples.
- Tornado GR.Mk 4s entered RAF service in September 1998.
- Both cockpits are fully compatible with night-vision goggles, allowing missions to be flown in complete darkness.
- Principal characteristic of the GR.Mk 4 is an additional ventral under-nose fairing.
- Help for navigation is provided by a global positioning system.

PROFILE

Making the best even better

With the Warsaw Pact threat almost entirely removed, a radical review of the RAF's front-line capabilities took place in the early 1990s. In the absence of funding to develop a new strike aircraft, a series of modifications allowed the Tornado to replace the retiring Buccaneer in the maritime strike role. Equipped with Sea Eagle anti-ship missiles, the GR.Mk 1Bs operate with 12 and 617 Sqns from Lossiemouth in Scotland.

Externally the new aircraft is virtually indistinguishable from the GR.Mk 1. The GR.Mk 4's internal layout is where most changes have been made. A new wider head-up display allows the pilot to fly the aircraft while also receiving additional information from the forward-looking infra-red (FLIR) equipment. Below this is a head-down display for systems relating to the aircraft.

Both crew members can plot their position with the aid of a global positioning system and view the terrain below via a thermal imaging pod. The GR.Mk 4 enter service in 1998.

Above: A total of 142 Tornado GR.Mk 1/1As will be converted to GR.Mk 4s, taking the RAF's strike capability into the 21st century.

The improvements breathed new life into Strike Command's Tornado fleet, making the aircraft the equal of the latest Russian and American types. The Tornado will eventually be replaced by the Typhoon.

Above: Replacing the Buccaneer in maritime service, the Tornado is equipped with Sea Eagle anti-ship missiles.

Tornado GR.Mk 1B

Type: maritime strike aircraft

Powerplant: two 71.16-kN (16,008-lb.-thrust) Turbo-Union RB.199-34R afterburning turbofans

Maximum speed: 1482 km/h (919 m.p.h.) at sea level

Combat radius: 1335 km (828 mi.)

Service ceiling: 24,000 m (78,720 ft.)

Weights: empty 13,600 kg (29,920 lb.); maximum take-off 27,210 kg (59,862 lb.)

Armament: two 27-mm Mauser cannon, two fuselage-mounted Sea Eagle anti-ship missiles, plus AIM-9L Sidewinder AAMs or other stores

Dimensions:

span (swept)	8.60 m (28 ft. 3 in.)
span (unswept)	13.90 m (45 ft. 7 in.)
length	16.70 m (54 ft. 9 in.)
height	5.79 m (20 ft.)
wing area	30.00 m² (323 sq. ft.)

GR.MK 1B TORNADO

Operated by No. 12 Squadron, RAF, this GR.Mk 1B was one of 26 former Batch 3 Tornado GR.Mk 1s which were converted. The first flight of the GR.Mk 1B occurred on 18 September 1993.

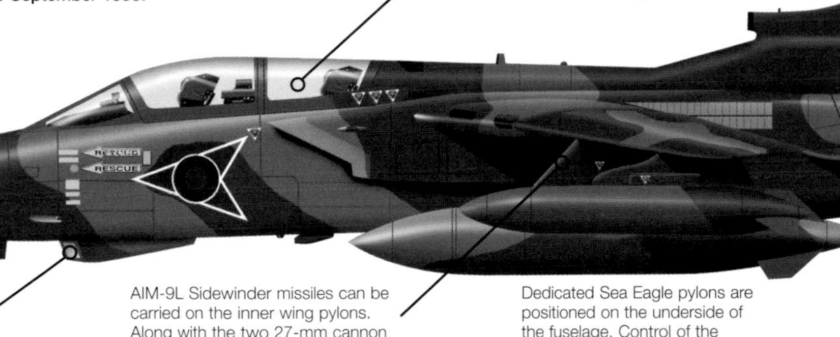

Matched against the latest military aircraft, the cockpit of the Tornado was becoming dated, so a number of improvements were implemented. The cockpit is now fully NVG-compatible and incorporates new head-up and head-down displays.

Unique to British Tornados is the fuel tank in the fin of the aircraft, which means the Tornado can strike targets at great distances. Additional 2250-litre (594-gal.) fuel tanks can be carried under the wings.

A distinguishing feature of the GR.Mk 4 is an extra under-nose fairing housing a GEC TICM II forward-looking infra-red unit.

AIM-9L Sidewinder missiles can be carried on the inner wing pylons. Along with the two 27-mm cannon in the nose, this offers a limited self-defence capability

Dedicated Sea Eagle pylons are positioned on the underside of the fuselage. Control of the missiles is facilitated by an extra panel in the rear cockpit.

Plans have been outlined for at least some GR.Mk 1Bs to be modified to carry the Flight Refuelling Mk 20B HDU pods that were previously used by the Victor fleet. This would let Tornados operate in the buddy refuelling role, extending the strike range of the aircraft.

COMBAT DATA

PILOT'S OFFICE: The pilot's cockpit (pictured below) features a new, wide-angle holographic head-up display onto which both FLIR imagery and normal flight symbology can be displayed simultaneously. Positioned below this is a Smiths Industries head-down display (HDD), used for navigational purposes.

NAVIGATOR'S OFFICE: Despite undergoing only a modest upgrade, the navigator's rear cockpit (pictured below) is equipped with an advanced global positioning system. Maritime strike variants (GR.Mk 1Bs) are fitted with a Sea Eagle missile panel, which allows the navigator to operate and fire the weapon.

The next generation

■ **HARRIER GR.Mk 7:** Constant upgrades have now made the Harrier one of the most capable combat aircraft in the world. It can undertake attack missions at night.

■ **JAGUAR GR.Mk 1A:** Improvements to its navigational suite and attack avionics have kept the Jaguar in front-line service with the Royal Air Force into the 21st century.

■ **TORNADO F.Mk 3 ADV:** As a result of first Gulf War experience, improvements to the ADV fleet included the addition of radar-absorbent materials (RAM) along the leading edges.

PIAGGIO

P.180 AVANTI

● Radical design ● Composite construction ● High performance

▲ *With its distinctive looks and high speed the Avanti would make an ideal aircraft for the rapid transport of top-ranking military officers and VIPs.*

First flown in September 1986, the Avanti was designed as a business aircraft. The distinctive airframe contains a host of innovative features which combine to provide the biggest possible cabin in an aircraft that also offers high speeds, long range and economy. Unfortunately, like the equally innovative Beech Starship, it has attracted few customers and the Italian air force has become its main operator.

PHOTO FILE

PIAGGIO P.180 AVANTI

▲ Radical shape
From all angles the P.180 is a stunningly unusual aircraft. The propellers counter-rotate.

▼ Military colours
Italian air force machines are finished in overall white, with a smart blue cheat line.

▲ Low foreplanes
Fixed foreplanes are mounted low down on the nose. They combine with the tailplane to produce lift and allow a small main wing area.

▼ Avanti airborne
The P.180 is extremely graceful and very fast. National markings are restricted to small fuselage and underwing roundels.

◀ Assembly line
Carbon-fibre reinforced plastic is used for the high-stress parts of the airframe, while Kevlar and epoxy materials are employed elsewhere. The fuselage is stretch-formed in large sections, with the inner surfaces matching exactly.

◀ Super streamlining
Piaggio's attention to detail is evident in every feature of the Avanti. The powerful turboprops are carefully faired and blend into a large, pointed spinner.

FACTS AND FIGURES

- Gates Learjet was temporarily a partner in the P.180 project, joining in 1983 and leaving in 1986 for financial reasons.
- A standard P.180, complete with colour glass cockpit, costs $4.84 million.
- Composite airframe parts are built by Sikorsky and Edo.
- The P.180 design was initiated in 1979 and Piaggio announced its amazing new aircraft in 1983.
- Piaggio began assembly of the first Avanti at its Finale Ligne plant in 1986.
- Italy's air force also flies the Piaggio P.166 and PD-808 transport aircraft.

PROFILE

Piaggio's adventurous Avanti

There were sound reasons behind the apparently radical features of the Avanti. The designers' chief goal was to make the cabin interior as large as possible, giving passengers maximum headroom. The main wing was therefore placed at the rear of the fuselage rather than in a conventional location further forward, where the main spar would have occupied valuable cabin space.

Normally, this wing location would demand an impossibly large tailplane, but a small fixed wing on the nose provides additional lift and makes it possible to control the aircraft's pitch with elevators which are no bigger than normal. In addition, the fuselage is subtly shaped to reduce drag, while the 'delta fin' strakes under the tail help maintain controllability at high angles of attack. At the same time, the unusual configuration helps to keep the aircraft's weight low.

Despite the outstanding performance and advanced glass cockpit, buyers have proved difficult to find. The only substantial operator is the Italian air force, which ordered six for communications and general transport duties. These aircraft are attached to various operational units and the first was delivered on 14 May 1994.

Above: Each main gear unit retracts rearwards into the lower fuselage. The nose unit retracts forwards and has twin wheels.

Below: Large flaps are mounted on both outboard and inboard sections on the wing trailing edges. The flaps deploy along substantial tracks.

P.180 Avanti

Type: light transport

Powerplant: two 1107-kW (1,485-hp.) Pratt & Whitney Canada PT6A-66 turboprops

Maximum speed: 732 km/h (454 m.p.h.) at 8625 m (28,300 ft.)

Range: 3150 km (1,950 mi.) at 11,890 m (39,000 ft.)

Service ceiling: 12,500 m (41,000 ft.)

Weights: empty 3402 kg (7,484 lb.); maximum take-off 5239 kg (11,525 lb.)

Accommodation: one or two pilots, plus up to nine passengers

Dimensions:		
	span	14.03 m (46 ft.)
	length	14.41 m (47 ft. 3 in.)
	height	3.94 m (12 ft. 11 in.)
	wing area	16 m² (172 sq. ft.)

P.180 AVANTI

Very few Avantis have been built and the type is represented here by the first prototype. A second aircraft joined I-PJAV in the air on 14 May 1987, and certification occurred in October 1990.

Two multi-function colour monitors display all the vital flight information. A colour display is also provided for the Collins WXR-480 weather radar.

A maximum load of nine passengers can enjoy the benefits of a galley, toilet and wardrobe. An alternative five-seat VIP interior is also available. Seats are of the armchair type, with multiple adjustments, and foldaway tables may be pulled out between them.

Each of the PT6A-66 turboprops drives a five-bladed Hartzell propeller. Some Italian air force machines have six-bladed propellers. The nacelles are constructed entirely from composites and represent the only break in the wing line.

Mounted high on the tail to clear the propeller wash, the sharply swept tailplane is electrically adjusted for trimming and also carries conventional elevators. The rudder is characterised by a very large trim tab.

I-PJAV

Fixed and carefully faired into the forward fuselage, the foreplane carries trailing-edge flaps. These are synchronised to operate with the wing flaps.

The wings are of high aspect ratio and of very limited area. This configuration minimises drag during high-speed flight. The main spar passes behind the passenger cabin.

Known as 'delta fins', the rear fuselage ventral strakes have no control surfaces but aid directional stability. The wings and tail section are manufactured by Piaggio in Genoa, while the forward fuselage is produced by Piaggio Aviation of Wichita.

ACTION DATA

MAXIMUM SPEED

Compared to other twin-turboprop light transports in military service, the Avanti has exceptional performance. It is capable of maximum and cruising speeds close to those of many jet transports and is also economical to operate.

P.180 AVANTI	732 km/h (454 m.p.h.)
SUPER KING AIR B200	545 km/h (338 m.p.h.)
TURBO CMDR 690	528 km/h (327 m.p.h.)

MAXIMUM PASSENGERS

As with their civilian counterparts, these aircraft rarely fly with a full passenger load. Five or six passengers would be typical and each therefore offers ample room. As a utility transport the P.180 is less useful, however, as it is a smaller aircraft.

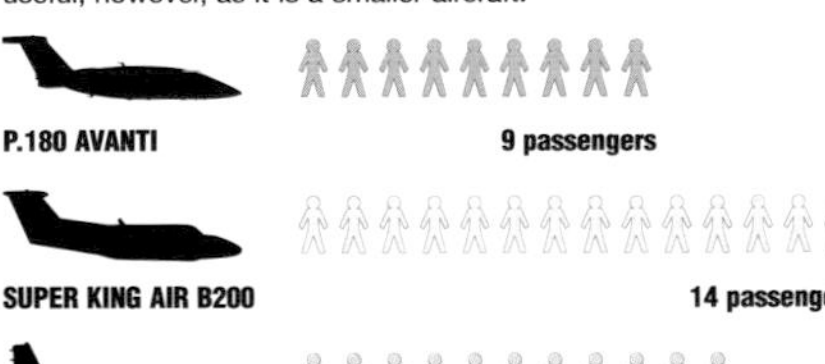

RANGE

Beechcraft's Super King Air B200 offers impressive range and many serve with the US forces as the C-12. The P.180 Avanti cannot equal the B200 for range, but far exceeds the capabilities of the Rockwell Turbo Commander 690.

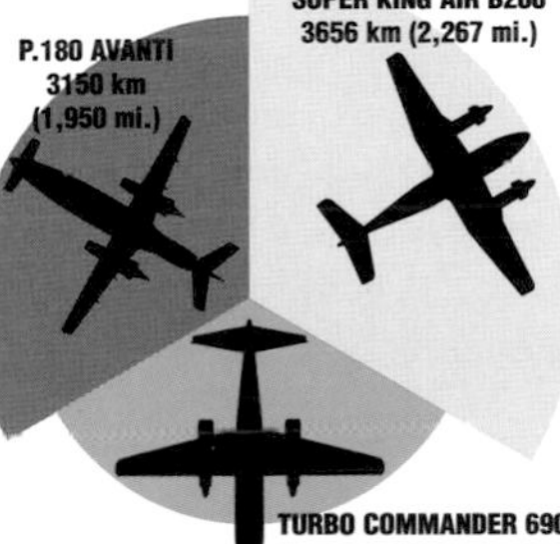

Military light twin-turboprops

BEECHCRAFT C-12: A variety of missions are performed by C-12s in US service. All variants, apart from the C-12J, are based on the B200.

BEECHCRAFT C-12J: Based on the 1900C airliner, the C-12J flies operational support tasks for the US Air National Guard.

EMBRAER EMB-121 XINGU: Brazil and France both fly the Xingu. The French aircraft are used for training and fast communications.

PIAGGIO P.166: Developed from the earlier and much smaller P.136 amphibian, several P.166s remain in Italian air force service.

PILATUS

PC-7/PC-9

● Tandem two-seat trainers ● Turboprop power ● Swiss built

▲ The PC-9 introduced an 857-kW (1,150-hp.) Pratt & Whitney Canada turboprop compared to the earlier PC-7's 485-kW (650-hp.) engine.

Using its 1950s designed P-3 piston-engined trainer as a starting point, Pilatus developed the PC-7 Turbo Trainer. The aircraft became a best-seller around the world and in 1984 it was joined in the air by the new PC-9. Although it looked very similar to the earlier machine, the PC-9 was in fact 90 per cent new. A more powerful engine, stepped cockpit and high performance make the PC-9 one of the world's most advanced and capable turboprop trainers.

PHOTO FILE

PILATUS PC-7/PC-9

▲ Civilian Pilatus in the US
At least four high-performance PC-7 sports planes are privately owned in the US. These two are pictured at Wisconsin's Oshkosh Air Show in 1986.

▲ Australian PC-9
By far the largest operator to date, the Royal Australian Air Force operates 67 PC-9s, which are designated PC-9As.

▼ PC-7 in Malaysia
The Royal Malaysian Air Force is a major PC-7 operator, and the aircraft shown below are members of its elite aerobatic team.

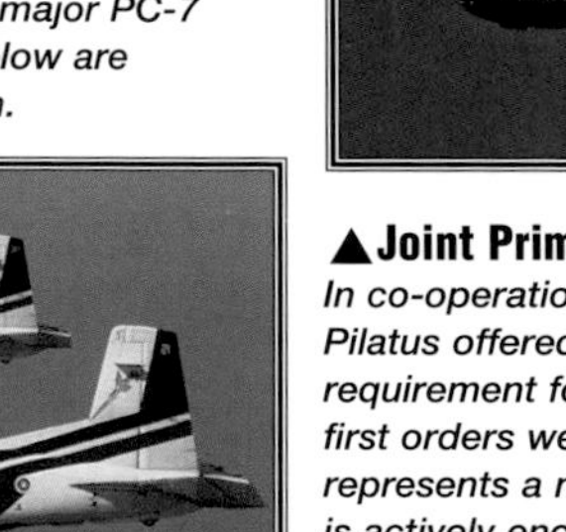

▲ Joint Primary Aircraft Training System
In co-operation with Raytheon Beech in the US, Pilatus offered the PC-9 Mk II to fulfil the JPATS requirement for the US Air Force and Navy. The first orders were placed in late 1995. This represents a major success for Pilatus since the US is actively encouraging exports.

BAe demonstrator ▶
BAe, teamed with Pilatus, offered the PC-9 to the RAF in its bid to find a Jet Provost replacement. The PC-9 lost out to the Shorts Tucano, possibly for political reasons.

FACTS AND FIGURES

- ➤ After BAe/Pilatus lost the RAF trainer contract, BAe was instrumental in winning a Saudi Arabian PC-9 order.
- ➤ In Germany, Holstenair operates a target-towing PC-9 for the Luftwaffe.
- ➤ From 1985 Pilatus offered Martin-Baker ejection seats as a retrofit for the PC-7.
- ➤ Swiss government regulations concerning the export of arms caused Pilatus to lose a Korean PC-9 order.
- ➤ Iran and Iraq used armed PC-7s against each other during their long conflict.
- ➤ The PC-7 Mk II was developed for South Africa and the aircraft were built by Atlas.

PROFILE

Pilatus' turboprop training twins

Installing a Pratt & Whitney Canada PT6A-20 turboprop in a Pilatus P-3 produced one of the world's earliest turboprop trainers. First flown in April 1966, the prototype suffered a landing accident, which caused the programme to be put on hold until 1973. A second P-3 was then modified and flew on 12 May 1975.

Incorporating a number of modifications to the basic P-3 airframe, the PC-7 Turbo Trainer was delivered to its launch customer, the Myanmar air force, in 1979. By early 1995 more than 440 aircraft had been delivered, the majority to military customers.

Comprehensively redesigned in the light of experience with the PC-7, the PC-9 was built from the outset with ejection seats allowing escape at sea level and speeds as low as 112 km/h (69 m.p.h.). The rear seat for the instructor was raised to give a good view over the student pilot's head.

A marketing agreement with BAe has seen the PC-9 offered as the ideal lead-in trainer to the Hawk, with a number of countries, including Saudi Arabia, using the aircraft in this way.

Following the award of the JPATS (Joint Primary Aircraft Training System) contract to the PC-9, US Navy pilots will also be following the PC-9/Hawk path. Total JPATS procurement will be 711 aircraft over 20 years. With Pilatus and its US partner Raytheon Beech encouraged to seek export orders, the future of the PC-9 is assured.

Above: Since the prototype's first flight in 1984, the PC-9 has been ordered by nine countries.

Above: The French Patrouille Martini aerobatic team used the PC-7 for displays in the late 1980s.

PC-9

Type: two-seat turboprop trainer

Powerplant: one 857-kW (1,150-hp.) Pratt & Whitney Canada PT6A-62 turboprop, flat rated at 708 kW (950 hp.)

Maximum speed: 556 km/h (345 m.p.h.)

Maximum climb rate: 1250 m/min (4,100 f.p.m.)

Range: 1642 km (1,018 mi.), or endurance to perform two one-hour missions

Service ceiling: 11,580 m (38,000 ft.)

Weights: empty 1685 kg (3,707 lb.); normal take-off for aerobatics 2250 kg (4,950 lb.); maximum take-off 3200 kg (7,040 lb.)

Dimensions:

span	10.19 m (33 ft. 5 in.)
length	10.18 m (33 ft. 5 in.)
height	3.26 m (10 ft. 8 in.)
wing area	16.29 m² (175 sq. ft.)

PC-9

This PC-9 is in the colours of the Myanmar air force, one of the most recent customers for the high-performance trainer. This machine is unarmed, with the only armed aircraft in the series being South Africa's PC 7 Mk II Astra.

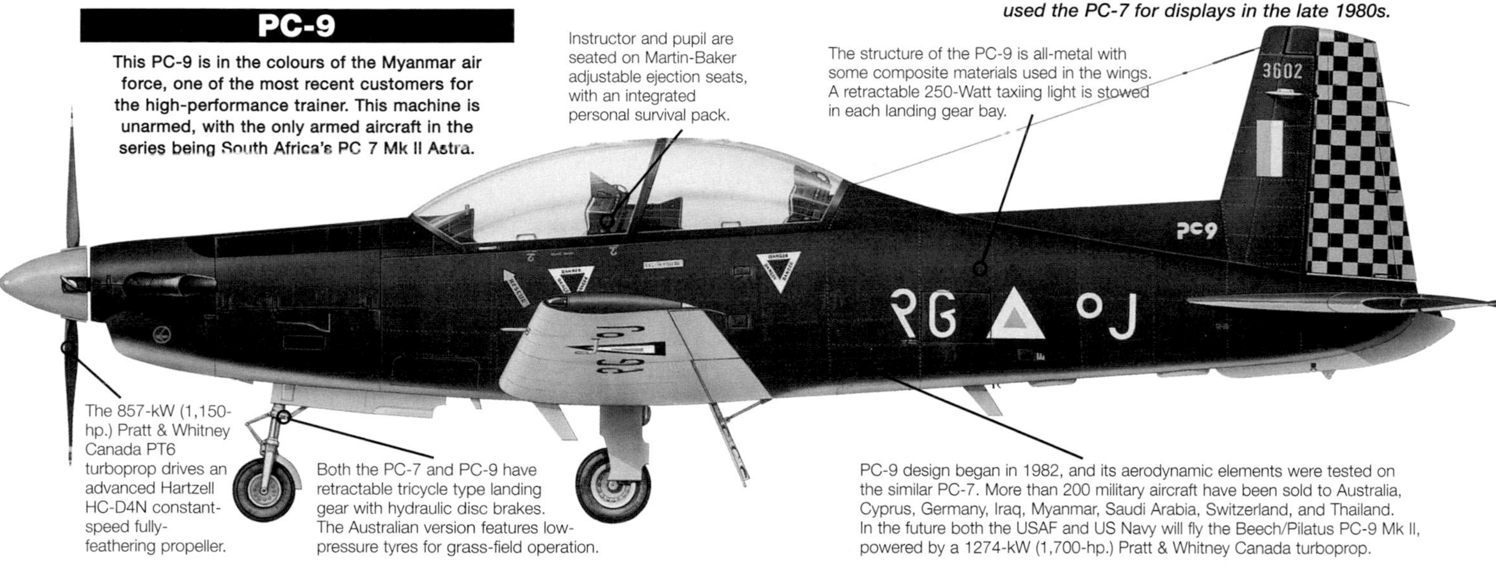

Instructor and pupil are seated on Martin-Baker adjustable ejection seats, with an integrated personal survival pack.

The structure of the PC-9 is all-metal with some composite materials used in the wings. A retractable 250-Watt taxiing light is stowed in each landing gear bay.

The 857-kW (1,150-hp.) Pratt & Whitney Canada PT6 turboprop drives an advanced Hartzell HC-D4N constant-speed fully-feathering propeller.

Both the PC-7 and PC-9 have retractable tricycle type landing gear with hydraulic disc brakes. The Australian version features low-pressure tyres for grass-field operation.

PC-9 design began in 1982, and its aerodynamic elements were tested on the similar PC-7. More than 200 military aircraft have been sold to Australia, Cyprus, Germany, Iraq, Myanmar, Saudi Arabia, Switzerland, and Thailand. In the future both the USAF and US Navy will fly the Beech/Pilatus PC-9 Mk II, powered by a 1274-kW (1,700-hp.) Pratt & Whitney Canada turboprop.

ACTION DATA

MAXIMUM SPEED

All three aircraft were designed to compete in the same marketplace and all are equally capable in terms of speed. Air forces demand jet-like speeds and handling at low cost.

PC-9	556 km/h (345 m.p.h.)
EMB-312H SUPER TUCANO	557 km/h (346 m.p.h.)
PZL-130 ORLIK	560 km/h (347 m.p.h.)

RATE OF CLIMB

EMBRAER's Super Tucano falls short on climb rate since it is a much heavier aircraft with similar power. The Orlik has suffered a protracted development period, although the introduction of US engine technology has produced a fine aircraft which should be capable of competing with the PC-9 on equal terms.

PC-9	EMB-312H SUPER TUCANO	PZL-130 ORLIK
1250 m/min (4,100 f.p.m.)	895 m/min (3,283 f.p.m.)	1236 m/min (4,054 f.p.m.)

RANGE

Poland's PZL-130 excels in this range comparison. The EMB-312H's range is much shorter, although the aircraft does offer the versatility of a range of missions outside the capabilities of its competitors. The Orlik is closely matched to the PC-9, but poses little threat since Pilatus is able to offer a complete training system.

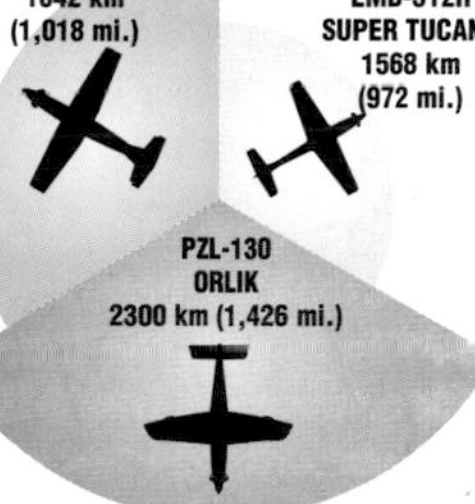

Turboprop trainers

■ **SHORT TUCANO:** The RAF's licence-built version of EMBRAER's successful trainer, the Tucano T.Mk 1, has replaced the Jet Provost.

■ **DAEWOO KTX-1:** One hundred indigenous KTX-1 Yeo-Myoung (Dawn) trainers have been ordered by the Republic of Korea Air Force.

■ **BEECHCRAFT T-34C TURBINE MENTOR:** Redeveloped from an earlier piston-engined design, the T-34C serves with the US Navy.

■ **ENAER TURBO PILLAN:** Once known as the Aucan, this is the updated variant of the Chilean air force's original Pillan.

PILATUS/BRITTEN-NORMAN

DEFENDER

● Military Islander variant ● Piston and turbine versions

Civil operators of the Pilatus/Britten-Norman Islander are usually attracted by the aircraft's low cost, ease of maintenance and minimal support requirements. The same qualities are equally attractive to military operators, and the manufacturer has developed military variants to exploit the type's combination of long endurance and STOL ability. The military variants are known as Defenders and fill a wide variety of roles.

▲ *Both large air-to-air radar and smaller air-to-surface systems have been fitted to Defenders. These aircraft provide affordable coverage for smaller nations with limited budgets.*

PHOTO FILE

PILATUS/BRITTEN-NORMAN DEFENDER

▼ Rockets away!
Defenders have been widely exported, and have been optimised for the military role with four underwing hardpoints for various stores, including rockets.

▲ AEW Defender and MSSA
The AEW Defender testbed, G-TEMI, was later refitted with a Westinghouse APG-66SR radar, to become the Multi-Sensor Surveillance Aircraft.

▼ Maritime Defender
The Maritime Defender is an all-weather, day or night maritime coastal patrol aircraft and is available in piston or turbine form. A nose-mounted sector scan radar of the customer's choice is a standard fitting.

▲ Radar-equipped CASTOR
Corps Airborne Stand-Off Radar, or CASTOR, was a 1984 attempt to provide the British Army with a battlefield surveillance aircraft.

Popular with smaller nations ▶
The island state of Mauritania has an air force of just 12 aircraft, including six Defenders that can be fitted with rockets. The aircraft have a dual transport and counter-insurgency role.

FACTS AND FIGURES

- Originally a Britten-Norman design, the Islander/Defender family is now built by the Swiss company Pilatus/Britten-Norman.
- British Army Air Corps Turbine Defenders are designated Islander AL.Mk 1s.
- One RAF Islander CC.Mk 2A retains the ability to fire a torpedo.
- The BN-2T-4 Defender 4000 is a new version with a longer-span wing and a 100 per cent better payload capability.
- CASTOR Defenders were intended to operate with USAF E-8 J-STARS aircraft.
- Mexico's Presidential Flight is equipped with a Defender.

PROFILE

Low-budget muscle for small air forces

Like the Islander, the Defender is available in both BN-2 piston-engined and BN-2T turboprop versions. The aircraft can be fitted with equipment for electronic warfare, search and rescue, border surveillance and fisheries patrol. It can also be armed with machine-guns and rocket pods. In fact, the reduced size and weight of modern electronics mean that the Defender can be equipped with sensors that provide the surveillance capability of much bigger aircraft.

One variant is the Multi-Sensor Surveillance Aircraft (MSSA), which was developed together with Westinghouse in the United States. This combines a Defender airframe with a version of the F-16 fighter's radar and an infra-red sensor.

The latest model is the BN-2T-4 Defender 4000, which has the enlarged wing of the Trislander, an increased fuel capacity and double the payload. In the BN-2T-4S version, the engines also drive 200-amp generators which provide electrical power for surveillance equipment.

Above: Botswana took delivery of both piston-engined and turbine-powered Defenders. This aircraft has four underwing hardpoints fitted.

Right: Seen here prior to delivery and still carrying their British delivery registrations, these Defenders were destined for Ghana's air force. Ghana also ordered Turbine Defenders.

BN-2T-4 Defender 4000

Type: twin-turbine multi-role transport

Powerplant: two 298-kW (400-hp.) Allison B250-17F turboprops flat rated at 238.5 kW (320 hp.)

Maximum speed: 326 km/h (202 m.p.h.) at sea level

Endurance: 8 hours

Service ceiling: 7620 m (25,000 ft.)

Weights: empty 2223 kg (4,890 lb.); maximum take-off 3856 kg (8,483 lb.)

Accommodation: up to 9 passengers plus pilot, or equivalent weight in mission equipment and associated crewmembers

Dimensions:

span	16.15 m (53 ft.)
length	12.37 m (40 ft. 7 in.)
height	4.18 m (13 ft. 8 in.)
wing area	31.31 m² (337 sq. ft.)

AEW DEFENDER

G-TEMI was the AEW (Airborne Early Warning) Defender demonstrator flown in the mid-1980s and later converted to MSSA standard as G-MSSA. An example of the latter has been sold to Turkey.

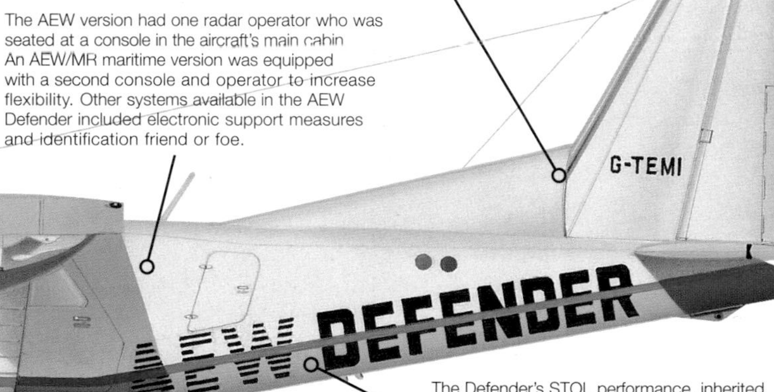

Marketed as an affordable airborne early warning (AEW) platform, the Defender featured a Thorn-EMI Skymaster radar in a large nose radome. In the 1990s a Westinghouse APG-66 radar was installed.

Turbine Islander/Defenders are powered by two 298-kW (400-hp.)Allison B250-17F turboprops, derivatives of the well-known 250-C turboshaft helicopter powerplant. They replace the Islander's Textron Lycoming O-540 or IO-540 flat-six piston engines.

The AEW version had one radar operator who was seated at a console in the aircraft's main cabin. An AEW/MR maritime version was equipped with a second console and operator to increase flexibility. Other systems available in the AEW Defender included electronic support measures and identification friend or foe.

To maintain directional stability with the bulbous radome fitted, the AEW Defender and MSSA aircraft had a fillet added forward of the tailfin. They also had the longer span wings which were introduced on the Defender 4000.

The Defender's STOL performance, inherited from the Islander, allowed it to be operated from forward, unprepared airstrips. Compared to many other AEW aircraft, the Defender had a smaller radar cross-section when airborne.

ACTION DATA

RANGE

In terms of its range capability, the Defender performs better than the Dornier Do 28D and DHC-6 Twin Otter. Defenders are able to carry extra fuel both internally and in external fuel tanks.

TAKE-OFF RUN

All three types are dedicated STOL designs and have good short-field performance. The Defender's take-off run at maximum weight is comparable to that of both the Twin Otter and the Do 28D Skyservant.

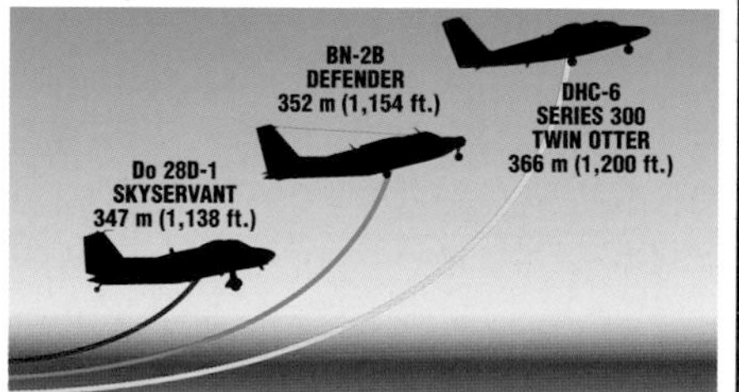

POWER

The piston-engined Defender has a modest power rating, which was addressed in the Turbine Defender. However, the Lycoming LTP-101 engine which was originally selected proved to be too powerful. The Do 28D is a piston-engined design and the DHC-6 is a turboprop.

Do 28D-1 SKYSERVANT 566 kW (754 hp.)

BN-2B DEFENDER 448 kW (640 hp.)

DHC-6 SERIES 300 TWIN OTTER 924 kW (1,238 hp.)

Britten-Norman's STOL family

BN-2/2A/2B ISLANDER: Flown for the first time in 1965, the Islander nine-seater has been in production for 30 years in four countries.

BN-2A Mk III TRISLANDER: Introduced in 1970, this stretched, 18-seat, tri-motored BN-2 variant was built in limited numbers.

BN-2T TURBINE ISLANDER: To improve the Islander's performance, turboprop engines were fitted in 1980.

BN-3 NYMPH: This all-metal light aircraft flew in 1969, but failed to enter production before the Britten-Norman became bankrupt.

PZL

I-22/M-93 Iryda

● Twin-engined jet trainer ● Polish design ● Export potential

While the Soviet's other Warsaw Pact allies adopted the Czech-built L-29 Delfin as their basic jet training aircraft, Poland chose to develop the indigenous TS-11 Iskra. When this first-generation local design needed replacing in the 1970s, Poland's highly developed PZL organisation came up with another new design, the Iskra-22, or I-22 Iryda. With the end of the Cold War, Poland has high export hopes for its new trainer.

▲ *Development of the I-22/M-93 series began in 1977. With the end of the Cold War, PZL now anticipates a worldwide market for the Iryda, but faces tough competition.*

Photo File

PZL I-22/M-93 Iryda

▼ First production M-93K

0204 was the first Iryda that was built to the initial Polish air force service standard and flew in July 1994. This aircraft entered service with the 58th Air School Regiment.

▲ Numerous variants

In addition to the M-93V, various other versions have been announced, including the M-93R two-seat reconnaissance aircraft and the M-93M maritime attack and reconnaissance platform.

Rolls-Royce power ▶

With airbrakes deployed, the fifth Iryda touches down. By this stage SP-PWE had been re-engined with Rolls-Royce Vipers for the export market. Designated M-93V, it flew in 1994.

◀ Advanced trainer

As the Iryda is expected to be used by the Polish air force for all aspects of pilot training, a weapon-carrying ability is an important feature.

Strength a strong point ▶

The I-22's name implies strength as Iryda (iridium) is a steel-grey metallic element with a very high melting point. The name Iryda is shared by a planned M-96 variant with improved aerodynamics.

Facts and Figures

- An ex-Vietnamese air force Northrop F-5 and Cessna A-37 were allegedly used in the development of the I-22.
- Including prototypes and 1996 orders, 25 Irydas had been built or ordered.
- The first I-22 deliveries were to the 58th Air School Regiment at Deblin-Irena.
- Proposed I-22/M-93 variants included two-seat reconnaissance and single-seat fighter/attack aircraft.
- At least two of the first 25 aircraft have been used as static test airframes.
- The PZL-Mielec factory was founded in 1938 and has built 15,000 aircraft.

PROFILE

Home-grown advanced jet trainer

Launched in 1977 as a replacement for the TS-11 and Lim-6 (MiG 17) tactical and advanced trainers, the I-22 was to be a combat-capable two-seater. Development has been prolonged, however, and the prototype did not fly until March 1985 and then crashed in 1987.

Four more aircraft flew between 1988 and 1991, the year in which the Polish air force announced its first order for nine aircraft. Five had been delivered by 1994, when it was decided to improve what was judged to be an underpowered design by fitting new engines, ejection seats and avionics.

The Polish air force did consider buying ex-German Luftwaffe Alpha Jet trainers (to which the I-22 bears a strong resemblance), but this idea was abandoned. Instead, the I-22's 10.76-kN (2,420-lb.-thrust) PZL-5 engines were replaced by two new 14.71-kN (3,300-lb.-thrust) IL K-15 turbojets to produce the M-93K. A re-engined example flew in 1994 and this has become the main production variant. Twelve were ordered by the Polish air force and the surviving I-22s will be brought up to the new standard.

In an effort to secure foreign sales, the fifth I-22 has been fitted with two Rolls-Royce Vipers, as the M-93V. A number of other variants have also been discussed.

Above: The third I-22 takes to the air with a load of assorted underwing stores. External loads are limited to 1100 kg (2,420 lb.).

Above: SP-PWB was the second I-22 prototype, and first flew in 1988. The crash of the first prototype and the political situation in Poland prolonged I-22/M-93 development.

M-93K Iryda

Type: two-seat basic and advanced trainer

Powerplant: two 14.71-kN (3,300-lb-thrust) Instytut Lotnictwa K-15 turbojets

Maximum speed: 950 km/h (589 m.p.h.) at 5000 m (18,000 ft.)

Maximum climb rate: 2520 m/min (8,265 f.p.m.) at sea level

Combat radius: 250 km (155 mi.) at 500 m (1,600 ft.) at maximum take-off weight

Service ceiling: 13,700 m (44,396 ft.)

Weights: empty equipped 4650 kg (10,230 lb.); maximum take-off 8700 kg (19,140 lb.)

Armament: one 23-mm twin-barrelled cannon in ventral pack, plus up to 1100 kg (2,420 lb.) of weapons on external pylons, including bombs, rockets, gun pods and air-to-air missiles

Dimensions:		
	span	9.60 m (31 ft. 6 in.)
	length	13.22 m (43 ft. 4 in.)
	height	4.30 m (14 ft. 2 in.)
	wing area	19.92 m² (214 sq. ft.)

I-22 IRYDA

Aircraft '02' was the prototype of the I-22/M-93 series. After being lost in a crash on 31 January 1987, it was followed by four more airframes, the first of which flew in 1988.

Among the changes made to the I-22 to bring it up to M-93K standard were the installation of Western systems, including avionics, an inertial navigation system (INS) and Martin-Baker PL10LR zero/zero ejection seats.

PZL designed the Iryda to cover the full spectrum of pilot training, operating in all weathers from unprepared airstrips and carrying a variety of ordnance types. The airframe is able to withstand battle damage and is quick and inexpensive to repair.

The I-22 has an all-metal light alloy stressed skin structure and a two-spar wing with integral fuel tanks. The engine bays have titanium heatshields.

The I-22's elevators and rudder are manually (rod) actuated. The flaps are hydraulic, although they can be pneumatically operated in emergencies. Hydraulic airbrakes are fitted in the upper fuselage.

02

A twin-barrelled GSz-23L 23-mm cannon pack installed in a bay under the rear cockpit is standard on the M-93Ks. Up to 200 rounds of ammunition can be carried in the fuselage.

Two underwing pylons are fitted on either side of the aircraft. They may contain camera pods, fuel tanks or, for advanced training flights, an offensive load. In combat, air-to-air missiles can be carried for self-defence.

After initial flight trials of the I-22, powered by PZL-5s, showed the aircraft to be underpowered, two more powerful K-15 engines were substituted. For export, PZL has flown a Rolls-Royce Viper-powered variant.

ACTION DATA

MAXIMUM SPEED

The BAe Hawk has a marginal speed advantage over the Alpha Jet and a much higher top speed than the Iryda. New engines improved the Iryda's performance, especially its top speed.

I-22 IRYDA 840 km/h (520 m.p.h.)

HAWK T.Mk 1 1038 km/h (644 m.p.h.)

ALPHA JET E 916 km/h (568 m.p.h.)

CLIMB RATE

The twin-engined Alpha Jet E had a considerable power-to-weight advantage over the single-engined Hawk T.Mk 1. In its original form the under-powered I-22 had an unimpressive performance, but this was rectified in later aircraft by fitting bigger engines.

I-22 IRYDA 1500 m/min (4,920 f.p.m.)

HAWK T.Mk 1 2835 m/min (9,300 f.p.m.)

ALPHA JET E 3660 m/min (12,000 f.p.m.)

Post-war PZL products

■ **M-15 BELPHEGOR:** Production of the jet-powered M-15 agricultural aircraft totalled 120. It ended in 1981, after the Belphegor proved to be uneconomical to operate.

■ **PZL-104 WILGA:** This radial-engined, light, general-purpose aircraft first flew in the early 1960s and remains in production. Roles include training and crop spraying.

■ **PZL-106 KRUK:** One of PZL's three dedicated crop-spraying/dusting designs, the piston-engined Kruk and turboprop Turbo-Kruk have secured export orders.

■ **PZL-230 SKORPION:** This turbofan-powered single-seat small agile battlefield attack (SABA) aircraft was proposed to the Polish air force in the 1990s, but did not proceed to prototype stage.

PZL

PZL-130 ORLIK

● Indigenous Polish trainer ● Jet-like performance

Flown for the first time in October 1984, the PZL-130 was conceived as part of a complete instruction system. As well as the aircraft itself, there was a simulator and an automatic inspection unit intended to diagnose faults with its systems or engine. The original aircraft was flown with two different piston engines, but after flight tests the Polish air force decided that it needed turboprop power. As a result, PZL has developed several versions of the PZL-130T.

▲ *Although it has suffered several setbacks and has taken a long time to develop, the indigenous Turbo Orlik basic turboprop trainer is now serving the Polish air force in large numbers.*

PHOTO FILE

PZL PZL-130 ORLIK

▼ Pre-production
A small batch of pre-production Turbo Orliks was built in 1990–91. These all featured different powerplants in an attempt to determine the most suitable engine for air force use.

▲ Canadian force
A distinctive maple leaf on the tail identifies this aircraft as a pre-production example powered by a Pratt & Whitney Canada PT6A turboprop. This engine is used in the rival Swiss Pilatus PC-9 trainer.

Production differences ▶
In service, Orliks wear this attractive two-tone grey colour scheme. Differences from the prototype include a redesigned canopy.

◀ East meets West
When it was conceived during the Communism days in Eastern Europe, few would have envisaged that this aircraft would incorporate Western components.

Number three ▶
First flying in 1985 this aircraft was the third prototype of the original series and became the first turboprop conversion to take to the air, two years later.

FACTS AND FIGURES

- Two different engines are specified for the 130 Turbo Orlik, a Walter M601T or Pratt & Whitney Canada PT6A-62.
- An initial order for 12 aircraft was placed by the Deblin Training Academy.
- Development of the piston-engined variant was abandoned in 1990.
- A third pre-production Turbo Orlik flew in 1991, an incredible 10 years after design on the aircraft was first begun.
- Export orders have been sought but none has been achieved so far.
- The first turboprop conversion was destroyed in a crash in January 1987.

PROFILE

Poland's Spotted Eaglet

After flight tests of two pre-production Orliks (Spotted Eaglet), one powered by a 246-kW Vedeneyev M-14PM radial from the Soviet Union, and the other by one of PZL's own Kalisz K8-AAs, the piston-engined version was abandoned in 1990. This was partly because of the unreliable supply of the Russian engines but also through the advent of something better.

Using the existing airframe, PZL developed the Turbo Orlik. The first such machine was the third prototype piston Orlik fitted with a Pratt & Whitney Canada PT6A which flew for the first time in July 1986, but crashed the following January. A new airframe was fitted with a 560-kW (750-hp.) Motorlet M601E and flown in January 1989.

Subsequent prototypes included both PT6A and M601-powered versions, and in September 1991 PZL flew the first of 48 P-130TBs ordered by the Polish air force. The aircraft can be used for a wide range of training missions, and its six underwing hardpoints can carry a useful selection of armament.

After its long development, the P-130 finally entered service with the Polish air force in 1992. PZL has continued to develop the PT6A-powered versions, offering a range of models with engines varying in power from 410 kW (550 hp.) to 708 kW (950 hp.).

Left: All aircraft are delivered fully assembled from the PZL factory and are specifically made to order. Examples destined for overseas are certified by the Polish Ministry of Defence and Airworthiness.

Above: The most powerful Orlik is the PZL-130TC. Test pilots were reluctant to fly this machine after accidents in trials.

130 TB Turbo Orlik

Type: two-seat tandem basic trainer

Powerplant: one 560-kW (750-hp.) Motorlet M601E turboprop engine

Maximum speed: 501 km/h (310 m.p.h.)

Cruising speed: 454 km/h (281 m.p.h.)

Initial climb rate: 972 m/min (3,190 f.p.m.)

Range: 1905 km (1,180 mi.)

Service ceiling: 10,000 m (33,000 ft.)

Weights: empty 1450 kg (3,190 lb.); loaded 2700 kg (5,930 lb.)

External payload: 800 kg (1,760 lb.)

Load limits: + 6.5 *g*, -3 *g*

Dimensions:

	span	9.00 m (29 ft. 6 in.)
	length	9.00 m (29 ft. 6 in.)
	height	3.53 m (11 ft. 7 in.)
	wing area	13 m² (140 sq. ft.)

PZL-130 ORLIK

SP-PCA was the first Orlik to fly, taking to the air in October 1983. It was soon followed by a second, and later a third example, though by this time interest in the piston-engined version was waning.

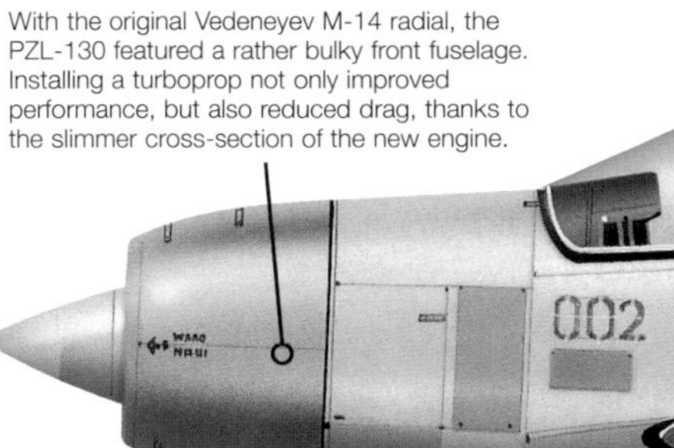

With the original Vedeneyev M-14 radial, the PZL-130 featured a rather bulky front fuselage. Installing a turboprop not only improved performance, but also reduced drag, thanks to the slimmer cross-section of the new engine.

A tandem layout is incorporated, in common with many other modern basic trainers, with the rear seat set quite far back. The cockpit is well laid out and spacious. Full dual controls are featured and both crewmen sit on British Martin-Baker ejection seats which are fully automatic. A special command system enables the rear occupant to initiate the ejection sequence.

In line with many of its competitors, the aircraft is of all-metal, stressed-skin construction. The Orlik forms one element of the System 130 concept, the others being pilot simulator training and automatic diagnosis for ground crew. PZL designed the aircraft for ease of maintenance, to ensure maximum use of the fleet.

Although the primary role of the aircraft is that of a trainer, a wide variety of external stores can be carried. In a war scenario, the Orlik would primarily be used for light-attack/close-support work.

All control surfaces are hydraulically powered and very light, giving the aircraft superb handling characteristics. PZL intended the Spotted Eaglet for both military and civilian operators and the aircraft is fully aerobatic.

ACTION DATA

POWER

An interesting aspect of the Orlik is that its performance differs greatly depending on the engine fitted. The 130TM, with its M601 engine, is not as powerful as current Western types, though it can be specified with a much more potent Pratt & Whitney PT6A-25.

PZL-130TM 560 kW (750 hp.)

PC-9 857 kW (1,150 hp.)

TUCANO T.Mk 1 820 kW (1,100 hp.)

SERVICE CEILING

Despite having a less powerful engine, the Orlik has excellent performance and can reach an altitude of 10000 m with few problems. Its service ceiling is, surprisingly, greater than that of the much more powerful Shorts Tucano T.Mk 1.

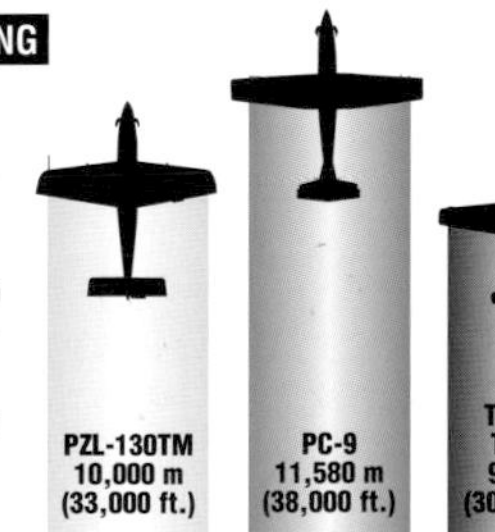

CLIMB RATE

Not too long ago, a climb rate of 900 m/min was considered only attainable by jets. Improvements in technology and the advent of powerful turboprop engines have ensured that the latest generation of basic trainers can offer jet-like performance without the considerable cost.

Indigenous trainers from Poland

■ **PZL TS-8 BIES:** Roughly equivalent to the North American T-28, the Bies (fiend) entered service in 1958. It established several world records that remained unbeaten for 25 years

■ **PZL TS-11 ISKRA:** Intended as a more advanced replacement for the TS-8, this aircraft represented a considerable coup for the Polish aviation industry, with some 500 built.

■ **P.Z.L IS-22 IRYDA:** Unlike other Eastern European countries which purchased the Aero L-39 Albatros, Poland chose to procure its own advanced trainer, resulting in the IS-22.

REPUBLIC F-84 THUNDERJET

● Ground attack ● Straight wings ● Korean War veteran

When the first F-84 Thunderjets reached Korea in December 1950, the USAF found itself with a fighter not quite ideal for air-to-air action but unmatched as a bomber and ground-attack platform. In a sense, the F-84 Thunderjet always played second fiddle; it was developed as 'insurance' early in the jet age and it remained in widespread service across Europe long after newer, faster jets stole the headlines.

▲ *Heading to the Korean war zone aboard a US Navy aircraft-carrier, Thunderjets and their pilots wait out the long cruise before their aircraft can be unloaded at the docks in Japan.*

PHOTO FILE

REPUBLIC F-84 THUNDERJET

▲ The jet age
The XP-84 was rolled out in December 1945. Its clean lines were possible because the airframe was designed around an axial-flow engine.

▼ No runway required
Because runways are so vulnerable, some F-84s were fitted with a solid-fuel booster rocket, enabling them to be launched from the back of a lorry.

▼ Rocket attack
This aircraft fires off a full load of ground-attack rockets on a practice range. The technique was used widely during the Korean War.

Star performers ▶
The 'Thunderbirds', the US Air Force's aerobatic team, flew F-84Gs from its inception in 1953 until the type was phased out in favour of swept-wing F-84Fs in 1955. Pilots praised the excellent handling of Republic's Thunderjet.

Tunnel vision ▶
The proposed XF-103 interceptor was fitted with a periscope, and the pilot flew the aircraft by looking through a sight.

FACTS AND FIGURES

- The F-84 was the first new American fighter to fly after the end of World War II in 1945.
- The first flight was made on 28 February 1946 at Edwards AFB in California.
- A record speed of 983 km/h (609 mph) was achieved on 6 September 1946.
- Thunderjets entered USAF service during the summer of 1947, and were initially known as P-84Bs; 'P' stood for pursuit.
- The F-84's first combat mission in the Korean War was on 6 December 1950.
- F-84s destroyed 105 MiG-15, mainly during ground-attack operations.

PROFILE

Straight-winged warrior

The straight-winged Republic F-84 Thunderjet was a solid and versatile jet fighter that poured from the factory production line at a time when aviation was being revolutionised by other jets with swept-back wings. The F-84 was nevertheless a tough and reliable combat aircraft that blazed a trail of glory in Korea and equipped NATO nations for many years.

Straight-winged F-84D, F-84E and F-84G fighters flew thousands of fighter-bomber missions in Korea and shot down a few MiG-15s. Others served as escort fighters with Strategic Air Command. The 'ultimate' straight-winged Thunderjet, the F-84G, was more powerful than earlier models and was equipped for in-flight refuelling from the beginning. These fighters were the first to deploy in large numbers across oceans, and established several records for mass ferry flights across the Atlantic and Pacific.

The basic design of the F-84 was so good that it led to a swept-winged version, which also served with distinction.

Faced with the need to bolster the defences of Europe, America supplied its NATO allies with 1936 examples of the Thunderjet. Here, an early Dutch model flies a low-level patrol.

Later models of the F-84 Thunderjet were equipped with tip tanks that allowed the aircraft to operate at greater range with no loss in speed.

The last of the straight-winged F-84s, the F-84G was the first single-seat fighter to have the capability of deploying nuclear weapons.

Extensive modifications were incorporated into the Republic F-84 Thunderjet series. Most noticeable was the increase in the length of the fuselage.

F-84E Thunderjet

Type: single-seat jet fighter-bomber

Powerplant: one 22.2-kN (5000-lb-thrust) Allison J35-A-17 turbojet

Maximum speed: 987 km/h (612 mph)

Initial climb rate: 1847 m/min (6060 fpm)

Range: 3138 km (1945 miles)

Service ceiling: 13,173 m (43,200 ft)

Weights: empty 4629 kg (10,183 lb); maximum take-off 10,189 kg (22,416 lb)

Armament: six 12.7-mm (.50-cal.) machine guns; plus up to 2041 kg (5000 lb) of bombs, or 32 HVAR rockets

Dimensions:

	span	11.09 m (36 ft 4 in)
	length	11.76 m (38 ft 7 in)
	height	3.91 m (12 ft 9 in)
	wing area	24.15 m² (260 sq ft)

F-84G THUNDERJET

Simple in design and layout, the Thunderjet offered the USAF an aircraft that could perform numerous operations during wartime. It earned the title of 'Champ of the Fighter-Bombers'.

The cockpit was enclosed under a sliding canopy. Later models were fitted with bracing struts to increase the strength of the hood against bird strikes. This also considerably eased construction of the canopy.

Having experienced developmental problems with the swept-winged F-84F, on the G model Republic re-introduced the straight wing to the USAF fighter fleet. Originally intended as purely an interim design, the F-84G was produced in the largest numbers and served with a number of NATO operators.

Six M-3 machine guns were positioned above the intake in the nose. Loading of the guns was accomplished via an upward-hinging door.

The F-84 was the first fighter to be fitted with an in-flight refuelling receptacle, which was positioned within the starboard tip tank. Tanker aircraft were the KB-29Ps of SAC.

Being equipped with an Allison J35 engine increased the F-84G's top speed to 1000 km/h (620 mph). This allowed the aircraft to be used for fighter and attack missions.

COMBAT DATA

MAXIMUM SPEED

Though powered by an improved engine, the Thunderjet's maximum speed was limited by the type's straight-winged design. The Russians held the lead in fighter design with their MiG-15 'Fagot', aircraft which came as an unpleasant surprise to the USAF in Korea.

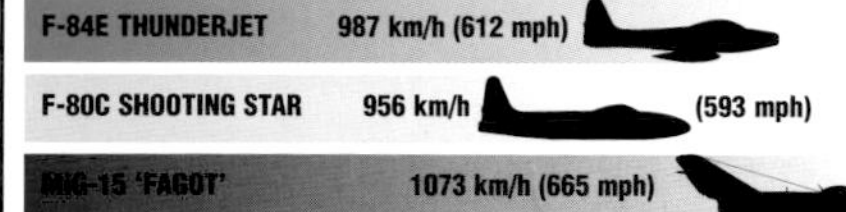

CLIMB RATE

With its ability to out-climb the Thunderjet, the MiG-15 was able to out-fight the F-84 whenever a dogfight occurred. Because of this, the F-84 was restricted to ground attack duties for which an escort of fighters could be provided.

THRUST

Early jet engines were often limited in their power output, and the F-84E Thunderjet offered low performance compared to its contemporaries. The earlier F-80C Shooting Star had increased thrust but was unable to perform the many attack duties of the F-84E Thunderjet.

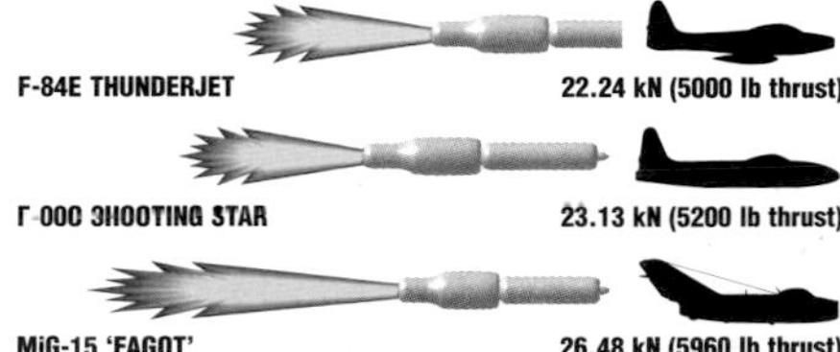

Thunder over Europe

■ **DENMARK:** Denmark received its aircraft as part of the NATO build-up after World War II. The Thunderjet was the first Danish fighter to enter service after the war.

■ **PORTUGAL:** Operating well into the 1970s, the Thunderjet flew with numerous NATO allies including Belgium, Italy and Portugal. It was eventually replaced by the Mirage and F-104.

■ **TURKEY:** This brightly coloured example flew with the Turkish air force display team. Examples were operated in the ground-attack role and on fighter duties.

REPUBLIC

F-84F THUNDERSTREAK

● NATO ground attacker ● Tactical nuclear bomber ● Reconnaissance

Republic's F-84F Thunderstreak hit the scene when the straight-wing F-84 was rebuilt with swept wings, reconfigured air intake and canopy, and an improved engine. The resulting fighter-bomber served the United States and 12 other nations, mostly in NATO, for over a decade. This subsonic warplane was heavy and was never more than an adequate performer, but its versatility ensured a long career.

▲ *The Republic F-84 was a mainstay of NATO fighter strength in the 1950s and 1960s. Tasked with the vital tactical nuclear delivery role in the 1960s, it was the post-war Luftwaffe's first jet.*

PHOTO FILE

REPUBLIC F-84F THUNDERSTREAK

▲ Photo jet
The RF-84F was a photo reconnaissance variant, with side-mounted intakes to allow for the large camera-filled nose section.

Rocket strike ▶
The Thunderstreak could launch all 24 of its 7-cm (2.76-in) rockets in one salvo. These weapons were very powerful, if not too accurate.

▲ Deadly arsenal
The Thunderstreak could deliver a shattering array of weaponry, including rockets, 20-mm cannon fire, napalm and nuclear bombs.

▼ Hooked up
Aerial refuelling was vital to the nuclear-strike role. Despite this, pilots knew that most missions would be 'one way'.

▲ Fire-bomb practice
The F-84F never dropped napalm in anger, unlike the straight-winged F-84G, which did so in Korea. This aircraft is unloading over a Nevada range in 1954.

Tanker's eye view ▶
This refuelling method requires the fighter merely to fly straight and level, as the boom operator does all the difficult work from the tanker.

FACTS AND FIGURES

- The YF-96, essentially the prototype for the F-84F, first flew on 3 June 1950.
- The first F-84F flew in 1951, but engine snags delayed service delivery until 1955.
- In all 2713 F-84Fs were built: 2476 by Republic and 237 by General Motors' Kansas City Division.
- At the height of the Cold War in 1965, 57 per cent of the fighter-bombers in Western Europe were Thunderstreaks.
- The YF-84J test ship, based on an F-84F, had a much more powerful engine.
- The Italian air force aerobatic team flew F-84Fs between 1957 and 1959.

PROFILE

NATO's tactical nuclear striker

The rocket-armed F-84F was an extremely potent tactical fighter in the 1950s and 1960s. Few would have guessed that the aircraft would still be providing useful service to NATO in the early 1980s, flying tactical reconnaissance missions for the Greek and Turkish air forces.

Developmental problems were rampant when Curtiss-Wright built a licensed British Sapphire engine for a swept-wing F-84, which was at first designated YF-96. The engine never yielded the 34.7 kN (7,804 lb thrust) once promised, but the F-84F proved successful, partly because it was tough and strong, and could deliver a potent load of bombs.

Early hopes that the Thunderstreak might prove to be a MiG-killer were forlorn: the F-84F introduced a new standard of precision as a fighter-bomber, but other performance shortfalls made it an adequate dogfighter at best.

Although it was a little heavy on the controls, the F-84F gave its pilot a roomy cockpit with fair visibility. In some units pilots relentlessly practised a 'lob' technique to deliver tactical atomic bombs. In nuclear war, their mission would have taken them one-way to Russia or Eastern Europe. Most F-84F outfits in the United States and NATO had a conventional mission, however, as did the Air National Guard squadrons which used this fighter-bomber late in its career.

The F-84F wing had a pronounced 'anhedral', angled downward from the wingroot, giving lively handling characteristics.

F-84Fs were usually fitted with two very large tanks when flying in the nuclear-strike role. The nuclear bomb went on the aircraft's centre pylon.

Despite having more thrust than its straight-winged predecessor, the F-84F was not much faster due to the drag of its deeper fuselage.

F-84F Thunderstreak

Type: single-seat fighter-bomber

Powerplant: one 32.12-kN (7,224-lb-thrust) Wright/Buick J65-W-3 Sapphire turbojet engine

Maximum speed: 1118 km/h (695 mph) at sea level

Combat radius: high altitude with two drop-tanks 1304 km (810 miles)

Service ceiling: 14,020 m (46,000 ft)

Weights: empty 6273 kg (13,830 lb); loaded 12,700 kg (28,000 lb)

Armament: six 12.7-mm (0.5-in) Browning M3 machine guns, up to 2722 kg (6,000 lb) of external bombs and rockets including tactical nuclear weapons

Dimensions:		
	span	10.24 m (33 ft 7 in)
	length	13.23 m (43 ft 5 in)
	height	4.38 m (14 ft 4 in)
	wing area	30.19 m² (325 sq ft)

F-84F THUNDERSTREAK

This is a Republic F-84F Thunderstreak of the United States Air Force, serving in the tactical nuclear-strike role, as indicated by the 'mushroom cloud' badge just under the canopy.

The wing of the Thunderstreak was swept sharply back at 38.5°. It was very broad in chord, and incorporated large leading-edge slats and large trailing-edge flaps.

Two very powerful perforated airbrakes were mounted just behind the wingroots.

USAF F-84Fs were left in a natural polished metal finish, but most NATO air forces camouflaged their aircraft, especially when they 'went nuclear'.

The Sapphire engine was first chosen for the RAF's Hawker Hunter fighter, but was prone to flame-outs when the aircraft fired its guns.

The ventral fairing under the jetpipe housed an emergency brake parachute.

COMBAT DATA

MAXIMUM SPEED

Although on paper the Thunderstreak was as fast as both the MiG-15 and the Sabre, it was never able to match the other two swept-wing jets in combat, as its pilots encountered severe and sometimes fatal handling problems in high-*g* manoeuvring.

F-84F THUNDERSTREAK	1118 km/h (695 mph)
F-86 SABRE	1118 km/h (695 mph)
MiG-15bis 'FAGOT'	1100 km/h (684 mph)

FERRY RANGE

The swept-wing F-84's deep fuselage could hold a great deal of fuel, and with underwing tanks it had probably the longest range of any tactical fighter of the early 1950s. This, together with its speed, made it suitable for the deep penetration nuclear strike mission to which it was assigned.

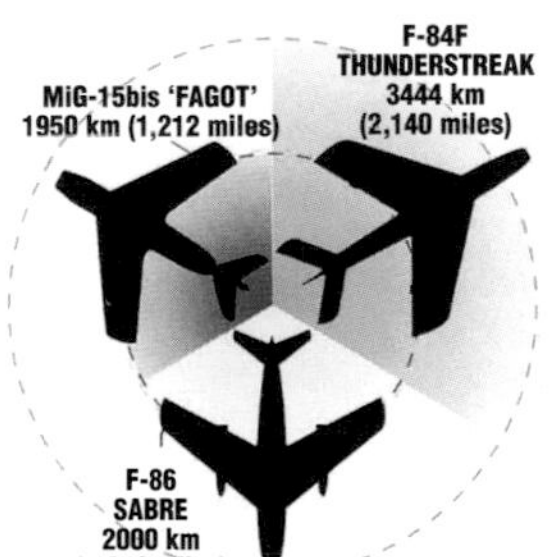

ARMAMENT

As with most Republic fighter designs, the Thunderstreak was a big, heavy and tough machine, able to carry and deliver a heavy weapons load with considerable precision. In common with most American fighters of the period, however, its gun fit was less powerful than was standard in European warplanes.

Cold War nuclear attack mission

TACTICAL NUCLEAR STRIKE: The F-84F's most important mission in the event of war would have been to make tactical nuclear strikes against military targets deep inside Eastern Europe. These would have been low-level, high-speed missions with little prospect of survival.

PENETRATING THE DEFENCES: The mission profile was dictated by the Warsaw Pact's extensive air-defence network. By flying fast and low, the Thunderstreak pilot limited the amount of time he might be illuminated by enemy radar systems.

ATTACK PROFILE: Toss-bombing with parachute-retarded weapons maximized the range from which the F-84 could attack, giving the pilot more chance to elude the ensuing nuclear blast.

ON TARGET: The F-84F was designed to take out key targets such as headquarters, communication centres, supply centres and military airfields.

REPUBLIC
F-105 THUNDERCHIEF

● Fighter-bomber ● Heavy ordnance load ● MiG-killer

On a bombing mission to Hanoi, Republic F-105 Thunderchief pilots faced considerable danger. Surface-to-air missiles (SAMs), anti-aircraft guns and MiG fighters were all intent on downing the Thunderchief before it reached its target. Geography, however, gave the F-105 pilot one ally; a high ridge known as 'Thud Ridge' which extended from the Laotian border almost to Hanoi, along which targets could be approached in relative safety.

▲ *During the arduous Rolling Thunder bombing campaign which lasted from 1965 to 1968, the US Air Force's F-105D Thunderchiefs bore the brunt of the missions. The aircraft were mainly employed in large strike packages, attacking strategic targets.*

PHOTO FILE

REPUBLIC F-105 THUNDERCHIEF

◀ **Early 'Thuds'**
Some of the first F-105Ds to reach Vietnam retained their buzz-number below the cockpit. During 1965 a programme of camouflage application began.

▲ **Into combat**
All F-105D units were based in Thailand and undertook long transit flights to reach targets in North Vietnam.

▲ **Takhli Thunder**
'RU'-tailcodes indicate that this aircraft was based at Takhli Royal Thai Air Force Base.

◀ **Rolling Thunder**
Seen at the height of Rolling Thunder operations during 1967, these fully camouflaged F-105s typify the many hundreds engaged in combat.

◀ **Air-to-air**
Seen through the sight of a second F-105D, a Thunderchief is engaged by a MiG-17.

▲ **Essential refuelling**
Such was the length of F-105 missions that air-to-air refuelling was a feature of most sorties.

FACTS AND FIGURES

➤ During much of the Vietnam War, F-105 'fighters' bombed strategic targets while B-52 'bombers' flew tactical missions.

➤ Two F-105 pilots were awarded the Medal of Honor for their courage.

➤ F-105 pilots were required to complete 100 missions before leaving Vietnam.

➤ According to one analysis, an F-105 pilot would almost certainly be shot down by the time of his 68th sortie.

➤ F-105Ds shot down 25 MiGs, using cannon and AIM-9 Sidewinder missiles.

➤ The value of all aircraft lost in Vietnam was estimated at US$3,129,948,000.

PROFILE

Fighting 'Thuds' over Vietnam

Almost one-third of all Republic F-105 Thunderchiefs came to the end of their lives in the fiercely defended skies over North Vietnam, with a total of 397 being lost during the conflict. It was hostile terrain, except for the jagged, 100-km (62-mile) ridge line which aircrews called 'Thud Ridge' after the nickname of their F-105s.

An F-105, or 'Thud' heading north from Thailand with a typical load of eight 340-kg (750-lb) bombs would be able to attack its target successfully only by outwitting the enemy's missiles, MiGs, and anti-aircraft fire. Typically, the F-105 pilot refuelled from a tanker, communicated with a command and control aircraft or a forward air controller (FAC), and then plunged into the hell of enemy airspace. Many aircraft fell and a host of pilots died fighting the most comprehensive anti-aircraft defences assembled up to that time.

Often, the pilot's approach to the target included hiding behind 'Thud Ridge' for a portion of the trip. This enabled the F-105 to attack targets like Kep airfield near Hanoi with a degree of surprise. It was some of the most dangerous flying in the history of air warfare, but the F-105 was a fine aircraft and its well-trained pilots fought valiantly, attacking ground targets and destroying MiG-17s in air-to-air combat.

Decades after the conflict, the F-105 is still highly regarded by all who flew it.

Above: This 355th Tactical Fighter Wing (TFW) aircraft carries a load of M117 and Mk 82 bombs, some with extended fuses.

Below: Preparing for a 1962 weapons meet at Nellis Air Force Base, Nevada, this F-105 demonstrates the combat readiness of USAF aircrews and their aircraft.

F-105D Thunderchief

Type: single-seat tactical fighter

Powerplant: one 117.92-kN 26,532-lb-thrust) Pratt & Whitney J75-P-19W afterburning turbojet engine

Maximum speed: 2237 km/h (1390 mph) at 10,975 m (36,000 ft)

Initial climb rate: 10,515 m/min (34,498 fpm)

Combat range: 2975 km (1849 miles)

Service ceiling: 15,850 m (52,000 ft)

Weights: empty 12,474 kg (27,500 ft); maximum take-off 23,834 kg (52,545 ft)

Armament: one 20-mm M61A1 Vulcan cannon with 1028 rounds plus, typically, eight 340-kg (750-lb) bombs on a bombing mission to Hanoi or a maximum of 6350 kg (14,000 lb) of ordnance

Dimensions:		
	span	10.65 m (34 ft 11 in)
	length	19.58 m (64 ft 3 in)
	height	5.99 m (19 ft 8 in)
	wing area	35.76 m² (385 sq ft)

F-105D Thunderchief

Two USAF tactical fighter wings flew the F-105 in combat over Vietnam. The aircraft arrived in-theatre, and began operations, wearing bright unit markings over their natural metal finish.

An ejection seat was vital for combat operations. Almost 400 F-105s went down over Vietnam, with several pilots being the subject of successful and dramatic rescue attempts. Others were less fortunate.

This early configuration with single M117 bombs on the outboard pylons was soon replaced by the normal load of two tanks, six M117s on the centreline pylon, an electronic countermeasures pod on one outboard pylon and an AIM-9 on the other.

Even though it offered 117.92 kN (26,532 lb thrust), the J75 engine left the F-105D underpowered. Afterburner was needed to keep a heavily laden 'Thud' on the tanker at altitude.

U.S.AIR FORCE FH-398 24398

Several F-105D pilots put the faithful M61 20-mm, six-barrelled cannon to good use. The majority of F-105 MiG-17 kills were achieved with the cannon, although at least three involved AIM-9 Sidewinder shots.

A 1703-litre (375-gallon) drop tank was carried on each inboard wing pylon for most missions. In-flight refuelling was also necessary, but once topped up the F-105D could remain on station for long periods, with its large ordnance load giving good combat persistence.

The F-105 could absorb extensive combat damage. One aircraft returned with an accidentally fired AIM-9 embedded in the tailpipe!

COMBAT DATA

MAXIMUM SPEED

Until the McDonnell Douglas F-4 began to reach the Vietnamese theatre in numbers, the F-105D was one of the USAF's fastest combat aircraft. These figures are for speed 'clean' at altitude, but the F-105D was easily supersonic, bombed-up, at sea level.

F-105D THUNDERCHIEF 2237 km/h (1390 mph)

F-100D SUPER SABRE 1390 km/h (864 mph)

F-4E PHANTOM II 2390 km/h (1485 mph)

CLIMB RATE

Even by today's standards the F-4E offered outstanding climb performance. The powerful Thunderchief was a better performer than the older North American F-100D and was able to use its performance in evading enemy defences.

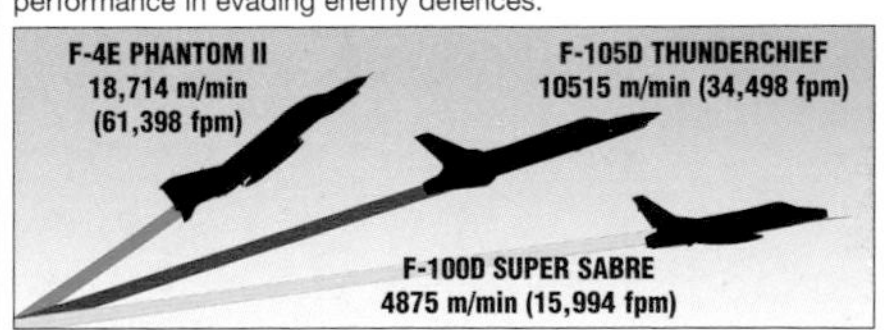

ARMAMENT

All three of these tactical aircraft featured gun armament. That on the F-4E was rushed into service in this model of Phantom after all-missile-armed F-4s had highlighted the need for guns during close-in air-to-air combat.

'Thud' combat versatility

WEAPONS AND TACTICS: Having entered the war mainly as a 'dumb' bomber, the F-105 acquired new weapons and tactics.

BULLPUP OPERATIONS: F-105Ds employed the AGM-12A/B Bullpup missile against the Thanh Hoa Bridge, with little success.

PAUL DOUMER BRIDGE: Alternatively known as The Hanoi Railroad and Highway Bridge, the Doumer Bridge was an obvious and vital target against which many F-105s were committed. Although the 'Thuds' caused some damage, F-4Ds armed with laser-guided bombs were needed to complete the job.

CLOUD BOMBING: Bombing jungle targets through cloud cover was a common practice. The radar-equipped EB-66 acted as pathfinder.

ROCKWELL B-1A

● Mach 2 bomber prototype ● Four built ● Predecessor of B-1B Lancer

Rockwell's B-1A was the great white hope of the late 1970s while the Cold War was raging. This was a 'swing-wing' bomber, capable of supersonic speed and hauling heavy bombs, that would finally, belatedly, replace the B-52 Stratofortress. However, those who complained that the B-52 should have been retired long before were premature if they expected the B-1A to replace it. President Jimmy Carter had other ideas.

▲ *Rolled out on 26 October 1974 and first flown on 23 December, the first of four B-1A prototypes was 74-0158. The expense of the programme was the major factor in its cancellation.*

PHOTO FILE

ROCKWELL B-1A

▼ Mach 2 top speed
The Rockwell B-1A was designed from the outset to be capable of twice the speed of sound at altitude.

▲ Crew escape capsule
Like the F-111 before it, the B-1 employed a crew escape capsule rather than ejection seats to allow the crew to leave the aircraft in an emergency at high speed. Normal ejection at high speeds would be fatal.

Swing wings ▶
A key feature of the B-1 was its swing wings, fully forward (15° sweep) for low-speed flight and landing, and swept to 67° for high-speed dashes.

▼ Cockpit layout
The B-1 featured fighter-type control sticks, vertical scale flight instruments and TV screens for a forward-looking infra-red image.

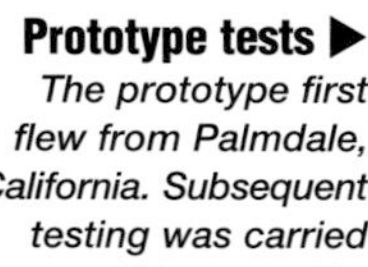

Prototype tests ▶
The prototype first flew from Palmdale, California. Subsequent testing was carried out at Edwards AFB.

FACTS AND FIGURES

- ➤ The prototype B-1A first flew on 23 December 1974 and made 79 test flights totalling 405 flight hours.
- ➤ The second B-1A crashed on its 127th flight on 29 August 1984, killing the pilot.
- ➤ B-1As had a crew of four: two pilots and offensive and defensive systems officers.
- ➤ On 19 April 1976 the US Secretary of Defense, Donald Rumsfeld, flew a B-1A with a Rockwell test pilot.
- ➤ The second and fourth B-1As were used as test aircraft for B-1B development.
- ➤ On 5 October 1978, the second B-1A briefly hit a speed of Mach 2.22.

PROFILE

SAC's ill-fated Mach 2 bomber

The Rockwell B-1A was the bomber of the 1970s that paved the way for the Rockwell B-1B Lancer, 100 of which were built in the 1980s.

However, the B-1A differed from the Lancer in several important ways. It was designed to fly at Mach 2, bomb from high altitude and have only a limited low-level capability. It had greater wing sweep and bomb-carrying capacity and had a very different avionics fit.

From 1974 until 1977, three glossy-white B-1As flying at Edwards Air Force Base, California, were believed to be prototypes of a new Strategic Air Command bomber, one that would supplant the ageing Boeing B-52 Stratofortress which was scheduled to retire in 1975.

A contract for the Advanced Manned Strategic Aircraft (AMSA) was awarded in 1970, with the first B-1A flying in 1974.

In 1977, President Carter struck what appeared to be a fatal blow by cancelling the B-1A programme. Concerns were raised regarding the huge cost of the 240 aircraft that SAC had requested. It was concluded that the job of striking at the Soviet Union could be carried out by B-52s armed with 'stand-off' weapons. Besides, any new manned bomber would have to be optimized for low-level flight. When Ronald Reagan became president in 1981, he revived the B-1 to create just such an aircraft, the B-1B.

Above: Unusually, the first flight of the prototype B-1A was also the first flight of the YF101 turbofan. New engines are more often tested in an existing airframe before being flown in a new aircraft type.

Below: The B-1A's undercarriage retracted into the fuselage between the engine nacelles. Each main leg was supported by a four-wheel bogie.

B-1A

Type: strategic bomber

Powerplant: four 136.93-kN (30,797-lb-thrust) General Electric F101-GE-100 turbofan engines with afterburning

Maximum speed: Mach 2.22 or 2351 km/h (1,461 mph) at 15,240 m (50,000 ft)

Range: 9815 km (6,099 miles)

Service ceiling: 12,000 m (39,370 ft)

Weights: empty approx. 72,575 kg (160,000 lb); maximum take-off 176,810 kg (389,800 lb)

Armament: maximum of 52,160 kg (114,993 lb) of stores, including up to 24 1016-kg (2,240-lb) AGM-69A Short-Range Attack Missiles (SRAMs), Air-Launched Cruise Missiles (ALCMs) and decoy missiles

Dimensions:

span (swept)	23.84 m (78 ft 3 in)
span (unswept)	41.67 m (136 ft 9 in)
length	45.78 m (150 ft 2 in)
height	10.24 m (33 ft 7 in)
wing area	181.2 m² (1,950 sq ft)

B-1A

Glossy-white 74-0158 was the first of three B-1A prototypes built and test flown before cancellation in 1977. A fourth example flew in 1979 after the Carter Administration agreed to allow testing to continue.

In common with prototype aircraft under test, the first B-1 was fitted with a 'candy-striped' instrumentation boom on the tip of the nose radome.

Two of the three 4.57-m (12-ft) long weapons bays were located ahead of the wings, the third being above the end of the engine nacelle. Fuel tankage was located in the wings and the rear fuselage. The B-1A was also able to refuel in the air.

The high-altitude bombing role of the B-1A was reflected in the 'anti-flash' white colour scheme applied to the prototypes. Anti-flash schemes are intended to reflect heat from a nuclear blast, protecting the airframe and crew.

An 'all-moving' tailplane was fitted. Below this, in the rear fuselage, was a large avionics bay. The B-1A was equipped with a comprehensive electronic countermeasures suite to provide some protection against Russian surface-to-air missiles and fighters. The B-1B relies on flying at low level for defence.

The first three prototypes carried the serials 74-0158, -0159 and -0160. The fourth aircraft, 76-0174, did not fly until 1979, after the B-1A programme was cancelled.

U.S. AIR FORCE

40158

A blue ribbon decorated with stars and highlighting the Strategic Air Command emblem was wrapped around the nose.

Movable foreplanes either side of the nose below the cockpit were part of the Low-Altitude Ride Control (LARC) system. This was designed to make the often bumpy conditions during high-speed flight at low altitude more bearable.

Power for the B-1A was provided by four General Electric F101-GE-100 afterburning turbofans. This engine was test flown in such aircraft as the F-16 fighter and was the basis for the later F110 turbofan.

COMBAT DATA

MAXIMUM SPEED

The B-1A's Mach 2 capability was sacrificed in the B-1B in order to improve other performance features. Wing sweep was reduced and engine air intakes were simplified. Both types outperformed the ageing B-52, however.

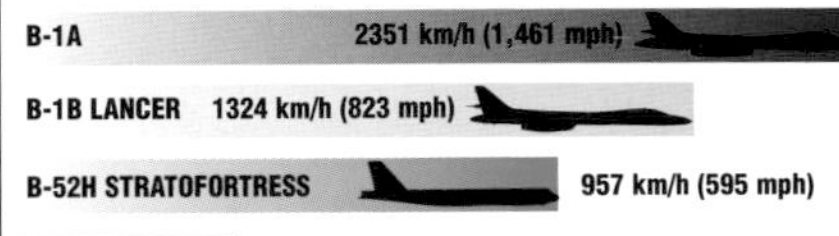

ARMAMENT

The B-1B was required to carry an even larger load than that of the B-1A and a wider variety of weapons. The B-52 can only carry about half this load, but over a greater range.

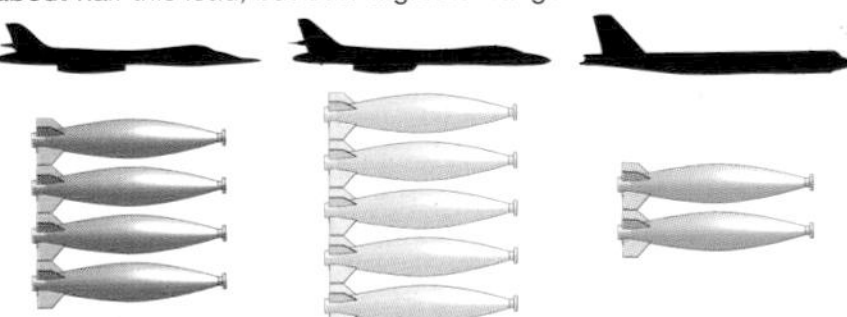

B-1A 52,160 kg (114,993 lb) | B-1B LANCER 56,699 kg (125,000 lb) | B-52H STRATOFORTRESS 22,680 kg (50,000 lb)

RANGE

The B-52's exceptional range is hard to better in an aircraft such as the B-1. The B-52 was intended to carry a relatively light nuclear bombload over very long ranges. While the B-1A was short on range, the B-1B was an improvement.

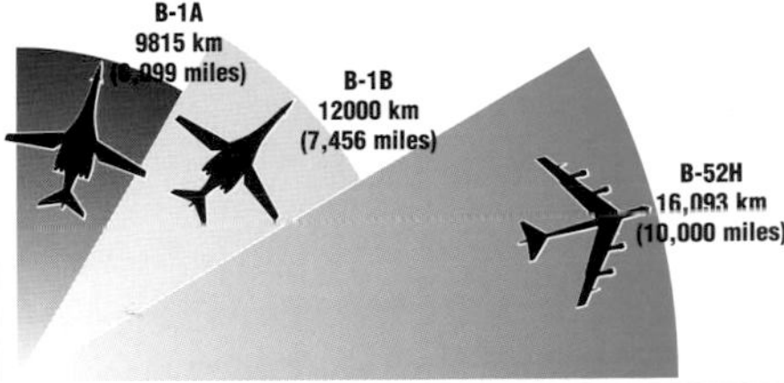

USAF jet bomber prototypes

CONVAIR XB-46: Straight-winged, four-engined and the USAF's fastest bomber when it first flew, the B-46 did not reach production.

CONVAIR YB-60: Based on the B-36, the B-60 was Convair's 1950s bomber contender in the competition won by the Boeing B-52.

NORTH AMERICAN XB-70 VALKYRIE: Intended to replace the B-52, the Mach 3 XB-70 was cancelled in the late 1960s. Two were built.

NORTHROP YRB-49A: One of the Northrop 'flying wing' family, the six-engined RB-49 would have been used as a reconnaissance bomber.

ROCKWELL

B-1B LANCER

● Strategic nuclear bomber ● Supersonic swing wing ● Cruise carrier

▲ *The B-1B combines stealth features with highly sophisticated defensive avionics. It has the ability to carry more bombs than the old B-52, and can fly low-level attack missions at high speed.*

It may lack the glamour of the stealthy B-2 flying wing or the reverence accorded to the 50-year-old B-52 Stratofortress, but the Rockwell B-1B Lancer is a highly advanced supersonic bomber. With its tremendous capacity to carry immense loads of nuclear and conventional weaponry, the Lancer has now become America's primary low-level, supersonic, nuclear strike asset.

PHOTO FILE

ROCKWELL B-1B LANCER

Fast dash ▶
With its wings swept, the Lancer can exceed Mach 1 at height, and gives a comfortable low-level ride at near-sonic speeds.

▲ Sleek and deadly
The long nose of the B-1B houses the Westinghouse AN/APQ-164 attack radar, derived from the F-16's APG-66. Most of the other electronic gear is classified.

▲ Low and slow
The high-lift devices on the B-1B's wing and blended fuselage give the big bomber very smooth handling. The flight control system is a mix of traditional hydraulics, with fly-by-wire outboard spoilers.

◀ High tail
Like the Russian Tu-160, the B-1B has a high-set tail to avoid the engine efflux. The bulge under the tail houses the defensive tail warning components of the AN/ALQ-161 system.

▲ Loading the bomb
The main weapons for the B-1B are the SRAM nuclear missile and the B28, B61 and B83 free-fall nuclear bombs. Future weapons options include cruise missiles and advanced precision-guided conventional munitions.

▼ Sweeping wings
Fuel is moved automatically to counter the large changes in trim as the wings change position. The variable geometry allows the B-1 to operate from relatively short runways.

FACTS AND FIGURES

➤ The all-white B-1A flew at Palmdale, California, on 23 December 1974.

➤ On 4 September 1984, the first B-1B was rolled out at Rockwell's Palmdale plant.

➤ The B-1B made its first flight on 18 October 1984, 15 years after design work began.

➤ One B-1B crashed in trials when the crew overrode the fuel transfer computer and unbalanced the aircraft.

➤ The first B-1Bs were assigned to the 96th Bomb Wing at Dyess AFB, Texas.

➤ The four crew sit in Weber-built ACES II (Advanced Concept Ejection Seats).

PROFILE

Low-level strategic striker

Making a low-level penetration of enemy territory, the B-1B crew flies 'zipped up', shielded from thermonuclear flash-blindness by blast curtains equipped with PLZT (polarised lead zirconium titanate).

The B-1B incorporates a number of stealth features, and has a radar cross-section one-fourth that of a B-52. This gives the Lancer an excellent chance of penetrating enemy defences and dropping its bombs without being detected.

Pilot and co-pilot sit side-by-side in a cockpit with both digital and analogue instruments. The B-1B is flown like a fighter, using a stick and rudder pedals.

Crew members 3 and 4, known as the OSO and DSO (offensive and defensive systems operators), sit side-by-side behind the pilots. They have small windows but cannot see a great deal outside the aircraft.

The B-1 entered service primarily as a carrier of free-fall nuclear bombs, with a maximum load of 24 B61 devices. With minor modifications it can carry a heavy load of cruise missiles, and as the ageing B-52 fleet is retired the huge swing-wing bomber will probably become a cruise missile carrier.

Left: The evolution of the B-1B has not been easy. There have been many problems bringing into service such an advanced aircraft, especially involving the defensive ECM (electronic countermeasures) system and the engines.

Below: The B-1's origins date from the 1960s, when it was realised that Soviet air defences would imperil any high-flying aircraft, even the planned Mach 3-capable B-70 Valkyrie. But switching to low level presented designers with a whole new set of problems.

B-1B Lancer

Type: four-crew strategic bomber

Powerplant: four 133.57-kN (29,964-lb.-thrust) General Electric F101-GE-102 turbofans

Maximum operational speed: Mach 0.99 or 1207 km/h (748 m.p.h.), although the aircraft can reach Mach 1.2

Range: 11,675 km (7,239 mi.)

Service ceiling: more than 15,000 m (49,200 ft.)

Weights: empty 87,090 kg (191,598 lb.); loaded 216,368 kg (476,010 lb.)

Armament: eight cruise missiles or 12 B28 nuclear bombs, or 24 B61/B83 nuclear bombs; theoretical maximum conventional weapons load of 60,782 kg (133,720 lb.)

Dimensions:

span (unswept)	41.66 m (137 ft.)
span (swept)	23.84 m (78 ft.)
length	47.80 m (157 ft.)
height	10.24 m (34 ft.)
wing area	181.10 m² (1,949 sq. ft.)

B-1B LANCER

The 95-strong B-1B force is operated by the US Air Force's Air Combat Command. This aircraft is assigned to the 28th Bomb Wing at Ellsworth AFB.

The wing has seven-segment leading-edge flaps and six-segment trailing-edge flaps. There are no ailerons, and roll control is effected by spoilers.

The engine intakes have been designed to shield the engine compressor fans from hostile radar beams. Since the compressor would otherwise give a strong radar return, this feature automatically reduces the bomber's signature.

All USAF strategic aircraft now carry low-visibility markings, with black lettering and reduced-size coloured unit emblems.

An advanced terrain-following radar system enables the huge bomber to make blind low-level attacks.

The original B-1A had an ejection capsule like the F-111, but the B-1B has separate crew compartments and individual ejection seats for the pilots and systems operators.

The B-1B has a pair of small composite vanes under the cockpit. These provide yaw and pitch damping, smoothing the ride at low level.

The fuselage structure is mainly aluminium and titanium alloy, with some composite glass fibre.

There are three internal weapon bays, two forward of the wing and one aft, covered by a large hydraulic-powered door. The bay can house the Common Strategic Rotary Launcher (CSRL) also used in the B-2 and B-52.

B-1 nuclear strike

STAND-OFF ATTACK: B-1s were designed to be armed with free-fall bombs, which could be 'tossed' several kilometres, or with SRAM nuclear missiles, with ranges of 50 km (30 mi.) at low level or more than 200 km (125 mi.) at altitude.

HIGH-LEVEL STRIKE: The original attack profile envisaged for the B-1A called for the aircraft to attack at high speed and from high level. But surface-to-air missiles would have made this suicidal long before the first metal was cut on the prototype.

LAUNCH FROM SAFETY: The advent of the air-launched cruise missile meant that nuclear bombers could attack from ranges of 2000 km (1,240 mi) or more and still hit targets with pinpoint accuracy.

LOW-LEVEL PENETRATION: The B-1's swing wings meant that it was a superb performer at low level, and it entered service as a low-level penetration bomber.

COMBAT DATA

CONVENTIONAL WEAPONS LOAD

Although the B-1B can carry up to 60 tonnes of conventional weaponry in its three bomb-bays and on 12 underwing weapons stations, operationally it will probably be limited to 85 Mk 82 227-kg general-purpose bombs or 20 AGM-86C conventionally-armed air-launched cruise missiles. As the B-52 force is retired, Lancers will acquire the ability to deliver a variety of precision-guided munitions as well as Harpoon anti-ship missiles.

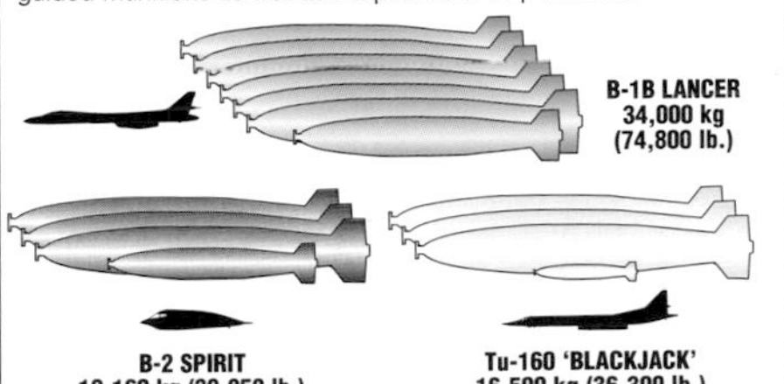

ROCKWELL

OV-10 BRONCO

● Forward air control ● Vietnam veteran ● Counter-insurgency

Rockwell's OV-10 Bronco was a product from early lessons learned in the Vietnam War. Designed as a COIN (counter-insurgency) aircraft, it evolved into an armed, agile forward air control (FAC) machine directing fighter-bombers to their targets. The Bronco began as a US Air Force warplane, but performed its final service in the Persian Gulf War, where the US Marine Corps used it over the battlefield to great effect.

▲ *Forward air control is a demanding mission, in which pilots must call in strikes while they are exposed to gunfire. The excellent view from the Bronco is appreciated by FAC officers.*

PHOTO FILE

ROCKWELL OV-10 BRONCO

▲ Night striker
Marine Corps OV-10Ds have been updated for the night observation role. They are armed with the M197 20-mm cannon, which is aimed by an AAS-37 infra-red tracker and laser designator pod.

▲ USAF retirement
Repeatedly declared obsolete, the OV-10 was finally retired from the USAF's inventory. It has been replaced by the Fairchild OA-10.

◀ Setting off
Despite its age, the Bronco was popular with crews, who enjoyed the excitement of low flying in a simple aircraft.

Rocket launcher ▶
Standard armament for the FAC mission in Vietnam was the rocket pod, usually containing phosphorus markers.

▼ Strike pair
Armed with powerful fuel-air explosive bombs and machine-guns, the Bronco has a potent tactical strike capability.

▲ Marine favourite
The Bronco was favoured by the Marines, who see close support as a key mission. They also used the type for clandestine special forces insertions.

FACTS AND FIGURES

- ➤ Eleven companies participated in the early 1960s FAC aircraft competition.
- ➤ The Bronco prototype first flew on 16 July 1965 at Columbus, Ohio.
- ➤ The Marine Corps and USAF took delivery of their first Broncos on the same day, 23 February 1968.
- ➤ In Vietnam, the US Navy briefly operated a light-attack squadron, the 'Black Ponies', equipped with 18 armed Broncos.
- ➤ Two OV-10s were shot down during Operation Desert Storm.
- ➤ A Bronco was shot down in Venezuela in November 1992 during a coup attempt.

PROFILE

Tree-top flying on the front line

After almost two decades of soldiering, seeing combat from Vietnam to the Persian Gulf, the familiar, twin-boomed shape of the OV-10 Bronco is no longer seen in military colours – except, possibly, in Venezuela, where a few may still be in service. Nowadays, you can see Broncos in Montana working with the US Forest Service, or in Virginia flying law enforcement missions.

The OV-10 was ordered in 1964 and reached Vietnam in 1969. Bronco variants served in Germany (which used a turbojet-boosted model for target towing), Indonesia, Morocco and Venezuela. The most advanced version was the Marine Corps OV-10D-Plus, which incorporated night observation capability and forward-looking infra-red sensors and was employed on covert special forces insertion missions as well as forward air control.

By the 1990s, many in the Corps were arguing that the OV-10 was too slow to survive in modern combat, when it might fall victim to shoulder-mounted heat-seeking missiles, but there was strong protest within Marine ranks when in 1993 the decision was made to retire the Bronco.

The OV-10 was the subject of much debate, and the future of forward air control missions by fixed-wing aircraft is still contested.

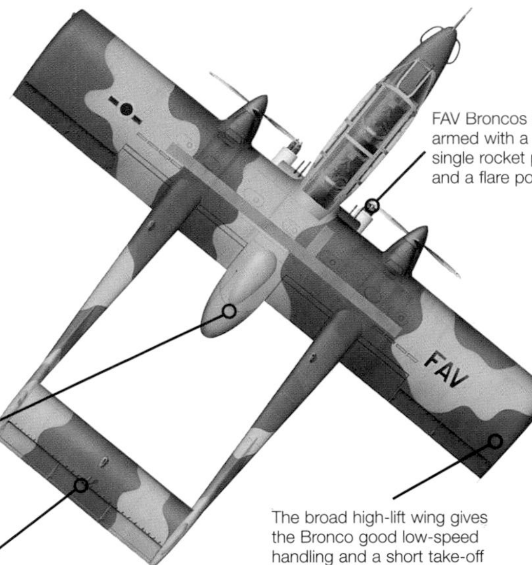

FAV Broncos are armed with a single rocket pod and a flare pod.

The Bronco normally operates with a two-man crew, sitting in tandem.

The tailplane is a fixed-incidence unit with an inset elevator, providing excellent control at low speeds.

The broad high-lift wing gives the Bronco good low-speed handling and a short take-off capability. It can fly slowly enough to escort helicopters.

Uprated engines with infra-red suppressing exhaust ducts were fitted to the OV-10D in an attempt to reduce vulnerability to shoulder-launched heat-seeking surface-to-air missiles.

The long bulged canopy and short nose allows an excellent view of the target area. Both crew members have ejection seats.

Venezuelan Broncos are painted in a jungle colour scheme similar to US aircraft during the Vietnam War. The FAV operates in the surveillance role near the Colombian border.

The central fuselage pod can accommodate two stretchers and a medical attendant, or five paratroopers.

A 568-litre (150-gal.) drop-tank can be carried, in addition to the 976 litres (250 gal.) of internal fuel.

M60 machine-guns are mounted in pairs in each sponson.

The undercarriage is designed to permit operation from tactical airstrips just behind the front line.

OV-10A BRONCO

The OV-10s of the Fuerza Aerea Venezuela (FAV) serve with two squadrons, the 'Geronimos' of 151 Escuadron and 'Zorros' of 152 Escuadron.

OV-10D Bronco

Type: two-seat forward air control aircraft

Powerplant: two Garrett 533-kW (715-hp.) T76-G-420/421 turboprops

Maximum speed: 452 km/h (280 m.p.h.)

Range: 2300 km (1,426 mi.)

Service ceiling: 7315 m (24,000 ft.)

Weights: empty 3161 kg (6,954 lb.); loaded 6552 kg (14,414 lb.)

Armament: one or two GPU-2/A lightweight gun pods containing an M197 Gatling gun coupled to a single-ended ammunition feed system with 300 rounds; high-explosive air-to-surface rocket pods

Dimensions:		
	span	12.67 m (40 ft.)
	length	13.41 m (42 ft.)
	height	4.62 m (15 ft.)
	wing area	27.03 m² (291 sq. ft.)

COMBAT DATA

MAXIMUM SPEED

The Bronco and the US Army Mohawk were designed as military aircraft. Both served extensively in Vietnam, where they had a considerable performance advantage over the Cessna O-2, a twin-engined 'push-pull' light plane that was minimally adapted from the commercial Cessna Model 337 Skymaster.

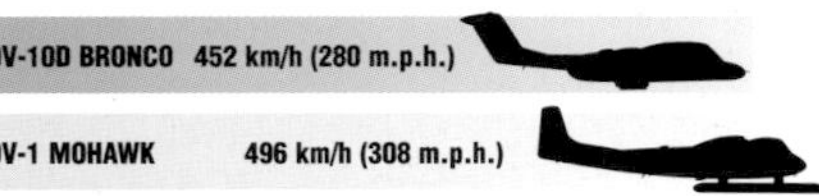

RANGE

All three of the observation aircraft were used to support US and South Vietnamese ground troops. They were deployed to American bases all over Southeast Asia, and the excellent range each displayed meant that they could provide overhead observation wherever US troops were in action.

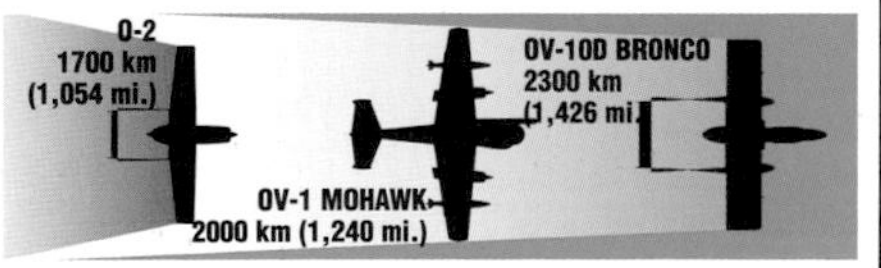

ENDURANCE

The ability to stay in the air for long periods is a definite asset in a forward air control machine. Directing support missions for units cut off on mountain tops or in isolated fire bases, or co-ordinating the rescue of pilots shot down in enemy territory could call for a FAC to stay in the air for several hours.

OV-10D BRONCO	OV-1 MOHAWK	O-2
7 hours 40 minutes	6 hours 30 minutes	6 hours

Forward observation in action

UNDER FIRE: Ground troops are advancing on a suspected enemy position when they come under artillery fire. Taking cover, they look for the enemy.

CALLING FOR HELP: The ground troops call the Forward Air Controller. The only information they can give is the general direction of fire. However, modern infantry are often equipped with locating radar, which tracks the shells in flight and makes a fairly accurate estimate of the position of the enemy battery.

LOCATING THE ENEMY: High above, an observer in an OV-10 follows the vector of the incoming shells, eventually spotting the enemy guns about 10 km away.

GROUND ATTACK: The observer calls in patrolling F/A-18 Hornets, which destroy the enemy artillery battery with a salvo of high-explosive air-to-ground rockets.

SAAB 105

● Saab private venture ● Trainer/ground attack ● Austrian air defence

Designed as a trainer and light attack aircraft for the Swedish air force, the Saab 105 has also been produced as an air defence fighter which is able to carry Sidewinder missiles. Other variants include a specialised reconnaissance aircraft and a four-seat liaison machine. After more than three decades of service, the Saab 105 is currently undergoing a major upgrade and the type looks set to serve well into the 21st century.

▲ *An entire family of highly successful light combat aircraft has evolved from the Saab private-venture trainer/business jet design.*

PHOTO FILE

SAAB 105

Nose modifications ▶
In addition to its highly modified camera nose, the Sk 60C retains an attack capability.

◀ Initial variant
All 150 Sk 60As ordered by the Swedish air force had been delivered by 1968. These aircraft have formed the basis of all subsequent variants. In 1997 about 140 remained in service.

Dispersed attacker ▶
Sk 60Cs taxi at a dispersed airfield site in northern Sweden. The lead aircraft is armed with a dozen 135-mm rockets.

◀ Defending Austria
Saab 105OEs were Austria's sole air defence assets until delivery of Saab Drakens in 1987.

Offensive export ▶
Saab developed the 105XT as a more powerful attack variant for export. This aircraft is firing rockets.

FACTS AND FIGURES

- Saab designed the 105 as a replacement for the Vampire and the various piston-engined trainers of the Swedish air force.
- Karl-Erik Fernberg piloted the 105's first flight on 1 July 1963.
- By the summer of 1998 the 115th, and final, Sk 60 will have been re-engined.
- Most Sk 60 modifications have been carried out by the Swedish government's maintenance organisations.
- The first students began training on the Sk 60 on 17 July 1967.
- Sk 60B/C aircraft can carry 30-mm ADEN cannon pods.

PROFILE

Saab's most versatile product

Five variants of the Saab 105 are in service with the Swedish air force. The Sk 60A was the original trainer, the Sk 60B added a ground attack capability and the Sk 60C is equipped with a nose-mounted reconnaissance camera and an infra-red search unit. A further trainer variant is the Sk 60D, with commercial avionics, which is used for the airline training of reserve officers. The ejection seats have been removed and two extra seats are installed in the rear cockpit. The Sk 60E also has four seats but is used as a liaison aircraft.

Forty of the 105XT model, with J85 turbojets, additional fuel capacity, strengthened wings and improved avionics, were built for Austria. Designated Saab 105OE in Austrian service, they can carry Sidewinder air-to-air missiles for air defence or camera pods for reconnaissance.

Most of the Swedish air force's remaining 105s are being modernised to extend their service lives to at least 2010.

In the late 1980s the SK 60s were fitted with new wings and ejection seats. Structural modifications also enabled them to carry out higher-*g* manoeuvres.

An upgrade programme started in 1995 to replace the original engines with 8.45-kN (1,900-lb.-thrust) Williams-Rolls FJ44 turbofans. The new powerplant will make the aircraft quieter and easier to maintain, as well as improving performance.

Left: A huge Perspex canopy provides excellent visibility. Of value in the training role, this feature is also useful to the crew of the armed Sk 60C, seen here fitted with two ADEN gunpods.

Left: This brightly coloured demonstrator shows off the 105's agility. Sweden's 'Team 60' aerobatic team use the Sk 60 as their display aircraft.

Sk 60B

Type: trainer and light attack aircraft

Powerplant: two 7.29-kN (1,640-lb.-thrust) Turboméca Aubisque turbofans

Maximum speed: 765 km/h (474 m.p.h.) at 6000 m (19,700 ft.)

Climb rate: 1050 m/min (3,445 f.p.m.)

Service range: 1400 km (868 mi.)

Service ceiling: 12,000 m (39,350 ft.)

Weights: empty 2510 kg (5,522 lb.); maximum take-off 4500 kg (9,900 lb.)

Armament: up to 700 kg (1,540 lb.) of bombs, rockets and air-to-air or air-to-ground missiles on six underwing hardpoints

Dimensions:

span	9.50 m	(31 ft. 2 in.)
length	10.50 m	(35 ft. 5 in.)
height	2.70 m	(8 ft. 10 in.)
wing area	16.30 m²	(175 sq. ft.)

Sk 60C

Sk 60s serve with four squadrons of F5 and with 5 divisionen of F16 of the Swedish air force. All aircraft wear F5 unit identification, regardless of where they are based, since they are held in a central maintenance pool.

Combining the attack role of the Sk 60B with a useful tactical reconnaissance capability, the Sk 60C has an extended nose which houses a Fairchild KB-18 panoramic camera and its associated clear windows. The fairing beneath the nose houses an infra-red search unit.

Saab designed the ejection seats of the 105. In four-seat configurations, these may be replaced by upholstered seats or more basic units, suitable for use with parachute and rescue packs.

Upwards- and downwards-hinging doors cover the engine compartment. With both sets of doors open, the majority of the engine's primary systems are revealed, allowing easy maintenance from ground level.

The large number on the tail identifies individual aircraft, while the nose number identifies the unit. Dayglo patches on the wing improve conspicuity.

Saab originally planned a four-seat business jet version of the 105. Although this never materialised, as a consequence the cockpit is very spacious.

Twin, hydraulically-actuated airbrakes are mounted behind the main landing gear doors. One is fitted on either side of the lower fuselage.

Early test flights showed that extensive redesign of the engine intakes and exhausts was necessary. To accommodate these major changes, the underside of the wingroot had to be altered. In addition, a great deal of work was necessary to rectify early engine reliability problems.

COMBAT DATA

THRUST

The Sk 60B appears to lack power when compared to the other two widely used light attack/trainer aircraft. The Saab machine's performance is, however, adequate and it offers the increased reliability and safety of twin-engined operations.

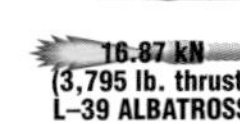

14.58 kN (3,280 lb. thrust) Sk 60B

15.17 kN (3,413 lb. thrust) STRIKEMASTER Mk 88

16.87 kN (3,795 lb. thrust) L-39 ALBATROSS

ORDNANCE

The Saab 105 is a very lightweight aircraft and is therefore restricted to a comparatively light weapon load. Saab has done its utmost to maximise the 105's potential in the attack role, however, by providing compatibility with a wide range of stores, including guided missiles.

Sk 60B 700 kg (1,540 lb.)

STRIKEMASTER Mk 88 1361 kg (2,994 lb.)

L-39 ALBATROSS 1000 kg (2,200 lb.)

CLIMB RATE

In a comparison of climb rates the Sk 60B cannot compete with the Strikemaster or Aero L-39. The ongoing Aubisque engine replacement programme will provide an improvement in performance, however, and neither of the other aircraft is as cost-effective as the Sk 60B.

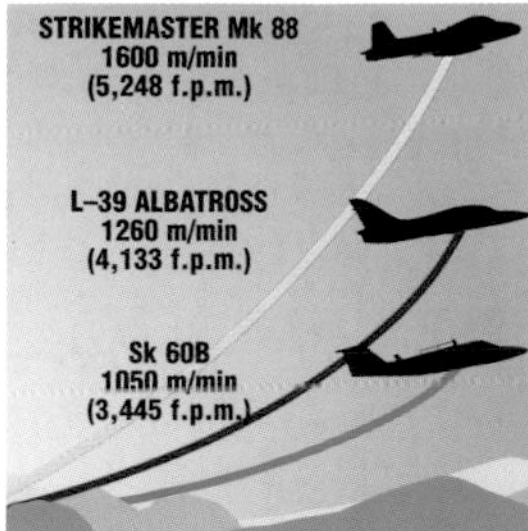

Side-by-side two-seat training jets

CANADAIR CL-41 TUTOR: Another private venture design which resulted in considerable sales, the Tutor was adopted by the Canadian forces and was also exported to Malaysia.

CESSNA T-37: Several hundred T-37s were delivered to the USAF from 1957. A number of aircraft were exported, including 34 to Chile.

BAC (HUNTING) JET PROVOST: Having adapted its piston-engined Provost design to turbojet power, Hunting was able to supply the RAF with its standard primary jet trainer.

Saab

J 35 Draken

● Double-delta design ● Attack fighter ● Tactical reconnaissance

Sweden took a revolutionary leap forward with the Saab J 35 Draken. Offering an innovative double-delta wing, surprisingly low cost and multi-role prowess, the Draken (Dragon) symbolizes Saab's boldness and independence. The Draken was futuristic when it entered service in 1960, and is still formidable approaching retirement today. This excellent aircraft flew in 17 versions, winning acclaim in military roles ranging from Mach 2 interceptor to combat trainer.

▲ *The Draken was the keystone of Sweden's air defence system, combining conscript ground crews with first-class modern equipment.*

Photo File

Saab J 35 Draken

▲ Scandinavian defender
In spite of the Draken's quality, export success was limited. It was sold to all Scandinavian air forces except Norway, with Denmark the only NATO user.

▲ Falconers
The Draken was one of the few jets to be armed with the Hughes Falcon series of missiles, built in Sweden as Rb 26 and Rb 28, in both radar and infra-red versions.

▲ Dragon's lair
Drakens are based at normal airfields, but in emergencies the Swedish air force would disperse them to well-camouflaged roadside hides.

▲ Uprated Draken
The improved J 35D featured an uprated engine based on the Avon 300, a 'zero-zero' ejection seat, extended air intakes and a badly needed increase in internal fuel capacity.

▼ Afterburner take-off
The Draken engine is based on the Rolls-Royce Avon, as used in the Lightning. Take-offs using afterburner have the same dramatic character.

Facts and Figures

- First prototype of the Saab J 35 Draken made its initial flight on 25 October 1955.
- The Draken was vectored to its targets by Sweden's STRIL-60 datalink system.
- The J 35D, first flown on 27 December 1960, had an improved engine and better avionics than earlier versions.
- During 1964, four Drakens formed the Swedish 'Acro Delta' aerobatic team.
- Austria was the last export customer for the Draken, acquiring 24 modified J 35Ds.
- F10 Wing at Angelholm is the last Swedish air force Draken unit, operating the two remaining squadrons.

PROFILE

Sweden's double-delta dragon

Saab's amazing Draken is still unique, four decades after its first flight. Paving new aerodynamic ground with the double-delta wing, tested in 1952 on the subscale Saab 210, the Draken was ready to fly in 1956. By March 1960 the Draken, with its British-designed engine, Swedish electronics and American Falcon missiles, was 'standing alert' with the Swedish air force's F13 Wing at Norrkoping.

Many new Drakens came along over the years. The J 35B was primarily an interceptor, first flown on 29 November 1959. The J 35D had a more powerful engine. The S 35E was a dedicated reconnaissance version, and the Sk 35C was a two-seat trainer.

The 'ultimate' Draken was the J 35F, which equipped eight wings of the Swedish air force. It had improved radar, a single cannon and an infra-red sensor to pick out a target nearly 30 km (19 miles) away. Upgraded as the J 35J, it remained operational in small numbers into the 1990s.

Armed with Sidewinder and Falcon missiles and its hard-hitting 30-mm (1.18-in) cannon, the Draken remains a potent fighter. New pilots still ask to fly this old jet.

Early Drakens carried a pair of British-developed ADEN 30-mm (1.18-in) cannon in the leading edges of the wings, but later variants such as the J 35F have only one gun.

Drakens are powered by Swedish-built variants of the Rolls-Royce Avon, delivering some 8 tonnes (9 tons) of thrust.

The distinctive 'double-delta' wing plan has reduced supersonic drag compared to pure deltas, and also performs better at low airspeeds.

Each of the Draken's control surfaces was operated by two separate hydraulic jacks.

J 35J Draken

Type: single-seat interceptor

Powerplant: one 78.46-kN (17,647-lb-thrust) Volvo Flygmotor RM6C turbojet (Rolls-Royce RB.146 Avon 300 fitted with Volvo-designed afterburner)

Maximum speed: Mach 2 or 2125 km/h (1,320 mph) at 11,000 m (36,089 ft)

Combat radius: 720 km (447 miles)

Service ceiling: 20,000 m (65,617 ft)

Weights: empty 8250 kg (18,188 lb); loaded 12,270 kg (27,051 lb)

Armament: one 30-mm (1.18-in) ADEN M/55 cannon with 90 rounds, two Rb 27 radar missiles and four Rb 28 Falcon or Rb 24 Sidewinder infra-red missiles, or 2900 kg (6,393 lb) of ordnance

Dimensions:	span	9.40 m (30 ft 10 in)
	length	15.35 m (50 ft 4 in)
	height	3.89 m (12 ft 9 in)
	wing area	49.20 m² (530 sq ft)

UBWG 1

J 35F DRAKEN

The J 35F was the most capable Draken, 230 of which were produced for Sweden. Though approaching its last days, some upgraded versions still remain in service with the F10 wing.

The Draken has had various colour schemes in Swedish service. Those remaining in service are all-over air defence grey. The Draken started life in a natural polished metal finish, some receiving this 'splinter' camouflage in the 1960s and 1970s.

The cockpit is narrow, cramped, and uses very old control technology. Yet it remains popular with pilots, possibly because it is a challenge to fly.

The limited rear view from the cockpit was a feature the Draken shared with most of its contemporaries.

The Draken had one of the most advanced fire-control systems of its day, combining the Ericsson PS-01a radar with an infra-red sensor. The sensor could detect targets as far away as 27 km (18 miles).

There are eight stores stations: two fuselage and six underwing.

A small auxiliary tailwheel under the jetpipe was needed to prevent 'tail scrapes' when the Draken landed.

COMBAT DATA

CLIMB RATE

The Draken had an excellent initial climb rate, making it well suited to the role of quick-reacting bomber-interceptor. It could easily outperform contemporary MiG designs, but was unable to catch the Lightning, which with two Rolls-Royce Avon engines had twice the power of the Swedish jet.

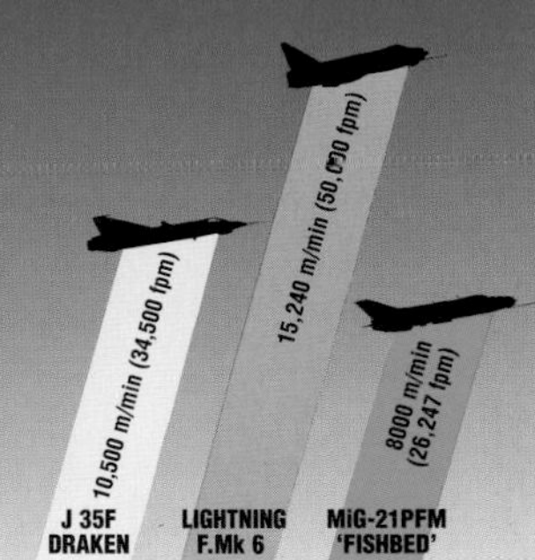

MAXIMUM SPEED

Most fighters of the late 1950s could comfortably break Mach 2. The Draken was almost as fast as the smaller and lighter MiG-21, but fell behind the much bigger and far more powerful Lightning flown by Britain's Royal Air Force.

J 35F DRAKEN 2125 km/h (1,320 mph)

LIGHTNING F.Mk 6 2400 km/h (1,491 mph)

MiG-21bis 'FISHBED' 2230 km/h (1,386 mph)

ARMAMENT

The Drakon was one of the first jets designed as a weapons system, with detection, fire control and weaponry all in one integrated unit. It was vastly more sophisticated than its MiG contemporary, and carried a bigger and better-balanced weapons fit than the Lightning.

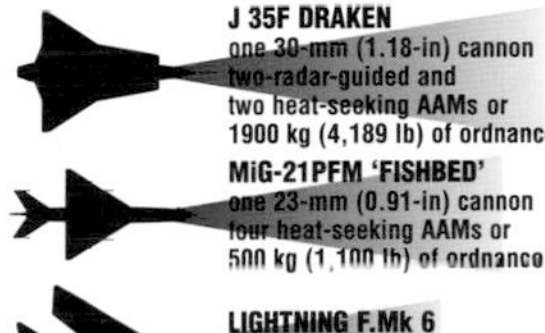

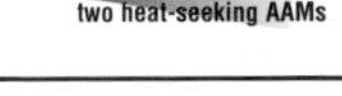

Mach 2 trailblazers

■ ENGLISH ELECTRIC LIGHTNING: Britain's first Mach 2 fighter was as dramatic in its own way as the Draken. Based on the P.1 experimental plane of the early 1950s, the Lightning used immense power to achieve supersonic performance.

■ LOCKHEED F-104 STARFIGHTER: Known as 'the missile with a man in it', the Starfighter, like the Draken, was powered by a single powerful engine. It flew for the first time in February 1954, a year before the Draken prototype.

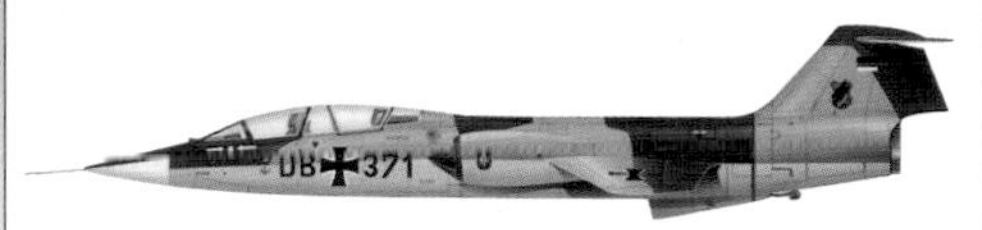

■ DASSAULT MIRAGE III: Also a delta-winged design, the Mirage III flew in 1956, a year after the Draken. Unfettered by the strict Swedish neutrality which limited Saab's sales of its equally effective design, the French exported Mirages widely.

Saab

J 35J Draken

● Upgraded version ● Highway fighter ● Double-delta

Delays to the original schedule for delivery of the Draken's replacement, the JAS 39 Gripen, led the Swedish air force to embark on an upgrade programme to keep two squadrons of J 35s operational until the Gripen was introduced. The aircraft selected were the best examples of the final air defence variant, the J 35F. With improved avionics and two additional wing pylons, the resulting J 35J served with the air force's 10 Wing alongside the Viggen.

▲ *Sweden's neutral situation has ensured that all its defence requirements are met without outside assistance. Here a pilot boards his aircraft on an air defence mission.*

PHOTO FILE

Saab J 35J Draken

'Dragon trainer' ▶
A development of the J 35A was the Sk 35C pilot trainer; the instructor sits in the rear.

▼ Landing roll-out
Reduction of the landing run is accomplished with a drag 'chute and fuselage airbrakes.

◀ Air-to-air armament
The large wing area allows for a varied stores option, which could include Sweden's own AIM-9 Sidewinder derivative and, for longer range combat, the indigenous Rb 27 missile.

▼ Draken overhaul
As the Swedish aircraft were fitted with upgraded avionics an overall grey scheme was applied reflecting current camouflage trends.

▲ Border patrol
Austria received 24 aircraft during 1985. The war in former Yugoslavia ensured that they saw constant use patrolling Austria's border against any violations.

FACTS AND FIGURES

- ➤ Modifications to the J 35J consist of two additional pylons under the intake ducts as well as improved avionics.
- ➤ The undercarriage of the J 35J is narrow enough to operate from Swedish roads.
- ➤ The pilot of the Draken is seated in a reclined ejection seat as in the F-16.
- ➤ Despite a cramped cockpit with old technology the Draken was a much sought after posting within the air force.
- ➤ The Austrian Air Force is the only current operator of Drakens.
- ➤ A few early variants of the Draken still fly in Sweden for trials work.

PROFILE

The Nordic Dragon

Right: The Austrian air force chose the Draken instead of surplus Lightnings from the Saudi Arabian air force.

At least 64 J 35Fs were selected for the J 35J upgrade. This involved splitting the airframe in two. The front section was returned to Saab for modification while the rear part of the airframe was overhauled by FFV.

Externally, the most obvious difference is the extra missile pylon installed under each of the inboard wing sections. These can be used for short-range Sidewinder air-to-air missiles, allowing the original two wing and two fuselage pylons to be used for up to four fuel tanks, or a combination of fuel tanks and two Falcon air-to-air missiles.

Other important changes involved improvements to the aircraft's sensors and systems. New wiring was installed, the radar and infra-red tracker were modernised, and some additional cockpit instruments were also installed. New transponders and IFF systems were fitted. Originally given the designation J 35F-Ny (Ny from the Swedish for modified), the reworked aircraft were subsequently given the new 'J' suffix. They were returned to service over a 55-month period starting in March 1987. During subsequent major overhauls, they were painted in a new two-tone grey colour scheme similar to that worn by many of the Swedish air force's Viggens.

J 35J DRAKEN

This J 35J wears the colourful markings applied to the F10 display pilot's aircraft. The creature displayed on the wings represents a dragon. Flying with the last Draken unit the design has proved a huge success.

The 'double-delta' design of the Draken wing allows good control at low speed. Lower speed improves the safety margin when landing at forward operational locations.

A single ADEN 30-mm cannon is positioned in the starboard wing root where it is easily accessible to ground crews. Gun gas is removed from the intakes by the natural airflow across the airframe.

Operating away from conventional airfields requires the Draken to have a small landing run. This is accomplished by the addition of a drag parachute at the base of the rudder and upper and lower fuselage-mounted airbrakes.

Despite the age of the Draken its cockpit was a sought-after position for Swedish fighter pilots, who were enthralled by the aircraft's performance, agility and high pilot workload. The bulged canopy gives adequate vision except to the rear.

The J 35J is fitted with a modified S71N Infra-Red Search and Track set under the nose. It has a range of about 16 miles under normal conditions which makes it a useful emission-free supplement to the radar.

The narrow tracked undercarriage is designed to allow easy operation from highway strips.

J 35J Draken

Type: single-seat interceptor

Powerplant: one 78.51-kN (17,660-lb.-thrust) Volvo Flygmotor RM6C afterburning turbojet

Maximum speed: over 2126 km/h (1,138 m.p.h.) at 10,975 m (36,000 ft.)

Initial climb rate: 10,500 m/min (34,500 f.p.m.)

Range: 720 km (446 mi.) combat radius with two drop tanks and two 454-kg (1.000-lb.) bombs

Service ceiling: 19,995 m (65,600 ft.)

Weights: empty 8250 kg (18,150 lb.), maximum take-off 15,000 kg (33,000 lb.)

Armament: one 30-mm cannon plus two Sidewinder and two Falcon air-to-air missiles

Dimensions:

span	9.40 m	(30 ft. 9 in.)
length	15.35 m	(50 ft. 4 in.)
height	3.89 m	(12 ft. 9 in.)
wing area	49.20 m²	(529 sq. ft.)

COMBAT DATA

THRUST

The use of a licence-built Rolls-Royce engine fitted with a Swedish-designed afterburner allowed an exceptional thrust capability, although it didn't compare with the British twin-engined Lightning. Thrust is small compared with more modern designs.

J 35J DRAKEN 78.51 kN (17,660 lb. thrust)

LIGHTNING F.Mk 6 145.5 kN (16,730 lb. thrust)

MIRAGE 50M 70.82 kN (15,930 lb. thrust)

RANGE

The Flygvapen has always placed emphasis on the range of its combat aircraft, trusted with defending the skies against all intruders over inhospitable terrain. The J35s ferry range was excellent. When compared with France's Mirage or the Lightning, the J35 excelled.

J 35J DRAKEN 2890 km (1,796 mi.)

LIGHTNING F.Mk 6 1200 km (746 mi.)

MIRAGE 50M 1315 km (817 mi.)

CEILING

At high altitude the Draken was found to be a stable platform because of the 'cranked delta' wing design. Changes within the 'J' model brought a slight reduction in ceiling. Compared with contemporary aircraft the Draken design has proved extremely reliable.

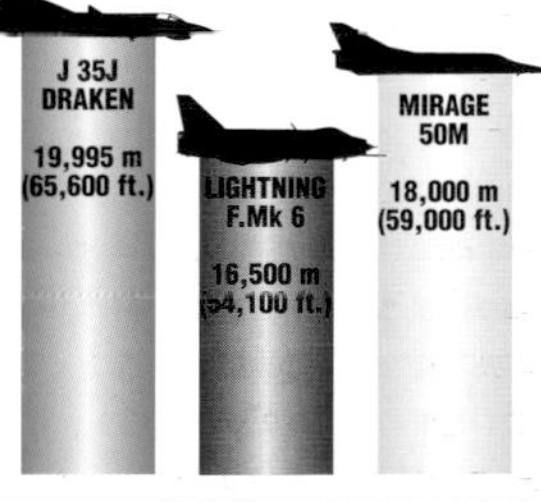

Draken developments

■ **J 35B DRAKEN:** To promote the Swedish military air service a formation team of four Drakens called the 'Acro Deltas' were fitted with smoke oil tanks and lines for formation aerobatics.

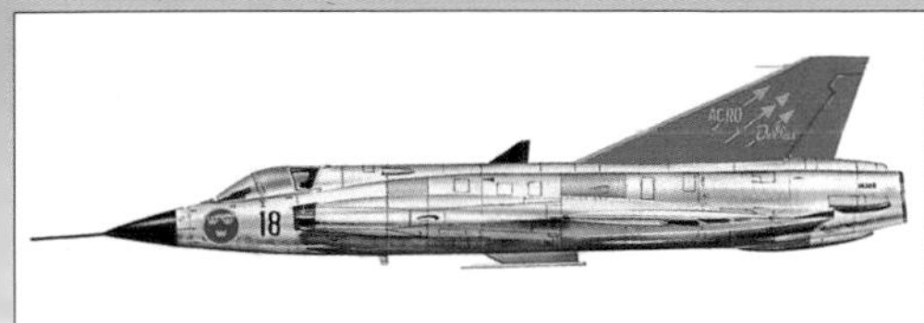

■ **J 35F DRAKEN:** Known as the F 35, the Draken's primary role in Danish service was ground attack. Some airframes were fitted with a camera nose for day photo-reconnaissance missions.

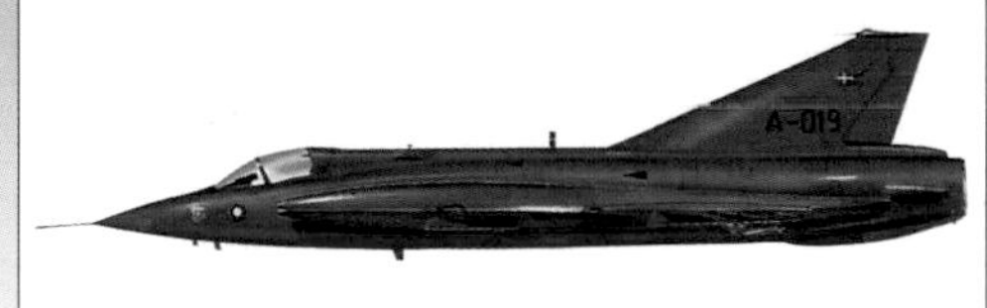

■ **J 35XS DRAKEN:** Finland modified its Drakens to allow installation of two cannon, and initial variants lacked the capability to carry the Falcon missile.

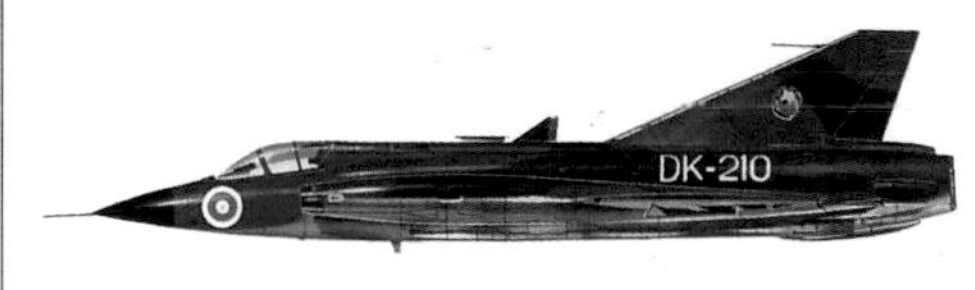

SAAB

AJ/AJS 37 VIGGEN

● Double-delta canard wing ● Multi-role strike fighter

It has been flying for nearly three decades, but the Saab 37 Viggen remains one of the most striking combat aircraft in the world. It is not just a fighter, it is a combat system built around one of the first of the modern 'canard', or tail-first, designs. As an interceptor, a ground attacker, a maritime striker, a reconnaissance platform or a trainer, the Viggen is an amazing warplane which upholds Sweden's tradition of independent, trailblazing aviation design.

▲ *The first ground-attack Viggen unit converted to the type at Satenas in 1971. The fighter variant entered service at Norrköping in 1978, replacing the Draken.*

PHOTO FILE

SAAB AJ/AJS 37 VIGGEN

▼ Unique appearance

The Viggen was the first modern fighter to be built with the now common 'canard' configuration, with control fins at the front of the airframe, pre-dating today's superfighters by two decades.

▲ Low-level strike

Armed for the low-level strike role, these AJ 37s are equipped with free-fall bombs, BOZ self-protection jamming pods and chaff and flare dispensers.

▲ Chunky nose

The classic profile of the Viggen gives an impression of strength and toughness. The cockpit area can withstand high-speed birdstrikes.

▲ Ship killer

The Rb 04 missile was once the main weapon of the AJS 37 for anti-ship attacks. It is now obsolete and has been replaced by the highly lethal Rb 15 missile.

Short take-off ▶

The Viggen has excellent short take-off capability, which makes the type ideal for operating from temporary bases on motorways.

▲ Clean cockpit

The AJ 37 cockpit is a very well-equipped design, with Doppler navigation, radar warning, ECM and head-up display systems.

FACTS AND FIGURES

- An uneventful flight test programme followed the Viggen's first flight on 8 February 1967.
- The Viggen carries about 600 kg of electronics gear in 50 'black boxes'.
- The Viggen fleet was grounded during 1981 due to an engine fatigue problem.
- The SF 37 single-seat reconnaissance version, a replacement for the Draken, first flew on 21 May 1973.
- The prototype Viggen two-seat trainer took to the sky on 2 July 1970.
- Australia, Austria, Britain, India and Norway all considered Viggen purchases.

PROFILE

The thunderbolt of Thor

Viggen is a thunderbolt in Nordic mythology, the hammer of the god Thor. Viggen the aircraft is, like Thor's hammer, a lethal weapon. Its primary purpose is to make an attack on Sweden so costly that any aggressor will bypass this customarily neutral nation.

The Viggen first appeared as the AJ 37 ground-attack aircraft in 1967. From the start its appearance was unusual, but the revolutionary wing form had a serious purpose. The extra lift from the forward-mounted canard wings gives the Viggen fine short-field performance, allowing the powerful double delta to operate from unprepared surfaces, including roadways. This capability allows the Viggen force to be dispersed and hidden in time of war.

The Viggen incorporated many advanced features which have now become standard, including a head-up display and a navigation/attack computer for accurate delivery of ordnance. One hundred and nine AJ 37s were built out of a total Viggen production run of 330. All remaining AJ 37s have been upgraded to AJS 37 standard, incorporating new avionics and weapons.

Saab knew that the Viggen had to be affordable, as effective as any potential opposition and built to cope with Swedish weather. It also needed to be simple to maintain, as all Flygvapen ground crew are conscripts.

AJ 37 Viggen

Type: single-seat all-weather attack aircraft

Powerplant: one 115.72-kN (25,960-lb.-thrust) Volvo Flygmotor RM8A turbojet

Maximum speed: Mach 2 or 2124 km/h (1,317 m.p.h.)

Combat radius: more than 1000 km (600 mi.)

Service ceiling: 18,300 m (60,000 ft.)

Weights: empty 11,800 kg (25,960 lb.); loaded 20,500 kg (45,100 lb.)

Armament: 6000 kg (13,200 lb.) of ordnance including bombs, air-to-surface or anti-ship missiles, air-to-air missiles, Bofors rocket pods or 30-mm ADEN gun pods

Dimensions:		
	span	10.60 m (35 ft.)
	length	16.30 m (53 ft.)
	height	5.80 m (19 ft.)
	wing area	46 m² (495 sq. ft.)

AJ 37 VIGGEN

F7 wing, consisting of three Attackflygdivisions of AJ 37 Viggens, was the first to receive the type in 1972. The wing formerly included a JA 37 squadron.

Unlike the fighter variant, the AJ 37 has no fixed gun. It can carry pod-mounted 30-mm ADEN cannon.

Ground-attack Viggens are easily identifiable since they lack the 'kinked' rudder fitted to the air-superiority fighter variant.

The reconnaissance SF 37 has a special camera-equipped nose section.

The intakes are of the fixed type, as all-out speed is not so important in the ground-attack role.

The distinctive 'splinter' camouflage is applied to most Viggen variants, though the JA 37 fighters are now painted grey.

The Ericsson PS-37 radar is capable of ground mapping, air-to-ground ranging and ground proximity warning, and even has a limited air-to-air capability.

The canard foreplane is a fixed unit designed to generate lift, notably on take-off. It has its own moving trailing-edge flap.

The Viggen has a tandem mainwheel arrangement to allow operation from rough surfaces. This configuration gives good performance when taxiing in snow.

COMBAT DATA

MAXIMUM SPEED

The Viggen's clean airframe, powerful engine and efficient delta wings make it one of the fastest attack jets currently in service. It is considerably faster than near contemporaries like the Anglo-French Jaguar and the MiG-27, which were designed to perform the same strike role.

AJ 37 VIGGEN	2124 km/h (1,317 m.p.h.)
JAGUAR GR.Mk.1	1700 km/h (1,054 m.p.h.)
MiG-27 'FLOGGER-D'	1880 km/h (1,166 m.p.h.)

TAKE-OFF RUN

The virtue of the Viggen's large canard foreplanes and the extra lift they provide at low speeds is most aptly demonstrated by the Swedish jet's superb short-field performance. Its rivals can also take off in a short distance, but as soon as they carry any sort of warload they need a much longer runway.

AJ 37 VIGGEN	400 m (1,312 ft.)
JAGUAR GR.Mk 1	880 m (2,886 ft.)
MiG-27 'FLOGGER-D'	950 m (6,000 ft.)

LOW-LEVEL COMBAT RADIUS

Fighting through the thick, resistant air at sea level forces a fighter's fuel consumption up dramatically. Although the Viggen has a ferry range in excess of 2500 km (1,550 mi.), on a strike mission flown entirely at low level its range is cut by at least 60 per cent. If part of the mission is flown at height, the aircraft's combat radius is extended to around 1000 km (600 mi.).

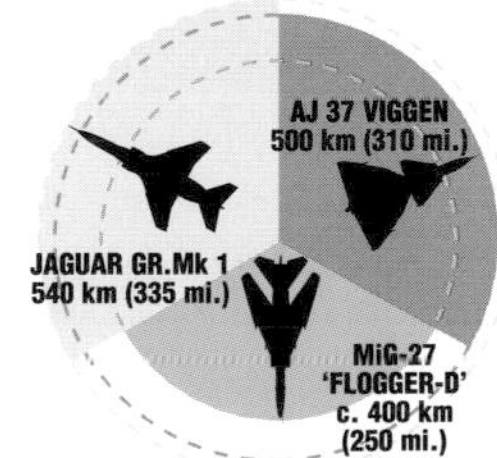

Viggen anti-ship strike

TARGET DETECTION: The Viggen's PS-37 radar can detect surface targets from at least 50 km (30 mi.) – more than 100 km (60 mi.) at altitude. Target data is fed to the missile's guidance system before launch.

INERTIAL GUIDANCE: The Rb 04 missile and its successor, the Rb 15, drops to approximately 20 m (60 ft.) above the water and flies by inertial guidance to the general target location.

ACTIVE RADAR: As it approaches the target, the missile activates its onboard radar. Once it has locked on, it drops to sea-skimming level to ensure that it strikes the target's hull.

LAUNCH PHASE

MID-COURSE PHASE

TERMINAL PHASE

SAAB

JAS 39 GRIPEN

● **High-tech multi-role lightweight** ● **Sweden's 21st-century defender**

Saab's JAS 39 Gripen is a sensational fighter – one of the best in the world. With its canard layout and delta wing, hi-tech features and ability to operate from short airfields, Sweden's new warplane is also as fast and manoeuvrable as any plane in its class. First flown on 9 December 1988, the Gripen (Griffin) bears comparison with any of the latest generation of advanced fighters built for the 21st century, keeping Saab at the forefront of fighter design.

▲ *Saab has long been in the forefront of aviation development, and the Gripen is equipped with the best of everything, including the latest Martin-Baker ejection seats, seen testing here.*

PHOTO FILE

SAAB JAS 39 GRIPEN

▲ Reconnaissance
With a centreline camera pod, the Gripen will also carry out low-level reconnaissance missions.

Strike mission ▶
Armed with the Rb 75 and Rb 15 missiles and extra fuel tanks, the Gripen is perfectly equipped for a long-range anti-shipping mission.

▲ Single engine
Unlike most of its competitors in the super-fighter stakes, the Gripen is powered by a single engine. However, its small size and light weight mean that its performance does not suffer by comparison.

▲ Pilot's-eye view
The Gripen has a very advanced cockpit, featuring a head-up display and three multi-function screens.

▼ Dogfighter
Armed with Sidewinder missiles and a powerful cannon, and not weighed down by underwing fuel tanks, the Gripen is a potent dogfighter.

▲ Air defender
Gripens will be armed with four advanced medium-range missiles and two Sidewinders. Equipped with the powerful PS-05 radar they should be able to intercept any bomber currently in service.

FACTS AND FIGURES

- Rollout of the first Gripen, on 26 April 1987, marked Saab's 50th anniversary.
- Gripens have shown their ability to fly from airfields or roadways as short as 800 m (2,625 ft.) in length.
- Gripens will be produced at a rate of 20 to 30 per year until at least the year 2015.
- A milestone was reached on 21 April 1993 when Gripens logged their 1,000th test flight.
- Sweden has been producing its own fighters since World War II.
- The first Gripen prototype was lost in a landing accident on 2 February 1989.

PROFILE

Swedish superfighter for every mission

The sophistication of Sweden's aircraft industry is evident in this advanced, multi-role fighter, which promises as much as any warplane built in America, Europe or Russia. Thirty per cent smaller than an F-16, the Saab JAS 39 Gripen is a bantamweight – but in aerial combat it will be a superstar. The pilot has advanced avionics at his disposal and is pushed through the stratosphere by a Volvo-built version of the tried and tested General Electric F404 powerplant.

Even though the programme has been hampered by two spectacular aircraft losses – from which the same pilot twice ejected successfully – the two-seat JAS 39B will soon join the growing fleet of Gripens.

Gripens have already started augmenting highly capable Viggens in the Swedish air force. In the post-Cold War international climate, the government in Stockholm is hoping for export sales of this superbly performing and very promising lightweight fighter which is available years before the EF 2000 or F-22.

Blasting off from a runway, the Gripen sets off on patrol. Like previous Swedish jet fighters, the Gripen will often operate from remote semi-prepared strips.

The Gripen has one of the smallest head-on profiles around. This is a useful combat asset, making the aircraft less easy to see or shoot down.

The Gripen has large canard foreplanes, which smooth the airflow over the wings and give enhanced low-speed manoeuvrability. They also act as airbrakes when landing.

The delta-canard configuration gives a good combination of high speed and load-carrying capability. The wing features leading-edge flaps, driven by the computerised flight control system.

JAS 39A GRIPEN

Number '02' was the first production JAS 39 Gripen to be handed over to the Swedish air force in June 1993, when it flew to its new base at Satenas escorted by Saab Viggens.

The fuselage is approximately 30 per cent composite materials. The structure proved to be far stronger than designers had predicted when it was tested. The Gripen's airframe can withstand 9*g* manoeuvres.

The view from the Gripen cockpit is superb, and pilots will have a great all-round view in a dogfight.

The Ericsson PS-05 is a lightweight multi-mode pulse-Doppler radar designed to perform air search and surface-attack functions.

The Gripen carries a 27-mm Mauser cannon under the port centre fuselage. This weapon is also used by the Tornado.

Power is provided by a single Volvo RM12 turbofan, which is a licence-built General Electric F404. This is the same engine that powers the McDonnell Douglas F/A-18 Hornet.

JAS 39 Gripen

Type: single-seat high-performance fighter

Powerplant: one 54.0-kN (12,150-lb. thrust) Volvo Flygmotor RM12 turbofan (General Electric F404-GE-400); 80.49 kN (18,110-lb. thrust) with afterburning

Maximum speed: 2126 km/h (1,321 m.p.h.) at 11,000 m (36,000 ft.)

Service ceiling: over 14,000 m (46,000 ft.)

Weights: empty 6622 kg (14,600 lb.); loaded 8300 kg (18,298 lb.)

Armament: one 27-mm Mauser BK27 cannon; two wingtip Rb 74 (AIM-9L Sidewinder) or other air-to-air missiles; underwing air-to-ground or Saab Rb 15F anti-shipping missiles

Dimensions:

span	8.00 m (26 ft. 3 in.)
length	14.10 m (46 ft. 3 in.)
height	4.70 m (15 ft. 5 in.)
wing area (est.)	80 m² (267 sq. ft.)

COMBAT DATA

MAXIMUM SPEED

All the current generation of fighters are supersonic with a similar 'clean' top speed, allowing them to make rapid intercepts of enemy aircraft as far away as possible from the area they are defending. But their speed is more than matched by their agility and handling, especially at subsonic speeds.

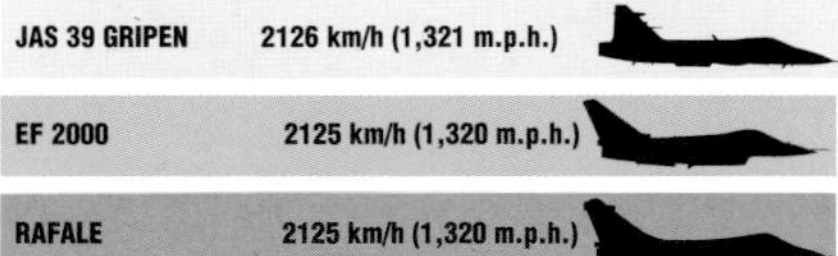

JAS 39 GRIPEN	2126 km/h (1,321 m.p.h.)
EF 2000	2125 km/h (1,320 m.p.h.)
RAFALE	2125 km/h (1,320 m.p.h.)

ENGINE POWER

The Gripen is unusual in being powered by a single engine. Both its European rivals are powered by two compact and advanced-design powerplants, delivering a great deal more thrust in total. But they are larger, heavier aircraft, and the Gripen's performance does not suffer by comparison.

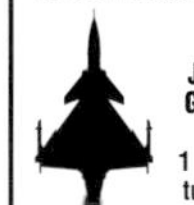

JAS 39 GRIPEN	EF 2000	RAFALE
1 x Volvo turbofan delivering 80.49 KN (18,110 lb.) of thrust with afterburning	2 x Eurojet turbofans delivering 180.20 kN (40,545 lb.) of thrust with afterburning	2 x SNECMA turbofans delivering 174.07 kN (39,165 lb.) of thrust with afterburning

BOMBLOAD

The Gripen was designed from the outset as a multi-role aircraft and, although much less powerful than its rivals, it is capable of lifting just as great a warload. It has been cleared to carry anti-ship missiles, guided air-to-surface missiles, bombs, guided bombs, cluster bombs and unguided high-explosive air-to-surface rockets.

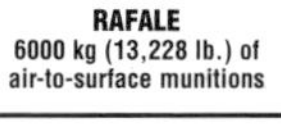

JAS 39 GRIPEN	EF 2000	RAFALE
6500 kg (14,330 lb.) of air-to-surface munitions	6500 kg (14,330 lb.) of air-to-surface munitions	6000 kg (13,228 lb.) of air-to-surface munitions

Sweden's tradition of aeronautical excellence

■ **Saab 21R:** Based on a wartime fighter with a pusher propeller, the 21R of 1947 was the first jet designed and built in Sweden.

■ **Saab 29:** Flown in September 1948, the Tunnan was the first swept-wing fighter to enter large-scale production in Europe.

■ **Saab 32:** The Lansen of 1952 was an elegant transonic design, contemporary with and comparable to the very capable Hawker Hunter.

■ **Saab 35:** The prototype of the 'double-delta' Draken flew in 1955. It was to become one of the world's first Mach 2-capable fighters.

■ **Saab 37:** The multi-role Viggen of 1967 anticipated by a quarter of a century the current trend for canard-winged combat jets.

SAAB

TP 100 & 340 AEW&C

● **Regional airliner** ● **Airborne early warning** ● **VIP transport**

▲ *Like its NATO equivalents, Sweden's AEW&C aircraft have armed guards placed around the aircraft when making public appearances.*

With its strong stance of neutrality Sweden has found its airspace violated in the past by both NATO and Russian aircraft. Reluctant to purchase a foreign airborne early warning and control design, Saab undertook the conversion of a twin-turboprop regional airliner. The addition of numerous blisters and a roof-mounted fairing have seen the Saab 340 transformed into a highly capable aircraft for defending Sweden's airspace.

PHOTO FILE

SAAB TP 100 & 340 AEW&C

◀ **Eye on the future**
Swedish defence officials had long been interested in providing their armed forces with a reliable command and control platform. The Saab 340 proved to be the ideal aircraft for the role.

◀ **Advanced avionics**
Using their Ericsson Erieye side-looking radar, operators can detect targets up to 300 km (200 mi.) away. The operators are also able to send information to orbiting friendly fighters on interception duty.

▼ **Radar research**
With its complete radar fit installed, the Saab 340 AEW&C entered operational service with Sweden's Flygvapen in early 1995.

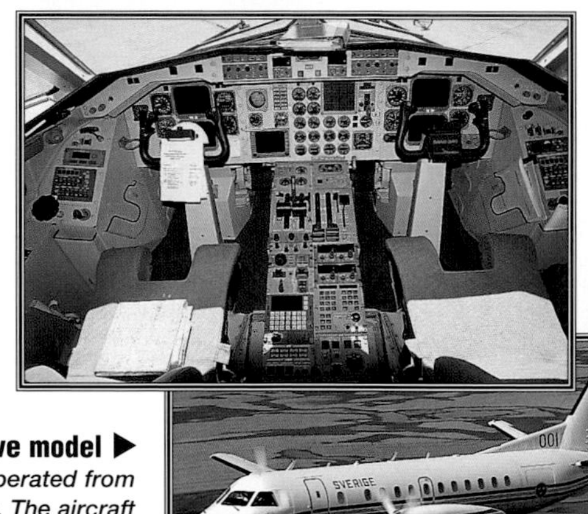

Fabulous flight deck ▶
Developed from a regional transport airliner, the flight deck of the Saab 340 is equipped with multi-function displays and advanced flight controls for the pilots. This considerably reduces crew fatigue on long-standing patrols.

Executive model ▶
Designated the Tp 100, one example is operated from Stockholm-Tullinge as part of Sweden's Royal Flight. The aircraft wears a smart patriotic colour scheme and is suitably equipped internally. The aircraft is often used as a transport for government ministers attending meetings across Europe.

FACTS AND FIGURES

- The Saab 340 was originally developed in partnership with the American Fairchild aviation company.
- At present, Sweden is the only customer for the AEW&C variant.
- In November 1985 Fairchild dropped out of the development of the aircraft.
- The specialised radar-equipped Saab 340 is dubbed the 340 AEW&C, as it has a command and control role.
- Sweden first flew the AEW&C variant on 17 January 1994.
- Possible future customers for the radar variant include Australia.

PROFILE

Sweden's airborne watcher

Ever conscious of airborne trespass, Sweden regularly dispatched interceptors to shepherd away inquisitive intruders. Located within the heart of the Cold War arena, Swedish airspace was regularly violated by NATO and Warsaw Pact aircraft.

Responding to these never-ceasing intrusions, Sweden developed an air force that was equipped with fighters that could rise from a standard highway to intercept the high flying intruders 24 hours a day, 365 days a year. A key addition to their command network was an airborne command and control aircraft as insurance for the future.

Initially working in partnership with Fairchild of America, Saab had already developed a highly capable turboprop airliner. After the withdrawal of American assistance, the aircraft was renamed the Saab 340. Quick to see the future potential in the design, the Flygvapen became the first military customer for the aircraft.

Equipped with an Ericsson Erieye side-looking airborne radar (SLAR) in a canoe fairing above the fuselage, the Saab 340 AEW&C as it is now known, has become a valuable asset within Sweden's defence strategy.

The aircraft completed its flight testing phase in early 1995, amd five more examples were delivered to the Swedish air force.

Overseas interest in the 340 AEW&C has been shown from Australia although firm orders have yet to be received.

Left: Proving the concept of the sideways-looking airborne radar was the responsibility of Fairchild Merlin. The aircraft wore a complex splinter-camouflage during its testing phase.

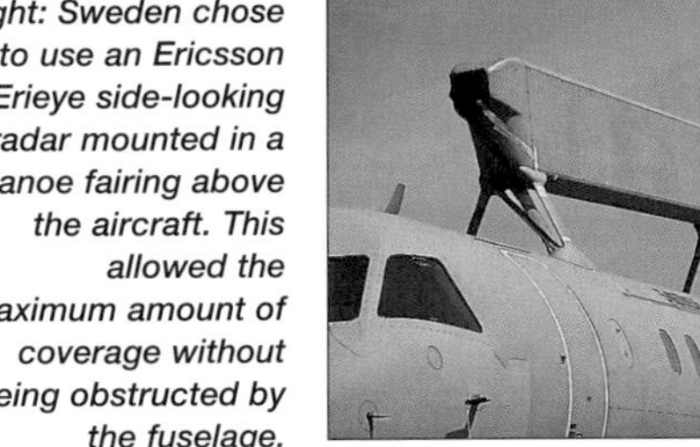

Right: Sweden chose to use an Ericsson Erieye side-looking radar mounted in a canoe fairing above the aircraft. This allowed the maximum amount of coverage without being obstructed by the fuselage.

340B

Type: twin-engined VIP transport/airborne command and control aircraft

Powerplant: two 1394-kW (1,870-hp.) General Electric CT7-9B turboprops

Maximum cruising speed: 522 km/h (324 m.p.h.)

Initial climb rate: 610 m/min (2,000 f.p.m.)

Range: 1807 km (1,120 mi.)

Service ceiling: 7620 m (25,000 ft.)

Weights: operational empty 8036 kg (17,679 lb.); maximum take-off 13,063 kg (28,739 lb.)

Accommodation: two pilots and 35 systems operators

Dimensions:

span	21.44 m (70 ft. 4 in.)
length	19.73 m (64 ft. 9 in.)
height	6.87 m (22 ft. 5 in.)
wing area	41.81 m² (450 sq. ft.)

340 AEW&C

Equipped with a fuselage-mounted SLAR, the Saab 340 AEW&C is proving to be a highly capable command and control platform. At present the prototype remains on operational test duties.

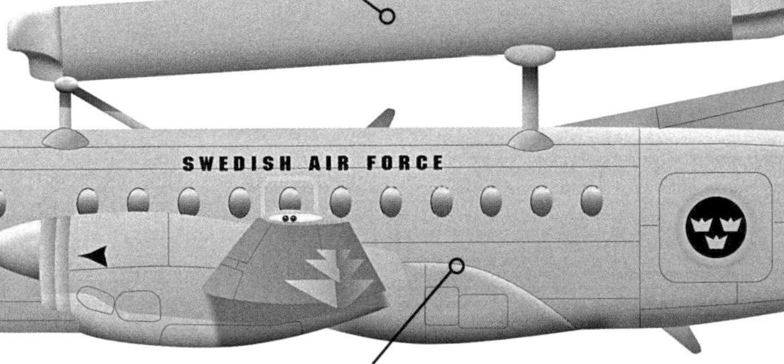

By positioning the radar in a canoe fairing above the fuselage, unrestricted coverage can be achieved. During testing, the detection range of the Ericsson Erieye radar has been measured at over 300 km (200 mi.) against small airborne targets.

Since it has proved to be highly successful the Swedish air force has placed an order for five examples of the Saab 340 AEW&C. They will operate alongside Saab Viggens and Gripens.

The well equipped flight deck provides accommodation for two pilots and one observer. Positioned on the roof of the cockpit is an escape hatch.

A door positioned on the forward fuselage allows access to the flight deck. This is fitted with a small set of integral steps.

The additional weight of the radar equipment did not result in additional strengthening being required for the airframe of the Saab 340.

To compensate for the aerodynamic drag caused by the canoe fairing, additional finlets were installed at the rear of the fuselage to ease handling.

LOW-COST WATCHERS

UNITED STATES: The US Coast Guard operates a fleet of aircraft under the designation of HU-25 Guardians (pictured below). The aircraft, derived from the French Dassault Falcon 20, have been progressively upgraded to include an external SLAR mounted on the fuselage. Civilian roles for the Guardian are concerned with drug interdiction and pollution monitoring.

BRAZIL: Unable to afford the expense of large, sophisticated, radar control aircraft, many countries have opted for a low-cost alternative. Initially marketed as a regional civil airliner the EMB-111 Bandeirante (below), now sports a large nose-mounted radar and under-wing hardpoints. With the addition of wingtip fuel tanks, mission endurance is increased to nine hours.

Sweden's airborne warriors

JAS 39 GRIPEN: Defending Sweden's neutrality, the Gripen represents the new cutting edge within the Flygvapen.

J 35 DRAKEN: First flying in 1955, the unique wing design of the Draken gave the aircraft an incredible performance.

SK 60: Used for both training and attack roles, the Saab 105, as it is more widely known, is also operated by Austria.

JA 37 VIGGEN: The backbone of Sweden's air defence system is the Viggen which has been produced in a host of variants.

SEPECAT

JAGUAR GR.MK 1/GR.MK 1B

● **Anglo-French single-seat attack aircraft** ● **Gulf War veteran**

One of the early successes of Anglo-French collaboration, the Jaguar fighter-bomber has been a mainstay of the RAF's first-line squadrons over the last three decades. With improved weaponry and avionics the Jaguar has developed into a useful tactical ground-attack and reconnaissance aircraft, despite a modest performance compared to some of its contemporaries.

▲ *It was thought that the Jaguar was in the twilight of its career when both French and RAF aircraft were sent to the Gulf to participate in Operation Desert Storm. Since then a new RAF version, the GR.Mk 1B, has entered service equipped with the TIALD imaging and laser pod.*

PHOTO FILE

SEPECAT JAGUAR GR.MK 1/GR.MK 1B

B-24 bombload ▶
This GR.Mk 1 carries eight 454-kg (1,000-lb.) bombs, equivalent to the tonnage carried by a wartime B-24 Liberator bomber. A more normal load includes chaff and flare pods, fuel tanks and a pair of infra-red missiles.

Multi-role aircraft ▶
When originally delivered to the RAF, Jaguars were tasked with nuclear strike, reconnaissance and conventional attack. Only the latter role is still performed.

◀ The 'front office'
This pilot's eye view of a single-seater's cockpit shows that it is fairly typical of a jet fighter-bomber of the 1970s.

▲ Motorway take-off
Demonstrating its ability to operate from dispersed sites, this Jaguar lifts off from a stretch of motorway with a load of cluster bombs.

▼ T.Mk 2 two-seater
The two-seat conversion trainer version of the GR.Mk 1 features a longer nose with the crew seated in tandem under separate canopies.

FACTS AND FIGURES

- During the Cold War there were up to five RAF 'Jag' squadrons in Germany, the theoretical 'front line' in a major conflict.
- A Jaguar was once accidentally shot down by an RAF Phantom in Germany.
- Jaguars in the Gulf were armed with iron bombs, cluster bombs and rockets.
- During Operation Desert Storm, 12 RAF Jaguars flew 618 war sorties during January and February 1991.
- The home base of the RAF's Jaguars is RAF Coltishall, home to three squadrons.
- An RAF Jaguar once survived a high-speed wire strike at an altitude of just 10 m (33 ft.).

PROFILE

The RAF's feline mud-mover

Throwing a fast fighter-bomber through mountains at night, without radar, alone and unaided by a navigator may seem a recipe for disaster, but this is what RAF Jaguar pilots do on a regular basis. They know that the Jaguar, with more than 25 years of service behind it, is a tried and tested weapon that will not let them down.

When it came to a real war situation in the Gulf in 1991, the Jaguar showed that it was able to fly missions as well as many aircraft that are considerably younger.

A Franco/British project, the result of collaboration between the British Aircraft Corporation (now British Aerospace) and Dassault-Breguet, the SEPECAT Jaguar was first flown on 8 September 1968 as a single-seat attack aircraft with limited all-weather capability. It was intended to serve both the Armée de l'Air and the RAF; the French Jaguar A entered service first, in May 1972.

The RAF took delivery of its first GR.Mk 1 in May 1973. A well-equipped tactical strike-fighter, its equipment included an inertial navigation system, a head-up display and laser rangefinder. From 1983 navigation upgrades resulted in the GR.Mk 1A. Some were able to perform a secondary reconnaissance role.

The GR.Mk 1B and two-seat T.Mk 2B were introduced in 1995, equipped with the TIALD (Thermal Imaging and Laser Designation) pod. This allows a Jaguar to deliver its own laser-guided weapons.

Jaguars are fitted with a retractable inflight-refuelling probe which greatly increases their range capability.

Jaguars were the first RAF attack aircraft sent to the Gulf after the Iraqi invasion of Kuwait.

RAF aircraft are equipped with 'zero-zero' ejection seats. These can be used at 'zero height' and 'zero forward speed'.

XZ364 is armed for a typical Gulf mission with four 454-kg (1,000-lb.) bombs, a jamming pod under the port wing, a chaff dispenser under the starboard and AIM-9 missiles for self-defence.

Jaguar GR.Mk 1A

Type: single-seat attack bomber

Powerplant: two 35.77-kN (8,048-lb. thrust) Rolls-Royce/ Turboméca Adour Mk 104 afterburning turbofans

Maximum speed: Mach 1.5 or 1690 km/h (1,050 m.p.h.) at altitude

Combat radius: 852 km (529 m.p.h.) on internal fuel

Service ceiling: 14,020 m (46,000 ft.)

Weights: empty 7000 kg (15,432 lb.); maximum take-off 15,442 kg (34,044 lb.)

Armament: two 30-mm ADEN cannon plus provision for two AIM-9L Sidewinder air-to-air missiles on overwing pylons, plus up to 4534 kg (9,996 lb.) of underwing stores on five pylons

Dimensions:		
	span	8.69 m (28 ft. 6 in.)
	length	15.52 m (50 ft. 11 in.)
	height	4.92 m (16 ft. 2 in.)
	wing area	24.18 m² (260 sq. ft.)

JAGUAR GR.MK 1A

XZ364 'Sadman' was one of a detachment of Jaguars from the RAF Coltishall Jaguar Wing based at Muharraq, Bahrain, and one of two RAF 'Jags' that flew 47 missions each in the Gulf during 1991.

Like the RAF Tornado bombers and Buccaneers in the Gulf, Jaguars were painted in a temporary 'desert pink' camouflage.

The fin fairing contains a radar warning receiver which warns the pilot when he is 'illuminated' by enemy radar.

The Jaguar is unusual in being able to carry a pair of air-to-air missiles on overwing pylons. RAF Jaguars use AIM-9 Sidewinders.

Nose art was a feature of RAF aircraft during the Gulf conflict. This one features a caricature of former Iraqi leader Saddam Hussein. The bomb symbols below the cockpit each represent missions flown.

RAF single-seat Jaguars are fitted with the 'chisel-nose' containing a Ferranti Laser Rangefinder and Marked Target Seeker (LRMTS).

Continuing the Rolls-Royce tradition of naming its engines after rivers, the Jaguar's Anglo-French Rolls-Royce/Turboméca Adour turbofans are named after a river in France.

COMBAT DATA

MAXIMUM SPEED

For ground-attack aircraft, speed at ground level is far more important than absolute maximum speed. All three aircraft have similar performance at lower levels.

JAGUAR GR.Mk 1A	1690 km/h (1050 m.p.h.)
MiG-27K 'FLOGGER-D'	1885 km/h (1,171 m.p.h.)
F-1	1700 km/h (1,056 m.p.h.)

ARMAMENT

The Jaguar is an excellent attack aircraft with the ability to carry a useful bombload, including laser-guided bombs, deep into enemy territory. The F-1 carries far less than the MiG-27 or the Jaguar.

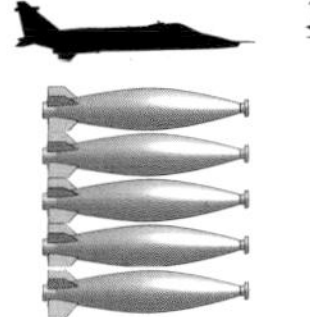
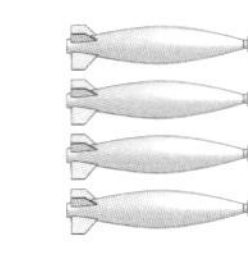
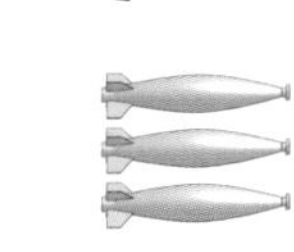

JAGUAR GR.Mk 1A	MiG-27K 'FLOGGER-D'	F-1
2 x 30-mm cannon	1 x 30-mm cannon	1 x 20-mm cannon
4534 kg (10,000 lb.)	4000 kg (8,800 lb.)	2721 kg (6,000 lb.)

COMBAT RADIUS

With a typical bombload the Jaguar can strike deeper into enemy territory than the MiG-27 or the F-1. This capability was shown to good effect in the Gulf War when RAF and French Jaguars attacked targets deep inside Iraq.

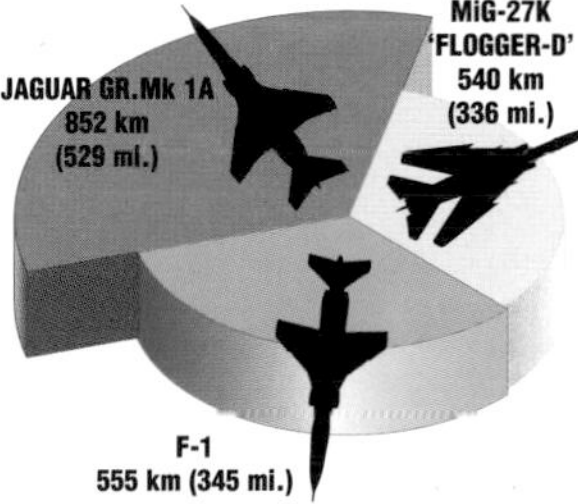

Jaguar ground attack

IN THE GULF AND BEYOND: Typical ordnance loads during the Gulf War included general-purpose iron bombs, cluster bombs and rocket pods. Since then the RAF has equipped a number of single- and two-seat Jaguars with the TIALD pod which was used briefly by Tornados during Operation Desert Storm. This allows Jaguars to deliver highly accurate laser-guided munitions autonomously as well as to 'illuminate' targets for other aircraft.

1 TIALD ATTACK: The attacking Jaguar illuminates' the target with a laser beam, the reflected light forming a cone-shaped 'bucket' into which the laser-guided bomb (LGB) is dropped.

2 PRECISION GUIDANCE: The LGB homes in on the source of the reflected light for pinpoint accuracy.

CRV-7 ROCKETS IN THE GULF: After it was decided that attacks would be made at medium rather than low level for safety, changes were made to the types of weapon used.

MACH 4 SPEED: The CRV-7 rocket, fired from a 240-kg (530-lb.) 19-tube pod, is accurate up to 6000 m (19,685 ft.).

SHENYANG J-6 'FARMER'

● MiG-19 copy ● Built in huge numbers ● 40-year-old design

▲ Although it appears to be little more than a copy of the Mikoyan-Gurevich MiG-19, the Shenyang J-6 has single-handedly helped to establish China as a major producer of military aircraft.

Chinese production of the Soviet MiG-19 began at Shenyang and Nanchang in the late 1950s. The first aircraft actually to fly were assembled from Soviet parts. The first true Chinese-built J-6 followed in September 1959, with series production beginning soon after. The original J-6 was a copy of the MiG-19P all-weather fighter, but in 1961 production switched to the MiG-19S day-fighter variant. This variant has been widely exported.

PHOTO FILE

SHENYANG J-6 'FARMER'

Sales success ▶
China saw the potential of the MiG-19 and was able to offer the aircraft at an unbelievably low price to other countries. Even more attractive is its simplicity and abundant spares situation.

◀ Longevity
Even today, large numbers of this 40-year-old design are in service.

▼ J-6 Xin
The word xin, meaning 'new', is applied to an upgraded variant with an air-intercept radar.

▼ Sub-continent Shenyangs
Pakistan was the first nation outside China to receive the F-6. Deliveries commenced shortly after the 1971 conflict with India.

Time warp ▶
Looking like a Frontal Aviation base in the 1950s, this scene actually dates from the 1980s. The Chinese pilots are even wearing leather helmets.

FACTS AND FIGURES

- ➤ All Pakistani air force F-6s have been retrofitted with British Martin-Baker ejection seats for better safety.
- ➤ The ground attack A-5 Fantan is based on a heavily modified F-6 airframe.
- ➤ Production of the J-6 was disrupted by the Cultural Revolution in the late 1960s.
- ➤ F-6s have been exported to Pakistan, Egypt, Vietnam, Bangladesh, Cuba, Tanzania and Somalia among others.
- ➤ In Chinese service the aircraft fulfils fighter, attack and reconnaissance roles.
- ➤ Nearly 5000 J-6s were produced, more than double the number of MiG-19s.

PROFILE

China's flying time capsule

During the 1960s, in addition to the J-6 fighter Shenyang produced a JJ-6 two-seat trainer and even a reconnaissance aircraft known as the J-Z6, based on the MiG-19R. The two-seater has been exported as the FT-6 to Bangladesh, North Korea, Vietnam and Zambia.

Although the J-6 became the standard fighter of the Chinese air force from 1962, the Cultural Revolution of the late 1960s badly hampered production. As a result, it was 1973 before the first new model was delivered. Designated J-6III, it was a high-speed day fighter with cropped wings and more powerful engines.

The J-6C was an improved version of the basic J-6 and featured, among other things, a relocated brake parachute. China's Guizhou factory used this variant as the basis for the all-weather J-6A. It has a revised nose profile with a new radar and carries PL-2 missiles.

As F-6s, J-6s were exported to several countries, including Albania, Egypt, Iran, Iraq, Pakistan, Somalia, and Tanzania, as well as the four countries already listed as customers for the FT-6. Pakistan bought 120 F-6s and subsequently modified them with new avionics, Sidewinder missiles and a large fuel tank under the fuselage.

Above: Some ex-Pakistani F-6s were transferred to the Bangladesh Defence Force Air Wing. By 1994 only a handful were still flying.

Above: Most 'Farmers' operated by the Pakistan air force wear this two-tone grey camouflage, though others sport an air-defence grey scheme or remain unpainted.

F-6 'Farmer C'

Type: single-seat fighter

Powerplant: two 31.88-KN (7,170-lb.-thrust) Limming (LM) Wopen-6 afterburning turbojets

Maximum speed: 1540 km/h (955 m.p.h.)

Initial climb rate: 9145 m/min (30,000 f.p.m.)

Combat radius: 685 km (425 mi.)

Range: 1390 km (862 mi.)

Service ceiling: 17,900 m (58,700 ft.)

Weights: empty 5760 kg (12,672 lb.); maximum take-off 10,000 kg (22,000 lb.) (est)

Armament: three 30-mm cannon

Dimensions:

	span	9.20 m (30 ft. 2 in.)
	length	14.90 m (48 ft. 10 in.)
	height	3.88 m (12 ft. 9 in.)
	wing area	25 m^2 (269 sq. ft.)

FT-6 'FARMER'

One of the many nations to purchase F-6s was Egypt. For conversion training on to single-seat F-6s, FT-6 trainers were also acquired. A small number of them were rumoured still to be active in the mid-1990s.

In common with early Mikoyan-Gurevich jet fighters, the F-6 features a large splitter plate at the mouth of the intake. This is contoured for more effective air flow to the twin turbojet engines.

A flat, almost razor-straight canopy profile identifies the two-seat 'Farmer'. The twin Shenyang ejection seats are woefully outclassed and are mounted high up, requiring tall pilots to wear old style leather flying helmets instead of modern 'bone domes'.

In comparison with the fighter variant, the two-seater is longer, with a fuselage plug of 84 cm (33 in.) forward of the wings. The rear cockpit is fitted in place of a fuel cell, and in an effort to restore fuel capacity the wing-root cannon were deleted and additional tanks substituted. Fit and finish are exceptional for an old design.

Large low-mounted stabilisers were fitted to the MiG-19 instead of the high-mounted units seen on its predecessors. The entire unit is able to move up and down. A small fairing at the base of the fin houses the relocated brake parachute.

Based on the airframe of the enhanced J-6C fighter variant, the trainer's improvements include nosewheel braking and tubeless tyres.

Conceived during the 1950s, the FT-6 suffers from the inadequate range that plagues all jets dating from this period. On most sorties drop tanks are fitted under the wings.

Twin Wopen WP-6 turbojets power the FT-6 variant. They are rated at 31.88 kN (7,170 lb. thrust) with afterburning and by modern standards are extremely crude and fuel thirsty.

COMBAT DATA

THRUST

Among the 1950s generation supersonic fighters still in service, the F-6 is not particularly powerful, especially considering that it is powered by two heavy turbojets. The slightly later MiG-21 had much greater performance despite having less thrust.

F-6 'FARMER' 63.76 kN (14,340 lb. thrust)

MIG-21 PFM 'FISHBED-F' 60.57 kN (13,625 lb. thrust)

F-104G STARFIGHTER 70.28 kN (15,810 lb. thrust)

MAXIMUM SPEED

Even today, these early supersonic fighters remain among the best-performing aircraft ever built, although the Starfighter was marred by poor handling. The F-6 retains the excellent performance of the MiG-19 but is a far more capable machine.

F-6 'FARMER' 1540 km/h (955 m.p.h.)

MIG-21 PFM 'FISHBED-F' 2125 km/h (1,318 m.p.h.)

F-104G STARFIGHTER 2338 km/h (1,450 m.p.h.)

RANGE

Drawbacks of the J/F-6 are numerous, especially range. The twin turbojets have horrendous fuel consumption and thus sorties are often very short, even with drop tanks fitted. Pakistani machines are sometimes fitted with an additional conformal tank under the fuselage in an effort to extend endurance.

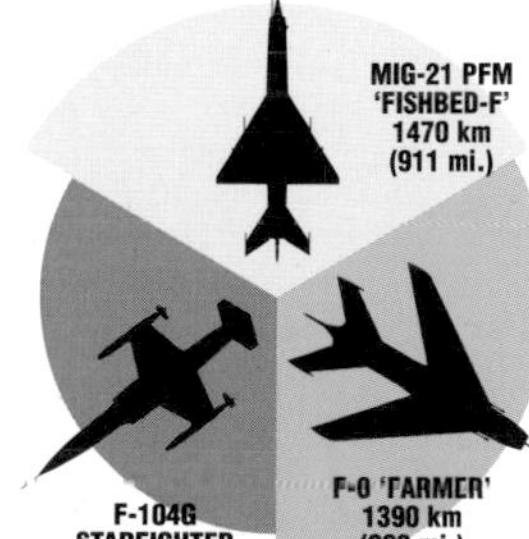

Indigenous combat jets of the People's Republic

■ **NANCHANG Q-5 'FANTAN':** Based on the airframe of the J-6, this dedicated ground attack aircraft features a redesigned nose housing an attack radar, and small fuselage air intakes.

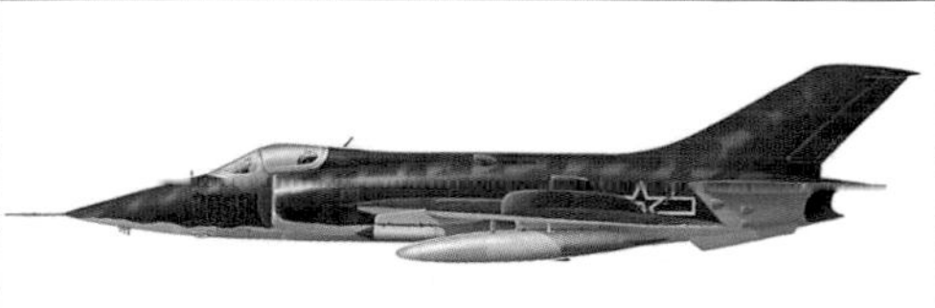

■ **SHENYANG J-8II 'FINBACK-B':** Developed in conjunction with Grumman Aerospace, this promising aircraft was cancelled after the Tiananmen Square massacre of 1989.

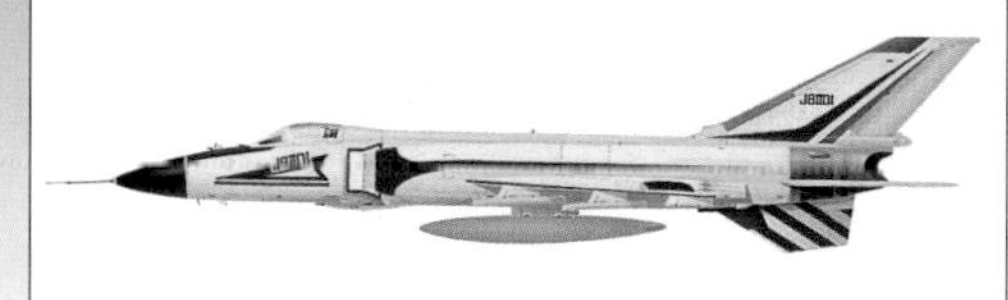

■ **GUIZHOU JJ-7/FT-7:** Externally identical to Soviet-built MiG-21UMs, complete with bulged dorsal spine and broad fin, these aircraft serve as advanced trainers with the PLA AF.

SHENYANG

J-8 'FINBACK'

● Interceptor ● Ten-year test programme ● MiG-21 development

First flown in June 1984, the F-8II was a development of the original Shenyang J-8, which had flown for the first time nearly 15 years earlier. Where the earlier aircraft had a configuration similar to that of the MiG-21, the F-8II has fuselage-side air intakes like those of the MiG-23 for its twin turbojets. It retains the J-8's combination of delta wings and sharply swept tailfin, but adds a folding fin below the tail.

▲ *China's self-imposed reliance on indigenous products has often led to problems in its aviation industry. The J-8 is no exception, and its development is in serious doubt.*

PHOTO FILE

SHENYANG J-8 'FINBACK'

▼ Missiles from abroad
In 1987 Grumman received a contract to upgrade the avionics and missiles for the J-8. Political events prevented this contract from being completed, at great technological cost to China.

▲ A big fighter
Based loosely on the MiG-21 'Fishbed', the J-8 'Finback' is a considerably larger machine.

Familiar lines ▶
A wing plan similar to the MiG-21's is evident in this view of a J-8 'Finback' seen participating in a Chinese Armed Forces Air Display.

◀ Future 'Finbacks'
An improved version of the J-8 was developed as the J-8II 'Finback-B', incorporating upgraded avionics and more powerful engines.

Chinese counterfeit ▶
When viewing the aircraft, features of the MiG-21 and MiG-23 became apparent. They are the result of the inventive nature of the Chinese aviation industry, and the acquisition of different Soviet fighters from various sources.

FACTS AND FIGURES

- The J-8 originated from a 1964 PLA requirement for a fighter with superior performance to that of the MiG-21.
- In its configuration the J-8 'Finback' is described as a scaled-up MiG-21.
- Two prototypes were delivered, the first of which flew on 5 July 1969.
- Flight testing of the J-8 'Finback' lasted 10 years, because of various political interruptions to its development.
- An improved all-weather variant is equipped with an SR-4 radar.
- The improved 'Finback-B' first flew on 12 June 1984.

PROFILE

China on its own

Code-named 'Finback-B' by NATO and originally known as the J-8II, the F-8II does not seem to have entered Chinese air force service. As a result, the F that replaces J in the designation of export versions of fighters has become standard.

With side intakes instead of the nose intake of the J-8, the F-8II has room for a much more capable radar. Changes to export versions include the addition of a head-up display as part of a digital avionics suite.

A planned development using US avionics in a programme called Peace Pearl was halted after the 1989 Tiananmen Square massacre in Beijing. Under a contract awarded in 1987, Grumman had been working to integrate a version of the F-16's radar, along with other new systems. The aircraft would also have had a bubble canopy and an American ejection seat.

Even so, work on the fighter did not stop, and Shenyang went on to fly the first F-8IIM in March 1996. The flight came only two years after drawings had been delivered, which constituted a record for the Chinese aircraft industry.

Recently, the future of the 'Finback-B' has been placed in further doubt by the purchase by the People's Republic of China of 24 Sukhoi Su-27 'Flankers'. The huge expense of these aircraft has restricted funding for the F-8II.

Left: No air force outside China operates the J-8. The recent purchase of Su-27 'Flankers' has placed the future of the fighter in serious doubt.

Above: When it was displayed at the 1989 Paris Air Salon, the J-8 'Finback' created much interest among Western observers, but no orders were received for the aircraft.

J-8 'Finback'

Type: single-seat interceptor

Powerplant: two 65.90-kN (14,825-lb.-thrust) Liyang (LMC) Wopen-13A II turbojets with afterburner

Maximum speed: 2338 km/h (1,450 m.p.h.)

Initial climb rate: 12,000 m/min (39,400 f.p.m.)

Range: 2200 km (1,365 mi.)

Service ceiling: 20,200 m (66,300 ft.)

Weights: empty 9820 kg (21,604 lb.); maximum take-off 17,800 kg (39,160 lb.)

Armament: one 23-mm ventral cannon with 200 rounds; plus various AAMs or 57-mm rockets

Dimensions:

span	9.34 m (30 ft. 8 in.)
length	21.59 m (70 ft. 10 in.)
height	5.41 m (17 ft. 9 in.)
wing area	42.20 m² (454 sq. ft.)

F-8II 'FINBACK-B'

The F-8II was developed from the earlier J-8 'Finback-A'. The aircraft's future is now in serious doubt after the withdrawal of American support and China's purchase of the Su-27 'Flanker'.

A bubble canopy was installed on later models at the request of pilots who found that vision to the rear of the aircraft was restricted. A modern ejection seat is fitted, as is a simple head-up-display.

The new side-mounted intakes of the 'Finback-B' give the aircraft greater airflow than the original nose intake, which fed a pair of the less powerful Wopen WP 7B turbojets. This design change was influenced by China's acquisition of several Egyptian MiG-23 'Floggers' during the late 1980s.

The 'Finback' is usually armed with a single 23-mm twin-barrelled cannon and a range of air-to-air missiles. Most Chinese copies of Russian weapons can be fitted. China also produces a missile that closely resembles the AIM-9L Sidewinder, plus a Sparrow copy. These, too, can be attached to the outer pylons.

An exact copy of the MiG-21 'Fishbed' fin is fitted to the F-8II. The wings follow a similar pattern but are increased in span and are equipped with extra hardpoints for missiles.

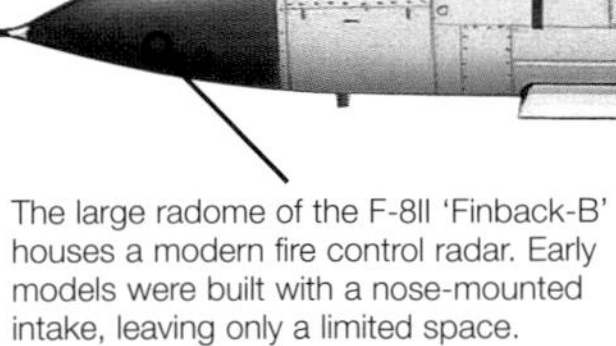

The large radome of the F-8II 'Finback-B' houses a modern fire control radar. Early models were built with a nose-mounted intake, leaving only a limited space.

Inspired by the Russian MiG-23/27 'Flogger', a folding fin is fitted on the lower fuselage to improve the directional stability of the aircraft.

COMBAT DATA

MAXIMUM SPEED

Using copied designs, China has often improved the capabilities of the Russian aircraft it has adopted. The gradual increase in speed of the various aircraft indicates that the manufacturers are constantly upgrading the types.

F-8II 'FINBACK-B'	2338 km/h (1,450 m.p.h.)
F-6 'FARMER'	1540 km/h (955 m.p.h.)
F-5 'FRESCO'	1145 km/h (710 m.p.h.)

COMBAT RADIUS

The size of the 'Finback' allows the aircraft to carry an exceptionally large fuel load, which can be improved even further by the addition of extra fuel tanks. The small dimensions of the F-5 'Fresco' restrict its fuel load, although additional tanks can be used, as on the 'Farmer'.

F-8II 'FINBACK-B' 800 km (500 mi.)

F-5 'FRESCO' 700 km (435 mi.)

F-6 'FARMER' 685 km (425 mi.)

CLIMB RATE

Equipped with two afterburning turbojets, the F-8's climb rate is exceptional compared to that of some previous Chinese fighters. This performance can be accomplished with a relatively large payload of weapons.

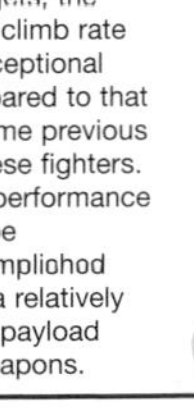

F-8II 'FINBACK-B' 12000 m/min (39,400 f.p.m.)

F-6 'FARMER' 9145 m/min (30,000 f.p.m.)

F-5 'FRESCO' 3900 m/min (12,800 f.p.m.)

Chinese copycats

XIAN F-7M AIRGUARD: Basically developed from the MiG-21, the F-7M was given an increased wingspan by Xian.

NANCHANG A-5M FANTAN: Exported to Pakistan, the A-5M 'Fantan' is used for ground attack duties using bombs and rockets.

SHENYANG J-6: After an agreement in 1958, China was allowed to produce a licensed copy of the MiG-19 'Farmer' for its air force.

SHENYANG J-8I: Known as the 'Flipper', this aircraft was the first indigenous fighter produced by China. It saw limited service.

ShinMaywa

SS-2

● Long-range flying-boat ● Search and rescue ● Maritime patrol

Introduced in 1967, the ShinMaywa SS-2 is one of the last great flying-boats. This aircraft served Japan's Maritime Self-Defence Force so well that in 1992 it was returned to production. Easily recognised with its watertight hull, high wing and T-tail, the ShinMaywa has been built in seaplane and amphibian versions and operates wherever water is found. This hard-working aircraft is successful and very popular with crews.

▲ *Flying-boats are a dying breed, and it is a tribute to the SS-2 that it has been put back into production. The combination of large size, long endurance (thanks to its turboprops) and the ability to land on the sea are ideal for search-and-rescue missions.*

PHOTO FILE

ShinMaywa SS-2

◀ Water-bomber
Eight tonnes of water smothers the flames. The SS-2 shows much promise as a firefighting aircraft, with the ability to scoop up water from lakes or the sea to replenish its tanks.

▲ High wing
The high wing, designed to keep the propellers out of the sea, means that mechanics need platforms to carry out maintenance.

▼ Rescue colours
The later search-and-rescue mission SS-2 was painted with bright orange nose and tail. The old anti-submarine PS-1s were grey and white.

▲ Coastal patrol
The SS-2 spends its time on long, slow patrols around Japan's coastline, ready to mount rescues at a moment's notice.

Amphibian ▶
The later variants of the SS-2 had a wheeled undercarriage capable of landing on runways, unlike earlier models, which were pure flying-boats.

FACTS AND FIGURES

- ➤ The original SS-2 prototype went aloft for the first time on 5 October 1967.
- ➤ In its rescue configuration, the ShinMaywa can carry 20 seated survivors or 12 patients on stretchers.
- ➤ The amphibian SS-2A version was first flown on 16 October 1974.
- ➤ One SS-2 was converted for firefighting, using equipment from Comair in Canada.
- ➤ The US Navy retired the Martin P5M Marlin, its last flying-boat, two years before the first flight of the SS-2.
- ➤ ShinMaywa was formerly known as Kawanishi.

PROFILE

Japan's famous flying-boat

The ShinMaywa SS-2 flying-boat was ordered into production in 1966, and 23 aircraft were built for anti-submarine patrol duties using the military designation PS-1. During the Cold War, the threat from the Soviet Union's submarine force was viewed with alarm in Japan. These naval aircraft, from the same builder as the 'Emily' flying-boat of World War II, flew thousands of missions guarding against the threat until their retirement in 1989.

Because of its obvious utility to a nation of islands surrounded by ocean, the ShinMaywa remains in service and re-entered production in the 1990s, now designated US-1. The seafaring capability of this aircraft makes it a 'guardian angel' to those in peril, and it is credited with several hundred rescues. Its comprehensive rescue equipment includes flares, float lights, droppable life raft containers, maritime markers and even a lifeboat with an outboard motor. The SS-2 with amphibious gear and more powerful engines is almost certainly the most hi-tech seaplane ever built, and will serve for many years.

It may look like an ungainly beast, but the SS-2 has advanced lift devices. Using upper surface blowing and slats, it can take off in only 80 metres and fly at very low speeds.

Like most maritime patrol aircraft, the SS-2 has a long, straight wing and four engines. The torpedo armament of the earlier versions was carried between the engines.

Most of the fuel capacity of the SS-2 is contained in large tanks between the wing spars.

The SS-2 is almost unique in having a hidden fifth engine. The T-58, installed in the top of the fuselage, blows hot air through ducts to the wing and tail surfaces to help lift performance.

SS-2

Japan remains the sole operator of the SS-2. This aircraft of the 75th Kokutai (squadron) entered service in 1976, and has saved many lives in rescues.

The fuselage carries all the essential rescue equipment along with the normal crew of nine.

For the rescue mission, the SS-2 can carry 12 stretchers or 20 seated survivors. The cabin can also store a rubber dinghy, which can be deployed through twin doors in the hull.

The nose houses a powerful search radar, although the sonar equipment fitted to the older anti-submarine aircraft has been deleted.

The hull of the SS-2 has a suppression system to deflect spray clear of the engines on take-off.

The boat-shaped hull of the SS-2 is an ingenious design, allowing very short take-offs despite its large size.

A rare feature of the SS-2 is its slatted tail. The 'T-tail' design helps keep this area clear of the sea.

SS-2

Type: anti-submarine aircraft (crew of 10); search-and-rescue aircraft (crew of nine)

Powerplant: four 2605-kW (2,850-hp.) Ishikawajima-built General Electric T64-IHI-10J turboprops; one 1014-kW (1,359-hp.) Ishikawajima-built General Electric T58-IHI-10J turboshaft

Maximum speed: 520 km/h (340 m.p.h.) at 3,040 m (10,000 ft.)

Range: 3800 km (2,360 mi.)

Service ceiling: 7195 m (29,500 ft.)

Weights: empty 25,500 kg (56,200 lb.); loaded 45,000 kg (100,000 lb.)

Dimensions:

span	33.15 m (107 ft. 3 in.)
length	33.46 m (109 ft. 11 in.)
height	9.95 m (31 ft. 10 in.)
wing area	135.82 m² (1,460 sq. ft.)

COMBAT DATA

RANGE

Designed for long-duration patrols, the big ShinMaywa boat has an extended range only bettered by the exceptional Russian Beriev Be-12. At normal cruise speeds the SS-1 and US-1 can stay aloft for at least nine hours at a time. Its turboprop engines give excellent fuel efficiency, increasing endurance.

Be-12 'MAIL' 5500 km (3,400 mi.)
ALBATROSS 2760 km (1,700 mi.)
SS-2 3800 km (2,360 mi.)

RESCUE CAPACITY

Flying-boats, with their high speed and long range, are particularly well-suited to mounting rescues far out into the ocean. Although their rescue capacity is no greater than that of the biggest of the current generation of helicopters, any fixed-wing aircraft is so much faster than a rotary-winged machine that it can make two or three trips in the time that a helicopter makes a single journey speeding recovery time. It is only the lack of hovering capability that stops the flying-boat from being the ideal rescue machine.

Be-12 'MAIL' 8 stretchers
ALBATROSS 10 stretchers
SS-2 12 stretchers

MAXIMUM SPEED

Turboprop power has revolutionised the performance of flying-boats. The Grumman Albatross is one of the best of the piston-engined boats, yet it would be left far in the ShinMaywa's wake.

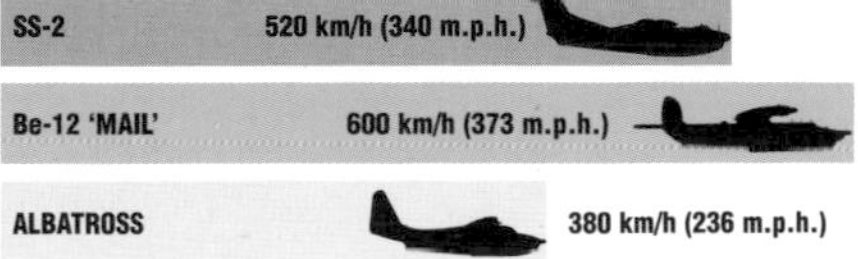

The Kawanishi connection

■ KAWANISHI H6K 'MAVIS': Built by one of Japan's oldest flying-boat makers, the Sikorsky-inspired 'Mavis' was the Imperial Navy's main patrol-boat in the first years of World War II.

■ KAWANISHI H8K 'EMILY': One of the biggest jumps in flying-boat technology ever devised, the 'Emily' was a heavily-armed boat which entered service as World War II started.

■ SHINMAYWA: The Kawanishi company was renamed Shin Meiwa (now ShinMaywa) in 1949. Their first post-war design was the piston-engined XS, which foreshadowed the PS-1.

SIAI-MARCHETTI

SF.260

● Training and light attack aircraft ● 1960s design ● Turbine version

Designed by Stello Frati as a three-seat civilian aircraft for the Aviamilano company, the SF.260, as it became known, was put into production by SIAI-Marchetti. After disappointing sales in the civilian market, the aircraft's potential for training or light ground-attack duties was realised. Now in service with 19 air arms around the world, the SF.260 is ideal as a low-cost attack aircraft for less wealthy countries. It is currently available in turboprop form.

▲ *Aviamilano flew the SF.260 as a two-seat type in 1964. Still in production (by SIAI-Marchetti, part of Agusta) more than 30 years later, the popular trainer has found numerous military buyers.*

PHOTO FILE

SIAI-MARCHETTI SF.260

◀ EFS contender
In the early 1990s, Agusta proposed the SF.260 in answer to the USAF's Enhanced Flight Screener (EFS) requirement for a replacement for the Cessna T-41A.

▼ Turbine-powered SF.260TP
Offering improved performance over its piston-engined counterpart, the Allison 250-powered SF.260TP has found six military customers.

▼ Pilot trainers
Belgium's 35 SF.260s are a mixture of military SF.260Ms and civil SF.260Ds.

▼ Somalian COIN
Until the mid-1990s, Somalia operated four SF.260Ws on counter-insurgency (COIN) duties.

◀ Aerobatic Belgian
In 1996, this colourful SF.260MB was a member of the 'Swallows', the Belgian national aerobatic team. ST-35 also carries the air force's 50th anniversary markings.

FACTS AND FIGURES

- ➤ By 1996, more than 900 SF.260s of all versions (including turboprops) had been ordered, most for military customers.
- ➤ In 1992, the first Turkish air force example built locally by TAI was delivered.
- ➤ The prototype SF.260M was first flown on 10 October 1970.
- ➤ Zimbabwe's SF.260TP turboprops were delivered as piston-engined, armed trainer SF.260WCs and converted locally.
- ➤ A search and surveillance SF.260SW Sea Warrior version with radar is available.
- ➤ In 1996, 20 countries continued to operate the SF.260 in various versions.

PROFILE

From sporty single to Warrior

With sleek lines and superb aerobatic qualities, the SF.260 recovered from a lack of interest in the civil market (as a result of its comparatively high cost) to become a great success in the military sector, with sales of more than 900. The first military version was the primary/basic training SF.260M which initially flew in October 1970. A strengthened airframe and more advanced equipment fit meant sales to five different air arms were forthcoming.

On the back of this success, SIAI-Marchetti developed the SF.260W Warrior. This aircraft retained the same training capability, but also featured two or four underwing hardpoints capable of carrying up to 300 kg (660 lb.) of ordnance. This versatility made the SF.260W ideal for a variety of roles such as air support, forward air control, armed reconnaissance and low-level strike. It achieved significant sales to a number of smaller air arms as a cost-effective multi-role aircraft.

Above: Zambia has a small fleet of piston-engined SF.260MZs. The basic military SF.260 lacked the SF.260W's strengthened airframe.

The turboprop-powered SF.260TP is the latest military version. Among five customers are Ethiopia and Sri Lanka, who have used this version in the counter-insurgency role.

Below: This pair of Sri Lankan SF.260TPs operate with No. 1 Flying Training Wing. Hardpoints allow carriage of light ordnance.

SF.260W Warrior

Type: single-engined light trainer and tactical support aircraft

Powerplant: one 194-kW (260-hp.) Avco Lycoming O-540-E4A5 piston engine

Maximum speed: 305 km/h (189 m.p.h.) at sea level

Range: 1104 km (684 mi.) with maximum internal fuel

Service ceiling: 4480 m (14,700 ft.)

Weights: empty 770 kg (1,694 lb.); maximum take-off 1300 kg (2,860 lb.)

Armament: two or four podded 7.62-mm (.30 cal.) machine-guns or up to 300 kg (660 lb.) of bombs or reconnaissance pods

Dimensions:		
	span	8.35 m (27 ft. 5 in.)
	length	7.10 m (23 ft. 4 in.)
	height	2.41 m (7 ft. 11 in.)
	wing area	10.10 m² (109 sq. ft.)

SF.260WT Warrior

Tunisia operated a mixed fleet of SF.260CTs and WTs in the training and COIN roles in 1996. Aircraft 401 is one of the latter and carries the markings of the Tunisian air force.

Piston-engined SF.260s are powered by either a normally-aspirated Avco (now Textron) Lycoming O-540 air-cooled, flat-six, or a fuel-injected AEIO-540. Both variants are rated at 194 kW (260 hp.).

A distinctive feature of the SF.260 family is the wingtip fuel tanks, each able to hold 72 litres (20 gal.). Two or four underwing hardpoints on the SF.260W are able to carry up to 300 kg (660 lb.) of stores between them, including gun pods, bombs, camera pods and supply containers.

Originally designed as a two-seater, the SF.260 was soon available with a third seat, to the rear of the cockpit. While the SF.260M is essentially a training aircraft with improved cockpit instrumentation, the strengthened SF.260W Warrior adds other roles, including close support, forward air control (FAC), armed reconnaissance and liaison.

A cantilever, low-wing monoplane, the SF.260 has an all-metal stressed-skin structure. The original design introduced Frise-type ailerons and electrically-operated flaps. The aircraft's landing gear is also electrically retracted.

Relatively high costs have resulted in only limited civilian SF.260 sales. In the US, the type was marketed as the Waco Meteor but, again, sales were disappointing and SIAI-Marchetti concentrated on developing military variants.

ACTION DATA

STORES LOAD

All three types are able to carry a variety of stores, including various types of ordnance and reconnaissance equipment. A load of 300 kg (660 lb.) is typical of these small aircraft, although the UTVA-75 is limited to just 200 kg (440 lb.).

SF.260W WARRIOR 300 kg (660 lb.)
RALLYE 235 GUERRIER 300 kg (660 lb.)
UTVA-75 200 kg (440 lb.)

MAXIMUM CRUISING SPEED

From the outset, the SF.260 was designed as a relatively fast sporting aircraft. This performance made the type attractive to military operators in a variety of roles, especially pilot training. Speed was also a useful attribute in the forward air control role.

SF.260W WARRIOR 281 km/h (189 m.p.h.)
RALLYE 235 GUERRIER 245 km/h (152 m.p.h.)
UTVA-75 185 km/h (115 m.p.h.)

TAKE-OFF DISTANCE TO 15-M HEIGHT

Compared to the SOCATA Rallye and UTVA-75, the SF.260 has a modest take-off distance performance of 825 m. The former designs are more useful aircraft when flown from confined airstrips.

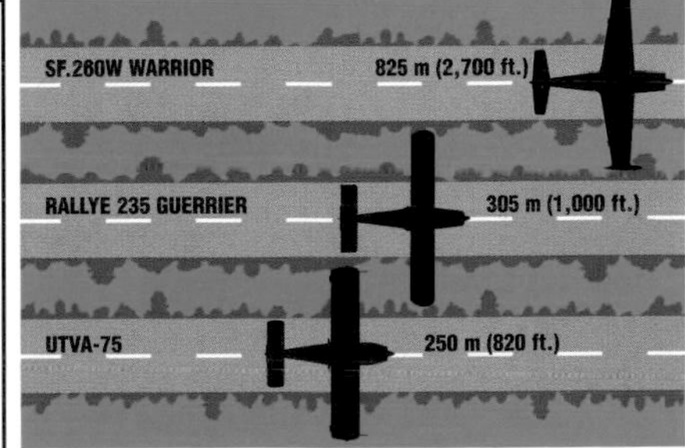

Post-war armed piston-engined trainers

NORTH AMERICAN T-6 TEXAN: Famous as a wartime pilot trainer, the versatile Texan (Harvard in RAF and Commonwealth service) was often adapted as a weapons trainer.

HUNTING PERCIVAL PROVOST: As well as serving with the RAF, the Provost trainer of 1950 was sold in armed Mk 52 and Mk 53 versions to Rhodesia, Eire, Burma, Iraq and Sudan.

SOCATA RALLYE 235G GUERRIER: A military version of the 235E, the Guerrier had a strengthened airframe and underwing hardpoints. Only one example was completed.

AEROSPATIALE TB 30B EPSILON: Togo took delivery of an armed version of the French air force's two-seat basic trainer in 1986. Underwing pylons have a 300-kg (660-lb.) capacity.

SIKORSKY

S-61/SH-3 SEA KING

● **Anti-submarine helicopter** ● **In service for 30 years**

As a true rotorcraft pioneer, Sikorsky was quick to realize the potential of the helicopter for anti-submarine warfare (ASW) operations. With its HSS-1 Sea Bat already in service, Sikorsky designed the HSS-2 Sea King as its turbine-engined replacement. The company could not have envisioned that the Sea King would become one of the world's most important helicopters, in service with the US Navy (USN) and many export customers.

▲ *One of the world's best known helicopters, the Sikorsky S-61 is also one of the longest-serving. Although now a rare sight in US Navy colours, the type continues to fly with other air arms.*

PHOTO FILE

SIKORSKY S-61/SH-3 SEA KING

▼ Topex

An SH-3H, belonging to HS-9 from Carrier Air Wing 8 aboard the USS Nimitz*, flies in company with a Brazilian Navy machine during the annual 'Topex' anti-submarine warfare exercise in the Atlantic.*

▲ Space rescue

Sea Kings were used for recovering astronauts after the Apollo *lunar landings.*

Dual-role helicopter ▶

In the early 1970s the USN needed a helicopter to perform both plane guard and ASW duties aboard its attack carriers and the SH-3 proved ideal.

▼ Enduring design

Despite being in service for more than 40 years, the S-61's outward appearance has surprisingly changed very little, though the latest versions are considerably more capable than early variants.

▼ Helicopters for the White House

Possibly the most glamorous of all S-61s are the VH-3Ds in use as VIP transports for the US president and government officials.

FACTS AND FIGURES

- ➤ Sea Kings were heavily involved in Vietnam, rescuing many downed USN pilots during the long conflict.
- ➤ A small number of RH-3A minesweeper variants entered service in 1964.
- ➤ The Royal Canadian Navy was the first export customer, ordering 41 of the type.
- ➤ Aeronautiche Giovanni Agusta acquired a licence to assemble Sea Kings for the Italian air force and navy.
- ➤ Argentina is unique in that it operates both Sikorsky- and Agusta-built examples.
- ➤ The SH-3 has been replaced by aboard USN carriers by the SH-60F Sea Hawk.

PROFILE

Backbone of the world's navies

Known by Sikorsky as the S-61 and by the US Navy as the SH-3, the Sea King still serves in considerable numbers, having flown for the first time on 11 March 1959.

Combining the roles of submarine hunter and killer thanks to its Bendix AQS-10 dipping sonar, Ryan APN-130 radar, and torpedo or depth bomb weapon load, the SH-3A was an instant success. The few remaining USN Sea Kings have all been upgraded to SH-3H standard. The design has also formed the basis of the much-modified Westland Sea King.

In addition to its ASW machines, the USN also flew nine examples of the specialized RH-3A minesweeping version of the basic SH-3, while a number of combat search and rescue HH-3 aircraft, also based on the SH-3 airframe, were built for the US Air Force.

Export customers included Argentina, Brazil, Canada, Denmark, Iran, Italy, Japan, Malaysia, Peru, Spain, and the UK. Several of these deals have included production licences.

Above: SH-3s can actually be refuelled in flight, although the usual method is somewhat different from that shown here!

Below: In Italian naval service, the Agusta SH-3Ds wear this dark sea grey colour scheme with high visibility Day-Glo noses and tail bands.

SPECIFICATION
SH-3H Sea King

Type: anti-submarine and plane guard shipboard helicopter

Powerplant: two 1044-kW (1,400-hp) General Electric T58-GE-10 turboshafts

Maximum speed: 267 km/h (166 mph)

Cruising speed: 219 km/h (136 mph)

Initial climb rate: 670 m/min (2,198 fpm)

Range: 1005 km (624 miles)

Service ceiling: 4480 m (14,698 ft)

Weights: empty 4428 kg (9,762 lb); loaded 9525 kg (21,000 lb)

Accommodation: two pilots and two systems operators

Dimensions:

rotor diameter	18.90 m (62 ft)
length	22.15 m (72 ft 8 in)
height	5.13 m (16 ft 10 in)
rotor disc area	280.47 m² (3,019 sq ft)

SH-3H SEA KING

This SH-3H of HS-7 'Shamrocks' served aboard the USS *John F. Kennedy* (CV-67) during the carrier's 1983–84 Atlantic cruise.

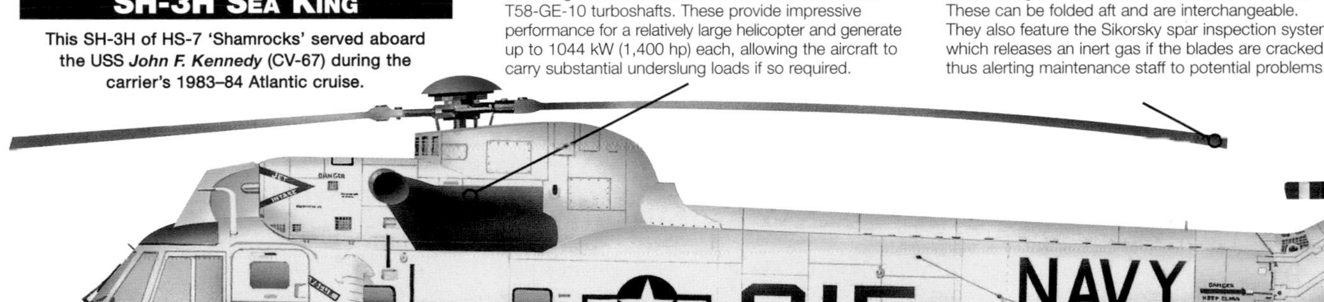

Powering the SH-3H variant are two General Electric T58-GE-10 turboshafts. These provide impressive performance for a relatively large helicopter and generate up to 1044 kW (1,400 hp) each, allowing the aircraft to carry substantial underslung loads if so required.

All Sea Kings are fitted with five-blade main rotors. These can be folded aft and are interchangeable. They also feature the Sikorsky spar inspection system, which releases an inert gas if the blades are cracked, thus alerting maintenance staff to potential problems.

All Sikorsky S-61s are amphibious and are capable of landing on water for brief periods if necessary. The underside of the fuselage is sculpted to act as a watertight hull.

Equipment unique to the USN 'H' variant includes an AQS-13B sonar, a Canadian Marconi surveillance radar, and towed magnetic anomaly detector for hunting submarines.

The anti-torque tail rotor is fitted on the port side and also features five blades. A single stabilizer is fitted on the opposite side. The entire tail section is movable and can hinge to starboard for accessibility and stowage below carrier decks.

ACTION DATA

POWER

Even when it entered service, the Sikorsky Sea King was a powerful machine, able to lift substantial loads. In later years Westland built its own version with more powerful engines.

RANGE

When employed for plane guard or search-and-rescue duties the Sea King does not operate far afield. In the ASW role Sea Kings work with longer-ranged fixed-wing aircraft. The bigger Aérospatiale Super Frelon is primarily a tactical transport helicopter

SH-3H SEA KING 1005 km (624 miles)

SEA KING HAS.MK5 1230 km (764 miles)

SA 321G SUPER FRELON 1020 km (634 miles)

CLIMB RATE

Despite being fitted with more powerful engines, the Westland Sea King performs less well than its slightly older Sikorsky cousin. The lumbering Super Frelon is very slow by comparison.

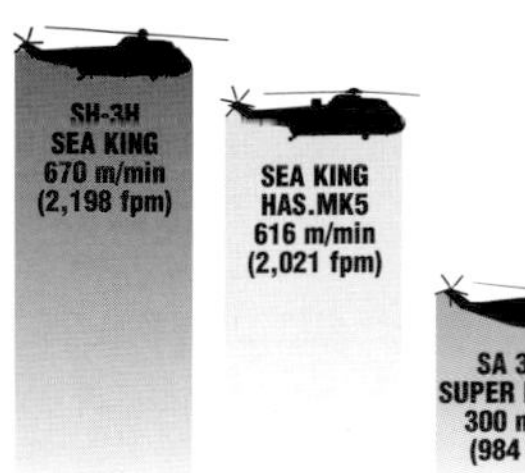

Sea King goes foreign

■ **BRAZILIAN NAVY SH-3D:** A number of machines were delivered to the Brazilian Navy and operated by 1° Esquadro de Helicopteros Anti-submarinos from Sao Pedro de Aldoida.

■ **JMSDF HSS-2B:** Mitsubishi of Japan acquired a licence to build Sea Kings and Japan's Maritime Self-Defence Force uses the type for anti-submarine warfare and rescue duties.

■ **SPANISH SH-3D:** This smart example is one of a batch of ex-USN machines transferred to Spain. These have been upgraded to SH-3H standard and serve with Escuadrilla 001.

SIKORSKY

S-65/CH-53

● **Heavylift transport helicopter** ● **Combat rescue** ● **Minesweeper**

One of the rotary-wing marvels of the Vietnam era, the Sikorsky S-65 was the largest helicopter built outside the USSR. Its dynamic parts (rotor, gearboxes and control system) were developed from those of the earlier S-64 SkyCrane and made extensive use of titanium. Fitted with folding rotor blades for shipboard stowage and given the designation CH-53 Sea Stallion by the US Marines, the S-65 emerged as the world's most capable assault transport.

▲ *Powerful and adaptable, the CH-53 revolutionised Western helicopter operations when introduced in the 1960s, and has proved extremely capable in a variety of land-based and seaborne roles.*

PHOTO FILE

SIKORSKY S-65/CH-53

◀ **Grenada attack**
The CH-53 saw action in the US invasion of Grenada, landing large numbers of Marines. The CH-53 fleet suffered no casualties in the operation, although UH-60s and AH-1s were shot down.

▲ **Heavy lifter**
The CH-53 was one of the few helicopters in Vietnam that could recover damaged aircraft, such as this Grumman A-6D.

▲ **Vietnam airlift**
The CH-53 won its laurels in Southeast Asia, flying in difficult 'hot and high' conditions and constantly threatened by ground fire. It is seen here delivering Marines to the besieged base at Khe Sanh.

◀ **Green Marine**
In Marine Corps service, the CH-53 is based on 'Tarawa'-class assault ships. It is the largest troop lifting asset available to the USMC.

▼ **Soldiering on**
Although succeeded in the 1980s by the more powerful CH-53E Super Stallion, the CH-53D remains in widespread service.

FACTS AND FIGURES

- US Air Force CH-53 cargo-haulers and HH-53B/C 'Super Jollies' began reaching Vietnam in 1967.
- The interior of the CH-53 is fitted with rollers for easy movement of cargo.
- Air Force special operations HH-53Hs and MH-53Js are rebuilds of HH-53B/Cs.
- Germany has the biggest fleet of S-65s outside the USA. VFW-Fokker licence-built 110 of the helicopters for the army.
- RH-53Ds were used as transports in the hostage rescue attempt in Iran in 1980.
- Marine pilots demonstrated that the S-65 could perform loops and rolls.

PROFILE

Sikorsky's strong lifter

The US Marine Corps had been strong believers in the value of the helicopter since Korea, and during the Vietnam War it was the Marines who were the inspiration for the largest and most powerful helicopter in the world outside the Soviet Union. From their earliest battles in 1965 they counted on the box-shaped, heavylift S-65 to haul ammunition, troops and supplies from logistics bases right out to the battle area. To the Marines who use air power as an adjunct to ground forces, the S-65 provided a new standard of speed and mobility in battle.

The CH-53A was the only version of the Sikorsky S-65 for some time after the first flight on 11 October 1964. In time, however, others saw the value of the powerful machine. US Navy MH- and RH-53s were used to sweep mines at sea; the US Air Force's HH-53 'Super Jolly' is a dedicated combat rescue machine. Other important operators include Austria, Germany and Israel. The Marines' 'ultimate' twin-engine S-65 was the CH-53D, which has since been supplanted by the much more powerful three-engined CH-53E, which is an entirely new machine.

The CH-53 is still used in the aircrew rescue role, and carried out a successful mission in Bosnia.

The MH-53J's rotor blades and tailboom have a power folding mechanism, which reduces the time needed to prepare the helicopter for air transport aboard the C-5 Galaxy.

An extensive avionics fit includes terrain-following radar and forward-looking infra-red sensors.

Special forces CH-53s have a crew of four: two pilots and two parajumpers, who act as loadmasters, winchmen, medics and gunners.

The tailboom folds to take up less space on confined carrier decks. The fixed tailplane acts as a stabiliser, providing improved pitch control.

Two external 1703-litre (450-gal.) drop-tanks more than double the MH-53's maximum range to nearly 900 km (1,060 mi.).

CH-53A

Type: twin-engine cargo helicopter

Powerplant: two 2127-kW (2,852-hp.) General Electric T64-GE-3, -6, -6B, or -12 turboshafts driving a six-bladed main rotor

Maximum speed: 305 km/h (189 m.p.h.) at sea level

Range: 870 km (540 mi.)

Weights: empty 10690 kg (23,567 lb.); loaded 18370 kg (40,500 lb.)

Accommodation: 55 troops, 24 stretchers and four attendants, or 3629 kg (8,000 lb.) of cargo loaded through full section rear ramp/doors; US Air Force rescue versions carry up to three 7.62-mm Miniguns

Dimensions:

main rotor diameter	22.02 m (72 ft. 3 in.)
length	20.47 m (67 ft. 2 in.)
height	7.6 m (24 ft. 11 in.)
rotor disc area	378.1 m² (4,070 sq. ft.)

MH-53J 'PAVE LOW III'

The US Air Force has long used the H-53 as a rescue helicopter. The latest variant is the MH-53J, in service with the special operations squadrons of the US Air Force.

Twin General Electric T64 turboshafts are mounted in pods on each side of the central gearbox.

The MH-53J's engines can be fitted with sand filters over the inlets and infra-red suppressors over the jetpipes.

The long inflight-refuelling probe extends forward, well clear of the rotor blades, when in use.

The tail bumper is fully retractable and the four-bladed tail rotor is slightly canted to port.

Special operations MH-53s have mounts for heavy machine-guns or multi-barrel Miniguns in the side doors and on the rear ramp.

COMBAT DATA

MAXIMUM SPEED

Big helicopters can be fitted with large rotor blades and powerful engines, and tend to be faster than their smaller brethren. The CH-53 is no exception. Even when carrying a heavy load, it remains one of the fastest helicopters in the world.

CH-53	305 km/h (189 m.p.h.)
Mi-26 'HALO'	295 km/h (183 m.p.h.)
SA 321 SUPER FRELON	248 km/h (154 m.p.h.)

RANGE

Although they cannot match the reach of fixed-wing machines, the CH-53 and its rivals have very long ranges for helicopters. Large size usually means the ability to carry large loads of fuel, which translates into the ability to fly quite long distances.

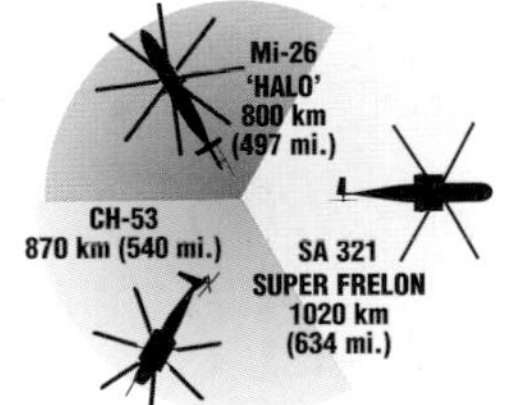

PAYLOAD

Large helicopters are designed to carry heavy loads. The CH-53 was for many years the West's most powerful helicopter, only replaced by the much modified and more powerful CH-53E. Though it cannot match Russia's giants for sheer lifting ability, the CH-53 is better in a tactical situation, being more agile.

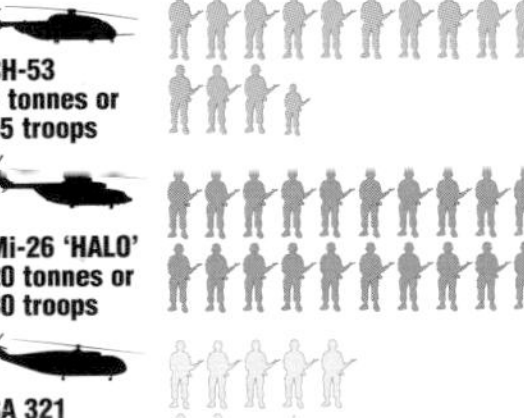

S-65s in service

MARINE ASSAULT: The CH-53 was designed primarily for the United States Marine Corps, which uses the type as its primary heavylift assault helicopter. Current versions can carry a 9-tonne payload.

GERMAN LOAD-LIFTER: The largest user of the big twin-engined Sikorsky outside the USA is the German army. The first of a fleet of 112 aircraft, all but two assembled or built by VFW Fokker, entered service in March 1973.

AIR FORCE RESCUE: The Sikorsky's size and speed made it ideal for combat rescue, and as the HH-53 it entered service with the US Air Force in Vietnam. Current versions are among the most sophisticated helicopters now flying.

SIKORSKY

UH-60 BLACK HAWK

● **Tactical assault helicopter** ● **First Gulf War transporter**

▲ *Carrying troops into battle demands a tough, fast helicopter. The UH-60 entered service in this role at the end of 1979, and has been a great success.*

Sikorsky's UH-60 Black Hawk is one of the most important combat helicopters in service today. Replacing the famous Bell Huey as the US Army's workhorse, the UH-60 was designed to haul a squad of 11 fully equipped infantrymen into battle. The same basic airframe has also been developed for special forces, combat rescue, air–sea rescue and anti-submarine operations.

PHOTO FILE

SIKORSKY UH-60 BLACK HAWK

▲ Squad carrier
The UH-60 can carry a larger squad of soldiers than the UH-1 it replaced, and in much greater comfort and protection.

Troops out ▶
The UH-60's doors are designed to allow an infantry squad to get into action in the minimum possible time.

▼ Weight lifter
Although designed as a troop carrier, the UH-60 can also carry a significant cargo load both internally and slung on hooks externally.

▲ Air assault
One of the conditions for the bulk of the equipment supplied to the Air Assault divisions of the US Army is that it should be Black Hawk-portable.

▼ Medical evacuation
A flying ambulance comes in to land at a desert airstrip, the soldier on the ground guiding the pilot through the fog of rotor-blown sand.

▲ Rope down
Special forces soldiers can abseil down from the UH-60 very quickly. This is useful in tight situations where the pilot cannot land safely.

FACTS AND FIGURES

- ➤ The original UH-60A prototype first flew on 17 October 1974.
- ➤ Black Hawks entered service with the 101st Airborne Division in 1979.
- ➤ Although the US Marine Corps has not adopted the UH-60, it flies nine VH-60N presidential transport helicopters.
- ➤ Black Hawks moved more than a million soldiers during the 1991 Gulf War.
- ➤ In a tragic 'friendly fire' mishap, F-15 fighters shot down two US Army UH-60s in Iraq on 14 April 1994, killing 26.
- ➤ The Army is developing a UH-60Q medical evacuation model of the Black Hawk.

PROFILE

Sikorsky's flying troop-truck

Known to the manufacturer as the Sikorsky S-70, the remarkable UH-60 Black Hawk provides soldiers with speed and mobility in the middle of the action, freeing them from terrain obstacles.

While combat troops enter and leave the battle zone aboard the UH-60, versions of the helicopter carry out electronic warfare duties, fight with special operations forces, or perform ambulance or VIP transport duties.

Pilots in the UH-60 have excellent visibility and armour protection as they fly in and out of landing zones. An exhaust suppression system reduces their vulnerability to heat-seeking battlefield missiles.

The UH-60 fought in Grenada, Panama, Iraq and Afghanistan, and appears little changed after more than two decades of Army duty. In fact, the UH-60 has been continuously upgraded with more powerful engines and other improvements. The latest UH-60L has the power to lift a military Hum-Vee tactical vehicle loaded with TOW anti-tank missiles.

The UH-60 was designed with all the years of experience of battle in Vietnam in mind. The low profile of the airframe makes it a difficult target, and safer if it crashes.

As a precaution against battle damage, the UH-60's engines are as widely spaced as possible.

The fuselage plan is noticeably broad and long, giving a generous internal capacity while allowing a very flat profile.

The UH-6's rotor system features swept tips, giving enhanced performance and allowing heavy loads to be lifted in 'hot and high' conditions.

UH-60A Black Hawk

Type: utility helicopter

Powerplant: two 1261-kW (1,691-hp) General Electric T700-GE-700, -701 or -401 turboshafts

Maximum speed: 296 km/h (184 mph)

Range: 600 km (373 miles)

Weights: (Army UH-60) empty 4819 kg (10,624 lb); loaded 9185 kg (20,249 lb). (Navy SH-60) empty 6191 kg (13,649 lb); loaded 9926 kg (21,883 lb)

Armament: usually two 7.62-mm (0.3-in) door guns

Dimensions:

rotor diameter	16.36 m (53 ft 8 in)
length	19.76 m
height	5.13 m
rotor disc area	210.10 m² (2,261 sq ft)

UH-60A BLACK HAWK

The UH-60A, the first of many versions of the Black Hawk family, saw action during the invasion of Grenada in 1981. The Black Hawk has since been in action in Lebanon, Somalia and the Gulf War.

The UH-60's rotor-head and blades were designed to withstand hits from large machine-gun rounds. The gearbox that drives it can run for half an hour after losing its entire oil supply.

The Black Hawk has an exhaust suppression system which dissipates hot engine gases. This makes the helicopter less of a target for heat-seeking infra-red missiles.

The transparent panels in the nose are essential for safe landing in confined spaces.

In an assault landing, the UH-60 comes in fast. Its undercarriage is designed to absorb vertical impacts of up to 45 km/h (28 mph).

Although the Black Hawk can carry armament, it is essentially a troop carrier. Its cabin and hatches are designed to allow a squad of infantry to get into action fast.

Sikorsky's designers intentionally built the tail rotor at an angle. This design feature means that lift is generated at the tail, allowing heavier loads at the rear of the cabin than would otherwise be possible.

COMBAT DATA

RANGE

PUMA 574 km (354 miles)
UH-60A BLACK HAWK 600 km (373 miles)
Mi-8 'HIP' 900 km (559 miles)

The Mi-8's greater size and fuel-carrying capacity give it an advantage over the Black Hawk when operating on internal fuel only. But the UH-60 can be fitted with stub wings, onto which can be mounted weaponry or external fuel tanks. With four tanks fitted, the efficient Sikorsky helicopter has a ferry range of more than 2000 km (1,240 miles).

MAXIMUM SPEED

The Black Hawk's powerful engines and slender aerodynamic cross-section make it one of the fastest helicopters around. It is quicker than most of its rivals, and this, allied to its great agility, makes it a superb platform for mounting helicopter assaults.

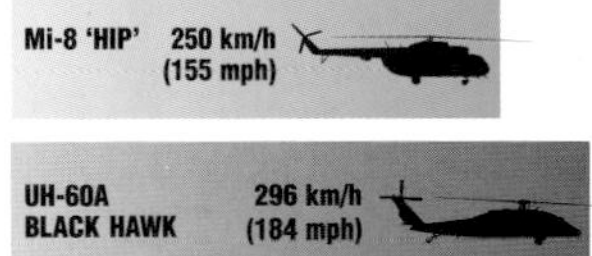

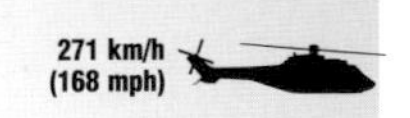

Mi-8 'HIP'	250 km/h (155 mph)
UH-60A BLACK HAWK	296 km/h (184 mph)
PUMA	271 km/h (168 mph)

PAYLOAD

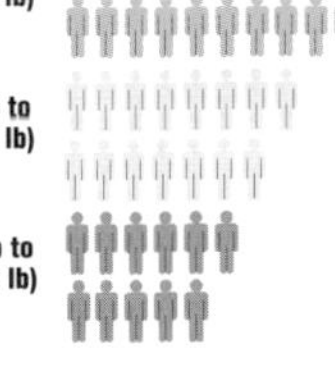

Mi-8 'HIP'	28 troops or up to 4000 kg (8,818 lb) of cargo
PUMA	15 troops or up to 3200 kg (7,055 lb) of cargo
UH-60A BLACK HAWK	11 troops or up to 3700 kg (8,157 lb) of cargo

Although the UH-60 is nominally an 11-seater, it can carry up to 20 troops in an emergency. The Black Hawk has enough power to lift the same kind of loads as its bigger Russian and European rivals, yet retains the agility of a much smaller machine.

Airborne helicopter assault in the 1991 Gulf War

GULF DEPLOYMENT: The Black Hawk was the most numerous helicopter in the Gulf, with over 350 serving with major US Army formations.

LOW-LEVEL FLIGHT: The biggest users of UH-60s were the 1st Cavalry Division and the 02nd and 101st Airborne divisions.

COALITION SPEARHEAD: Black Hawks were at the forefront of the Coalition offensive, taking spearhead troops deep into Iraqi-held territory.

SADDAM DEFEATED: By attacking in helicopters, elite US Army airborne troops were able to outflank Iraq's battlefield defences.

SLINGSBY

T.67/T-3A FIREFLY

● Military trainer ● Aerobatic ● Glass-fibre construction

Founded by Fred T. Slingsby in the 1930s, the Slingsby company became famous for producing highly respected gliders and sailplanes. By the 1980s the company's interests had diversified into other fields, and it was its experience in glass-fibre technology which lead to its success with the T.67 aerobatic trainer. Originally popular in the civil market, the aircraft has also achieved significant military sales in the more powerful T.67M form.

▲ *Low operating costs and impressive performance have led to significant orders from both civil and military customers. Glass-fibre construction also reduces maintenance costs.*

PHOTO FILE

SLINGSBY T.67/T-3A FIREFLY

◀ **Clear canopy**
The single-piece canopy fitted to the T.67 gives the pilot excellent visibility, which is useful for aerobatics.

▼ **Large span**
A long wingspan plus large ailerons give the T.67 superb stability and control, particularly during aerobatics.

Island trainers ▶
Four T.67M-200s were acquired by the Royal Hong Kong Auxiliary Air Force as trainers.

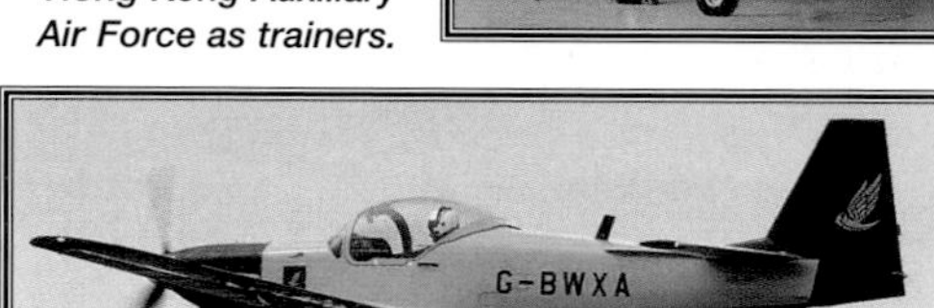

▲ **High visibility**
The Joint Elementary Flying Training School (JEFTS) T.67s are colourfully painted to be easily visible.

◀ **Training school**
Based at RAF Barkston Heath, the JEFTS operates 18 T.67Ms under a civilian contract, currently held by Hunting, for the RAF, Royal Navy and Army Air Corps.

FACTS AND FIGURES

- ➤ Developed from the Fournier RF-6B, the T.67B gained British CAA certification on 18 September 1984.
- ➤ Slingsby also designs and manufactures hovercraft in composite materials.
- ➤ Dutch airline KLM operates nine T.67s for training future aircrew.
- ➤ Initial production cost for the USAF's 113 T-3A Fireflys was US$54.8 million, plus options for air conditioning and radios.
- ➤ Northrop Grumman is the sub-contractor for final T-3A assembly at Hondo, Texas.
- ➤ The T.67M Firefly, G-BKAM, first flew on 5 December 1982.

PROFILE

Elementary trainer for the 21st century

In 1979 the newly reformed French Fournier company granted a licence to Slingsby for the manufacture of the RF-6B wooden trainer/tourer. Named T.67A, an initial series of 10 was built before Slingsby decided its experience in glass-fibre design could be integrated into the aircraft, producing a new and superior product.

Having re-engineered the RF-6B in glass-reinforced plastic (GRP), the T.67M (indicating its 'military' role) first flew from the company's Kirkbymoorside factory in 1982. Civil versions, named T.67B/C, achieved steady sales but it was the military interest which persuaded the company that the type had greater potential in this field.

Launched at the end of 1982, the T.67M Mk II Firefly was a dedicated military trainer with a new rear-hinged cockpit canopy, available with either 119-kW (160-hp.) or 149-kW (200-hp.) engines. Customers for this version to date have included the RAF and Royal Navy, and Norway's Flying Academy. A number of airlines in the UK and Japan also use the type for training. However, the type's greatest success has come in winning the USAF's Enhanced Flight Screener competition to replace the ageing T-41. Fitted with a 194-kW (260-hp.) engine and designated T-3A, 113 examples have been delivered, securing a healthy future for the company.

Above: Seen prior to its entry into USAF service, this T-3A displays the 'RA' tailcode of Randolph AFB, Texas.

Below: Seen in the colours of Hunting Aircraft Ltd, this T.67M Firefly 2 deploys full landing flap for a short-field landing at its Topcliffe base.

T-3A Firefly

Type: two-seat military basic trainer

Powerplant: one 194-kW (260-hp.) Textron Lycoming AEIO-540-D4A5 flat-six piston engine

Maximum speed: 281 km/h (174 m.p.h.)

Maximum cruising speed: 259 km/h (161 m.p.h.)

Endurance: 5 hr 20 min (with 20 min reserve)

Initial climb rate: 480 m/min (1,575 f.p.m.)

Range: 755 km (470 mi.) (with 30 min reserve)

Weights: empty 807 kg (1,775 lb.); maximum take-off 1145 kg (2,520 lb.)

Accommodation: two seats side by side

Dimensions:

span	10.59 m (34 ft. 9 in.)
length	7.57 m (24 ft. 10 in.)
height	2.36 m (7 ft. 9 in.)
wing area	12.63 m² (136 sq. ft.)

T.67M-200 FIREFLY

Four T.67s were acquired by Hong Kong as training aircraft. Registered HKG-10 to -13, they have now been sold because of the handover of the colony to China.

Royal Hong Kong Auxiliary Air Force T.67s were painted in a high-visibility white-and-orange paint scheme. Two of these aircraft have since been sold to Hunting in the UK for training duties with the JEFTS.

The heated and ventilated cockpit seats two pilots side by side. The canopy hinges upwards and to the rear, with a fixed windscreen to the front.

Control is provided by mass-balanced elevators and ailerons, with the elevators having a manually operated trim tab fitted. Strakes are situated forward of the tailplane roots to aid safer spinning.

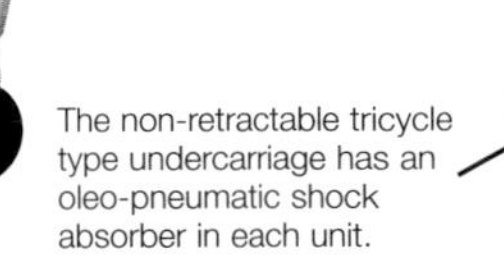

Power is provided by a 149-kW (200-hp.) Textron Lycoming AEIO-360-A1E piston engine driving a Hoffman three-bladed propeller.

The non-retractable tricycle type undercarriage has an oleo-pneumatic shock absorber in each unit.

The aircraft has a good avionics suite including an artificial horizon, turn co-ordinator, rate-of-climb indicator, outside temperature gauge and an accelerometer. Full IFR equipment is optional.

The aircraft structure is of glass-fibre-reinforced plastic, making the airframe strong enough for stresses of $+6/-3$ g. There is a stainless steel firewall between the cockpit and the engine to protect the pilots. The wings are covered with a double skin, made up of a corrugated inner layer bonded to a plain outer.

ACTION DATA

POWER

The Bulldog is the most powerful of these three training types, giving it better aerobatic and acceleration characteristics. More powerful versions of the Firefly can compete with the Bulldog on equal terms.

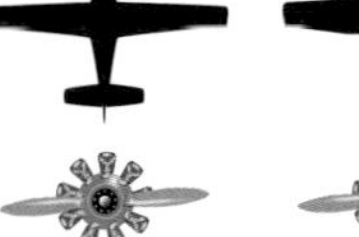

T.67M Mk II FIREFLY 119 kW (160 hp.)
T-41A MESCALERO 108 kW (145 hp.)
BULLDOG T.Mk 1 149 kW (200 hp.)

MAXIMUM SPEED

Despite having a less powerful engine, the Firefly has a better turn of speed than the Bulldog thanks to its more aerodynamic shape and lighter weight. The larger T-41 is a 1950s design and is slower.

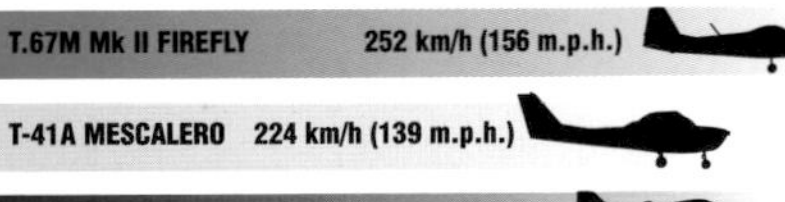

CLIMB RATE

The use of lightweight glass-fibre-reinforced plastic in the T.67's structure allows the aircraft to outclimb its two competitors. It also has a long wing span creating greater lift and aiding climb rate. The T-41 is a four-seat design, and this extra weight hinders climb performance.

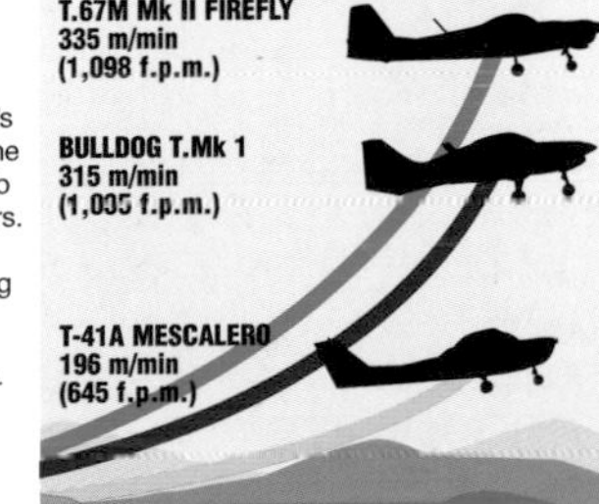

Slingsby post-war designs

■ **SLINGSBY KIRBY CADET:** Designed to an Air Ministry specification for a two-seat glider, the Kirby Cadet first flew in 1946.

■ **MOTOR TUTOR:** Devised by fitting a Tutor glider airframe with an undercarriage and an Aeronca engine, only three examples were built.

■ **T.61 FALKE:** This side-by-side two-seat trainer was based on the Scheibe SF-24A. Licence-production began in 1970.

■ **T.59 KESTREL:** Based on the German Glasflügel Kestrel, 109 T-59s were produced by Slingsby between 1971 and 1974.

Sud-Ouest

Vautour

● 1950s all-weather fighter and bomber ● In action with Israel

Sud-Ouest's Vautour was a versatile twin-jet produced in both single-seat and two-seat versions. For several years after entering service in 1956 it was France's only all-weather fighter, and it remained operational in this role until 1973. There were also light bomber and strike versions. The only other operator was the Israeli air force, which used the Vautour during the 1967 Six-Day War against Egypt, Iraq, Jordan and Syria.

▲ *Although ordered in large numbers by the French air force, only 140 were delivered and a significant proportion of these ended up in Israel. Like Britain and Canada, France chose to build its own all-weather fighter rather than buy American F-86 Sabres.*

Photo File

Sud-Ouest Vautour

Radar testing ▶

This two-seat Vautour found a new lease of life as the testbed aircraft for the Thomson-CSF RDM Cyrano 500 radar fitted to the Mirage 2000.

▲ Vautour IIB bomber

The bomber version of the Vautour was a two-seater, with the pilot sitting under the canopy, as in the IIA ground-attack version, but with his bomb-aimer positioned on a seat in the transparent nose of the aircraft.

▼ Second prototype

The second Vautour, S.O.4050-02, was completed as a single-seat, ground-attack aircraft powered by two Atar 101D turbojets. It first flew on 16 December 1963.

▲ Brand-new Vautour IIA

This early aircraft clearly shows the tandem main undercarriage and the engine nacelle-mounted outriggers.

◀ Underwing stores

Two pylons on each wing could be used to carry bombs, rockets or fuel drop-tanks.

Facts and Figures

- ➤ Pre-production Vautours were built with Rolls-Royce Avon and Armstrong Siddeley Sapphire engines.
- ➤ French air force Vautours have also been used as air-to-air refuelling tankers.
- ➤ Only 30 of 300 French air force Vautour IIAs originally ordered were built.
- ➤ When it entered service in 1956 the Vautour IIN was the Armée de l'Air's only all-weather/night fighter.
- ➤ The first Vautour was fitted with engines producing 23.54 kN (5,294 lb thrust) each.
- ➤ Vautours were produced by Sud-Ouest for three years from 1956 to 1959.

PROFILE

Versatile 1950s fighter-bomber

France's aircraft industry recovered remarkably well after World War II. Together with the Dassault series of jets came new military aircraft from the national aircraft industry, among them being Sud-Ouest's S.O.4050 Vautour.

The first version to fly, in 1952, was the IIN all-weather/night fighter. It carried a radar in the nose, four 30-mm (1.18-in) cannon or 240 air-to-air rockets in the forward fuselage and additional rockets or missiles under the wings. Next came the IIA, a single-seat, ground-attack aircraft armed with four cannon and up to six 450-kg (992-lb) bombs carried internally. The IIB was a two-seat bomber. It carried no guns, but had a glazed nose for bomb aiming. Some were modified as IIBR reconnaissance bombers.

Israel bought up to 25 IIAs together with a number of IINs in 1960. These were used in combat during the Six-Day War. After taking part in pre-emptive strikes against airfields on 5 June that left 309 Egyptian aircraft destroyed on the ground, Vautours were used against targets in Iraq and to support the ground troops advancing towards the Suez Canal.

The Armée de l'Air retained their Vautour IINs until 1973, when they started to be replaced by Mirage F.1Cs. This example carries the markings of 30e Escadre de Chasse.

Fuel drop-tanks were often carried on the inboard pair of wing pylons to increase the Vautour's range.

Two SNECMA Atar turbojet engines powered all production Vautours.

Camouflage was a feature of the Vautour towards the end of its career with the Israeli air force.

Vautour IIA

Type: single-seat ground-attack fighter

Powerplant: two 34.32-kN (7,719-lb-thrust) SNECMA Atar 101E-3 turbojet engines

Maximum speed: 1105 km/h (687 mph)

Maximum climb rate: 3600 m/min (11,811 fpm)

Range: 2575 km (1,600 miles)

Service ceiling: over 15,000 m (49,210 ft)

Weights: empty 10,000 kg (22,046 lb); maximum take-off 20,000 kg (44,092 lb)

Armament: four DEFA 30-mm (1.18-in) cannon, up to 240 rockets or 10 bombs in the fuselage bomb-bay, 76 MATRA M.116E rockets or 24 120-mm (4.72-in) rockets or two 450-kg (992-lb) bombs

Dimensions:

	span	15.09 m (49 ft 6 in)
	length	15.57 m (51 ft 1 in)
	height	4.50 m (14 ft 9 in)
	wing area	45.00 m² (484 sq ft)

VAUTOUR IIN

One of five Vautour IIN night fighters exported to Israel in 1960, '67' may have been among a number of Israeli Vautours converted for an electronic countermeasures role later in its career.

All crew positions were pressurized and equipped with ejection seats. In the IIN the backseater operated the radar, while in the IIB the second crewmember was the bomb-aimer.

As the Vautour used a high-mounted wing, the main undercarriage consisted of two main legs positioned in tandem and retracting into the fuselage. Outriggers retracted into the engine nacelles.

Some Vautour IINs were fitted with slab tailplanes after entering service with the Armée de l'Air and were redesignated II1Ns.

Nose radar was fitted to the IIN model, the only production Vautour variant so equipped.

The primary armament of the Vautour IIN consisted of four 30-mm (1.18-in) DEFA cannon mounted in the nose. These were also carried by the IIA, but were deleted in the IIB.

COMBAT DATA

MAXIMUM SPEED

The Vautour and the Canberra had excellent speeds for the mid-1950s when they entered service, and both could also climb to an impressive altitude. The later Yak-28, however, was a far quicker interdictor with its powerful RD 11 turbojet engines.

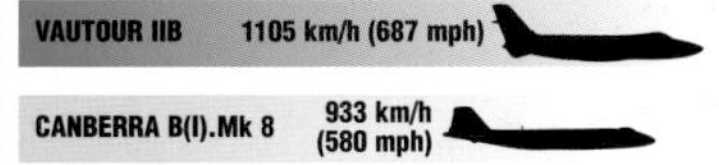

Aircraft	Speed
VAUTOUR IIB	1105 km/h (687 mph)
CANBERRA B(I).Mk 8	933 km/h (580 mph)
Yak-28B 'BREWER'	1900 km/h (1,181 mph)

RANGE

As air-to-air refuelling was in its infancy during the late 1950s range was especially important. Both the Vautour and the Yak-28 had good reach, but this was noticeably reduced when a full load of bombs was carried. The Canberra could not match the range of its rivals.

Aircraft	Range
CANBERRA B(I).Mk 8	1287 km (800 miles)
Yak-28B 'BREWER'	1950 km (1,212 miles)
VAUTOUR IIB	2575 km (1,600 miles)

BOMBLOAD

The Vautour and the Canberra could both carry a similar weight of bombs. The Canberra was highly versatile and was equipped with four cannon and had the ability to carry nuclear weapons. The Vautour was often employed in the ground-attack role.

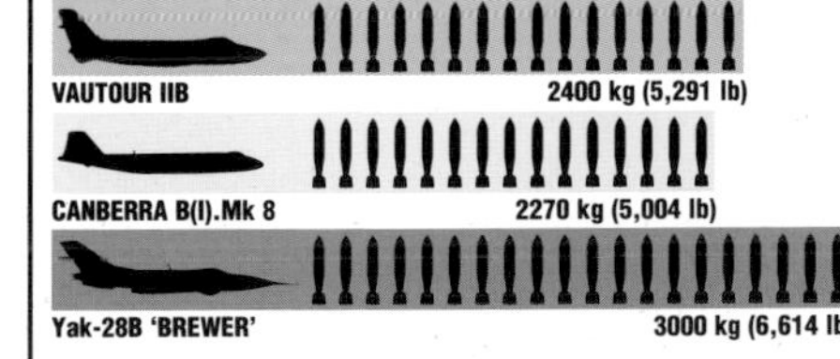

Aircraft	Bombload
VAUTOUR IIB	2400 kg (5,291 lb)
CANBERRA B(I).Mk 8	2270 kg (5,004 lb)
Yak-28B 'BREWER'	3000 kg (6,614 lb)

The Six-Day War

'BADGERS' ON THE GROUND: In the opening hours of the war, Israel launched pre-emptive strikes against neighbouring states, including Egypt where Soviet-built Tu-16s were caught on the ground.

TANKS IN THE SINAI DESERT: Vautours were also used tactically in support of ground forces. Major tank battles between Israel and Egypt took place in the Sinai Desert, with Vautours making bombing runs over enemy tank columns.

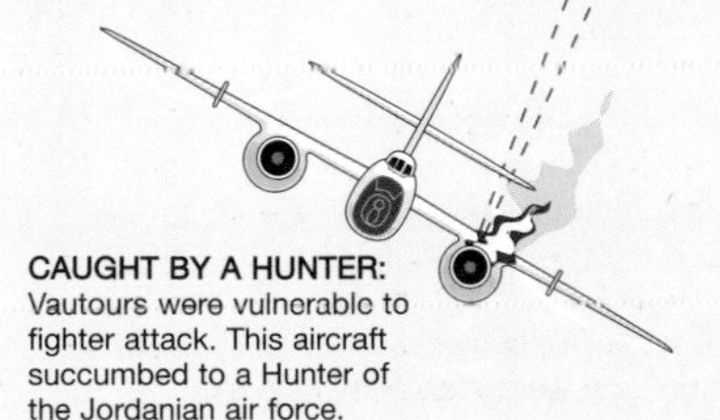

CAUGHT BY A HUNTER: Vautours were vulnerable to fighter attack. This aircraft succumbed to a Hunter of the Jordanian air force.

SUKHOI

SU-15 'FLAGON'

● Supersonic ● Twin-jet interceptor ● Delta-winged fighter

▲ A high-performance interceptor fighter built to replace the Sukhoi Su-11, the more powerful Su-15 was first revealed to the public at the 1967 Soviet Aviation Day in Moscow.

Sukhoi developed the Su-15 as a response to the threat from projected American bombers. Equipped with a high standard of avionics for automated interceptions with long-range missiles, the Sukhoi Su-15 was progressively upgraded, receiving new wings, engines, optional cannon pods and improved radar. Less well-known than rival MiGs, the Su-15 is now infamous for destroying a Korean Boeing 747.

PHOTO FILE

SUKHOI SU-15 'FLAGON'

▼ STOL research

This Su-15VD short take-off and landing version had three additional lift engines in the fuselage.

▲ Modified delta

Production Su-15s had a redesigned outer wing, with the leading edge reduced to 45° and greater span.

Missiles ▶

The Su-15's nose radar was used for long-distance auto-interceptions and firing of underwing air-to-air missiles.

▼ Twin turbojet

With a large diameter nose radar, the Su-15's two afterburning R-11F2SU-300 turbojets had side fuselage air intakes. These were canted outwards and raked back in plan view.

▲ Fighter cockpit

The Su-15 was equipped for all-weather operation, including SAU-58 autopilot, an Iskra-K blind-landing system and 'Taifun' interception radar.

FACTS AND FIGURES

- An exceptionally 'clean' fighter, the Su-15 could climb to 11 km (6.8 miles) at combat weight in 2½ minutes.
- The Su-15 was developed to counter the USAF bomber threat in the early 1960s.
- The first public showing was by a Soviet air force aerobatic team in 1967.
- The very long nose probe of the 'Flagon' housed pitch and yaw transducers which provided data for a fire-control computer.
- Su-15s shot down a KAL Boeing 707 in April 1978 and a 747 in September 1983.
- A dual trainer (Su-15UM) had a second cockpit in place of the No. 1 fuel tank.

PROFILE

Sukhoi's deadly 'Flagon'

Designed to fully meet the demanding requirement for an all-weather interceptor that would be able to remain operational in the most adverse conditions, the Sukhoi Su-15 was a conventional interceptor. The Sukhoi Design Bureau decided not to adopt a variable geometry wing, which was internationally favoured at that time. Instead, the Su-15 emerged as a needle-nosed single-seater incorporating some 'tried and tested' systems and equipment, including Tumanskii engines. The radar was new, as were the intended weapons.

Flight-testing of the Su-15 began in 1964, but a lengthy development period delayed its Soviet air force service debut until the early 1970s. The type was given the NATO reporting code name 'Flagon'. Among the variants that emerged were the Su-15UM tandem two-seat trainer ('Flagon-C') and the Su-15VD, with additional lift engines. Three of these were installed in the rear fuselage to provide data on V/STOL performance.

A compound delta wing was used on the principal interceptor version, the Su-15 'Flagon-D'. Armed with both missiles and guns, it was capable of a maximum 'dash' speed of Mach 2.59. Two final versions, designated 'Flagon-E' and 'F', also entered service.

The first prototype Su-15 was rebuilt for STOL research. It had a modified wing and three additional engines; one was in the forward bay, with two in tandem to the rear. It was first flown in 1966.

Su-15TM 'Flagon-F'

Type: all-weather interceptor fighter

Powerplant: two Tumanskii R-11 F2SU-300 turbojets giving 78.00 kN (17,196 lb thrust) (112.00 kN/24,692 lb thrust with afterburner)

Maximum speed: 2230 km/h (1,385 mph) at 13000 m (42,750 ft)

Range: 1380 km (860 miles)

Service ceiling: 16600 m (55,000 ft)

Weights: empty 10874 kg (24,000 lb); loaded 17194 kg (37,900 lb); maximum 17660 kg (38,900 lb)

Armament: four wing hardpoints for two R-98M and two R-60T AAMs and two underfuselage UPK-23-250 gun pods

Dimensions:		
	span	9.34 m (30 ft 8 in)
	length	20.54 m (67 ft 5 in)
	height	5.79 m (19 ft)
	wing area	36.6 m² (394 sq ft)

SU-15TM 'FLAGON-F'

The twin-turbojet, delta-winged Su-15 was first flown on 30 May 1962. It took nearly 10 years of development before it was fully operational as an all-weather air-defence fighter. More than 1500 had been built when production ended in 1979.

The swept-back fin and tailplane are of conventional all-metal construction, as are the all-moving tailplane and standard rudder.

Standard armament for the Su-15 was the R-98M AA-3 'Anab' missile. This was used in both infra-red homing and radar versions, and had a range of around 24 km (15 miles) and speed of around Mach 2.5.

The original conical radar nose radome was replaced in the later versions by one of ogival shape and housed the improved 'Taifun-M' interception radar. The entire avionics system could be linked to ground control stations for automated interceptions.

Forward fuselage is circular in section, with a bubble cockpit canopy. The side ram-type air intakes are rectangular with blow-in auxiliary intakes ahead of the wing.

The two afterburning Tumanskii turbojets are mounted side by side in the rear fuselage and have protruding variable-area nozzles below the rudder. Each engine drives separate electrical and hydraulic systems.

The aircraft had a tricycle-type undercarriage with single wheels on each leg. The nosewheel retracts forwards and the mainwheels retract inwards into the wings.

Underwing external stores were carried by a single pylon on early versions and two pylons on later 'Flagons'. To supplement the AA-3 missile, four infra-red close-range R-60 AA-8 'Aphid' air-to-air missiles could also be fitted on twin PD-62 pylons. There is provision for UPK gun pods under the fuselage.

Rectangular, door-type air brakes were fitted, one on each side of the fuselage, forward of the tailplane.

Death of KE007

1 NAVIGATION ERROR: Korean Air Flight 007 to Seoul set out from Anchorage, Alaska, but apparently strayed off course, heading towards the Soviet missile base at Petropavlovsk.

Anchorage

USSR

Petropavlovsk missile base test site

MiG-23s scrambled

KE007 destroyed

Su-15

USS *Badger*

Seoul

JAPAN

CHINA

2 INTRUDER: The 747 was mistaken for a USAF RC-135 which was in the area on a snooping mission. The intrusion into Soviet airspace prompted a huge reaction by the entire Soviet air defence chain, including the launch of Su-15s and MiG-23s.

3 SHOOT DOWN: After an unsuccessful attempt by two MiG-23s, an Su-15 acquired the target. Despite numerous radio calls to the 747, the aircraft continued on towards the Soviet Union's most important military bases on Sakhalin Island. Finally, the Su-15 pilot fired AA-3 missiles and destroyed KAL Flight 007, killing more than 260 passengers.

Key

- Area of Soviet airspace
- Limit of remote-control air-to-ground beacon
- Normal route for KAL flight
- Airway reporting points
- Flight path of KE007
- Supposed flight path after shoot-down
- Alleged flight path of the USAF's RC-135

COMBAT DATA

MAXIMUM SPEED

The Su-15's powerful twin R-13 turbojet engines propel the Su-15 well beyond Mach 2. Most jets of the 1960s era have an excellent turn of speed, but tend to lack the manoeuvrability of today's superfighters.

Aircraft	Speed
Su-15TM 'FLAGON-F'	2230 km/h (1,386 mph)
F-106A DELTA DART	2454 km/h (1,525 mph)
MIRAGE IIIE	2230 km/h (1,386 mph)

RANGE

All three aircraft were designed as interceptors to be used against attacking high-level bombers. Although they possessed respectable range for the 1960s, the use of afterburner drastically reduced their range. The use of airborne refuelling was important for longer range interception.

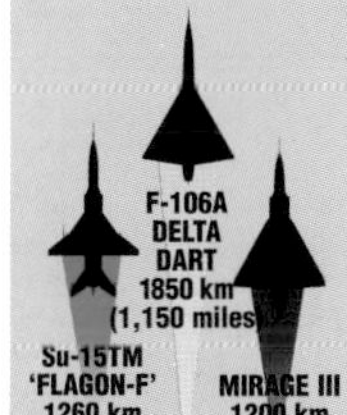

ARMAMENT

Standard armament for the later versions of the 'Flagon' was two medium-range and four short-range missiles. Like many 1960s fighters an integral cannon was omitted from the design, but the Su-15 often carried two 23-mm (0.91-in) GSh-23L cannon pods under the fuselage. The F-106 housed its weapons in an internal bay, allowing it to retain its aerodynamic shape.

SUKHOI

SU-17 'FITTER'

● Strike fighter ● Swing wing ● Afghan war veteran

Although overshadowed by Russia's better-known MiGs, the Sukhoi family of ground-attack aircraft have proved capable, sturdy and reliable in service, and have seen extensive combat with many countries around the world. The Su-17 'Fitter-C' and Su-22 'Fitter-K' combine modern, variable-sweep wings with the rugged features of earlier Sukhoi warplanes in a package liked by the pilots who fly it.

▲ *The Su-17 has evolved from a simple tactical fighter with limitations into a very capable strike machine. The latest versions can carry sophisticated precision-guided bombs and missiles.*

PHOTO FILE

SUKHOI SU-17 'FITTER'

▲ Libyan 'Fitter'
The Su-22s exported to Libya are armed with the K-13 'Atoll' infra-red missile, equivalent to early-model Sidewinders. The Su-22 lacks the modern avionics and weaponry of Russia's newer Su-17M-4.

▲ Nose cone
The shock cone in the nose is fixed, unlike the one in the earlier Su-7. It houses a laser rangefinder which may also be a marked target seeker.

▼ Low pass
An Su-17 pilot enjoys a high-speed pass over his home airfield at Templin.

▲ Redundant
The retirement of the Luftwaffe's Su-22s was resented by their pilots, who thought the aircraft was as good as the Tornado.

▲ Well equipped
This 'Fitter' is equipped with flare dispensers above the wingroots, a UV-32 rocket pod, an infra-red R-60 dogfight missile and the SPPU-22 wing cannon pod.

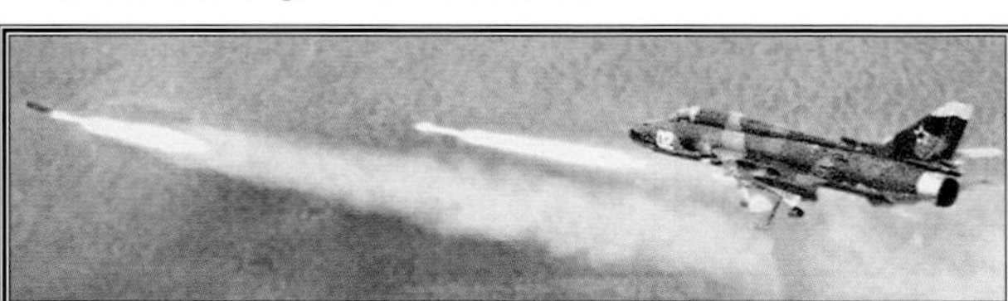

◀ Rocket blast
The Su-17's usual armament is the powerful UV-32 rocket pod, often used in Afghanistan for attacking rebel positions in caves.

FACTS AND FIGURES

- ➤ The prototype swing-wing Su-17 made its first flight on 2 August 1966.
- ➤ In a 1981 air-to-air engagement, a pair of Libyan Su-22s proved no match for US Navy F-14 Tomcats and were shot down.
- ➤ In the late 1980s Pakistan air force F-16s had tangles with intruding Afghan Su-22s.
- ➤ With wings swept forward, an Su-17 or Su-22 has a 100 km/h (62 m.p.h.) slower landing speed than earlier Sukhoi jets.
- ➤ An Afghan air force Su-22 pilot defected to Pakistan with his aircraft.
- ➤ All the Su-22s inherited by the Luftwaffe from East Germany have been retired.

PROFILE

Sukhoi's strike master

The original Sukhoi Su-7 'Fitter' was a swept-wing contemporary of the MiG-21. While Sukhoi jets were highly prized for their handling, their robust and rugged airframe and outright performance, they lacked the range to carry a heavy bombload over a long distance. The solution: variable-geometry wings, which can remain in the swept-forward position for low-speed performance when landing and taking off but can be swept back (as much as 62°) for high speed in combat.

Entering service with Frontal Aviation in the late 1960s, swing-wing 'Fitters' were upgraded several times to carry more fuel, weapons and better avionics. The aircraft was exported, as the Su-22, to Warsaw Pact air forces and to more than a dozen countries, from Afghanistan through Peru to the Yemen.

'Fitters' carried out thousands of attack missions in Afghanistan, flying precision strikes against the Mujahideen. More recently, they were in action in Peru in a border war with Ecuador, and in the Russian campaign in Chechnya. With the two-seat 'Fitter-E' and 'Fitter-G' providing excellent training, the Su-17 family will be around for many years to come.

Dismissed by many as a revamped Su-7, the Su-17 is a capable aircraft with good performance at low level. The 'Fitter' is popular with its pilots and is nicknamed 'Swallow' by Russian crew.

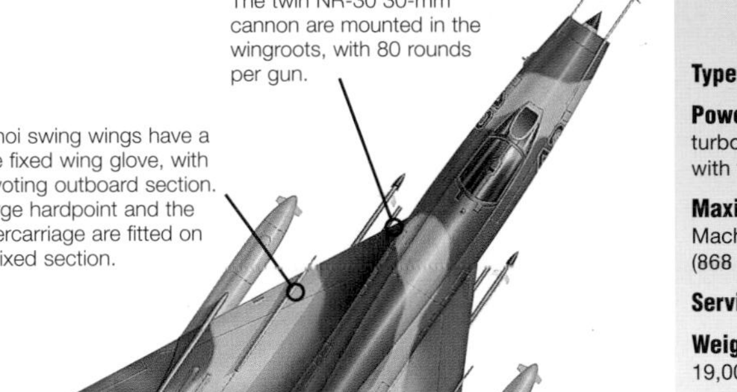

The twin NR-30 30-mm cannon are mounted in the wingroots, with 80 rounds per gun.

Sukhoi swing wings have a large fixed wing glove, with a pivoting outboard section. A large hardpoint and the undercarriage are fitted on the fixed section.

Like all the Sukhois of the 1950s and 1960s, the Su-17 has large wing fences.

The Lyul'ka turbojet is cooled through a number of vents and intakes, including a large vent at the base of the fin.

Su-22M-4 'Fitter'

Type: single-seat attack fighter

Powerplant: one Tumanskii R-29B augmented turbofan, rated at 122.34 kN (5,659 lb. thrust) with full afterburner

Maximum speed: 2335 km/h (1,448 m.p.h.) or Mach 2,20 at high altitude; 1400 km/h (868 m.p.h.) at sea level

Service ceiling: 15,200 m (49,869 ft.)

Weights: empty 11,000 kg (24,251 lb.); loaded 19,000 kg (41,887 lb.)

Armament: two 30-mm NR-30 or related cannon plus about 5000 kg (11,023 lb.) of weapons on two tandem pairs of pylons under the fuselage or under the wing

Dimensions:

span	14.00 m (46 ft.)
length	18.90 m (61 ft.)
height	5.18 m (17 ft.)
wing area	40.10 m² (431 sq. ft.)

Su-17 'FITTER-H'

Frontal Aviation of the Soviet air force was the largest user of the Su-17. This late model 'Fitter-H' version, with a pronounced dorsal spine, was based at Bagram in Afghanistan during the 1980s Soviet occupation.

A special TV-style display is installed in some Su-17s for the use of TV-guided weapons.

The pilot aims his weapons using a head-up display and ASP-17BC gunsight.

The Su-17M-4 introduced further avionics updates including a mission computer and a navigation system that comprised Doppler, radio compass, inertial navigation system and improved IFF equipment.

Flare pods can be fitted to the fuselage to decoy infra-red missiles.

Underwing armament can also include TV-guided and laser-guided bombs, and the AS-11 'Kilter' anti-radar missile.

Although the Su-17 had better range/payload than the Su 7 series, external fuel tanks are commonly fitted for all but short-range missions.

The rearward facing 'bullet' fairing covers an aerial for the 'Sirena' radar warning receiver.

COMBAT DATA

SEA-LEVEL SPEED

The 'Fitter' was designed as a Mach 2-capable fighter, and although current versions no longer carry any of the aerodynamic refinements necessary for such speeds they are still very fast at low level. However, achieving high speed requires plenty of afterburner, which uses fuel at such a rate that it cuts endurance to a matter of minutes.

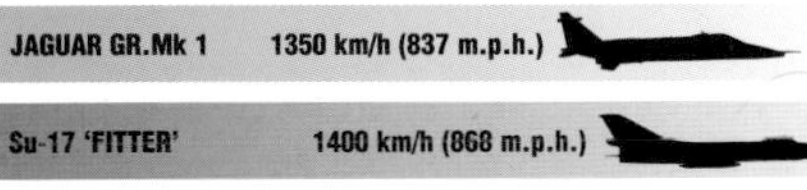

BOMBLOAD

The theoretical maximum bombload is almost never carried. Although a fighter like the Su-17 can lift over four tons of bombs, a normal combat load might consist of 1000 kg (454 lb.) of bombs, air-to-surface missiles and podded or unpodded rockets, ranging in calibre from 57 mm to 300 mm.

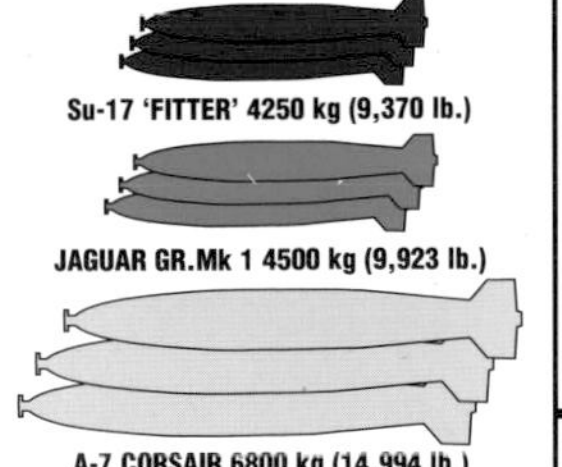

COMBAT RADIUS

Flying through the dense air at sea level requires a great deal of power, and although a jet might be capable of flying thousands of kilometres at economical speeds, on a lo-lo-lo mission it is much more limited. The 'Fitter' has always been somewhat 'short-legged', but it still has a useful tactical range.

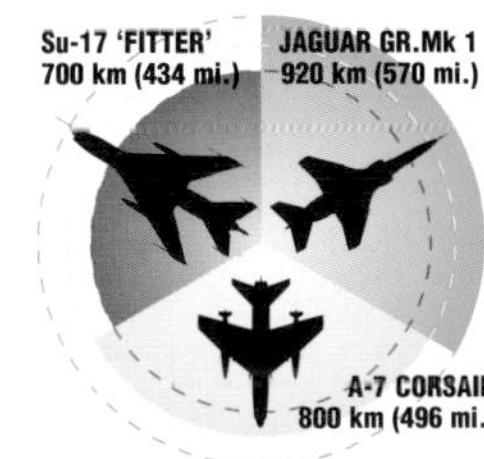

Sukhoi's dynasty of fighters

Su-7 'FITTER': First seen in 1956, it was the standard Soviet fighter bomber in the 1960s and was the foundation of a line of combat aircraft.

Su-9/11 'FISHPOT': This had a small delta wing and radar in the intake cone. It equipped 25 per cent of the Soviet air defence force in the 1970s.

Su-15 'FLAGON': Supplementing the 'Fishpot', the very fast 'Flagon' was of similar configuration but had two engines and a large nose radar.

Su-17 'FITTER': Originally known as the Su-7IG, the swing-wing adaptation of the 'Fitter' first entered service in the early 1970s.

Su-27 'FLANKER': In the 1980s Sukhoi stepped away from previous designs and introduced the 'Flanker', arguably the world's best fighter.

SUKHOI

SU-24 'FENCER'

● Low-level strike ● Electronic warfare ● Nuclear bomber

Fast, long-ranged and deadly accurate, the Su-24 'Fencer' was the first Soviet warplane with an avionics system which integrated navigation, bombsight and weapons control via a central computer. An advanced swing-wing bomber, the Su-24 could mount high-speed nuclear strikes deep into NATO territory from far behind the Iron Curtain. The Su-24 also proved its high-level bombing capability during operations over Afghanistan.

▲ *From bases in Poland or East Germany, the Su-24 could have hit air bases in eastern Britain. The huge increase in capability introduced by this aircraft caused NATO planners considerable headaches.*

PHOTO FILE

SUKHOI SU-24 'FENCER'

◀ Reconnaissance bird

The Su-24MR is equipped with advanced cameras and infra-red systems for the reconnaissance role. Electronic sensors can also be carried in pods.

▼ Wings forward

With its broad wings forward, the Su-24 can land at a sedate 230 km/h (143 m.p.h.). Full-span flaps and a slotted leading edge allow low-speed flight.

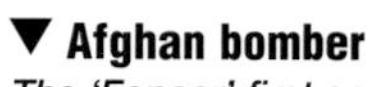

▼ Afghan bomber

The 'Fencer' first saw action in Afghanistan, flying long-range strikes in the Panjshir Valley from bases in the USSR.

▲ Anti-ship missile

Long-range naval strikes were another Su-24 speciality. This aircraft is armed with the lethal AS-11 'Kilter' missile, which has a 150-kg (330-lb.) warhead.

'Fencer-E' ▶

The reconnaissance 'Fencer-E' has dielectric panels on the nose sides. These cover the Shtik side-looking radar system, which has a moving target indicator and can be used to produce maps.

FACTS AND FIGURES

- ➤ The 'Fencer' was derived from a prototype that first flew in June 1967.
- ➤ The Su-24 entered squadron service in 1974 and appeared outside the USSR in 1979.
- ➤ The Su-24 was the first aircraft with the superb Severin K-36D ejection seat.
- ➤ About 700 'Fencers' of all versions have been manufactured.
- ➤ The reconnaissance 'Fencer-E' can use its cameras from altitudes of 150–2000 m (500–6,500 ft.).
- ➤ The Su-24 used laser-guided bombs to destroy bridges in Chechnya.

PROFILE

Sukhoi's long-armed striker

With side-by-side seating for its two-man crew and variable-geometry wings which can be swept back for high-speed flight, the powerful Su-24 has often been compared with the larger General Dynamics F-111. Like the American jet, the 'Fencer' is a long-range strike aircraft, but it also exists in reconnaissance and electronic warfare versions.

Improved Su-24s now in service make extensive use of smart weapons technology, including laser and TV designator/tracker systems. Like the F-111 and the smaller Tornado, the 'Fencer' can fly virtually all of a typical combat mission at treetop altitude, evading enemy radar and air defences and attacking with remarkable accuracy. Some versions of the 'Fencer' add in-flight refuelling capability, giving them strategic range.

Ironically, while the US Air Force is retiring the F-111 for economy reasons, the Sukhoi Su-24 is employed more widely than ever, as the forces of the former USSR are struggling to fund a replacement. This will probably be Sukhoi's Su-27IB strike fighter.

Seen here over the Baltic from a Swedish fighter, the 'Fencer' is a formidable machine. The loss of most Su-24s to other republics is keenly felt by the Russian forces.

'Fencer' has a twin nosewheel to allow operation from short unpaved runways at high all-up weights. A large mudguard is fitted behind the wheels to prevent the engines from ingesting snow.

The first 'Fencers' had a 30-mm cannon in the lower starboard fuselage, but this is replaced by cameras in the 'Fencer-E'.

Su-24 'Fencer-C'

Powerplant: two NPO Saturn (Lyul'ka) AL-21F-3A turbojets each rated at 76.49 kN (17,160 lb. thrust) dry and 110.33 kN (24,750 lb. thrust) with afterburning

Maximum speed: 2320 km/h (1,438 m.p.h.) at 11,000 m (33,600 ft.)

Service ceiling: 17,500 m (57,400 ft.)

Weights: empty 19,000 kg (41,800 lb.); loaded 36,000 kg (79,200 lb.)

Armament: one GSH-6-23m 23-mm cannon; provision for TN-1000 and TN-1200 nuclear bombs or for up to 8800 kg (19,360 lb.) of conventional bombs and missiles

Dimensions:

span (spread)	17.63 m (34 ft.)
span (swept)	10.36 m (21 ft.)
length	24.53 m (80 ft.)
height	6.19 m (20 ft.)
wing area	42 m² (452 sq. ft.)

Su-24 'Fencer-C'

The 'Fencer-C' differed from the earlier 'Fencer-B' in having radar warning receiver fairings just above the intake doors. This version serves with Russia and Kazakhstan, and the later 'Fencer-D' with the Ukraine.

The pilot looks through a PPV head-up display, supplied with data from the PNS-24M navigation system. This allows him to aim weapons accurately, aided by the Kaira laser and TV sighting system.

The crew sit side-by-side on K-36 ejector seats, which can be command-fired by either crew member. The canopy is a two-piece upward-hinging unit.

Outboard pylons can swivel to keep the wing stores facing into the airstream during wing sweep. An air-to-air missile, usually an R-60, can be carried under the outboard pylon.

The all moving tail is responsible for roll control as the aircraft has no ailerons. The cylindrical fairing on the rear of the tail houses the large brakechute.

The 'Fencer' has a forward-looking attack radar and a downward-facing terrain-following radar.

Almost any Russian air-to-surface weapon can be carried.

Power is provided by a pair of afterburning AL-21F turbojets.

Su-24 WEAPONS

AA-8 (R-60) MISSILE

The R-60 missile is a short-range infra-red homing weapon. The Su-24 usually carries at least one of these under the wing for self-defence against enemy fighters.

FAB-500 BOMB

The FAB-500 is the standard general-purpose Russian free-fall bomb. It is filled with 214 kg (471 lb.) of Torpex high-explosive, detonated by various types of fuses.

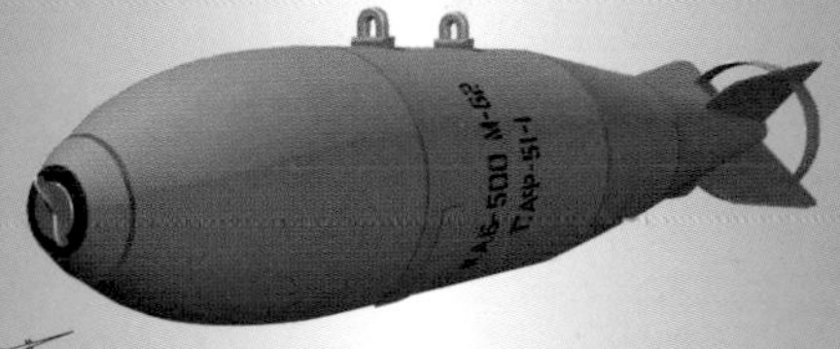

S-24 ROCKET

Designed to destroy large fixed installations such as aircraft shelters and missile launchers, the S-24 is unusual in that it relies only on fins for guidance. The weapon has a very powerful warhead. It is also carried by MiG-29 and Su-30 fighter-bombers.

Killing radar sites with 'Kegler'

1 TARGET ACQUIRED: The crew will have a general location of the target, and may get an exact fix from a 'Fencer-F' or other aircraft.

2 MISSILE AWAY: When the systems operator acquires the radar signal on his ESM system, he fires the AS-12 'Kegler' anti-radar missile, at up to 70 km (40 mi.) from the transmitter.

3 POP-UP AND DIVE: The missile can either be launched from high level for more range, or can pop-up from low-level and search.

4 RADAR DESTROYED: 'Kegler' flies down the radar beam, using inertial navigation until it acquires the signal. Travelling at Mach 4, the radar operator has very little time to turn off his equipment before the missile hits.

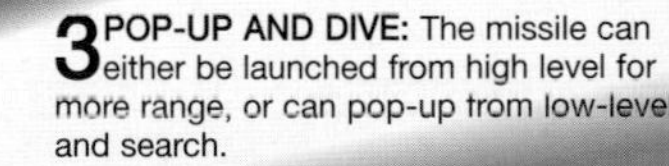

SUKHOI

SU-27 'FLANKER'

● Soviet superfighter ● Long-range interceptor ● Superb dogfighter

The Sukhoi Su-27 'Flanker' was the greatest success in the last days of the Soviet aviation industry. Holder of 27 absolute records, it is one of the great jet fighters. The Su-27 is not as heavy as it looks: it is exceptionally manoeuvrable and one of the most agile aircraft in the world. Small wonder, then, that the Su-27 performs with pride for international audiences with the 'Russian Knights' aerobatic team.

▲ *Members of the 'Russian Knights' aviation display team pose with General Antoshkin, commander of the Moscow Military District, in front of one of their Su-27s. The 'Flanker' is one of the most powerful fighters ever used to perform team aerobatics.*

SUKHOI SU-27 'FLANKER'

▲ Superpower superfighter
The Su-27's two Lyul'ka AL-31F turbofans are about the same size and diameter as the F100 jets used in the American F-15. But at nearly 13 tons of thrust the Russian engines are more powerful, yet consume less fuel.

Old-style cockpit ▶
First generation 'Flankers' use old-style instruments. However, the display from the powerful lookdown/shootdown radar (top right) makes the big Russian fighter a deadly opponent in air combat.

▲ Long-range warrior
For Soviet Frontal Aviation, as for its post-Soviet successors, the Su-27 was the long-range counterpart to the MiG-29. It specialises in long-range intercepts, escorting strike aircraft and counter-air missions against enemy air forces.

▲ Quick reaction
Immensely powerful and with sophisticated aerodynamics, the Su-27 can get aloft after a take-off run of only 500 m (1,640 ft.). Once in the air it climbs faster than any other fighter in the world, being rivalled only by the McDonnell Douglas F-15 Eagle.

◀ Naval 'Flanker'
The heavily-armed Su-27K is a navalised variant of the standard Su-27, and was designed to operate from the carrier Admiral Kuznetsov.

FACTS AND FIGURES

- The 'Flanker' prototype, known as the T-10, made its first flight on 20 May 1977.
- The Su-27 uses what Sukhoi calls an 'integrated airframe', with wing and fuselage blended to form a single 'lifting body'.
- The two-seat Su-27KU began as a demonstrator for carrier operations.
- The side-by-side two-seater is viewed as a possible replacement for the Su-24 'Fencer' as a long-range strike aircraft.
- Su-27s are operated by former Soviet states, but China is the only export user.
- A new-technology version, the Su-35, is being promoted for possible foreign sales.

PROFILE

The best fighter in the world

Looks are misleading. The Su-27 looks like a bigger MiG-29. But the 'Flanker' is not just the big brother of the 'Fulcrum'; it is an advanced design which demonstrates that the Sukhoi design bureau is neck-and-neck in the race for excellence with the better-known MiG organisation.

Chosen as the principal fighter of Soviet air forces, the 'Flanker' is beyond question an aerodynamic miracle. It was first seen in the West as a blurred image on grainy film, but the veil of secrecy has now lifted. In visits to air shows abroad the Sukhoi's incredible agility, including its tail-sitting 'Cobra' manoeuvre, has never been matched by any other performer. This is a pilot's aircraft: the man in the cockpit can fling this ship all over the sky.

Some experts say that the radar and missiles are not as advanced as the basic design of the aircraft, but Russian technology has improved greatly over the last decade and it would be a mistake to underestimate the Su-27.

The 'Flanker' is one of the fastest and most agile fighters in the world. It is the standard by which modern combat jets are judged.

In these post-Soviet days the Su-27s used by the 'Russian Knights' are colourfully painted in the markings of the old Imperial Russian Air Force.

The sharply-swept wing leading-edge extensions provide extra lift at high angles of attack, and contribute to the Su-27's extraordinary agility.

The 'Flanker' bears a marked resemblance to the smaller MiG-29 because both aircraft use an advanced wing designed at TsAGI, the Central Aerodynamics Institute, which is the Russian equivalent of NASA.

Su-27 'Flanker-B'

Type: high-performance interceptor and fighter

Powerplant: two NPO Saturn (Lyul'ka) AL-31F turbofans each rated at 79.43 kN (17,872-lb. thrust), increasing to 122.58 kN (27,581-lb. thrust) with afterburning

Maximum speed: Mach 2.35 or 2350 km/h (1,460 m.p.h.)

Service ceiling: 18,000 m (59,000 ft.)

Weights: empty 17,700 kg (39,022 lb.); loaded 33,000 kg (72,753 lb.)

Armament: one GSh-30-1 30-mm cannon with 149 rounds; six AA-10 'Alamo' medium-range and four AA-11 'Archer' short-range missiles

Dimensions:	span	14.70 m (48 ft. 3 in.)
	length	21.90 m (71 ft. 10 in.)
	height	5.93 m (19 ft. 5 in.)
	wing area	46.50 m² (501 sq. ft.)

Su-27UB 'Flanker-C'

This 'Flanker-C' of the 234th 'Proskurovskii' Guards Fighter Regiment wears the colours of the 'Russian Knights'. Based at Kubinka, the team has demonstrated its extraordinary aircraft worldwide.

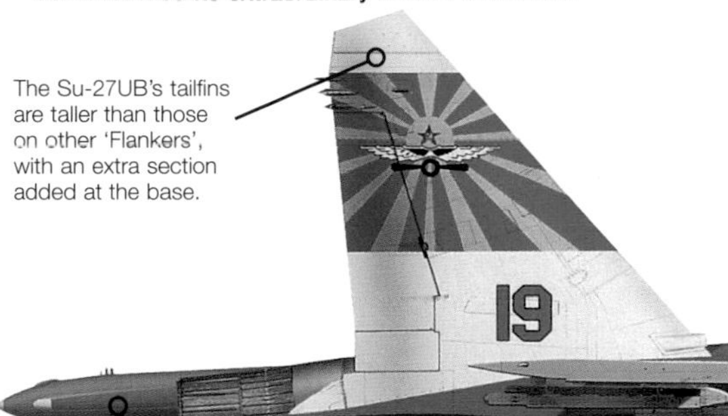

The Su-27UB's tailfins are taller than those on other 'Flankers', with an extra section added at the base.

Although primarily designed as a two-seat trainer, with a stepped cockpit giving both the trainee and instructor good forward visibility, the Su-27UB has full combat capability.

On combat 'Flankers', the long fuselage protrusion houses an aft-looking radar.

The ventral fins fitted to all 'Flankers' greatly improve spin recovery.

The air intakes are fitted with a mesh debris screen which remains closed until the nosewheel has lifted off the ground.

A glazed ball mounted in front of the windscreen houses a laser rangefinder and an infra-red search and track system, which can detect enemy aircraft at up to 70 km (43 mi.).

COMBAT DATA

MAXIMUM SPEED

The 'Flanker' is one of the fastest jets around, if not quite as speedy as the American F-15 Eagle. At lower speeds, however, the Russian jet's powerful engines and advanced aerodynamics give it a slight handling advantage. The smaller F/A-18, as it is purely an interceptor, is not quite as fast.

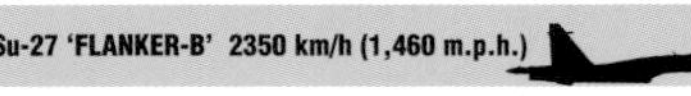

Su-27 'FLANKER-B' 2350 km/h (1,460 m.p.h.)

F-15 EAGLE 2500 km/h (1,553 m.p.h.)

F/A-18 1900 km/h (1,181 m.p.h.)

SERVICE CEILING

Once again, the 'Flanker' and the Eagle are closely matched. The Su-27 was one of the first Soviet jets to be equipped with an effective lookdown/shootdown radar, and operating at such heights means that it can protect an immense amount of air space. Both aircraft can zoom climb to intercept high-flying reconnaissance aircraft.

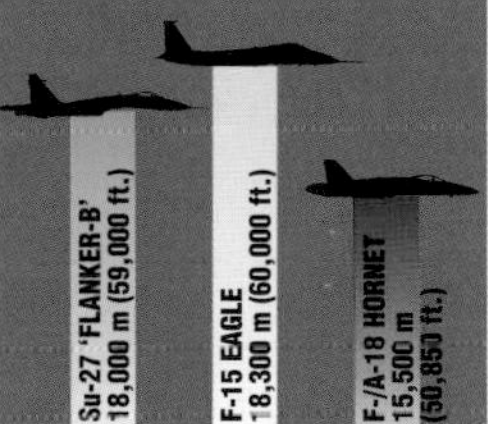

COMBAT RADIUS

The 'Flanker' has a slightly smaller range than the F-15. However, the Russian jet achieves its long range on internal fuel alone; the American fighter needs auxiliary drop-tanks or conformal tanks to reach its intercept limits. All three types are able to be air-to-air refuelled to increase their range.

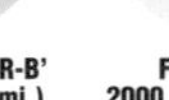

Su-27 'FLANKER-B' 1500 km (932 mi.)

F-15 EAGLE 2000 km (1,243 mi.)

F/A-18 HORNET 1000 km (621 mi.)

The Pugachev 'Cobra'

AEROBATIC PASS: First revealed at the Paris Air Show by Sukhoi's great test pilot Viktor Pugachev, the 'Cobra' is an astonishing manoeuvre no Western fighter can match.

NOSE HARD BACK: As the 'Flanker' makes a low-level pass, the pilot pulls the nose back sharply while the fighter carries on forwards.

STRIKING SNAKE: From the vertical or even beyond, the fighter's nose snaps back and then forwards like a striking snake. Loss of height in the manoeuvre is minimal.

COMBAT USE: The Cobra is more than an air show trick; it enables the 'Flanker' pilot to take a snap missile shot at an aircraft directly above or even behind his fighter.

SUKHOI

SU-27K/SU-33 'FLANKER'

● **Ship-based interceptor** ● **Heavy missile load** ● **In service**

Having previously operated only helicopters and the vertical take-off Yak-38 'Forger', the Soviet navy had an urgent requirement for a carrier-capable aircraft to equip its planned force of four new aircraft-carriers. Sukhoi responded with the powerful Su-27K 'Flanker-D' (sometimes known as the Su-33), an adaptation of the standard Su-27 'Flanker-B'. The aircraft has entered service, although only one carrier has been completed.

▲ *By considerably modifying the land-based 'Flanker-B', Sukhoi produced a highly effective carrier-based interceptor which entered service on the* Admiral Kuznetsov.

PHOTO FILE

SUKHOI SU-27K/SU-33 'FLANKER'

◀ **Sukhois on deck**
Visible behind this Su-27K is an Su-25, several of which have been modified for carrier training.

▼ **Folding 'Flanker'**
Folding wings and tailplanes allow the large Su-27K to be stored on the carrier deck.

▼ **No 'cat' carrier**
After deciding that a steam catapult could not be developed within the required timescale, the Soviet navy opted for a combination of a ski-ramp and deck restraints, which hold the aircraft against retractable thrust deflectors while it runs up to full power.

▼ **'Blue 109'**
This aircraft was the last of the Su-27K prototypes, which were known as T10Ks. It was the closest prototype to production form and was deployed on the Kuznetsov*'s first cruise.*

◀ **Extra missiles**
Two additional underwing hardpoints allow the carriage of two extra missiles. This gives the Su-27K a formidable eight-shot BVR capability when armed with the R-27 missile.

FACTS AND FIGURES

- Victor Pugachev, flying an Su-27K, performed the first Soviet landing on a conventional carrier in November 1989.
- Several Su-27s were used to test features of the new Su-27K.
- Production 'Flanker-Ds' are known as Su-33s by Sukhoi.
- In spite of Sukhoi's use of the Su-33 designation, the Su-27K is not a development of the advanced Su-35.
- The Su-27K is unable to operate at full weight from a carrier deck.
- Early take-off tests were performed on a land-based ski-ramp.

PROFILE

'Flanker' joins the navy

A fleet of four carriers was to be built for the Soviet navy, the first of which, the *Tbilisi,* was launched on 5 December 1985. Each carrier was to be equipped with an Airborne Early Warning and Control System (AWACS) platform, as well as a dedicated air defence aircraft derived from the Su-27 'Flanker-B' and a multi-role strike version of the MiG-29 known as the MiG-29K.

Budgetary problems after the break-up of the Soviet Union led to the completion of only one carrier, the *Tbilisi,* which entered service as the *Admiral Kuznetsov.* Consequently, production of the Su-27K was reduced from a potential 72 to a maximum of just 20.

In addition, the Su-27K found itself in competition with the MiG-29K, since only one aircraft type was to be ordered for the sole carrier. With its strong political position, Sukhoi was able to secure orders for its air-combat dedicated Su-27K, even though the multi-role MiG might have been the better choice for a single-type air wing.

Nevertheless, the 'Flanker-D' represents a highly capable aircraft, with powerful radar, a heavy air-to-air missile load and excellent range. Its lack of strike capability is being addressed in service and the aircraft seems likely to have gained a podded reconnaissance system.

This unusual angle shows the muzzle of the 30-mm cannon in the starboard leading-edge root extension (LERX) and the Su-27K's retractable refuelling probe to port below the cockpit.

Analogue fly-by-wire (FBW) controls are retained by the Su-27K. The canard-equipped Su-35 has a digital FBW system and is therefore a more capable aircraft.

Su-27 'Flanker-D'

Type: carrier-based interceptor and air defence fighter

Powerplant: two 122.59-kN (28,170-lb.-thrust) Saturn Lyul'ka AL-31F afterburning turbofans

Maximum speed: 2300 km/h (1,426 m.p.h.)

Range: 3000 km (1,805 mi.) clean

Service ceiling: 17,000 m (55,800 ft.)

Weights: maximum carrier launch weight 29,940 kg (65,868 lb.)

Armament: one 30-mm cannon, plus up to eight R-27 (AA-10 'Alamo') air-to-air missiles, or a combination of R-27s and R-73 (AA-11 'Archer') air-to-air missiles

Dimensions:

span	14.70 m (48 ft. 3 in.)
length	21.19 m (69 ft. 6 in.)
height	5.85 m (19 ft. 3 in.)
wing area	46.50 m² (500 sq. ft.)

SU-27K 'FLANKER-D'

Only one squadron flies the production Su-27K, the 1st Squadron of the Severomorsk Regiment of the AV-MF (Russian Naval Aviation). This aircraft was present during the type's first operational tour.

In order to fit the retractable in-flight refuelling probe, Sukhoi had to move the Infra-Red Search and Tracking (IRST) sensor slightly to starboard from its usual centreline position. The sensor allows the passive acquisition and tracking of targets by their heat signature.

Cockpit modifications were kept to a minimum in the Su-27K. The only additional equipment was that relating to a more precise landing approach system, plus tail hook and wing fold controls.

A typical load for the Su-27K is represented here. The AA-10 'Alamo' missiles provide a beyond-visual-range (BVR) kill capability and the smaller AA-11 'Archer' are used for close-in dogfighting.

In order to prevent tail scraping on take-off, the tailcone of the Su-27K was considerably shortened. This also allows slower landing speeds and a shorter landing run, but requires forward repositioning of the chaff and flare dispensers, which were also reduced in number.

'Slot Back' radar is common to both the Su-27 and MiG-29. The unit has excellent range performance and power, but scanning capacity is poor, with multiple targets causing problems. The Su-27K relies on AWACS or Ground Controlled Intercept (GCI) support.

A substantial square-section arrester hook was introduced on the first Su-27K prototype. The undercarriage is also modified to withstand carrier landings and twin nosewheels are fitted.

COMBAT DATA

THRUST

Powerful engines are vital for the heavy 'Flanker-D' to operate from carriers without catapults. The lighter MiG-29K was less powerful but offered comparable performance.

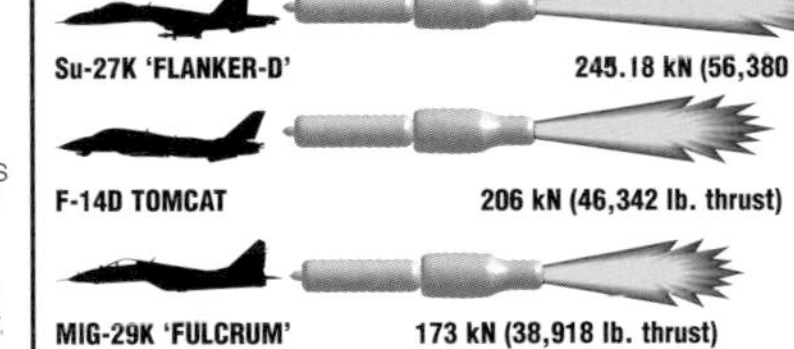

SERVICE CEILING

Reports suggest that the Su-27K has a slightly lower service ceiling than the Su-27 'Flanker-B'. It has a greater ceiling than its nearest Western counterpart, the F-14D, however, and is about 20 km/h (12 m.p.h.) faster than the standard 'Flanker-B'.

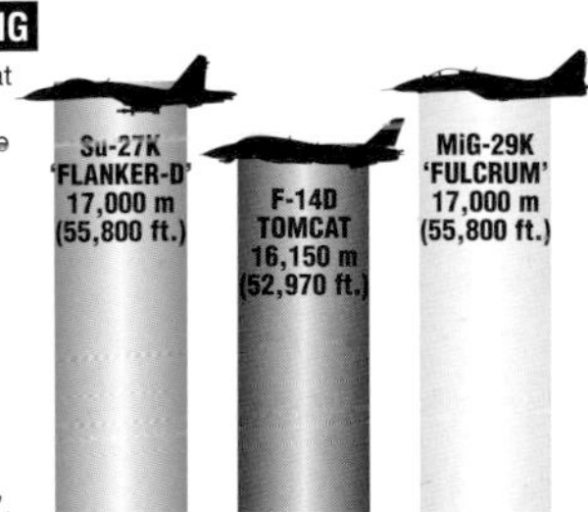

RANGE

Long range is essential for the fleet defence role, in which missiles and aircraft must be intercepted long before they reach the naval battle group. Only the Su-27K is able to achieve a 3000-km (1,860-mi.) range without external fuel tanks taking up valuable pylons.

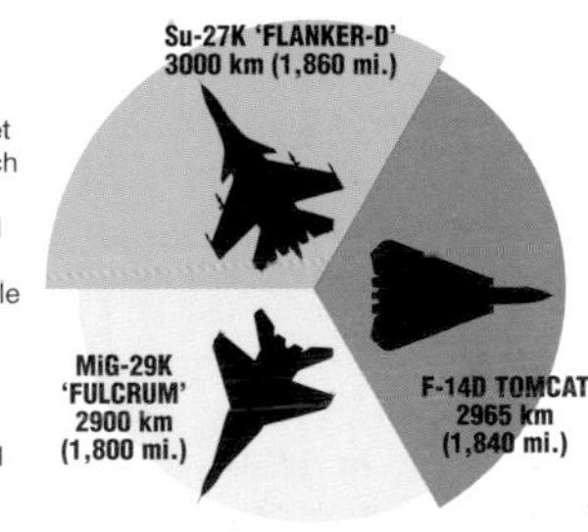

'Flanker-D' at sea

DECK MANOEUVRES: Wing and tailplane folding is necessary to make the large Su-27K easier to handle on deck. To avoid collisions, flying surfaces are kept folded as long as possible.

FULL THRUST FOR TAKE-OFF: With the deck restraints engaged, the aircraft's AL-31F turbofans are wound up to full afterburning thrust. Retractable deflector plates move up behind the 'Flanker-D' to prevent damage from jet thrust.

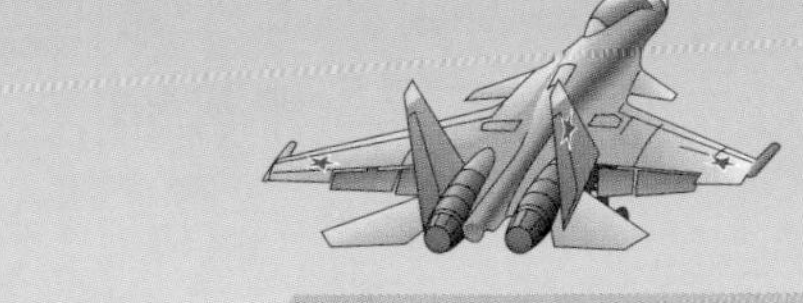

SKI-RAMP: A conventional take-off by the 'Flanker-D' would be impossible if the *Admiral Kuznetsov* was not equipped with a ski-ramp. The aircraft leaves the ramp at a speed of about 148 km/h (92 m.p.h.) and at an angle of attack of 14°. The take-off run is a mere 100 m (300 ft.) when lightly loaded, or 180 m (600 ft.) at maximum launch weight. The aircraft launch is at full power.

SUKHOI

SU-34 'FLANKER'

● Advanced strike aircraft ● Long-range ● Side-by-side seating

Possibly one of the world's most admired and distinctive warplanes, the Su-27IB/Su-32FN/Su-34 is a formidable maritime strike aircraft. While some confusion exists, even among Sukhoi officials, as to the aircraft's true designation, there is no doubt about its incredible capabilities. Although a chronic shortage of funding continues to dog the programme, it seems likely that the Su-32FN will eventually enter service.

▲ *The number of different variants that have already been derived from the original Su-27 interceptor is a credit to the versatility of this exceptional Russian design.*

PHOTO FILE

SUKHOI SU-34 'FLANKER'

▼ Long range
The Su-34 has a completely redesigned forward fuselage with side-by-side seating and full dual controls. It also has twin nose wheels and a longer wheelbase.

▲ Uncertain future
Despite funding problems, the Su-34 entered operational service in the mid-1990s.

▲ Flying 'Platypus'
The characteristic flattened nose profile has led to the universal nickname of 'Platypus'.

▲ Big brute
A pre-production Su-27IB inside the hangar at Kubinka dwarfs the MiG-29 'Fulcrum' in the background.

◀ Carrier trainer?
Taken by TASS, this photo apparently shows the Su-27IB poised for touchdown on the carrier Kuznetsov. *Note the lack of an arrester hook, however.*

FACTS AND FIGURES

- Sukhoi confirmed the Su-27IB designation after it was revealed accidentally by TASS photographers.
- Buddy refuelling is likely to be an important part of Su-27IB operations.
- A food heater and toilet are fitted in the cockpit of the Su-27IB.
- For its ASW role, the Su-32FN carries a magnetic anomaly detector and a pod containing up to 72 sonobuoys.
- By 1997 an order for 12 Su-32FNs had been placed by an unnamed country.
- Unit price of the Su-32FN in 1997 was quoted at roughly US $36 million.

PROFILE

Fearsome 'Flanker'

The heavier weight of the Su-32FN/Su-34 has resulted in a redesign of the undercarriage. This has given the aircraft a distinctive tail-up attitude on the ground, in contrast to fighter variants which are known as 'Cranes' because of their drooping noses.

A considerable redesign of the basic Su-27 'Flanker' produced the T10V-1 prototype in the early 1990s. Referred to originally as the Su-27KU, the aircraft appeared to be a carrier trainer, but when the true designation of Su-27IB became known, it was clear that the machine was destined for the strike role.

Features of the new machine included a side-by-side two-seat cockpit, situated in a completely new nose section. The entire undercarriage was strengthened and the machine optimised for low-level attack/maritime strike in all weathers.

When the Su-27IB was revised for production, twin-wheel main undercarriage bogies were introduced, along with a 'glass cockpit' and compatibility with a wide range of weapons. Intended primarily as a replacement for the Su-24 'Fencer', the Su-27IB is known to the Sukhoi design bureau as the Su-34.

An attack 'Flanker' appeared for the first time in the West at the 1995 Paris Air Salon. The aircraft was described as a maritime attack variant of the Su-27IB, designated Su-32FN. The programme was halted in 1997 because of a lack of resources at Sukhoi, by which time the machine was described as an export version of the Su-27IB. By June 1997, however, the Su-32FN was back in action at the Paris Air Salon.

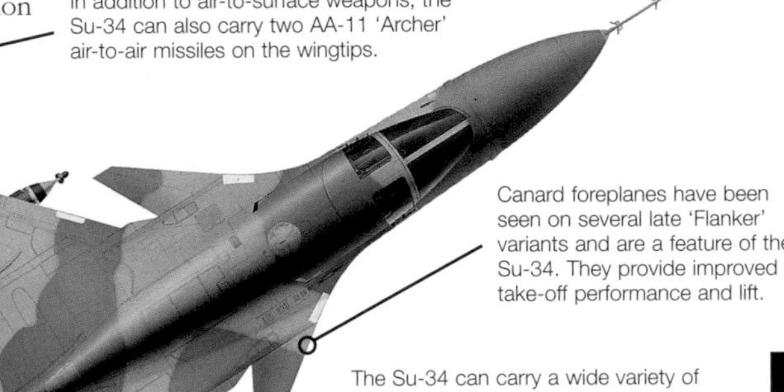

In addition to air-to-surface weapons, the Su-34 can also carry two AA-11 'Archer' air-to-air missiles on the wingtips.

Canard foreplanes have been seen on several late 'Flanker' variants and are a feature of the Su-34. They provide improved take-off performance and lift.

The Su-34 can carry a wide variety of external stores, virtually the entire inventory of Russian air-to-surface weapons. They include 100-kg (220-lb.) and 250-kg (550 lb.) bombs, SL25 laser-guided rockets, CBUs and, it is rumoured, long-range stand-off missiles.

Su-34 'FLANKER'

This particular aircraft, originally referred to as the Su-27KU, or carrier trainer, was later designated Su-27IB, signifying a strike role. It was first seen at the 1992 Moscow Aeroshow.

Strike variants of the 'Flanker' have a completely redesigned forward fuselage, an all-glass cockpit with side-by-side seating and full dual flight controls.

Although the rear fuselage is similar to that of the tandem-seat Su-27, the tailcone has been completely recontoured and is presumed to house a rearward-facing radar related to the N012 fitted to the Su-27M, along with twin braking chutes.

Unlike the single seat and tandem-seat versions, the Su-34 features a new-profile, flat nose with a dielectric tip for the new attack radar.

Second generation 'Flankers' like the Su-34 boast a retractable in-flight refuelling probe, to extend their already formidable combat radius further.

Production Su-34s feature a redesigned nose gear along with tandem main gears, which help distinguish them from earlier 'Flanker' variants.

Despite the new forward fuselage, the rest of the airframe remains essentially unaltered from the original Su-27 Interceptor, including the twin tails, unlike the Su-27UB and Su-35 variants which have new fins.

Su-32FN/Su-34 'Flanker'

Type: two-seat long-range maritime strike aircraft

Powerplant: two 130.42-kN (29,340-lb.-thrust) NPO Saturn Lyul'ka AL31FM afterburning turbofans

Maximum speed: 1800 km/h (1,116 m.p.h.)

Range: 3680 km (2,280 mi.) at altitude

Service ceiling: 15,000 m (49,000 ft.)

Weights: maximum take-off weight 44,360 kg (97,590 lb.); normal take-off weight 42,000 kg (92,400 lb.)

Armament: up to 8000 kg (17,600 lb.), including 100-/250-kg (220-/550-lb.) bombs, 1500-kg (3,300 lb.) ASM-M missiles and KGMU cluster bomb dispensers

Dimensions:	span	14.75 m (81 ft. 4 in.)
	length	23.95 m (92 ft. 6 in.)
	height	6.5 m (21 ft. 4 in.)
	wing area (est.)	62 m² (516 sq. ft.)

COMBAT DATA

THRUST

New generation strike aircraft have powerful, fuel-efficient turbofan engines and greater range than many of their predecessors. The Su-34 is no exception, its Lyul'ka AF-31s putting out a total of 245.18 kN (58,680 lb. thrust), much more than those of previous generation attack aircraft such as the Sukhoi Su-24 'Fencer'.

Su-32FN 'FLANKER'	F-15E EAGLE	Su-24M 'FENCER-D'
245.18 kN (56,680 lb. thrust)	258.90 kN (58,250 lb. thrust)	219.66 kN (49,414 lb. thrust)

BOMBLOAD

The maritime strike variant of the 'Flanker' can carry a wide variety of external stores, up to 8000 kg. This is no improvement on its predecessor, the Su-24, nor is it very impressive in comparison with the smaller and lighter F-15E, which can carry much more ordnance.

Aircraft	Bombload
Su-32FN 'FLANKER'	0000 kg (17,600 lb.)
F-15E EAGLE	11,113 kg (24,450 lb.)
Su-24M 'FENCER-D'	8000 kg (17,600 lb.)

MAXIMUM SPEED AT ALTITUDE

All three aircraft have supersonic capability, and although the performance of the Su-34 represents a considerable improvement over the 'Fencer' it is still out-performed in many respects by the McDonnell Douglas F-15E, a much older design than the Sukhoi.

Aircraft	Speed
Su-32FN 'FLANKER'	1800 km/h (1,116 m.p.h.)
F-15E EAGLE	2655 km/h (1,646 m.p.h.)
Su-24M 'FENCER-D'	1435 km/h (890 m.p.h.)

Modern maritime strike aircraft

BAe SEA HARRIER FA.Mk 2: The new generation Sea Harrier provides the Royal Navy with an effective maritime strike force.

McD D F/A-18 HORNET: The Hornet continues to be one of the most capable and versatile strike aircraft in front-line service.

PANAVIA TORNADO IDS: For anti-ship work, the principal users of the Tornado are the RAF and the German Marineflieger.

SEPECAT JAGUAR: India is among several Jaguar users. In addition to ground attack, its aircraft also perform maritime strike duties.

TRANSALL C.160

● **Franco-German tactical transport** ● **Sigint and civil variants**

One of Europe's earliest multinational aircraft programmes was started in 1959 as a collaboration between France and Germany to develop a new military transport. Nord-Aviation, HFB and VFW formed Transport Allianz, or Transall. The resulting aircraft, designed to replace the Nord Noratlas, carries a payload of 16,000 kg (35,200 lb.). The prototype flew in February 1963, and deliveries to the French and German air forces began in 1967.

▲ *Built to replace the Nord Noratlas, Transalls have, until recently, single-handedly filled the tactical transport requirement for the German and French air forces.*

PHOTO FILE

TRANSALL C.160

▲ Fire-bomber role

This Luftwaffe C.160 demonstrates a secondary fire-fighting capability, with tanks fitted in the cargo bay. The rear loading ramp must be lowered for this role.

▲ Paradropping

The main door on the right-hand side of the aircraft, behind the main wing, is used by paratroopers.

▲ Turkish Transall

Turkey's C.160s operate alongside a smaller number of C-130 Hercules and ageing C-47 transports.

▲ French relief flights

This Armée de l'Air C.160F, in a white colour scheme, has seen service in a humanitarian role.

Updated C.160D ▶

The threat presented by heat-seeking missiles was addressed in the C.160 fleet by fitting missile defence systems, such as flares.

FACTS AND FIGURES

- ➤ Of the C.160NGs built for the French, 10 are fitted with a hose-drum unit in the port undercarriage sponson for the IFR role.
- ➤ The four French C.160H ASTARTE aircraft are fitted with IFR probes.
- ➤ The C.160SE electronic surveillance version was proposed but never built.
- ➤ Two C.160G GABRIEL electronic intelligence (Elint) aircraft replaced similarly equipped Noratlases.
- ➤ Some French Transalls are based overseas in Senegal and New Caledonia.
- ➤ The Transall programme is now controlled by Aérospatiale and DASA.

PROFILE

Transport Allianz collaboration

Initial production of the C.160 included 110 for Germany and 50 for France. All were completed by 1972, but France later bought another 29 new-generation C.160NGs with additional fuel tanks, in-flight refuelling (IFR) probes and new avionics. Ten are fitted with hoses allowing them to refuel tactical aircraft. An upgrade programme was started in the early 1990s to modernise the earlier aircraft and add defences against missiles.

Two of the newer aircraft were completed as C.160G GABRIEL signals intelligence variants. They have a number of additional antennas to pick up emissions from radar and other systems. A further four, designated C.160H ASTARTES, were equipped to communicate with ballistic missile submarines. They use long trailing antennas to transmit very low frequency (VLF) radio signals which carry coded messages that can be received underwater. All six of these special mission versions have refuelling probes and hoses.

Germany sold 20 of its C.160s to Turkey, and the remainder operate as the Luftwaffe's main transport aircraft, equipping three wings. South Africa bought nine C.160Zs as part of the original production batch, but these were retired in the early 1990s.

Below: This Swiss-registered C.160 was used by the Red Cross. Other civil examples included four postal aircraft in Air France colours.

Above: The C.160NG (nouvelle génération) is distinguished by its in-flight refuelling probe above the cockpit.

C.160F

Type: military transport

Powerplant: two 4548-kW (6,100-hp.) Rolls-Royce Tyne RTy.20 Mk 22 turboprops

Maximum speed: 536 km/h (332 m.p.h.) at 4500 m (14,760 ft.)

Range: 4500 km (2,790 mi.) with 8000-kg (17,600-lb.) payload or 1182 km (733 mi.) with 16,000 kg (35,200 lb.)

Weights: empty 28,758 kg (63,268 lb.); maximum take-off 49,100 kg (108,020 lb.)

Payload: 93 troops, 88 paratroops or up to 16,000 kg (35,200 lb.) of cargo

Dimensions:

span	40.00 m (131 ft. 3 in.)
length	32.40 m (106 ft. 3 in.)
height	11.65 m (38 ft. 3 in.)
wing area	160.10 m² (1,723 sq. ft.)

C.160D

This is one of 110 C.160s delivered to the German air force. More than 200 C.160s were built, initially for Germany and France, but new aircraft were also delivered to South Africa.

The flightdeck crew of the C.160 consists of a pilot, co-pilot and flight engineer. The aircraft is fully pressurised and air-conditioned in flight and on the ground.

Two Rolls-Royce Tyne turboprops power all Transall C.160s. This powerplant has also been used in the Atlantic maritime patrol aircraft. Two four-bladed British Aerospace Dynamics propellers are fitted.

The main cabin of the Transall will hold up to 93 troops, 61 to 88 fully equipped paratroops or 62 stretchers and four attendants. Other typical loads include armoured vehicles up to 16,000 kg (35,200 lb.) in weight.

Among the projected versions that did not enter production was the C.160AAA (avion d'alerte avancée). This would have filled an airborne early warning role, with large radomes fitted in the nose and tail, in a similar fashion to the ill-fated British Aerospace Nimrod AEW.Mk 3.

In common with most tactical transport types, the C.160 has a rear loading ramp. This forms the underside of the upswept rear fuselage.

The French air force's C.160H variant is used to communicate with missile-armed nuclear submarines in a similar role to the US Navy's E-6 Mercury. The cargo hold carries VLF communications equipment and associated crew.

ACTION DATA

LOAD CAPACITY

Despite being only a twin-engined aircraft, the C.160 has a creditable load-carrying capacity. However, its performance with a full load aboard would not be as impressive.

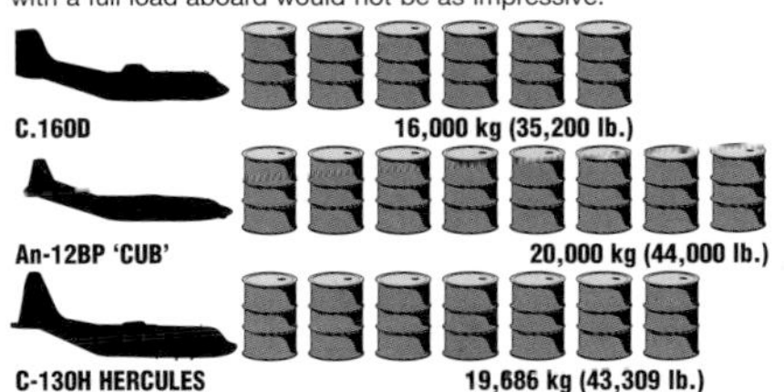

LANDING RUN

Being a smaller aircraft, the Transall has a shorter landing run than the larger types. Short take-off and landing runs are important for tactical transport aircraft which are required to use hastily prepared landing strips constructed in confined areas, possibly under enemy fire.

C.160D 640 m (2,100 ft.)
An-12BP 'CUB' 804 m (2,635 ft.)
C-130H HERCULES 838 m (2,750 ft.)

RANGE

A negative factor of the Transall's small size is its correspondingly short range, approximately a third of that of the C-130 and An-12. This shortcoming was addressed in the C.160NG, which introduced in-flight refuelling. While later versions of the C-130 have also been equipped with IFR, An-12s have never been fitted with this feature.

C.160D 1182 km (733 mi.)
An-12BP 'CUB' 3600 km (2,232 mi.)
C-130H HERCULES 3539 km (2,194 mi.)

C.160s in military and civil service

■ **C.160D:** The Luftwaffe has been the largest operator of the Transall. It is its principal transport machine and still equips three wings. Search and rescue is a secondary role for these aircraft.

■ **C.160P:** Air France operated four C.160Ps converted from French air force C.160Fs in 1970. Flown under contract to the French post office, they transported mail.

■ **C.160T:** In the early 1970s Turkey took delivery of 20 ex-German air force C.160Ds. These were redesignated C.160Ts and had a modified camouflage scheme applied.

TUPOLEV

TU-4 'BULL'

● Post-war strategic bomber ● Chinese-built turboprop versions

By the second half of 1944, when three US B-29 bombers landed at Vladivostok after running low on fuel, the Tupolev design bureau was already working on an equivalent to the Superfortress. The United States had refused to supply its latest bomber to the Soviet Union, so the three examples were dismantled and analysed. It then took more than 1000 draughtsmen to prepare plans to build a direct copy of the aircraft.

▲ *A direct copy of the United States' own B-29 Superfortress, the Tu-4 was based on three B-29s which crash-landed in the eastern Soviet Union, only to be restored and flown to Moscow for study.*

PHOTO FILE

TUPOLEV TU-4 'BULL'

◀ **Chinese AWACS**
In China about 20 Tu-4s were used in the bombing, airborne early warning and drone launching/directing roles.

▼ **Prototype 'Bull'**
The first Tu-4, then known as the B-4, took to the air on 19 May 1947 flown by N. Rybko.

▲ **Reconnaissance version**
The Tu-4R variant carried fuel in its forward bomb-bay, and cameras in the rear bay for strategic photographic missions.

◀ **Weapons fit**
Tu-4s carried Soviet weapons, comprising five 23-mm (0.91-in) twin NS-23 gun turrets and modifications to allow 8000 kg (17,637 lb) of free-fall bombs.

Powerplants ▶
The basic Tu-4 had primitive ASh-73TK engines. This drone-carrying Chinese aircraft uses AI-20 turboprops. In Russia, Tu-4LI flying laboratories tested engines for the Tu-95 and Il-18.

FACTS AND FIGURES

- Prior to building the Tu-4 as Stalin ordered, Tupolev had planned its own strategic bomber, 'Project 64'.
- In copying the B-29, Tupolev converted 105,000 parts to metric sizing.
- Production of the 'Bull' ended in 1951, with around 900 eventually built.
- The Tu-4N tanker variants tested numerous types of refuelling system, typically flying with 'probed' MiG-17s.
- A single Tu-4 was converted into the Tu-4T assault aircraft for 28 paratroops
- The Tupolev OKB proposed a turbopr version, to be known as the Tu-94.

PROFILE

Tupolev's own Superfortress

Starting in January 1945, it took Tupolev nearly two years and 20 prototypes to prepare the Tu-4 for production. Deliveries of the Tu-4 started in 1948, and the type remained in service as a bomber until the late 1950s. Surviving examples were then used as tankers, radar trainers and transport aircraft.

Developments of the basic Tu-4 included the Tu-80 and Tu-85 bombers. The single Tu-80 had increased fuel capacity and low-drag gun turrets, while the much bigger Tu-85, first flown in January 1950, could carry still more fuel and had more powerful engines for a range of 13,000 km (8,078 miles). Only two were built.

There were also one-off transport prototypes with new, circular-section fuselages. The Tu-70 was designed as a 72-passenger airliner, while the Tu-75 was intended to carry troops or military hardware.

The 'Bull' was also supplied to China, and in the late 1990s a few Tu-4s were believed to remain in Chinese service.

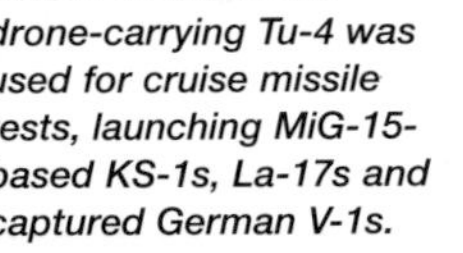

Above: Equipped with Kobalt blind bombing radar and powered gun turrets, the 'Bull' was the Soviets' first truly modern bomber aircraft.

Re-engined with Zhuzhou WJ-6 turboprops, they are used as drone carriers and equipment testbeds. A few were fitted with radar for the airborne early warning and control role.

Below: This Chinese drone-carrying Tu-4 was used for cruise missile tests, launching MiG-15-based KS-1s, La-17s and captured German V-1s.

Tu-4 'Bull'

Type: four-engined, long-range strategic bomber

Powerplant: four 1320-kW (1,770-hp) Shvetsov ASh-73TK air-cooled piston engines

Maximum speed: 558 km/h (347 mph) at 10,000 m (32,808 ft)

Initial climb rate: 5000 m (16,404 ft) in 18.2 min

Range: 5100 km (3,169 miles) with 2000-kg (4,409-lb) bombload

Service ceiling: 11,200 m (36,745 ft)

Weights: empty 35,270 kg (77,757 lb); maximum take-off 54,500 kg (120,152 lb)

Armament: ten 23-mm (0.91-in) NS-23 cannon, plus up to 8000 kg (17,637 lb) of bombs

Dimensions:		
	span	43.05 m (141 ft 3 in)
	length	30.18 m (99 ft)
	height	8.95 m (29 ft 4 in)
	wing area	161.70 m² (1,741 sq ft)

TU-4 'BULL'

This Tu-4, 'Red 01', is currently preserved at the Monino aerospace museum near Moscow. It seems likely it was one of the first to be built, possibly from the pre-production batch of 20 ordered in 1945.

Tu-4 pilots found they had some difficulty with internal cockpit reflections and optical distortion as a result of the glazed forward fuselage. The original restored B-29s were flown to Moscow by test pilots Reydel and Marunov. Tupolev fitted its own Soviet VHF radio and IFF (Identification Friend or Foe) to the 'Bull'.

Power for the Tu-4 'Bull' was provided by four ASh-73TK engines each with TK-19 turbochargers and 5-m (16-ft 5-in) diameter VZV-A5 propeller units.

The definitive production defensive armament fit for the 'Bull' was five powered turrets each with two 23-mm (0.91-in) twin-barrelled NS-23 cannon. Those turrets mounted above and below the fuselage were remotely controlled; the tail position was manned.

Produced more quickly than the Tu-4, the Tu-70 VIP passenger transport utilized the entire wings and engines of a captured B-29. This aircraft ultimately had a fuselage holding a crew of six and 72 seats. It had the service designation Tu-12.

Unlike the B-29, it seems that the 'Bull' was never equipped to carry nuclear weapons, but its two bomb-bays were able to carry a useful load of up to 8 tonnes (8.8 tons) of conventional bombs.

Between the two large bomb-bays was a retractable Kobalt blind bombing radar, which was fitted to the Tu-4 from 1948. At the same time, the early Tu-4s were retrofitted with new gun turrets.

Original production included the 'reconnaissance dedicated' Tu-4R with no offensive weapons, an increased fuel load for long-range missions, and a camera group fitted in the rear bomb-bay.

ACTION DATA

MAXIMUM SPEED

Tupolev's 'Bull' was unable to match the high performance of its inspiration, the American Boeing B-29. Unlike the Tu-4 and the Renzan, the Superfortress saw much active service during the war. Let down in terms of speed by its inferior engines, the Tu-4 was, nonetheless, a great leap forward in aviation for the Soviet Union.

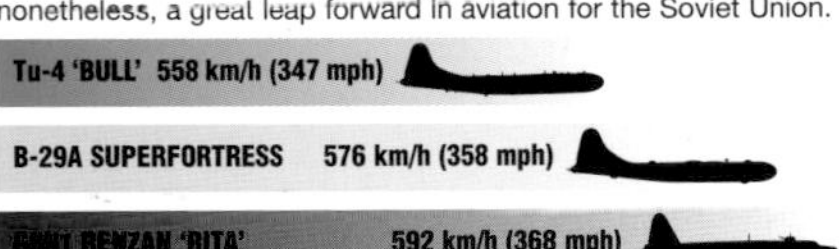

RANGE

The hastily prepared Nakajima Renzan from Japan could not match the range of the Tu-4 or the Boeing B-29. The Tu-4's range was increased greatly after initial flight testing, when internal tankage was increased from a 3480 kg (7,672 lb) to 11,300 kg (24,912 lb).

SERVICE CEILING

Surprisingly, the Tu-4 had a greater altitude capability than the Boeing Superfortress. This made it an ideal reconnaissance platform and flying laboratory. However, with a full load of 16 500-kg (1,100-lb) bombs, the type's operational ceiling and range would both decrease.

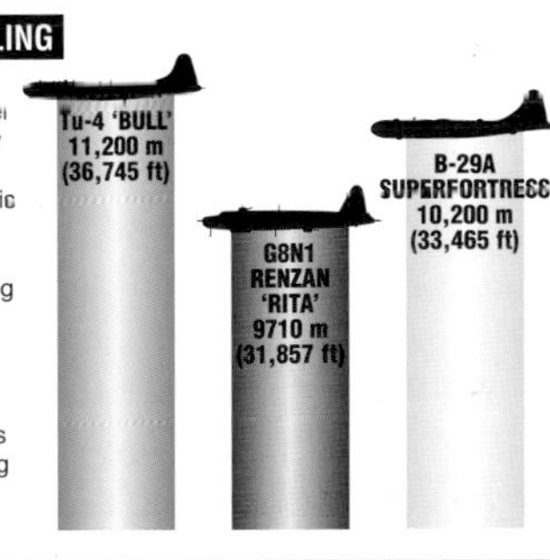

Tupolev's Superfortress derivatives

■ **Tu-70 'CART':** The Tu-70 pressurized VIP passenger transport flew six months before the Tu-4. One aircraft was used by high-ranking Soviet air force (VVS) officials.

■ **Tu-75 'CART':** Entirely Soviet-built, the sole Tu-75 unpressurized military transport featured 50 per cent more fuel capacity, folding seats for up to 120 troops and a cargo ramp/conveyor.

■ **Tu-80:** An attempt at improving the B-29, 1949's Tu-80 had modified gun turrets and was comparable to the US B-50, with a communication tunnel and 12000-kg (26,500 lb) bombload.

■ **Tu-85 'BARGE':** Succeeding the Tu-80, the Tu-85 was abandoned in favour of the mighty 'Bear'. Itself a fine machine, the nuclear-capable Tu-85's range was bettered only by the B-36.

TUPOLEV

TU-16 'BADGER'

● Tanker ● Anti-ship missile launcher ● Reconnaissance role

Still in service after more than 50 years, the Tu-16 'Badger' remains a vital part of Russia's Long Range Aviation, serving as a tanker, electronic jammer and reconnaissance aircraft. The 'Badger' was also sold overseas, and remains in service in China, Ukraine and the Middle East. Despite its age, the 'Badger' is still a very useful aircraft and will almost certainly be flying somewhere in the world for many years.

▲ *The Tu-16 has proved capable of adapting to many roles. With the shortage of cash to fund a replacement in Russia, it will remain an important aircraft for many years to come.*

PHOTO FILE

TUPOLEV TU-16 'BADGER'

▼ Desert launch

Egypt still operates a handful of 'Badgers' based at Cairo West air base. They are equipped with the ageing 'Kelt' missile.

▲ Ocean snooper

This 'Badger-F' was spotted near a NATO surface fleet during an exercise. A small number of these dedicated reconnaissance aircraft serve with Russian naval aviation.

Chinese 'Badger' ▶

Probably one of the B-6 export aircraft subsequently delivered to Iraq, this aircraft was equipped to deliver the C-601 'Silkworm' missile. This system is large and slow, and a lot less dangerous than the Mach 3-capable AS-6 'Kingfish' missile normally used by the aircraft in Russian service.

▲ On patrol

This 'Badger-G' is one of the earlier model 'Gs' with missile-carrying ability but no ventral radar fairing.

Missile launcher ▶

A 'Badger-G Mod' carries an AS-6 missile. It has a range of 300 km (185 mi.) and can carry a nuclear warhead.

FACTS AND FIGURES

- 'Badgers' are believed to be in service in Belarus, China, Egypt, Iraq, Russia (naval aviation and air force) and the Ukraine.
- A small number of Tu-16PP 'Badger-Js' remain in service in the jamming role.
- 'Badgers' originally employed a wingtip-to-wingtip refuelling technique.
- About 20 Tu-16N tankers serve with the Russian air force (VVS) and six with the naval air force (AV-MF).
- Ukraine's Tu-16s serve with 251 HBAP at Belaya Tserkov and 260 HBAP at Stryy.
- F-117 bombers attacked three Iraqi 'Badgers' on the ground in the first Gulf War.

PROFILE

Half a century of 'Badger' power

Despite being obsolete in its original role of nuclear free-fall bombing, the Tu-16 'Badger' is still doing sterling work in the hands of a small number of pilots, most notably in Russia and China. The Tu-16 airframe was highly adaptable, and was soon pressed into service in the first Soviet air-to-air refuelling squadrons, a role in which the aircraft remains to this day, designated Tu-16N. Another role that the Tu-16 retained was as an airborne missile launcher, at first carrying the KS-1 'Komet' missile and then the faster KS-15. Chinese-built 'Badgers', known as Xian H-6s, carry the C-601 anti-ship cruise missile, and also carry out test and development work. Other roles for the Badger are in electronic warfare, using chaff launchers and various active jammers (Tu-16PP 'Badger-J') and in long-range reconnaissance (Tu-16P 'Badger-F').

About 100 'Badgers' are still flying in China, with about the same number flying in Russia, and around 50 in the Ukraine. Quite how long the 'Badger' will remain in service is hard to determine, but the absence of any obvious replacement suggests that the aircraft could well survive to celebrate its fiftieth birthday.

Left: 'Badgers' used to be a common sight flying near every NATO exercise, but fuel availability constraints mean that the aircraft now rarely fly even at home.

Above: Some 'Badger' variants retain a manned tail gun turret and are among the last aircraft to do so.

The radar system in the nose is believed to be the system known to NATO as 'Short Horn'.

The few remaining Tu-16 tankers have replaced the old wingtip fuelling system with a probe-and-drogue system located in the capacious bomb bay.

Earlier Tu-16s were powered by the Mikulin AM-3 turbojet, but most current versions use the Tumanskii RD-3M engine rated at 93 kN thrust.

Tu-16 'Badger-G'

Type: twin-engined long-range anti-ship missile carrier

Powerplant: two 93-kN (20,920-lb.-thrust) Mikulin AM-3M turbojet engines

Maximum speed: 1050 km/h (651 m.p.h.) at 6000 m (19,700 ft.)

Endurance: 5 hours with maximum load

Range: 7200 km (3,675 mi.)

Service ceiling: 15,000 m (49,200 ft.)

Weights: empty 37,200 kg (81,840 lb.); maximum take-off 75,800 kg (166,760 lb.)

Armament: two K-26 missiles plus six 23-mm cannon in tail, dorsal and ventral turrets

Dimensions:

span	32.99 m (108 ft. 3 in.)
length	36.80 m (120 ft. 8 in.)
height	10.36 m (34 ft.)

TU-16 'BADGER-L'

The Tu-16PM is a dedicated electronic intelligence gatherer, with special electronic aids replacing the rear gun turret. The nose has a small thimble radome, and the aircraft retains its dorsal and ventral turrets.

A useful defensive armament is retained in the form of two NR-23 cannon in the dorsal and ventral turrets. The fit of this 'Badger' variant varies widely, but most have a camera window in the port forward fuselage.

The fin-tip has a dielectric antenna, probably used to relay high-frequency radio communications to surface vessels.

The nose of this Tu-16 has the pentagonal excellence award painted under the cockpit.

The underwing pods house electronic information-gathering equipment, and are also fitted to the earlier 'Badger-F'.

Like most Soviet designs from the 1950s, the Tu-16 has large overwing fences to reduce spanwise airflow and induced drag.

The extended tailcone is believed to house electronic counter-measures gear or very low frequency radio equipment for communications with submarines.

COMBAT DATA

MAXIMUM SPEED

Jet engines gave the 'Badger' higher speed than the bombers it replaced. The Tu-22, a smaller design with bigger engines, was faster still, but short ranged. The remarkable Tu-95/142 'Bear' was almost as fast by virtue of its swept wing and enormous propellers.

Tu-16 'BADGER-G'	1050 km/h (651 m.p.h.)
Tu-142M 'BEAR-F'	925 km/h (574 m.p.h.)
Tu-22 'BLINDER-A'	1480 km/h (918 m.p.h.)

COMBAT RADIUS

Range was an important feature of the early jet bombers, and the Tu-16 was one of many Soviet designs from the 1950s to suffer from the lack of efficient engines. For this reason, Tupolev designed the Tu-95 with the massive NK-12 turboprop engine.

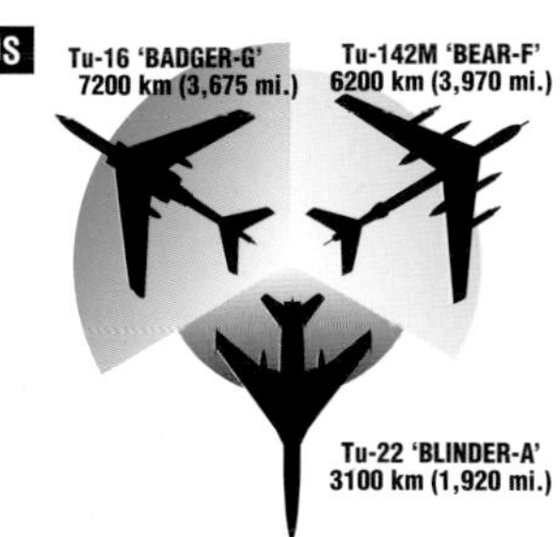

SERVICE CEILING

'Badgers' fly at high altitude for long-range operations and to make radar searches for hostile ships more effective. The launch of the AS-6 is also better performed at height. The Tu-22 had an even better ceiling.

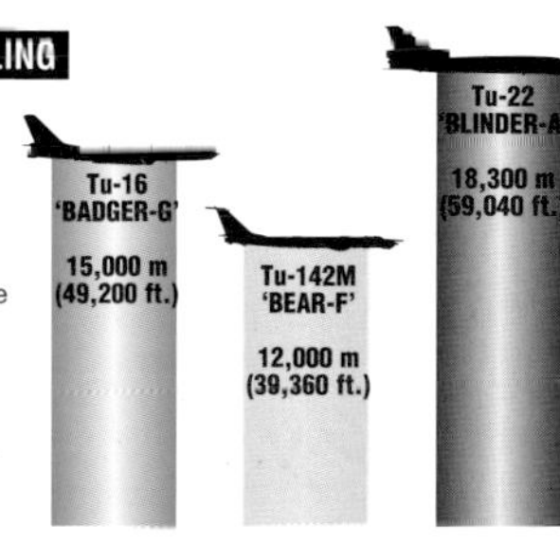

'Badger' missions

JAMMING: The 'Badger-J' has an on-board chaff-cutting system and active jammers, so that it can saturate a radar with false signals at exactly the right wavelength.

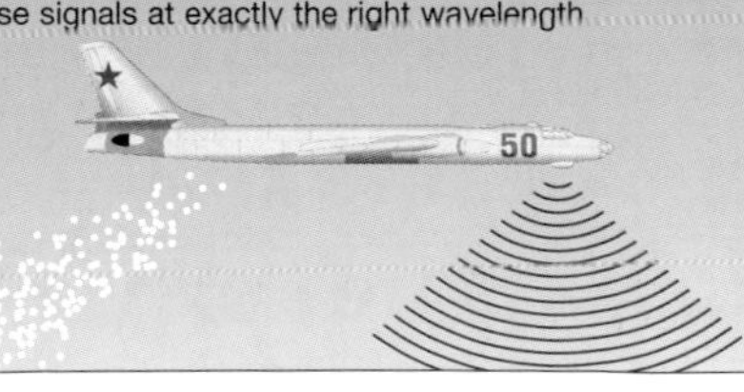

TANKER: The Soviet forces eventually settled on a probe-and-drogue technique similar to that used by most Western air forces and the US Navy. The thirsty MiG-31 interceptor needs frequent top-ups to remain on-station.

MISSILE ATTACK: A Chinese H-6 launches a C-601 cruise missile. This weapon is a relatively slow and high flying system, and is less of a threat than the new C-801. However, it has a very heavy payload and is still a potent weapon.

TUPOLEV

TU-22 'BLINDER'

● Supersonic strike ● Missile carrier ● Tail-engined design

The Tupolev Tu-22 'Blinder' is now an obsolete design, but its sleek airframe was highly advanced when it entered service, and a few are still flying. One of the fastest bombers of its time, the 'Blinder' was designed with fighter-like aerodynamics, and could dash through hostile defences to deliver a heavy load of conventional or nuclear weapons. Export 'Blinders' saw action in Africa and in the Iran-Iraq War, on long-range strikes.

▲ *The Tu-22 was designed in an era when supersonic jet bombers were a potent new threat. Combined with nuclear-tipped AS-4 missiles and powerful ECM equipment, the 'Blinder' was a powerful anti-ship strike aircraft facing NATO.*

PHOTO FILE

TUPOLEV TU-22 'BLINDER'

▼ Ready for scrap
About 200 Tu-22s remained in service in the early 1990s, but many have been scrapped to comply with the CFE (Conventional Forces in Europe) disarmament treaty.

▲ Blinder trainer
The Tu-22UB is a special conversion training variant with a second cockpit raised aft of the front cockpit. Only a few remain in service.

◀ Fast touchdown
Landing a Tu-22 needed care and a strong brake parachute due to its high touchdown speed.

▲ Engine change
The prototype Tu-22 flew with AM-3 engines, but these were replaced by Koliesov VD-7M turbojets.

▼ Formation leader
This Tu-22 leads a flight of MiG-21s in a display. The 'Blinder' was rarely seen outside the Soviet Union, except when shadowing NATO ships.

FACTS AND FIGURES

- ➤ The 'Blinder' first flew in 1959 and was seen publicly at the Tushino aviation display in 1961.
- ➤ Iraqi 'Blinders' were used in supersonic toss attacks against Iranian cities.
- ➤ The Tu-22 was used by Libya to attack N'Djamena airport in Chad in 1986.
- ➤ Some 400 'Blinders' were built in the 1960s, but virtually all of them have now been retired.
- ➤ The Ukraine has about 35 'Blinders' flying with operational units.
- ➤ Soviet 'Blinders' were used to bomb Mujahideen positions in the Afghan War.

PROFILE

Tupolev's supersonic Striker

An impressive design, the Tu-22 'Blinder' remains an almost unique example of a tail-engined jet bomber. Intended to fly many of the missions of the slower, more vulnerable Tu-16 'Badger', the Tu-22 was designed with an area-ruled fuselage and sharply swept wing to reduce supersonic drag. Although its speed was impressive it suffered from a lack of range, and later versions were fitted with a refuelling probe to remedy this. A radar-guided cannon turret was installed in the tail.

Other unusual features were the downward-firing ejection seats for the crew, a tailskid to prevent the tail hitting the runway and the large 'Down Beat' missile guidance radar in the 'Blinder B', used in association with the AS-4 'Kitchen' air-to-surface missile.

Soviet 'Blinders' flew as bombers, missile carriers, maritime strike aircraft and as reconnaissance platforms. Russia and the Ukraine operated the type into the 1990s, but the only exports were to Libya and Iraq. Libya used a 'Blinder' in a high-level attack on N'Djamena airport in Chad dropping four bombs, all of which hit the target. Iraqi Tu-22s saw action during the long war with Iran, but most were destroyed by Coalition raids during Operation Desert Storm.

Now retired, the 'Blinder' will be remembered as a symbol of the USSR's Cold War might.

Tu-22s were frequently spotted close to NATO exercises in the Baltic and North Sea. 'Blinder-C' was a dedicated maritime reconnaissance variant equipped with long-range cameras.

The 'Blinder' was designed as a Tu-16 replacement, but the older Tupolev was a more versatile design in many ways.

Tu-22 'Blinder'

Type: supersonic bomber

Powerplant: two 156.9-kN (35,289-lb-thrust) RKBM (Koliesov) VD-7M turbojets with afterburning engines

Maximum speed: 1480 km/h (920 mph) at 12,000 m (39,370 ft)

Combat radius: 3100 km (1,926 miles)

Service ceiling: 18,300 m (60,039 ft)

Weights: basic empty about 40,000 kg (88,185 lb); maximum take-off about 83,900 kg (184,968 lb)

Armament: up to 9070 kg (19,996 lb) of nuclear or conventional bombs or missiles including AS-4 'Kitchen' air-to-surface missiles carried in recessed bays by some variants; one 23-mm (0.91-in) NR-23 cannon in tail barbette

Dimensions:

span	23.75 m (77 ft 11 in)
length	10.67 m (35 ft)
height	10.67 m (35 ft)
wing area	144.00 m² (1,550 sq ft)

Tu-22 'Blinder'

The Tu-22 entered service with the VVS (Soviet air force) in 1960, and flew with the air forces of the Russian Federation and the Ukraine, and possibly Libya and Iraq.

The crew consisted of pilot, co-pilot and navigator. The pilot's ejector seat fires upwards, but the other crewmember's seats fire downwards.

Soviet Tu-22's were left with a polished metal finish, but Libyan examples had striped camouflage.

The VD-7 engine has a ring on the leading edge, which can be moved forward on take-off to expose an annular slot air intake. Tail mounting the engines allowed the wing design to be kept very clean, and allowed easier maintenance.

The Tu-22's refuelling probe has a small triangular guard on the underside to prevent damage to the nose cone during air-to-air refuelling.

'Blinder-B' has a slightly enlarged nose radome to accommodate the large 'Down Beat' radar. Other variants had cameras and electronic warfare equipment installed in the nose.

The small badge under the cockpit is an excellence award to the ground crew for efficiency in maintaining the aircraft in a high state of readiness.

Offensive weapons were accommodated in an internal bomb-bay. The AS-4 missile was carried in the fuselage in a semi-recessed position which replaced the bomb-bay.

Like many transonic Soviet designs, the Tu-22 had large wing fences to reduce induced drag. The highly swept wing gave very light handling at high speed, but landing speeds were very fast, which made a brakechute a vital feature.

Defensive armament consisted of a 23-mm (0.91-in) cannon with automatic radar tracking from the 'Bee Hind' fire-control radar above it.

Anti-ship strike operations

1 MISSILE LAUNCH: The Tu-22 releases its AS-4 missile with an approximate target location. This could be provided by a submarine or a maritime reconnaissance aircraft. The missile climbs to high altitude to cruise at maximum efficiency.

2 MID-COURSE GUIDANCE: The missile is fed updated information from a Tu-95 'Bear', which picks up enemy shipping with its 'Big Bulge' targeting radar.

3 FINAL DIVE: The missile dives at the target from high altitude, building up very high speed. It acquires the target with its own terminal homing radar. AS-4 was often fitted with a 350-kiloton yield nuclear warhead.

COMBAT DATA

MAXIMUM SPEED

The Tu-22 had a high dash speed, but even this was surpassed by the B-58 and Mirage IV. The B-58 Hustler could maintain its terrific speed for more than an hour, unlike the short-ranged Tu-22 which guzzled fuel at a high rate.

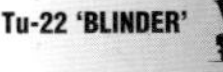

Tu-22 'BLINDER'	1480 km/h (920mph)
B-58 HUSTLER	2228 km/h (1,384 mph)
MIRAGE IV	2340 km/h (1,454 mph)

TUPOLEV

TU-22M 'BACKFIRE'

● Strategic bomber ● Missile carrier ● Reconnaissance

Fast, long-ranged and hard hitting, the Tu-22M remains one of the most capable bombers in the world. This large swing-wing bomber is tasked primarily with long-range missile strikes against shipping, serving with units of Russian naval aviation (AVMF). Equipped with powerful sensors and large supersonic missiles, the Tu-22M is even more important now that Russia has very few of its Tu-160s still in service.

▲ *Together with the Tu-160 'Blackjack', the 'Backfire' makes up Russia's modern long-range bombing fleet. As a replacement for the Tu-22 'Blinder', the 'Backfire' serves in large numbers – 250 in total, with around 150 employed by the naval air arm. It may well drop decoy drones to confuse enemy air defences.*

PHOTO FILE

TUPOLEV TU-22M 'BACKFIRE'

▲ Ultimate bomber
The Tu-22M-3 is the most advanced and formidable 'Backfire' development, with new radar, engines, intakes and more advanced electronic countermeasures systems.

▲ Anti-shipping strike
This Tu-22M is armed with the AS-4 'Kitchen' anti-ship missile. The 11-m (36-ft.) missile has a range of over 400 km (250 mi.) and can be nuclear armed.

▲ Maritime patrol and reconnaissance
The Tu-22M-3 'Backfire-C' is employed by the Russian navy for long-range destruction of enemy naval fleets. The M-3 can also carry six AS-16 'Kickback' attack missiles internally, plus four more externally. Defence is provided by a 23-mm tail gun.

▲ Interception
This Tu-22M-2 'Backfire-B' was intercepted over the Baltic by a Swedish Saab Draken fighter.

High-speed attack ▶
The Tu-22M-3 sweeps back its long wings for a rapid bomb run over the enemy fleet's shipping.

FACTS AND FIGURES

- ➤ For short landings the Tu-22M can deploy a large brake parachute, stored in the rear fuselage.
- ➤ The Tu-22M can carry external rocket packs to decrease take-off distance.
- ➤ The 'Backfire' can lift a maximum of 69 FAB-250 conventional bombs.
- ➤ Tu-22M-3s were first used operationally on bombing missions in the Soviet war in Afghanistan in October 1988.
- ➤ Video cameras are used on the Tu-22M for bomb aiming from high altitude.
- ➤ An inflatable LAS-5M dinghy is carried behind the cabin for emergencies.

PROFILE

Soviet swing-wing striker

First known in the West as the Tu-26, the Tu-22M 'Backfire' was developed at the same time as the Su-7IG variable-geometry prototype, and may have benefited from the same research by Soviet aerodynamicists. It is possible that early prototypes (Tu-22M-1) were in fact radically modified Tu-22 'Blinder' airframes, hence the Tu-22M designation. Alternatively, the name may have been adopted simply to confuse Western analysts.

Development began around 1965, and the production Tu-22M-2 'Backfire-B' first flew in 1975. This machine featured a four-man crew, revised undercarriage and two GSh-23 twin-barrel 23-mm cannon in the tail. Typically this aircraft would be armed with up to three Kh-22 (AS-4 'Kitchen') missiles. After arms limitation treaties the bombers' refuelling probes were removed to reduce their strategic capability.

The later Tu-22M-3 'Backfire-C' introduced a recontoured nose, Kh-15 (AS-16 'Kickback') short-range attack missiles, single GSh-23 cannon, improved wedge intakes and two new NK-25 turbofans. The M-3 first entered service with the Black Sea fleet in 1985, replacing the M-2 in production. A dedicated electronic warfare version, the Tu-22M-4, is also rumoured to exist.

For years the Tu-22M was a subject of debate. NATO argued with the Warsaw Pact about its role, and even its real name.

Although no flight refuelling probe is normally carried, one can be bolted on quickly if required for a long-range mission.

Large variable-geometry wings are swept forward for cruise and swept back for a high-speed dash over the target.

The aircraft shown here carries only one of a possible three Kh-22 anti-ship missiles. Alternatively, up to 10 Kh-15s could be carried, or a combination of both weapons.

Two Kuznetsov KKBM NK-25 afterburning turbofans propel the Tu-22M-3 to 2125 km/h (1,317 m.p.h.) at an altitude of 11,000 m (33,000 ft.). Fuel reserves provide a 12000-km (7,440-mi.) ferry range and a 4000-km (2,480-mi.) combat radius.

For defence, a single GSh-23 twin-barrel 23-mm cannon and associated guidance radar are mounted in the tail.

Tu-22M-3 'Backfire'

Type: long-range medium bomber and maritime strike/reconnaissance aircraft

Powerplant: two 245.18-kN (55,000-lb.-thrust) Kuznetsov KKBM NK-25 turbofans with afterburning

Maximum speed: (clean and level) 2125 km/h (1,317 m.p.h.)

Service ceiling: 18,000 m (59,000 ft.)

Weights: maximum take-off 130,000 kg (286,000 lb.)

Armament: 12,000 kg (26,400 lb.) in weapons bay; 12,000 kg (26,400 lb.) on external pylons; three Kh-22 missiles or 10 Kh-15 missiles or bombs, plus one GSh-23 twin barrel 23-mm cannon in tail

Dimensions:

span	34.30 m (112 ft. 6 in.)
length	39.60 m (129 ft. 10 in.)
height	10.80 m (35 ft. 5 in.)
wing area	170 m² (1,829 sq. ft.)

TU-22M-3 'BACKFIRE-C'

This Tupolev Tu-22M-3 'Backfire-C' is a Russian navy aircraft configured for a long-range anti-shipping mission. The Russian navy has large numbers of 'Backfires', and as newer types begin to enter service with the other air forces, more will be transferred to the AVMF squadrons.

The Tu-22M-3 introduces not only more powerful turbofans, but reconfigured high-performance ramp-type intakes similar in shape to those on the Russian MiG-25 'Foxbat'.

The large missile targeting and navigation radar in the nose is codenamed 'Down Beat' and is coupled with very advanced electronic systems.

The 'Backfire-C' carries a crew of four, comprising a pilot and co-pilot side-by-side in front and two further crewmembers behind. All four have ejection seats under gull-wing doors.

For conventional missions 12,000 kg (26,400 lb.) of bombs can be carried in the weapons bay and another 12,000 kg (26,400 lb.) on underwing racks. The heaviest weapon is the FAB-3000 3000-kg (6,600-lb.) bomb.

The main undercarriage consists of two heavy-duty six-wheeled units, retracting neatly into the lower fuselage for storage.

COMBAT DATA

MAXIMUM SPEED

Optimised for long-distance missions, the Tu-22M compensates for its slow speed with a very long range and heavy weapons load. The Mirage and FB-111 were designed for shorter missions.

Tu-22M-3 'BACKFIRE-C'	2125 km/h (1,317 m.p.h.)
FB-111A	2334 km/h (1,447 m.p.h.)
MIRAGE IVP	2338 km/h (1,450 m.p.h.)

AS-4 'KITCHEN'

Known in the West as the AS-4 'Kitchen', the Kh-22 anti-shipping missile has a range of over 400 km and can carry either a 350-kiloton nuclear warhead or a 1000-kg (2,200-lb.) high-explosive warhead. It makes very steep attacks at extremely high speed.

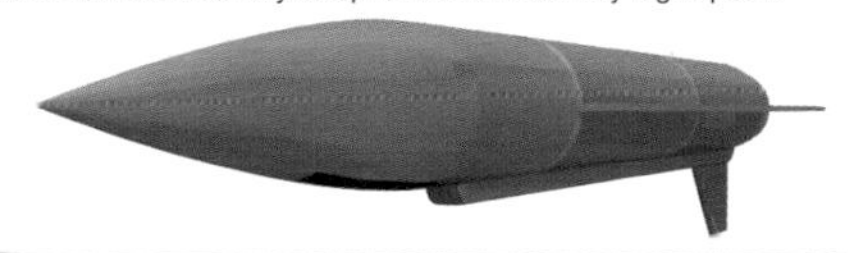

'Backfire' over Afghanistan

STRIKE THE PANSHJIR: 'Backfire' squadrons based in the USSR could easily reach distant Afghanistan. They often headed for the Panshjir valley, north-east of Kabul. The Tu-22Ms were tasked with the destruction of towns, villages and the concealed guerrilla bases of Afghan rebels.

ROUTE IN: The 'Backfires' crossed into Afghanistan over high mountain ranges, often using them to help mask their presence.

SAFE FROM ATTACK: Flying high and fitted with decoy flares and chaff launchers, the Tu-22M was safe from the Afghans' Stinger missile system.

NO WARNING: Bombing from high altitude, the Tu-22M attacks were silent until the bombs were dropped. The 'Backfires' released conventional 'iron' bombs weighing 1500 kg (3,300 lb.), 500 kg (1,100 lb.) and 250 kg (550 lb.). From October 1988 the improved M-3 model joined the earlier M-2 over Afghanistan.

TUPOLEV

TU-95 'BEAR A/B/C/G'

● Intercontinental bomber ● Long career ● Unique design

Having beaten off a stiff challenge from Myasishchev's jet-powered M-4 'Bison', Tupolev's Type 95 was developed into the Tu-95M 'Bear-A' bomber. As the potential of the aircraft was recognized, new variants were quickly developed. Both the 'Bear-B' and 'Bear-G' were rebuilds of the Tu-95M, while a number of new-build 'Bear-Cs' also entered service. All were dedicated missile carriers and a few remain in service.

▲ *A familiar sight to many Western pilots during the Cold War period, the huge Tu-95 could be seen and heard for great distances, simulating its deadly mission against NATO forces.*

PHOTO FILE

TUPOLEV TU-95 'BEAR A/B/C/G'

▲ Soviet Union's big stick
Intercepted by a US Navy F-8 Crusader, this Tu-95 'Bear-A' was the original strategic bomber variant. The lower fuselage and rudder were often painted in anti-flash white in later years.

▼ Painted undersurfaces
Some 'Bears' were given black-painted undercarriage nacelles and wing trailing edge surfaces in an attempt to hide exhaust stains.

Might of the motherland ▶
For more than 20 years Tupolev's giant bomber represented the pinnacle of Soviet military power. Able to roam far and wide, it justifiably caused great concern among NATO countries.

◀ Flying Guinea pig
One Tu-95 was used in trials as a mother ship for a high-speed reconnaissance aircraft. The project was cancelled and the 'Bear' later put on display.

Elint role ▶
Among the early variants was the intelligence-gathering Tu-95KM 'Bear-C'. Most of these aircraft were later rebuilt as 'Bear-G' dedicated cruise-missile carriers.

FACTS AND FIGURES

- ➤ In 1953 the first Tu-95 crashed during a test flight after an engine fell off. All but three of the crew escaped.
- ➤ Most Tu-95s had been scrapped by the 1990s, in accordance with SALT treaties.
- ➤ A single Tu-96, high-altitude variant was built, but did not enter service.
- ➤ Some design features of the Tu-95 can be traced back to the Tu-4, an exact copy of the B-29 Superfortress.
- ➤ Production of the Tu-95 began in 1954 and ended in 1959, with 173 being built.
- ➤ Escape for the pilots was by means of a special lift, located near the nose gear.

PROFILE

Tupolev's Cold War Giant

Tupolev was authorized to proceed with its Type 95 on 11 July 1951. The new aircraft proved the concept of the swept-wing turboprop-powered bomber, but it also showed that more development work was necessary to produce an operational machine.

Two prototypes, 95/I and 95/II, were subsequently completed and these were to pave the way for the Tu-95M with increased fuel capacity and revised operational equipment.

Known in the West as the 'Bear-A', the Tu-95M (M for modernized) was a basic free-fall nuclear bomber. Many of these machines were converted to Tu-95K 'Bear-B' standard, with provision for firing the giant AS-3 'Kangaroo' missile.

From 1960, a number of new-build, multi-role Tu-95KM 'Bear-Cs' were joined by several machines modified from earlier airframes, while an early 1970s project designed to produce a cruise-missile carrying aircraft resulted in several 'Bear-As' and 'Bear-Bs' being substantially reconfigured to Tu-95K-22 'Bear-G' standard, with chin-mounted 'Crown Drum' missile guidance radar.

Above: These 'Bears' are carrying huge Kh-20/AS-3 'Kangaroo' missiles during an air show near Moscow.

Below: A swept wing, combined with huge turboprop engines, resulted in outstanding performance.

Tu-95KM 'Bear-C'

Type: Long-range intelligence gathering aircraft and stand-off cruise missile platform

Powerplant: four 11,033-kW (14,795-hp) Kuznetsov NK-12MV turboprop engines

Maximum speed: 860 km/h (534 mph)

Cruising speed: 750 km/h (466 mph)

Combat radius: 6080 km (3,778 miles)

Range: 12,500 km (7,767 miles)

Service ceiling: 11,600 m (38,058 ft)

Weights: empty 81,200 kg (179,015 lb); loaded 182,000 kg (401,241 lb)

Armament: six 23-mm (0.91-in) cannon

Dimensions:

	span	50.04 m (164 ft 2 in)
	length	46.17 m (151 ft 6 in)
	height	12.50 m (41 ft)
	wing area	283.70 m² (3,054 sq ft)

TU-95KM 'BEAR-C'

This particular example represents a Tu-95KM 'Bear-C'. All these aircraft were rebuilt from the original bombers and were used both for Elint gathering and as cruise missile platforms.

The standard crew complement in early Tu-95s was two pilots, two navigators, a flight engineer and radio operator/gunner. Most of the crew were housed in the pressurized nose section and could escape via a special emergency lift.

Earlier strategic bombers had insufficient performance, so the Kuznetsov bureau was given the task of designing a suitable engine for the Tu-95. The massive NK-12 turboprop which resulted was, and still is, one of the most powerful in the world.

Extensive tests were conducted in order to come up with an aircraft which was turboprop-powered, but offered jet-like performance. Tupolev's answer was to sweep the wing 35° to achieve the necessary targets. For reduced drag, the main undercarriage was fitted to the inner engine nacelles.

Barely visible in this illustration is the rear dorsal turret, which was a feature of early 'Bear' variants. This was based on a system dating back to the B-29 and was fully retractable. It was deleted on some aircraft.

Like the wings and horizontal stabilizers, the tail was also swept back, albeit at a modest angle. Most 'Bear' variants were fitted with twin 23-mm (0.91-in) cannon in a tail turret. Aircraft converted into Tu-95KM 'Bear-C's later had the turret faired over and replaced by an elongated conical section, housing electronic countermeasures (ECM) equipment.

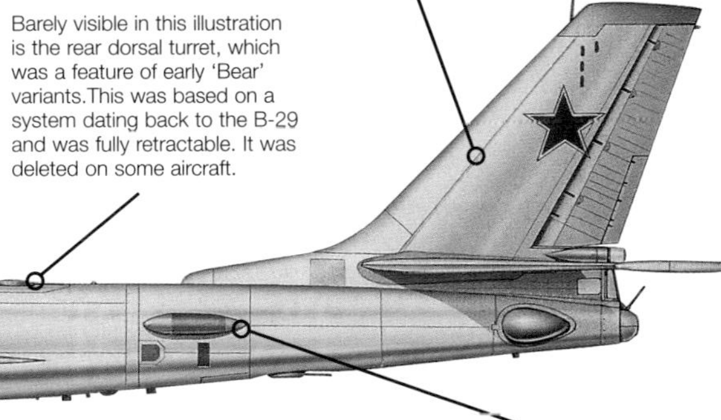

In order to cope with the immense torque of the NK-12 engines, giant four-bladed contra-rotating propellers were fitted.

Single main wheels were fitted to the 'Bear's' predecessor, the Tu-85. To cope with the increased weight of the Tu-95, tandem units were introduced.

Distinguishing features of the Tu-95KM were the twin Elint blisters located on either side of the rear fuselage. Below them were camera ports, indicating a reconnaissance role for this variant.

ACTION DATA

MAXIMUM SPEED

With its slow-turning turboprops, the 'Bear' was one of the slowest strategic bombers, although this factor resulted in great fuel economy and efficiency in comparison with jet-powered bombers such as the B-52 Stratofortress and M-4 'Bison'.

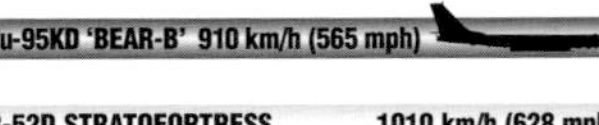

RANGE

Although the Tu 95 may have been slow, combining the turboprop engines with a swept wing resulted in an incredible range, the aircraft being able to cover huge distances with few problems. Both he B-52 and M-4 could not quite match the endurance of the 'Bear'.

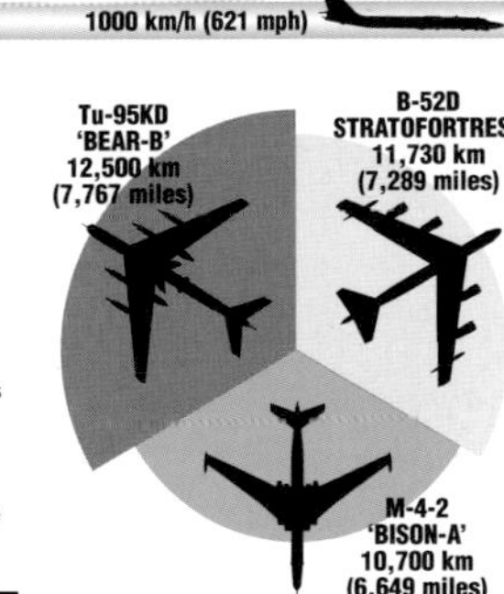

SERVICE CEILING

In addition to its range and fuel economy, the Tu-95 could also operate at greater altitudes than either the Boeing B 52 or M-4. High altitude interceptors and bomber destroyers had to be developed specifically to challenge these bombers.

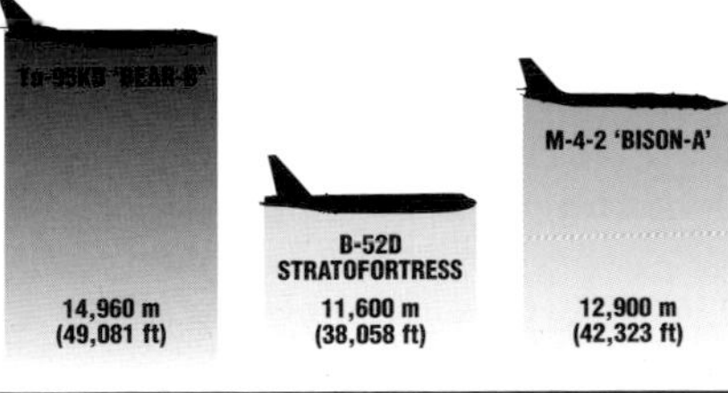

'Bear' derivatives

■ **TUPOLEV Tu-116:** In the late 1950s, the Soviet Union lacked a suitable VIP transport aircraft for Nikita Khrushchev and other government leaders. An interim solution was found by modifying two Tu-95 bombers with plush interiors.

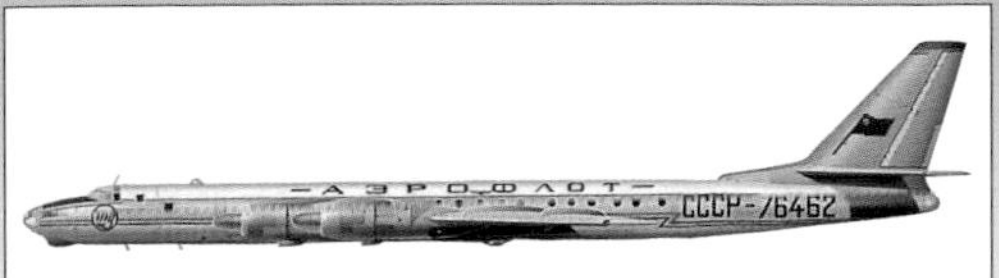

■ **TUPOLEV Tu-114 'CLEAT':** Design began on the Tu-114 before the Tu-116 took to the air and this aircraft featured an entirely new and larger fuselage, mated to the wings and tail surfaces of the 'Bear'. It entered service with Aeroflot in 1961.

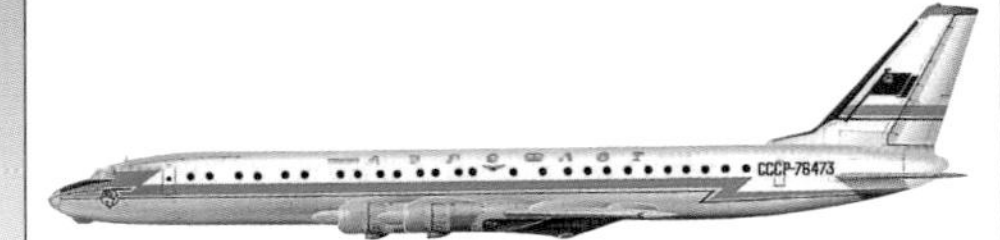

■ **TUPOLEV Tu-126 'MOSS':** A military derivative of the Tu-114, the 'Moss' provided the V-VF (Soviet air force) with a long-range airborne early warning (AEW) aircraft. The type was replaced during the 1980s, by the more capable A-50 'Mainstay'.

TUPOLEV

TU-95 'BEAR-D/E'

● Powerful strategic bomber ● Ultra-long-range maritime patrol

One of the most majestic sights in aviation is the Russian 'Bear' bomber, cruising at high altitude with bare metal surfaces gleaming in the sun and vapour streaming back from its huge engines. This incredible giant has served Russia valiantly for more than 40 years. Now almost all 'Bears' except the newest versions are close to retirement, and the big Tupolev bomber is becoming an increasingly rare sight.

▲ *The 'Bear-D' was usually not far from any NATO exercise, and frequently flew down the North Sea coast of Britain testing the reaction times of the RAF's Lightning and Phantom interceptors.*

PHOTO FILE

TUPOLEV TU-95 'BEAR-D/E'

▼ A classic bomber
'Bear' sums up the Tu-95's power and strength superbly well: never was a NATO reporting name more aptly chosen.

▲ Pre-jumbo giant
The 'Bear' was used as the basis for the amazing Tupolev Tu-114, the largest and longest-ranged airliner before the Boeing 747. It could carry more than 200 passengers.

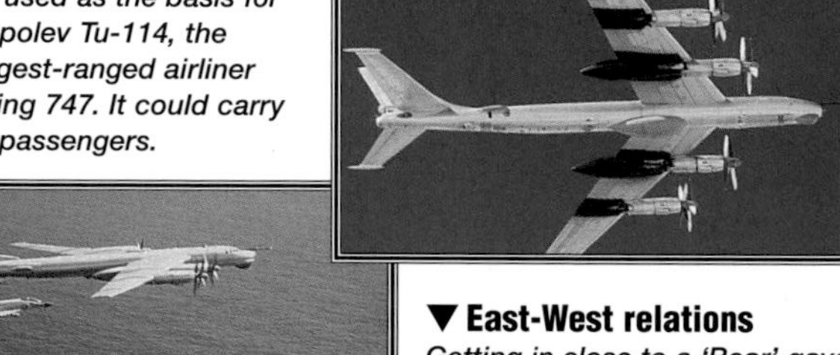

◀ Maritime scout
The 'Bear-D' was the most frequently encountered variant, growling over the world's oceans to gather maritime intelligence for the Soviet navy.

▼ East-West relations
Getting in close to a 'Bear' gave NATO pilots and Tupolev crews a chance for some good-natured rivalry – never forgetting that in war the rivalry would have been deadly.

▲ Eye in the sky
NATO navies could expect to pick up a shadowing 'Bear' almost anywhere in the world. In war, the bomber's task would have been to guide Soviet missiles onto US carriers. Other 'Bears' carried nuclear-tipped weaponry such as AS-3 missiles.

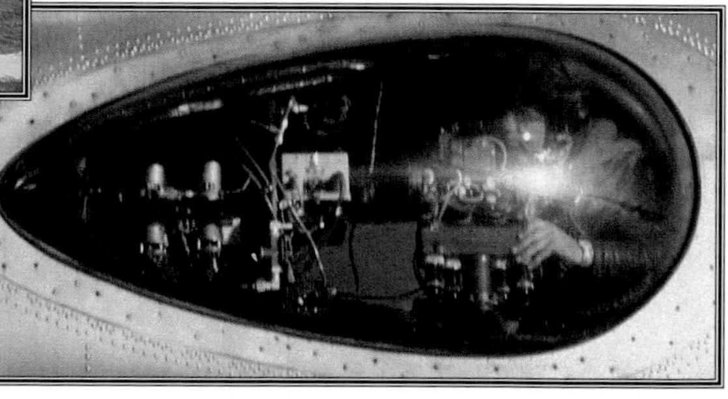

FACTS AND FIGURES

- ➤ Bombers are designated Tu-95; maritime reconnaissance and anti-submarine warfare variants are designated Tu-142.
- ➤ The 'Bear' prototype flew on 12 November 1952.
- ➤ The Indian navy operates a small number of naval 'Bears', known as Tu-142Ms.
- ➤ The 'Bear'-based Tu-114 airliner was the biggest aircraft in the world when it flew on commercial routes in the early 1960s.
- ➤ 'Bears' covered the world from bases in Cuba, Somalia, Angola and Vietnam.
- ➤ Over 400 'Bears' have been built in the type's four-decade production run.

PROFILE

In the shadow of the 'Bear'

The 'Bear' was a truly international performer. The combination of its vast range and the Soviet Union's many bases in client states meant that there was almost no part of the world's oceans that could not be photographed, or attacked.

Now in its fifth decade, the Tupolev Tu-95 'Bear' is one of the most visually stunning aircraft ever built. It is unique in having swept wings and turboprop engines, which use jet power to drive enormous contra-rotating propellers. Tupolev decided this was the only practical way to achieve long range and high-altitude flight for bombing and intelligence-gathering duties, given the limitations of early Soviet jet engines. The huge turboprops made the 'Bear' almost as fast as many jet bombers. The pilots in the big maritime patroller's flight deck are at the controls of one of the biggest and heaviest military planes in history. A dozen versions of the 'Bear' were built, the 'Bear-D' acting first as a missile-guidance platform and then as a photo-reconnaissance machine when missiles no longer needed target updating. In the reconnaissance role, the 'Bear' could even communicate with Soviet satellites. The rarer Tu-95MR 'Bear-E' was a similar update of 'Bear-As', incorporating electronic intelligence-gathering equipment.

For decades, 'Bears' flew along the fringes of the West, shadowing NATO's fleets and prying out the secrets and testing the reaction times of opposing air defence systems. As long as they were in the danger zone they were invariably intercepted and escorted by Allied fighters.

The 'Bear-D' remains in limited service with about 15 examples on strength. The sight of a 'Bear', once a common occurrence, is now rare indeed.

NATO fighter pilots have had a lot of practice intercepting 'Bears', and most Western knowledge of the type has come from such regular encounters.

Tu-95RT 'Bear-D'

Type: long-range maritime reconnaissance/missile guidance aircraft

Powerplant: four 11,186-kW (15,000-hp.) Kuznetsov NK-12MV turboprops

Maximum speed: 925 km/h (573 m.p.h.) at 9000 m (29,500 ft.); cruising speed 710 km/h (440 m.p.h.)

Range: 13,500 km (8,730 mi.)

Service ceiling: 12,500 m (41,000 ft.)

Weights: empty 80,000 kg (176,000 lb.); loaded 188,000 kg (413,600 lb.)

Armament: two 23-mm cannon in manned tail turret (other 'Bears' had up to six cannon and a wide variety of bombs, cruise missiles, torpedoes and depth charges)

Dimensions:

Dimensions:	span	51.10 m (167 ft. 7 in.)
	length	49.50 m (162 ft. 4 in.)
	height	12.12 m (39 ft. 8 in.)
	wing area	297 m² (3,196 sq. ft.)

TU-95RT 'BEAR-D'

The mighty Tupolev 'Bear' was designed as a conventional bomber. Very early in its career, however, it was given a new role as a long-range target acquisition and maritime reconnaissance aircraft, finding targets for missile guidance.

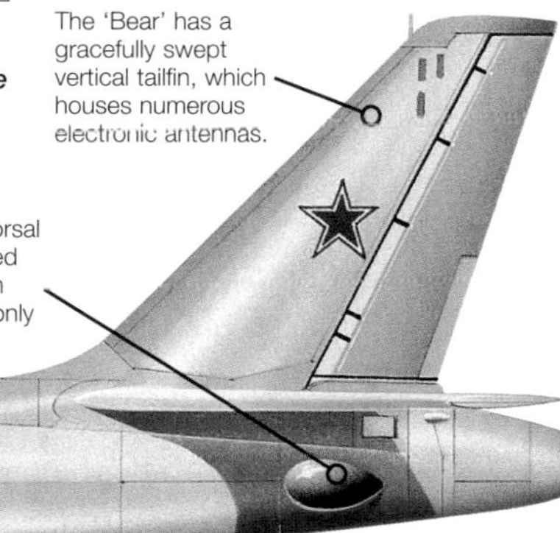

The fuselage of the Tu-95 contains a unique aircrew escape system, in which a conveyer-belt style floor section carries the pilots to safety through an escape hatch. The tail gunner has a floor hatch.

The 'Bear' is powered by four massive Kuznetsov NK-12M turboprops, the most powerful engines of their type ever built. They drive massive contra-rotating propellers.

Huge engine power and a graceful swept wing push the 'Bear' faster than any other propeller-driven aircraft, achieving jet-like speeds in excess of 900 km/h (560 m.p.h.). Jet power was considered for the 'Bear' but never adopted.

The defensive armament of the 'Bear-C' included retractable dorsal and ventral turrets and a manned tail turret, each with two 23-mm cannon. The 'Bear-D' retained only the rear gun turret.

The 'Bear' has a gracefully swept vertical tailfin, which houses numerous electronic antennas.

The addition of a refuelling probe meant that the 'Bear's' already massive range could be extended indefinitely.

The blister under the nose housed a missile-guidance radar associated with the AS-3 Kangaroo cruise missile. The radar was kept in the RT version but bomb and missile capability was deleted.

Big Bulge is a very powerful radar, able to detect a large ship at over 250-km (155-mi.) range.

The blisters on the rear fuselage of the 'Bear' house electronic intelligence-gathering sensors. A reconnaissance camera port is also visible under the rear of the Elint blister.

COMBAT DATA

RANGE

B-52 STRATOFORTRESS 16,000 km (9,900 mi.)

P-3 ORION 7600 km (4,700 mi.)

Tu-95 'BEAR-D' 13,500 km (8,400 mi.)

The key to effective maritime reconnaissance and strike capability is long range and endurance. The Boeing B-52 is the 'Bear's' only rival in this regard, especially when carrying a heavy weapons load. More conventional maritime patrollers such as the Lockheed P-3 Orion are not in the same league.

Long eyes of the Soviet fleet

THE RED FLEET: Soviet naval doctrine called for the elimination of American carrier battle groups. As a result, Red Fleet warships were very heavily armed with large, long-range missiles with heavy conventional or nuclear warheads.

MID-COURSE GUIDANCE: The largest of the Soviet anti-ship missiles had very long ranges, far beyond any possibility of guidance from their launch platforms. For maximum accuracy they relied on mid-course targeting updates from the 'Bear'.

TARGET LOCATION: In its Cold War maritime role, the 'Bear' was tasked with locating American carrier battle groups either visually or by radar, and transmitting that location to the Soviet fleet.

TUPOLEV

Tu-128 'FIDDLER'

● Heavy interceptor ● Ultra-long range ● World's largest fighter

The Tu-128 was developed in the late 1950s to defend the Soviet Union against the threat of B-52 bombers armed with long-range stand-off missiles. This enormous interceptor was based on an unsuccessful bomber design, the Tu-98 'Backfin', and carried long-range missiles designed specifically for it. The Tu-128's highly specialized role meant that only limited numbers were built, and it has now been replaced by the MiG-31 and Su-27.

▲ *Defending the Soviet Union's borders was a huge task and required large numbers of sensors, thousands of missile sites and highly specialized long-range interceptors such as the Tu-128.*

PHOTO FILE

TUPOLEV Tu-128 'FIDDLER'

▼ Guided missiles
The sole armament of the Tu-128 was the R-4 air-to-air missile, which was unique to the type and was available in both radar-guided (R-4R) or infra-red (R-4T) versions.

▲ Threats from the West
The Tu-128 was developed specifically to intercept airborne threats from America, including the naval A-5 Vigilante and B-70.

◄ Unrivalled range
The long-ranged 'Fiddler' could patrol along interception lines at ranges of between 600 and 965 km (373 and 600 miles) from base.

▼ Improved interceptor
Introduced into service in 1979, the Tu-128M had a more capable RP-5M Smerch-M fire-control radar as well as four new R-4PM and R-4TM missiles.

▲ PVO protector
Tu-128s served with the PVO from 1961 until 1988, and were also used for long-range bomber escort.

FACTS AND FIGURES

- In the West the 'Fiddler' is also often referred to, incorrectly, as the Tu-28; in fact only the factory code is 'Type 28'.
- Development of the Tu-128 began after the failure of the Lavochkin La-250.
- Test pilots for the Tu-128 included would-be cosmonaut G. Beregovi.
- The Tu-128UT trainer version had a third cockpit buried in the bulged, radar-less, part-glazed nosecone.
- Tu-128 backseat weapons operators trained on the specialized Tu-124Sh 'Cookpot'.
- An early Tu-128 was damaged during its attack on an Il-28M target drone.

PROFILE

Facing the Western threat

Probably no more than 200 Tu-128s were built for the Soviet home defence fighter force (PVO) and frontal aviation air regiments (VVS); not many survived in service into the 1990s. The aircraft's huge size enabled it to carry all the equipment needed to intercept bombers before they could penetrate to within their missiles' effective range.

A powerful radar scanner in the nose enabled the Tu-128 to locate intruders at long ranges. Twin afterburning engines enabled it to reach speeds of up to 2085 km/h (1,296 mph) and it could take off with enough fuel for patrols lasting up to six hours.

Just as important were its weapons. The R-4 missile, designated AA-5 'Ash' by NATO, had 60-km (37-mile) range in its active radar-homing (ARH) version and delivered a 65-kg (143-lb) high-explosive warhead. The R-4 missile was also available with an infra-red seeker, and two missiles of each type were usually carried. Although the ARH version weighed 580 kg (1,279 lb) and the IR version 545 kg (1,202 lb), the 'Fiddler' carried all four comfortably under its huge 17.5-m (57-ft 5-in) wingspan.

Above: When the Tu-128 design emerged it was similar in size, shape, power and weight to the failed Tu-98 bomber.

Right: Two separate missile homing systems made the Tu-128 more able to defeat enemy jamming.

Five variants saw service: the Tu-128, the Tu-128UT trainer, the LORAN-equipped Tu-128Ch, the Tu-128A with Smerch-A radar and the final production Tu-128M.

Tu-128M 'Fiddler'

Type: two-seat ultra-long-range interceptor and escort fighter

Powerplant: two 104.9-kN (23,539-lb-thrust) Lyul'ka AL-7F-4 afterburning turbojets

Maximum speed: 2085 km/h (1,296 mph) at 11,000 m (36,089 ft)

Range: 2565 km (1,594 miles) with allowances for combat

Combat radius: 600–965 km (373–600 miles) on patrol

Service ceiling: 20,000 m (65,617 ft)

Weights: empty 25,960 kg (57,232 lb); maximum take-off (Tu-128) 43,000 kg (94,800 lb)

Armament: two R-4PM and two R-4TM air-to-air missiles (AA-5 'Ash')

Dimensions:		
	span	17.67 m (58 ft)
	length	30.49 m (100 ft)
	height	7.00 m (23 ft)
	wing area	96.94 m² (1,043 sq ft)

Tu-128Ch 'Fiddler'

Serving with the Soviet PVO, the Tu-128 was the largest fighter-type aircraft ever built. The last have now been replaced by the MiG-31 'Foxhound'

Both crewmembers entered via an 11-rung ladder. The pressurized cockpit had alternate red/white lighting and KT-1 ejection seats, and was protected by a heavy duty upward-hinged metal canopy with a bullet-proof V-windscreen.

Fuel was carried in eight central fuselage tanks and twin wing tanks. With a total fuel capacity of 14,850 kg (32,739 lb), external tanks and air-to-air refuelling were considered unnecessary.

Four wing pylons carried R-4T (later R-4TM) infra-red and R-4R (later R-4PM) radar guided air-to-air missiles. Generally, the IR weapons were carried inboard, with the radar-guided weapons outboard. The weapons had to be loaded using a specially built powered trolley because they were so heavy.

The Tu-128 was originally designed to use new VD-19 turbojets, but was eventually powered by the AL-7Fs of the unsuccessful Tu-98 'Backfin' bomber. Later versions introduced improved AL-7F-4 turbojets.

The fuselage and tail were similar in configuration to the older Tupolev Tu-98, but lacked the tail turret gun armament of the bomber. Instead, the tail held an enormous 50 m² (538 sq ft) brake parachute within a thermally insulated container just beneath the lower fuselage.

94

The large radome contained an RP-5 radar as part of the Smerch fire-control system. The prototype aircraft had a large ventral fairing containing a receiver antenna for target echo-reception.

Avionics included an AP-7P autopilot, an NVU-B1 navigational complex and a Put-4 flight-control system giving semi-automatic level flight guidance, airfield homing, altitude/heading hold, auto-runway approach and auto-return to a pre-programmed position.

As on the Tu-22 and early Tupolev airliners, the main undercarriage retracted backwards into giant wing trailing-edge bullet fairings.

COMBAT DATA

MISSILE RANGE

The Tu-128M had excellent range and was equipped with long-range missiles allowing it to strike from a distance. The F-106A had AIM-4 medium-range missiles, but they were unreliable. The Su-15 also carried infra-red and radar guided missiles, the AA-3 'Anab'.

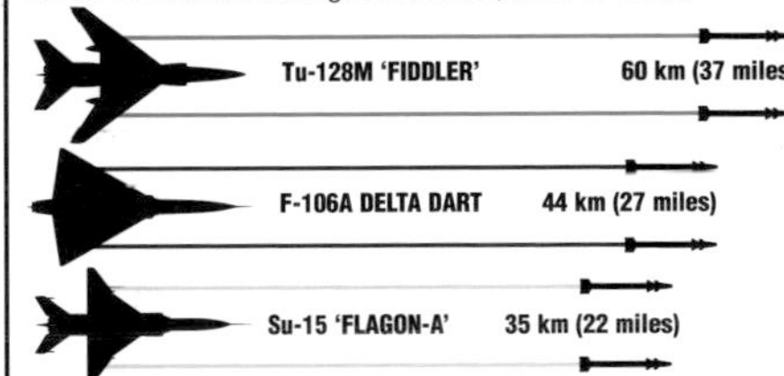

MAXIMUM SPEED

Carrying huge quantities of fuel for its engines, a second crewmember and a heavy radar and missiles, the Tu-128M was not an agile performer compared to Russia's smaller MiG-21 and Su-15. However, it was fast enough to intercept an incoming B-52 or Vulcan, and even some fighter aircraft.

Tu-128M 'FIDDLER'	2085 km/h (1,296 mph)
F-106A DELTA DART	2136 km/h (1,327 mph)
Su-15 'FLAGON-A'	2230 km/h (1,386 mph)

COMBAT RADIUS

The Su-15 was an all-out performance machine, with speed and a large radar as the design priorities rather than range. The F-106A was a dedicated air defence aircraft and had medium range and moderate performance. Neither aircraft could match the range of the Tu-128M, which patrolled 900 km (560 miles) from base.

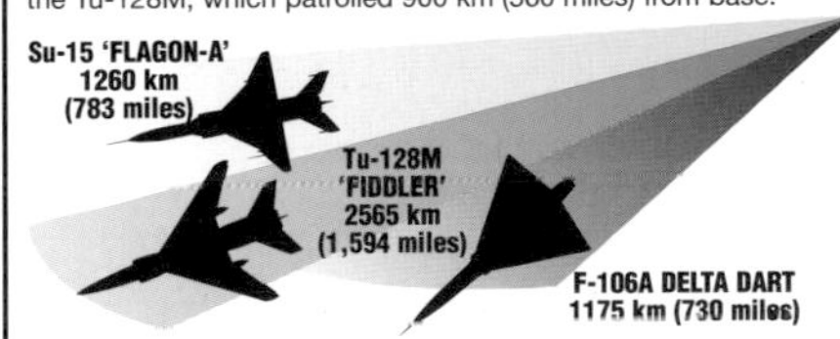

Soviet interceptors

■ **MiG-21 'FISHBED':** In January 1963 the first examples of this classic combat aircraft took their place in the front line of Soviet air defence. Early aircraft were known as the 'Fishbed-C'.

■ **MiG-23 'FLOGGER':** Initial production models of the MiG-23, with limited capability, entered service late in 1970. By 1976, 2000 of the improved MiG-23M were in service.

■ **MiG-25 'FOXBAT':** In February 1962 authorization was granted to begin production of the 'Foxbat' to counter the threat posed by the B-70 and A-12. First deliveries were in 1973.

■ **Su-27 'FLANKER':** Now distributed among the states of the former Soviet Union, the 'Flanker' represents the pinnacle of Russian interceptor development.

Vickers

Valiant

● First of the V-bombers ● Nuclear and conventional ● Four jet engines

After World War II Britain required a jet-powered, high-flying bomber which was capable of penetrating enemy air defences and delivering a nuclear weapon at long range. In 1947 an official requirement was declared, which led to the procurement of the V-bomber force. Due to the urgent need, the simplest, and therefore the most rapidly available, of the proposals was immediately chosen, and so the Vickers Valiant was born.

▲ *Few problems were encountered on introducing the Valiant into service. The addition of a flight refuelling probe solved an early shortfall in range. The ground and air crew were quickly trained in nuclear procedures.*

PHOTO FILE

Vickers Valiant

Night-time preparations ▶
Groundcrew prepare a Valiant B(PR).Mk 1 for a night mission. This variant of the versatile Valiant flew as a strategic photographic-reconnaissance platform.

▼ Valiant prototype
Vickers modified the engine air intakes to the 'spectacle' type, allowing more air to reach the increasingly powerful engines.

▼ Graceful Valiant
An aerodynamically simple but very attractive design allowed the Valiant to enter service earlier than the other two V-bombers.

▼ 'Anti-flash' white
Experts thought that a bright, shiny paint scheme would reflect the radiation of a nuclear blast, protecting the bomber crew from its harmful effects.

On finals ▶
This No. 7 Squadron Valiant, with its large flaps deployed, is ready to land. The squadron relinquished its Valiants in July 1960.

FACTS AND FIGURES

- ➤ Rolls-Royce Avon turbojets powered the first prototype; Armstrong Siddeley Sapphires powered the second.
- ➤ A grass airfield was used for the Valiant's first flight in 1951.
- ➤ Super-Sprite rockets were tested on one Valiant for assisted take-offs.
- ➤ Valiants dropped nuclear weapons during tests over Maralinga, Australia, and over Christmas Island.
- ➤ Only one B.Mk 2, known as the 'black bomber', was built.
- ➤ Valiants dropped conventional bombs in anger during the Suez crisis.

PROFILE

Establishing the nuclear deterrent

Although the Valiant was the least advanced of the V-bombers, it was was nevertheless a very able aircraft which represented a great leap in capability for the RAF.

Having flown for the first time on 18 May 1951, the first prototype was lost in January 1952 when there was an in-flight fire in the left engine bay. The second prototype was rapidly completed, but the production bomber had already been ordered off the drawing board, and the first Valiant squadron, No. 138, received its aircraft in early 1955.

Valiants gave exceptional service in their designed role, and also as strategic reconnaissance platforms and tankers. Unfortunately, a switch to low-level duties caused catastrophic structural failures and the rapid withdrawal of the aircraft in January 1965.

Despite the problems which were caused by these changing roles and faulty alloys in the wing spars, the Valiant was a superb bomber.

Above: Several B.Mk 1 and B(PR).Mk 1 aircraft were converted to tankers and designated B(K).Mk 1 and BPR(K).Mk 1, respectively.

Below: Only one Valiant B.Mk 2 was completed, being optimized for low-level attack. A strengthened wing structure used the space previously occupied by the retracted main undercarriage.

Valiant B.Mk 1

Type: long-range bomber

Powerplant: four 44.7-kN (10,054-lb-thrust) Rolls-Royce Avon RA.28 turbojets

Maximum speed: 912 km/h (576 mph) at 9145 m (30,000 ft)

Initial climb rate: 1219 m/min (4,000 fpm)

Maximum range: 7242 km (4,500 miles) with underwing fuel tanks

Service ceiling: 16,460 m (54,000 ft)

Weights: empty 34,419 kg (75,881 lb); maximum take-off 63,503 kg (140,000 lb)

Armament: one 4536-kg (10,000-lb) nuclear bomb or up to 21 454-kg (1,000-lb) conventional bombs

Dimensions:		
	span	34.85 m (114 ft 4 in)
	length	32.99 m (108 ft 3 in)
	height	9.80 m (32 ft 2 in)
	wing area	219.43 m² (2,362 sq ft)

VALIANT B.MK 1

Very few Valiants were finished in this tactical camouflage scheme before fatigue cracks, brought on by low-level flights, caused the rapid grounding and scrapping of the fleet.

Only the pilot and co-pilot were provided with ejection seats, with the other three crewmembers escaping by parachute from the door below the cockpit. Two extra personnel were carried during the tanker role.

When the Valiant was designed, British thinking was that engines should be mounted in the wingroots. This was true of all the operational V-bombers. American designers preferred to fit podded engines, which were slung on pylons beneath the wings.

Mounting the wings at the shoulders of the fuselage produced a large volume of space in the fuselage for the bomb-bay. It also meant that the engines were attached high on the airframe, and the tailplane had to be high-set to avoid the efflux.

Improvements in Soviet air defence led to the Valiant force moving to low-level operations for safety from interception. The stresses of low-level flight caused the wing spars to crack and the premature withdrawal of the entire Valiant fleet.

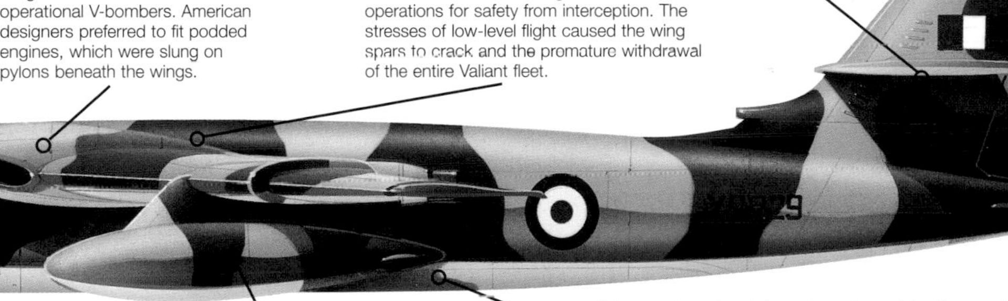

Principal among the Valiant's bombing aids was the H_2S bombing radar from World War II, but in its improved Mk 9 form.

A large fuel tank could be carried beneath each wing, although these were not always fitted.

A large-volume bomb-bay allowed a variety of conventional and nuclear stores, including the American-supplied B43 weapon, to be carried. The bomb doors opened into the fuselage, reducing drag and allowing high speed to be maintained over the target.

COMBAT DATA

MAXIMUM SPEED

Military planners believed that high speed and high altitude were the keys to the successful penetration of enemy airspace. Fighter pilots found it difficult to aim guns at bombers while flying through the buffeting encountered at speeds just below the speed of sound.

VALIANT B.Mk 1	912 km/h (567 mph)
M-4 'BISON-A'	998 km/h (620 mph)
B-47E-II STRATOJET	975 km/h (606 mph)

MAXIMUM BOMBLOAD

In the conventional bombing role the Valiant carried a heavier load than these contemporaries. For nuclear strikes the bomb-bay capacity was significant, as nuclear devices were often large. The Valiant was equipped with a huge weapons bay.

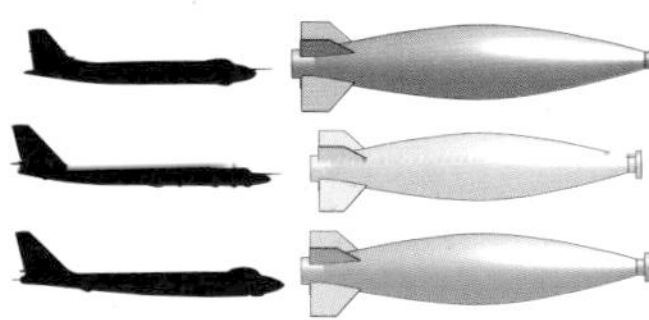

RANGE

The Myasishchev M-4 'Bison' had long range at the expense of weapons load and never achieved its design promise. Boeing's B-47 Stratojet used six turbojet engines, but paved the way for the B-52. The Valiant did not quite meet the original range requirements, but nonetheless flew long missions

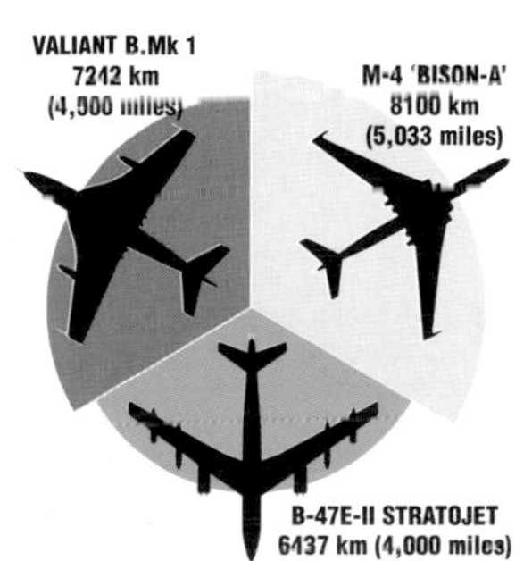

Britain's V-bomber force

AVRO VULCAN B.Mk 2: Fitted with a semi-recessed Blue Steel missile and wearing the markings of the illustrious No. 617 'Dambusters' Squadron, this Vulcan has toned-down national markings on its anti-flash paintwork.

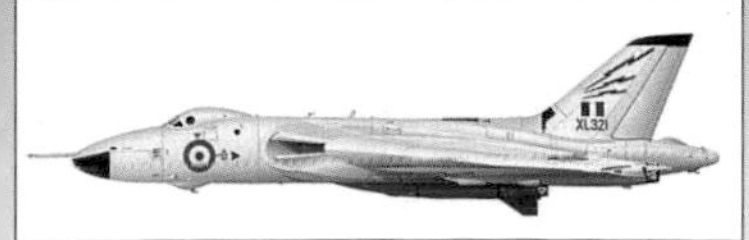

AVRO VULCAN B.Mk 2: Combining tactical green/grey camouflage with white undersides, this aircraft dates from 1964. The Vulcan had a similar bombload to the Valiant, but the Victor could carry 15,876 kg (35,000 lb) of conventional bombs.

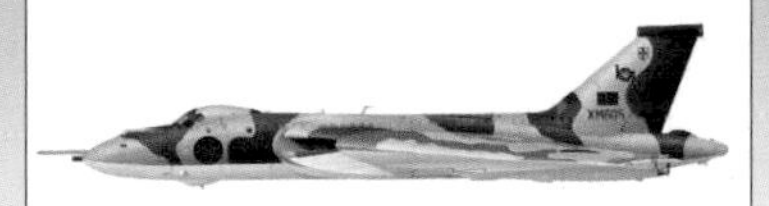

HANDLEY PAGE VICTOR B.Mk 1: Although these aircraft wore colours in keeping with the nuclear strike role, some flew area bombing missions against terrorist camps in the Malayan jungle, armed with conventional weapons.

HANDLEY PAGE VICTOR B.Mk 2R: These special aircraft were equipped to fire the Avro Blue Steel stand-off missile. A series of small fairings, clustered around the tailcone, accommodated the Blue Steel avionics.

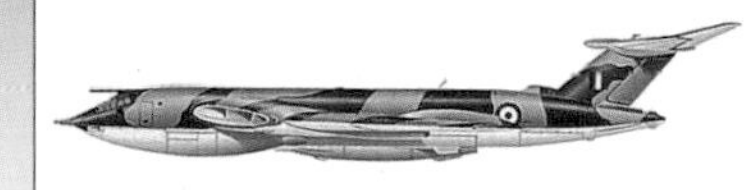

VOUGHT

A-7 CORSAIR II (USN)

● Vietnam veteran ● Subsonic bomber ● Carrier deployments

There is a saying in aviation, 'if something looks right, it flies right.' Taking into account the stubby appearance of the A-7 Corsair II, one may think the aircraft was therefore a poor performer. In fact the Corsair II proved to be one of the most capable attack aircraft in the US Navy. Replacing the diminutive Douglas A-4 Skyhawk, the Corsair II provided a quantum leap in technology that the US Navy was quick to exploit.

▲ *A typical carrier-deck scene as a US Navy A-7 Corsair is re-armed and prepared for flight. The aircraft achieved an excellent maintenance record whenever operating on deployment.*

PHOTO FILE

VOUGHT A-7 CORSAIR II (USN)

◀ **High visibility**
Upon entering service, Navy Corsairs proudly displayed colourful squadron markings on their tails and wings.

▼ **Leemoore line-up**
Early A-7As are positioned prior to inspection by naval ground crews at Leemoore Naval Air Station. One aircraft already has its starboard avionics access panel open.

▼ **On the approach**
Trailing its tailhook, a Corsair II returns to the carrier from a combat sortie with empty bomb racks.

▲ **Compact Corsair**
Carrier operations have always been restricted by space. With its folding-wing, a 'Golden Dragons' A-7 Corsair II can taxi while aboard ship.

▲ **Carrier attack**
A true naval attack aircraft in every way, this Corsair II displays its folding wings and enormous warload. The Corsair II has been used around the world by the US Navy for attack duties and flew its last combat missions during the Gulf War of 1991.

FACTS AND FIGURES

- ➤ The A-7 Corsair II was designed as a replacement for the A-4 Skyhawk in the attack role.
- ➤ Vought named the Corsair II after the World War II F4U naval fighter.
- ➤ The first combat mission for the Corsair II took place in December 1967.
- ➤ In all, 395 A-7As, A-7Bs and A-7Es took part in the Vietnam War. They flew with a total of 27 US Navy squadrons.
- ➤ The improved A-7E entered service off the Vietnam coast in May 1970.
- ➤ Altogether, 54 US Navy A-7s were lost to enemy fire.

PROFILE

Vought's venerable warrior

Often overshadowed aboard the aircraft carrier by the sleek fighters nestled alongside it, Vought's A-7 Corsair II hid its enormous capabilities beneath a short bulky fuselage. Observers seeing the aircraft for the first time often mocked the design, but to naval pilots the A-7 presented them with an ideal attack platform from which to deliver a wide range of bombs and air-to-air missiles.

The A-7A flew its first combat mission in Vietnam in 1967 with VA-147, more commonly known as the 'Argonauts'. Operating aboard USS *Ranger*, the first combat deployment included a cadre of Air Force officers assigned to test the A-7A's combat potential.

A few years later, the US Air Force would request the Vought company to develop a land-based equivalent for it.

Despite its success, the Corsair II encountered problems in service. Pilots found the aircraft had a tendency to suck up catapult steam during launches, which resulted in more than a few accidents.

Above: With its nose leg extended, a Corsair II from USS Coral Sea *returns to its home port after a cruise.*

Yet the Corsair II achieved the reputation of being one of the most able attack aircraft ever.

Improvements to the avionics allowed the A-7 Corsair II to remain in the front line with the US Navy for more than 20 years, before being retired in 1991.

Below: The striking capability of the naval carrier is depicted in this view of four Corsair IIs over-flying their home carrier.

A-7E Corsair II

Type: single-seat carrier-based attack aircraft

Powerplant: one 66.6-kN (14,979-lb-thrust) Rolls-Royce Allison TF41-A-2 turbofan

Maximum speed: 1123 km/h (698 mph) at sea level

Initial climb rate: 4572 m/min (15,000 fpm)

Combat radius: 1151 km (715 miles)

Service ceiling: 12,800 m (41,995 ft)

Weights: empty 8988 kg (19,815 lb); maximum take-off 19,050 kg (41,998 lb)

Armament: one M61A1 Vulcan six-barrel 20-mm (0.79-in) cannon, plus up to 6804 kg (15,000 lb) of ordnance

Dimensions:		
	span	11.81 m (38 ft 9 in)
	length	14.06 m (46 ft 2 in)
	height	4.88 m (16 ft)
	wing area	34.83 m² (375 sq ft)

A-7B Corsair II

This early A-7B bears the 'AB' tail-code of carrier air wing CVW-1. The wing flew from the USS *John F. Kennedy* (CV-67), a 'Kitty Hawk'-class carrier which was assigned to the Atlantic Fleet.

Having built numerous attack aircraft for the US Navy, the Vought designers listened to advice and gave the pilot exceptional visibility with the Corsair II. An upward-hinging canopy was provided. The pilot was seated on an Escapac ejection seat.

A moderately swept wing was adopted for the Corsair II and six pylons were installed under the wings roughly in line with the centre of gravity, to reduce pitching movements during weapons release.

This particular aircraft was part of attack squadron VA-46 'Clansmen', whose home base was at Cecil Field, Florida. The unit's tartan trim can be seen on the fin of the Corsair II.

Positioned on the lower port fuselage was a single six-barrelled cannon. This was provided with 500 rounds of ammunition housed behind the cockpit.

To allow stowage beneath aircraft carrier decks, the outer wings of the Corsair could be folded. The aircraft could taxi around the carrier deck like this. The wings would be unfolded prior to launch.

The airframe configuration adopted was unusual, but well suited to undertaking attack missions at high subsonic speeds, both at high and medium altitudes.

Colourful Corsairs

'BLUE BLAZERS': An early A-7A, as it appeared in the colours of VA-93. This particular example was based at Atsugi in Japan, but was assigned to the USS *Midway*.

BICENTENNIAL BIRD: Celebrating America's Independence this Corsair flew in a patriotic red, white and blue colour scheme. The aircraft remained in these colours during 1976.

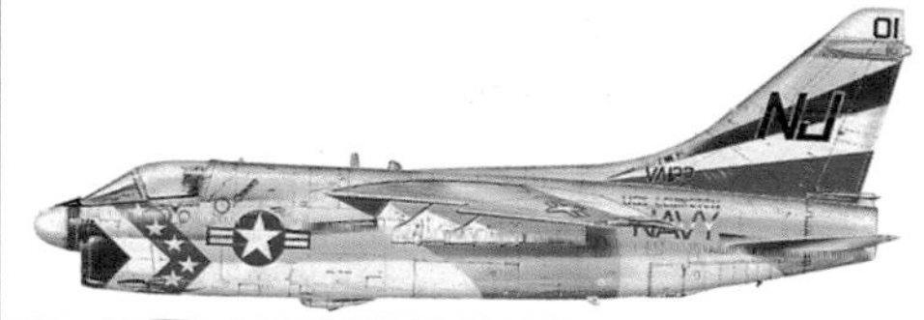

CAMOUFLAGE CORSAIR: One of several A-7Es which adopted a low-visibility trial paint scheme for the US Navy. This particular example operated aboard USS *Enterprise*.

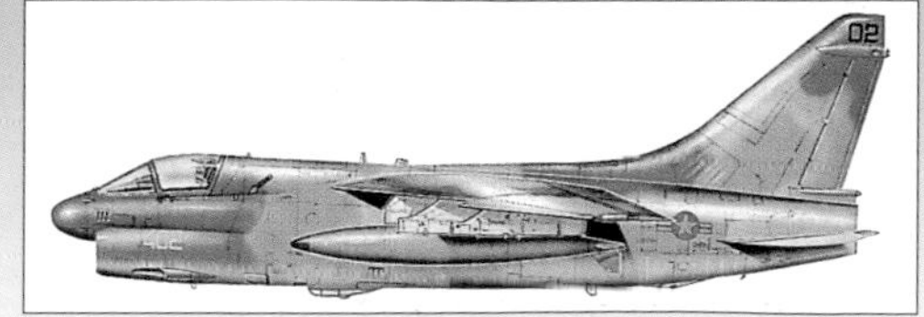

US NAVY ATTACK JETS

GRUMMAN A-6 INTRUDER: Providing the United States Navy with heavy attack capability, the A-6 Intruder (pictured below) could undertake solo precision attack missions in all weathers. Constantly upgraded with new avionics, the A-6 Intruder saw heavy combat use in Vietnam. The aircraft was so complex that a dedicated weapons officer accompanied the pilot. One specialized variant – the KA-6D – was a dedicated tanker. This often supported A-7 Corsair IIs on their missions. Despite early problems with its complex radar, the A-6 Intruder proved itself to be a highly capable attack platform.

DOUGLAS A-4 SKYHAWK: Often called the 'Scooter' because of the way it flew off carrier decks, the A-4 Skyhawk (pictured below) was so small that folding wings were not required on the aircraft. Having entered service in October 1956, the Skyhawk was found to be limited in capability and, by the early 1960s, the US Navy and Marine Corps were already planning a replacement for the aircraft. Although improvements in attack capability were introduced, the

small size of the design restricted the Skyhawk's use. The limited future potential of the Skyhawk having been established, a request for a more capable attack aircraft was developed. The winning design was ultimately Vought's A-7 Corsair II. Despite its removal from carrier operations, the Skyhawk remained in service with the USMC as a forward-air-control aircraft. For this role, two-seat trainers were specially adapted. The US Navy and USMC also used the Skyhawk extensively in Vietnam.

VOUGHT

A-7 (USAF)

● **Combat-proven** ● **Single seat** ● **Subsonic attack aircraft**

It is dated today, but for 30 years the snub-nosed A-7 fought in every conflict the United States was involved in and established a dominant position as the world's best single-seat subsonic attack aircraft. The USAF adopted this fine warplane in the mid-1960s after it had been developed by Vought and the US Navy. Pilots called it the 'SLUF' (Short Little Ugly Fella) and loved it with a passion. Over eight years 459 'SLUFs' were delivered to the US Air Force.

▲ *Groundcrew prepare an A-7 for a training mission. The naval origins of the aircraft are given away by its strong main landing gear and long nosewheel strut.*

PHOTO FILE

VOUGHT A-7 (USAF)

▼ **A vertical take**

The YA-7F, with a new engine and strengthened airframe, offered much higher performance than the standard A-7.

▲ **Missile away**

A Maverick missile leaves a US Air Force A-7 during armament trials.

A-7 formation ▶

These A-7s are finished in the Vietnam-style camouflage of greens and brown over white.

▲ **Eight pylons**

Six underwing and two fuselage pylons give the A-7 the ability to carry a huge load of weapons. The fuselage pylons normally carry Sidewinder missiles for self-defence.

▼ **Flying high**

This aircraft carries practice bombs at high altitude. Any operational flying would be done at much lower levels.

FACTS AND FIGURES

- ➤ The A-7 is credited with having an especially roomy and comfortable cockpit area.
- ➤ The USAF test-flew Navy A-7s from 27 September 1965.
- ➤ The first Air Force A-7 made its initial flight on 26 September 1968.
- ➤ Without being catapulted from an aircraft carrier, the A-7 had a typical take-off run of 1707 m (5,600 ft).
- ➤ Originally designed for the Navy, the A-7 was known as the Corsair II.
- ➤ In Vietnam, a pilot refuelled in flight three times and was aloft for nine hours.

PROFILE

The 'Short Little Ugly Fella'

Once the US Air Force got its version of the A-7 to Vietnam, ground commanders wanted it to throw against the enemy because the A-7 offered a new standard of bombing accuracy. The A-7 also had the 'legs' to rove in enemy territory – no target was too far away or too small to hit with pinpoint precision.

The navigation and weapons delivery system on the A-7 are primitive by today's standards, but in 1967 they were the world's most advanced. Pilots were delighted that they could actually 'pickle' a bomb on a specific building, or on the centre of a bridge, even if the target was in a congested area. The development of laser-guided and other precision weapons was occurring at the same time as the A-7 was appearing on carrier decks, and over time it gained the ability to carry 'smart' bombs.

The USAF used the A-7 in the Sandy mission, escorting rescue helicopters picking up downed airmen in enemy terrain and as a bomber. The A-7 also became a staple with the Air National Guard, which picked up Air Force single-seaters and purchased a handful of two-seat ships.

Left: With US Air Force funding Vought fitted an A-7 with an afterburning engine and modern avionics. This YA-7F did not progress beyond the prototype stage.

Right: USAF A-7s have a 6804-kg (15,000-lb) warload. Here the aircraft carries ten 454-kg (1,000-lb) bombs and two Sidewinder air-to-air missiles.

A-7D

Type: single-seat attack aircraft

Powerplant: one 64.51-kN (14,510-lb-thrust) Allison T41-A-1, US-built version of the Rolls-Royce Spey engine

Maximum speed: 1062 km/h (660 mph)

Ferry range: 5858 km (3,640 miles)

Combat radius: 885 km (550 miles)

Service ceiling: 12,800 m (42,000 ft)

Weights: empty 6861 kg (15,127 lb); maximum take-off 19,011 kg (41,912 lb)

Armament: 20-mm (0.79-in) General Electric M61A1 cannon with 1000 rounds; up to 6804 kg (15,000 lb) of bombs or missiles on six wing and two fuselage pylons

Dimensions:		
	span	11.81 m (38 ft 9 in)
	length	14.07 m (46 ft 2 in)
	height	4.90 m (16 ft 1 in)
	wing area	34.84 m² (375 sq ft)

A-7D

Finished in its original colours, this aircraft belonged to the 355th Tactical Fighter Wing and was based in Arizona at Davis-Monthan AFB. It carries twenty-four 227-kg (500-lb) bombs and two AIM-9s.

The inflight refuelling receptacle is mounted behind and to the left of the cockpit. It is compatible with the USAF's flying-boom system.

The stores pylons are clustered under the fixed inner wing section. On the original naval model the outer section was folded for stowing aboard aircraft-carriers.

A load of Mk 82 low-drag 227-kg (500-lb) bombs equips this A-7. In Air National Guard service the aircraft was given a much more potent night-attack capability.

The Tactical Air Command shield is carried on the fin and other colourful markings adorn the aircraft. Such markings are increasingly rare since low-visibility colour schemes have become popular.

This fairing covers the six rotating barrels of the 20-mm (0.79-in) M61 Gatling gun. The weapon fires at 6000 rounds per minute.

An Allison TF41 turbofan engine powers the A-7 to high subsonic speeds. It is very fuel-efficient and gives the A-7 its long-range characteristics and load-carrying ability. The engine was built under licence from Rolls-Royce.

ACTION DATA

SPEED

These attack aircraft are closely matched in speed. While the A-6 and Buccaneer have twin engines, the A-7 achieves its slight superiority on only one. Both the former aircraft are also around 9072 kg (20,000 lb) heavier, but carry similar weapon loads.

A-7D	1062 km/h (660 mph)
A-6E INTRUDER	1041 km/h (647 mph)
BUCCANEER S.Mk 2B	1036 km/h (644 mph)

BOMB LOAD

All three aircraft carry a similar bomb load. The A-7, however, is a smaller, lighter and faster aircraft, and is therefore more economical to operate and maybe less vulnerable in combat.

A-7D	6804 kg (15,000 lb)
A-6E INTRUDER	8147 kg (17,960 lb)
BUCCANEER S.Mk 2B	7242 kg (15,965 lb)

CLIMB RATE

Attack aircraft, which spend much of their time at low level, are often required to make rapid climbs in the course of an attack or during evasive action. Again, the lighter A-7 outperforms the Intruder and Buccaneer.

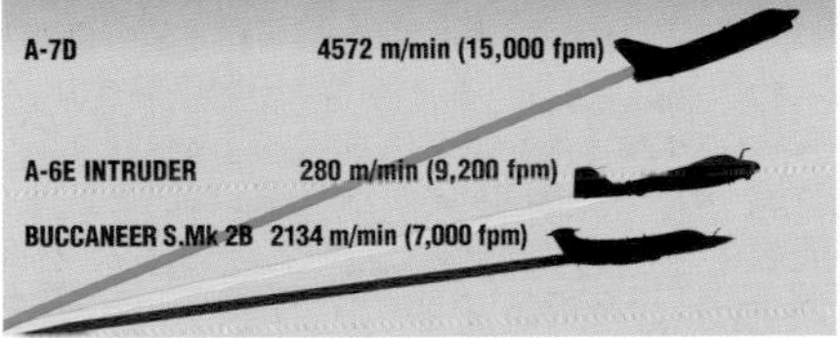

The Vought dynasty

VOUGHT OS2U KINGFISHER: Designed as a scout/observation aircraft, the OS2U also served in the anti-submarine and SAR roles.

VOUGHT F4U CORSAIR: Many experts regard the F4U as the finest fighter of World War II. It was flown by several Navy and Marine aces.

VOUGHT F7U CUTLASS: The F7U first flew in 1948 and was hated by pilots. It later introduced the Sparrow AAM into service.

VOUGHT F-8 CRUSADER: One of the best naval fighters ever, the F-8 could reach 1798 km/h (1,117 mph) and had an extremely long range.

VOUGHT

F4U CORSAIR

● Carrier- and land-based ● MiG-killer ● Korean War

▲ Marine Corps Corsair operations were flown from US Navy carriers and from shore bases. Together with the USAF's P-51 Mustang, the Corsair bore the brunt of the close support operations in the opening months of the war.

After their successes with the F4U Corsair in the Pacific during World War II, the US Navy and Marine Corps took Vought's 'Whispering Death' to war again in 1950. This time it was used in the night-fighter and close support roles during the 'police action' in Korea. The United States was so reliant on the Corsair that it was put back into production for the Marines as the AU-1. In this age of the jet's ascendancy, the 'big props' still had a role.

PHOTO FILE

VOUGHT F4U CORSAIR

▲ **Dedicated ground attack**
Originally known as F4U-6, the AU-1 had a single-stage supercharger to improve low-level performance.

▼ **Night-fighter**
F4U-5Ns were fitted with a wing-mounted radar and equipped USMC night-fighter units. Twin air intakes fed the supercharger on the R-2800 engine.

▲ **F4U-4 with 'Tiny Tim' aboard**
This Marine Corps machine carries a 227-kg (500-lb) bomb and a large 'Tiny Tim' unguided rocket. Other typical loads included a 1136-litre (300-US gal) drop-tank and 907 kg (2,000 lb) of bombs.

▼ **Korean winter at Yonpo**
The 1st Marine Air Wing F4U-5s flew close support missions from Yonpo in the winter of 1950/51.

◀ **Running into the target**
Seen in a typical low-level close support pose, this F4U-4 carries a standard load of eight 12.7-mm (0.5-in) rockets. The heaviest loads were carried by the AU-1 variant.

FACTS AND FIGURES

- During carrier landings and take-offs, Corsair pilots left the cockpit canopies open for a quick escape in an emergency.
- The famous 'Flying Nightmares', VMF(N)-513, flew F4U-5Ns on night missions.
- Land-based F4Us were often maintained outdoors in primitive conditions.
- During the war, AU-1s flew with all-up weights as high as 8799 kg (19,398 lb), including 2268 kg (5,000 lb) of underwing ordnance and fuel.
- Corsairs were able to loiter over targets, unlike the early short-ranged jets.
- Including Korean War production, 12,571 Corsairs were built.

PROFILE

Gull-wing fighters return to war

Although it was a US Navy carrier-based F4U unit that opened the Korean campaign only eight days after the war began, it was the Marine Corps that flew the bulk of Corsair missions over Korea. Corsairs remained in intensive use for three years, from 1950 until the last day of the war on 27 June 1953.

With a radial engine that was far less vulnerable to small-arms fire, the Corsair was better suited than the USAF's P-51s to ground attack missions. This was to be its main role in Korea – close support of USMC ground forces. Missions were flown from US Navy carriers 'on station' in the Yellow Sea and from shore bases, with units often alternating between the two.

Corsair variants in action over Korea included the F4U-4 (which had first appeared in 1945 and introduced four 20-mm/0.79-in cannon in the -4B), the F4U-5 (including the radar-equipped -5N and 'winterized' -5NL) and the AU-1. First proposed by Vought in 1950 and boasting extra armour, a modified engine and greatly increased weapon load, the Corsair, as the AU-1, was put back into production 10 years after its first flight. By October 1952 111 AU-1s had been built.

Left: Apart from detail improvements, the Corsair's airframe remained largely unchanged since World War II.

Below: An F4U-4 leaves the deck of a US Navy carrier. This major production version was intended to replace F4U-1s from 1945.

F4U-5N Corsair

Type: single-seat night fighter and ground-attack aircraft

Powerplant: one 1715-kW (2,300-hp) Pratt & Whitney R-2800-32W radial engine

Maximum speed: 756 km/h (470 mph) at 8169 m (26,800 ft)

Cruising speed: 365 km/h (227 mph)

Climb rate: 1152 m/min (3,780 fpm)

Service ceiling: 12,619 m (41,400 ft)

Weights: empty 4392 kg (9,683 lb); maximum take-off 6398 kg (14,105 lb)

Armament: four 20-mm (0.79-in) cannon, plus up to 907 kg (2,000 lb) of bombs, rockets and external fuel

Dimensions:		
	span	12.50 m (41 ft)
	length	10.21 m (33 ft 6 in)
	height	4.50 m (15 ft 9 in)
	wing area	29.17 m² (314 sq ft)

F4U-4B CORSAIR

BuNo. 97201 was flown by Captain Jesse Folmar, of VMA-312 aboard USS *Sicily*, when he claimed the only Corsair versus MiG kill. After successfully engaging the MiG he was himself shot down by four other MiGs. Folmar was rescued by an SA-16 amphibian.

The F4U-4 was powered by the proven Pratt & Whitney R-2800 Double Wasp 18-cylinder two-row radial engine, rated at 1566 kW (2,100 hp). The F4U-5 and AU-1 used a 1715-kW (2300-hp) version, although the latter had only a single-stage supercharger as it was intended for low-altitude operations.

The F4U-4 retained some fabric covering of the wing surfaces. This was replaced with an all-metal wing covering in the F4U-5 which reduced drag considerably.

Due to the conditions of the harsh Korean winter, the Dash-5NL variant had wing and tail de-icer boots and de-icer shoes fitted to the propeller. The windscreen had improved thermal de-icing.

WR

9 MARINES VMA-312

F4U4B MARINES 97201

Although earlier variants were armed with six 12.7-mm (0.5-in) machine guns, the F4U-4B, -5 and AU-1 were fitted with four 20-mm (0.79-in) cannon.

Late Corsair versions had increased load-carrying capability on underwing pylons. The AU-1 had six hardpoints under each wing for up to 2268 kg (5,000 lb) of bombs, rockets and fuel tanks. The normal maximum load was 1815 kg (4,000 lb).

By the 1950s the standard naval colour scheme was an all-over coat of 'midnight blue'.

ACTION DATA

MAXIMUM SPEED

The Dash-5 variant of the Corsair was one of the fastest propeller-driven fighters built – even faster than some versions of the twin-engined Tigercat. However, jets such as the F3D were on the way.

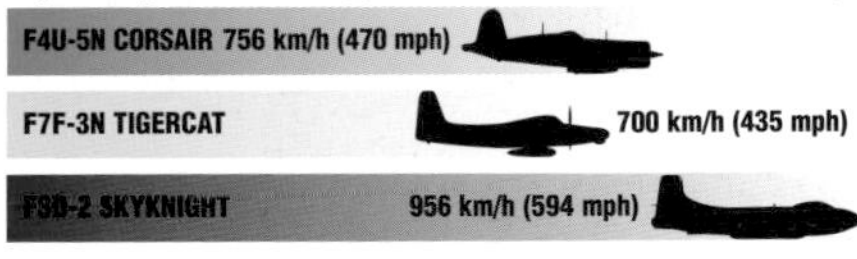

ARMAMENT

The American forces were slow to adopt cannon armament during World War II, but by the late 1940s they had introduced it. Four 20-mm (0.79-in) cannon were common.

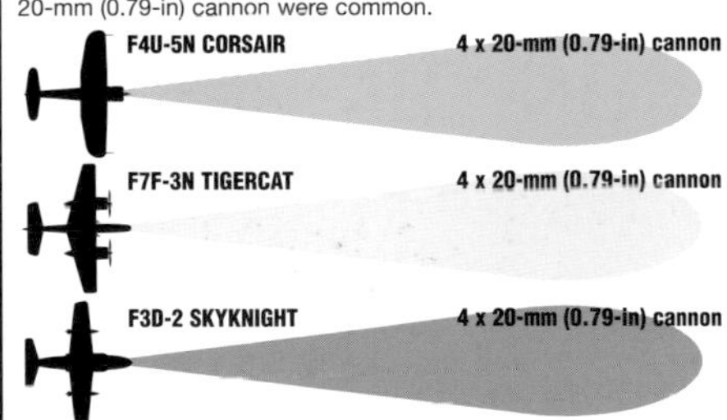

KILLS

These kills by Marine pilots flying the three principal US night-fighter types of the war show that propeller-driven types such as the Corsair were still useful, at least against slower targets such as Po-2s.

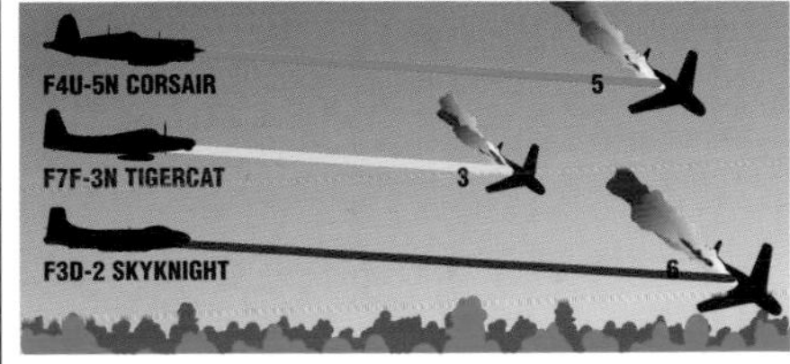

Corsairs in action over Korea

MIG-KILLER: USMC pilot Jesse Folmar made the only MiG kill by a Corsair in Korea, shooting down a MiG-15 on 10 September 1952.

NIGHT ATTACK: Corsairs in Korea were perhaps at their most deadly in the night-time close-support role. Radar-equipped F4U-5Ns hit Chinese supply trucks.

SLOW SPEED ADVANTAGE: Corsairs were able to shoot down Po-2 and Yak-18 aircraft which were too slow targets for jet fighters.

Vought F-8 Crusader

● Fleet air defence ● Vietnam MiG killer ● Variable-incidence wing

▲ Just as the US Navy was looking forward to receiving the heavy, complex F-4B, the F-8 was proving that a simple cannon-armed aircraft was ideal for taking on MiG-21s in a dogfight.

Crusader jocks boasted that their manoeuvrable, cannon-armed jet was hotter than anything in the skies and scoffed when 'experts' said that missiles would make their fighters obsolete. In battle, the pilots were proved correct when their fighter was able to dogfight with Vietnamese MiGs on equal terms. The Crusader was the best-loved fighter in the post-war US Navy and remained in service in France until 2000.

Photo File

Vought F-8 Crusader

▲ Folded up

Wings folded and starboard flap down, an F-8 is prepared for combat. Crusaders shot down 18 MiGs with Sidewinders over Vietnam.

▲ Raised wing

The Crusader has a variable-incidence wing, which reduces speed when the aircraft lands.

◀ Two-seater

One XF8U was converted to a two-seater, with only two cannon but a second set of controls. It first flew in 1962, but did not see active service.

▲ French fighters

Armed with MATRA missiles, the Crusader provided the French navy with its only fighter asset until 2000.

Air to ground ▶

The F-8 was quite capable of bombing as well as air defence, but this capability was seldom used as the US Navy had plenty of A-4 and A-7 bombers.

▼ Philippine defender

The Philippine air force was the only other user, but its F-8Hs are now retired. Like the French Crusaders, the F-8H had boundary-layer control and improved avionics.

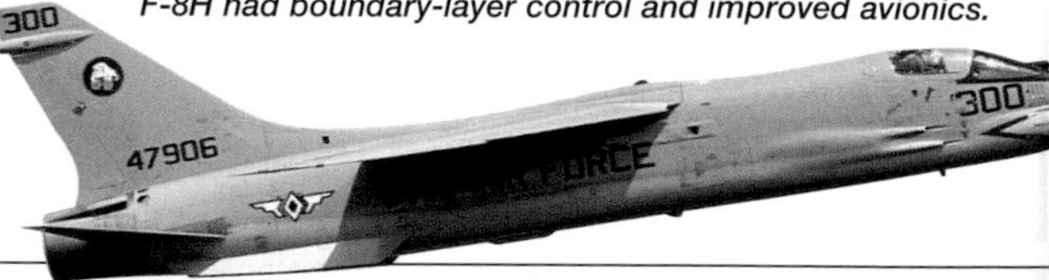

Facts and Figures

- ➤ Test pilot John Konrad flew the XF8U-1 prototype on its maiden flight on 25 March 1955.
- ➤ The Philippines air force acquired F-8H Crusaders in the 1980s.
- ➤ Vought's XF8U-3 Crusader III was not ordered into production.
- ➤ RF-8A photo Crusaders helped to spot new Soviet bases in Cuba during the Missile Crisis of 1962.
- ➤ Seventy-one US Navy and Marine Corps squadrons operated F-8 Crusaders.
- ➤ Crusaders could also carry the AGM-12 Bullpup missile for ground attack.

PROFILE

MiG killing with the US Navy

One of the first supersonic fighters, Vought's F-8 Crusader (originally F8U) pushed back the boundaries of naval aviation in the 1950s and battled with MiGs in Vietnam a decade later.

Pilots saw the F-8 as the ultimate dogfighter: light, manoeuvrable and packing heavy cannon armament. Unlike many of its contemporaries in Vietnam, notably the F-4 Phantom, the F-8 eschewed missiles, complex avionics and radar in favour of old-fashioned guns and thrust, and pilots loved it.

With its supersonic 'area rule' shape and powerful J57 engine, the Crusader set many speed records and was clearly the world's best carrier-based fighter when it went to war in Vietnam. In action near Hanoi, Crusaders shot down 18 MiG-17s and MiG-21s without a single air-to-air loss. It also took on an extra duty as a carrier-based reconnaissance platform.

With its variable-incidence wing raised for low-speed flight, an F-8 refuels from a Skyraider. French F-8(FN)s had even better low-speed handling than the US versions.

Some Crusaders acquired air-to-ground capability and served the US Marine Corps well during the Tet fighting of 1968. France used this superb jet on its light carriers *Foch* and *Clemenceau*. These last few F-8s flew until 2000 when the Rafale M entered service.

Another innovative feature of the F-8 was the dogtooth, which provided vortexes to improve control at high alpha. The wing also had large leading-edge flaps.

F-8E Crusaders had a small tail-warning radar system, located in the fintip. The top of the fin contained a VHF aerial covered by a fairing.

F-8E Crusader

Type: single-seat naval fighter (F-8E)

Powerplant: one 80.07-kN (18,009-lb-thrust) Pratt & Whitney J57-P-20A afterburning turbojet engine

Maximum speed: 1802 km/h (1,120 mph) or Mach 1.7 at 12,192 m (40,000 ft)

Initial rate of climb: 8290 m/min (27,198 fpm)

Range: 1660 km (1,031 miles)

Service ceiling: 17,983 m (59,000 ft)

Weights: empty 9038 kg (19,925 lb); maximum (with external stores) 15,422 kg (34,000 lb)

Armament: four 20-mm (0.79-in) Mk 12 cannon with 144 rounds per gun; up to four AIM-9 Sidewinders AAMs; or 16 113-kg (250-lb) or eight 227-kg (500-lb) bombs; or eight Zuni rockets; or two AGM-12A or AGM-12B Bullpup attack missiles

Dimensions:	span	10.87 m (35 ft 8 in)
	length	16.61 m (54 ft 6 in)
	height	4.80 m (15 ft 9 in)
	wing area	32.52 m² (350 sq ft)

F8U-1E CRUSADER

Known after 1962 as the F-8B, this Crusader variant had APS-67 radar providing a limited all-weather capability; 130 of this variant were built by Vought.

The F8U-2N version had an illuminating radar in the nose for the AIM-9C radar-guided Sidewinder missile. Earlier versions had a simple ranging radar. Crusader pilots sat on Martin-Baker Mk 5 ejector seats.

The variable-incidence wing allowed a lower nose attitude for a given angle of attack, providing the pilot with a good view of the deck when landing. The wing was hinged at the back, and raised by hydraulic jacks.

The large main fuel tank was fitted in the rear fuselage, just ahead of the engine. Air was ducted to the engine through the nose, over the mainwheel bay and under the wing. Later F-8s fitted for Bullpup air-to-surface missiles had a distinct 'hump' over the mid-fuselage, which housed the electronics guidance system.

Four 20-mm (0.79-in) Mk 12 cannon were fitted in the lower fuselage, fed from ammunition tanks behind the pilot. These were replaced by cameras in the reconnaissance RF-8A.

Two AIM-9B Sidewinders were carried on rails on the fuselage sides. Zuni air-to-ground rockets could also be fitted.

Power was provided by the same J57 engine used in the F-100 and F-102 land-based fighters. F-8Js received the more powerful 87.39-kN (19,655-lb-thrust) J57-P-420 engine.

COMBAT DATA

MAXIMUM SPEED

The Crusader was very fast for a naval fighter and could even outrun most land-based types. The very short-range MiG-21s which it faced in Vietnam were slightly faster, but only at high level.

F-8C CRUSADER 1802 km/h (1,120 mph)

MiG-21F 'FISHBED' 2000 km/h (1,243 miles)

SEA VIXEN FAW.Mk 1 1050 km/h (652 miles)

ARMAMENT

Gun armament was seen as obsolete when Crusaders first went to war, a view rapidly ignored by the pilots when the unreliability of early missiles became apparent. Despite this, the Crusader actually scored most of its kills with Sidewinders. The first MiG-21s were gun-armed only, then missile-armed. Like the F-8, it could also carry free-flight rockets for air-to-air use.

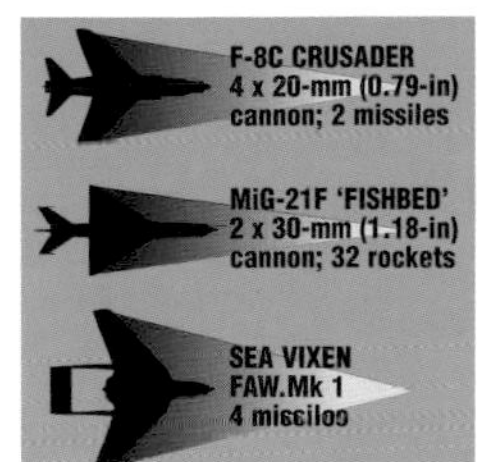

RANGE

Designed as a naval fighter from its inception, the F-8 had long range. The MiG-21 was designed as a short-range 'point-defence' interceptor, and was always dogged by a lack of fuel.

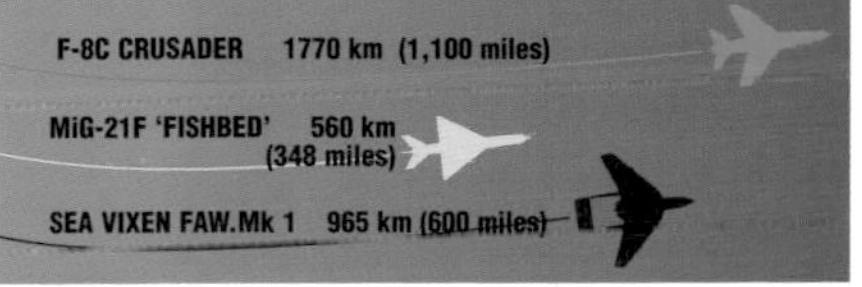

Death of a Crusader

HARD TOUCHDOWN: During a landing on the carrier USS *Franklin D. Roosevelt* in 1961, Lieutenant J. Kryway misjudged his approach and broke the starboard undercarriage of his F-8.

BLOWING UP: The crash ruptured the engine and fuel tank bays, causing the stricken aircraft to catch fire, then blow up. Lieutenant Kryway was already starting his ejection.

OVER THE SIDE: With all control lost, the doomed F-8 went over the side of the ship. Here, the canopy is just beginning to lift off the cockpit as part of the ejection sequence.

BLASTED TO SAFETY: With only milliseconds to spare, Kryway is blasted to safety by his Martin-Baker ejection seat. He was rescued shortly after and survived.

VOUGHT

F-8E(FN) CRUSADER

● Carrier fighter ● Variable-incidence wing ● Superb dogfighter

One of the most spectacular fighters ever, the Vought F-8 Crusader was chosen by the French Aéronavale in the early 1960s. At that time, the Crusader had already chalked up a superb record with the American Fleet and was soon to wage a near-perfect campaign against North Vietnamese MiGs. Entering French service in 1967, the Crusader became the backbone of France's naval air power aboard the aircraft-carriers ***Clemenceau*** and ***Foch***.

▲ *For all its success, the Crusader attracted few export orders and is now a very rare aircraft. The Aéronavale retired its ageing fighters in 1999, replacing them with Rafale Ms.*

PHOTO FILE

VOUGHT F-8E(FN) CRUSADER

◀ Quad launcher
One of the weaknesses of many fighters in the early 1960s was their lack of weapon load, with only two missiles carried. The F-8E solved the problem by having a new twin missile rail on each side of the fuselage and four cannon.

▼ Turning tight
The F-8E has excellent manoeuvrability, and pilots can out-turn many more modern fighters.

▲ Navy blue
In the early years the F-8E was painted light-grey, but the aircraft now wear this all-over blue paint scheme to blend in with the sea.

▼ Sidewinder aboard
Unusually for a French aircraft, this F-8E of 14F carries an American-made Sidewinder missile in place of the usual MATRA weapons.

▼ Raised wing
The flash of red paint above the fuselage shows the variable-incidence wing in the raised position.

FACTS AND FIGURES

- ➤ France acquired 42 single-seat Crusaders, but it cancelled plans for six two-seat variants.
- ➤ A Crusader can fly at about twice the speed of a bullet fired from a pistol.
- ➤ The test prototype for the French navy made its first flight in February 1964.
- ➤ The F-8E(FN) lands 50 km/h (30 m.p.h.) slower than American Crusaders, to permit duty on smaller French aircraft-carriers.
- ➤ The first production F-8E(FN) made its initial flight in June 1964.
- ➤ Pilots considered the Crusader difficult to fly, but a real pleasure when mastered.

PROFILE

Gunfighter of the Aéronavale

French officers made a dramatic choice when they turned to America for the F-8E(FN) Crusader in 1964; a quantum leap forward when chosen to replace the propeller-driven F4U-5N Corsair and jet Aquilon (developed Sea Venom). With minor changes to the wing and boundary layer systems fitted to the Crusaders in American service, the F-8E(FN) became a stunning performer in French hands. Even today, with the new-generation Rafale having entered service as a repacement, many regard the Crusader as one of the finest fighters they ever flew.

Although the Crusader can drop bombs and attack ground targets, the Aéronavale chose to use the F-8E(FN) strictly as an air-to-air fighter. These Crusaders supported Allied operations in the Persian Gulf in 1987, although they were never employed in combat. Once a world-class air warrior, the F-8E(FN), which lacks a multi-mode radar and long-range missiles, is now outclassed, and has been replaced in service by the naval Rafale M.

Left: The F-8E could carry the MATRA R.530 radar-guided missile. In firing trials this weapon had a poor record.

Right: The Aéronavale conducted acceptance trials of the F-8E onboard the American carrier USS Shangri La.

F-8E(FN) Crusader

Type: single-seat carrier-based fighter

Powerplant: one 47.60-kN (10,700-lb.-thrust) Pratt & Whitney J57-P-20A turbojet engine

Maximum speed: 1827 km/h (1,133 m.p.h.) at 10,975 m (36,000 ft.)

Cruising speed: 901 km/h (559 m.p.h.)

Range: 2253 km (1,397 mi.)

Service ceiling: 17,680 m (58,000 ft.)

Weights: empty 9038 kg (19,884 lb.); maximum take-off 15,420 kg (33,924 lb.)

Armament: four Colt-Browning Mk 12 20-mm cannon, plus two to four MATRA R.530 or 550 air-to-air missiles or two to four AIM-9 Sidewinder air-to-air missiles

Dimensions:		
	span	10.87 m (35 ft. 8 in.)
	length	16.61 m (54 ft. 6 in.)
	height	4.80 m (15 ft. 9 in.)
	wing area	32.51 m² (350 sq. ft.)

F-8E(FN) Crusader

Now operated only by 12F at Landivisiau, the F-8E is one of very few American types used by the French forces since 1960. The Aéronavale was the last operator of the F-8E, which has also been retired by the US Navy and the Philippines.

The F-8E had a short-range radar for ranging use only. It could not detect aircraft at long range over water or search for targets at low altitude.

For escape from the aircraft, the F-8E was fitted with a Martin-Baker ejection seat. The Crusader had a comfortable cockpit for its era but rearward visibility was quite poor.

The F-8E was the only jet fighter ever with a variable-incidence wing. The wing used boundary layer control for extra lift during take-off and landing. Bullpup or Zuni rockets could be carried for ground attack, but the Aéronavale did not equip their aircraft with them.

Power was provided by a single J57 engine, as used in the B-52, U-2, B-57 and KC-135. The fixed intake limited the aircraft's speed to less than Mach 2. The F-8 has an all-moving tailplane.

Armament consisted of four Colt 20-mm cannon, with two MATRA 550 Magic infra-red homing missiles. In the 1960s Sidewinder or R.530 were carried.

The F-8E, like the RF-8A, had ventral fins fitted.

Variable incidence in action

ANGLE OF ATTACK: Wings generate lift according to the angle of attack – the angle at which the wing meets the oncoming airflow. The lift generated increases with the angle of attack up to about 20° when the wing stalls.

MOVING WING: The Crusader pilot can increase the incidence of the wing (the angle at which it is mounted on the airframe). This is carried out by a large hydraulic jack in the fuselage. For a given incidence the aircraft's attitude can be lowered, providing better cockpit visibility without losing lift.

LOWER NOSE: The Crusader has more lift for a given airspeed, and the pilot can fly with a lower nose attitude. This gives him a better view of the deck on approach.

COMBAT DATA

MAXIMUM SPEED

The Crusader was a relatively small fighter with only a single engine, and was not as fast as the Phantom or MiG-21. However, in a subsonic dogfight, it was just as fast as any other fighter, and its legendary agility gave it the edge over many MiG-21s.

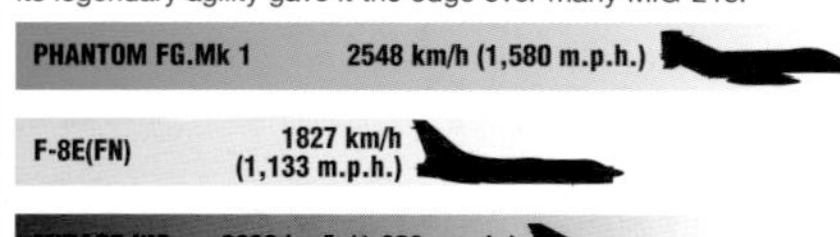

CEILING

On the power of one J57, the F-8E could climb to a very respectable altitude. The Phantom had twice the power and was one of the finest interceptors of its day. However, fuel and weapon load often meant a much lower ceiling was attained in flight.

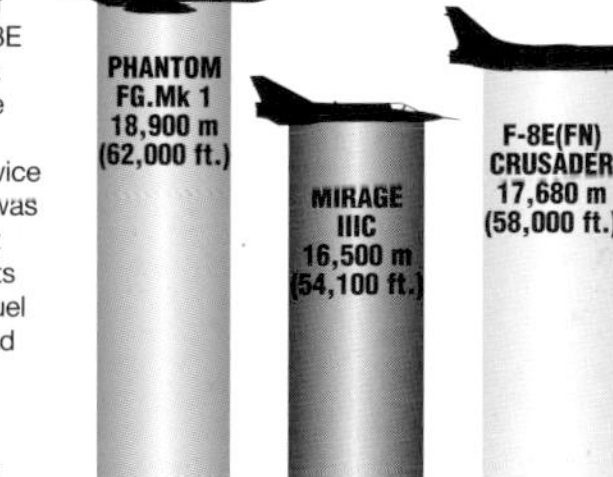

RANGE

Naval fighters require range, and the F-8E had a good performance. Range is highly dependant on the use of afterburner, which gives a huge increase in thrust but uses fuel up at a massive rate. The Phantom consumed fuel quickly as it had twin engines.

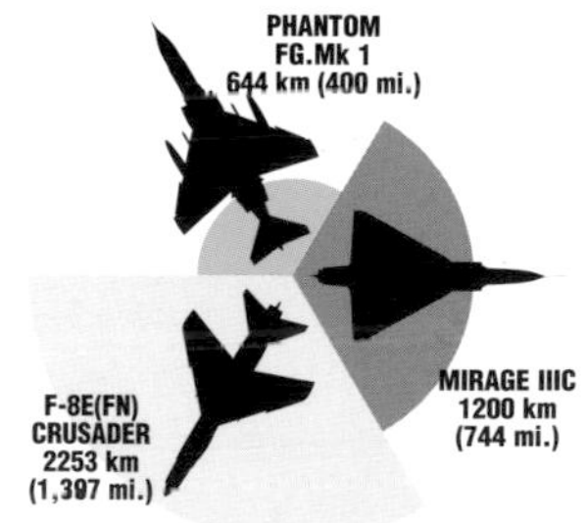

YAKOVLEV

YAK-28 'BREWER'/'FIREBAR'

● Late 1950s design ● Bomber and interceptor ● Long service

Code-named 'Brewer-A' by NATO, the original Yak-28 was a twin-engine supersonic tactical bomber developed from the earlier trouble-plagued Yak-26. The Yak-28 made its public debut at the 1961 Aviation Day flypast. A two-seat interceptor version called 'Firebar' and reconnaissance and electronic counter-measures versions of 'Brewer' followed. Few, if any, are left; some may still be in service with trials and training units.

▲ *'Firebar' first flew in 1960 as a two-seat, low- to medium-level interceptor derivative of 'Brewer'. The nose was redesigned to hold a radar set, the former bomb-bay was fitted with fuel tanks and air-to-air missiles were carried.*

PHOTO FILE

YAKOVLEV YAK-28 'BREWER'/'FIREBAR'

▼ Bicycle landing gear
With a tandem fuselage-mounted main undercarriage, as shown here, wingtip outrigger wheels were needed to support the wings.

Conversion trainer ▶
'Maestro' was the NATO code name given to the Yak-28U unarmed conversion trainer variant that had its second cockpit forward of the main canopy.

▲ Unofficial service
Somewhat strangely, the 'Firebar' did not officially enter service with the Soviet air defence force (PVO); most units received the Sukhoi Su-15 'Flagon'. However, it is known that about 200 Yak-28s served with Arctic-based regiments as late as 1980.

▲ Practice alert
This TASS photograph dated 1979 shows a Yak-28U conversion trainer and crew during a practice alert. Note the 'Brewer' bombers parked in the background.

▼ Northern latitudes
A Yak-28P, with the early-style shorter, fatter radome, during winter weather in northern Russia. Yak-28PMs had a longer radome with a more capable radar set.

FACTS AND FIGURES

- Early versions of the 'Brewer' had a bombing radar fitted; later versions used ground stations for guidance to a target.
- The Yak-28 prototype (the Yak-129) flew for the first time on 5 March 1958.
- 'Brewers' carried either an NR-23 23-mm cannon or the two-barrel GSh-23Ya.
- Radar-equipped 'Brewer-As' had to be raised off the ground to provide access to the bomb-bay for loading.
- Reconnaissance 'Brewer-Ds' carried cameras, radar and infrared detectors.
- The Yak-28-64 fighter was a failed redesign to compete with the Su-15.

PROFILE

'Brewer' of 1960s Soviet vintage

Powered by big turbojets carried in large underwing pods, the original Yak-28 had a glazed nose for the navigator/bombardier and was flown by a single pilot. It carried a 2995-kg (6,600-lb) bombload, and had a 23-mm (0.91-in) cannon in the right side of the forward fuselage.

The configuration enabled it to be adapted for various other roles. 'Brewer-B' and 'Brewer-C' were improved attack aircraft with additional equipment, while 'Brewer-D' was a reconnaissance version with cameras and other equipment such as infrared sensors and radar carried in the bomb-bay.

In 1970, the 'Brewer-E' became the first Soviet electronic countermeasures (ECM) escort aircraft to be deployed. Carrying an ECM pack in the bomb-bay, along with many additional antennas and fairings, it could use chaff launchers or anti-radar missiles to suppress defences.

The Yak-28P 'Firebar', which entered service in the early 1960s, was a two-seat interceptor with a radome replacing the glazed nose of the earlier versions. It carried no guns, and the bomb-bay was used to house additional fuel tanks. There was also a trainer version, the Yak-28U 'Maestro'.

Above: Distinguished by its glazed nose, the 'Brewer' was the first member of the Yak-28 family to enter service. It could carry a hefty bombload and was fitted with a cannon for self-defence and ground strafing. Two fuel tanks (not fitted to these aircraft) could be attached to the outer wings to increase fuel capacity.

Above: The last examples of the Yak-28 family in use are Yak-28PP 'Brewer-E' electronic warfare (EW) aircraft. These were deployed by Russia until at least 1994, after the Ukraine absorbed all examples of the Sukhoi Su-24MP, its intended replacement.

Yak-28PM 'Firebar'

Type: two-seat all-weather interceptor

Powerplant: two 60.02-kN (13,500-lb-thrust) Tumanskii R-11-AF2-300 afterburning turbojets

Maximum speed: 2105 km/h (1,308 mph) at 10,668 m (35,000 ft)

Initial climb rate: 8498 m/min (27,880 fpm)

Combat radius: 925 km (575 miles)

Service ceiling: 15,996 m (52,480 ft)

Range: 2575 km (1,600 miles)

Weights: empty 7734 kg (17,050 lb); loaded 15,867 kg (34,980 lb)

Armament: Two R-8 ('Anab') infra-red and two R-3 ('Atoll') infra-red/semi-active radar-homing air-to-air missiles

Dimensions:	span	11.68 m (38 ft 4 in)
	length	21.46 m (70 ft 5 in)
	height	3.94 m (12 ft 11 in)
	wing area	35.21 m² (379 sq ft)

YAK-28PM 'FIREBAR'

Delivered between 1965 and 1968, the Yak-28PMs were improved versions of the original Yak-28P interceptor. Total production of both variants totalled 435.

The nose radome contained an Orel radar set; Orel-DM in the Yak-28PM. This had improved power and discrimination over earlier models.

The two crew (pilot and navigator) in the 'Firebar' were housed in tandem under a four-piece sliding canopy. The 'Brewer' had a single-seat cockpit and a navigator's station in the nose.

Two afterburning Tumanskii R-11-AF2-300 turbojets powered the Yak-28, one in a nacelle under each wing. R-11s were also installed in Sukhoi Su-15s and early model MiG-21s.

The Yak-28 design can be traced back through the Yak-25, -26 and -27 to the single-engine Yak-50, itself an abortive attempt to produce a fighter to compete with the MiG-15.

The high-set tail was used to provide an undisturbed air flow over the tailplane, away from the disturbed air lower down.

The 'Brewer' bombers had a glazed nose for a navigator/bombardier station. This had successively lighter framing on later variants.

Yak-28Ps carried two R-8 infrared air-to-air missiles (NATO code name 'Anab'); the Yak-28PM added two smaller R-3 ('Atoll') infra-red or semi-active radar-homing missiles.

Similar to Soviet air defence aircraft, 'Firebars' carried minimal markings (a red star and two-digit aircraft code) and wore an unpainted metal finish.

ACTION DATA

SPEED

Compared with other interceptors of the mid-1960s, the 'Firebar' had a slightly slower top speed at just under Mach 2. The RAF's Lightning was one of the fastest aircraft of the day.

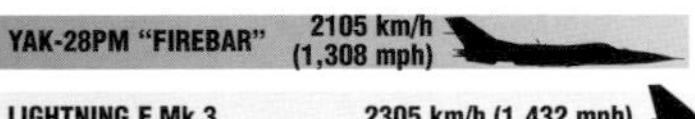

WEAPONS

The F-4 was the US Navy's most modern interceptor of the mid-1960s and had an impressive missile load. The Lightning was relatively lightly equipped, with half as many air-to-air missiles as the 'Firebar'.

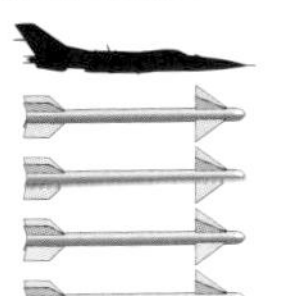

YAK-28PM "FIREBAR"
4 x air-to-air missiles

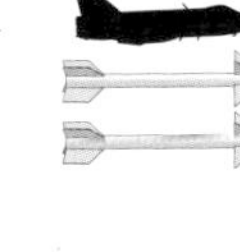

LIGHTNING F.Mk 3
2 x air-to-air missiles

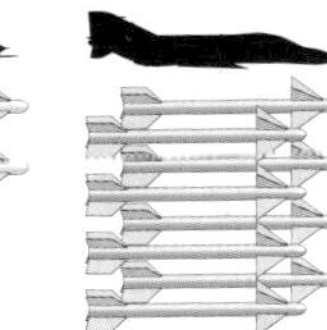

F-4J PHANTOM II
8 x air-to-air missiles

RANGE

Range was never a strong point of the Lightning, unlike the F-4. The Yak-28 also had good range, especially when the limitations of what was a dated design were considered. A handicap was the Yak's inability to refuel in the air, something that the Phantom was equipped to do; early versions of the Lightning were not.

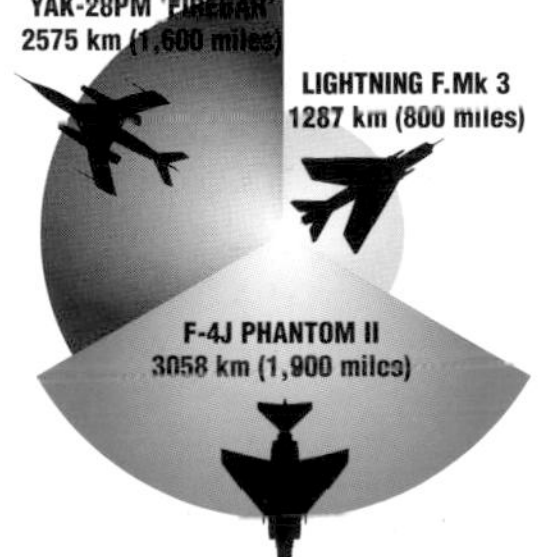

Yak-28s in action

MULTI-ROLE AIRCRAFT: The Yak-28 family comprised different versions that could perform a variety of tasks over a battlefield.

TACTICAL BOMBING: Its three-ton bomb load and a 23-mm (0.91-in) cannon equipped the 'Brewer' bomber versions well for close support missions.

AIR DEFENCE AND ESCORT: 'Firebar' fighters could be used to escort strategic bombers and support aircraft.

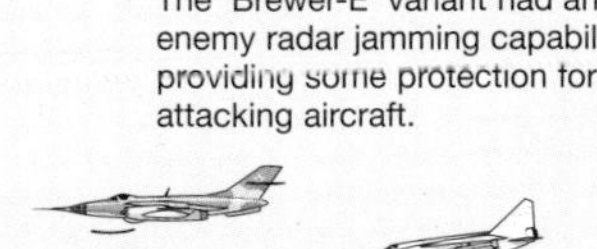

ELECTRONIC WARFARE: The 'Brewer-E' variant had an enemy radar jamming capability, providing some protection for attacking aircraft.

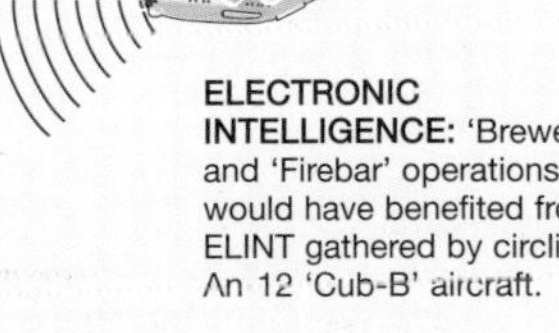

ELECTRONIC INTELLIGENCE: 'Brewer' and 'Firebar' operations would have benefited from ELINT gathered by circling An 12 'Cub-B' aircraft.

YAKOVLEV

YAK-38 'FORGER'

● Vertical take-off ● Fleet air defence ● Maritime strike

Since 1976, the Yak-38 'Forger' has been Moscow's equivalent of the famous Harrier, but uses three powerplants instead of the Harrier's one for vectored-thrust performance. The vertical take-off jet was designed to spring from the decks of 'Kiev'-class carriers to defend the Russian fleet from Western patrol aircraft and saw service on Russia's last 'Kiev' carrier, ***Gorshkov***.

▲ *The Yak-38 gave the Soviet navy experience with high-performance jets at sea, and was a useful stepping stone towards the fixed-wing naval fighters now coming into service with the Russian navy.*

PHOTO FILE

YAKOVLEV YAK-38 'FORGER'

◀ Conversion trainer

The 'Forger-B' is the two-seat trainer variant of the Yak-38. This was a much-needed aircraft as the standard Yak-38 was always a very tricky aircraft to learn to fly. The trainer aircraft lacks underwing pylons, radar or infra-red systems, and is therefore not combat-capable.

◀ 'Freestyle'

The Yak-141 'Freestyle' is the follow-on to the Yak-38, with advanced avionics and increased speed and range. It has not been produced in quantity, and needs a foreign buyer.

▲ On deck

The 'Forger' was not an impressive aircraft by itself, but the overall 'Kiev'-class package was capable and a real threat.

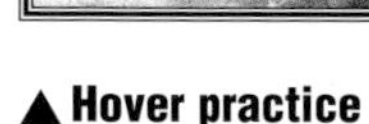

▲ Hover practice

This Yak-38 is hovering, with the lift-engine intake doors opened just behind the cockpit, and jet blast churning the sea.

Pacific fleet ▶

The Yak-38 could be seen all over the world as Soviet sea power expanded. The carrier Novorossiysk, *based in Vladivostok, flew its 'Forgers' all over the Pacific.*

FACTS AND FIGURES

- The Yak-36 'Freehand' of 1967 was the test ship for the better-looking 'Forger'.
- The Yak-38 first carried out sea trials on board the *Kiev* in the Black Sea.
- About 90 'Forgers' were built, but at least 37 have been lost in accidents (with 32 pilots ejecting safely).
- Each aircraft carrier had 12 single-seaters and a pair of two-seat trainers.
- Of four 'Kiev'-class carriers, only one remains in service with Yak-38s.
- The advanced Yakovlev Yak-141 'Freestyle', a supersonic replacement for the 'Forger', has not entered service.

PROFILE

Soviet naval 'jump-jet' fighter

The Yak-38 'Forger' stirred excitement in the West when first seen aboard the *Kiev* in the Mediterranean. Using a main turbojet with twin rotating nozzles plus tandem lift jets behind its cockpit, the 'Forger' performed well in its specialised domain as a V/STOL (Vertical/Short Take-off and Landing) naval fighter.

The Yak-38 was never designed to be in the class of conventional naval fighters; it was aimed at warding off NATO maritime patrol and strike aircraft such as the P-3 Orion and BAe Nimrod. Its radar has only a very limited range, and it carried only the short-range infra-red 'Atoll' missile and cannon. It had limited strike capability, with armament including the unguided UV-32 rocket pod and the short-range AS-7 'Kerry' tactical missile. Neither was suited to attacking a well-defended warship.

The 'Forger' was tested, not very successfully, in Afghanistan. Its main value to the Soviet navy was to give experience in operating jets at sea.

The Yak-36 could not carry a major warload and was no match for land-based fighters, but it was more than capable of destroying enemy bombers and anti-submarine aircraft.

The cockpit has a head-up display, but is otherwise very simple and quite cluttered compared to modern fighter aircraft.

Fences were later fitted to the upper fuselage above the intakes to improve the airflow.

Four pylons under the fixed portions of the wings can carry up to 2000 kg (4,400 lb.) of stores, including bombs, missiles and cannon pods.

The short-span wing folds for shipboard stowage, with a hinge between the flap and ailerons. A 600-litre (160-gal.) fuel tank can be fitted under each wing.

The traditional Yak-38 paint scheme was a naval blue, but this has been changed to a sea grey on the 'Forgers' remaining in service.

YAK-38 'FORGER-A'

The Yak-38 served aboard the 'Kiev'-class aircraft carriers *Kiev*, *Minsk*, *Novorossiysk* and *Baku* (now renamed *Admiral Gorshkov*). This Yak-38 carries the badge of the Red Banner Northern Fleet.

The air intake at the base of the fin directs cooling air into the aircraft's rear electronics bay.

The Yak-38 is unique in having an automatic ejection system, which is used in the dangerous transition phase when taking off or landing.

Twin Koliesov RD-36 lift engines are mounted behind the cockpit. They are not used during wingborne flight.

The Yak-38 radar is a simple model, with a surface search mode and capable of giving range data for infra red missiles.

Auxiliary blow-in doors were added to the intake walls, to improve engine air flow while in the hover.

The Yak-38 uses a Harrier-like system of autostabilisers with reaction control jets in the wingtips, nose and tail.

The main Soyuz R-27 thrust engine exhausts through twin vectoring nozzles under the tail.

Yak-38 'Forger-A'

Type: single-seat VTOL fighter

Powerplant: one 66.68-kN (15,000-lb.-thrust) MNPK 'Soyuz' (Tumanskii) R-27V-300 turbojet; two 31.87-kN RKBM (Koliesov) RD-36-35FVR lift jets

Maximum speed: 1009 km/h (625 m.p.h.) in 'clean' condition at 11,000 m (36,000 ft.)

Service ceiling: 12,000 m (39,000 ft.)

Weights: empty 7485 kg (16,467 lb.); loaded 13,000 kg (28,600 lb.)

Armament: up to 2000 kg (4,400 lb.) of underwing stores or four AA-8 'Aphid' air-to-air missiles

Dimensions:		
	span	7.32 m (24 ft.)
	length	15.50 m (51 ft.)
	height	4.37 m (14 ft.)
	wing area	18.50 m² (199 sq. ft.)

COMBAT DATA

MAXIMUM SPEED

When it first appeared, Western experts assumed that the Yak-38 was capable of travelling faster than sound, but it has since been discovered that the Russian jet is subsonic, and somewhat slower than Britain's Sea Harrier.

Yak-38 'FORGER'	1009 km\h (625 m.p.h.)
SUPER ETENDARD	1380 km\h (856 m.p.h.)
SEA HARRIER FRS.Mk 1	1185 km\h (738 m.p.h.)

COMBAT RADIUS

The penalty for carrying extra weight in the shape of lift engines, which also take up valuable space in the fuselage, is a noticeable deficiency in range. The 'Forger' could not match earlier versions of the Harrier, and while the British jet's capability has been greatly enhanced the Yak's range has remained limited.

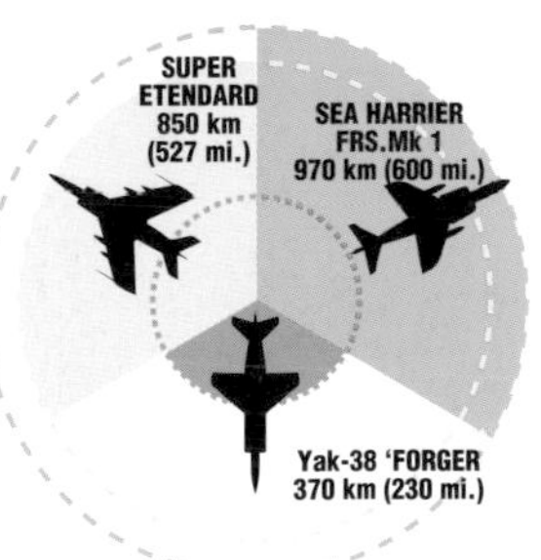

WEAPONS LOAD

The primary task of the 'Forger' was to destroy Western maritime and anti-submarine warfare aircraft, and although it has been given some air-to-surface capability it cannot strike as hard as land-based fighters. But, although limited, the Yak can match the French Etendard, although it is much less capable than the latest Sea Harrier.

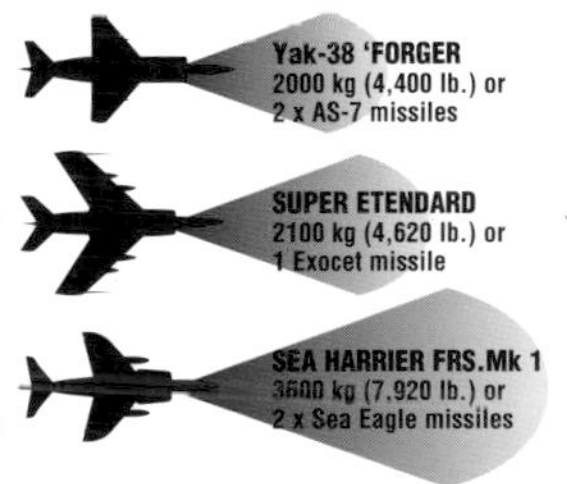

Soviet carrier evolution

■ **HELICOPTER CARRIER:** The 'Moskva' class appeared in the early 1960s. It was a cross between a carrier and a cruiser, and could only operate helicopters.

■ **'FORGER' CARRIER:** Carriers of the 40,000-ton 'Kiev' class had a through-deck, which enabled them to operate with a dozen Yak-38s as well as anti-submarine helicopters.

■ **SUPERCARRIER:** The last gasp of Soviet naval expansion was the supercarrier *Kuznetsov*, which was designed to operate with advanced fighters like the Su-33 'Flanker'. It has proved to be far too expensive, however, for financially challenged Russia to contemplate putting into service.

Index